PEDIATRIC NEUROLOGY

CLINICAL AND IMAGING CASE STUDIES

Hugo A. Arroyo, MD
Honorary Consultant, Department of Neurology
Hospital de Pediatría Juan P Garrahan
Faculty of Medicine and Ex-Director, Pediatric Neurology Postgraduate Program
Universidad de Buenos Aires
Buenos Aires, Argentina

Alcy R. Torres, MD
Clinical Professor of Pediatrics and Neurology
Director of Pediatric Brain Injury Program
Boston University Chobanian & Avedisian School of Medicine
Boston, Massachusetts, USA

Jorge Vidaurre, MD
Professor of Pediatrics and Neurology
The Ohio State University
Director of Pediatric Clinical Neurophysiology Program and EEG Laboratory
Nationwide Children's Hospital
Columbus, Ohio, USA

Carlos A. Rugilo, MD
Neuroradiologist
Chief of MRI
Hospital de Pediatría Juan P Garrahan
Buenos Aires, Argentina

Mai-Lan Ho, MD
Professor, Vice Chair, and Medical Director of Radiology
Physician Director of Radiology Informatics
Division Director of Neuroradiology
University of Missouri
Columbia, Missouri, USA

ELSEVIER

Elsevier
1600 John F. Kennedy Blvd.
Ste 1800
Philadelphia, PA 19103-2899

PEDIATRIC NEUROLOGY: CLINICAL AND IMAGING CASE STUDIES

ISBN: 978-0-443-28722-0

Content Strategist: Mary Hegeler
Senior Content Development Specialist: Suddha Satwa Sen
Publishing Services Manager: Deepthi Unni
Project Manager: Manchu Mohan
Design Direction: Ryan Cook

Printed in India.

Last digit is the print number: 9 8 7 6 5 4 3 2 1

Dedicated to all the patients and colleagues who inspired us to write this book.

CONTRIBUTIORS

Rocio E. Alamo, MD
Pediatrician, Pediatric Neurologist
FLENI, CABA
Buenos Aires, Argentina

Lennyn Albán, MD
Neuroradiology
Hospital Metropolitano
Quito, Pichincha, Ecuador

Xènia Alonso Curcó, MD
Pediatric Neurologist
Department of Neurology
Sant Joan de Déu Hospiital
Barcelona, Spain

Diana Ángulo Manchola, MD
Pediatrician, Pediatric Neurologist
Department of Pediatric Neurology
FLENI. CABA
Buenos Aires, Argentina

Suresh Kumar Angurana, MD
Department of Pediatrics
PGIMER
Chandigarh, India

Juan Ignacio Appendino, MD
Pediatric Neurologist, Epileptologist
Department of Pediatrics
Hospital Italiano de Buenos Aires
Buenos Aires, Argentina

Juan Pablo Appendino, MD, CSCN (EEG), FAES
Pediatric Neurologist, Epileptologist
Professor
College of Medicine, University of Saskatchewan
Division Head of Neurology
Department of Pediatrics
Jim Pattison Children's Hospital
Saskatoon, Saskatchewan, Canada

Hugo A. Arroyo, MD
Honorary Consultant, Department of Neurology
Hospital de Pediatría Juan P Garrahan
Faculty of Medicine and Ex-Director, Pediatric Neurology Postgraduate Program
Universidad de Buenos Aires
Buenos Aires, Argentina

Federico Baltar, MD
Pediatric Neurologist
Pediatric Neurology Academic Unit
School of Medicine, University of the Republic
Montevideo, Uruguay

Leslie A. Benson, MD
Pediatric Neuroimmunologist
Department of Neurology
Boston Children's Hospital
Boston, Massachusetts, USA

Gerard T. Berry, MD
Professor, Harvard Medical School
Department of Genetics & Metabolism
Boston Children's Hospital
Boston, Massachusetts, USA

Chandana Bhagwat, MD, DM
Consultant
Department of Pediatric Neurology
MGM Institute of Health Sciences
Mumbai, India

M. Celeste Buompadre, MD
Pediatric Neurologist
Department of Pediatric Neurology
Hospital de Pediatría Juan P Garrahan
Buenos Aires, Argentina

Jaume Campistol, DM, PhD
Pediatric Neurologist
Department of Neurology
Hospital Sant Joan de Deu
Barcelona, Spain

Santiago Campos-Miño, MD, MSc
Professor
Department of Pediatrics
Universidad Internacional del Ecuador
Director of Clinical Research
Hospital Metropolitano
Quito, Ecuador

Martín D. Carnevale, MD
Neuroradiologist, Radiologist
Department of Radiology
FLENI, CABA
Buenos Aires, Argentina

Alfredo Cerisola, MD
Associate Professor
Pediatric Neurology Academic Unit
School of Medicine, UDELAR
Montevideo, Uruguay

Quentin Yau Ching Wong, BSocSc (Psychology), MPsyMed
Research Department
Hong Kong Children's Hospital
Hong Kong, China

Micaela Chinigioli, MD
Pediatrician, Pediatric Neurologist
Department of Pediatric Neurology
FLENI, CABA
Buenos Aires, Argentina

Gökalp Çıkman, MD
Pediatric Radiologist
Department of Radiology
Mardin Training and Research Hospital
Mardin, Turkey

Daniel J. Clark, MD, PhD
Assistant Professor
Division of Neurology
Cincinnati Children's Hospital Medical Center
Cincinnati, Ohio, USA

Marta Conti, MD
Pediatric Neurologist
Department of Child Neurology
Epilepsy and Movement Disorders
Bambino Gesù Children's Hospital, IRCCS, Piazza
Rome, Italy

Paolo Curatolo, MD
Pediatric Neurologist
Professor
Department of Systems Medicine
Tor Vergata University
Rome, Italy

Russell C. Dale, PhD, MRCP, MBChB
Professor
Clinical School
University of Sydney
Sydney, New South Wales, Australia

Luca de Palma, MD
Neurology, Epilepsy and Movement Disorders Unit
Full Member of European Reference Network EpiCARE
Bambino Gesù Children's Hospital, IRCCS, Piazza
Rome, Italy

Angela De Dominicis, MD
Department of Neurology, Epilepsy and Movement Disorders
Full Member of European Reference Network EpiCARE
Bambino Gesù Children's Hospital, IRCCS, Piazza
Rome, Italy

Brigid Dwyer, MD
Assistant Professor
Department of Neurology
Boston University Chobanian & Avedisian School of Medicine
Boston, Massachusetts, USA

Mohamed El-Dib, MD
Director of Neonatal Neurocritical Care
Department of Pediatrics, Division of Newborn
Brigham and Women's Hospital
Associate Professor
Department of Pediatrics
Harvard Medical School
Boston, Massachusetts, USA

Aisling B. Fagan, FRCR, MB, BCh, BAO
Consultant Radiologist
Department of Radiology
Children's Health Ireland
Dublin, Ireland
Radiology Fellow
Department of Radiology
Great Ormond Street Hospital
London, United Kingdom

Gabriel González Rabelino, MD
Professor and Director
Pediatric Neurology Academic Unit
Pereira Rossell Hospital Center School of Medicine
UDELAR
Montevideo, Uruguay

Mai-Lan Ho, MD
Professor of Radiology
Vice Chair of Clinical Radiology
Vice Chair of Operations and Innovation
Medical Director of Radiology
Physician Director of Radiology Informatics
Division Director of Neuroradiology
University of Missouri
Columbia, Missouri, USA

Kam Lun Ellis Hon, MBBS, MD, FAAP, FCCM, FHKAM, FHKCPaed
Clinical Professional Consultant and Professor of Practice
Department of Paediatrics
The Chinese University of Hong Kong Medical Center
Honorary Consultant
Department of Paediatrics and Adolescent Medicine
The Hong Kong Children's Hospital
Hong Kong, China

Terrie Inder, MBChB, MD
Director, Center for Newborn Research
Department of Pediatrics
Rady Children's Health of Orange County
Professor
Department of Pediatrics
University of California, Irvine
Orange, California, USA

Camilo Jaimes, MD, MPH
Chief, Pediatric Neuroradiology
Department of Radiology
Mass General Brigham
Assistant Professor of Radiology
Harvard Medical School
Boston, Massachusetts, USA

Seh-Hyun Kim, MD, PhD
Assistant Professor
Department of Pediatrics
Seoul National University Children's Hospital
Seoul, Republic of Korea

Karen Ka Yan Leung, MBBS, MSc, FRCPCH
Pediatric Intensive Care
Department of Paediatrics and Adolescent Medicine
Hong Kong Children's Hospital
Kowloon, Hong Kong, China

Katherine Liu, MD
Resident Physician
Department of Medicine
University of Alberta
Edmonton, Alberta, Canada

Natarie D. Liu, MD, FRCPC, BSc
Pediatric Neurologist, Epileptologist
Assistant Professor
University of Alberta
Department of Pediatrics
Stollery Children's Hospital
Edmonton, Alberta, Canada

Mariana Loos, MD
Pediatric Neurologist
Department of Pediatric Neurology
Hospital de Pediatría Juan P Garrahan
Buenos Aires, Argentina

Concetta Luisi, MD
Neurologist
Full Member of European Reference Network
EpiCARE
Department of Neurology, Epilepsy and Movement Disorders
Bambino Gesù Children's Hospital, IRCCS Piazza
Rome, Italy

Minette K. Manalo, MD
Pediatric Epilepsy Fellow
Division of Pediatric Neurology and Epilepsy
Alberta Children's Hospital, Cumming School of Medicine, University of Calgary
Calgary, Alberta, Canada

Kshitij Mankad, MBBS, FRCR
Imaging Lead
Consultant Paediatric Neuroradiologist
Department of Radiology
Great Ormond Street Hospital
London, United Kingdom

Jordi Muchart, MD
Clinical Lead, Pediatric Neuroradiology
Department of Diagnostic Imaging
Sant Joan de Déu Children's Hospital, University of Barcelona
Barcelona, Spain

Giusy Carfi Pavia, MD
Department of Neurology, Epilepsy and Movement Disorders
Full Member of European Reference Network
EpiCARE
Bambino Gesù Children's Hospital, IRCCS, Piazza
Rome, Italy

Chiara Pepi, MD
Child Neurologist
Department of Neuroscience
Bambino Gesù Children's Hospital, IRCCS, Piazza
Rome, Italy

Nicola Pietrafusa, MD
Department of Neurology, Epilepsy and Movement Disorders
Full Member of European Reference Network
EpiCARE
Bambino Gesù Children's Hospital, IRCCS, Piazza
Rome, Italy

Ludovica Piscitello, MD
Department of Neurology, Epilepsy and Movement Disorders
Full Member of European Reference Network
EpiCARE
Bambino Gesù Children's Hospital, IRCCS, Piazza
Rome, Italy

Daniel J. Pomerantz, MD, FACMG
Instructor
Department of Pediatrics, Medical Genetics & Metabolism
Massachusetts General Hospital
Boston, Massachusetts, USA

Douglas G. Postels, MD, MS
Professor
Department of Pediatric Neurology
Children's National Hospital
Washington, District of Columbia, USA
Consultant
Department of Paediatrics
Queen Elizabeth Central Hospital
Blantyre, Malawi

Juan Carlos Pérez-Poveda, MD
Assistant Professor of Neuropediatrics
Department of Pediatrics
Pontifical Xavierian University
Chief of Neuropediatrics
Department of Pediatrics
Clinica Infantil Colsubsidio
Bogotá, D.C., Colombia

Lance H. Rodan, MD
Assistant Professor
Department of Pediatrics, Genetics and Genomics
Harvard Medical School
Attending Physician
Department of Neurology
Boston Children's Hospital
Boston, Massachusetts, USA

Marcelo Bayardo Román, MD
Attending Physician
Department of Pediatrics
Pediatric Neurology Metropolitan Hospital
Quito, Pichincha, Ecuador

Carlos A. Rugilo, MD
Neuroradiologist
Chief of MRI
Hospital de Pediatría Juan P Garrahan
Buenos Aires, Argentina

Arushi Gahlot Saini, MD, DM, MNAMS
Associate Professor
Department of Pediatrics
Postgraduate Institute of Medical Education and Research
Chandigarh, India

Morris H. Scantlebury, MD
Professor
Department of Pediatrics
Professor
Department of Clinical Neuroscience
University of Calgary
Calgary, Alberta, Canada

Angeles Schteinschnaider, MD
Head
Department of Neuropediatrics
FLENI CABA
Buenos Aires, Argentina

Esma Şengenç, MD
Department of Pediatric Neurology
Biruni University Hospital
Istanbul, Turkey

Bindu N. Setty, MD
Clinical Associate Professor
Department of Radiology
Boston University
Boston, Massachusetts, USA

Nicola Specchio, MD, PhD
Chair of Neurology, Epilepsy and Movement Disorders
Department of Neuroscience
Full Member of European Reference Network
EpiCARE
Bambino Gesù Children's Hospital, IRCCS, Piazza
Rome, Italy

Renu Suthar, MD, DM
Pediatric Neurologist
Adjunct Professor
Department of Pediatrics
PGIMER
Chandigarh, India

Alcy R. Torres, MD
Clinical Professor of Pediatrics and Neurology
Director of Pediatric Brain Injury Program
Boston University Chobanian & Avedisian School of Medicine
Boston, Massachusetts, USA

Marina Trivisano, MD, PhD
Pediatric Neurologist
Neurology, Epilepsy and Movement Disorders Unit
Full Member of European Reference Network
EpiCARE
Bambino Gesù Children's Hospital, IRCCS, Piazza
Rome, Italy

Álvaro Emilio Turcatti, MD
Neuroradiologist
Department of Radiology
Hospital Británico
Montevideo, Uruguay

Jorge Vidaurre, MD
Professor of Pediatrics and Neurology
The Ohio State University
Director, Pediatric Clinical Neurophysiology Program and EEG Laboratory
Nationwide Children's Hospital
Columbus, Ohio, USA

Federico Vigevano, MD
Professor of Neurology
Director, Department of Neurological Sciences and Rehabilitation Medicine
Bambino Gesù Children's Hospital, IRCCS
Rome, Italy

Jeff L. Waugh, MD, PhD
Director, Pediatric Movement Disorders Program
Department of Pediatrics
University of Texas Southwestern
Dallas, Texas, USA

Elizabeth Wilson, MD
Assistant Professor
Department of Neurology
Cincinnati Children's Hospital Medical Center
Cincinnati, Ohio, USA

PREFACE

While practicing at various medical centers, we have all participated in clinical rounds regarding complex patient cases and questions for diagnosis and treatment. Such multidisciplinary conferences offer the possibility for attendees to contribute their diverse knowledge and skill sets toward maximal clinical, academic, and educational impact. Often, these discussions touch upon not only the scientific issues but also the humanitarian aspects of child and family care.

Patient rounds tend to follow a characteristic format. Medical trainees present the patient information, an attending physician reviews the possible differential diagnoses, and a radiologist discusses the imaging findings. Next, the group synthesizes available data to develop a working diagnosis and next steps in management. Although such interactions are generally not documented in patient clinical notes, they often lead to profound interdisciplinary realizations and inspiring research topics in academic medicine.

The great neuroscientist Santiago Ramón y Cajal said that "any man could, if he were so inclined, be the sculptor of his own brain." In this spirit, we decided to model this book on real-life clinical case presentations and discussions. Such an approach diverges from conventional texts, which present information in a traditional pedagogical fashion. Instead, we aim to highlight the process of interactive multidisciplinary learning. Each section follows multiple patients in their diagnostic journey, beginning with the history and physical exam, proceeding to diagnostic workup, discussing clinical and imaging differential diagnoses and red flags, and concluding with the final diagnosis and discussion.

Pediatric neurology has profoundly evolved over the past several decades. Varied and challenging diagnoses at each stage of life—fetus, infant, child, and adolescent—have been revolutionized by advances in medical imaging. In particular, magnetic resonance imaging (MRI) offers exquisite characterization of the developing central nervous system without exposure to ionizing radiation. MRI has elucidated a stunning variety of neurologic disorders in children, including congenital malformations, tumors, infections, autoimmune diseases, and vascular conditions. Our book highlights the rich collaborations between child neurologists and neuroradiologists, with nearly every case requiring imaging to make the diagnosis.

In the modern era, our widespread use of virtual and hybrid technologies enables connectivity among people across the world. Similarly, the editors and authors of each chapter represent prestigious worldwide experts recruited from multiple countries and continents to contribute to this series. We hope that you, the reader, enjoy this novel international collaboration and approach to child neurology and imaging.

Hugo A. Arroyo
Alcy R. Torres
Jorge Vidaurre
Carlos A. Rugilo
Mai-Lan Ho

ABBREVIATIONS

%	Percent or percentile
ACA	Anterior cerebral artery
ADC	Apparent diffusion coefficient
ADEM	Acute disseminated encephalomyelitis
ADHD	Attention-deficit/hyperactivity disorder
ALL	Acute lymphocytic leukemia
ANEC	Acute necrotizing encephalopathy of childhood
ARCA	Autosomal recessive cerebellar ataxias
ASL	Arterial spin labeling
ATTP	Alpha-tocopherol transfer protein
AVED	Ataxia with vitamin E deficiency
AVM	Arteriovenous malformations
AVN	Avascular necrosis
BG	Basal ganglia
BOSD	Bottom of the sulcus dysplasia
CA	Cerebellar atrophy
CADASIL	Autosomal dominant cerebral arteriopathy with subcortical infarcts and leukoencephalopathy
CBC	Complete blood count
CCM	Cavernous malformation
CGA	Conceptional gestational age
CHD	Congenital heart disease
Cho	Choline
CLOVES	Congenital lipomatous overgrowth, vascular malformations, epidermal nevus, spinal/skeletal anomalies
CMV	Cytomegalovirus
CNS	Central nervous system
CP	Cerebral palsy
Cr	Creatine
CSF	Cerebrospinal fluid
CSVT	Cerebral sinovenous thrombosis
CT	Computed tomography
CTA	Computed tomography angiography
CTV	Computed tomography venography
DEE-SWAS	Developmental and epileptic encephalopathy with spike and wave activation in sleep
DIC	Disseminated intravascular coagulation
DNET	Dysembryoplastic neuroepithelial tumor
DWI	Diffusion-weighted imaging
ECG	Electrocardiogram
EEG	Electroencephalography
FCD	Focal cortical dysplasia
FLAIR	Fluid-attenuated inversion recovery
GCS	Glasgow Coma Scale
GRE	Gradient recalled echo
HIE	Hypoxic-ischemic encephalopathy
HME	Hemimegalencephaly
HS	Hemorrhagic stroke
HUS	Hemolytic uremic syndrome
ICA	Internal carotid artery
ITP	Immune thrombocytopenic purpura
IV	Intravenous
Lac	Lactate
Lip	Lipid
MCA	Middle cerebral artery
MELAS	Mitochondrial encephalopathy, lactic acidosis, and stroke-like episodes
MI	Myoinositol
MODS	Multiple organ dysfunction syndrome
MOGAD	Myelin oligodendrocyte glycoprotein-associated antibody disease
MRA	Magnetic resonance arteriography
MRI	Magnetic resonance imaging
MRS	Magnetic resonance spectroscopy
MRV	Magnetic resonance venography
MTS	Mesial temporal sclerosis
MTX	Methotrexate
NAA	N-acetylaspartate
NIHSS	National Institutes of Health Stroke Scale
NMDARE	Anti-NMDA receptor encephalitis
NMOSD	Neuromyelitis optica spectrum disorder
PCA	Posterior cerebral artery
PCH	Pontocerebellar hypoplasia
PCR	Polymerase chain reaction
PICA	Posterior inferior cerebellar artery
PICU	Pediatric intensive care unit
PRES	Posterior reversible encephalopathy syndrome
RBC	Red blood cell
RCVS	Reversible cerebral vasoconstriction syndrome

SARA	Scale for the Assessment and Rating of Ataxia
SARS-CoV-2	Severe acute respiratory syndrome coronavirus-2
SCA	Spinocerebellar ataxia
SCD	Sickle cell disease
SD	Standard deviation
SEEG	Stereo EEG
SSPE	Subacute sclerosing panencephalitis
STEC	Shiga toxin (Stx)–producing *Escherichia coli*
STIR	Short tau inversion recovery
SWI	Susceptibility-weighted imaging
SWS	Sturge-Weber syndrome
TE	Time to echo
TOF	Time of flight
TSC	Tuberous sclerosis complex
US	Ultrasound
WBC	White blood cell
XA	Angiography
XR	Radiography

CONTENTS

SECTION 1

Headache

Hugo A. Arroyo, Alcy R. Torres, Jorge Vidaurre, Carlos A. Rugilo, Mai-Lan Ho

INTRODUCTION

Headache is one of the most frequent symptoms in children, and one of the most common reasons for general pediatrician referral to specialists, as well as a growing reason for consultation in the emergency department. Most headaches are primary, such as migraine and tension headache. In some cases headache may be secondary to an underlying neurological disorder necessitating accurate diagnosis and treatment.

There is a broad differential diagnosis with paucity of biological markers in pediatric headache. This creates challenges for clinicians in deciding whether to refer patients to specialists and order complex diagnostic workups. The need to evaluate for serious illnesses in a timely manner needs to be balanced against unindicated testing that overburdens the health care system and exposes children to unnecessary harm.

The International Headache Society has published the updated Classification of Headache Disorders (ICHD, Third Edition), noting key differences between children and adults. However, less scientific data exist for pediatric patients, with greater clinical variability, wider differential diagnoses, and more challenging diagnostic workups.

In this chapter we describe clinical and imaging red flags in children with headache that should prompt diagnostic testing. History suggestive of a serious neurological disease and/or abnormal neurological examination are clear indicators for neuroimaging. When ordering an imaging study, providing a detailed and relevant history to the radiologist greatly increases the likelihood of a timely and accurate diagnosis. Overall, close communication and collaboration between neurologists and radiologists are central to ensuring appropriate diagnosis and management.

SUGGESTED READINGS

Alexiou GA, Argyropoulou MI. Neuroimaging in childhood headache: a systematic review. *Pediatr Radiol.* 2013;43:777–784. https://doi.org/10.1007/s00247-013-2692-3.

Goadsby PJ, Evers S. International classification of headache disorders – ICHD-4 alpha. *Cephalalgia.* 2020;40(9):887–888. https://doi:10.1177/0333102420919098.

Headache Classification Committee of the International Headache Society (IHS) the international classification of headache disorders, 3rd edition. *Cephalalgia.* 2018;38(1):1–211. https://doi.org/10.1177/0333102417738202.

Perry MC, Yaeger SK, Toto RL, Suresh S, Hickey RW. A modern epidemic: increasing pediatric emergency department visits and admissions for headache. *Pediatr Neurol.* 2018;89:19–25. https://doi.org/10.1016/j.pediatrneurol.2018.07.015.

Zhou AZ, Marin JR, Hickey RW, Ramgopal S. Serious diagnoses for headaches after ED discharge. *Pediatrics.* 2020;146(5). https://doi.org/10.1542/peds.2020-1647.

When Sinuses Are the Cause of a Headache

HISTORY AND PHYSICAL

A 14-year-old male presents with a history of seasonal allergies and headache since the age of 12. Initially, headaches were sporadic, but recently pain has been frequent and intense. The pain is located on the forehead and eyes without radiation. It is not associated with any food intake, and patient denies visual aura. Pain is oppressive and can reach an intensity of 8/10, worse if the patient leans forward. Pain does not clearly change when lying down, coughing, or performing other Valsalva maneuvers. There is no history of photophobia, phonophobia, nausea, or vomiting. Mother comments that sometimes his eyelids and forehead are swollen. He has no history of fever, trauma, or toxic exposures. Patient was previously seen by his pediatrician, who prescribed nasal drops and fluticasone propionate inhaler. As the headaches did not improve, the patient was referred to neurology.

Systems review is positive for frequent nasal congestion on the left. Patient is not taking vitamins, hormones, antibiotics, or other medicines. He also denies the use of recreational drugs including cocaine. There is no history of significant weight gain in the past year, anxiety, or depression. He has no allergies to medications. Vaccinations are complete.

There is no family history of migraine headaches, aneurysms, or brain tumors. Maternal grandfather with meningioma treated by surgery, maternal aunt with pituitary adenoma, younger brother with ADHD.

Physical examination shows weight 70 kg, height 175 cm, head circumference 55 cm, blood pressure 110/70, pulse 88, temperature 37.8°C. On general head examination, patient is normocephalic, without neck stiffness or lymphadenopathy. Current headache level is 6/10, with mild pain on percussion of frontal bone and left maxillary sinus. Nasal examination shows mucosal edema and hyperemia in addition to yellowish discharge on the left side. Cardiorespiratory and abdominal examinations are normal.

Neurological examination shows normal mental status for age. Cranial nerves and fundoscopy are normal. Motor, sensory, cerebellar, and gait examinations are normal.

DIAGNOSTIC WORKUP

Paranasal sinus X-ray reveals opacification of the left maxillary sinus.

CT scan confirms maxillary and ethmoid sinus inflammatory disease without associated bone alterations.

MRI shows air-fluid level in the left maxillary sinus indicative of acute inflammation (Fig. 1.1).

CLINICAL DIFFERENTIAL DIAGNOSIS

Migraine, cluster headache, chronic paroxysmal hemicrania, SUNCT/SUNA (short-lasting, unilateral, neuralgiform headaches with conjunctival tearing and injection/cranial autonomic features), and hemicrania continua. Headaches are distinguished by duration, stereotyped circadian cycles, and response to indomethacin.

Tension headache can cause pain in the forehead and back of neck.

"Salt-and-pepper pains" of the eyes may indicate an evolving brainstem infarction.

Purulent nasal discharge and sinonasal inflammation are suggestive of acute rhinosinusitis.

IMAGING DIFFERENTIAL DIAGNOSIS

Mucocele is caused by obstruction of sinus exit foramina with sinus expansion and wall thinning/remodeling (Fig. 1.2). Infection (mucopyocele) is a dreaded complication.

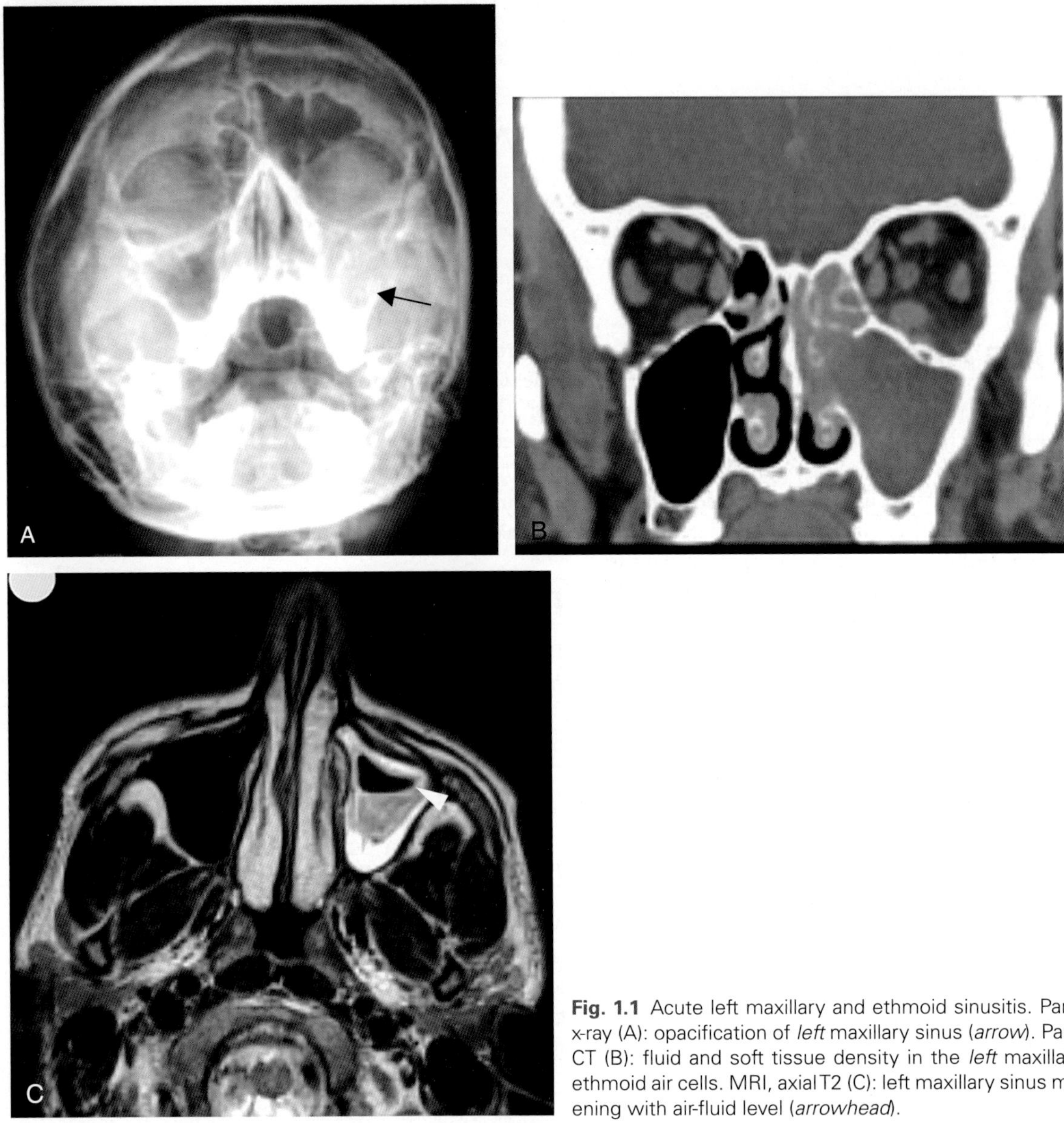

Fig. 1.1 Acute left maxillary and ethmoid sinusitis. Paranasal sinus x-ray (A): opacification of *left* maxillary sinus (*arrow*). Paranasal sinus CT (B): fluid and soft tissue density in the *left* maxillary sinus and ethmoid air cells. MRI, axial T2 (C): left maxillary sinus mucosal thickening with air-fluid level (*arrowhead*).

Sinusitis with secretions can demonstrate varying MRI signals depending on fluid, protein, and fungal contents.

Benign and malignant paranasal sinus masses can be characterized by imaging features, including calcifications, expansion, contrast enhancement, bone erosion, and spread (direct extension, perineural spread, satellite lymphadenopathy).

FINAL DIAGNOSIS

Sinusitis.

DISCUSSION

Diagnosis of sinusitis is clinical. Imaging can help confirm the diagnosis or further evaluate disease severity,

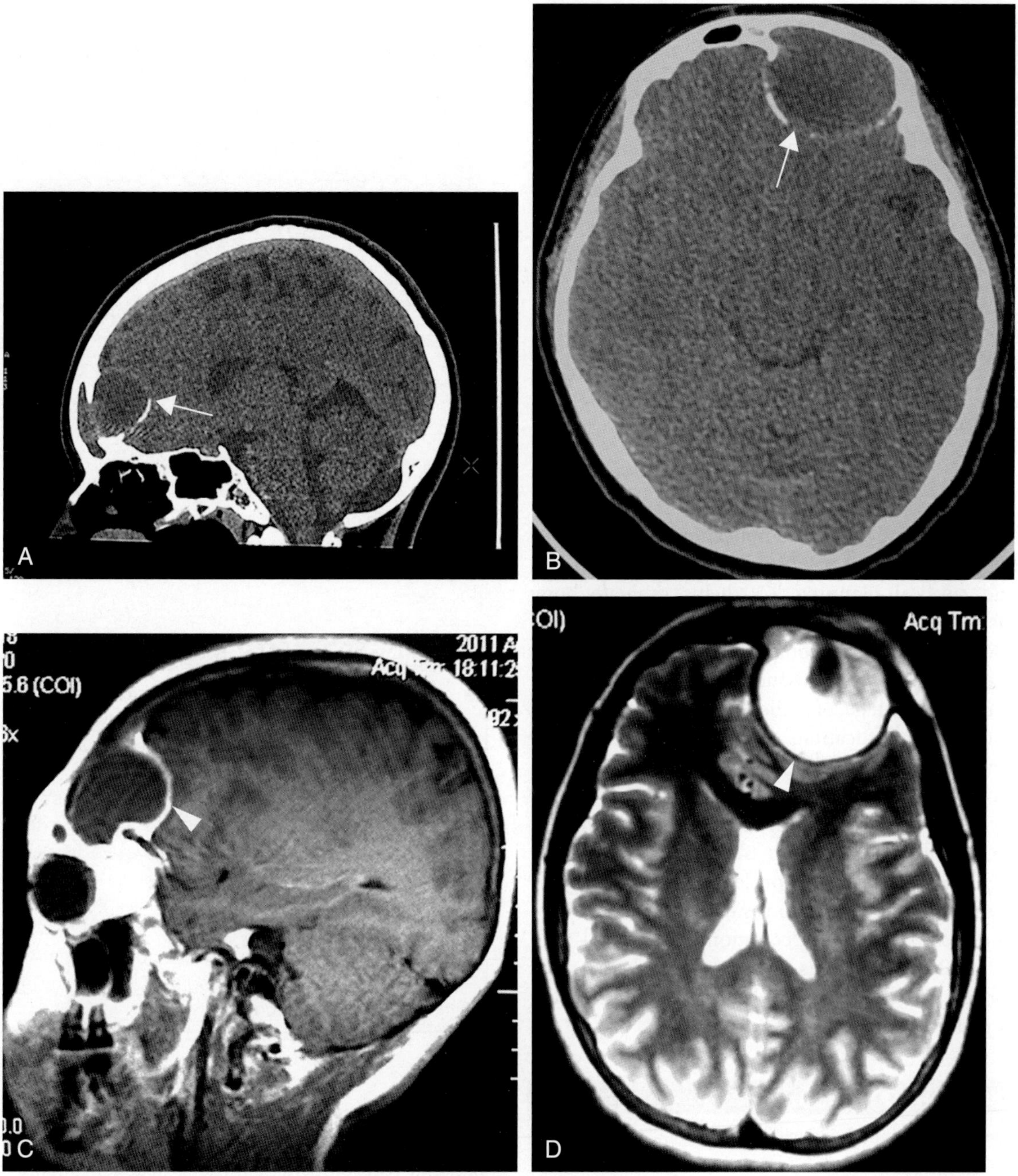

Fig. 1.2 Mucocele. (A and B) Noncontrast CT, sagittal and axial, and (C and D) MRI, sagittal T1 postcontrast and axial T2: opacification and expansion of the *left* frontal sinus with surrounding bone thinning and protrusion into the anterior cranial fossa (*arrows*, *arrowheads*).

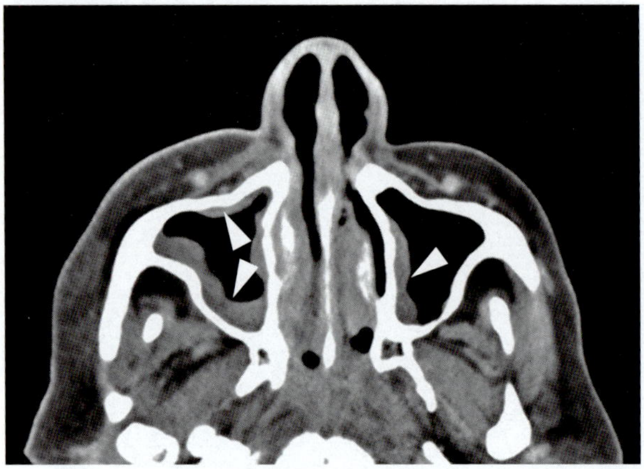

Fig. 1.3 Incidental sinonasal mucosal disease. Paranasal sinus CT: patchy mucosal thickening and retention cysts in both maxillary sinuses (*arrowheads*).

response to treatment, or complications. Sinus radiograph is sufficient for basic diagnosis. For rapid screening and surgical planning, CT helps evaluate bony sinonasal anatomy. MRI can be considered in the setting of suspected intracranial complications or invasive fungal sinusitis requiring soft tissue detail.

A large percentage of children with imaging tests done for other indications show incidental sinonasal abnormalities, including mucosal thickening and retention cysts. These abnormalities can be caused by chronic upper respiratory infection or allergic inflammation, which may not require treatment if asymptomatic (Fig. 1.3). However, the presence of air-fluid levels or aerosolized bubbly secretions suggests an acute infectious process that is more commonly associated with headache. Chronic sinusitis can manifest with paranasal sinus atelectasis (decreased size) and/or wall thickening (hyperostosis) (Fig. 1.4).

CLINICAL RED FLAGS

- Diagnosis of sinus headaches is clinical. Examine the nostrils, eyes, and face for important diagnostic clues of sinonasal inflammation.
- Migraine is the most common cause of headaches, even in patients with sinus disease. Ask about specific headache features and family history.

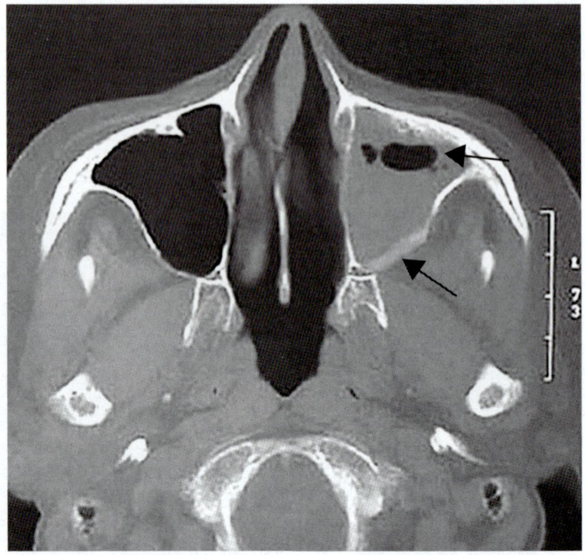

Fig. 1.4 Acute on chronic sinusitis. Paranasal sinus CT: left maxillary sinus mucosal thickening and aerosolized secretions with slight volume reduction and wall hyperostosis (*arrows*).

IMAGING RED FLAGS

- Sinusitis can be complicated by intracranial extension, with spread of infection through small transosseous veins, resulting in purulent empyema, venous sinus thrombosis, and/or cerebritis (Fig. 1.5).
- In immunosuppressed patients, hypointense T2 signal and mucosal nonenhancement with extrasinus inflammation raise concern for invasive fungal infection. Mucormycosis and aspergillosis infections can progress rapidly with vascular invasion, thrombosis, and necrosis (Fig. 1.6).
- In children, frontal sinusitis can be associated with osteomyelitis and involvement of the overlying soft tissues (Pott puffy tumor) (Fig. 1.7).

CONCLUSIONS

Patients with sinusitis can have headaches from other causes, such as migraine. Primary headaches should be suspected in patients with chronic symptoms and a normal neurologic examination. For surgical management of sinusitis, patients can be referred to otolaryngology.

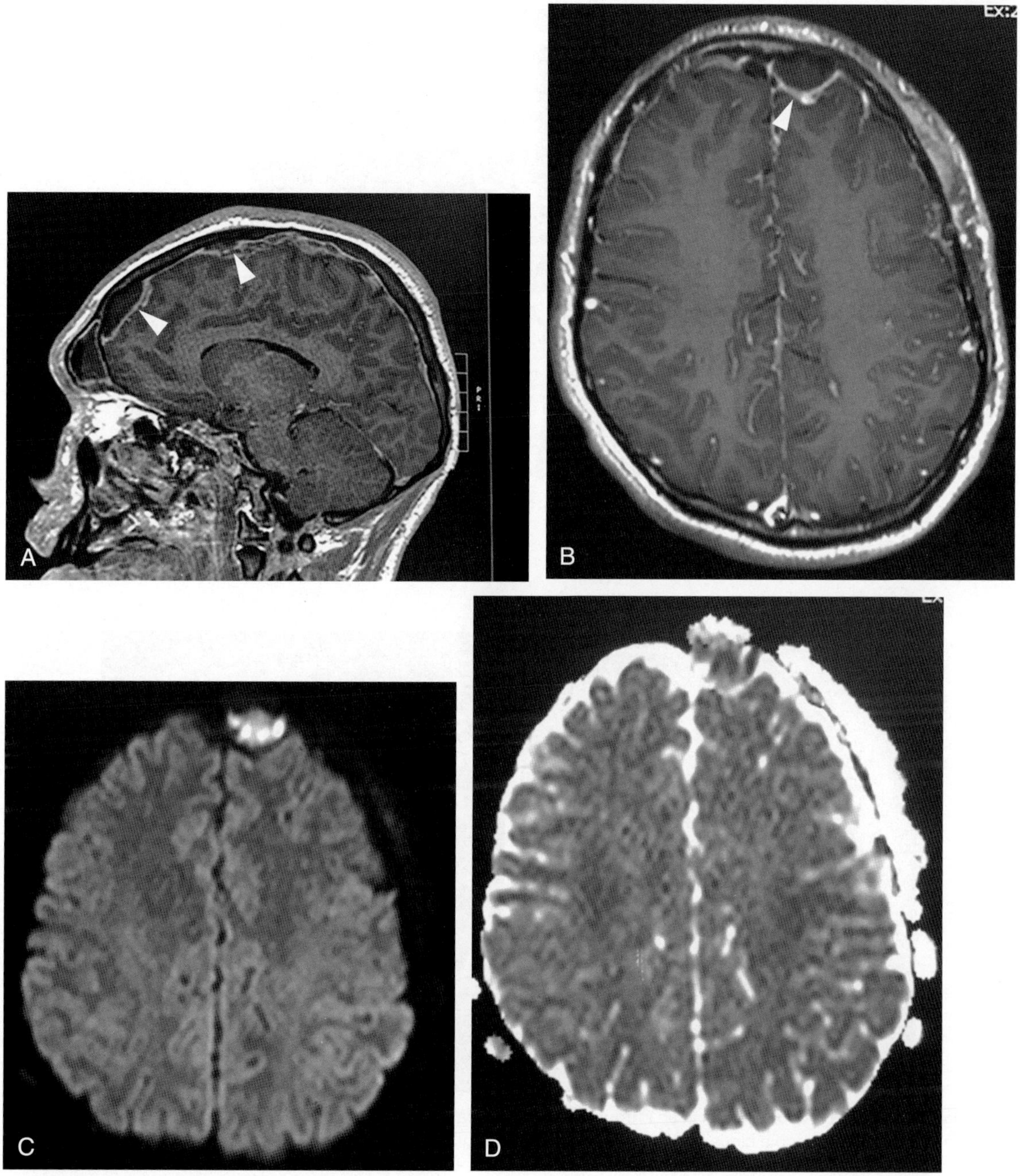

Fig. 1.5 Frontal sinusitis complicated by epidural empyema and superior sagittal sinus thrombus. MRI, (A) sagittal (*arrowheads*) and (B) axial T1 with gadolinium: *left* frontal sinusitis with subjacent epidural abscess (*arrowhead*) demonstrating rim enhancement and (C and D) restricted diffusion on DWI and ADC. (E) MRV shows partial thrombosis in the superior sagittal sinus (*arrows*). *ADC*, Apparent diffusion coefficient; *DWI*, diffusion weighted imaging; *MRV*, magnetic resonance venography.

Continued

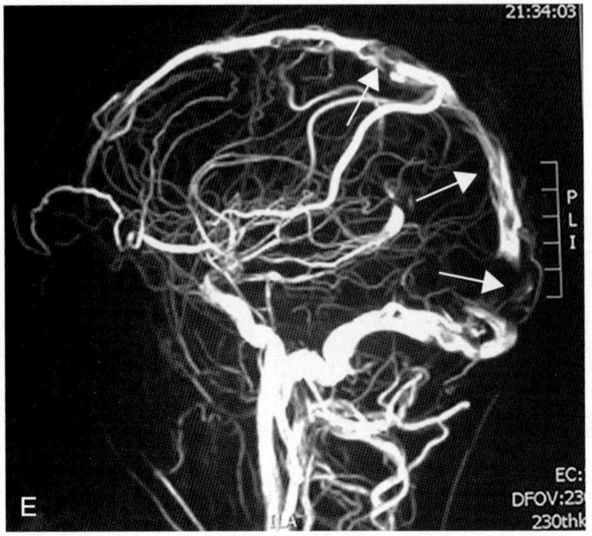

Fig. 1.5 cont'd

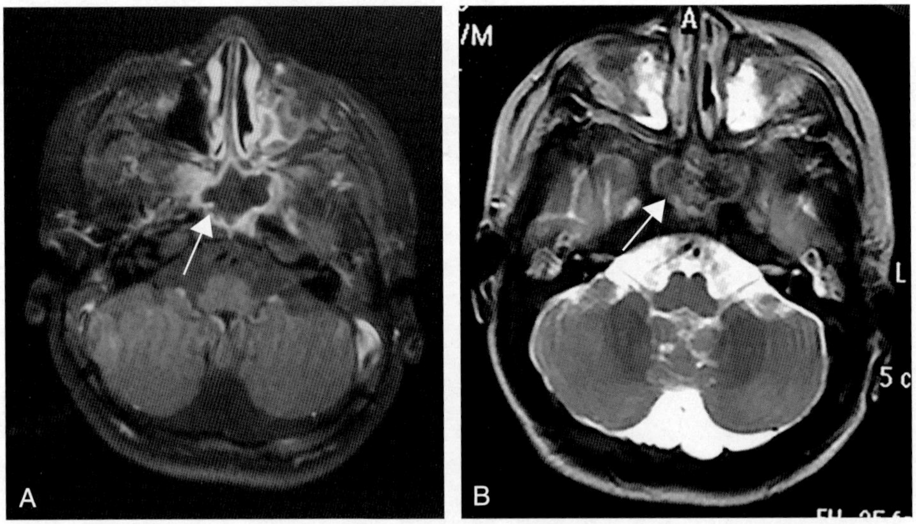

Fig. 1.6 Invasive mucormycosis in an immunosuppressed patient. MRI, (A) axial T1 fat saturation with gadolinium and (B) T2: sphenoid sinusitis with low T2 signal content and hypoenhancement (*arrows*).

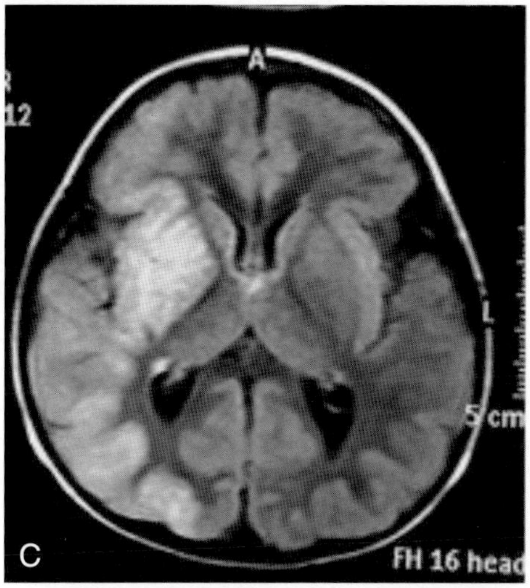

Fig. 1.6 cont'd (C) Follow-up 48 hours later with axial FLAIR showing right middle cerebral artery territory infarct. *FLAIR*, Fluid-attenuated inversion recovery.

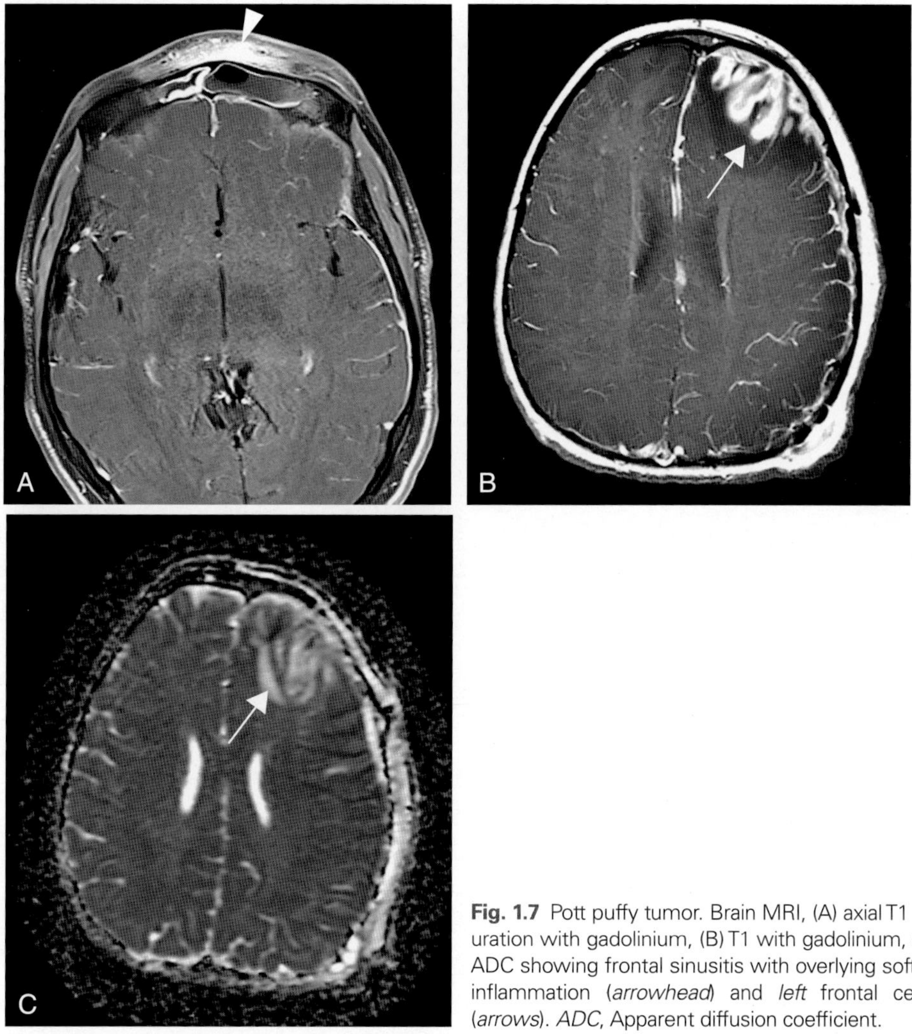

Fig. 1.7 Pott puffy tumor. Brain MRI, (A) axial T1 fat saturation with gadolinium, (B) T1 with gadolinium, and (C) ADC showing frontal sinusitis with overlying soft tissue inflammation (*arrowhead*) and *left* frontal cerebritis (*arrows*). *ADC*, Apparent diffusion coefficient.

REFERENCES

Buehring I, Friedrich B, Schaaf J, Schmidt H, Ahrens P, Zielen S. Chronic sinusitis refractory to standard management in patients with humoral immunodeficiencies. *Clin Exp Immunol.* 1997;109(3):468–472. https://doi.org/10.1046/j.1365–2249.1997.4831379.x.

Diament M. The diagnosis of sinusitis in infants and children: x-ray, computed tomography, and magnetic resonance imaging diagnostic imaging of pediatric sinusitis. *J Allergy Clin Immunol.* 1992;90(3):442–444. https://doi.org/10.1016/0091-6749(92)90166-y.

Goldsmith AJ, Rosenfeld RM. Treatment of pediatric sinusitis. *Pediatr Clin North Am.* 2003;50(2):413–426. https://doi.org/10.1016/s0031-3955(03)00027-0.

Manning SC, Biavati MJ, Phillips DL. Correlation of clinical sinusitis signs and symptoms to imaging findings in pediatric patients. *Int J Pediatr Otorhinolaryngol.* 1996;37(1):65–74. https://doi.org/10.1016/0165-5876(96)01381-x.

Smith BC, George LC, Svider PF, et al. Rhinogenic headache in pediatric and adolescent patients: an evidence-based review. *Int Forum Allergy Rhinol.* 2019;9(5):443–451. https://doi.org/10.1002/alr.22268.

Case 2

The Brain Also Suffers From Obesity

HISTORY AND PHYSICAL

A 17-year-old female patient comes to the emergency room with a headache of 5 weeks' evolution. She describes the headache as pulsatile with a severity of 6-7/10, bilateral frontal in location, with retroorbital pressure and photophobia but no phonophobia, nausea, or vomiting. She also reports blurred and tunnel vision, mainly when bending over to tie her shoes, and intermittent pulsatile tinnitus. She has no history of medications, contraceptives, or vitamins and unremarkable personal and family history. Physical examination, including vital signs, is normal. Body mass index is above the 95th percentile. Neurological examination is significant for 3+ papilledema showing significant optic disc protrusion. Vision acuity is 20/20 in both eyes, but campimetry demonstrated an enlarged blind spot.

DIAGNOSTIC WORKUP

MRI shows partially empty sella with a concave superior margin of the pituitary gland (Fig. 2.1), as well as dilated optic nerve sheaths with inversion of the optic discs compatible with papilledema and increased intracranial pressure (Fig. 2.2). There is no evidence for dural sinus thrombosis or meningitis.

In the emergency room, a lumbar puncture (LP) shows an opening pressure of 29 cm H_2O and a closing pressure of 18 cm H_2O. CSF is negative for cytology and cultures.

CLINICAL DIFFERENTIAL DIAGNOSIS

Primary headaches: Tension headache and migraine have characteristic clinical features and normal CSF pressures.

Drug overuse headache: Patients on chronic analgesics.

Idiopathic intracranial hypertension (IIH): Obesity, cranial nerve (CN) palsies as "false localizing signs," and papilledema.

Secondary intracranial hypertension: various etiologies including cerebral edema, venous thrombosis, hydrocephalus, infection, and tumor. Neuroimaging is valuable to distinguish from IIH.

IMAGING DIFFERENTIAL DIAGNOSIS

Dural sinus thrombosis presents with filling defects in the venous sinuses, and parenchymal venous infarcts if advanced.

Empty sella can be an incidental imaging finding in patients with normal CSF pressure and incompetence of the diaphragma sellae.

FINAL DIAGNOSIS

Idiopathic intracranial hypertension.

DISCUSSION

IIH or pseudotumor cerebri describes the condition of increased intracranial pressure in the absence of a mass or other primary etiology. The incidence is higher in obese females, but prepubertally affects males and females in equal numbers. The most frequent symptom is a high-pressure headache, which can worsen with Valsalva maneuvers and lying down. Other possible symptoms and signs include diplopia, pulsatile tinnitus, visual dimness, nausea, vomiting, CN signs (often VI), and papilledema.

Diagnostic criteria for IIH:

A. Papilledema.

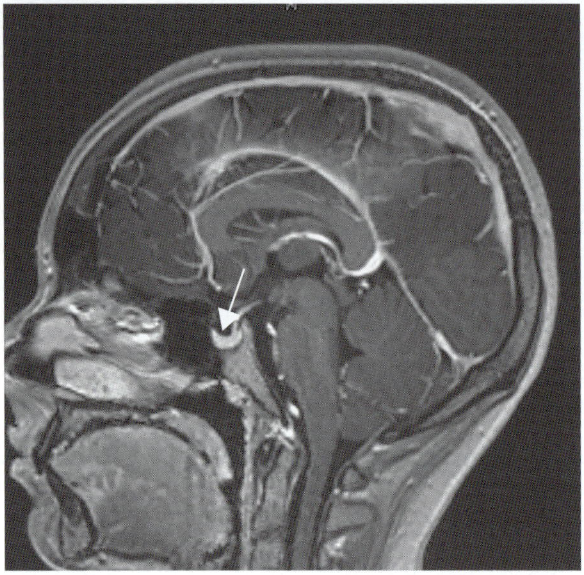

Fig. 2.1 Partially empty sella. Brain MRI, sagittal T1 with gadolinium, demonstrates a concave superior surface of the pituitary gland (*arrow*).

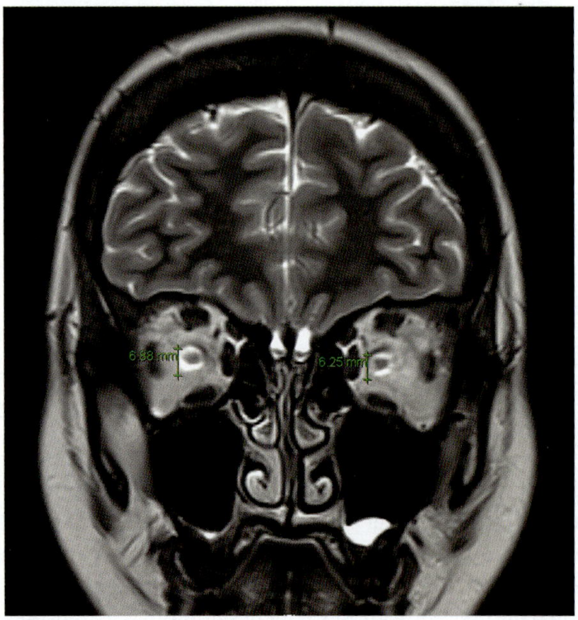

Fig. 2.2 Optic nerve sheath dilation. Brain MRI, coronal T2, shows engorged optic nerve sheaths (green) measured 3 mm posterior to the globe.

B. Normal neuroimaging using MRI with and without gadolinium, or CT with contrast if MRI is not available. Signs of increased intracranial pressure may be present but without an underlying mass.

C. Normal neurological examination, except for CN signs.

D. CSF testing normal.

E. Elevated CSF opening pressure (>25 cm H_2O in adults and >28 cm H_2O in children, or 25 cm H_2O if nonsedated and not obese) with appropriate pressure collection.

Diagnosis is definite if criteria A to E are fulfilled. Diagnosis is considered probable if criteria A to D are fulfilled, but CSF pressure is lower than the threshold for definitive diagnosis.

In absence of papilledema, criteria B to E must be present, and in addition, patient must have CN VI palsy (uni- or bilateral).

In absence of papilledema and CN VI deficits, diagnosis can be suspected but not confirmed, and neuroimaging must show signs of elevated intracranial pressure.

CLINICAL RED FLAGS

- Progressive headache, aggravated by Valsalva maneuver or lying down.
- Headaches awakening from sleep, with or without vomiting.
- Headache with visual obscurations, diplopia, papilledema.
- Headache with focal neurological signs, especially CN VI palsy.

IMAGING RED FLAGS

MRI findings consistent with diagnosis of IIH:

- Empty or partially empty sella turcica (can be an incidental finding in isolation).
- Enlarged and/or tortuous optic nerve sheaths.
- Posterior scleral flattening (Fig. 2.3).
- Optic disc edema or inversion, sometimes with contrast enhancement or diffusion restriction (Fig. 2.4).
- Venous sinus pseudostenosis, classically at the junction of the sigmoid and transverse sinuses (Fig. 2.5).

CONCLUSIONS

Given the nonspecificity of clinical and imaging features, it is important to keep a high index of suspicion for diagnosing IIH, especially in obese females. Early intervention can prevent vision loss and other complications. Treatment options include weight loss, high-volume LP, acetazolamide, topiramate, CSF shunting, and venous sinus stenting.

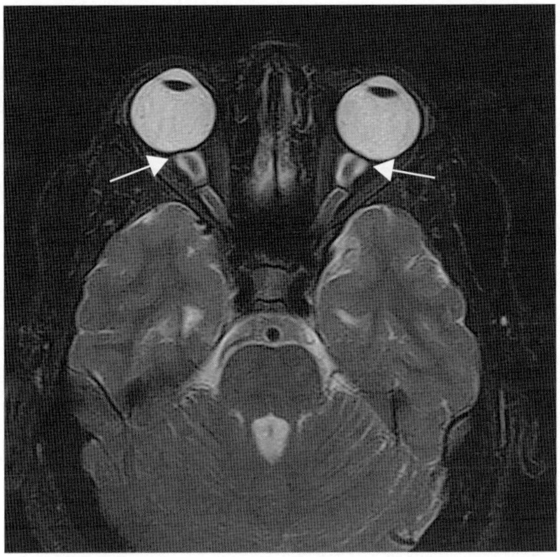

Fig. 2.3 Flattened posterior sclerae. Orbit MRI, axial T2 with fat suppression, shows dilated optic nerve sheaths with flattened posterior globes and optic disc inversion (*arrows*).

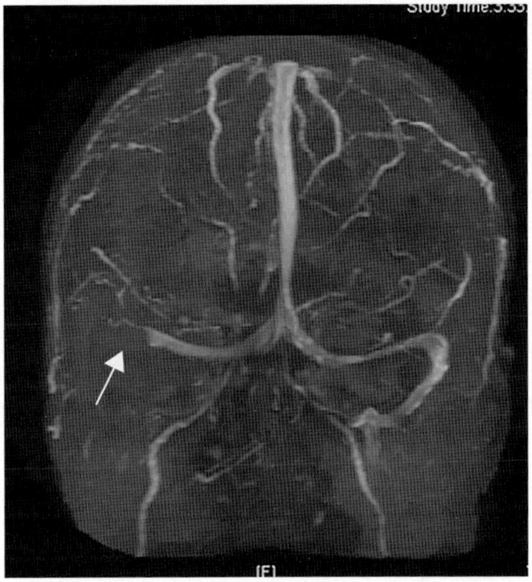

Fig. 2.5 Right transverse-sigmoid sinus pseudostenosis (*arrow*).

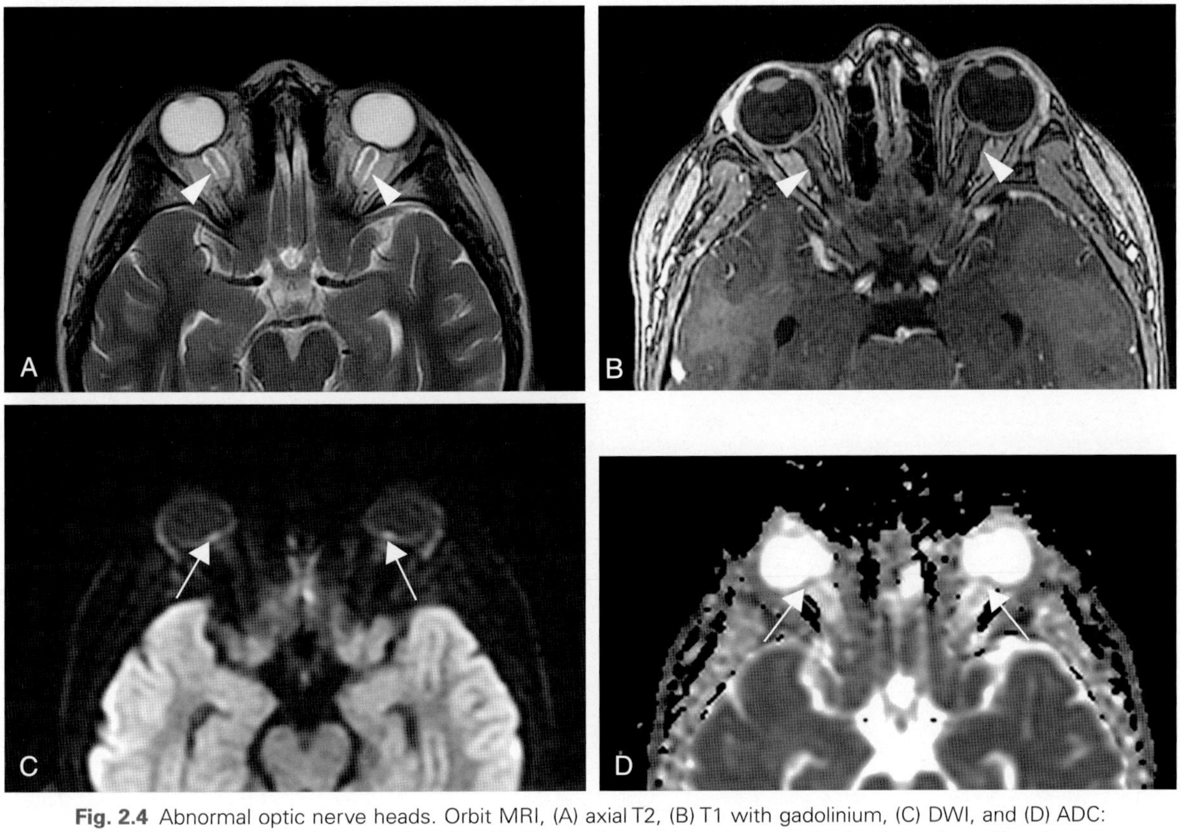

Fig. 2.4 Abnormal optic nerve heads. Orbit MRI, (A) axial T2, (B) T1 with gadolinium, (C) DWI, and (D) ADC: dilated optic nerve sheaths (*arrowheads*) with flattened posterior sclerae, optic disc inversion with enhancement and restricted diffusion (*arrows*).

REFERENCES

Dsouza S, Aylward BS, Rogers DL, Aylward SC. Presenting symptomatology and risk factors in pediatric secondary intracranial hypertension due to venous sinus thrombosis. *Pediatr Neurol.* 2019;101:53–56. https://doi.org/10.1016/j.pediatrneurol.2019.04.016.

Friedman DI, Liu GT, Digre KB. Revised diagnostic criteria for the pseudotumor cerebri syndrome in adults and children. *Neurology.* 2013;81(13):1159–1165. https://doi.org/10.1212/wnl.0b013e3182a55f17.

Hamedani AG, Witonsky KFR, Cosico M, et al. Headache characteristics in children with pseudotumor cerebri syndrome, elevated opening pressure without papilledema, and normal opening pressure: a retrospective cohort study. *Headache.* 2018;58(9):1339–1346. https://doi.org/10.1111/head.13362.

Matthews Y-Y, Dean F, Lim MJ, et al. Pseudotumor cerebri syndrome in childhood: incidence, clinical profile and risk factors in a national prospective population-based cohort study. *Arch Dis Child.* 2017;102(8):715–721. https://doi.org/10.1136/archdischild-2016-312238.

Moavero R, Sforza G, Papetti L, et al. Clinical features of pediatric idiopathic intracranial hypertension and applicability of new ICHD-3 criteria. *Front Neurol.* 2018;9. https://doi.org/10.3389/fneur.2018.00819.

Vieira D, Masruha M, Gonçalves A, et al. Idiopathic intracranial hypertension with and without papilloedema in a consecutive series of patients with chronic migraine. *Cephalalgia.* 2008;28(6):609–613. https://doi.org/10.1111/j.1468-2982.2008.01564.x.

When the Hindbrain Causes Headache

HISTORY AND PHYSICAL

A 10-year-old previously healthy girl presents with headaches for the past 6 months. Headaches occur one to two times per week, with variable duration from several minutes to a few hours. They are bilateral in location, often occipital, and of moderate intensity (6-7/10) with no clear triggers. Symptoms improve spontaneously or with ibuprofen in prolonged cases. There is no associated vomiting, nausea, photophobia, phonophobia, or aura. No antecedent fever, trauma, or toxin exposure. Psychiatric evaluation excludes anxiety and depression. Family history is negative for migraine and recurrent headaches. Physical examination is normal. Patient returns 3 months later, following an episode of laryngotracheitis. She reports intense headaches during coughing spells and Valsalva maneuvers, different from the prior headaches. At this time, the headaches are more localized to the occipital region and remain variable in duration, from very brief to 1 hour. Again, the clinical and neurological examination is normal.

DIAGNOSTIC WORKUP

MRI demonstrates dysmorphic cerebellar tonsils located 10 mm below the foramen magnum (McRae line) and cervical cord syrinx (Fig. 3.1A–C). Phase contrast study confirms CSF flow obstruction at the level of the foramen magnum, both ventrally and dorsally (Fig. 3.1D).

CLINICAL DIFFERENTIAL DIAGNOSIS

Primary cough headache
Chiari I malformation
Intracranial hypotension
Intracranial hypertension
Intracranial hemorrhage
Brain tumor

IMAGING DIFFERENTIAL DIAGNOSIS

Inferior displacement of the cerebellar tonsils can be observed in a variety of normal and pathologic conditions. Cerebellar tonsillar ectopia refers to normal morphology but low positioning of the tonsils below the skull base. Though the normal measurements vary with age, most cases lie within approximately 5 mm of the basion-opisthion or McRae line (Fig. 3.2), with the normal spectrum varying by age.

Chiari I malformation refers to a developmental posterior fossa anomaly with descent and dysplasia of the cerebellar vermis and tonsils, creating a pointed appearance. In severe cases, there can be mass effect on the brainstem with a dorsal cervicomedullary kink. Simple Chiari I malformations are amenable to surgical decompression with suboccipital craniectomy. Complex Chiari I malformations are associated with additional bony abnormalities such as clival hypoplasia (Fig. 3.3), platybasia, craniosynostosis (Fig. 3.4), and odontoid variants (Figs. 3.5 and 3.6), which can affect the surgical approach.

CSF pressure disorders, including both intracranial hypotension and intracranial hypertension, can present with low-lying cerebellar tonsils (Fig. 3.7). Intracranial mass effect from hydrocephalus (Fig. 3.8), hemorrhage, or tumor (Fig. 3.9) can also cause the cerebellum to herniate inferiorly.

In all cases of cerebellar abnormalities, CSF flow through the craniocervical junction can be impaired with obliteration of subarachnoid spaces. Sagittal high-resolution volumetric T2 sequences or phase-contrast imaging to evaluate CSF flow are helpful. When CSF obstruction is present, a syrinx (fluid collection) may develop in the spinal cord, usually in the cervical region (Fig. 3.1C). Some

(Text continues on p. 21)

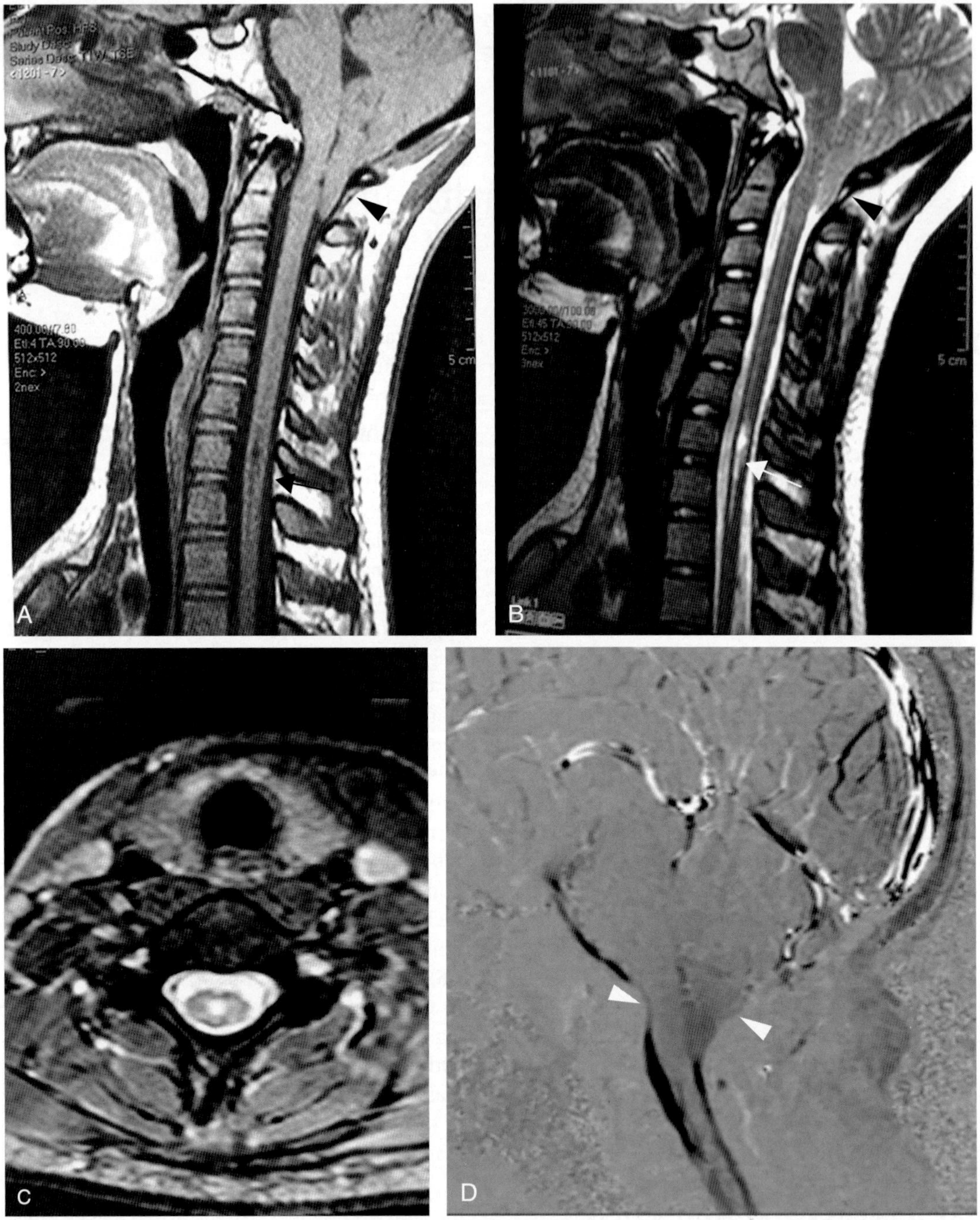

Fig. 3.1 Chiari I malformation with cervical cord syrinx. (A) Craniocervical junction MRI, (B) sagittal T1 and T2: dysmorphic cerebellar vermis and tonsils located 10 mm below skull base (*arrowheads*), with cervical cord syrinx from C7 to T1 (*arrows*). (C) Axial T2 shows cervical cord syrinx. (D) Sagittal phase contrast shows obstructed ventral and dorsal CSF flow through the craniocervical junction (*arrowheads*). *CSF*, Cerebrospinal fluid.

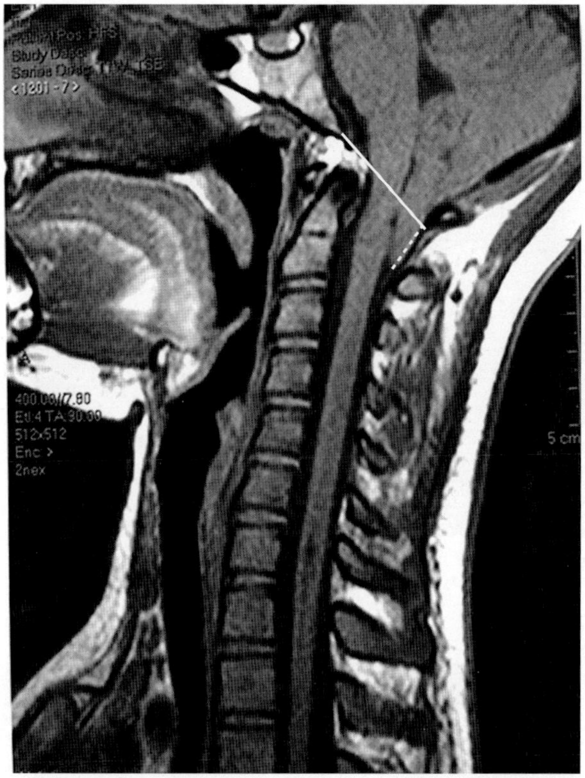

Fig. 3.2 McRae line. Craniocervical junction MRI, sagittal T1 shows tonsillar descent (*dotted line*) below the basion-opisthion line (*solid line*) connecting the anterior and posterior margins of the foramen magnum.

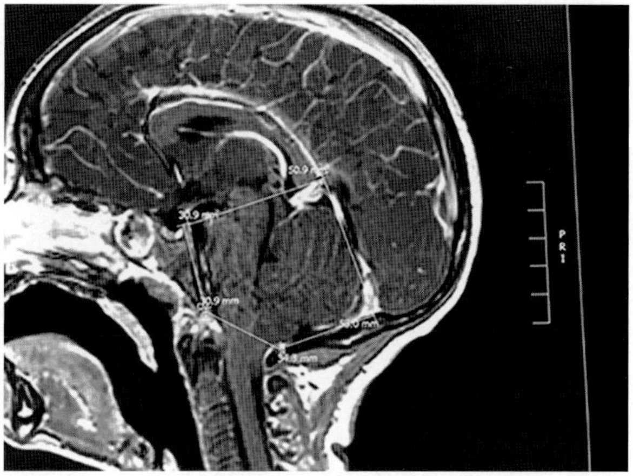

Fig. 3.3 Chiari I malformation secondary to clival hypoplasia. Brain MRI, sagittal T1 with gadolinium shows Chiari I malformation. The posterior fossa pentagon connecting the clivus, McRae line, supraocciput, tentorium, and tentorium-clivus line (*lines*) shows a foreshortened and vertically oriented clivus.

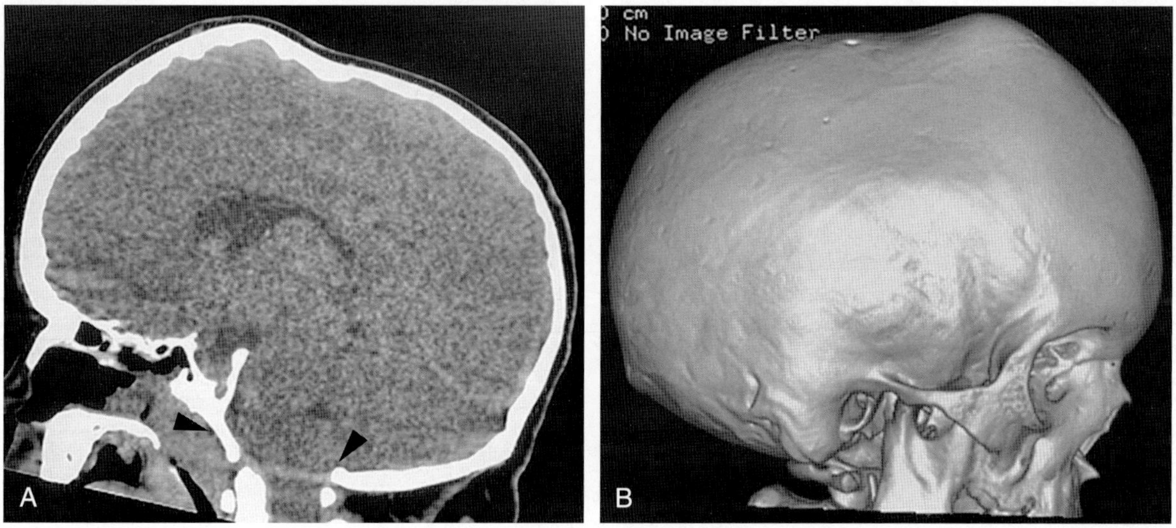

Fig. 3.4 Syndromic craniosynostosis due to Apert syndrome. Head CT, sagittal (A), and 3D reconstruction (B) show multisuture craniosynostosis with turribrachycephaly, skull base hypoplasia, decreased posterior fossa volume, and cerebellar crowding (*arrowhead*). Brain MRI, sagittal T1 (C) and T2 (D) show posterior fossa hypoplasia and crowding of the craniocervical junction (*arrows*).

Continued

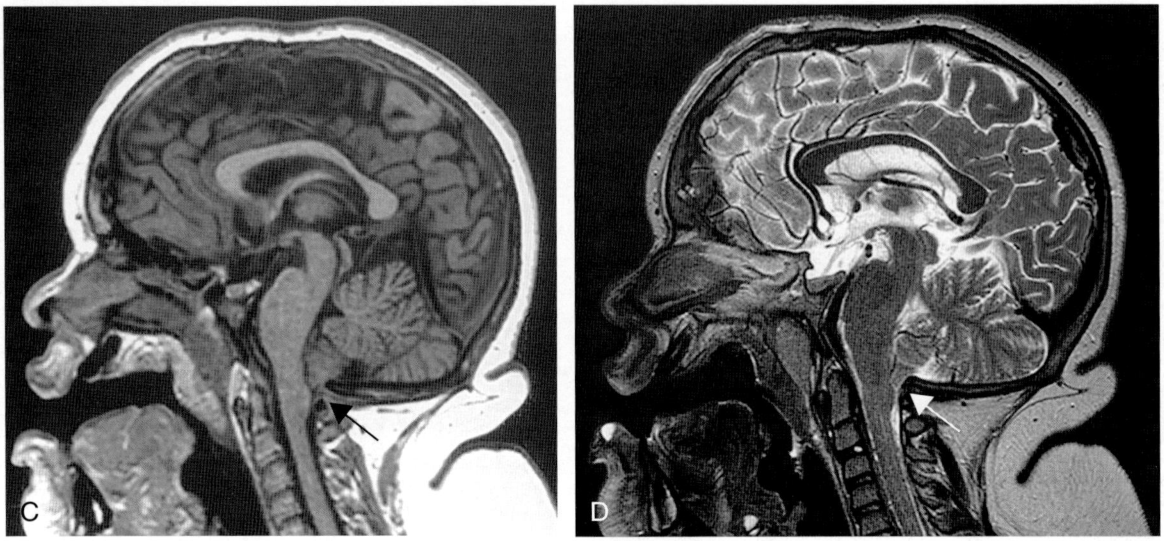

Fig. 3.4 cont'd

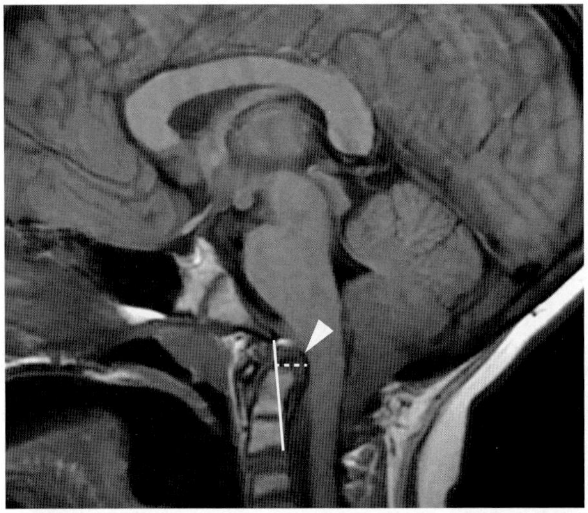

Fig. 3.5 Complex Chiari I with platybasia and odontoid retroversion. Brain MRI, sagittal T1 shows platybasia and odontoid retroversion (*arrowhead*) more than 9 mm behind the pBC2 line (maximum perpendicular distance from the line of the basion to the infero-posterior point of the vertebral body of C2) (*dotted and solid lines*). There is secondary posterior fossa crowding with dysmorphic pointed cerebellar tonsils.

Fig. 3.6 Complex Chiari I with platybasia and basilar invagination. Craniocervical junction MRI, sagittal T2 shows platybasia with Wackenheim clivus angle of 100 degrees (*solid lines*). Basilar invagination (*arrow*) extends more than 3 mm above Chamberlain line from the back of hard palate to opisthion (*dotted lines*). There is a secondary Chiari I malformation with pointed cerebellar tonsils and cervical cord presyrinx (*arrowhead*).

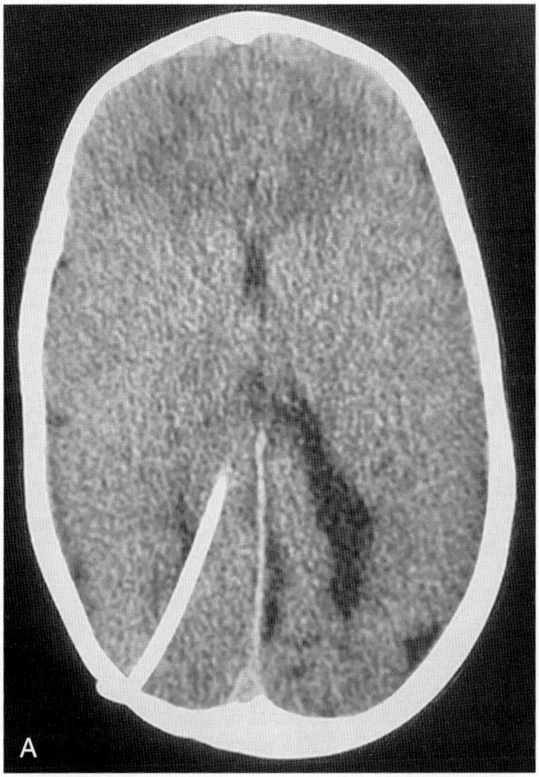

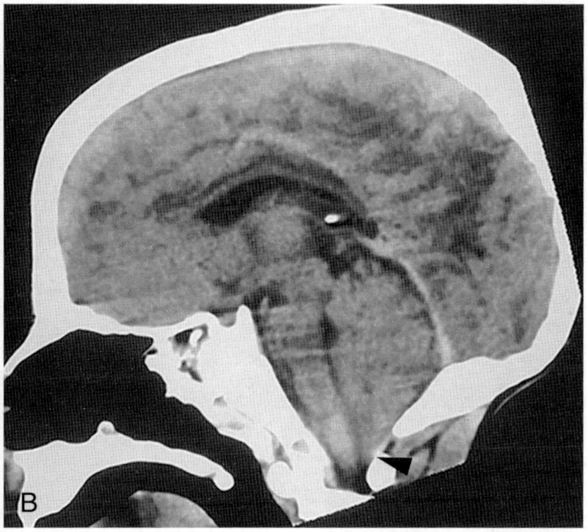

Fig. 3.7 Overshunting with slit ventricle syndrome. Head CT, axial (A), shows shunted hydrocephalus with partial collapse of the lateral ventricles. Sagittal view (B) shows low-lying cerebellar tonsils and brainstem with obliteration of subarachnoid spaces at the foramen magnum (*arrowhead*).

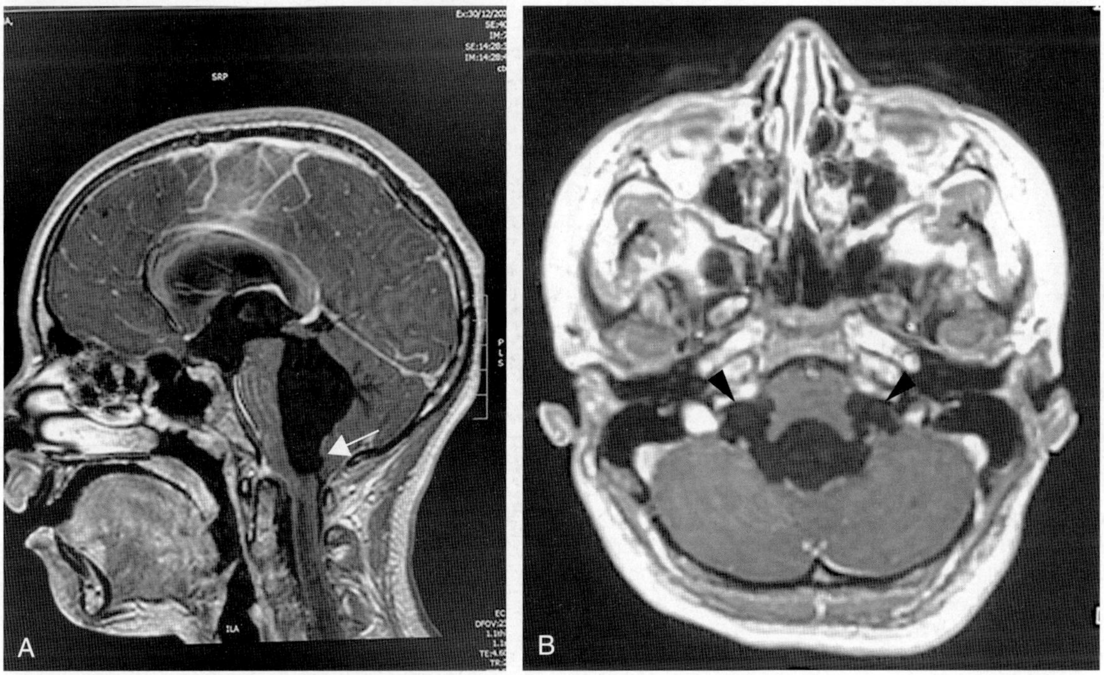

Fig. 3.8 Communicating hydrocephalus. Brain MRI, sagittal (A) and axial (B) T1 with gadolinium show tetraventricular hydrocephalus with ballooned fourth ventricle (*arrow*) and foramina of Luschka diverticulae (*arrowheads*). There is secondary compression of the cerebellar vermis and hemispheres with descent of the cerebellar tonsils, obstruction of the foramen magnum, and cervical cord syrinx.

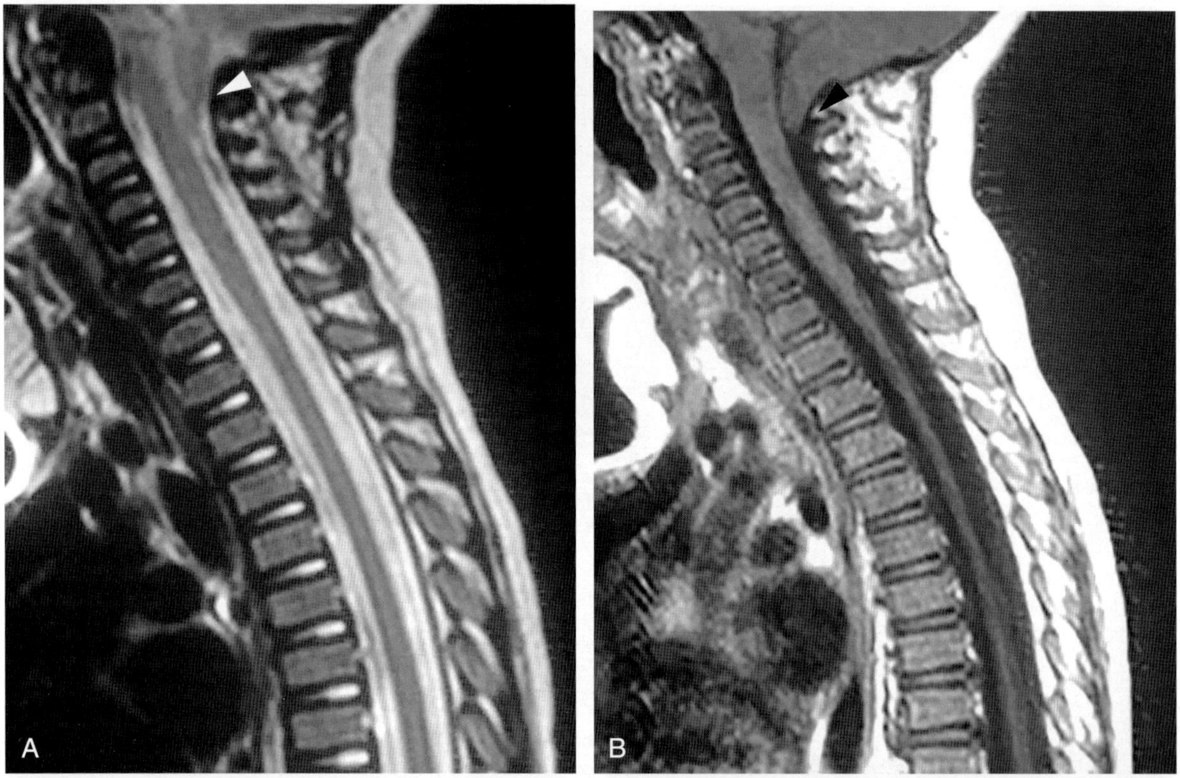

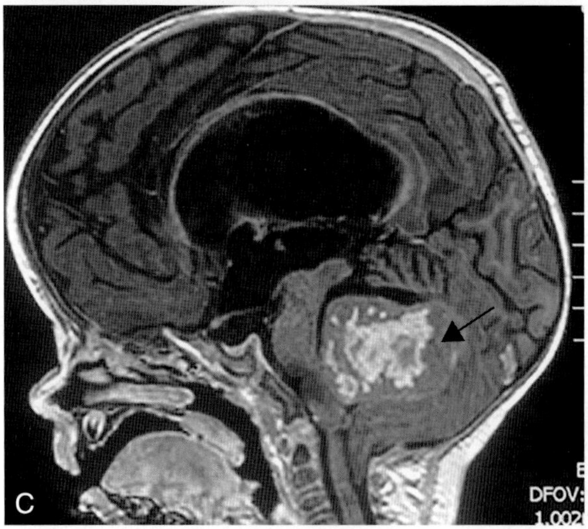

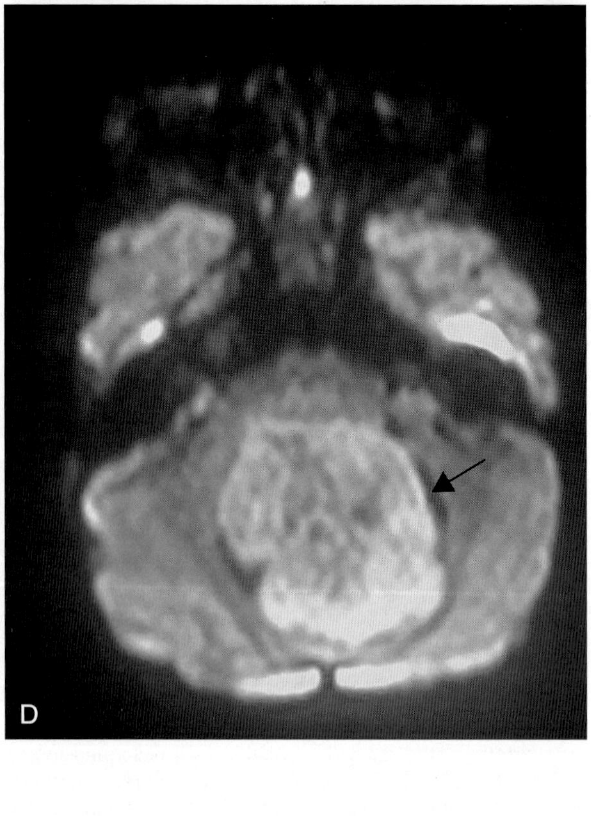

Fig. 3.9 Group 3 medulloblastoma. Cervical spine MRI, sagittal T2 (A) and T1 (B) show posterior fossa mass effect with inferior cerebellar herniation and obliteration of the foramen magnum (*arrowheads*). Brain MRI, sagittal T1 with gadolinium (C), and axial DWI (D) show a fourth ventricular mass with heterogeneous contrast enhancement and diffusion restriction (*arrows*) causing obstructive hydrocephalus. *DWI*, Diffusion weighted imaging.

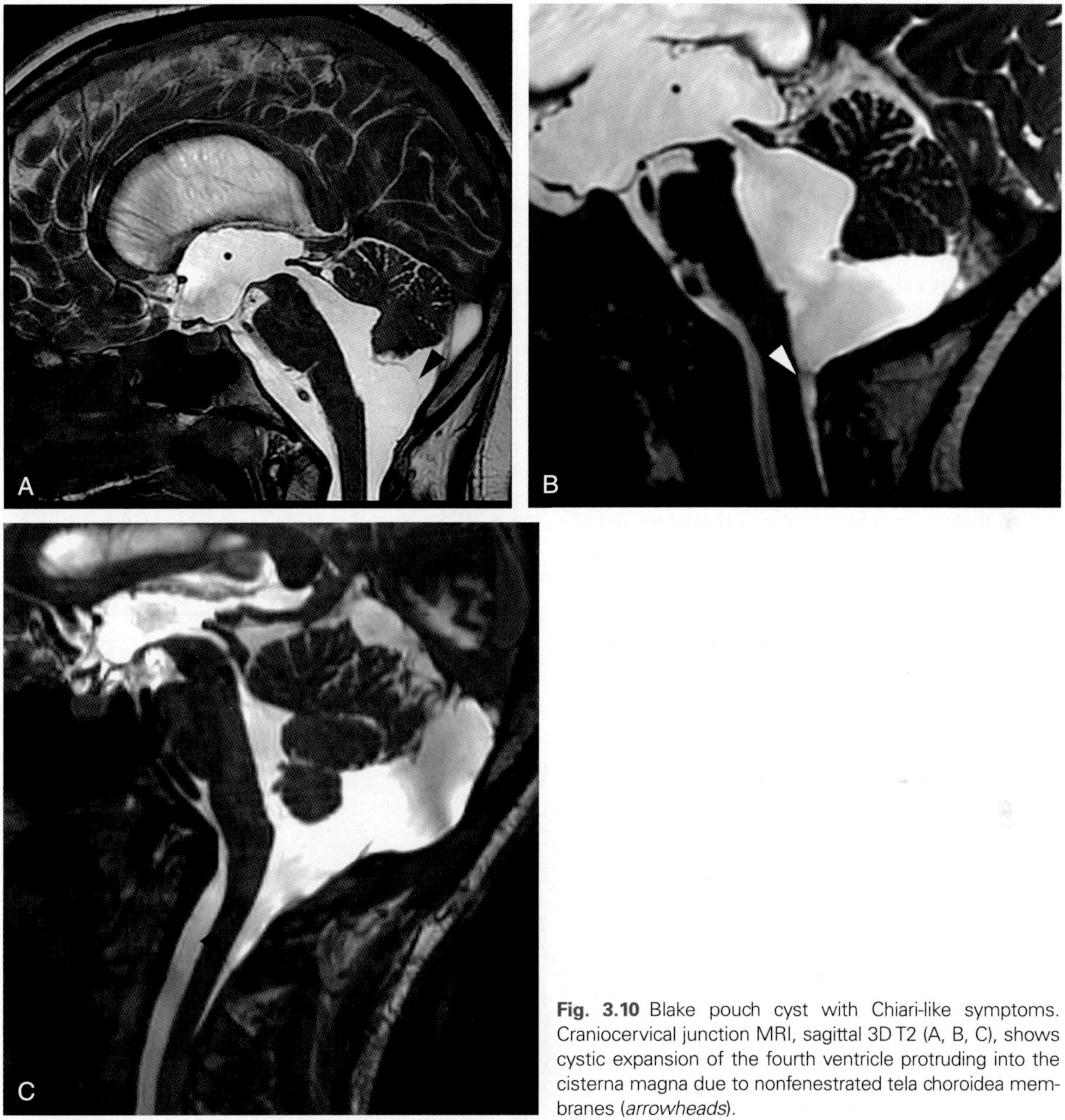

Fig. 3.10 Blake pouch cyst with Chiari-like symptoms. Craniocervical junction MRI, sagittal 3D T2 (A, B, C), shows cystic expansion of the fourth ventricle protruding into the cisterna magna due to nonfenestrated tela choroidea membranes (*arrowheads*).

disorders can mimic Chiari I–like symptoms, such as Blake pouch cyst, in which cystic expansion of the nonfenestrated fourth ventricle protrudes into the cisterna magna (Fig. 3.10).

FINAL DIAGNOSIS

Chiari I malformation.

DISCUSSION

Chiari malformations reflect a wide spectrum of entities with very different etiologies, pathophysiology, and clinical features. The various subtypes have in common the presence of developmental posterior fossa deformities affecting the brainstem and cerebellum. The widespread use of brain MRI has led to increased frequency of identification, from 1% to 3.6%. Of note, diagnosis is clinical, and the MRI findings can be incidental diagnosis without associated symptoms in up to 50% of cases.

Chiari II and III malformations are etiologically distinct and associated with open spinal dysraphisms: lumbosacral myelomeningocele and cervicooccipital meningocele, respectively. In Chiari II and III, additional brain abnormalities result from developmentally low CSF pressures with resultant biomechanical effects. These can include callosal dysgenesis, stenogyria, polymicrogyria, periventricular heterotopia, massa intermedia enlargement, tectal beaking, and upward and downward cerebellar herniation.

Symptoms are highly variable, ranging from headache and neck pain to signs of brainstem compression, cerebellar syndrome, and myelopathy. Approximately 25% of Chiari 1 patients develop syrinx, a fluid collection in the spinal cord that can produce motor and sensory deficits and urinary incontinence. Scoliosis is another frequent complication, especially in patients with syrinx.

CLINICAL RED FLAGS

- Headache caused by coughing or Valsalva maneuvers.
- Occipital or suboccipital headache.
- Cranial nerve or spinal cord involvement.
- Early-onset swallowing disorders.
- Symptoms of intracranial hypertension: waking at night, projectile vomiting, diplopia, papilledema.

IMAGING RED FLAGS

- In children, Chiari I malformation can sometimes resolve spontaneously with growth (Fig. 3.11).
- Following surgical decompression, imaging is performed to confirm normalization of tonsillar morphology, CSF flow obstruction, and syrinx. In some cases the obstruction persists after suboccipital decompression (Fig. 3.12).
- In equivocal cases, high-resolution imaging of the posterior fossa can be used to exclude or detect Chiari I malformation.

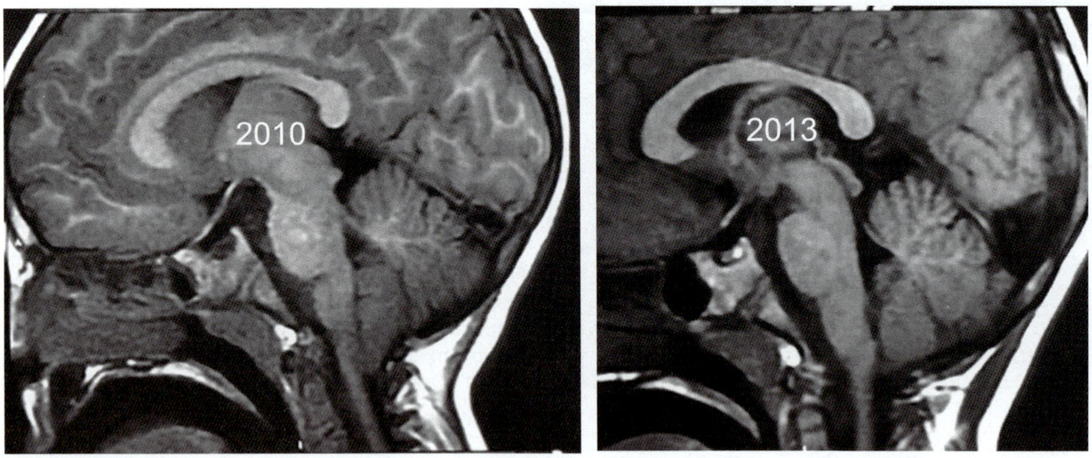

Fig. 3.11 Spontaneous temporal resolution of Chiari I. Brain MRI, sagittal T1 shows spontaneous resolution of posterior fossa crowding and cerebellar tonsillar deformity.

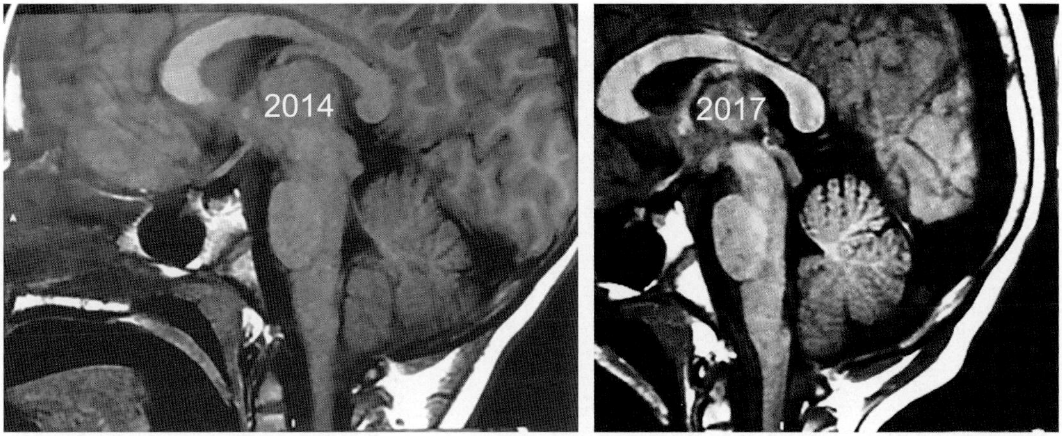

Fig. 3.11 cont'd

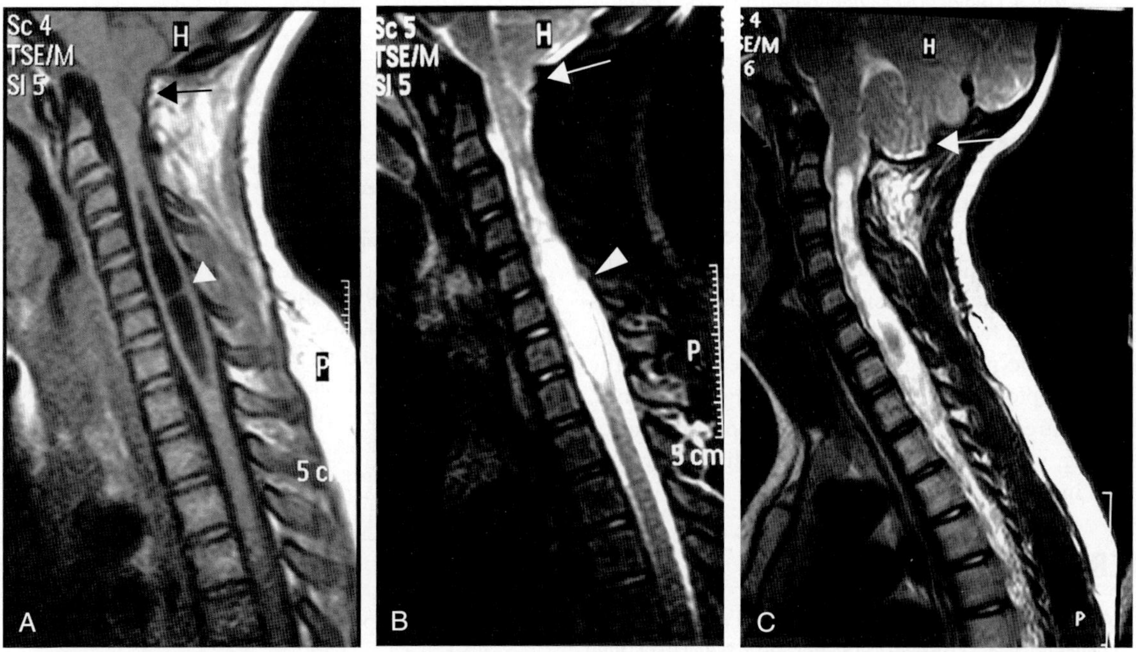

Fig. 3.12 Postoperative complications of Chiari I decompression. Cervical spine MRI, sagittal T1 (A) and STIR (B) show dysmorphic pointed cerebellar tonsils (*arrows*) below the skull base with effaced subarachnoid spaces and cervical cord syrinx (*arrowheads*). Postoperative MRI, sagittal T2 of the cervical spine (C) and

Continued

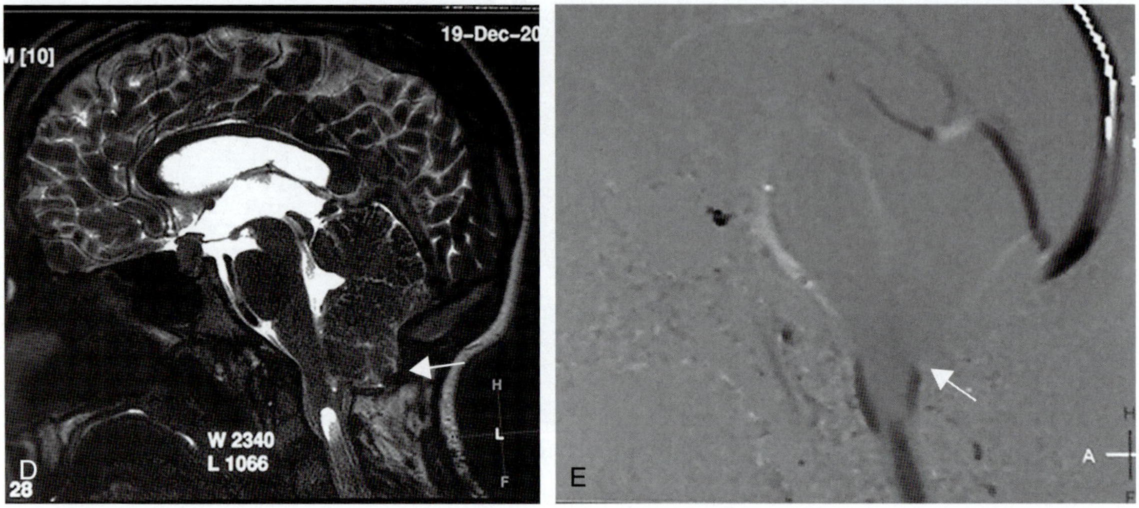

Fig. 3.12 cont'd brain (D) show suboccipital craniectomy with persistent herniation of the cerebellum (*arrow*) and cord syrinx. Sagittal phase-contrast (E) shows continued obstruction of CSF flow through the dorsal craniocervical junction (*arrow*). *CSF*, Cerebrospinal fluid; *STIR*, short tau inversion recovery.

CONCLUSIONS

Episodic suboccipital headaches that increase with cough or Valsalva maneuvers should raise clinical suspicion for Chiari malformation. Widespread use of MRI in children has made it possible to identify the characteristic imaging features of this disorder. It is the role of the pediatric neurologist to determine whether the patient's symptoms are related to the imaging findings. Chiari features on imaging may be asymptomatic or self-resolve with age; therefore careful clinical evaluation and imaging follow-up are crucial.

REFERENCES

Aiken AH, Hoots JA, Saindane AM, Hudgins PA. Incidence of cerebellar tonsillar ectopia in idiopathic intracranial hypertension: a mimic of the Chiari I malformation. *Am J Neuroradiol.* 2012;33(10):1901–1906. https://doi.org/10.3174/ajnr.a3068.

Bear JJ, Gelfand AA, Goadsby PJ, Bass N. Occipital headaches and neuroimaging in children. *Neurology.* 2017;89(5):469–474. https://doi.org/10.1212/wnl.0000000000004186.

Ciaramitaro P, Ferraris M, Massaro F, Garbossa D. Clinical diagnosis—part I: what is really caused by Chiari I. *Childs Nerv Syst.* 2019;35(10):1673–1679. https://doi.org/10.1007/s00381-019-04206-z.

Di Rocco C. Should we stop using the term "malformation" for Chiari type I? *Childs Nerv Syst.* 2019;35(10):1649–1650. https://doi.org/10.1007/s00381-019-04311-z.

Irwin SL, Gelfand AA. Occipital headaches and neuroimaging in children. *Curr Pain Headache Rep.* 2018;22(9). https://doi.org/10.1007/s11916-018-0712-6.

Sadler B, Kuensting T, Strahle J, et al. Prevalence and impact of underlying diagnosis and comorbidities on Chiari 1 malformation. *Pediatr Neurol.* 2020;106:32–37. https://doi.org/10.1016/j.pediatrneurol.2019.12.005.

Case 4

The Brain Also Faints

HISTORY AND PHYSICAL

A 16-year-old right-handed girl presents with recurrent headaches intensifying over the past month. Since 13 years of age, she has experienced monthly headaches of variable duration (2–8 hours). She describes these as bifrontal with some very intense pulsatile episodes, up to 8/10 severity but mostly mild (3–4/10) and not interfering with her activities of daily living. Analgesics usually address the pain. She reports associated photophobia but never phonophobia. She also denies nausea, vomiting, abdominal pain, and changes with posture or Valsalva maneuver.

During the last month, her headaches have become frequent and almost daily, frontal and occipital in location, of moderate intensity or sometimes greater. This is accompanied by nausea but not vomiting and shows a decreased response to analgesics. She denies any visual changes, difficulty eating, or other symptoms. Her headache becomes more intense after exercising in dance class with intense cephalic rotation: "my long hair looks like the blades of a windmill." She also reports tinnitus and cervical pain, with relief when lying down and worsening when standing up. She is currently in her second year of high school with excellent school performance and has attended dancing school since she was 12 years old. She has no history of fever, trauma, or toxic exposures. No symptoms of depression or anxiety. No relevant personal or family history.

Clinical examination shows normal vital signs and body measurements. Patient has a marfanoid appearance, with mild discomfort in the neck and trapezius muscles on palpation, as well as joint hyperlaxity. Neurological examination shows moderate neck stiffness and mild incoordination in heel-toe walking. Headache clearly improves when placed in the Trendelenburg position.

DIAGNOSTIC WORKUP

Brain MRI images with contrast showed bilateral subdural hygromas and smooth linear dural enhancement, engorged pituitary gland, decreased mammillary-pontine distance, low-lying posterior fossa structures with flattening of the basis pontis against the clivus and low-lying cerebellar tonsils (Fig. 4.1).

Next, a spinal MRI was performed in search of a fistula. The lumbar spine showed a left perineural diverticulum with cerebrospinal fluid (CSF) fistula toward the paraspinal veins and paravertebral plexuses (Fig. 4.2). Based on the imaging findings, no lumbar puncture was performed, since this could worsen the symptoms by further reducing the CSF volume.

CLINICAL DIFFERENTIAL DIAGNOSES

Primary headache, including tension headache and migraine.

Postural orthostatic tachycardia syndrome is an intolerance to orthostasis with a measured increase in heart rate by at least 30 beats per minute (bpm) compared to resting rate, or a rate greater than 120 bpm with orthostasis. Headache may be associated with other symptoms: dizziness, blurred vision, presyncope-syncope chest pain or discomfort, anxiety, flushing, fatigue, dyspnea, heat intolerance, feeling cold, excessive sweating, nausea, instability, noise sensitivity, light sensitivity, and exercise intolerance.

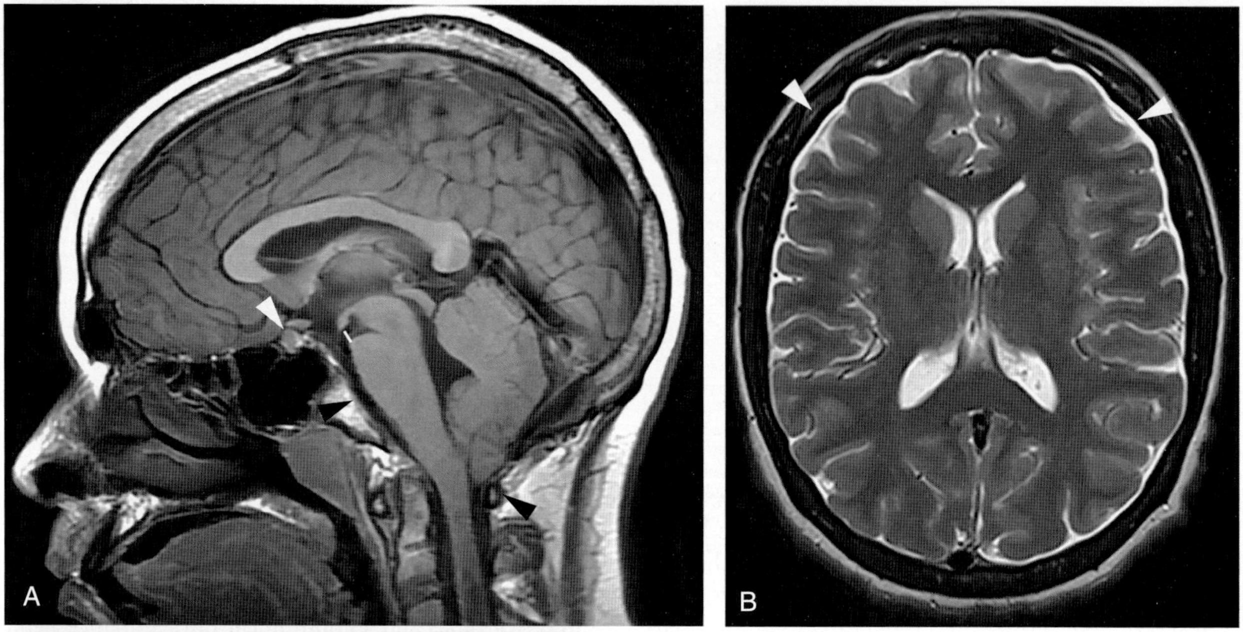

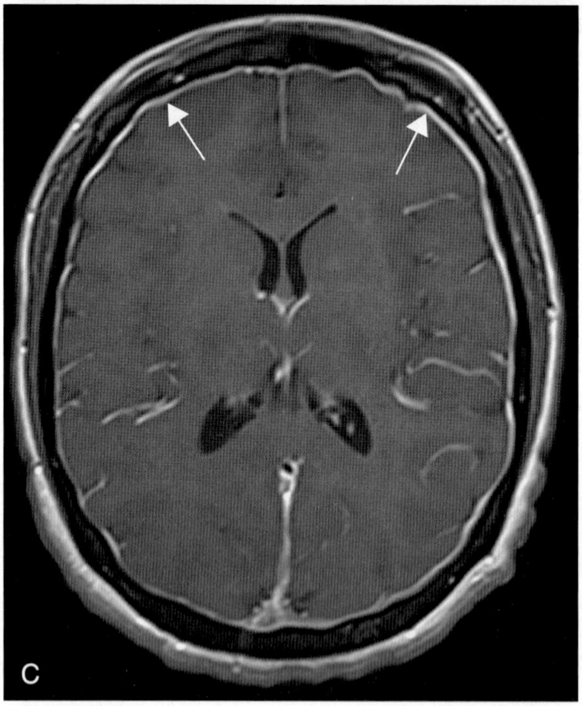

Fig. 4.1 CSF hypotension. Brain MRI, (A) sagittal T1 shows mild engorgement of the pituitary gland (*white arrowhead*), decreased mammillary-pontine distance (*line*), descent of the posterior fossa structures with flattening of the basis pontis against the clivus and cerebellar tonsillar ectopia (*black arrowheads*). (B) Axial T2 and (C) T1 with gadolinium show thin subdural hygromas (*arrowheads*) and smooth linear dural enhancement (*arrows*). *CSF*, Cerebrospinal fluid.

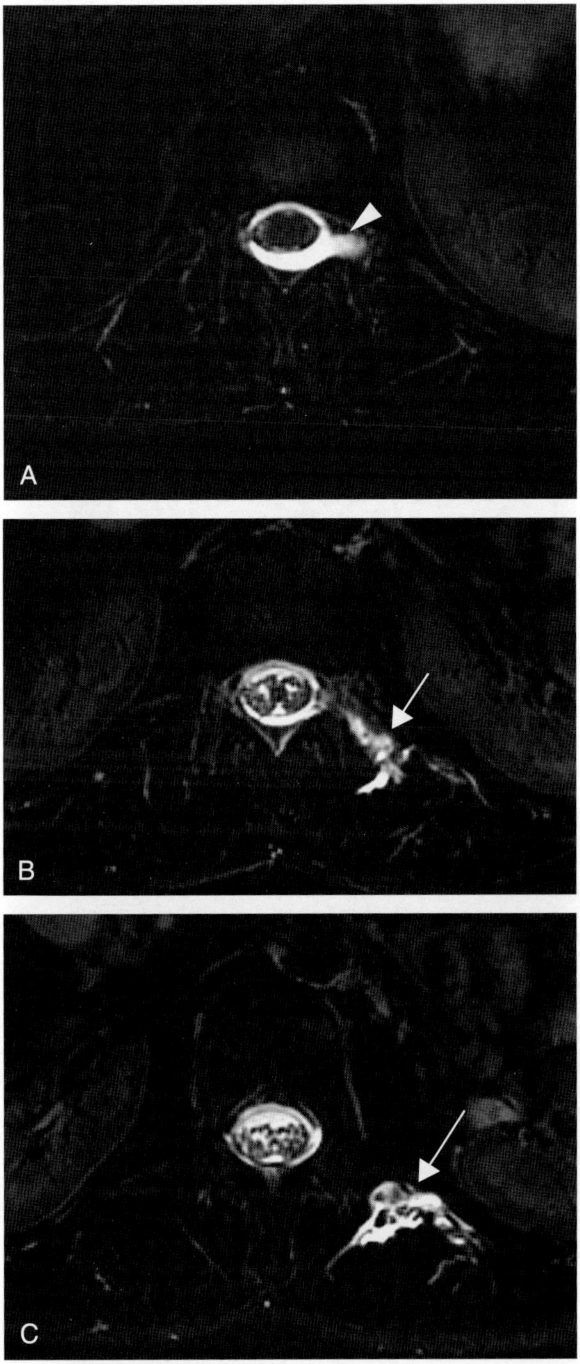

Fig. 4.2 Cerebrospinal fluid—venous fistula. Lumbar spine MRI, axial T2 sequence with fat suppression, shows (A) left perineural diverticulum (*arrowhead*) with (B and C) fistulization to paraspinal veins and paravertebral plexuses (*arrows*).

IMAGING DIFFERENTIAL DIAGNOSES

Diffuse pachymeningeal enhancement: craniotomy, infection, inflammation, post-LP.

Unilateral or asymmetric dural enhancement: idiopathic hypertrophic pachymeningitis (Fig. 4.3).

Enlarged pituitary gland: hormonal variation (prepubertal age and pregnancy), pathological causes (adenomas, hyperplasia, hypophysitis).

Bilateral subdural collections: abusive head trauma with hematomas of varying ages, bridging vein injury, retinal hemorrhages (Fig. 4.4).

FINAL DIAGNOSIS

Spontaneous intracranial hypotension due to CSF-venous fistula.

DISCUSSION

Spontaneous intracranial hypotension (SIH) is a rare and underdiagnosed cause of headache in children and adolescents and should be considered a differential diagnosis for headache. A typical clinical feature is worsening when sitting or standing and improvement with lying down. Other symptoms may include nausea, tinnitus, photophobia, and neck pain. More severe manifestations can include disturbance of consciousness, seizures, personality changes, and diplopia. Based on the ICHD criteria, opening pressure of LP should be less than 6 cm H_2O of water while sitting for definitive diagnosis, but pressures may be normal or variable even in the same patient. If imaging features are characteristic, there is no need to confirm with CSF pressures.

Although imaging is normal in up to 20% of cases, distinctive features of low CSF pressure include "brain sag" with low-lying brainstem, cerebellar tonsils, splenium, and optic chiasm; decreased ventricular volumes; subdural collections; pachymeningeal thickening; engorged pituitary gland; and distended venous sinuses.

High-resolution imaging of the neuraxis with contrast and fat-suppressed sequences can help identify extradural CSF collections and/or fistulas, particularly in the presence of a large-volume (fast) leak. The presence of dural ectasia, diverticula, or perineural cysts (Fig. 4.5), even without localization of an obvious fistula,

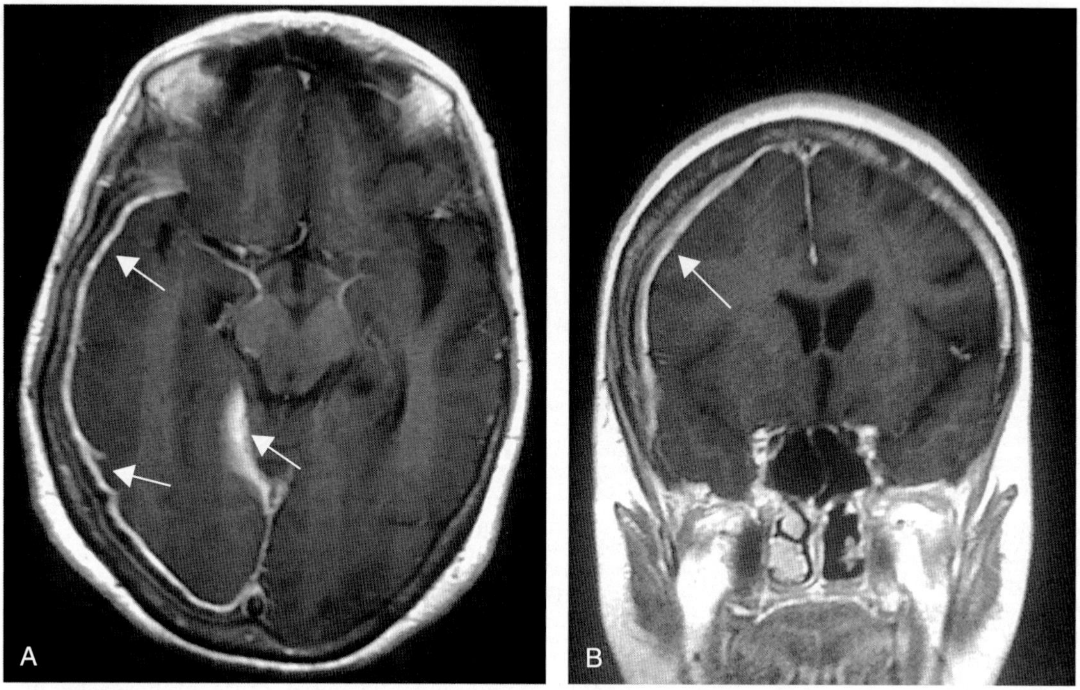

Fig. 4.3 Idiopathic hypertrophic pachymeningitis. Brain MRI, (A) axial and (B) coronal T1 with gadolinium show smooth pachymeningeal thickening and enhancement along the right posterior cerebral hemisphere and tentorium cerebelli (*arrows*).

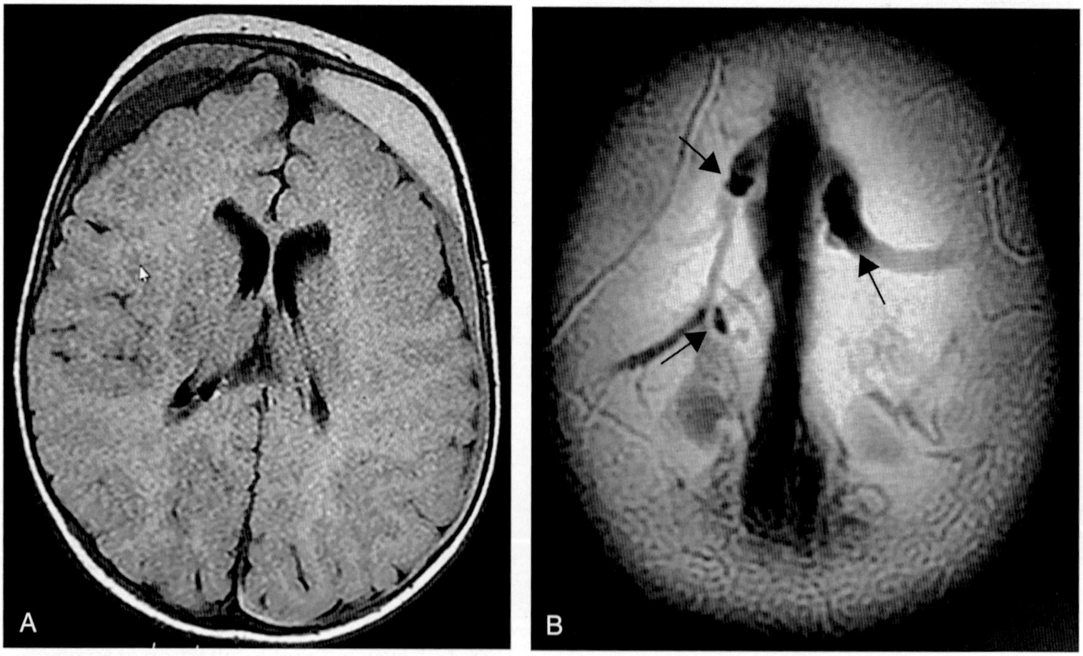

Fig. 4.4 Abusive head trauma. Brain MRI, (A) axial T1 shows bifrontal subdural collections of varying intensities. (B) Axial T2-weighted imaging shows irregular and thrombosed bridging veins draining into the superior sagittal sinus (*arrows*). (C) Orbit MRI, axial T2 shows small bilateral retinal hemorrhages (*arrowheads*).

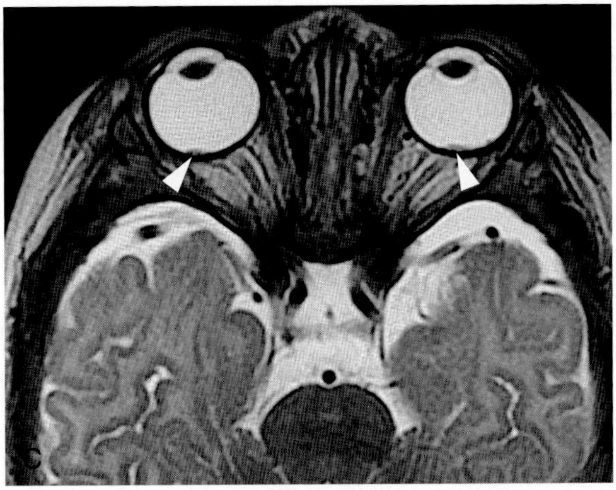

Fig. 4.4 cont'd

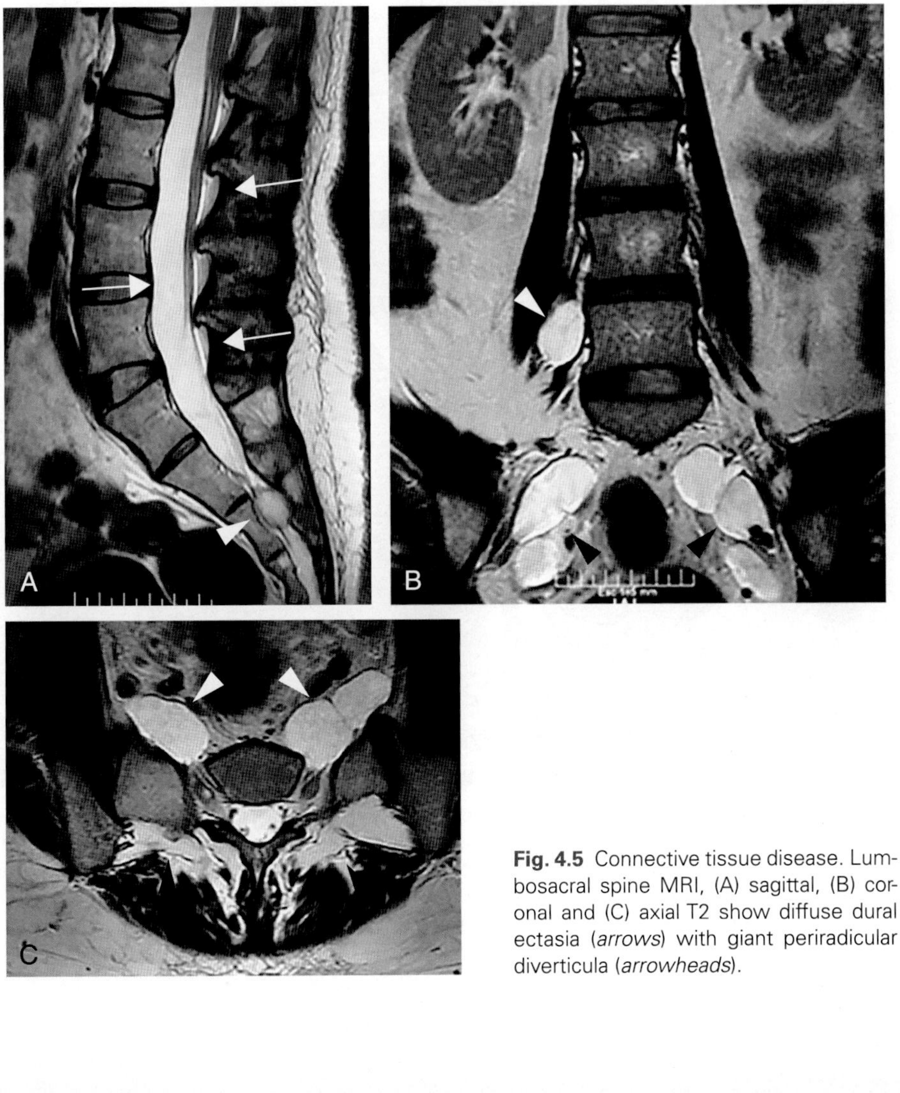

Fig. 4.5 Connective tissue disease. Lumbosacral spine MRI, (A) sagittal, (B) coronal and (C) axial T2 show diffuse dural ectasia (*arrows*) with giant periradicular diverticula (*arrowheads*).

suggests the diagnosis of CSF hypotension due to caudal CSF accumulation or occult fistula. CSF fistulas at the skull base are not necessarily a cause of SIH; continue searching for larger-volume CSF leaks in the remainder of the neuraxis.

Small-volume (slow) leaks may be negative on conventional imaging and require more invasive procedures such as digital subtraction myelography, dynamic CT myelography, or MRI with intrathecal gadolinium injection. Treatment may be medical and/or surgical, depending on the location and severity of the fistula.

Secondary intracranial hypotension can be caused by several etiologies. Connective tissue disorders such as Marfan syndrome, Ehlers-Danlos syndrome, neurofibromatosis type 1, and meningeal diverticula are common predisposing causes. Hypotensive headaches can be experienced for several days following an LP. Abrupt cephalic movements related to ligamentous laxity can also be associated.

CLINICAL RED FLAGS

- Patient with primary headache who presents with changes in frequency and/or intensity.
- Clear orthostatic symptoms and postural headache changes (increasing when standing, decreasing or absent when lying down).
- History of abrupt cervicocephalic movements, hyperlaxity, and/or marfanoid appearance.

IMAGING RED FLAGS

- When a patient with intracranial hypotension shows abrupt changes in headache or neurologic signs, complications such as venous sinus thrombosis should be considered.
- Distinction of primary from secondary intracranial hypotension (Fig. 4.6) relies on identification of a CSF leak or fistula in the brain (Fig. 4.7) or spine. In spine MRI studies, it is common to find mild dorsal edema in the upper cervical spine (Fig. 4.8), which is a false localizing sign due to lower anatomical containment in this region.

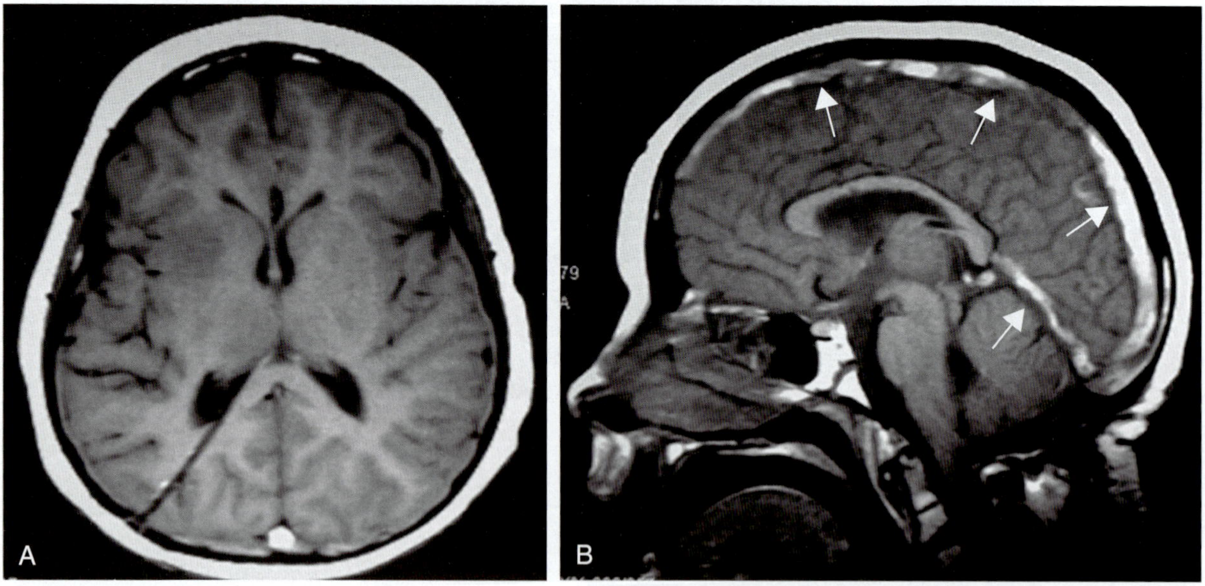

Fig. 4.6 Secondary intracranial hypotension from overshunting. Brain MRI, (A) axial T1 showing shunted hydrocephalus. (B) Sagittal T1 shows diffusely hyperintense signal from thrombus in the superior sagittal and straight sinuses (*arrows*). (C) Axial FLAIR shows bilateral subdural fluid collections and venous infarcts in the right thalamus and external capsule (*arrowheads*). (D) Coronal MR venography shows absent flow signal in the superior sagittal, straight, and transverse sinuses with collateral drainage by extracranial veins. *FLAIR*, Fluid-attenuated inversion recovery.

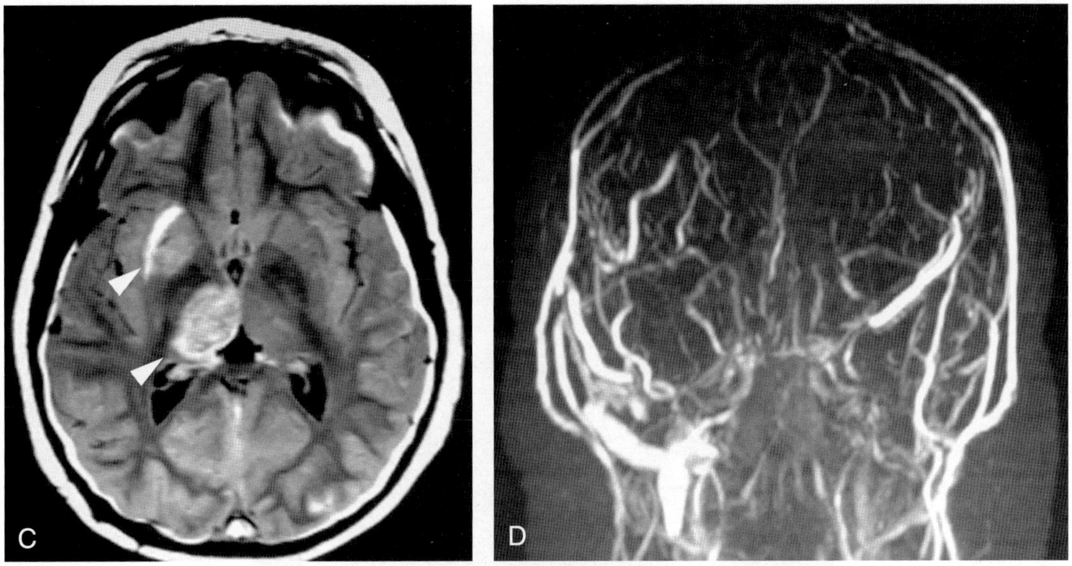

Fig. 4.6 cont'd

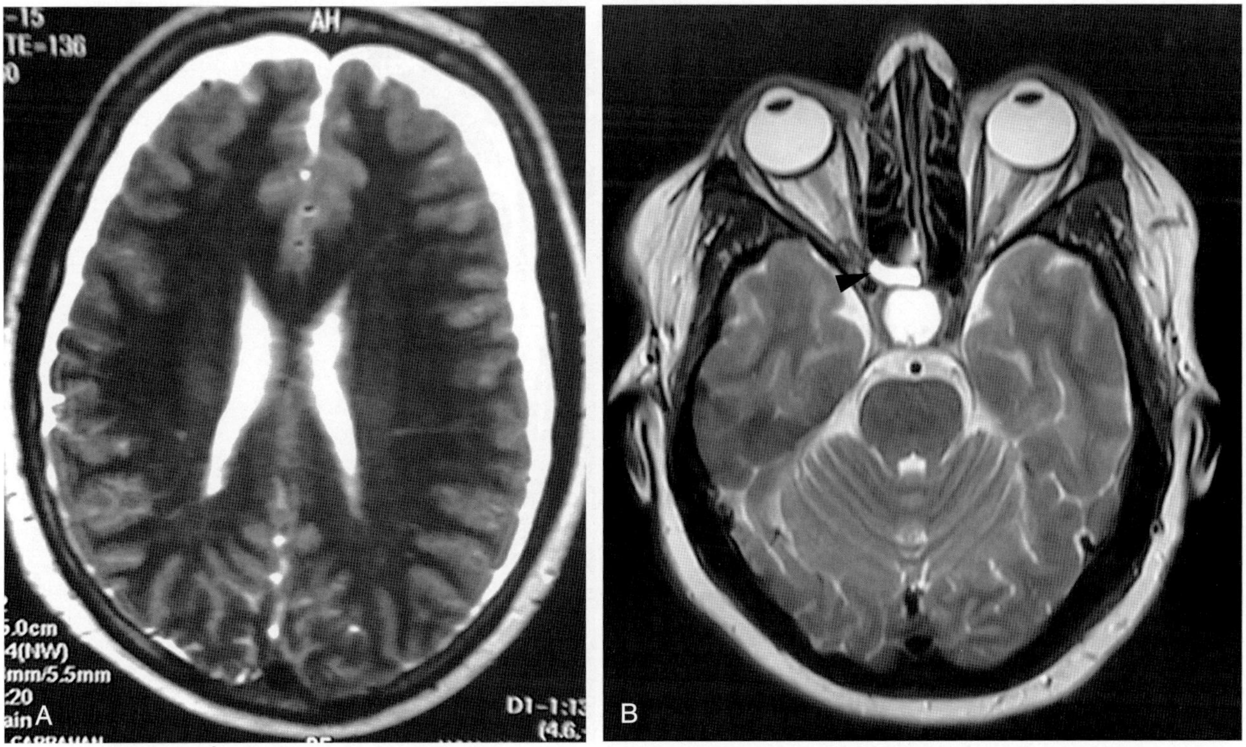

Fig. 4.7 Secondary intracranial hypotension with CSF leak in sphenoid sinus. Brain MRI, (A and B) axial T2 shows bilateral subdural fluid collections and partially empty sella with CSF leakage into the right sphenoid sinus (*arrowhead*). (C) Coronal T1 with gadolinium shows diffuse smooth pachymeningeal enhancement (*arrows*). *CSF*, Cerebrospinal fluid.

Continued

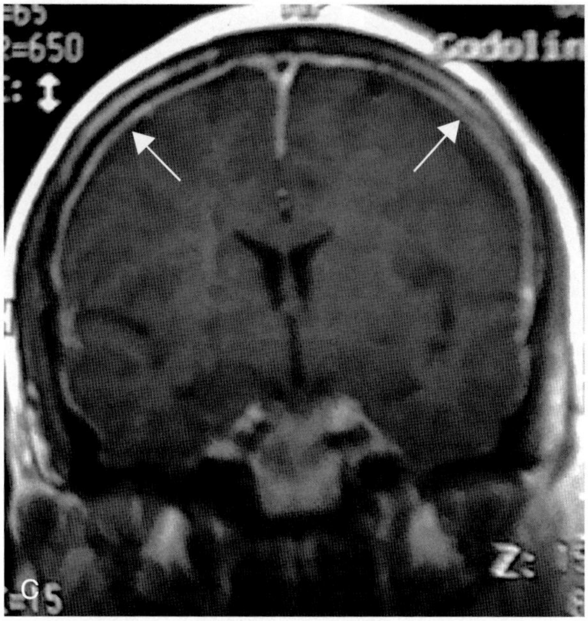

Fig. 4.7 cont'd

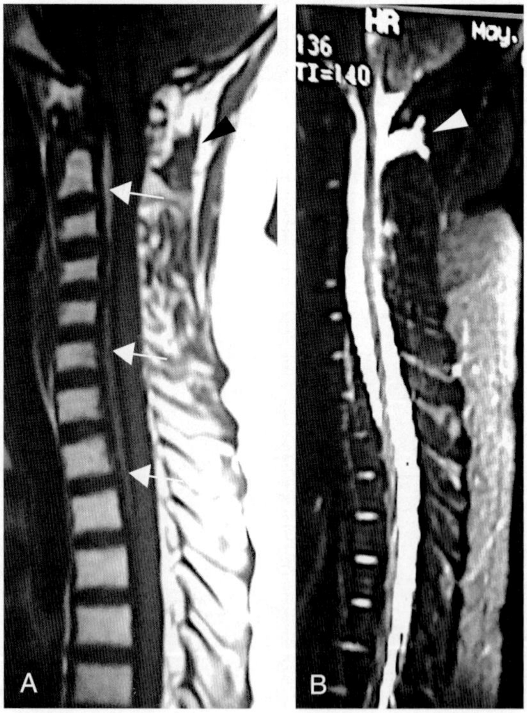

Fig. 4.8 Spinal CSF leak with false localizing sign at C1-C2. Cervicothoracic spine MRI, (A) sagittal T1 and (B) STIR show ventral epidural fluid (*arrows*) and edema between spinous processes of C1 and C2 (*arrowheads*). *CSF*, Cerebrospinal fluid; *STIR*, short tau inversion recovery.

CONCLUSIONS

Children or adolescents with headache who show orthostatic changes, possibly with a history of trauma or hyperlaxity, should be evaluated for intracranial hypotension syndrome. MRI may show signs of CSF hypotension, but identifying the precise site of leakage can be challenging due to the diverse potential spaces and mechanisms.

REFERENCES

Harder S, Griebel RW, Lemire EG, Kriegler S, Gitlin J, Seshia SS. Spinal CSF leaks: mimicker of primary headache disorder in a child. *Can J Neurol Sci*. 2012;39(3):388–392. https://doi.org/10.1017/s0317167100013573.

Johnson JN, Mack KJ, Kuntz NL, Brands CK, Porter CJ, Fischer PR. Postural orthostatic tachycardia syndrome: a clinical review. *Pediatr Neurol*. 2010;42(2):77–85. https://doi.org/10.1016/j.pediatrneurol.2009.07.002.

Prats Viñas JM, García Ribes A, Suinaga Errasti I. Hipotensión intracraneal espontánea como causa de cefalea persistente en un caso pediátrico. *Rev Neurol*. 2011;53(5):317–318. https://doi.org/10.33588/rn.5305.2011149.

Schievink WI, Maya MM, Louy C, Moser FG, Sloninsky L. Spontaneous intracranial hypotension in childhood and adolescence. *J Pediatr*. 2013;163(2). https://doi.org/10.1016/j.jpeds.2013.01.055.

Yoganathan S, Mariappan R, Sudhakar SV, et al. An unusual cause of chronic headache in an adolescent boy: a case report. *Neuropediatrics*. 2019;50(6):395–399. https://doi.org/10.1055/s-0039-1694974.

Case 5

The Worst Headache of My Life

HISTORY AND PHYSICAL

A 17-year-old male with a history of obesity, Cushing syndrome, and arterial hypertension comes to the emergency room for severe headache starting 3 hours before sexual intercourse. Patient describes a history of occasional headaches, but never like this one, which qualifies as "the worst headache of his life." Pain intensifies during intercourse and is located in the left parietal region, with a sensation of pressure and a severity of 10/10. Patient shows agitation, confusion, nausea, and vomiting. Family history: father with arterial hypertension, mother with obesity and diabetes, paternal grandfather with stroke. Vital signs: weight 110 kg, height 170 cm, head circumference 58 cm, blood pressure 190/110, pulse 120, axillary temperature 37°C. Neurological examination: nuchal rigidity, left horizontal nystagmus, alteration of right upper visual field. Fundoscopy shows papilledema and bilateral subhyaloid retinal hemorrhages.

Head CT is normal without acute hemorrhage, hydrocephalus, or mass. LP performed 7 hours after headache onset shows an opening pressure of 25 cm H_2O. CSF is xanthochromic with leukocytes 3 mm^3, red blood cells 4700 mm^3, protein 49 mg/dL, glucose 56 mg/dL. Gram-negative stains and cultures are negative at 72 hours.

DIAGNOSTIC WORKUP

MRI at 24 hours after headache onset reveals FLAIR-hyperintense signal in the occipital horn of left lateral ventricle and along the subarachnoid spaces of the interhemispheric fissure (Fig. 5.1). There is no abnormal contrast enhancement. MR angiography and cerebral angiography are both normal.

CLINICAL DIFFERENTIAL DIAGNOSIS

Primary headache related to sexual activity: bilateral and progressive pain.

Migraine: unilateral, nausea/vomiting, photo/phonophobia.

Cluster headaches: periods of attacks, ipsilateral autonomic symptoms.

Autonomic headaches: unilateral neuralgiform headache, paroxysmal hemicrania, and reversible vasoconstriction syndrome.

Meningitis: fever, meningeal signs, stiff neck.

Hypertensive encephalopathy: persistent during hypertensive crises.

Stroke: acute neurological deficit with arterial territory infarct on neuroimaging.

IMAGING DIFFERENTIAL DIAGNOSIS

Infectious meningitis: Contrast enhancement on MRI T1 and FLAIR sequences with gadolinium. Patterns can be regional or diffuse, with thick empyema/abscess formation in bacterial infections, thin smooth enhancement in viral or parasitic infections, and basilar nodular enhancement for fungal/tuberculous infections (Fig. 5.2).

Leptomeningeal carcinomatosis: Irregular enhancement on MRI T1 and FLAIR sequences with gadolinium. In benign or low-grade tumors, leptomeningeal dissemination may be absent or nonenhancing. Evaluate the posterior fossa, basal cisterns, and CNs for subtle leptomeningeal disease (Fig. 5.3).

Pseudosubarachnoid hemorrhage: CT imaging appearance created by hypodense cerebral edema and/or ischemia with crowding of subarachnoid spaces. Vascular congestion due to compression and stasis may also contribute to extraaxial hyperdensity (Fig. 5.4).

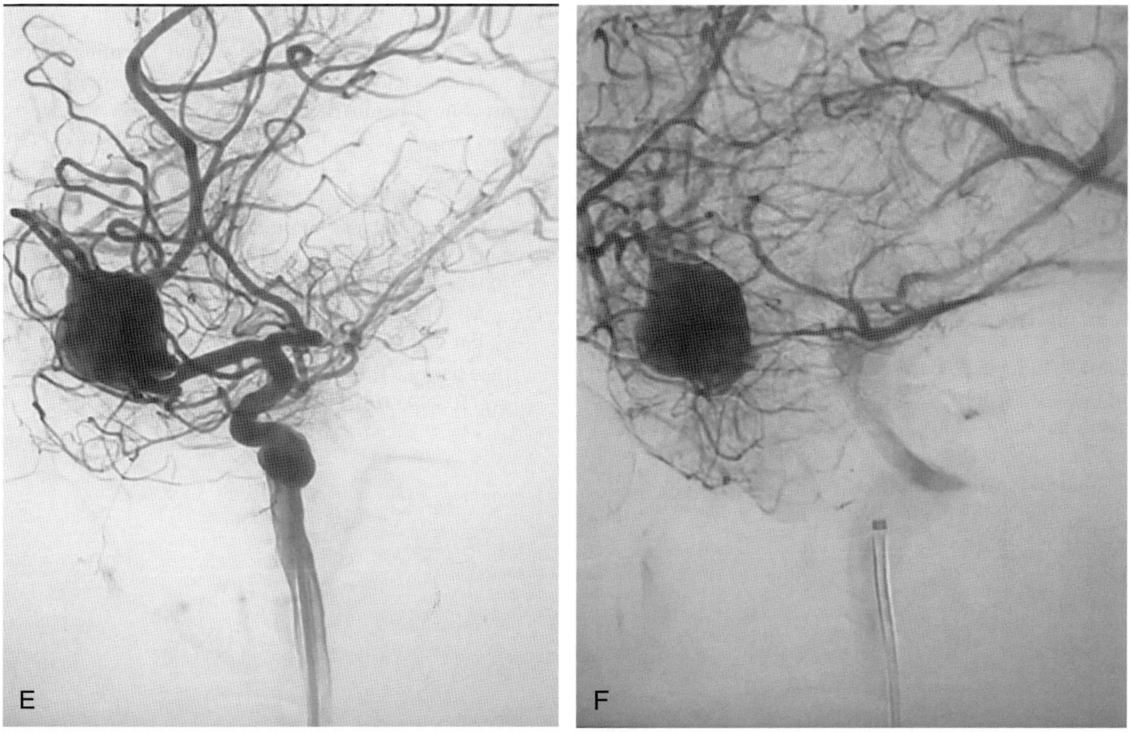

Fig. 5.7 cont'd

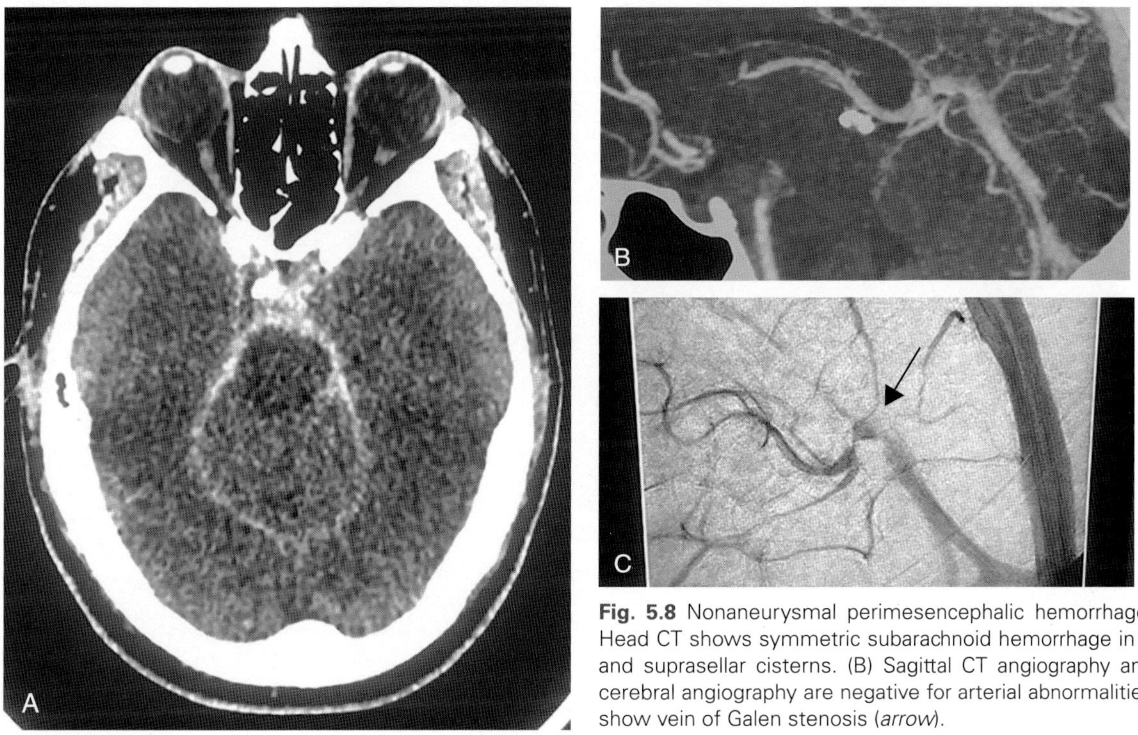

Fig. 5.8 Nonaneurysmal perimesencephalic hemorrhage. (A) Head CT shows symmetric subarachnoid hemorrhage in basal and suprasellar cisterns. (B) Sagittal CT angiography and (C) cerebral angiography are negative for arterial abnormalities but show vein of Galen stenosis (*arrow*).

CONCLUSIONS

Isolated subarachnoid hemorrhage is rare in children, but represents a neurological emergency. It most frequently occurs in the setting of trauma, ruptured aneurysms, or vascular malformations. Neuroimaging (CT and/or MRI) are typically diagnostic, but LP can also be performed in concerning cases.

REFERENCES

Chaudhari PP, Pineda J, Bachur RG, Khemani RG. Epidemiology of critical interventions in children with traumatic intracranial hemorrhage. *Pediatr Emerg Care*. 2018;37(4). https://doi.org/10.1097/pec.0000000000002352.

Das JM, Zito PM. *Nimodipine. StatPearls*. National Center for Biotechnology Information; 2023. https://www.ncbi.nlm.nih.gov/books/NBK534870/.

Epstein D, Freund Y, Marcusohn E, et al. Association between ionized calcium level and neurological outcome in endovascularly treated patients with spontaneous subarachnoid hemorrhage: a retrospective cohort study. *Neurocrit Care*. 2021;35(3):723–737. https://doi.org/10.1007/s12028-021-01214-3.

Garrido E, Metayer T, Borha A, et al. Intracranial aneurysms in pediatric population: a two-center audit. *Childs Nerv Syst*. 2021;37(8):2567–2575. https://doi.org/10.1007/s00381-021-05151-6.

Oruç M, Dündar AS, Okumuş H, Görmez M, Şamdancı ET, Celbiş O. Shaken baby syndrome resulting in death: a case series. *Turk J Pediatr*. 2021;63(1):31–36. https://doi.org/10.24953/turkjped.2021.01.004.

Case 6

Not All Hemiparesis Is a Stroke

HISTORY AND PHYSICAL

A 17-year-old right-handed male consults for a daily and persistent headache over 2 weeks. Headaches are predominantly left unilateral, with retroorbital and throbbing pain. They are associated with photophobia, phonophobia, and nausea and vomiting. In addition, he reports blurred vision in the left eye without tearing or conjunctival injection.

On the day of presentation, the headache is severe (8–9/10) and associated with sudden-onset paresthesias in the right hemibody. The paresthesias rapidly spread from fingers to hand, arm, and face. This is accompanied by dysarthria and word-finding difficulties. Symptoms worsen over a 10-minute period, to the point where he is unable to feel his face and right arm. These symptoms resolve within an hour, but he subsequently develops paresthesias and slight weakness in his right arm, lasting 2 hours. He recalls a similar but milder episode 6 months earlier. Family history is negative for migraine, stroke, or other illnesses.

In the emergency department, the patient is oriented in time and space. He is able to follow orders but not comfortably. The neurological examination shows mild dysarthria but preserved language function with good understanding, repetition, and meaning of words. The young man does not have any sensory deficits, but strength in the hand and right arm is approximately 4/5, and deep reflexes are difficult to obtain. No facial or lower limb weakness is observed. The rest of the exam is normal.

DIAGNOSTIC WORKUP

MRI stroke protocol performed 2 hours after the onset of symptoms is negative for acute infarct but shows asymmetric decrease in left cerebral perfusion and cortical venous susceptibility (Fig. 6.1).

CLINICAL DIFFERENTIAL DIAGNOSIS

Stroke and transient ischemic attack: Strokes, especially of the hemorrhagic type, can present with headaches. Urgent investigation is required, including MRI with stroke protocol and laboratory tests to evaluate for risk factors.

Focal seizures with Todd paralysis: Paralysis after a focal seizure is usually sudden, and most patients have a history of prior motor seizures.

Hemiplegic migraine: Development of neurological symptoms in hemiplegic migraine is progressive (usually more than 20 minutes). Clinical and radiologic abnormalities are generally reversible. Hemiplegic migraine occurs around the first or second decade of life.

Alternating hemiplegia of childhood: Children with this disorder have intermittent episodes of hemiplegia affecting one or both sides. Age of onset is usually before 18 months.

Tumors and hydrocephalus: Space-occupying lesions can present with headaches and motor deficits. These generally follow a subacute time course, though a longer deterioration is possible.

Sturge-Weber syndrome (SWS): Children with SWS have headache, seizures, and hemiplegic episodes. Type 3 SWS affects the brain without facial vascular malformations. Type 1 to 2 SWS are easier to diagnose due to the overlying facial port-wine stains.

Infection: Meningoencephalitis can manifest with asymmetric focal deficits and headaches. Patients present with fever and CSF abnormalities.

Mitochondrial disorders: Cerebral autosomal dominant arteriopathy with subcortical infarcts and leukoencephalopathy (CADASIL) and mitochondrial encephalopathy with lactic acidosis and stroke-like episodes (MELAS) can cause headaches and motor deficits, typically self-resolving.

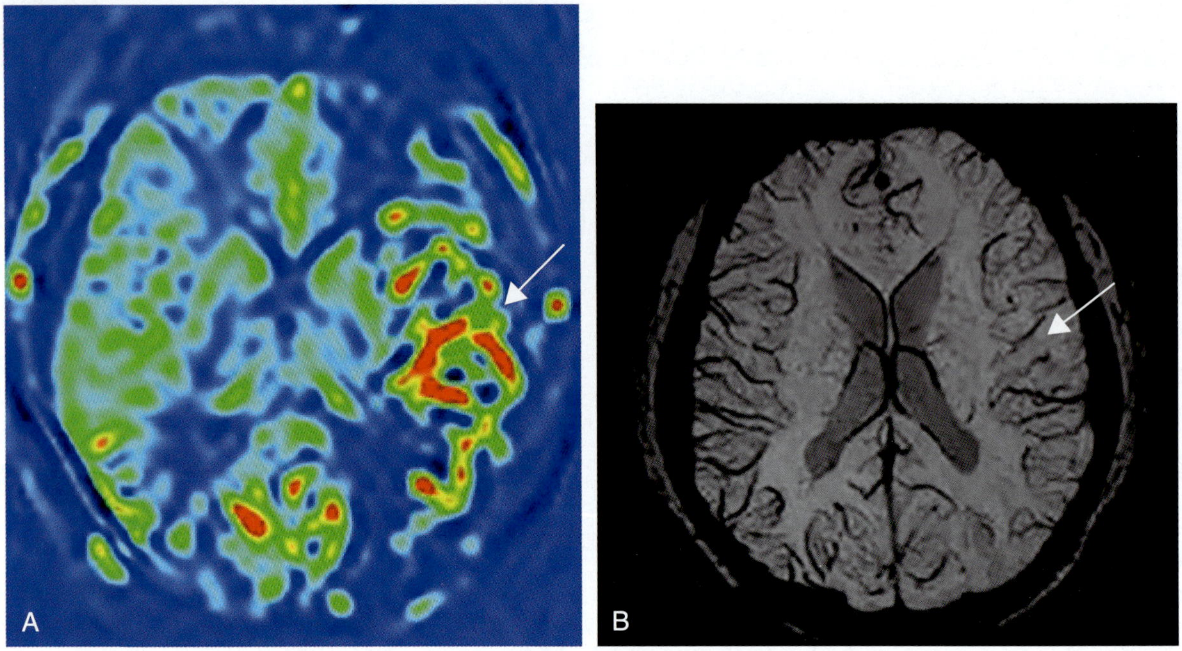

Fig. 6.1 Hemiplegic migraine. Brain MRI, (A) arterial spin labeling (ASL) demonstrates decreased perfusion throughout the *left* cerebral hemisphere with increased signal in overlying arteries, reflecting arterial transit artifact (*arrow*). (B) Susceptibility-weighted imaging (SWI) shows decreased asymmetric signal in *left* hemispheric cortical veins (*arrow*).

IMAGING DIFFERENTIAL DIAGNOSIS

Stroke: Arterial (Fig. 6.2) and venous strokes can present with decreased perfusion in vascular distributions but not involving an entire hemisphere. A global anoxic event can produce bilateral infarcts, but again not in a hemispheric distribution.

Periictal state: Abnormal perfusion with hyperperfusion in the periictal period and hypoperfusion in the interictal period can be observed on noncontrast perfusion sequences such as arterial spin labeling (ASL).

Tumors: Depending on histology and grade, tumors can demonstrate focal alterations of perfusion.

Sturge-Weber syndrome: Slow-flow superficial vascular malformations may involve a segment or hemisphere of the brain, with early leptomeningeal enhancement progressing to cerebral atrophy and parallel "railroad track" cortical calcification. Perfusion is usually regionally elevated in early stages (or during a seizure) and decreased in later stages (Fig. 6.3).

FINAL DIAGNOSIS

Hemiplegic migraine.

DISCUSSION

Diagnosis of hemiplegic migraine depends on careful history taking and examination. Focal neurological symptoms develop gradually and are typically accompanied by headache. Some patients may present with encephalopathy, psychosis, or migrainous infarction. Sensory-motor deficits are reversible. Electroencephalogram (EEG) performed during the attack may show continuous unilateral delta slowing. Exclusion of symptomatic causes, such as stroke, is necessary. Therefore the use of neuroimaging is important to rule out structural lesions. During an episode, neuroimaging is generally normal, but newer MRI techniques such as gadolinium-free arterial spin labeling (ASL) can demonstrate perfusion abnormalities in the form of hyper- or

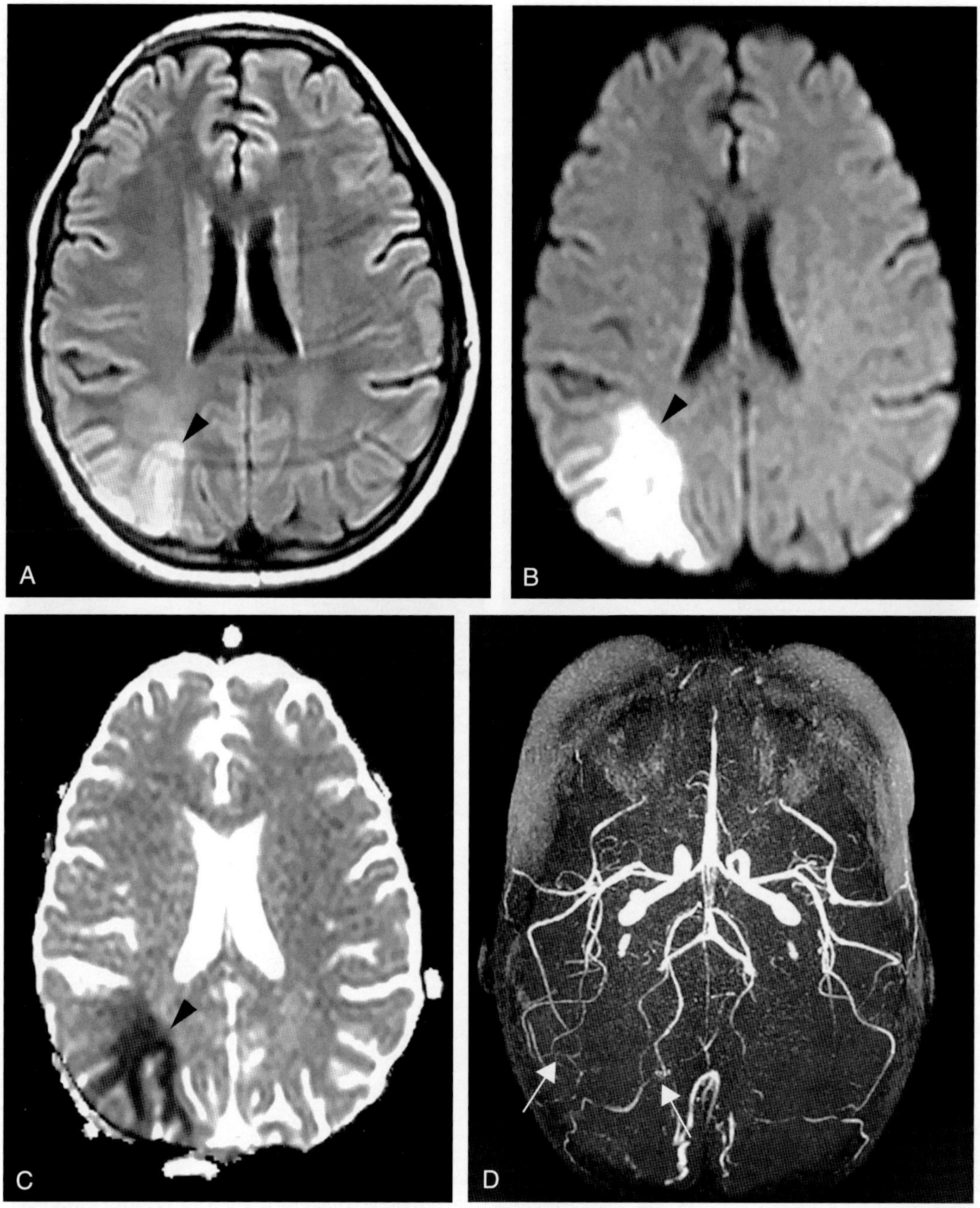

Fig. 6.2 Acute stroke with autoregulation. Brain MRI, (A) axial FLAIR, (B) DWI, and (C) ADC show right parietal infarct with restricted diffusion in the cortex and subcortical white matter (*arrowheads*). (D) MR angiography shows dilation of the distal right middle and posterior cerebral artery branches (*arrows*), reflective of cerebral autoregulation. *ADC*, Apparent diffusion coefficient; *DWI*, diffusion weighted imaging; *FLAIR*, fluid-attenuated inversion recovery.

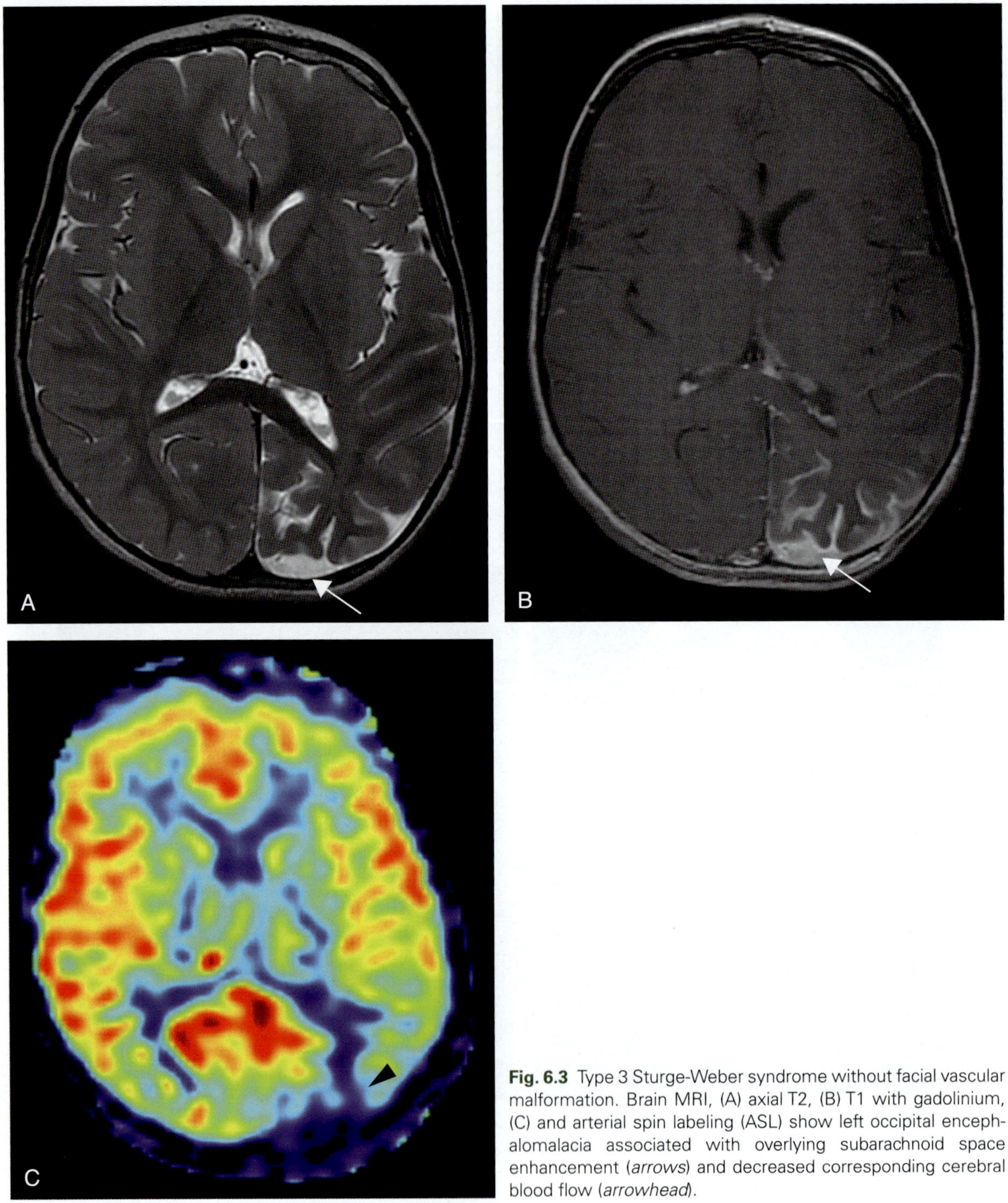

Fig. 6.3 Type 3 Sturge-Weber syndrome without facial vascular malformation. Brain MRI, (A) axial T2, (B) T1 with gadolinium, (C) and arterial spin labeling (ASL) show left occipital encephalomalacia associated with overlying subarachnoid space enhancement (*arrows*) and decreased corresponding cerebral blood flow (*arrowhead*).

hypoperfusion with subsequent complete resolution. Cytotoxic edema and evidence of hypometabolism in the affected hemisphere may be present on multimodal imaging.

CLINICAL RED FLAGS

- Onset of sensory or motor deficits associated with headache.
- Family history of hemiplegic migraine.

IMAGING RED FLAGS

- Asymmetric perfusion in a nonvascular distribution.
- Hemispheric cortical edema or restricted diffusion (severe cases).
- Asymmetric cortical veins on susceptibility-weighted imaging
- Asymmetric arteries and/or veins on angiography.
- Transient imaging abnormalities that resolve spontaneously.

CONCLUSIONS

Hemiplegic migraine should be considered in patients with headache and focal neurological deficits after ruling out other acute causes. Hemiplegic migraine can be familial and inherited (three major genes identified: *CACNA1A*, *ATP1A2*, *SCN1A*) or sporadic with no family history. Treatment is supportive, and symptoms almost always resolve completely, though preventive medications can be trialed for recurrent cases.

REFERENCES

Bansal V, Kumar S, Sharma S, Sharma S, Sood RG. Usefulness of pulsed arterial spin labeling magnetic resonance imaging in new-onset seizure patients and its comparison with dynamic susceptibility contrast magnetic resonance imaging. *J Neurosci Rural Pract.* 2017;8(4):569–574. https://doi.org/10.4103/jnrp.jnrp_141_17.

Lai T-H, Hong C-T. Prolonged symptoms in sporadic hemiplegic migraine: aura or migrainous infarction? *Acta Neurol Taiwan.* 2012;21(3):129–132.

Ohmura K, Suzuki Y, Saito Y, Wada T, Goto M, Seto S. Sporadic hemiplegic migraine presenting as an acute encephalopathy. *Brain Dev.* 2012;34(8):691–695. https://doi.org/10.1016/j.braindev.2011.11.002.

Russell MB, Ducros A. Sporadic and familial hemiplegic migraine: pathophysiological mechanisms, clinical characteristics, diagnosis, and management. *Lancet Neurol.* 2011;10(5):457–470. https://doi.org/10.1016/s1474-4422(11)70048-5.

Soldozy S, Galindo J, Snyder H, et al. Clinical utility of arterial spin labeling imaging in disorders of the nervous system. *Neurosurg Focus.* 2019;47(6). https://doi.org/10.3171/2019.9.focus19567.

Case 7

Children Can Also Have Microstrokes

HISTORY AND PHYSICAL

A 12-year-old girl presents with episodic recurrent headaches since 10 years of age, which are throbbing in quality, 8/10 in intensity. The headaches are accompanied by phonophobia, photophobia, nausea, and vomiting, and sometimes a preceding visual aura. Episodes last 2 to 4 hours, with no obvious trigger, and improve with pain relievers or a short nap. Patient has no relevant prior medical history, no known exposure to trauma or toxins, no mood disorders, and good school performance. Family history: mother and maternal grandmother report similar headache episodes. Grandmother has cognitive impairment. Two maternal uncles have a history of stroke. Clinical examination: vital signs and height appropriate for age, neurological examination normal. Basic labs are negative for systemic abnormalities. Given the frequency of symptoms, migraine with aura was initially diagnosed and patient was treated with cyproheptadine, flunarizine, and topiramate, with minimal improvement.

DIAGNOSTIC WORKUP

Brain MRI reveals frontoinsular cortical atrophy and bilateral symmetric T2 hyperintense signal in the subcortical and periventricular white matter with extension to internal and external capsules (Fig. 7.1).

Metabolic studies are normal: lactic acid, pyruvate, ammonium, creatine phosphokinase (CPK), carnitine, acylcarnitine, adrenal and pituitary hormones, lysosomal enzymes, very long chain fatty acids in blood, amino acids in blood and urine, organic acids and acylglycines in urine. Other studies including EEG, auditory and visual evoked potentials, and peripheral nerve conduction velocity are also normal.

Patient continues to experience headaches of variable frequency, some preceded by facial sensory symptoms. At 15 years of age, following an episode of prolonged headache, she presents with hemiparesis and right hemihypoesthesia. Extensive workup excludes vascular, metabolic, inflammatory, cardiac, and mitochondrial diseases.

Repeat brain MRI shows progression of confluent hyperintensities in the subcortical white matter, with predominance in the temporal poles and posterior periventricular regions, and additional lesions in the optic pathway, thalami, and pontine tegmentum. A small left thalamic lesion shows restricted diffusion indicative of an early acute lacunar infarct. MRI angiography is normal (Fig. 7.2).

Genetic testing confirms *NOTCH3* gene mutation in both the patient and mother.

CLINICAL DIFFERENTIAL DIAGNOSIS

Numerous pathologies in children are associated with recurrent headaches and stroke, including primary and secondary CNS vasculitis, SWS, moyamoya syndrome, and mitochondrial diseases (MELAS).

White matter abnormalities can be seen with migraine (Fig. 7.3), demyelinating diseases, leukodystrophies, and metabolic diseases (homocystinuria, Fabry disease).

IMAGING DIFFERENTIAL DIAGNOSIS

Many diseases can affect white matter in pediatrics, but few involve the temporal subcortical white matter. The differential diagnosis includes congenital cytomegalovirus (CMV) infection (Fig. 7.4), Alexander disease, megalencephalic leukoencephalopathy, and congenital muscular dystrophies (Fig. 7.5).

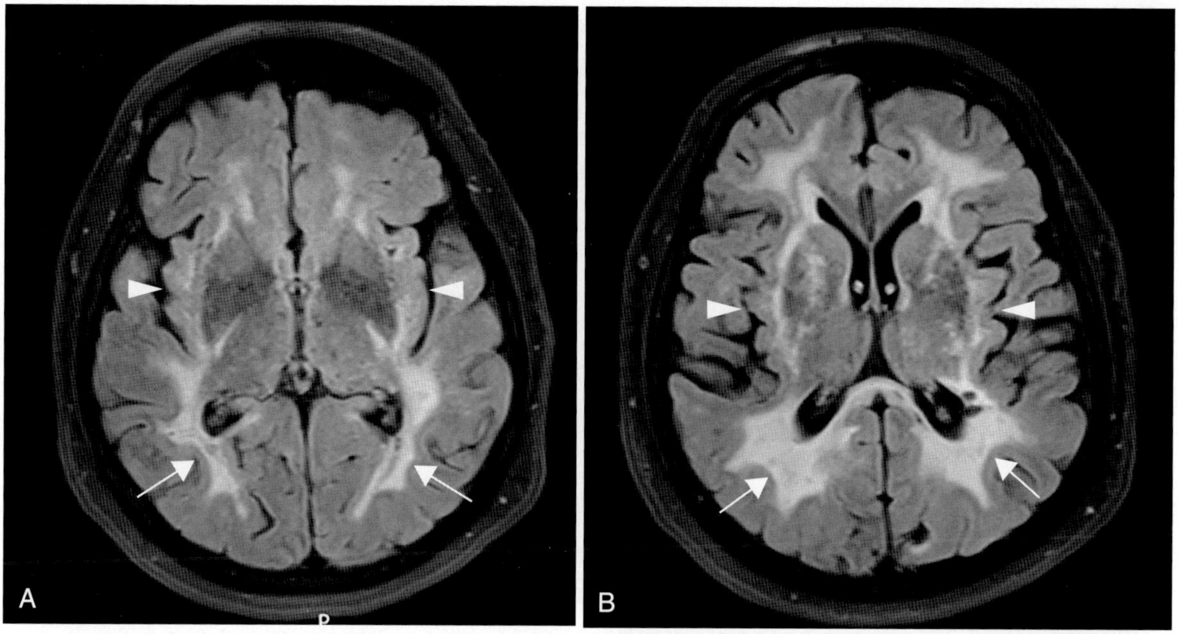

Fig. 7.1 Oligosymptomatic CADASIL with nonspecific hyperintensities in white matter. (A and B) Brain MRI, axial FLAIR, shows mild insular atrophy (*arrowheads*) with confluent bilateral hyperintensity of periventricular white matter (*arrows*) extending into internal and external capsules. *CADASIL*, Cerebral autosomal dominant arteriopathy with subcortical infarcts and leukoencephalopathy; *FLAIR*, fluid-attenuated inversion recovery.

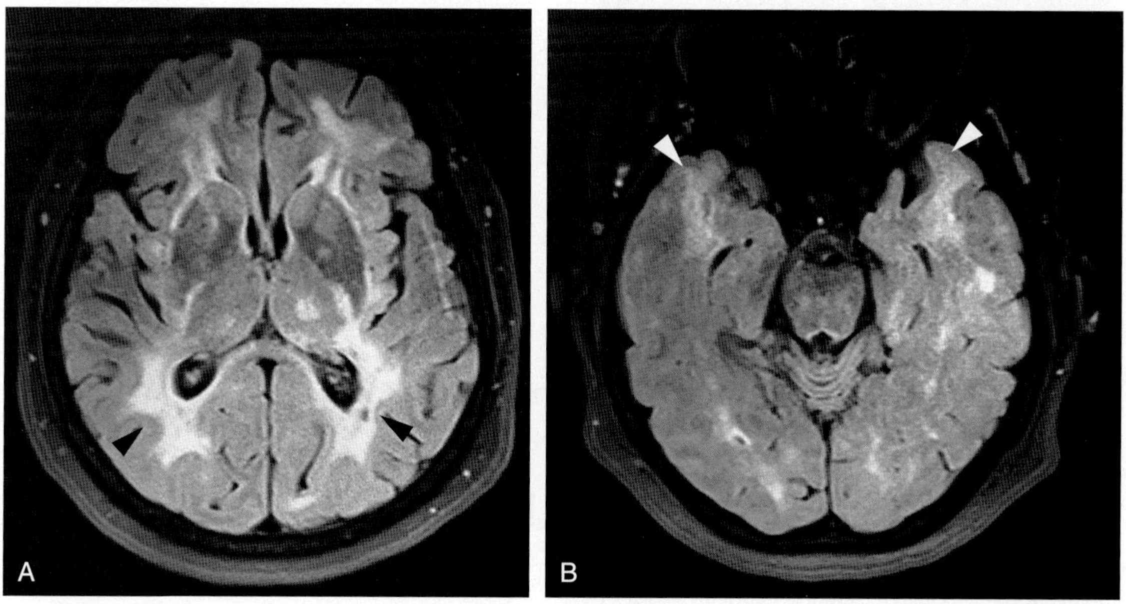

Fig. 7.2 Follow-up CADASIL with acute lacunar infarction. (A and B) Brain MRI, axial FLAIR, shows progression of confluent hyperintensities in periventricular white matter, with subcortical predominance in anterior temporal (*white arrowheads*) and parietal lobes (*black arrowheads*), and additional lesions in the optic radiations, thalami, and pons. (C) Axial DWI and (D) ADC show restricted diffusion in the left thalamus corresponding to an acute lacunar infarction (*arrows*). (E) MR angiography is normal. *ADC*, Apparent diffusion coefficient; *CADASIL*, cerebral autosomal dominant arteriopathy with subcortical infarcts and leukoencephalopathy; *DWI*, diffusion-weighted imaging; *FLAIR*, fluid-attenuated inversion recovery.

Continued

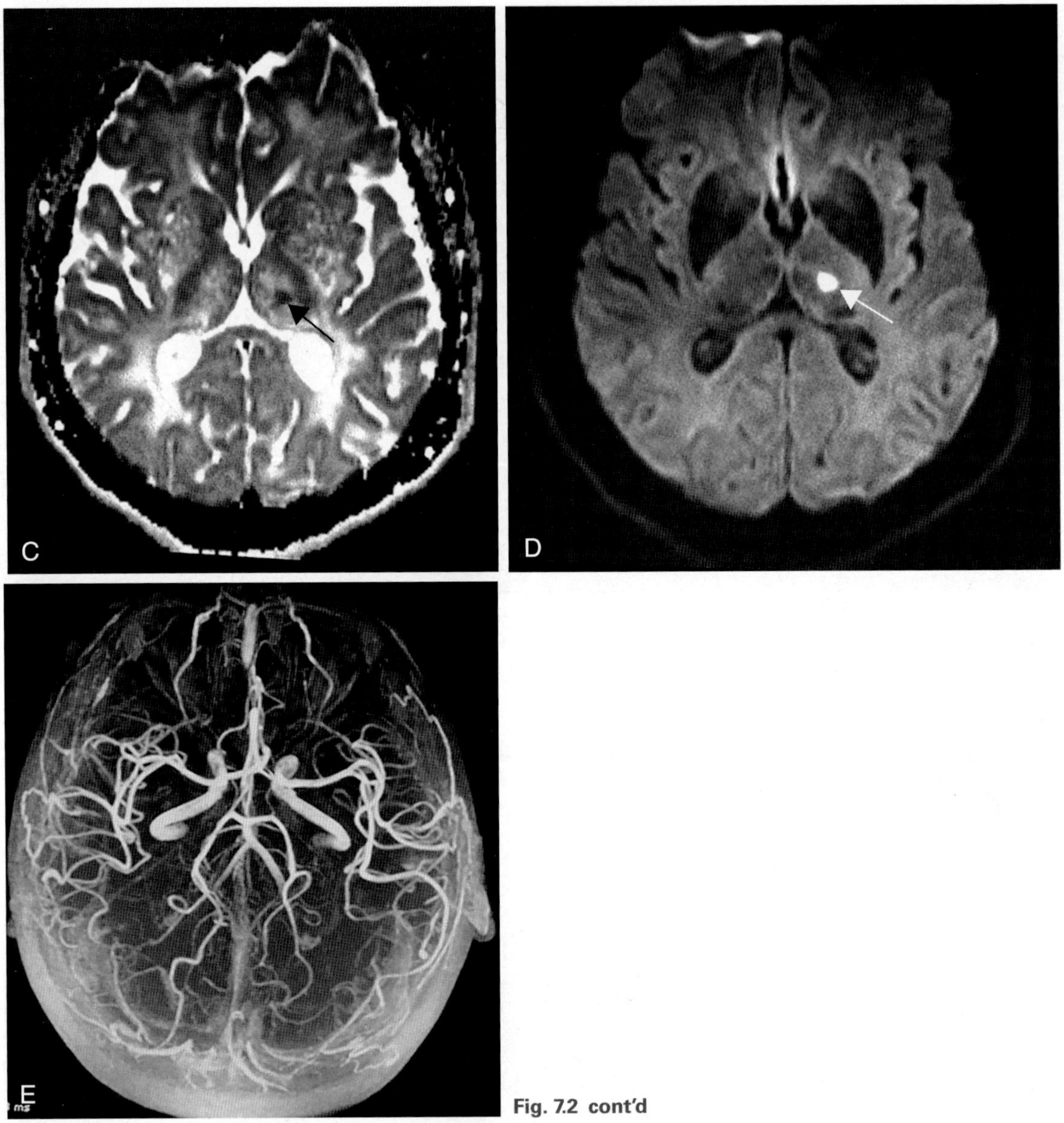

Fig. 7.2 cont'd

External capsule involvement can be seen early in cerebral autosomal dominant arteriopathy with subcortical infarcts and leukoencephalopathy (CADASIL). It has also occasionally been described in status epilepticus, extrapontine myelinolysis, and acute necrotizing encephalopathy.

Advanced CADASIL can demonstrate microhemorrhages and confluent white matter involvement of the centrum semiovale, corpus callosum, posterior fossa, and spinal cord (Figs. 7.6–7.8).

FINAL DIAGNOSIS

CADASIL.

DISCUSSION

CADASIL is caused by mutations in *NOTCH3*, a gene that encodes a transmembrane protein involved in cell differentiation and signaling, resulting in systemic small vessel arteriopathy. It typically manifests in young adults with a history of migraine with aura, recurrent ischemic strokes, and cognitive impairment progressing over time to dementia. CADASIL can present earlier in childhood and should be considered in pediatric patients with recurrent headaches, particularly those with atypical migraines or a family history of early stroke or dementia.

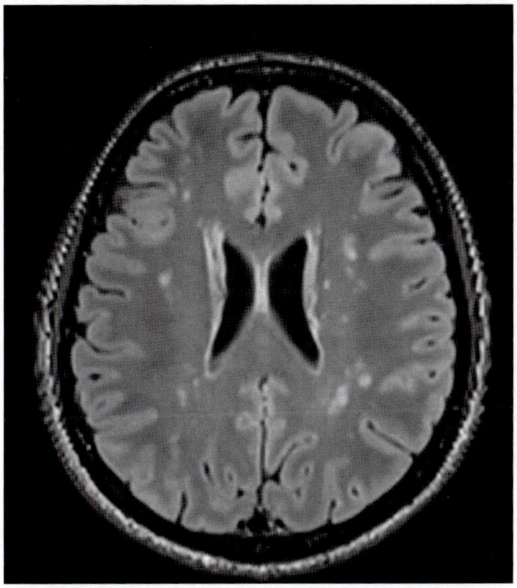

Fig. 7.3 Migraine. Brain MRI, axial FLAIR, shows scattered small hyperintense foci throughout the subcortical white matter. *FLAIR*, Fluid-attenuated inversion recovery.

Brain MRI shows multifocal and progressively confluent symmetric T2/FLAIR hyperintense lesions in the frontotemporal white matter with involvement of subcortical U fibers, periventricular regions, external/internal capsules, and basal ganglia. Ischemic lesions can present acutely, especially small lacunar infarcts in white matter or deep gray structures. Corpus callosal lesions can also be seen, often with full-thickness involvement and associated parenchymal thinning (Fig. 7.7). Advanced cases manifest with diffuse white matter involvement, atrophy, and brainstem and cerebellar lesions. MRI angiography is typically normal, since the disease involves small arteries. Rarely, CADASIL can also involve the spinal cord (Fig. 7.8).

CLINICAL RED FLAGS

- Atypical migraine that is nonresponsive or minimally responsive to treatment.
- Family history of migraine with aura or stroke.

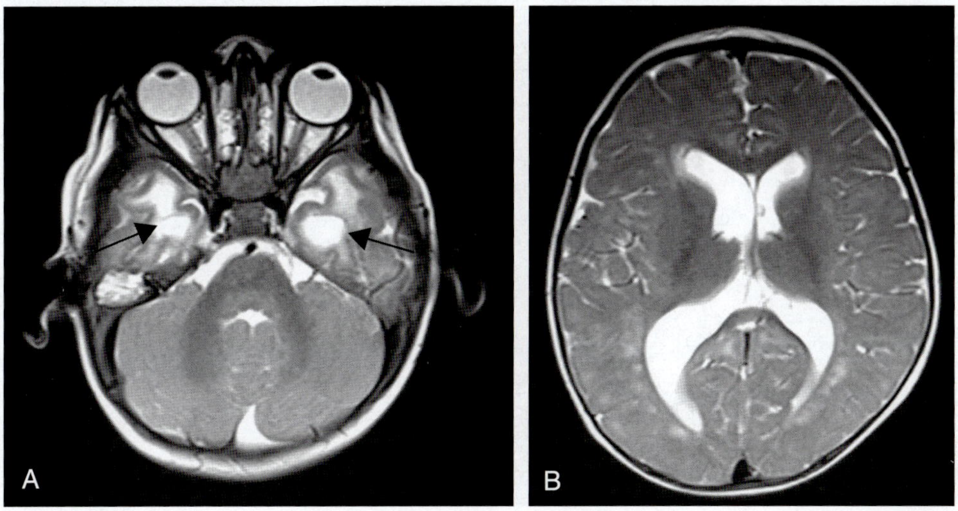

Fig. 7.4 Congenital CMV infection. Brain MRI, axial T2, shows (A) bitemporal white matter hyperintensity with cystic dilation of temporal horns (*arrows*). (B) Multifocal hyperintense signal in periventricular white matter with asymmetric ex vacuo ventriculomegaly. *CMV*, Cytomegalovirus.

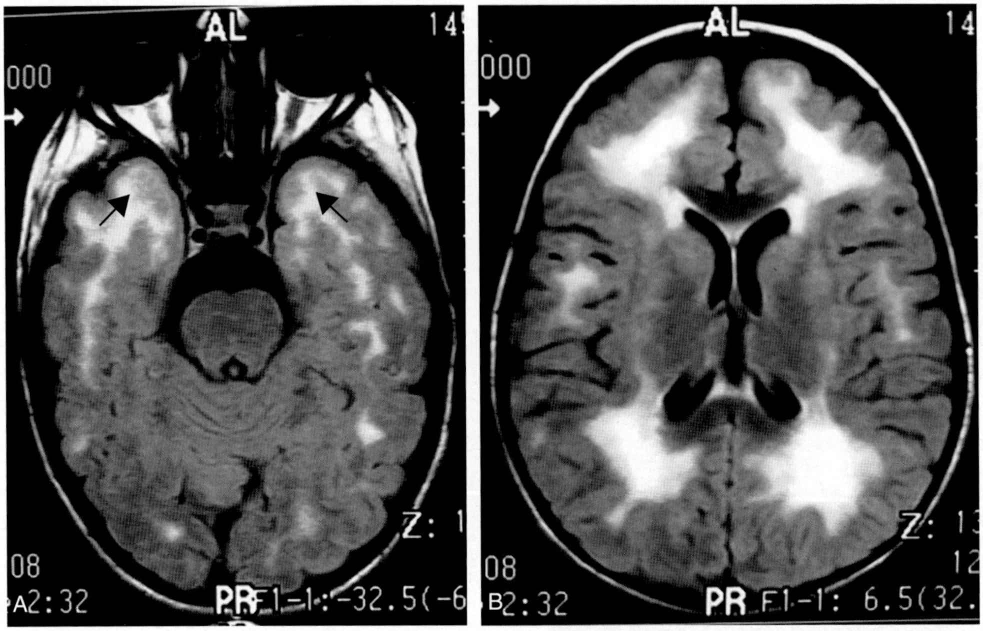

Fig. 7.5 Congenital muscular dystrophy. Brain MRI, axial FLAIR, shows (A and B) cobblestone cortex and bilateral symmetric hyperintensities throughout periventricular and subcortical white matter with involvement of temporal lobes (*arrows*), frontal and parietal poles. *FLAIR*, Fluid-attenuated inversion recovery.

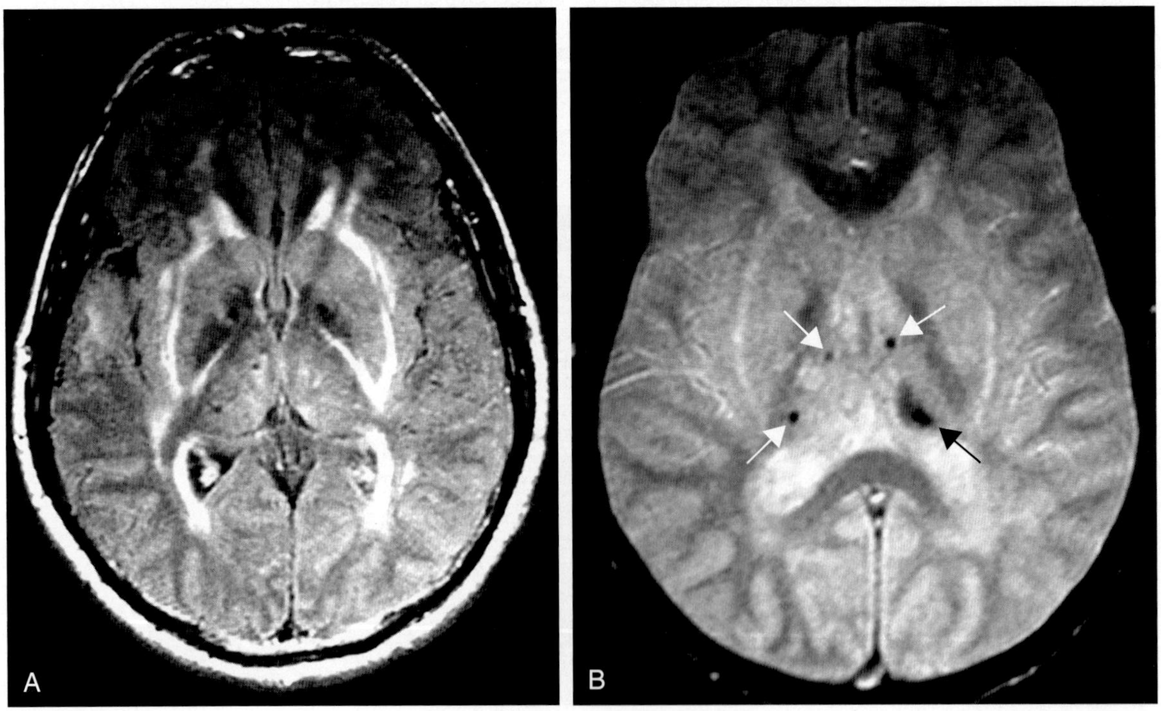

Fig. 7.6 CADASIL with chronic microbleeds. Brain MRI, (A) axial FLAIR, shows symmetric confluent hyperintensities in periventricular white matter with extension to external capsules and posterior limbs of internal capsules. (B) Axial GRE shows multiple punctate microhemorrhages in bilateral thalami (*arrows*). *CADASIL*, Cerebral autosomal dominant arteriopathy with subcortical infarcts and leukoencephalopathy; *FLAIR*, fluid-attenuated inversion recovery; *GRE*, gradient recalled echo.

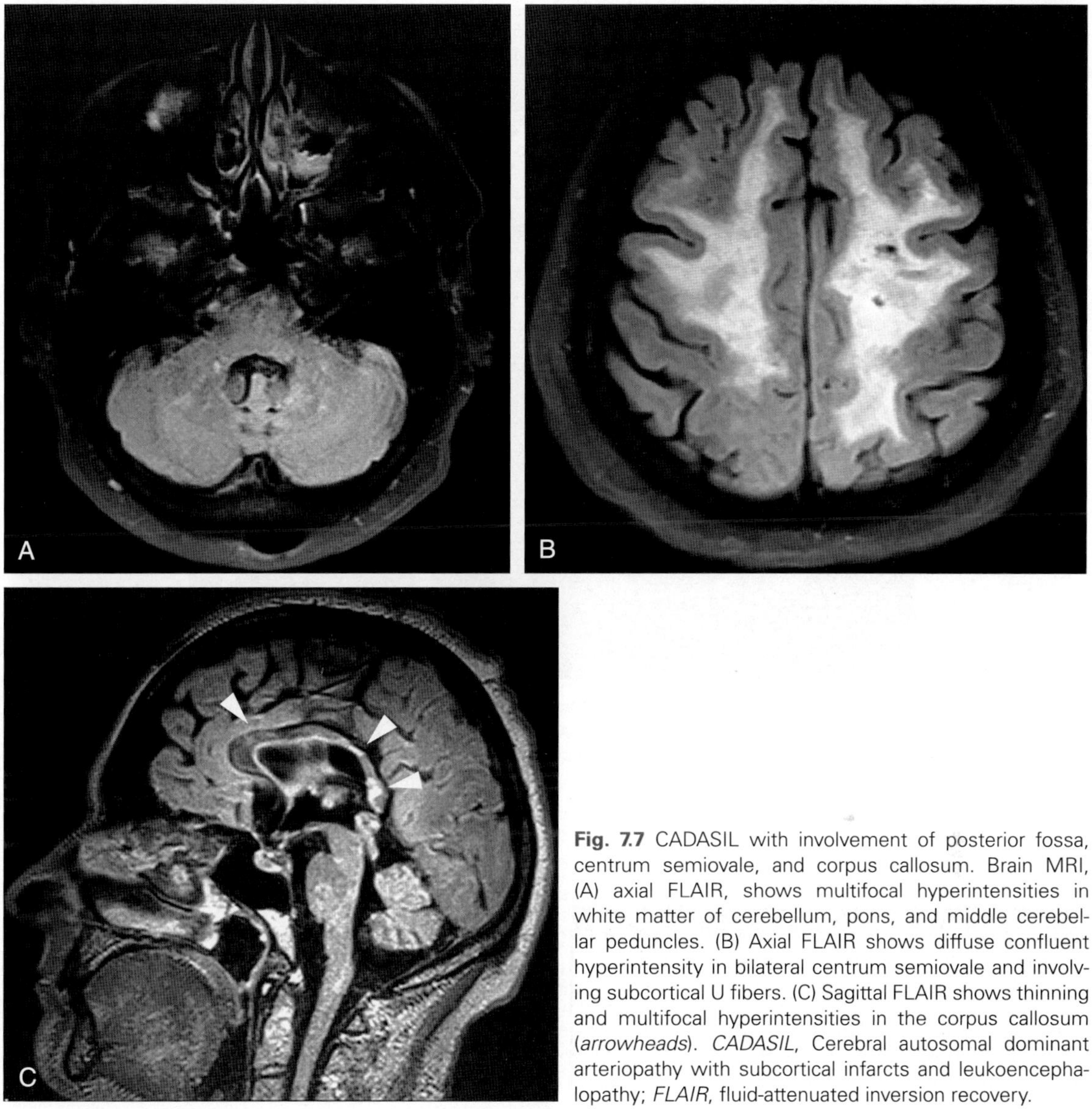

Fig. 7.7 CADASIL with involvement of posterior fossa, centrum semiovale, and corpus callosum. Brain MRI, (A) axial FLAIR, shows multifocal hyperintensities in white matter of cerebellum, pons, and middle cerebellar peduncles. (B) Axial FLAIR shows diffuse confluent hyperintensity in bilateral centrum semiovale and involving subcortical U fibers. (C) Sagittal FLAIR shows thinning and multifocal hyperintensities in the corpus callosum (*arrowheads*). *CADASIL*, Cerebral autosomal dominant arteriopathy with subcortical infarcts and leukoencephalopathy; *FLAIR*, fluid-attenuated inversion recovery.

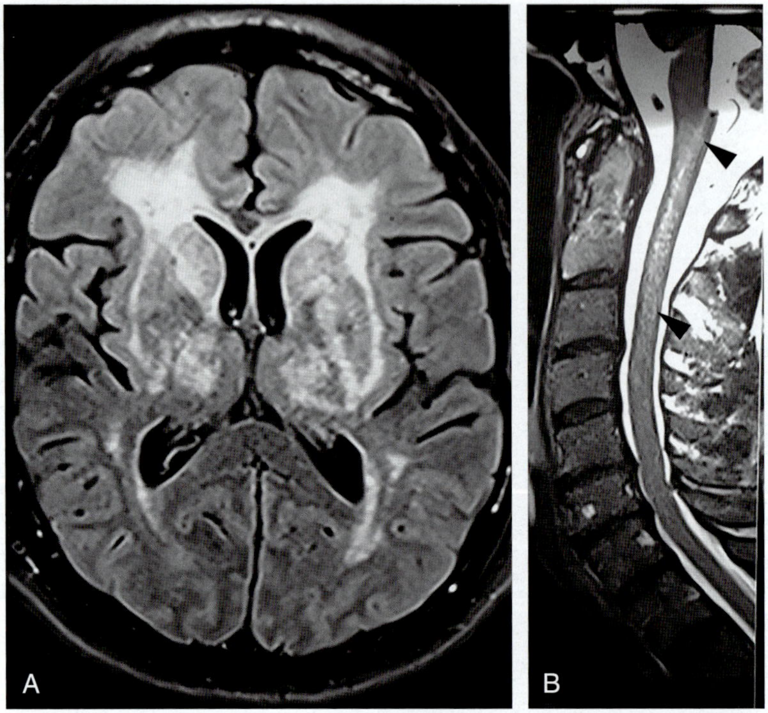

Fig. 7.8 CADASIL with spinal involvement. Brain MRI, (A) axial FLAIR, shows symmetric and partially confluent hyperintensities in the frontal periventricular and subcortical white matter with extension into corpus callosum, internal/external capsules, and basal ganglia. Cervical spine MRI, (B) sagittal T2, shows long-segment central hyperintense signal in the upper cervical cord (*arrowheads*). *CADASIL*, Cerebral autosomal dominant arteriopathy with subcortical infarcts and leukoencephalopathy; *FLAIR*, fluid-attenuated inversion recovery.

IMAGING RED FLAGS

- In a child or adolescent with atypical migraine, excessive white matter lesions on imaging should raise the possibility of CADASIL, with genetic testing and appropriate management. In some cases, CADASIL can be associated with reversible or recurrent acute encephalopathy (Fig. 7.9).

CONCLUSIONS

Children and adolescents with white matter abnormalities on MRI invoke a wide differential diagnosis. Frequent or prolonged episodes of atypical migraine with aura, ischemic strokes, and family history of migraine and/or stroke should suggest the diagnosis of CADASIL. Management includes antithrombotic agents to minimize the risk of future strokes.

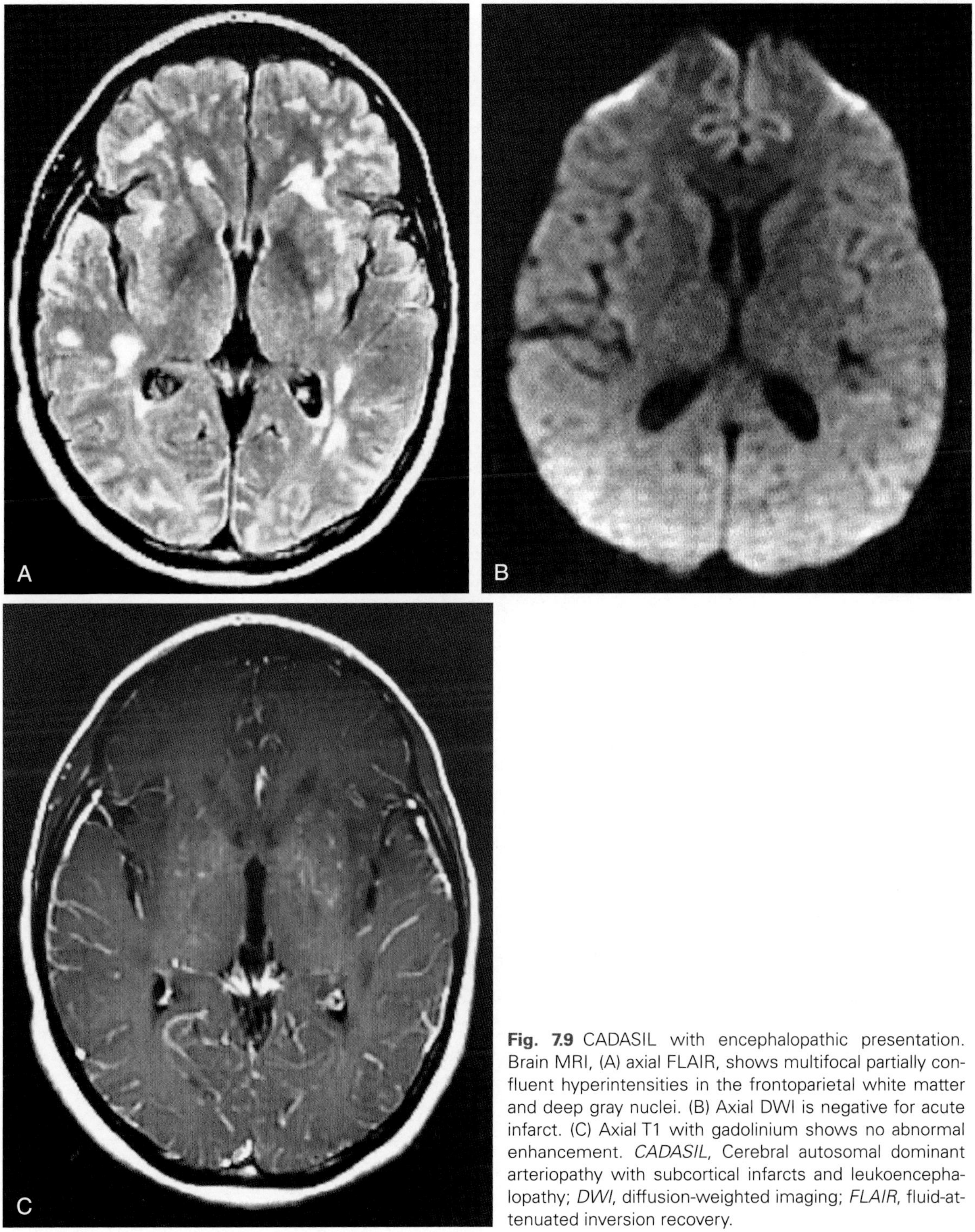

Fig. 7.9 CADASIL with encephalopathic presentation. Brain MRI, (A) axial FLAIR, shows multifocal partially confluent hyperintensities in the frontoparietal white matter and deep gray nuclei. (B) Axial DWI is negative for acute infarct. (C) Axial T1 with gadolinium shows no abnormal enhancement. *CADASIL*, Cerebral autosomal dominant arteriopathy with subcortical infarcts and leukoencephalopathy; *DWI*, diffusion-weighted imaging; *FLAIR*, fluid-attenuated inversion recovery.

REFERENCES

Benabu Y, Beland M, Ferguson N, Maranda B, Boucher R-M. Genetically proven cerebral autosomal-dominant arteriopathy with subcortical infarcts and leukoencephalopathy (CADASIL) in a 3-year-old. *Pediatr Radiol.* 2013;43(9):1227–1230. https://doi.org/10.1007/s00247-013-2658-5.

Cleves C, Friedman NR, Rothner AD, Hussain MS. Genetically confirmed CADASIL in a pediatric patient. *Pediatrics.* 2010;126(6):e1603–e1607. https://doi.org/10.1542/peds.2010-0714.

Golomb MR, Sokol DK, Walsh LE, Christensen CK, Garg BP. Recurrent hemiplegia, normal MRI, and NOTCH3 mutation in a 14-year-old: is this early CADASIL? *Neurology.* 2004;62(12):2331–2332. https://doi.org/10.1212/01.wnl.0000130333.32410.2b.

Granild-Jensen J, Jensen UB, Schwartz M, Hansen US. Cerebral autosomal dominant arteriopathy with subcortical infarcts and leukoencephalopathy resulting in stroke in an 11-year-old male. *Dev Med Child Neurol.* 2009;51(9):754–757. https://doi.org/10.1111/j.1469-8749.2008.03241.x.

Hartley J, Westmacott R, Decker J, Shroff M, Yoon G. Childhood-onset CADASIL: clinical, imaging, and neurocognitive features. *J Child Neurol.* 2010;25(5):623–627. https://doi.org/10.1177/0883073810361382.

Hirabayashi S, Wada T, Kondo Y, Arima K. Autosomal dominant leukoencephalopathy with mild clinical symptoms due to cerebrovascular dysfunctions: a new disease entity? *Brain Dev.* 2008;30(2):146–150. https://doi.org/10.1016/j.braindev.2007.06.003.

SECTION 2

Neonatal Neurology

Seh Hyun Kim, Mohamed El-Dib, Terrie Inder

Significant improvements in obstetrical and neonatal care have decreased mortality rates in high-risk infants admitted to neonatal intensive care units (NICUs). Improved survival has led to the recognition of a broader spectrum of neurological disorders, including encephalopathy of prematurity, hypoxic-ischemic encephalopathy (HIE), intraventricular hemorrhage, cerebellar hemorrhage, and stroke.

Brain injury in the neonatal period increases the risk of mortality and adverse neurodevelopmental outcomes, including cerebral palsy, cognitive impairments, and epilepsy. Alongside this recognition of neurological conditions, there has been an increased focus on neonatal neurocritical care including acute brain monitoring, with electroencephalography (EEG), near-infrared spectroscopy, and neuroimaging in NICUs.

In this chapter, we describe four common neurologic disorders of the newborn: (1) hypoxic ischemic encephalopathy; (2) periventricular leukomalacia; (3) neonatal arterial ischemic stroke; and (4) posthemorrhagic ventricular dilatation. These conditions require the use of appropriate imaging modalities, such as cranial ultrasonography, magnetic resonance imaging, and magnetic resonance angiography for diagnosis and treatment. These conditions highlight the importance of collaboration between neonatologists, neurologists, and radiologists to optimize outcomes in the neonatal period.

SUGGESTED READINGS

El-Dib M, Limbrick Jr DD, Inder T, et al. Management of post-hemorrhagic ventricular dilatation in the infant born preterm. *J Pediatr*. 2020;226:16–27.e3.

Gotardo JW, Volkmer NFV, Stangler GP, Dornelles AD, Bohrer BBA, Carvalho CG. Impact of peri-intraventricular hemorrhage and periventricular leukomalacia in the neurodevelopment of preterms: a systematic review and meta-analysis. *PLoS One*. 2019;14:e0223427.

Lehman LL, Rivkin MJ. Perinatal arterial ischemic stroke: presentation, risk factors, evaluation, and outcome. *Pediatr Neurol*. 2014;51:760–768.

Miller SP, Ramaswamy V, Michelson D, et al. Patterns of brain injury in term neonatal encephalopathy. *J Pediatr*. 2005;146:453–460.

Volpe JJ, Inder TE, Darras BT, et al. *Volpe's Neurology of the Newborn*. 6th ed. Elsevier; 2017.

Full-Term Infant With Seizure

HISTORY AND PHYSICAL

A male infant was born by cesarean section at 40^{+2} weeks of gestation for nonreassuring fetal heart tracing. Birth weight was 3530 g. Meconium-stained amniotic fluid, nuchal cord, fetal tachycardia, and maternal chorioamnionitis were present during birth. Prenatal labs were negative for Group B streptococcus, hepatitis B surface antigen, gonorrhea and chlamydia, HIV, and syphilis, and showed immunity to rubella. There was no family history of neurologic disorders or seizures. He required positive pressure ventilation for 2 minutes in the delivery room with Apgar scores of 1, 3, and 5 at 1, 5, and 10 minutes, respectively. He then received supplemental oxygen in the neonatal intensive care unit (NICU) and developed seizures after 6 hours of life. Amplitude integrated EEG showed seizure activity, and blood gas analysis showed metabolic acidosis. Hence, therapeutic hypothermia was started with seizure medications, intubation due to recurrent apnea, and hypoglycemia. Seizures were controlled with administration of phenobarbital, fosphenytoin, midazolam, and levetiracetam.

DIAGNOSTIC WORKUP

Head ultrasound (US) was reported as normal at 2 and 7 days after birth. Brain MRI on day 5 showed global hypoxia-ischemia with cerebral edema. There was diffuse T2 hyperintensity with loss of gray-white matter differentiation, especially involving the left basal ganglia (Fig. 8.1). Diffusion-weighted images demonstrated increasing restricted diffusion with relative sparing of the cerebellum (Fig. 8.2).

CLINICAL DIFFERENTIAL DIAGNOSES

The differential diagnosis for neonatal seizures includes hypoxic-ischemic encephalopathy (HIE), intracranial hemorrhage, intracranial infection, developmental defects, hypoglycemia, hypocalcemia, metabolic disorders, and epilepsy syndromes. In a prospective cohort of 426 neonates with seizure who underwent continuous EEG, the most common seizure etiologies were HIE in 38%, ischemic stroke in 18%, neonatal-onset epilepsy in 13%, intracranial hemorrhage in 11%, neonatal genetic epilepsy syndrome in 6%, congenital cerebral malformation in 4%, and benign nonfamilial neonatal convulsions in 3%.

IMAGING DIFFERENTIAL DIAGNOSES

Hypoxic-ischemic encephalopathy

Neonatal metabolic encephalopathies: organic acidemias, urea cycle defects, and aminoacidemias including maple syrup urine disease

Congenital malformations

Central nervous system infection

FINAL DIAGNOSIS

Hypoxic-ischemic encephalopathy

DISCUSSION

The incidence of HIE is 2 to 3 per 1000 live-term births in developed countries. The major causes of serious ischemia are intrauterine asphyxia, postnatal cardiac insufficiency, and postnatal circulatory insufficiency. Maternal clinical factors associated with neonatal encephalopathy include obesity, diabetes, fetal growth restriction,

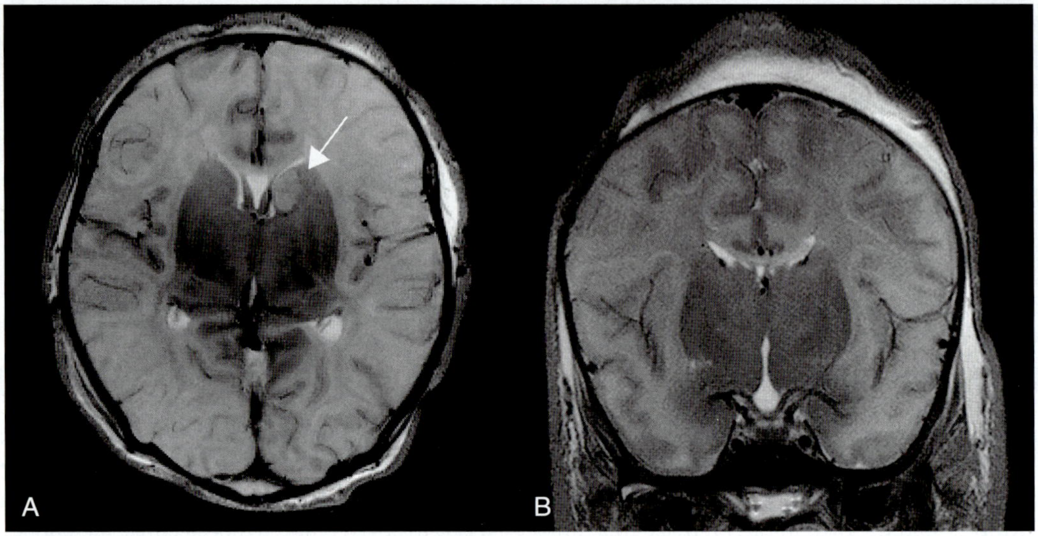

Fig. 8.1 Hypoxic-ischemic encephalopathy. Brain MRI, (A) axial and (B) coronal T2 show severe cerebral edema with diffuse T2 hyperintensity and loss of gray-white matter differentiation. There is focal T2 hyperintensity involving the *left* basal ganglia (*arrow*).

hypertension, and clinical chorioamnionitis. Symptoms of neonatal encephalopathy include decreased level of consciousness, abnormality of muscle tone and power, respiratory depression, disturbances of cranial nerve function, and seizures. Low Apgar scores and metabolic acidosis are associated with neurologic dysfunction. Therapeutic hypothermia initiated within the first 6 hours of life is the only treatment proven to reduce the risk of death and neurodevelopmental impairment.

Head US is the most utilized neuroimaging modality in the NICU. However, US is limited in evaluating cerebral injury in HIE. Brain MRI is preferred and is a useful tool to predict neurodevelopmental outcomes. In the first week after birth, diffusion-weighted (DWI) MRI of the brain may assist physicians in making management decisions for infants with HIE. Because pseudonormalization occurs 7 to 8 days after birth, the optimal time for detection of DWI abnormality in the term infant is 2 to 3 days after birth.

CLINICAL RED FLAGS

Decreased level of consciousness
Abnormality of muscle tone and power
Respiratory depression
Disturbances of cranial nerve function
Seizures
Low Apgar scores
Metabolic acidosis

IMAGING RED FLAGS

In infants with HIE, involvement of the basal ganglia and thalami is strongly associated with severe encephalopathy, including a decreased level of alertness (Fig. 8.3). Diffusion-weighted MRI is most sensitive for detecting acute ischemic injury.

Major intracranial hemorrhage can affect the brain parenchyma or extra-axial spaces (epidural, subdural, subarachnoid, subpial) (Fig. 8.4).

Cerebral sinovenous thrombosis has poor neurodevelopmental outcomes including neurological and motor impairments, epilepsy, or death. Since factors predisposing to cerebral sinus venous thrombosis can overlap with those predisposing to HIE, both conditions can coexist (Fig. 8.5).

The classic pattern of neonatal hypoglycemia classically affects the posterior cerebral cortex, with restricted diffusion in the parietal and occipital lobes (Fig. 8.6).

CONCLUSIONS

Clinicians should consider HIE when a full-term infant with fetal distress develops neonatal seizures. Therapeutic hypothermia initiated within the first 6 hours of life is the only proven treatment for HIE. There are several neuroimaging modalities for evaluating HIE; however, brain MRI is preferred and helps predict neurodevelopmental outcomes.

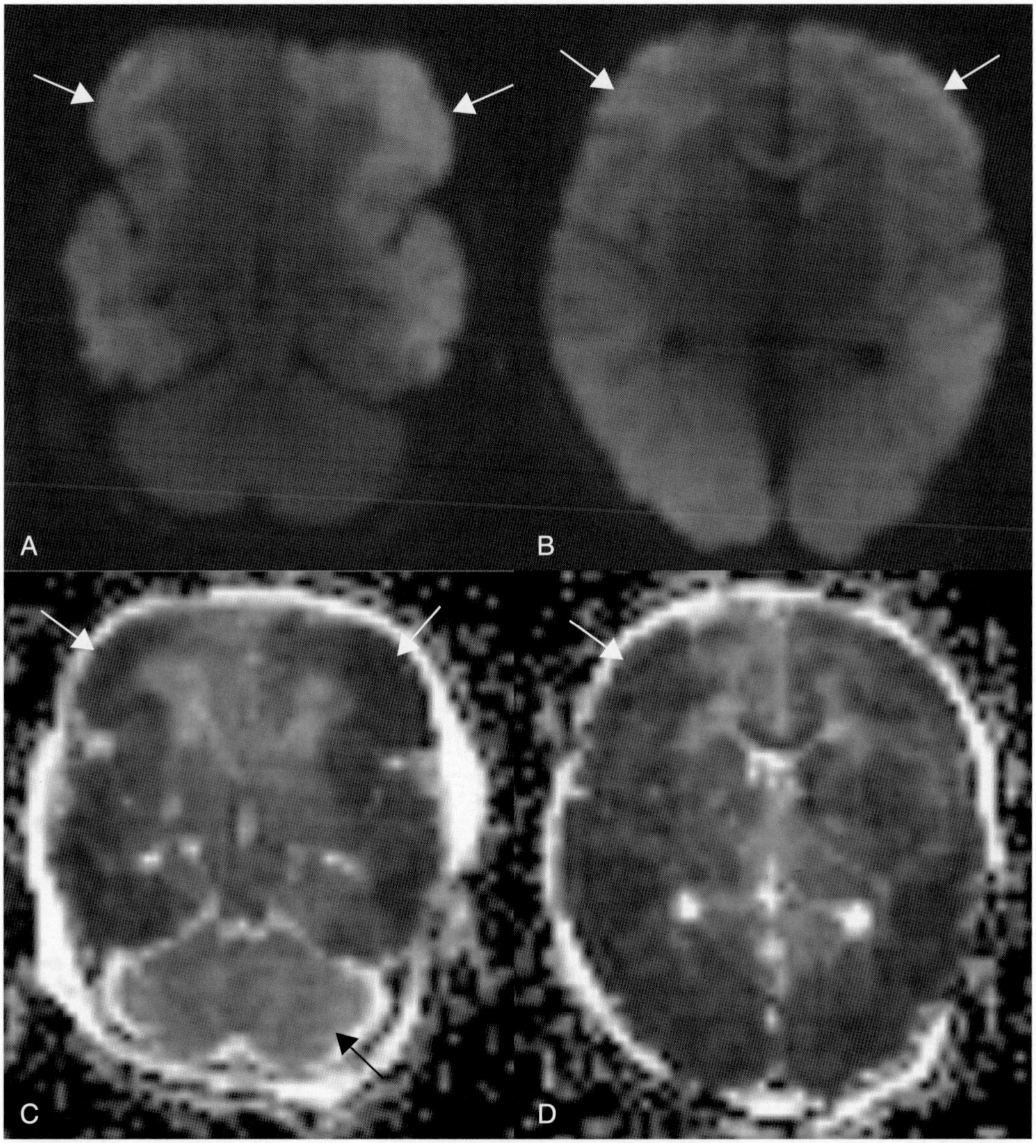

Fig. 8.2 Hypoxic-ischemic encephalopathy. Brain MRI, (A and B) axial DWI, and (C and D) axial ADC show profound restricted diffusion throughout the cortex (*white arrows*), white matter, and deep gray structures. There is relative sparing of the cerebellum (*black arrow*). *ADC*, Apparent diffusion coefficient; *DWI*, diffusion-weighted imaging.

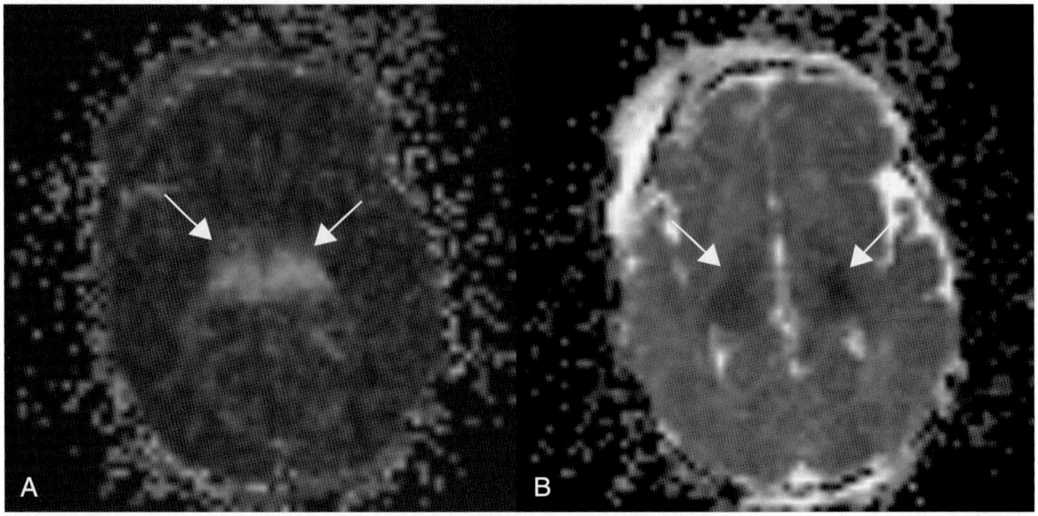

Fig. 8.3 Hypoxic-ischemic encephalopathy. Brain MRI, (A) axial DWI and (B) ADC show restricted diffusion in the deep gray nuclei, particularly thalami (*arrows*). *ADC,* Apparent diffusion coefficient; *DWI,* diffusion-weighted imaging.

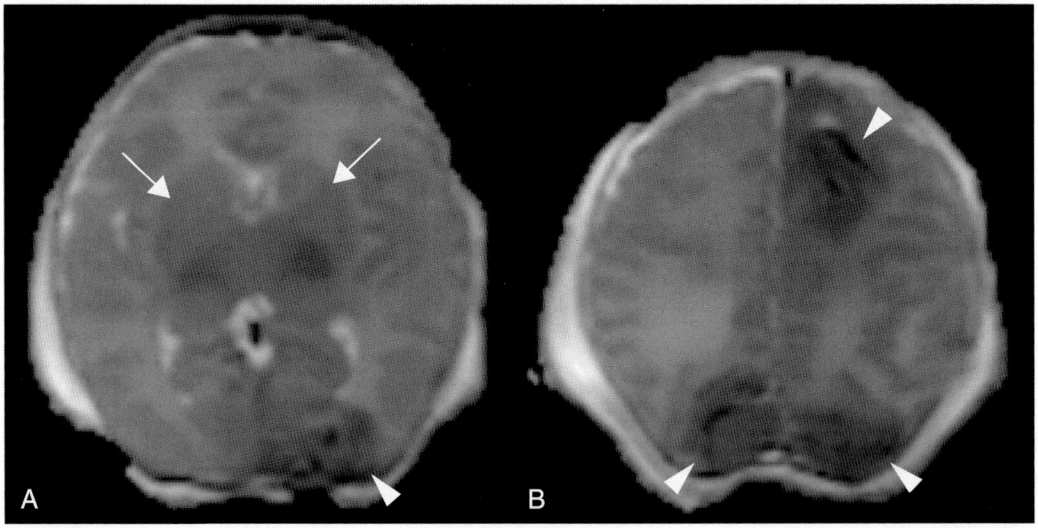

Fig. 8.4 Subpial hemorrhage. Brain MRI, (A and B) axial ADC, shows restricted diffusion in the bilateral basal ganglia and thalami (*arrows*). There are triangular subpial hemorrhages in the occipital lobes and *left* frontal lobe, with subjacent parenchymal reduced diffusivity (*arrowheads*). *ADC,* Apparent diffusion coefficient.

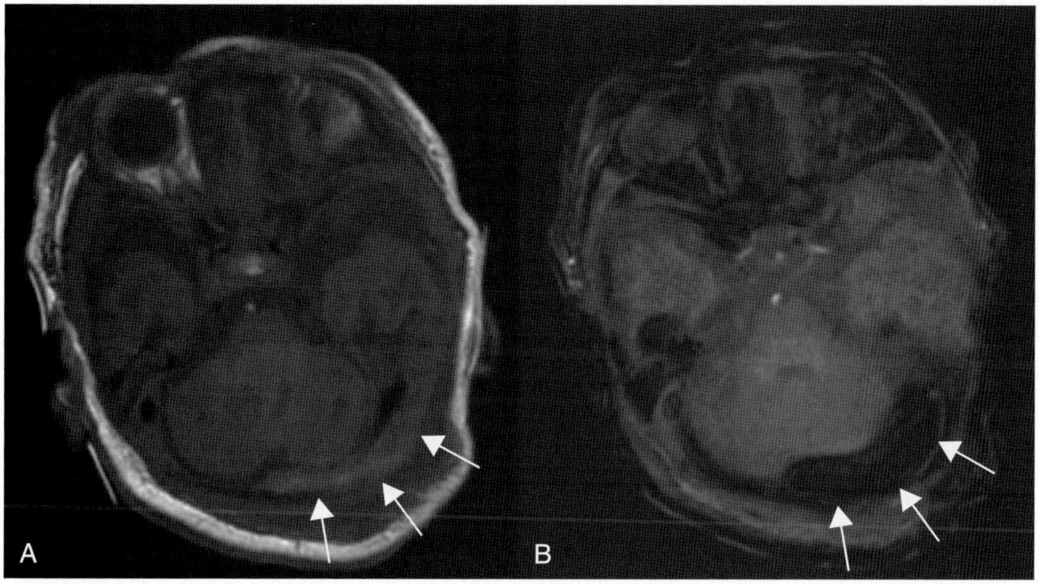

Fig. 8.5 Cerebral sinovenous thrombosis. Brain MRI, (A) axial T1, and (B) SWI, show expansile T1 hyperintensity and susceptibility in the left transverse sinus (*arrows*). *SWI*, Susceptibility-weighted imaging.

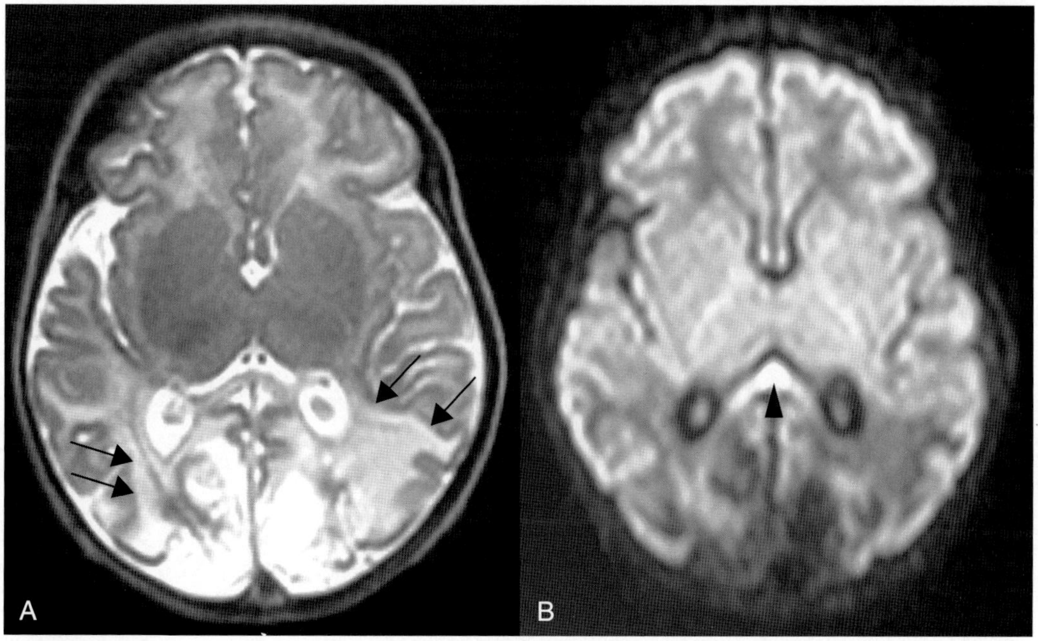

Fig. 8.6 Neonatal hypoglycemia. Brain MRI, (A) axial T2, and (B) DWI, show symmetric T2 hyperintensity in the bilateral occipital lobes (*arrows*). There is also focal diffusion restriction in the splenium of the corpus callosum (*arrowhead*), which can be seen in the setting of seizures and metabolic disturbances. *DWI*, Diffusion-weighted imaging.

REFERENCES

Berfelo FJ, Kersbergen KJ, van Ommen CH, et al. Neonatal cerebral sinovenous thrombosis from symptom to outcome. *Stroke*. 2010;41:1382–1388. https://doi.org/10.1161/STROKEAHA.110.583542.

Cowan F, Rutherford M, Groenendaal F, et al. Origin and timing of brain lesions in term infants with neonatal encephalopathy. *Lancet*. 2003;361:736–742. https://doi.org/10.1016/S0140-6736(03)12658-X.

Miller SP, Ramaswamy V, Michelson D, et al. Patterns of brain injury in term neonatal encephalopathy. *J Pediatr*. 2005;146:453–460. https://doi.org/10.1016/j.jpeds.2004.12.026.

Munster CB, El-Shibiny H, Szakmar E, et al. Magnetic resonance venography to evaluate cerebral sinovenous thrombosis in infants receiving therapeutic hypothermia. *Pediatr Res*. 2023;93:985–989. https://doi.org/10.1038/s41390-022-02195-5.

Volpe JJ, Inder TE, Darras BT, et al. *Volpe's Neurology of the Newborn*. 6th ed. Elsevier; 2017.

Case 9

Preterm Infant With Ventricular Dilatation

HISTORY AND PHYSICAL

A female infant was born at 31^{+5} weeks of gestation by spontaneous vaginal delivery in the setting of premature rupture of membranes, preterm labor, and meconium-stained amniotic fluid. Prenatal US was normal. Birth weight was 1780 g. The patient had intermittent apnea requiring positive-pressure ventilation in the first few minutes of birth but did not require prolonged positive-pressure ventilation. Her exam at 3 days of life was appropriate for age with soft, flat fontanelles. At 1 week of life, she developed decreased consciousness, periodic breathing, bulging fontanelles, and rapidly increasing head circumference.

DIAGNOSTIC WORKUP

Head US on 1 day after birth was normal. However, US 3 days after birth showed right greater than left intraventricular hemorrhage with ventriculomegaly (Fig. 9.1), which increased at 1-week follow-up (Fig. 9.2). Term equivalent brain magnetic resonance imaging (MRI) showed diffuse hemorrhagic hydrocephalus with evolving porencephalic cyst (Fig. 9.3).

CLINICAL DIFFERENTIAL DIAGNOSES

Causes of congenital hydrocephalus include intraventricular hemorrhage, aqueductal stenosis (Fig. 9.4), lumbosacral myelomeningocele with Chiari II malformation, communicating hydrocephalus, and Dandy-Walker malformation.

IMAGING DIFFERENTIAL DIAGNOSES

Ventricular dilatation in the preterm infant is most often caused by one of two major mechanisms: posthemorrhagic ventricular dilatation (PHVD) and/or ex vacuo ventricular dilatation due to parenchymal volume loss. The morphology of the ventricles can assist in diagnosis. Ventricular dilatation due to PHVD shows ballooned ventricular morphology and crowding of the extra-axial spaces. Proportional dilatation of the ventricles and extra-axial spaces with low parenchymal volumes indicates brain atrophy.

FINAL DIAGNOSIS

Posthemorrhagic ventricular dilatation

DISCUSSION

PHVD represents progressive ventricular dilatation caused by intraventricular hemorrhage (IVH). PHVD affects up to 50% of infants with severe IVH and remains a clinically significant complication of germinal matrix-IVH (GMH-IVH) in preterm infants. There is a high risk for adverse neurodevelopmental outcomes. Diagnostic metrics include ventricular size on HUS and assessments of elevated intracranial pressure such as tense fontanelles, ocular sunset phenomena, and measurements of head circumference. On US, the ventricular index of lateral ventricles, anterior horn width, and thalamo-occipital distance are common measurements for evaluation of ventricular size (Fig. 9.5). Brain MRI provides a more comprehensive evaluation but is less accessible and more involved than US. There are diverse clinical symptoms depending on the severity of the hemorrhage, which can include altered consciousness, altered motility, hypotonia, respiratory disturbance, generalized tonic seizures, and flaccid quadriparesis. However, clinically silent GMH-IVH is the most common presentation. Intervention for PHVD usually starts with lumbar puncture and/or ventricular shunting to decompress

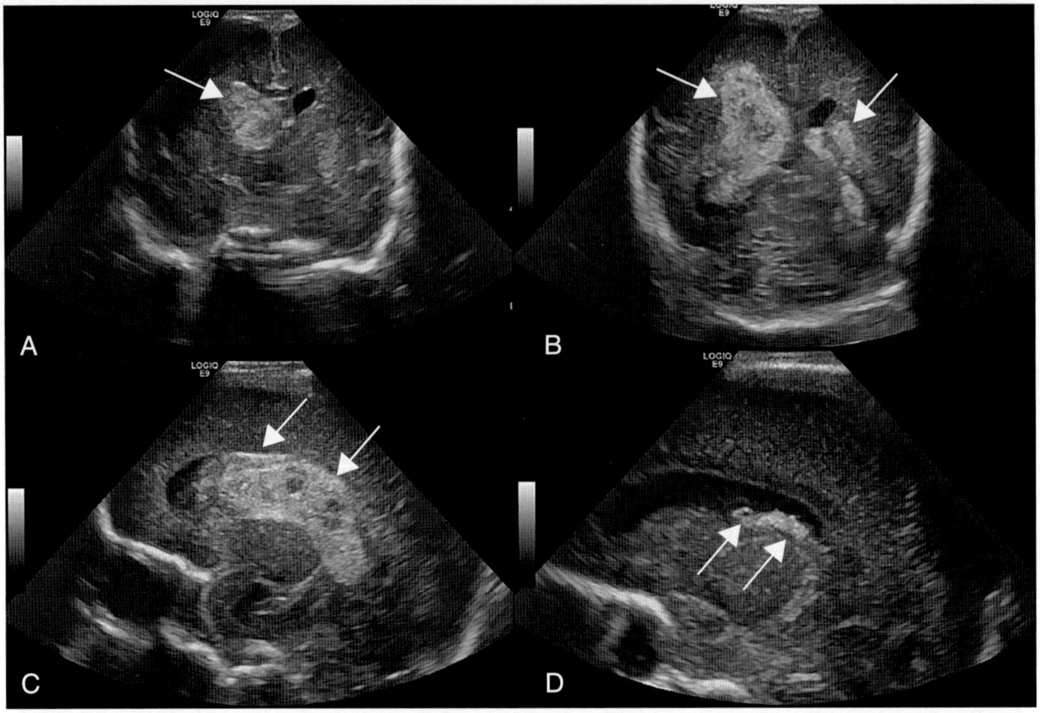

Fig. 9.1 Intraventricular hemorrhage. (A and B) Head ultrasound (US) 3 days after birth with coronal and (C and D) sagittal views show *right* greater than *left* intraventricular hemorrhage (*arrows*) with mild ventriculomegaly.

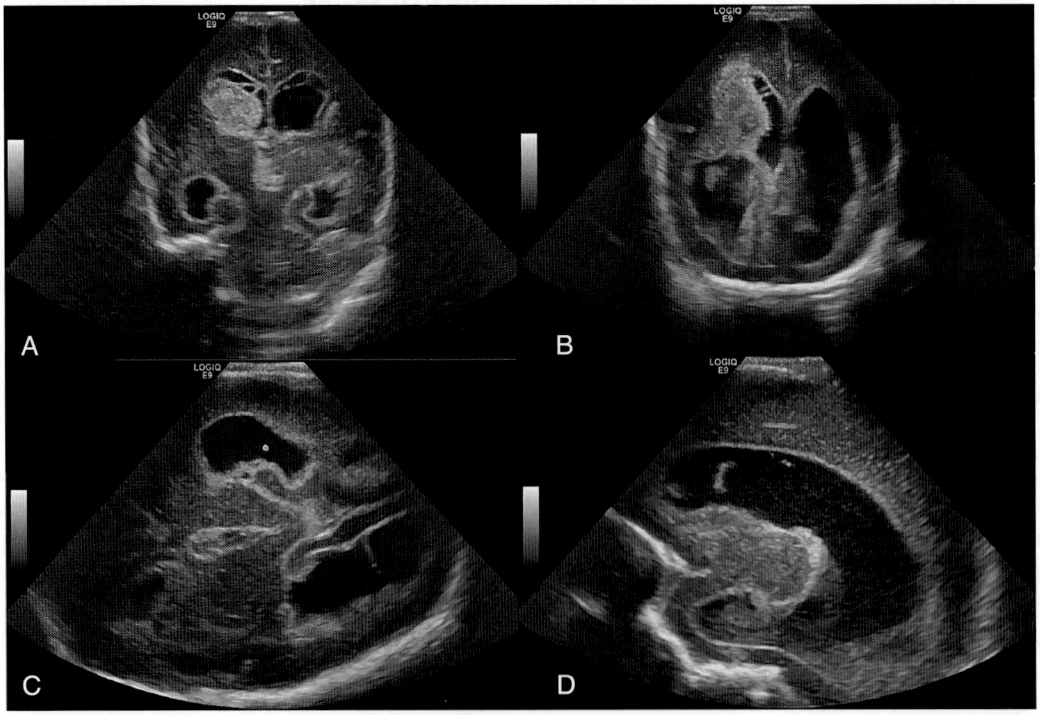

Fig. 9.2 Follow-up intraventricular hemorrhage. (A and B) US 1 week after birth with coronal and (C and D) sagittal views show right greater than left intraventricular hemorrhage with increasing moderate ventriculomegaly.

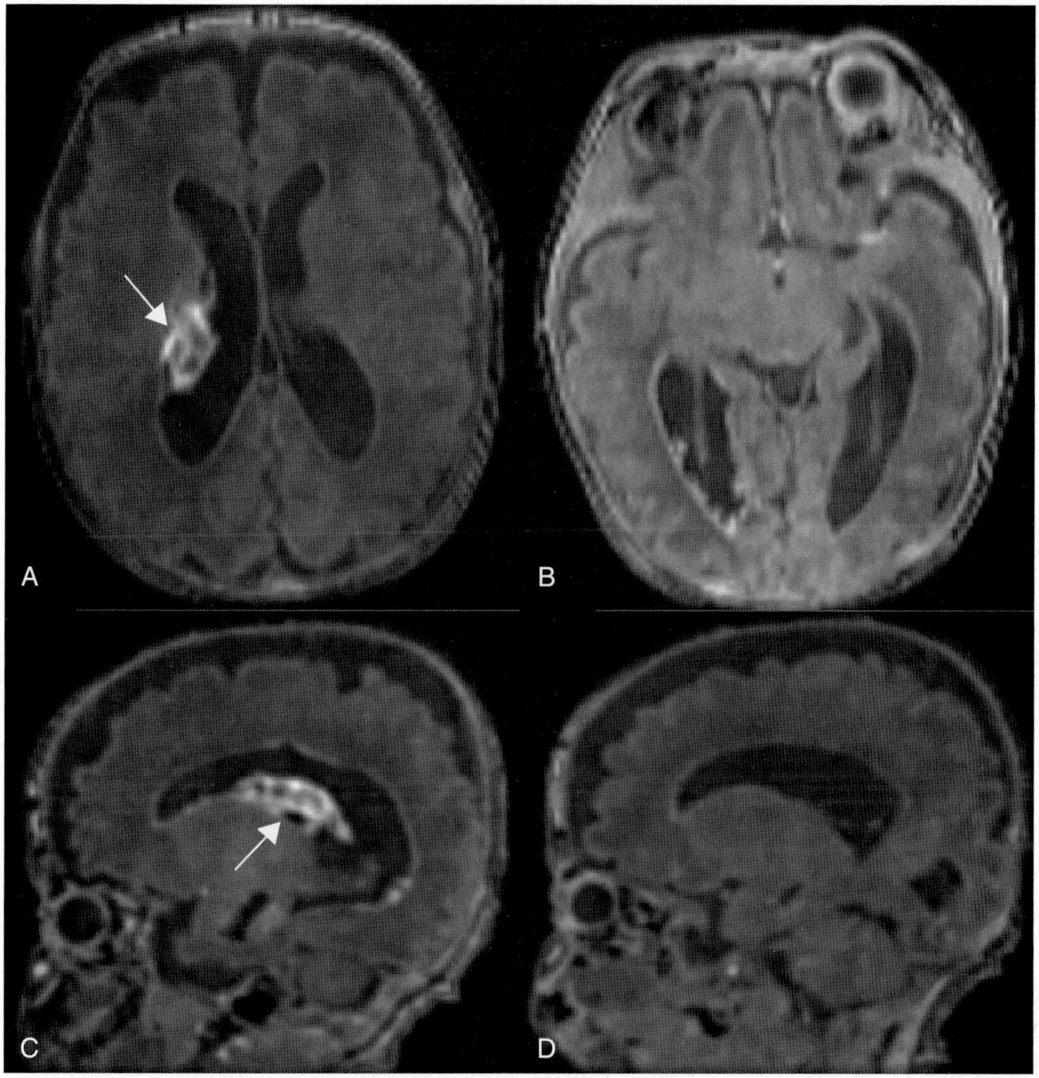

Fig. 9.3 Posthemorrhagic ventricular dilatation (PHVD). Brain MRI, (A and B) axial T1 and (C and D) sagittal T1 show right intraventricular hemorrhage (*arrows*). There is brain volume loss with enlargement of the ventricles and subarachnoid spaces.

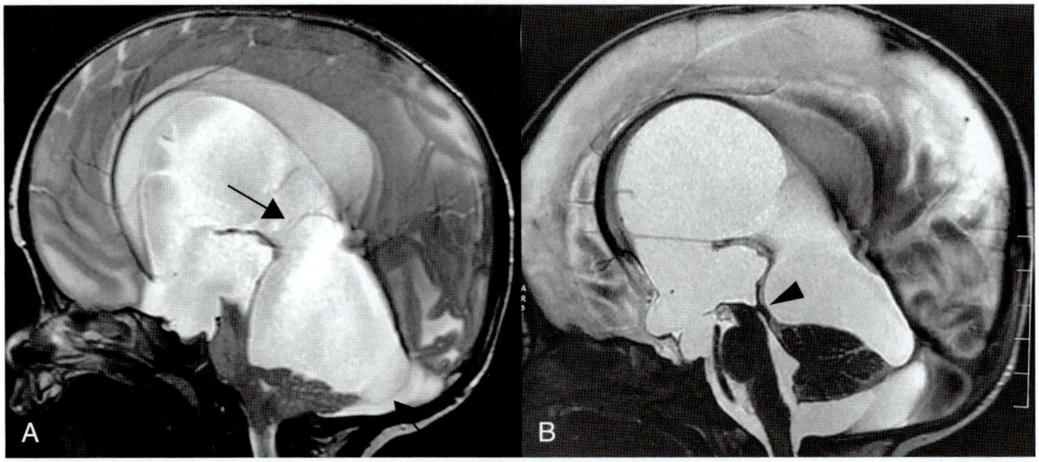

Fig. 9.4 Aqueductal stenosis. Brain MRI, (A) sagittal T2 before and (B) after shunting show severe hydrocephalus with large atrial diverticula (*arrow*) compressing the infratentorial structures. After shunting, there was decreased ventricular size revealing an underlying aqueductal stenosis (*black arrowhead*).

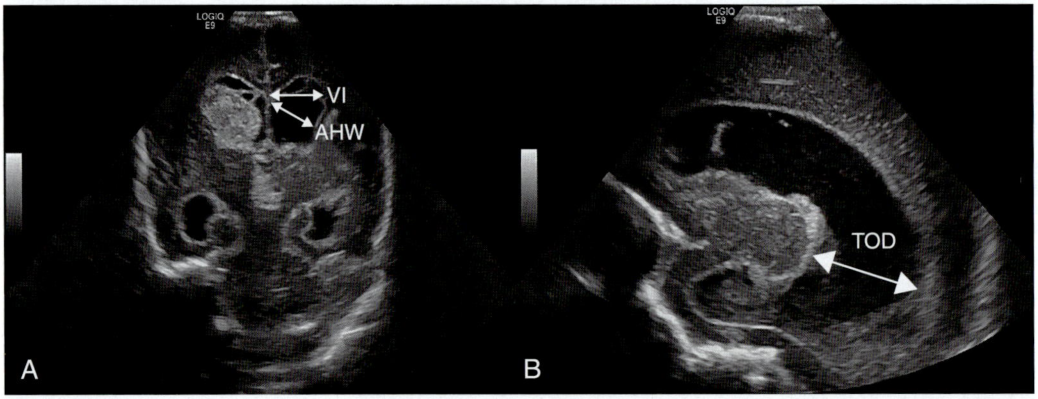

Fig. 9.5 Ventricular metrics. Head US, (A) coronal and (B) sagittal, showing measurement of metrics, including ventricular index (*VI*), anterior horn width (*AHW*), and thalamo-occipital distance (*TOD*).

hydrocephalus. CSF diversion options include external ventricular drain, ventricular access device, ventriculoperitoneal shunt, and endoscopic third ventriculostomy. Complications include parenchymal injury due to IVH and ischemic insults such as white matter injury.

CLINICAL RED FLAGS

Altered level of consciousness
Respiratory disturbance
Generalized tonic seizures
Decerebrate posturing
Pupils fixed to light
Eyes fixed to vestibular stimulation
Flaccid quadriparesis

IMAGING RED FLAGS

White matter injury (periventricular leukomalacia [PVL]).
Arterial infarction.
Brain MRI helps prognosticate based on the degree and presence of parenchymal injury. Among infants with extensive lesions, 30 of 38 (81%) died, and of the eight survivors, seven had subsequent motor deficits.

CONCLUSIONS

PHVD frequently begins within 1 to 3 weeks after the onset of severe IVH. Hemorrhage can be detected by screening US, with brain MRI used for detailed evaluation. There are several CSF diversion interventions for PHVD. Because IVH-GMH and PHVD can have silent symptoms, clinicians should be aware of the risks in preterm infants and screen for injury using US.

REFERENCES

El-Dib M, Limbrick Jr DD, Inder T, et al. Management of post-hemorrhagic ventricular dilatation in the infant born preterm. *J Pediatr*. 2020;226. 16–27.e3. https://doi.org/10.1016/j.jpeds.2020.07.079.

Khanafer-Larocque I, Soraisham A, Stritzke A, et al. Intraventricular hemorrhage: risk factors and association with patent ductus arteriosus treatment in extremely preterm neonates. *Front Pediatr*. 2019;7:408. https://doi.org/10.3389/fped.2019.00408.

Leijser LM, Scott JN, Roychoudhury S, et al. Post-hemorrhagic ventricular dilatation: inter-observer reliability of ventricular size measurements in extremely preterm infants. *Pediatr Res*. 2021;90:403–410. https://doi.org/10.1038/s41390-020-01245-0.

Volpe JJ, Inder TE, Darras BT, et al. *Volpe's Neurology of the Newborn*. 6th ed. Elsevier; 2017.

Case 10

Infants Can Have Strokes Too

HISTORY AND PHYSICAL

A male infant was born at 39 weeks of gestation by planned cesarean section delivery for macrosomia. Mother had a pregnancy history of diet-controlled gestational diabetes mellitus and preeclampsia. Prenatal US was normal. Birth weight was 3935 g. The infant emerged with a vigorous cry and a good tone for gestational age. Respiratory support was not provided in the delivery room. Heart rate was greater than 100 during delivery room observation and interventions. Apgar scores at 1 and 5 minutes were 8 and 9, respectively. The patient had difficulties with breastfeeding from the first day of birth. He developed a seizure on day 3 of life, which lasted 90 seconds with myoclonic jerking of his right arm and leg. There were no abnormal facial movements, eye deviation, eyelid fluttering, or lip smacking. There was no family history of seizures. His exam was otherwise appropriate for his age with soft, flat fontanelles.

DIAGNOSTIC WORKUP

Head US at 3 days after birth was normal. Brain MRI without contrast on day 4 showed confluent restricted diffusion consistent with an acute ischemic infarct involving the left middle and inferior frontal gyri (Fig. 10.1).

CLINICAL DIFFERENTIAL DIAGNOSES

The most common clinical symptom of neonatal arterial ischemic stroke (NAIS) in term infants is seizures, especially focal seizures with onset after 12 hours of life. The timing is different than in HIE, for which seizures most often occur in the first 12 hours. In one study, the mean time of seizure onset in NAIS was 27.8 hours versus 5.1 hours in HIE. Other differential diagnoses for neonatal seizure include intracranial hemorrhage, intracranial infection, developmental defects, hypoglycemia, hypocalcemia, metabolic disorders, and epilepsy syndromes.

IMAGING DIFFERENTIAL DIAGNOSES

HIE shows global diffusion changes that evolve to cytotoxic edema over several days, with symmetric geographic involvement depending on the severity and duration of injury.

In NAIS, acute vessel occlusion leads to restricted diffusion and cytotoxic edema within several hours in an arterial distribution.

Cerebral sinus venous thrombosis yields vasogenic edema in bilateral superficial and/or deep distributions.

FINAL DIAGNOSIS

Neonatal arterial ischemic stroke.

DISCUSSION

NAIS can be associated with mortality and adverse neurodevelopmental outcomes. Symptomatic perinatal stroke occurs in about 1 in 4000 full-term infants. Maternal risk factors for NAIS include smoking, preeclampsia, thrombophilia, fever, infection, prolonged rupture of membranes, and intrapartum complications. Neonatal risk factors for NAIS include male infant, 5-minute Apgar score less than 7, prolonged resuscitation, hypoglycemia, sepsis, congenital heart disease, vascular abnormality, and thrombophilia. The most common initial clinical sign of NAIS is a focal seizure occurring in the first 24 hours of life without other overt neurological signs. Laboratory studies should be performed to rule out seizure etiologies requiring prompt

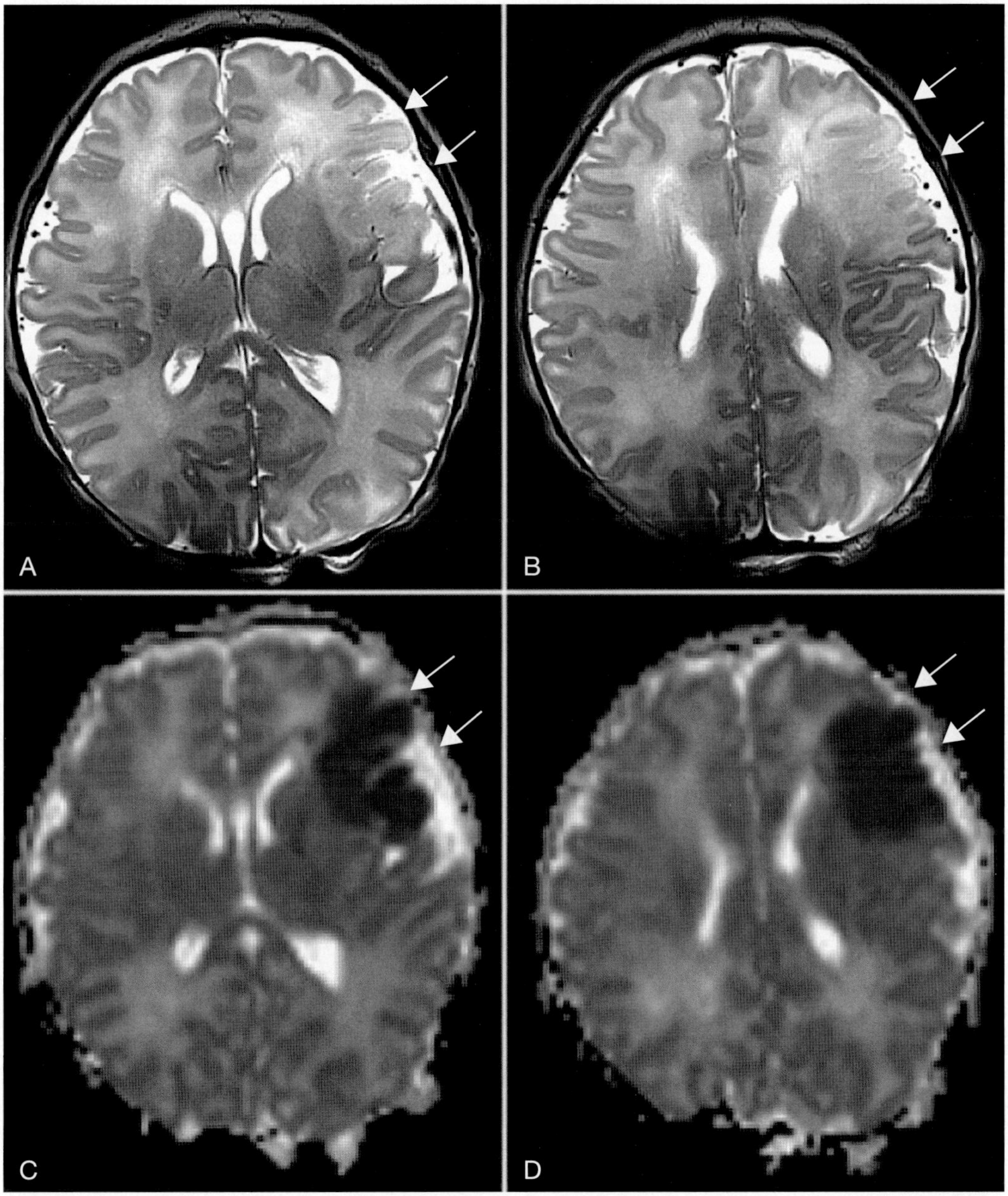

Fig. 10.1 Perinatal arterial ischemic stroke. Brain MRI, (A and B) axial T2, and (C and D) axial ADC, show cytotoxic edema and restricted diffusion in the *left* frontal cortex in the superior MCA territory (*arrows*). *ADC*, Apparent diffusion coefficient; *MCA*, middle cerebral artery.

and often specific intervention, such as hypoglycemia, infection, electrolyte, or metabolic abnormalities. Initial neuroimaging assessment is often performed with head US, but brain MRI provides definitive characterization.

In NAIS, approximately 75% of lesions are unilateral and usually involve the middle cerebral artery (MCA) territory, with 65% on the left. Management includes supportive therapy with fluid/electrolyte management and maintenance of cardiorespiratory function. Use of anticoagulant and antiplatelet therapies is controversial. Long-term neurodevelopment is normal in 19% to 41% of infants with perinatal ischemic infarction. However, hemiparesis occurs in 25% to 35% of surviving full-term infants with established unilateral cerebral infarction.

CLINICAL RED FLAGS

Focal seizure with onset after 12 hours of life
Altered mental status
Abnormal tone
Hemiparesis
Respiratory difficulties
Feeding difficulties

IMAGING RED FLAGS

In NAIS, the likelihood of hemiparesis depends on the extent of the lesion and involvement of the contralateral hemisphere. Hemiparesis occurs in nearly 100% of cases with proximal MCA occlusion. If lenticulostriate or cortical branches are affected, the likelihood of hemiparesis is less than 10%. When the hemisphere contralateral to the infarction is involved even mildly, the likelihood of hemiparesis also approaches 100%.

CONCLUSIONS

NAIS is strongly suspected when an infant develops focal seizure with onset after 12 hours of life. Neuroimaging studies should be done to evaluate the extent of ischemia. There are several neuroimaging modalities that can be used for diagnosis, but no definitive measures to prevent or treat NAIS. Physical, occupational, and language-based therapies can maximize neurodevelopmental outcomes.

REFERENCES

Govaert P, Ramenghi L, Taal R, de Vries L, Deveber G. Diagnosis of perinatal stroke I: definitions, differential diagnosis and registration. *Acta Paediatr.* 2009;98:1556–1567. https://doi.org/10.1111/j.1651-2227.2009.01461.x.

Lehman LL, Rivkin MJ. Perinatal arterial ischemic stroke: presentation, risk factors, evaluation, and outcome. *Pediatr Neurol.* 2014;51:760–768. https://doi.org/10.1016/j.pediatrneurol.2014.07.031.

Nelson KB, Lynch JK. Stroke in newborn infants. *Lancet Neurol.* 2004;3:150–158. https://doi.org/10.1016/S1474-4422(04)00679-9.

Volpe JJ, Inder TE, Darras BT, et al. *Volpe's Neurology of the Newborn.* 6th ed. Elsevier; 2017.

Case 11

Preterm Infant With Hypotonia

HISTORY AND PHYSICAL

A male infant was born at 33^{+1} weeks of gestation by emergency cesarean section in the setting of breech positioning, hypotonia, and prolonged bradycardia of 60 beats/minute. Birth weight was 1860 g. The baby was born in breech presentation, and Apgar scores at 1 and 5 minutes were 2 and 4, respectively. In the delivery room, the infant experienced significant respiratory distress prompting intubation. Neurologic examination showed hypotonia and few spontaneous movements including eye opening. EEG demonstrated continuous low-voltage patterns.

DIAGNOSTIC WORKUP

Head US on day 2 of life showed prominent extra-axial spaces. Brain MRI at 18 days showed confluent restricted diffusion throughout the cerebral white matter with medullar venous injury (Fig. 11.1). Follow-up MRI at 45 days showed development of large areas of cystic encephalomalacia with global volume loss (Fig. 11.2).

CLINICAL DIFFERENTIAL DIAGNOSES

Differential diagnoses for neonatal hypotonia include hypoxic-ischemic encephalopathy, intracranial hemorrhage, cerebral malformations, chromosomal abnormalities, intracranial infection, peroxisomal disorders, inborn errors of metabolism, and maternal drug use. The diagnostic algorithm should include history and physical examination, neuroimaging, neurogenetic and biochemical testing, and muscle and nerve investigations.

IMAGING DIFFERENTIAL DIAGNOSES

Periventricular leukomalacia (PVL) consists of two distinct pathologic components: focal necrosis and diffuse cellular injury involving preoligodendrocytes in cerebral white matter with astrogliosis and microgliosis.

Global hypoxia-ischemia is more common in term infants.

Metabolic brain disorders such as molybdenum cofactor deficiency (Fig. 11.3) and bilirubin encephalopathy (Fig. 11.4).

FINAL DIAGNOSIS

Periventricular leukomalacia.

DISCUSSION

Encephalopathy of prematurity describes the complex injuries in the preterm brain caused by developmental and acquired factors. The hallmark imaging feature is PVL with white matter necrosis, reactive gliosis, and microglial activation. In one systematic review, the incidence of white matter abnormalities was estimated at 39.6% for infants born under 28 weeks of gestation, 27.4% under 32 weeks of gestation, and 7.3% under 37 weeks of gestation. The major pathogenic causes of PVL are cerebral ischemia and systemic infection/inflammation. Perinatal risk factors include fetal metabolic acidosis, systemic fetal inflammation, respiratory insufficiency, cardiac insufficiency, and conditions that lead to elevated concentrations of inflammation-related proteins in the circulation, such as necrotizing enterocolitis. Serial head US is valuable in diagnosing PVL and characterizing the evolving cystic changes. Brain MRI is more sensitive for noncystic forms of PVL with white matter signal changes and medullary venous congestion. Unfavorable long-term neurodevelopmental outcomes include motor deficits, spastic diplegia, and a variety of cognitive, behavioral, attentional, and socialization defects.

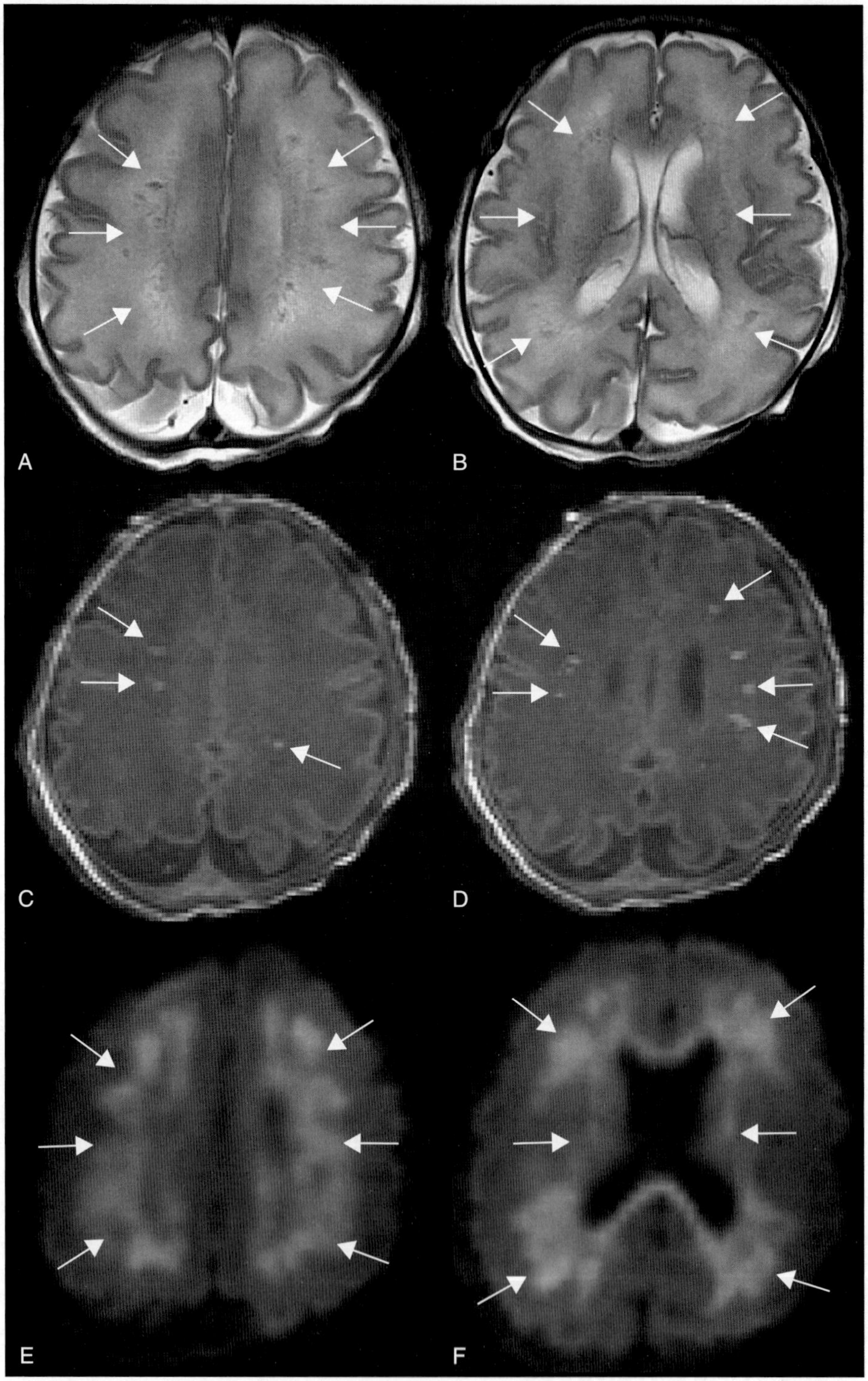

Fig. 11.1 Periventricular leukomalacia and medullary venous thrombosis. Brain MRI, (A and B) axial T2, (C and D) T1, and (E and F) DWI show confluent white matter edema with radiating linear and punctate areas of medullary venous injury (*arrows*). *DWI*, Diffusion-weighted imaging.

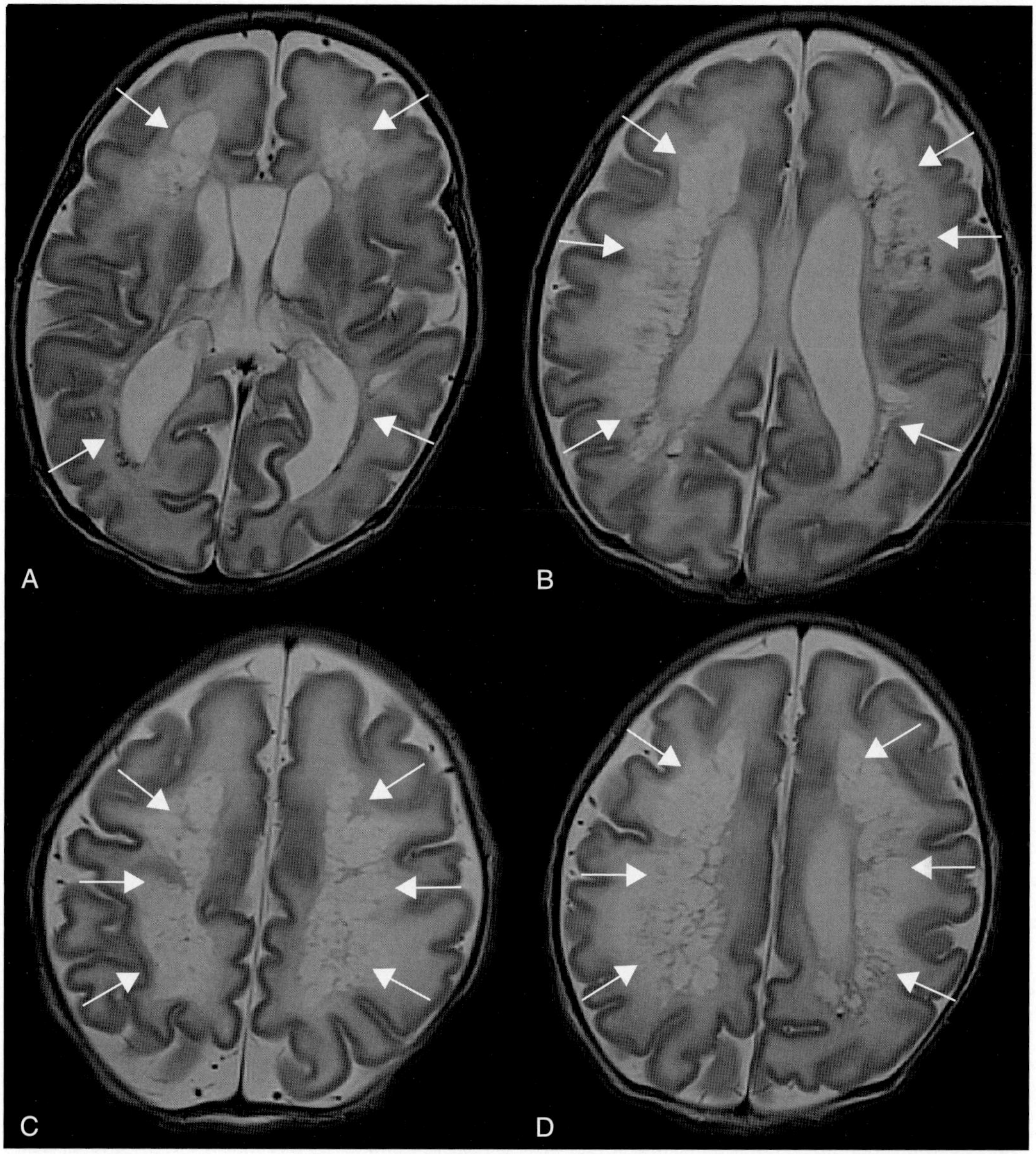

Fig. 11.2 Follow-up of periventricular leukomalacia. Brain MRI, (A–D) axial T2, shows multicystic encephalomalacia (*arrows*).

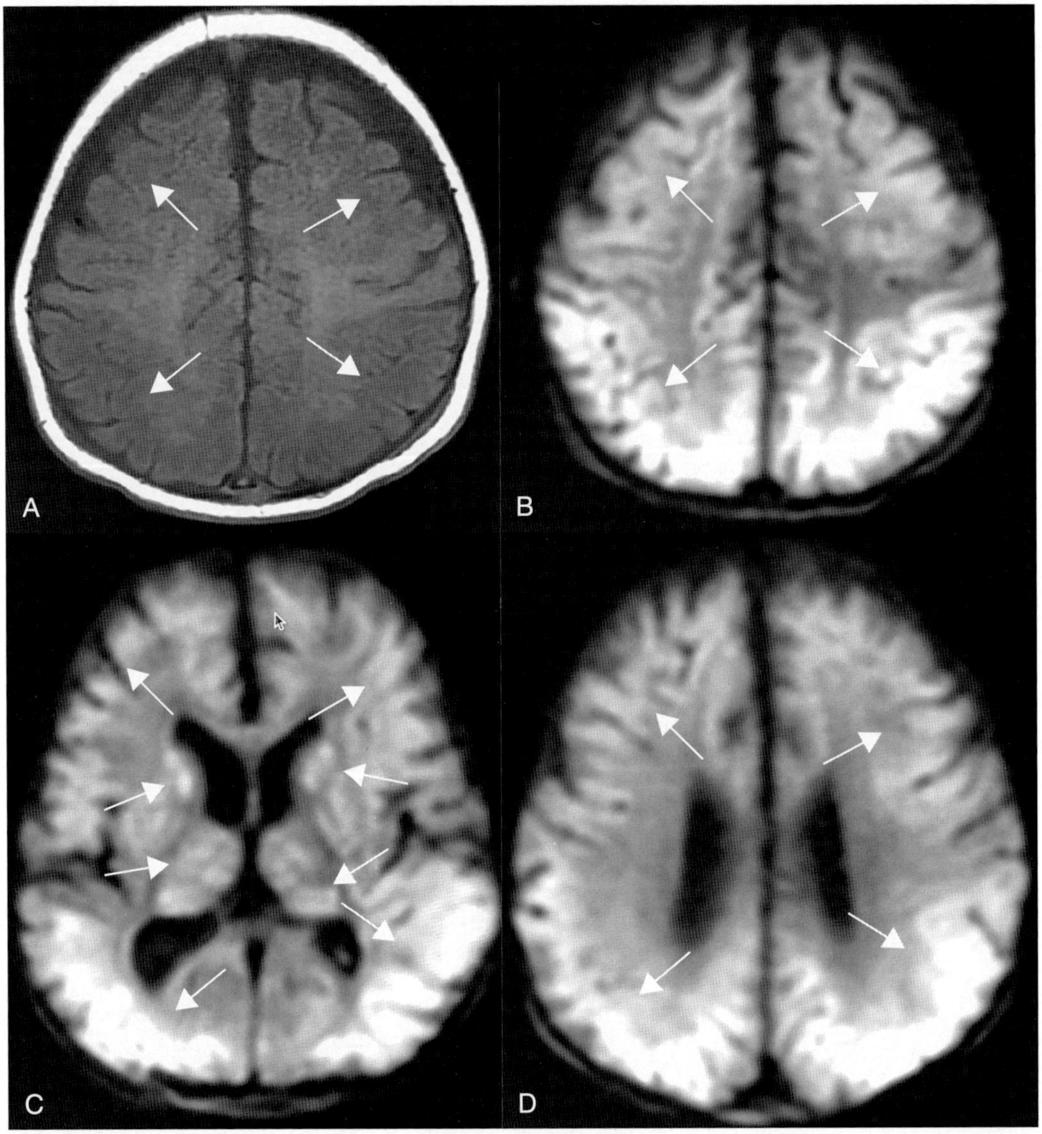

Fig. 11.3 Molybdenum cofactor deficiency. Brain MRI, (A) axial T1 and (B–D) DWI show edema and diffusion restriction of the cortex and deep gray structures (*arrows*). *DWI*, Diffusion-weighted imaging.

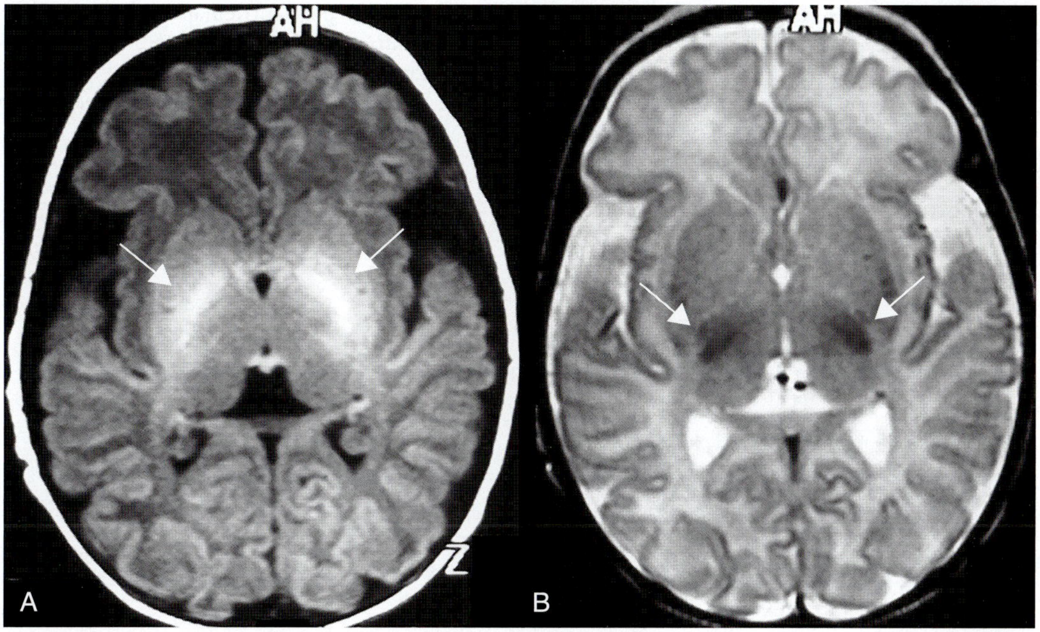

Fig. 11.4 Bilirubin encephalopathy. Brain MRI, (A) axial T1 and (B) T2, show symmetric T1 hyperintensity and T2 hypointensity of the globi pallidi and subthalamic nuclei (*arrows*).

CLINICAL RED FLAGS

Periodic breathing at term equivalent
Absent light pupillary reaction at 32 to 34 weeks
Hypotonia in the upper extremities at term equivalent
Seizure

IMAGING RED FLAGS

Neurological disturbances associated with PVL relate to the degree of white matter injury and associated deficits of cerebral cortex (especially sensorimotor and visual), thalamus, basal ganglia, and cerebellum.

Identification of white matter lesions can be accomplished by serial head US and/or brain MRI.

CONCLUSIONS

Neonatal hypotonia can be clinically challenging given the broad differential diagnosis. Careful history and neuroimaging evaluation are important. Because PVL has a major impact on neurodevelopment and is difficult to prevent, clinicians should manage cases carefully with newborn resuscitation, ventilation, glucose management, and seizure management as indicated.

REFERENCES

Gotardo JW, Volkmer NFV, Stangler GP, Dornelles AD, Bohrer BBA, Carvalho CG. Impact of peri-intraventricular hemorrhage and periventricular leukomalacia in the neurodevelopment of preterms: a systematic review and metaanalysis. *PloS One*. 2019;14:e0223427. https://doi.org/10.1371/journal.pone.0223427.

Sparks SE. Neonatal hypotonia. *Clin Perinatol*. 2015;42:363–371. ix. https://doi.org/10.1016/j.clp.2015.02.008.

Staudt M, Pavlova M, Böhm S, Grodd W, Krägeloh-Mann I. Pyramidal tract damage correlates with motor dysfunction in bilateral periventricular leukomalacia (PVL). *Neuropediatrics*. 2003;34:182–188. https://doi.org/10.1055/s-2003-42206.

Volpe JJ, Inder TE, Darras BT, et al. *Volpe's Neurology of the Newborn*. 6th ed. Elsevier; 2017.

SECTION 3

Cerebral Palsy

Xènia Alonso Curcó, Federico Baltar, Jordi Muchart, Emilio Turcatti, Alfredo Cerisola

INTRODUCTION

Cerebral palsy (CP) describes a clinical spectrum of limitations in development of movement, posture, and motor function, occurring in the developing fetal or infant brain. Clinical features evolve with age and may lead to a deterioration of motor function, even though the underlying condition is nonprogressive. Motor disorders are often accompanied by disturbances of sensation, perception, cognition, communication, behavior, epilepsy, and/or secondary musculoskeletal problems. CP can be classified in several ways:

A. topography (unilateral or bilateral)
B. predominant tone/movement disorder (spastic [80%], dyskinetic—including dystonic and choreoathetoid—[15%], or ataxic [5%] forms)
C. functional level (considering gross motor function, manual ability, communication, and ability to eat and drink)
D. associated disorders

Radiologic abnormalities are not included in these criteria, and a normal imaging examination does not exclude the diagnosis. Nevertheless, imaging findings are abnormal in more than 80% to 90% of children with CP. Neuroimaging can be helpful in revealing etiology, timing, and structural-functional relationships.

Several imaging classification systems have been proposed, most recently the MRI Classification System (MRICS) by the Surveillance of CP in Europe (SCPE) group. MRICS consists of five major groups: (A) maldevelopments, (B) predominant white matter injury, (C) predominant grey matter injury, (D) miscellaneous, and (E) normal findings. Etiologies are diverse and depend on the timing of injury during brain development. In the first and second trimesters of pregnancy, cortical neurogenesis disturbances result in malformations of cortical development such as lissencephaly, and pachygyria. Early in the third trimester, the white matter and residual germinal matrix are more susceptible to injury such as periventricular leukomalacia, intraventricular hemorrhage, and periventricular hemorrhagic infarction. The etiology of CP in the late third trimester may involve cortical and/or deep gray matter injury, along with brainstem and cerebellum. Large arterial territory infarcts occur mainly in term babies during the perinatal period. It is important to note that different patterns of injury can coexist, in which case the predominant imaging pattern should be used for classification. MRI performed after the age of 2-3 years is better at detecting lesions, once myelination is complete.

SUGGESTED READINGS

Crichton A, Ditchfield M, Gwini S, et al. Brain magnetic resonance imaging is a predictor of bimanual performance and executive function in children with unilateral cerebral palsy. *Dev Med Child Neurol.* 2020;62(5):615–624. doi:10.1111/dmcn.14462.

Himmelmann K, Horber V, De La Cruz J, et al. MRI classification system (MRICS) for children with cerebral palsy: development, reliability, and recommendations. *Dev Med Child Neurol.* 2017;59(1):57–64. doi:10.1111/dmcn.13166.

Rosenbaum P, Paneth N, Leviton A, et al. A report: the definition and classification of cerebral palsy April 2006 [published correction appears in Dev Med Child Neurol. 2007 Jun;49(6):480]. *Dev Med Child Neurol Suppl.* 2007;109:8–14.

My Baby Is Left-Handed

HISTORY AND PHYSICAL

A 2-year-old boy was referred for use of only his left hand and clumsiness when walking. Pregnancy was complicated by gestational diabetes with good metabolic control. He was born by vaginal delivery without complications at 40 weeks of gestational age. He had motor delays and walked independently at 18 months of age, as well as expressive and receptive language delays. Social milestones were normal for age. Physical examination revealed spasticity of the right arm and leg with associated hyperreflexia and Babinski sign. The left side was neurologically normal. He walked with internal rotation of the right foot and circumduction with associated elbow flexion and forearm pronation.

DIAGNOSTIC WORKUP

MRI showed left periventricular white matter signal abnormalities corresponding to gliosis, associated with ex vacuo ventricular dilation. Traversing linear susceptibility was compatible with medullary venous injury (Fig. 12.1).

CLINICAL DIFFERENTIAL DIAGNOSES

Causes of congenital hemiparesis include large artery infarcts, small artery infarcts, and malformations of cortical development.

Mutations in type IV collagen (*COL4A1* or *COL4A2* genes) are associated with familial hemorrhagic strokes, congenital porencephalic cysts, and multisystem cardiac, ocular, muscular, and/or renal findings.

IMAGING DIFFERENTIAL DIAGNOSES

Perinatal large artery infarcts classically show cystic encephalomalacia affecting the cortex and subcortical white matter in the territory of the affected artery (Fig. 12.2). Perinatal hemorrhagic stroke can be easily diagnosed with susceptibility-weighted MRI for detection of remote parenchymal hemorrhage.

Small artery lacunar infarcts are more localized, with a rounded or triangular morphology. Basal ganglia involvement is common with lenticulostriate artery infarcts.

Periventricular leukomalacia is associated with preterm birth and can demonstrate diffuse or asymmetric white matter injury, intraventricular hemorrhage, and ex vacuo ventricular dilation (Fig. 12.3).

FINAL DIAGNOSIS

Unilateral spastic cerebral palsy (CP), due to periventricular venous infarction.

DISCUSSION

Perinatal cerebrovascular accidents classically present with motor impairment, which may go unnoticed in the first few months of life unless Prechtl Qualitative Assessment of General Movements is performed. This is the most common type of perinatal stroke with an estimated incidence of 40/100,000.

Periventricular venous infarcts are associated with injury to deep medullary veins, which radiate through the white matter and drain to ependymal veins in the ventricular system. Slow flow and thrombosis of these veins can lead to venous ischemia with infarction and hemorrhagic necrosis. This has been associated with multiple factors, including gestational diabetes, small-for-gestational-age infants, first pregnancy, advanced maternal age, and genetic factors.

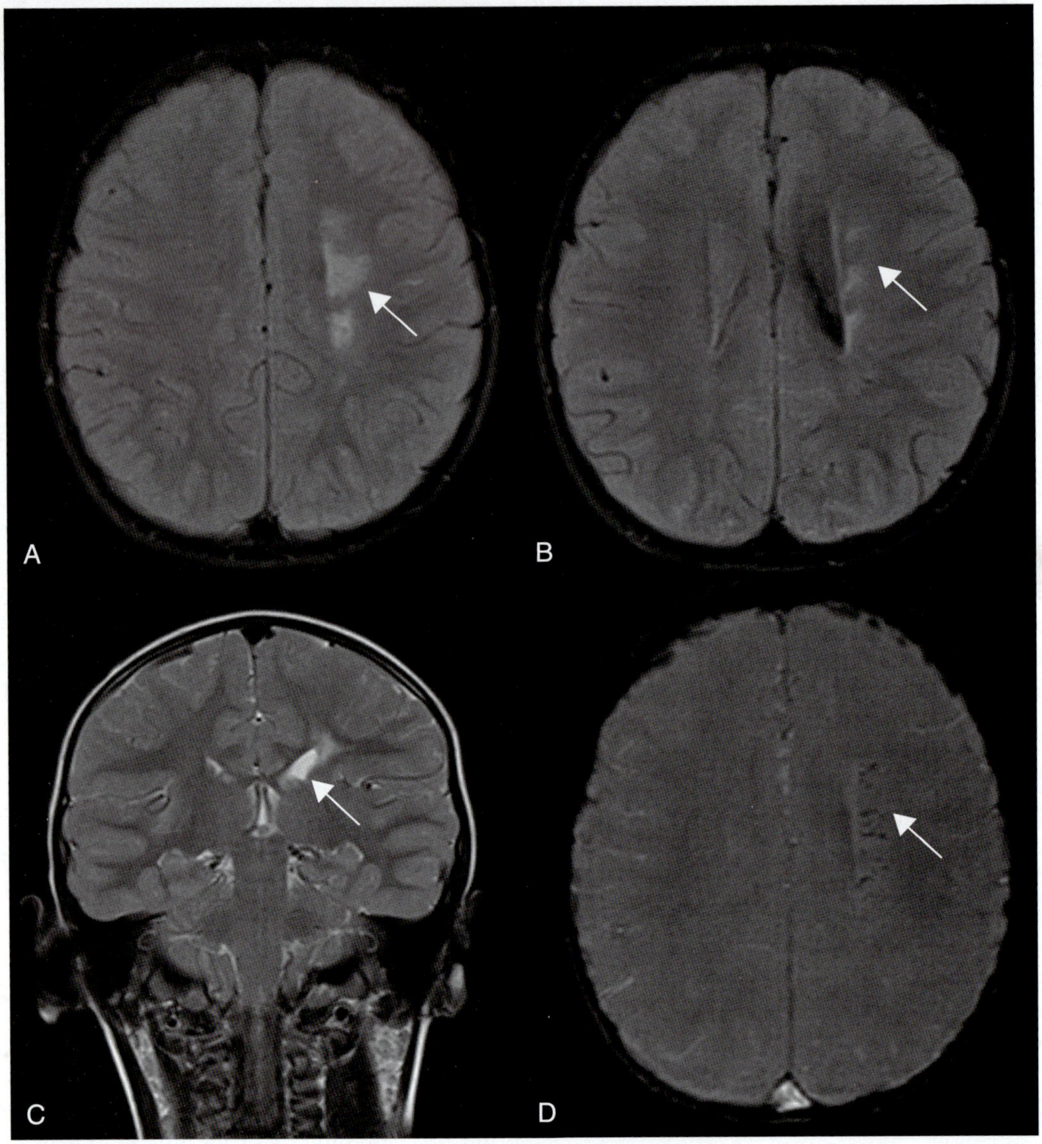

Fig. 12.1 Left medullary venous thrombosis. Brain MRI, (A and B) axial FLAIR, (C) coronal T2, and (D) SWI show hyperintense signal and volume loss in the left periventricular white matter, associated with ex vacuo ventricular dilatation and medullary venous thrombosis (*arrows*). *FLAIR*, Fluid-attenuated inversion recovery; *SWI*, susceptibility-weighted imaging.

CLINICAL RED FLAGS

- Early hand preference and asymmetric reaching before 3 years of age raise concern for hemiparesis.
- Many perinatal cerebrovascular accidents occur in the absence of antenatal risk factors and are asymptomatic early on.
- Early diagnosis is essential to begin neurorehabilitation.

IMAGING RED FLAGS

- There is a wide spectrum of causes of congenital hemiparesis, and brain MRI helps elucidate etiology.
- Periventricular white matter changes should suggest medullary venous infarcts.
- Susceptibility-weighted MRI can identify prior thrombosis and hemorrhage.

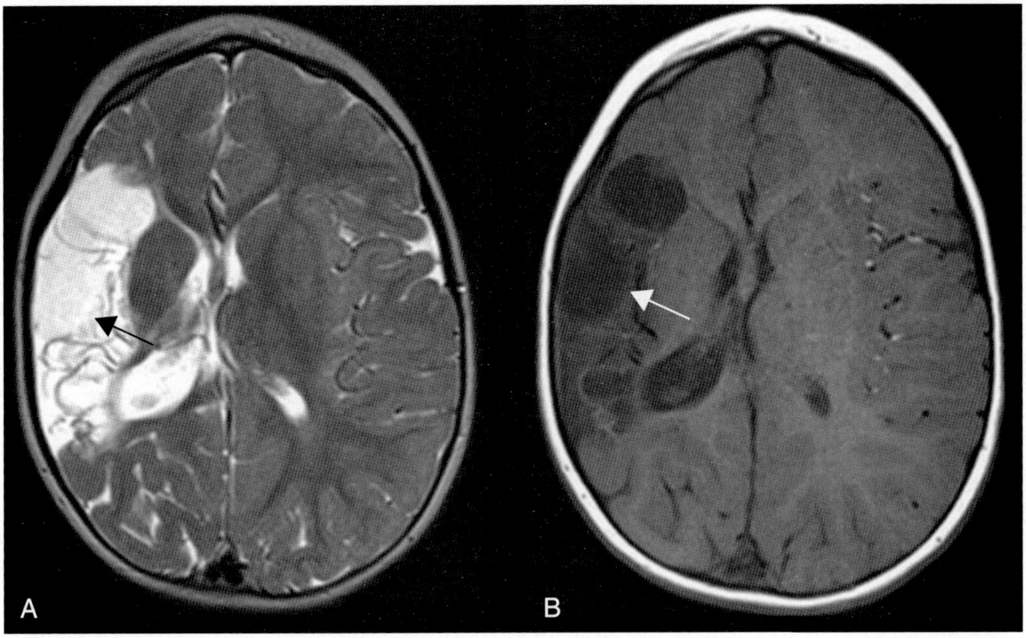

Fig. 12.2 Right MCA infarct. Brain MRI, (A) axial T2 and (B) T1 show right MCA territory cystic encephalomalacia (*arrows*) with ex vacuo dilation of the right lateral ventricle. *MCA*, Middle cerebral artery.

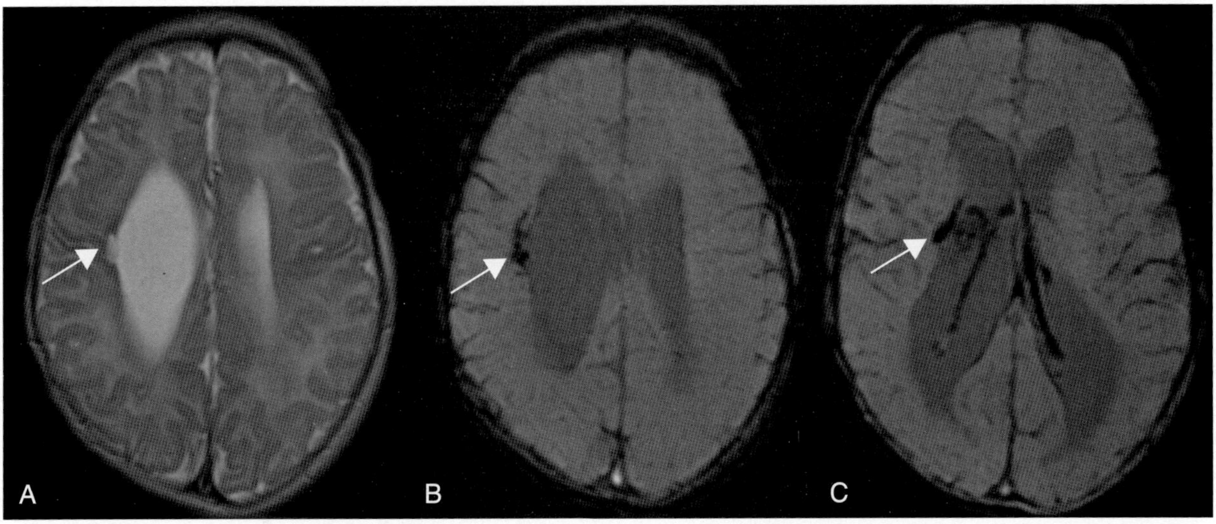

Fig. 12.3 Asymmetric periventricular leukomalacia. Brain MRI, (A) axial T2 shows right greater than left white matter hyperintense signal and volume loss with ex vacuo ventricular dilatation (*arrow*). (B–C) Axial SWI shows intraventricular hemorrhage staining the caudothalamic grooves (*arrows*) and choroid plexus. *SWI*, Susceptibility-weighted imaging.

CONCLUSIONS

Perinatal stroke presents as unilateral CP in a previously healthy infant. Therapy should focus on early neurorehabilitation.

REFERENCES

Benders MJ, Kersbergen KJ, de Vries LS. Neuroimaging of white matter injury, intraventricular and cerebellar hemorrhage. *Clin Perinatol.* 2014;41(1):69–82. doi:10.1016/j.clp.2013.09.005.

de Vries LS. Congenital hemiplegia: not only caused by presumed perinatal arterial stroke. *Ann Neurol.* 2008;63(4):413–415. doi:10.1002/ana.21374.

Dunbar M, Kirton A. Perinatal stroke: mechanisms, management, and outcomes of early cerebrovascular brain injury. *Lancet Child Adolesc Health.* 2018;2(9):666–676. doi:10.1016/S2352-4642(18)30173-1.

Fluss J, Dinomais M, Chabrier S. Perinatal stroke syndromes: Similarities and diversities in aetiology, outcome and management. *Eur J Paediatr Neurol.* 2019;23(3):368–383. doi:10.1016/j.ejpn.2019.02.013.

Kirton A, Shroff M, Pontigon AM, deVeber G. Risk factors and presentations of periventricular venous infarction vs arterial presumed perinatal ischemic stroke. *Arch Neurol.* 2010;67(7):842–848. doi:10.1001/archneurol.2010.140.

Reid SM, Dagia CD, Ditchfield MR, Carlin JB, Reddihough DS. Population-based studies of brain imaging patterns in cerebral palsy. *Dev Med Child Neurol.* 2014;56(3):222–232. doi:10.1111/dmcn.1222.

Srivastava R, Kirton A. Perinatal stroke: a practical approach to diagnosis and management. *Neoreviews.* 2021;22(3):e163–e176. doi:10.1542/neo.22-3-e163.

The Infant With Asymmetric Posture

HISTORY AND PHYSICAL

A 15-month-old boy was brought in for difficulties using his left hand. He was born full term with no complications during pregnancy or delivery. At 5 months of age, his parents observed that his left hand remained fisted, and his thumb adducted. He had mild motor delays, walking with assistance at 15 months and favoring the use of his right hand. Language and social skills were normal. On physical examination, he exclusively used his right hand to grab objects while keeping his left hand fisted. He had left hemiparesis with hyperreflexia and upgoing plantar responses.

DIAGNOSTIC WORKUP

Brain MRI demonstrated right perisylvian polymicrogyria (Fig. 13.1).

CLINICAL DIFFERENTIAL DIAGNOSES

Causes of congenital hemiparesis include perinatal large artery infarcts, small artery infarcts, and periventricular leukomalacia.

IMAGING DIFFERENTIAL DIAGNOSES

Polymicrogyria is a malformation of cortical development that manifests on MRI as multiple small gyri and sulci with diffuse gray-white junctional irregularity. The finding is best appreciated when comparing the affected region to normal contralateral gyri (if unilateral) or age-matched controls. Depending on the imaging plane and resolution, polymicrogyria may appear fine and small, thick and bumpy, or saw-toothed.

Antenatal infections, such as cytomegalovirus (CMV), can result in white matter injury, subependymal cysts, calcifications, ventriculomegaly, polymicrogyria, and cerebellar abnormalities depending on the timing of infection.

Schizencephaly is an early developmental insult that results in a transmantle defect from the ependymal surface of the ventricle through the pial surface of the cortex. The gray matter lining is disorganized and dysplastic, with a polymicrogyric appearance. Schizencephalic clefts are typically classified as unilateral (60%) or bilateral (40%) and as open lip (with intervening cerebrospinal fluid gap) versus closed lip (Fig. 13.2).

Lissencephaly refers to neuronal undermigration with decreased gyration and sulcation, forming rudimentary disorganized and thickened gyri (agyria-pachygyria-band heterotopia spectrum) (Fig. 13.3).

FINAL DIAGNOSIS

Left unilateral spastic cerebral palsy (CP), due to right perisylvian polymicrogyria.

DISCUSSION

In a multicenter study of 3818 children with CP, 1320 (34.6%) received imaging with a predominant white matter injury pattern in 47.3%, followed by predominant gray matter injury in 30.2%, maldevelopments in 9.5%, miscellaneous in 7.1%, and normal findings in 6.1% of cases.

Malformations of cortical development are caused by genetic or environmental factors that inhibit neuronal/glial proliferation, migration, and/or cortical organization depending on the timing of injury. Etiologies include genetic mutations, infection, hemorrhage, exogenous toxins (alcohol and other drugs), and endogenous toxins (metabolic disorders). Polymicrogyria is related to postmigrational cortical disorganization resulting in multiple small and disorganized

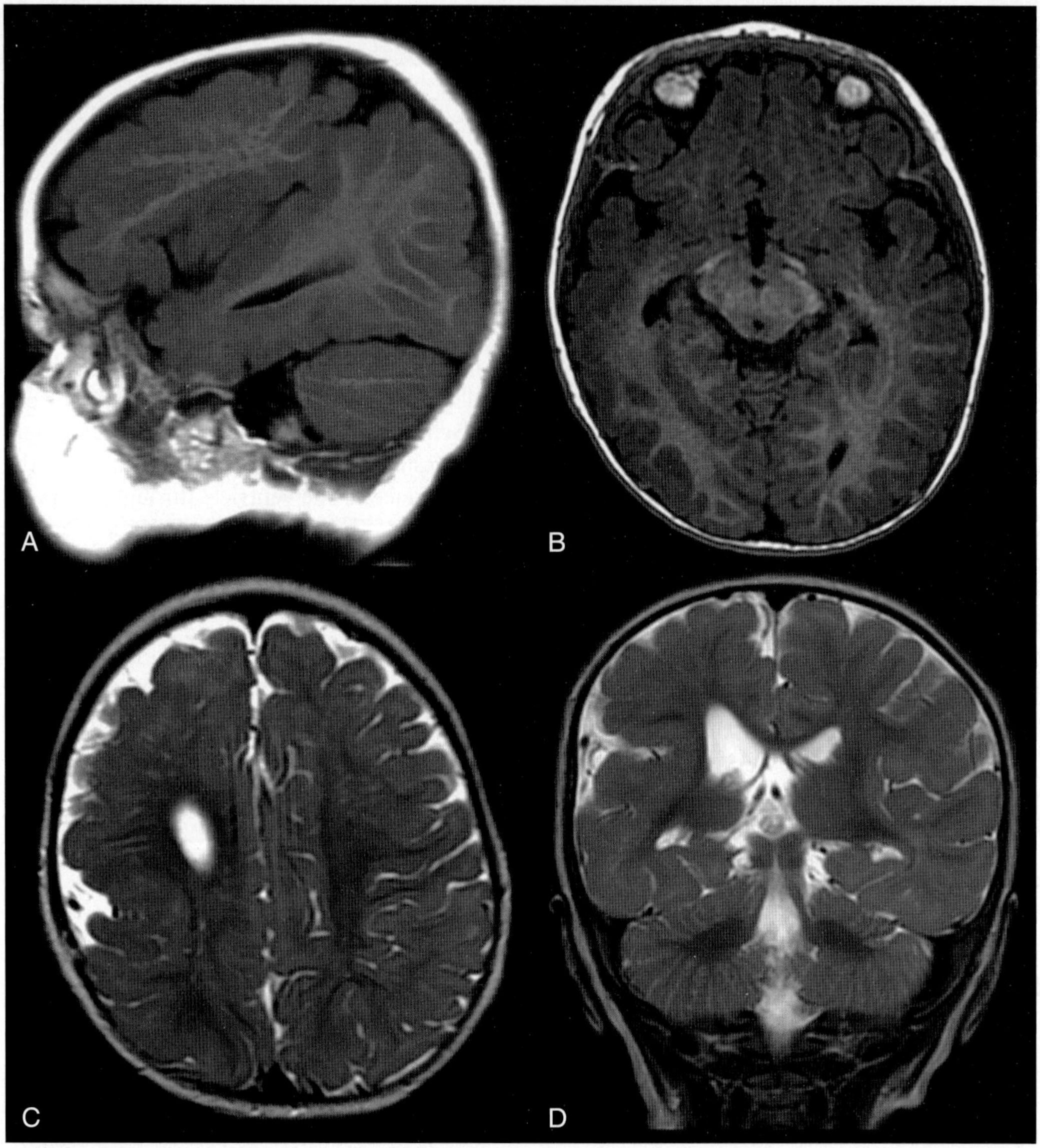

Fig. 13.1 Right perisylvian polymicrogyria. Brain MRI, (A and B) sagittal and axial T1 and (C and D) axial and coronal T2 show abnormally shallow right Sylvian fissure with thickened and irregular cortex over the frontal, temporal, and parietal lobes.

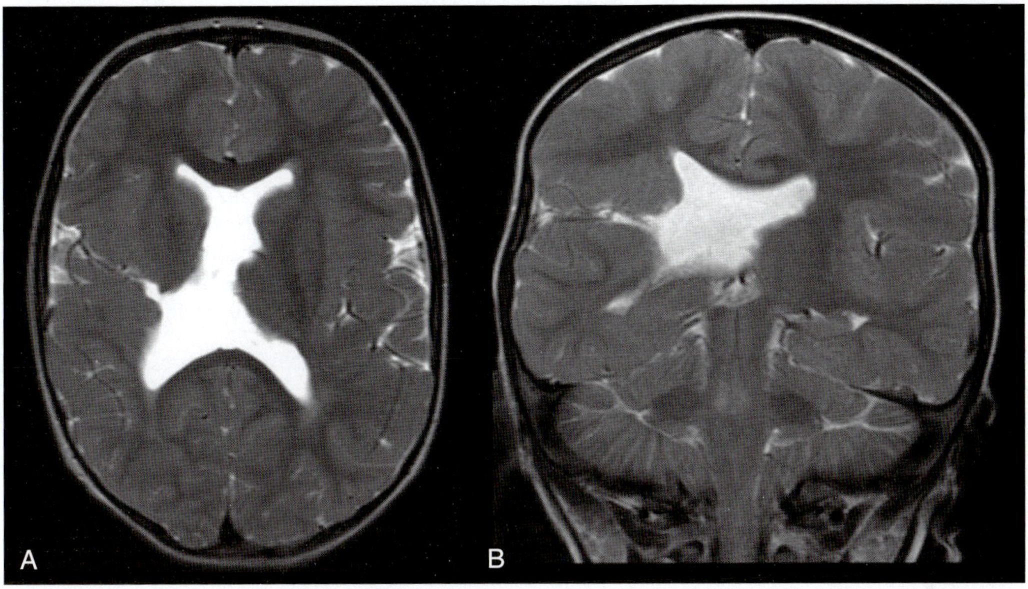

Fig. 13.2 Right closed-lip schizencephaly. Brain MRI, (A) axial and (B) coronal T2 show a right cerebral hemispheric cleft lined by irregular gray matter.

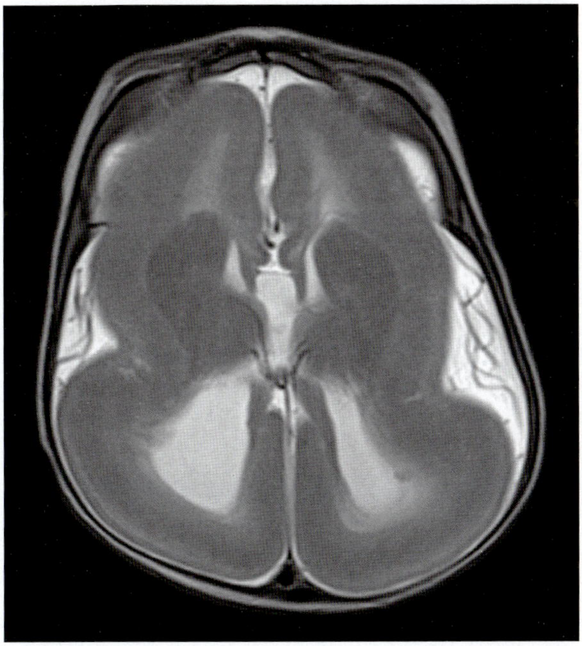

Fig. 13.3 Agyria. Brain MRI, axial T2 shows smooth cerebral surface with morphology showing minimal gyration and sulcation. The cortical layers are disorganized with a thin hypointense cellular layer, subcortical hyperintense cell-sparse zone, and hypointense inner layer of unmigrated heterotopic cells.

gyri and sulci. Malformations can be focal, diffuse, unilateral, or bilateral, with sporadic cases frequently located in and adjacent to the Sylvian fissure (perisylvian distribution).

CLINICAL RED FLAGS

- Signs of unilateral CP in an infant (hemiparesis or asymmetry in movement or posture) should alert physicians to a contralateral brain lesion. Clinical motor impairment may be subtle. Causes of hemiparesis are diverse, therefore neuroimaging is an effective tool to clarify the diagnosis.

IMAGING RED FLAGS

- Polymicrogyria may not be appreciated on imaging in infants and young children due to incomplete myelination limiting evaluation of the gray–white junction. Thus, in the setting of persistent unilateral spastic CP, a repeat MRI at 2 to 3 years of age should be considered even if the initial MRI was read as normal.
- High-resolution 3D volumetric MRI or 2D sequences in multiple planes (axial, sagittal, coronal) may be necessary to detect subtle cortical abnormalities.

CONCLUSIONS

Unilateral spastic CP should be suspected in infants with asymmetric posture. MRI is useful for determining the underlying diagnosis.

REFERENCES

Barkovich AJ. Current concepts of polymicrogyria. *Neuroradiology*. 2010;52(6):479–487. doi:10.1007/s00234-009-0644-2.

Fenton LZ. Imaging of congenital malformations of the brain. *Clin Perinatol.* 2022;49(3):587–601. doi:10.1016/j.clp.2022.05.002.

Horber V, Sellier E, Horridge K, et al. The Origin of the cerebral palsies: contribution of population-based neuroimaging data. *Neuropediatrics*. 2020;51(2):113–119. doi:10.1055/s-0039-3402007.

Khandelwal A, Aggarwal A, Sharma A, Malik A, Bose A. Magnetic resonance imaging of malformations of cortical development: a comprehensive review. *World Neurosurg.* 2022;159:70–79. doi:10.1016/j.wneu.2021.12.011.

Leventer RJ, Jansen A, Pilz DT, et al. Clinical and imaging heterogeneity of polymicrogyria: a study of 328 patients. *Brain.* 2010;133(Pt 5):1415–1427. doi:10.1093/brain/awq078.

te Velde A, Morgan C, Novak I, Tantsis E, Badawi N. Early diagnosis and classification of cerebral palsy: an historical perspective and barriers to an early diagnosis. *J Clin Med.* 2019;8(10):1599. doi:10.3390/jcm8101599.

Return to the Perinatal History

HISTORY AND PHYSICAL

A 2-year-9-month-old male was referred to neurology for evaluation of global developmental delay and microcephaly. He was born full term with uncomplicated pregnancy and delivery. However, his head circumference was 32 cm (below 3rd percentile for age) and his birth weight was 3060 g (below 50th percentile). Postnatal blood testing confirmed the diagnosis of congenital cytomegalovirus (CMV) infection. Auditory evoked potentials detected sensorineural hearing loss. He received oral valganciclovir for 6 months. At the time of neurological examination, his head circumference was 44 cm (below first percentile), and he could not sit by himself. He had truncal hypotonia and spastic quadriparesis, right greater than left. He also demonstrated generalized hyperreflexia and bilateral upgoing plantar responses.

DIAGNOSTIC WORKUP

Head ultrasound at 5 weeks showed abnormal gyration, diffuse white matter signal abnormality, and a left germinolytic cyst (Fig. 14.1).

MRI showed diffuse white matter T2 abnormalities and migrational defects with abnormal cortical sulcation and gyration (Fig. 14.2).

CLINICAL DIFFERENTIAL DIAGNOSES

Congenital CMV infection is defined by the presence of clinical and/or biological signs with supportive findings at neuroimaging. The most frequent neonatal signs are hepatosplenomegaly (60%), microcephaly (53%), jaundice (67%), petechiae (76%), and at least one neurological abnormality (68%). Laboratory abnormalities include increased liver transaminases (83%), thrombocytopenia (77%), hyperbilirubinemia (69%), hemolysis (51%), and elevated cerebrospinal fluid proteins (46%). Imaging abnormalities are present in 70% of symptomatic newborns, with intracerebral calcifications being the most commonly described feature.

Causes of microcephaly include perinatal toxoplasmosis, rubeola, CMV, herpes simplex (TORCH) infections; some genetic syndromes; and maternal toxins such as alcohol, tobacco, drugs, or antiepileptics.

IMAGING DIFFERENTIAL DIAGNOSES

MRI in congenital CMV shows periventricular calcifications, white matter abnormalities, and ventriculomegaly. Polymicrogyria is the most frequently associated cortex abnormality.

Congenital toxoplasmosis can produce a similar appearance, though with more diffuse cerebral calcifications and less common polymicrogyria.

FINAL DIAGNOSIS

Bilateral cerebral palsy (CP) and sensorineural hearing loss, due to congenital CMV infection.

DISCUSSION

The overall prevalence of congenital CMV infection among patients with CP is 10.9%, while the prevalence of CP among patients diagnosed with congenital CMV infection is 26%.

Congenital CMV is the most commonly reported congenital infection, affecting 0.7% of newborns. Approximately 30% to 40% of mothers with primary CMV infection during pregnancy give birth to affected infants. The incidence of neonates with CMV-specific symptoms at birth is reported at 10% to 15%. Of these, 40% to 60% develop permanent sequelae, particularly

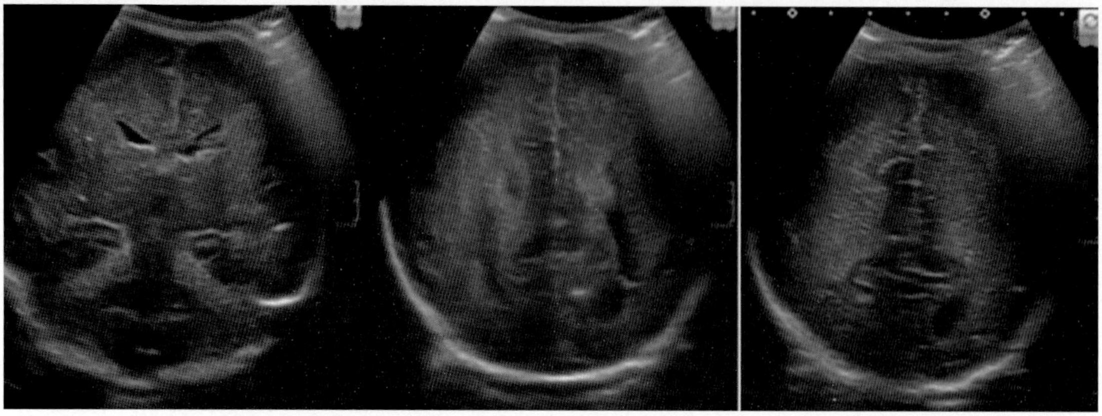

Fig. 14.1 Congenital CMV. Coronal head ultrasound shows shallow sylvian fissures, diffuse white matter hyperechogenicity, and left germinolytic cyst. *CMV*, Cytomegalovirus.

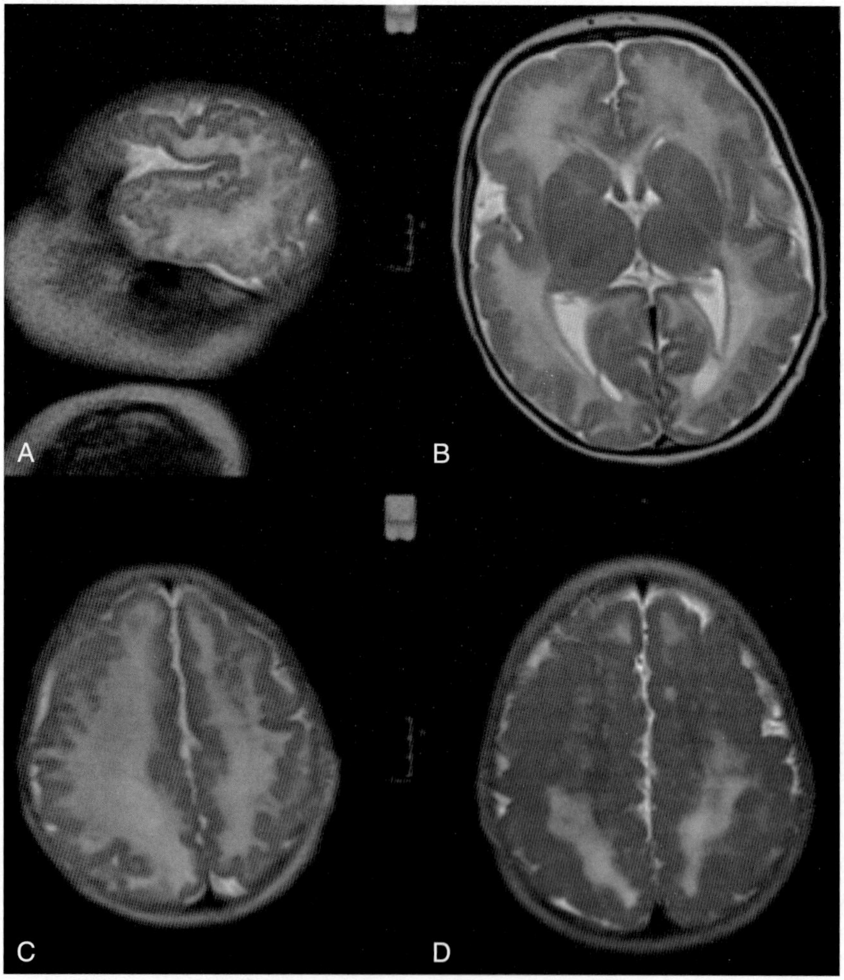

Fig. 14.2 Congenital CMV. Brain MRI, (A) sagittal T2 and (B and C) axial T2 MRI at 5 months and (D) axial T2 MRI at 23 months show shallow Sylvian fissures with extensive polymicrogyria and diffuse white matter abnormalities that decrease with progressive age and myelination. *CMV*, Cytomegalovirus.

sensorineural hearing loss followed by cognitive impairment, retinitis, and CP.

Imaging findings depend on the developmental timing of infection and the extent of brain damage. Early injury may show diffuse cortical abnormalities (agyria/lissencephaly and cortical thinning), ex vacuo ventriculomegaly with periventricular calcifications, delayed myelination and white matter abnormalities, and cerebellar hypoplasia (Fig. 14.2). Later injury results in less severe abnormalities, usually white matter signal changes, which can improve with postnatal myelination. In the anterior temporal lobes, white matter can be edematous with cystic dilation of the temporal horns.

Education of pregnant women about the prevention of CMV infection is key, as a vaccine has not yet been developed. Neonatal screening for CMV is also routine in many countries. Currently, antiviral treatment is only recommended for symptomatic patients.

CLINICAL RED FLAGS

- The presence of congenital microcephaly and auditory deficits should prompt investigation for congenital CMV infection.
- Viral isolation in the urine and/or saliva within the first 2 to 3 weeks after birth is considered the gold standard for diagnosis.
- After the neonatal period, testing of dried blood spot (DBS) from the newborn screening card can be performed using polymerase chain reaction (PCR) assay for CMV.

IMAGING RED FLAGS

- Focal, patchy, or confluent white matter abnormalities, particularly in the posterior white matter with sparing of periventricular and subcortical white matter
- Malformations of cortical development
- Periventricular and basal ganglia calcifications
- Anterior temporal lobe edema and cysts
- Volume loss with ex vacuo ventriculomegaly

CONCLUSIONS

Congenital CMV is associated with more severe hearing impairment, intellectual disability, and motor disability when compared to other causes of CP. Patients should receive a complete neurological evaluation and perinatal workup. Neuroimaging findings help characterize structural brain abnormalities and predict outcome.

REFERENCES

Alarcon A, Martinez-Biarge M, Cabañas F, Hernanz A, Quero J, Garcia-Alix A. Clinical, biochemical, and neuroimaging findings predict long-term neurodevelopmental outcome in symptomatic congenital cytomegalovirus infection. *J Pediatr.* 2013;163(3):828-34.e1. doi:10.1016/j.jpeds.2013.03.014.

Dakovic I, da Graça Andrada M, Folha T, et al. Clinical features of cerebral palsy in children with symptomatic congenital cytomegalovirus infection. *Eur J Paediatr Neurol.* 2014;18(5):618–623. doi:10.1016/j.ejpn.2014.04.007.

Fink KR, Thapa MM, Ishak GE, Pruthi S. Neuroimaging of pediatric central nervous system cytomegalovirus infection. *Radiographics.* 2010;30(7):1779–1796. doi:10.1148/rg.307105043.

Ong LT, Fan SWD. The association between congenital cytomegalovirus infection and cerebral palsy: a systematic review and meta-analysis. *J Paediatr Child Health.* 2022;58(12):2156–2162. doi:10.1111/jpc.16244.

Rawlinson WD, Boppana SB, Fowler KB, et al. Congenital cytomegalovirus infection in pregnancy and the neonate: consensus recommendations for prevention, diagnosis, and therapy. *Lancet Infect Dis.* 2017;17(6):e177–e188. doi:10.1016/S1473-3099(17)30143-3.

Smithers-Sheedy H, Raynes-Greenow C, Badawi N, et al. Congenital cytomegalovirus among children with cerebral palsy. *J Pediatr.* 2017;181:267-271.e1. doi:10.1016/j.jpeds.2016.10.024.

van der Knaap MS, Vermeulen G, Barkhof F, Hart AA, Loeber JG, Weel JF. Pattern of white matter abnormalities at MR imaging: use of polymerase chain reaction testing of Guthrie cards to link pattern with congenital cytomegalovirus infection [published correction appears in *Radiology.* 2004 May;231(2):605]. *Radiology.* 2004;230(2):529–536. doi:10.1148/radiol.2302021459.

Case 15

Pay Attention to Preterm Babies

HISTORY AND PHYSICAL

A 17-month-old boy was referred to neurology after being adopted by Spanish parents. He was born in Romania at 32 weeks of postmenstrual age (PMA), with limited prenatal care and a history of placenta previa. His birth weight was 1480 g, and he spent 3 months in the neonatal intensive care unit. Upon examination, he demonstrated left-hand preference, truncal hypotonia, generalized hyperreflexia, bilateral leg spasticity, and bilateral upgoing toes with plantar responses. He walked on his tiptoes with assistance.

DIAGNOSTIC WORKUP

Brain MRI showed posterior periventricular and deep white matter signal abnormality and volume loss. There was associated cortical thinning and angular ex vacuo ventricular enlargement (Fig. 15.1).

CLINICAL DIFFERENTIAL DIAGNOSES

About 50% of patients with cerebral palsy (CP) have clearly identified perinatal risk factors. Symptoms can be subtle, with diagnosis delayed during the first 2 years of life. However, nonspecific abnormalities of motor development can improve and resolve with age.

Several genetic/metabolic disorders can mimic CP, including hereditary spastic paraplegia and Pelizaeus-Merzbacher disease. Neuroimaging can help determine the underlying etiology.

IMAGING DIFFERENTIAL DIAGNOSES

Hypoxic-ischemic injury is seen in term babies. Complete prolonged anoxia affects the developing basal ganglia and corticospinal tracts, and possibly hippocampal formations and cerebellum. Milder partial hypoxia can affect the vascular watershed zones.

Congenital infections, such as cytomegalovirus (CMV), can affect the white matter with multifocal abnormalities, malformations of cortical development, periventricular and basal ganglia calcifications, and anterior temporal lobe edema/cysts.

FINAL DIAGNOSIS

Bilateral CP (spastic diplegia), due to periventricular leukomalacia.

DISCUSSION

For preterm infants with known risk factors, evaluation for CP is recommended during the first 5 months of corrected age. The combination of Prechtl General Movement Assessment (GMA), Hammersmith Infant Neurologic Examination (HINE), and brain MRI achieves more than 95% accuracy.

Periventricular leukomalacia (PVL) is present on brain MRI in 19% to 45% of preterm infants, particularly between ages of 24 and 34 weeks PMA. The most prevalent pathological lesion is focal necrosis of the periventricular white matter, involving myelin precursors. Microscopic necrosis usually evolves into glial cicatricial lesions (the most common mechanism of injury), while macroscopic necrosis can lead to cystic lesions (observed in 10% of PVL cases). Finally, diffuse gliosis can occur without evidence of necrosis. The severity of CP depends on the degree of parenchymal volume loss with resulting cystic encephalomalacia. Focal cysts can be associated with bilateral CP and spastic monoplegia or diplegia, while more widespread cysts result in spastic quadriplegia. There is also a reduction of neurons in the cortex and deep gray matter, which leads to combined motor and cognitive impairment.

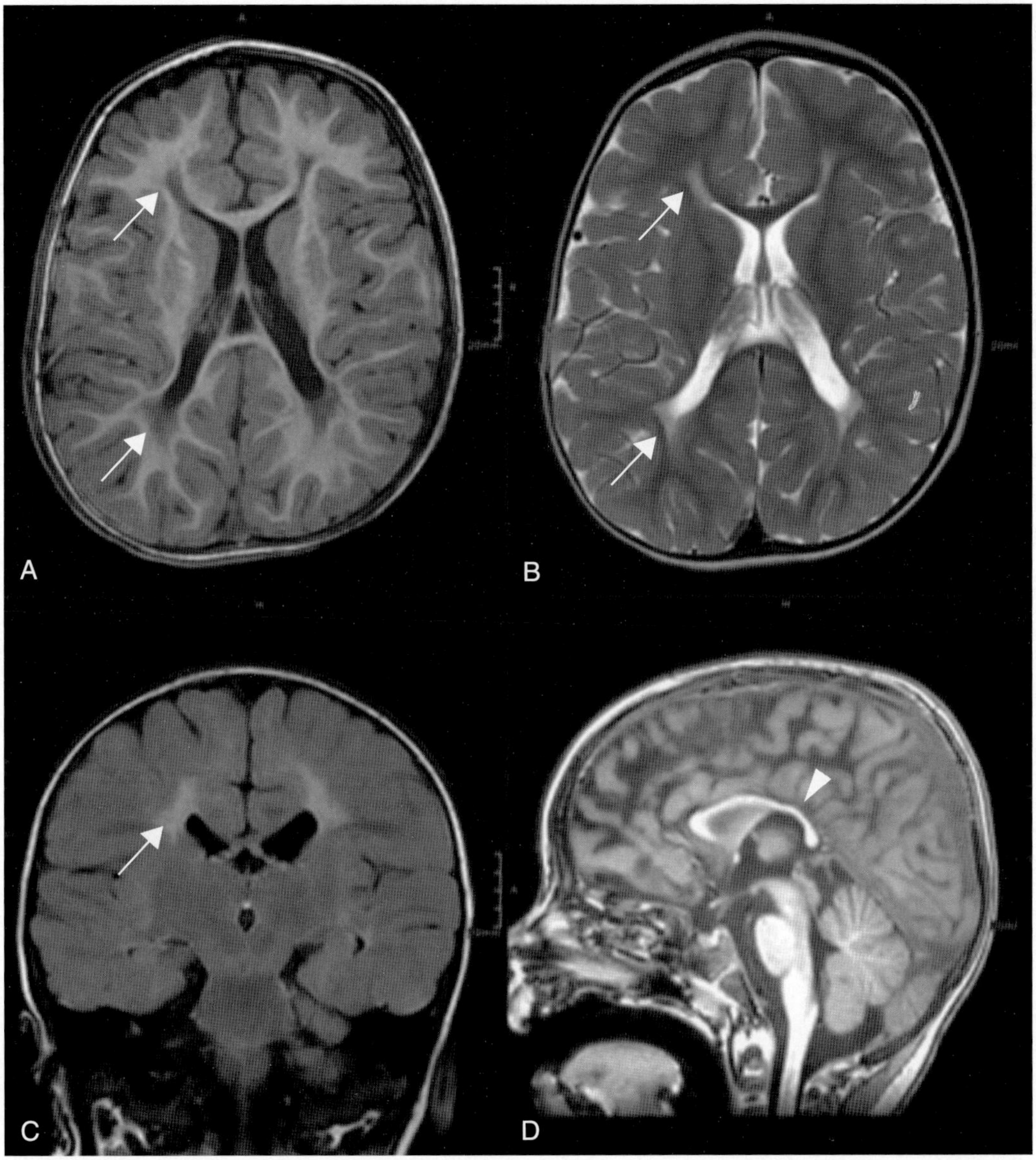

Fig. 15.1 Periventricular leukomalacia. Brain MRI, axial T1 (A), axial T2 (B), coronal FLAIR (C), sagittal T1 (D) show periventricular white matter signal and volume loss (*arrows*), along with thinning of the corpus callosum (*arrowhead*) and basal ganglia atrophy. *FLAIR*, Fluid-attenuated inversion recovery.

CLINICAL RED FLAGS

- Preterm newborns with perinatal risk factors should have a dedicated workup for CP. Symptoms can be very subtle during the first months of life.
- Children without any risk factors at birth should be assessed for CP when there is delayed or atypical motor development.
- In spastic diplegia, all four limbs are involved, with greater predominance of the lower extremities.

IMAGING RED FLAGS

- Abnormal signal and volume loss in the periventricular and deep white matter, with angular ex vacuo dilation of the ventricles.

CONCLUSIONS

In an infant with preterm birth or other perinatal risk factors, motor impairment combined with an abnormal MRI should prompt workup and early intervention for CP.

REFERENCES

Appleton RE, Gupta R. Cerebral palsy: not always what it seems. *Arch Dis Child.* 2019;104(8):809–814. doi:10.1136/archdischild-2018-315633.

Novak I, Morgan C, Adde L, et al. Early, accurate diagnosis and early intervention in cerebral palsy: advances in diagnosis and treatment [published correction appears in *JAMA Pediatr.* 2017 Sep 1;171(9):919]. *JAMA Pediatr.* 2017;171(9):897–907. doi:10.1001/jamapediatrics.2017.1689.

Reid SM, Dagia CD, Ditchfield MR, Carlin JB, Reddihough DS. Population-based studies of brain imaging patterns in cerebral palsy. *Dev Med Child Neurol.* 2014;56(3):222–232. doi:10.1111/dmcn.1222.

Volpe JJ. Brain injury in premature infants: a complex amalgam of destructive and developmental disturbances. *Lancet Neurol.* 2009;8(1):110–124. doi:10.1016/S1474-4422(08)70294-1.

SECTION 4

Epilepsy

Juan Ignacio Appendino, Katherine Liu, Natarie D. Liu, Minette K. Manalo, Juan Carlos Pérez-Poveda, Morris H. Scantlebury, Juan Pablo Appendino

INTRODUCTION

Epilepsy is a chronic neurological disorder characterized by recurrent spontaneous or reflex seizures with a sudden abnormal surge of synchronized electrical activity in the brain. Epilepsy can be caused by a variety of etiologies including brain injury, malformation, stroke, metabolic or genetic disorders, and tumors. It affects people of all ages and can have a significant impact on quality of life. Identifying a focal lesional cause can lead to surgical remediation.

One of the most important diagnostic tools for epilepsy is brain MRI, which enables diagnostic evaluation of structure and function as well as interventional planning without exposure to ionizing radiation. The use of high-resolution 3D volumetric sequences helps identify focal structural abnormalities with multiplanar reconstructions. In this chapter, we aim to demonstrate the important role of MRI in the diagnosis and treatment of epilepsy, discussing a wide variety of etiologies with associated imaging findings that facilitate diagnosis and management.

SUGGESTED READINGS

Barkovich AJ, Koch BL, Moore KR. *Diagnostic Imaging.* Amirsys Publishing, Inc.; 2015.

Barkovich AJ, Raybaud C. *Pediatric Neuroimaging.* Wolters Kluwer; 2019.

Bernasconi A, Cendes F, Theodore WH, et al. Recommendations for the use of structural magnetic resonance imaging in the care of patients with epilepsy: a consensus report from the International League Against Epilepsy Neuroimaging Task Force. *Epilepsia.* 2019;60(6):1054–1068. doi:10.1111/epi.15612.

Moore KR. *Diagnostic Imaging: Pediatric Neuroradiology E-Book.* Elsevier Health Sciences; 2019.

Ironing Out the Cause of Seizures

HISTORY AND PHYSICAL

A 12-year-old girl had a prolonged history of severe global developmental delay, stereotyped behaviors, nocturnal awakenings, and occasional staring spells. During infancy, she was diagnosed with global developmental delay and hypotonia. At 4 years, she presented with repetitive behaviors diagnosed as stereotypies. At the age of 7, she experienced nocturnal awakenings and occasional staring spells. Overnight electroencephalography (EEG) showed occasional bifrontal interictal discharges with right-sided predominance (Fig. 16.1). She was started on oxcarbazepine which improved her symptoms and behavior.

On physical examination, there was hypertelorism with bilateral down-slanted eyes and epicanthal folds. She was nonverbal, and her motor exam revealed axial hypotonia, distal hypertonia, and increased deep tendon reflexes. She walked with an ataxic gait. Skin examination was normal.

DIAGNOSTIC WORK-UP

Due to dysmorphic features and a history of developmental delay, metabolic testing, karyotype, comparative genomic hybridization (CGH) microarray, methyl CpG binding protein (MECP2), and Angelman syndrome tests were ordered and were normal.

MRI at 6 and 9 years showed restricted diffusion, T2 hypointensity, and susceptibility in the bilateral globus pallidus and substantia nigra (Figs. 16.2 and 16.3). There was global cerebral and cerebellar atrophy with prominence of sulci and folia.

Multiple EEGs showed bilateral independent epileptiform discharges over the left and right frontal and central head regions, with mild slowing of background activity.

Whole exome sequencing showed a pathogenic variant in the *WDR45* gene.

CLINICAL DIFFERENTIAL DIAGNOSIS

Rett syndrome can be seen in girls with global developmental delay, stereotypies, and seizures. It is caused by pathogenic variants in the *MECP2* gene, and symptoms usually start before 1 year of age. There is progressive loss of purposeful hand dexterity and development of stereotyped hand movements, speech and language regression, and progressive gait abnormalities. MRI shows nonspecific global brain atrophy.

Metabolic epilepsies can be seen with developmental delay, regression, and seizures in late infancy and childhood. These include disorders of creatine biosynthesis and transport (Fig. 16.4), mitochondrial disorders (Fig. 16.5), pyruvate dehydrogenase deficiency (PDH) (Fig. 16.6), peroxisomal disorders, and lysosomal storage disorders (Fig. 16.7).

IMAGING DIFFERENTIAL DIAGNOSIS

The basal ganglia are highly vulnerable to metabolic, chemical, and/or ischemic abnormalities due to their high glucose/oxygen demands with rich mitochondrial density and vascular supply.

Basal ganglia T2/fluid-attenuated inversion recovery (FLAIR) hyperintensity can be seen with edema and resulting gliosis from toxic and metabolic etiologies, such as late-onset methylmalonic acidemia (MMA), cerebral creatine deficiency syndromes, and PDH.

Basal ganglia susceptibility with prominent T2-hypointense signal can be seen in diseases of iron, calcium, or hemosiderin deposition (Figs. 16.2 and 16.3), for example, neurodegeneration with brain iron accumulation. There may be corresponding T1 hyperintensity

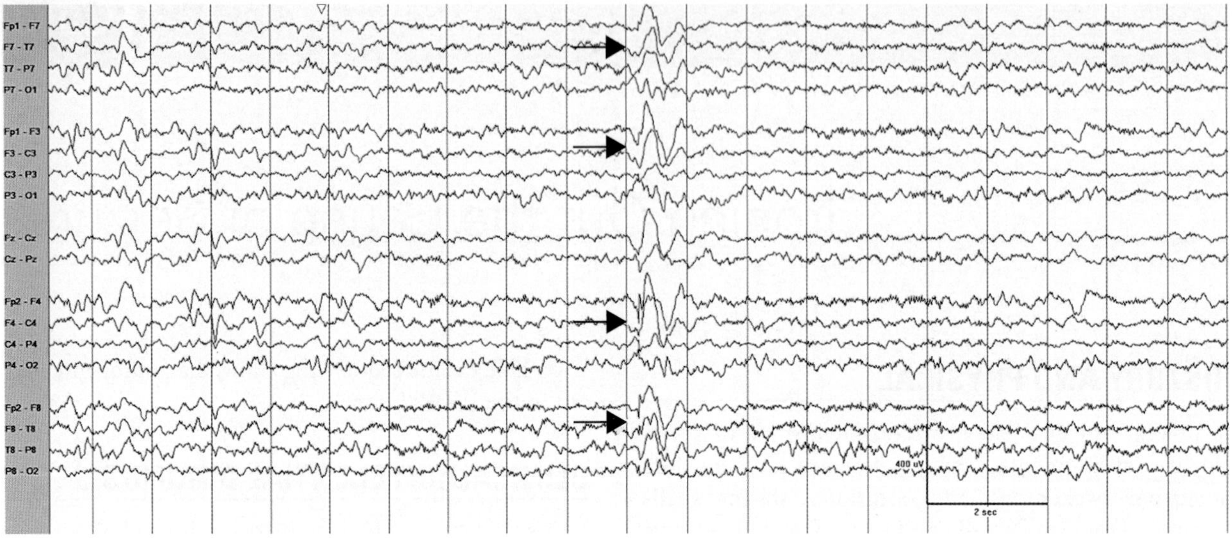

Fig. 16.1 Electroencephalography (EEG) showing right greater than left frontal interictal discharges (*arrows*). Parameters: LFF 1Hz; HFF 70Hz; Notch on; Sensitivity 20 uV/mm; Paper speed: 30 mm/sec. *HFF*, High-frequency filter; *LFF*, low-frequency filter.

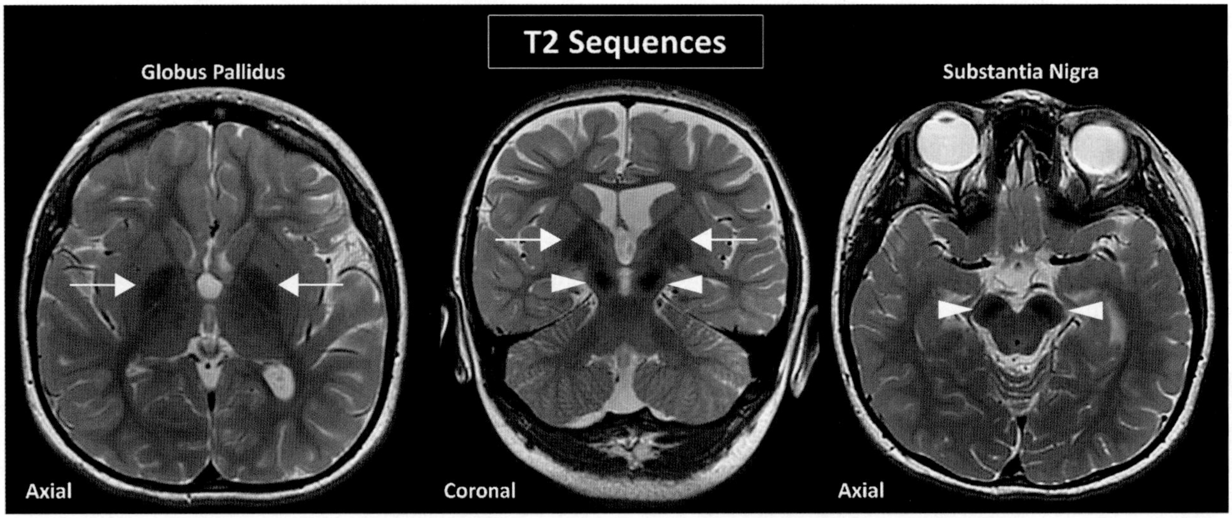

Fig. 16.2 Beta-propeller protein-associated neurodegeneration. Brain MRI showing decreased T2 signal in the globus pallidus (*arrows*) and substantia nigra (*arrowheads*).

when the deposits include bilirubin (kernicterus), manganese (total parenteral nutrition, liver failure), and certain forms of calcium. T2-hypointense and T1-hyperintense thalamic signal can also be seen with lysosomal storage disorders such as neuronal ceroid lipofuscinosis, GM gangliosidosis, aspartylglucosaminuria, and fucosidosis (Fig. 16.7). Predominant striatal involvement and white matter abnormalities may signify organic acidemia, glutaric aciduria (Fig. 16.8), propionic acidemia, mitochondrial disorders, and Wilson disease.

FINAL DIAGNOSIS

Beta-propeller protein-associated neurodegeneration (BPAN).

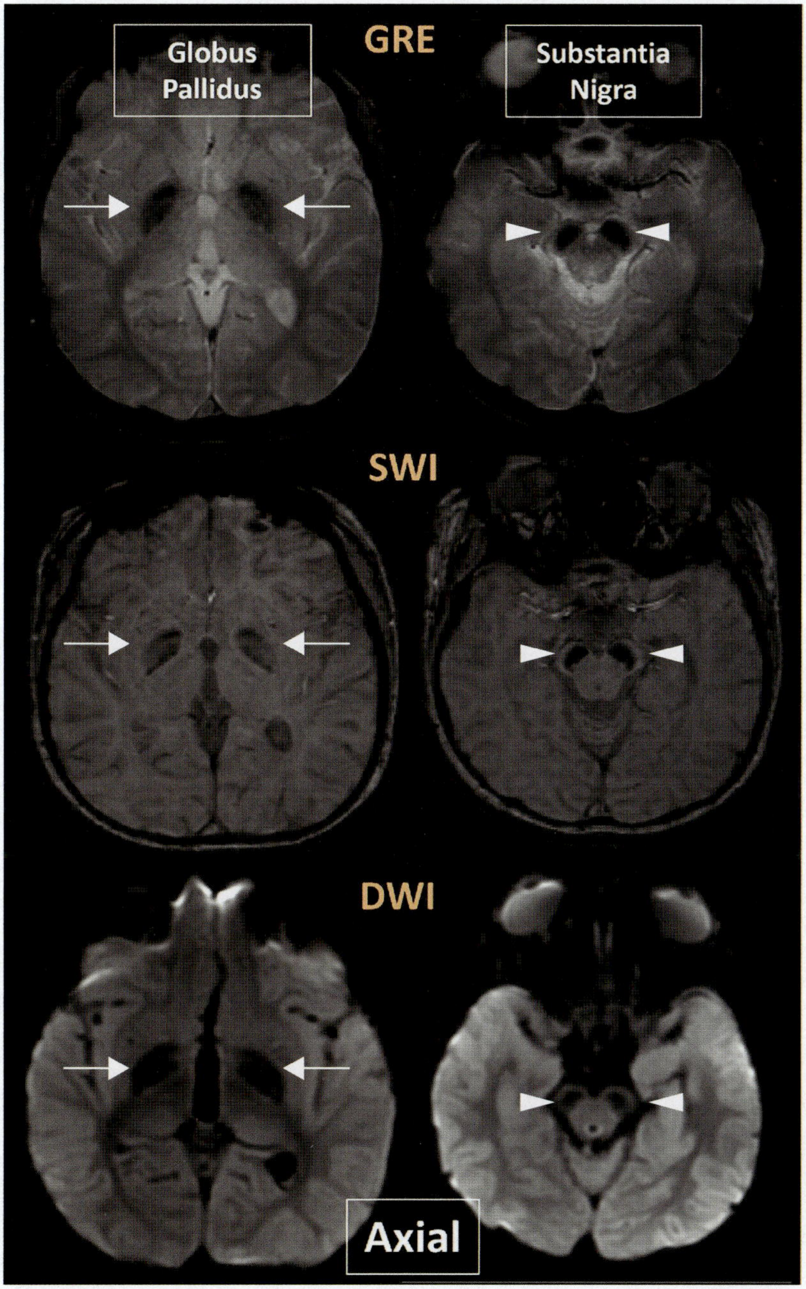

Fig. 16.3 Beta-propeller protein-associated neurodegeneration. Brain MRI showing susceptibility in the globus pallidus (*arrows*) and substantia nigra (*arrowheads*).

DISCUSSION

BPAN is a rare and progressive metabolic disorder caused by mutation of WD-repeat domain 45 (WDR45) gene located on Xp11.23, resulting in abnormal iron deposition in the deep gray nuclei. It is a biphasic disease, with clinical presentations differing in childhood and adulthood. During childhood, the disease can present as global developmental delay, intellectual disability, expressive

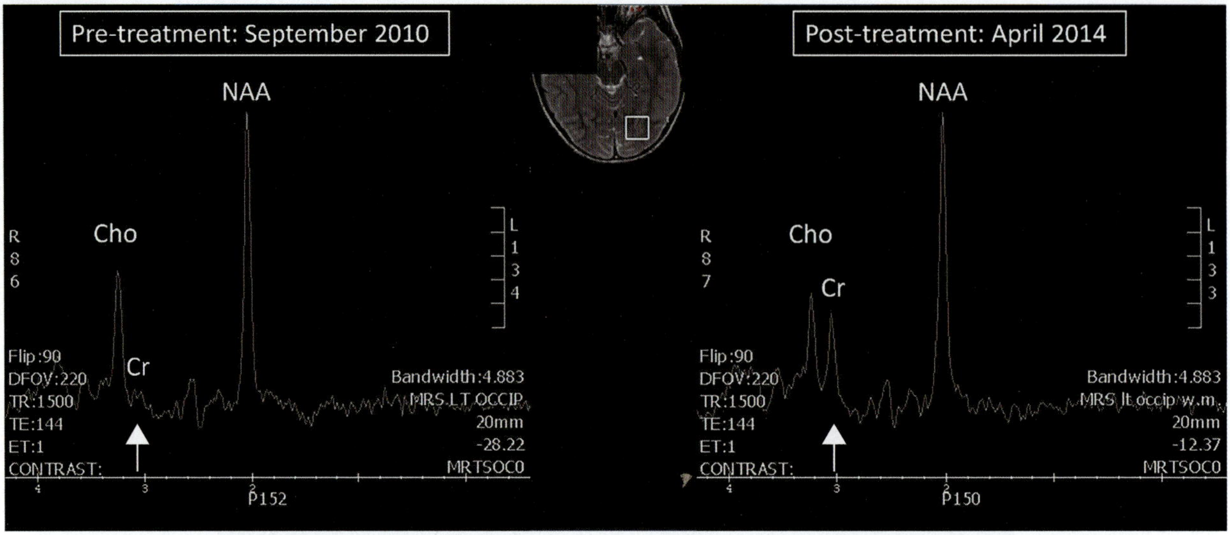

Fig. 16.4 Cerebral creatine deficiency due to *GAMT* gene mutation encoding guanidinoacetate methyltransferase. Pretreatment MRS at intermediate echo show lack of creatine in the brain (*arrow*) leading to global developmental delay and seizures. Dietary treatment with oral creatine monohydrate, ornithine supplementation, and dietary protein restriction of arginine increased cerebral creatine content (*arrow*) and decreased seizure burden.

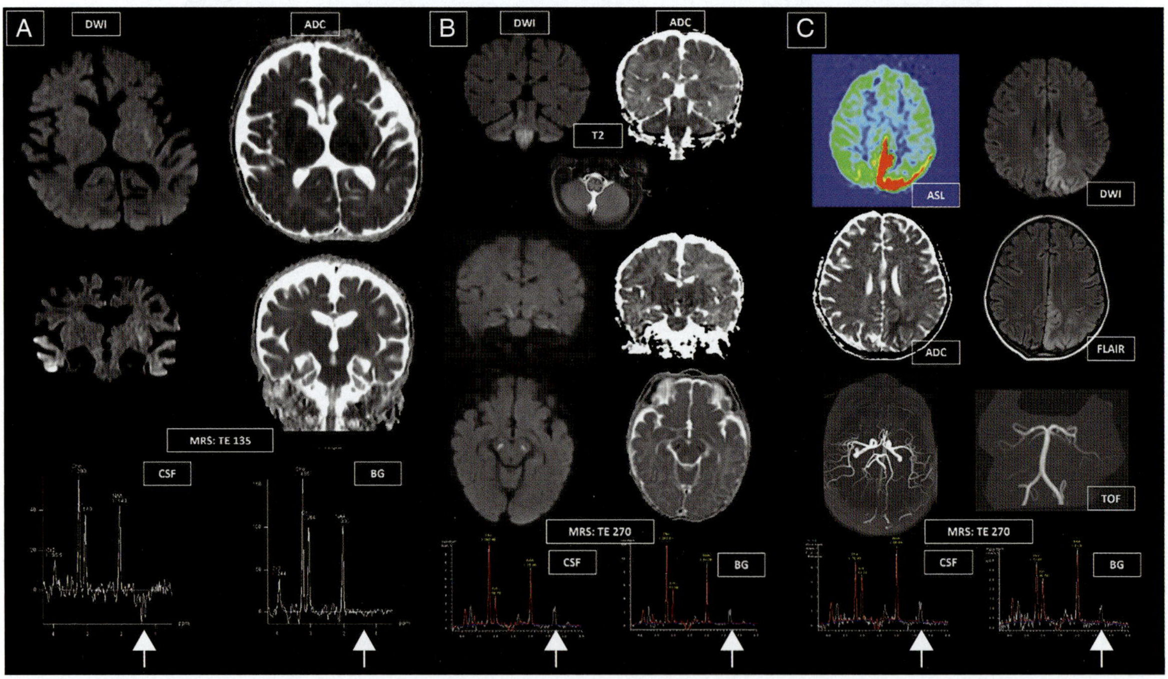

Fig. 16.5 Mitochondrial disorders. (A) 4-month-old infant with ongoing epilepsia partialis continua (EPC) secondary to polymerase gamma (*POLG*) deficiency. There is diffusion restriction in the left internal capsule. MRS at intermediate echo shows a large lactate peak in CSF but not parenchyma (*arrows*). (B) 9-month-old with Leigh disease due to a pathogenic variant in *NDUFS4*. There is restricted diffusion in the corticospinal tracts and substantia nigra. MRS at long echo shows increased lactate peak in both CSF and basal ganglia (*arrows*). (C) 9-year-old patient with MELAS due to pathogenic variant in *MT-TL1* with 67% blood heteroplasmy (severe disease). There is restricted diffusion, cytotoxic edema on FLAIR, increased perfusion on ASL, and dilated vessels on MRA in the left posterior quadrant, indicating a stroke-like episode due to mitochondrial dysfunction. MRS at long echo shows increased lactate peak in both CSF and basal ganglia (*arrows*). *ASL*, Arterial spin labeling; *CSF*, cerebrospinal fluid; *FLAIR*, fluid-attenuated inversion recovery; *MELAS*, mitochondrial encephalopathy, lactic acidosis, and stroke-like episodes; *MRA*, magnetic resonance angiography; *TOF*, time of flight.

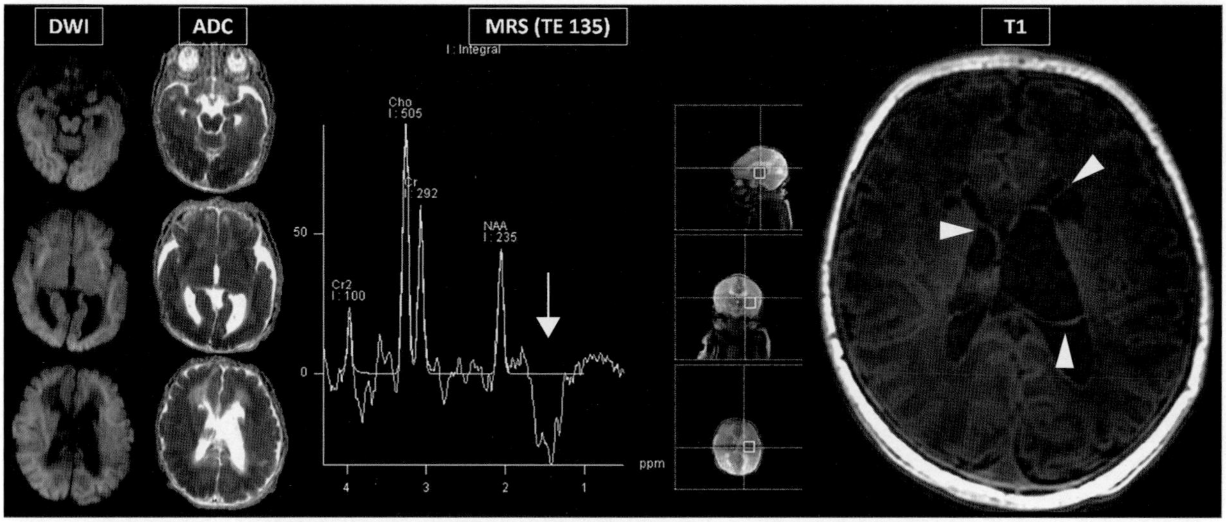

Fig. 16.6 Pyruvate dehydrogenase complex deficiency due to pathogenic variant in *PDHA1* gene leading to pyruvate dehydrogenase E1 subunit alpha deficiency. Patient presented with neonatal seizures at 6 days and poor feeding in the first week of life. Brain MRI shows global diffusion restriction despite normal birth history. MRS of the basal ganglia at intermediate echo shows a large lactate peak (*arrow*). Axial T1 sequence shows ventricular cysts and septations (*arrowheads*). The patient responded to classical ketogenic diet.

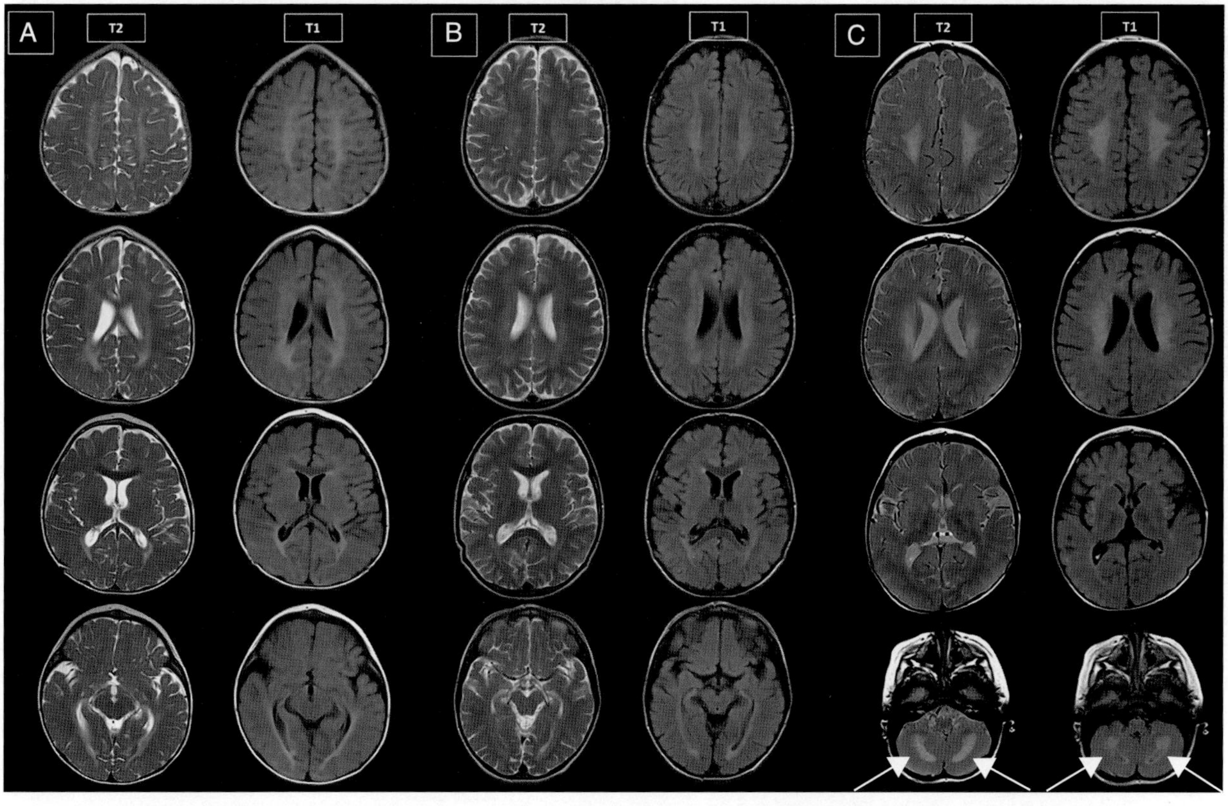

Fig. 16.7 Lysosomal storage disorders. (A) GM1 gangliosidosis. MRI at 27 months shows diffuse white matter changes and mild thalamic T2 hypointensity. (B) Neuronal ceroid lipofuscinosis, late infantile subtype. MRI at 3 years shows diffuse white matter changes and mild thalamic T2 hypointensity. (C) Krabbe disease. MRI at 15 months shows diffuse white matter changes and faint thalamic T2 hypointensity.

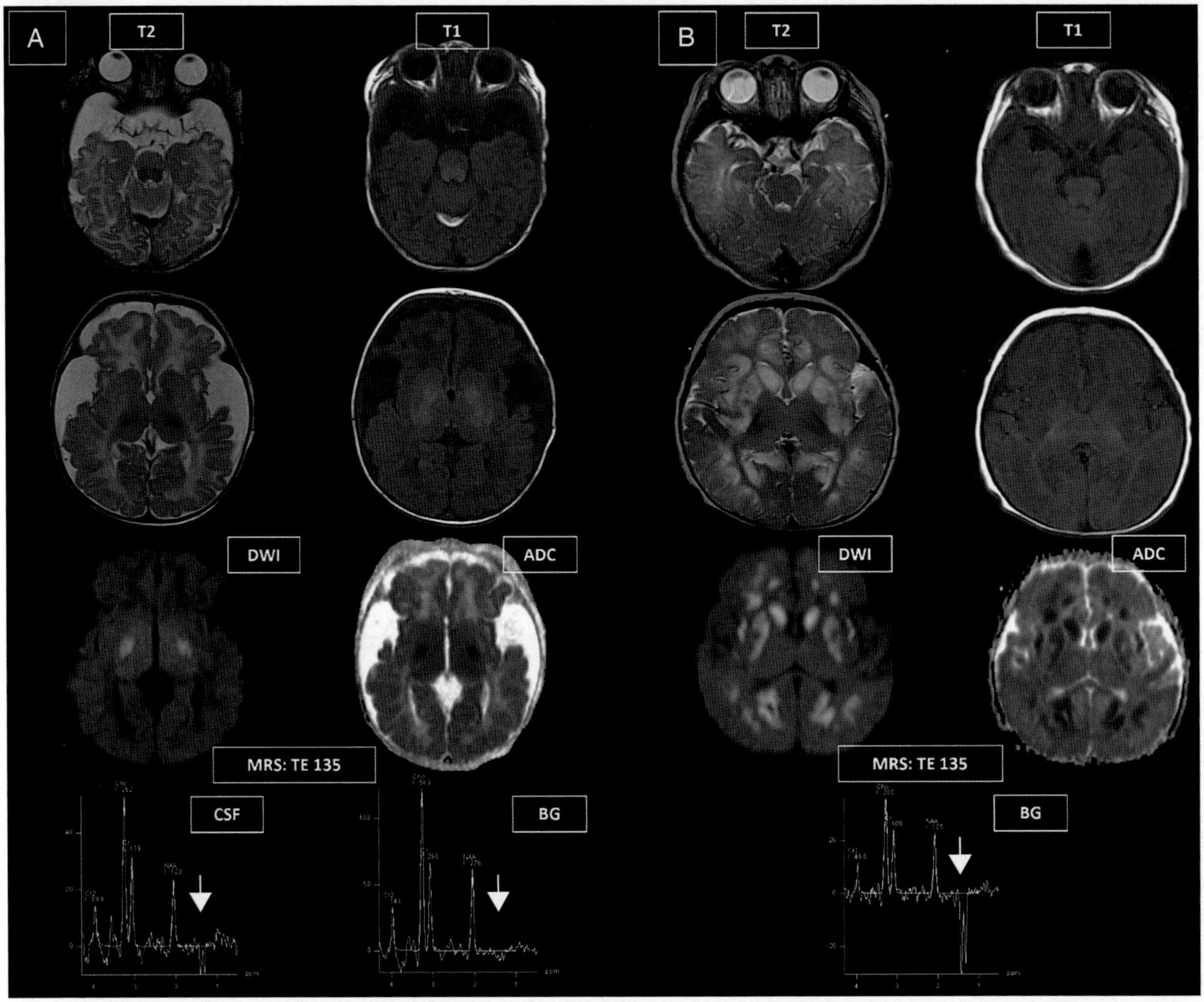

Fig. 16.8 Glutaric aciduria/acidemia (GA). (A) GA type 1 (GA-1) presents with seizures and severe encephalopathy in the newborn period. Brain MRI shows underopercularization of the Sylvian fissures with enlarged subarachnoid spaces and acute restricted diffusion in the internal capsules. MRS at intermediate echo shows small lactate peaks (*arrows*), more so in CSF than basal ganglia. (B) GA type 2 (GA-2) shows fewer structural abnormalities but widespread acute diffusion restriction of white matter and basal ganglia (BG) with large lactate peak on MRS at intermediate echo (*arrows*). *CSF*, Cerebrospinal fluid; *MRS*, magnetic resonance spectroscopy.

language impairment, and epilepsy. Epilepsy onset can be seen as early as 2 months, and patients can exhibit multiple seizure types. EEG may show multifocal or bilateral spike and spike-and-wave complexes, as well as diffuse high-amplitude beta activity. BPAN can also present with developmental and epileptic encephalopathies, ataxia, incoordination, sleep dysfunction, and stereotyped hand movements. In adulthood, dyskinesia, progressive dystonia, parkinsonism, and dementia are seen.

MRI can be normal in early childhood, but iron deposition will begin to manifest with susceptibility in the substantia nigra and globi pallidi. On T1-weighted images, a halo sign may be present in the substantia nigra and cerebral peduncles. There may also be global atrophy of the cerebrum, cerebellum, and corpus callosum.

CLINICAL RED FLAGS

- Seizures, intellectual disability, cognitive decline, and developmental regression raise concern for a metabolic disorder. Other suspicious features include abnormal movements, gait disturbances, multisystem involvement, symptoms worsening with certain medications or fasting/high-protein meals, dysmorphic features, parental consanguinity, and a family history of unexplained neonatal death.
- Neurophysiological findings include unexplained slowing of EEG background activity or paroxysmal responses during low-frequency photic stimulation.

IMAGING RED FLAGS

- Different brain regions have varying susceptibility to injury, which may help in the diagnosis of specific metabolic disorders. Children with suspected inborn errors of metabolism should undergo MRI with T1-weighted imaging with and without contrast (for structural assessment and acute inflammation), T2/FLAIR (for white matter and basal ganglia signal), diffusion imaging (for acute energy failure), susceptibility-weighted imaging (SWI) or gradient echo (GRE) (for metal deposition), and magnetic resonance spectroscopy (MRS) (for metabolites).
- The pattern of involvement of brain MRI is important for differential diagnosis. White matter abnormalities can indicate hypomyelination or inborn errors of metabolism. Gray matter involvement can involve the cortex, deep gray matter, or both as in mitochondrial disorders, Canavan disease, urea cycle disorders, glutaric aciduria type 1, and Wilson disease.

CONCLUSIONS

Suspicion for metabolic epilepsy is based on a combination of abnormal findings:

- Clinical: Seizures in developmentally delayed patients or with developmental regression.
- EEG: Slow background, unusual EEG features.
- MRI: Delayed myelination, gray and white matter diffusion restrictions, abnormal MRS.
- Laboratory testing: Increased or decreased metabolites such as lactate, ammonia, glucose.

REFERENCES

Almannai M, Al Mahmoud RA, Mekki M, El-Hattab AW. Metabolic seizures. *Front Neurol.* 2021;12:640371. doi:10.3389/fneur.2021.640371.

Barkovich AJ, Koch BL, Moore KR. *Diagnostic Imaging.* Amirsys Publishing, Inc.; 2015.

Biswas A, Malhotra M, Mankad K, et al. Clinico-radiological phenotyping and diagnostic pathways in childhood neurometabolic disorders: a practical introductory guide. *Transl Pediatr.* 2021;10(4):1201–1230. doi:10.21037/tp-20-335.

Chard M, Appendino JP, Bello-Espinosa LE, et al. Single-center experience with beta-propeller protein-associated neurodegeneration (BPAN): expanding the phenotypic spectrum. *Mol Genet Metab Rep.* 2019;20:100483. doi:10.1016/j.ymgmr.2019.100483.

Ibrahim M, Parmar HA, Hoefling N, Srinivasan A. Inborn errors of metabolism: combining clinical and radiologic clues to solve the mystery. *AJR Am J Roentgenol.* 2014;203(3):W315–W327. doi:10.2214/AJR.13.11154.

Lehéricy S, Roze E, Goizet C, Mochel F. MRI of neurodegeneration with brain iron accumulation. *Curr Opin Neurol.* 2020;33(4):462–473. doi:10.1097/WCO.0000000000000844.

Sharma S, Prasad AN. Inborn errors of metabolism and epilepsy: current understanding, diagnosis, and treatment approaches. *Int J Mol Sci.* 2017;18(7):1384. doi:10.3390/ijms18071384.

Case 17

Long-Term Epilepsy-Associated Tumors

HISTORY AND PHYSICAL

A previously healthy 10-year-old girl presented for 10 months of dystonic painful left limb posturing followed by transient left hemiplegia. Events occurred in the mornings upon awakening, consisting of 3 minutes of dystonic posturing of her left limbs and hemiface, followed by left-sided weakness. There was no impairment of awareness, although mild dyslalia was present during and a few seconds after the events. She also complained of intermittent pain in the left lower limb. Physical examination was otherwise normal.

DIAGNOSTIC WORKUP

EEG: showed normal background activity with frequent spikes and sharp waves over the left centro-temporal-frontal head regions (maximal amplitude at electrodes T7-C3-F3), at times with bilateral synchronic activity including centro-frontal areas (F4-C4) (Fig. 17.1).

MRI with contrast (Fig. 17.2) showed a right frontal mass with T2-hyperintense signal and bubbly appearance. Multivoxel spectroscopy showed decreased N-acetyl-aspartate (neuronal marker) without an increase in the choline peak (cell membrane marker) in the area of interest. No other abnormal metabolites were present.

Electroencephalogram (EEG) showed focal epilepsy in the left centro-temporo-frontal region and treatment with levetiracetam was initiated.

The patient went to surgery, and the resected tissue showed a nodular lesion consisting of neuronal cells with mucoid matrix. Immunohistochemistry showed positive results for synaptophysin and glial fibrillary acidic protein (GFAP) (in astrocytes) and negative neurofilament, CD34, and p53. Proliferative index (Ki-67 Ventana, clone 30-9) was 2% to 3%.

CLINICAL DIFFERENTIAL DIAGNOSES

Focal epilepsies in children are often due to focal cortical dysplasia (FCD). FCD manifests with seizures earlier in life that are highly refractory to antiseizure medications (ASMs) and can be often complicated by status epilepticus. FCDs can be associated with mesial temporal sclerosis, vascular malformations, low-grade neoplasms, and neurocutaneous syndromes.

Hemiplegic migraine is an epilepsy mimic that can occur familially or sporadically. Patients experience transient episodes of hemiplegia that can last hours or even days, often in association with chronic headaches. Genetic testing can reveal pathogenic variants in ion transporters such as *ATP1A2*, *CACNA1A*, or *SCN1A* genes, usually with autosomal dominant inheritance.

Vascular malformations can present with focal motor or sensory symptoms including cranial nerve palsies, monoparesis, or hemiparesis–hemiplegia. Headaches may also occur, particularly in the setting of hemorrhagic transformation.

IMAGING DIFFERENTIAL DIAGNOSES

Cortically based solid/cystic masses include various low-grade glioneuronal tumors. Ganglioglioma often shows contrast enhancement and calcification, with greater mass effect and larger cysts (Fig. 17.3).

Pleomorphic xanthoastrocytoma (PXA) has a more homogeneous solid appearance with prominent contrast enhancement, surrounding vasogenic edema, and a possible "dural tail" sign due to invasion of the leptomeninges (Fig. 17.4).

Focal cortical dysplasias (FCD) are non-enhancing dysplastic lesions with disorganized architecture that may manifest as gray-white blurring.

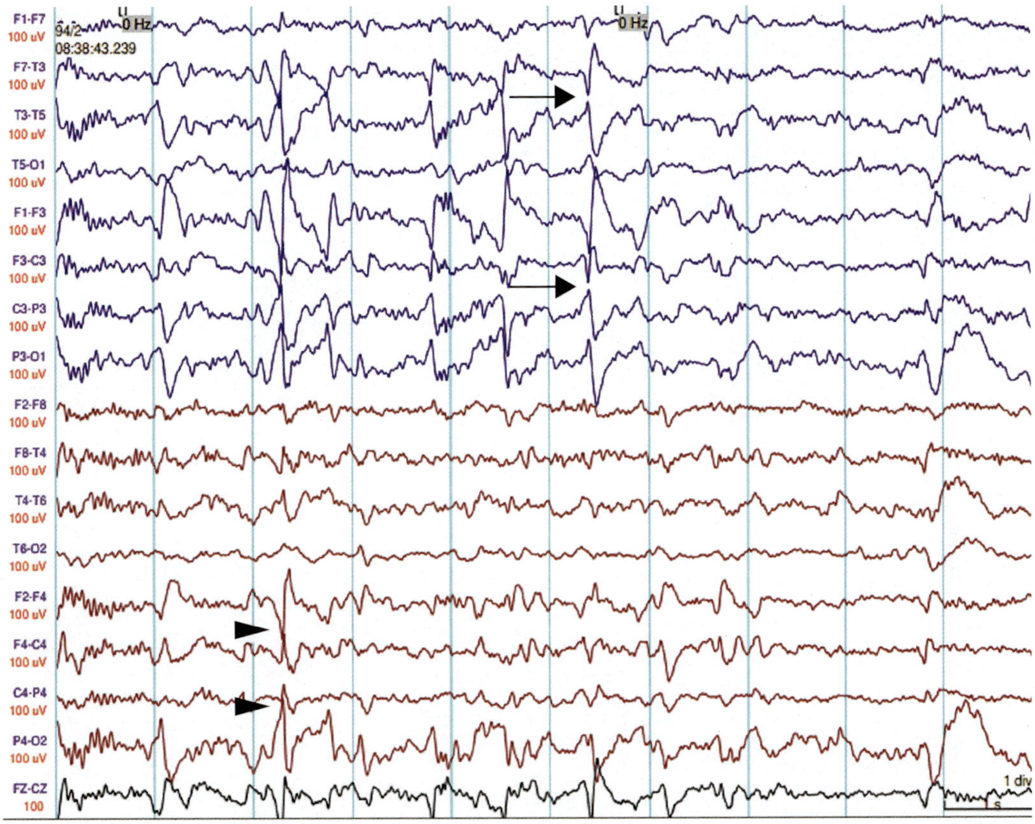

Fig. 17.1 Sleep EEG shows normal background activity with paroxysmal interictal discharges as spikes, sharps, and subsequent slow waves over the left central-temporal areas with an electrical field over the frontal and parietal areas (*arrows*) and occasional bilateral synchronous discharges (*arrowheads*). *EEG*, Electroencephalography.

FINAL DIAGNOSIS

Dysembryoplastic neuro-epithelial tumor (DNET).

DISCUSSION

Long-term epilepsy-associated tumors (LEATs) refer to tumors associated with chronic epilepsy (greater than 2 years) that are generally refractory to antiseizure medications. Most of these tumors are low-grade, cortically based, and arise in children, with DNET and ganglioglioma being the most common histologies. Around 50% of patients may also have associated FCDs.

DNETs are low-grade glioneuronal tumors (WHO grade 1) that involve the cerebral cortex and subcortical white matter. Temporal lobes are the most common location, followed by the frontal lobes. On CT, they appear hypodense with cystic components and variable calcifications. On MRI, there is T1-hypointense and T2-hyperintense signal with a bubbly appearance and FLAIR-hyperintense rim.

CLINICAL RED FLAGS

- Paroxysmal symptoms or signs, such as clonic or tonic movements followed by hemiparesis/hemiplegia, are suspicious for epilepsy. Transient unilateral weakness is known as Todd paralysis and increases the suspicion of a postictal state. Seizures usually cause cortical hyperexcitability with "positive" neurological symptoms and signs (e.g., tingling, pins and needles, dystonic posturing). Rarely, negative symptoms or signs (numbness, weakness, hypotonia) can be the sole ictal manifestation. EEG and brain MRI should be ordered to evaluate for focal epilepsy and structural brain lesions. Common causes include cortically located tumors, FCD, ischemia, or trauma. Genetic etiologies are possible but usually cause multifocal seizures.

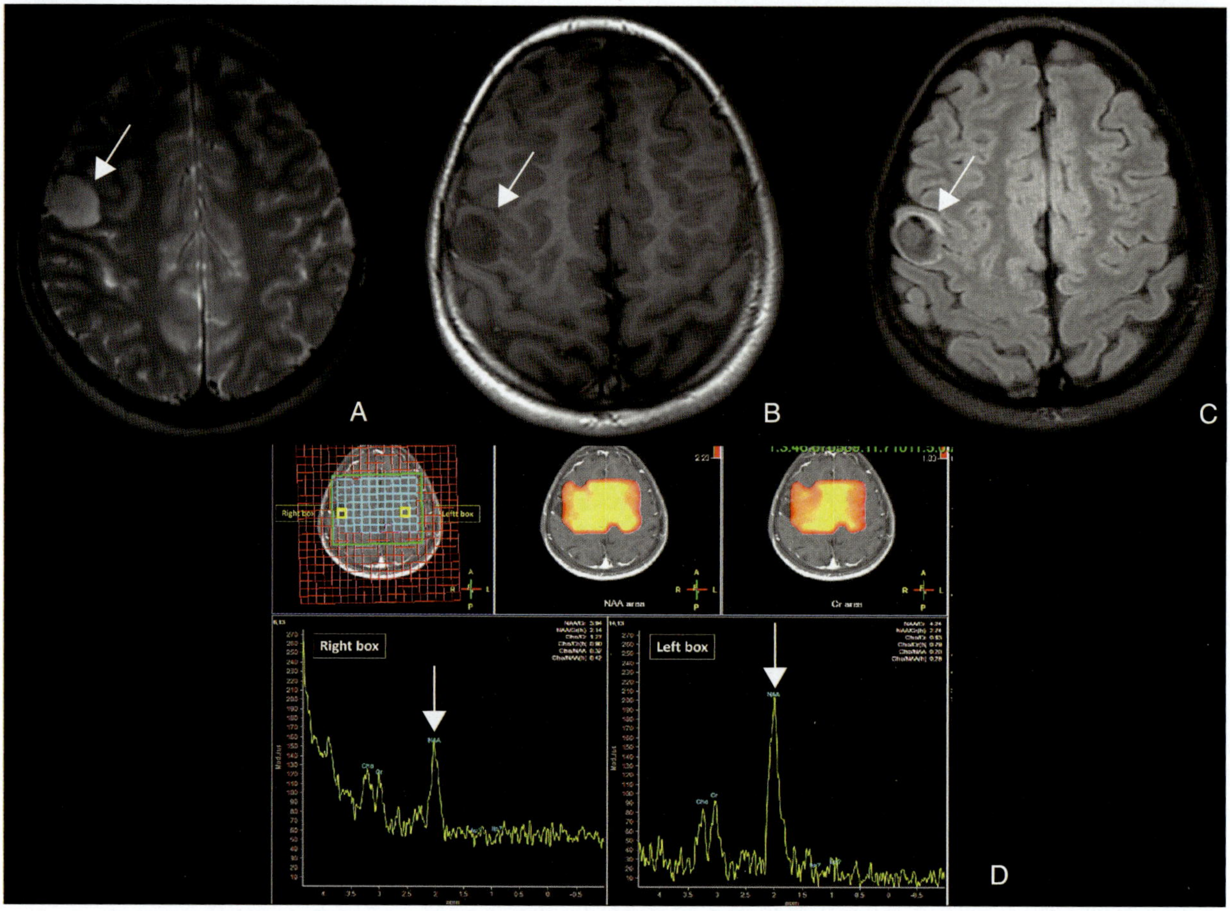

Fig. 17.2 DNET. Brain MRI, (A) axial T2 shows hyperintense, well-circumscribed, rounded lesion in the right lateral precentral gyrus cortex and subcortical white matter (*arrow*). (B) Axial T1 shows corresponding hypointense signal (*arrow*). (C) Axial FLAIR shows internal signal suppression with bubbly cysts and surrounding hyperintense rim (*arrow*). (D) Multivoxel spectroscopy shows decreased NAA (*arrows*) within the lesion (*right box*) compared with contralateral normal brain tissue (*left box*). *DNET*, Dysembryoplastic neuro-epithelial tumor; *FLAIR*, fluid-attenuated inversion recovery; *NAA*, N-acetylaspartate.

IMAGING RED FLAGS

- DNETs are cortically based tumors with a bubbly cystic appearance, variable calcifications, and a FLAIR-hyperintense rim. Other tumors can show variable signal, contrast enhancement, and mass effect.

CONCLUSIONS

Focal epilepsy in children requires neuroimaging, preferably brain MRI to evaluate for a structural lesion. Long-term epilepsy-related tumors include DNET and other low-grade tumors. Due to slow growth and low recurrence rate, total surgical resection is preferred when possible.

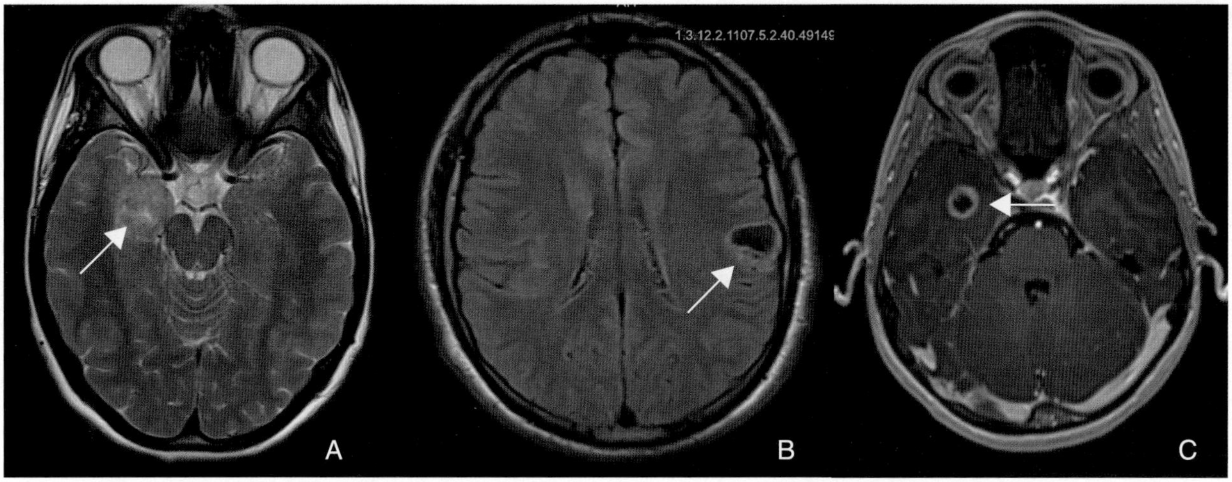

Fig. 17.3 Gangliogliomas. Brain MRI, (A) axial T2 shows right mesial temporal lesion with expansile cortical and subcortical hyperintensity (*arrow*). (B) Axial FLAIR shows left lateral precentral cortical/subcortical mass with solid and cystic components (*arrow*). (C) Axial postcontrast T1 shows right mesial temporal irregular ring-enhancing solid and cystic mass (*arrow*). *FLAIR*, Fluid-attenuated inversion recovery. (Cases courtesy Mai-Lan Ho, MD.)

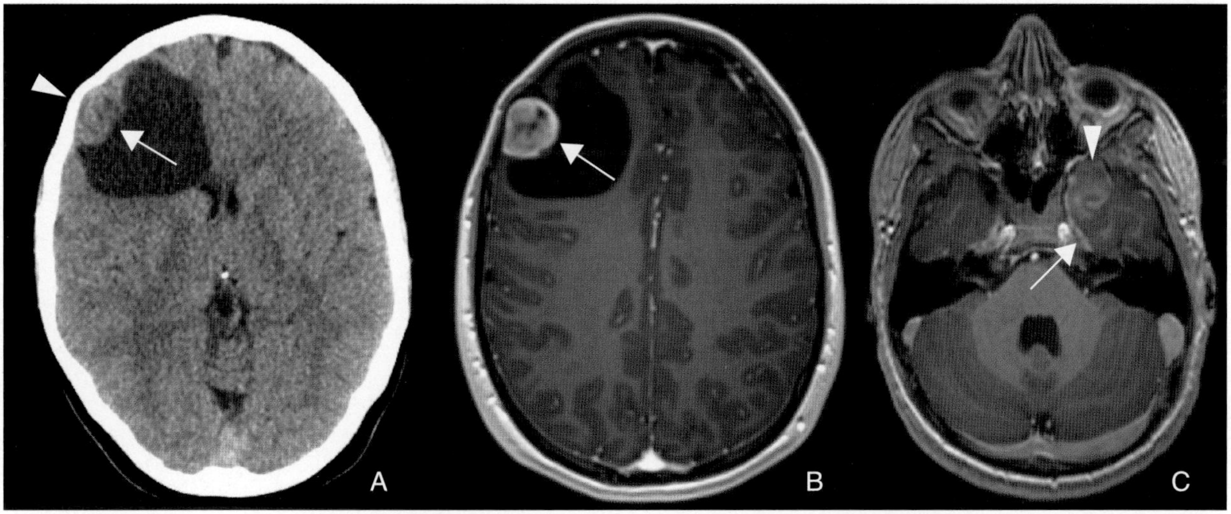

Fig. 17.4 Pleomorphic xanthoastrocytomas. (A) Head CT without contrast shows large right frontal cyst with hyperdense mural nodule (*arrow*) scalloping the inner table of calvarium (*arrowhead*). Brain MRI, (B) axial postcontrast T1 shows avidly enhancing solid nodule (*arrow*). Brain MRI, (C) axial postcontrast T1 shows left amygdala heterogeneously enhancing mass with scalloping of the sphenoid wing (*arrowhead*) and adjacent dural tail (*arrow*). (Cases courtesy Mai-Lan Ho, MD.)

REFERENCES

Blümcke I, Thom M, Aronica E, et al. The clinicopathologic spectrum of focal cortical dysplasias: a consensus classification proposed by an ad hoc Task Force of the ILAE Diagnostic Methods Commission. *Epilepsia.* 2011;52(1):158–174. doi:10.1111/j.1528-1167.2010.02777.x.

Chávez López EK, Aparicio J, Valera C, et al. Pre-surgical evaluation challenges and long-term outcome in children operated on for low grade epilepsy associated brain tumors. *Eur J Paediatr Neurol.* 2022;41:55–62. doi:10.1016/j.ejpn.2022.10.001.

Jen JC. Familial Hemiplegic Migraine. In: Adam MP, Feldman J, Mirzaa GM et al, eds. *GeneReviews®*. Seattle, WA: University of Washington; July 17, 2001 Seattle.

Louis DN, Perry A, Wesseling P, et al. The 2021 WHO classification of tumors of the central nervous system: a summary. *Neuro Oncol.* 2021;23(8):1231–1251. doi:10.1093/neuonc/noab106.

Sukheeja D, Mehta J. Dysembryoplastic neuroepithelial tumor: a rare brain tumor not to be misdiagnosed. *Asian J Neurosurg.* 2016;11(2):174. doi:10.4103/1793-5482.175643.

Case 18

Focus on the Etiology

HISTORY AND PHYSICAL

A 6-week-old boy presented with 1 week of episodic bilateral arm flexion and upward eye rolling. These episodes occurred in clusters (4–5 seizures/cluster, 3 times a day). There was no associated developmental regression. Birth history was notable for the use of vaginal forceps, but he was born full-term with no complications. Family history was unremarkable. During presentation, a full septic workup was performed with no abnormalities. Prolonged video-EEG captured multiple epileptic spasms associated with electrodecremental responses. Associated symptoms consisted of flexion and subtle upward tonic eye deviation (Fig. 18.1A). There was also right-dominant hypsarrhythmia and several focal seizures originating in the right temporal region. Clinically, these were either monosymptomatic or were characterized by left arm extension (Fig. 18.1B). Occasional intermittent theta activity was observed in the right posterior quadrant.

DIAGNOSTIC WORKUP

Head CT was normal. Brain MRI showed asymmetric gyration in the right posterior quadrant, with thickening of right middle and inferior temporal cortex, blurring of gray-white matter interface, and decreased white matter volume. These findings were suggestive of focal cortical dysplasia (FCD) involving the right posterior temporal lobe (Fig. 18.2).

Genetic epilepsy panel revealed a missense pathogenic variant in *NPRL3* (p.Arg92Gln) in addition to an exon 4 to 8 duplication. Both missense variants were inherited from the asymptomatic father (with a normal brain MRI) and paternal grandfather. The patient's *NPRL3* abnormality was responsible for GATOR1 complex dysfunction, which in turn caused disinhibition of mTORC1. Pathogenic variants in *NPRL3* have been associated with focal epilepsies, with the presence of FCD suggesting a second-hit somatic mutation.

CLINICAL DIFFERENTIAL DIAGNOSIS

Infantile epileptic spasms (previously known as West) syndrome (IESS) is a developmental epileptic encephalopathy characterized by epileptic spasms in infancy, a highly chaotic EEG pattern termed *hypsarrhythmia*, and developmental arrest or regression. Over 200 causative factors have been associated including structural, metabolic, toxic, and genetic etiologies. Structural etiologies account for the majority of cases but can overlap with other conditions.

IMAGING DIFFERENTIAL DIAGNOSIS

The abnormalities found in neuroimaging in this patient with epileptic spasms and focal seizures were suggestive of FCD. FCDs are histologically classified by the International League Against Epilepsy (ILAE) into type I (cortical lamination disorders: A = abundant microcolumns; B = abnormal layering; C = vertical and horizontal abnormalities); type II (cortical dysplastic neuron disorder: A = dysmorphic neurons; B = dysmorphic neurons and balloon cells). The best surgical response is seen with transmantle or bottom-of-the-sulcus dysplasias (BOSD) classified as type IIB (Fig. 18.3). FCDs associated with other lesions are classified as type III (Fig. 18.4).

Onset of seizures in patients with FCD type II often occurs in the first weeks of life. Pathologically, FCDs are often indistinguishable from tubers associated with tuberous sclerosis complex (TSC) (Fig. 18.5). Genetic testing reveals somatic or germline abnormalities of mTOR-related cellular growth and proliferation.

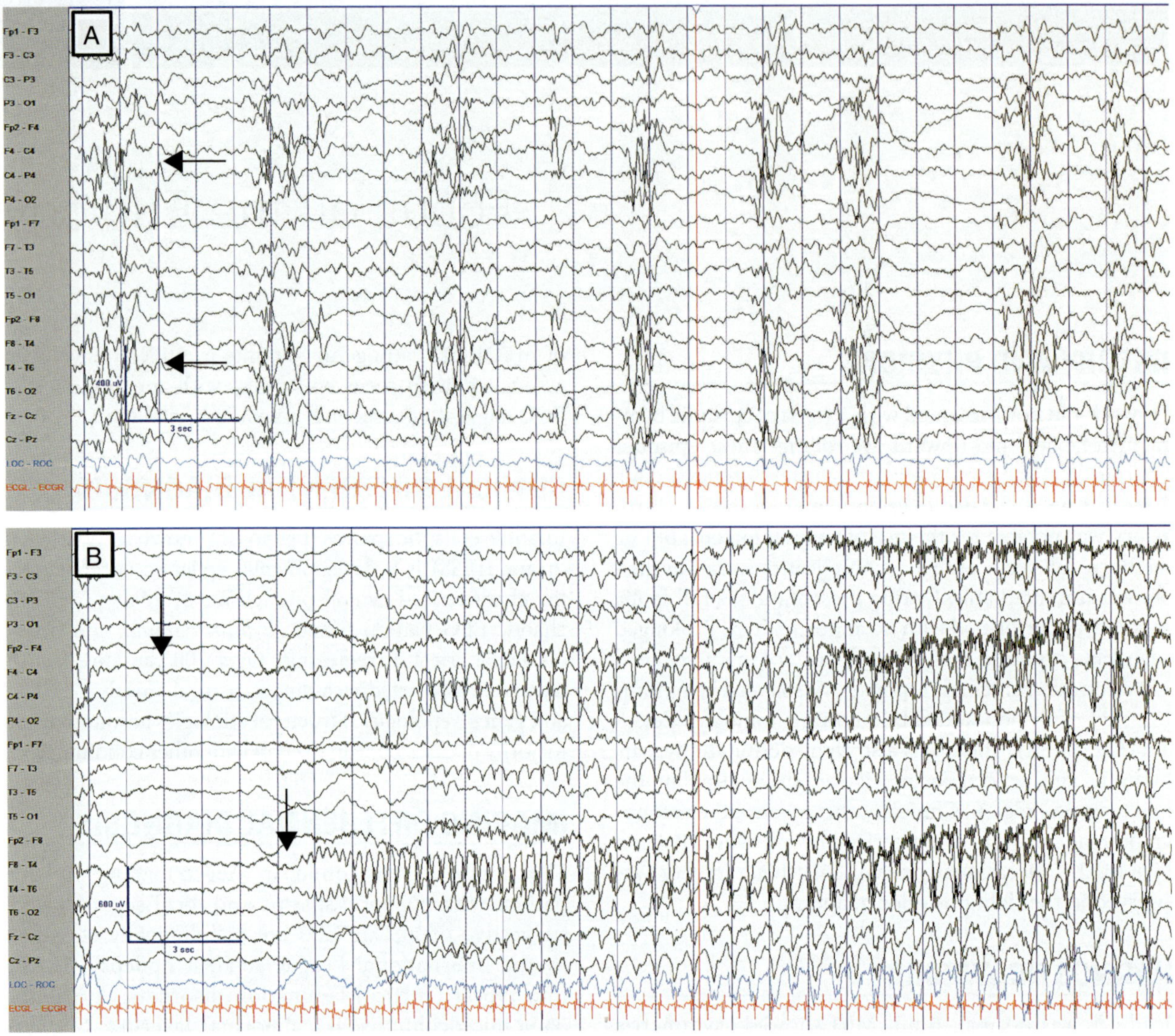

Fig. 18.1 Electroencephalography (EEG) in a 6-week-old male with infantile epileptic spasms. (A) Hypsarrhythmia during sleep, maximal in the right hemisphere (*arrows*). (B) Nonconvulsive focal seizure with onset in the right central and mid-posterior temporal lobe, electrodes C4 - T4 (*arrows*).

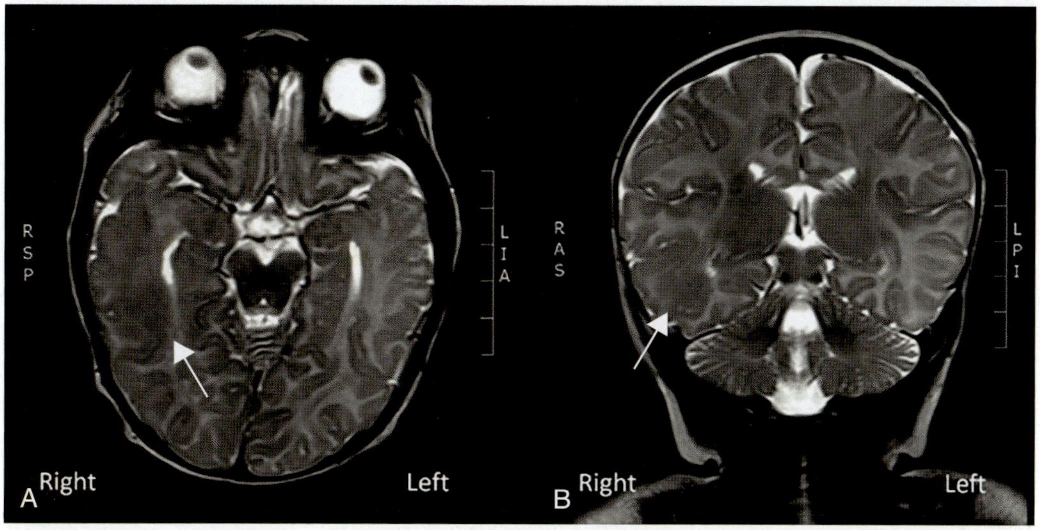

Fig. 18.2 Infantile epileptic spasms syndrome. Brain MRI, (A) axial and (B) coronal T2 show aberrant sulcation and gray-white blurring in the right temporal lobe (*arrows*) with asymmetric white matter signal and volume.

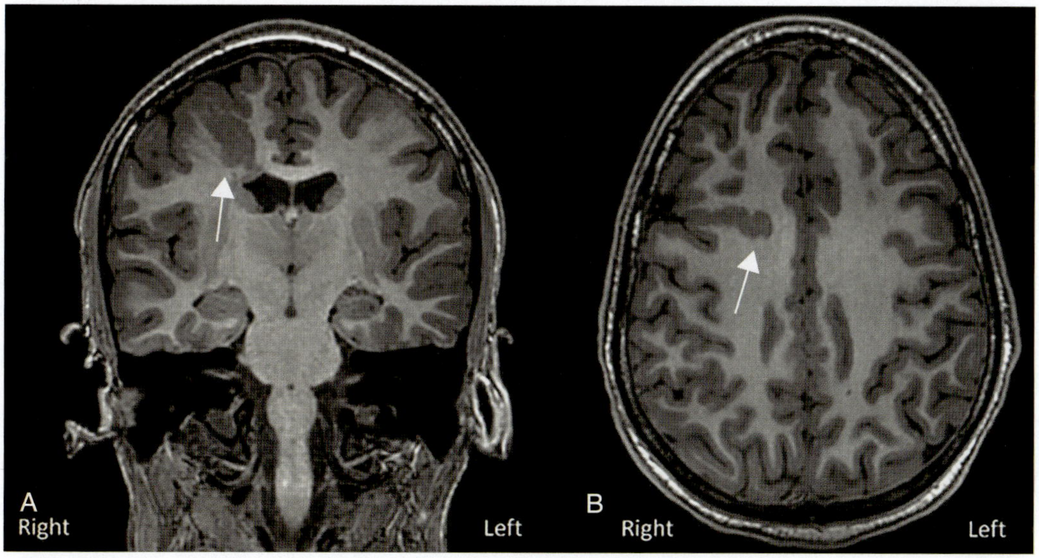

Fig. 18.3 Type IIb FCD. Brain MRI, (A) coronal and (B) axial T1 show aberrant and deep sulcation in the right frontal lobe with transmantle signal abnormality (*arrows*). *FCD,* Focal cortical dysplasia.

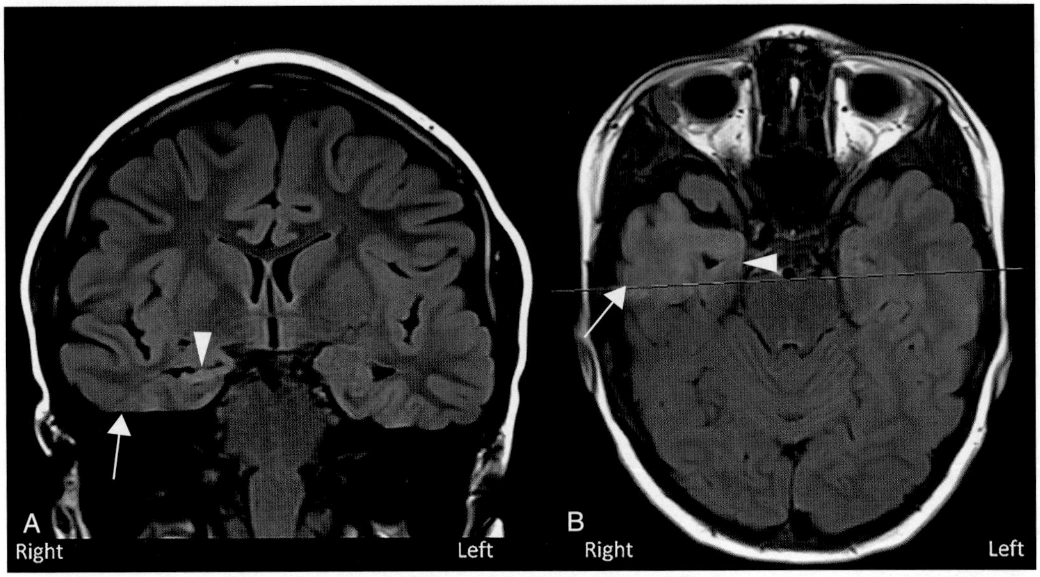

Fig. 18.4 Type IIIa FCD. Brain MRI, (A) coronal and (B) axial FLAIR showing expansile gray-white blurring (*arrows*) associated with mesial temporal sclerosis (*arrowheads*). *FCD*, Focal cortical dysplasia; *FLAIR*, fluid-attenuated inversion recovery.

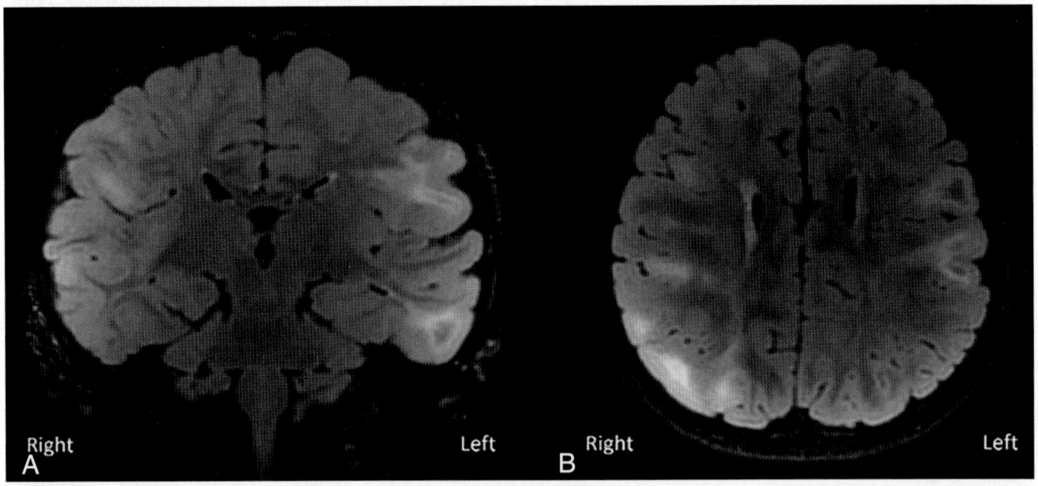

Fig. 18.5 Tuberous sclerosis complex. Brain MRI, (A) coronal and (B) axial FLAIR showing multifocal cortical/subcortical tubers with transmantle white matter signal. *FLAIR*, Fluid-attenuated inversion recovery.

FINAL DIAGNOSIS

Focal cortical dysplasia with infantile epileptic spasms syndrome.

DISCUSSION

When a focal structural lesion is present, surgery for IESS has been associated with a seizure-free outcome in 60% to 80% of patients. In this case, medical management was trialed due to the patient's young age. Vigabatrin was utilized due to the mutation affecting mTORC1 function, as vigabatrin has been shown to inhibit mTOR pathway activation in a mouse model of TSC. The patient experienced complete resolution of spasms and focal seizures, with his most recent EEG showing normal background with rare right temporal interictal discharges and mild intermittent slowing over the right posterior hemisphere. The patient is now 3 years old, seizure free on topiramate, and developing normally with only mild expressive language delays.

CLINICAL RED FLAGS

- Asymmetric hypsarrhythmia, spasms, and focal seizures suggest a focal structural lesion, worthy of surgical consideration.

IMAGING RED FLAGS

In an infant with epileptic spasms and focal EEG features, brain MRI is necessary to evaluate for a structural anomaly. Subtle dysplasias can be identified by careful evaluation for asymmetries in sulcation, cortical thickness, gray-white distinction, and white matter volume.

CONCLUSIONS

IESS can be caused by multiple etiologies. Accurate identification of etiology can significantly impact treatment, including surgical resection or targeted therapies, with improved long-term outcomes.

REFERENCES

Janicot R, Shao LR, Stafstrom CE. Infantile spasms: an update on pre-clinical models and EEG mechanisms. *Children (Basel)*. 2020;7(1):5. doi:10.3390/children7010005.

Karvelas G, Lortie A, Scantlebury MH, Duy PT, Cossette P, Carmant L. A retrospective study on aetiology based outcome of infantile spasms. *Seizure*. 2009;18(3):197–201. doi:10.1016/j.seizure.2008.09.006.

Moosa AN, Velayudam KV, Erdemir G. Electroclinical features in epilepsy surgery candidates with epileptic spasms. *J Clin Neurophysiol*. 2022;39(7):552–560. doi:10.1097/WNP.0000000000000907.

Najm I, Lal D, Alonso Vanegas M, et al. The ILAE consensus classification of focal cortical dysplasia: an update proposed by an ad hoc task force of the ILAE diagnostic methods commission. *Epilepsia*. 2022;63(8):1899–1919. doi:10.1111/epi.17301.

Wang S, Liu C, Zhang H, et al. Lesional intractable epileptic spasms in children: electroclinical localization and postoperative outcomes. *Front Neurol*. 2022;13:922778. doi:10.3389/fneur.2022.922778.

Weckhuysen S, Marsan E, Lambrecq V, et al. Involvement of GATOR complex genes in familial focal epilepsies and focal cortical dysplasia. *Epilepsia*. 2016;57(6):994–1003. doi:10.1111/epi.13391.

Zhang B, McDaniel SS, Rensing NR, Wong M. Vigabatrin inhibits seizures and mTOR pathway activation in a mouse model of tuberous sclerosis complex. *PLoS One*. 2013;8(2):e57445. doi:10.1371/journal.pone.0057445.

Zuberi SM, Wirrell E, Yozawitz E, et al. ILAE classification and definition of epilepsy syndromes with onset in neonates and infants: position statement by the ILAE Task Force on Nosology and Definitions. *Epilepsia*. 2022;63(6):1349–1397. doi:10.1111/epi.17239.

Case 19

Skin Is the Window to the Brain

HISTORY AND PHYSICAL

A 48-day-old girl presented to the emergency department with a first-time seizure. Immediately after breastfeeding, she vomited and became unresponsive. Her head and eyes deviated to the left, followed by bilateral arm and leg shaking for 20 minutes. A 20 mg/kg fosphenytoin load was given. Neurological examination showed mildly decreased axial tone with mild head lag and slip-through on vertical suspension. There was a hypopigmented lesion on the right forehead with irregular borders (Fig. 19.1).

The patient was otherwise healthy and born following an uncomplicated full-term pregnancy at 39 weeks via elective cesarean section to a G3P2 mother with no complications during delivery. Development was appropriate for age. The parents were originally from Ethiopia, with two other healthy children and no family history of consanguinity, seizures, or developmental delay.

The patient's seizures were refractory to levetiracetam bolus, requiring loading doses of lorazepam and fosphenytoin. Intermittent and at times prolonged seizures continued, requiring daily lorazepam rescue doses and maintenance of levetiracetam, phenobarbital, and lacosamide. Despite all antiseizure medications, she required a brief midazolam infusion in the pediatric intensive care unit.

DIAGNOSTIC WORKUP

Initial labs, cultures, and CSF analysis were unremarkable. Head CT was also normal. Brain MRI showed subtle right hemispheric asymmetry of T1, T2, and diffusion signal with cortical thickening (Fig. 19.2). Repeat brain MRI 20 days later showed more prominent gray-white differentiation suggestive of diffuse cortical dysplasia (Fig. 19.3). Additional investigations and prolonged video-EEG monitoring were performed (Fig. 19.4).

The patient proceeded to neurosurgery for a right functional hemispherotomy at 69 days of life. Pathology reported extensive cortical dysplasia including cortical thinning with radial and tangential dyslamination, numerous enlarged dysmorphic neurons with extension into subcortical white matter, and extensive gliosis.

CLINICAL DIFFERENTIAL DIAGNOSES

Seizures in the neonatal and early infant period can show stereotyped features, forced posturing, and lack of improvement with repositioning. There are multiple

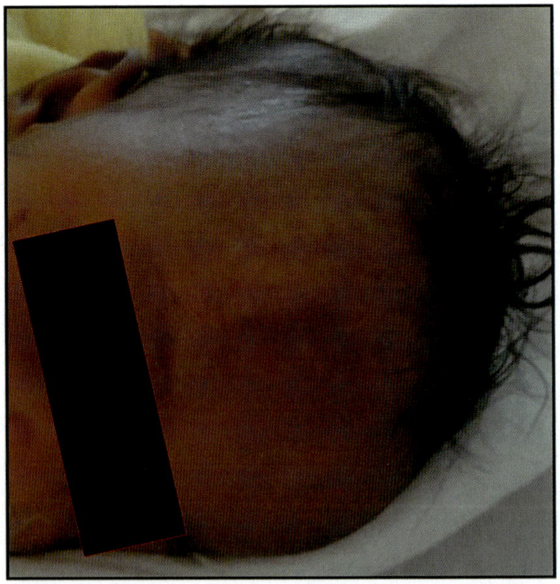

Fig. 19.1 Hypomelanosis of Ito. Hypopigmentation may appear as striations, swirls, patches, or whorls at birth or during the first year of life. Lesions can involve the trunk, limbs, and/or head.

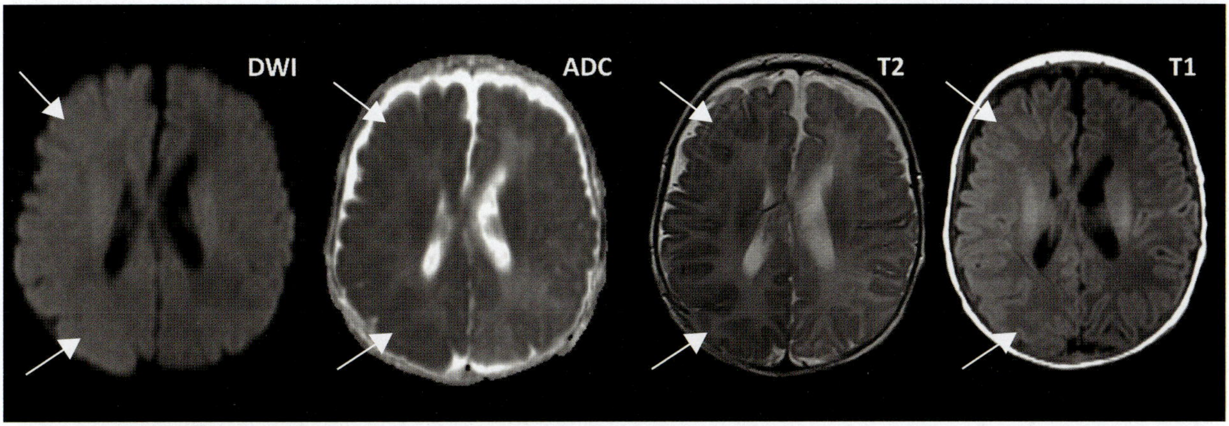

Fig. 19.2 Hemimegalencephaly. Brain MRI shows asymmetric right cerebral signal with cortical thickening and white matter signal abnormality (*arrows*).

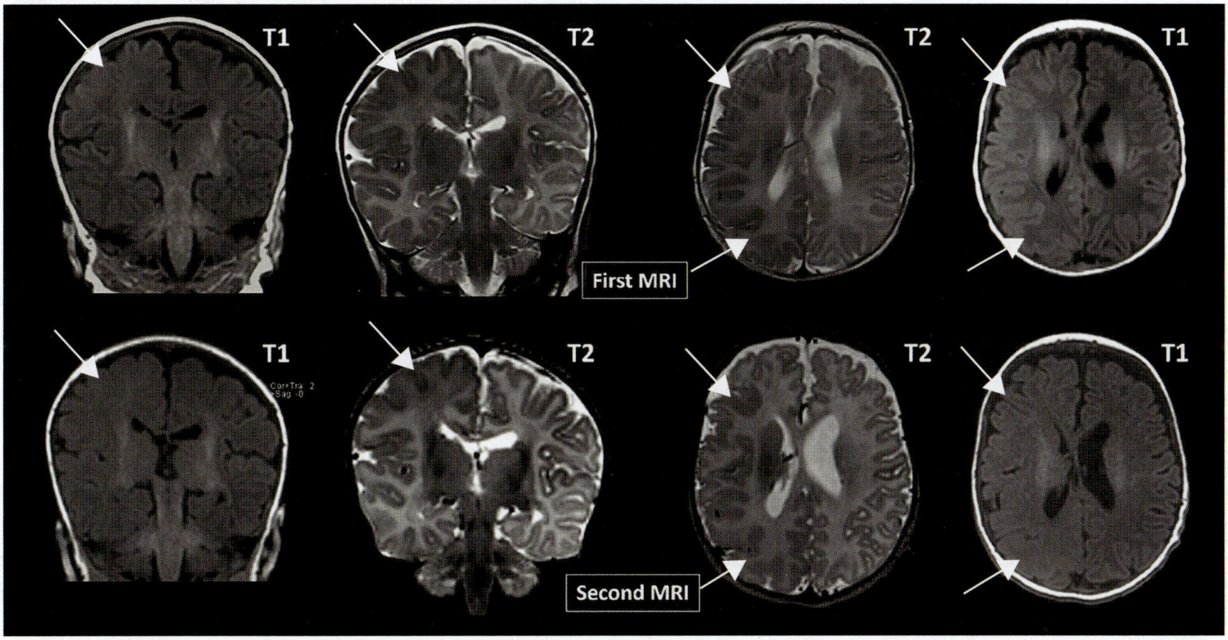

Fig. 19.3 Hemimegalencephaly. Brain MRI on day 2 and day 20 of admission show persistent asymmetric right cerebral findings (*arrows*). There is mild interval volume loss with more prominent cortical irregularity on the follow-up examination.

causes including inborn errors of metabolism, intracranial or intraparenchymal hemorrhage, cerebral ischemia, infections, congenital brain malformations, genetic epilepsy syndromes, and developmental or epileptic encephalopathies.

Seizure mimics include gastro-esophageal reflux disorder, benign neonatal sleep myoclonus, excessive startle, and benign clonic movements.

Careful history and physical examination, laboratory testing, EEG, and neuroimaging should be performed to identify etiology and guide appropriate management.

IMAGING DIFFERENTIAL DIAGNOSES

Focal cortical dysplasia (FCD) or hemimegalencephaly (HME) are characterized by focal or hemispheric

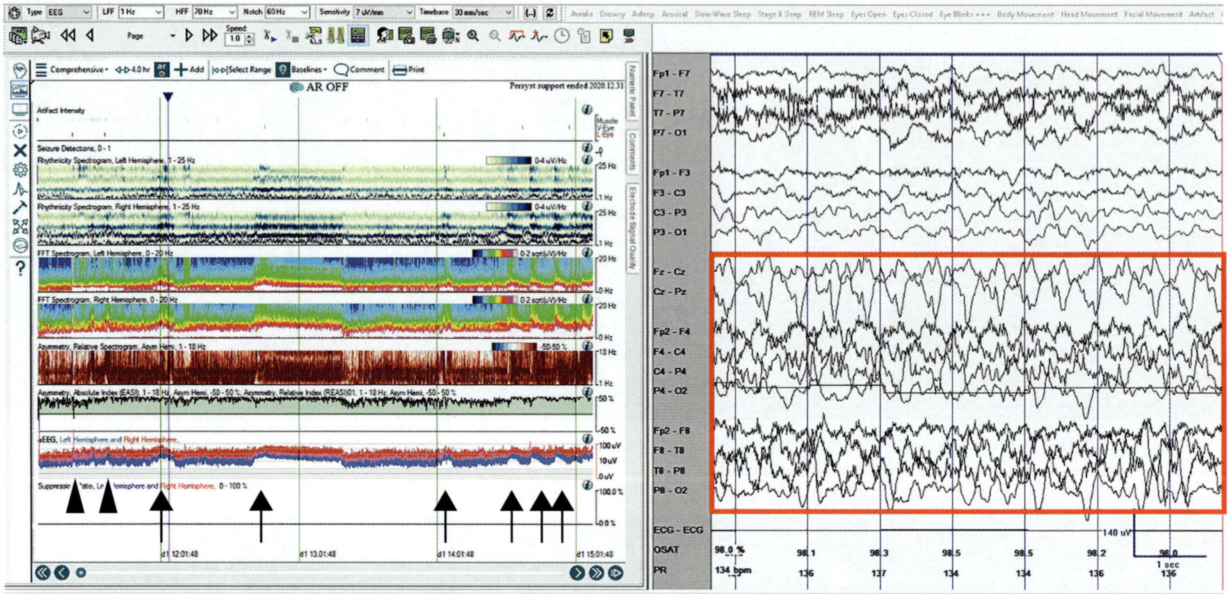

Fig. 19.4 1-hour epoch of EEG trends (*left*) and 7-second epoch of regular EEG (*right*) at 2 months of age showing ongoing seizures despite aggressive antiseizure therapy. Frequent seizures were recorded over the right hemisphere (*red rectangle*). These were often brief and minimally noticeable on the EEG trends (*arrowheads*), but other episodes were very prolonged and almost 1 hour in length (*arrows*). *EEG*, Electroencephalography.

abnormalities in sulcation, gray-white matter differentiation, and white matter volume (Fig. 19.5).

Asymmetric cerebral hemispheric signal changes can also be seen in the setting of status epilepticus, hypoxic-ischemic injury, infarction, infection, tumors (gliomatosis or lymphoma), autoimmune disorders (Rasmussen encephalitis), and neurocutaneous disorders (Sturge-Weber, nevus sebaceous, CLOVES [congenital lipomatous overgrowth, vascular malformations, epidermal nevi, skeletal and spinal anomalies] syndrome) (Fig. 19.6A and B).

FINAL DIAGNOSIS

Hemimegalencephaly associated with hypomelanosis of Ito.

DISCUSSION

HME is a rare congenital malformation of the brain involving overgrowth of one cerebral hemisphere. It usually presents with focal and unilateral seizures, typically in the first few months of life and refractory to medical treatment, contralateral hemiparesis, and severe psychomotor delays. HME may be associated with ipsilateral facial or somatic hemihypertrophy. HME can occur in isolation or in association with neurocutaneous syndromes, such as epidermal nevus syndrome, Proteus syndrome, and hypomelanosis of Ito.

HME is caused by anomalies in neuronal proliferation leading to cell overgrowth and migration abnormalities with gray and white matter malformations, occurring as early as the third week of gestation. It is hypothesized that HME forms due to somatic mutations in genes such as *AKT3*, *P13K*, or *MTOR* that lead to hyperactivation of the mTOR signaling cascade, which plays important roles in regulating cell division, growth, and survival.

MRI is the method of choice for studying brain malformations in HME. Key features include increased volume of the affected hemisphere with ventriculomegaly. Depending on the timing of the somatic mutation, more or less of the brain can be affected. Usually, the white matter abnormalities can include disorganization with T2 hyperintensity and T1 hypointensity in a myelinated patient, volume increase, and a hamartomatous appearance. Gray matter abnormalities include

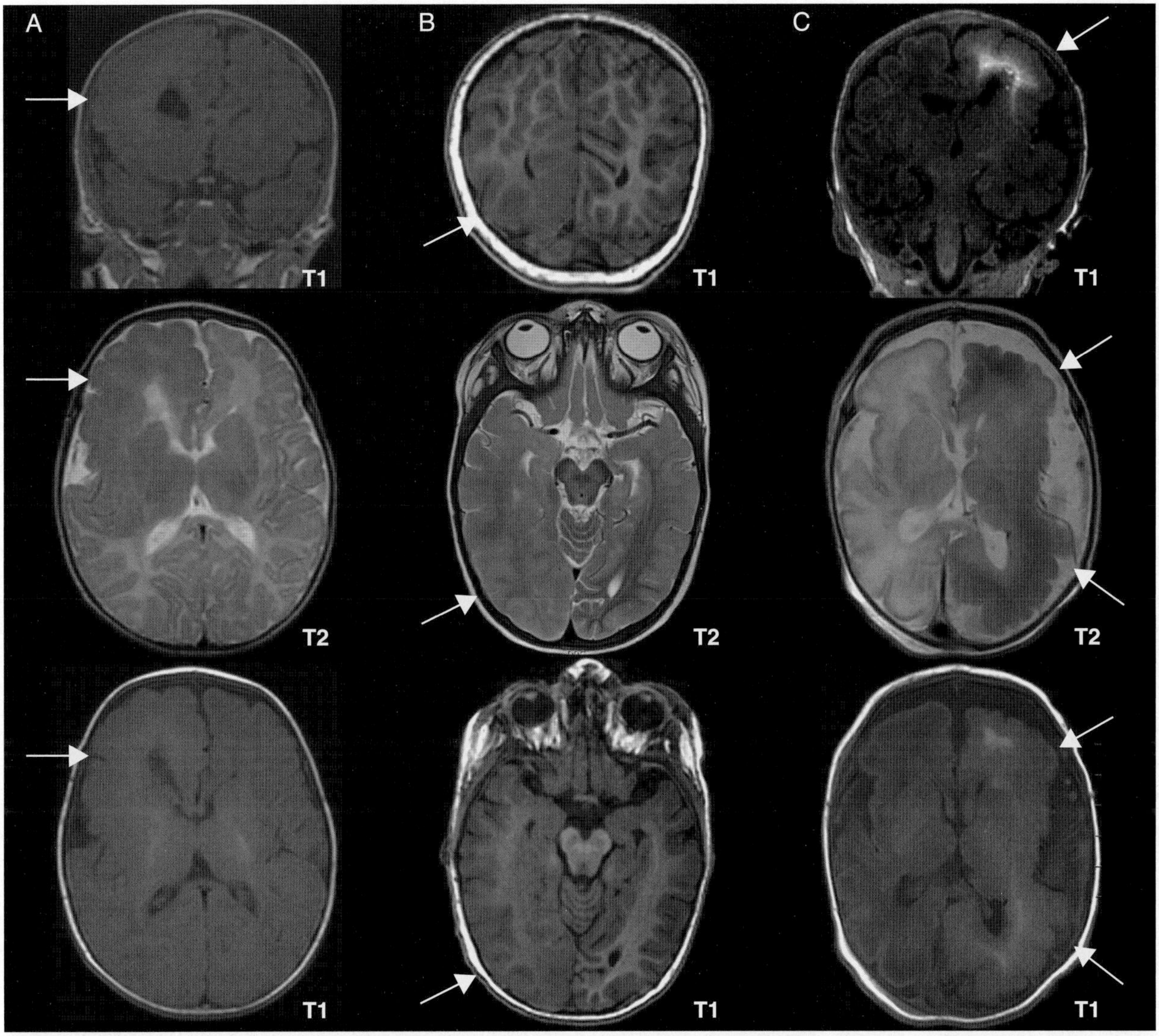

Fig. 19.5 Spectrum of megalencephaly. (A) 2-month-old with right fronto-insular megalencephaly (*arrows*). (B) 18-month-old with right temporo-occipital megalencephaly (*arrows*). (C) Preterm 33-week infant with left HME (*arrows*). Affected regions show increased volume, abnormal white matter signal, gray-white blurring, and cortical malformations. *HME*, Hemimegalencephaly.

polymicrogyria, pachygyria, or agyria, as well as loss of gray-white differentiation.

Hypomelanosis of Ito is the third most common neurocutaneous disorder, characterized by hypopigmented macules arranged in sharply demarcated whorls, streaks, and patches following the migrational lines of Blaschko. Areas of hypopigmentation can be unilateral or bilateral and usually involve the trunk and limbs, less commonly the head. Extracutaneous findings are found in 75% of cases, most commonly affecting the central nervous, musculoskeletal, and cardiovascular systems. Most cases are sporadic without evidence of genetic transmission. The clinical appearance of the lesions is due to pigmentary mosaicism, in which de novo postzygotic chromosomal or genetic aberrations result in distinct cell lines with different pigmentations.

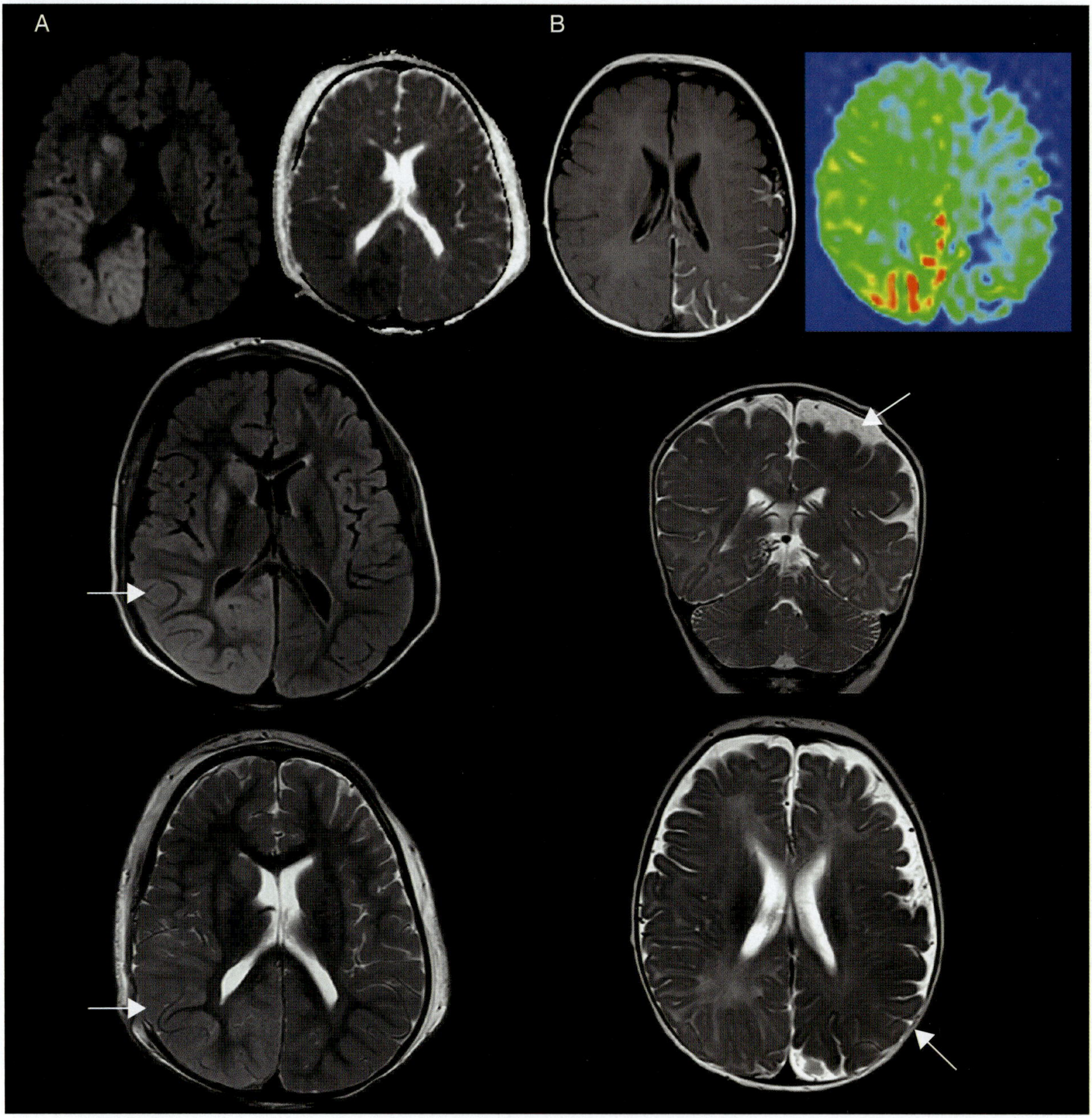

Fig. 19.6A (A) 8-year-old with asymmetric hypoxic-ischemic injury. Brain MRI, axial DWI, ADC, FLAIR, and T2 show restricted diffusion and T2/FLAIR-hyperintense signal in the right posterior cortex (*arrows*) and basal ganglia. (B) 4-month-old with Sturge-Weber syndrome. Brain MRI, axial T1 postcontrast, ASL, coronal T2, and axial T2 show leptomeningeal enhancement, cerebral atrophy (*arrows*), and decreased perfusion on ASL in the left posterior quadrant. *ASL*, Arterial spin labeling; *FLAIR*, fluid-attenuated inversion recovery.

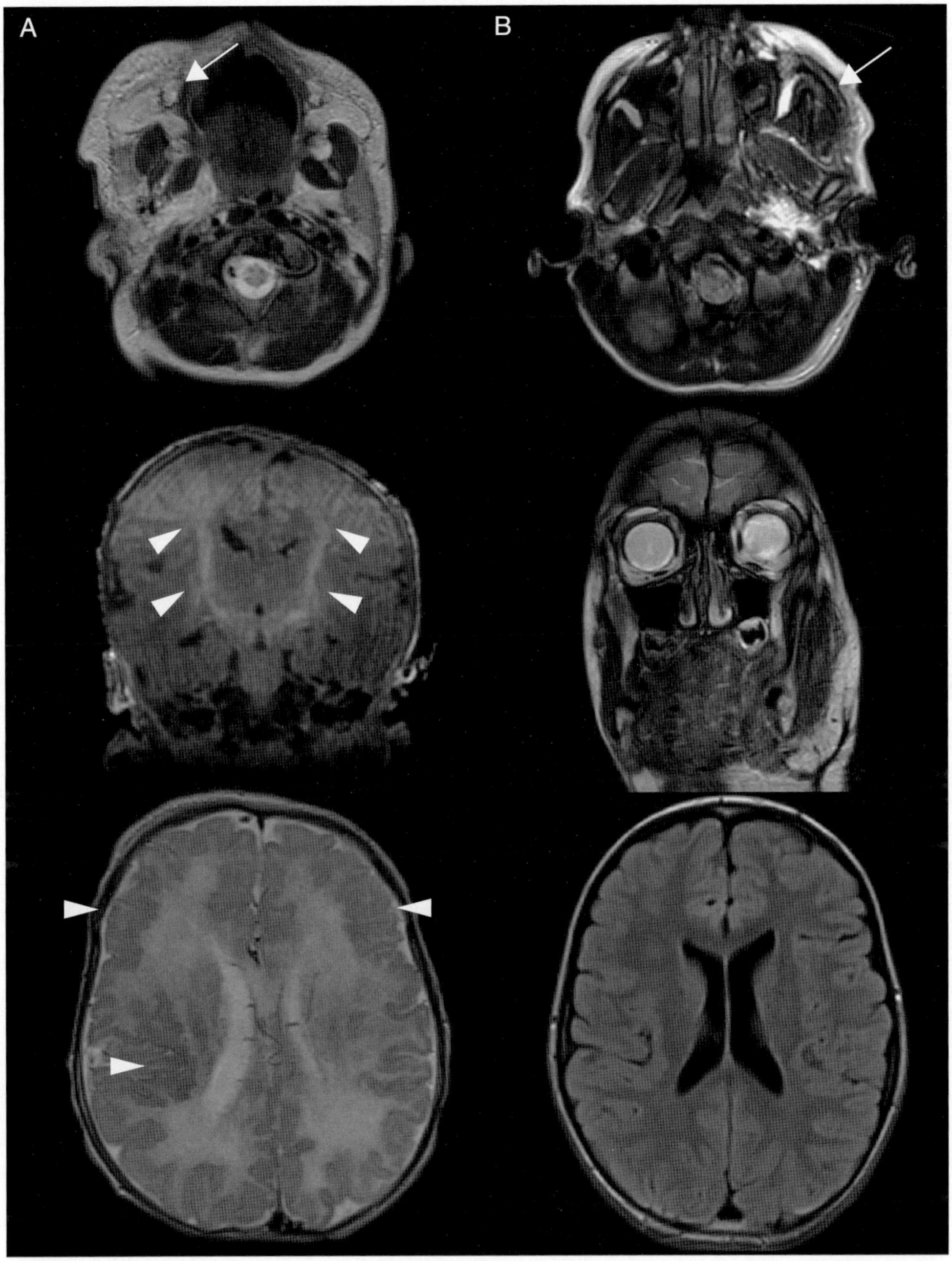

Fig. 19.6B CLOVES syndrome with facial overgrowth (*arrows*). (A) 2-day-old term infant with right greater than left megalencephaly, abnormal white matter, and polymicrogyria (*arrowheads*). (B) 8-year-old with minimally larger left cerebral hemisphere.

CLINICAL RED FLAGS

- Seizures in the first year of life, particularly focal and drug-resistant.
- Hypopigmented lesions following Blaschko lines.
- Psychomotor retardation.

IMAGING RED FLAGS

MRI is the preferred imaging modality to detect the cortical malformations seen in HME. Characteristic findings include unilateral lobar or hemispheric enlargement and white matter signal abnormalities. Diffusion changes can be seen postictally, particularly after prolonged or multiple brief seizures. Other MRI features include gyral abnormalities (such as polymicrogyria, pachygyria, or agyria), shallow sulci, midline distortion, asymmetric corpus callosum, thickened cortex, asymmetry, ventricular deformation, and the "occipital sign" (marked displacement of an enlarged occipital lobe to the contralateral side) (Fig. 19.5).

CONCLUSIONS

Seizures in infancy that are refractory to medical treatment should raise suspicion for congenital brain malformations such as FCD or HME. Malformations can occur in isolation or as part of a neurocutaneous syndrome, such as hypomelanosis of Ito. Brain MRI is key to characterizing the nature of structural abnormalities and planning for surgery in drug-resistant individuals. Functional hemispherotomy is preferred over anatomic hemispherectomy due to a lower rate of complications. When performed before 1 year of age, patients can show improvements in global development, particularly speech and quality of life. This patient received a functional right hemispherotomy with partial resection of the right temporal lobe and has been seizure free for the past 5 years. She has persistent left spastic hemiplegia but retains the ability to walk and run, and is attending an adapted school program for reading and speech.

REFERENCES

Chamli A, Litaiem N. Hypomelanosis of Ito. *StatPearls*. Treasure Island, FL: StatPearls Publishing; June 20, 2023.

Crino PB. mTOR signaling in epilepsy: insights from malformations of cortical development. *Cold Spring Harb Perspect Med*. 2015;5(4):a022442. doi:10.1101/cshperspect.a022442.

Dmytriw AA, Sawlani V, Shankar J. Diffusion-weighted imaging of the brain: beyond stroke. *Can Assoc Radiol J*. 2017;68(2):131–146. doi:10.1016/j.carj.2016.10.001.

Flores-Sarnat L. Hemimegalencephaly: part 1. Genetic, clinical, and imaging aspects. *J Child Neurol*. 2002;17(5):373–384. doi:10.1177/088307380201700512.

Garcia CAB, Carvalho SCS, Yang X, et al. mTOR pathway somatic variants and the molecular pathogenesis of hemimegalencephaly. *Epilepsia Open*. 2020;5(1):97–106. doi:10.1002/epi4.12377.

Paladin F, Chiron C, Dulac O, Plouin P, Ponsot G. Electroencephalographic aspects of hemimegalencephaly. *Dev Med Child Neurol*. 1989;31(3):377–383.

Pavone P, Praticò AD, Ruggieri M, Falsaperla R. Hypomelanosis of Ito: a round on the frequency and type of epileptic complications. *Neurol Sci*. 2015;36(7):1173–1180. doi:10.1007/s10072-014-2049-1.

Santos AC, Escorsi-Rosset S, Simao GN, et al. Hemispheric dysplasia and hemimegalencephaly: imaging definitions. *Childs Nerv Syst*. 2014;30(11):1813–1821. doi:10.1007/s00381-014-2476-6.

Case 20

Secondary Seizures

HISTORY AND PHYSICAL

A 15-year-old right-handed boy consulted for left-sided hemiclonic motor seizures that evolved into bilateral tonic-clonic motor seizures. These were refractory to antiseizure medications (ASMs), and he subsequently developed episodes of convulsive status epilepticus that were also refractory. His past medical and family history was normal. He was very active in sports and excelled academically.

Postictal neurological examination demonstrated left-sided hemiparesis, with increased deep tendon reflexes in his left upper and lower extremities, and upgoing plantar response. Eleven months later, the patient started having nocturnal seizures with left hemiclonic rhythmic jerks and impairment of awareness.

DIAGNOSTIC WORKUP

Head CT showed right middle cerebral artery territory hypodensity (Fig. 20.1). Cerebral angiography and carotid Doppler US were normal.

A prolonged video-EEG demonstrated continuous slow activity over the right hemisphere with frequent sharps, spikes, and slow waves over the right frontal region (Fig. 20.2).

Transthoracic echocardiogram showed a mural thrombus in the left anterior mitral leaflet. Coagulation studies demonstrated protein C deficiency.

CLINICAL DIFFERENTIAL DIAGNOSIS

The differential diagnosis for acute-onset focal seizures or status epilepticus, encephalopathy, and hypotonic hemiplegia is broad and includes acute ischemic causes, either arterial (Fig. 20.3) or venous stroke. Additional vascular causes include Sturge-Weber, moyamoya, arteriovenous malformations (AVMs), and vasculopathies. Inflammatory conditions include CNS demyelination and Rasmussen encephalitis. Tumors, infection, hemorrhage, and metabolic disorders may also cause transient weakness with seizures.

Pediatric stroke mimics include genetic conditions and inborn errors of metabolism (Fig. 20.4) including hemiplegic migraine, hypokalemic periodic paralysis, and mitochondrial disorders (*POLG* [DNA polymerase gamma]-related disorders and mitochondrial encephalopathy, lactic acidosis, and stroke-like episodes [MELAS]). Many of these disorders are associated with subsequent development of epilepsy.

IMAGING DIFFERENTIAL DIAGNOSES

Arterial ischemic stroke in a previously healthy teenager has several possible etiologies including small, medium, and large vessel vasculitis (systemic or isolated to the central nervous system), cardiogenic thromboembolism, and hypercoagulability.

Head CT is the primary imaging modality used in the emergency setting, but brain MRI provides more detailed information without ionizing radiation exposure. Increased signal on diffusion-weighted imaging (DWI) and decreased signal on apparent diffusion coefficient (ADC) are seen with cytotoxic edema due to acute arterial stroke (Fig. 20.3). Other vascular etiologies include venous infarction, which manifests with vasogenic edema (T2-shine-through, increased signal on both DWI and ADC) in a superficial or deep distribution, which can be complicated by hemorrhagic conversion. High-flow vascular malformations include AVM and arteriovenous fistula (AVF), which can rupture and cause hemorrhagic strokes (Fig. 20.4).

Stroke mimics are nonvascular conditions that present with an acute neurological deficit simulating ischemic stroke, seen in nearly 20% of cases prior to imaging. Etiologies include epilepsy with postictal paralysis, MELAS

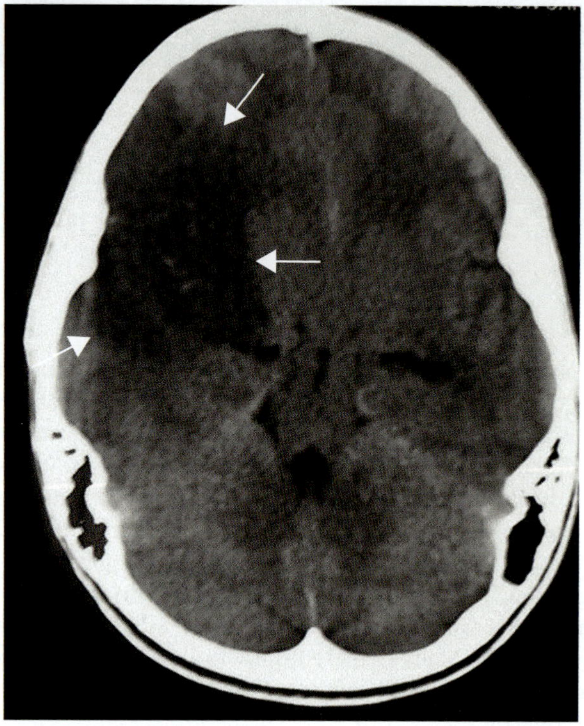

Fig. 20.1 Right superior MCA infarct. Head *CT* shows cytotoxic edema involving the right frontal and anterior temporal cortex and white matter (*arrows*). *MCA*, Middle cerebral artery.

with stroke-like episodes (Fig. 20.5), posterior reversible encephalopathy syndrome (PRES), and tumors.

FINAL DIAGNOSIS

Middle cerebral artery infarct with status epilepticus.

DISCUSSION

Pediatric ischemic stroke is a rare condition, especially in neonates. Patients who present with focal seizures during the early post-stroke period (first 6 hours) have the most significant risk of developing post-stroke epilepsy, though an elevated risk persists even 10 to 20 years post-stroke (Fig. 20.6). It is theorized that early acute seizures can potentiate ischemia-related neurodegeneration and contribute to the development of post-stroke epilepsy. In severe cases, surgery may be required to control seizures. Following left hemispherectomy at 18 months, the patient has remained seizure-free for over 4 years without antiseizure medications.

Identifying stroke etiology is key to predicting recurrence risk, particularly in patients with immune or metabolic etiologies, coagulation defects, or cardiac disease (congenital or acquired). Laboratory workup including

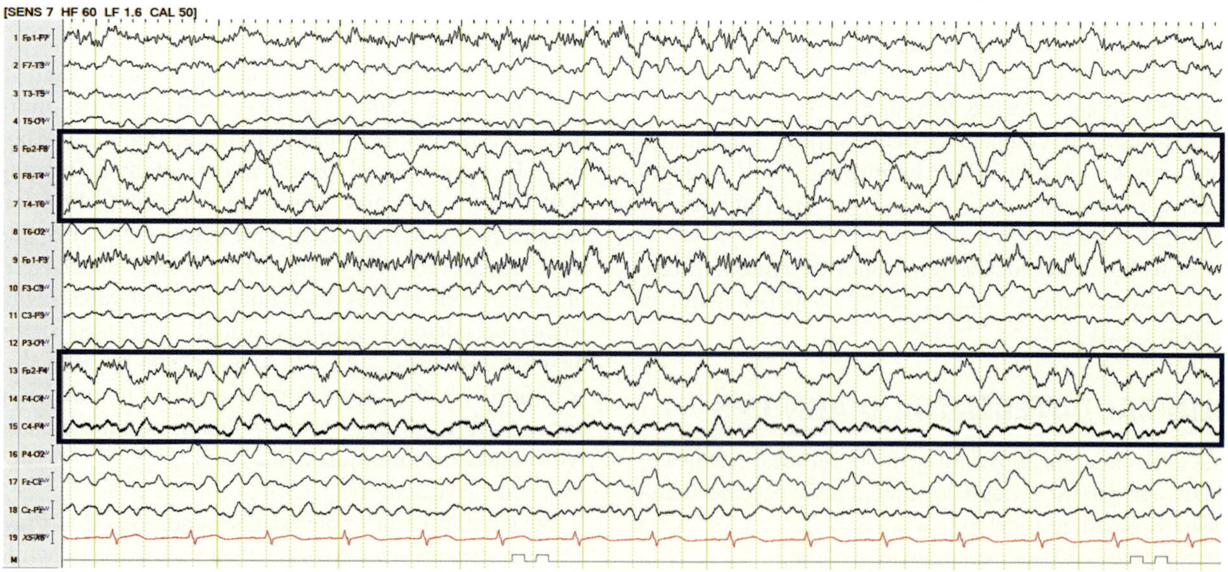

Fig. 20.2 Electroencephalography (EEG) shows continuous slowing in the right hemisphere with frontotemporal predominance (*black rectangles*).

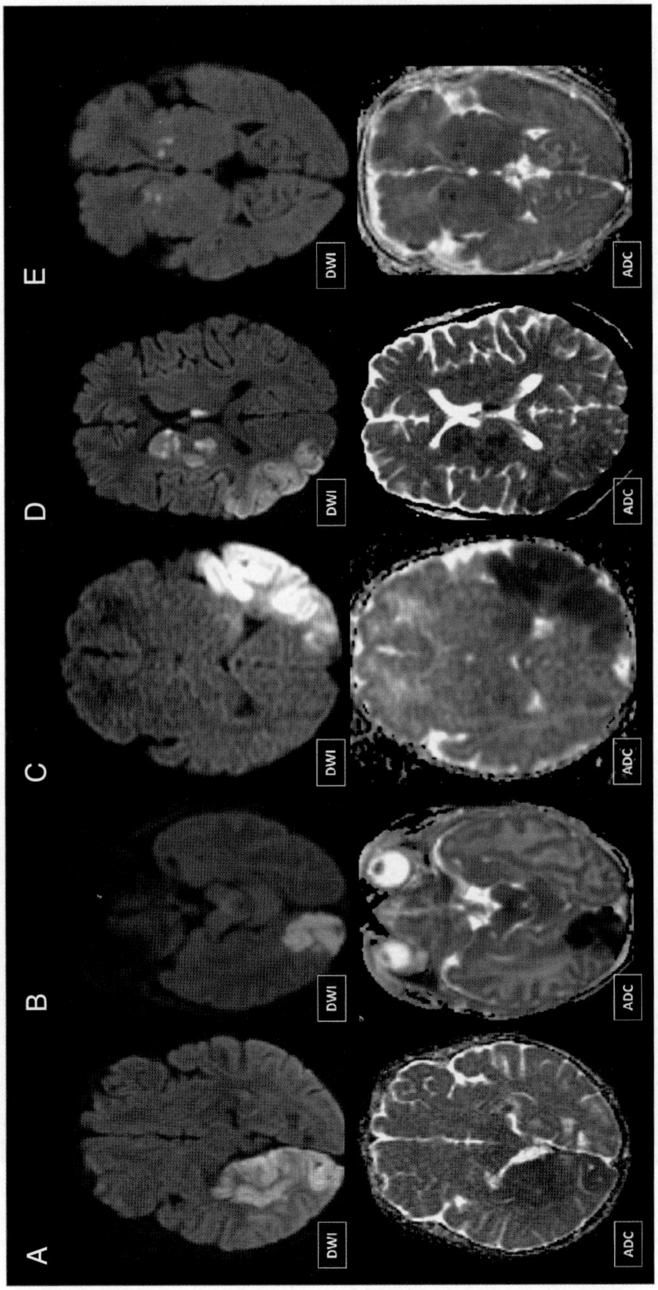

Fig. 20.3 Acute ischemic strokes with restricted diffusion. (A) Complete right PCA territory infarct. (B) Distal right PCA territory infarct involving the occipital pole. (C) Left inferior MCA territory infarct. (D) Embolic infarcts in multiple arterial distributions secondary to metastatic undifferentiated pulmonary sarcoma. (E) Neonate with *Streptococcus* meningoencephalitis and bilateral basal ganglia microinfarcts suggesting mycotic vasculitis. *MCA*, Middle cerebral artery; *PCA*, posterior cerebral artery.

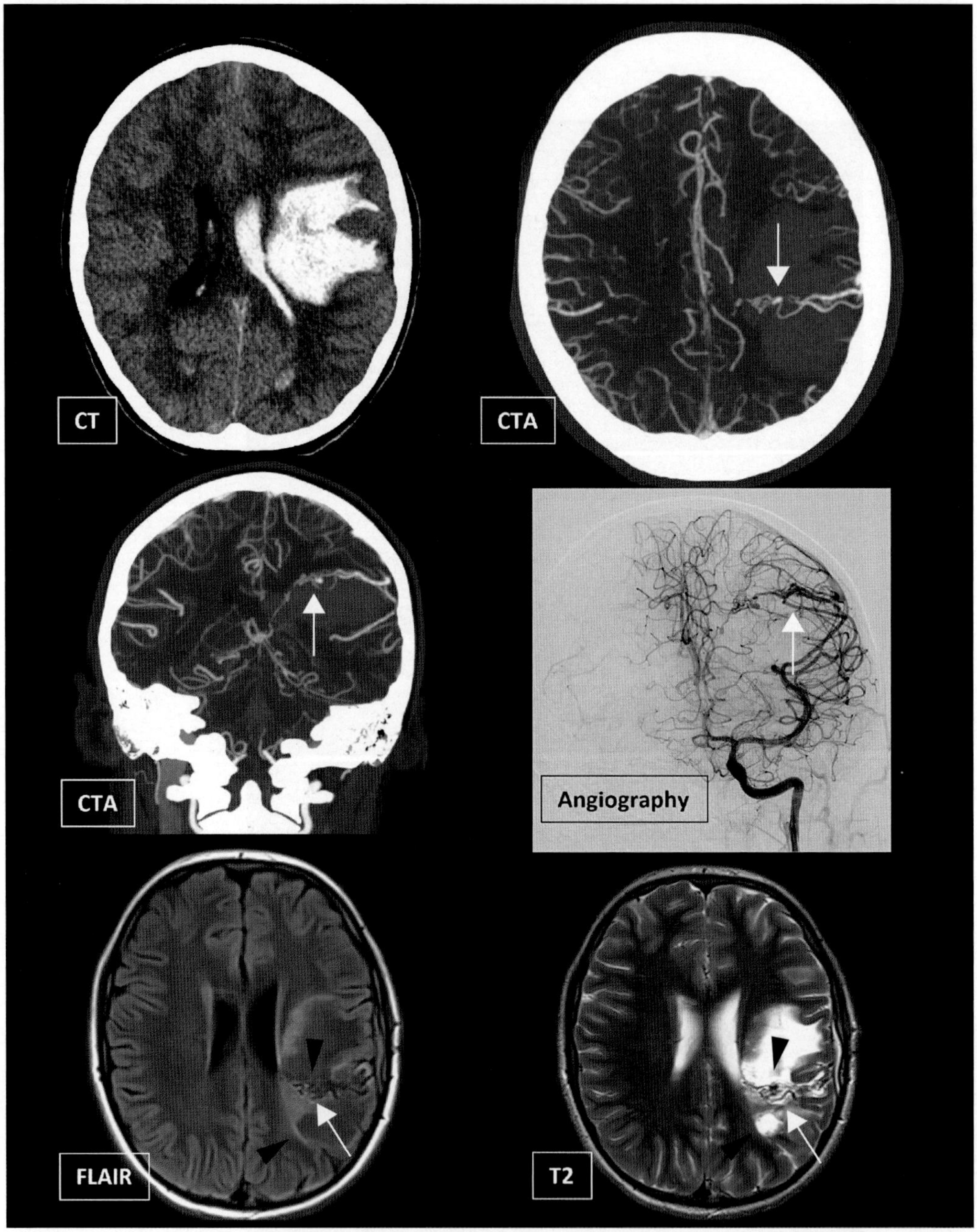

Fig. 20.4 Ruptured arteriovenous malformation. A 12-year-old female with acute onset encephalopathy and dense right hemiparesis after a 5-minute focal motor tonic-clonic seizure. Head CT shows left cerebral hemorrhagic stroke with intraventricular extension. Head CTA shows underlying AVM (*arrows*). Cerebral angiography with Onyx embolization was performed at 24 hours. Follow-up brain MRI shows involution of the AVM (*arrows*) with surrounding parenchymal gliosis (*arrowheads*). *AVM*, Arteriovenous malformation.

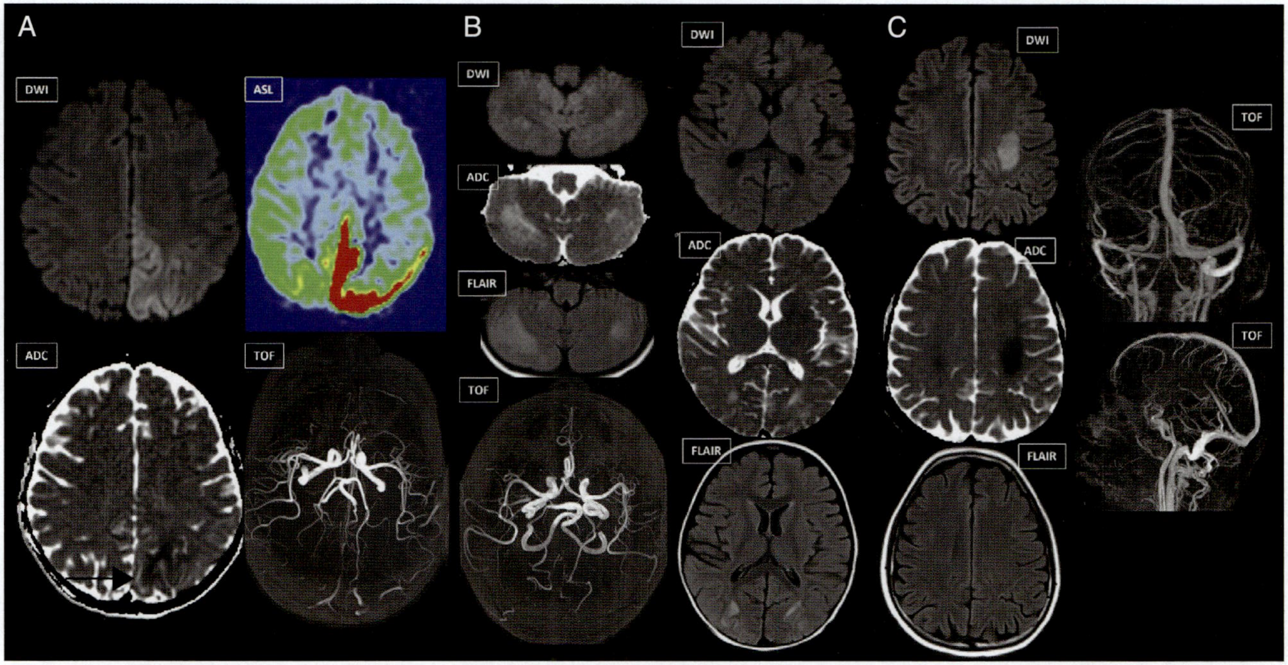

Fig. 20.5 Stroke mimics. (A) MELAS shows restricted diffusion, elevated perfusion, and arterial dilation in the left posterior quadrant in a nonvascular territory. (B) PRES. Bilateral parietal and cerebellar white matter FLAIR hyperintensity and facilitated diffusion with normal MRA. (C) Methotrexate leukoencephalopathy with patchy restricted diffusion in the left greater than right centrum semiovale and normal MRV. *FLAIR*, Fluid-attenuated inversion recovery; *MELAS*, mitochondrial encephalopathy, lactic acidosis, and stroke-like episodes; *MRA*, magnetic resonance angiography; *MRV*, magnetic resonance venography; *PRES*, posterior reversible encephalopathy syndrome; *TOF*, time-of-flight.

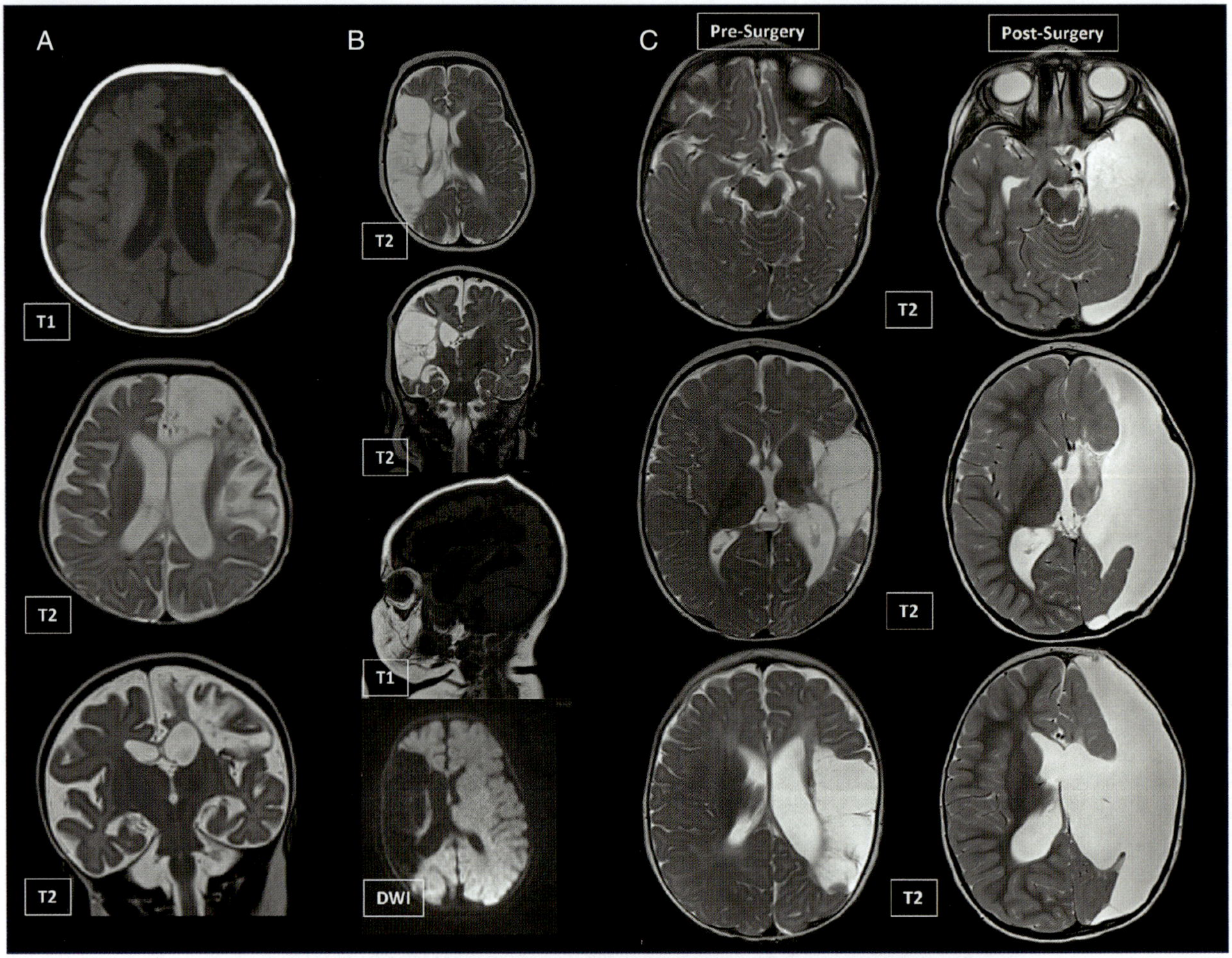

Fig. 20.6 Perinatal strokes. (A) Left ACA and MCA territory infarcts with cystic encephalomalacia, cortical laminar necrosis, and ex vacuo dilatation of the left lateral ventricle. (B) Right MCA territory infarct with cystic encephalomalacia. (C) Left MCA territory stroke with cystic encephalomalacia, treated with functional hemispherectomy. *ACA*, Anterior cerebral artery; *MCA*, middle cerebral artery.

functional assays for protein C and S deficiency and antithrombin III should be performed, as well as polymerase chain reaction (PCR) for factor V Leiden mutation and prothrombin G20210A mutation. Additional tests include homocysteine and antiphospholipid antibodies, routine coagulation panel, complete blood count (CBC), and D-dimer levels. Transthoracic or transesophageal echocardiogram can detect cardiac defects and thrombi. Electrocardiogram (EKG) can detect atrial fibrillation and other arrhythmias that can predispose to a thromboembolic disorder.

CLINICAL RED FLAGS

- New-onset seizures associated with focal neurological deficits.
- History of complex congenital heart disease, coagulation defects, or metabolic disorders.

IMAGING RED FLAGS

- Acute hypodensity on brain CT or diffusion restriction on MRI in an arterial distribution.

CONCLUSIONS

Healthy children and adolescents with abrupt onset of status epilepticus require comprehensive evaluation including neuroimaging. Following a stroke, treatment of underlying thrombus by intraarterial or intravenous anticoagulation and ASMs is indicated. Approximately 25% of children will develop epilepsy within 6 months, and 30% during the first decade.

REFERENCES

Beslow LA, Helbig I, Fox CK. Long-term risk of epilepsy after pediatric stroke and potential genetic vulnerabilities. *Stroke.* 2021;52(11):3541–3542. doi:10.1161/STROKEAHA.121.036376.

Fox CK, Mackay MT, Dowling MM, et al. Prolonged or recurrent acute seizures after pediatric arterial ischemic stroke are associated with increasing epilepsy risk. *Dev Med Child Neurol.* 2017;59(1):38–44. doi:10.1111/dmcn.13198.

Polat İ, Yiş U, Ayanoğlu M, et al. Risk factors of post-stroke epilepsy in children: experience from a tertiary center and a brief review of the literature. *J Stroke Cerebrovasc Dis.* 2021;30(1):105438. doi:10.1016/j.jstrokecerebrovasdis.2020.105438.

Senst B, Tadi P, Basit H, Jan A. Hypercoagulability. *StatPearls.* Treasure Island, FL: StatPearls Publishing; August 22, 2023.

Singh RK, Zecavati N, Singh J, et al. Seizures in acute childhood stroke. *J Pediatr.* 2012;160(2):291–296. doi:10.1016/j.jpeds.2011.07.048.

Sundelin HEK, Tomson T, Zelano J, Söderling J, Bang P, Ludvigsson JF. Pediatric ischemic stroke and epilepsy: a nationwide cohort study. *Stroke.* 2021;52(11):3532–3540. doi:10.1161/STROKEAHA.121.034796.

SECTION 5

Central Nervous System Vascular Disease

M. Celeste Buompadre, Gabriel González Rabelino, Carlos A. Rugilo, Hugo A. Arroyo

INTRODUCTION

Pediatric stroke is an important cause of mortality and long-term morbidity in children. Many patients suffer from delayed diagnosis and the potential for recurrence. Early clinical suspicion and use of imaging aids diagnosis and therapeutic options.

Imaging by CT and/or MRI helps identify brain structural abnormalities shortly after symptom onset. This helps differentiate true strokes from other etiologies that manifest with similar symptoms, especially hemiplegia, aphasia, and seizures. Evaluation of vascular anatomy and perfusion is critical for diagnosis in acute ischemic or hemorrhagic stroke (HS) and other intracranial vasculopathies.

Childhood vascular neurologic disease is distinct from that in adults, due to the varying risk factors from fetal life through adolescence. Hemorrhagic presentations are more frequent. Vasculopathies and congenital heart disease (CHD) are the most common risk factors for ischemic stroke. A superimposed "second hit," such as infection or anemia, may trigger the initial presentation.

Clinical trials and research data in adult stroke provide some guidance for pediatric care but are not directly translatable. Due to the low incidence of pediatric stroke, multidisciplinary working groups with national/international registries are needed to establish diagnostic and treatment guidelines.

We present a series of pediatric stroke cases with neuroimaging to demonstrate the broad spectrum of potential mechanisms and etiologies.

SUGGESTED READINGS

Ferriero DM, Fullerton HJ, Bernard TJ, et al. Management of stroke in neonates and children: a scientific statement from the American Heart Association/American Stroke Association. *Stroke.* 2019;50(3). https://doi.org/10.1161/str.0000000000000183.

Ganesan Vijeva K. *Stroke and Cerebrovascular Disease in Childhood.* Mac Keith Press; 2011.

González G, Arroyo HA. *Accidente cerebrovascular en la infancia y adolescencia.* Ediciones Journal; 2011.

Medley TL, Miteff C, Andrews I, et al. Australian clinical consensus guideline: the diagnosis and acute management of childhood stroke. *Int J Stroke.* 2019;14(1):94–106. https://doi.org/10.1177/1747493018799958.

Sacco RL, Kasner SE, Broderick JP, et al. An updated definition of stroke for the 21st century: a statement for healthcare professionals from the American Heart Association/American Stroke Association. *Stroke.* 2013;44(7):2064–2089. https://doi.org/10.1161/str.0b013e318296aeca.

Case 21

Postinfectious Stroke

HISTORY AND PHYSICAL

An 8-year-old boy arrived in the emergency department with sudden-onset dysarthria and right hemiparesis, which evolved over 6 hours to complete right hemiplegia. During the week prior to presentation, he experienced fever, odynophagia, and exanthema that improved within 48 hours. He denied antecedent headache, trauma, recent vaccinations, and travel. His prenatal and birth history were normal, with no developmental issues or other medical/family history. On neurological examination, he was fully oriented but dysarthric with 2/5 weakness throughout the right upper and lower extremities, and 3+ reflexes with upgoing toes on the right. Sensation was intact.

DIAGNOSTIC WORKUP

Head CT showed patchy hypodensity in the left basal ganglia, external and internal capsules, and frontal operculum (Broca area) (Fig. 21.1). Brain MRI confirmed acute infarction with T2/fluid-attenuated inversion recovery (FLAIR) hyperintense cytotoxic edema and restricted diffusion (Fig. 21.2). MR angiography (MRA) demonstrated irregular stenosis of the left internal carotid artery (ICA) terminus, M1, and A1 segments (Fig. 21.3). Digital subtraction angiography showed corresponding luminal narrowing without obvious dissection flap or collateral vessels. Blood and CSF testing was normal with no signs of coagulopathy or infection. Echocardiogram was normal. The patient was treated with aspirin and steroids, with residual hemiparesis after 6 months. Follow-up MRA at 9 months showed improved but persistent mild stenosis of the involved vessels (Fig. 21.4).

CLINICAL DIFFERENTIAL DIAGNOSIS

Hemiplegic migraine (familial or sporadic): usually presents with aura of progressive visual and sensory disturbances and unilateral paresthesias, followed by language disturbances and hemiparesis. The deficit lasts from minutes to hours, followed by headache with nausea, vomiting, and photophobia.

Postictal hemiparesis (Todd phenomenon): occurs following seizure, with duration of less than 24 hours.

Hemorrhagic stroke or venous thrombosis: symptoms of intracranial hypertension or encephalopathy.

Central nervous system infection (meningoencephalitis): elevated CSF and blood inflammatory markers and positive cultures.

IMAGING DIFFERENTIAL DIAGNOSIS

Post-varicella (varicella zoster virus, VZV) arteriopathy: Variant of focal cerebral arteriopathy (FCA) with a history of varicella infection in the last 12 months or positive PCR in CSF.

Intracranial arterial dissection: Rare but classically seen in young boys following trauma. Usually affects the internal carotid or vertebral artery with spiraling or tapered luminal narrowing, and can predispose to distal thromboembolism (Figs. 21.5 and 21.6).

Moyamoya disease or syndrome: Progressive obliterative arteriopathy of distal ICA, M1, and A1 with "puff-of-smoke" lenticulostriate, leptomeningeal, and basal collaterals, which are particularly well characterized by cerebral angiography (Fig. 21.7).

Primary or secondary CNS vasculitis (Fig. 21.8): Multifocal infarcts and vascular irregularity.

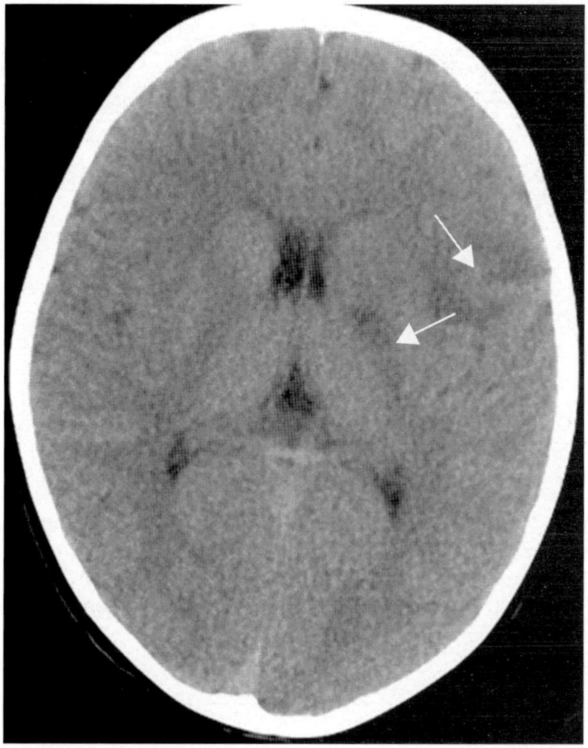

Fig. 21.1 Focal cerebral arteriopathy. Head CT shows patchy hypodensity in the left frontal operculum, internal/external capsules, and basal ganglia consistent with acute infarcts (*arrows*).

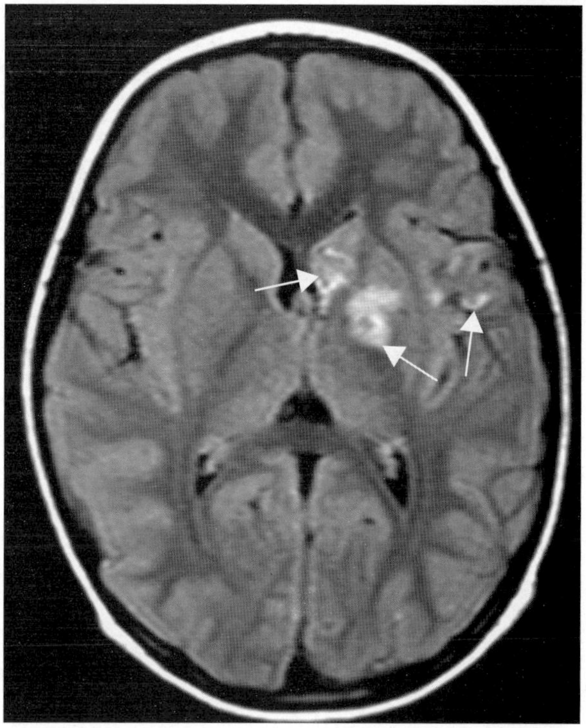

Fig. 21.2 Focal cerebral arteriopathy. Brain MRI, axial FLAIR, shows patchy cytotoxic edema in the left MCA distribution (*arrows*). *FLAIR*, Fluid-attenuated inversion recovery; *MCA*, middle cerebral artery.

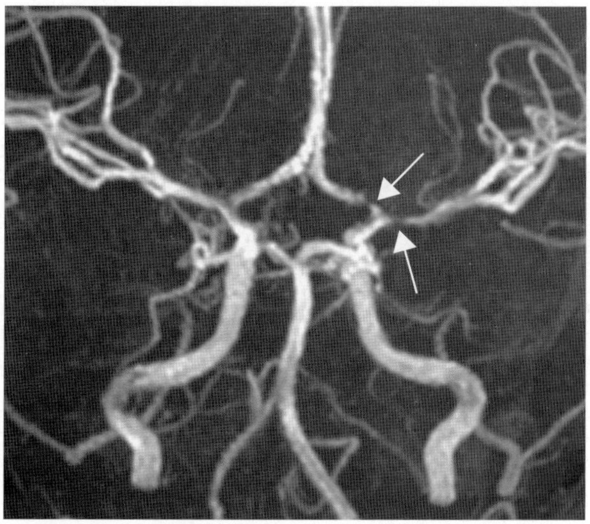

Fig. 21.3 Focal cerebral arteriopathy. Brain MRA shows irregular stenoses of the left ICA terminus, M1 and A1 (*arrows*). *ICA*, Internal carotid artery; *MRA*, magnetic resonance angiography.

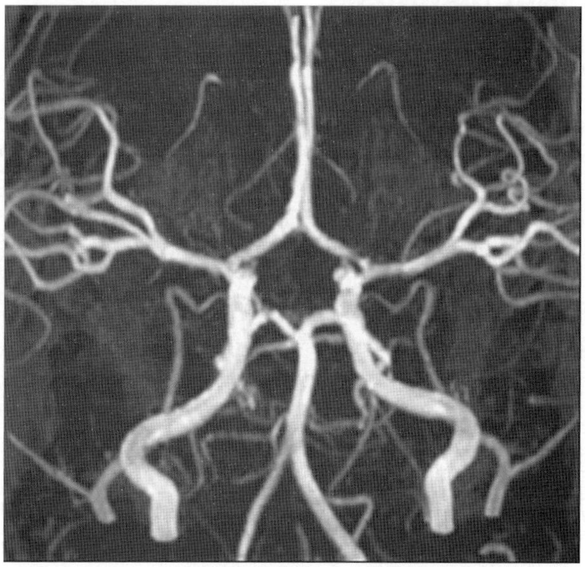

Fig. 21.4 Focal cerebral arteriopathy. Follow-up brain MRA after 9 months shows improved but persistent mild stenosis of the left distal ICA, M1, and A1. *ICA*, Internal carotid artery; *MRA*, magnetic resonance angiography.

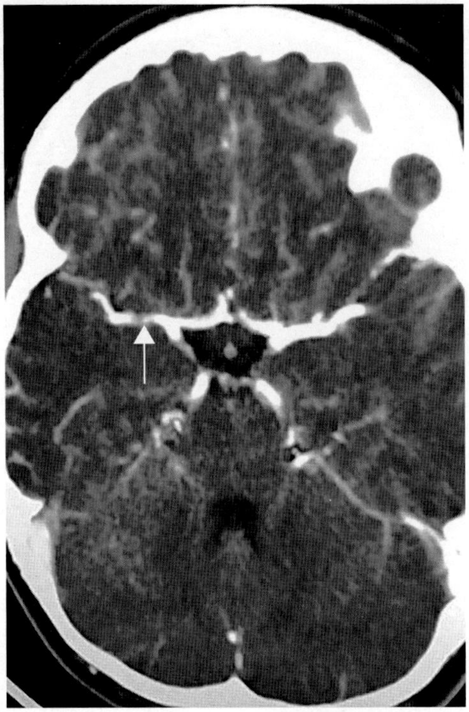

Fig. 21.5 Thromboembolism. Head CTA shows tapered narrowing of the right ICA terminus and M1 with focal filling defect (*arrow*).

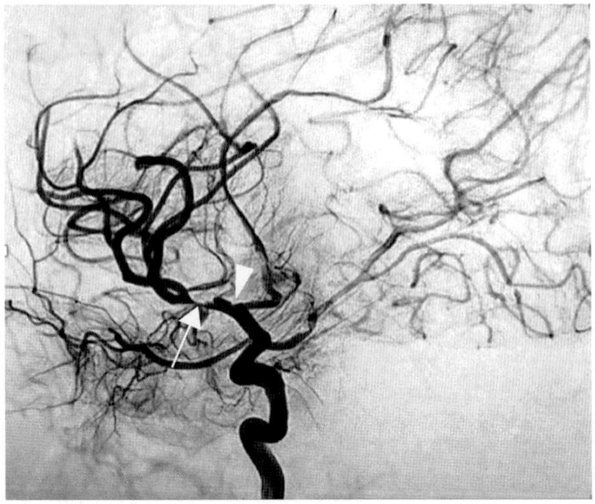

Fig. 21.6 Thromboembolism. Cerebral angiography, sagittal view, shows irregular stenosis and outpouching of right distal ICA (*arrowhead*) with severe stenosis of A1 and M1 (*arrow*) involving the lentriculostriate artery origins. *ICA*, Internal carotid artery.

FINAL DIAGNOSIS

Focal cerebral arteriopathy.

DISCUSSION

Approximately 30% to 50% of pediatric arterial ischemic strokes are due to focal cerebral arteriopathy (FCA), previously known as transient cerebral arteriopathy due to the typically self-limiting course. FCA accounts for 7% to 10% of cerebral arterial infarctions and 25% of arteriopathies in children. Imaging reveals segmental stenosis and/or thrombosis with surrounding wall enhancement suggestive of inflammation. Proposed mechanisms include direct viral infection or post-infectious inflammation and thrombosis. If there is a history of varicella infection in the last 12 months or positive PCR in CSF, FCA is further classified as post-varicella arteriopathy.

The diagnostic criteria for FCA are:

1. Unilateral stenosis of distal ICA, A1, M1, or sometimes P1.
2. Lack of radiological progression after 6 months of treatment. Progression after 6 months can be seen in moyamoya and vasculitis, whereas FCA progresses only within the first 3 months after presentation (Figs. 21.3 and 21.4).

Antecedent infections increase the risk of parenchymal infarct by a factor of 6.3. Viral causes include parvovirus B_{19}, cytomegalovirus (CMV), enterovirus, and herpesviruses; as well as atypical bacteria, including *Mycoplasma pneumoniae* and *Borrelia burgdorferi*, which have been associated with FCA. At imaging, visible arteriopathy is associated with a 20% to 30% elevated risk of disease recurrence and worse long-term outcomes.

Treatment in the hyperacute stage with thrombolysis or thrombectomy is controversial and not proven to significantly alter outcomes in FCA, given the wall inflammation and self-limiting course. There is a risk of vessel rupture and hemorrhage in both FCA and other clinical vasculopathies. After the acute phase, antithrombotic (aspirin) and antiinflammatory therapy (corticosteroids) are recommended to reduce the risk of progression and recurrence. Antiviral drugs such as acyclovir can be used if there is an underlying herpesvirus infection.

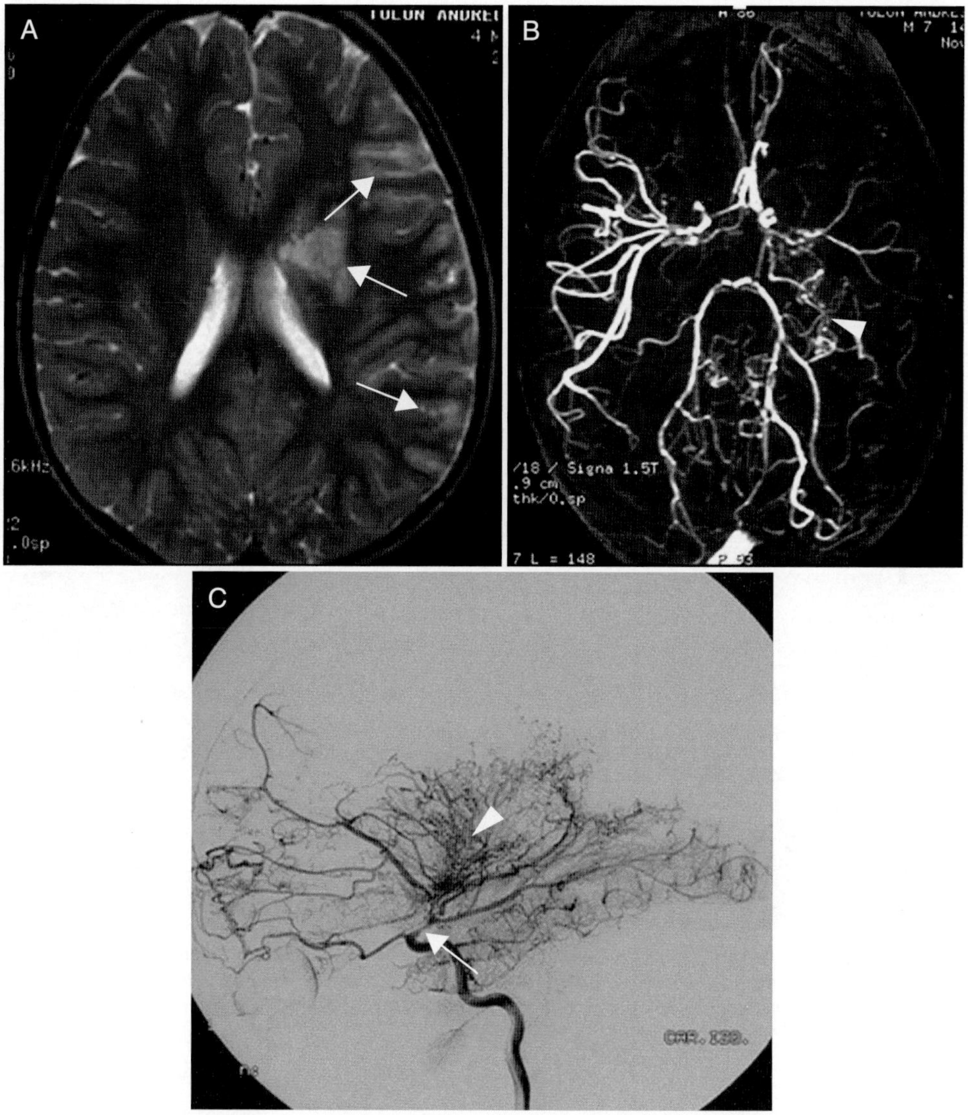

Fig. 21.7 Moyamoya disease. (A) Brain MRI, axial T2, shows left MCA territory infarcts (*arrows*). (B) MRA: Left greater than right ICA, M1, and A1 stenoses with corkscrew collateral vessels (*arrowhead*). (C) Cerebral angiography of left ICA shows irregular distal ICA and M1 stenoses (*arrow*) with proliferation of anomalous lenticulostriate arteries (*arrowhead*). *ICA*, Internal carotid artery; *MCA*, middle cerebral artery; *MRA*, magnetic resonance angiography.

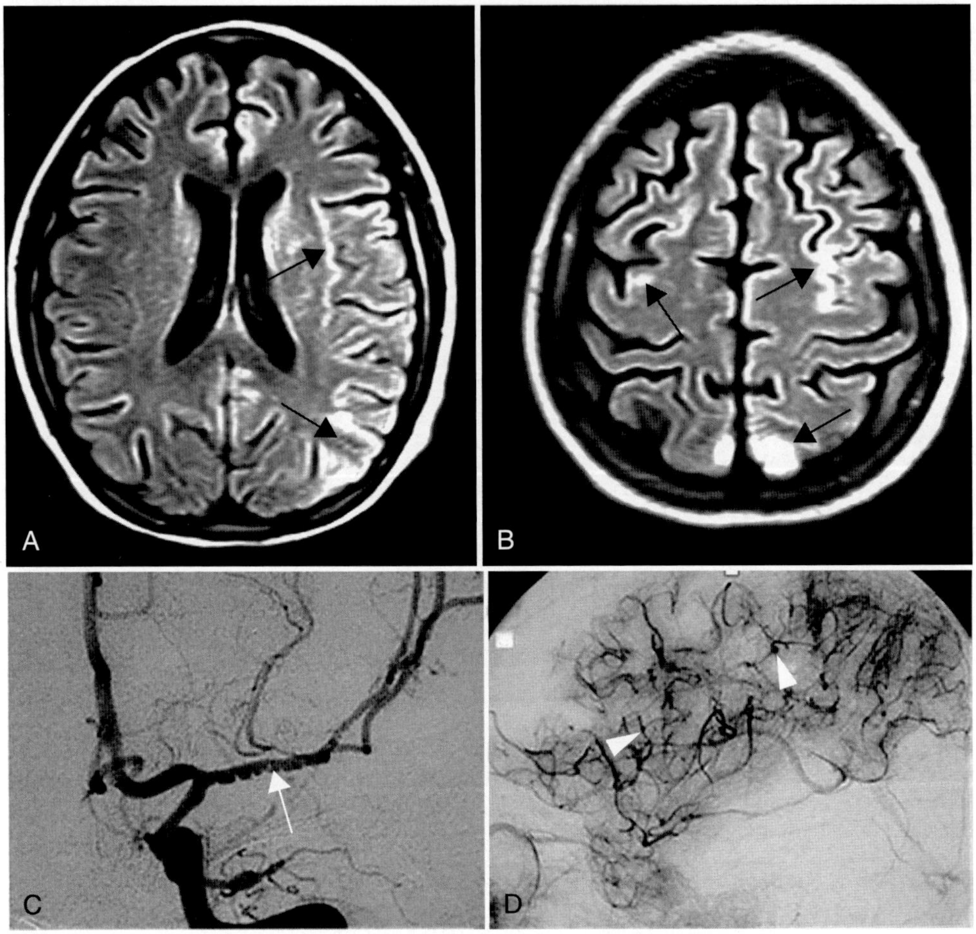

Fig. 21.8 Vasculitis. Brain MRI, (A and B) axial FLAIR, shows left greater than right cerebral peripheral infarcts in multiple vascular territories (*arrows*). *FLAIR*, Fluid-attenuated inversion recovery. (C and D) Cerebral angiography shows left ICA stenosis, M1 beading (*arrow*), and multifocal branch vessel irregularity (*arrowheads*).

CLINICAL RED FLAGS

- Acute hemiparesis concerning for cerebral infarction. Clinical progression or stuttering course is more suggestive of a thrombotic than embolic etiology.
- Preceding history of fever, viral infection, or varicella zoster. FCA presentation is typically focal and monophasic, though there is an increased risk for recurrence.

IMAGING RED FLAGS

- Unilateral basal ganglia involvement with narrowing and thrombosis of the distal ICA, M1, and A1, and lacking other features of dissection, moyamoya, or vasculitis. Imaging findings should not progress after 6 months of treatment.

CONCLUSIONS

FCA is a common cause of pediatric basal ganglia infarction with hemiparesis and should be suspected with a history of setting of antecedent infection. Imaging aids in classification of the type and distribution of arteriopathy.

REFERENCES

Amlie-Lefond C. Evaluation and acute management of ischemic stroke in infants and children. *Continuum (Minneap Minn)*. 2018;24(1, Child Neurology):150–170. https://doi.org/10.1212/CON.0000000000000559.

Cellerini M, Princiotta C, Menozzi R, Capurri G, Russo R, Bergui M. Letter-to-the editor: focal cerebral arteriopathy and acute ischaemic stroke in children: a diagnostic-therapeutical conundrum. *Eur J Radiol*. 2021;142:109846. https://doi.org/10.1016/j.ejrad.2021.109846.

Chabrier S, Sébire G, Fluss J. Transient cerebral arteriopathy, postvaricella arteriopathy, and focal cerebral arteriopathy or the unique susceptibility of the M1 segment in children with stroke. *Stroke*. 2016;47(10):2439–2441. https://doi.org/10.1161/STROKEAHA.116.014606.

Fearn ND, Mackay MT. Focal cerebral arteriopathy and childhood stroke. *Curr Opin Neurol*. 2020;33(1):37–46. https://doi.org/10.1097/WCO.0000000000000787.

Fullerton HJ, Stence N, Hills NK, et al. Focal cerebral arteriopathy of childhood: novel severity score and natural history. *Stroke*. 2018;49(11):2590–2596. https://doi.org/10.1161/STROKEAHA.118.021556.

Oesch G, Perez FA, Wainwright MS, Shaw DWW. Amlie-Lefond C. Focal cerebral arteriopathy of childhood: clinical and imaging correlates. *Stroke*. 2021;52(7):2258–2265. https://doi.org/10.1161/STROKEAHA.120.031880.

Pizzatto R, Resende LL, Lobo CFT, et al. Arteriopathy in pediatric stroke: an underestimated clinical entity. *Arq Neuropsiquiatr*. 2021;79(4):321–333. https://doi.org/10.1590/0004-282X-ANP-2020-0105.

Rafay MF, Shapiro KA, Surmava AM, et al. Spectrum of cerebral arteriopathies in children with arterial ischemic stroke. *Neurology*. 2020;94(23):e2479–e2490. https://doi.org/10.1212/WNL.0000000000009557.

Steinlin M, Bigi S, Stojanovski B, et al. Focal cerebral arteriopathy: do steroids improve outcome? *Stroke*. 2017;48(9):2375–2382. https://doi.org/10.1161/STROKEAHA.117.016818.

Case 22

Hidden Impact

HISTORY AND PHYSICAL

A 3-year-old previously healthy male was referred to the emergency department with a sudden-onset unsteady gait that persisted for 8 hours. He had no headache or neck pain and no recent history of infections, vaccinations, or toxic exposures. However, 3 days earlier, he had been a restrained passenger in a car that suddenly stopped. There was no family history of migraine, gait disturbances, psychiatric disorders, or early-onset stroke. Physical examination on admission showed a weight of 16 kg (50th–75th percentile), height 85 cm (5th–10th percentile), head circumference 51 cm (75th–90th percentile), blood pressure 91/46 mmHg (50th percentile), and pulse 88 bpm. The patient was fully alert and oriented. Cranial nerve examination, fundoscopy, and motor and sensory examination were all normal. Cerebellar examination revealed gait and limb ataxia. Language and speech were normal. Deep tendon reflexes were normal.

DIAGNOSTIC WORKUP

Head CT performed at 11 hours after symptom onset was unrevealing. Brain MRI 28 hours after onset showed an acute right anterior cerebellar infarct in the territory of the superior cerebellar artery (SCA) (Fig. 22.1A–C). Neck MRA showed mild right vertebral artery irregularity (Fig. 22.1D). Lumbar puncture and CSF cultures were normal. Blood tests and prothrombotic studies were normal. Toxins in urine were negative. On day 4 of admission, the patient recovered completely. He was started on anticoagulant therapy and discharged after 1 week on antiplatelet therapy.

Follow-up brain MRI 4 months later showed a new asymptomatic (silent) infarct in the left PICA (posterior inferior cerebellar artery) territory (Fig. 22.2). CT angiography was performed and showed bilateral vertebral artery irregularity and pseudoaneurysms (Fig. 22.3). The patient was switched to oral anticoagulant therapy for 6 months, followed by aspirin for 2 more years, with no further findings on imaging.

CLINICAL DIFFERENTIAL DIAGNOSIS

The most common cause of acute ataxia in children is acute cerebellar ataxia following viral or bacterial illness, which is thought to be an autoimmune process with cross-reactivity of pathogenic antibodies. This is most commonly described with varicella or Epstein-Barr virus, characterized by rapid-onset ataxia during the acute or convalescent phase of disease. Lumbar puncture usually reveals mild pleocytosis.

Other etiologies of ataxia include toxins (alcohol, barbiturates, antiepileptic drugs) and trauma.

Neuroinflammatory disorders, such as acute disseminated encephalomyelitis (ADEM), usually present with encephalopathic features such as impaired consciousness and other neurological symptoms such as motor deficits. Miller-Fisher syndrome is a cranial nerve variant of Guillain-Barré syndrome characterized by postinfectious acute ataxia, areflexia, and ophthalmoplegia. Cerebrospinal fluid shows albuminocytological dissociation, and anti-GQ1b antibody may be positive.

Metabolic disorders that can present with episodic ataxia include urea cycle disorders, mitochondrial disorders, and congenital disorders of glycosylation.

IMAGING DIFFERENTIAL DIAGNOSIS

Cerebellitis: MRI findings of acute cerebellitis have been categorized into bihemispheric cerebellitis, hemicerebellitis, and cerebellitis with encephalitis. There is edema of the involved regions and no or minimal linear contrast enhancement (Fig. 22.4). Typically, the deep

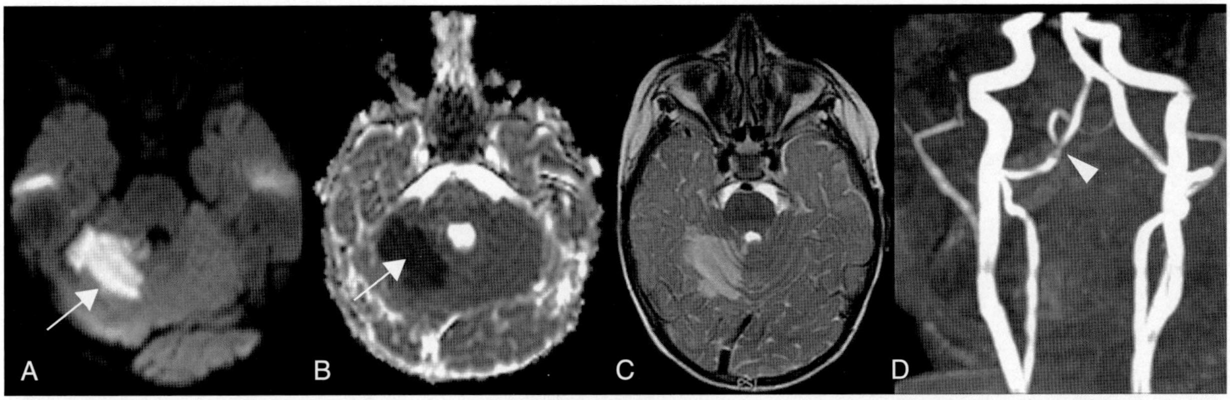

Fig. 22.1 Brain MRI, (A) diffusion-weighted imaging (DWI), (B) apparent diffusion coefficient (ADC) map and (C) T2 show acute right SCA territory infarct (*arrows*). (D) Neck MRA shows multifocal irregularity of the right vertebral artery (*arrowhead*). *SCA*, Superior cerebellar artery.

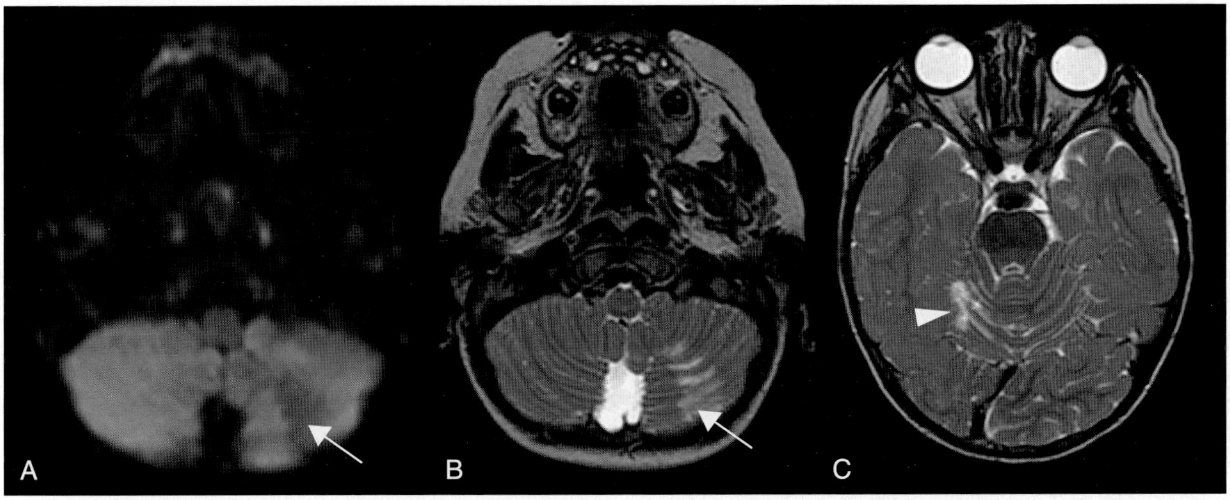

Fig. 22.2 Follow-up brain MRI, (A) axial DWI and (B) T2, show interval left PICA territory infarct (*arrows*) and (C) evolution of prior right SCA infarct (*arrowhead*). *DWI*, Diffusion-weighted imaging; *PICA*, posterior inferior cerebellar artery; *SCA*, superior cerebellar artery.

gray nuclei are spared, in contrast to metabolic disorders that disproportionately involve gray matter structures.

ADEM: Multifocal white and gray matter involvement with edema and no/minimal contrast enhancement. Lesions associated with ADEM are typically bilateral but may be asymmetric and poorly delineated, particularly in the white matter. The periventricular regions are generally spared. Brainstem and spinal cord abnormalities are common (Fig. 22.5).

Miller-Fisher syndrome: Brain MRI shows nerve root enhancement, sometimes accompanied by signal abnormalities in the brainstem and spinal cord.

FINAL DIAGNOSIS

Bilateral vertebral artery dissections.

DISCUSSION

Childhood arterial ischemic stroke (AIS) has an incidence ranging from 1.7 to 3 per 100,000 children per year. Roughly 15% to 22% of cases involve the posterior circulation. The clinical presentation is variable with nonspecific presenting symptoms, including ataxia, vertigo, vomiting, and altered consciousness. These atypical

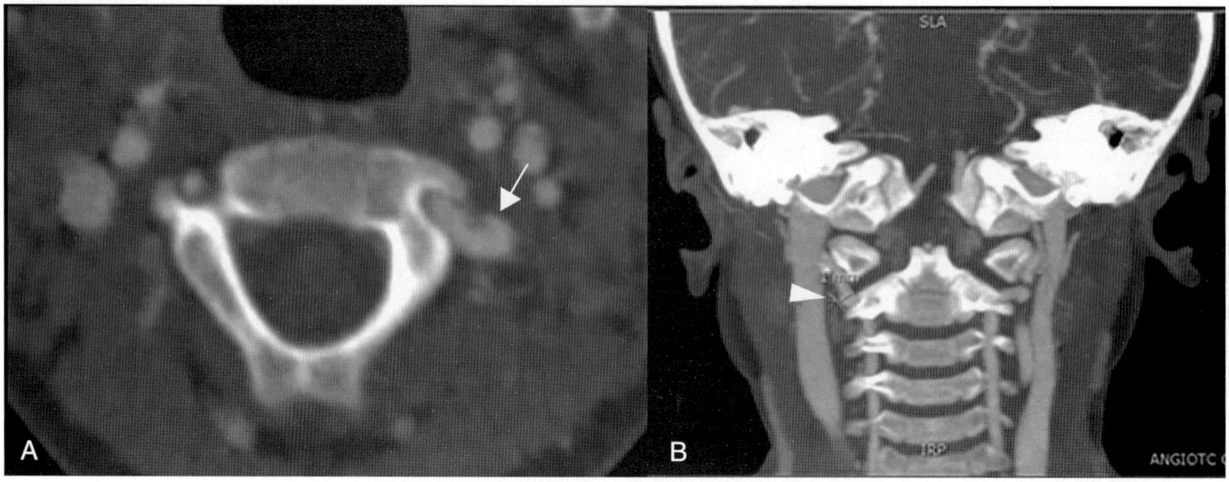

Fig. 22.3 Neck CTA shows irregularity and pseudoaneurysms of the (A) left (*arrow*) and (B) right (*arrowhead*) vertebral arteries.

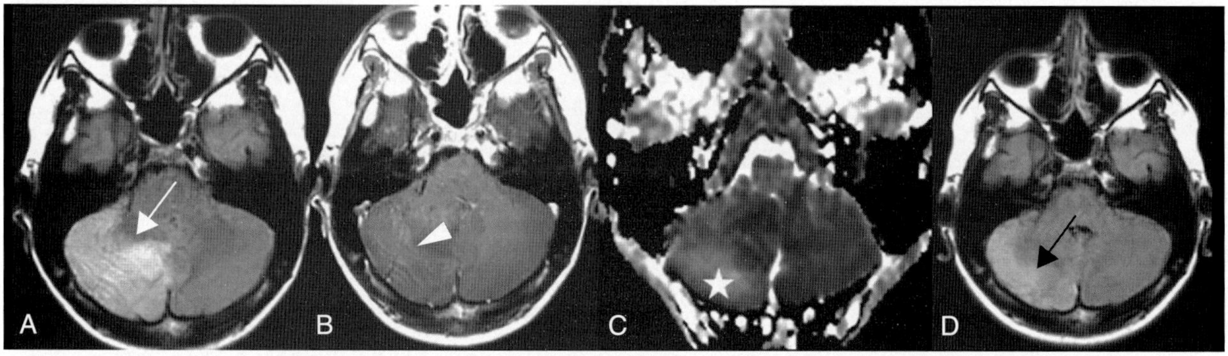

Fig. 22.4 Cerebellitis. Brain MRI, (A) axial FLAIR, (B) postcontrast T1, and (C) ADC show right cerebellar hemispheric edema (*arrow*), thin linear enhancement (*arrowhead*), and facilitated diffusion (*star*) in the right cerebellar hemisphere. Follow-up MRI 3 months later, axial FLAIR (D), shows residual encephalomalacia in the right cerebellum (*black arrow*). *ADC*, Apparent diffusion coefficient; *FLAIR*, fluid-attenuated inversion recovery.

symptoms frequently lead to mistaken or delayed diagnosis in children. Furthermore, head CT in the emergency department has limited value in posterior fossa evaluation.

One of the most frequent risk factors for posterior circulation stroke is vertebral artery dissection, which may be either traumatic or spontaneous in origin. Traumatic dissection is typically seen after blunt force trauma, which may be minimal (e.g., coughing, vomiting, sports, cervical manipulation) if a predisposing arteriopathy is present. Imaging criteria for arterial dissection include (1) angiographic double lumen, intimal flap, pseudoaneurysm, or intramural hematoma on T1 fat-suppressed MRI; (2) segmental arterial narrowing or occlusion, with a history of antecedent trauma or neck pain within 6 weeks; (3) segmental narrowing or occlusion of the vertebral artery at the C2 level, even without known traumatic history. Vertebral artery dissection predominantly affects the distal V2 (35%) or V3 segments (34%). The risk of recurrence in this population is as high as 20%, and current practice guidelines recommend anticoagulant therapy for at least 6 months.

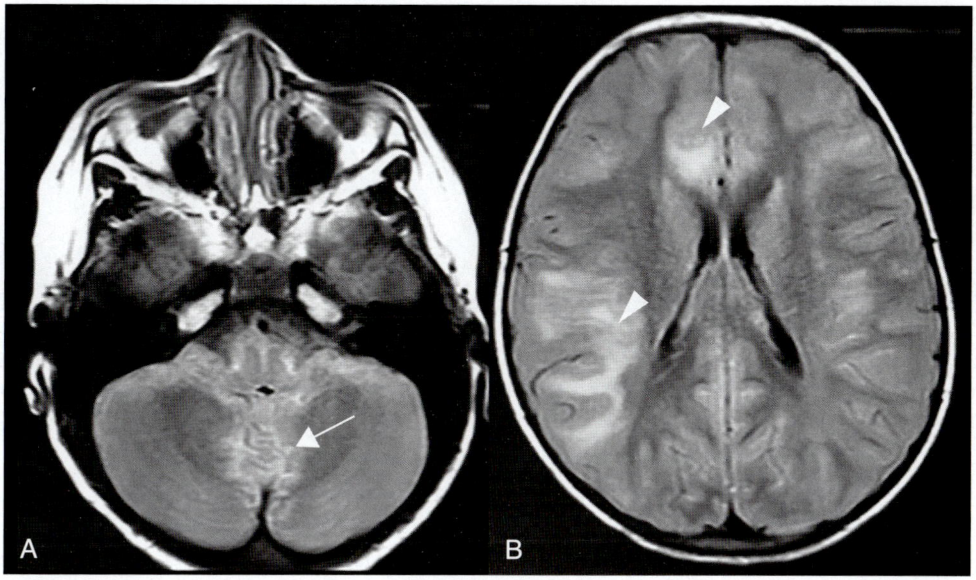

Fig. 22.5 ADEM. Brain MRI, axial FLAIR, showing (A) brainstem and cerebellar vermian (*arrow*) and (B): multifocal subcortical white and gray matter hyperintensity (*arrowheads*) in both cerebral hemispheres. *ADEM*, Acute disseminated encephalomyelitis; *FLAIR*, fluid-attenuated inversion recovery.

CLINICAL RED FLAGS

- Acute ataxia following blunt trauma, which can be major or minor.
- Acute and severe headache, especially along the posterior head or with focal neurological deficits.
- Patients with connective tissue disorders or arteriopathies.
- Signs of increased intracranial pressure (ICP) or herniation.

IMAGING RED FLAGS

- In the acute setting, CT angiography provides rapid and accurate assessment of arterial narrowing or occlusion. Intimal flaps and dissecting aneurysms can also be identified with high spatial resolution.
- MRI of arterial dissection shows variable signal of the intramural hematoma, based on the relative age of blood products. The T1 hyperintensity of subacute methemoglobin can persist for months.
- Contrast-enhanced neck MRA can be used to better assess caliber of cervical vessels, decreasing artifacts from stenosis and slow flow seen with noncontrast MRA.
- Cerebral angiography is still considered the gold standard for diagnosis but is invasive and associated with high radiation exposure.
- Congenital cervical spine anomalies can predispose to arterial injury including basilar impression, congenital craniovertebral junction defects, Down syndrome, and Klippel-Feil syndrome. Flexion-extension radiographs, CT, or MRI may provide information about bony anatomy and/or ligamentous stability.

Neuroimaging is important to rule out stroke mimics such as migraine, seizure, infection (Fig. 22.6), vascular malformation, tumor, and posterior reversible leukoencephalopathy syndrome.

CONCLUSIONS

Pediatric posterior circulation stroke often presents with nonspecific symptoms, such as dizziness, nausea, vomiting, and headache. A high index of suspicion is required in order to avoid missed or delayed diagnosis.

Neuroimaging, especially MRI, plays a key role in diagnosis and follow-up. For children with suspected dissection, MRI and MRA are the best initial imaging studies to provide mapping of the infarct volume and associated arterial abnormalities. For neck angiography, axial T1-weighted imaging with fat suppression for intramural hematoma can be helpful, and contrast-enhanced imaging can better evaluate vessel patency. Repeat

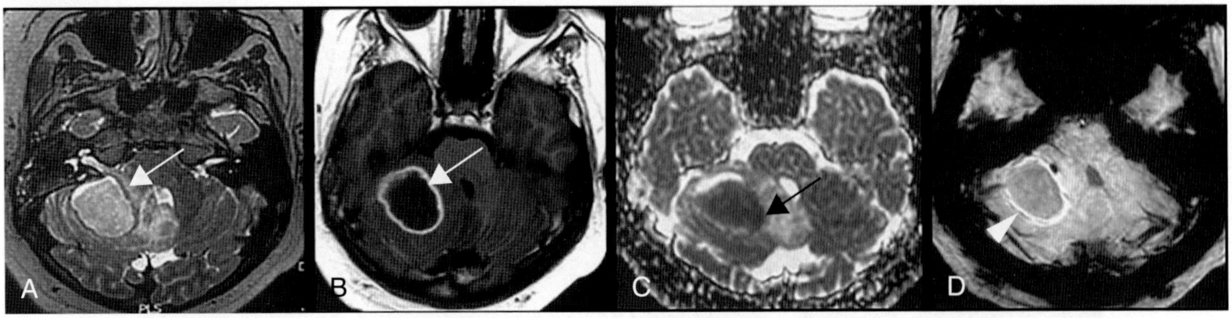

Fig. 22.6 Cerebellar abscess. Brain MRI, (A) axial T2, (B) postcontrast T1, (C) ADC, and (D) SWI show right cerebellar abscess with rim enhancement (*white arrows*), internal restricted diffusion (*black arrow*) and surrounding vasogenic edema. Susceptibility shows dual rim sign with inner hyperintense granulation tissue and outer fibrocollagenous capsule (*arrowhead*). *ADC*, Apparent diffusion coefficient; *SWI*, susceptibility-weighted imaging.

imaging is warranted if the child experiences recurrent disease.

Large infarctions may be complicated by cerebellar edema, herniation, and death. Therefore it is crucial to closely monitor patients within the first 72 hours after stroke onset. The risk of recurrence is higher in posterior circulation strokes than in anterior circulation strokes.

REFERENCES

Carey S, Wrogemann J, Booth FA, Rafay MF. Epidemiology, clinical presentation, and prognosis of posterior circulation ischemic stroke in children. *Pediatr Neurol.* 2017;74:41–50. https://doi.org/10.1016/j.pediatrneurol.2017.05.007.

Fink M, Slavova N, Grunt S, et al. Posterior arterial ischemic stroke in childhood. *Stroke.* 2019;50(9):2329–2335. https://doi.org/10.1161/STROKEAHA.119.025154.

Rodallec MH, Marteau V, Gerber S, Desmottes L, Zins M. Craniocervical arterial dissection: spectrum of imaging findings and differential diagnosis. *Radiographics.* 2008; 28(6):1711–1728. https://doi.org/10.1148/rg.286085512.

Shellhaas RA, Smith SE, O'Tool E, Licht DJ, Ichord RN. Mimics of childhood stroke: characteristics of a prospective cohort. *Pediatrics.* 2006;118(2):704–709. https://doi.org/10.1542/peds.2005-2676.

Case 23

From Heart to Brain

HISTORY AND PHYSICAL

A 2-month-old infant male prenatally diagnosed with transposition of the great arteries experienced neonatal seizures that were treated with phenobarbital. He then underwent an arterial switch operation, left ventricular outflow tract repair, and ventricular septal defect closure. In the immediate postoperative period, the patient presented with fluid-refractory hypotension. Three days after surgery, after sedatives were titrated down, he developed abrupt-onset stereotyped episodes of eye opening, mydriasis, and left lower limb clonic movements lasting several seconds. On neurological examination, he was awake and ventilated on low doses of sedative agents. Cranial nerve examination showed symmetric and reactive pupils. Motor and sensory examinations were normal, including deep tendon reflexes.

DIAGNOSTIC WORKUP

EEG showed paroxysms of sharp waves in both temporal lobes, with a wider initial amplitude on the right followed by voltage attenuation.

Head ultrasound was normal. Head CT performed 2 hours after seizure onset revealed multifocal cytotoxic edema in the right greater than left cerebral gray and white matter (Fig. 23.1).

Brain MRI performed on day 16 exhibited evolution of infarcts with T2-hyperintense gliosis and volume loss (Fig. 23.2A and B). On diffusion-weighted imaging, there was restricted diffusion in the splenium of corpus callosum and right thalamus related to seizure activity (Fig. 23.2C).

CLINICAL DIFFERENTIAL DIAGNOSIS

Neurologic complications are common in children with CHD and can present with seizures following cardiac surgery. Reversible causes of seizure, such as hypoglycemia and electrolyte disturbances, should be excluded. Perioperative hypoxia-ischemia can lead to global cerebral hypoperfusion and postoperative reperfusion injury. Other vascular causes include vaso-occlusive insults and bland, fat, or air emboli from cardiopulmonary bypass. Extracorporeal membrane oxygenation (ECMO) may injure the brain through ischemic and/or hemorrhagic mechanisms. Systemic heparinization increases the risk of intracranial hemorrhage, either primary or secondary. Brain abscess is a rare complication of cyanotic heart disease with right-to-left shunts.

Acquired heart disease is most commonly caused by infection or parainfectious autoimmune conditions. Viral myocarditis and rheumatic heart disease predispose to embolism and cerebral ischemia.

IMAGING DIFFERENTIAL DIAGNOSIS

Mild cases of hypoxic-ischemic encephalopathy (HIE) due to brief and partial limitations of blood flow or oxygen can demonstrate damage to the cerebral and cerebellar watershed zones (Fig. 23.3). Moderate-to-severe HIE is seen with complete and prolonged loss of blood flow or oxygen. This selectively affects the most actively developing and hypermetabolic areas of the brain, including perirolandic and occipital cortex, basal ganglia, and limbic structures. In the first 1 to 2 days of injury, diffusion-weighted imaging (DWI) is positive, followed by T1 shortening from dysmyelination and then T2-hyperintense edema. Over time, areas of damaged brain evolve into apoptosis and/or necrosis with encephalomalacia.

Neonatal hypoglycemia causes selective injury to the posterior cerebrum (parietal and occipital lobes), including both gray and white matter, and can potentiate HIE.

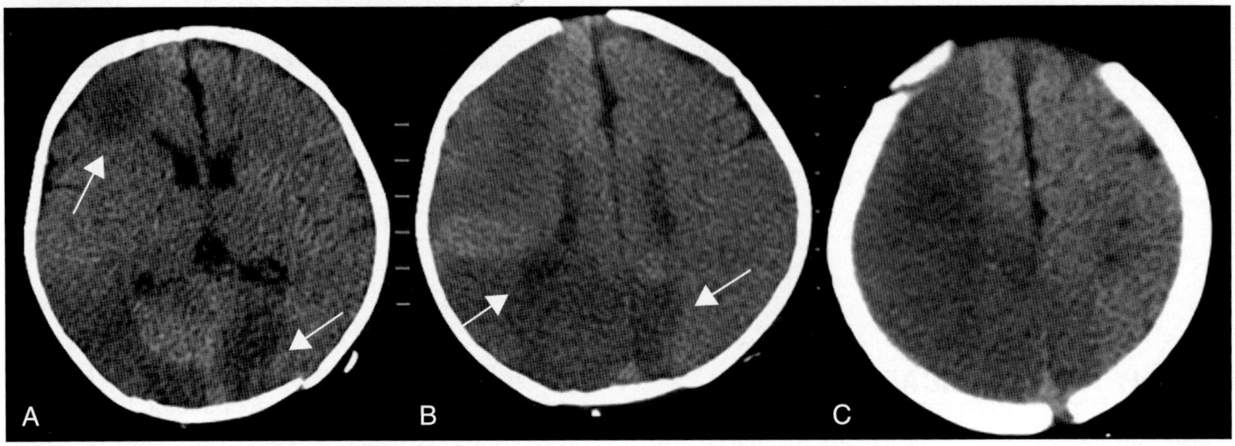

Fig. 23.1 (A–C) Cardioembolic stroke. Head CT shows multifocal cytotoxic edema in the right greater than left cerebral gray and white matter (*arrows*).

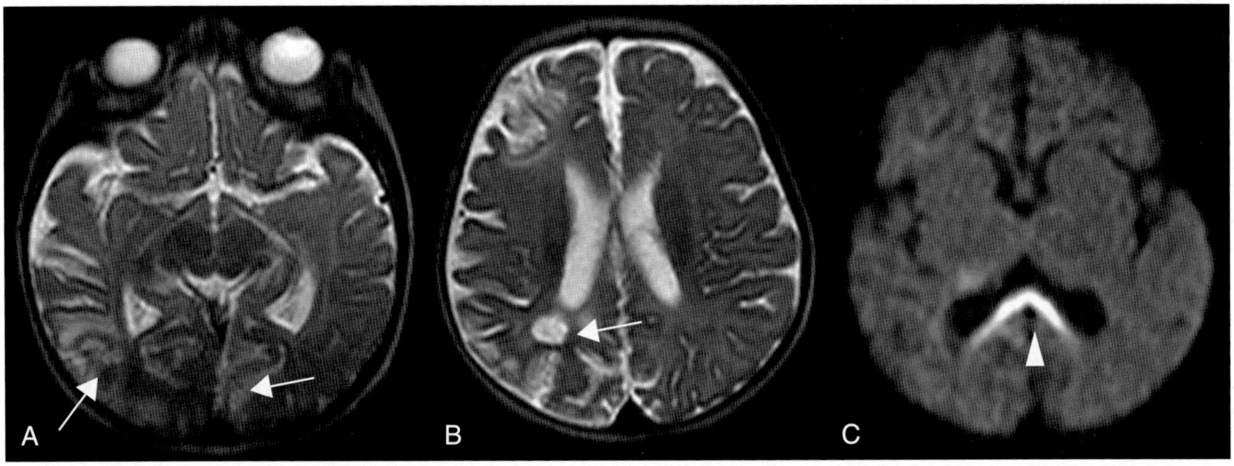

Figure 23.2 Cardioembolic stroke. Brain MRI, (A and B) axial T2, shows multifocal hyperintensities corresponding to areas of gliosis (*arrows*). DWI (C) shows restricted diffusion of the callosal splenium (*arrowhead*) and right thalamus. *DWI*, Diffusion-weighted imaging.

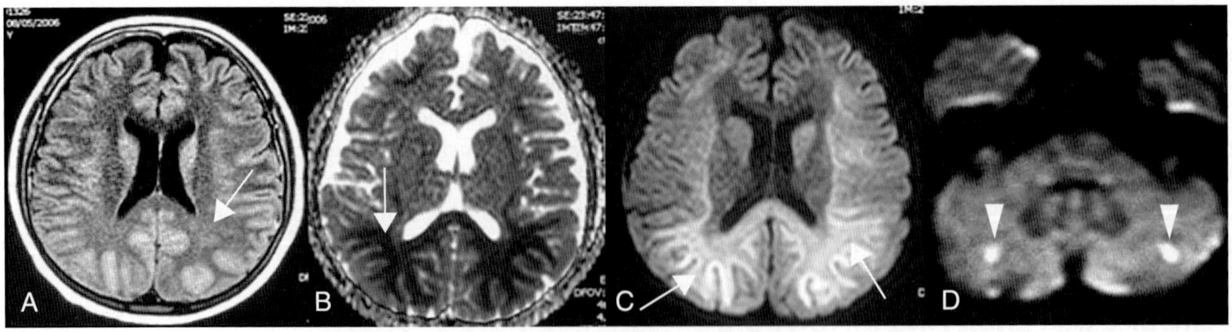

Fig. 23.3 Hypoxic-ischemic injury. Brain MRI, (A) axial FLAIR, (B) ADC, and (C and D) DWI show acute restricted diffusion and FLAIR hyperintensity in the cerebral (*arrows*) and cerebellar (*arrowheads*) watershed territories. *ADC*, Apparent diffusion coefficient; *DWI*, diffusion-weighted imaging; *FLAIR*, fluid-attenuated inversion recovery.

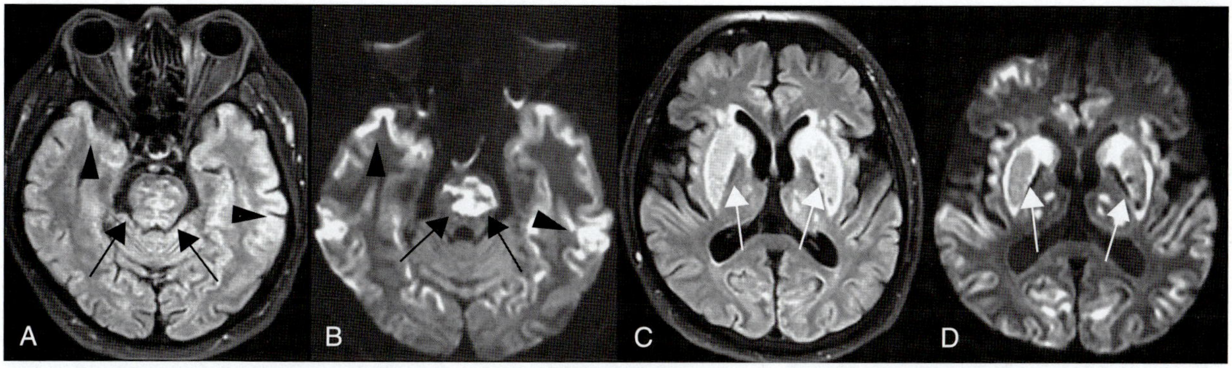

Fig. 23.4 Acute osmotic demyelination. Brain MRI, (A and C) axial FLAIR, and (B and D) DWI show bilateral symmetric hyperintensities in the central pons (*black arrows*) with sparing of the periphery and corticospinal tracts. Extrapontine involvement includes the basal ganglia and thalami (*white arrows*) and cerebral cortex and subcortical white matter (*black arrowheads*). *DWI*, Diffusion-weighted imaging; *FLAIR*, fluid-attenuated inversion recovery.

Osmotic myelinolysis can manifest in the central pons, with sparing of the peripheral brainstem and corticospinal tracts producing a "trident," "bat-wing," or "snake eyes" appearance. Extrapontine involvement can be seen in the basal ganglia, cerebellar peduncles, cerebral white matter, and cortex. Diffusion and enhancement characteristics vary (Fig. 23.4).

FINAL DIAGNOSIS

Cardioembolic stroke.

DISCUSSION

CHD is a risk factor for pediatric stroke in 24% of neonates and 29% of older children. Acquired heart disease (cardiomyopathy, arrhythmia, endocarditis) is the other major etiology of cardioembolic stroke. Most pediatric cardioembolic strokes occur after cardiac instrumentation, with the highest risk during the first postprocedural year. The clinical presentation can include focal neurological deficit, altered consciousness, seizures, or headache.

Head CT can show multifocal hypodensities of cytotoxic edema and hyperdensities with hemorrhagic transformation. MRI reveals multiple bilateral infarcts, often involving arterial borderzones, as well as associated macro- and microhemorrhages. MRA may show vascular occlusion (Fig. 23.5) and/or narrowing.

Around 27% of children with cardioembolic stroke experience recurrence within 10 years after the sentinel event. Pediatric stroke treatment guidelines recommend antithrombotic therapy as prevention, despite the 24% risk of hemorrhagic transformation. Overall, antithrombotic therapy has a positive effect on outcomes in most patient subgroups, particularly those with single-ventricle physiology.

CLINICAL RED FLAGS

- Children with higher Pediatric National Institute of Health Stroke Severity (NIHSS) scores >20 and prolonged initial seizures >5 minutes are at greatly increased risk for malignant cerebral infarctions, in which massive cerebral edema can lead to increased intracranial pressure and cerebral herniation. This is a life-threatening emergency that requires decompressive hemicraniectomy to minimize morbidity and mortality.
- Congenital heart disease and genetic syndromes can be associated with arterial anomalies, including cerebral and spinal aneurysms and vascular malformations, predisposing to ischemic and/or hemorrhagic stroke.

IMAGING RED FLAGS

- MCA infarcts involving >50% of the MCA territory are considered to be malignant. An Alberta Stroke Program Early CT Score (ASPECTS) ≤7 on initial head CT is predictive of worse functional outcomes and hemorrhagic transformation.

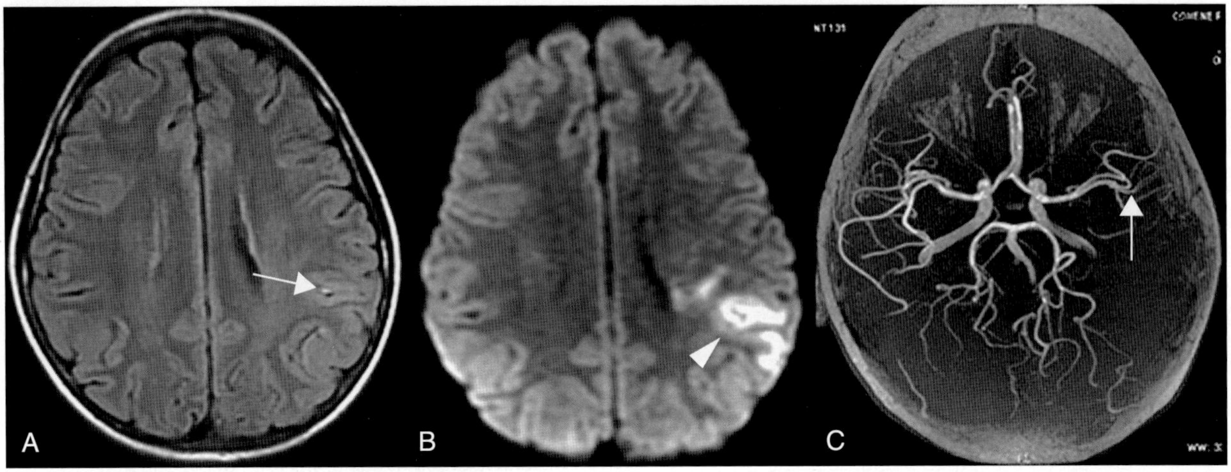

Fig. 23.5 Acute embolic stroke. Brain MRI, (A) axial FLAIR, and (B) DWI show acute infarct in the left inferior MCA territory with restricted diffusion (*arrowhead*) and faint cytotoxic edema. There is focal intravascular signal intensity from arterial thrombus with lack of distal opacification on MRA (*arrows*) (C). *DWI*, Diffusion-weighted imaging; *FLAIR*, fluid-attenuated inversion recovery.

CONCLUSIONS

Congenital and acquired heart disease are common causes of pediatric stroke, particularly following cardiac intervention. Early recognition of symptoms is important in order to initiate early antithrombotic treatment and avoid recurrence. MRI is the best imaging tool to diagnose stroke, but features on head CT can be suggestive.

REFERENCES

Dowling MM, Hynan LS, Lo W, et al. International paediatric stroke study: stroke associated with cardiac disorders. *Int J Stroke*. 2013;8(Suppl A100):39–44. https://doi.org/10.1111/j.1747-4949.2012.00925.x.

Pulcine E, Seed M, Brandão LR, et al. Hemorrhagic transformation and stroke recurrence in children with cardiac disease receiving antithrombotic therapy for secondary stroke prevention. *J Thromb Haemost*. 2021;19(10):2428–2439. https://doi.org/10.1111/jth.15428.

Rodan L, McCrindle BW, Manlhiot C, et al. Stroke recurrence in children with congenital heart disease. *Ann Neurol*. 2012;72(1):103–111. https://doi.org/10.1002/ana.23574.

Shah S, Murthy SB, Whitehead WE, Jea A, Nassif LM. Decompressive hemicraniectomy in pediatric patients with malignant middle cerebral artery infarction: case series and review of the literature. *World Neurosurg*. 2013;80(1–2):126–133. https://doi.org/10.1016/j.wneu.2013.06.001.

Ziesmann MT, Nash M, Booth FA, Rafay MF. Cardioembolic stroke in children: a clinical presentation and outcome study. *Pediatr Neurol*. 2014;51(4):494–502. https://doi.org/10.1016/j.pediatrneurol.2014.06.013.

Case 24

Asymmetric Worsening

HISTORY AND PHYSICAL

A 3-year-old boy presented with progressively decreased mobility of the right arm. Birth and development were normal for age, and family history was negative. His symptoms started after an episode of prolonged crying, followed by vomiting. One day later, he showed irritability, dysarthria, and right hemiplegia. His parents reported a similar episode 6 months earlier that occurred in the context of febrile illness. At hospital admission, the patient was irritable. Neurological exam revealed mild right hemiparesis. Reflexes were 3+ on the right and 2+ on the left, without clonus. Plantar responses were downgoing.

DIAGNOSTIC WORKUP

Extensive coagulopathy workup showed mildly hypochromic microcytic anemia. Echocardiography was normal. Head CT was unrevealing.

Brain MRI showed subtle atrophy of the left cerebral hemisphere with overlying FLAIR-hyperintense leptomeningeal vessels ("ivy sign"). There were scattered acute left cerebral microinfarcts on a background of chronic bilateral white matter FLAIR hyperintensities (Fig. 24.1).

Magnetic resonance angiography (MRA) showed irregular stenosis of the left greater than right distal ICA, left MCA, and both anterior cerebral arteries (ACAs) (Fig. 24.2).

Head CTA and cerebral angiography showed left greater than right distal ICA stenosis with tortuous bilateral lenticulostriate moyamoya collaterals (Fig. 24.3).

CLINICAL DIFFERENTIAL DIAGNOSIS

Right hemiparesis in the setting of fever can be seen with a transient ischemic attack, defined as temporary neurological symptoms without imaging evidence of infarction and resolving fully within 24 hours.

Recurrent strokes can be caused by central cardioembolism and various vasculopathies, including transient cerebral arteriopathy, arterial dissection, primary or secondary CNS vasculitis, and moyamoya disease (primary) or syndrome (secondary).

IMAGING DIFFERENTIAL DIAGNOSIS

Cardioembolic infarcts can show multiple bilateral watershed infarcts of various ages, with vessel occlusions that can recanalize over time (Fig. 24.4).

Vasculopathy can show vessel wall enhancement in various patterns, often with circumferential involvement and a segmental distribution. When there is associated luminal narrowing (negative remodeling), cerebral ischemia may result (Fig. 24.5).

Rasmussen encephalitis is an autoimmune disorder associated with progressive asymmetric periinsular atrophy.

Vasospasm with transient arterial narrowing can occur following subarachnoid hemorrhage, meningitis, or vasoactive drug use. Vascular stenoses are irregular and often multifocal, with reversibility over time or following injection of vasodilators.

FINAL DIAGNOSIS

Moyamoya disease.

DISCUSSION

Moyamoya is an obliterative arteriopathy with progressive stenosis and occlusion of the terminal ICA, extending to MCA and ACA. Involvement can be unilateral, but often becomes bilateral and asymmetric over time.

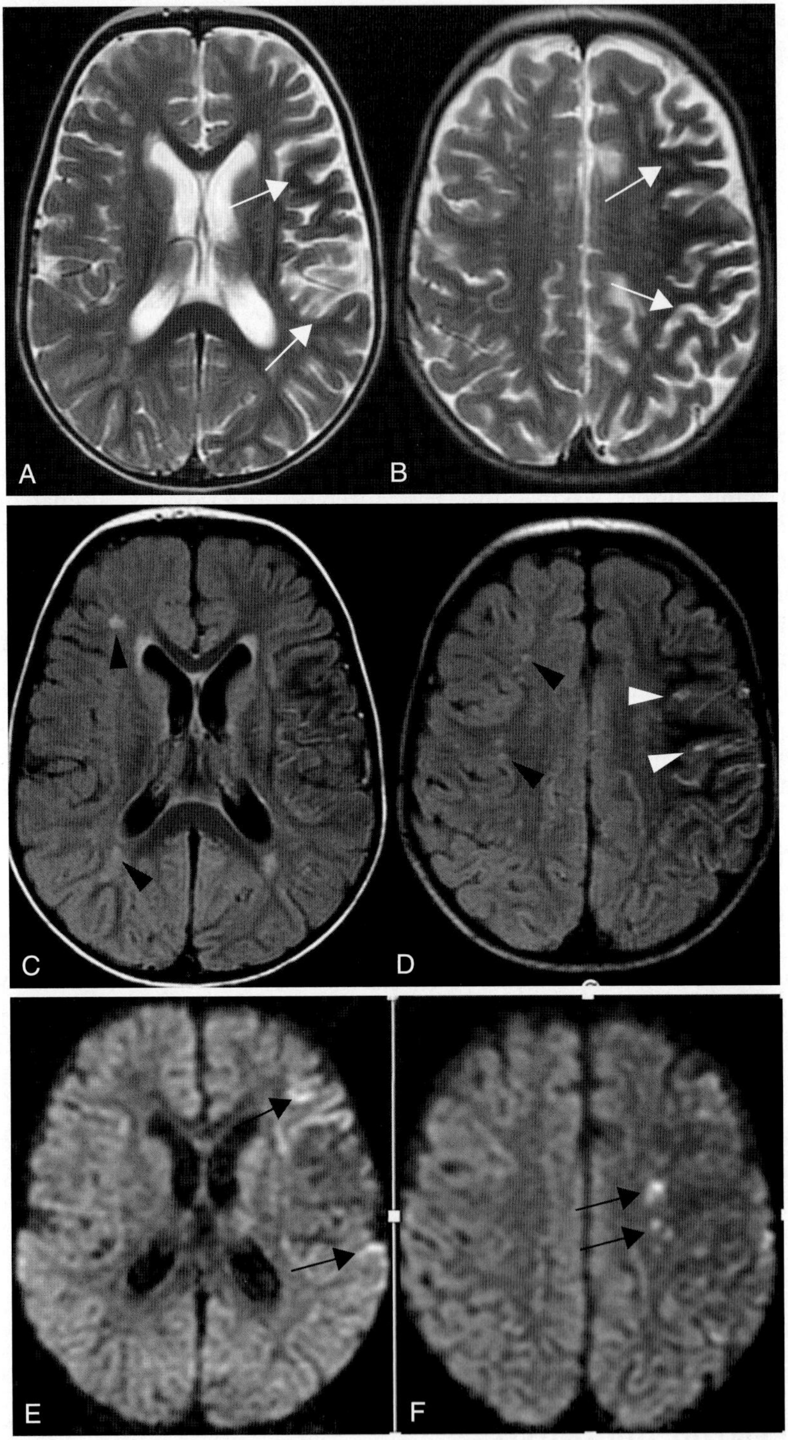

Fig. 24.1 Moyamoya disease. Brain MRI, (A and B) axial T2, (C and D) FLAIR, and (E and F) DWI, show mild atrophy of the left cerebral hemisphere (*white arrows*) with overlying FLAIR-hyperintense leptomeningeal collaterals (*white arrowheads*). There are multiple acute left cerebral microinfarcts with restricted diffusion (*black arrows*) on a background of chronic bilateral white matter changes (*black arrowheads*). *DWI*, Diffusion-weighted imaging; *FLAIR*, fluid-attenuated inversion recovery.

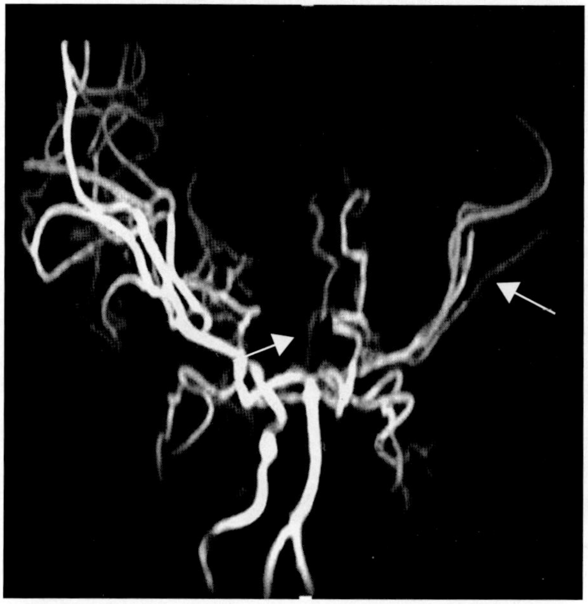

Fig. 24.2 Moyamoya disease. Coronal brain MRA shows irregular narrowing of the left greater than right distal ICAs, left MCA, and both ACAs (*white arrows*). *ACAs*, Anterior cerebral arteries; *ICAs*, internal carotid arteries; *MCA*, middle cerebral artery.

Formation of the characteristic moyamoya collaterals creates a "puff of smoke" appearance in the lenticulostriate distribution, and the "ivy" sign with leptomeningeal involvement. Clinical symptoms include recurrent stroke, transient ischemic attack, seizure, headache, and movement disorders. Children may develop symptoms of cerebral ischemia after minor vasoactive stressors such as hyperventilation, vigorous exercise, crying, playing wind instruments, or eating hot foods. Hemorrhagic strokes become more common with increasing age.

The diagnosis is made by noninvasive or invasive cerebral angiography, showing stenosis or occlusion of the terminal ICA, proximal ACA and/or MCA with development of abnormal tortuous collaterals in at least one hemisphere (Fig. 24.6). Perfusion and cerebrovascular reserve assessment can be performed using transcranial Doppler ultrasound, CT, or MRI perfusion (Fig. 24.7).

Many genetic variants and rare diseases are associated with moyamoya. Known moyamoya susceptibility genes include *RNF213*, *MTHFR*, *TCN2*, *HDAC9*, *HLA-DQA2*, and *HLA-B*.

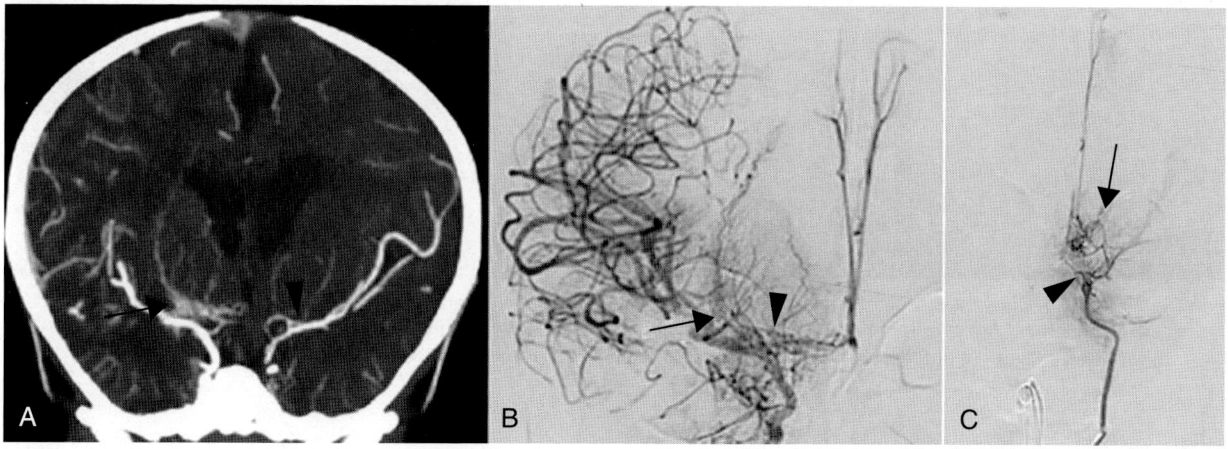

Fig. 24.3 Moyamoya disease. (A) Coronal head CTA, (B) cerebral angiography of the right and left (C) internal carotid arteries show stenosis of both distal ICAs, A1, and M1 (*arrowheads*) with tortuous lenticulostriate moyamoya vessels bilaterally (*arrows*). *ICA*, Internal carotid artery.

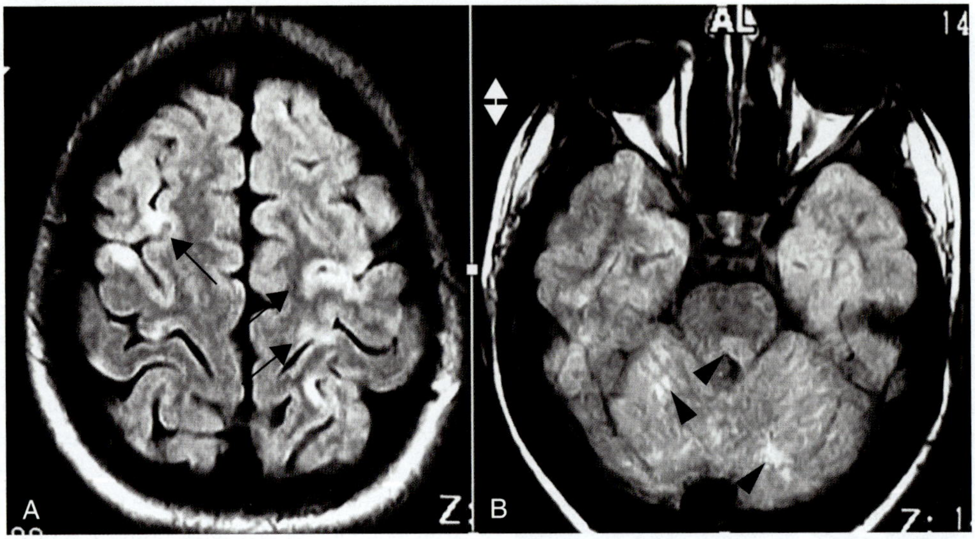

Fig. 24.4 Cardioembolism in a boy with congenital cardiomyopathy. Brain MRI, (A and B) axial FLAIR shows multiple bilateral cerebral cortical infarcts (*arrows*), along with cerebellar and brainstem lesions (*arrowheads*). *FLAIR*, Fluid-attenuated inversion recovery.

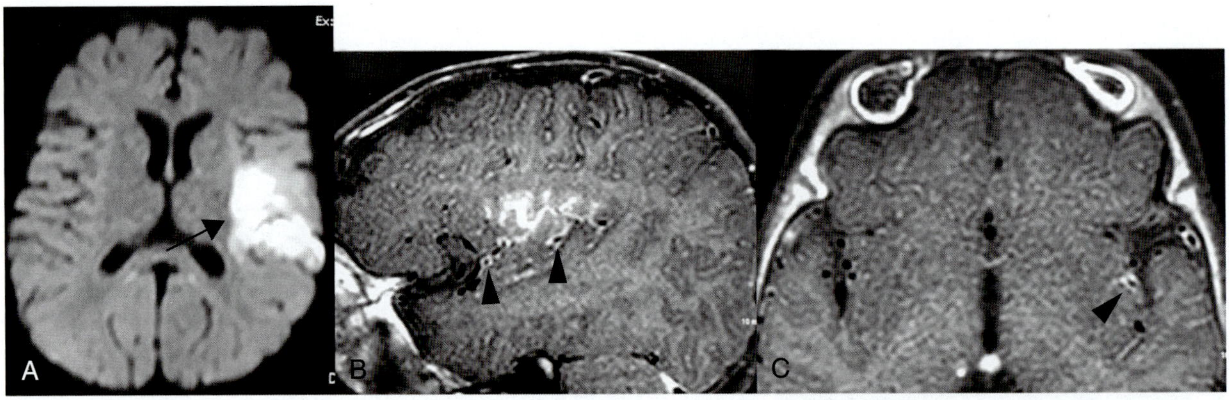

Fig. 24.5 Cerebral vasculitis. Brain MRI, axial DWI (A) and sagittal (B) and axial (C) vessel wall imaging show acute left MCA infarct (*arrow*) with circumferential wall enhancement of the left MCA branches (*arrowheads*). *DWI*, Diffusion-weighted imaging; *ICA*, internal carotid artery; *MCA*, middle cerebral artery.

CLINICAL RED FLAGS

- Recurrent transient ischemic attacks.
- Focal seizures.
- Associated genetic syndromes, neurocutaneous, hematological, cardiac, and metabolic disorders.

IMAGING RED FLAGS

- Asymmetric cerebral ischemia, particularly of different ages with cortical/subcortical and borderzone involvement.

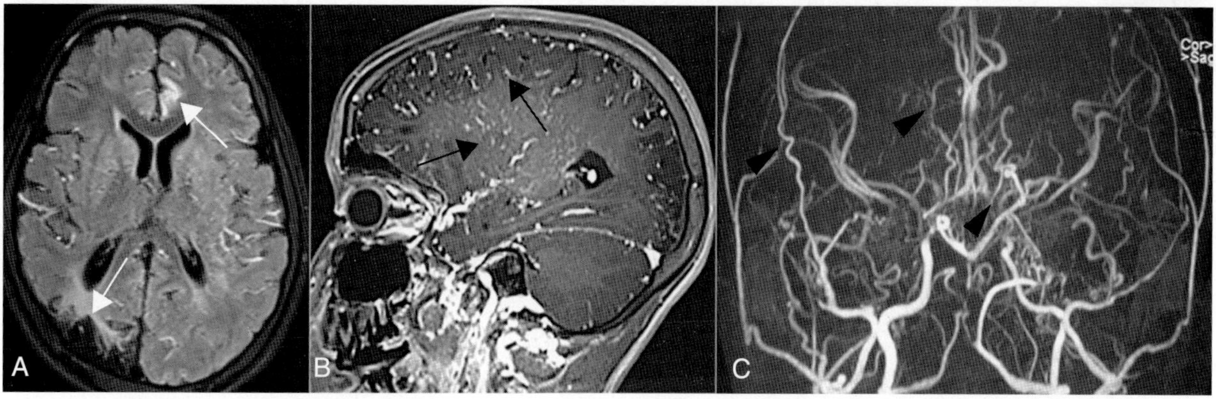

Fig. 24.6 Brain MRI, (A) axial postcontrast FLAIR, (B) sagittal postcontrast T1, and (C) coronal MRA show bilateral cerebral microinfarcts of varying ages (*white arrows*) with enhancing moyamoya collaterals (*black arrows*). Angiography shows bilateral terminal ICA stenoses with lenticulostriate, basal, and leptomeningeal collaterals (*arrowheads*). *FLAIR*, Fluid-attenuated inversion recovery; *ICA*, internal carotid artery.

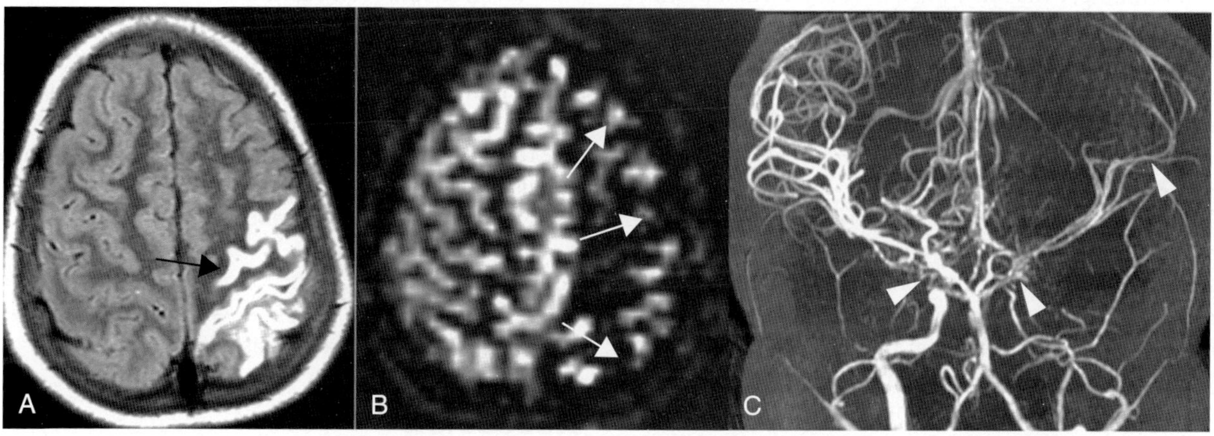

Fig. 24.7 Brain MRI. (A) axial postcontrast FLAIR, (B) arterial spin labeling perfusion, and (C) coronal MRA show a left inferior MCA territory infarct (*black arrow*) with surrounding ischemic penumbra (*white arrows*). There is diffuse narrowing of the distal ICA, MCA and ACA branches (*arrowheads*). *FLAIR*, Fluid-attenuated inversion recovery; *ICA*, internal carotid artery; *MCA*, middle cerebral artery.

CONCLUSIONS

In East Asian countries, moyamoya disease (primary or idiopathic) is the most frequent cause of stroke in children. Incidence in the West is much less common and usually represents moyamoya syndrome associated with various causes such as Down syndrome, neurofibromatosis type 1, sickle cell disease, prior radiation, and congenital heart disease. Since there are no established treatments to slow disease progression, antiplatelet therapy to prevent strokes and direct (bypass) or indirect (synangiosis) revascularization to increase leptomeningeal collateralization are the mainstays of management.

REFERENCES

Bersano A, Khan N, Fuentes B, et al. European Stroke Organisation (ESO) guidelines on moyamoya angiopathy endorsed by Vascular European Reference Network (VASCERN). *Eur Stroke J.* 2023;8(1):55–84. https://doi.org/10.1177/23969873221144089.

Dlamini N, Muthusami P, Amlie-Lefond C. Childhood moyamoya: looking back to the future. *Pediatr Neurol.* 2019;91:11–19. https://doi.org/10.1016/j.pediatrneurol.2018.10.006.

Remember the Veins

HISTORY AND PHYSICAL

A 13-month-old girl was evaluated in the emergency department for gastroenteritis and dehydration and discharged after 48 hours. Twenty days later, she returned with vomiting, irritability, and loss of ambulation. Family history was unremarkable. General examination showed a sick and irritable infant. Neurological exam showed right greater than left esotropia and generalized hypotonia with hyperreflexia. The anterior fontanelle was bulging.

DIAGNOSTIC WORKUP

Head CTV (Fig. 25.1) and brain MRI (Fig. 25.2) showed superior sagittal sinus thrombosis. Blood count showed microcytosis with a hemoglobin level of 7.5 g/dl. Lumbar puncture showed normal pressures and CSF composition. The patient received anticoagulation for 5 months, with clear clinical improvement and normalization of the venous angiogram at 4 months (Fig. 25.3). She was also started on iron supplementation for her microcytic anemia.

CLINICAL DIFFERENTIAL DIAGNOSIS

Central nervous system infection can present with neurologic deterioration but should have associated meningeal signs, fever, and/or CSF abnormalities.

Idiopathic intracranial hypertension can produce false localizing signs (irritability, vomiting, cranial nerve VI paralysis). Lumbar puncture should show high CSF pressures, and papilledema may be seen at fundoscopy.

Brain tumors and other intracranial masses can produce secondary intracranial hypertension with mass effect and herniation in severe cases.

IMAGING DIFFERENTIAL DIAGNOSIS

Lemierre syndrome involves septic thrombophlebitis secondary to head and neck infections. The inciting infection should be identified, and the neck veins are often involved first (Fig. 25.4).

On a noncontrast examination, posttraumatic subdural hematomas can appear hyperdense and track eccentrically along the dural reflections and sinuses (Fig. 25.5).

Arachnoid granulations (Fig. 25.6A) and congenital venous sinus hypoplasia (Fig. 25.6B) should not be confused with true venous thrombosis.

FINAL DIAGNOSIS

Cerebral sinovenous thrombosis (CSVT).

DISCUSSION

CSVT is a serious and underdiagnosed condition in children and should be suspected when there are clinical signs of increased intracranial pressure (ICP) with associated risk factors.

Predisposing conditions include local or systemic infections, dehydration, renal failure, head trauma, neoplasms, hematological disorders (anemia, thrombophilia), and chronic diseases such as inflammatory bowel disease, nephrotic syndrome, systemic lupus erythematosus, and thyrotoxicosis.

Brain MRI and magnetic resonance venography (MRV) are best for characterizing the various features of CSVT. In the emergent setting, noncontrast head CT can show corresponding hyperdensity and evaluate for intracranial mass effect, while CTV can demonstrate intraluminal filling defects.

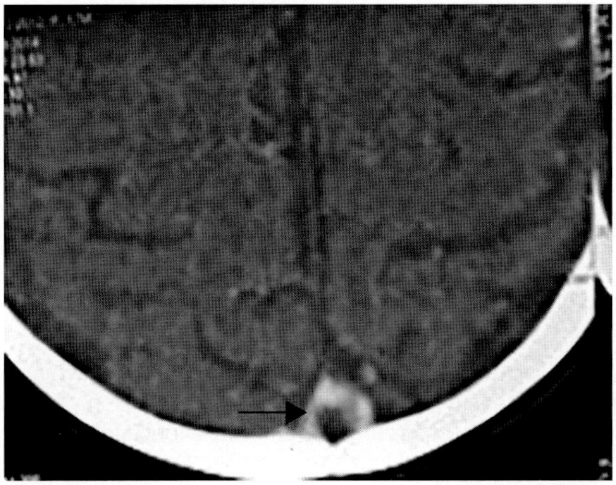

Fig. 25.1 Sagittal sinus thrombosis. Head CT with contrast shows central filling defect in the posterior superior sagittal sinus (*arrow*).

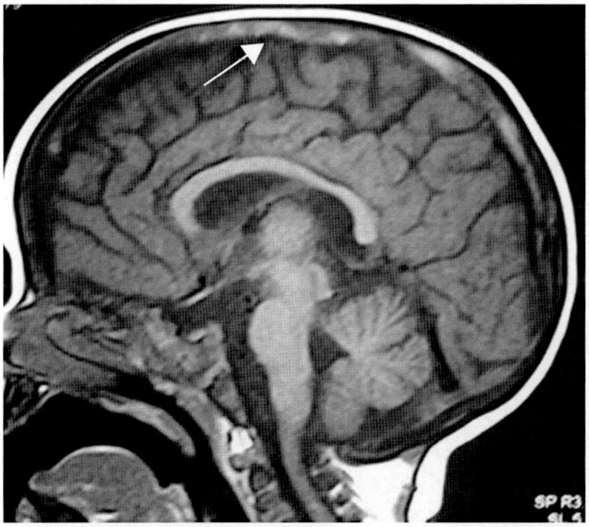

Fig. 25.2 Sagittal sinus thrombosis. Brain MRI, sagittal T1, shows expansile hyperintensity in the superior sagittal sinus (*arrow*).

CSVT in children can involve multiple vessels, particularly the superficial sinovenous system including cortical veins, superior sagittal sinus in 35% to 50%, and transverse sinuses in 70% of cases.

Most guidelines recommend anticoagulation for treatment of pediatric CSVT if there is no significant hemorrhagic transformation, over a period of at least 3 months. In CSVT associated with significant hemorrhage, imaging surveillance is recommended for 5 to 7 days. If there is extension of thrombus, anticoagulation

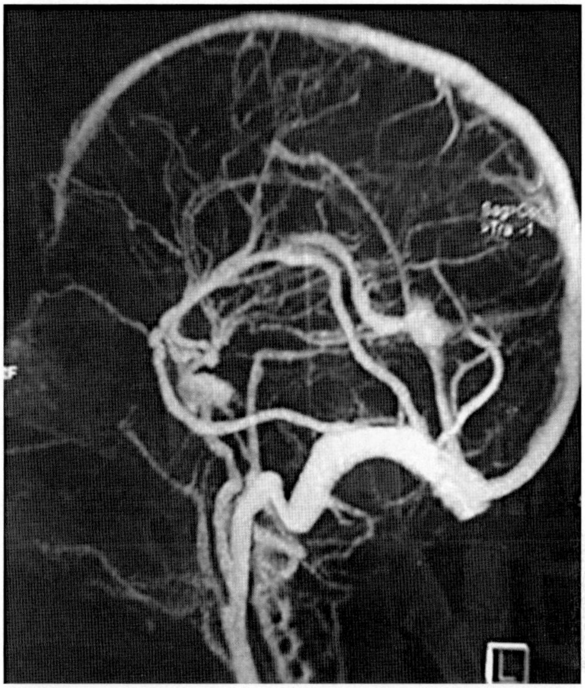

Fig. 25.3 Follow-up sagittal sinus thrombosis. Sagittal brain MRV shows recanalization of the superior sagittal sinus. *MRV*, Magnetic resonance venography.

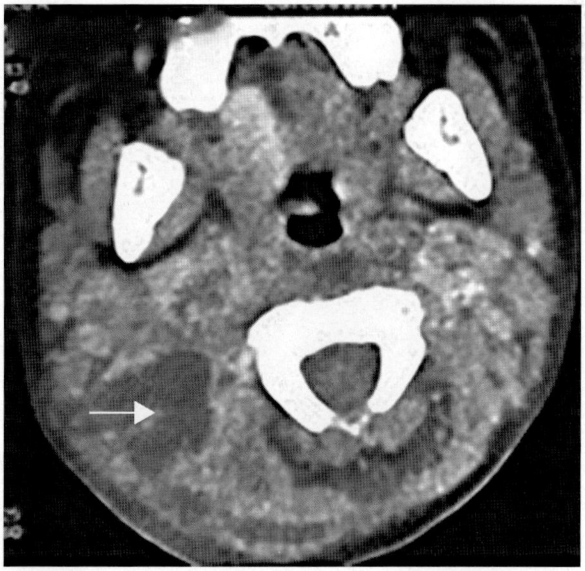

Fig. 25.4 Lemierre syndrome. Neck CT with contrast: right posterior neck abscess (*arrow*) associated with septic thrombophlebitis of the internal jugular vein.

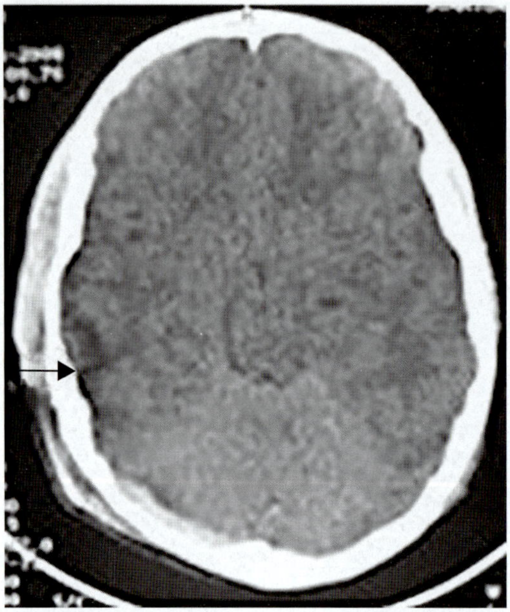

Fig. 25.5 Subacute subdural hematoma. Head CT shows right scalp edema and holohemispheric mixed-density crescentic hematoma (*arrow*) with small underlying parenchymal contusion.

should be continued, especially when there are comorbidities associated with recurrent risk of thrombosis.

The overall mortality of CSVT is about 10% with approximately 10% to 20% of children experiencing recurrences. Complications occur in approximately one-half of neonates and one-third of older children.

CLINICAL RED FLAGS

- Signs can be nonspecific and subtle, acute or subacute.
- Neonates may present with seizures, lethargy, vomiting, and/or feeding intolerance.
- Older children may show features of intracranial hypertension, including headaches, vomiting, visual disturbances, seizures, or other focal deficits.

IMAGING RED FLAGS

- Cordlike abnormalities (CT hyperdensity, MRI T1 hyperintensity, and susceptibility) on noncontrast imaging.
- Venous filling defects on angiography.
- Venous infarcts with vasogenic edema and/or hemorrhage.

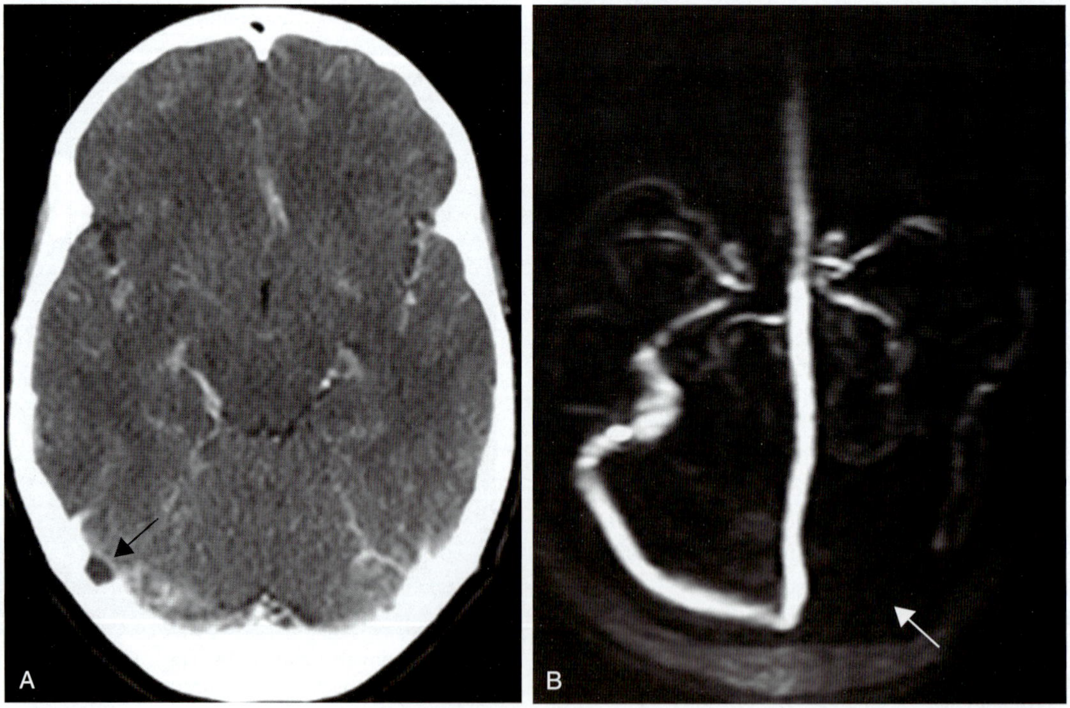

Fig. 25.6 Large arachnoid granulation. (A) Head CT with contrast shows prominent hypodensity in the right posterior temporal region with inner table remodeling and focal indentation of the dominant transverse sinus (*arrow*). (B) Hypoplastic left transverse sinus (*arrow*) without evidence of thrombosis on other sequences.

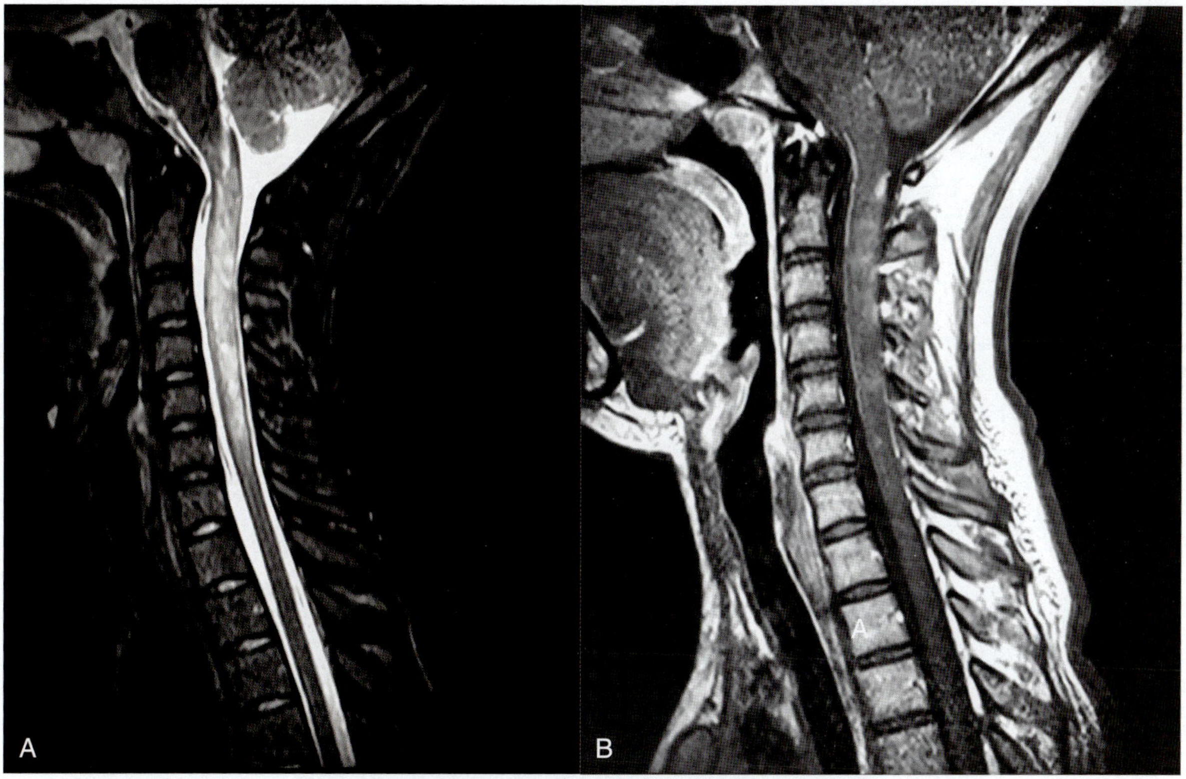

Fig. 26.3 Neuromyelitis optica spectrum disorder. (A) Sagittal T2 and (B) postcontrast T1 images show longitudinally extensive cervical cord edema with patchy enhancement.

pain sensation, and loss of bladder and bowel function. Spinal angiography may identify vascular malformations or occlusions for intervention. Systemic anticoagulation, thrombolytics, and/or corticosteroids may be helpful.

CLINICAL RED FLAGS

- Acute/hyperacute neurologic signs and symptoms of spinal cord dysfunction.
- Acute neck or abdominal pain followed by motor dysfunction.
- Recent interventions such as aortic surgery, orthopedic surgery, catheter placement.
- Normal CSF serology.

IMAGING RED FLAGS

- Early imaging of spinal cord infarct may be unremarkable, particularly if diffusion-weighted imaging is not acquired.
- Cord edema typically develops 24 to 48 hours after clinical onset, with T2-hyperintense signal. Abnormalities most commonly affect the anterior horns, but can also involve the posterior horns, central gray matter, or entire cord cross-section.
- Contrast enhancement may be observed in the subacute stage following blood–spinal cord barrier breakdown, usually several days after the initial presentation.
- There may be associated marrow signal abnormalities suggestive of vertebral infarction and/or disc abnormalities concerning for fibrocartilaginous embolism (Fig. 26.2).

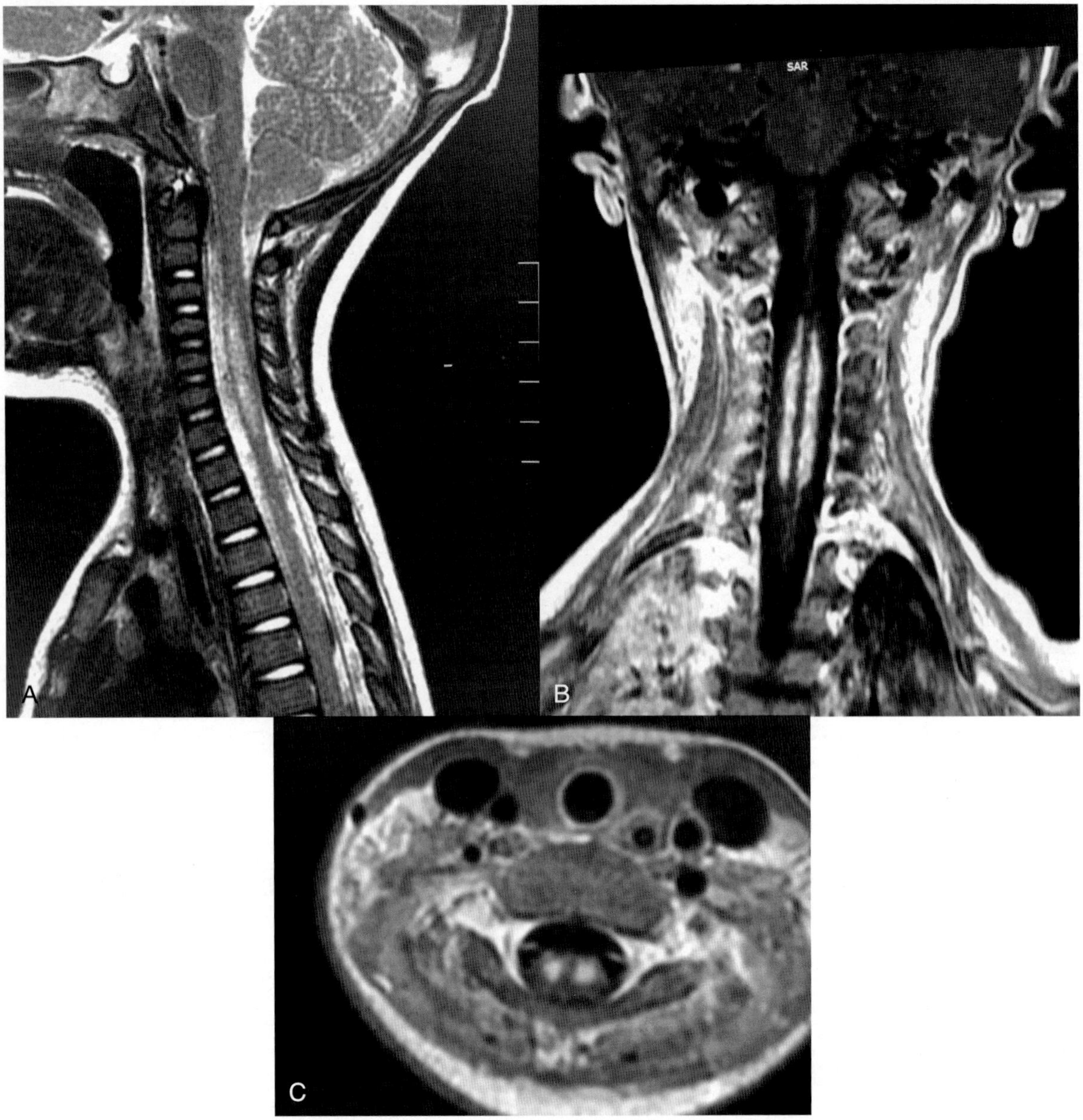

Fig. 26.4 Enterovirus D-68 myelitis. Spine MRI, (A) sagittal T2 shows long-segment edema in the cervical cord central gray matter. (B) Coronal and (C) axial postcontrast T1 images show intense enhancement of the anterior horns and exiting ventral nerve roots (radiculomyelitis).

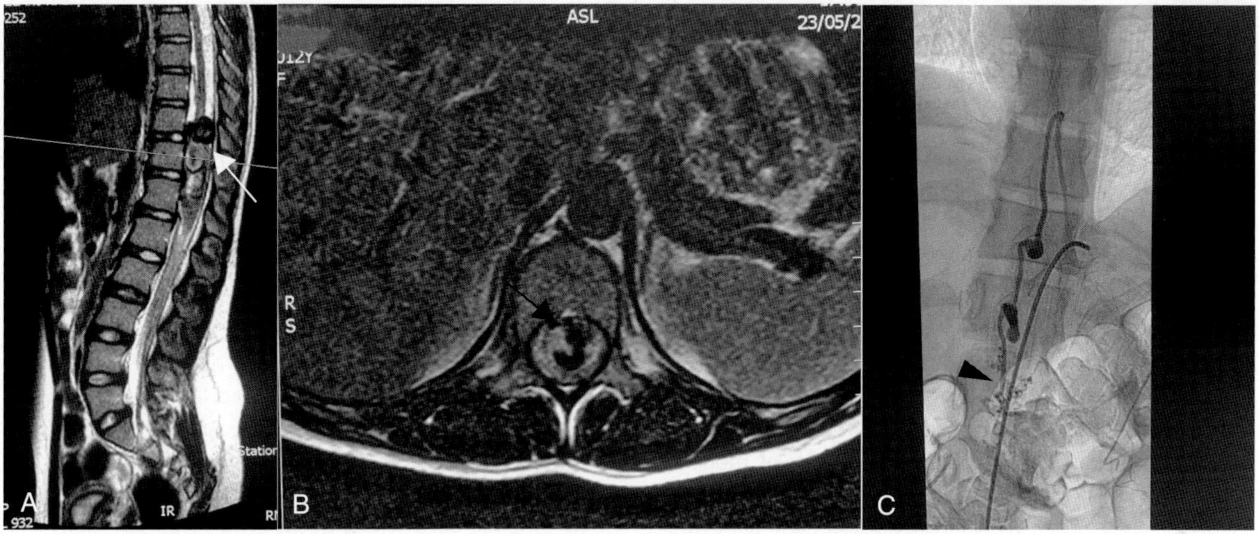

Fig. 26.5 Spinal perimedullary arteriovenous fistula in Osler-Weber-Rendu disease (hereditary hemorrhagic telangiectasia). Spine MRI, (A) sagittal and (B) axial T2, show engorged tortuous vessels within and surrounding the lower thoracic cord with regional edema and mass effect (*arrows*). (C) Spinal angiogram shows a partially thrombosed aneurysm of the feeding anterior spinal artery, communicating directly with several tortuous and dilated draining veins (*arrowhead*).

CONCLUSIONS

Spinal cord infarction in children and adolescents is an uncommon entity with severe morbidity and mortality. The clinical picture can mimic other myelopathies (transverse myelitis, hemorrhage, contusion), making definitive diagnosis challenging. Rapid identification of risk factors and concerning imaging features can facilitate timely diagnosis and management.

REFERENCES

Arroyo H, Buompadre MC. Infarto Isquémico de Médula Espinal. In: González G, Arroyo H, eds. *Accidente Cerebrovascular en la Infancia y Adolescencia*. Ediciones Journal; 2011.

Arroyo HA. Mielopatías agudas no traumáticas en niños y adolescentes [Acute non-traumatic myelopathy in children and adolescents]. *Rev Neurol.* 2013;57 Suppl 1:S129–S138.

Murphy OC, Pardo CA. Acute flaccid myelitis: a clinical review. *Semin Neurol.* 2020;40(2):211–218. https://doi.org/10.1055/s-0040-1705123.

Nance JR, Golomb MR. Ischemic spinal cord infarction in children without vertebral fracture. *Pediatr Neurol.* 2007;36(4):209–216. https://doi.org/10.1016/j.pediatrneurol.2007.01.006.

Quinn JN, Breit H, Dafer RM. Spinal cord infarction due to fibrocartilaginous embolism: a report of 3 cases. *J Stroke Cerebrovasc Dis.* 2019;28(6):e66–e67. https://doi.org/10.1016/j.jstrokecerebrovasdis.2019.03.012.

Case 27

High Flow, High Pain

HISTORY AND PHYSICAL

An 11-year-old previously healthy girl was admitted to the emergency department with a 3-day history of moderate occipital pain associated with vomiting. There was no recent history of infections, vaccinations, head trauma, or toxic exposures. Family history was negative for migraine or chronic headache, psychiatric disorders, or early-onset stroke. Physical examination showed weight 32 kg (50th–75th percentile), height 126 cm (25th–50th percentile), head circumference 54 cm (75th–90th percentile), blood pressure 100/62 mm/Hg (50th percentile), and pulse 88 bpm.

On admission, her headache increased to 8/10. While in the hospital, she became lethargic with a marked decrease in consciousness and a Glasgow Coma scale of 13. During neurologic evaluation, she was not oriented to a person or location and had difficulty following instructions. Cranial nerve, motor exam, and deep tendon reflexes were normal.

DIAGNOSTIC WORKUP

Head CT performed immediately after admission revealed an acute left anterior temporal hematoma with surrounding vasogenic edema (Fig. 27.1). Head CTA revealed a ruptured giant left MCA bifurcation arteriovenous malformation (AVM) measuring 2.5 cm, with superficial venous drainage via the vein of Labbé (Fig. 27.2). Cerebral angiography confirmed the diagnosis of AVM (Fig. 27.3). The patient underwent two angiographic embolizations with no further bleeding. Follow-up MRI showed development of parenchymal encephalomalacia and siderosis surrounding the AVM with a small residual nidus (Fig. 27.4).

CLINICAL DIFFERENTIAL DIAGNOSIS

Acute severe headache is the hallmark of hemorrhagic stroke (HS). Thunderclap headache, particularly if accompanied by nausea/vomiting or other neurological symptoms, should be considered HS until otherwise proven. Underlying lesions include ruptured aneurysms or AVMs. Patients can present with nonspecific encephalopathy and altered consciousness. Progressive neurological deficits can occur with brain parenchymal or cranial nerve compression.

Systemic causes of subarachnoid hemorrhage include leukemia, idiopathic thrombocytopenic purpura, hemorrhagic disease of the newborn, hemophilia, and other bleeding diatheses. Seizures, meningeal signs, and fever can occur and can be distinguished from infectious meningitis by CSF testing.

IMAGING DIFFERENTIAL DIAGNOSIS

Cavernous malformations (CCMs): Approximately 85% of brain CCMs are supratentorial in children (92% cerebral, 8% basal ganglia). The remainder are located infratentorially (57% brainstem, 43% cerebellar). Rarely, CCMs can also occur in the spinal cord. CT can show hyperdense areas of hemorrhage and calcification in larger lesions (Fig. 27.5A). Brain MRI, especially susceptibility-weighted sequences, has the greatest sensitivity for micro- and macrohemorrhages (Fig. 27.5B). MRI screening is recommended for first-degree relatives of patients with CCMs with two or more affected family members.

Aneurysm: The most common location is the ICA terminus, seen in 29% to 54% of children with aneurysms, primarily in the juvenile to adolescent age group. Noncontrast head CT is used to evaluate for acute subarachnoid hemorrhage. CTA or MRA helps identify underlying cerebral aneurysms and vascular malformations (Fig. 27.6A). In young infants, head ultrasound may also identify large vascular abnormalities. Dissecting and fusiform aneurysms are more common in children than adults. Cerebral angiography is the gold

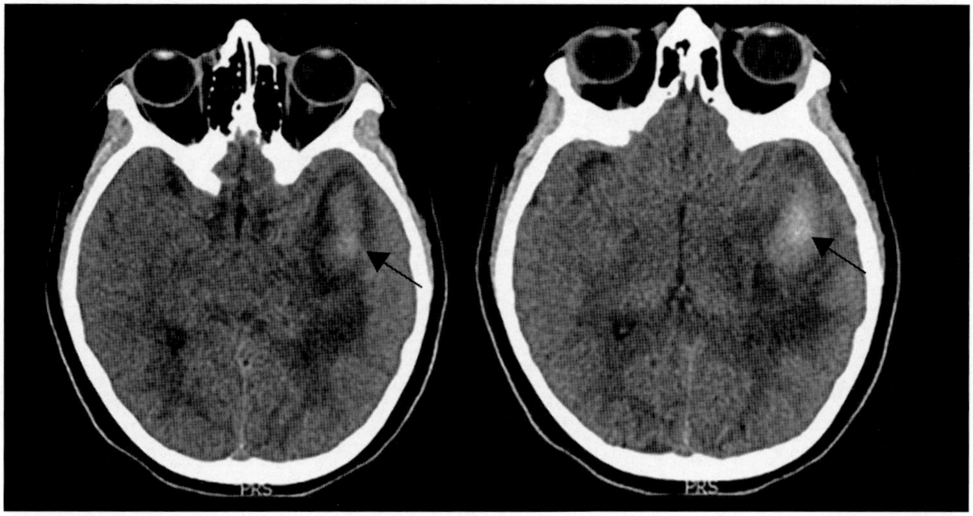

Fig. 27.1 Ruptured arteriovenous malformation. Head CT shows acute left anterior temporal hematoma with surrounding vasogenic edema (*black arrows*).

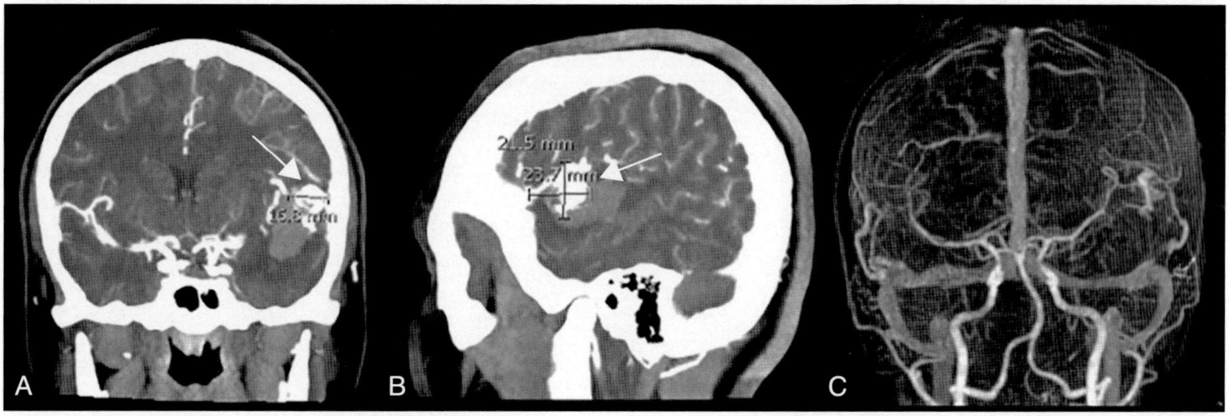

Fig. 27.2 Ruptured arteriovenous malformation. Head CTA, (A) coronal, (B) sagittal, and coronal MIP show ruptured giant left MCA bifurcation arteriovenous malformation (*white arrows*). *MCA*, Middle carotid artery; *MIP*, maximum intensity projection.

standard for detection of smaller vascular abnormalities and provides access for minimally invasive therapies (Fig. 27.6B).

Developmental venous anomalies: Rarely symptomatic unless transitional (arterialized) or associated with bleeding cavernous malformation. CT, MR, or cerebral angiography can demonstrate the aberrant venous drainage in a "caput medusae" pattern.

Other genetic arteriopathies: Hereditary hemorrhagic telangiectasia is associated with systemic vascular malformations in the lung, liver, and brain. Connective tissue disorders, for example *COL4A1* and *COL4A2* mutations, can predispose to early-onset and recurrent HS.

Coagulopathies account for a small percentage of HS but represent a significant risk factor. In conditions such as hemophilia and acute leukemia associated with thrombocytopenia, massive intracranial hemorrhage is often the cause of death (Fig. 27.7).

Hemorrhagic tumors can be diagnostically challenging. At imaging, marked heterogeneity, excessive associated edema, and areas of internal enhancement suggest an underlying mass lesion (Fig. 27.8).

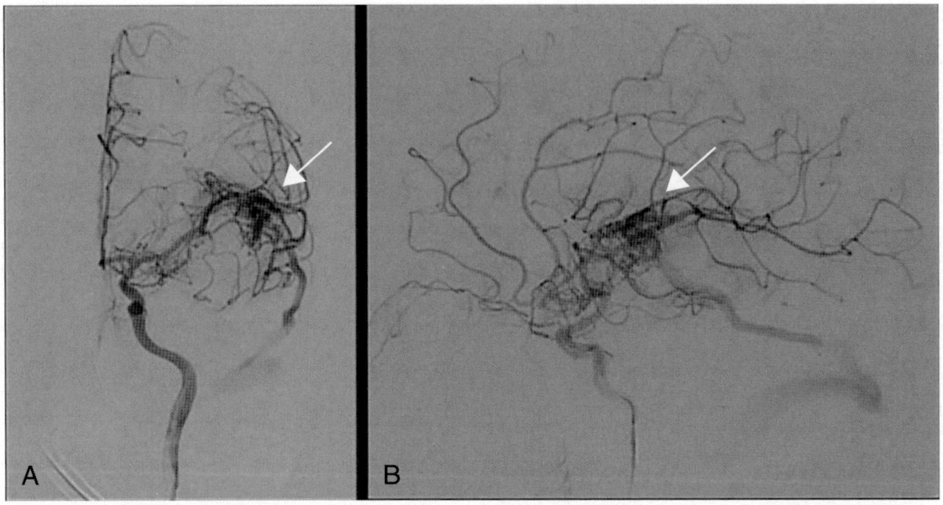

Fig. 27.3 Ruptured arteriovenous malformation. (A and B): Cerebral angiography, (A) anteroposterior (AP) and (B) lateral views, shows the left MCA arteriovenous malformation (*white arrows*) with contrast blush and venous drainage to the vein of Labbé. *MCA*, Middle carotid artery.

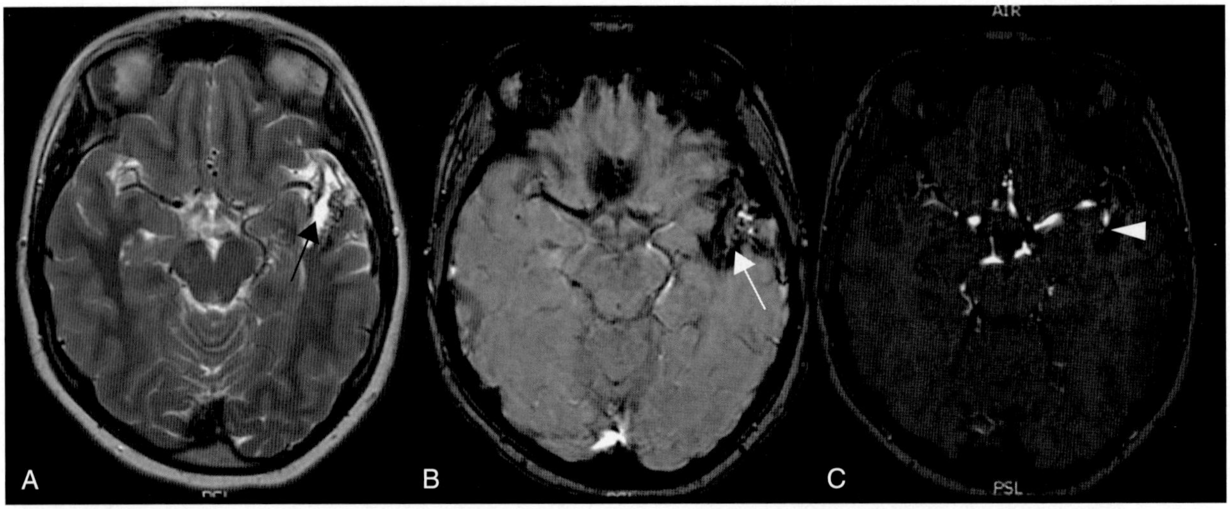

Fig. 27.4 Follow-up ruptured arteriovenous malformation. Brain MRI, (A) axial T2 and (B) SWI show parenchymal encephalomalacia (*black arrow*) and siderosis (*white arrow*). (C) Brain MRA shows small residual nidus (*white arrowhead*). *MRA*, Magnetic resonance angiography; *SWI*, susceptibility weighted imaging.

FINAL DIAGNOSIS

Hemorrhagic stroke (HS) due to ruptured AVM.

DISCUSSION

HS (intraparenchymal and/or subarachnoid hemorrhages) accounts for roughly half of pediatric stroke cases, with an incidence of 10 to 20 million children/year.

Etiologies differ from the adult population. There is a predominance of hematologic causes in the first year of life, while structural lesions such as vascular malformations are more commonly present in older children and adolescents.

Headache is the most frequent presenting symptom in 46% to 80% of children. Other symptoms include vomiting in 21% to 64%, altered mental status in 37% to 50%, seizures in 37% to 54%, focal neurological deficits

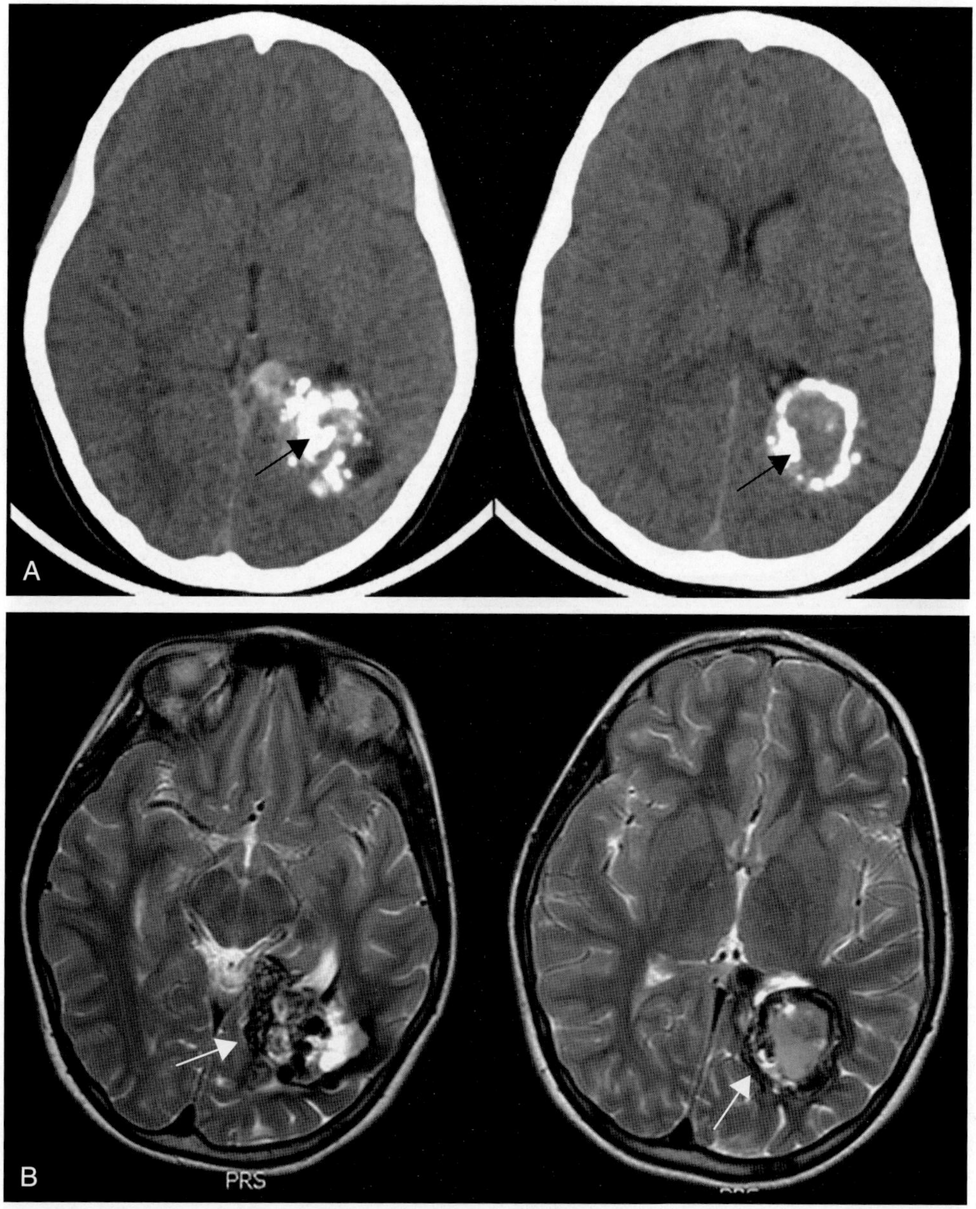

Fig. 27.5 Giant CCM. Head CT (A) shows a large left periatrial lesion with multiple hyperdense locules and coarse calcifications (*black arrows*). Brain MRI, axial T2 (B) shows popcorn-like lesion (*white arrows*) with prominent locules of susceptibility and blood products of various ages. *CCM*, Cavernous malformations.

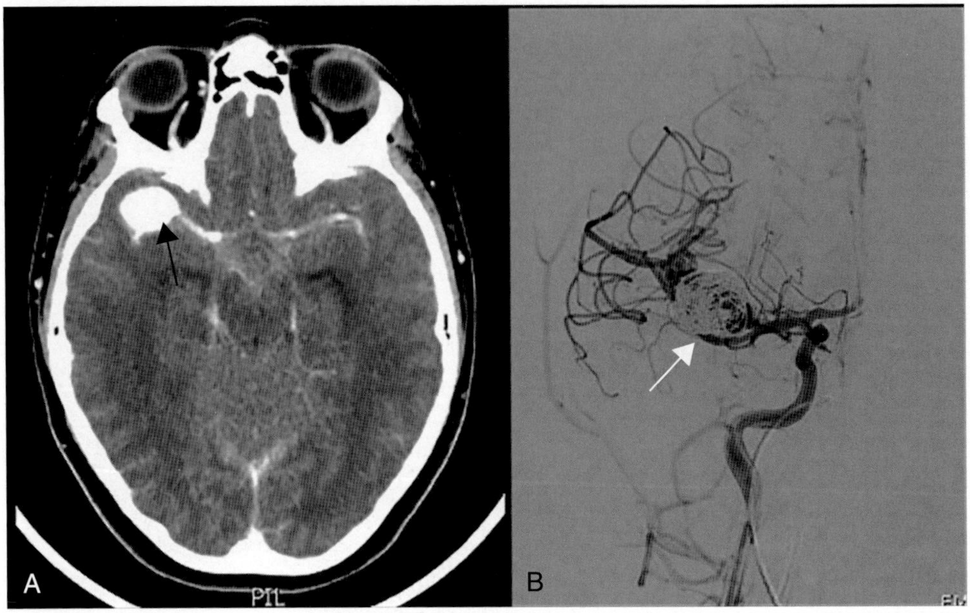

Fig. 27.6 (A and B) Giant aneurysm. (A) Head CTA, axial, shows a large right MCA aneurysm (*black arrow*). (B) Cerebral angiography, coronal, shows aneurysm post-embolization with mild extrinsic narrowing of the residual lumen (*white arrow*). *MCA*, Middle cerebral artery.

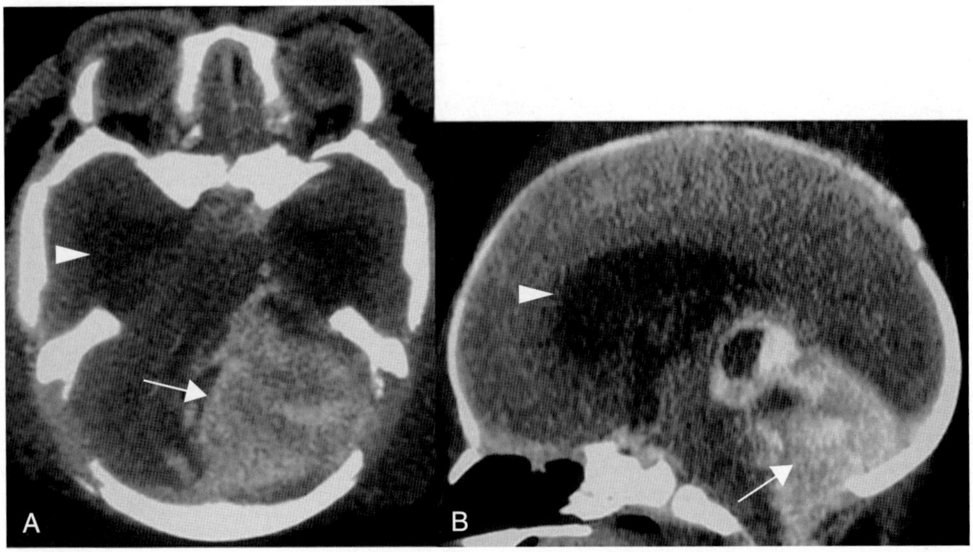

Fig. 27.7 Neonate with hemophilia. Head CT, (A) axial and (B) sagittal, show large left cerebellar hematoma (*arrows*) with brainstem compression and acute obstructive hydrocephalus (*arrowheads*).

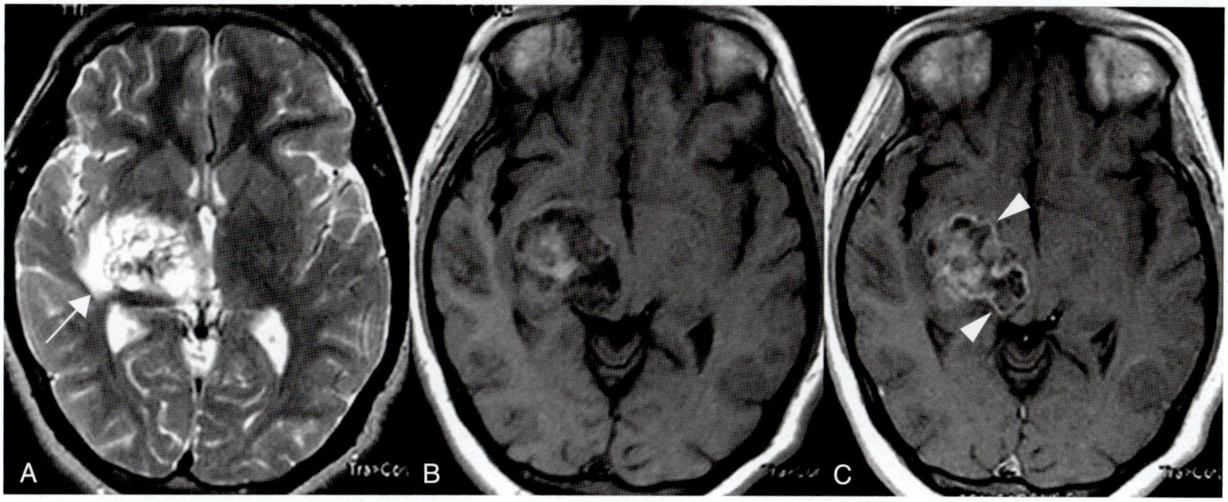

Fig. 27.8 Hemorrhagic tumor. Brain MRI, (A) axial T2 and (B) T1 without and (C) with contrast, show solid/cystic mass centered in the right thalamus with heterogeneous internal contrast enhancement (*arrowhead*), hemorrhagic transformation, and surrounding edema (*arrow*).

in 16% to 50%, and loss of consciousness in 3% to 5% of children.

CT is the first-line modality for screening of children with suspected hemorrhage. CTA or MRA can be used to detect underlying vascular abnormalities. Cerebral angiography is the gold standard for identifying small vascular abnormalities and providing access for minimally invasive therapy.

Children with intracranial hemorrhage (ICH) require admission to the intensive care unit. Management should include correction of bleeding diatheses and surgical intervention in the setting of clinical deterioration (Glasgow Coma Scale <8), large hematoma with herniation (>2% brain volume), posterior fossa location, and/or hydrocephalus.

CLINICAL RED FLAGS

- Patients with HS should be admitted to the intensive care unit to achieve normotensive or even hypertensive state to maintain cerebral perfusion.
- Intracranial pressure is a common problem due to mass effect and/or hydrocephalus.

IMAGING RED FLAGS

- CTA or MRA are noninvasive first-line imaging modalities but may miss smaller vascular lesions. If initial imaging is negative, cerebral angiography is recommended to evaluate for subtle aneurysms or vascular malformations.
- After treatment, follow-up imaging is indicated to evaluate for residual or recurrent vascular abnormality.
- The "spot sign" on CTA indicates active arterial extravasation with a risk of hematoma expansion.
- Noncontrast CT sensitivity is limited in the posterior fossa due to streak artifact from skull base. Patients with anemia can also show false negatives due to reduced density of blood products.

CONCLUSIONS

HS is a severe acute condition with high morbidity and mortality. Large hematoma volume, altered mental status within 6 hours of presentation, infratentorial location, Glasgow Coma Scale ≤7 on admission, associated aneurysm, age <3 years, and underlying hematological disorders are poor prognostic factors. Imaging helps identify the underlying cause to determine the diagnosis and appropriate management.

REFERENCES

Al-Jarallah A, Al-Rifai MT, Riela AR, Roach ES. Nontraumatic brain hemorrhage in children: etiology and presentation. *J Child Neurol.* 2000;15(5):284–289. https://doi.org/10.1177/088307380001500503.

Elhadi AM, Zabramski JM, Almefty KK, et al. Spontaneous subarachnoid hemorrhage of unknown origin: hospital course and long-term clinical and angiographic follow-up. *J Neurosurg.* 2015;122(3):663–670. https://doi.org/10.3171/2014.10.JNS14175.

Fullerton HJ, Achrol AS, Johnston SC, et al. Long-term hemorrhage risk in children versus adults with brain arteriovenous malformations. *Stroke.* 2005;36(10):2099–2104. https://doi.org/10.1161/01.STR.0000181746.77149.2b.

Jordan LC, Hillis AE. Hemorrhagic stroke in children. *Pediatr Neurol.* 2007;36(2):73–80. https://doi.org/10.1016/j.pediatrneurol.2006.09.017.

Khalaf A, Iv M, Fullerton H, Wintermark M. Pediatric stroke imaging. *Pediatr Neurol.* 2018;86:5–18. https://doi.org/10.1016/j.pediatrneurol.2018.05.008.

Kumar R, Shukla D, Mahapatra AK. Spontaneous intracranial hemorrhage in children. *Pediatr Neurosurg.* 2009;45(1):37–45. https://doi.org/10.1159/000202622.

Lori J, Argye H. Hemorrhagic stroke in children. *Pediatr Neurol.* 2007;36(2):73–80.

SECTION 6

Neurodegenerative Diseases

Jaume Campistol, Jordi Muchart

INTRODUCTION

Neurodegenerative diseases of childhood have different forms of presentation and it can be clinically challenging to identify regression. In the early stages, it is usually very difficult to establish the progressive nature of disease, as the time course may be very slow. Other more common pathologies in pediatrics can produce a similar picture and must first be excluded.

In general, following a transient stage of normality or with a previous history of delayed psychomotor development, obvious motor, cognitive, or global deterioration can be observed. Seizures and dementia are considered characteristic features of gray matter involvement, while spasticity and ataxia indicate white matter involvement. Progressive dementia, seizures, ataxia, tone and motor disorders, sensory defects, retinal alterations, and even extra-neurological manifestations may coexist.

The final diagnosis is based on clinical symptoms, including careful assessment of family and clinical history and detailed neurological examination. Frequently, complementary tests such as neuroimaging and genetic testing are needed.

SUGGESTED READINGS

Aicardi J, Arzimanoglou A. *Diseases of the Nervous System in Childhood*. 4rd ed. Mac Keith Press; 2019.

Gordon-Lipkin E, Fatemi A. Current therapeutic approaches in leukodystrophies: a review. *J Child Neurol*. 2018;33(13):861–868. https://doi.org/10.1177/0883073818792313.

Kovacs GG. Concepts and classification of neurodegenerative diseases. *Handb Clin Neurol*. 2017;145:301–307. https://doi.org/10.1016/B978-0-12-802395-2.00021-3.

Swaiman K, Ashwal S, Ferriero DM, et al. *Swaiman's Pediatric Neurology:Principles and Practice*. Elseveir; 2018.

van der Knaap MS, Bugiani M. Leukodystrophies: a proposed classification system based on pathological changes and pathogenetic mechanisms. *Acta Neuropathol*. 2017;134(3):351–382. https://doi.org/10.1007/s00401-017-1739-1.

Waldman AT. Leukodystrophies. *Continuum (Minneap Minn)*. 2018;24(1, Child Neurology):130–149. https://doi.org/10.1212/CON.0000000000000560.

A Child Who Drops Very Quickly in His School Performance

HISTORY AND PHYSICAL

A 10-year-old boy with a history of second-degree consanguinity started experiencing learning difficulties 6 months before consultation. The problem was attributed to attention deficit without hyperactivity disorder and was addressed by educators and school guidelines. One year later, he started to fall to the ground with amnesia after episodes. Physical examination was normal. A vitamin deficiency was suspected, and he was treated with methylphenidate and vitamin therapy (B_6) for 6 months.

Basic plasma analysis and EEG were requested, which were normal. However, his symptoms did not improve, and he was referred to child neurology. The neurological examination revealed spasticity with hyperreflexia, positive Babinski, bradypsychia, and brown staining of the skin, conjunctivae, and gums.

DIAGNOSTIC WORKUP

Hormonal analysis was requested with a thyroid study and basal cortisol and long-chain fatty acids, confirming a decrease in basal cortisol.

Brain MRI showed diffuse white matter T2 hyperintensity and T1 hypointensity, predominantly posteriorly. Confluent, symmetrical areas of T2 hyperintensity were predominantly in the splenium of the corpus callosum. Over time, these extended into the parieto-occipital periventricular white matter (Fig. 28.1) with volume loss and secondary atrophy of the corpus callosum and thalami (Fig. 28.2).

Laboratory testing for very long-chain fatty acids and sensory evoked potentials was immediately requested.

CLINICAL DIFFERENTIAL DIAGNOSIS

The initial presentation of pediatric neurodegenerative disorders can be mistaken for attention deficit disorder, learning disorder, or other behavioral disturbance. Visual, hearing, and motor problems can be very subtle in the early stages of the disease. Cognitive deficits become evident as the disease progresses. In 90% of untreated patients, there is a loss of all neurological functions (motor, cognitive, language, and behavioral) over a time range of 6 months to 3 years.

Many patients can manifest symptoms of adrenocortical insufficiency at the onset of symptoms, which should alert the physician to order laboratory testing and make a differential diagnosis.

Of course, we also have to consider other differential diagnoses with childhood-adolescent-onset neurodegenerative diseases such as metachromatic leukodystrophy (MLD), juvenile Krabbe disease, and other lysosomal storage diseases.

IMAGING DIFFERENTIAL DIAGNOSIS

Peroxisomal acyl-CoA oxidase deficiency: Much rarer with some similar MRI features. The typical findings are progressive white matter abnormalities, atrophy, and contrast enhancement in the centrum semiovale. Polymicrogyria has sometimes been described.

Metachromatic leukodystrophy: Characteristic imaging features include deep white matter involvement with perivenular sparing and late involvement of subcortical U fibers, accompanied by global atrophy over time.

Krabbe disease (Fig. 28.3): As with many leukodystrophies, Krabbe disease shows distinct imaging features and ages of onset for different clinical subtypes. The subtypes that can resemble X-linked adrenoleukodystrophy (ALD) are the juvenile and adult forms, with deep white matter and/or isolated corticospinal tract involvement.

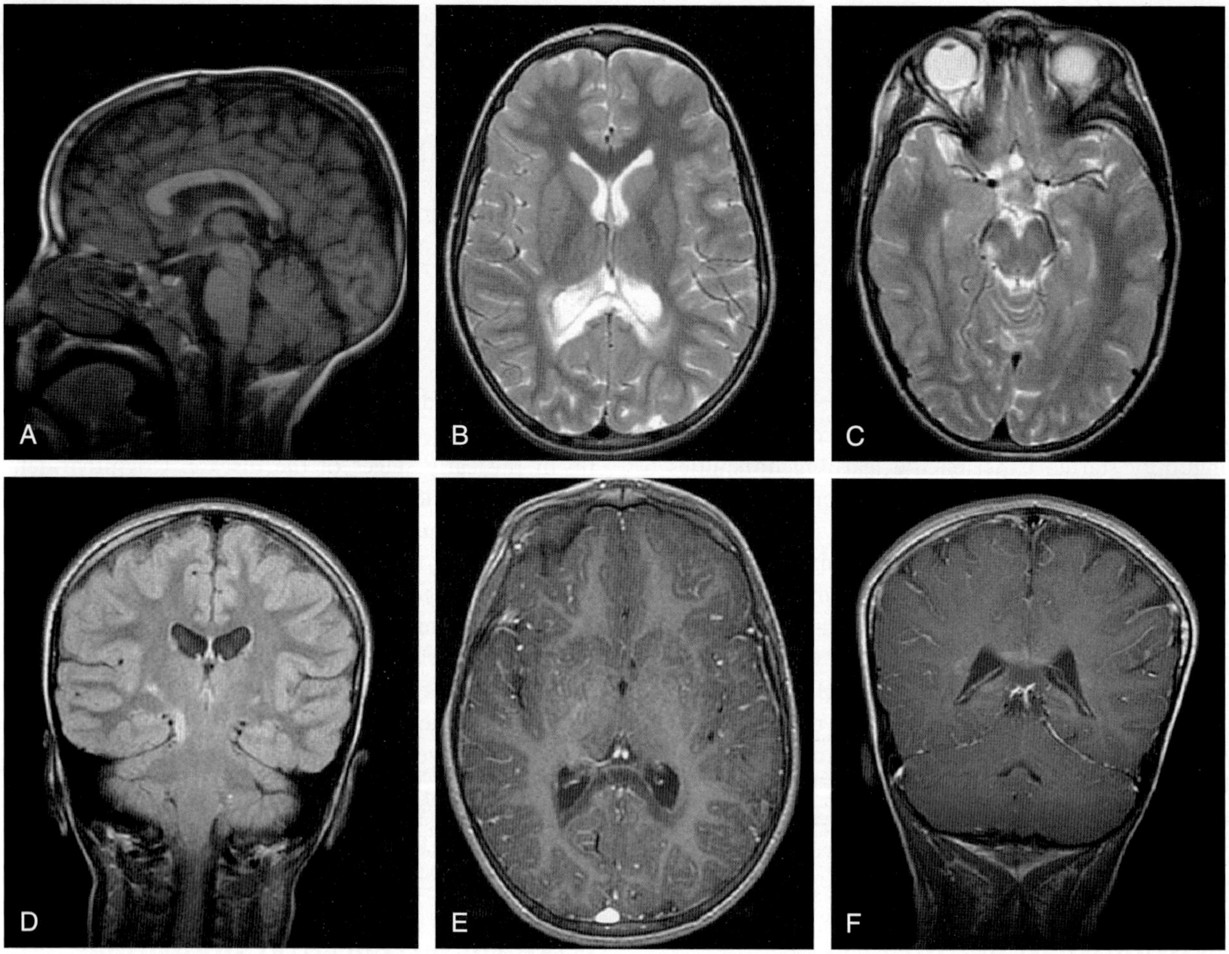

Fig. 28.1 Boy with X-linked adrenoleukodystrophy. Brain MRI, (A) sagittal T1, (B and C) axial T2, (D) coronal FLAIR, (E) axial T1 with contrast, (F) coronal T1 with contrast show signal abnormality of the splenium of corpus callosum, right corticospinal tract, and posterior periventricular white matter with leading-edge enhancement.

FINAL DIAGNOSIS

X-linked ALD with mutation in *ABCD1* gene.

DISCUSSION

ALD is an X-linked disease. Pathogenic variants in the *ABCD1* gene, which encodes a peroxisomal membrane transporter, result in defective transport and accumulation of very long-chain fatty acids with resultant brain toxicity. The incidence of the disease is estimated between 1 in 10,000 and 1 in 17,000 live births. Diagnosis is based on four sets of characteristics:

Clinical examination: Presenting hypotonia is observed in the early-onset forms during the neonatal or childhood periods. Progressive cognitive dysfunction includes learning, language, and attention problems. Psychiatric symptoms may include anxiety, depression, and social withdrawal. Motor symptoms can appear later with delay or regression due to compromise of the pyramidal tracts, causing spasticity, gait disturbances, dystonia, and chronic pain.

Brain MRI: Neuroimaging is important for screening, diagnosis, and monitoring of patients. When hematopoietic stem cell transplantation is being considered, the Loes severity score can help predict disease

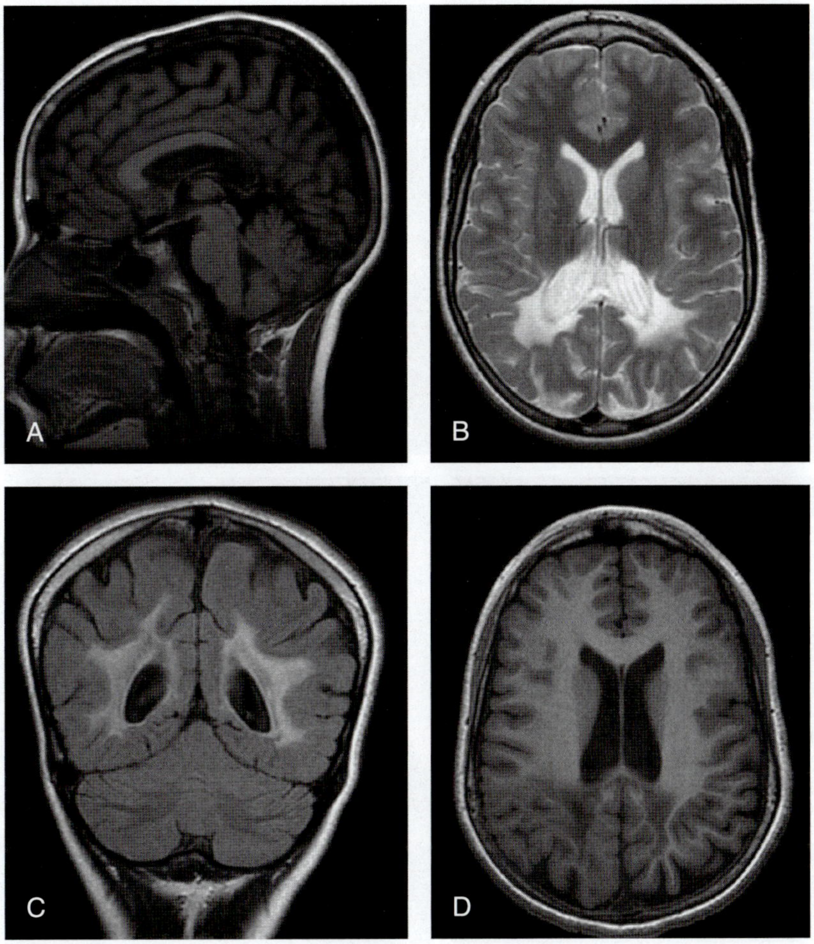

Fig. 28.2 Boy with X-linked adrenoleukodystrophy. Brain MRI, (A) sagittal T1, (B) axial T2, (C) coronal FLAIR, (D) axial T1 show abnormal signal and atrophy in the splenium of corpus callosum and posterior periventricular white matter.

course and select suitable transplant candidates. The classic features are diffuse white matter abnormality, initially involving the deep white matter (usually posteriorly) with perivascular sparing. Fifteen percent of patients show a reverse pattern with predominant involvement of frontal white matter (Fig. 28.4). Isolated involvement of the corticospinal tracts can also occur (Fig. 28.5). Leading-edge contrast enhancement is compatible with areas of active demyelination. In the chronic stage, disease can extend to the subcortical U fibers, which are spared earlier in the disease process. There is progressive brain atrophy, cystic degeneration, and calcification.

Laboratory testing: Confirmation of elevated very long-chain fatty acids: hexacosanoic acid, hexacosanoic acid: docosahexaenoic acid ratio; hexacosanoic acid: tetracosanoic acid ratio.

Molecular testing: Mutation of *ABCD1* gene.

CLINICAL RED FLAGS

- Progressive neurocognitive compromise in a previously healthy male, with childhood onset at 4–10 years, with no other explanation and few initial motor manifestations.
- Rapid progression of cognitive and sensory impairment, over a period of months to a few years, with added psychiatric and motor manifestations.
- Adrenal insufficiency, with increased skin pigmentation due to elevated ACTH, usually precedes neurological symptoms or occurs together with other symptoms.

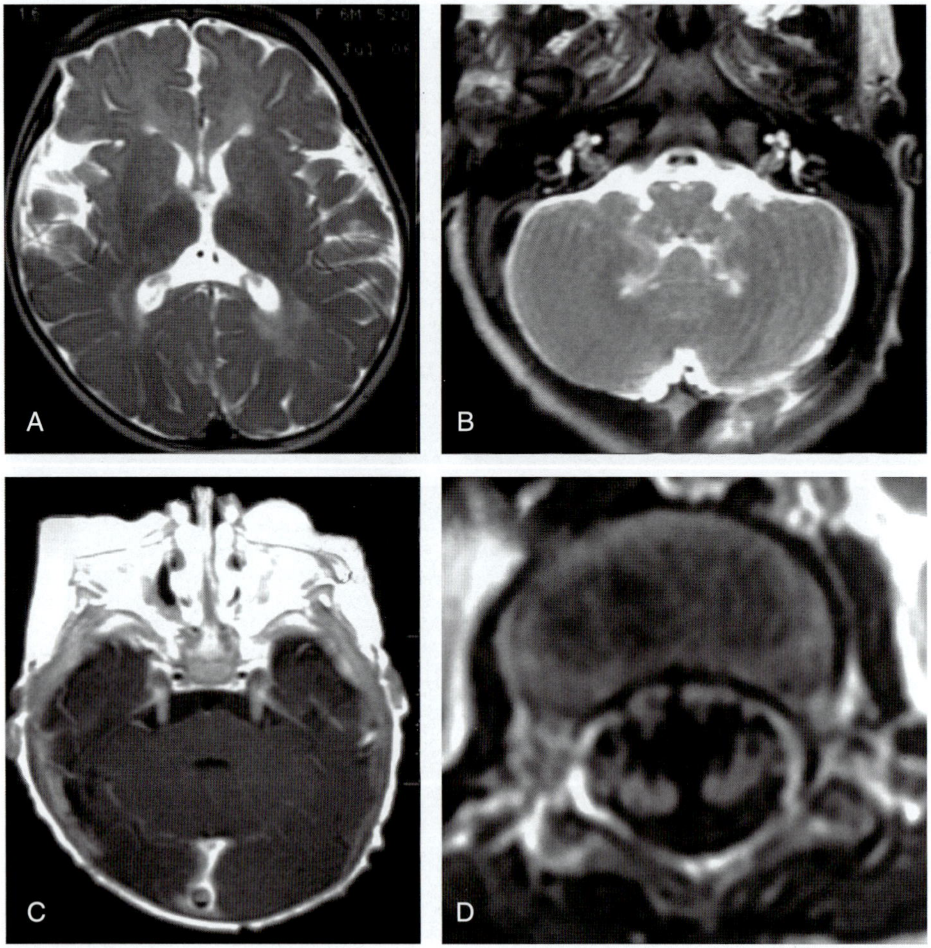

Fig. 28.3 Infant girl with Krabbe disease. Brain MRI, (A and B) axial T2 and brain and spine MRI, (C and D) axial T1 with contrast show confluent T2 hyperintense signal in the periventricular white matter, dentate nuclei, corticospinal tracts, and dorsal brainstem nuclei. The cranial and spinal nerves are diffusely enlarged and enhancing.

IMAGING RED FLAGS

- White matter lesions extending from splenium of the corpus callosum toward deep parietal and occipital white matter.
- Progressive tissue loss of affected areas and secondary Wallerian degeneration.
- Leading-edge enhancement with sparing of perivascular regions and subcortical U fibers.

CONCLUSIONS

Consider ALD in a previously healthy male patient with slow cognitive decline at onset, with progressive motor/psychiatric symptoms and skin hyperpigmentation. Neuroimaging findings can be highly suggestive but should be confirmed by biochemical and genetic testing. Early diagnosis is important for optimal management and establishment of disease-modifying therapies.

REFERENCES

Ashrafi MR, Amanat M, Garshasbi M, et al. An update on clinical, pathological, diagnostic, and therapeutic perspectives of childhood leukodystrophies. *Expert Rev Neurother.* 2020;20(1):65–84. https://doi.org/10.1080/14737175.2020.1699060.

Eichler F, Duncan C, Musolino PL, et al. Hematopoietic stem-cell gene therapy for cerebral adrenoleukodystrophy. *N Engl*

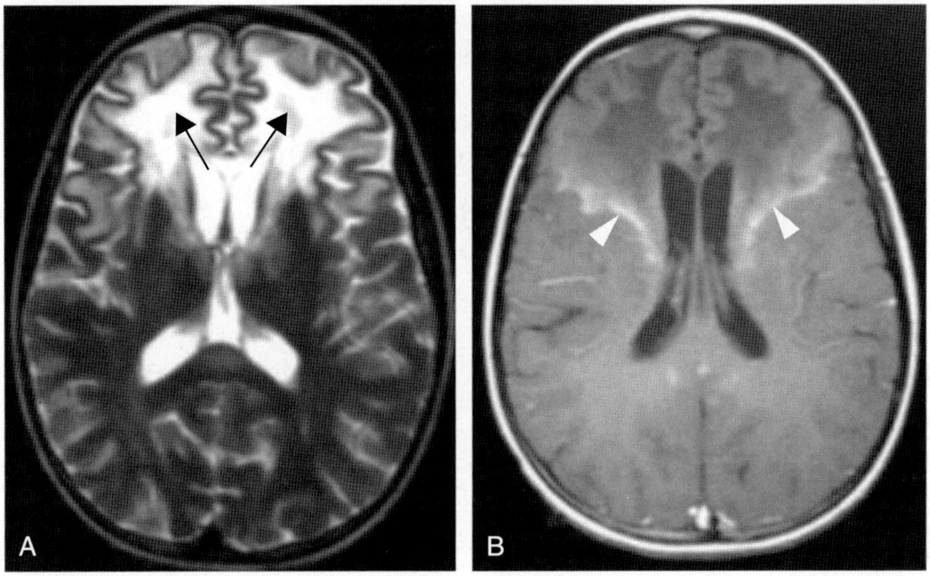

Fig. 28.4 Frontal variant of X-linked adrenoleukodystrophy. Brain MRI, (A) axial T2, (B) axial T1 with contrast show symmetric confluent hyperintensity in the anterior white matter (*arrows*) with leading-edge enhancement (*arrowheads*).

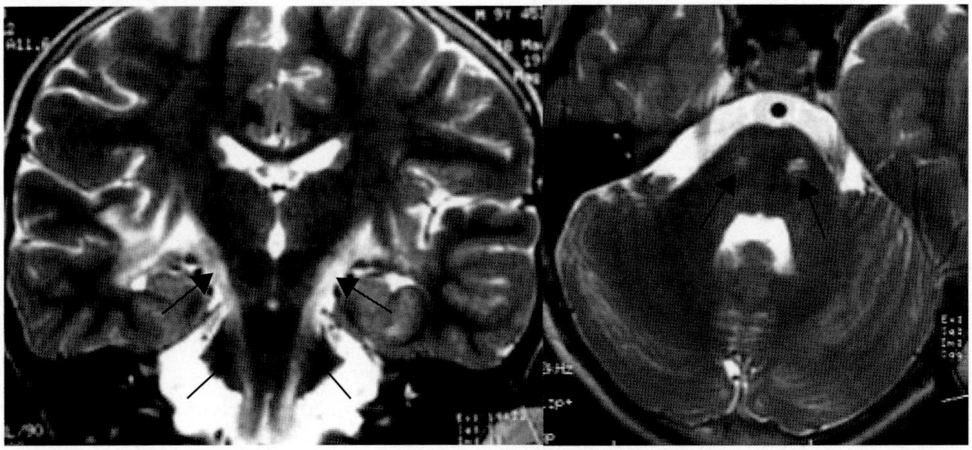

Fig. 28.5 Boy with X-linked adrenoleukodystrophy. Brain MRI, (A) coronal and (B) axial T2 show hyperintense signal in the corticospinal tracts (*arrows*).

J Med. 2017;377(17):1630–1638. https://doi.org/10.1056/NEJMoa1700554.

van der Knaap MS, Bugiani M. Leukodystrophies: a proposed classification system based on pathological changes and pathogenetic mechanisms. *Acta Neuropathol*. 2017;134(3):351–382. https://doi.org/10.1007/s00401-017-1739-1.

Van Haren K, Bonkowsky JL, Bernard G, et al. Consensus statement on preventive and symptomatic care of leukodystrophy patients. *Mol Genet Metab*. 2015;114(4):516–526. https://doi.org/10.1016/j.ymgme.2014.12.433.

Wiesinger C, Eichler FS, Berger J. The genetic landscape of X-linked adrenoleukodystrophy: inheritance, mutations, modifier genes, and diagnosis. *Appl Clin Genet*. 2015;8:109–121. https://doi.org/10.2147/TACG.S49590.

Case 29

Head Circumference Is Increasing While the Child Is Deteriorating

HISTORY AND PHYSICAL

A 2-month-old infant with no prior history manifested with new-onset loss of muscle tone and difficulties with head control. His physical examination was normal, and he was referred to an early intervention program. After 2 months of therapy, no improvements were noted, notable hypotonia persisted, and head control did not improve in the pull-to-sit maneuver. Neurological evaluation at 4 months showed a large head circumference (macrocephaly + 3 SD) that had developed since birth, little visual contact, global hypotonia with preserved reflexes, and general apathy. Fundoscopic examination revealed mild optic nerve pallor. There were no signs of increased intracranial pressure, and head ultrasound was normal. Blood work was also normal, including creatine kinase. Brain MRI and more detailed blood and urine testing were requested.

DIAGNOSTIC WORKUP

Brain MRI showed megalencephaly and cerebral white matter abnormality with centripetal progression, starting from subcortical white matter and moving toward the periventricular white matter, internal capsules, and corpus callosum. The brainstem tracts, basal ganglia, and cerebellum were also involved, with sparing of the lentiform nuclei. Involved areas showed initial edema that later evolved to atrophy. MR spectroscopy (MRS) of the affected areas showed increased N-acetylaspartate and decreased choline peaks (Fig. 29.1).

CLINICAL DIFFERENTIAL DIAGNOSES

Alexander disease: Macrocephaly, frontal bossing, neurological impairment, and epilepsy. Leukodystrophy is predominantly frontal, without elevation of N-acetylaspartate in urine or on MRS. Brain biopsy confirms the presence of Rosenthal fibers. Molecular testing shows mutations in the *GFAP* gene.

Glutaric aciduria type 1: Nonprogressive macrocephaly and dystonic tetraparesis. There is high urine excretion of glutaric and hydroxyglutaric acid. Genetic testing shows mutations in the *GCDH* gene, located at 19p13.2 and encoding the enzyme glutaryl CoA dehydrogenase.

Neurometabolic diseases (gangliosidosis, mucopolysaccharidosis, megalencephalic leukoencephalopathy with subcortical cysts).

Neurogenetic syndromes (fragile X, PTEN mutations, macrocephaly-polydactyly-polymicrogyria-hydrocephalus)

Neurocutaneous syndromes (RASopathies)

Brain tumors

Child abuse

IMAGING DIFFERENTIAL DIAGNOSIS

Alexander disease (Fig. 29.2): Infantile Alexander disease typically presents with frontal white matter edema, followed by cyst formation. There is macrocephaly with rapid neurologic deterioration in both the infantile and neonatal variants.

Megalencephalic leukoencephalopathy with subcortical cysts (Fig. 29.3): There is diffuse white matter edema that evolves to subcortical cysts. The subcortical white matter is spared, especially posteriorly.

FINAL DIAGNOSIS

Canavan disease due to *ASPA* gene mutation with aspartoacylase deficiency.

DISCUSSION

Canavan disease is a neurodegenerative disorder associated with spongiform degeneration of the brain white

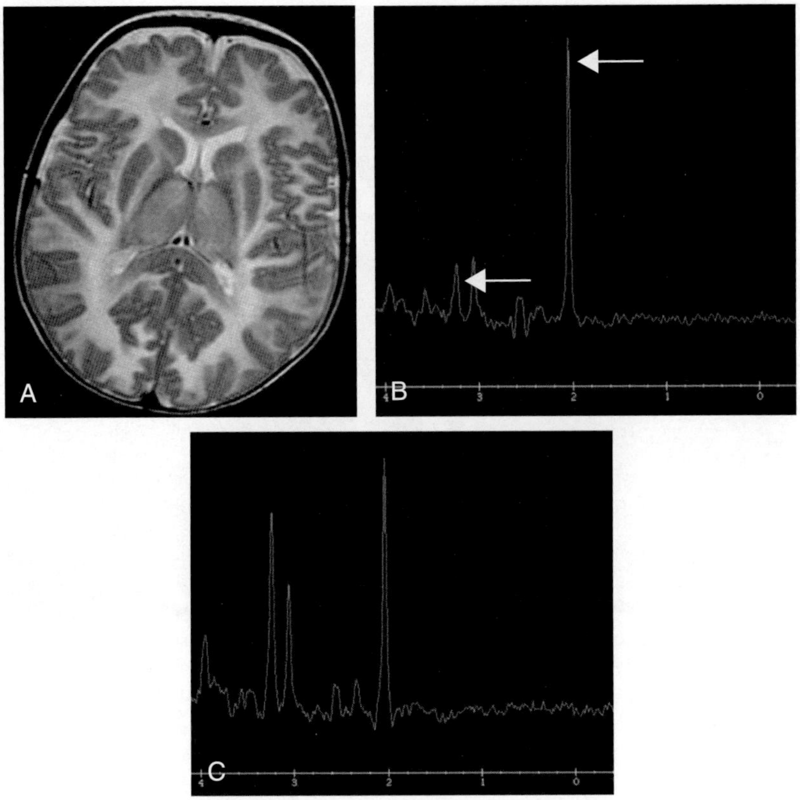

Fig. 29.1 Infant with Canavan disease. Brain MRI, (A) axial T2, shows diffuse white matter abnormality and involvement of the thalami. There is relative sparing of the lentiform nuclei. (B) MR spectroscopy with intermediate echo time shows increased N-acetylaspartate (*right arrow*) and decreased choline (*left arrow*) compared to (C) normal MRS.

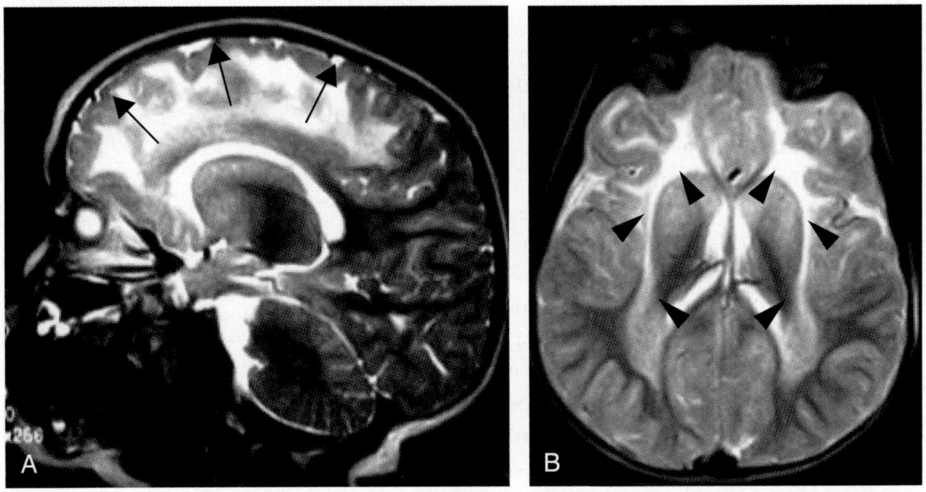

Fig. 29.2 Alexander disease. Brain MRI, (A) sagittal T2 and (B) axial T2 show diffuse white matter hyperintensity in the lobar and subcortical frontal white matter (*arrows*). There is also involvement of the external and extreme capsules, posterior periventricular white matter, and basal ganglia (*arrowheads*).

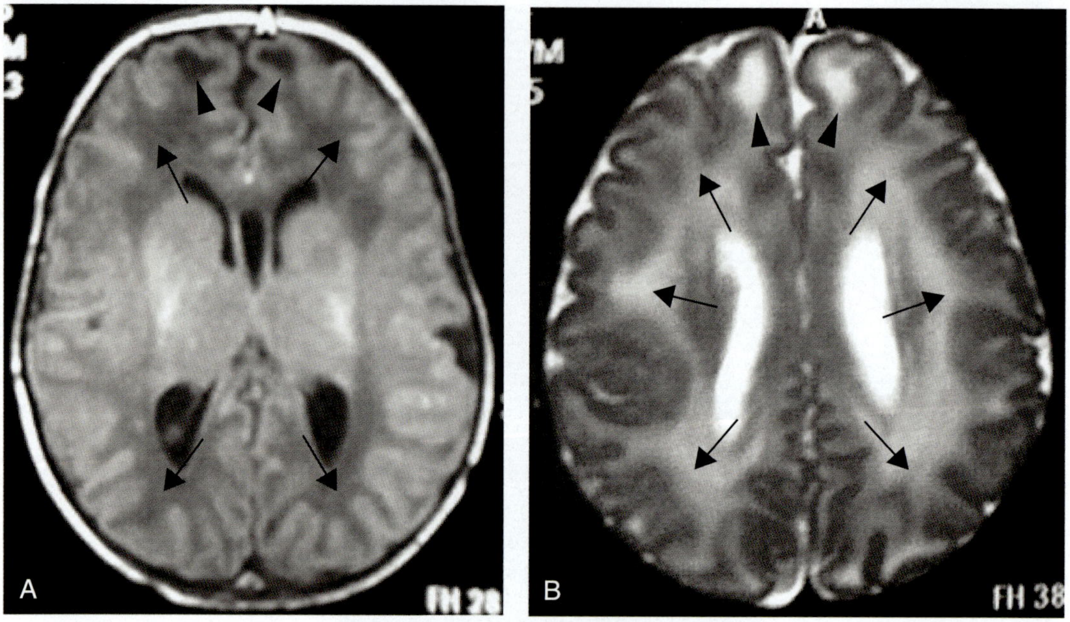

Fig. 29.3 Megalencephalic leukoencephalopathy with subcortical cysts. Brain MRI, (A) axial T1 and (B) T2 show diffuse T1 hypointensity and T2 hyperintensity in the white matter of both cerebral hemispheres (*arrows*). There are developing cysts in the frontal subcortical white matter (*arrowheads*).

matter. It is an autosomal recessive hereditary disease that usually manifests in infancy with growth arrest, progressive macrocephaly, irritability, swallowing difficulties, opisthotonus, spasticity, and blindness. Patients usually die before the age of 5 years. Elevated N-acetylaspartate (NAA) can be detected in urine, CSF, and brain parenchyma. The enzymatic deficiency in aspartoacylase can be measured in skin fibroblast samples, with mutations in the *ASPA* gene (17p13-ter). At pathology, the brain appears enlarged and spongiform, with generalized vacuolization and numerous fluid-filled cavities throughout the white matter. This likely reflects neuronal damage due to accumulation of NAA, which interferes with conversion of lignoceric acid to cerebronic and glutamic acid for myelin synthesis. Brain MRI reveals a centripetal pattern of demyelination, beginning in the subcortical U fibers and progressing to the periventricular regions. MRS can detect the essentially pathognomonic elevation in NAA. Early diagnosis is important for genetic counseling and enrollment in clinical trials. Treatment is symptomatic, with emerging enzyme replacement and gene therapies.

CLINICAL RED FLAGS

- Progressive macrocephaly starting in the infant period without an obvious cause.
- Progressive psychomotor impairment with poor head control, absence of eye tracking, and sucking/swallowing problems.
- Elevated NAA in urine.

IMAGING RED FLAGS

- Megalencephaly and diffuse white matter edema. Early involvement of subcortical U fibers with progressive centripetal extension. Globus pallidus and thalami are usually affected, while the lentiform nuclei are spared.
- MRS showing high N-acetylaspartate and low choline.

CONCLUSIONS

Infantile Canavan disease classically presents with the triad of hypotonia, delayed head control, and macrocephaly between 3 and 5 months of life with poor visual monitoring and sucking/swallowing difficulties. The later-onset juvenile form shows slow regression or juvenile forms. Elevation of N-acetylaspartate in urine can be detected by gas chromatography–mass spectrometry and is confirmed by enzymatic or genetic testing. Brain MRI findings with leukodystrophy and elevated NAA on spectroscopy are characteristic.

REFERENCES

Barkovich JA, Raybaud C. *Pediatric Neuroimaging*. Lippincott Williams & Wilkins; 2018.

Bley A, Denecke J, Kohlschütter A, et al. The natural history of Canavan disease: 23 new cases and comparison with patients from literature. *Orphanet J Rare Dis*. 2021;16(1):227. https://doi.org/10.1186/s13023-020-01659-3.

Hoshino H, Kubota M. Canavan disease: clinical features and recent advances in research. *Pediatr Int*. 2014;56(4):477–483. https://doi.org/10.1111/ped.12422.

Lotun A, Gessler DJ, Gao G. Canavan disease as a model for gene therapy-mediated myelin repair. *Front Cell Neurosci*. 2021;15:661928. https://doi.org/10.3389/fncel.2021.661928.

Pleasure D, Guo F, Chechneva O, et al. Pathophysiology and treatment of Canavan disease. *Neurochem Res*. 2020;45(3):561–565. https://doi.org/10.1007/s11064-018-2693-6.

van der Knaap MS, Val J. *Magnetic Resonance of Myelination and Myelin Disorders*. Springer; 2005.

Case 30

The Infant Who Loses Ambulation

HISTORY AND PHYSICAL

A 2-year-old girl with no prior history presented with a new gait disorder. At daycare, she experienced progressive worsening of motor clumsiness and psychomotor skills, without cognitive impairment. She was noted to walk poorly and fall easily, with no abnormalities identified on orthopedic examination. Neurologic examination revealed truncal ataxia with osteotendinous hyporeflexia and extremity hypertonia. Sensory examination was normal and language function was preserved. Basic blood and urine analyses were normal. CSF was notable for elevated protein of 112 mg/dL (normal 15–45). Neurophysiology revealed a demyelinating peripheral neuropathy with reduced motor and sensory nerve conduction velocities. Head CT and brain MRI showed diffuse cerebral white matter abnormality. The diagnosis was confirmed by skin biopsy for fibroblasts with enzymatic and molecular testing.

DIAGNOSTIC WORKUP

Brain MRI shows confluent and symmetric involvement of the periventricular and deep white matter, including splenium of corpus callosum, with initial preservation of the subcortical U fibers. With disease progression, there is linear sparing of perivascular regions in a "tigroid" pattern (Fig. 30.1). With gadolinium administration, cranial and spinal nerve enhancement can be demonstrated (Fig. 30.2).

CLINICAL DIFFERENTIAL DIAGNOSIS

Genetic leukodystrophies can be inherited in an autosomal dominant, autosomal recessive, or X-linked fashion. These are generally childhood-onset conditions with predominant motor involvement, including hypotonia and pyramidal and cerebellar signs. Cognitive deterioration is usually slow, with a low incidence of seizures. Brain MRI shows predominant involvement of white matter.

Certain leukodystrophies are linked to specific metabolic defects, for example globoid cell leukodystrophy (Krabbe disease), multiple sulfatase deficiency, saposin B deficiency, mucolipidoses, fucosidosis, and hexosaminidase A deficiency. Metabolic workup and molecular testing will provide a definitive diagnosis.

Neurotransmitter defects, dopamine-responsive dystonia, and infantile cerebral palsy can have similar clinical features.

IMAGING DIFFERENTIAL DIAGNOSIS

Krabbe disease: As with many leukodystrophies, Krabbe disease shows distinct imaging features and ages of onset for different clinical subtypes. The subtypes that can resemble X-linked ALD are the juvenile and adult forms, with deep white matter and/or isolated corticospinal tract involvement.

Acute demyelination: Diffuse demyelination can be bilateral and symmetric but occurs acutely following an osmotic or infectious insult.

Gangliosidoses: In the gangliosidoses, there are diffuse white matter abnormalities with heterogeneous signal intensity of the thalami and basal ganglia. The thalami show bilateral and symmetric hyperdensity on CT, hyperintensity on T1-weighted, and hypointensity on T2-weighted MRI (Fig. 30.3).

FINAL DIAGNOSIS

Early infantile metachromatic leukodystrophy (MLD) due to *ARSA* gene mutation with arylsulfatase A deficiency.

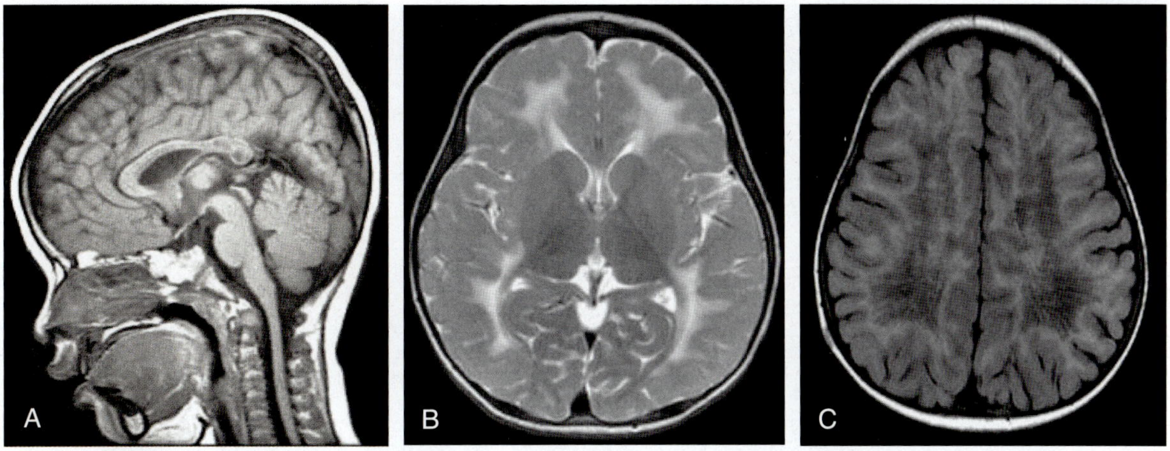

Fig. 30.1 Metachromatic leukodystrophy. Brain MRI, (A) sagittal T1, (B) axial T2, (C) axial T1 show abnormal signal in the corpus callosum and periventricular white matter with sparing of subcortical fibers and perivascular spaces creating a "tigroid" pattern.

DISCUSSION

MLD is an autosomal recessive neurodegenerative disease due to mutations in the *ARSA* gene (22q13), yielding defects in the enzyme ARSA. This leads to failed catabolism of sulfatide, an essential sphingolipid component of myelin and cell membranes. The incidence is 1:40,000 with three age ranges at presentation: early childhood (50–60%), juvenile (20–30%), and adult (15–20%). The early infantile form, which is most common, begins before 30 months of age with abdominal pain, progressive gait disorder, and instability. This progresses to loss of walking and sitting ability, global regression, cognitive compromise, and epileptic seizures. In the early stages, deep tendon reflexes are difficult to evoke due to the peripheral neuropathy. Later manifestations include hypertonia, spasticity and hyperreflexia, optic atrophy, nystagmus, language regression with dysarthria and aphasia. Rigidity with opisthotonus, arm flexion, and leg stiffness with club feet are common in the later stages. In almost all cases, there is hyperproteinorrachia in CSF. Neuroimaging features are characteristic of posterior white matter predominance in the early stages, progressing to anterior and diffuse involvement. Diagnosis is confirmed by demonstration of metachromatic material in urine, measurement of ARSA in fibroblasts, and genetic mutation in the *ARSA* gene. Genetic counseling and prenatal diagnosis are important, as no curative treatment is yet widely available. Bone marrow or umbilical cord blood transplantation and gene therapy with lentiviral hematopoietic stem cells are therapeutic options.

CLINICAL RED FLAGS

- Young children who experience progressive gait disorder with hypotonia, weakness, motor clumsiness, spasticity, ataxia, and pyramidal signs.
- Demyelinating peripheral neuropathy with reduced motor and sensory nerve conduction velocities.
- Hyperproteinorrachia in CSF.
- Decreased ARSA enzymatic activity in fibroblasts and mutation in the *ARSA* gene.

IMAGING RED FLAGS

- Centrifugal involvement from periventricular white matter toward cortex.
- Perivascular sparing in a "tigroid" pattern.
- Initial involvement of the splenium.
- No enhancement in the affected areas.

CONCLUSIONS

Late infantile MLD is a neurodegenerative leukodystrophy that usually presents before 30 months of age. Presenting findings include weakness, hypotonia, clumsiness, frequent falls, toe walking, and dysarthria. As the disease progresses, language, cognitive, and gross and

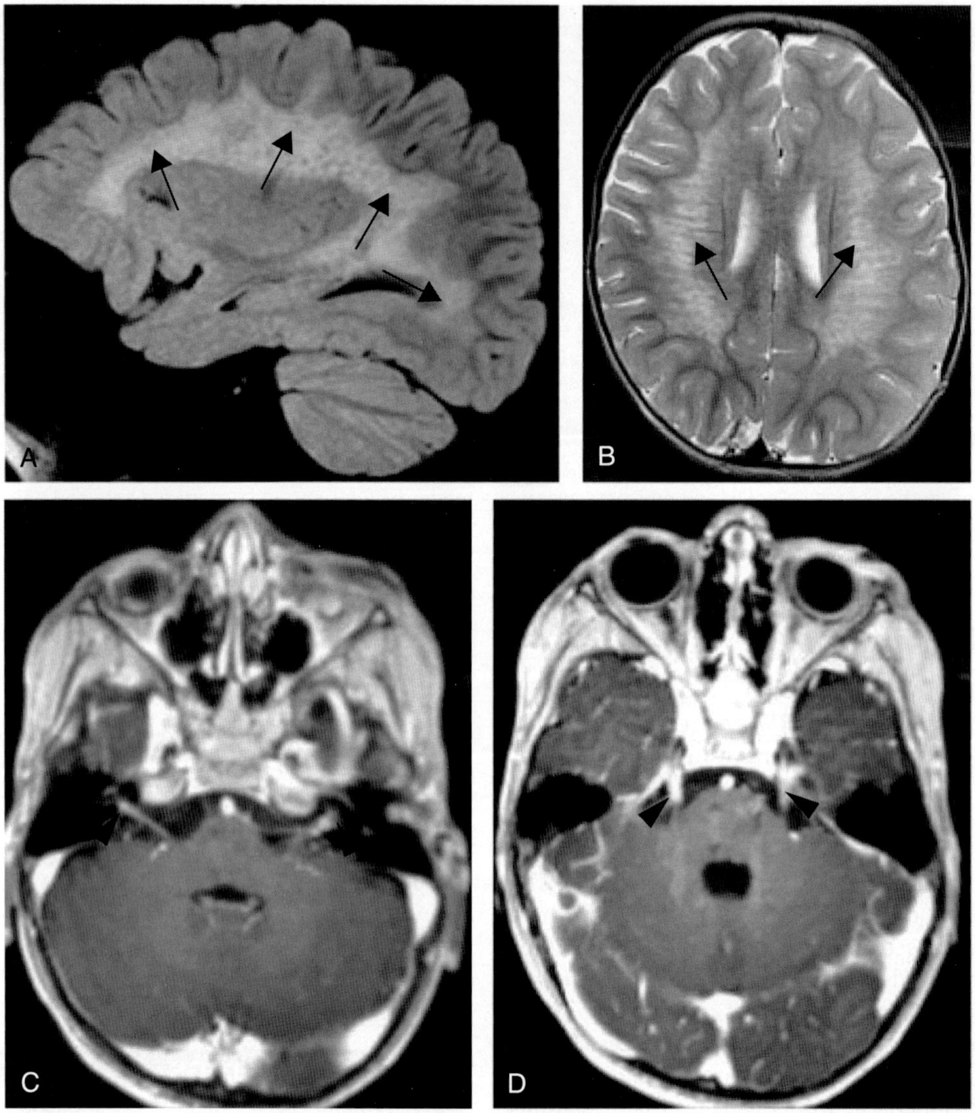

Fig. 30.2 Metachromatic leukodystrophy. Brain MRI, (A) sagittal FLAIR, (B) axial T2, (C and D) axial T1 with contrast show diffuse T2/FLAIR white matter hyperintensity with sparing of the perivascular regions (*arrows*) creating a "tigroid" pattern. The cranial nerves are diffusely enlarged and enhancing (*arrowheads*). *FLAIR*, Fluid-attenuated inversion recovery.

fine motor skills deteriorate. Later signs include spasticity, pain, seizures, and vision and hearing problems. In the final stages, children develop tonic spasms, decerebrate posturing, and progressive deterioration. Neuroimaging findings are suggestive, and enzymatic and genetic testing are confirmatory. Genetic counseling and assessment of therapeutic options are key in the early stages of disease.

REFERENCES

Cesani M, Lorioli L, Grossi S, et al. Mutation update of ARSA and PSAP genes causing metachromatic leukodystrophy. *Hum Mutat*. 2016;37(1):16–27. https://doi.org/10.1002/humu.22919.

Fumagalli F, Zambon AA, Rancoita PMV, et al. Metachromatic leukodystrophy: a single-center longitudinal study of 45 patients. *J Inherit Metab Dis*. 2021;44(5):1151–1164. https://doi.org/10.1002/jimd.12388.

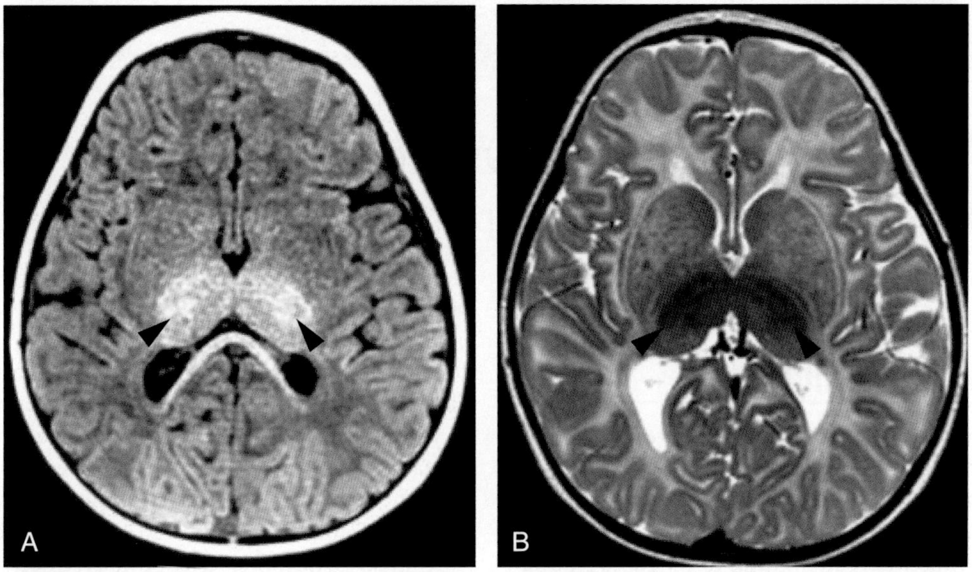

Fig. 30.3 GM1 gangliosidosis. Brain MRI, (A) axial T1 and (B) T2 show diffuse white matter dysmyelination with bilateral thalamic signal changes, which appear as T1 hyperintense and T2 hypointense (*arrowheads*). The basal ganglia also show heterogeneous signal.

Rosenberg JB, Kaminsky SM, Aubourg P, Crystal RG, Sondhi D. Gene therapy for metachromatic leukodystrophy. *J Neurosci Res*. 2016;94(11):1169–1179. https://doi.org/10.1002/jnr.23792.

van der Knaap MS, Bugiani M. Leukodystrophies: a proposed classification system based on pathological changes and pathogenetic mechanisms. *Acta Neuropathol*. 2017;134(3): 351–382. https://doi.org/10.1007/s00401-017-1739-1.

van Rappard DF, Boelens JJ, van Egmond ME, et al. Efficacy of hematopoietic cell transplantation in metachromatic leukodystrophy: the Dutch experience. *Blood*. 2016;127(24): 3098–4101. https://doi.org/10.1182/blood-2016-03-708479.

van Rappard DF, Boelens JJ, Wolf NI. Metachromatic leukodystrophy: disease spectrum and approaches for treatment. *Best Pract Res Clin Endocrinol Metab*. 2015;29(2):261–373. https://doi.org/10.1016/j.beem.2014.10.001.

Waldman AT. Leukodystrophies. *Continuum (Minneap Minn)*. 2018;24(1):130–149. Child Neurology. https://doi.org/10.1212/CON.0000000000000560.

Case 31

Child With Nystagmus, Dystonia, and Developmental Failure

HISTORY AND PHYSICAL

A male patient with no family history presented with psychomotor retardation from the first months of life with slow acquisition of milestones, marked axial hypotonia, and horizontal rotatory nystagmus associated with head tremor when attempting to fix gaze. He was initially diagnosed with infantile cerebral palsy and started on rehabilitation.

DIAGNOSTIC WORKUP

Basic laboratory tests and ophthalmological examination were normal. Metabolic studies were normal. Peripheral nerve conduction studies, electroretinography, and CSF study were also normal. Visual, auditory, and somatosensory evoked potentials were abnormal, reflecting central involvement. Head CT showed hypoattenuation of the white matter. Brain MRI was highly abnormal, with a lack of normal age-appropriate myelination, resembling the appearance of a newborn brain (Fig. 31.1). On follow-up, progressive brain atrophy developed. Genetic studies were confirmatory.

CLINICAL DIFFERENTIAL DIAGNOSES

Other hypomyelinating diseases with similar clinical and radiological characteristics are known as Pelizaeus-Merzbacher-like disease. These express autosomal recessive inheritance with other mutations such as *GJC2*, *AIMP1*, or *HSPD*. *GJC2* / *GJA12* (1q41-q42) encodes a protein (connexin 47) expressed in oligodendrocytes. Disease severity is less than in the X-linked form, with peripheral neuropathy and epilepsy and fewer cognitive deficits. In the classic form, brain MRI shows partial myelination of the corticospinal tracts. The connatal form is the most severe, with early onset and near-total absence of brain myelin that evolves to death in less than 2 years. Milder atypical forms associated with *SPG2* mutations present with spastic paraplegia.

Other genetic leukodystrophies include Krabbe disease, Canavan disease, MLD, Alexander disease, Cockayne syndrome, trichothiodystrophy with photosensitivity or Tay syndrome, hypomyelination with atrophy of the basal ganglia and cerebellum, or hypomyelination with congenital cataracts. Clinical onset can be insidious and progression so slow that some patients are misdiagnosed as having cerebral palsy.

Other metabolic pathologies include Leigh, Leber, and Zellweger disease, Sjögren-Larson syndrome, multiple sclerosis, congenital muscular dystrophy, and rhizomelic chondrodysplasia punctata.

IMAGING DIFFERENTIAL DIAGNOSIS

Some forms of trichothiodystrophy: MRI patterns can be very similar, although in trichothiodystrophy there are coarse calcium deposits seen by CT or MRI with susceptibility-weighted imaging (SWI).

Salla disease: Severe myelin deficiency and reduction of white matter volume. MRS can show sialic acid, which co-resonates with N-acetylaspartate at 2.02 ppm.

4H leukodystrophy: Hypomyelination along with hypogonadotropic hypogonadism and hypodontia.

Other hypomyelinating disorders: Look for additional clinical findings to narrow the diagnosis, then perform genetic testing for confirmation (Fig. 31.2).

FINAL DIAGNOSIS

Pelizaeus-Merzbacher disease due to *PLP* mutation.

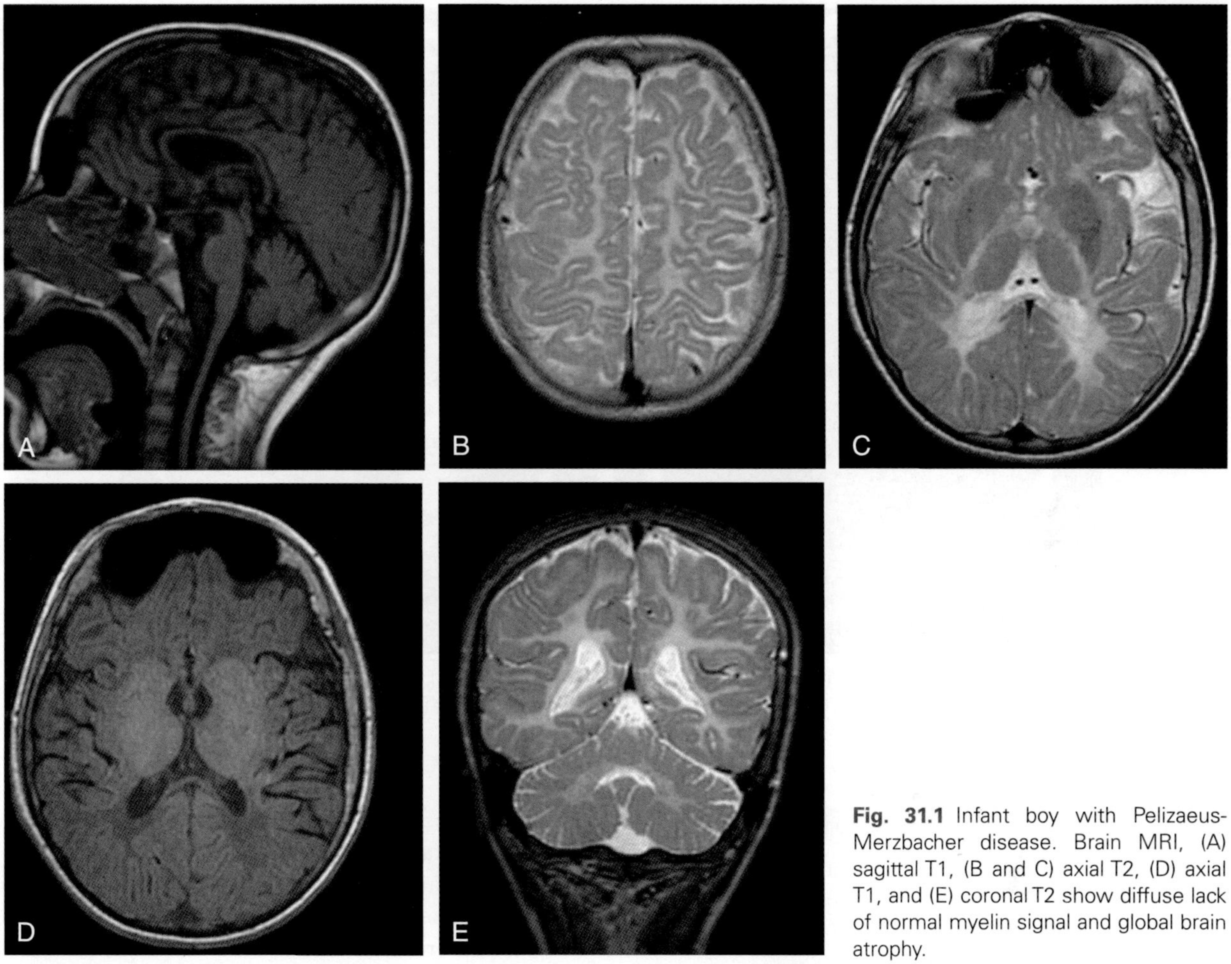

Fig. 31.1 Infant boy with Pelizaeus-Merzbacher disease. Brain MRI, (A) sagittal T1, (B and C) axial T2, (D) axial T1, and (E) coronal T2 show diffuse lack of normal myelin signal and global brain atrophy.

DISCUSSION

Classical Pelizaeus-Merzbacher disease is suspected in a male patient with delayed motor development in the first months of life, ophthalmologic signs (nystagmus, which can disappear after 2–3 years), and neurologic manifestations (hypotonia, choreoathetosis, ataxia, spasticity). Most patients show stabilization or even slight improvement up to 10 to 12 years. This is followed by slow regression with dystonia, increased ataxia and spasticity, and optic atrophy. Visual, auditory, and somatosensory evoked potentials are abnormal reflecting central nervous system involvement, while peripheral nerve conduction and CSF studies are normal. Head CT can show mild hypoattenuation and atrophy of the white matter. Brain MRI demonstrates a near-complete absence of myelination, with diffusely hyperintense T2 and hypointense T1 signal. MRS can show a corresponding reduction of NAA and elevation of choline. Neuropathology demonstrates structurally abnormal myelin with swelling and involution. There is axonal degeneration with relative preservation of oligodendrocytes. Molecular testing (*PLP, SPG2*) is confirmatory. Only symptomatic treatments are currently available, though research is being done into stem cell transplantation and gene therapy.

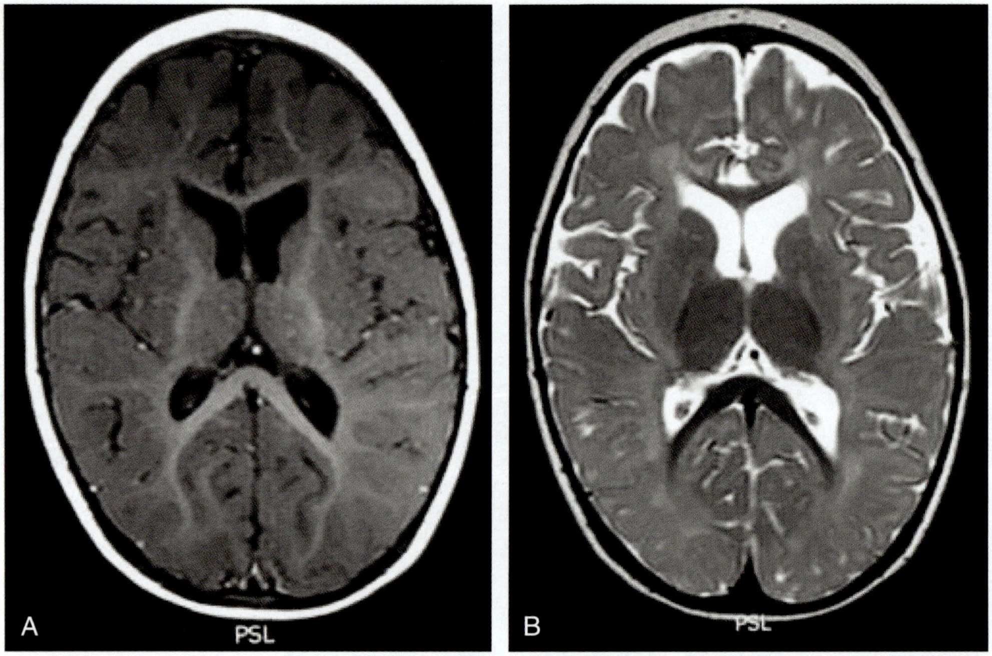

Fig. 31.2 Infant with *MCT8* mutation causing hypothyroidism. Brain MRI, (A) axial T1 and (B) axial T2, show heterogeneous and delayed myelination. *MCT8*, Monocarboxylate transporter 8.

CLINICAL RED FLAGS

- Child with delayed motor development in the first months of life, with ophthalmological signs (rotatory nystagmus) and neurological manifestations (hypotonia, choreoathetosis, ataxia, spasticity).
- Brainstem auditory evoked potentials (BAEP) with absence of II to V waves.
- Genetic testing confirms the diagnosis.

IMAGING RED FLAGS

- Newborn appearance of the brain at older ages.
- Diffuse and persistent hypomyelination.
- No cystic degeneration or destruction.

CONCLUSIONS

Classic Pelizaeus-Merzbacher disease is an X-linked recessive hypomyelinating leukodystrophy in which myelin does not form properly in the central nervous system, due to deletions or mutations in the gene for the proteolipid protein PLP1 (Xq22). Atypical cases (Pelizaeus-Merzbacher-like) have different mutations that can show autosomal dominant inheritance, affect females, and arise later in life with less severe symptoms. Diagnosis is based on clinical presentation, brain MRI findings, and confirmatory molecular testing including sequencing of the *PLP1* gene.

REFERENCES

Grossi S, Regis S, Biancheri R, et al. Molecular genetic analysis of the PLP1 gene in 38 families with PLP1-related disorders: identification and functional characterization of 11 novel PLP1 mutations. *Orphanet J Rare Dis.* 2011;6:40. https://doi.org/10.1186/1750-1172-6-40.

Hobson GM, Garbern JY. Pelizaeus-Merzbacher disease, Pelizaeus-Merzbacher-like disease 1, and related hypomyelinating disorders. *Semin Neurol.* 2012;32(1):62–67. https://doi.org/10.1055/s-0032-1306388.

Osorio MJ, Rowitch DH, Tesar P, Wernig M, Windrem MS, Goldman SA. Concise review: stem cell-based treatment of Pelizaeus-Merzbacher disease. *Stem Cells.* 2017;35(2):311–315. https://doi.org/10.1002/stem.2530.

Sarret C, Lemaire JJ, Tonduti D, et al. Time-course of myelination and atrophy on cerebral imaging in 35 patients with PLP1-related disorders. *Dev Med Child Neurol.* 2016;58(7):706–713. https://doi.org/10.1111/dmcn.13025.

Steenweg ME, Vanderver A, Blaser S, et al. Magnetic resonance imaging pattern recognition in hypomyelinating disorders. *Brain.* 2010;133(10):2971–2982. https://doi.org/10.1093/brain/awq257 Erratum in: *Brain.* 2013; 136(Pt 9):2923.

Wolf NI, Ffrench-Constant C, van der Knaap MS. Hypomyelinating leukodystrophies: unravelling myelin biology. *Nat Rev Neurol.* 2021;17(2):88–103. https://doi.org/10.1038/s41582-020-00432-1.

Case 32

Infant With Brittle Hair, Seizures, and Neurological Deterioration

HISTORY AND PHYSICAL

A male infant with no prior history developed generalized tonic-clonic seizures with multifocal EEG changes at 2 months of life. He also demonstrated feeding difficulties with poor weight gain. Physical examination revealed global developmental delay with axial hypotonia. He started treatment with sodium valproate and oxcarbazepine. One month later, he had persistent epileptic seizures and low weight/height for his age with microcephaly. There was notable axial hypotonia with delayed motor milestones. In addition, he had unusual hair in both temporal regions with a poor, brittle, silvery appearance that fell out easily. On microscopy, the hair showed findings of pili torti and trichorexis nodosa. Blood work showed very low values of copper at 34 ug/L (normal 620–1544) and ceruloplasmin at 35 mg/L (normal 200–470). Brain MRI and genetic testing were ordered.

DIAGNOSTIC WORKUP

Skeletal survey showed widened metaphyses with osteoporosis and multiple fractures (Fig. 32.1).

Brain MRI showed abnormal myelination and white matter lesions with involvement of the neostriatum. There was tortuosity and elongation of major cerebral arteries (Fig. 32.2).

CLINICAL DIFFERENTIAL DIAGNOSIS

Early brain injury
Epileptic or developmental encephalopathies
Gray matter neurodegenerative diseases such as neuronal ceroid lipofuscinosis
Mitochondrial disorders such as Alpers disease

IMAGING DIFFERENTIAL DIAGNOSIS

Abusive head trauma: Can present with subdural hematohygromas and other injuries of the central nervous and skeletal systems. Evaluate for mechanical injuries (Fig. 32.3).

Glutaric aciduria type 1: Bilateral abnormalities of the deep gray nuclei, progressing from edema to atrophy. The Sylvian fissures are underopercularized with shallow morphology and prominent CSF spaces. This increases the risk of cortical vein rupture with minor trauma, resulting in subdural hemorrhages (Fig. 32.4).

FINAL DIAGNOSIS

Menkes disease due to *ATP7A* gene mutation.

DISCUSSION

Menkes disease, also known as kinky hair disease, is an X-linked recessive disease reported in 1 per 75,000 births. It is caused by mutations of the *ATP7A* gene (Xq13.3), which encodes a copper-transporting ATPase. Disordered copper metabolism with deficient transport to cell organelles results in degeneration of gray matter and cerebellum with neuronal loss and gliosis, as well as tortuous and dysplastic arteries. Secondary deficiency of several copper-dependent enzymes, including cytochrome c oxidase and lysine oxidase, yields bone and connective tissue abnormalities. Concentrations of copper and ceruloplasmin are very low in plasma, liver, and brain and elevated in intestinal mucosa and kidneys due to failed absorption. Skin fibroblasts demonstrate increased copper sensitivity and copper-binding proteins.

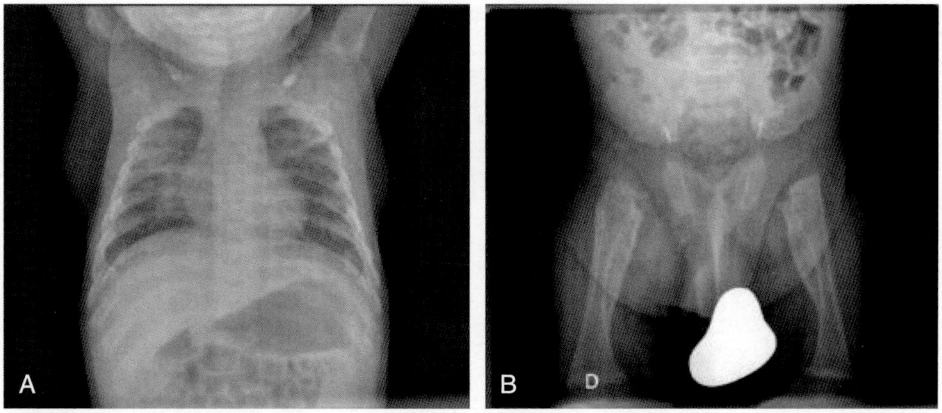

Fig. 32.1 Menkes disease. (A and B) Skeletal survey shows broad ribs and metaphyseal spurs.

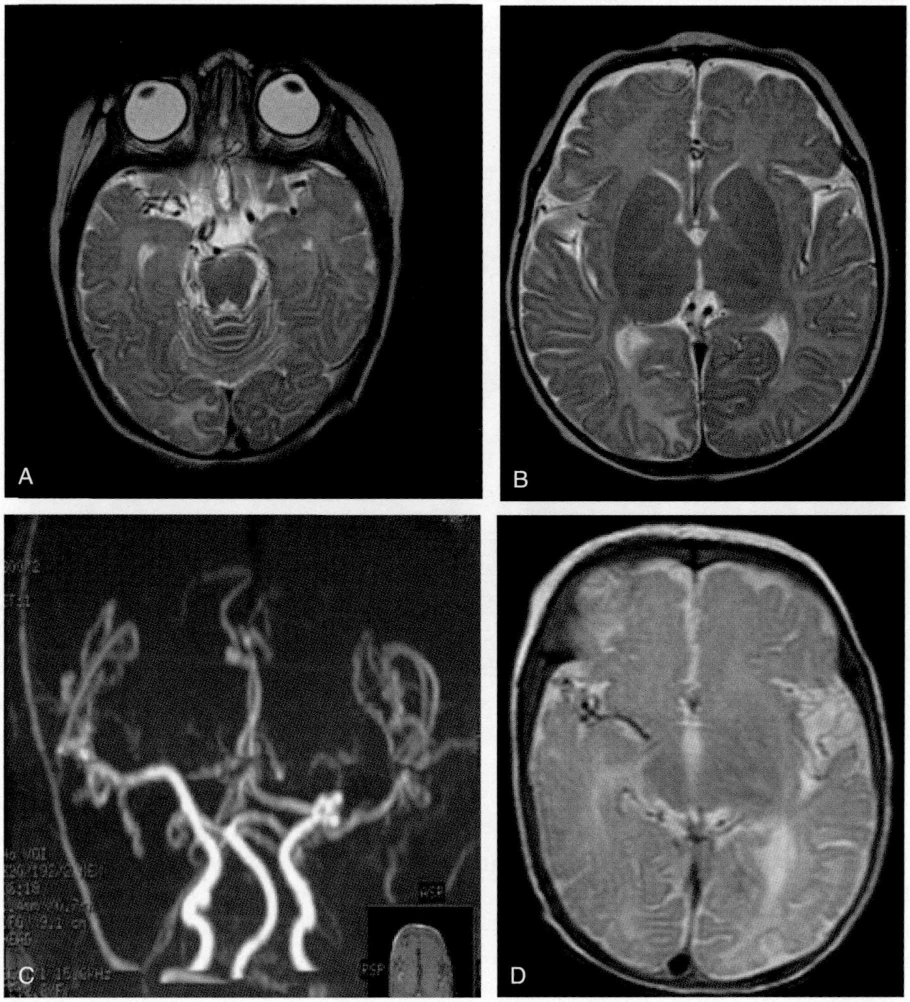

Fig. 32.2 Menkes disease. Brain MRI, (A and B) axial T2, (C) MRA at 6 months, and (D) axial T2 at 18 months show delayed myelination, tortuous cerebral arteries, and wide Sylvian fissures.

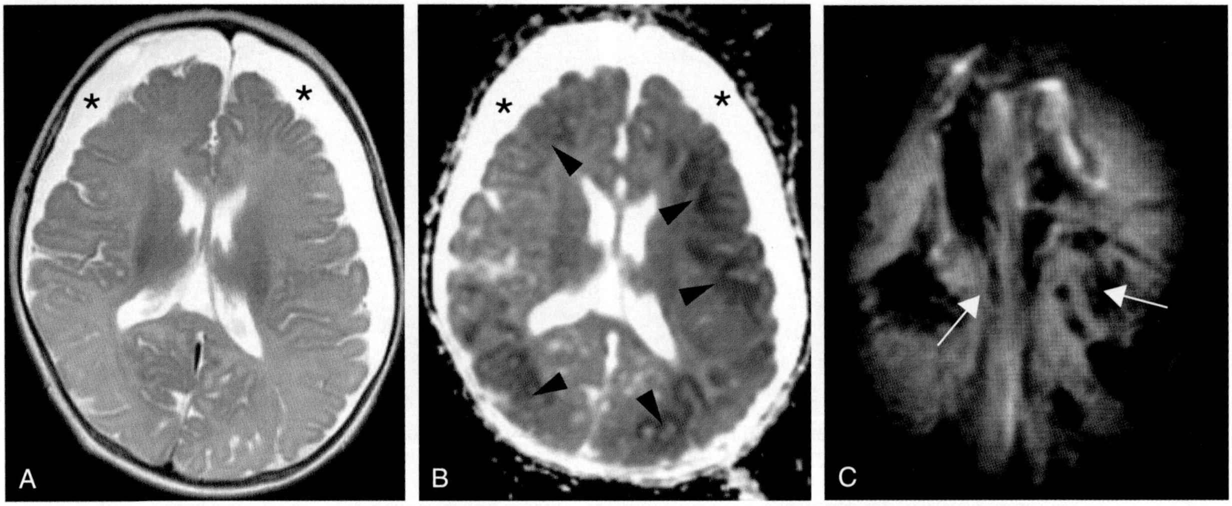

Fig. 32.3 Abusive head trauma. Brain MRI, (A) axial T2 and (B) ADC show bilateral subdural fluid collections (*asterisks*) with cortical restricted diffusion (*arrowheads*) indicating hypoxic-ischemic injury. (C) Axial SWI shows irregular and thrombosed cortical and bridging veins ("lollipop" and "tadpole" signs) (*arrows*).

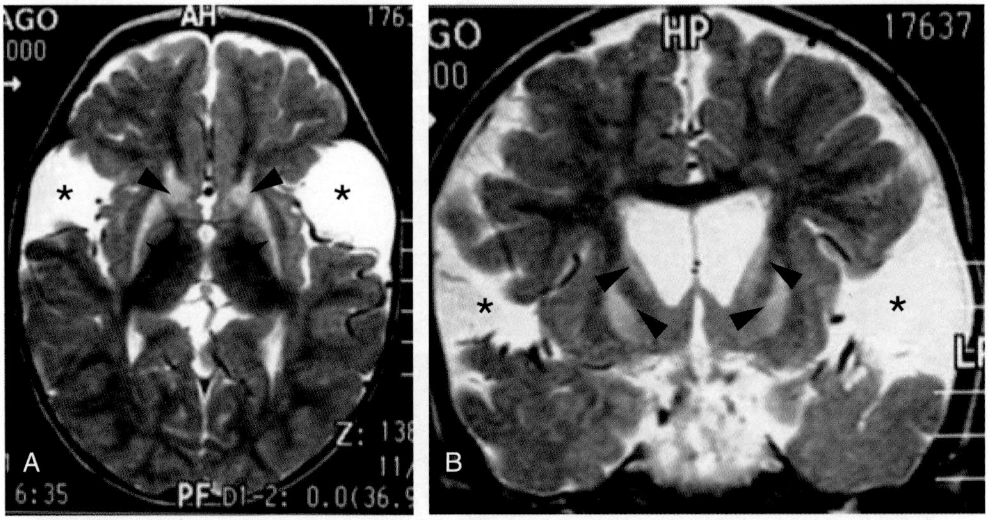

Fig. 32.4 Glutaric aciduria type 1. Brain MRI, (A) axial and (B) coronal T2 show underopercularization with gaping Sylvian fissures (*asterisks*) and atrophic hyperintense striatal nuclei (*arrowheads*).

Phenotypes can be very diverse even with identical mutations. Clinical manifestations may present in the neonatal or early infantile period, with slowed neurological and weight/height development, followed by seizures and even refractory spasms. Progressive neurological impairment develops with hypotonia and hypothermia. Facies are cherubic with sparse hair that turns brittle gray or silver and microscopically reveal pili torti, trichorexis nodosa, and moniletrix.

Skeletal survey shows osteoporosis and striking cortical hyperostosis with diaphyseal periosteal reaction and wormian bones in the cranial vault. Neuroimaging shows diffuse brain atrophy, defective myelination, and subdural hygromas and/or hematomas. Genetic testing for *ATP7A* mutations is confirmatory. The type and severity of the pathogenic variant determine the response to copper histidinate treatment. Without treatment, the disease is rapidly progressive with death in the first years of life.

CLINICAL RED FLAGS

- Clinical manifestations in the neonatal or early infantile period with stagnation of weight, height, and neurological development.
- Rapidly progressive neurological impairment with refractory epilepsy, hypotonia, hypothermia, and sparse hair turning brittle gray or silver.
- Low concentrations of copper and ceruloplasmin in plasma.
- Genetic testing is confirmatory.

IMAGING RED FLAGS

- Progressive brain atrophy.
- Defective myelination.
- Subdural hygromas and/or hematomas.
- Tortuous and elongated cerebral arteries.
- Skeletal survey: wormian bones, widened metaphyses, cortical hyperostosis.

CONCLUSIONS

Menkes disease is an X-linked recessive disease caused by mutations in the *ATP7A* gene, affecting copper metabolism. It is characterized by poor, sparse, and kinky hair, growth retardation, and progressive brain deterioration with refractory epilepsy. Children with Menkes syndrome usually experience symptoms in the first months of life. Early treatment with copper histidinate may slightly extend life expectancy and prevent further neurological damage.

REFERENCES

Gandhi R, Kakkar R, Rajan S, Bhangale R, Desai S. Menkes kinky hair syndrome: a rare neurodegenerative disease. *Case Rep Radiol.* 2012;2012:684309. https://doi.org/10.1155/2012/684309.

HomN Tümer Z. Menkes disease and the Occipital Horn syndrome. In: Royce P, Steinmann B, eds. *Connective Tissue and Its Heritable Disorders.* 2nd ed. Wiley-Liss; 2002:651–685.

Kaler SG, DiStasio AT. *ATP7A*-related copper transport disorders. [updated 2021 Apr 15]. In: Adam MP, Feldman J, Mirzaa GM et al, eds. *GeneReviews®*. Seattle: University of Washington; 2003:1993–2023.

Kodama H, Fujisawa C, Bhadhprasit W. Inherited copper transport disorders: biochemical mechanisms, diagnosis, and treatment. *Curr Drug Metab.* 2012;13(3):237–250. https://doi.org/10.2174/138920012799320455.

Prasad AN, Levin S, Rupar CA, Prasad C. Menkes disease and infantile epilepsy. *Brain Dev.* 2011;33(10):866–876. https://doi.org/10.1016/j.braindev.2011.08.002.

Zlatic S, Comstra HS, Gokhale A, Petris MJ, Faundez V. Molecular basis of neurodegeneration and neurodevelopmental defects in Menkes disease. *Neurobiol Dis.* 2015;81:154–161. https://doi.org/10.1016/j.nbd.2014.12.024.

SECTION 7

Neurometabolic Disorders

Daniel J. Pomerantz, Lance H. Rodan, Gerard T. Berry

Neurological manifestations are common in inborn errors of metabolism (IEM). Inborn errors of metabolism can be broadly classified into four major categories, including (1) disorders of intermediary metabolism (e.g., organic acidurias, urea cycle disorders); (2) large molecule disorders (e.g., lysosomal and peroxisomal disorders); (3) disorders of energy metabolism (e.g., primary mitochondrial disorders); and (4) miscellaneous disorders (e.g., purine/pyrimidine disorders, neurotransmitter disorders, disorders of heavy metal or vitamin metabolism).

Brain MRI pattern recognition is important in both the diagnosis and management of IEMs. There are several distinct patterns of abnormalities on brain MRI.

SYMMETRIC T2 HYPERINTENSITY AND/OR DIFFUSION RESTRICTION IN DEEP GRAY STRUCTURES

This pattern is commonly seen in primary mitochondrial disorders including Leigh disease (Fig. 7.1), pyruvate dehydrogenase deficiency, biotin-thiamine responsive basal ganglia disease, as well as organic acidurias such as glutaric aciduria type 1.

ABNORMAL CEREBRAL WHITE MATTER

Many IEMs affect the cerebral white matter. A number of lysosomal disorders are associated with chronically progressive white matter disease (leukodystrophy), including Krabbe disease and metachromatic leukodystrophy (Fig. 7.2).

The mucopolysaccharidoses often present with glycosaminolycan deposition distending the perivascular spaces with surrounding white matter gliosis.

Salla disease and fucosidosis may be associated with cerebral hypomyelination.

The peroxisomal disorders, X-linked adrenoleukodystrophy, and Zellweger spectrum may also have cerebral white matter involvement.

Glycine encephalopathy and maple syrup urine disease (MSUD) can both cause diffusion restriction of actively myelinating regions in the neonatal period.

Organic acidurias, such as propionic acidemia and Canavan disease, can also be associated with prominent white matter signal abnormalities.

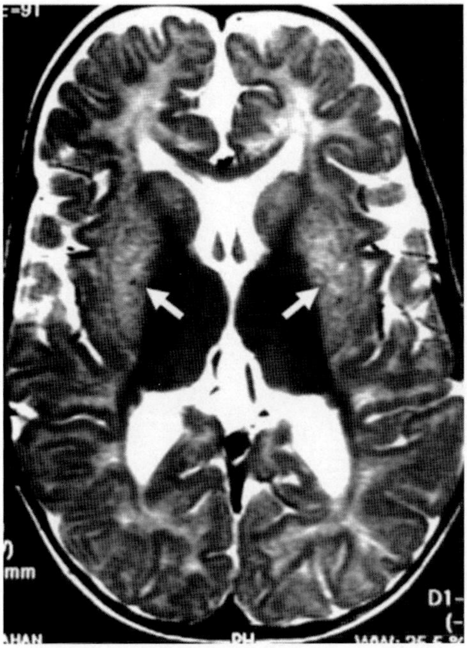

Fig. 7.1 Mitochondrial disease. Axial T2 shows bilateral and symmetric hyperintensities of the lentiform nuclei (*arrows*).

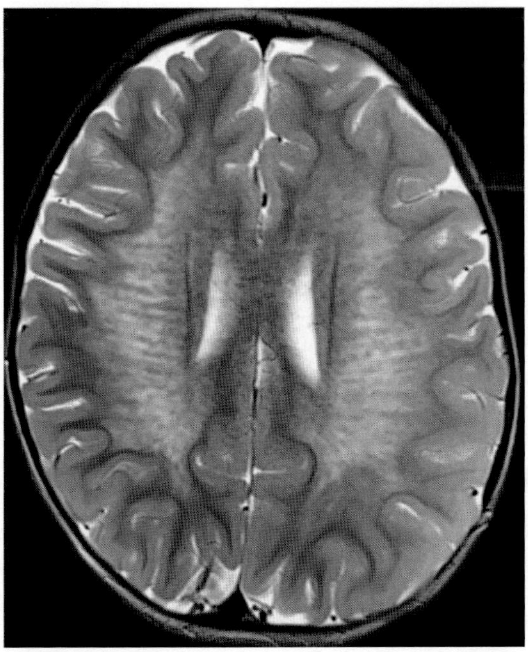

Fig. 7.2 Metachromatic leukodystrophy. Axial T2 shows diffuse white matter hyperintensity with perivascular sparing creating a "tigroid pattern."

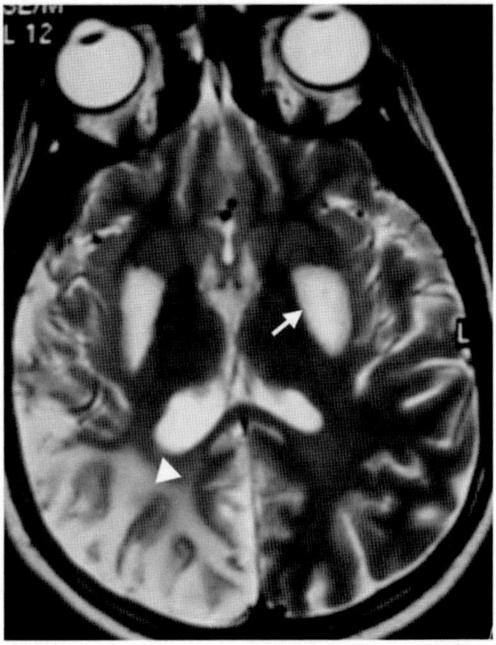

Fig. 7.3 MELAS. Axial T2 shows hyperintensity in the posterior putamina (*arrow*) and right temporo-occipital cortex and subcortical white matter (*arrowhead*). *MELAS*, Mitochondrial encephalopathy, lactic acidosis, and stroke-like episodes.

Mitochondrial disorders can have significant white matter involvement progressing to cavitation/cystic degeneration. This pattern is seen in Kearns-Sayre syndrome, mitochondrial neurogastrointestinal encephalopathy syndrome (MNGIE), and some complex 1 disorders.

STROKE OR STROKE-LIKE LESIONS

Acute or subacute stroke-like lesions affecting the cortex and subcortical white matter in nonvascular territories can be seen in mitochondrial disorders with mitochondrial encephalopathy, lactic acidosis, and stroke-like episodes (MELAS) phenotype (e.g., mt-tRNA disorders, Polymerase Gamma (POLG)-related disorders) (Fig. 7.3). Stroke-like episodes can be associated with vasculopathies and channelopathies in Menkes disease and congenital disorders of glycosylation. Decompensated urea cycle disorders can produce focal regions of cerebral injury and edema that can mimic a stroke. Secondary metabolic strokes can occur in the setting of acute energy decompensation, beginning with neuronal failure and edema and progressing to capillary occlusion.

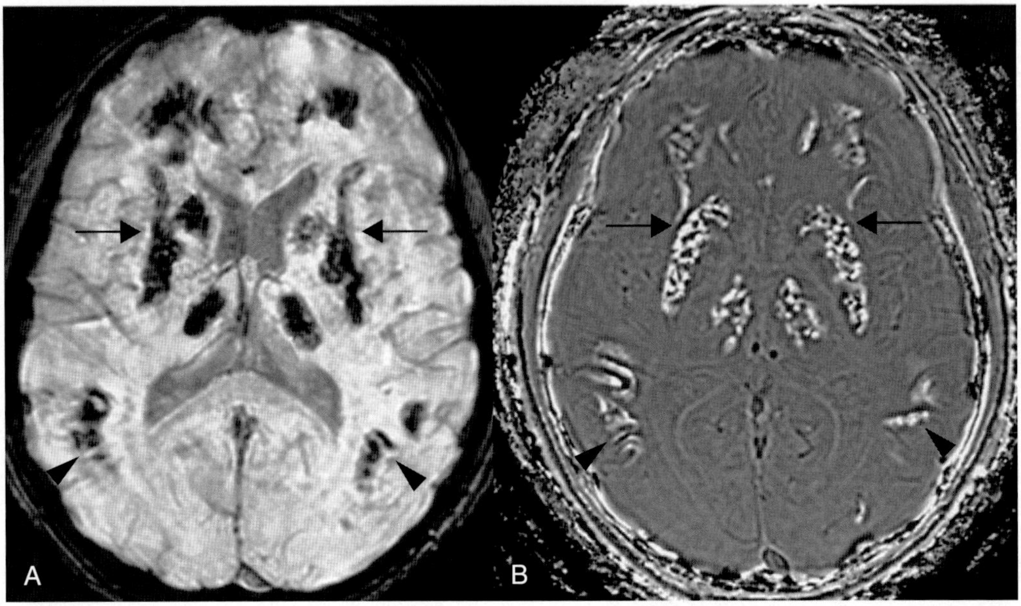

Fig. 7.4 Fahr disease. Axial SWI and phase map show coarse calcifications in the basal ganglia (*arrows*) and subcortical white matter (*arrowheads*). *SWI*, Susceptibility-weighted imaging.

Arterial ischemic stroke can be seen in homocystinurias, congenital disorders of glycosylation, cystinosis, and Fabry disease.

BRAIN MINERALIZATION

Iron accumulation in the deep gray nuclei can be seen in neurodegeneration with brain iron accumulation (NBIA) disorders.

Brain calcification can be seen in a variety of disorders, including Fahr syndrome (familial basal ganglia calcification) (Fig. 7.4), Cockayne syndrome, Aicardi-Goutières syndrome, mitochondrial disorders, carbonic anhydrase II deficiency, cerebral folate deficiency, and disorders of calcium homeostasis, among others.

Wilson disease is associated with the accumulation of copper within the brain; in addition to mineralization, there is typically T2 hyperintensity of the basal ganglia and brainstem. Menkes disease results from copper deficiency with friable vessels, subdural hematohygromas, and strokes.

Brain manganese disorders can occur due to defects in transporter genes, causing overload or deficiency with deep gray structures. Typically, there is increasing T1 hyperintensity with greater manganese content.

OTHER NEUROIMAGING PATTERNS

Brain malformations can be seen in pyruvate dehydrogenase deficiency, some mitochondrial disorders (e.g. fumarase deficiency), peroxisomal disorders, Smith-Lemli-Opitz syndrome, and severe forms of multiple acyl-CoA dehydrogenase deficiency and carnitine palmitoyltransferase 2 (CPT-II) deficiency. Glutaric aciduria type 1 is classically associated with widened Sylvian fissures.

Nonspecific global cerebral and/or cerebellar atrophy can be seen in several IEMs.

Many IEMs can show unremarkable brain imaging including most of the neurotransmitter disorders, *GLUT1* deficiency, purine/pyrimidine disorders, etc.

MR SPECTROSCOPY

MR spectroscopy (MRS) quantifies metabolites in a brain region of interest and may demonstrate characteristic peaks in certain IEMs, such as a glycine peak at 3.55 parts per million (ppm) in glycine encephalopathy and a branched-chain ketoacid peak at 0.9 ppm in MSUD. Mitochondrial and pyruvate disorders during acute energy crisis can produce an abnormal lactate

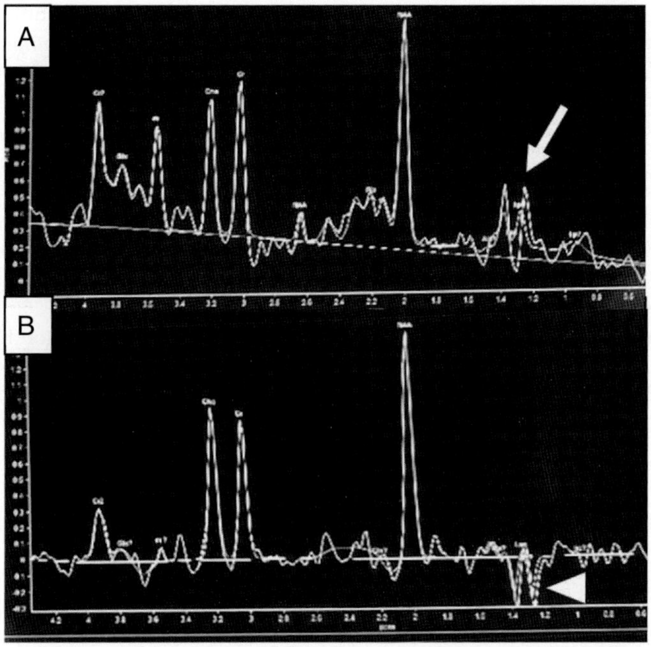

Fig. 7.5 Acute brain injury. Magnetic resonance spectroscopy (MRS) with echo time (TE) of (A) 30 ms and (B) TE 144 ms shows a small lactate doublet peak at 1.33 ppm that is above baseline at the short TE (*arrow*) and below baseline at medium TE (*arrowhead*) due to J-coupling of the methyl group.

peak at 1.3 ppm. The lactate doublet lies above baseline in short and long-echo MRS, and below the baseline in intermediate-echo MRS, due to J-coupling of the methyl group (Fig. 7.5). A reduced creatine peak can suggest an inborn error of creatine metabolism or biosynthesis. Finally, an increased N-acetylaspartate (NAA) peak can be seen in Canavan disease due to lack of conversion by aspartoacylase.

SUGGESTED READINGS

Ferreira CR, van Karnebeek CDM. Inborn errors of metabolism. *Handbook of Clinical Neurology*. 2019:449–481. doi:10.1016/b978-0-444-64029-1.00022-9 Published online.

Gonçalves FG, Alves CA, Heuer B, et al. Primary mitochondrial disorders of the pediatric central nervous system: neuroimaging findings. *RadioGraphics*. 2020;40(7):2042–2067. doi:10.1148/rg.2020200052.

Gropman AL, Anderson A. Novel imaging technologies for genetic diagnoses in the inborn errors of metabolism. *Journal of Translational Genetics and Genomics*. 2020:429–445. doi:10.20517/jtgg.2020.09 Published online.

Liserre R, Pinelli L, Gasparotti R. MR spectroscopy in pediatric neuroradiology. *Translational Pediatrics*. 2021;10(4):1169–1200. doi:10.21037/tp-20-445.

Ortigoza-Escobar JD. A proposed diagnostic algorithm for inborn errors of metabolism presenting with movements disorders. *Frontiers in Neurology*. 2020;11. doi:10.3389/fneur.2020.582160.

Poretti A, Blaser SI, Lequin MH, et al. Neonatal neuroimaging findings in inborn errors of metabolism. *Journal of Magnetic Resonance Imaging*. 2012;37(2):294–312. doi:10.1002/jmri.23693.

Reddy N, Calloni SF, Vernon HJ, Boltshauser E, Huisman TA, Soares BP. Neuroimaging findings of organic acidemias and aminoacidopathies. *RadioGraphics*. 2018;38(3):912–931. doi:10.1148/rg.2018170042.

Widened Sylvian Fissures and Basal Ganglia

HISTORY AND PHYSICAL

A 12-month-old male patient of Yemeni descent presented to the emergency room after 48 hours of fever, poor oral intake, and impaired movements. He was reportedly in his normal state of health until 2 days earlier, when he developed a fever, cough, and rhinorrhea. Six hours prior to presentation, he was noted to appear increasingly more lethargic and refused to bear weight or reach for things. His parents said that he "felt really stiff" and seemed "really tired despite waking up from his nap."

History was notable as follows: The child was born in Yemen to consanguineous parents and did not receive newborn screening. The parents reported he was born at full term and was noted to have a "large head" without a history of neurodevelopmental delays. He was noted to avoid eating meat despite the rest of his family doing so. There was a reported family history of multiple cousins dying of "meningitis" in early infancy. His parents had recently been battling upper respiratory infections as well. He was up to date on vaccinations. He was not on any medications and had no prior medical history or known allergies. On general examination, he was febrile, appeared mildly dehydrated, and was grossly macrocephalic. He had a reduced level of consciousness and was minimally responsive to pain with IV insertion. He was observed to have spontaneous dystonic posturing of his arms and legs. Plantar response was upgoing bilaterally. Initial viral screen in the emergency room was positive for influenza B despite a reported history of influenza vaccination.

DIAGNOSTIC WORKUP

Brain MRI demonstrated widening of Sylvian fissures and symmetrical T2 hyperintensity of the basal ganglia (Fig. 33.1). Blood, urine, and CSF cultures were negative for bacteria. White blood count, including neutrophil count and lymphocyte count, was appropriately elevated. Biochemical testing demonstrated elevated glutaric acid and 3-hydroxyglutaric acid on urine organic acids. Confirmatory genetic testing demonstrated a homozygous pathogenic variant in the *GCDH* gene.

CLINICAL DIFFERENTIAL DIAGNOSES

The history of acute encephalopathy in an infant raises concern for infection (e.g., encephalitis, meningitis, sepsis), toxic ingestion, possible nonaccidental injury, and inborn errors of metabolism (IEMs).

IMAGING DIFFERENTIAL DIAGNOSES

In terms of IEMs, bilateral basal ganglia T2 hyperintensity raises the possibility of a primary mitochondrial disorder, pyruvate dehydrogenase complex deficiency, biotin-thiamine-responsive basal ganglia disease, and organic acidurias.

Widened Sylvian fissures are a common finding in glutaric aciduria type 1 but can be seen to a lesser extent in benign enlargement of the extra-axial spaces (BESS) and other genetic disorders.

FINAL DIAGNOSIS

Glutaric aciduria type 1.

DISCUSSION

Glutaric aciduria type 1 (GA-1) is an autosomal recessive cerebral organic aciduria that results from dysfunction of the glutaryl-CoA dehydrogenase enzyme. This disorder is associated with the accumulation of abnormal metabolites, glutaric acid, and 3-hydroxyglutaric acid, which are derived from oxidation of lysine, tryptophan, and hydroxylysine.

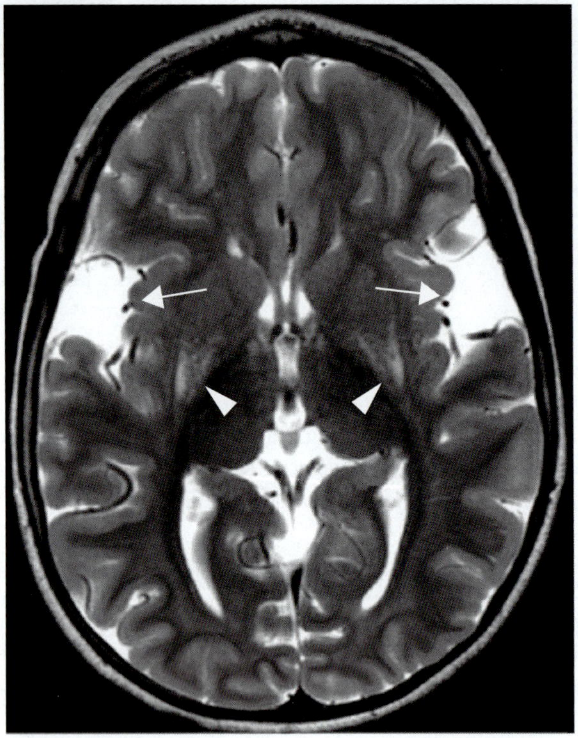

Fig. 33.1 Glutaric aciduria type 1. Brain MRI, axial T2 shows widened, square-shaped Sylvian fissures (*arrows*) with bilateral hyperintensity and volume loss of posterior putamina and globi pallidi (*arrowheads*).

Glutaric aciduria type 1 classically presents between ages 6 months and 6 years with acute metabolic brain injury. The latter is often provoked by a febrile illness or other major stressor. Brain MRI often demonstrates enlarged Sylvian fissures, T2 hyperintensity and diffusion restriction of basal ganglia (classically striatum), and occasionally abnormal cerebral white matter and subdural hemorrhage.

Survivors of metabolic brain injury are typically left with severe spasticity and dystonia. Studies have shown that long-term neurological outcomes are best preserved by early identification and management. The current best practice for achieving these goals requires identifying patients in the presymptomatic period via newborn screening. Newborn screening focuses on screening for elevated glutarylcarnitine (C5DC) in the blood, followed by confirmatory testing with urine organic acids, plasma acylcarnitine profile, and GCDH gene testing. Presymptomatic patients are treated with a protein-restricted diet, particularly low in lysine and tryptophan; this is accomplished by supplementing with a metabolic formula that is low in tryptophan and lysine and enriched in arginine. Patients are also treated with levocarnitine to facilitate the excretion of toxic metabolites. Finally, during illnesses, intact protein is further restricted, calories are increased, and levocarnitine dosing is increased to mitigate the risk of metabolic brain injury.

CLINICAL RED FLAGS

- Acute encephalopathy, often provoked by illness
- Macrocephaly
- Subdural hemorrhage and concern for nonaccidental injury
- Dystonia and spasticity that can mimic cerebral palsy, but history not consistent with cerebral palsy
- Consanguinity (especially Amish and Yemini populations for GA-1)

IMAGING RED FLAGS

- Bilateral T2 hyperintensity ± diffusion restriction of basal ganglia (predominantly striatum)
- Enlarged Sylvian fissures
- White matter abnormalities and subdural hemorrhages

CONCLUSIONS

GA-1 is a cerebral organic aciduria that can present with acute metabolic brain injury between 6 months and 6 years of age. Most individuals are macrocephalic from birth. Imaging during a metabolic crisis may demonstrate symmetric T2 hyperintensity and diffusion restriction of the basal ganglia (predominantly striatum). Early presymptomatic identification and treatment are critical to ensure good long-term outcomes.

REFERENCES

Larson A, Goodman S. *Glutaric Acidemia Type 1 - GeneReviews® - NCBI bookshelf.* National Center for Biotechnology Information; 2019. https://www.ncbi.nlm.nih.gov/books/NBK546575/.

Panigrahy A, Nelson MD, Blüml S. Magnetic resonance spectroscopy in pediatric neuroradiology: clinical and research applications. *Pediatric Radiology*. 2010;40(1):3–30. doi:10.1007/s00247-009-1450-z.

Strauss KA, Williams KB, Carson VJ, et al. Glutaric acidemia type 1: treatment and outcome of 168 patients over three decades. *Molecular Genetics and Metabolism*. 2020;131(3):325–340. doi:10.1016/j.ymgme.2020.09.007.

Intramyelinic Edema in Infancy

HISTORY AND PHYSICAL

A 4-day-old, full-term male was born by vaginal delivery to a mother with no significant medical history. There were no complications during pregnancy or with delivery. The baby was discharged from the newborn nursery on day 2 of life. The patient had newborn screening performed at 25 hours of life and before discharge. After discharge, he fed well with no specific concerns. Starting on day 4 of life, his mother noted he was slowing with feeds and had been producing less urine. He also seemed more irritable, but not lethargic.

Newborn screening results were reported on day 4 of life and raised high concern for an inborn error of metabolism (IEM), prompting referral to the pediatric emergency room for further evaluation. In the emergency room, the patient was febrile and generally alert but with a weak cry; there was concern for dehydration. His limbs were hypertonic and his urine was noted to be cloudy.

DIAGNOSTIC WORKUP

Newborn screening from day 1 of life demonstrated elevated leucine at 574.74 uM and elevated valine at 438.15 uM, concerning for maple syrup urine disease (MSUD).

A full sepsis workup was initiated. Urine culture was positive for Enterococcus. Blood and CSF cultures were negative. The patient was also found to have an increased anion gap metabolic acidosis (anion gap 37, bicarbonate of 10). He had 4+ ketonuria. Serum beta-hydroxybutyrate was 4.98. Sodium was elevated to 152. He was hypoglycemic with a blood glucose of 33 mg/dl. The patient was started on IV ampicillin and gentamicin. Breastfeeds were immediately discontinued, and IV D12.5 + ½ normal saline at 1.5 X maintenance IV rate was initiated. A nasogastric tube was placed and Ketonex formula (deficient in branched-chain amino acids leucine, valine, and isoleucine) was initiated alongside valine and isoleucine supplementation. The patient was also started on IV thiamine supplementation.

Plasma amino acids at day 4 of life upon arrival to the hospital demonstrated dramatically elevated leucine to 2599 umol/L, with commensurate elevations in isoleucine and valine. Hemodialysis was initiated. Urine organic acids showed marked excretion of branched-chain ketoacids 2-ketoisocaproic, 2-keto-3-methylvaleric, 2-ketoisovaleric, and 2-hydroxyisovaleric acids. CSF amino acids also demonstrated marked elevations in branched-chain amino acids.

Brain MRI demonstrated T2 hyperintensity with diffusion restriction affecting actively myelinating structures (perirolandic white matter, posterior segments of internal capsules, corticospinal tracts, cerebellar white matter (Fig. 34.1A–E). Magnetic resonance spectroscopy showed branched-chain ketoacid peak at 0.9 ppm (Fig. 34.1F).

Confirmatory genetic testing revealed compound heterozygous pathogenic variants in the *BCKDHA* gene consistent with classical MSUD. The patient was ultimately taken off hemodialysis within 24 hours and stabilized on an appropriate diet restricted in branched-chain amino acids.

CLINICAL DIFFERENTIAL DIAGNOSES

Infection (e.g., meningitis, encephalitis, sepsis), dehydration, errors in making infant formula, and IEM.

IMAGING DIFFERENTIAL DIAGNOSES

Diffusion restriction of actively myelinating structures in a neonate can be seen in hypoxic-ischemic injury,

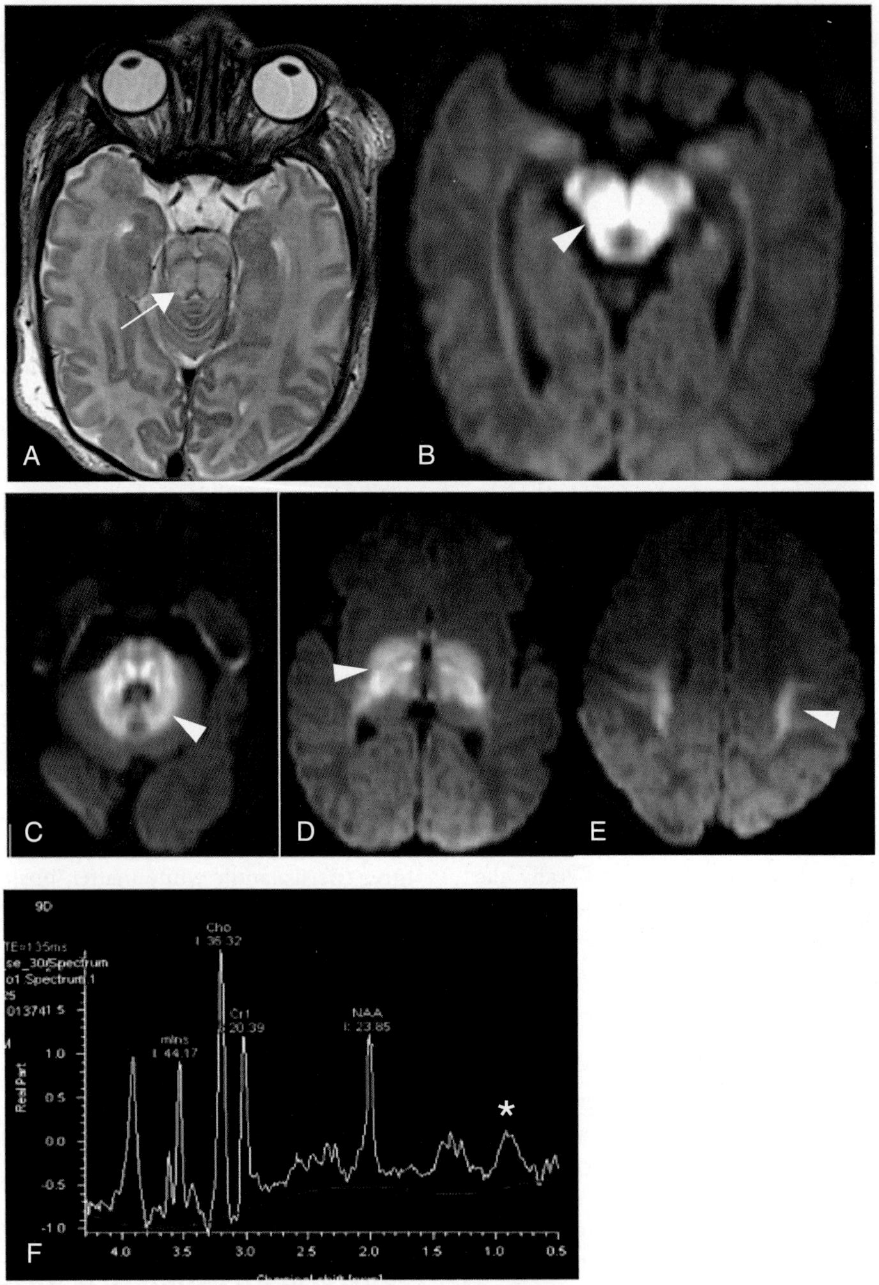

Fig. 34.1 Maple syrup urine disease. Brain MRI, (A) axial T2 demonstrates brainstem hyperintensity due to intramyelinic edema (*arrow*). (B–E) DWI shows diffusion restriction in bilateral corticospinal tracts, deep gray matter, brainstem, and cerebellum (*arrowheads*). (F) MRS shows branched-chain ketoacid peak at 0.9 ppm (*asterisk*). *DWI*, Diffusion-weighted imaging; *MRS*, magnetic resonance spectroscopy.

certain infections (e.g., parechovirus), infant formula preparation errors/hypernatremia, and IEMs including MSUD, glycine encephalopathy, decompensated urea cycle disorders.

FINAL DIAGNOSIS

Maple syrup urine disease.

DISCUSSION

Maple syrup urine disease results from dysfunction of the branched-chain amino acid dehydrogenase complex. It has an autosomal recessive inheritance and can result from biallelic mutations in one of several genes (*BCKDHA*, *BCKDHB*, *DBT*). Symptoms typically include acute encephalopathy in untreated individuals. Individuals may also develop acute dystonia during a crisis. Untreated, progressive, and fatal cerebral edema may develop. There may be a maple syrup odor to the skin, urine, and cerumen. Biochemically, the disorder is associated with elevations in branched-chain leucine, isoleucine, and valine on plasma amino acids. There is also a pathognomonic elevation of alloisoleucine. Urine organic acids demonstrate elevations in branched-chain ketoacids. During acute metabolic decompensation, ketoacidosis and hyponatremia (elevated leucine can provoke syndrome of inappropriate antidiuretic hormone secretion [SIADH]) may also develop.

Studies have shown that long-term outcomes are dependent on early identification and management. The current best practice for achieving these goals requires identifying patients in the presymptomatic period via newborn screening. Newborn screening focuses on screening for elevated leucine on dried blood spot. This should be followed by confirmatory testing with plasma amino acids, urine organic acids, and molecular genetic testing.

Presymptomatic patients are treated for life with a protein-restricted diet, particularly of branched-chain amino acids. This is accomplished by using a metabolic formula that is low in leucine, isoleucine, and valine and supplementing with small calculated amounts of valine and isoleucine. Some forms of MSUD are responsive to high dosing of thiamine supplementation, since thiamine is a cofactor for the branched-chain ketoacid dehydrogenase enzyme. During acute episodes, intact protein is further restricted and calories may be increased. With very severe or refractory decompensations, hemodialysis may be considered.

CLINICAL RED FLAGS

- Acute encephalopathy
- Acute dystonic posturing
- Maple syrup odor to urine and/or ear cerumen
- Consanguinity (especially Amish and Mennonite populations for MSUD)

IMAGING RED FLAGS

- Diffusion restriction of actively myelinating white matter tracts
- Diffuse cerebral and cerebellar edema
- Elevated MRS peak at 0.9 ppm, corresponding to branched-chain ketoacids

CONCLUSIONS

Maple syrup urine disease is an aminoacidopathy that can present with acute encephalopathy in untreated individuals at any age. There may be acute dystonia during a crisis, as well as a maple syrup odor to the skin, urine, and cerumen. During a metabolic crisis, there may be diffusion restriction and edema of white matter. MR spectroscopy may demonstrate a pathognomonic peak at 0.9 ppm. Early clinical diagnosis and treatment are critical for optimizing long-term outcomes.

REFERENCES

Jan W, Zimmerman RA, Wang ZJ, Berry GT, Kaplan PB, Kaye EM. MR diffusion imaging and MR spectroscopy of maple syrup urine disease during acute metabolic decompensation. *Neuroradiology*. 2003;45(6):393–399. doi:10.1007/s00234-003-0955-7.

Panigrahy A, Nelson MD, Blüml S. Magnetic resonance spectroscopy in pediatric neuroradiology: clinical and research applications. *Pediatric Radiology*. 2010;40(1):3–30. doi:10.1007/s00247-009-1450-z.

Saudubray J-M, García-Cazorla Á. Clinical approach to inborn errors of metabolism in paediatrics. In: Saudubray J-M, Baumgartner MR, García-Cazorla Á, Walter J, eds. *Inborn Metabolic Diseases: Diagnosis and Treatment*. 7th ed. Springer; 2022:3–123.

Strauss KA, Puffenberger EG, Carson VJ. *Maple syrup urine disease - GeneReviews® - NCBI bookshelf*. National Center for Biotechnology Information; 2006. https://www.ncbi.nlm.nih.gov/books/NBK1319/.

Case 35

Stroke-Like Episodes

HISTORY AND PHYSICAL

A 23-year-old female with a known history of mitochondrial encephalomyopathy, lactic acidosis, and stroke-like episodes (MELAS) presented with 1 day of fever, reduced oral intake, and acute left-sided hemiparesis of 1-hour duration.

DIAGNOSTIC WORKUP

Plasma lactic acid was elevated to 6.7 umol/L. Plasma bicarbonate was 9 with an anion gap of 20. Brain MRI demonstrated multiple T2-hyperintense lesions in the bilateral frontal and parietal cortex and subcortical white matter, greater on the right side and in a nonvascular distribution (Fig. 35.1).

CLINICAL DIFFERENTIAL DIAGNOSIS

The differential diagnoses for acute stroke in a child are broad and include cardiac etiologies (e.g., congenital heart disease, valvular disease, arrhythmias), vasculopathies (e.g., dissection, inflammatory disorders), and prothrombotic conditions.

Metabolic stroke-like episodes can be seen in MELAS and, rarely, in Menkes disease and congenital disorders of glycosylation.

Arterial ischemic (vascular) stroke can be seen in homocystinurias, congenital disorders of glycosylation, cystinosis, and Fabry disease.

IMAGING DIFFERENTIAL DIAGNOSIS

A focal cortical lesion could also be seen with infarction, infection, cortical dysplasia, and glioma.

In MELAS, lesions usually involve the cortex and subcortical white matter, particularly occipital and parietal lobes. Lesions involve nonvascular territories and can self-resolve or migrate over time. In the acute phase, there is a lactate peak on MRS and increased perfusion due to cerebral autoregulation in the setting of decreased mitochondrial oxygen extraction.

FINAL DIAGNOSIS

Mitochondrial encephalomyopathy, lactic acidosis, and stroke-like episodes.

DISCUSSION

MELAS is a specific phenotype seen in a number of distinct mitochondrial mutations affecting both mtDNA and nuclear DNA. The most common genetic etiology is the m.3243A>G variant in the mitochondrial *MT-TL1* gene. The nuclear gene *POLG* is another common etiology.

Most affected individuals develop clinical features of MELAS between the ages of 2 and 40 years with clinical manifestations including stroke-like episodes and variable acute and chronic encephalopathy, epilepsy, myopathy, lactic acidosis, fatigue, visual problems, hearing loss, short stature, cardiac conduction abnormalities, gastrointestinal (GI) dysfunction, and diabetes mellitus.

Neuroimaging classically demonstrates cerebral edema in a nonvascular distribution (Fig. 35.1) during acute "stroke-like" episodes. While management is largely supportive, an intravenous arginine bolus (500 mg/kg for children or 10 g/m^2 body surface area for adults) within 3 hours of symptom onset is recommended by some groups, followed by the administration of a similar dosage of intravenous arginine as a continuous infusion over 24 hours for the next 3 to 5 days. L-arginine may also be continued chronically,

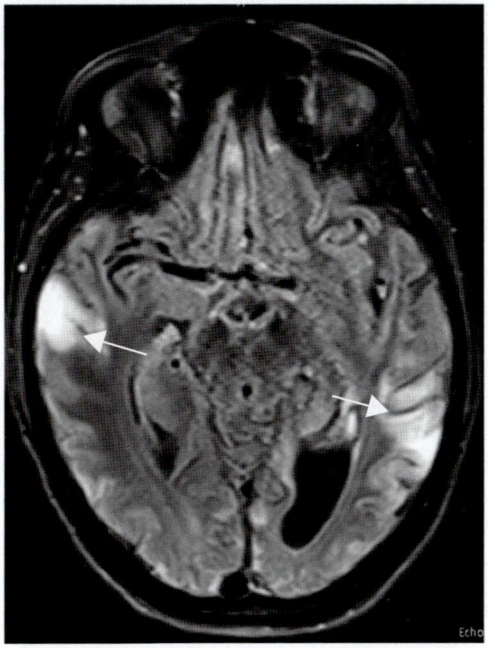

Fig. 35.1 MELAS. Brain MRI, axial FLAIR shows multifocal cortical and subcortical hyperintensities from stroke-like episodes (*arrows*). *FLAIR*, Fluid-attenuated inversion recovery; *MELAS*, mitochondrial encephalopathy, lactic acidosis, and stroke-like episodes.

possibly reducing the frequency and severity of further stroke-like events. Mitochondrial cofactors can also be supplemented.

CLINICAL RED FLAGS

- Stroke-like episodes
- Unexplained lactic acidosis
- Short stature, headaches, hemiparesis, epilepsy, ptosis, ophthalmoplegia, myopathy, diabetes, hearing loss, cardiomyopathy/arrhythmia, vision loss, gastrointestinal dysmotility

IMAGING RED FLAGS

- Cortical and subcortical involvement crossing multiple vascular territories
- Location in parieto-occipital lobes
- Multifocal lesions of different ages involving various brain regions
- Diffusion restriction
- Lactate peak on MRS
- Deep gray signal or calcification
- Chronic volume loss

CONCLUSIONS

MELAS is a phenotype seen in various mitochondrial disorders with stroke-like lesions in nonvascular territories. While the management of MELAS is primarily supportive, there may be benefit in treatment with arginine during acute stroke-like episodes, and more chronically to reduce the frequency and severity of events.

REFERENCES

Cheng W, Zhang Y, He L. MRI features of stroke-like episodes in mitochondrial encephalomyopathy with lactic acidosis and stroke-like episodes. *Frontiers in Neurology*. 2022;13. doi:10.3389/fneur.2022.843386.

Chinnery PF. *Primary mitochondrial disorders Overview - GeneReviews® - NCBI Bookshelf*. National Center for Biotechnology Information; June 8, 2000. https://www.ncbi.nlm.nih.gov/books/NBK1224/.

El-Hattab AW, Almannai M, Scaglia F. *Melas - GeneReviews® - NCBI Bookshelf*. National Center for Biotechnology Information; February 27, 2001. https://www.ncbi.nlm.nih.gov/books/NBK1233/.

Case 36

Severe Neonatal Communicating Hydrocephalus

HISTORY AND PHYSICAL

A 20-week ultrasound of a female fetus showed severe ventriculomegaly. The mother was referred for genetic and metabolic evaluation. There was no significant prior family history of hydrocephalus, neurodevelopmental disorder, or infantile death.

DIAGNOSTIC WORKUP

Nontargeted carrier screening of the parents demonstrated that both were carriers for carnitine palmitoyltransferase (CPT-II) deficiency. Amniocentesis confirmed that the fetus was compound heterozygous for the familial mutations (c.1816_1817del/p.Val606Leufs*2 and c.110_111dupGC/p.S38fs*36), confirming a diagnosis of severe congenital CPT-II deficiency. The patient was delivered at 38 weeks' gestation and was started immediately on metabolic supplementation, including intravenous high-dextrose infusion and orogastric tube feeds with 4g/kg triheptanoin and polycal therapy.

Postnatal brain MRI and MRS confirmed the presence of a Dandy–Walker malformation, severe hydrocephalus, cerebellar vermis hypoplasia, polymicrogyria, and thinning of the cortex and corpus callosum (Fig. 36.1). There was no lactate peak on MRS. Echocardiogram, cardiac telemetry, and abdominal imaging remained normal during hospitalization.

Metabolic labs demonstrated only mild elevation of transaminases and ammonia that resolved within the first week of life. There was no hypoglycemia or elevation of creatinine phosphokinase (CPK). Initial plasma acylcarnitine profile at 24 hours of life demonstrated an elevated C16 level of 12.4 nmol/mL (nl <0.35 nmol/mL).

The triheptanoin dosage was increased to 7 g/kg mixed, combined with Vivonex-10 formula and Polycal after the first 24 hours of life, with gradual reintroduction of long-chain fats with walnut oil over 3 weeks. Plasma C16 levels decreased to 3 to 4 nmol/mL with treatment. After stabilization, a VP shunt was placed. The patient was ultimately discharged from the neonatal intensive care unit (NICU) at nine weeks of life.

CLINICAL DIFFERENTIAL DIAGNOSIS

Hydrocephalus can be seen in the congenital form of CPT-II deficiency, as well as cobalamin C deficiency, many nonmetabolic genetic disorders (e.g., L1CAM syndrome), and acquired conditions (preterm intraventricular hemorrhage).

Brain malformations including polymicrogyria can be seen in certain inborn errors of metabolism (IEMs) including congenital CPT-II deficiency, severe multiple acyl-CoA dehydrogenase deficiency, some mitochondrial disorders (e.g., fumarase deficiency), peroxisomal biogenic disorders (e.g., Zellweger spectrum), and disorders of O-mannosylation of alpha-dystroglycan (e.g., Walker-Warburg syndrome).

Corpus callosum abnormalities can be seen with pyruvate dehydrogenase complex deficiency, Smith-Lemli-Opitz syndrome, and glycine encephalopathy.

Dandy-Walker malformations have a large differential diagnosis, although rarely associated with IEMs. Cerebellar hypoplasia is characteristic of congenital disorder of glycosylation type 1A.

IMAGING DIFFERENTIAL DIAGNOSIS

Hydrocephalus should be distinguished from ex vacuo ventricular enlargement due to cerebral atrophy. While CT is used in the urgent setting to evaluate for hemorrhage and increased intracranial pressure, brain MRI allows more detailed diagnosis. Acute hydrocephalus often shows

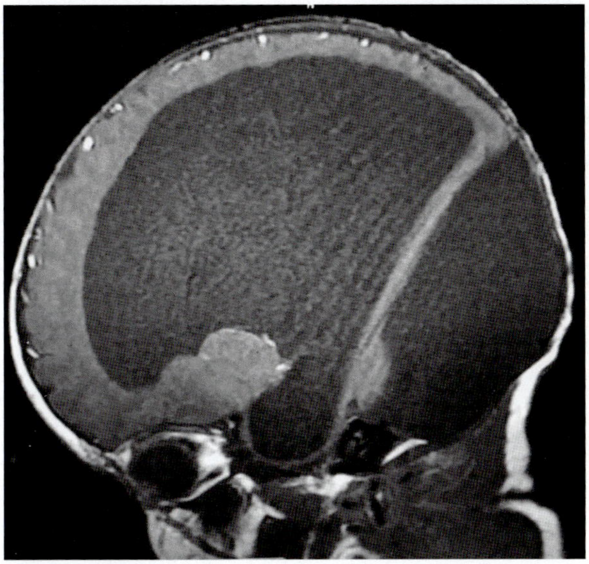

Fig. 36.1 Neonatal carnitine palmitoyltransferase type II deficiency. Brain MRI, sagittal T1 shows severe communicating hydrocephalus with cortical malformations and cerebellar hypoplasia.

rounding of ventricular horns and recesses, interstitial edema, effacement of sulci and subarachnoid spaces, and upward displacement of the corpus callosum.

Acute edema and restricted diffusion with a diffuse or symmetric pattern raise suspicion for a metabolic or mitochondrial etiology. Early-onset metabolic disorders can produce a variety of congenital brain malformations. In CPT-II deficiency, pachygyria, polymicrogyria, cystic dysplasia, and posterior fossa anomalies often coexist with hydrocephalus.

FINAL DIAGNOSIS

Neonatal onset carnitine palmitoyltransferase II (NO-CPT-II).

DISCUSSION

Carnitine palmitoyltransferase II (CPT-II) deficiency is an autosomal recessive disorder of the carnitine cycle that secondarily impairs fatty acid beta-oxidation. It most commonly presents with exercise- and illness-induced rhabdomyolysis in older children and adults. There is a very rare and lethal form of the disorder with severe enzyme deficiency (as in this case with biallelic truncating variants) that manifests congenitally with brain and renal malformations and presents in the neonatal period with liver failure, hypoglycemia, cardiomyopathy, and arrhythmia. Due to the prenatal genetic diagnosis, early management was possible, including initiation of triheptanoin to stabilize the patient for VP shunt placement. Triheptanoin is a synthetic medium-chain triglyceride composed of three odd-chain 7-carbon fatty acids (heptanoate) on a glycerol backbone. This both bypasses the metabolic block in fatty acid oxidation in this disorder and serves as an anaplerotic compound (oxidized to form propionyl CoA).

CLINICAL RED FLAGS

- Neonatal encephalopathy
- Congenital renal malformations
- Cardiomyopathy and arrhythmia
- Hypoglycemia
- Elevated CPK
- Neonatal liver failure
- Elevated C16 and C18:1 on plasma acylcarnitine profile

IMAGING RED FLAGS

- Cortical malformations
- Congenital hydrocephalus

CONCLUSIONS

Neonatal CPT-II deficiency is a very rare disorder that manifests in the neonatal period with congenital brain anomalies, renal dysgenesis, and metabolic crisis and is associated with encephalopathy, cardiomyopathy/arrhythmia, liver failure, and myopathy. It is typically lethal, although prenatal diagnosis and early management may improve survival.

REFERENCES

Dinçer A, Özek MM. Radiologic evaluation of pediatric hydrocephalus. *Child's Nervous System*. 2011;27(10):1543–1562. doi:10.1007/s00381-011-1559-x.

Mador-House R, Liu Z, Dyack S. Detection of early onset carnitine palmitoyltransferase II deficiency by newborn screening: should CPT II deficiency be a primary disease target? *International Journal of Neonatal Screening*. 2021;7(3):55. doi:10.3390/ijns7030055.

Malik S, Paldiwal AA, Korday CS, Jadhav SS. Neonatal carnitine palmitoyltransferase II deficiency: a lethal entity. *Journal of Clinical and Diagnostic Research*. 2015;9(10). doi:10.7860/jcdr/2015/13600.6560.

Tajima G, Hara K, Yuasa M. Carnitine palmitoyltransferase II deficiency with a focus on newborn screening. *Journal of Human Genetics*. 2018;64(2):87–98. doi:10.1038/s10038-018-0530-z.

Vockley J, Burton B, Berry G, et al. Effects of triheptanoin (UX007) in patients with long-chain fatty acid oxidation disorders: results from an open-label, long-term extension study. *Journal of Inherited Metabolic Disease*. 2020;44(1):253–263. doi:10.1002/jimd.12313.

SECTION 8

Neuroinfections in Childhood

Arushi Gahlot Saini, Suresh Kumar Angurana, Daniel J. Clark, Renu Suthar, Chandana Bhagwat, Douglas G. Postels, Jorge Vidaurre

INTRODUCTION

Central nervous system (CNS) infections are one of the most devastating insults to the pediatric brain, often presenting as serious medical emergencies and resulting in significant morbidity and mortality. They have varying etiology, clinical presentation, treatment course, and prognosis. Early diagnosis and institution of appropriate treatment help in reducing complications.

In the acute setting, it is necessary to distinguish CNS infection from other causes of CNS inflammation, especially demyelination, autoimmune, and inflammatory encephalitis. Clinical risk factors and physical examination can be helpful. Cerebrospinal fluid (CSF) examination helps in differentiating viral, bacterial, and mycobacterial causes. Additional CSF testing can include parasites, viral culture, polymerase chain reaction (PCR), antigen testing, serology, and autoimmune antibodies. Neuroimaging provides vital clues to the underlying pathology, extent of involvement, presence of complications, and response to treatment.

In this chapter, we describe the clinical and imaging features of commonly acquired pediatric CNS infections that warrant prompt diagnostic testing and management. Acute febrile encephalopathy and abnormal neurological signs are urgent indications for neuroimaging, as CNS infections often present with a complicated course. Neuroimaging supplemented by clinical history and examination often suggests the diagnosis and guides confirmatory testing. It is important to be aware of both typical and atypical clinical and neuroimaging patterns of the common acquired CNS infections in children.

SUGGESTED READINGS

Abdalkader M, Xie J, Cervantes-Arslanian A, Takahashi C, Mian AZ. Imaging of intracranial infections. *Seminars in Neurology*. 2019;39(03):322–333. doi:10.1055/s-0039-1693161.

Alam AM, Gillespie CS, Goodall J, et al. Neurological manifestations of scrub typhus infection: A systematic review and meta-analysis of clinical features and case fatality. *PLOS Neglected Tropical Diseases*. 2022;16(11). doi:10.1371/journal.pntd.0010952.

Hwee TP, Koh Cheng T. Imaging of congenital/childhood central nervous system infections. *Neuroimaging Clinics of North America*. 2023;33(1):207–224. doi:10.1016/j.nic.2022.07.017.

Nguyen I, Urbanczyk K, Mtui E, Li S. Intracranial CNS infections: A literature review and radiology case studies. *Seminars in Ultrasound, CT and MRI*. 2020;41(1):106–120. doi:10.1053/j.sult.2019.09.003.

Norris AH, Shrestha NK, Allison GM, et al. 2018 Infectious Diseases Society of America Clinical Practice guideline for the management of outpatient parenteral antimicrobial Therapya. *Clinical Infectious Diseases*. 2018;68(1). doi:10.1093/cid/ciy745.

Tunkel AR, Hasbun R, Bhimraj A, et al. 2017 Infectious Diseases Society of America's Clinical practice guidelines for healthcare-associated ventriculitis and meningitis*. *Clinical Infectious Diseases*. 2017;64(6). doi:10.1093/cid/ciw861.

Limbic Encephalitis: A Double Hit

HISTORY AND PHYSICAL

A 4-year-old right-handed boy presented to the emergency department with fever, twitching of the left side of his face, and altered sensorium for two days. On day one, he complained of an altered sensation on the left side of his face that lasted for 30 minutes. This was followed by multiple episodes of focal-onset motor seizures affecting the left face. Subsequently, he became lethargic and confused. There was no relevant family history. His perinatal history was normal and he attained age-appropriate developmental milestones. Immunizations were up to date. He had a prior history of febrile seizures at one year of age.

Physical examination showed a fever of 101°F and a Glasgow Coma score of 11. Neurological examination demonstrated neck stiffness, left hemiparesis (3/5), brisk deep tendon reflexes, and extensor plantar response bilaterally. Due to the history of acute febrile encephalopathy with left hemiparesis, he was admitted for suspicion of CNS infection and started on empirical intravenous acyclovir, ceftriaxone, and antiseizure medications. He showed improvement after one week of treatment.

In the third week of illness, he developed new-onset generalized hyperkinetic movement disorder, insomnia, and behavioral problems, without fever or seizures at this time.

DIAGNOSTIC WORKUP

Brain MRI with contrast showed diffusion restriction and T2/fluid-attenuated inversion recovery (FLAIR) hyperintense signal in the bilateral thalami, insulae, insular and perirolandic cortex, and white matter (Fig. 37.1). There was no associated contrast enhancement or susceptibility.

Follow-up MRI in the third week showed development of gliosis in the previously affected areas, without new lesions identified (Fig. 37.2).

Hematological and biochemical testing were normal. Cerebrospinal fluid examination (CSF) showed 10 cells (lymphocytes), glucose 80 mg/dL, protein 48 mg/dL, and sterile culture. Serum antibodies for dengue, scrub typhus, and Japanese encephalitis (JE) were negative. Herpes virus DNA was detected in the CSF by PCR. Due to the onset of new neurological symptoms in the second week of illness, CSF was collected and sent for anti-N-methyl-D-aspartate (NMDA) receptor antibodies showing an elevated titer (Fig. 37.3).

CLINICAL DIFFERENTIAL DIAGNOSES

Acute encephalitis syndrome (AES) is characterized by acute onset of fever, change in mental status lasting for more than 24 hours (lethargy, personality change, disorientation, inability to talk, alteration in sleep-wake cycle, or coma), and new-onset seizures. Common causes of AES include herpesviruses, enteroviruses, paramyxoviruses, and influenza viruses. There is clinical overlap in presentation, so CSF viral serology or DNA/RNA testing is required for confirmation. Herpes simplex virus encephalitis (HSE) is the most common cause of sporadic encephalitis in children worldwide. In adolescents and young adults, this is related to reactivation of latent oropharyngeally transmitted herpesvirus in the trigeminal nerve, while neonates can present with more widespread brain infection due to vertical transmission during birth.

Limbic encephalitis can be seen with parainfectious conditions, demyelinating diseases, cytokine exacerbation causing acute leukoencephalopathy, and autoimmune conditions such as anti-NMDA receptor encephalitis.

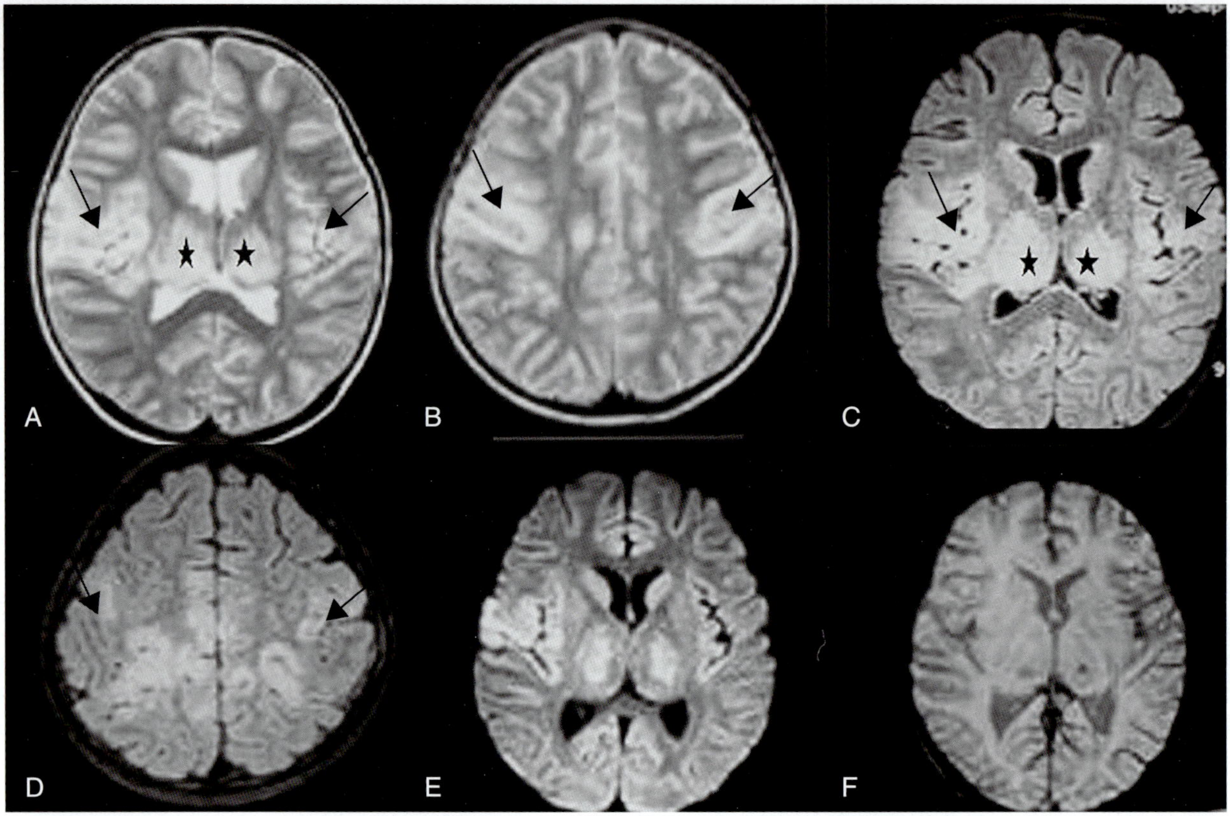

Fig. 37.1 Herpes encephalitis. (A and B) Axial T2 and (C and D) FLAIR MRI show hyperintensity involving bilateral insular and perirolandic cortex (*arrows*) and thalami (*stars*). (E) There is associated diffusion restriction with (F) foci of hemorrhage on SWI. *FLAIR*, Fluid-attenuated inversion recovery; *SWI*, susceptibility-weighted imaging.

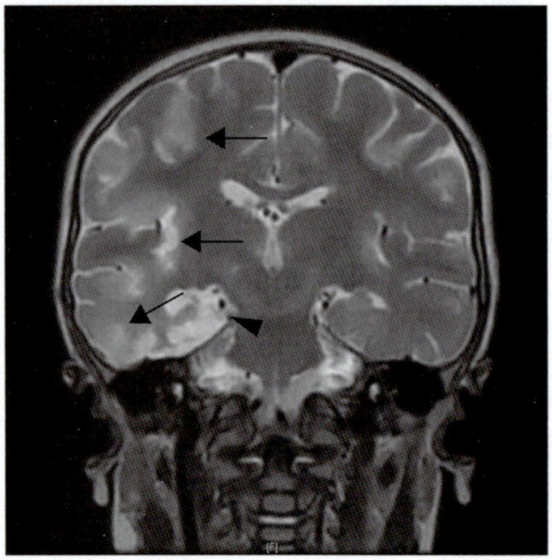

Fig. 37.2 Follow-up herpes encephalitis. Coronal T2 shows patchy encephalomalacia in the right greater than left periinsular regions (*arrows*) and hippocampi (*arrowhead*).

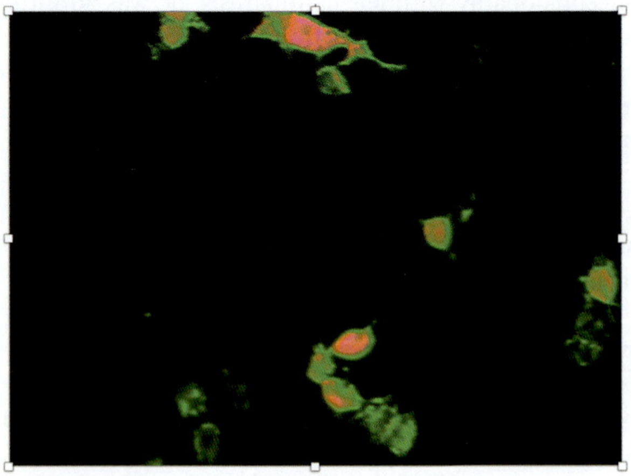

Fig. 37.3 Photomicrograph showing indirect immunofluorescence on transfected cell lines expressing NMDAR with strong granular cytoplasmic fluorescence [Magnification × 400]. *NMDAR*, Anti-NMDA receptor encephalitis.

Rarely, metabolic disorders such as uremia, hepatic failure, and urea cycle defects can cause similar symptoms.

IMAGING DIFFERENTIAL DIAGNOSES

Brain sites of involvement are suggestive of different viral etiologies:

Frontal/temporal lobes and limbic structures (insula, hippocampi, cingulate cortex): herpesviruses (HSV-1, HSV-2, HHV-6) (Fig. 37.4), JE, rabies, enteroviruses, and dengue.

Thalami and brainstem: Japanese encephalitis (Fig. 37.5), West Nile virus, Epstein-Barr virus (EBV), dengue, and influenza (H1N1).

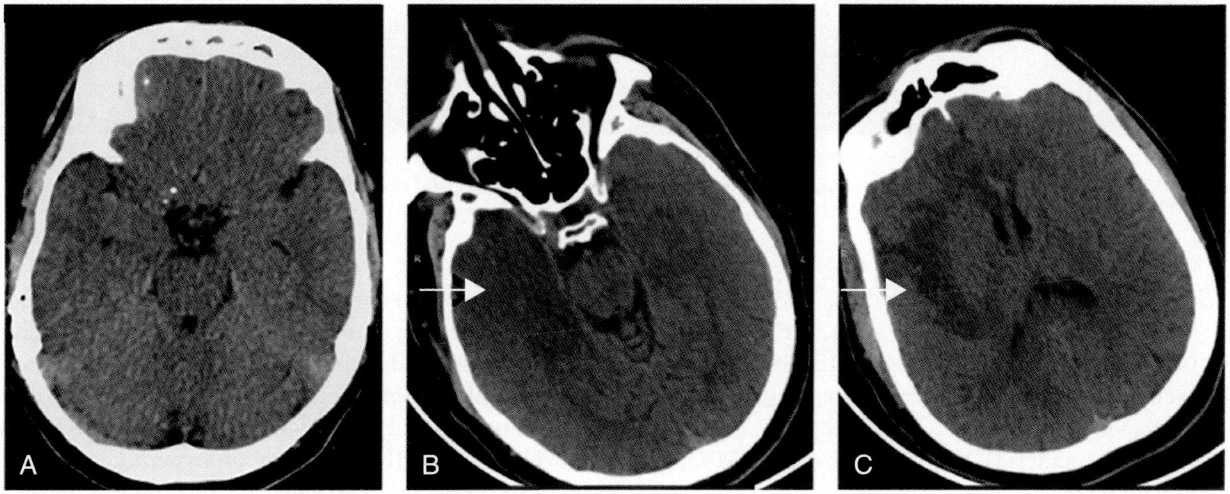

Fig. 37.4 Herpes encephalitis. Head CT is (A) normal in early disease, with (B–C) right temporal and insular hypodensities developing after 5 to 7 days (*arrows*).

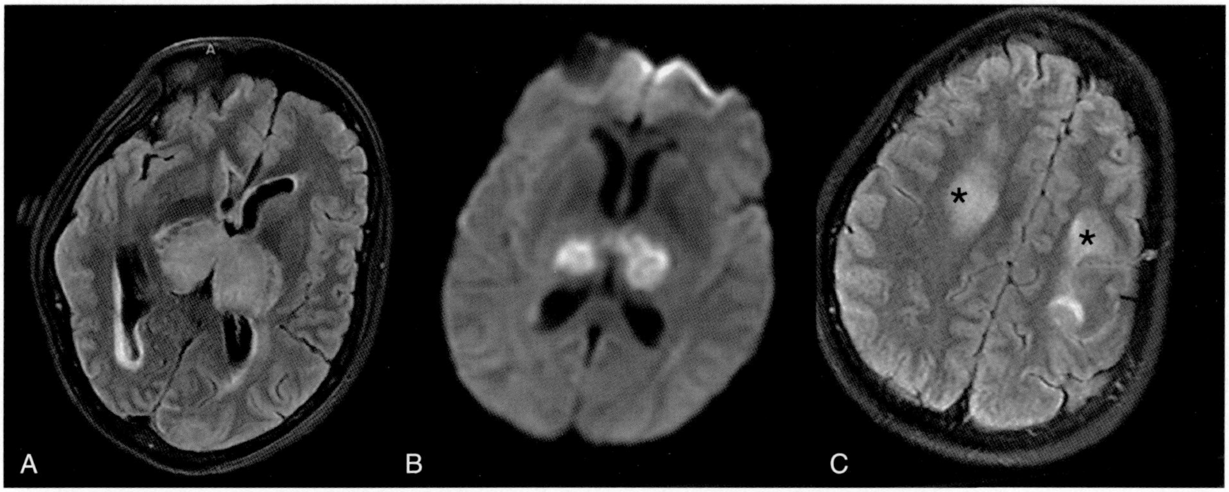

Fig. 37.5 Japanese encephalitis. Brain MRI shows bilateral thalamic (A) FLAIR hyperintensity and (B) diffusion restriction with (C) perirolandic edema (*asterisks*). *FLAIR*, Fluid-attenuated inversion recovery.

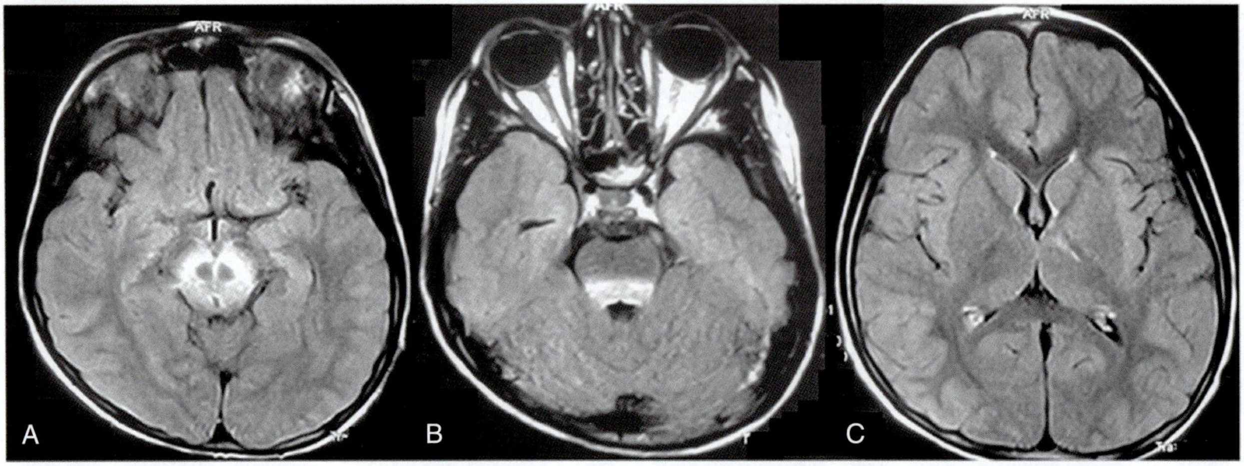

Fig. 37.6 Enterovirus encephalitis. Brain MRI, axial FLAIR, shows bilateral hyperintensities in (A) midbrain and (B) dorsal pons with (C) relative sparing of the basal ganglia and cortex. *FLAIR*, Fluid-attenuated inversion recovery.

Basal ganglia: Japanese encephalitis, EBV, congenital human immunodeficiency virus (HIV), measles (subacute sclerosing panencephalitis [SSPE]).

Periventricular and subcortical white matter: chikungunya virus.

Diffuse white matter: HIV, cytomegalovirus (CMV), fulminant SSPE.

Dorsal brainstem: enteroviruses (Fig. 37.6), rabies (Fig. 37.7), adenoviruses.

Spinal cord: enteroviruses, varicella zoster virus (VZV), dengue

FINAL DIAGNOSIS

Herpes encephalitis complicated by anti-NMDA receptor encephalitis (NMDARE).

DISCUSSION

Herpes simplex virus encephalitis (HSE) commonly presents with an acute encephalitic syndrome with edema, necrosis, and/or hemorrhage. Relapses following the initial infection can be caused by ongoing viral infection or autoimmune reaction. Viral-mediated injury exposes the neuronal antigens to the systemic immune system and leads to the development of autoimmunity.

Anti-NMDA receptor (NMDAR) antibodies can be generated after HSV and other viral CNS infections. Children usually present with new-onset cognitive deficits, sleep and speech impairment (mutism), mood changes, seizures, and extrapyramidal symptoms (chorea and/or dystonia) after resolution of acute infection.

Any child who presents with a biphasic disease course should be initiated on antiviral therapy and investigated for NMDARE. The presence of hyperkinetic movement disorder, absence of new necrotic lesions on MRI, absence of viral DNA in the CSF, and positive anti-NMDAR antibodies in the CSF support a secondary autoimmune process. Electroencephalography (EEG) can show slowing and focal discharges or rarely "extreme delta brush" pattern (named because of its resemblance to the neonatal EEG pattern known as delta brush). First-line treatment includes immunomodulation with high-dose pulsed methylprednisolone and intravenous immunoglobulin. Second-line therapy includes cyclophosphamide, rituximab, or plasmapheresis, followed by maintenance immune therapy if required.

CLINICAL RED FLAGS

- Patients with encephalitis who present with acute neurological deficits after the acute infectious period.
- Viral encephalitis can trigger NMDARE due to acute exposure to neuronal antigens.
- Fresh-onset behavioral and speech problems, insomnia, and hyperkinetic movement disorder are often the clues to underlying NMDARE.
- Seizures are less common in autoimmune encephalitis than in relapsed HSE.

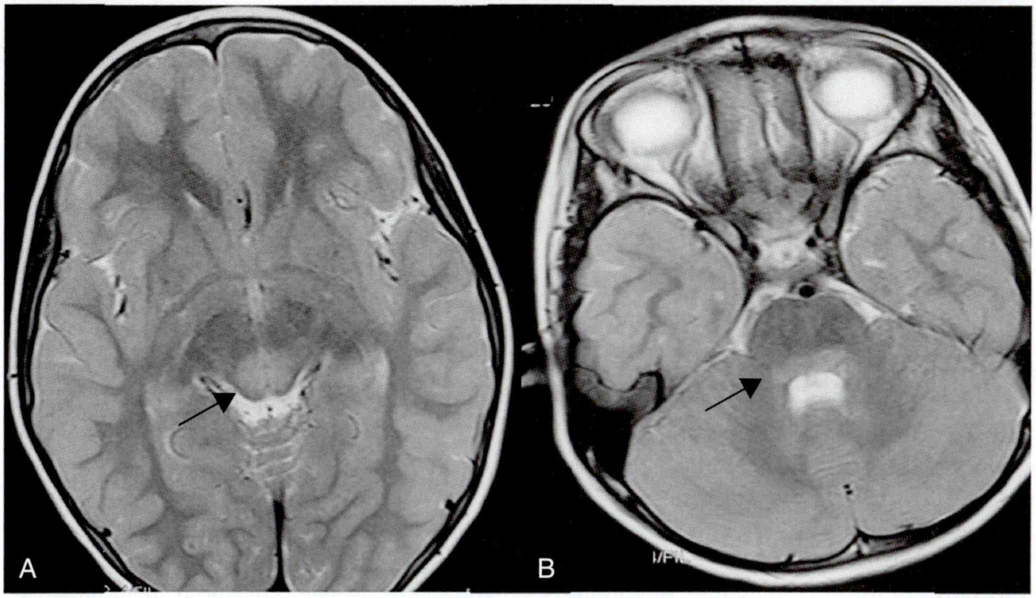

Fig. 37.7 Rabies encephalitis. Brain MRI, axial T2, shows hyperintensities in (A) midbrain tectum and periaqueductal gray matter and (B) dorsal pons (*arrows*).

IMAGING RED FLAGS

- When a patient with AES presents with near-normal imaging and CSF, consider autoimmune encephalitis.
- Relapsed viral encephalitis often shows new and progressive areas of involvement.

CONCLUSIONS

A child who presents with biphasic symptoms following acute viral encephalitis should be evaluated for both viral and autoimmune relapse. The absence of CSF pleocytosis and viral DNA, no new lesions on imaging, and new marked behavioral abnormalities and movement disorders point towards NMDARE. Prompt diagnosis and management will reduce mortality and morbidity.

REFERENCES

Hardy D. Autoimmune Encephalitis in Children. *Pediatric Neurology*. 2022;132:56–66.

Huang Q, Xie Y, Hu Z, Tang X. Anti-N-methyl-D-aspartate receptor encephalitis: A review of pathogenic mechanisms, treatment, prognosis. *Brain Research*. 2019:15;1727:146549. doi:10.1016/j.brainres.2019.146549.

Nosadini M, Mohammad SS, Corazza F, et al. Herpes simplex virus-induced anti-N-methyl-d-aspartate receptor encephalitis: a systematic literature review with analysis of 43 cases. *Developmental Medicine and Child Neurology*. 2023;59:796–805. doi:10.37473/fic/10.47936/encephalitis.2023.00101.

Prithvi A, Kesavan S, Saini AG, Suthar R, Mahadevan A. Little Children, Bigger Problems: Anti-N-Methyl D-Aspartate Receptor Encephalitis. *Indian Journal of Pediatrics*. 2019;86(11):1048–1050. doi:10.1007/s12098-019-03000-8.

Suthar R, Saini AG, Sankhyan N, Sahu JK, Singhi P. Childhood Anti-NMDA Receptor Encephalitis. *Indian Journal of Pediatrics*. 2016;83(7):628–633. doi:10.1007/s12098-015-1988-8.

Venkatesan A, Tunkel AR, Bloch KC, Lauring AS, Sejvar J, Bitnun A, Stahl JP, Mailles A, Drebot M, Rupprecht CE, Yoder J, Cope JR, Wilson MR, Whitley RJ, Sullivan J, Granerod J, Jones C, Eastwood K, Ward KN, Durrheim DN, Solbrig MV, Guo-Dong L, Glaser CA. International Encephalitis Consortium. Case definitions, diagnostic algorithms, and priorities in encephalitis: consensus statement of the international encephalitis consortium. *Clinical Infectious Disease*. 2013;57:1114–1128. doi:10.1093/cid/cit458.

Zhang S, Yang Y, Liu W, Li Z, Li J, Zhou D. Clinical Characteristics of Anti-N-Methyl-d-Aspartate Receptor Encephalitis Overlapping with Demyelinating Diseases: A Review. *Frontiers in Immunology*. 2022;13:857443. doi:10.3389/fimmu.2022.857443.

Case 38

Complications of the Pandemic

HISTORY AND PHYSICAL

A 7-year-old male presented with fever for the past three days, followed by multiple generalized tonic seizures and altered sensorium. There was no recent history of respiratory symptoms or known exposure to severe acute respiratory syndrome coronavirus-2 (SARS-CoV-2) infection. Birth history was unremarkable. At 2 months of age, he had one episode of unprovoked seizure for which he received antiseizure medications for 3 months. He was the second child of 4 siblings and showed mild developmental delay.

On examination, he was febrile with tachycardia (120/min) and normal blood pressure. Anthropometry was normal for age. He had mild pallor, a Glasgow Coma Scale of 10, right facial palsy, normal tone, brisk deep tendon reflexes, extensor plantar responses, normally reacting pupils, and absence of papilledema. He was empirically started on intravenous ceftriaxone, acyclovir, and phenytoin.

DIAGNOSTIC WORKUP

MRI brain on day 1 of hospitalization showed bilateral asymmetrical hyperintense lesions involving the thalamus, midbrain, and pons on T2 weighted images with diffusion restriction (Fig. 38.1).

Complete blood count, renal and liver function tests were normal. Blood culture was sterile. Cerebrospinal fluid examination (CSF) showed 3 cells/mm^3, glucose 67 mg%, protein 68 mg%, sterile culture, and negative PCR for HSV-1 and Japanese encephalitis (JE) viruses. Serum ammonia was 58 mmol/L and lactate was 1.4 mmol/L.

Nasopharyngeal swab PCR was positive for SARS-CoV-2. SARS-CoV-2 serology was negative. The patient was treated with intravenous methylprednisolone (30 mg/kg/day) for 5 days, resulting in gradual improvement of sensorium and discharge after a hospital stay of 10 days.

CLINICAL DIFFERENTIAL DIAGNOSES

Acute febrile encephalopathy can be seen with infectious etiologies, such as acute viral encephalitis (HSV) and acute pyogenic bacterial meningitis. Severe acute respiratory syndrome coronavirus-2 (SARS-CoV-2) can directly affect the CNS.

Autoimmune disorders include acute necrotizing encephalopathy of childhood (ANEC), demyelinating diseases, and febrile infection-related status epilepticus (FIRES).

Metabolic encephalopathies (urea cycle, organic acidemias, mitochondrial disorders) can be triggered by febrile illness.

IMAGING DIFFERENTIAL DIAGNOSES

Bilateral thalamic and brainstem involvement can be seen in viral infections like JE (Fig. 38.2), rabies encephalitis (Fig. 38.3), dengue, and West Nile virus.

Metabolic or toxic causes can be considered such as Leigh syndrome (Fig. 38.4), Wilson disease, pediatric Wernicke encephalopathy, Reye syndrome, osmotic myelinolysis, and hemolytic-uremic syndrome.

FINAL DIAGNOSIS

Acute necrotizing encephalopathy of childhood (ANEC) associated with SARS-CoV-2 infection.

DISCUSSION

SARS-CoV-2 infection is usually asymptomatic or mild in children with mainly respiratory symptoms. However,

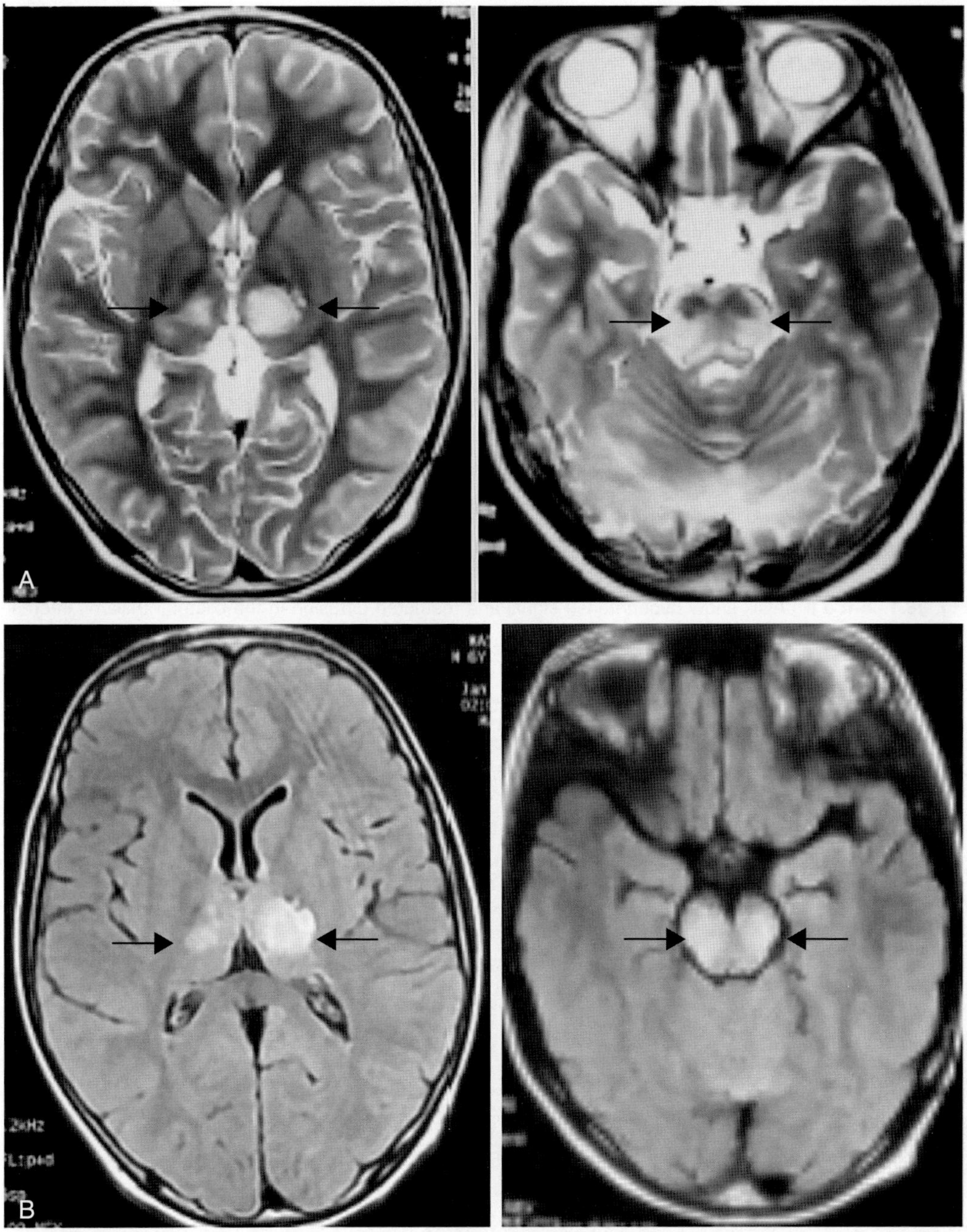

Fig. 38.1 Acute necrotizing encephalopathy of childhood. Brain MRI, (A) axial T2, (B) FLAIR, and

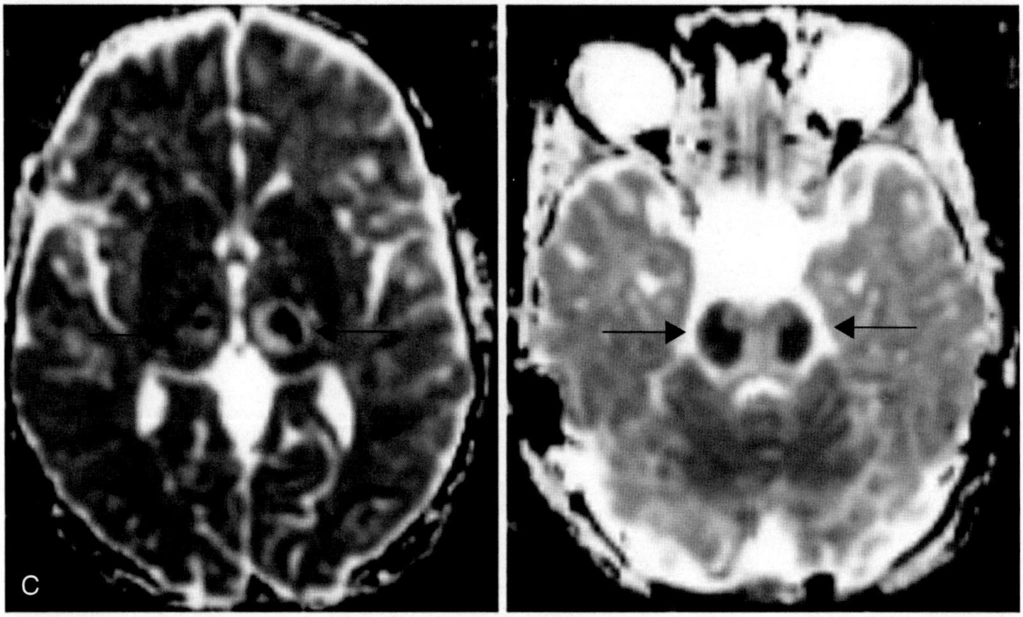

Fig. 38.1 cont'd (C) ADC show hyperintense signal and restricted diffusion in the bilateral thalami, internal capsules, and pons (*arrows*).

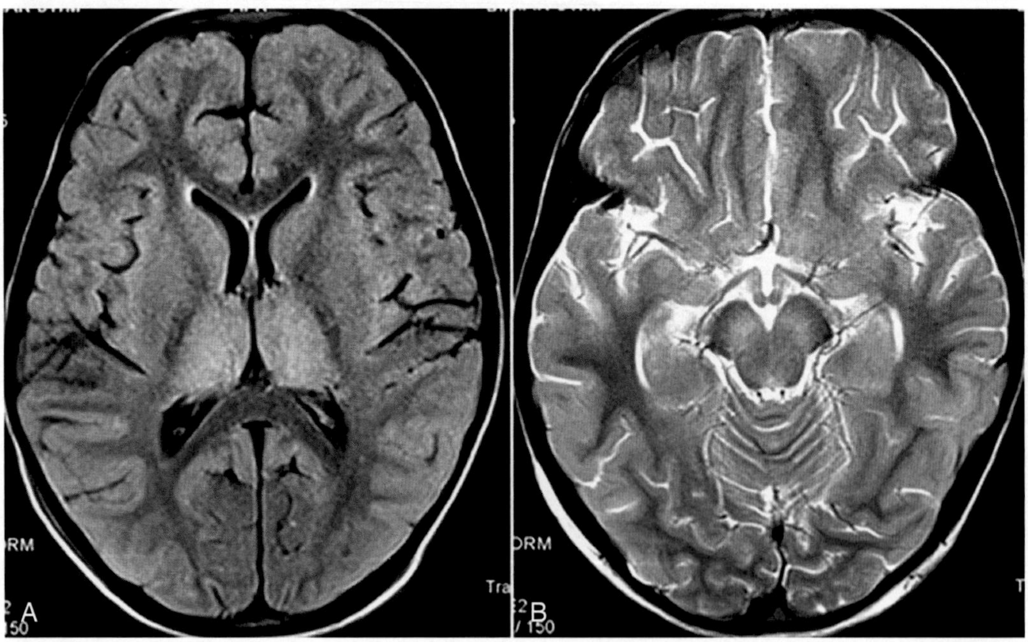

Fig. 38.2 Japanese encephalitis. Brain MRI, (A) axial FLAIR and (B) T2 with bilateral thalamic and substantia nigra hyperintensities. *FLAIR*, Fluid-attenuated inversion recovery.

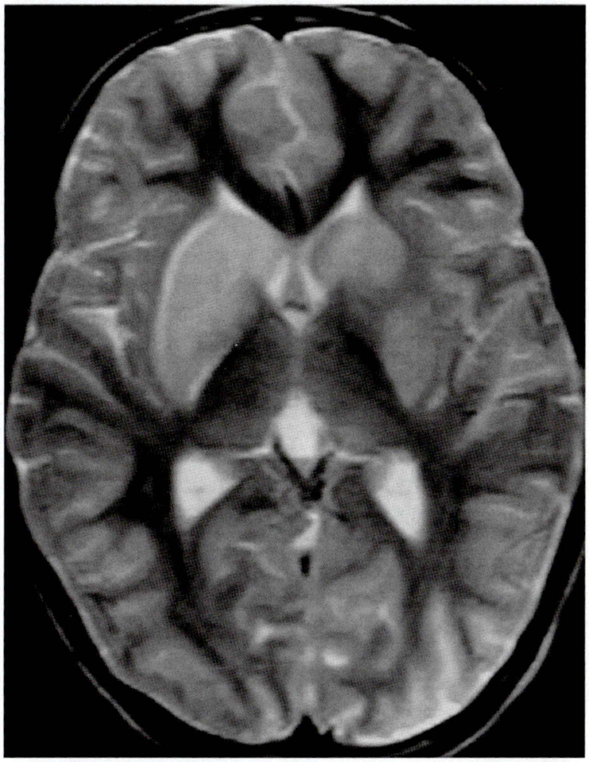

Fig. 38.3 Rabies encephalitis. Brain MRI, axial T2 shows hyperintensities involving lentiform nuclei and medial thalami.

there can be additional neurological manifestations including anosmia, ageusia, seizures, meningoencephalitis, encephalopathy, cerebral edema, cerebrovascular disease, Guillain-Barre syndrome, transverse myelitis, and acute disseminated encephalomyelitis (ADEM).

ANEC is an uncommon manifestation of SARS-CoV-2 infection in children. It is a rare and severe syndrome characterized by seizures and rapid deterioration of consciousness. ANEC has high mortality (10-40%) and poor neurological outcome, with complete recovery documented in <10% of cases. Common triggers include viral infections such as influenza, human herpesvirus-6, human herpesvirus-7, parainfluenza, varicella, enterovirus, novel human reovirus, rotavirus, herpes simplex virus, rubella, coxsackie A9, and measles. Dysregulation of cytokine production, especially interleukin-6 (IL-6), is believed to be the underlying mechanism rather than direct viral invasion. Other causes are mycoplasma infection, autoimmune conditions, and genetic (*RANBP2* mutation).

Characteristic imaging findings of ANEC include bilateral symmetric involvement of thalami, putamen,

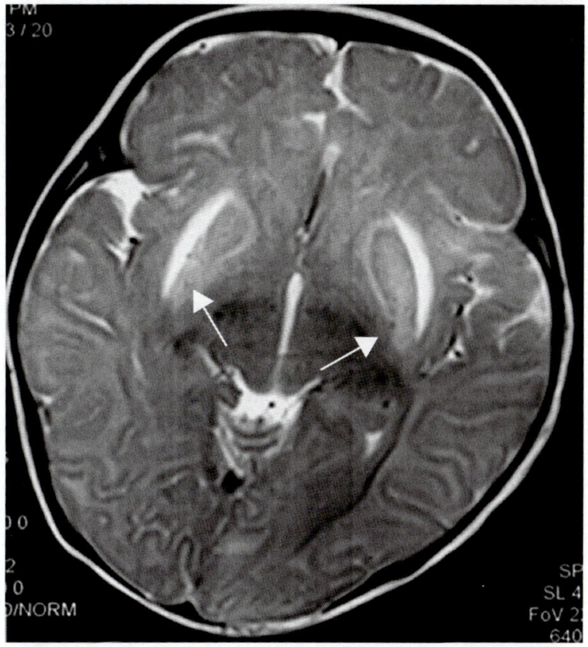

Fig. 38.4 Leigh syndrome. Brain MRI, axial T2 shows bilateral hyperintensities involving putamina and internal capsules (*arrows*).

internal capsule, brainstem, cerebellum, and periventricular white matter. Treatment of ANEC is largely supportive. Immunotherapy (steroids, intravenous immunoglobulin, plasma exchange, and IL-6 antagonists) may be beneficial. The outcome is usually poor with high mortality and severe neurological sequelae among survivors.

CLINICAL RED FLAGS

- Any child with acute febrile or afebrile illness, multiple seizures, and rapidly progressing encephalopathy
Persistent fever or multifocal neurological involvement

IMAGING RED FLAGS

- Involvement of bilateral thalami and brainstem, possibly with hemorrhagic transformation

CONCLUSIONS

ANEC is a rare and serious parainfectious neurological disorder, usually triggered by viral infections such as SARS-CoV-2. Clinical presentation includes febrile illness with seizures and rapid deterioration of consciousness. Neuroimaging can show bilateral symmetrical lesions involving the thalamus and brainstem, sometimes with hemorrhagic transformation. Treatment is mainly supportive with immunomodulation (corticosteroids, intravenous immunoglobulin, plasma exchange, and IL-6 antagonists).

REFERENCES

Bentes Almeida A, Dos Santos Walter J, Pessoa Natalia L, Costa Thais A, Garcia Oliveira Gabriela F, Martins Oliveira Diniz L, Ribeiro Torres Bruna C, Teixeira Daniela C, Mendes Renata B, Avelar Ana BA, Campos Marcos A, Geessien Kroon Erna, Paiva Drumond Betania. Neuro-COVID-19 With or Without the Multisystem Inflammatory Syndrome (MIS-C): A Single-Center Study: COVID-19: Neurologic Manifestations in Children. *Journal of Molecular Neuroscience*. 2023;1–9. doi:10.1007/s12031-023-02109-y.

Ho JHY, Lee CYM, Chiong YK, Aoyama R, Fan LJ, Tan AHS, Han VX. SARS-CoV-2-Related Acute Necrotizing Encephalopathy of Childhood with Good Response to Tocilizumab in an Adolescent. *Pediatric Neurology*. 2023;139:65–69. doi:10.1016/j.pediatrneurol.2022.11.010.

Khanna PC, Iyer RS, Chaturvedi A, Thapa MM, Chaturvedi A, Ishak GE, Shaw DW. Imaging bithalamic pathology in the pediatric brain: demystifying a diagnostic conundrum. *American Journal of Roentgenology*. 2011;197(6):1449–1459. doi:10.2214/AJR.11.6702.

Kumar S, Navid A, Sharma R, Suthar R, Vyas S, Angurana SK. Acute Necrotizing Encephalopathy of Childhood: A Rare Neurological Manifestation of Dengue. *Annals of Indian Academy of Neurology*. 2021;24(5):828–831. doi:10.4103/aian.AIAN_809_20.

Takia L, Saini L, Keshavan S, Angurana SK, Nallasamy K, Suthar R, Verma S, Singh P, Goyal K, Ratho RK, Jayashree M. Acute Necrotizing Encephalopathy of Childhood with H1N1 Infection. *Journal of Pediatric Intensive Care*. 2020;9(3):222–222. doi:10.1055/s-0040-1705182.

Wang PY, Yang MT, Liang JS. Acute necrotizing encephalopathy caused by SARS-CoV-2 in a child. *Pediatrics and Neonatology*. 2022;63(6):642–644. doi:10.1016/j.pedneo.2022.06.003.

Parasites in the Brain

HISTORY AND PHYSICAL

An 11-year-old boy presented to the emergency department with a history of fever for one week, followed by headache, vomiting, and left eye squint for the past three weeks. He also had three episodes of generalized seizures. His father worked as a farmer. He did not report systemic symptoms or recent exposure to infection, pets, or domestic animals. There was no history of consumption of raw milk or pork, recent travel, or recurrent infections.

On examination, his heart rate was 67, and his blood pressure was 135/95 mm Hg. He had a few palpable, discrete non-tender subcutaneous nodules <1 cm distributed over the abdominal wall, axilla, and infrascapular area (Fig. 39.1A). Neurological examination showed diminished sensorium. He was conscious but not oriented to time, place, and person, with incoherent speech. There was left eye esotropia due to left sixth cranial nerve and seventh cranial nerve upper motor neuron palsies. He had brisk deep tendon reflexes, extensor plantar responses, meningeal signs, and bilateral papilledema. Bradycardia, hypertension, and papilledema raised concern for increased intracranial pressure (ICP) and he was treated with head elevation, sedation, and antiseizure medications.

DIAGNOSTIC WORKUP

Head CT showed tiny calcified lesions distributed over both cerebral hemispheres with surrounding edema. Contrast-enhanced brain MRI showed multiple well-defined, 1 to 5 mm, "cyst with dot" ring-enhancing lesions throughout the cerebral hemispheres, deep gray nuclei, brainstem, and cerebellum (Figs. 39.1 and 39.2).

Chest radiograph, gastric aspirate for acid-fast bacilli, and Mantoux test were negative. Serology was negative for HIV and strongly positive for cysticercosis. Ultrasound of subcutaneous nodules showed hypoechoic lesions with eccentric hyperechoic nodules embedded in abdominal wall muscles.

CLINICAL DIFFERENTIAL DIAGNOSES

Fever and increased intracranial pressure (ICP) can be seen with cerebral infection.

Disseminated cysticercosis can present with cerebral, ocular and soft tissue lesions.

Tubercular meningitis, disseminated or miliary CNS tuberculosis (TB) can be considered due to meningeal signs. Ocular examination may show choroidal tubercles.

Bacterial infections can develop brain abscesses and purulent empyemas.

In immunocompromised patients, invasive fungal infections include aspergillosis or mucormycosis.

Toxoplasmosis and brucellosis can also involve the central nervous system.

IMAGING DIFFERENTIAL DIAGNOSIS

Multiple ring-enhancing lesions of the brain can be seen in infectious, neoplastic, inflammatory, and vascular disorders.

Infectious causes include bacterial, fungal, tuberculous, and parasitic.

Inflammatory causes include neurosarcoidosis and Behçet disease.

FINAL DIAGNOSIS

Disseminated cysticercosis including neurocysticercosis (NCC).

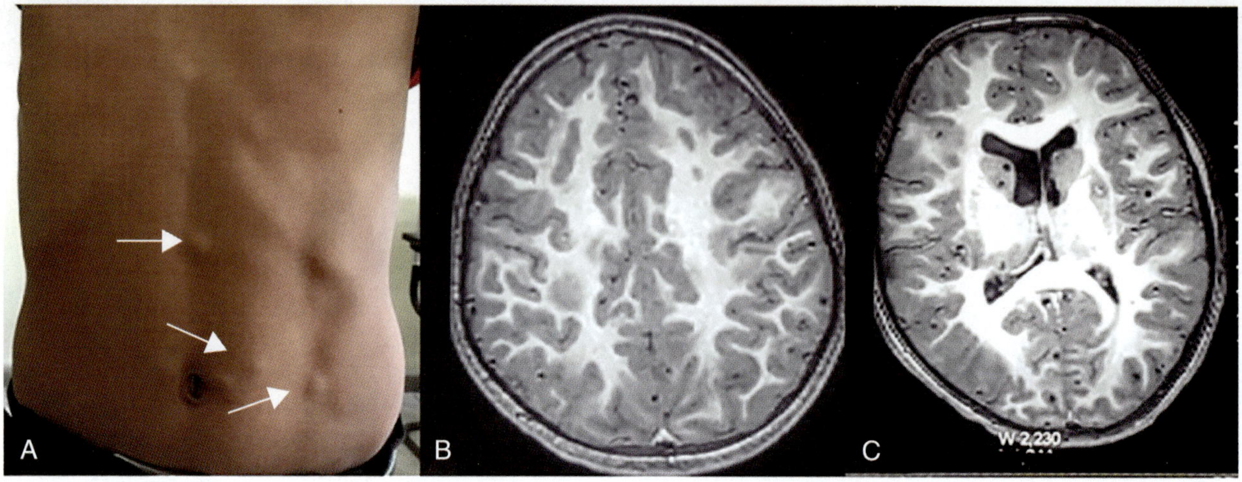

Fig. 39.1 Disseminated cysticercosis. (A) Clinical photograph showing subcutaneous nodules over anterior abdominal wall and right flank (*arrows*). (B and C) Neurocysticercosis. Brain MRI, axial T1, shows multiple punctate hypointense lesions throughout the cerebral cortex and deep gray matter.

DISCUSSION

Neurocysticercosis is the single most common cause of acquired epileptic seizures in the developing world. The parasitic infestation is caused by fecal-oral contamination with ingestion of eggs from the pork tapeworm *Taenia solium*. Disseminated cysticercosis is a rare manifestation with numerous cysticerci scattered throughout the body including brain, muscles, soft tissues, and eyes. Disease can present with minimal symptoms in the latent (non-encephalitic) form, or fulminant neurologic features following parasite exposure with inflammatory encephalitis. Multiple lesions can create a "starry sky" or "starry night" appearance. Imaging features are characteristic that can be supported by ELISA, electro-immunoblot, PCR, or tissue biopsy. A short course of steroids plus antihelminthic therapy is the mainstay of treatment. When encephalitis is severe, steroids may be used first, as parasite death and antigen exposure to the CNS can worsen neuroinflammation. If orbital cysticercosis is present, high-dose therapy can lead to cyst rupture with catastrophic vision loss. Therefore, hospitalization with careful monitoring is required during the treatment course.

CLINICAL RED FLAGS

- Headache, vomiting, and papilledema suggest increased ICP.
- Stage and severity of brain and ocular involvement determine appropriate therapy.

IMAGING RED FLAGS

- Enhancement and edema raise concern for cyst degeneration and inflammation.
- Involvement of ventricles and CSF can lead to hydrocephalus.

CONCLUSIONS

NCC with disseminated cysticercosis is a rare and serious disease with widespread involvement of the brain, eyes, muscles, and other organs. The Escobar pathological stages include vesicular (viable parasite with intact membrane and no host reaction), colloidal vesicular (parasite death with turbid cyst fluid and surrounding inflammation), granular nodular (cyst retraction with decreasing enhancement and edema), and nodular calcified (end-stage quiescence). Lesions can show punctate, ringlike, or "cyst with dot" appearance reflecting the parasitic scolex. The disease stage and severity determine appropriate therapy with cysticidal agents, steroids, antiseizure medications, and management of ICP.

REFERENCES

Del Brutto OH, Garcia HH. The many facets of disseminated parenchymal brain cysticercosis: A differential diagnosis with important therapeutic implications. *PLoS Neglected*

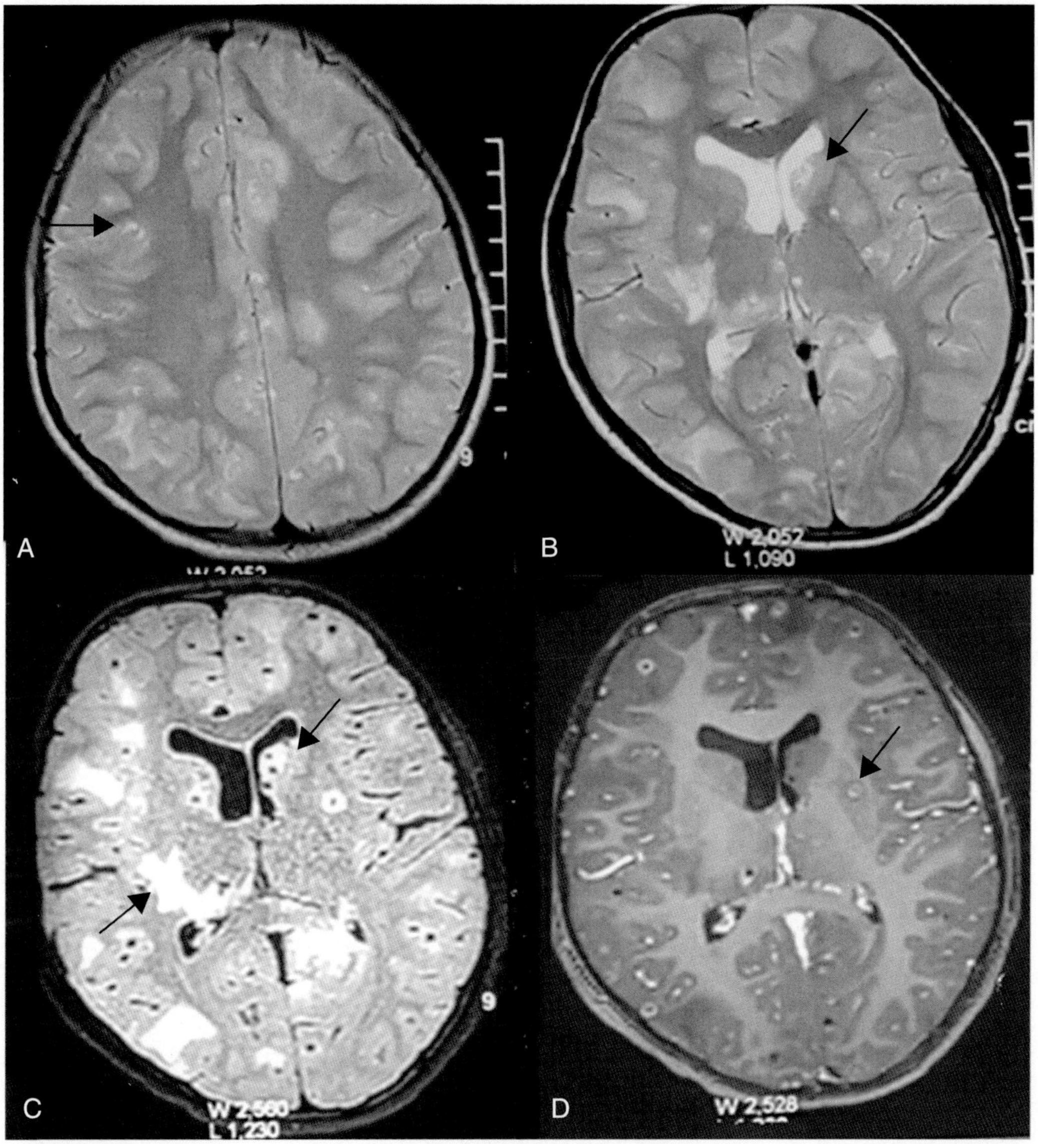

Fig. 39.2 Neurocysticercosis. Brain MRI, (A and B) Axial T2, (C) FLAIR, and (D) postcontrast T1 show multifocal "cyst with dot" enhancement, calcification, and perilesional edema (*arrows*). *FLAIR*, Fluid-attenuated inversion recovery.

Tropical Diseases. 2021;15(11):e0009883. doi:10.1371/journal.pntd.0009883.

Ganaraja HV, Mahadevan A, Saini J, Nalini A, Pal PK, Satishchandra P, Netravathi M. Disseminated Cysticercosis in Indian Scenario-Experience from a Teaching University Hospital. *Neurology India*. 2022;70(3):1032–1040. doi:10.4103/0028-3886.349634.

Ghosal A, Bhattacharya K, Shobhana A, Saraff R. Nightmares with a starry sky-Treating neurocysticercal encephalitis, how far to go. *Tropical Parasitology*. 2020;10(2):158–162. doi:10.4103/tp.TP_65_20.

Singhi P, Saini AG. Pediatric neurocysticercosis: current challenges and prospects. *Pediatric Health Medicine and Therapeutics*. 2016;8;7:5–16. doi:10.2147/PHMT.S79058.

Wangda K, Kumar N, Garg RK, Malhotra HS, Rizvi I, Uniyal R, Pandey S, Malhotra KP, Verma R, Sharma PK, Parihar A, Jain A. Value of whole-body MRI for the assessment of response to albendazole in disseminated neurocysticercosis: a prospective follow-up study. *Transactions of the Royal Society of Tropical Medicine and Hygiene.* 2023;117(4):271–278. doi:10.1093/trstmh/trac097.

White AC Jr, Coyle CM, Rajshekhar V, Singh G, Hauser WA, Mohanty A, Garcia HH, Nash TE. Diagnosis and treatment of neurocysticercosis: 2017 clinical practice guidelines by the Infectious Diseases Society of America (IDSA) and the American Society of Tropical Medicine and Hygiene (ASTMH). *American Journal of Tropical Medicine and Hygiene.* 2018;98(4):945–966. doi:10.4269/ajtmh.18-88751.

Zou Y, Wang F, Wang HB, Wu WW, Fan CK, Zhang HY, Wang L, Tian XJ, Li W, Huang MJ. Disseminated cysticercosis in China with complex and variable clinical manifestations: a case series. *BMC Infectious Disease.* 2019;19(1):543. doi:10.1186/s12879-019-4171-4.

Endemic Infection: Lying in Wait

HISTORY AND PHYSICAL

An 11-year-old boy presented with a low-grade fever for one month, followed by headache for the past 15 days and altered sensorium over the past week. On day 15 of fever, he experienced an episode of transient right-sided weakness that resolved within 24 hours. The headache was occasionally associated with projectile vomiting and transient relief. Patient and family history were noncontributory.

Clinical examination showed normal vital signs and anthropometry. Blood pressure in supine position was mildly elevated for age. The patient appeared sleepy but arousable. He had neck stiffness, Brudzinski sign, and bilateral Kernig signs. There was no papilledema, restriction of eye movement, facial or motor weakness. The rest of the systemic examination was unremarkable, without organomegaly or lymphadenopathy.

DIAGNOSTIC WORKUP

Lumbar puncture showed elevated CSF pressure with 179 cells (lymphocytes), normal glucose (63 mg/dL), elevated protein (97 mg/dL), and absence of acid-fast bacilli on Ziehl-Neelsen staining. Gram stain, bacterial cultures, and PCR for mycobacterium were negative. Intradermal Mantoux skin test was reactive and showed an induration of 15 × 15 mm. Serology for HIV was negative.

Head CT showed bilateral basal ganglia infarcts, basal exudates, hydrocephalus, and cerebellar tuberculomas (Fig. 40.1). Brain MRI with contrast revealed thick meningeal enhancement along the basal cisterns and bilateral cerebral convexities, basal ganglia infarcts, and moderate obstructive hydrocephalus (Fig. 40.2).

CLINICAL DIFFERENTIAL DIAGNOSIS

Chronic neurologic symptoms with fever, increased ICP, and meningismus can be seen in:

Infection: Tuberculosis, HIV with opportunistic infections, cryptococcosis, neurobrucellosis, invasive fungal infection, granulomatous amebic encephalitis in an immunocompromised host

Vascular: CNS vasculopathies

Tumors: primary CNS malignancies and metastases

IMAGING DIFFERENTIAL DIAGNOSIS

Meningeal enhancement: Tuberculosis, sarcoidosis, IgG4-related disease, leptomeningeal carcinomatosis.

Basal exudates: Tuberculosis, neurobrucellosis, granulomatous amebic encephalitis.

Hydrocephalus: Meningitis, tumors, aqueductal stenosis.

FINAL DIAGNOSIS

Tuberculous meningitis (TBM) with intracranial tuberculomas.

DISCUSSION

In endemic regions, CNS TB has a prevalence of 2 per 100,000 people and a mortality rate of 40% among hospitalized patients. *Mycobacterium tuberculosis* is spread via the respiratory tract to the lungs, from which it can disseminate hematogenously to the CNS. Lesions may rupture into the ventricular system and subarachnoid space, with subsequent inflammatory reaction forming thick gelatinous exudates, especially over the brainstem, basal cisterns, and Sylvian fissures. This in turn blocks the flow of CSF with resultant hydrocephalus (Fig. 40.3). Infarcts can occur secondary to perivascular involvement (Fig. 40.4).

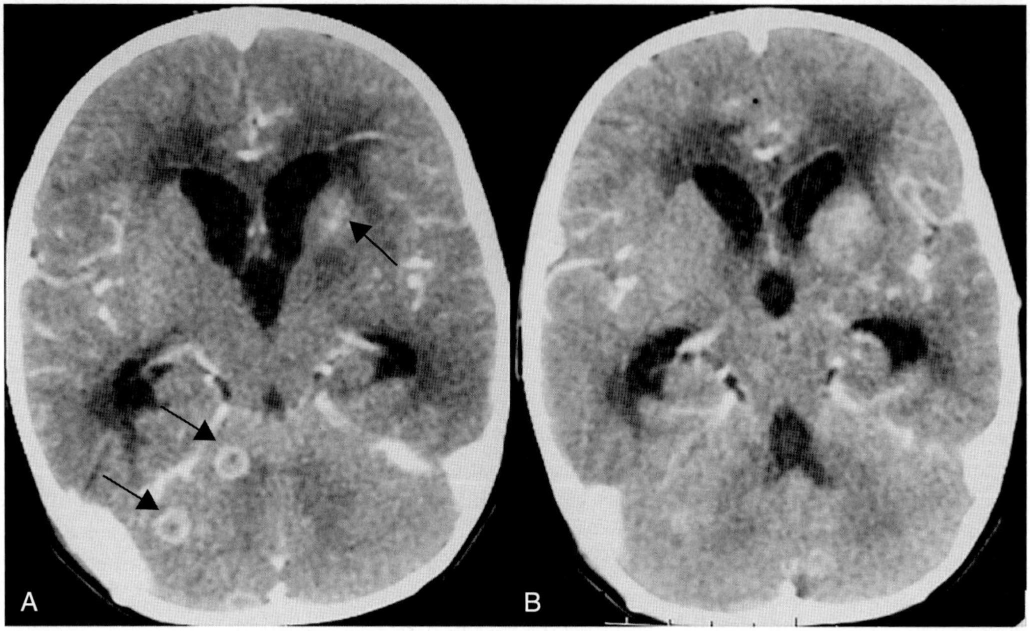

Fig. 40.1 Tuberculous meningitis. Head CT with contrast (A and B) showing communicating hydrocephalus, ring-enhancing lesions (*arrows*) with surrounding vasogenic edema, and leptomeningeal enhancement.

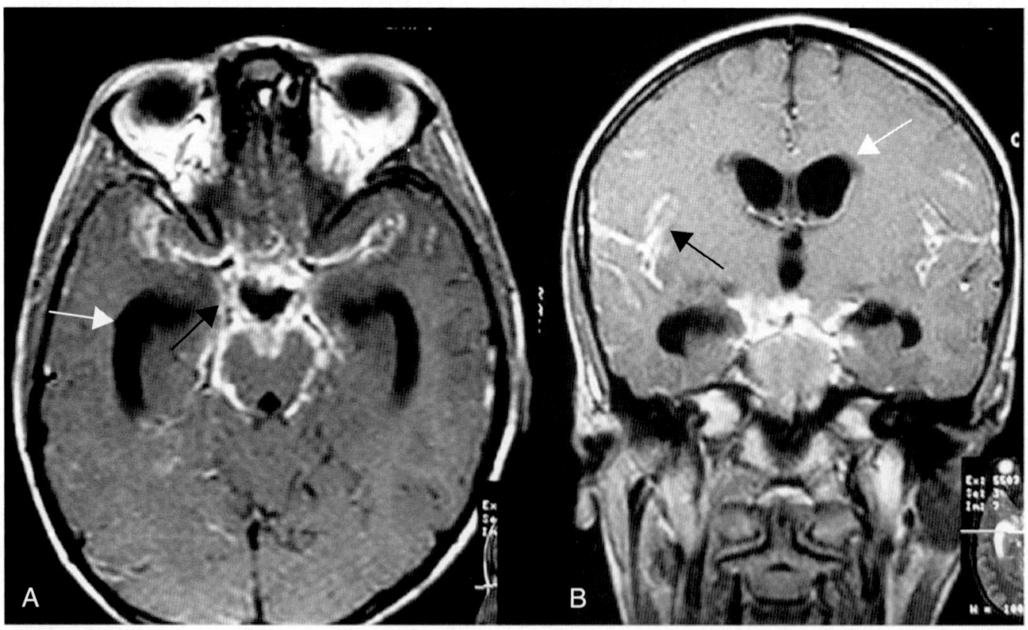

Fig. 40.2 Tuberculous meningitis. Brain MRI, (A) axial and (B) coronal postcontrast T1 show thick irregular meningeal enhancement along basal cisterns and insular regions (*black arrows*) with moderate communicating hydrocephalus (*white arrows*).

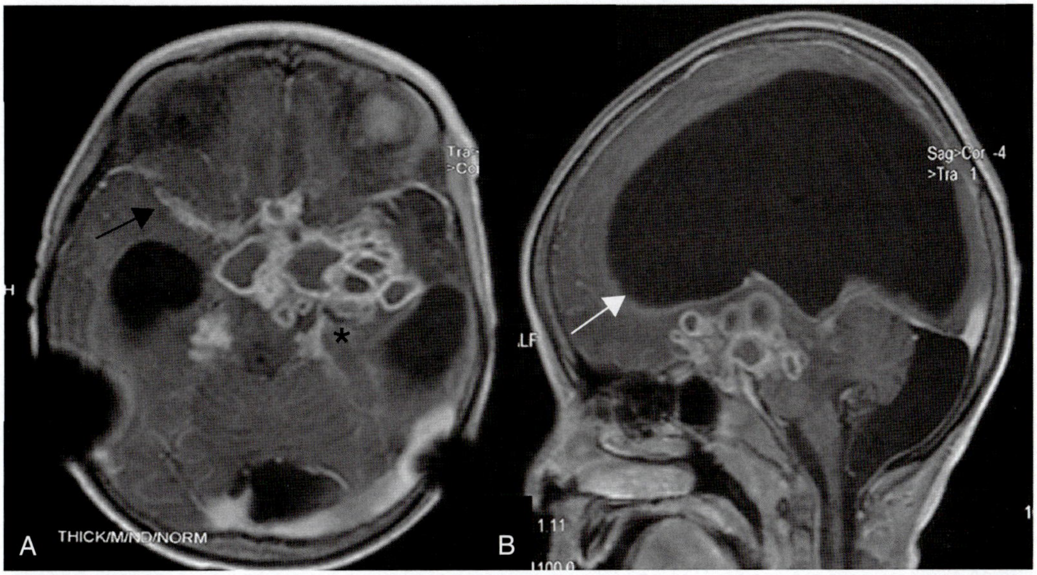

Fig. 40.3 Tuberculous meningitis. Brain MRI, (A) axial and (B) sagittal postcontrast T1 show multinodular enhancing tuberculomas in the basal cisterns (*asterisk*) with leptomeningeal enhancement (*black arrow*) and severe hydrocephalus (*white arrow*).

TBM commonly presents with subacute to chronic fever, malaise, headache, seizures, and meningismus. Headache, vomiting, bulging anterior fontanelle, diplopia, and papilledema suggest increased ICP and/or hydrocephalus. Over time, there may be progression of cranial nerve palsies, focal motor deficits, and encephalopathy. Complications include inflammatory vasculitis with strokes, hydrocephalus, tuberculoma or tubercular abscesses, vision loss, myeloradiculopathy, long-term cognitive defects, and epilepsy. Systemic complications consist of hyponatremia secondary to syndrome of inappropriate antidiuretic hormone secretion (SIADH), endocrinopathies due to pituitary involvement, drug-induced hepatitis, and peripheral neuropathy due to antitubercular therapy.

At imaging, basal meningeal exudates, infarcts, and tuberculomas (Fig. 40.3 and 40.4) can be seen. Concomitant HIV infection should be excluded as it is associated with a poorer prognosis. Evaluation of pulmonary disease is also important. Multidrug antitubercular therapy (ATT) for at least one year is the mainstay of management. Corticosteroids are given at the start of therapy to reduce inflammation. Sometimes, inflammatory reactions may occur weeks or months after the start of treatment and stopping steroids (paradoxical reaction), requiring further immunomodulation.

CLINICAL RED FLAGS

- Infants and young children have a higher risk of severe forms of TB, such as disseminated TB or TBM.
- Any child with subacute to chronic fever with neurological manifestations in an endemic region should be evaluated for TB.
- Presence of meningismus and CSF lymphocytosis support the clinical diagnosis.
- There may be a history of recent contact with another infected person.

IMAGING RED FLAGS

- Basal exudates, basal ganglia infarcts, and obstructive hydrocephalus are concerning for TBM (Fig. 40.3 and 40.4).
- Tuberculomas are often seen as conglomerate ring-enhancing lesions with surrounding edema (Fig. 40.3 and 40.4).
- Miliary TB is due to hematogeneous spread of infected tuberculous nodules (Fig. 40.5). This can be seen in infants and young children due to vertical transmission from the mother, or following dissemination of pulmonary TB.
- Spinal arachnoiditis is a rare manifestation with involvement of the cord surface, meninges, and nerve roots (Fig. 40.6).

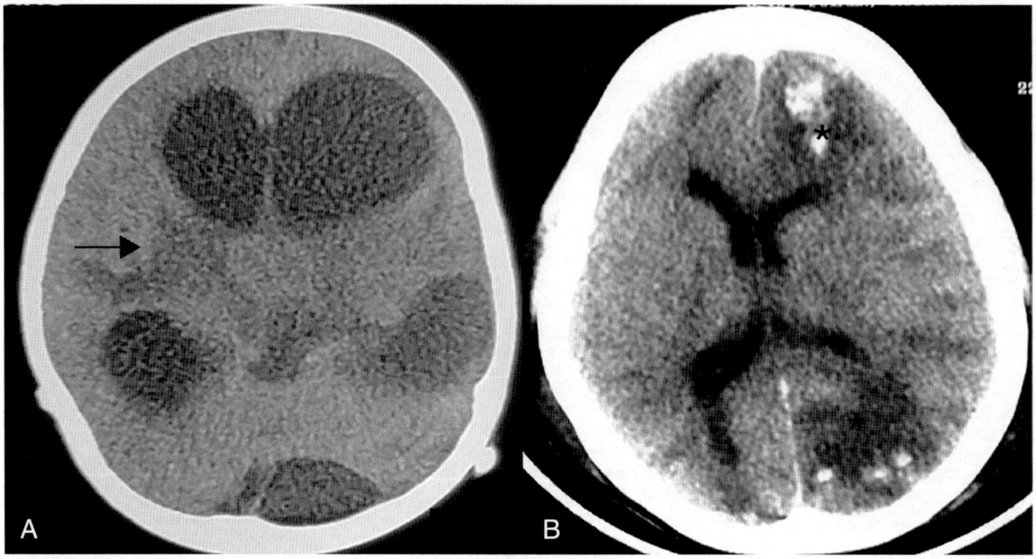

Fig. 40.4 Tuberculous meningitis. (A) Head CT without contrast showing severe communicating hydrocephalus and right basal ganglia hypodensity (*arrow*). (B) Head CT with contrast showing enhancing tuberculomas with vasogenic edema (*asterisks*). There is mild hydrocephalus and leptomeningeal enhancement.

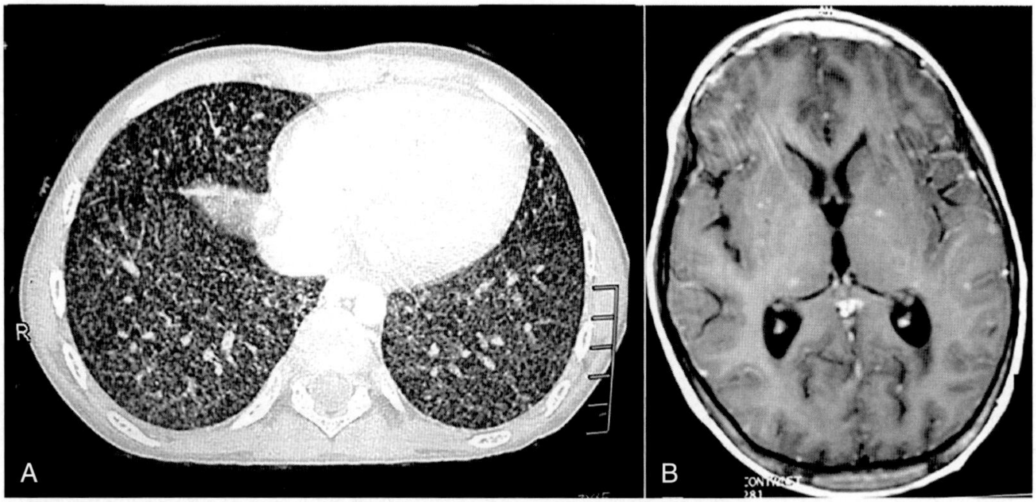

Fig. 40.5 Miliary tuberculosis. (A) Chest CT shows innumerable millimetric nodules throughout the bilateral lungs. (B) Brain MRI, axial postcontrast T1, shows tiny enhancing nodules throughout the brain and meninges.

CONCLUSIONS

In children with subacute to chronic febrile encephalopathy, TBM should be a leading consideration, especially in developing and endemic countries. CSF examination is crucial to the diagnosis and can show clear or straw-colored fluid with elevated pressures, cobweb formation, lymphocytic pleocytosis, low glucose, and elevated protein. Neuroimaging clues include the presence of basal exudates, infarcts, and hydrocephalus with or without leptomeningeal enhancement and ring-enhancing lesions (TB). Identification of organisms can be challenging, so probable diagnosis is made based on clinical features since timely initiation of ATT reduces mortality and morbidity.

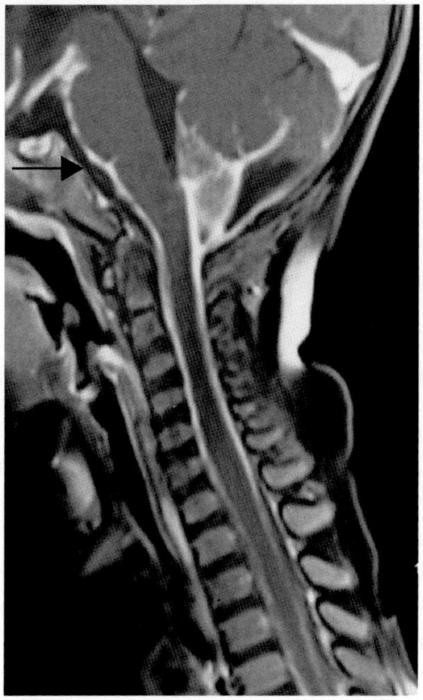

Fig. 40.6 Tuberculous arachnoiditis. Cervical spine MRI, sagittal postcontrast T1 shows thick irregular leptomeningeal enhancement coating the brain and cervical cord.

REFERENCES

Agarwal S, Saini AG, Dhawan S, Khadwal A, Sharma K, Singhi P. Comparative evaluation of IS6110 and protein antigen b PCR in cerebrospinal fluid for rapid diagnosis of tuberculous meningitis in children. *Journal of Medical Microbiology*. 2020;69(7):979–985. doi:10.1099/jmm.0.001220.

Daniel BD, Grace GA, Natrajan M. Tuberculous meningitis in children: Clinical management & outcome. *Indian Journal of Medical Research*. 2019;150(2):117–119. doi:10.4103/ijmr.IJMR_786_17.

Morais CG, Reis-Melo A, Oliveira J, Ribeiro A, Pinto-Carvalho I, Tavares M. Neuroimaging of central nervous system tuberculosis. *Acta Neurologica Taiwanica*. 2023;32(2):86–87. No doi provided.

Navarro-Flores A, Fernandez-Chinguel JE, Pacheco-Barrios N, Soriano-Moreno DR, Pacheco-Barrios K. Global morbidity and mortality of central nervous system tuberculosis: a systematic review and meta-analysis. *Journal of Neurology*. 2022;269(7):3482–3494. doi:10.1007/s00415-022-11052-8.

Sharma R, Saini AG, Katoch D, Bhatia V. Never Forget the Optic Fundi in Tuberculosis!. *Journal of Pediatrics*. 2018;195:305–306. doi:10.1016/j.jpeds.2017.11.035.

WHO consolidated guidelines on tuberculosis: Module 5: Management of tuberculosis in children and adolescents. Geneva: World Health Organization; 2022.

Case 41

Cerebral Malaria

HISTORY AND PHYSICAL

A 3-year-old previously healthy Malawian boy presented with nausea, fatigue, and headache followed by fever, loss of consciousness, and recurrent brief generalized seizures for one day. He was brought to a local health center where his malaria rapid diagnostic test was positive. He received intramuscular artesunate and was transported to a local referral hospital.

On examination, he was pale, febrile (39°C), tachycardic (150 beats per minute [bpm]), and comatose (Blantyre Coma Score [BCS] 1), with generalized hypotonia and hyperreflexia. Pupils were 3 mm bilaterally and slowly reactive. His resting gaze was deconjugate. Fundoscopic exam revealed macular whitening, flame hemorrhages, and papilledema (Fig. 41.1). His liver was palpable 2 cm below the right costal margin. Treatment with intravenous artesunate was continued. He was begun on intravenous ceftriaxone, and placed on maintenance fluids and supportive care.

DIAGNOSTIC WORKUP

Thick and thin blood smears showed *Plasmodium falciparum* asexual parasites with a density of 60,500/mm^3. White blood cell count was 13.5×10^{-19}/liter, hematocrit 20%, and platelet count 49×10^{-19}/liter. Both hyperlactatemia (9 mmol/liter) and hypoglycemia (2.1 mmol/liter) were present. Lumbar puncture opening pressure was 210 mm H_2O with clear CSF and white cell count of 2/high-power field (HPF). Cerebrospinal fluid protein and glucose were normal. Rapid HIV assay was negative.

Brain MRI revealed diffuse cerebral edema with cerebellar tonsillar herniation and effaced subarachnoid spaces (Fig. 41.2). Thirty-minute routine EEG showed an unreactive slow background with no sleep elements.

CLINICAL DIFFERENTIAL DIAGNOSIS

In endemic areas, cerebral malaria (CM) is the most common cause of febrile coma or acute febrile encephalopathy in children. Rapid diagnostic tests are typically used for screening tests, with peripheral blood smears performed to confirm asexual malaria parasitemia. People living in high-transmission areas may acquire partial immunity, with some eventually developing a state of asymptomatic parasitemia. It is therefore possible for a comatose febrile child to have a chronic asymptomatic parasitemia, followed by systemic or CNS coinfection (usually bacterial or viral) causing acute illness.

Malarial retinopathy is a confirmatory sign, as two-thirds of children with clinical CM have malarial retinopathy. However, recent studies show that many children without signs of malarial retinopathy (retinopathy-negative CM) can also be infected.

Other causes of non-malaria febrile coma in Africa include viral or bacterial meningoencephalitis, TBM, toxoplasmosis, and brucellosis. Bacterial meningoencephalitis usually manifests with elevated CSF white count. Focal findings on neurological examination can raise the possibility of focal abscess, tuberculoma, or empyema.

In the absence of fever, subacute-chronic neurologic symptoms can be seen with NCC and fungal infections, as well as tumors and autoimmune disorders.

IMAGING DIFFERENTIAL DIAGNOSIS

Cerebral edema and symmetric thalamic signal changes can be seen in a variety of disorders:

- Viral encephalitides (e.g., HSV, EBV, SARS-CoV-2, enterovirus, rabies, arboviruses)
- Autoimmune inflammatory conditions (e.g., acute disseminated encephalomyelitis)

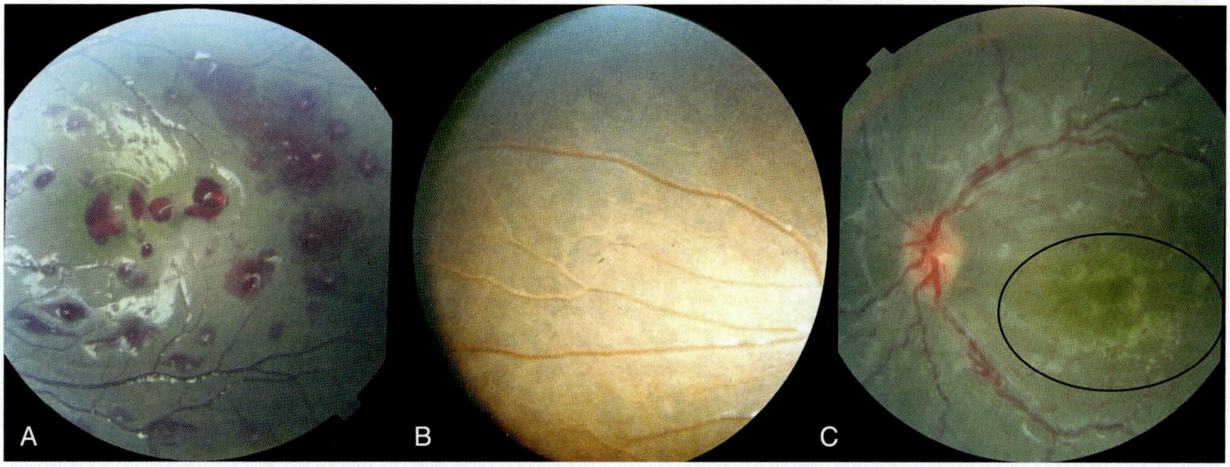

Fig. 41.1 Malarial retinopathy. (A) White-centered hemorrhages. (B) Vessel color changes in branching veins. (C) Perimacular whitening (*oval*). (Reproduced with permission from Taylor et al.)

- Posterior reversible encephalopathy syndrome (often comorbid with CM)
- Hypoxic-ischemic encephalopathy
- Neurometabolic diseases (e.g., Wilson's disease, Leigh syndrome, organic acidemias)

Other imaging features of CM can include focal or multifocal patchy/confluent T2/FLAIR hyperintensity and diffusion restriction, including the basal ganglia (Fig. 41.3), subcortical white matter (Fig. 41.4), and cortex.

FINAL DIAGNOSIS

Cerebral malaria.

DISCUSSION

Severe malaria yields end-organ dysfunction or serious hematological or metabolic abnormalities. Although anemia is the most common manifestation, CM is the most dreaded complication with a high mortality rate due to diffuse cerebral edema, herniation, brainstem compression, and respiratory arrest. Most cases occur in sub-Saharan Africa in children less than 5 years of age. Even with prompt treatment, the mortality rate is 15% to 25%. Among those that survive, 10% to 30% have neurologic deficits at the time of discharge, 25% to 50% have long-term neurocognitive/behavioral impairments, and 10% to 20% develop epilepsy. The diagnosis of CM is clinical and driven by epidemiology, history, physical exam, and malaria testing (rapid diagnostic tests, peripheral blood smears, PCR). Neuroimaging findings are nonspecific but may be used to rule out alternative etiologies.

CLINICAL RED FLAGS

The following factors increase mortality risk in CM:

- Blantyre Coma Score ≤1
- Leukocytosis
- Hypoglycemia (blood glucose <2.2 mmol/L or 40 mg/dL)
- Hyperlactatemia (blood lactate >5 mmol/L)

IMAGING RED FLAGS

- Diffuse cerebral edema with gray-white blurring, effacement of ventricles and subarachnoid spaces, cerebellar tonsillar herniation, brainstem compression.

CONCLUSIONS

Cerebral malaria is a common cause of febrile coma in endemic regions. Mortality risk is highest in children less than 5 years of age, or in those who have not yet acquired partial immunity. Although three *Plasmodium* species may cause CM, *Plasmodium falciparum*—transmitted to humans via the bites of female *Anopheles* mosquitos—is responsible for the vast majority of deaths in Africa. Affected children often present with rapid onset of seizures and coma. While the diagnosis is based

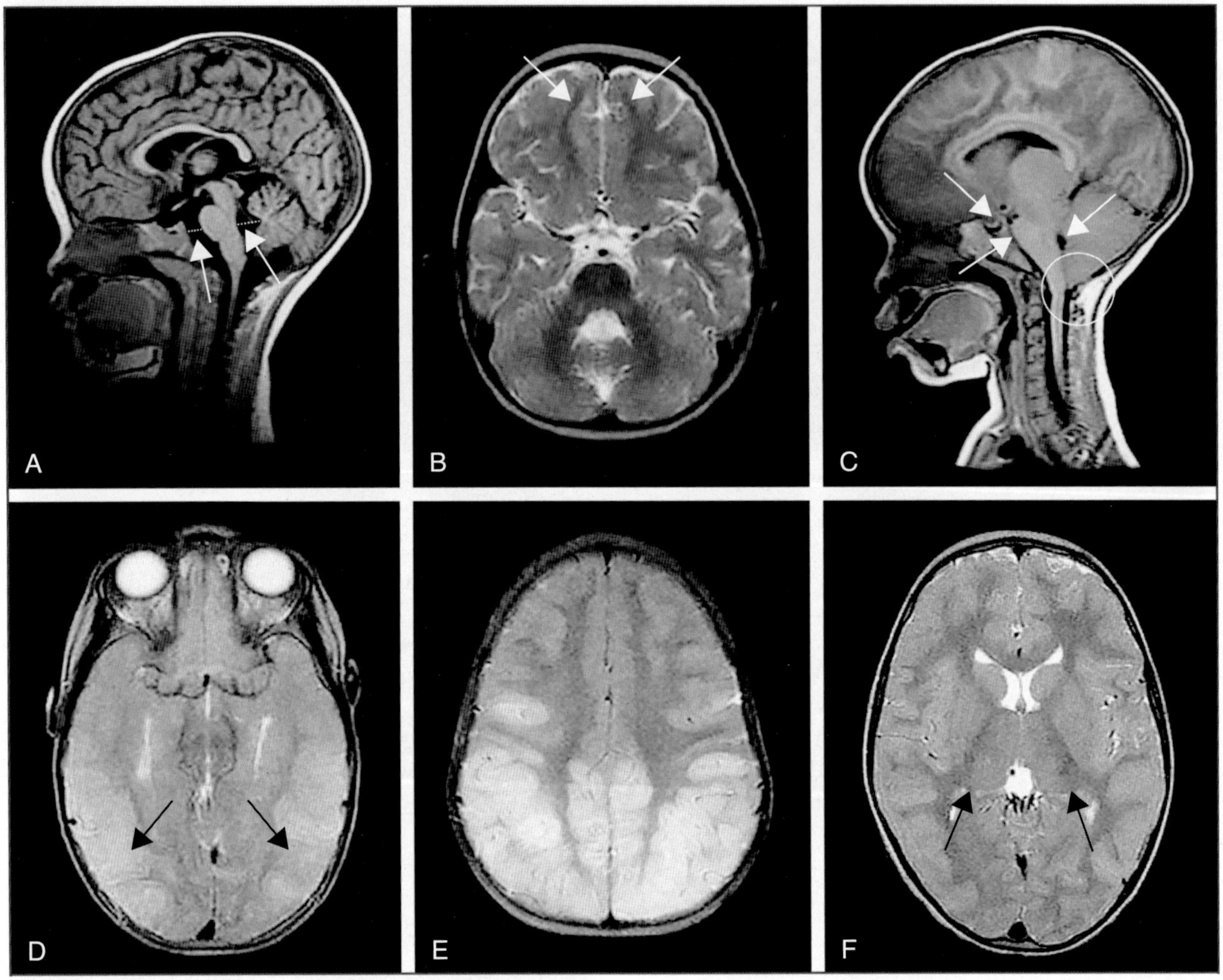

Fig. 41.2 Spectrum of brain MRI in cerebral malaria. (A) 14-month-old girl one month after infection. Sagittal T1 shows mild global volume loss and ex vacuo dilation of the prepontine cistern and fourth ventricle (*arrows*). (B) Axial T2 shows patchy edema in the bifrontal subcortical white matter (*arrows*), with crowding of sulci and basal cisterns. (C) Sagittal T1 with severe cerebral edema causing cerebellar tonsillar herniation (*circle*), effacement of prepontine cistern, compression of the fourth ventricle, and empty sella (*arrows*). (D) Follow-up axial T2 showing progression of cerebral edema with cortical swelling (*arrows*) and effacement of sulci and basal cisterns. (E) Involvement of the cortex is more severe posteriorly with swelling of the parieto-occipital cortex and (F) thalami (*arrows*). (Reproduced with permission from Seydel et al.)

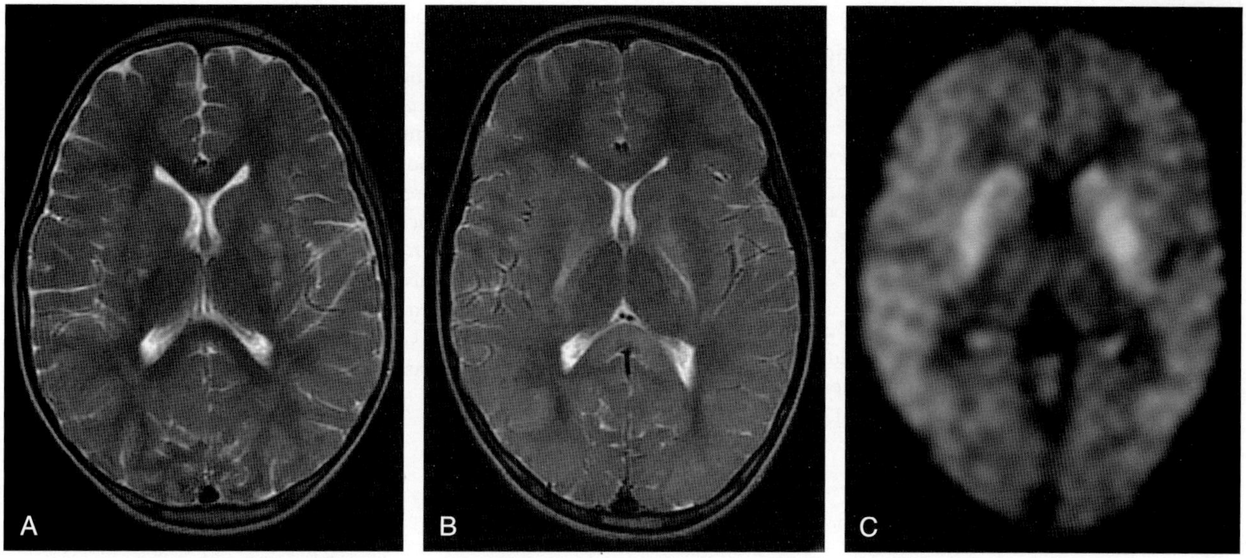

Fig. 41.3 Cerebral malaria involving basal ganglia. Brain MRI, (A) axial T2 with mild patchy basal ganglia edema. (B) Axial T2 with moderate basal ganglia edema. (C) Axial DWI with prominent basal ganglia restricted diffusion. *DWI*, Diffusion-weighted imaging. (Reproduced with permission from Potchen et al.)

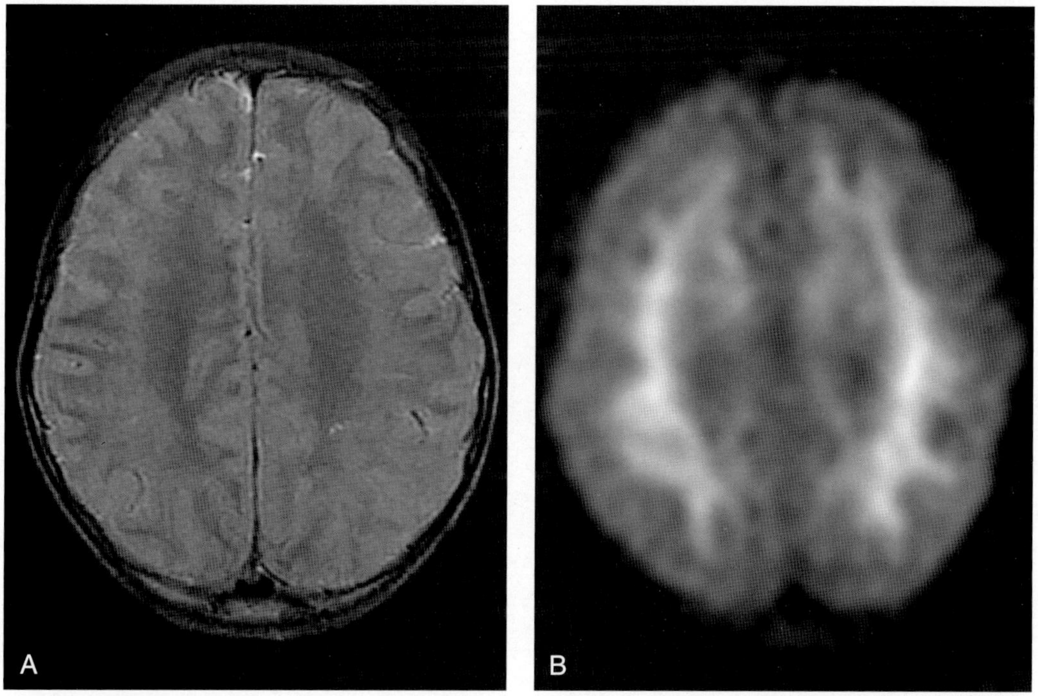

Fig. 41.4 Cerebral malaria involving white matter. Brain MRI, (A) axial T2 and (B) DWI with patchy subcortical edema and restricted diffusion. *DWI*, Diffusion-weighted imaging. (Reproduced with permission from Potchen et al.)

on clinical and laboratory findings, neuroimaging is important to rule out alternative etiologies and help determine prognosis.

REFERENCES

Idro R, Jenkins NE, Newton CR. Pathogenesis, Clinical Features, and Neurological Outcome of Cerebral Malaria. *The Lancet. Neurology*. 2005;4(12):827–840. doi:10.1016/S1474-4422(05)70247-7.

Potchen MJ, Kampondeni SD, Seydel KB, et al. Acute Brain MRI Findings in 120 Malawian Children with Cerebral Malaria: New Insights into an Ancient Disease. *American Journal of Neuroradiology*. 2012;33(9):1740–1746. doi:10.3174/ajnr.A3035.

Potchen MJ, Kampondeni SD, Seydel KB, et al. 1.5 Tesla Magnetic Resonance Imaging to Investigate Potential Etiologies of Brain Swelling in Pediatric Cerebral Malaria. *American Journal of Tropical Medicine and Hygiene*. 2018;98(2):497–504. doi:10.4269/ajtmh.17-0309.

Seydel KB, Kampondeni SD, Valim C, et al. Brain Swelling and Death in Children with Cerebral Malaria. *The New England Journal of Medicine*. 2015;372(12):1126–1137. doi:10.1056/NEJMoa1400116.

Taylor TE, Molyneux ME. The Pathogenesis of Pediatric Cerebral Malaria: Eye Exams, Autopsies, and Neuroimaging. *Annals of the New York Academy of Sciences*. 2015;1342(1):44–52. doi:10.1111/nyas.12690.

SECTION 9

Pediatric Brain Tumors

Gökalp Çıkman, Esma Şengenç, Aisling B. Fagan, Kshitij Mankad

INTRODUCTION

Central nervous system (CNS) tumors are the most common solid tumors in children. Brain tumors are still very rare overall, occurring in 5 of every 100,000 children. Between 54% and 70% of all childhood brain tumors originate in the posterior fossa, compared to 15% to 20% of adult brain tumors. Lesions can be benign or malignant; both types can be life-threatening depending on location. Pediatric brain tumors differ from those in adults in histology, location, and prognosis. Many children and adolescents who develop brain tumors will survive into adulthood but face long-term physical, psychological, social, and intellectual challenges.

Clinical features concerning for a brain tumor include increased intracranial pressure, such as headaches with red flags (new onset, waking up at night, nausea, vomiting, personality changes, double vision). Additional symptoms may include new-onset seizure, stroke-like events, or focal neurological deficits. The phenotype reflects a wide spectrum of tumor size, location, patterns of growth and metastasis, and complications.

Due to the broad differential diagnosis, neuroimaging is important to detect, characterize, and classify tumors and monitor growth, response to therapy, and complications. Brain MRI provides multiple options for soft tissue contrast, without the radiation exposure of CT. Imaging technology continues to advance with new methods to characterize tissue properties in correlation with histologic and molecular features.

Brain tumors are commonly treated with surgery and adjuvant therapies, such as chemotherapy and radiation. With the discovery of causative genetic mutations, there is an increased focus on targeted immunotherapy and molecular therapies that can modify the course of disease.

The fifth edition of the WHO Classification of Tumors of the CNS, published in 2021, is the sixth version of the international standard for the classification of brain and spinal cord tumors. Radiologic criteria are not formally included in this system; however, imaging is essential to localize and characterize tumors, enable locoregional and distant staging, and provide noninvasive longitudinal assessments. In this chapter, we will review key diagnostic considerations and neuroimaging findings for five classic pediatric brain tumors.

SUGGESTED READINGS

Cohen AR. Brain tumors in children. *New England Journal of Medicine.* 2022;386(20):1922–1931. doi:10.1056/nejmra2116344.

Roth C. Supratentorielle Hirntumoren im kindesalter. *Die Radiologie.* 2023;63(8):592–597. doi:10.1007/s00117-023-01158-z.

Tomita T. Pediatric neuroimaging in pre-CT era: back to the future. *Child's Nervous System.* 2023;39(10):2595-2604. doi:10.1007/s00381-023-06018-8

Udaka YT, Packer RJ. Pediatric brain tumors. *Neurologic Clinics.* 2018;36(3):533–556. doi:10.1016/j.ncl.2018.04.009.

Yang M, Wang J, Zhang L, Liu J. Update on MRI in pediatric intracranial germ cell tumors: the clinical and radiological features. *Frontiers in Pediatrics.* 2023;11. doi:10.3389/fped.2023.1141397.

Case 42

Posterior Fossa Emergency

HISTORY AND PHYSICAL

A 6-year-old previously healthy boy presented with a 20-day history of increasing headache, nausea, and vomiting upon awakening from sleep. He was admitted to the pediatric emergency unit with worsening double vision, gait disturbance, and back pain over two days. He was the only child of healthy, nonconsanguineous parents.

On physical examination, temperature was 36.3°C, pulse 100, respiratory rate 24/min, blood pressure 100/60, weight 19 kg (25%), height 114 cm (37%). On neurological examination, he was conscious and cooperative, with no signs of meningeal irritation. Papilledema was present on fundoscopy. Horizontal nystagmus was detected when looking to the left. Dysmetria, dysdiadochokinesia, and ataxic gait were also noted. Examination of other systems was unremarkable.

DIAGNOSTIC WORKUP

Routine laboratory tests were normal.

Head CT showed a hyperdense rounded mass in the fourth ventricle with obstructive hydrocephalus.

Brain MRI with contrast showed corresponding contrast enhancement and diffusion restriction, with leptomeningeal metastases in the brain (Fig. 42.1) and spine (Fig. 42.2).

CLINICAL DIFFERENTIAL DIAGNOSES

Clinical signs of brainstem and cerebellar dysfunction raise concern for posterior fossa pathology including neoplasms, infections, demyelinating, and vascular diseases.

IMAGING DIFFERENTIAL DIAGNOSES

Pediatric posterior fossa tumors can be intra- or extra-axial. Intra-axial lesions include medulloblastoma, ependymoma, astrocytoma, atypical teratoid-rhabdoid tumor (ATRT), teratoma, and hemangioblastoma.

Medulloblastoma is the most common malignant pediatric fossa tumor. There are four molecular subtypes, which show variable location, morphology, and hypercellular imaging characteristics, including hyperdensity on CT, iso- to hypointensity on T2, diffusion restriction on diffusion-weighted imaging (DWI), and contrast enhancement.

ATRT is more aggressive than medulloblastoma, often affecting young children less than four years of age, and appearing more heterogeneous at imaging with necrotic/hemorrhagic conversion, greater risk of regional dissemination and metastasis.

Pilocytic astrocytoma is the most common low-grade posterior fossa tumor. It frequently has both solid and cystic components, with prominent enhancement of the solid component and overall facilitated diffusion.

Ependymomas arise from the ependymal cells of the fourth ventricle and tend to insinuate along cerebrospinal fluid (CSF) spaces with a "toothpaste" morphology and cystic/hemorrhagic changes.

Brainstem gliomas can expand and infiltrate the brainstem. Low-grade ones generally have a well-marginated appearance, while high-grade ones are diffusely infiltrative with areas of enhancement and restricted diffusion.

Nonneoplastic disorders include giant perivascular spaces, demyelinating or autoimmune disease, vasculopathy, metabolic disease, infarct, and infection.

Extra-axial lesions can include dermoid/epidermoid cyst, neurenteric cyst, schwannoma, meningioma, and other skull base tumors.

FINAL DIAGNOSIS

Group 3 medulloblastoma with leptomeningeal metastasis.

DISCUSSION

Medulloblastoma is a WHO grade 4 CNS embryonal tumor and the most common malignant pediatric posterior fossa tumor. Imaging features of hyperdensity on CT, hypointensity on T2, and diffusion restriction on DWI reflect the high cellularity and nucleocytoplasmic ratio. Variable contrast enhancement, cystic changes, calcification, and hemorrhage can be present. The WHO classification includes four molecular subgroups with

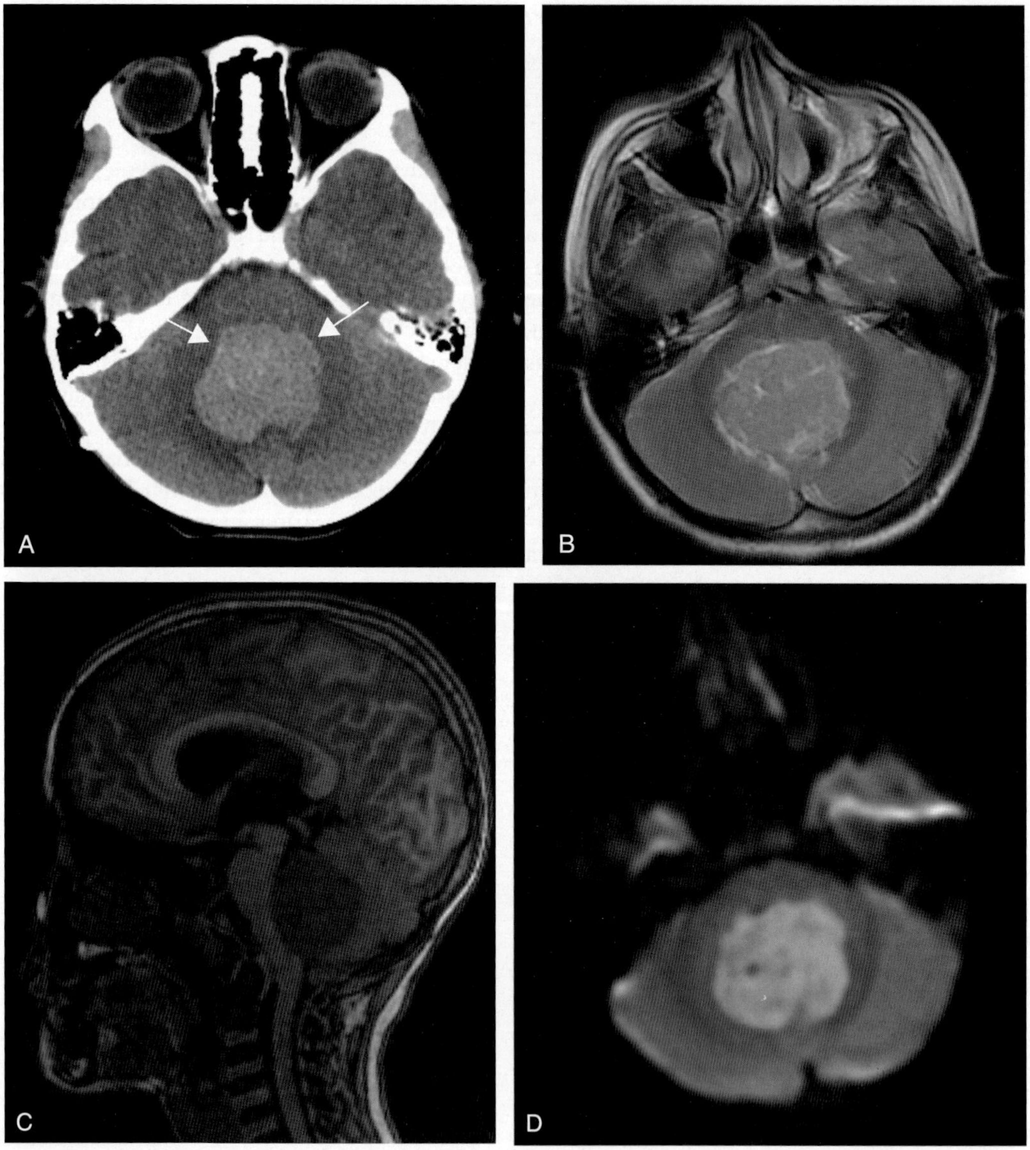

Fig. 42.1 Group 3 medulloblastoma with intracranial leptomeningeal metastasis. (A) Noncontrast head CT shows expansile, hyperdense mass in the fourth ventricle (*white arrows*). Brain MRI, (B) axial T2 demonstrates tumor isointense to cerebellar gray matter. (C) Sagittal T1 shows tumor compression of cerebellum and dorsal brainstem. (D) Axial DWI image shows prominent restricted diffusion. Axial postcontrast T1 shows (E) mild homogeneous tumor enhancement (*arrow*) and (F) left parietal nodular leptomeningeal metastasis (*arrow*). *DWI*, Diffusion-weighted imaging.

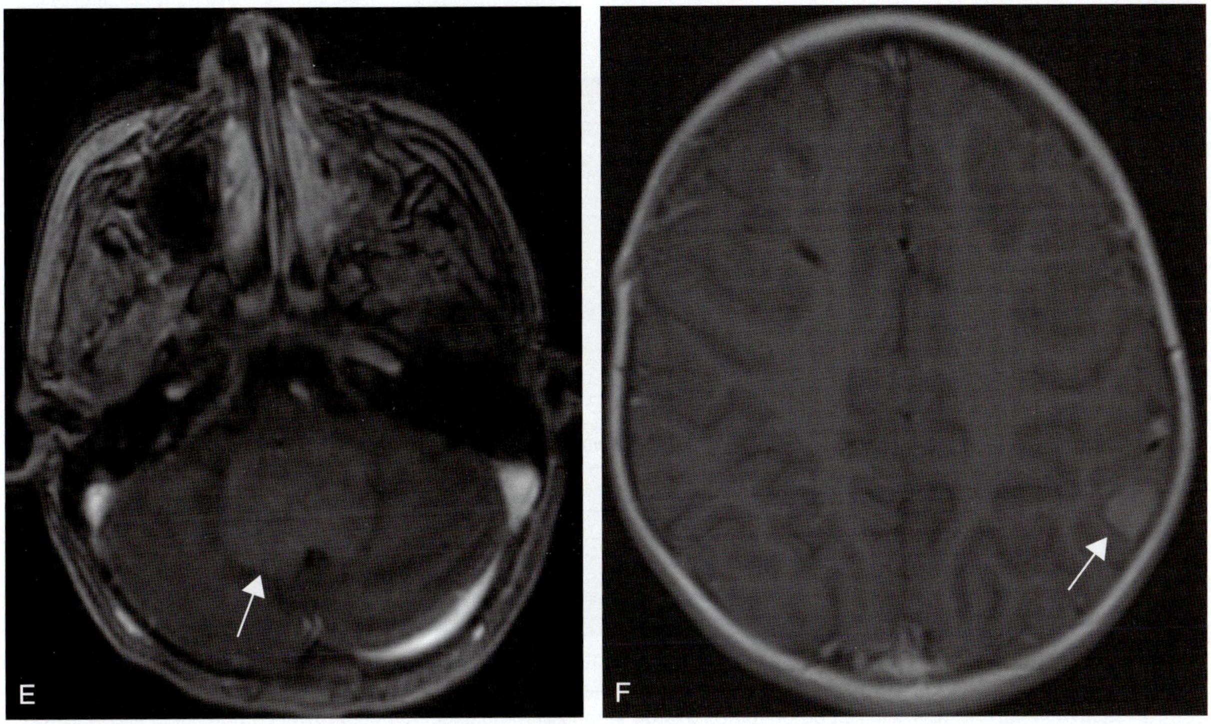

Fig. 42.1 cont'd

distinct clinical characteristics, embryonic precursor cells, radiologic phenotypes, and outcomes: wingless (Wnt), sonic hedgehog (Shh), group 3, and group 4. Wnt tumors arise at the cerebellopontine angle, Shh tumors arise in the cerebellar hemispheres with a desmoplastic nodular histology, and non-Wnt/Shh tumors arise in the fourth ventricle with mild enhancement for group 3 and minimal enhancement for group 4. On MR spectroscopy, medulloblastoma shows high levels of choline, taurine, and lipids and decreased N-acetylaspartate (NAA). Leptomeningeal metastases can be present at diagnosis, which tend to be nodular in group 3 and laminar in group 4. The standard treatment is maximally safe surgical resection followed by chemotherapy and craniospinal radiation. Follow-up imaging may show areas of residual treated tumor or posttreatment inflammatory changes.

CLINICAL RED FLAGS

- In infants, rapid increase in head circumference, intermittent lethargy, and tilting the head to one side.
- In children, worsening headache, vomiting, and neurological symptoms.
- Papilledema on fundoscopy is concerning for a space-occupying lesion.
- Changes in consciousness and coma are concerning for brainstem compression and hydrocephalus.

IMAGING RED FLAGS

- Leptomeningeal metastasis at presentation has a poor prognosis and requires treatment with chemotherapy and craniospinal radiation.
- Primary and metastatic tumors may show no or minimal enhancement (particularly groups 3–4), so DWI must be scrutinized (Fig. 42.3). High-resolution heavily T2-weighted imaging, such as steady-state free precession (SSFP), can also help increase contrast between CSF and brain parenchyma to detect small nodular tumor deposits.
- Bones (vertebrae, skull) and lymph nodes are the most common sites for systemic metastasis.

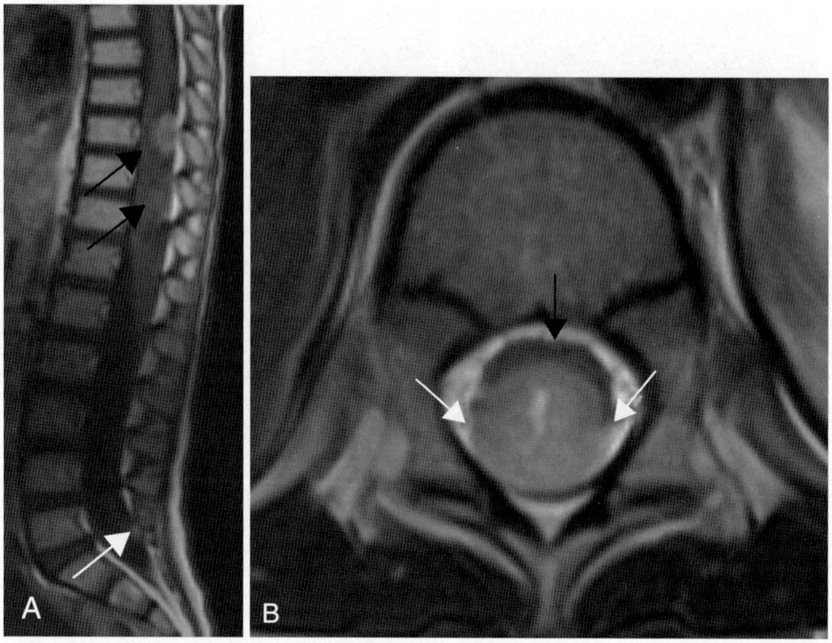

Fig. 42.2 Group 3 medulloblastoma with spinal leptomeningeal metastasis. Lumbar spine MRI, (A) sagittal postcontrast T1 shows enhancing drop metastases along the distal spinal cord (*black arrows*) and thecal sac (*white arrow*). (B) Axial T2 demonstrates a large intradural metastasis (*white arrows*) compressing and displacing the spinal cord anteriorly (*black arrow*).

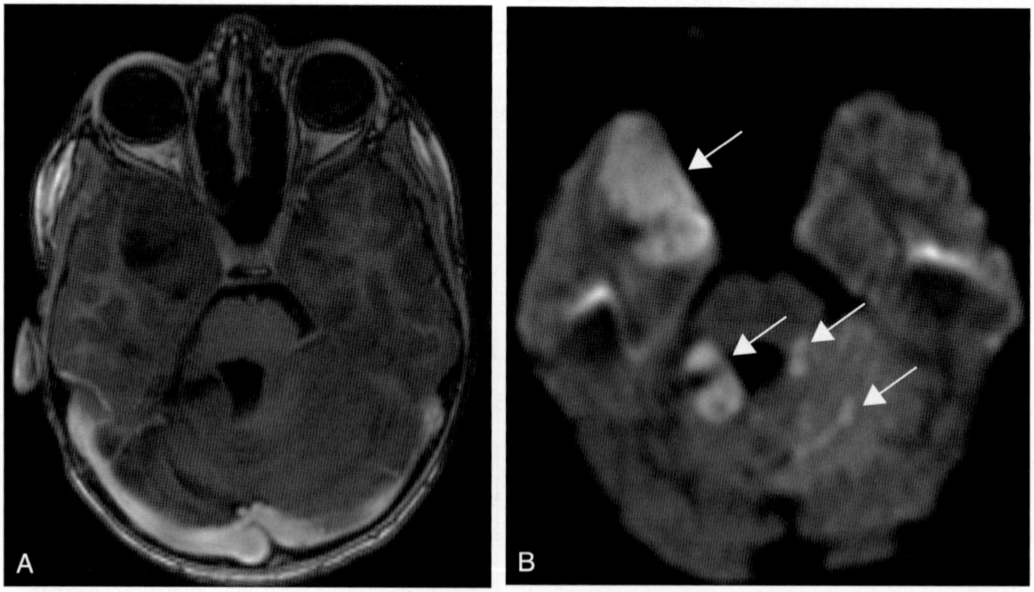

Fig. 42.3 Group 4 medulloblastoma with nonenhancing leptomeningeal metastasis. Brain MRI, (A and C) axial postcontrast T1 show several nonenhancing or minimally enhancing leptomeningeal metastases with (B and D) prominent restricted diffusion on DWI (*arrows*). *DWI*, Diffusion-weighted imaging.

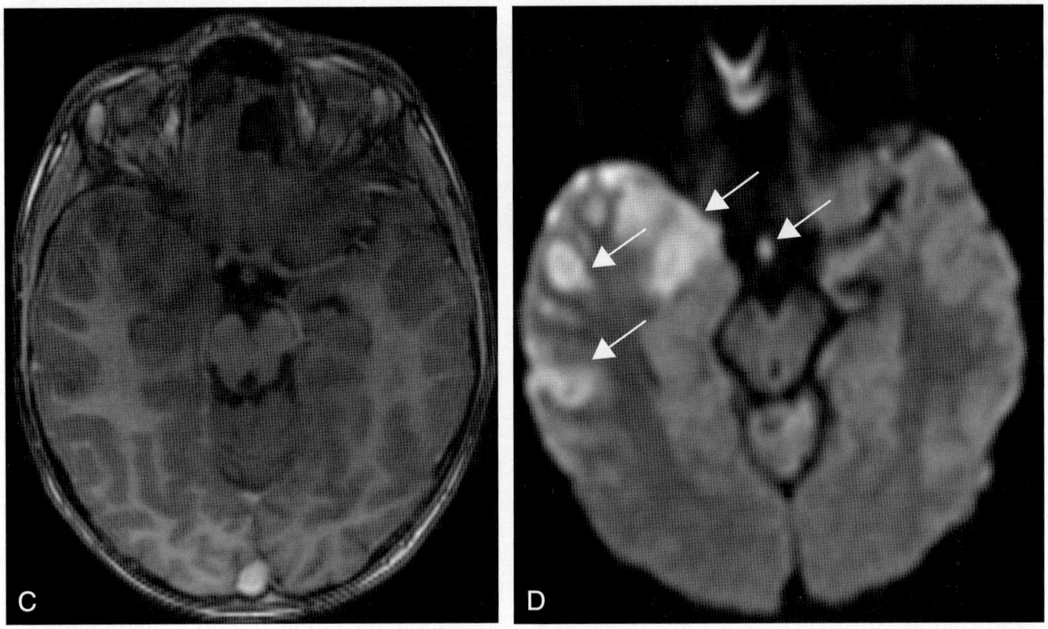

Fig. 42.3 cont'd

CONCLUSIONS

New-onset symptoms such as headache, nausea, and vomiting may be due to a space-occupying lesion that causes increased intracranial pressure. Atypical clinical history and worsening neurological findings should prompt imaging to identify an underlying mass.

REFERENCES

AlRayahi J, Zapotocky M, Ramaswamy V, et al. Pediatric brain tumor genetics: What radiologists need to know. *RadioGraphics.* 2018;38(7):2102–2122. doi:10.1148/rg.2018180109.

Culleton S, McKenna B, Dixon L, et al. Imaging pitfalls in paediatric posterior fossa neoplastic and non-neoplastic lesions. *Clinical Radiology.* 2021;76(5):391.e19-391.e31. doi:10.1016/j.crad.2020.12.011.

Koeller KK, Rushing EJ. From the archives of the AFIP: Medulloblastoma- A Comprehensive Review with Radiologic-Pathologic Correlation. *RadioGraphics.* 2003;23(6):1613–1637. doi:10.1148/rg.236035168.

Kool M, Korshunov A, Remke M, et al. Molecular subgroups of Medulloblastoma: An international meta-analysis of transcriptome, genetic aberrations, and clinical data of Wnt, shh, group 3, and group 4 medulloblastomas. *Acta Neuropathologica.* 2012;123(4):473–484. doi:10.1007/s00401-012-0958-8.

Soares BP, Poretti A, Huisman TAGM. Magnetic resonance imaging to diagnose leptomeningeal spread of medulloblastoma in children: Decreasing diagnostic uncertainty, moving in New Directions. *Pediatric Blood & Cancer.* 2017;64(8):9–10. doi:10.1002/pbc.26514.

Case 43

Sticky in the Sella

HISTORY AND PHYSICAL

A 9-year-old boy began drinking large amounts of water and urinating excessively for 3 months. This led to frequent interruptions at school and bedwetting at night. Over the past 3 weeks, his vision worsened and he had difficulty reading the school board from a distance. Medical history was unremarkable with no history of asphyxia, head trauma, surgery, encephalitis, tuberculosis, kidney disease, blood disease, visual impairment, deafness, or drug use. He was the third child of healthy, nonconsanguineous parents. The other two siblings, a 14-year-old girl and a 12-year-old boy, were both healthy.

Physical examination showed temperature 36.2°C, pulse 90, respiration rate 23/min, blood pressure 100/60, weight 22 kg (3%), and height 123 cm (5%). Head and neck examination was normal and assessments of respiratory, cardiovascular, gastrointestinal, and genitourinary systems were unremarkable. Bitemporal hemianopsia was detected on ophthalmologic examination.

DIAGNOSTIC WORKUP

Glucose and renal function tests were within normal limits. Urine volume was increased and a urine sample was lightly colored, with specific gravity between 1.001 and 1.005, and osmolality lower than plasma. Water restriction test and nasal 1-desamino-8-D-arginine vasopressin test confirmed central diabetes insipidus. Head CT showed a sellar and suprasellar mass with calcifications. Brain MRI showed an expansile cystic sellar and suprasellar mass replacing the pituitary gland and infundibulum. There was a mural nodule along the superior surface with uplifting and compression of the hypothalamus and optic chiasm (Fig. 43.1).

CLINICAL DIFFERENTIAL DIAGNOSES

Common endocrine presentations of hypothalamic and pituitary disorders are central (vasopressin deficient) diabetes insipidus, hypopituitarism, precocious puberty, delayed/early puberty, and amenorrhea.

In a patient with diabetes insipidus and bitemporal hemianopsia, consider masses of the sella and suprasellar region including tumors, inflammation, infection, and vascular lesions.

IMAGING DIFFERENTIAL DIAGNOSES

Pediatric sellar and suprasellar masses can include craniopharyngioma, optic-hypothalamic glioma, germ cell tumor, Langerhans cell histiocytosis, hypothalamic hamartoma, pituitary adenoma, Rathke cleft cyst, arachnoid cyst, inflammatory, and granulomatous disease.

Craniopharyngioma is a benign tumor originating from remnants of the Rathke pouch with admixed solid tissue, coarse calcifications, and complex cysts of varying size and composition. Tumor walls can be very adherent to surrounding brain parenchyma with associated vasogenic edema.

Optic pathway-hypothalamic gliomas are infiltrative tumors with T2-hyperintense signal, facilitated diffusion, and variable contrast enhancement.

Germ cell tumors are heterogeneous midline tumors that arise near the midline with heterogeneous solid-enhancing tissue and restricted diffusion, cystic/hemorrhagic changes, and calcifications. CSF dissemination is common.

Langerhans cell histiocytosis preferentially involves the infundibulum with a thickened appearance. Additional sites of osseous involvement may be present in the cranium, jaw, or skeleton with lytic and "beveled edge" appearance.

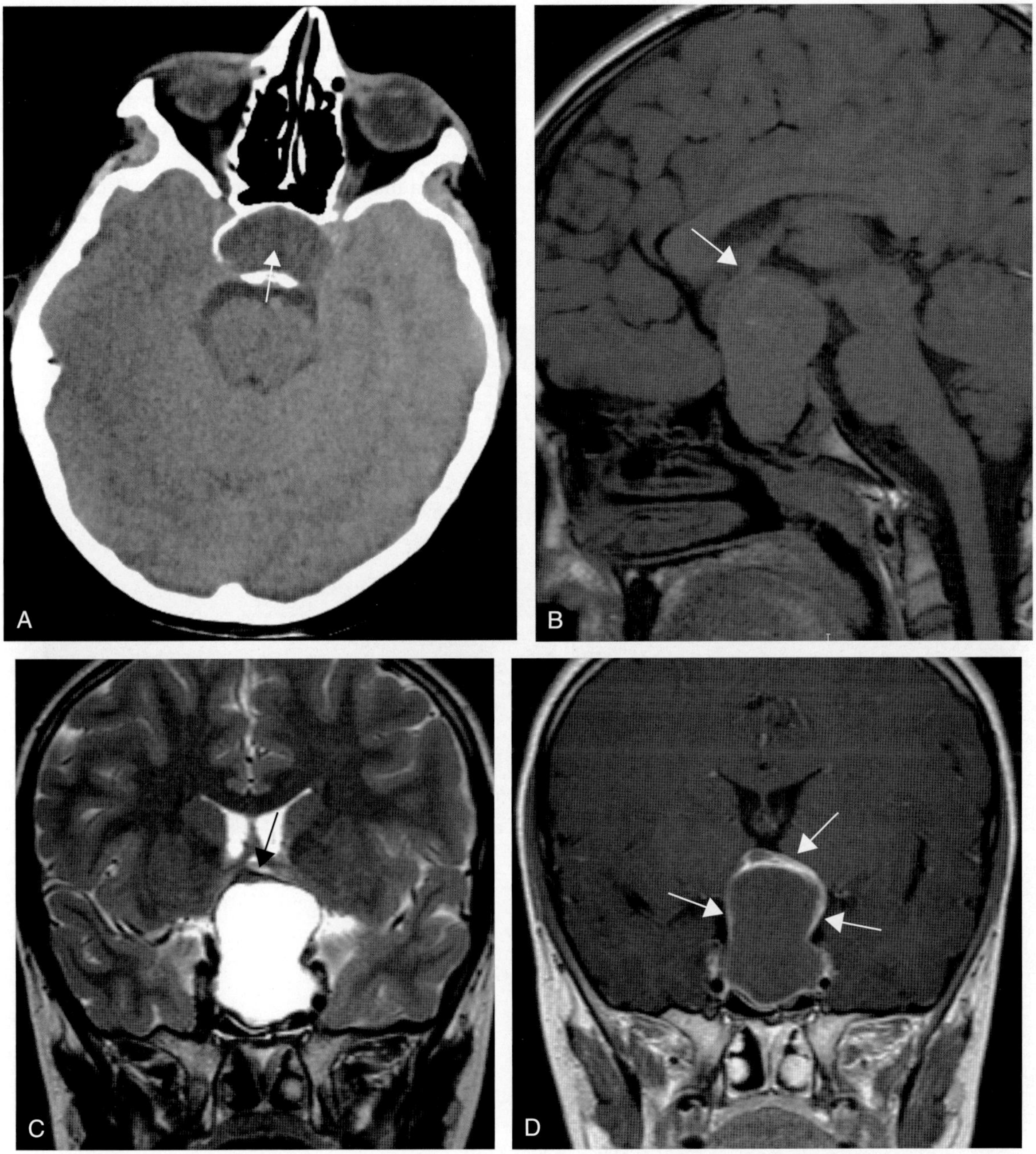

Fig. 43.1 Craniopharyngioma. (A) Noncontrast head CT shows an expansile hypodense sellar mass with surrounding bone remodeling. Brain MRI, (B) sagittal precontrast T1 demonstrates a lobulated sellar/suprasellar mass with uplifting of the optic chiasm (*arrow*). (C) Coronal T2 shows hyperintense cystic component with small superior solid nodule (*arrow*). (D) Postcontrast coronal T1 shows peripheral cyst wall and solid nodular enhancement (*arrows*).

Hypothalamic hamartomas are sessile or pedunculated masses of ectopic gray matter with similar signal characteristics but more disorganized appearance (Fig. 43.2).

Pituitary adenomas arise in pituitary parenchyma with relative hypoenhancement and can invade the suprasellar cistern, cavernous sinus, and/or clivus.

Rathke cleft cysts arise from the pars intermedia as small intrasellar or suprasellar complex cystic lesions with a proteinaceous mural nodule.

Arachnoid cysts are extra-axial CSF collections that can be congenital or secondary to prior infection or hemorrhage. When located in the suprasellar region, they can herniate down through the diaphragma sellae and compress the pituitary gland with an "empty sella" appearance.

Inflammatory conditions that can affect the pituitary gland include lymphocytic hypophysitis and autoimmune polyendocrinopathy. There may be thickening

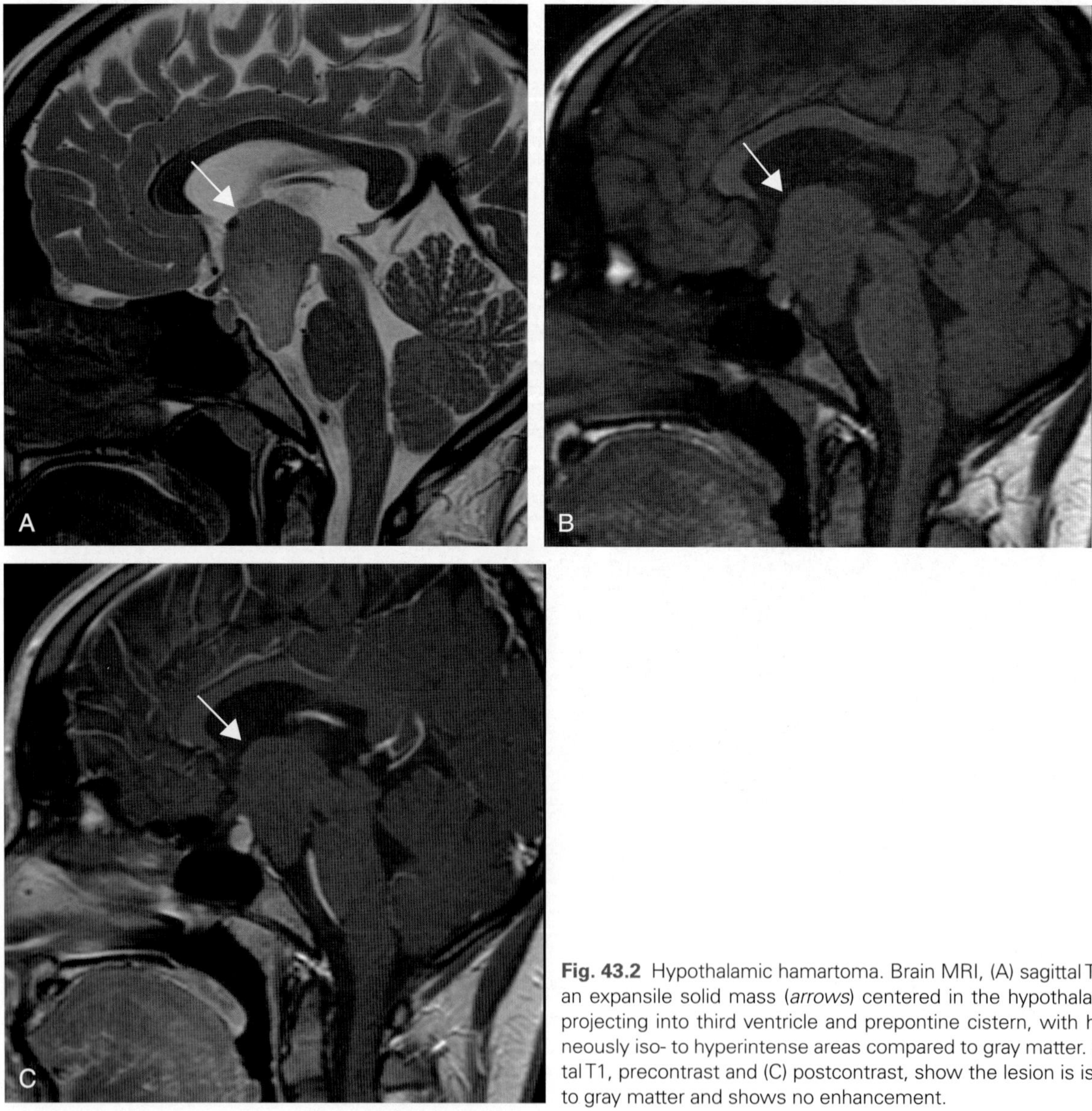

Fig. 43.2 Hypothalamic hamartoma. Brain MRI, (A) sagittal T2 shows an expansile solid mass (*arrows*) centered in the hypothalamus and projecting into third ventricle and prepontine cistern, with heterogeneously iso- to hyperintense areas compared to gray matter. (B) Sagittal T1, precontrast and (C) postcontrast, show the lesion is isointense to gray matter and shows no enhancement.

and hyperenhancement of the gland in early stages, and scarring and fibrosis in more chronic stages.

Tuberculosis and sarcoidosis can manifest with intra- or extra-axial granulomatous nodular deposits showing T2-hypointense signal, restricted diffusion, and enhancement.

FINAL DIAGNOSIS

Craniopharyngioma.

DISCUSSION

Central diabetes insipidus and bitemporal hemianopsia raise concern for a suprasellar mass compressing the hypothalamus, pituitary, and optic chiasm. Pathologies affecting this region include craniopharyngioma, optic-hypothalamic glioma, germ cell tumor, Langerhans cell histiocytosis, hypothalamic hamartoma, pituitary adenoma, Rathke cleft cyst, arachnoid cyst, inflammatory, and granulomatous disease.

Craniopharyngiomas constitute 3% to 5% of all childhood intracranial tumors and 50% of suprasellar tumors. They are more common in males, with an incidence peaking between the ages of 10 and 14 years. Headache, visual field defects, anterior and posterior pituitary gland dysfunction, hyperphagia, and obesity are the most common clinical symptoms.

At imaging, craniopharyngiomas follow the "90% rule": 90% suprasellar, 90% solid/cystic, 90% calcified, and 90% enhancing. There can be enhancing solid tissue, coarse calcifications, and complex cysts with varying proteinaceous content. Tumor walls can be very adherent to surrounding brain parenchyma with associated vasogenic edema. Tumor can enlarge and extend inferiorly into the sella, laterally into middle cranial fossa, anteriorly into anterior cranial fossa, posteriorly toward the brainstem, and superiorly to the third ventricle (Fig. 43.3).

Preoperative imaging aims to identify in detail the relation between the mass and the pituitary gland, stalk, optic chiasm, hypothalamus, and vascular structures in order to determine the optimal surgical approach. Initial management involves drainage of cystic components to decrease mass effect. Additional debulking can be performed but should seek to preserve hypothalamic function. Given the high local recurrence rate,

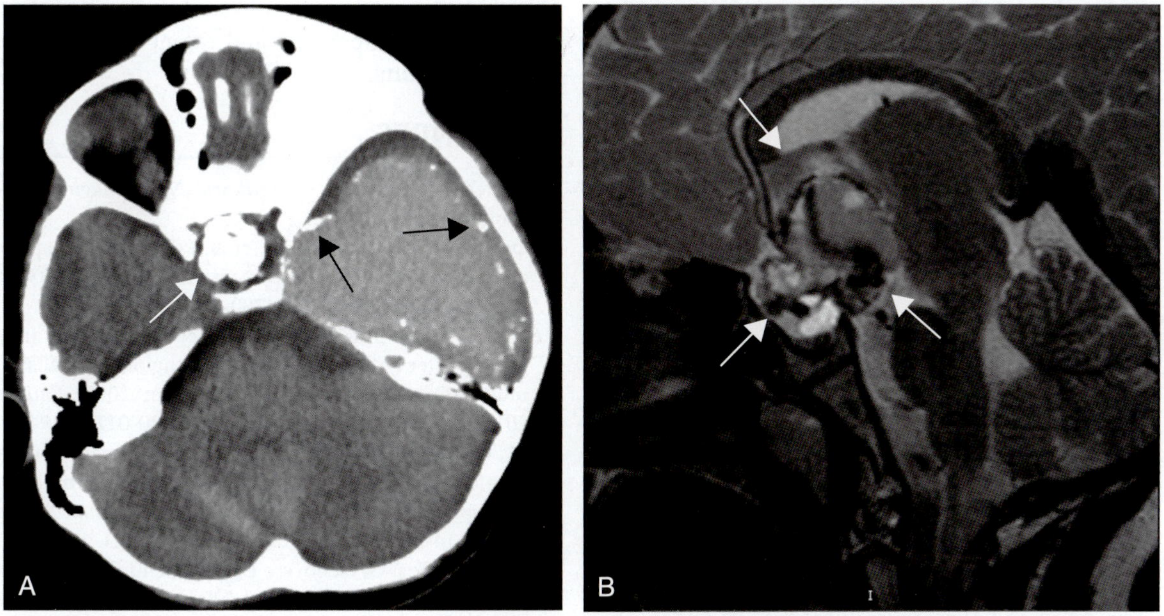

Fig. 43.3 Craniopharyngioma. (A) Noncontrast head CT shows soft tissue and popcorn calcification (*white arrow*) in the suprasellar cistern and a large hyperdense cystic component projecting into the left middle cranial fossa with thin mural calcifications (*black arrows*). Brain MRI, (B) sagittal T2 shows heterogeneous solid/cystic mass in the sella and suprasellar cistern (*arrows*). (C) Postcontrast axial T1 shows heterogeneous contrast enhancement of suprasellar solid tissue (*white arrows*) and hyperintense cystic component (*black arrow*). (D) Coronal T2 shows surrounding mass effect with effaced ventricles and rightward shift (*arrows*).

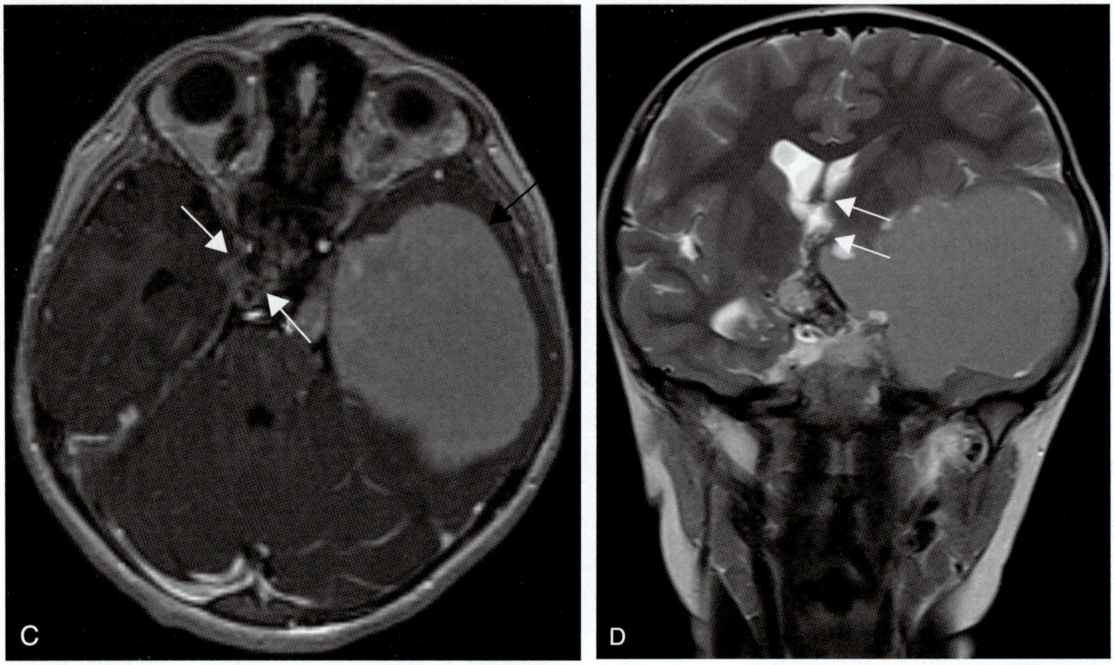

Fig. 43.3 cont'd

radiation—particularly proton therapy—is increasingly being used to treat residual disease in many centers across the world.

CLINICAL RED FLAGS

- Bitemporal hemianopsia raises concern for optic chiasm compression by a suprasellar mass.
- Growth failure, obesity, and delayed puberty should be evaluated endocrinologically.

IMAGING RED FLAGS

- Early imaging is important for tumor characterization and surgical planning relative to neurovascular structures, ventricles, brain parenchyma, and bone.

CONCLUSIONS

Pediatric sellar and suprasellar tumors vary widely in histology and clinical presentations. Nonspecific symptoms and young age may lead to delays in diagnosis. Clinical symptoms can include endocrine dysfunction and vision problems due to mass effect on the pituitary, hypothalamus, and optic pathway. Imaging is critical for assessing the composition and extent of the lesion for surgical planning.

REFERENCES

Barkovich AJ, Raybaud C. *Pediatric Neuroimaging*. 6th ed. Wolters Kluwer; 2019.

Drapeau A, Walz PC, Eide JG, et al. Pediatric craniopharyngioma. *Child's Nervous System*. 2019;35(11):2133–2145. doi:10.1007/s00381-019-04300-2.

Heinks K, Boekhoff S, Hoffmann A, et al. Quality of life and growth after childhood craniopharyngioma: results of the multinational trial kraniopharyngeom 2007. *Endocrine*. 2017;59(2):364–372. doi:10.1007/s12020-017-1489-9.

Hu W, Qiu B, Mei F, et al. Clinical impact of craniopharyngioma classification based on location origin: a multicenter retrospective study. *Annals of Translational Medicine*. 2021;9(14):1164–1174. doi:10.21037/atm-21-2924.

Maghnie M, Cosi G, Genovese E, et al. Central diabetes insipidus in children and young adults. *New England Journal of Medicine*. 2000;343(14):998–1007. doi:10.1056/nejm200010053431403.

Schroeder JW, Vezina LG. Pediatric sellar and suprasellar lesions. *Pediatric Radiology*. 2011;41(3):287–298. doi:10.1007/s00247-010-1968-0.

Midline Menace

HISTORY AND PHYSICAL

A 7-year-old girl experienced difficulty walking for 3 days, left eye esotropia, double vision, and speech impairment. She reported a headache for the preceding 2 weeks. She was the second child of nonconsanguineous parents and had no significant past medical history. Her 12-year-old brother was healthy.

Physical examination revealed temperature of 36.4°C, pulse 96, blood pressure 95/65, weight 22 kg (40%), and height 123 cm (58%). Examination of respiratory, cardiovascular, gastrointestinal, and genitourinary systems were unremarkable. No birthmarks were noted. Neurological examination revealed a conscious and cooperative patient without signs of meningeal irritation. She had limited lateral left gaze indicating a sixth nerve palsy. She also had left central seventh nerve palsy with lower facial paralysis and normal forehead movements. Speech was dysarthric. Dysmetria and dysdiadochokinesia were present. Gait was broad-based and ataxic. Romberg test was positive.

DIAGNOSTIC WORKUP

Routine laboratory testing was normal.

Brain MRI showed an expansile nonenhancing tumor infiltrating nearly the entire pons, without associated enhancement or diffusion restriction. There was partial encasement of the basilar artery and effacement of the floor of fourth ventricle. MRS was suggestive of low-grade neoplasia (Fig. 44.1).

CLINICAL DIFFERENTIAL DIAGNOSES

Brainstem and cerebellar dysfunction raise concern for posterior fossa disorders, including neoplastic, infectious, demyelinating or autoimmune, vascular, and traumatic pathologies.

IMAGING DIFFERENTIAL DIAGNOSES

Brainstem tumors include diffuse intrinsic pontine glioma (DIPG), lymphoma, hemangioblastoma, germ cell tumors, and gliomas.

Inflammatory conditions such as Langerhans cell histiocytosis can affect the posterior fossa with variable enhancement and white matter signal changes.

Autoimmune disorders such as Behçet disease and Bickerstaff encephalitis can preferentially affect the brainstem.

Infectious rhombencephalitis can be related to viral, bacterial, and parasitic pathogens.

Osmotic demyelination classically affects the central pons with sparing of the periphery and corticospinal tracts. Extrapontine myelinolysis can affect the basal ganglia and supratentorial white matter tracts. This occurs with rapid correction of hyponatremia or other systemic imbalances.

Patients with genetic disorders, such as neurofibromatosis type 1 or tuberous sclerosis, may develop dysplastic lesions in the brainstem and cerebellum.

Vascular malformations, such as cavernous malformations or arteriovenous malformations, can have central hemorrhage/enhancement and surrounding edema.

FINAL DIAGNOSIS

Diffuse intrinsic pontine glioma/diffuse midline glioma.

DISCUSSION

Diffuse intrinsic pontine gliomas (DIPG) represent 75% to 80% of pediatric brainstem tumors, with peak prevalence between the ages of 5 and 10 years. Children with DIPG have a rapid clinical course. Most symptoms begin within 4 weeks before seeking medical care. Classically, a pontine tumor manifests with pyramidal

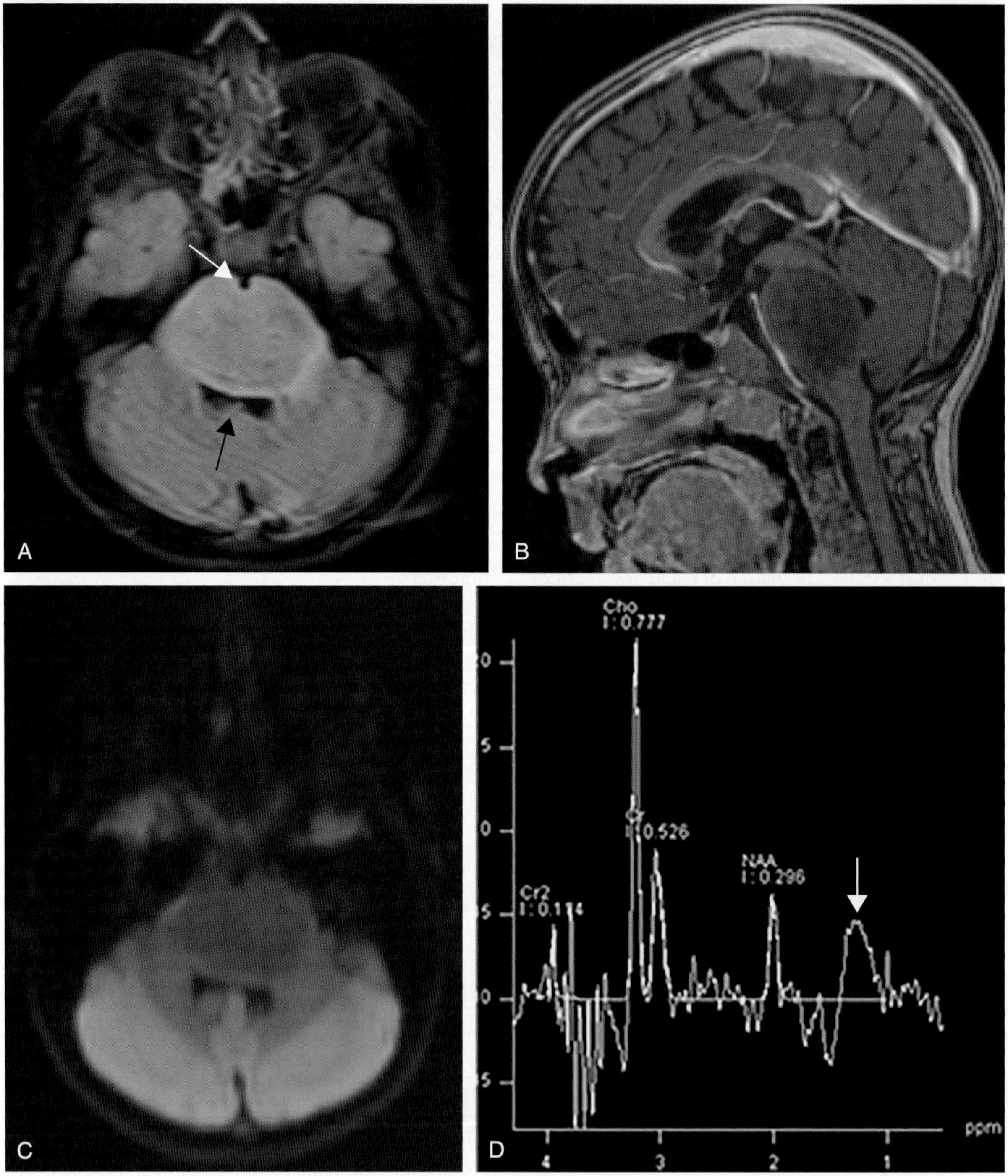

Fig. 44.1 Diffuse intrinsic pontine glioma. Brain MRI, (A) axial FLAIR shows a hyperintense expansile pontine mass with effacement of the floor of fourth ventricle dorsally (*black arrow*) and partial encasement of basilar artery ventrally (*white arrow*). (B) Sagittal postcontrast T1 shows no appreciable enhancement. (C) Axial DWI shows no diffusion restriction. (D) MRS (TE = 135 ms) shows moderate lactate peak (*arrow*), increased choline (Cho), and decreased NAA. *DWI*, Diffusion-weighted imaging; *FLAIR*, Fluid-attenuated inversion recovery; *MRS*, magnetic resonance spectroscopy; *NAA*, N-acetylaspartate.

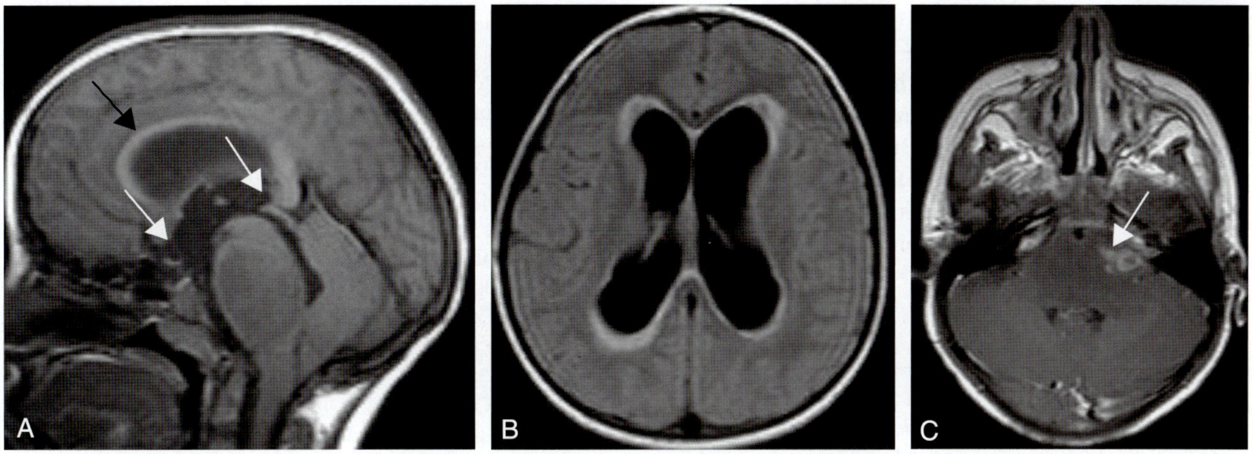

Fig. 44.2 Diffuse midline glioma with H3 K27M mutation. Brain MRI, (A) sagittal T1 shows expansile pontine tumor with obstructive hydrocephalus. There is enlargement of the third ventricle supraoptic and pineal recesses (*white arrows*) and upward bowing of the corpus callosum (*black arrow*). (B) Axial FLAIR shows moderate lateral ventriculomegaly and periventricular interstitial edema. (C) Axial postcontrast T1 shows heterogeneous contrast enhancement (*arrow*) in the left lateral tumor. *FLAIR*, Fluid-attenuated inversion recovery.

tract symptoms, cerebellar impairment (ataxia and nystagmus), and cranial nerve palsies. This classic triad in DIPG is present in about 50% of the patients. Hydrocephalus and signs of increased intracranial pressure are uncommon.

Radiological findings are the cornerstone for diagnosis, with characteristic brainstem expansion and mass effect on the fourth ventricle. Lower-grade lesions are fairly well circumscribed, localized, and nonenhancing with facilitated diffusion. Higher-grade tumors can be more expansile and infiltrative throughout the brain, with potential areas of contrast enhancement and restricted diffusion indicating hypercellularity. Higher apparent diffusion coefficient (ADC) values ($>1300 \times 10^{-6}$ mm^2/s) are associated with a median survival of 13 months, while lower ADC values ($<1300 \times 10^{-6}$ mm^2/s) have a median survival of 3 months. Larger lesions can partially encase the brainstem and cause hydrocephalus. Magnetic resonance spectroscopy (MRS) can show elevated choline and decreased NAA.

Brainstem biopsies are only performed for atypical tumors or for research/clinical trial purposes. Molecular testing for the histone H3 K27M mutation is seen in higher-grade diffuse midline glioma (DMG), which can manifest with multifocal involvement of the basal ganglia, brainstem, and spinal cord and increased risk of local recurrence and metastasis (Fig. 44.2).

Patients with DIPG have a median progression-free survival (PFS) and overall survival (OS) of 6 and 11 months, respectively. Palliative radiation is the first-line treatment. Several clinical trials of systemic and targeted therapies are ongoing, but none have yet been shown to improve patient survival.

CLINICAL RED FLAGS

- Acute ataxia in children can be caused by life-threatening illnesses such as infection, inflammation, tumors, toxic exposures, and stroke.
- Signs of increased intracranial pressure, meningeal irritation, positive toxicologic screen, or ischemic stroke require rapid imaging and workup.

IMAGING RED FLAGS

- In DIPG, tumor cellularity and ADC values have been correlated with prognosis.
- H3 K27M mutant tumors are more likely to be locally aggressive and show multifocal involvement throughout the neuraxis.
- Leptomeningeal disease at presentation is a poor prognostic sign.
- More aggressive tumors can demonstrate enhancement and restricted diffusion, infiltrate into the medulla and midbrain, and cause mass effect and hydrocephalus.

CONCLUSIONS

Rapid clinical deterioration with long tract signs, cranial nerve neuropathies, and cerebellar signs raise concern for brainstem pathology. Brain MRI is important for evaluating brainstem neoplasms and distinguishing them from nonneoplastic conditions such as infection, inflammation, and demyelination.

REFERENCES

Lober RM, Cho Y-J, Tang Y, et al. Diffusion-weighted MRI derived apparent diffusion coefficient identifies prognostically distinct subgroups of pediatric diffuse intrinsic pontine glioma. *Journal of Neuro-Oncology*. 2014;117(1):175–182. doi:10.1007/s11060-014-1375-8.

Louis DN, Perry A, Reifenberger G, et al. The 2016 World Health Organization classification of tumors of the central nervous system: a summary. *Acta Neuropathologica*. 2016;131(6):803–820. doi:10.1007/s00401-016-1545-1.

Louis DN, Perry A, Wesseling P, et al. The 2021 WHO classification of tumors of the central nervous system: a summary. *Neuro-Oncology*. 2021;23(8):1231–1251. doi:10.1093/neuonc/noab106.

Rechberger JS, Lu VM, Zhang L, Power EA, Daniels DJ. Clinical trials for diffuse intrinsic pontine glioma: the current state of affairs. *Child's Nervous System*. 2019;36(1):39–46. doi:10.1007/s00381-019-04363-1.

Vanan MI, Eisenstat DD. DIPG in children: what can we learn from the past? *Frontiers in Oncology*. 2015;5. doi:10.3389/fonc.2015.00237.

Vitanza NA, Monje M. Diffuse intrinsic pontine glioma: from diagnosis to next-generation clinical trials. *Current Treatment Options in Neurology*. 2019;21(8). doi:10.1007/s11940-019-0577-y.

Warren KE. Diffuse intrinsic pontine glioma: poised for progress. *Frontiers in Oncology*. 2012;2:1–9. doi:10.3389/fonc.2012.00205.

Case 45

Temporal Trouble

HISTORY AND PHYSICAL

A 10-year-old boy presented with sudden-onset seizures, characterized by staring and right-hand twitching. After the seizures, he was sleepy but otherwise neurologically intact. He had experienced headaches for several days before. Prior medical history included absence seizures without convulsive features at 2 years of age, controlled with sodium valproate. He had a normal birth history and was otherwise well.

The patient developed several additional episodes of seizures, upon which he was intubated and transferred to the intensive care unit for stabilization. Following extubation, his clinical examination was normal including cranial nerve examination and fundoscopy, and he was discharged.

Several weeks later, he returned with worsening seizures, now with an aura of epigastric discomfort and postictal confusion and short-term memory dysfunction.

DIAGNOSTIC WORKUP

EEG indicated seizures arising from the left temporal lobe. Empiric IV acyclovir was started without clinical response and with increasing seizure burden.

Lumbar puncture demonstrated acellular sterile CSF. Herpes virus (HSV) polymerase chain reaction (PCR) and antibody panel were negative.

Head CT at presentation showed subtle hypodensity in the left temporal lobe (Fig. 45.1a). MRI 6 days later (Fig. 45.1b) showed expansile T2 hyperintense signal in the left anterior temporal lobe cortex and white matter without enhancement, restricted diffusion, or hemorrhage.

Follow-up brain MRI 2 months later (Fig. 45.1c) showed interval increase in infiltrative and expansile abnormality in the temporal lobe. A biopsy was performed.

CLINICAL DIFFERENTIAL DIAGNOSES

Focal and worsening seizures can be seen with a variety of neoplastic, infectious, inflammatory, vascular, and dysplastic brain lesions.

Temporal lobe seizures can occur with tumors, herpes encephalitis, autoimmune limbic encephalitis, middle cerebral artery (MCA) territory stroke, and congenital malformations.

IMAGING DIFFERENTIAL DIAGNOSES

On imaging, postictal changes can produce mild cytotoxic edema of the involved cortex and subcortical white matter, which either resolves after the seizures end or progresses to cerebral atrophy with ongoing seizures. There is no or minimal associated mass effect.

Unilateral temporal lobe edema can be seen in viral encephalitides. Herpesvirus (HSV) can show unilateral or asymmetric bilateral involvement with restricted diffusion, hemorrhage, and cystic changes. Other viruses such as varicella-zoster virus (VZV) and autoimmune conditions such as anti-NMDA receptor encephalitis can also affect the limbic system.

Ill-defined expansion and infiltration of the brain parenchyma can be seen in congenital malformations, such as focal cortical dysplasia with cortical thickening and gray-white blurring, as well as diffuse gliomas, which show growth over time.

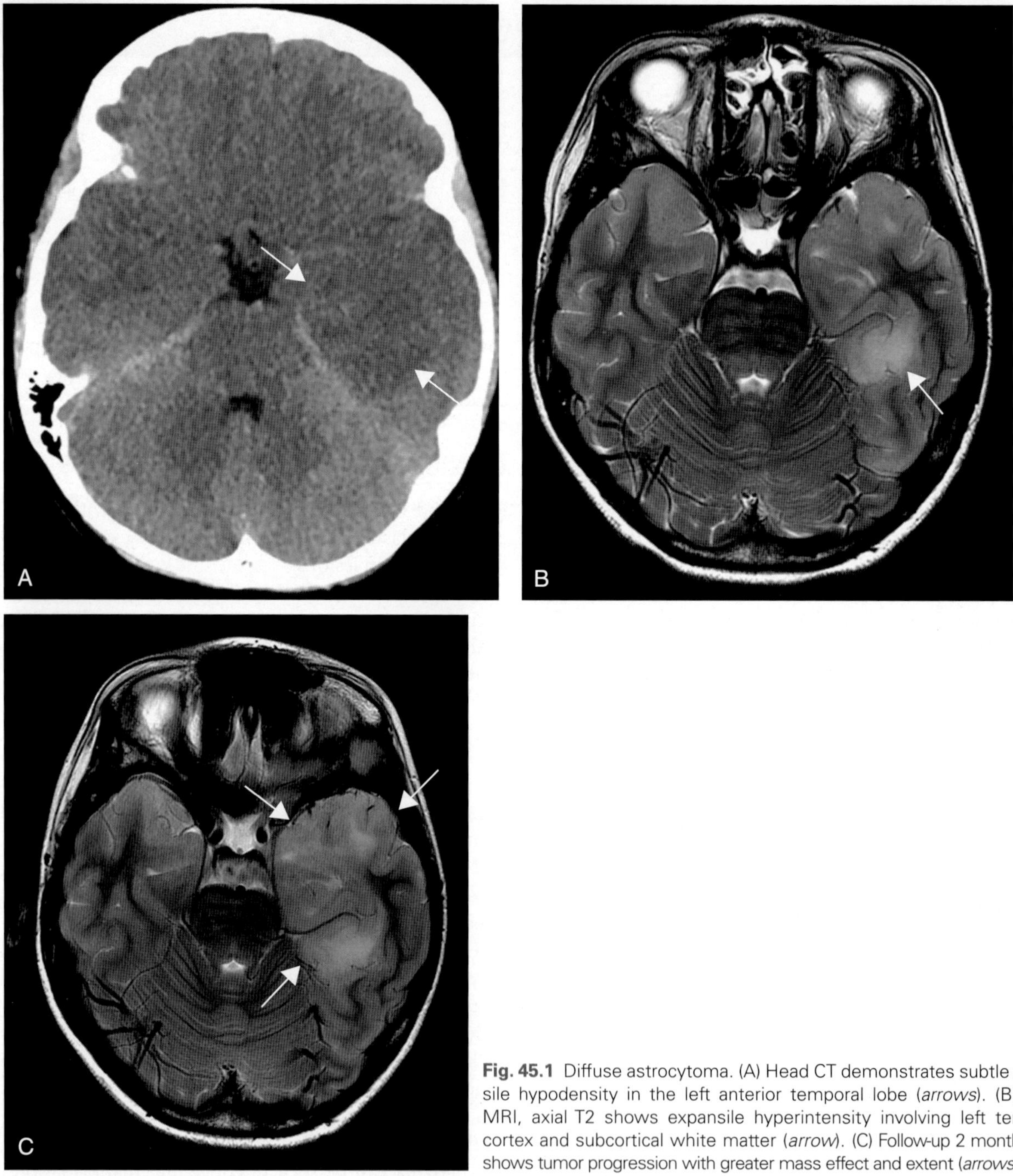

Fig. 45.1 Diffuse astrocytoma. (A) Head CT demonstrates subtle expansile hypodensity in the left anterior temporal lobe (*arrows*). (B) Brain MRI, axial T2 shows expansile hyperintensity involving left temporal cortex and subcortical white matter (*arrow*). (C) Follow-up 2 months later shows tumor progression with greater mass effect and extent (*arrows*).

FINAL DIAGNOSIS

Diffuse astrocytoma.

DISCUSSION

Focal and worsening seizures raise concern for a progressive neurologic disorder. Tumors should be a leading diagnostic concern when patients are refractory to antiseizure therapies and encephalitis treatments. For gliomas, the standard of care is maximal safe surgical resection followed by radiation and chemotherapy for high-grade tumors. Targeted therapies may be trialed for tumors with unique molecular markers.

CLINICAL RED FLAGS

- Lack of clinical response and increasing seizure burden on IV acyclovir.
- Negative CSF results and autoantibody screen.
- Acute onset and subacute progression of seizures.

IMAGING RED FLAGS

- Infiltrative, expansile, and eccentric signal abnormality extending contiguously along cortex and subcortical white matter.
- Growth on follow-up imaging.

CONCLUSIONS

Temporal lobe tumors can clinically mimic encephalitis but are unresponsive to medical therapy with expansile mass effect and progressive growth on imaging. Early imaging enables surgical resection and adjuvant therapy to improve long-term survival.

REFERENCES

Cellucci T, Van Mater H, Graus F, et al. Clinical approach to the diagnosis of autoimmune encephalitis in the pediatric patient. *Neurology - Neuroimmunology Neuroinflammation*. 2020;7(2). doi:10.1212/nxi.0000000000000663 Erratum in: Neurol Neuroimmunol Neuroinflamm. 2020 Apr 15;7(4).

Gerges N, Fontebasso AM, Albrecht S, Faury D, Jabado N. Pediatric high-grade astrocytomas: a distinct neuro-oncological paradigm. *Genome Medicine*. 2013;5(7):66. doi:10.1186/gm470.

Yang C-WR, Mason M, Parizel PM, Warne R. Magnetic resonance imaging patterns of paediatric brain infections: a pictorial review based on the Western Australian experience. *Insights into Imaging*. 2022;13(1). doi:10.1186/s13244-022-01298-1.

Case 46

Jumping Into Orbit

HISTORY AND PHYSICAL

A male infant presented immediately postpartum with redness and swelling of the eye, initially ascribed to a traumatic forceps delivery. He had a left periorbital hematoma and contralateral cephalohematoma. There was no other medical history or family history of eye anomalies. The ocular abnormality persisted over time, and ophthalmological assessment suggested a developmental anomaly of the globe. The periorbital tissues became progressively more swollen over time despite antibiotic therapy.

DIAGNOSTIC WORKUP

Brain MRI at presentation (Fig. 46.1) demonstrated a small left globe infiltrated by heterogeneous T2-hypointense and T1-hyperintense signal, with overlying periorbital fluid.

Head CT with contrast 2 weeks later (Fig. 46.2) demonstrated new left proptosis with growing hyperdense orbital mass showing diffuse choroidal invasion and focal extrascleral invasion with exophytic component in the retrobulbar space.

Brain MRI performed 3 weeks after presentation (Fig. 46.3) demonstrated continued growth of the orbital mass with T2-hypointense signal and heterogeneous enhancement indicating hypercellular tumor. There was extrascleral invasion along the lateral globe with encasement of the optic nerve, lateral rectus, and superior rectus-levator complex and mild remodeling of the bony orbit.

Urgent left enucleation was performed. Staging positron emission tomography (PET)-CT demonstrated an aggressive renal mass that was also resected.

Follow-up brain MRI scan performed 3 months post-enucleation showed massive local recurrence (Fig. 46.4). Massive orbital hemorrhage required multiple rounds of arterial embolization and chemotherapy.

CLINICAL DIFFERENTIAL DIAGNOSES

In an infant with periorbital edema and erythema, the differential includes infection, inflammation, trauma, vascular anomalies, and neoplasia. Prenatal and birth history are important to rule these conditions in or out.

Persistent fetal vasculature (PFV) occurs when fetal vessels fail to regress within the eye. Patients can present with leukocoria and microphthalmia. At fundoscopy and imaging, the persistent embryonic vessels and hyaloid canal can usually be visualized.

Slow-flow vascular malformations—such as varix, cavernous malformation, or lymphatic malformation—can present with recurrent orbital swelling and proptosis due to increased systemic pressures, trauma, and/or infection.

Hemangiomas are vascular tumors that can present at birth (congenital) or appear shortly after birth (infantile). Congenital hemangiomas develop before birth due to placental hypoxia, are GLUT1-positive, and involute after birth. Infantile hemangiomas grow in the first 1 to 2 years of life and respond to propranolol.

Orbital infection can be primary or secondary to sinusitis with subperiosteal spread of infection. Viral infections tend to be mild and self-limiting. Bacterial infections are more purulent but respond to antibiotics. Fungal infections may become invasive in immunocompromised hosts, with submucosal, extrasinus soft tissue, and/or bone involvement.

Nonspecific orbital inflammation can affect the globe and multiple orbital compartments and responds to steroids and immunosuppression.

Malignant orbital tumors can invade the globe and orbit, with surrounding soft tissue inflammation due to aggressive growth and neovascularization.

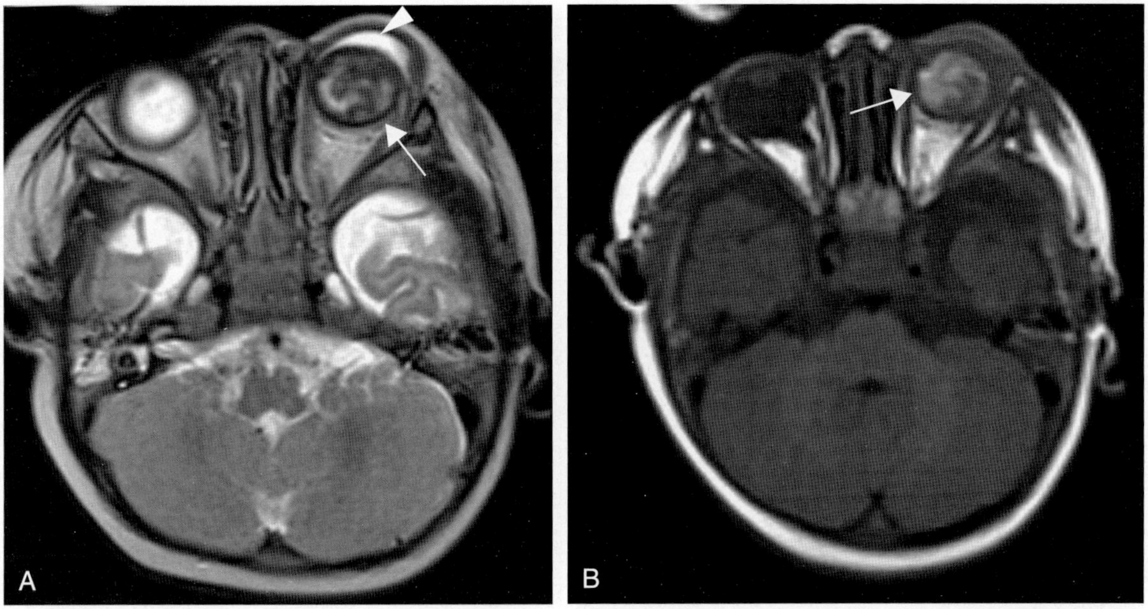

Fig. 46.1 Orbital rhabdoid metastasis. Brain MRI, (A) axial T2 demonstrates a small left globe with heterogeneous infiltration by T2-hypointense tissue (*arrow*) and overlying periorbital fluid (*arrowhead*). (B) Axial T1 demonstrates intrinsic hyperintensity (*arrow*) concerning for hemorrhage or proteinaceous material.

IMAGING DIFFERENTIAL DIAGNOSES

In an infant, small left globe can reflect congenital microphthalmia/anophthalmia or prenatal insult to the globe from infection, inflammation, trauma, or tumor.

Malignant orbital tumors include retinoblastoma originating from retinal cells; sarcomas arising from soft tissues (most commonly rhabdomyosarcoma); lymphoma and leukemia; and metastasis from distant primaries (neuroblastoma and rhabdoid tumors of the posterior fossa, sinonasal tract, or kidney). All of these are small round blue cell tumors with hypercellularity characterized by T2 hypointensity, enhancement, and restricted diffusion on MRI. There may be heterogeneous areas of cystic/necrotic change, hemorrhage, and/or calcification. The aggressive behavior is reflected by rapid growth on follow-up imaging, often with extension beyond the globe and involving multiple orbital compartments. There may be bone remodeling with erosion or periosteal reaction as well as soft tissue inflammatory changes that do not respond to antibiotic therapy.

Tissue biopsy is required to determine appropriate treatment. Depending on the degree of tumor involvement, surgical approaches include evisceration

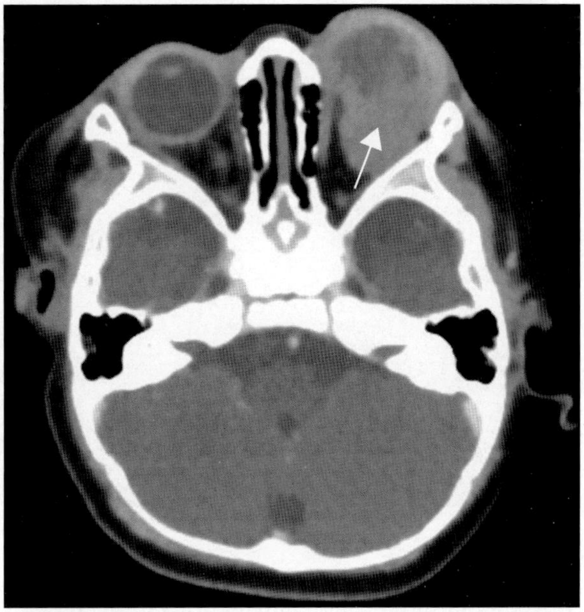

Fig. 46.2 Orbital rhabdoid metastasis. Postcontrast head CT 2 weeks after presentation shows growing mass (*arrow*) with new left proptosis, soft tissue infiltration of the globe, diffuse choroidal invasion with circumferential nodular tissue, and exophytic extension into the retrobulbar space with mild remodeling of the lateral orbital wall.

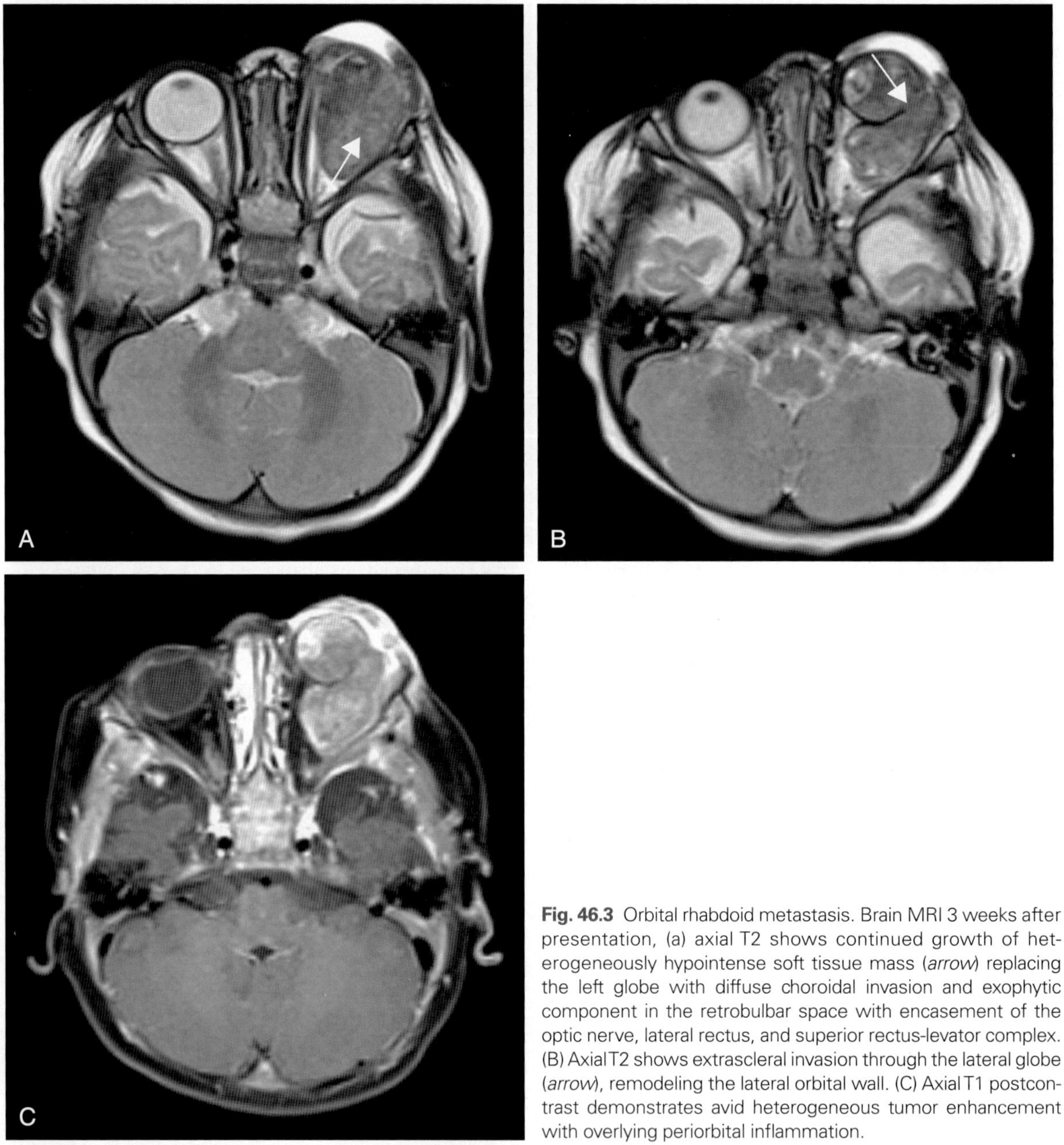

Fig. 46.3 Orbital rhabdoid metastasis. Brain MRI 3 weeks after presentation, (a) axial T2 shows continued growth of heterogeneously hypointense soft tissue mass (*arrow*) replacing the left globe with diffuse choroidal invasion and exophytic component in the retrobulbar space with encasement of the optic nerve, lateral rectus, and superior rectus-levator complex. (B) Axial T2 shows extrascleral invasion through the lateral globe (*arrow*), remodeling the lateral orbital wall. (C) Axial T1 postcontrast demonstrates avid heterogeneous tumor enhancement with overlying periorbital inflammation.

(resection of intraocular contents with preservation of sclera), enucleation (removal of entire globe including sclera and cornea), and exenteration (resection of all orbital soft tissues).

Benign orbital lesions include vascular malformations, such as lymphatic and venous malformations, vascular tumors including hemangiomas, and nonspecific orbital inflammation.

FINAL DIAGNOSIS

Orbital rhabdoid metastasis from renal primary.

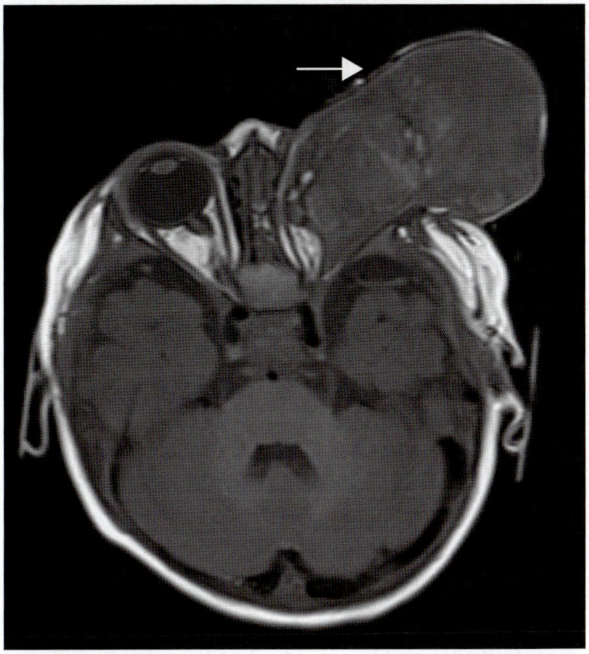

Fig. 46.4 Orbital rhabdoid metastasis recurrence. Brain MRI 3 months post-enucleation, axial T1 shows locally recurrent hemorrhagic mass (*arrow*) filling the surgical bed, remodeling bone, and projecting beyond the bony orbit.

DISCUSSION

Infantile orbital masses are difficult to evaluate and require a combination of clinical, ophthalmologic, and radiologic data. Soft tissue inflammation that does not respond to and worsens on antibiotic therapy raises concern for underlying neoplasia. Tumors of the orbit may arise from within the globe, soft tissues, or metastatic from a distant primary. At imaging, diffuse soft tissue infiltration, rapid progression, local recurrence, and distant metastasis are poor prognostic signs.

CLINICAL RED FLAGS

- Rapid progression of soft tissue swelling and proptosis
- Failure to improve on antibiotic therapy

IMAGING RED FLAGS

- Infiltrative and hypercellular soft tissue
- Rapid growth and invasion
- Extraorbital invasion, bone remodeling, soft tissue inflammation

CONCLUSIONS

Ocular tumors in children have a broad differential diagnosis including primary ocular, soft tissue, and metastatic masses. Small round blue cell tumors are hypercellular and aggressive histologies characterized by hyperdensity on CT and T2 hypointensity, restricted diffusion, and avid contrast enhancement on MRI. Examples include retinoblastoma, rhabdomyosarcoma, and metastatic rhabdoid tumors. Primary rhabdoid tumors can affect the kidneys, sinonasal tract, and posterior fossa with potential for metastasis.

REFERENCES

Haddad R, Font RL, Reeser F. Persistent hyperplastic primary vitreous: a clinicopathologic study of 62 cases and review of the literature. *Survey of Ophthalmology*. 1978;23(2):123–134. doi:10.1016/0039-6257(78)90091-7.

Purohit BS, Vargas MI, Ailianou A, et al. Orbital tumours and tumour-like lesions: exploring the armamentarium of multiparametric imaging. *Insights into Imaging*. 2015;7(1):43–68. doi:10.1007/s13244-015-0443-8.

SECTION 10

Other Autoimmune Disorders

Russell C. Dale

The current chapter covers important autoimmune CNS conditions beyond demyelination. CNS neuroinflammation is important due to its potentially reversible nature when the underlying etiology is recognized and treated promptly. Without treatment, these disorders can be highly destructive with life-threatening complications.

Biomarkers remain very important to disease recognition, and autoimmune neurology has benefited from the identification of autoantibody biomarkers that can define potentially treatable monophasic or relapsing disorders. Some conditions, however, do not yet have established biomarkers, and the diagnosis hinges on a combination of clinical and radiological phenotypes.

We focus on four clinical syndromes with important clinical presentations and characteristic neuroimaging phenotypes that can prompt suspicion for and diagnosis of these treatable conditions.

SUGGESTED READINGS

Mohammad SS, Dale RC. Principles and approaches to the treatment of immune-mediated movement disorders. *Eur J Paediatr Neurol.* 2018;22(2):292–300. https://doi.org/10.1016/j.ejpn.2017.11.010.

Wells E, Hacohen Y, Waldman A, et al. Neuroimmune disorders of the central nervous system in children in the molecular era. *Nat Rev Neurol.* 2018;14(7):433–445. https://doi.org/10.1038/s41582-018-0024-9.

Case 47

Insult to the Deep Gray Nuclei

HISTORY AND PHYSICAL

A previously well 4-year-old boy who had a fever and chesty cough for 2 weeks presented to the emergency department with increasing fatigue and inability to walk over 3 days. There was no relevant medical or family history. On examination, the boy was lying in bed and afebrile, with a notable reduction in spontaneous movements, and reduced facial expression but a full range of eye movements. His speech was intact but slow. He could follow commands after a delay, for example taking 4 seconds to fully open his eyes. There was increased tone of all four limbs, with rigidity but no spasticity, and normal tendon reflexes.

DIAGNOSTIC WORKUP

Brain MRI showed symmetric edema in the lentiform nuclei (Fig. 47.1), without diffusion restriction and with other structures spared. MR angiography was normal.

Cerebrospinal fluid examination showed mild CSF pleocytosis (22 monocytes per mm^3), slightly raised CSF protein (0.44 g/dl), and raised neopterin (137 pmol/L, normal <30), with a normal CSF lactate. Serum showed elevated mycoplasma IgM.

CLINICAL DIFFERENTIAL DIAGNOSES

For any acute-onset neurologic syndrome, differential diagnoses include acute CNS infection or inflammation (encephalitis, demyelination), acute drug toxicity, biochemical or metabolic derangement, or acute vascular event.

IMAGING DIFFERENTIAL DIAGNOSES

Symmetric involvement of the basal ganglia can occasionally be seen with arterial emboli or venous infarcts (Fig. 47.2).

Metabolic disorders including organic acidurias, aminoacidopathies, biotin-responsive basal ganglia disease, and mitochondrial disease can often involve the basal ganglia. These disorders often involve additional deep gray structures and white matter tracts, with diffusion restriction and elevated CSF lactate.

Inflammatory conditions require a combination of clinical history, CSF serology, and imaging features for diagnosis. Acute disseminated encephalomyelitis (ADEM) can have basal ganglia involvement but is typically patchy and asymmetric, involves white matter, and rarely presents with extrapyramidal features.

CNS infection can involve the basal ganglia, either due to direct CNS infection or a postinfectious autoimmune reaction. Direct infection can occur with enterovirus, Epstein-Barr virus, Group A streptococcus, and *Mycoplasma pneumoniae*. Postinfectious Sydenham chorea (with antibasal ganglia antibodies) and anti-N-methyl-D-aspartate receptor (NMDAR) limbic encephalitis do not usually present with akinesia or dystonia, but instead with chorea or complex hyperkinetic movement disorder.

FINAL DIAGNOSIS

Autoimmune basal ganglia encephalitis, likely triggered by mycoplasma infection.

DISCUSSION

The differential diagnosis of acute-onset movement disorders due to CNS inflammation or autoimmunity includes anti-NMDAR encephalitis, autoimmune basal ganglia encephalitis, Sydenham chorea, opsoclonus-myoclonus-ataxia syndrome (OMAS), and other rare autoimmune encephalitis syndromes (e.g., progressive encephalitis with rigidity and myoclonus [PERM]). These syndromes can be distinguished by a combination of

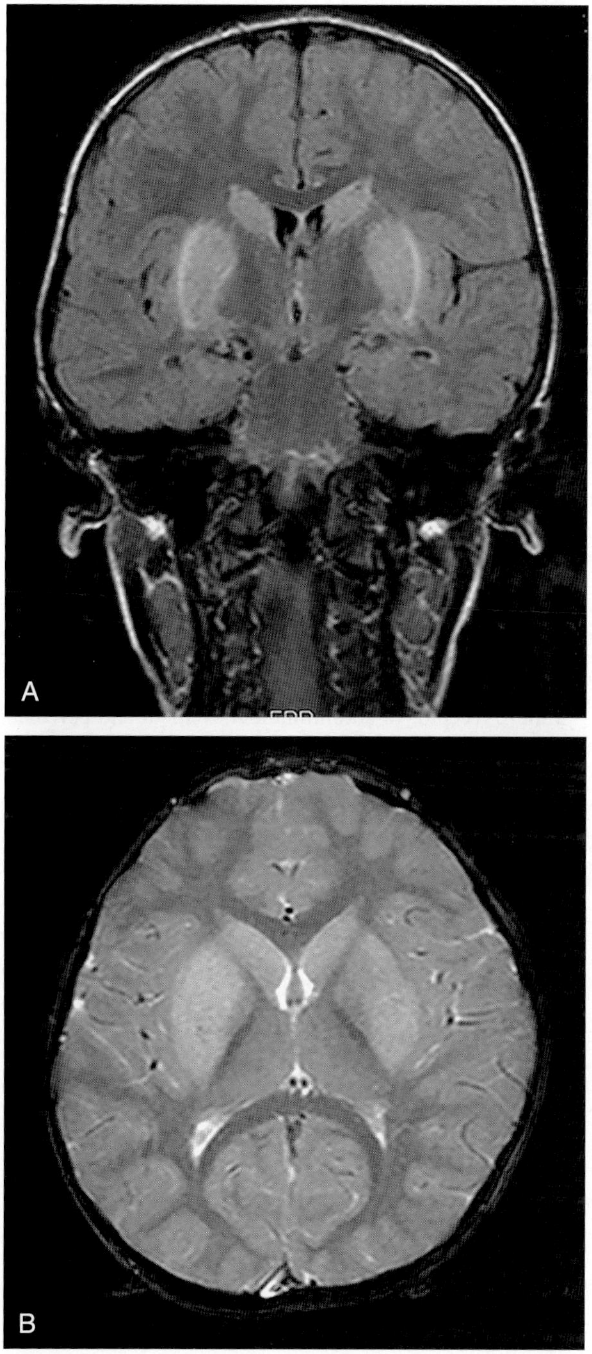

Fig. 47.1 Autoimmune basal ganglia encephalitis. Brain MRI, (A) coronal FLAIR and (B) axial T2 show edema in the bilateral lentiform nuclei. *FLAIR*, Fluid-attenuated inversion recovery.

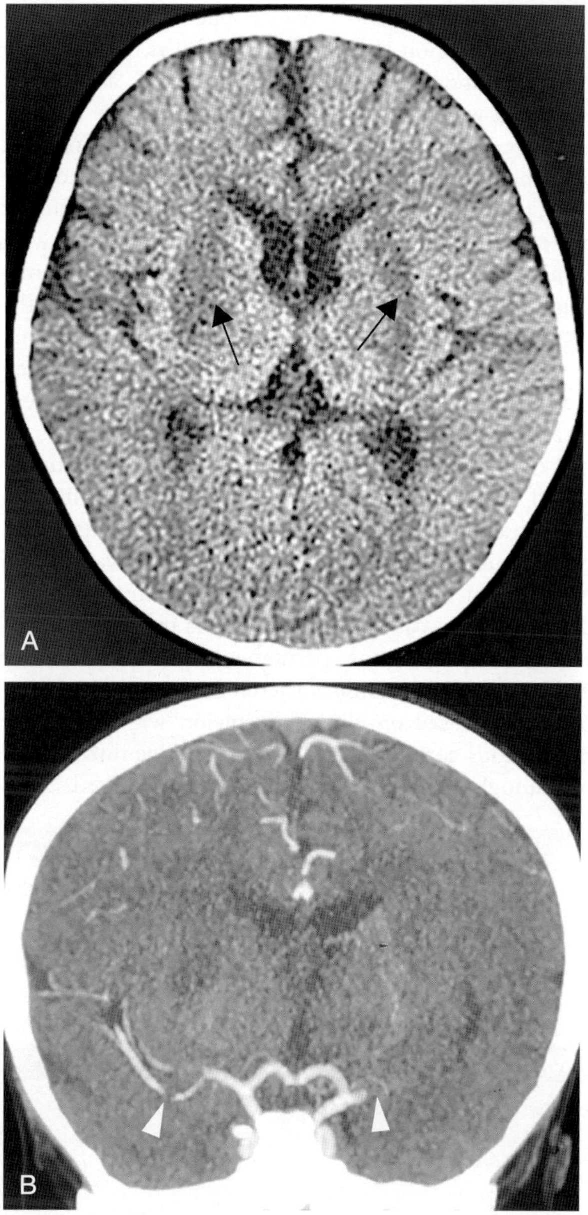

Fig. 47.2 Bilateral embolic strokes in a patient with cardiomyopathy. (A) Head CT, axial, shows bilateral putaminal hypodensities (*arrows*). (B) Head CTA, coronal MIP, shows left MCA cutoff and right MCA short-segment occlusion with distal irregular narrowing (*arrowheads*). *MCA*, Middle cerebral artery; *MIP*, maximum intensity projection.

specific biomarkers and clinical phenomenology. A high index of suspicion is paramount, and it is important to start immunosuppression once suspected, as delayed treatment worsens outcomes and may increase the risk of future relapse. Recording videos on smartphones can be helpful for expert diagnostics and second opinions.

Autoimmune basal ganglia encephalitis typically presents after acute infection in young children with an acute extrapyramidal movement disorder (dystonia, akinesia, or combined), psychiatric features, and lethargy or hypersomnia. Imaging shows symmetric edema of the caudate and putamen with sparing of other deep gray structures and brain regions. CSF can show features of CNS inflammation including pleocytosis in half of patients, elevated protein, oligoclonal bands, or raised neopterin. Dopamine-2 receptor autoantibodies can be found in blood or CSF in some patients and have pathogenic potential, though testing is not available on most commercially available panels. Left untreated, the disease process can cause basal ganglia injury with gliosis and atrophy, causing permanent dystonia and other movement abnormalities. Therefore, treatment should be started based on clinical suspicion with high-dose intravenous corticosteroids and adjunctive intravenous immunoglobulin or plasma exchange as required.

CLINICAL RED FLAGS

- New-onset acute encephalopathy in a previously well child.
- Symmetric extrapyramidal movement disorder with akinetic and dystonic features.

IMAGING RED FLAGS

- Symmetric edema of the lentiform nuclei.
- Absence of diffusion restriction.
- Sparing of other deep gray structures, white matter, and cortex.

CONCLUSIONS

Autoimmune basal ganglia encephalitis is a rare acute syndrome, significantly less common than anti-NMDAR encephalitis and myelin oligodendrocyte glycoprotein (MOG) antibody-associated disease. When young children present with acute basal ganglia findings, clinicians often mistakenly assume the diagnosis of mitochondrial (Leigh) disease. However, the lack of elevated CSF lactate, sparing of the globus pallidus and brainstem, and absence of diffusion restriction should alert the clinician to the possibility of basal ganglia encephalitis, particularly in the setting of a pure akinetic-dystonic syndrome. Rapid commencement of intravenous corticosteroids can result in clinical improvements within the first week and optimize long-term outcomes. Relapses occur in a minority of patients, sometimes triggered by infection, but are generally less severe than the initial episode.

REFERENCES

Dale RC, Merheb V, Pillai S, et al. Antibodies to surface dopamine-2 receptor in autoimmune movement and psychiatric disorders. *Brain*. 2012;135(11):3453–3468. https://doi.org/10.1093/brain/aws256.

Mohammad SS, Angiti RR, Biggin A, et al. Magnetic resonance imaging pattern recognition in childhood bilateral basal ganglia disorders [published correction appears in Brain Commun. 2021 Jan 09;3(1):fcaa236]. *Brain Commun*. 2020;2(2). https://doi.org/10.1093/braincomms/fcaa178.

Mohammad SS, Dale RC. Principles and approaches to the treatment of immune-mediated movement disorders. *Eur J Paediatr Neurol*. 2018;22(2):292–300. https://doi.org/10.1016/j.ejpn.2017.11.010.

Inflammatory Emesis

HISTORY AND PHYSICAL

A previously well 14-year-old African American female presented with anorexia, recurrent vomiting, and weight loss for 2 weeks. She had lost 9 kg in the preceding 2 weeks and was assessed by a child psychiatrist who did not identify body dysmorphology or other features of anorexia nervosa. Other than daily vomiting three to four times per day of undigested food and associated weight loss, there were no other symptoms. Gastroscopy was negative. Neurological examination was normal, including fundoscopy, which was negative for papilledema.

DIAGNOSTIC WORKUP

Brain MRI showed T2 hyperintense patchy signal in the thalami and medulla, particularly periaqueductal gray and dorsal medulla in the area postrema (Fig. 48.1).

Cerebrospinal fluid examination showed mild CSF pleocytosis (35 white cells per mm^3, including 12 polymorphonuclear cells), slightly elevated CSF protein (0.67 g/dl), and negative oligoclonal bands. Serum testing for aquaporin-4 antibodies (neuromyelitis optica immunoglobin G [NMO IgG]) was positive. The patient also had elevated antinuclear antibodies.

CLINICAL DIFFERENTIAL DIAGNOSES

Unexplained vomiting and severe weight loss without gastrointestinal or eating disorder suggest a CNS condition, likely inflammatory based on CSF testing. Increased intracranial pressure or functional neurological disorders can present this way, but are usually accompanied by more global symptoms.

IMAGING DIFFERENTIAL DIAGNOSES

Area postrema syndrome involves the area postrema (emetic center) in dorsal medulla along the floor of fourth ventricle. This location is strongly suggestive of neuromyelitis optica syndrome, associated with anti-aquaporin-4 autoantibodies that impair regulation of CNS water transport. Additional lesions can be found in the brain and spinal cord, particularly surrounding the ventricles and central canal.

FINAL DIAGNOSIS

Neuromyelitis optica spectrum disorder (NMOSD).

DISCUSSION

Recurrent and unexplained vomiting is an uncommon symptom in neurology. Area postrema syndrome presents with intractable and unresponsive nausea, vomiting, anorexia, and hiccups. This is a unique clinical diagnostic criterion of NMOSD, as compared to the more typical presentation with optic neuritis or longitudinal transverse myelitis. Given the fact that NMOSD is a severe and potentially destructive inflammatory CNS disorder, it is important to make this diagnosis and start immune therapy as soon as suspected, as relapsing disease is associated with high morbidity and mortality.

CLINICAL RED FLAGS

- Unexplained refractory vomiting and weight loss if other causes (gastrointestinal, psychological) have been ruled out.
- Females and black people are at higher risk.
- Comorbid autoimmune disorders such as systemic lupus erythematosus (SLE).

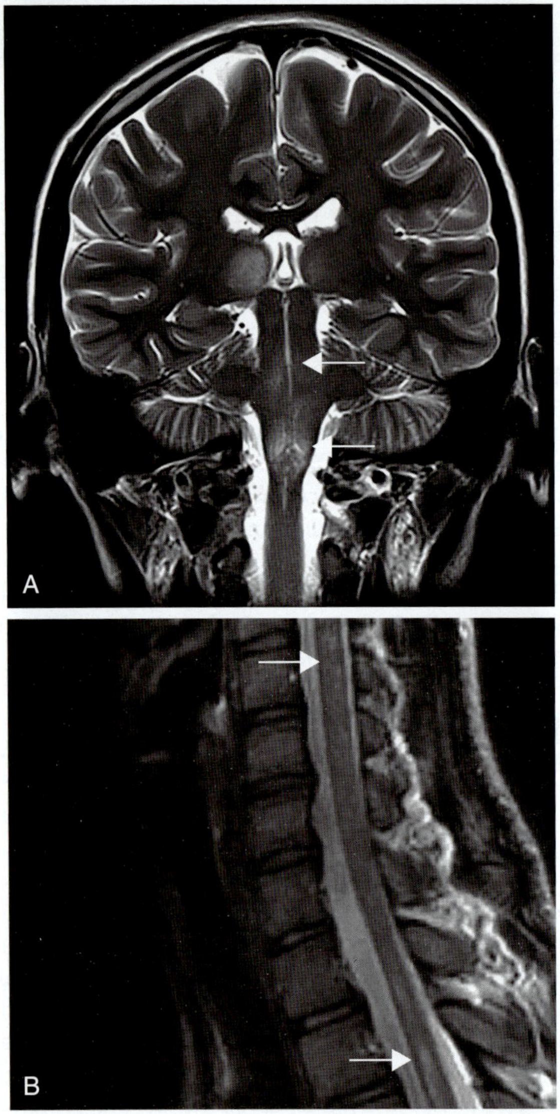

Fig. 48.1 Neuromyelitis optica spectrum disorder. Brain MRI, (A) coronal T2 shows patchy hyperintensity in the right greater than left thalami and medulla, including the periaqueductal gray and area postrema (*arrows*). Cervical spine MRI, (B) sagittal T2 shows patchy hyperintensity throughout the cord (*arrows*).

IMAGING RED FLAGS

- Inflammation of the dorsal medulla involving the area postrema.
- Cloudy brain lesions involving periventricular white matter.
- Optic neuritis, often bilateral.
- Longitudinally extensive transverse myelitis.

CONCLUSIONS

Area postrema syndrome is a rare but important syndrome to recognize. Area postrema inflammation is rarely complicated by demyelination and necrosis, so most patients show reversal of symptoms on immune therapy. However, the condition is a harbinger of NMOSD, and without chronic immune treatment, 50% of patients will progress to blindness (due to optic neuritis) or paralysis (due to myelitis) within 5 years. The presence of aquaporin-4 antibodies is associated with a relapsing course in the majority of patients, and spontaneous remission is very uncommon when compared to myelin oligodendrocyte glycoprotein antibody disease (MOGAD). Acute management can include corticosteroids and plasma exchange, followed by a chronic regimen such as rituximab redosing. There is an association with other systemic autoimmune disorders.

REFERENCES

Misu T, Fujihara K, Nakashima I, Sato S, Itoyama Y. Intractable hiccup and nausea with periaqueductal lesions in neuromyelitis optica. *Neurology*. 2005;65(9):1479–1482. https://doi.org/10.1212/01.wnl.0000183151.19351.82.

Wingerchuk DM, Banwell B, Bennett JL, et al. International consensus diagnostic criteria for neuromyelitis optica spectrum disorders. *Neurology*. 2015;85(2):177–189. https://doi.org/10.1212/wnl.0000000000001729.

Case 49

Postinfectious Ataxia

HISTORY AND PHYSICAL

A previously well 5-year-old boy presented with progressively worsening headache over 2 days, unsteadiness when walking, poor coordination, and slurred speech. On examination, he was drowsy with a Glasgow coma score of 13. Speech was slow and lacked rhythm, with a staccato tone. He was unable to walk unaided and veered from side to side. Even sitting on the bed was challenging with trunk unsteadiness. There was bilateral horizontal nystagmus, most notable on lateral gaze, although ocular movements were full. Reflexes were slightly brisk bilaterally, but plantars were downgoing. Fundoscopy revealed bilateral optic disc edema.

DIAGNOSTIC WORKUP

Brain MRI showed patchy cerebellar edema (Fig. 49.1) with sparing of the cerebrum. MR angiography was normal.

Lumbar puncture was not performed due to the concern for cerebellar tonsillar herniation.

CLINICAL DIFFERENTIAL DIAGNOSES

Rapidly worsening intracranial pressure and new-onset cerebellar syndrome can be seen with posterior fossa tumor, hemorrhage, hydrocephalus, metabolic decompensation, infection, or inflammation.

IMAGING DIFFERENTIAL DIAGNOSES

Isolated involvement of the cerebellum is classically seen in postinfectious cerebellitis. Other inflammatory disorders, such as opsoclonus-myoclonus-ataxia syndrome (OMAS), cause less mass effect and involve additional deep gray and supratentorial structures. Demyelinating disorders show additional supratentorial, optic nerve, and/or cord involvement. Some metabolic disorders can selectively involve the cerebellum but show progressive signal abnormality and atrophy.

FINAL DIAGNOSIS

Cerebellitis.

DISCUSSION

Cerebellitis is an inflammatory condition that can occur during or after infection with various pathogens including Epstein-Barr virus, group A streptococcus, and *Mycoplasma pneumoniae.* Paraneoplastic causes are also possible, including lymphoma and lung cancer.

In adults with autoimmune cerebellitis, antibodies against metabotropic glutamate receptor 5, septin-5, Homer-3 antibodies, and GluR1 antibodies can be found. Recent reports have also found autoantibodies against metabolomic glutamate receptor 1. GluR1 antibodies appear to have the strongest association with cerebellar inflammation in adults, with edema and/or atrophy at imaging and bilateral or unilateral involvement (Fig. 49.2). At present, there are few reports of antibody associations in children.

Complications of severe cerebellitis can include brainstem compression and tonsillar herniation, for which neurosurgical decompression can be lifesaving. High-dose methylprednisolone treatment can be used to reduce the presumed inflammation, with additional options including intravenous immunoglobulin and plasma exchange. Even with early treatment, a significant proportion of patients experience persistent deficits.

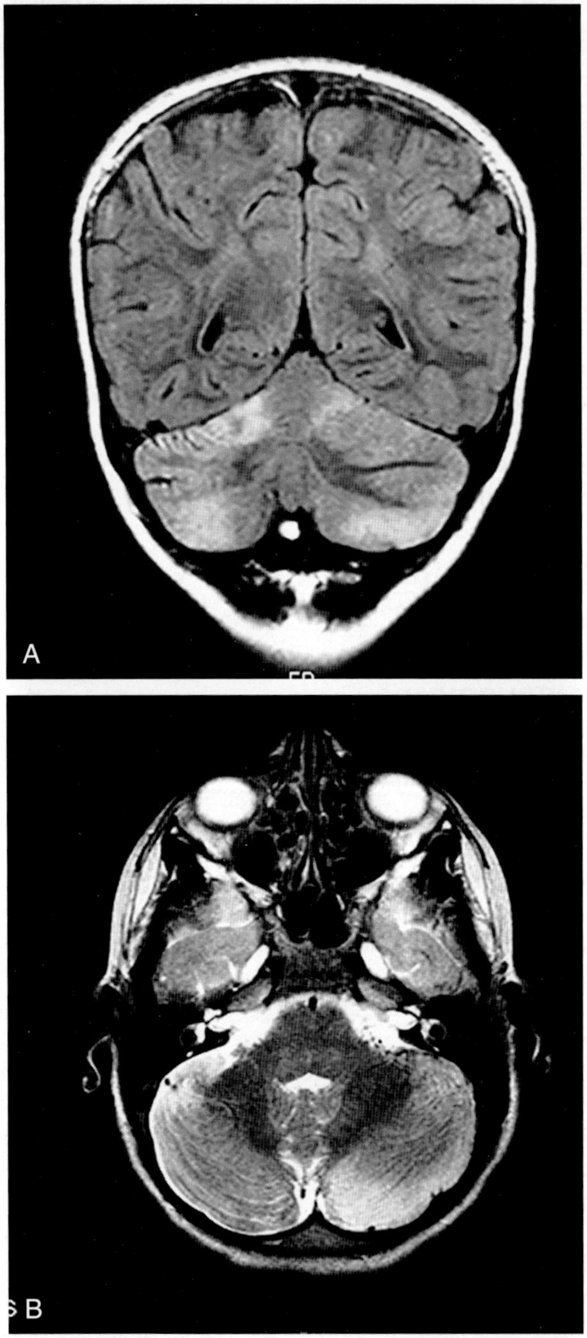

Fig. 49.1 Cerebellitis. Brain MRI, (A) coronal FLAIR and (B) axial T2 show patchy edema involving bilateral cerebellar hemispheres. *FLAIR*, Fluid-attenuated inversion recovery.

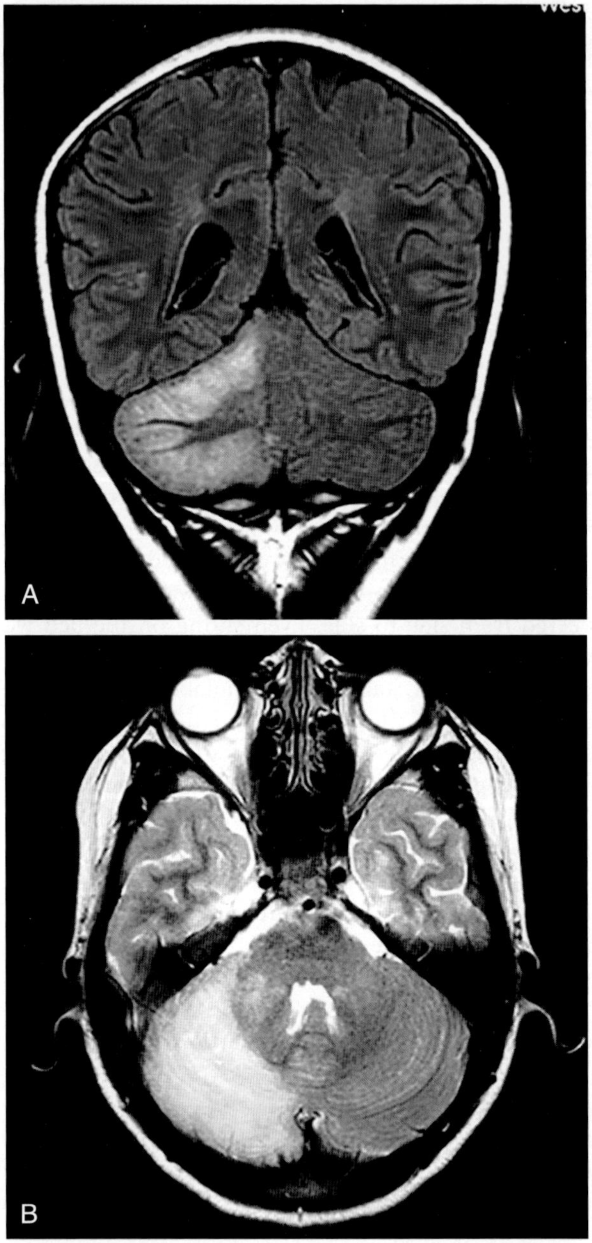

Fig. 49.2 Hemicerebellitis. Brain MRI, (A) coronal FLAIR and (B) axial T2 show edema in the cortex and subcortical white matter of the right cerebellum. *FLAIR*, Fluid-attenuated inversion recovery.

CLINICAL RED FLAGS

- Rapidly progressive headache and drowsiness (sometimes with vomiting) should alert the clinician to conditions of increased intracranial pressure.
- Rapidly progressive cerebellar syndromes involve trunk, limbs, speech, and nystagmus.

IMAGING RED FLAGS

- Isolated cerebellar edema.
- Spared supratentorial structures.
- Hydrocephalus, brainstem compression, tonsillar herniation.

CONCLUSIONS

Cerebellitis is a rare but important clinical syndrome to diagnose. Consider high-dose corticosteroids to reduce inflammation and edema, and surgical decompression if there is a risk of herniation.

REFERENCES

Honorat JA, Lopez-Chiriboga AS, Kryzer TJ, et al. Autoimmune septin-5 cerebellar ataxia [published correction appears in Neurology-Neuroimmunology Neuroinflammation. 2018 Dec 12;6(1):e534]. *Neurol Neuroimmunol Neuroinflamm*. 2018;5(5):e474. https://doi.org/10.1212/nxi.0000000000000474.

Kornreich L, Shkalim-Zemer V, Levinsky Y, Abdallah W, Ganelin-Cohen E, Straussberg R. Acute cerebellitis in children. *J Child Neurol*. 2016;31(8):991–997. https://doi.org/10.1177/0883073816634860.

Marignier R, Chenevier F, Rogemond V, et al. Metabotropic glutamate receptor type 1 autoantibody–associated cerebellitis. *Arch Neurol*. 2010;67(5):627–630. https://doi.org/10.1001/archneurol.2010.51.

Spatola M, Petit Pedrol M, Maudes E, et al. Clinical features, prognostic factors, and antibody effects in anti-mGluR1 encephalitis. *Neurology*. 2020;95(22):e3012–e3025. https://doi.org/10.1212/wnl.0000000000010854.

Case 50

Progressive Hemiseizures

HISTORY AND PHYSICAL

A previously well 6-year-old boy presented with steadily increasing twitching of the face and eyes for 3 months. These were initially thought to represent tics, but it became increasingly clear that he could not control the movements. On examination, the twitching involved the right orbital muscles and face, resulting in partial eye closure and hemi-grimacing. The motions were very jerky and arrhythmic, occurring every second or so, and appeared to continue in sleep. There was no associated pain or change in awareness or consciousness. 30-minute EEG showed left frontal epileptic discharges, occurring every second on average, with mild slowing in the same region, but no other abnormalities. Carbamazepine was started and increased to 15 mg/kg/day without clear effect.

Over the following 6 months, the focal facial seizures continued, and the child started to have focal clonic seizures affecting the right arm with some alteration of awareness. These seizures lasted 30 to 40 seconds and tended to occur in clusters, worsening with infection. Medical trials of lamotrigine, topiramate, clobazan, and clonazepam failed. In between seizures, during this period, the right arm and hand were less coordinated, resulting in changes in handwriting and dropping objects. School performance also deteriorated with reduced focus, concentration, and completion of tasks. His speech became less distinct, and he became quieter and less able to find words. Formal neurological examination revealed mild right-sided hemiplegia and a right hemianopia.

DIAGNOSTIC WORKUP

Brain MRI (Fig. 50.1) showed asymmetric volume loss in the left cerebral hemisphere, particularly periinsular region.

Cerebrospinal fluid examination showed intrathecal oligoclonal bands without pleocytosis. All peripheral blood investigations, including inflammatory markers and lupus serology, were normal.

Brain biopsy showed diffuse microglia and astrocyte gliosis, neuronal loss, and occasional perivascular lymphocytic infiltration. There was no evidence of viral inclusions.

CLINICAL DIFFERENTIAL DIAGNOSES

Insidious onset of seizures affecting the face followed by an evolving focal epilepsy syndrome is typical of epilepsia partialis continua (EPC). The history was subacute and progressive, suggesting a more chronic or persistent process.

The two most common causes are autoimmune encephalitis and *POLG* (polymerase gamma) mutation, a mitochondrial disorder that can be triggered by infections. EPC can also be due to a structural lesion, such as a tumor or cortical malformation.

IMAGING DIFFERENTIAL DIAGNOSES

Asymmetric atrophy in one cerebral hemisphere can be seen with Rasmussen encephalitis, Sturge-Weber syndrome, infarcts, asymmetric infection or trauma.

FINAL DIAGNOSIS

Rasmussen encephalitis.

DISCUSSION

EPC is most frequently caused by autoimmune encephalitis, such as Rasmussen encephalitis or gamma-aminobutyric acid type A (GABA-A) receptor antibody

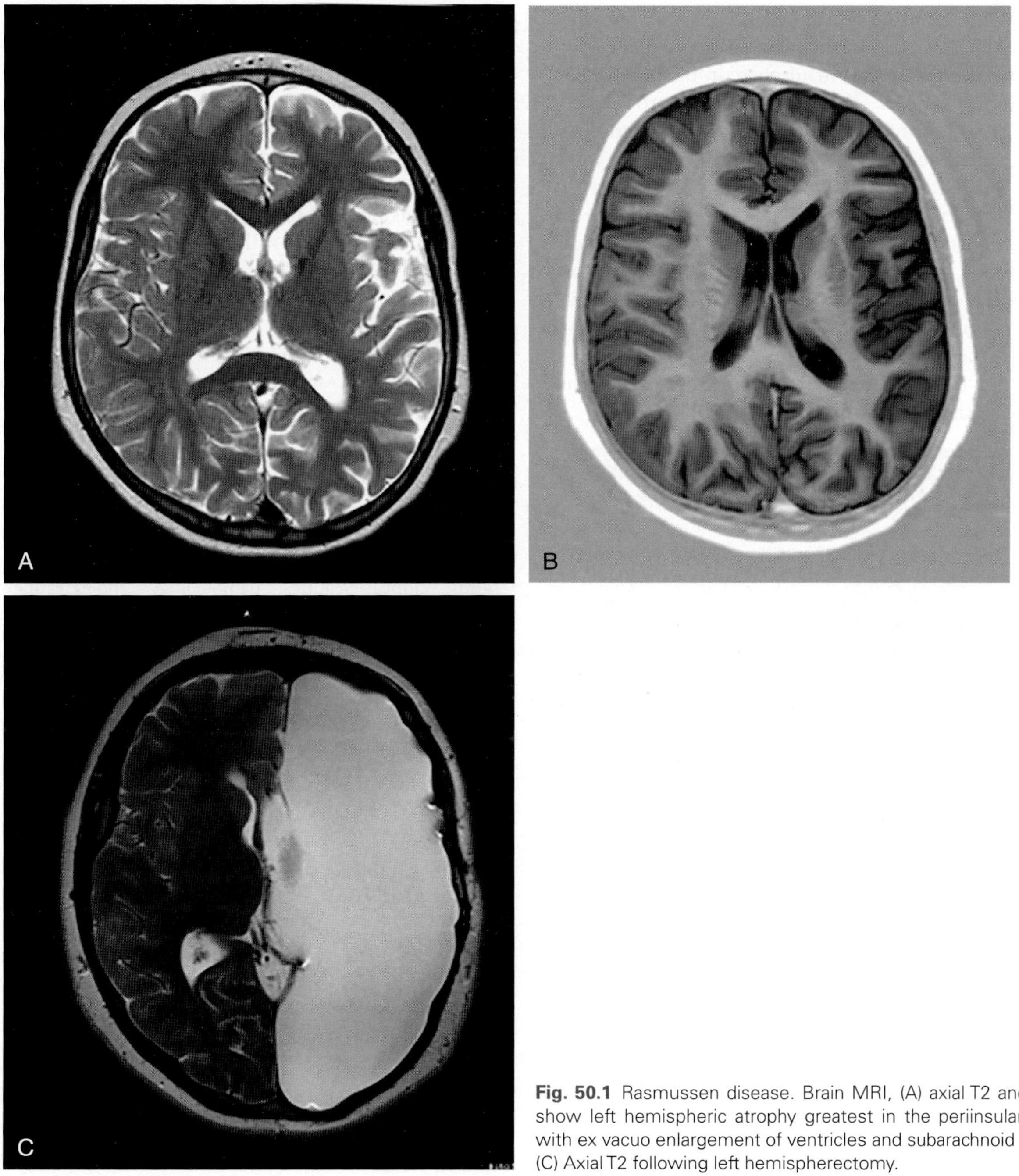

Fig. 50.1 Rasmussen disease. Brain MRI, (A) axial T2 and (B) T1 show left hemispheric atrophy greatest in the periinsular region with ex vacuo enlargement of ventricles and subarachnoid spaces. (C) Axial T2 following left hemispherectomy.

encephalitis. The imaging features of each are quite different, with Rasmussen showing progressive atrophy and signal of one cerebral hemisphere in the periinsular region, and GABA-A showing multifocal cortical/subcortical lesions. Clinically, Rasmussen shows progressive intractable and refractory epilepsy and hemiplegia with hemianopia.

Initial treatment options include antiepileptic medications, corticosteroids, and intravenous immunoglobulins. If these options fail, hemispherectomy or hemispherotomy can result in control of seizures, albeit with persistent neurologic deficits. When surgery is performed earlier in life, ideally before 1 year of age, neuroplasticity of the developing brain can help recover some of the lost function (Fig. 50.1).

CLINICAL RED FLAGS

- EPC is a rare disorder with a focused differential diagnosis.
- Refractory focal epilepsy and hemimotor syndrome are strongly suggestive of Rasmussen encephalitis.

IMAGING RED FLAGS

- Asymmetric and progressive unilateral cerebral atrophy.
- The frontal lobe and insular region are most commonly affected.

CONCLUSIONS

Rasmussen encephalitis is a clinico-radiological syndrome that is thought to reflect asymmetric autoimmune brain destruction. No associated autoantigen has been discovered, and a T-cell-mediated etiology is considered most likely. Immune suppression often fails, and most patients proceed to surgery. In some patients, the disease course stabilizes with age and residual deficits can be managed medically.

REFERENCES

Bien CG, Granata T, Antozzi C, et al. Pathogenesis, diagnosis and treatment of Rasmussen encephalitis: a European consensus statement. *Brain*. 2005;128(3):454–471. https://doi.org/10.1093/brain/awh415.

Bien CG, Widman G, Urbach H, et al. The natural history of Rasmussen's encephalitis. *Brain*. 2002;125(8):1751–1759. https://doi.org/10.1093/brain/awf176.

Varadkar S, Bien CG, Kruse CA, et al. Rasmussen's encephalitis: clinical features, pathobiology, and treatment advances. *Lancet Neurol*. 2014;13(2):195–205. https://doi.org/10.1016/s1474-4422(13)70260-6.

SECTION 11

Demyelinating Diseases of the Central Nervous System

Elizabeth Wilson, Camilo Jaimes, Leslie A. Benson

The past several decades have profoundly increased our recognition and knowledge of demyelinating disorders. We have begun to understand the unique aspects of disease in children and develop pediatric-centered data and treatment guidelines. Clinical presentation is variable and overlaps with infectious, rheumatologic, neoplastic, and primary psychiatric disorders. Patient outcomes also vary depending on the underlying etiology, initial treatment, and maintenance therapy. Thus, timely and accurate diagnosis is essential to inform prognosis and guide management decisions.

As biomarkers for these disorders are still limited, a combination of imaging and laboratory findings is required to reach a definitive diagnosis. MRI patterns are helpful in differentiating the various diagnostic possibilities and have been incorporated into diagnostic criteria, including the 2017 McDonald Criteria for Multiple Sclerosis, proposed criteria for the diagnosis of myelin oligodendrocyte glycoprotein-antibody disease (MOGAD) from the international MOGAD Panel, International Panel for NMO Diagnosis (IPND) diagnostic criteria, Graus criteria for diagnosis of autoimmune encephalitis, and proposed approach to the diagnosis of acute flaccid myelitis (AFM).

Accurate initial diagnosis is vital to guide appropriate clinical management with acute and chronic therapies. In this chapter, we describe clinical and imaging characteristics for a spectrum of pediatric demyelinating and autoimmune disorders and distinguish them from differential considerations, including infection, rheumatologic, and malignant processes.

SUGGESTED READINGS

Banwell B, Bennett JL, Marignier R, et al. Diagnosis of myelin oligodendrocyte glycoprotein antibody-associated disease: International MOGAD Panel proposed criteria. *Lancet Neurol.* 2023;22:268–282. https://doi.org/10.1016/S1474-4422(22)00431-8.

Graus F, Titulaer MJ, Balu R, et al. A clinical approach to diagnosis of autoimmune encephalitis. *Lancet Neurol.* 2016;15:391–404. https://doi.org/10.1016/S1474-4422(15)00401-9.

Murphy OC, Messacar K, Benson L, et al. Acute flaccid myelitis: cause, diagnosis, and management. *Lancet.* 2021;397:334–346. https://doi.org/10.1016/S0140-6736(20)32723-9.

Thompson AJ, Banwell BL, Barkhof F, et al. Diagnosis of multiple sclerosis: 2017 revisions of the McDonald criteria. *Lancet Neurol.* 2018;17:162–173. https://doi.org/10.1016/S1474-4422(17)30470-2.

Wingerchuk DM, Banwell B, Bennett JL, et al. International consensus diagnostic criteria for neuromyelitis optica spectrum disorders. *Neurology.* 2015;85:177–189. https://doi.org/10.1212/WNL.0000000000001729.

When the Central Nervous System Loses Color

HISTORY AND PHYSICAL

A 14-year-old female presented with left arm and leg weakness. One year before, she recalled an episode of abnormal vision without diplopia, blurry vision, or color desaturation. These symptoms lasted for a month and self-resolved. Two weeks earlier, she had vertigo triggered by position changes or rapid head movements, and this also self-resolved. One week prior to presentation, she awoke with left arm and leg weakness that persisted. She denied numbness, trauma, recent infectious symptoms, neck stiffness, insect bites, incontinence, and recent travel. On physical exam, she was found to have intact ocular movements. Sensation was intact to light touch, proprioception, and pinprick throughout. Reflexes were 2+ and symmetric bilaterally. She was found to have grade 4/5 weakness throughout the left upper and lower extremities. Gait was slightly broad-based and unsteady.

DIAGNOSTIC WORKUP

MRI brain was significant for numerous periventricular and subcortical T2/fluid-attenuated inversion recovery (FLAIR) hyperintensities (Fig. 51.1A and B). Lesions in the right precentral gyrus and superior frontal gyrus demonstrated incomplete ring and nodular enhancement, respectively (Fig. 51.1C and D). There was no restricted diffusion. The patient had extensive clinical workup ruling out infectious, metabolic, and rheumatologic etiologies, and tested negative for myelin oligodendrocyte glycoprotein (MOG) and aquaporin 4 (AQP4) antibodies. CSF studies were significant for lymphocyte predominant pleocytosis, elevated immunoglobin G (IgG) index, and >5 oligoclonal bands. She received 5 days of IV methylprednisolone with improvement and was started on disease-modifying therapy as an outpatient.

CLINICAL DIFFERENTIAL DIAGNOSES

Demyelinating diseases such as multiple sclerosis (MS), MOG-associated antibody disease (MOGAD), and neuromyelitis optica spectrum disorder (NMOSD) are in the differential. Acute disseminated encephalomyelitis (ADEM) was not a consideration, given the lack of encephalopathy with any of the episodes.

Nondemyelinating neuroinflammatory conditions can also present with recurrent and subacute focal neurologic deficits.

Ischemic events, hemiplegic migraine, alternating hemiplegia of childhood, and periodic paralysis can present with acute-onset unilateral weakness. In this case, onset of symptoms was more subacute, recurrent, and varied, making these etiologies less likely.

Infectious processes can cause intra- and/or extra-parenchymal lesions with a subacute onset.

IMAGING DIFFERENTIAL DIAGNOSES

Periventricular and subcortical enhancing T2/FLAIR-hyperintense lesions can be seen in a variety of acquired demyelinating syndromes including MOGAD, NMOSD, and MS. On imaging, these disorders can overlap significantly, but there are some distinguishing features.

NMOSD is most likely to present with optic neuritis or myelitis. Brain lesions are typically hyperintense on T2/FLAIR imaging and can be asymmetric, distributed along the ventricles and cerebral aqueduct (Fig. 51.2). Involvement of the area postrema in the caudal fourth ventricle is a more specific finding. NMOSD is often associated with AQP-4 antibodies, which bind water channels in areas with increased permeability of the blood-brain barrier. There may be contrast enhancement with a heterogeneous "cloud-like"

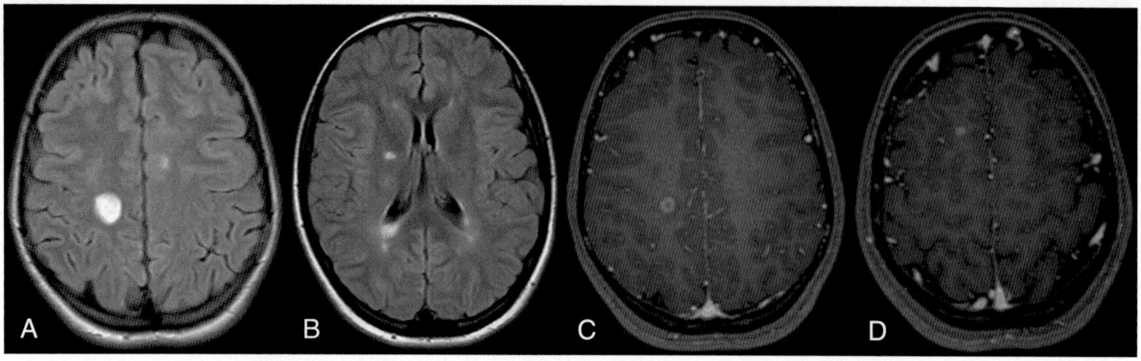

Fig. 51.1 Multiple sclerosis. Brain MRI, axial FLAIR, shows hyperintense juxtacortical lesions in the (A) bifrontal lobes and (B) multiple ovoid periventricular and deep white matter foci. (C) Postcontrast T1 shows active ring enhancement in the right precentral gyrus and (D) nodular enhancement in right superior frontal gyrus. *FLAIR*, Fluid-attenuated inversion recovery.

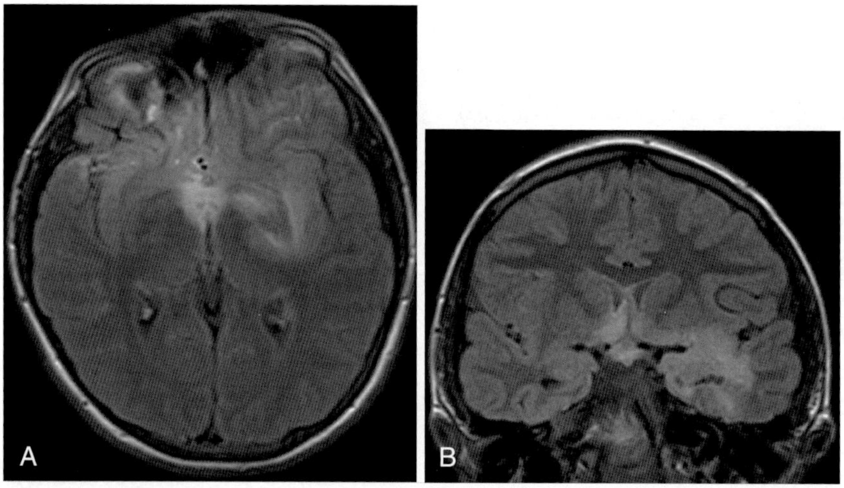

Fig. 51.2 NMOSD. Brain MRI, (A) axial and (B) coronal FLAIR show hyperintensity in the right greater than left hypothalamus surrounding the third ventricle and left anterior temporal lobe. *FLAIR*, Fluid-attenuated inversion recovery; *NMOSD*, neuromyelitis optica spectrum disorder.

or linear "pencil thin" appearance. When present, spinal lesions classically present as longitudinally extensive transverse myelitis (LETM), spanning three or more vertebral segments. Optic nerve lesions can also be longitudinally extensive and more often involve the chiasm.

A similar imaging pattern can be found in patients with MOGAD. These patients tend to present with T2/FLAIR-hyperintense lesions of the deep gray matter, infratentorial parenchyma (brainstem, cerebellar peduncles), optic nerves and conus medullaris. However, these lesions are typically larger, more numerous, and poorly demarcated (Fig. 51.3). The lesions may be symmetric, mimicking a leukodystrophy.

MS lesions are classically ovoid T2/FLAIR hyperintensities in the periventricular space oriented perpendicular to the ventricles (Dawson fingers) with a "central vein" sign on susceptibility-weighted imaging (SWI) (Fig. 51.4). These lesions can be enhancing in the acute phase with an incomplete ring or nodular pattern of active myelination. On SWI, a hypointense

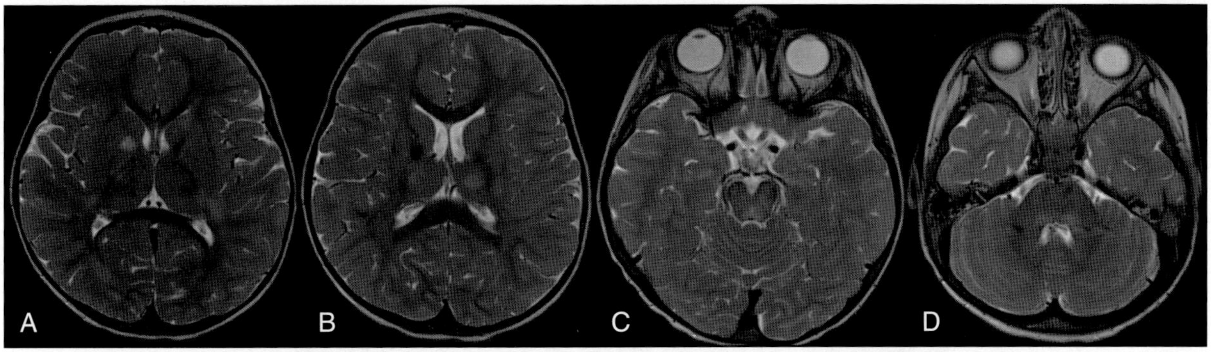

Fig. 51.3 MOGAD. Brain MRI, axial T2, shows multifocal hyperintense signal within the (A) bilateral cerebral white matter, corpus callosum, basal ganglia, (B) thalami, and posterior limbs of the internal capsules. Additionally, there are brainstem lesions, including (C) left cerebral peduncle and periaqueductal gray matter, (D) dorsal pons and middle cerebellar peduncles. There was no associated contrast enhancement or restricted diffusion. *MOGAD*, Myelin oligodendrocyte glycoprotein antibody associated disease.

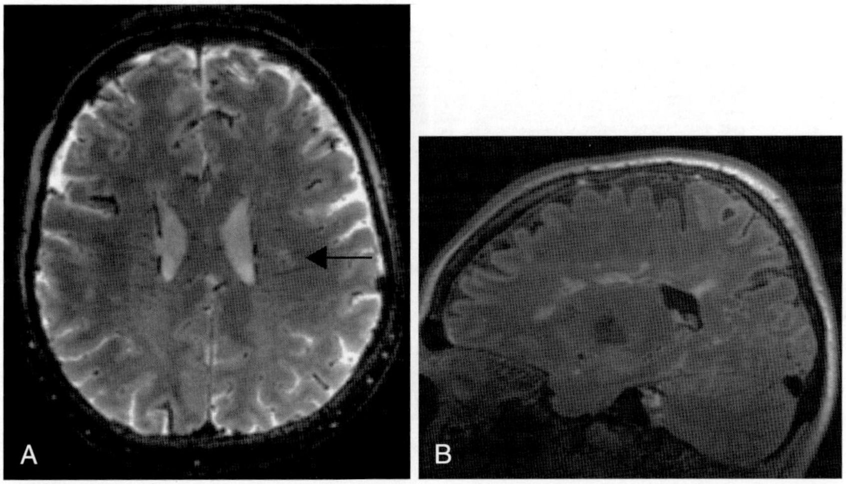

Fig. 51.4 Multiple sclerosis. Brain MRI, (A) axial SWI shows demyelinating plaque with central vein sign (*arrow*). (B) Sagittal FLAIR shows Dawson fingers radiating perpendicular to the corpus callosum along the expected courses of medullary veins. *FLAIR*, Fluid-attenuated inversion recovery; *SWI*, susceptibility-weighted imaging.

"paramagnetic rim" is suggestive of ongoing MS, correlating with the presence of peripheral activated macrophages on pathology (Fig. 51.5). Juxtacortical lesions involving the subcortical U fibers are also suggestive.

Focal hypointense and nonenhancing lesions on T1 ("black holes") are characteristic of chronic MS, representing tissue loss after a previous inflammatory event (Fig. 51.6).

Demyelinating lesions can sometimes appear tumefactive and difficult to differentiate from CNS tumors, such as lymphoma or glioma. Both lymphoma and MS involve the periventricular region, can be associated with CSF pleocytosis, and respond to steroid treatment.

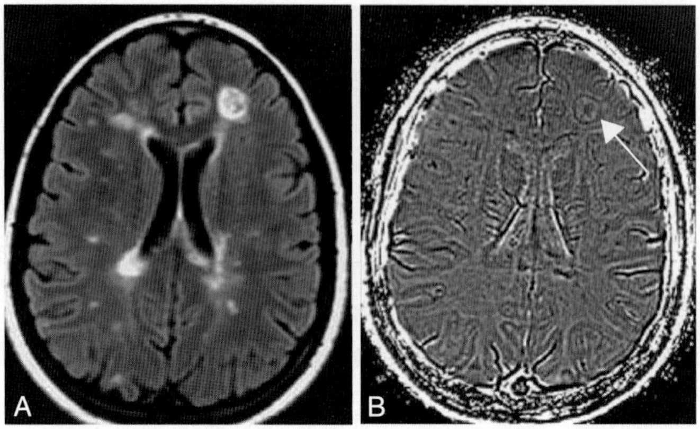

Fig. 51.5 Multiple sclerosis. Brain MRI, (A) axial FLAIR and (B) SWI phase map show multiple lesions in the lobar and periventricular white matter. Left frontal lobe lesion has a paramagnetic rim indicating inflammatory iron deposition (*arrow*). *FLAIR*, Fluid-attenuated inversion recovery; *SWI*, susceptibility-weighted imaging.

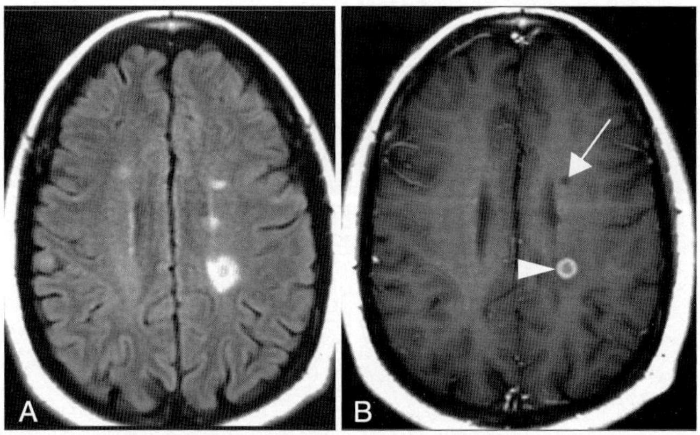

Fig. 51.6 Multiple sclerosis. Brain MRI, (A) axial FLAIR and (B) postcontrast T1 show multiple FLAIR-hyperintense lesions. Rim enhancement in the left posterior corona radiata (*arrowhead*) indicates acute demyelination. Nonenhancing T1-hypointense black hole in the left anterior corona radiata (*arrow*) indicates chronic demyelination.

If uncertainty remains, brain MRI with and without contrast should be repeated in a short time interval. MRS may be helpful as gliomas can show persistent elevation in choline and lactate with reduced N-acetylaspartate (NAA) peaks, while a demyelinating plaque would evolve over time with resolution of metabolic abnormalities after the acute period.

Other disorders with periventricular involvement include rheumatologic conditions such as neuro-Behcet, infectious processes such as bacterial ventriculitis and cytomegalovirus (CMV) ventriculitis, vasculopathies such as Susac syndrome, and leukodystrophies, including Alexander disease, X-linked adrenoleukodystrophy, and Krabbe disease.

FINAL DIAGNOSIS

Relapsing-remitting MS.

DISCUSSION

The 2021 MAGNIMS-CMSC-NAIMS consensus reiterates the importance of obtaining brain and spine MRI as part of the diagnostic workup for MS. The updated 2024 McDonald Criteria define the criteria for diagnosing MS, with clinical and imaging findings indicating dissemination in space and/or time. MRI markers include the central vein and paramagnetic rim signs. Dissemination in space can involve the periventricular, cortical/juxtacortical, optic nerve, infratentorial, and spinal cord compartments. Dissemination in time can be established clinically and/or radiologically. CSF biomarkers include oligoclonal bands and CSF kappa free light chains (KFLC).

CLINICAL RED FLAGS

- Recurrent neurologic deficits lasting over 24 hours that self-resolve.
- Clinical localization to multiple different areas of the CNS.

IMAGING RED FLAGS

- Presence of contrast-enhancing and nonenhancing lesions.
- Lesions disseminated in space and/or time, as per the 2024 McDonald Criteria.
- Ovoid, T2/FLAIR hyperintense lesions radiating perpendicular to the ventricles.
- Central vein and paramagnetic rim signs.
- Dawson fingers.
- Incomplete ring enhancement.

CONCLUSIONS

Neurologic deficits with enhancing and nonenhancing T2/FLAIR hyperintense lesions on brain MRI should raise suspicion for a demyelinating process. The imaging characteristics (location, size, enhancement) and biomarkers can help differentiate between MOGAD, NMOSD, and MS with implications for treatment. It is important to assess for mimics of demyelinating disease including malignancy, infection, and rheumatologic processes.

REFERENCES

DeAngelis LM. Primary central nervous system lymphoma imitates multiple sclerosis. *J Neurooncol.* 1990;9:177–181.

Dutra BG, da Rocha AJ, Nunes RH, Martins MAC. Neuromyelitis optica spectrum disorders: spectrum of MR imaging findings and their differential diagnosis. *Radiographics.* 2018;38:169–193. https://doi.org/10.1148/rg.2018170141.

Ferilli MAN, Valeriani M, Papi C, et al. Clinical and neuroimaging characteristics of MOG autoimmunity in children with acquired demyelinating syndromes. *Mult Scler Relat Disord.* 2021;50:1–7. https://doi.org/10.1016/j.msard.2021.102837.

Hartung HP, Graf J, Aktas O, Mares J, Barnett MH. Diagnosis of multiple sclerosis: revisions of the McDonald criteria 2017–continuity and change. *Curr Opin Neurol.* 2019;32:327–337. https://doi.org/10.1097/WCO.0000000000000699.

Ikeguchi R, Shimizu Y, Abe K, et al. Proton magnetic resonance spectroscopy differentiates tumefactive demyelinating lesions from gliomas. *Mult Scler Relat Disord.* 2018;26:77–84. https://doi.org/10.1016/j.msard.2018.08.025.

Wattjes MP, Ciccarelli O, Reich DS, et al. MAGNUMS-CMSC-NAIMS consensus recommendations on the use of MRI in patients with multiple sclerosis. *Lancet Neurol.* 2021;20:653–670. https://doi.org/10.1016/S1474-4422(21)00095-8.

Werneck LC, Scola RH, Arruda WO, Torres LF. Glioma and multiple sclerosis: case report. *Arq Neuropsiquiatr.* 2002;60:469–474.

Case 52

Altered Mentation and Myelitis

HISTORY AND PHYSICAL

A 4-year-old girl presented with prolonged fever, weight loss, leukocytosis, and vomiting for one month. She was diagnosed with croup 2 weeks prior to presentation and received MMR vaccination one week prior to presentation. Subsequently, she developed lethargy, irritability, abdominal pain, and musculoskeletal pain. She was initially diagnosed and treated for *Clostridium difficile* infection, but her fever returned about 3 weeks later. She was found to have elevated white blood cell (WBC), erythrocyte sedimentation rate (ESR), and C-reactive protein (CRP). She then reported bilateral eye pain and had difficulty walking, hyperphagia, constipation, and bladder issues. During her hospitalization, she continued to have hypersomnolence and developed hypopnea and desaturations during sleep. Exam was significant for encephalopathy, allodynia, lower extremity weakness, and diffuse hyperreflexia with upgoing toes.

DIAGNOSTIC WORKUP

Brain MRI with and without contrast revealed diffuse T2/FLAIR hyperintense signal abnormalities. There were patchy and confluent foci throughout all cerebral lobes. Involvement was most severe in the bilateral mesial temporal lobes. There was also involvement of the deep gray structures including the putamina and thalami, as well as brainstem structures including superior cerebellar peduncles and dorsal midbrain. White matter involvement included the periventricular regions, corona radiata, and centrum semiovale. The optic chiasm was thickened with similar signal alterations that extended posteriorly into the optic tract and inferiorly into the hypothalamus (Fig. 52.1). There was no associated diffusion restriction or contrast enhancement. MRS was normal.

Spinal MRI was significant for multifocal edema throughout the cord (Fig. 52.2). There was no associated enhancement.

The patient underwent an extensive workup and was found to have elevated inflammatory markers, including absolute neutrophil count (ANC), platelet (PLT), ESR, and CRP. Creatinine kinase (CK), complement, lactate dehydrogenase (LDH), and rheumatoid factor (RF) were normal. Broad infectious workup was negative. Hormonal screening was unrevealing including thyroid stimulating hormone (TSH). Autoimmune workup for systemic lupus erythematosus (SLE) and sarcoidosis with dsDNA and angiotensin-converting enzyme (ACE) was negative. Lumbar puncture (LP) revealed an elevated cell count (45) and protein (123). AQP-4 antibody testing was negative. Myelin oligodendrocyte glycoprotein (MOG) antibody obtained during a subsequent bout of optic neuritis was positive. She was started on steroids with significant clinical improvement, and treatment was tapered off over 2 months. Follow-up MRI 6 months later was normal. She had long-term sequelae including distal lower extremity spasticity and recurrent urinary tract infections.

CLINICAL DIFFERENTIAL DIAGNOSES

A patient presenting with subacute onset of fever, altered mental status, and signs of myelitis raises concern for various metabolic, infectious, endocrinologic, and autoimmune processes.

The presence of encephalopathy narrows the clinical differential from various causes of myelitis to those that may mimic acute disseminated encephalomyelitis (ADEM). These include thyroid (Hashimoto) encephalopathy and CNS infections, particularly given her fever: Epstein-Barr virus (EBV)/CMV, Lyme, HIV, human herpesvirus 6 (HHV-6), and Powassan virus.

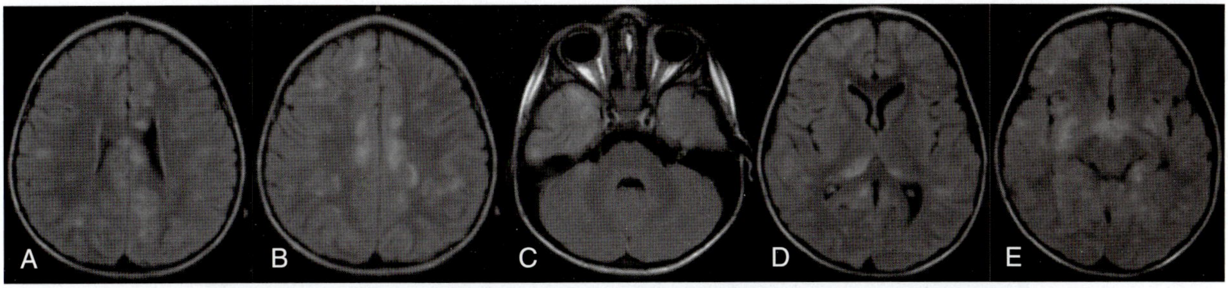

Fig. 52.1 ADEM. Brain MRI, axial FLAIR, shows patchy hyperintensity throughout the (A-B) cerebral cortex and subcortical white matter, (C) mesial temporal lobes, (D) thalami, and (E) optic pathway. *ADEM*, Acute disseminated encephalomyelitis; *FLAIR*, fluid-attenuated inversion recovery.

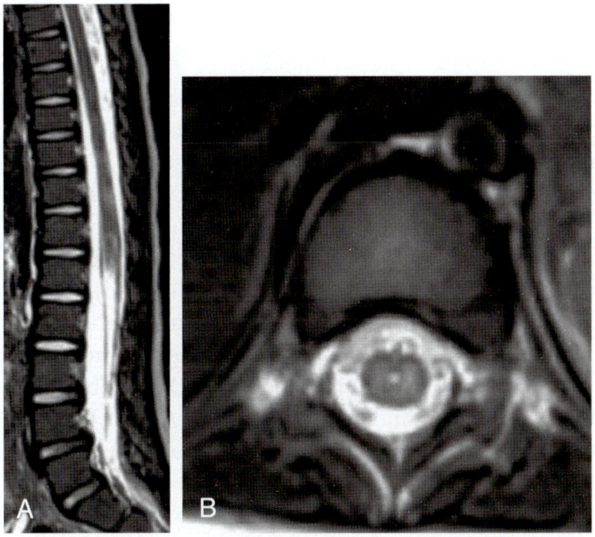

Fig. 52.2 ADEM. Spine MRI, (A) sagittal and (B) axial T2, show multifocal lesions involving the majority of the cord cross-section. No definite enhancement was seen. *ADEM*, Acute disseminated encephalomyelitis; *MOGAD*, myelin oligodendrocyte glycoprotein-antibody disease.

Multiple sclerosis (MS) can present with myelitis and optic neuritis but is much less likely to have associated encephalopathy with extensive cord, hypothalamic, and chiasm involvement.

Several autoimmune conditions can present with altered awareness, such as autoimmune encephalitis and Rasmussen encephalitis.

CNS vasculitis can present acutely with altered awareness and neurologic deficits.

IMAGING DIFFERENTIAL DIAGNOSES

There is a broad differential for multifocal T2/FLAIR-hyperintense lesions involving both white and gray matter. Autoimmune encephalitides can show cortical/subcortical abnormalities and meningeal enhancement. Limbic encephalitides affect limbic structures including hippocampus, amygdala, claustrum, and mesial temporal lobe. There may be additional involvement of basal ganglia, brainstem, and neocortex. Rasmussen encephalitis can present with more asymmetric abnormalities, including unilateral cerebral and basal ganglia atrophy, T2/FLAIR-hyperintense signal in cortex/subcortical white matter, and ex vacuo ventriculomegaly (Fig. 52.3).

Prolonged seizures can also yield cortical signal abnormalities. For example, new-onset refractory status epilepticus can present with bilateral peri-insular T2/FLAIR hyperintensities.

Involvement of the optic tract and spinal cord narrows the differential to ADEM (which can be secondary to MOG), neuromyelitis optica spectrum disorder (NMOSD), and MS.

ADEM typically has poorly demarcated lesions on MRI that can involve the deep gray structures, cortex, and deep white matter with periventricular sparing. Spinal cord lesions in ADEM are more often large, edematous, centrally located, and thoracic, compared to those of MS which more commonly affect the peripheral cervical cord and are short-segment.

The pattern of optic neuritis is also important. Patients with MOG-IgG are more likely to have bilateral optic neuritis involving the anterior optic nerve, with optic

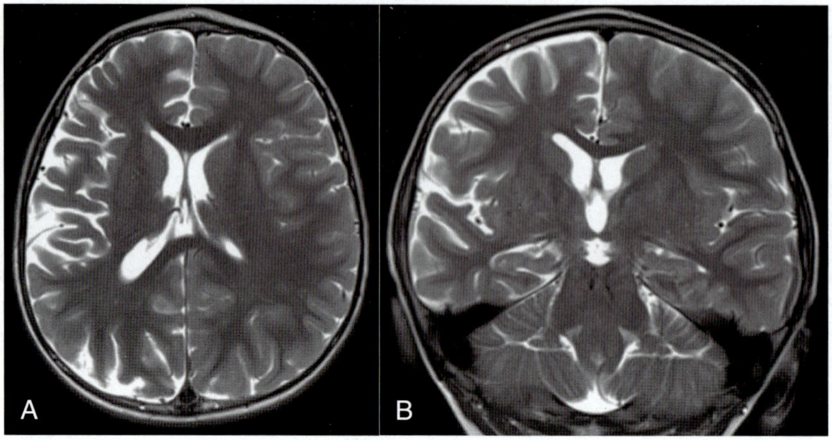

Fig. 52.3 Rasmussen encephalitis. Brain MRI, (A) axial and (B) coronal T2, show right peri-insular volume loss with ex vacuo dilatation of the lateral ventricle and subarachnoid spaces. There was no abnormal enhancement of the brain parenchyma, leptomeninges, or dura.

head edema and retrobulbar involvement. Patients with AQP-4 or NMOSD are more likely to have bilateral optic neuritis involving the posterior optic nerve or optic chiasm. All of the above can have longitudinally extensive myelitis. Classically, patients with MS have short segment, unilateral optic neuritis. Unfortunately, none of these patterns is 100% reliable, so early biomarker testing provides the best chance of differentiating these disorders.

Lesions in ADEM occasionally show diffusion restriction. Malignancy (such as CNS lymphoma), vasculitis, and infarct should be in the differential. MRS may be helpful to differentiate these possibilities.

FINAL DIAGNOSIS

MOG antibody-associated ADEM.

DISCUSSIONS

ADEM is a multifocal inflammatory demyelinating disease of the central nervous system. It is often associated with recent infection or vaccination and is clinically monophasic. The mechanism is thought to result from T-cell-mediated cross-activation against myelin proteins.

Diagnosis of ADEM as defined by the International Pediatric Multiple Sclerosis Study group requires: a first polyfocal clinical CNS event with presumed inflammatory demyelinating cause, encephalopathy, brain MRI abnormalities consistent with demyelination during the acute phase, and no new clinical or MRI findings 3 months or more after the clinical onset.

There are five imaging patterns that may be seen in ADEM. These include (1) small lesions (<5 mm); (2) large confluent white matter asymmetric lesions; (3) symmetric bithalamic involvement; (4) leukodystrophic pattern with diffuse bilateral and usually nonenhancing white matter lesions; and (5) acute hemorrhagic encephalomyelitis. The presence of MOG antibodies is associated with a higher risk of relapse. ADEM followed by optic neuritis is a recognized phenotype within the MOGAD (MOG antibody-associated disease) spectrum. In contrast, MS typically shows perivenular, juxtacortical, and callosal-septal lesions.

CLINICAL RED FLAGS

- Encephalopathy.
- Optic neuritis.
- Myelitis.

IMAGING RED FLAGS

- CNS lesions that resolve or dramatically improve on repeat imaging.
- Asymmetric CNS lesions.
- Bilateral optic neuritis.
- Demyelinating lesions in brainstem, cerebellum, and spinal cord.
- Longitudinally extensive myelitis.

CONCLUSIONS

The presence of optic neuritis, myelitis, and altered mental status with multifocal demyelinating lesions on MRI should raise suspicion for ADEM. There may be associated MOG antibodies in the CSF. ADEM is classically monophasic and can be difficult to distinguish at imaging from NMOSD and MS, which are clinically associated with a higher risk of relapse and require long-term immunotherapy. Follow-up imaging may be helpful to assess for resolution of lesions as well as assess for new lesions after a period of 6 months or more.

REFERENCES

Alper G, Heyman R, Wang L. Multiple sclerosis and acute disseminated encephalomyelitis diagnosed in children after long-term follow up: comparison of presenting features. *Dev Med Child Neurol.* 2009;51:480–486. https://doi.org/10.1111/j.1469-8749.2008.03136.x.

Banwell B, Bennett JL, Marignier R, et al. Diagnosis of myelin oligodendrocyte glycoprotein antibody-associated disease: International MOGAD panel proposed criteria. *Lancet Neurol.* 2023;22:268–282. https://doi.org/10.1016/S1474-4422(22)00431-8.

Baumann M, Bartels F, Finke C, et al. E.U. paediatric MOG consortium consensus: part 2—neuroimaging features of paediatric myelin oligodendrocyte glycoprotein antibody-associated disorders. *Eur J Paediatr Neurol.* 2020;29:14–21. https://doi.org/10.1016/j.ejpn.2020.10.002.

Boesen MS, Blinkenberg M, Thygesen LC, Ilginiene J, Langkilde AR. Magnetic resonance imaging criteria at onset to differentiate pediatric multiple sclerosis from acute disseminated encephalomyelitis: a nationwide cohort study. *Mult Scler Relat Disord.* 2022;62. https://doi.org/10.1016/j.msard.2022.103738.

Cai MT, Zhang YX, Zheng Y, Fang W, Ding MP. Callosal lesions on magnetic resonance imaging with multiple sclerosis, neuromyelitis optica spectrum disorder and acute disseminated encephalomyelitis. *Mult Scler Relat Disord.* 2019;32:41–45. https://doi.org/10.1016/j.msard.2019.04.019.

Esposito S, Di Pietro GM, Madini B, Mastrolia MV, Rigante D. A spectrum of inflammation and demyelination in acute disseminated encephalomyelitis (ADEM) of children. *Autoimmun Rev.* 2015;14:923–929. http://dx.doi.org/10.1016/j.autrev.2015.06.002.

Pohl D, Alper G, Van Haren K, et al. Acute disseminated encephalomyelitis: updates on an inflammatory CNS syndrome. *Neurology.* 2016;87:S38–S45. https://doi.org/10.1212/WNL.0000000000002825.

Case 53

When the Spinal Cord Takes Off Its Coat

HISTORY AND PHYSICAL

An 8-year-old boy presented with acute-onset and progressive lower extremity weakness in the setting of a rhinovirus/enterovirus positive respiratory test. On the day of admission, he developed difficulty walking and urge incontinence, without sensory symptoms. Weakness progressed and he developed respiratory failure requiring bilevel positive airway pressure (BiPAP). Neurologic exam revealed mild weakness in the distal upper extremities and more significant weakness in the lower extremities. Sensation and reflexes were intact and symmetric throughout. He was unable to stand without support and could not take any steps.

DIAGNOSTIC WORKUP

MRI of the spine was significant for mild focal T2 hyperintensity at the cervicothoracic junction. MRI brain was normal. Repeat MRI of the spine 3 days later revealed a larger and clearly demarcated lesion from C6 to T1, primarily involving the central cord (Fig. 53.1). There was no associated mass effect or abnormal enhancement.

Within 24 hours, the patient developed hypotonia, worsening distal weakness (left greater than right), areflexia in all extremities, and diffuse pain. Over the subsequent 3 days, a sensory level was identified around T5 to T8. Workup was significant for negative MOG and AQP-4 antibodies. CSF was without pleocytosis or protein elevation. He was initially treated with high-dose IV steroids, followed by intravenous immunoglobin (IVIG) after his weakness progressed. His exam improved and he was discharged on a steroid taper. At 3-month follow up, his residual deficits were mild intrinsic hand weakness, mildly decreased sensation to temperature in the lower extremities, hyperreflexia, and bilateral ankle clonus.

CLINICAL DIFFERENTIAL DIAGNOSES

The initial neurologic exam suggested an upper motor neuron process within the cervical cord, such as autoimmune myelitis (given weakness in the setting of preserved reflexes). The differential includes CNS demyelinating disorders (MOGAD, NMOSD, MS) and systemic autoimmune disorders (lupus Sjogren syndrome, antiphospholipid antibody syndrome, mixed connective tissue disease, sarcoidosis). Infectious causes of myelitis include EBV, CMV, poliovirus, herpes simplex virus (HSV), HIV, human T-lymphotropic virus type 1 (HTLV-1), Lyme, syphilis, tuberculosis, and schistosomiasis.

As the patient's course progressed, he developed areflexia more suggestive of lower motor neuron involvement, as can be seen in Guillain-Barré syndrome (Fig. 53.2) and acute flaccid myelitis (AFM). His asymmetric weakness and spinal MRI findings were concerning for possible AFM, particularly in the setting of a recent upper respiratory infection with positive entero/rhinovirus testing. While polio is the classic cause of acute flaccid paralysis, many nonpolio infections can cause lower motor neuron presentations (including enterovirus D-68 (Fig. 53.3) and A-71, coxsackievirus, echovirus, West Nile virus, adenovirus, herpesvirus, and flaviviruses). A clear sensory level is more suggestive of inflammatory myelitis than AFM. Of note, both myelitis and AFM are expected to have associated pleocytosis, but this finding may be delayed from clinical presentation.

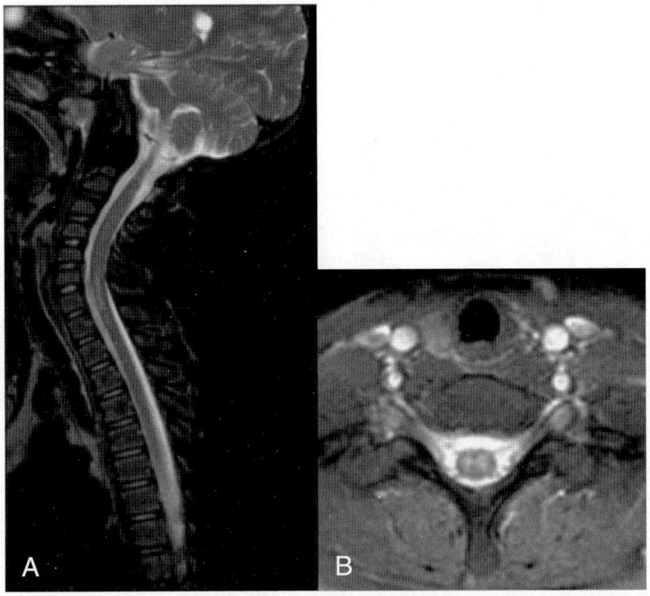

Fig. 53.1 Transverse myelitis. Spine MRI, (A) sagittal T2 shows focal cord hyperintensity from C6-T1 without associated enhancement or edema. (B) Axial T2 shows preferential involvement of the central gray matter.

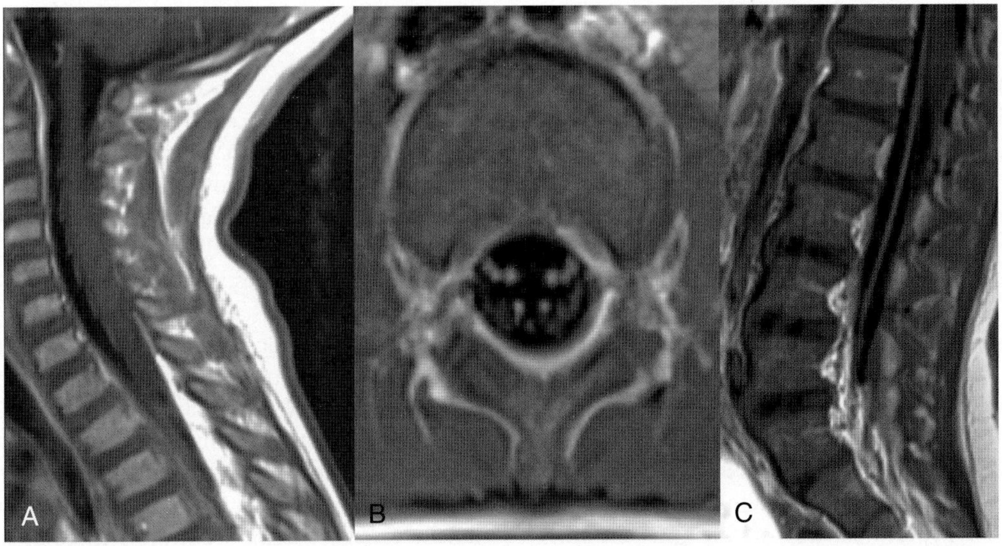

Fig. 53.2 Guillain-Barré syndrome. Spine MRI, (A) sagittal cervical and (B) axial and (C) sagittal lumbar post-contrast T1, shows smooth thickening and enhancement of nerve roots with preferential involvement of ventral motor roots.

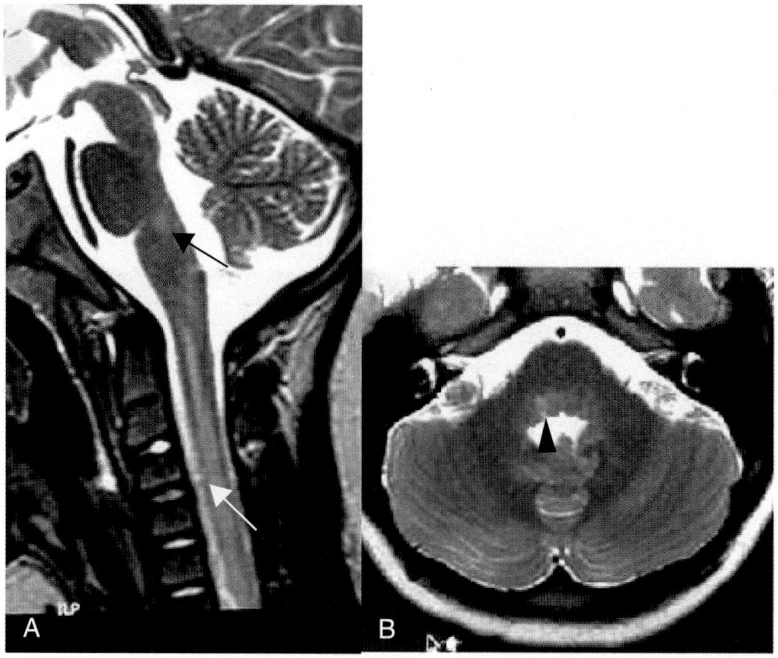

Fig. 53.3 Enterovirus D-68 rhombencephalomyelitis. Cervical spine MRI, (A) sagittal T2, shows longitudinally extensive myelitis with ill-defined brainstem and cord involvement (*arrows*). (B) Axial T2 shows asymmetric hyperintensity of the dorsal brainstem (*arrowhead*).

Other diagnoses less likely given clinical history and exam include trauma, ischemic and hemorrhagic myelopathy, spinal cord tumor, and abscess.

IMAGING DIFFERENTIAL DIAGNOSES

Edema involving spinal cord gray and white matter in children is suggestive of transverse myelitis. However, there is a wide differential diagnosis with few reliable biomarkers. Nutritional deficiencies (vitamins E and B_{12}, copper) can affect the dorsal and lateral columns. Spinal cord ischemia can be associated with vascular anomalies such as arteriovenous shunts, vasculitis such as Behcet disease, and fibrocartilaginous embolism. MRI reveals pencil-like T2 hyperintensities of the anterior horns of gray matter ("snake eye" or "owl eye" appearance) (Fig. 53.4). Diffusion-weighted imaging (DWI) changes are not sensitive or specific for distinguishing ischemia from infection.

If a patient with suspected myelitis does not improve with immunosuppression, underlying neoplasia should be considered (glioma, lymphoma, dermoid, hemangioblastoma, metastases). Gliomas can extend over multiple vertebral levels with eccentric location in the cord (Fig. 53.5). There may be associated enhancement, cysts, and/or syrinx. Lymphoma may also show T2 signal hyperintensity and contrast enhancement. Paraneoplastic processes should also be considered, including CRMP5, GAD, GFAP, and amphiphysin antibodies.

Demyelinating diseases include MS, NMOSD, and MOG. In MS, cervical or thoracic spine lesions do not extend more than two spinal segments, and involve the peripheral cord. NMOSD is the most common cause of longitudinally extensive myelitis. Spinal lesions are typically centrally located and extend over multiple vertebral segments. Patients with MOGAD may also have longitudinally extensive lesions, but these more often affect the lumbar spine (>2 spinal segments) and conus. MOGAD can closely mimic AFM with grey matter predilection and similar clinical syndrome. The grey matter involvement in MOGAD myelitis may manifest as nonenhancing T2 hyperintensity on sagittal images ("sagittal line") with involvement of the gray matter on axial images ("H sign"). Both MOGAD and NMOSD-associated myelitis can have

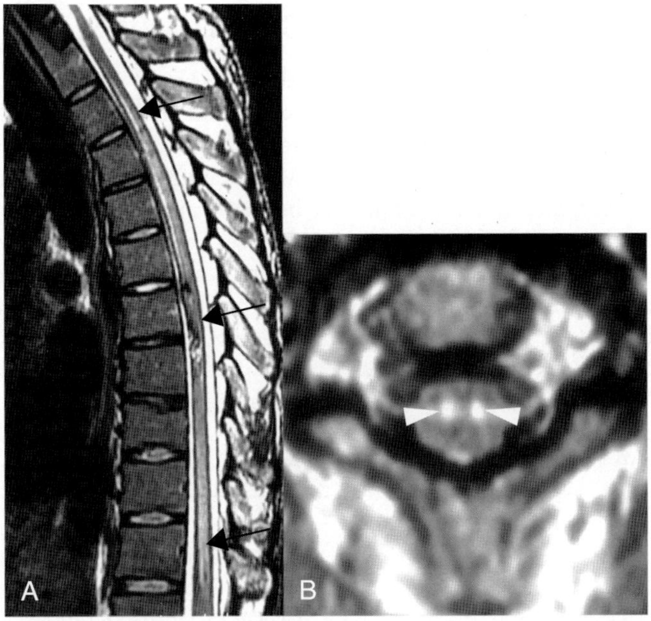

Fig. 53.4 Fibrocartilaginous embolism with hemorrhagic cord infarction. Spine MRI, (A) sagittal T2 and (B) axial T1 postcontrast show longitudinally extensive thoracic cord hyper- and hypointense signal indicating edema and hemorrhage (*arrows*). Multilevel disc desiccation and Schmorl nodes are present. There is selective involvement of the anterior horns of gray matter (*arrowheads*).

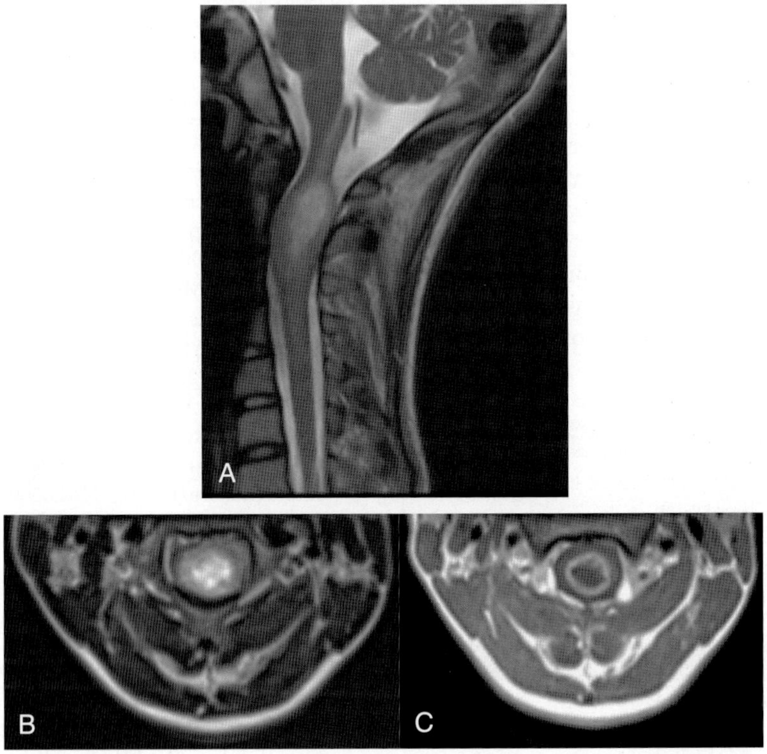

Fig. 53.5 Spinal cord glioma. Cervical spine MRI, (A) sagittal T2 and (B) axial T2 show expansile hyperintense intramedullary lesion at C1-C3 with (C) irregular ring enhancement on axial postcontrast T1.

associated enhancement. Other inflammatory causes of LETM include systemic lupus, sarcoidosis, and Sjogren syndrome.

In AFM, spinal cord signal abnormality is usually seen within the anterior horns of grey matter and extending over >3 vertebral segments, with the cervical region most commonly involved. Acute lesions are nonenhancing or minimally enhancing. Additionally, while demyelinating diseases may be associated with supratentorial lesions, AFM is classically limited to the spinal cord, brainstem, and cranial nerves.

Nerve root enhancement can be seen in AFM as well as idiopathic myelitis, ADEM, MOGAD, and rheumatologic processes such as sarcoidosis. Nerve root involvement is less commonly reported in MS, AQP-4-associated myelitis, and ischemic myelopathy.

FINAL DIAGNOSIS

Parainfectious transverse myelitis.

DISCUSSION

Myelitis may be an isolated event or the first presentation of an autoimmune disease. Treatment and outcomes depend on the underlying etiology. In addition to CSF and serum studies, MRI findings can help differentiate etiologies and exclude surgical emergencies, such as abscess or cord compression. A small percentage of acute myelitis lesions may not be visible on MRI at presentation. Advanced sequences that can increase sensitivity to subtle lesions include DWI, double inversion recovery, and phase-sensitive inversion recovery. Brain MRI should be performed during initial evaluation, as the presence of brain lesions increases the likelihood of demyelinating disease and future relapse.

CLINICAL RED FLAGS

- Acute to subacute-onset asymmetric limb weakness.
- Rapidly progressive weakness.
- Respiratory distress.
- Preserved sensation.

IMAGING RED FLAGS

- Anterior nerve root enhancement.
- Predominantly gray matter cord involvement.

CONCLUSIONS

There is a broad differential diagnosis for myelitis, which may result in delayed diagnosis and treatment. While serum and CSF studies are a vital part of the workup, MRI brain and spine without and with contrast should be performed to fully assess the pattern and extent of disease. Through careful consideration of imaging characteristics, the differential diagnosis can be narrowed and prompt treatment initiated. Consider specialized imaging sequences, such as DWI and inversion recovery, if there is an atypical clinical course or ongoing diagnostic uncertainty.

REFERENCES

Absoud M, Greenberg BM, Lim M, Lotze T, Thomas T, Deiva K. Pediatric transverse myelitis. *Neurology*. 2016;87:S46–S52. https://doi.org/10.1212/WNL.0000000000002820.

DeSena A, Graves D, Morriss MC, Greenberg BM. Transverse myelitis plus syndrome and acute disseminated encephalomyelitis plus syndrome: a case series of 5 children. *JAMA Neurol*. 2014;71:624–629. https://doi.org/10.1001/jamaneurol.2013.5323.

Gordon-Lipkin E, Muñoz LS, Klein JL, Dean J, Izbudak I, Pardo CA. Comparative quantitative clinical, neuroimaging, and functional profiles in children with acute flaccid myelitis at acute and convalescent stages of disease. *Dev Med Child Neurol*. 2019;61:366–375. https://doi.org/10.1111/dmcn.14030.

Group Transverse Myelitis Consortium Working. Proposed diagnostic criteria and nosology of acute transverse myelitis. *Neurology*. 2002;59:499–505. https://doi.org/10.1212/WNL.0000000000010979.

Murphy OC, Messacar K, Benson L, et al. Acute flaccid myelitis: cause, diagnosis, and management. *Lancet*. 2021;397:334–346. https://doi.org/10.1016/S0140-6736(20)32723-9.

Rinaldi S, Davies A, Fehmi J, et al. Overlapping central and peripheral nervous system syndromes in MOG antibody–associated disorders. *Neurol Neuroimmunol Neuroinflamm*. 2021;8:e924. https://doi.org/10.1212/NXI.0000000000000924.

Trebst C, Raab P, Voss EV, et al. Longitudinal extensive transverse myelitis—it's not all neuromyelitis optica. *Nat Rev Neurol*. 2011;7:688–698. https://doi.org/10.1038/nrneurol.2011.176.

Wang C, Narayan R, Greenberg B. Anti-myelin oligodendrocyte glycoprotein antibody associated with gray matter predominant transverse myelitis mimicking acute flaccid myelitis: a presentation of two cases. *Pediatr Neurol*. 2018;86:42–45. https://doi.org/10.1016/j.pediatrneurol.2018.06.003.

Case 54

When Emotional Lability Is Not Psychiatric

HISTORY AND PHYSICAL

A 9-year-old previously healthy boy presented with personality changes, fatigue, right facial weakness, drooling, and dysarthria over the course of 2 weeks. He became withdrawn and less interactive with his family. He did not have any recent illnesses, vaccination, travel, or insect bites. Upon presentation, he was perseverative, dysarthric, and had mild right facial droop with tongue deviation to the right. He also had right pronator drift, right upper extremity ataxia, and mild difficulty with tandem gait.

DIAGNOSTIC WORKUP

Brain MRI was significant for multifocal T2/FLAIR hyperintensities involving the bilateral frontotemporal lobes, particularly the inferior frontal lobes, mesial temporal lobes, and insulae (Fig. 54.1). There was no restricted diffusion, hemorrhage, or abnormal enhancement. Cranial nerves were normal.

Within 24 hours the patient developed hypotonia, worsening distal weakness (left greater than right), areflexia in all extremities, and diffuse pain. Blood testing for metabolic/endocrine abnormalities and serum inflammatory markers was unrevealing, aside from mildly elevated ESR. Autoimmune encephalitis and meningitis/encephalitis panels were negative. Rheumatologic testing showed positive antinuclear antibody (ANA) (titer 1:80). EBV, mycoplasma, and CMV IgG were positive, with negative IgM. CSF at presentation was significant for 23 WBCs (90% lymphocytes), with normal protein and glucose. Neopterin and IgG index were elevated and oligoclonal bands were positive. MOG and AQP-4 antibodies were negative. CT chest, abdomen, and pelvis did not reveal any evidence of malignancy. Over the subsequent 3 days, a sensory level was identified around T5 to T8. He was treated with IV methylprednisolone for 5 days, started on IVIG for 2 days with clinical improvement, then discharged on daily prednisone.

Repeat MRI 1 month later revealed decreased T2/FLAIR hyperintensities, with corresponding volume loss of the temporal lobes. He ultimately developed seizures with EEG significant for left temporal notched slowing, for which he was started on oxcarbazepine with good control. At 3-month follow up, his residual deficits were mild intrinsic hand weakness, mild decreased sensation to temperature in the lower extremities, hyperreflexia, and bilateral ankle clonus.

CLINICAL DIFFERENTIAL DIAGNOSES

Rapidly progressive mental status changes and cranial nerve deficits can be seen in infectious, rheumatologic, and autoimmune processes.

CNS infections include Lyme, Powassan, syphilis, HIV, HSV, varicella zoster, EBV, CMV, HHV-6, arbovirus, and fungi such as histoplasma and aspergillus.

Rheumatologic processes include Sjogren's disease, CNS lupus, sarcoidosis, and neuro-Behcet's.

Autoimmune encephalitides, such as limbic encephalitis and NMDAR receptor (NMDAR) encephalitis, can present with subacute changes in mental status. NMDAR encephalitis is more likely to be associated with speech dysfunction, seizures, movement disorders, and dysautonomia. Limbic encephalitis can be associated with several specific antibodies, including LGI1, $GABA_BR$, AMPAR, CASPR2, Hu, Ma2, and GAD. Both limbic encephalitis and NMDAR encephalitis may be associated with paraneoplastic processes, such as ovarian or testicular teratoma.

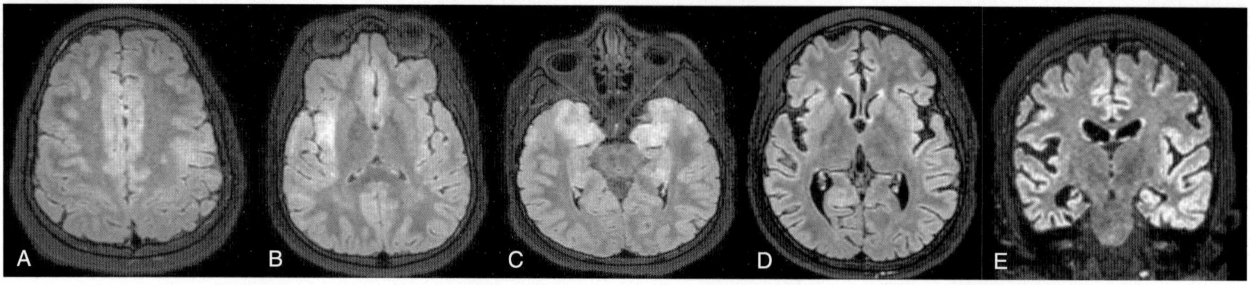

Fig. 54.1 Limbic encephalitis. Brain MRI, axial FLAIR, shows multifocal hyperintensities involving the (A) left frontal lobe, (B) right insula, and (C) bilateral mesial temporal lobes. Follow-up MRI shows decreased signal abnormalities with development of atrophy in the (D) insulae, (E) hippocampi and temporal lobes. *FLAIR*, Fluid-attenuated inversion recovery.

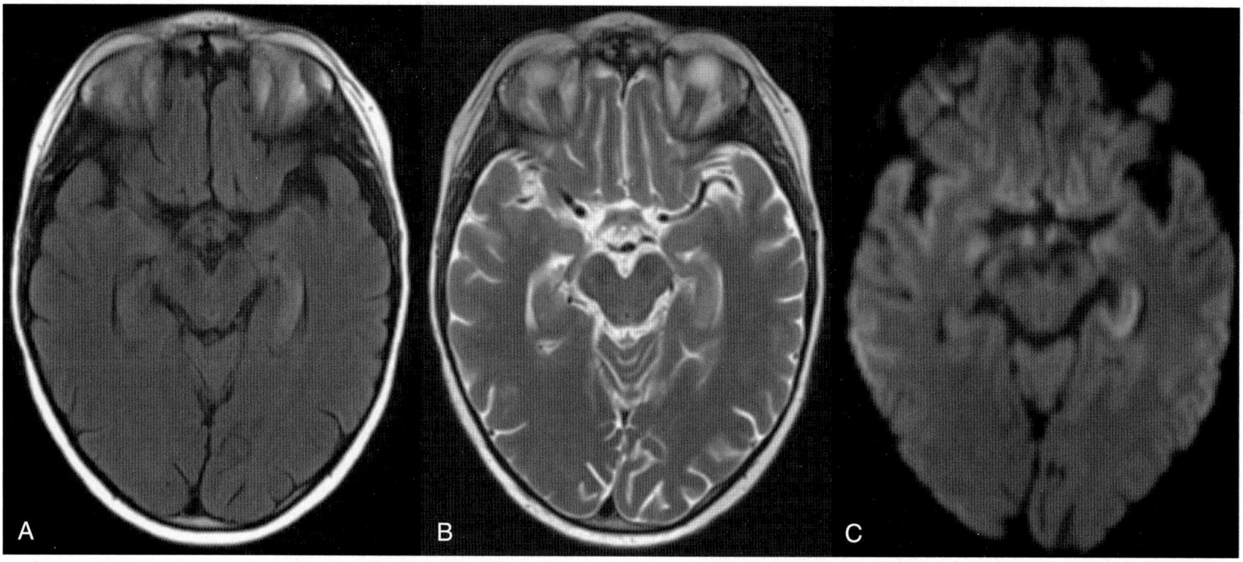

Fig. 54.2 HSV encephalitis. MRI brain, (A) axial FLAIR, (B) T2, and (C) DWI show hyperintense signal in the left hippocampus. *DWI*, Diffusion-weighted imaging; *FLAIR*, fluid-attenuated inversion recovery.

IMAGING DIFFERENTIAL DIAGNOSES

T2/FLAIR hyperintensities of the mesial temporal lobes can be seen in multiple conditions. The differential diagnosis includes infectious, metabolic, vascular, neoplastic/paraneoplastic, and autoimmune disorders.

HSV classically causes T2/FLAIR hyperintensities in the mesial temporal lobes as well as insulae, cingulate gyri, and frontal lobes with sparing of the lentiform nuclei (Fig. 54.2). DWI and SWI can be helpful for early detection of restricted diffusion and hemorrhage.

Congenital CMV can also yield bilateral temporal lobe signal abnormalities with white matter changes, temporal lobe cysts, and periventricular calcifications (Fig. 54.3), but typically presents at birth with chronic symptoms. Other infectious etiologies include varicella, tuberculosis, and neurosyphilis.

Malignancies such as gliomatosis can also involve the temporal lobes. However, tumor is more likely to be unilateral and may have associated enhancement, vasogenic edema, and necrosis. MRS can be helpful to show decreased NAA, increased choline, and elevated myoinositol in gliomas.

Metabolic etiologies involving the temporal lobes include mitochondrial encephalopathy, lactic acidosis and stroke-like episodes (MELAS), hyperammonemia, and Wilson's disease. MELAS is characterized by recurrent

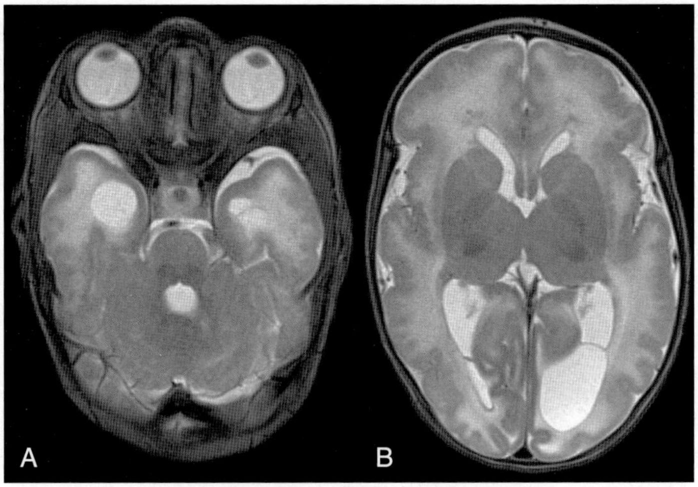

Fig. 54.3 Congenital cytomegalovirus. Brain MRI, axial T2, shows (A) bilateral temporal and (B) occipital horn subependymal cysts with polymicrogyria. There is diffuse white matter hyperintensity with punctate frontal periventricular hypointensities compatible with calcifications.

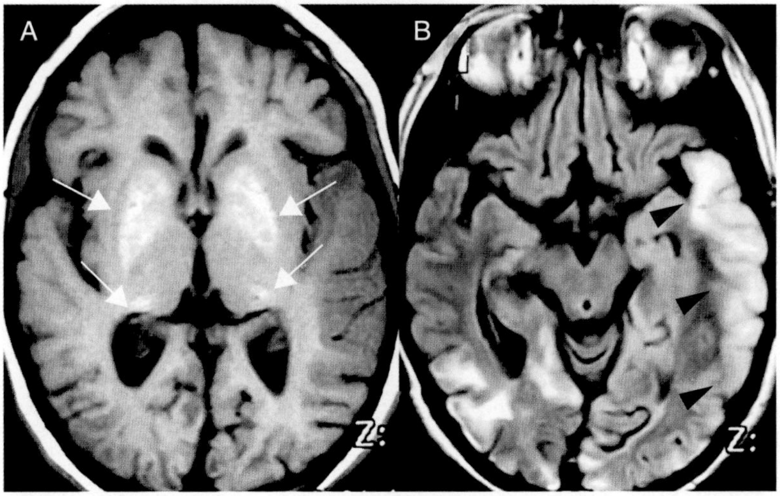

Fig. 54.4 MELAS. Brain MRI, (A) axial T1 and (B) FLAIR, show bilateral calcifications of the deep gray nuclei (*arrows*) and edema in the left greater than right temporal cortex (*arrowheads*). *FLAIR*, Fluid-attenuated inversion recovery; *MELAS*, mitochondrial encephalopathy, lactic acidosis, and strokelike episodes.

cortical/subcortical diffusion and signal abnormalities in non-vascular territories (Fig. 54.4) with spontaneous resolution. MRS can reveal a lactate peak during acute episodes. Hyperammonemia can involve the bilateral temporal lobes, insular cortex, and posterior cingulate gyri, with sparing of the occipital lobes and perirolandic cortex. Wilson's disease may also involve the temporal lobes but classically affects the deep gray structures.

Seizures can lead to T2/FLAIR hyperintensity or diffusion restriction in the temporal lobes (Fig. 54.5), which can resolve on follow-up imaging.

Megalencephalic leukoencephalopathy with subcortical cysts, caused by a mutation in *MLC1*, can be associated with T2/FLAIR white matter signal abnormalities that evolve to subcortical cysts in the temporal and frontoparietal lobes.

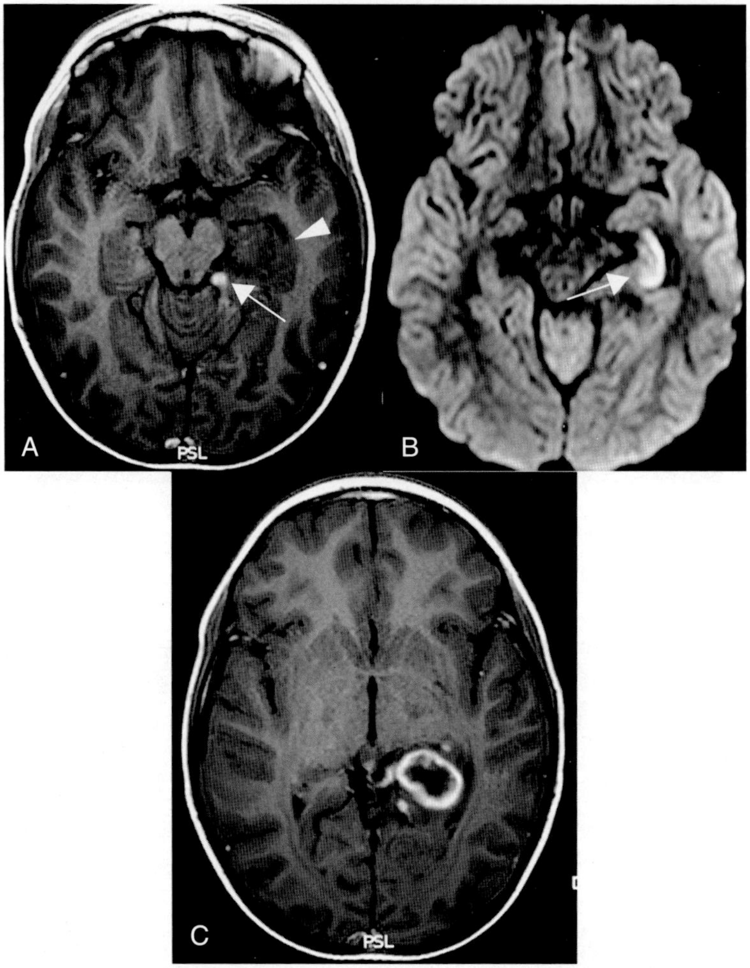

Fig. 54.5 Ganglioglioma causing seizure. Brain MRI, (A) axial postcontrast T1, shows enhancing focus in the left lingual gyrus (*arrow*) with edema of the left hippocampus (*arrowhead*). (B) Axial DWI shows restricted diffusion in the left hippocampal cortex (*arrow*). (C) 9-month follow-up postcontrast T1 shows enlargement of the tumor with central necrosis. *DWI*, Diffusion-weighted imaging.

Vascular etiologies should be considered with acute diffusion restriction in arterial territories. Cerebral autosomal dominant arteriopathy with subcortical infarcts and leukoencephalopathy (CADASIL) is caused by mutations in the *NOTCH3* gene. Progressive subcortical and lacunar infarcts develop over time and can lead to confluent T2/FLAIR hyperintensities in the anterior temporal lobes.

Autoimmune conditions including MOGAD and NMOSD often present with multifocal brain lesions and/or optic pathway involvement. In limbic encephalitis, T2/FLAIR hyperintensity of the mesial temporal lobes is often asymmetric or unilateral without significant enhancement.

FINAL DIAGNOSIS

Antibody-negative autoimmune limbic encephalitis.

DISCUSSION

Autoimmune limbic encephalitis is an inflammatory disease that classically presents with behavioral abnormalities, psychiatric symptoms, and seizures. MRI findings include increased T2/FLAIR signal abnormalities in the bilateral mesial temporal lobes, amygdala, cingulate gyri, insulae, and inferior frontal lobes without mass effect or enhancement. Initially, there may be associated edema, which resolves over months to years and may evolve to atrophy in the chronic stage. The diagnosis of autoimmune limbic encephalitis requires four criteria: (1) subacute onset of working memory deficits, seizures; or psychiatric symptoms; (2) bilateral abnormalities on T2/FLAIR MRI restricted to the mesial temporal lobes; (3) CSF pleocytosis or EEG with slow-wave activity involving the temporal lobes; and (4) reasonable exclusion of alternative causes. If autoimmune limbic encephalitis is diagnosed, further imaging with MRI or CT of the chest, abdomen, and pelvis should be considered to assess for occult malignancy. Brain fluorodeoxyglucose-positron emission tomography (FDG-PET) may be more sensitive for temporal lobe abnormalities if there is high clinical suspicion of limbic encephalitis and brain MRI is unremarkable. If there is a concern for clinical worsening, a repeat MRI is indicated to assess for alternative diagnoses such as glioma.

CLINICAL RED FLAGS

- Subacute onset of working memory deficits, seizures, or psychiatric symptoms.
- CSF pleocytosis.
- EEG with temporal slowing.

IMAGING RED FLAGS

- T2/FLAIR abnormalities affecting the mesial temporal lobes.

CONCLUSIONS

On brain MRI, there are various etiologies for temporal lobe signal abnormalities. It is important to assess for hemorrhage, cystic changes, white matter involvement, and diffusion restriction. Follow-up brain MRI may reveal atrophy of the previously inflamed regions. If clinical suspicion for limbic encephalitis is high, consider brain FDG-PET. Paraneoplastic etiologies can be further assessed using MRI or CT of the torso.

REFERENCES

Budhram A, Leung A, Nicolle MW, Burneo JG. Diagnosing autoimmune limbic encephalitis. *CMAJ*. 2019;191:E529–E534. https://doi.org/10.1503/cmaj.181548.

Carroll CG, Campbell WW. Multiple cranial neuropathies. *Semin Neurol*. 2009;29:053–065. https://doi.org/10.1055/s-0028-1124023.

Graus F, Titulaer MJ, Balu R, et al. A clinical approach to diagnosis of autoimmune encephalitis. *Lancet Neurol*. 2016;15:391–404. https://doi.org/10.1016/S1474-4422(15)00401-9.

Sureka J, Jakkani RK. Clinico-radiological spectrum of bilateral temporal lobe hyperintensity: a retrospective review. *Br J Radiol*. 2012;85:e782–e792. https://doi.org/10.1259/bjr/30039090.

Tüzün E, Dalmau J. Limbic encephalitis and variants: classification, diagnosis and treatment. *Neurologist*. 2007;13:261–271. https://doi.org/10.1097/NRL.0b013e31813e34a5.

Recurrent Discoordination

HISTORY AND PHYSICAL

A 5-year-old girl presented with headache and vomiting. She initially experienced mild sore throat and headache, which progressed to emesis and severe headaches over several days. Her speech slowed and she developed difficulties with articulation and word finding. She also appeared more clumsy than usual with slight gait ataxia. Consciousness was preserved.

DIAGNOSTIC WORKUP

Brain MRI showed extensive areas of abnormal T2/FLAIR hyperintensity in the cerebellar hemispheres, cerebellar peduncles, internal capsules, and periventricular white matter extending into the corona radiata (Fig. 55.1). There was also involvement of the left cerebral peduncle, left subthalamic region, and right occipital lobe. Postcontrast T1 imaging revealed "salt and pepper" enhancement within the regions of T2/FLAIR hyperintensity, most extensive within the cerebellum. DWI showed variable degrees of restricted diffusion within the lesions. MRI of the spine was normal.

LP was performed and revealed normal protein and glucose and 10 WBCs (88% lymphocytes). She had no oligoclonal bands and her IgG index was normal. She had a normal CBC except for slightly elevated white count of 10.8. ESR and CRP were normal. Antiphospholipid antibodies, von Willebrand factor antigen, lupus anticoagulant, ACE, ANA, SS_A, SS_B, antineutrophil cytoplasmic antibody (ANCA), and titers for CMV, varicella zoster virus (VZV), EBV, Mycoplasma, and Lyme ELISA and Western blot were all normal.

The patient was initially diagnosed with clinically isolated syndrome and treated with IV methylprednisone, but experienced clinical relapses during each taper attempt, even after the addition of monthly IVIG. Serial MRI showed radiologic progression concerning for chronic lymphocytic inflammation with pontine perivascular enhancement responsive to steroids (CLIPPERS), and brain biopsy was performed. This revealed mixed chronic inflammatory infiltrates with perivascular inflammation diffusely involving the white matter, gray matter, and leptomeninges. She underwent induction treatment with glucocorticoids and cyclophosphamide followed by mycophenolate mofetil, which slowed but did not halt her disease progression. She went on to develop progressive tremor, ataxia, dysarthria, dysconjugate gaze, and slowed speech and response time. Next-generation sequencing of CSF and brain tissue was unrevealing. She stabilized on natalizumab for 3 years but subsequently progressed both clinically and radiologically. CSF phenotyping and soluble biomarker analysis revealed activation of her innate immune system. *PRF1* gene sequencing identified a pathogenic mutation compatible with hemophagocytic lymphohistiocytosis (HLH). She was treated with intrathecal methotrexate and hydrocortisone and systemic dexamethasone with clinical improvement and normalization of CSF neopterin levels. She received a curative stem cell transplant at 10 years of age. At age 18 years, she has stable and permanent neurological deficits.

CLINICAL DIFFERENTIAL DIAGNOSES

The initial clinical presentation of headache, emesis, ataxia, and dysarthria has a broad differential including demyelinating, autoimmune, and infectious processes.

Symptoms were consistent with a clinically isolated event or first-time presentation of MS, MOG, or NMO, although these are less typically associated with severe headaches. She did not have altered mental status, excluding ADEM.

Infectious etiologies, such as viral or bacterial meningitis, could present with slowed processing speed and severe headache.

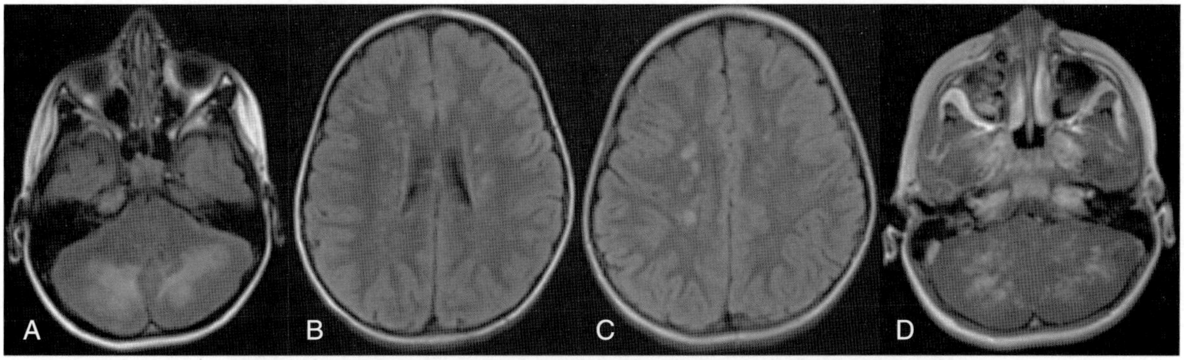

Fig. 55.1 Hemophagocytic lymphohistiocytosis. Brain MRI, (A–C) axial FLAIR, shows multifocal hyperintense signal within the cerebellar white matter, periventricular white matter, and corona radiata. (D) There is corresponding punctate and curvilinear enhancement on postcontrast T1. *FLAIR*, Fluid-attenuated inversion recovery.

Autoimmune parainfectious cerebellitis could present with dysarthria and ataxia.

IMAGING DIFFERENTIAL DIAGNOSES

An important consideration is chronic lymphocytic inflammation with pontine perivascular enhancement responsive to steroids (CLIPPERS) (Fig. 55.2). The diagnosis is defined by imaging characteristics, but can have various underlying etiologies such as HLH or malignancy. On MRI, the initial findings are infratentorial punctate and curvilinear enhancing lesions, predominating in the pons and cerebellum. Disease can spread to spinal cord and brain, involving both white and deep gray matter, but typically spares the cortex. Radiographic criteria include homogeneous contrast-enhancing nodules measuring <3 mm in diameter. There should not be significant ring enhancement, mass effect, or T2 signal beyond the areas of enhancement. Lesions should improve with steroid treatment.

CNS lymphoma may also show T1 hypointense, T2 iso- to hyperintense lesions with patchy enhancement. These are typically supratentorial and can have associated edema (Fig. 55.3). MRS will show increased Cho, decreased NAA, and slightly decreased Cr. PET can also reveal high metabolism of 18F-FDG in primary lesions, with decreased metabolism after treatment due to necrosis.

Lymphoid granulomatosis and GFAP astrocytopathy may also present with periventricular T2/FLAIR hyperintensities and ringlike enhancement, but the lesions classically extend radially from the periventricular surface. There may also be longitudinal cord signal changes.

Demyelinating disorders such as MS, MOGAD, and NMOSD can show enhancing T2/FLAIR hyperintensities in the periventricular and cortical regions.

Indolent infections that do not respond to immunosuppression include CMV, progressive multifocal leukoencephalopathy (PML) (Fig. 55.4), and HIV.

FINAL DIAGNOSIS

Hemophagocytic lymphohistiocytosis.

DISCUSSION

Severe CNS HLH is typically seen in older children with multifocal lesions in the brainstem and cerebellum. However, patients can also have normal MRI, isolated cortical atrophy, or isolated T2/FLAIR hyperintensities. When lesions are present, they tend to be bilateral and asymmetric. There may be dorsal pons involvement, as well as midbrain and medulla involvement. Leptomeningeal enhancement can appear diffuse, while parenchymal enhancement may be more discrete. There may also be associated microhemorrhages, calcifications, or diffusion restriction. There are rare reports of optic nerve involvement with thickening and enhancement.

There are three characteristic pathologic stages of CNS HLH. The first includes leptomeningeal infiltrates of lymphocytes and histiocytes, followed by parenchymal involvement with perivascular lymphohistiocytic infiltration, and finally diffuse lymphocyte and histiocyte infiltration of brain parenchyma, astrogliosis, white matter and cortical necrosis, and occasional calcifications (Fig. 55.5).

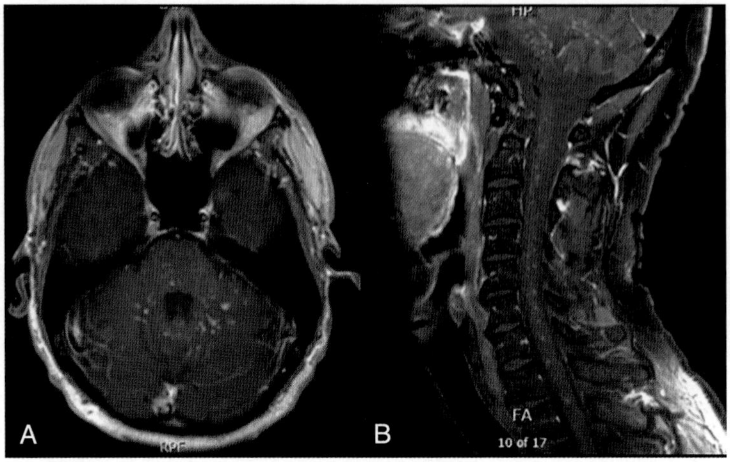

Fig. 55.2 Chronic lymphocytic inflammation with pontine perivascular enhancement responsive to steroids (CLIPPERS). Brain and cervical spine MRI, postcontrast T1, shows patchy enhancing punctate and curvilinear lesions throughout the pons, middle cerebellar peduncles, cerebellum, and cervical cord.

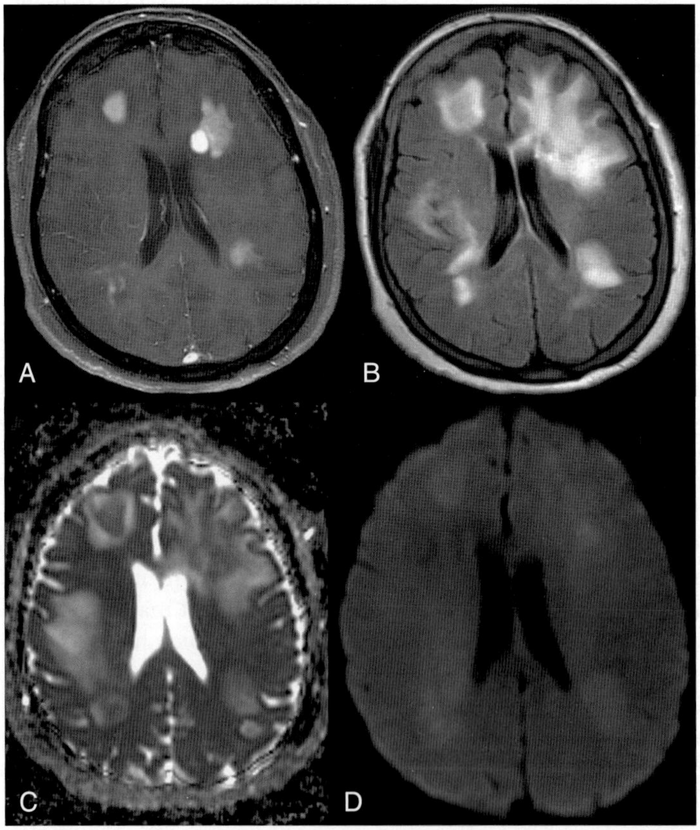

Fig. 55.3 CNS lymphoma. Brain MRI, (A) axial postcontrast T1, shows multifocal flocculent enhancement in the periventricular and deep white matter. (B) On axial FLAIR, there is associated vasogenic edema. (C) Axial ADC and (D) DWI show restricted diffusion. *ADC*, Apparent diffusion coefficient; *DWI*, diffusion-weighted imaging; *FLAIR*, fluid-attenuated inversion recovery.

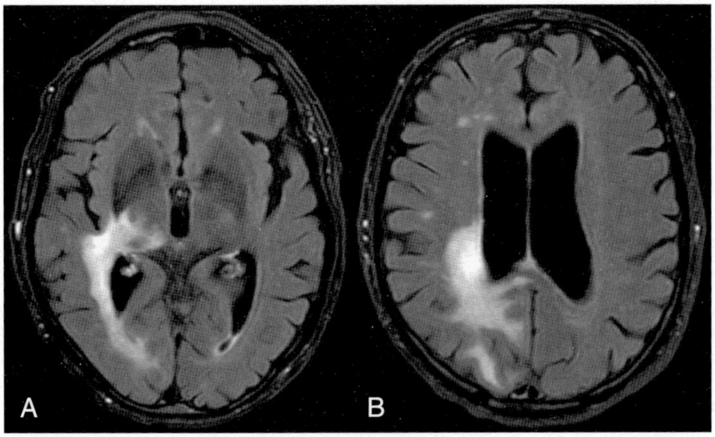

Fig. 55.4 Progressive multifocal leukoencephalopathy (PML). Brain MRI, (A-B), axial FLAIR, shows confluent subcortical and periventricular white matter lesions in the right posterior quadrant with minimal mass effect. *FLAIR*, Fluid-attenuated inversion recovery.

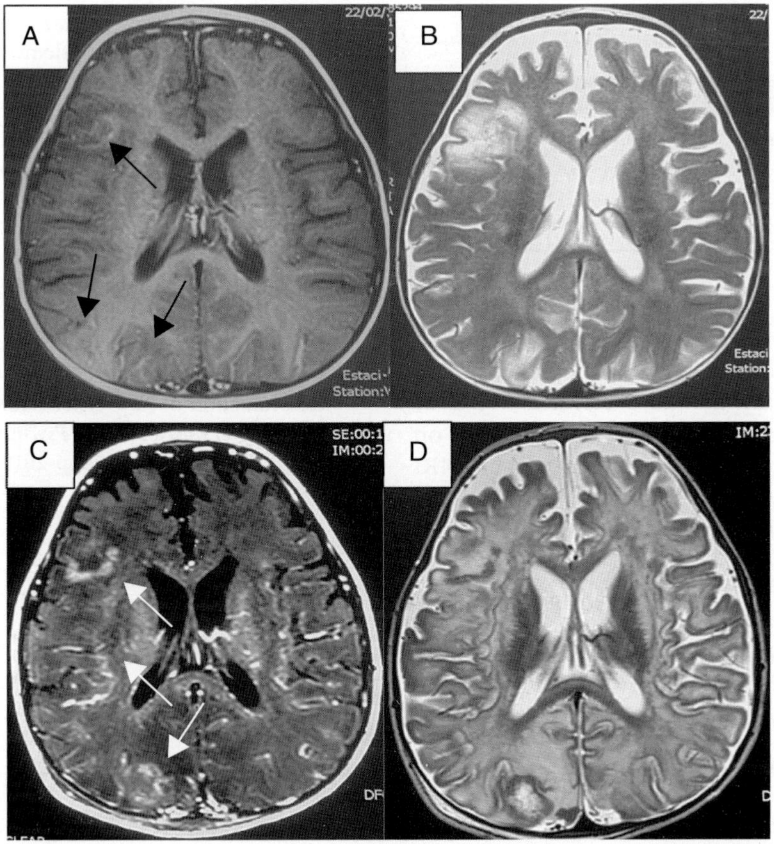

Fig. 55.5 Hemophagocytic lymphohistiocytosis. Brain MRI, (A) postcontrast T1 and (B) axial T2, show ill-defined cortical/subcortical lesions with edema, irregular peripheral enhancement, and T2 hypointensity in the right frontal and occipital lobes (*arrows*). 1-month follow-up brain MRI, (C) postcontrast T1 and (D) axial T2, shows evolution of lesions with expanding incomplete rim enhancement, calcification, and atrophy (*arrows*).

HLH is rare but life-threatening with uncontrolled CNS inflammation. Primary HLH is typically genetic (familial HLH, Griscelli Syndrome, Chediak-Higashi Syndrome, X-linked lymphoproliferative syndrome), usually autosomal recessive or X-linked. Genetic and functional testing can avoid the need for invasive testing such as brain biopsy. CNS involvement can be isolated, with no systemic features or markers, or may portend a systemic clinical syndrome. Secondary HLH is triggered by an underlying infection, autoimmune disease, or malignancy. The disease is fatal without treatment, but treatment of any underlying conditions, chemotherapy, immunosuppression, and stem cell transplant can be curative.

CLINICAL RED FLAGS

- Lack of response to steroids or other treatment.
- Significant systemic inflammation.
- Associated EBV infection, malignancy, or known genetic syndrome with predisposition to HLH.

IMAGING RED FLAGS

- CNS lesions not responsive to steroids.
- Multifocal FLAIR hyperintensities with enhancement, diffusion, and susceptibility.
- Leptomeningeal enhancement.

CONCLUSIONS

Children with CNS HLH prior to development of systemic involvement may not have elevated WBC or inflammatory markers and may only have findings on brain MRI, HLH functional, or genetic testing. MRI features may overlap with infection, demyelination, and neuroinflammatory disorders, which can delay diagnosis.

REFERENCES

Benson LA, Li H, Henderson LA, et al. Pediatric CNS-isolated hemophagocytic lymphohistiocytosis. *Neurol Neuroimm Neuroinflamm*. 2019;6:e560. https://doi.org/10.1212/NXI.0000000000000560.

Blincoe A, Heeg M, Campbell PK, et al. Neuroinflammatory disease as an isolated manifestation of hemophagocytic lymphohistiocytosis. *J Clin Immunol*. 2020;40:901–916. https://doi.org/10.1007/s10875-020-00814-6.

Cheng G, Zhang J. Imaging features (CT, MRI, MRS, and PET/CT) of primary central nervous system lymphoma in immunocompetent patients. *Neurol Sci*. 2019;40:535–542. https://doi.org/10.1007/s10072-018-3669-7.

Guandalini M, Butler A, Mandelstam S. Spectrum of imaging appearances in Australian children with central nervous system hemophagocytic lymphohistiocytosis. *J Clin Neurosci*. 2014;21:305–310. http://dx.doi.org/10.1016/j.jocn.2013.03.032.

Kimura A, Kato S, Takekoshi A, et al. Autoimmune glial fibrillary acidic protein astrocytopathy resembling isolated central nervous system lymphomatoid granulomatosis. *J Neuroimmunol*. 2021;361:577748. https://doi.org/10.1016/j.jneuroim.2021.577748.

Malik P, Antonini L, Mannam P, et al. MRI patterns in pediatric CNS hemophagocytic lymphohistiocytosis. *AJNR Am J Neuroradiol*. 2021;42:2077–2085. https://dx.doi.org/10.3174/ajnr.A7292.

Stredny CM, Blessing MM, Yi V, et al. Mimics of pediatric small vessel primary angiitis of the central nervous system. *Ann Neurol*. 2023;93(1):109–119. https://doi.org/10.1002/ana.26531.

Taieb G, Mulero P, Psimaras D, et al. CLIPPERS and its mimics: evaluation of new criteria for the diagnosis of CLIPPERS. *J Neurol Neurosurg Psychiatry*. 2019;90:1027–1038. https://doi.org/10.1136/jnnp-2018-318957.

SECTION 12

Neurocutaneous Syndromes

Nicola Specchio, Luca de Palma, Marina Trivisano, Chiara Pepi, Concetta Luisi, Marta Conti, Angela De Dominicis, Nicola Pietrafusa, Ludovica Piscitello, Giusy Carfì Pavia, Federico Vigevano, Paolo Curatolo

INTRODUCTION

Neurocutaneous syndromes (phakomatoses) encompass a range of genetic disorders that involve the nervous system and skin, which have a common ectodermal origin. At the time of this writing, more than 150 phakomatoses have been genetically characterized. Although the cutaneous manifestations are often apparent at clinical examination, neurological stigmata often require diagnostic imaging to characterize disturbances including malformations, benign and malignant neoplasia. Our emerging understanding of molecular mechanisms offers opportunities for earlier and more accurate patient diagnosis, genetic counseling for risk assessment and prognosis, and early institution of disease-modifying therapies. In this chapter, we describe clinical and imaging red flags in children with four key neurocutaneous disorders: tuberous sclerosis complex (TSC), neurofibromatosis type 1 (NF1), Sturge-Weber syndrome (SWS), and nevus sebaceous syndrome.

SUGGESTED READINGS

Curatolo P, Specchio N, Aronica E. Advances in the genetics and neuropathology of tuberous sclerosis complex: edging closer to targeted therapy. *Lancet Neurol.* 2022;21(9):843–856.

Flores-Sarnat L, Sarnat HB. Phenotype/genotype correlations in epidermal nevus syndrome as a neurocristopathy. *Handb Clin Neurol.* 2015;132:9–25.

Klar N, Cohen B, Lin D. Neurocutaneous syndromes. *Handb Clin Neurol.* 2016;135:565–589.

Poliner A, Fernandez FE, Blieden L, et al. Port-wine birthmarks: update on diagnosis, risk assessment for Sturge-Weber syndrome, and management. *Pediatr Rev.* 2022;43(9):507–516.

Specchio N, Pepi C, de Palma L, et al. Surgery for drug-resistant tuberous sclerosis complex-associated epilepsy: who, when, and what. *Epileptic Disord.* 2021;23(1):53–73.

Case 56

Spots Here, There, and Everywhere

HISTORY AND PHYSICAL

A 5-year-old girl was prenatally diagnosed with cardiac rhabdomyomas on fetal ultrasound. After birth, brain MRI showed multiple cortical/subcortical tubers and subependymal nodules. Genetic testing revealed a de novo *TSC2* gene mutation. On physical exam, she had several hypomelanotic spots and angiofibromas. Seizures began at one month of age with focal motor symptoms characterized by grimaces; asymmetric blinking (right>left) with oral automatisms; clonic jerks of the right eye, mouth, and occasionally arm; and epileptic spasms (ES). Psychomotor development was delayed with significant language impairment. Multiple antiseizure medications were trialed (valproic acid, levetiracetam vigabatrine, oxcarbazepine, carbamazepine, clonazepan, topiramate), without success.

DIAGNOSTIC WORKUP

Brain MRI demonstrated multiple bilateral cerebral cortical/subcortical tubers, radial migrational lines, and subependymal nodules (Fig. 56.1A and B). A dominant tuber in the left supramarginal gyrus (Fig. 56.1C and D) correlated with the patient's seizure semiology.

Interictal electroencephalogram (EEG) showed repetitive epileptiform abnormalities over the left frontotemporal region (Fig. 56.2A), as well as subclinical discharges with rhythmic slow waves over the left central region (Fig. 56.2B).

Intracranial stereo EEG lead placement was performed (Fig. 56.3A), confirming an ictal focus over the left posterior perisylvian region on a background of independent multifocal abnormalities (Fig. 56.3B).

Focal cortical resection was performed. Two years later, the patient was seizure free and her medication regimen was simplified (Carbamazepine withdrawn, Vigabatrin ongoing). Fig. 56.4 shows the intraoperative MRI and SEEG implantation.

CLINICAL DIFFERENTIAL DIAGNOSIS

Tuberous sclerosis (TSC) is a multisystem genetic disorder with distinctive cutaneous hallmarks including hypomelanotic macules, angiofibromas, cephalic fibrous plaques, shagreen patches, and ungual fibromas. Other multisystem findings can involve the eyes, brain, heart, kidneys, and lungs. Epilepsy is the most common and earliest clinical symptom, usually with spasms or focal seizures starting before one year of age. Other early-onset epilepsies in the differential include infantile ES syndrome, structural or genetic developmental, and epileptic encephalopathies.

IMAGING DIFFERENTIAL DIAGNOSIS

The radiologic presentation of TSC includes diffuse cortical/subcortical tubers, subependymal nodules, and giant-cell astrocytomas (Fig. 56.5) and radial migrational lines (Fig. 56.6). Histopathologic and molecular testing of tubers reveals somatic mutations affecting the inhibition of mammalian target of rapamycin (mTOR) pathway, in the spectrum of focal cortical dysplasia (FCD) type IIB and hemimegalencephaly (HME).

FINAL DIAGNOSIS

Tuberous sclerosis complex

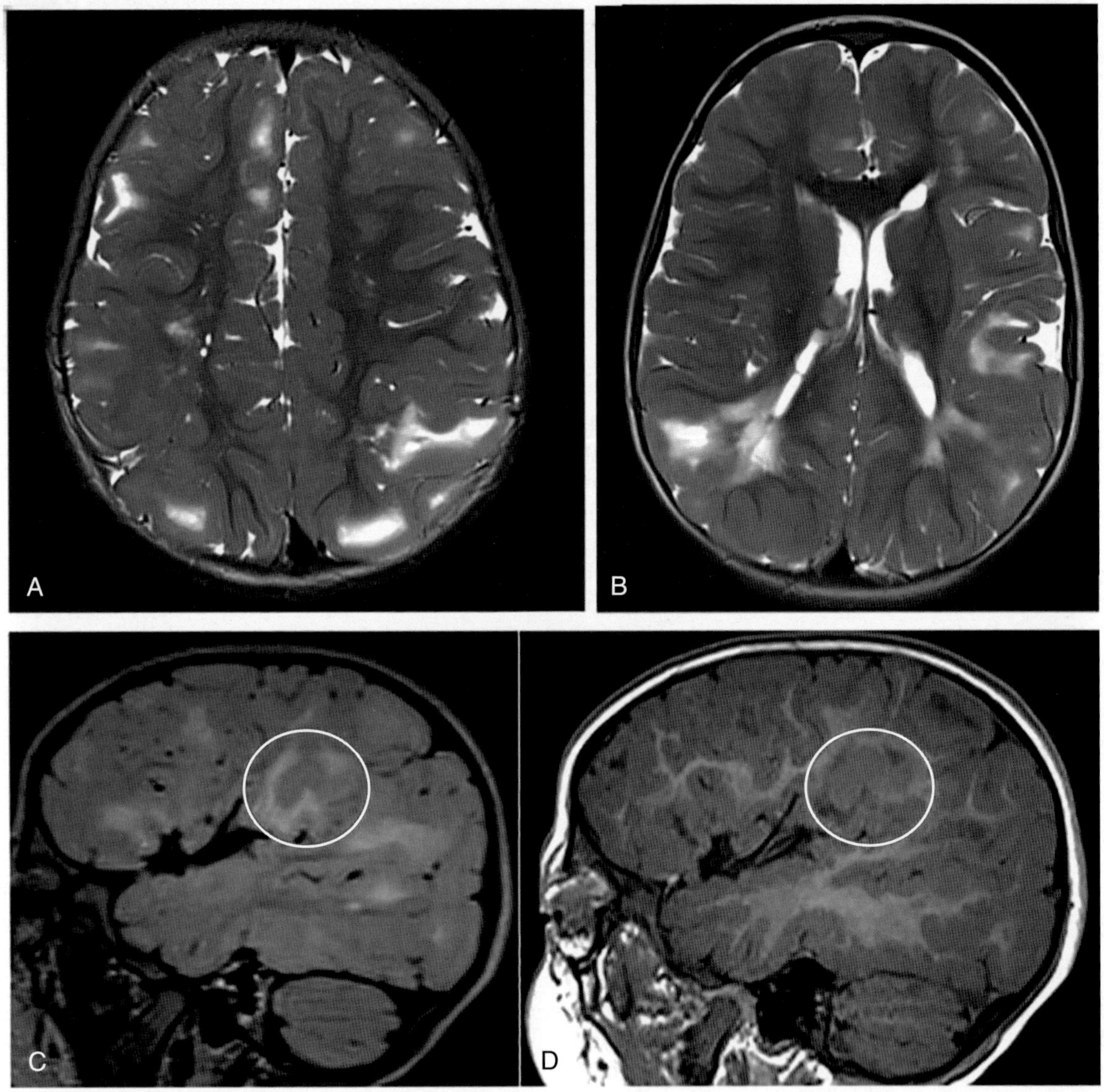

Fig. 56.1 Tuberous sclerosis complex. Brain MRI, (A and B) axial T2 shows multiple bilateral hyperintense cortical/subcortical tubers. (C) Sagittal FLAIR and (D) sagittal T1 show dominant tuber in the left supramarginal gyrus (*circles*). *FLAIR*, Fluid-attenuated inversion recovery.

DISCUSSION

TSC is an autosomal dominant neurocutaneous syndrome with an incidence of 1 in 6000 to 22,000 live births. Genetic mutations of *TSC1* or *TSC2* affect the conformation of the hamartin-tuberin heterodimer. This, in turn, results in excessive activation of the mTOR antiapoptosis pathway that controls cell growth and differentiation, metabolism, and autophagy. In the brain, this yields developmental hamartomatous malformations including cortical/subcortical tubers, radial migrational lines, and subependymal nodules which can develop into giant cell astrocytomas.

Epilepsy is the most common neurological manifestation, occurring in 80% to 90% of patients with TSC. Patients with TSC can experience several seizure types including focal and generalized motor, myoclonic, tonic, atonic, and tonic-clonic. TSC is also associated with a broad range of cognitive, behavioral, and psychiatric manifestations, known as tuberous sclerosis-associated neuropsychiatric disorders (TAND). In the literature, postsurgical seizure-freedom rates in patients with TSC range from 65% to 75%. Given the multifocality patients with TSC should be referred to a dedicated epilepsy center for tailored workup and presurgical evaluation by a multidisciplinary epilepsy team.

CLINICAL RED FLAGS

- Cutaneous findings, including hypomelanotic macules, fibromas, and plaques.
- Early-onset epilepsy with spasms of focal seizures.
- Renal angiomyolipomas.
- Cardiac rhabdomyomas.
- Pulmonary lymphangioleiomyomatosis.

IMAGING RED FLAGS

- Cortical/subcortical tubers.
- Radial migrational lines.
- Subependymal nodules.
- Subependymal giant cell astrocytomas.

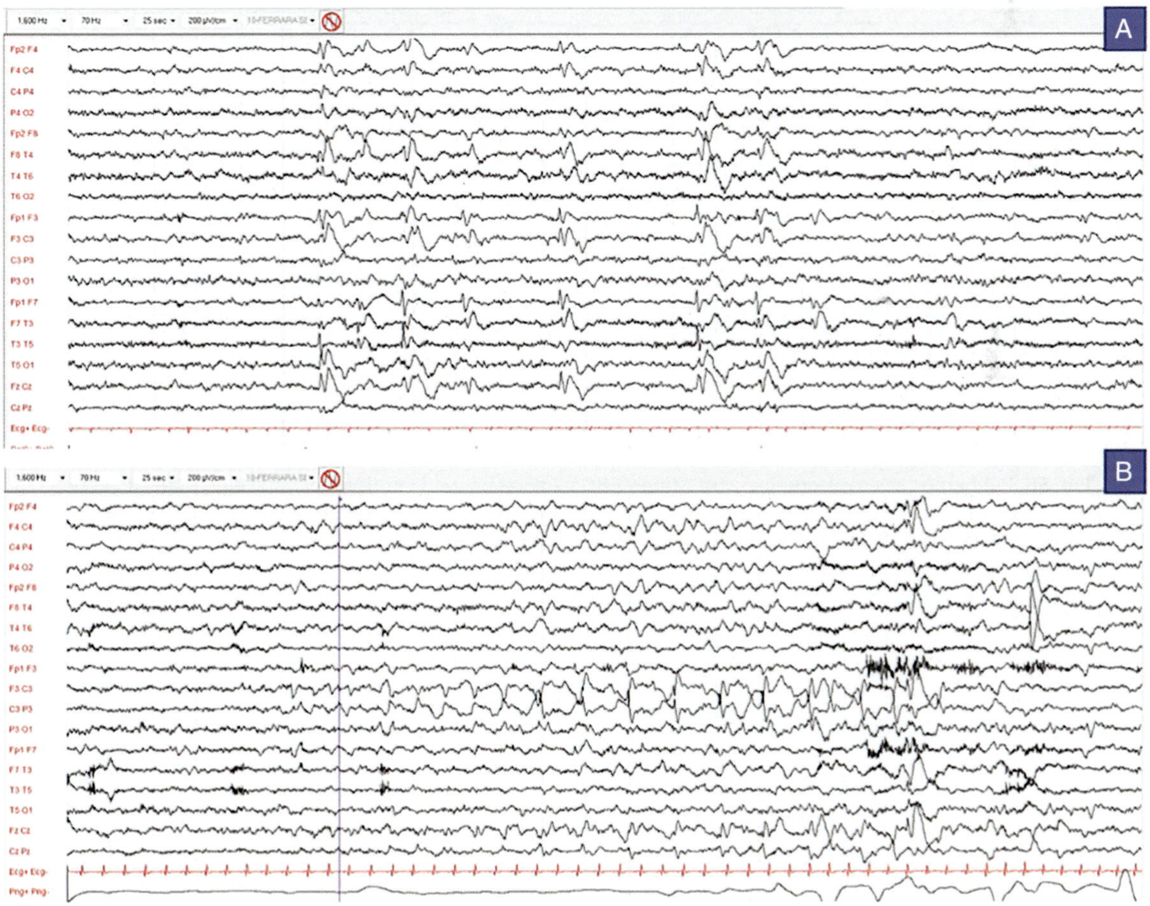

Fig. 56.2 Tuberous sclerosis complex. (A) Interictal awake EEG shows left frontotemporal repetitive epileptiform abnormalities with frequent contralateral spread. (B) Left central rhythmic interictal discharges. *EEG*, Electroencephalogram.

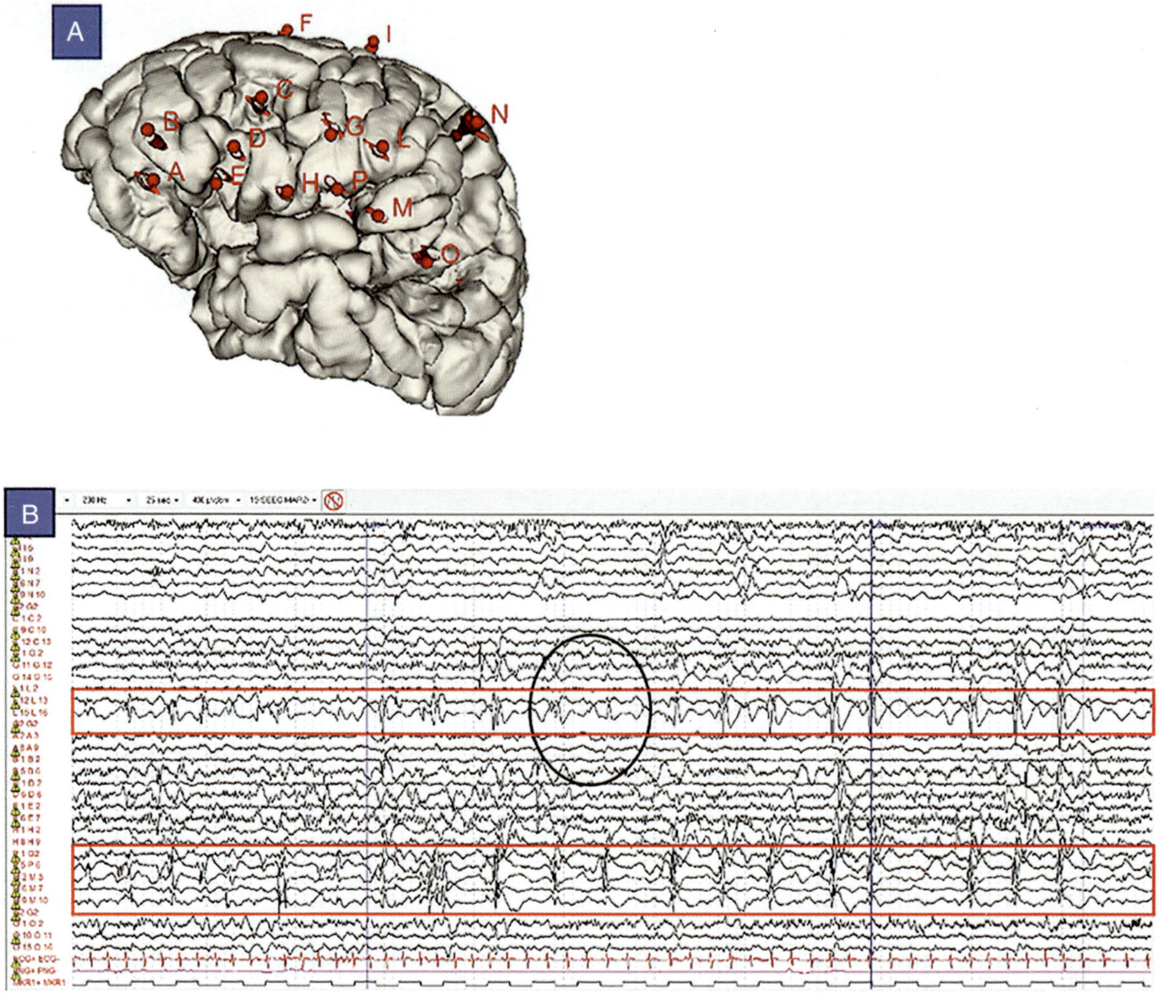

Fig. 56.3 Tuberous sclerosis complex. (A) Stereo-EEG exploration with left frontoparietal electrodes and one temporal control. (B) Focal clonic seizure with rhythmic spike-and-wave complexes over L, M and P electrodes (oval) corresponding to right eye clonic jerks. *EEG,* Electroencephalogram.

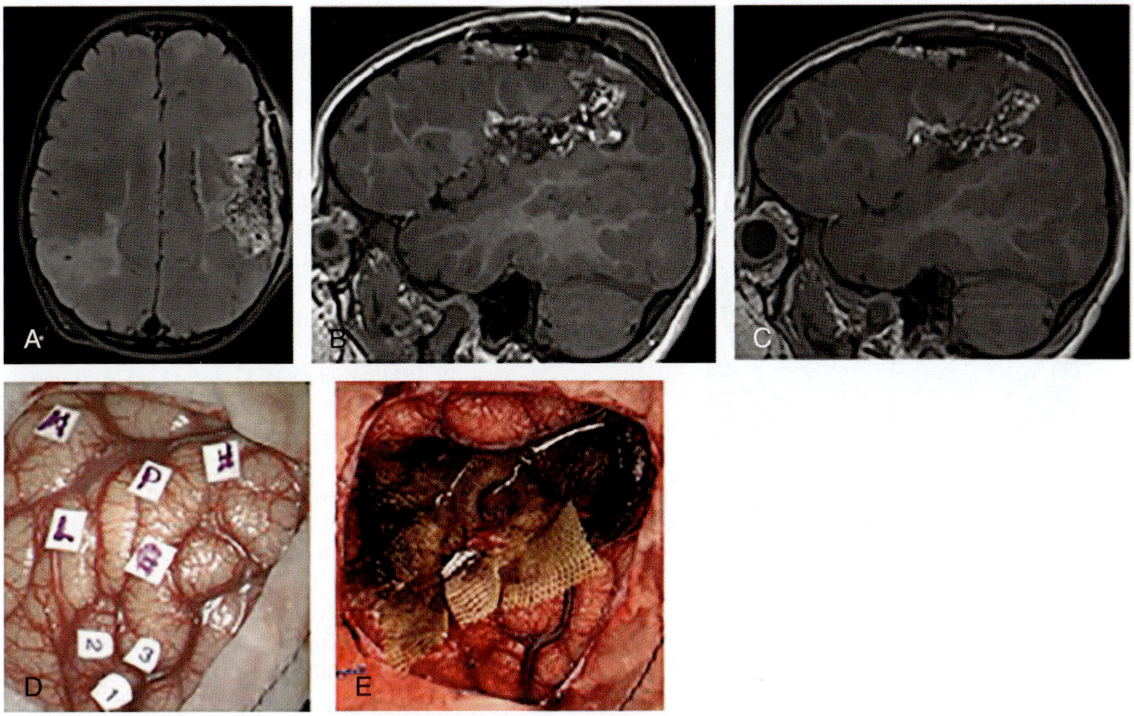

Fig. 56.4 Tuberous sclerosis complex. Intraoperative brain MRI, (A) axial FLAIR, (B–C), sagittal T1 showing resection of left posterior perisylvian tuber. (D) Intraoperative photos before and (E) after surgical resection of epileptogenic L, M, and P electrodes. *FLAIR*, Fluid-attenuated inversion recovery.

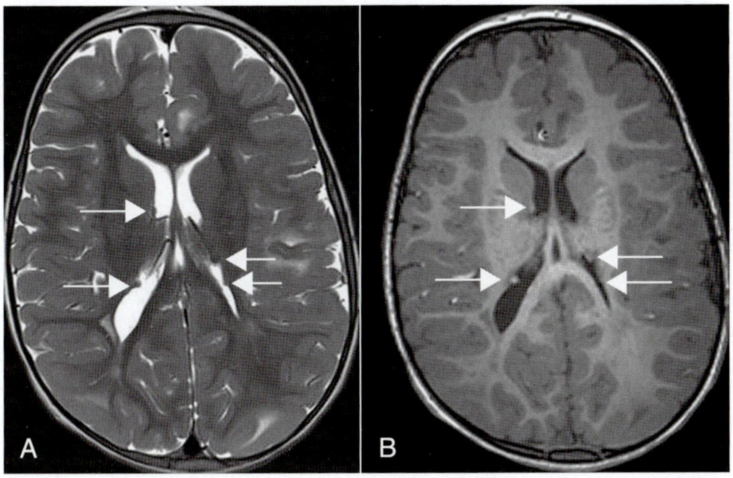

Fig. 56.5 Tuberous sclerosis complex. Brain MRI, (A) axial T2 and (B) axial T1 show small subependymal nodules outlining both lateral ventricles (*arrows*).

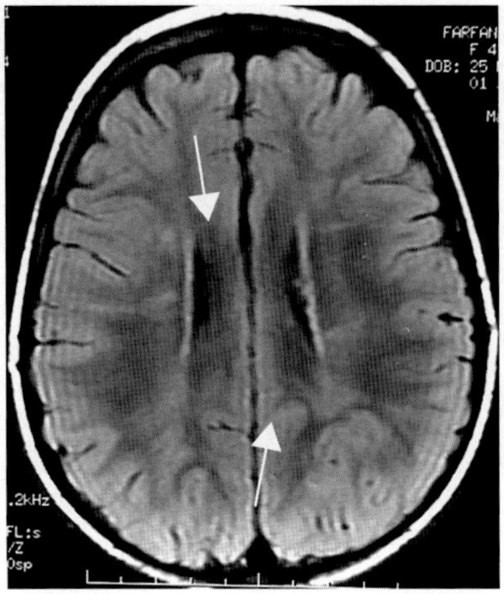

Fig. 56.6 Tuberous sclerosis complex. Brain MRI, axial FLAIR shows multiple radial migrational lines in both cerebral hemispheres (*arrows*). *FLAIR*, Fluid-attenuated inversion recovery.

CONCLUSIONS

TSC is one of the most common neurocutaneous syndromes, presenting early in children with recognizable clinical and radiological features. In patients with intractable epilepsy, early evaluation may identify a dominant tuber for surgical resection, which can help maximize long-term neurocognitive outcomes.

REFERENCES

Curatolo P, Moavero R, de Vries PJ. Neurological and neuropsychiatric aspects of tuberous sclerosis complex. *Lancet Neurol.* 2015;14(7):733–745.

Curatolo P, Nabbout R, Lagae L, et al. Management of epilepsy associated with tuberous sclerosis complex: updated clinical recommendations. *Eur J Paediatr Neurol.* 2018;22(5):738–748.

De Vries PJ, Whittemore VH, Leclezio L, et al. Tuberous Sclerosis Associated Neuropsychiatric Disorders (TAND) and the TAND checklist. *Pediatr Neurol.* 2015;52:25–35.

Ebrahimi-Fakhari D, Lisa Mann L, Poryo MGN, et al. Incidence of tuberous sclerosis and age at first diagnosis: new data and emerging trends from a national, prospective surveillance study. *Orphanet J Rare Dis.* 2018;13(1):117.

Northrup H, Krueger DA. International Tuberous Sclerosis Complex Consensus Group. Tuberous sclerosis complex diagnostic criteria update: recommendations of the 2012 international tuberous sclerosis complex consensus conference. *Pediatr Neurol.* 2013;49(4):243–254.

Specchio N, Pepi C, de Palma L, et al. Surgery for drug-resistant tuberous sclerosis complex-associated epilepsy: who, when, and what. *Epileptic Disord.* 2021;23(1):53–73.

Café au Lait: Tip of the Iceberg

HISTORY AND PHYSICAL

An 11-year-old girl presented to the epilepsy clinic. She was the first child of non-consanguineous parents, born at term with a history of placental abruption at 22 weeks gestational age. Family history was positive for neurofibromatosis (mother) and febrile convulsions (maternal uncle). At 11 months of age, she had febrile convulsions (10–12 episodes) with normal EEG. Her first afebrile seizure started at 5 years old and was characterized by gaze fixation, loss of consciousness, facial redness, and bilateral clonic jerking of limbs and eyelids. A seizure cluster (5 events) required rescue treatment in the emergency department. EEG at that time showed left temporo-occipital slowing and spikes during both sleep and wake states.

At 6 years of age, she presented with recurrent focal seizures of possible left posterior onset. Carbamazepine therapy was initiated. Due to persistence of focal seizures at follow-up, clobazan was added for better seizure control. She also received a diagnosis of attention deficit/hyperactivity disorder (ADHD).

Dermatology evaluation performed at 9 years of age detected facial plexiform neurofibroma, right lower limb neurofibroma, multiple café-au-lait spots of varying sizes (Fig. 57.1A), axillary and inguinal freckling (Fig. 57.1B). Ophthalmologic evaluation showed iris Lisch nodules (Fig. 57.1C).

Genetic testing showed the heterozygous pathogenic mutations c.7949dupT and p.Leu2650PhefsTer22 in *NF1* gene.

DIAGNOSTIC WORKUP

Brain MRI at 5 years of age showed multiple T2/fluid attenuated inversion recovery (FLAIR) hyperintense nonenhancing foci, most prominent in the bilateral basal ganglia. These gradually resolved on follow-up MRIs (Fig. 57.2).

An optic pathway glioma was present with expansion and signal abnormality of the anterior optic pathway (Fig. 57.3).

At 7 years of age, face/neck MRI showed transspatial plexiform neurofibromas involving the left perivertebral muscles and pterygopalatine fossa (Fig. 57.4).

CLINICAL DIFFERENTIAL DIAGNOSIS

Multisystem disorders with café-au-lait spots include various RASopathies such as neurofibromatosis type 1 (NF1), neurofibromatosis type 2 (NF2), Noonan syndrome, Noonan syndrome with multiple lentigines (LEOPARD), and Legius syndrome. In NF1, the café-au-lait spots have a smooth "coast of California" morphology. In NF2, patients demonstrate multiple schwannomas, meningiomas, and ependymomas (MISME), and juvenile posterior subcapsular cataracts. Noonan and LEOPARD syndromes often present with congenital heart disease, deafness, and more severe craniofacial anomalies. In Legius syndrome, the café-au-lait spots appear similar to NF1, but Lisch nodules and neurofibromas are absent. In McCune-Albright syndrome, caused by somatic mutations of *GNAS1*, café-au-lait spots tend to have more irregular margins ("coast of Maine").

IMAGING DIFFERENTIAL DIAGNOSIS

Imaging of NF1 requires distinction between unidentified bright objects (UBOs), which are dysplastic lesions; and true neoplastic lesions such as gliomas. Typically, UBOs are located in the white matter and basal ganglia, with minimal mass effect and no appreciable contrast enhancement. UBOs spontaneously decrease over time with myelin repair, usually resolving by the second

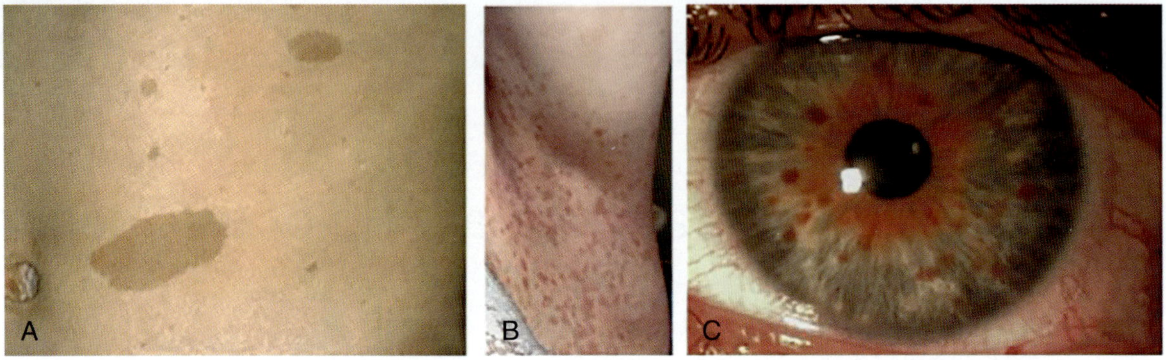

Fig. 57.1 Neurofibromatosis type 1. (A) Cafè-au-lait spots, (B) axillary freckling, and (C) Lisch nodules.

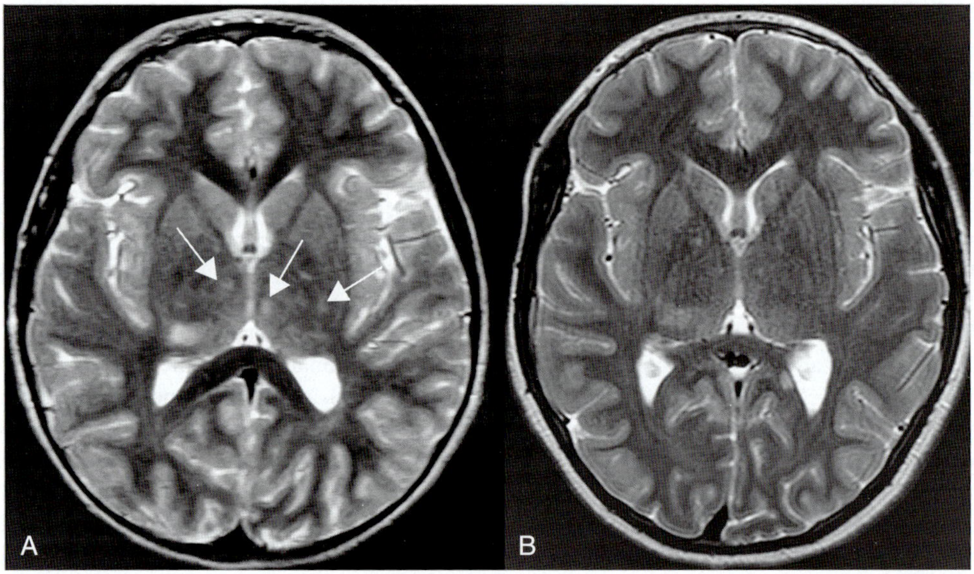

Fig. 57.2 Neurofibromatosis type 1. Brain MRI, axial T2 at (A) 5 years shows multifocal hyperintensities in the bilateral basal ganglia compatible with dysmyelination (*arrows*), with (B) partial involution and remyelination at 10 years.

decade of life. Imaging features concerning for neoplastic transformation include increasing mass effect and contrast enhancement over time.

Optic nerve gliomas are characteristic tumors in NF1 and usually begin in the anterior optic pathway, with better response to therapy and some case reports of spontaneous resolution. In contrast, sporadic optic gliomas are often limited to the chiasm, frequently present earlier with larger tumors, and have a higher risk of progression.

Plexiform neurofibromas are transspatial peripheral nerve sheath tumors that diffusely infiltrate multiple neural elements in the face, neck, and/or spine. They are usually benign, though malignant transformation can occur with new pain, rapid enlargement, soft tissue infiltration, and hypermetabolism. In contrast, schwannomas involve only the Schwann cell layer of the nerve sheath and tend to be well-circumscribed, with rare plexiform morphology.

FINAL DIAGNOSIS

Neurofibromatosis type 1.

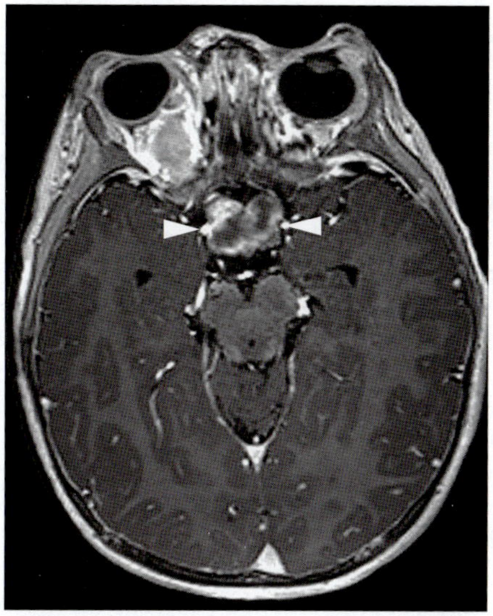

Fig. 57.3 Neurofibromatosis type 1. Brain MRI, axial postcontrast T1 shows optic pathway glioma with expansile heterogeneously enhancing infiltration of the optic pathway (*arrowheads*).

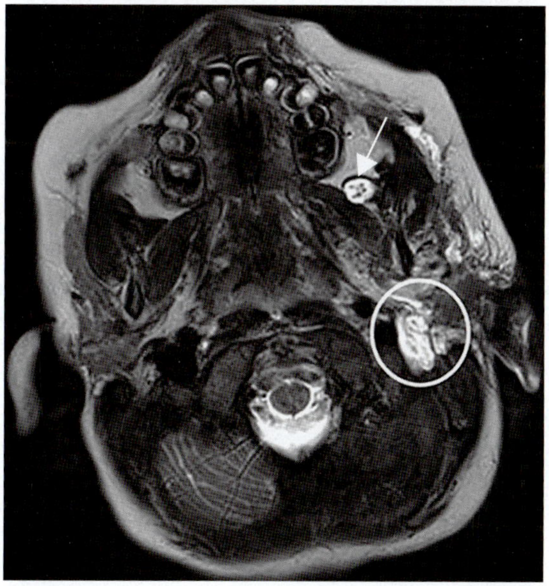

Fig. 57.4 Neurofibromatosis type 1. Brain MRI, axial T2 shows transspatial plexiform neurofibromas with multilocular targetoid lesions in the left perivertebral muscles (*circle*) and left pterygopalatine fossa (*arrow*).

DISCUSSION

NF1, also known as von Recklinghausen disease, is the most common multisystem neurocutaneous disorder, affecting 1 in 2500 to 3000 individuals worldwide. The *NF1* gene is located at 17q11.2 and its protein product, neurofibromin, is a negative regulator of the RAS-MAPK pathway. Dysfunction of neurofibromin leads to oncogenic constitutive MAPK activation, an autosomal dominant condition. Mutations are inherited from an affected parent in half of cases and caused by *de novo* mutations in the other half of patients. Penetrance is close to 100% but with broad phenotypic variability based on the severity of the mutation. Clinical manifestations include cutaneous signs, such as multiple café-au-lait spots, axillary and inguinal freckling, and multiple neurofibromas. About half of people with NF1 develop plexiform neurofibromas with transspatial involvement causing pain, neurologic deficits, and deformation of adjacent structures. Additional manifestations include macrocephaly, cerebral overgrowth, and dysmyelination; optic nerve and other central nervous system gliomas; malignant peripheral nerve sheath tumors; skeletal manifestations (kyphoscoliosis, tibial bowing, sphenoid wing dysplasia); vasculopathies; and gastrointestinal, endocrine, or pulmonary disease. Annual surveillance is recommended for early diagnosis and treatment (medical or surgical) of neurologic, ophthalmologic, skeletal, cardiovascular, and abdominal disease complications. In children, endocrine screening and evaluation for growth deficiency are also recommended. In addition to routine imaging surveillance, MRI can be helpful for workup of new neurologic signs or symptoms (focal deficits, headaches, seizures, sleep disturbances, pain).

CLINICAL RED FLAGS

Clinical diagnosis of NF1 requires at least one of the following features:

- Six or more café-au-lait spots (>5 mm in prepubertal individuals and >15 mm in postpubertal individuals). Macules are recognizable in almost all affected individuals at birth or within the first 2 years of life and tend to become lighter in adulthood.
- Freckling in the axillary or inguinal regions. These are present in 90% of individuals, classically appearing around the age of 6 and increasing until puberty.
- Two or more neurofibromas of any type or one plexiform neurofibroma. These typically present near puberty and may increase throughout life, with alternating periods of growth and relative stability.
- Optic pathway glioma.
- Two or more Lisch nodules (iris hamartomas), detectable by slit lamp examination in 90% of cases.

- Distinctive osseous lesions such as sphenoid wing dysplasia, tibial bowing, or long bone pseudoarthrosis.
- Positive family history for NF1 in a parent.
- Identification of a germline pathogenic variant in *NF1* gene.

Minor clinical features can include macrocephaly, growth deficiency, intellectual disability or behavioral problems, other skeletal features such as scoliosis or thoracic malformations (pectus excavatum or carinatum), pulmonary disease, and cardiovascular disease. NF1 is also associated with an increased risk of leukemia (especially juvenile myelomonocytic leukemia and myelodysplastic syndromes), gastrointestinal stromal tumors (6%), and adrenal or extra-adrenal pheochromocytoma (0.1%–5%). Rare NF1-associated systemic neoplasms include rhabdomyosarcoma, juvenile xanthogranuloma, melanoma, thyroid medullary carcinoma, and glomus tumors.

IMAGING RED FLAGS

- Foci of dysmyelination (spongiform myelinopathy at pathology) in NF1 appear as T2/FLAIR-hyperintense lesions, termed UBOs or focal areas of high signal intensity (FASI). These are present in more than half of children with NF1 and may occur throughout the white matter, basal ganglia, brainstem, and cerebellum. They are more detectable in childhood and tend to spontaneously regress over time due to myelin repair.
- Plexiform neurofibromas are peripheral nerve sheath tumors that involve all neural elements in a disorganized fashion, often with transspatial extent and targetoid morphology. Approximately one-third of plexiform neurofibromas are found in the head and neck. Multiple isolated cranial, spinal, or peripheral nerve neurofibromas are also common.
- Orbitotemporal NF1 presents with sphenoid wing dysplasia, temporal lobe herniation, plexiform neurofibromas, and orbital anomalies.
- Optic pathway gliomas are low-grade tumors involving the hypothalamus, optic nerves, chiasm, and/or optic radiations. They can be expansile and infiltrative lesions, with intraneural and/or perineural T2/FLAIR-hyperintense signal and contrast enhancement.

CONCLUSIONS

Clinical suspicion of NF1 usually begins with recognition of multiple café-au-lait spots. Detailed clinical and genetic workup with imaging surveillance enables earlier detection and treatment of complications.

REFERENCES

Calvez S, Levy R, Calvez R, et al. Focal areas of high signal intensity in children with neurofibromatosis type 1: expected evolution on MRI. *AJNR Am J Neuroradiol.* 2020;41(9):1733–1739.

Friedman JM. Neurofibromatosis. In: Adam MP, Everman DB, Mirzaa GM et al, eds. *GeneReviews®*. Seattle: University of Washington; 2022:1993–2023.

Khajavi M, Khoshsirat S, Ahangarnazari L, Majdinasab N. A brief report of plexiform neurofibroma. *Curr Probl Cancer.* 2018;42(2):256–260.

Miller DT, Freedenberg D, Schorry E, Ullrich NJ, Viskochil D, Korf BR; COUNCIL ON GENETICS; AMERICAN COLLEGE OF MEDICAL GENETICS AND GENOMICS. Health supervision for children with neurofibromatosis type 1. *Pediatrics.* 2019;143(5):e20190660.

Nix JS, Blakeley J, Rodriguez Fausto J. An update on the central nervous system manifestations of neurofibromatosis type 1. *Acta Neuropathol.* 2020;139(4):625–641.

Stewart DR, Korf BR, Nathanson KL, Stevenson DA, Yohay K. Care of adults with neurofibromatosis type 1: a clinical practice resource of the American College of Medical Genetics and Genomics (ACMG). *Genet Med.* 2018;20(7):671–682.

Theos A, Korf BR. American College of Physicians; American Physiological Society. Pathophysiology of neurofibromatosis type 1. *Ann Inter Med.* 2006;144(11):842–849.

Case 58

Mysteries of the Hairless Plaque

HISTORY AND PHYSICAL

A 7-year-old boy was born at term following an uneventful pregnancy, with no family history. Birth examination showed a flat, alopecic, xanthomatous lesion in the left temporo-occipital scalp, suggestive of nevus sebaceous (Fig. 58.1). Neurological examination revealed asymmetry of spontaneous movements with preferential use of the left arm, as well as mild motor delay. In the first year of life, he presented with language delay, oppositional behavior, and poor social interaction. Griffith developmental scale at the age of 14 months revealed a total developmental score of 60 (mild mental impairment). Seizures began at 6 months, with clusters lasting 2 to 3 minutes, characterized by sudden extensions of the upper limbs and trunk.

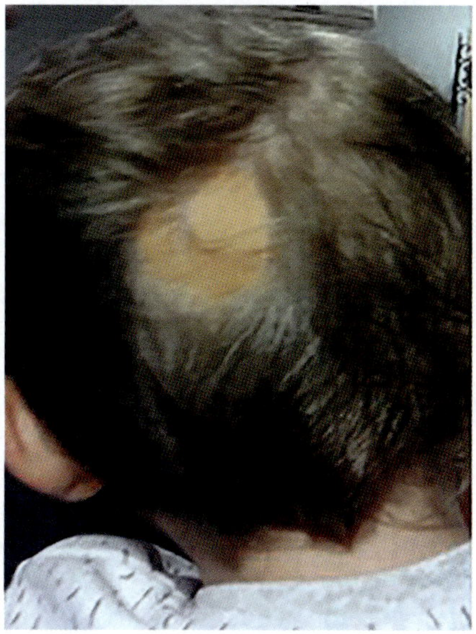

Fig. 58.1 Nevus sebaceous. Xanthomatous and alopecic lesion of the left posterior scalp.

DIAGNOSTIC WORKUP

Awake EEG showed continuous left temporo-occipital epileptiform abnormalities (Fig. 58.2A). Ictal video-EEG demonstrated periodic diffuse slow waves with superimposed fast activity lasting 20 to 30 seconds, associated with subtle ocular elevation (Fig. 58.2B).

Brain MRI showed left cerebral overgrowth with diffuse cortical dysplasia (Fig. 58.3).

At the age of 2 years, the patient underwent left temporooccipital resection. Histopathology documented FCD type Ia in the occipital region and hippocampal sclerosis type 1 with preserved cortical organization in the temporal lobe. During the next 5 years of follow-up, he was seizure-free without medications (Engel class Ia).

Custom next generation sequencing (NGS) panel on DNA extracted from the brain specimen and nevus sebaceous revealed a somatic *KRAS* gene mutation c.35G>T (p.Gly12Val), which was absent in blood.

CLINICAL DIFFERENTIAL DIAGNOSIS

Other neurocutaneous syndromes with hairless macules and nevi include incontinentia pigmenti and hypomelanosis of Ito.

Early-onset epilepsy can be seen with infantile epileptic spasms syndrome and structural or genetic epileptic encephalopathies.

IMAGING DIFFERENTIAL DIAGNOSIS

Widespread gray-white indistinction and early-onset epilepsy can be seen with various malformations of cortical development that involve congenital disruptions of neuronal migration.

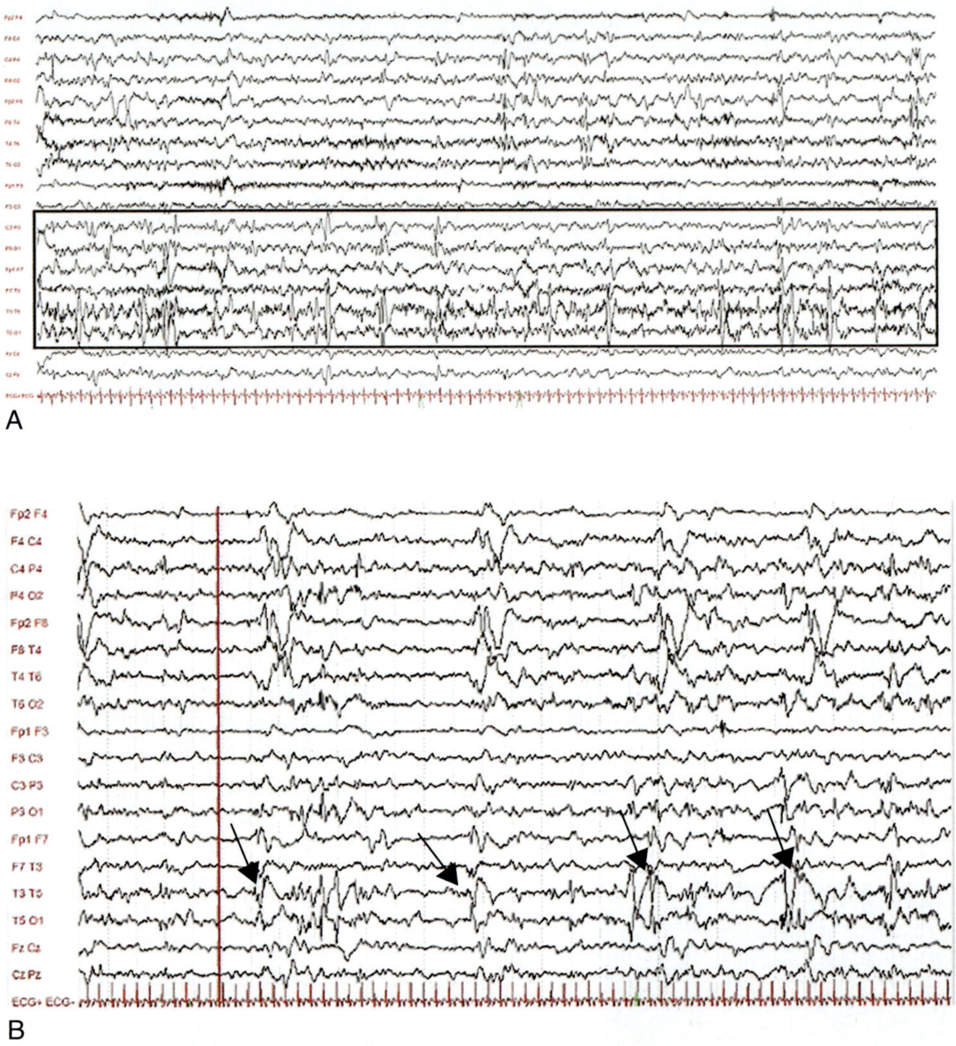

Fig. 58.2 (A) Awake EEG shows continuous left temporo-occipital (*rectangle)* slow waves and epileptiform abnormalities, with sporadic contralateral activity. *EEG*, Electroencephalogram. (B) Left temporo-occipital (*arrows*) periodic slow wave complexes (*arrows*) were associated with subtle eye elevation.

Hippocampal sclerosis can occur as a primary structural abnormality in temporal lobe epilepsy, or secondary to longstanding seizures arising from the ipsilateral cerebral hemisphere.

FINAL DIAGNOSIS

Nevus sebaceous syndrome (NSS).

DISCUSSION

NSS, also known as Schimmelpenning-Feuerstein-Mims syndrome) is a rare neurocutaneous disorder in which nevus sebaceous (NS) is found in association with congenital abnormalities of the brain, eyes, and/or skeleton. Usually occurring on the scalp or face, NS represents an epidermal nevus originating

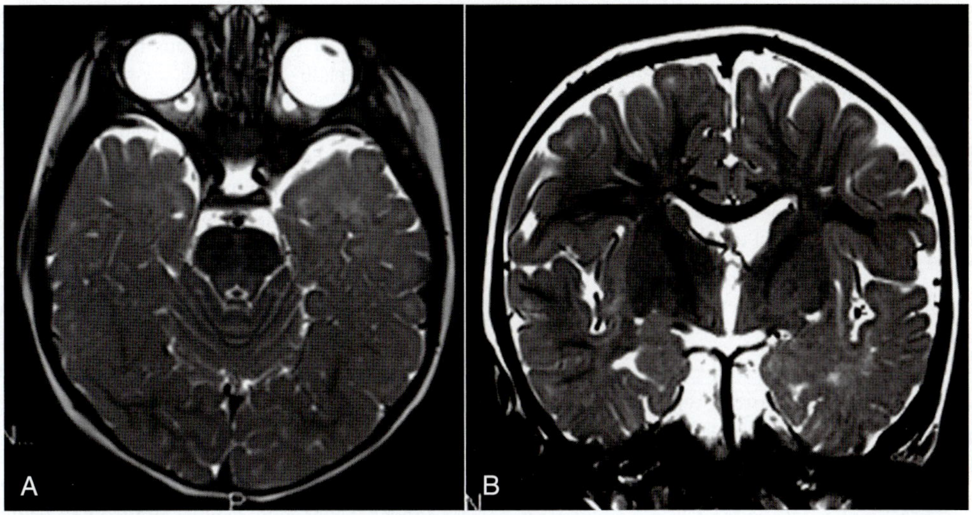

Fig. 58.3 Hemimegalencephaly. Brain MRI, (A) axial T2 and (B) coronal T2 show left hemimegalencephaly with asymmetric cerebral enlargement and gray-white blurring.

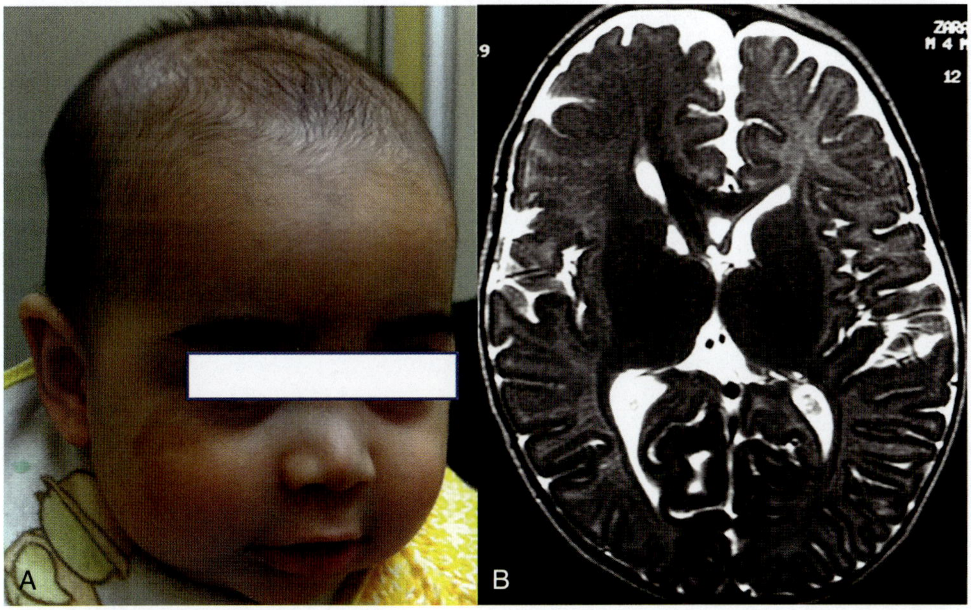

Fig. 58.4 Hemimegalencephaly. (A) Clinical photo shows right facial overgrowth and hyperpigmentation. (B) Brain MRI, axial T2 shows right cerebral overgrowth.

from the sebaceous glands with a waxy, yellow-orange, and alopecic appearance.

Somatic *HRAS*, *KRAS* and *NRAS* variants occurring during embryogenesis have been identified as pathogenic. Neurological involvement is evident in 5% to 15% of patients and can include intellectual disability, epileptic seizures (especially spasms), and hemiparesis. Epilepsy occurs in 38% to 96% of patients with NSS and neurological involvement. The most common brain malformation is hemimegalencephaly (HME) (Fig. 58.3 and 58.4), occurring in up to 72% of cases, and typically ipsilateral to the skin lesion.

CLINICAL RED FLAGS

- Epidermal nevus with waxy and alopecic appearance.
- Early-onset epilepsy within 6–8 months of life.

IMAGING RED FLAGS

- Diffuse or hemispheric malformations of cortical development, usually ipsilateral to the skin lesion.

CONCLUSIONS

NSS is a rare neurocutaneous disorder with unique cutaneous and cerebral stigmata. Epilepsy is a common manifestation, and early evaluation may enable resection of the abnormal brain regions with better patient outcomes.

REFERENCES

Asch SL, Sugarman J. Epidermal nevus syndromes: new insights into whorls and swirls. *Pediatr Dermatol.* 2018;35(1):21–29.

Davies D, Rogers M. Review of neurological manifestations in 196 patients with sebaceous naevi. *Australas J Dermatol.* 2002;43(1):20–23.

El Ezzi O, de Buys Roessingh AS, Michèle B, Captier G. Syndromic sebaceous nevus: current findings. *Int J Dermatol.* 2018;57(5):599–604.

Pavone L, Curatolo P, Rizzo R, et al. Epidermal nevus syndrome: a neurologic variant with hemimegalencephaly, gyral malformation, mental retardation, seizures, and facial hemihypertrophy. *Neurology.* 1991;41(2 [Pt 1]):266–271.

Rogers M. Epidermal nevi and the epidermal nevus syndromes: a review of 233 cases. *Pediatr Dermatol.* 1992;9(4):342–344.

Rogers M, McCrossin I, Commens C. Epidermal nevi and the Epidermal Nevus syndrome. *J Am Acad Dermatol.* 1989;20(3):476–488.

Winston KR, Kang J, Laoprasert P, Kleinschmidt-DeMasters BK. Hemispherectomy in a premature neonate with Linear Sebaceous Nevus Syndrome. *Pediatr Neurosurg.* 2008;44(2):159–164.

Case 59

Port-Wine and the Brain

HISTORY AND PHYSICAL

An 8-year-old boy was the first child of non-consanguineous parents, born at term after a normal pregnancy. Family history was negative for epilepsy or other neurodevelopmental disorders.

At birth, a port-wine stain (PWS) was identified on his left forehead, extending to his eyelid and nose (Fig. 59.1). Epilepsy began at 13 months of life, with clonic seizures of the upper right arm that were initially well controlled by phenobarbital and levetiracetam. After a period of sporadic seizures, he experienced a progressive increase in seizure frequency at 4 years. Seizures were mostly tonic or tonic-clonic, involving the left hemibody, with worsening during episodes of fever, infection, and sleep deprivation. Clobazam, carbamazepine, and valproate were trialed with poor efficacy and persistence of monthly seizures. At the time of presentation, the patient was nonverbal with clumsy autonomous walking, preferential left-hand usage, and autism spectrum disorder (ASD) features.

DIAGNOSTIC WORKUP

Brain MRI at 1 year of age showed abnormal leptomeningeal enhancement over the left posterior quadrant. At 6 years of age, a follow-up MRI showed interval volume loss and T2 hyperintensity of the brain parenchyma (Fig. 59.2). At 10 years of age, there was progressive leptomeningeal and choroid plexus enhancement with gyriform cortical calcifications (Fig. 59.3). EEG showed slowing over the left parieto-temporal-occipital region without epileptic abnormalities.

CLINICAL DIFFERENTIAL DIAGNOSIS

Many neurocutaneous syndromes are associated with vascular malformations. The characteristic lesion of Sturge-Weber syndrome (SWS) is the PWS, or nevus flammeus. This is a capillary malformation of the upper face and orbit with frequent brain involvement. A dermatologic evaluation can easily distinguish PWS at risk for SWS, in locations over the orbit and forehead. Patients lack clinical signs of high-flow vascular malformations such as warm regions, pulsatile lesions, and swelling.

Other vascular lesions of the skin include small incidental capillary malformations (nevus simplex), congenital hemangiomas, infantile hemangiomas (which can be segmental and associated with posterior fossa, hemangiomas, arterial, cardiovascular, eye, sternal and/or supraumbilical anomalies [PHACES]), arteriovenous malformations in Wyburn-Mason syndrome, and capillary/venous malformations with limb hypertrophy in Klippel-Trenaunay syndrome.

IMAGING DIFFERENTIAL DIAGNOSIS

The imaging differential diagnosis for vascular lesions of the brain and face includes various syndromes such as Klippel-Trenaunay, meningioangiomatosis, blue rubber bleb nevus, and Wyburn-Mason syndrome. The characteristic leptomeningeal enhancement and progressive brain atrophy, in association with overlying cutaneous and/or ophthalmological abnormalities, are diagnostic of SWS. In the late stages of disease, chronic venous ischemia can produce gyriform "tram-track" calcification of the cerebral cortex, associated with focal epilepsy.

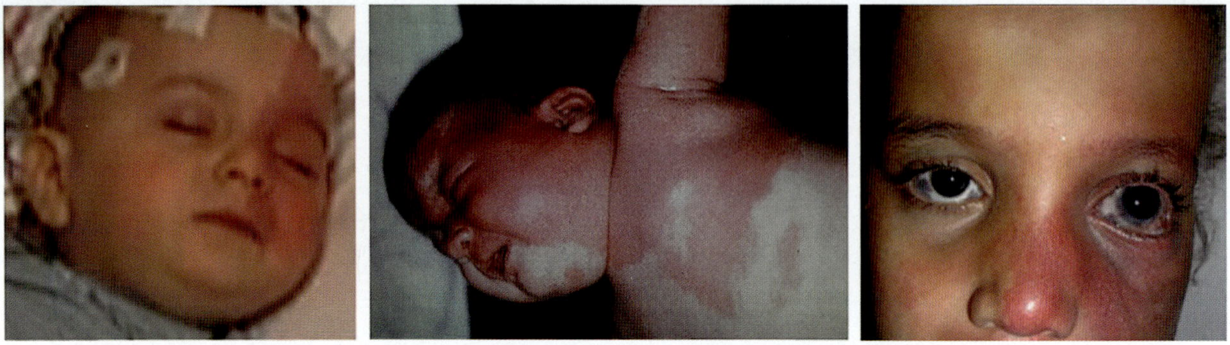

Fig. 59.1 Sturge-Weber syndrome. Serial photos from birth and childhood showing port-wine stains on the left forehead, orbit, nose, and chest.

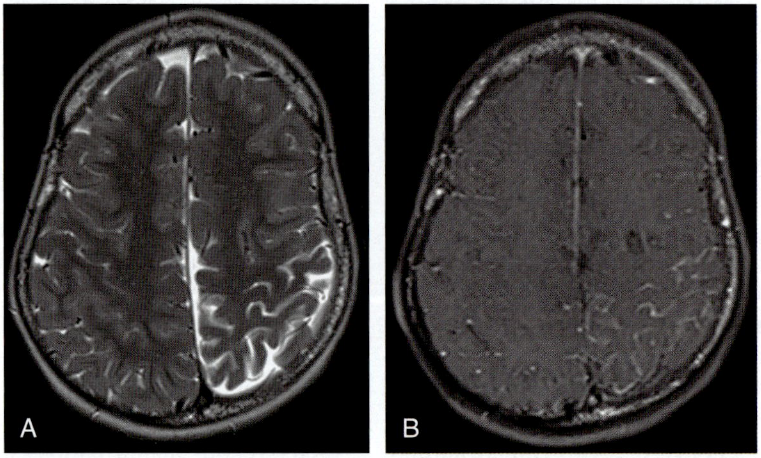

Fig. 59.2 Sturge-Weber syndrome. Brain MRI, (A) axial T2 and (B) postcontrast T1 show left posterior quadrant encephalomalacia with overlying enhancement in the subarachnoid space.

FINAL DIAGNOSIS

Sturge-Weber syndrome.

DISCUSSION

SWS, formerly known as encephalotrigeminal angiomatosis, is the third most common neurocutaneous syndrome after neurofibromatosis and tuberous sclerosis. It is a sporadic disease caused by somatic mutations in the *GNAQ* gene. Slow-flow capillary and venous malformations can affect the brain, eyes, and skin in a segmental distribution. In 10% of cases, brain involvement is isolated without cutaneous and ophthalmologic stigmata (type 3 SWS), therefore MRI is required for diagnosis. Epilepsy is the most common clinical manifestation, usually beginning by year 2 of life and refractory to multiple medications. Additional symptoms include hemiparesis, headache, and intellectual impairment. Prompt recognition is essential for appropriate management to optimize neurodevelopmental outcome and seizure control.

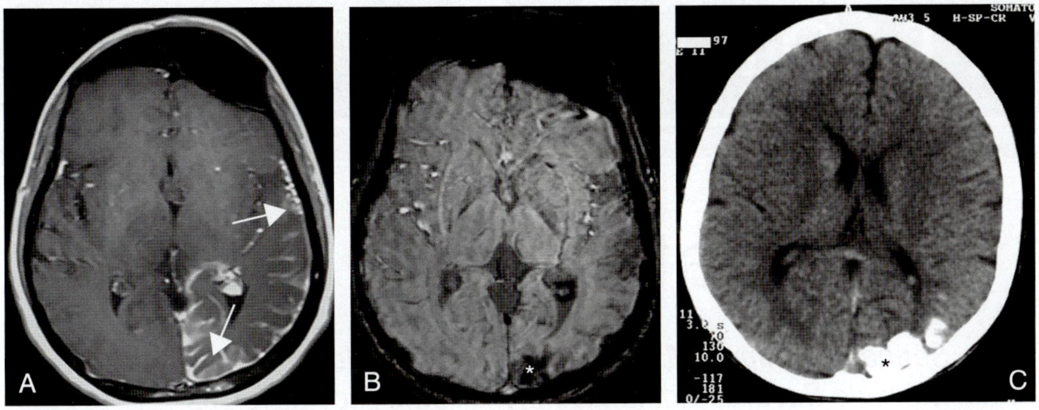

Fig. 59.3 Sturge-Weber syndrome. Brain MRI, (A) axial postcontrast T1 and (B) SWI and (C) head CT show left posterior quadrant atrophy with enhancement and susceptibility in the subarachnoid space (*arrows*), dilated medullary veins, hyperenhancing choroid plexus, and gyriform cortical calcifications in the occipital pole (*asterisks*).

CLINICAL RED FLAGS

- PWS is a capillary malformation of the upper face that is highly characteristic of SWS. It is typically a dark, solid, sharply demarcated erythematous patch involving the forehead, eyelid, and/or nose.

IMAGING RED FLAGS

- Brain imaging features differ depending on the stage of the disease. The characteristic cerebral slow-flow vascular malformation consists of hypoplastic and engorged superficial veins (formerly known as pial angioma).
- Early on, there is transient cerebral hyperperfusion with accelerated myelin maturation and leptomeningeal enhancement.
- Over time, inadequate cortical venous outflow leads to brain atrophy and decreased pial enhancement. There is compensatory increased drainage to deep veins via the medullary/subependymal veins and enlarged choroid plexus.
- In chronic stages, venous ischemia yields gyriform "tram-track" calcification of the cerebral cortex.

CONCLUSIONS

Clinical suspicion of SWS typically begins with recognition of PWS at or shortly after birth. Ophthalmologic exam can help detect associated ocular malformations. Patients with forehead and/or orbital involvement should be imaged using brain MRI with contrast to detect the typical slow-flow vascular malformations, which evolve over time with progressive venous ischemia, encephalomalacia, and cortical calcifications causing seizures. Delayed imaging may be more sensitive as these findings evolve with age.

REFERENCES

Comi AM. Update on Sturge-Weber syndrome: diagnosis, treatment, quantitative measures, and controversies. *Lymphat Res Biol.* 2007;5(4):257–264.

Comi AM. Sturge-Weber syndrome. *Handb Clin Neurol.* 2015;132:157–168.

Klar N, Cohen B, Lin D. Neurocutaneous syndromes. *Handb Clin Neurol.* 2016;135:565–589.

Nozaki T, Nosaka S, Miyazaki O, et al. Syndromes associated with vascular tumors and malformations: a pictorial review. *Radiographics.* 2013;33(1):175–195.

Poliner A, Fernandez Faith E, Blieden L, et al. Port-wine birthmarks: update on diagnosis, risk assessment for Sturge-Weber syndrome, and management. *Pediatr Rev.* 2022;43(9):507–516.

Shirley MD, Tang H, Gallione CJ, et al. Sturge-Weber syndrome and port-wine stains caused by somatic mutation in GNAQ. *N Engl J Med.* 2013;368(21):1971–1979.

Singh AK, Keenaghan M. *Sturge-Weber Syndrome.* StatPearls; 2022.

Thomas-Sohl KA, Vaslow DF, Maria Bernard L. Sturge-Weber syndrome: a review. *Pediatr Neurol.* 2004;30(5):303–310.

SECTION 13

Traumatic Brain Injury

Santiago Campos-Miño, Brigid Dwyer, Bindu N. Setty, Marcelo Bayardo Román, Lennyn Albán, Alcy R. Torres

INTRODUCTION

Traumatic brain injury (TBI) is a serious public health problem, with an estimated 223,000 hospitalizations in the United States in 2019 and an average of approximately 190 deaths per day. Falls are one of the leading causes of emergency department visits, hospitalizations, and deaths, with over 25% of cases involving young children (0–4 years). TBI is the leading cause of pediatric disability; in a European study, about one-third of children with moderate-severe TBI required rehabilitation. Clinical complaints span the somatic, cognitive, and affective domains. Symptoms can include impairments of attention, working memory, memory encoding and retrieval, naming, comprehension, repetition, and visuospatial processing. Motor weakness, sensory loss, ataxia, spasticity, and issues such as headache and seizure are also major contributors to loss of independence and productivity.

The effects of TBI can vary significantly depending on the severity of injury. Children with mild TBI generally experience short-term symptoms and resolution of symptoms within a few weeks. Those with moderate or severe TBI may have chronic and lifelong effects. Severe TBI is especially likely to impart a large societal and economic toll, estimated to be $76.5 billion per year in 2010. Injuries requiring hospitalization (including fatal TBIs) comprise 90% of TBI-related medical costs.

In this chapter, we describe clinical and imaging red flags in children with TBI that should prompt diagnostic testing. Focal neurological symptoms, persistent loss of consciousness or post-traumatic confusion, and abnormal neurological examination are key indicators for neuroimaging.

SUGGESTED READINGS

Ben Abdeljelil A, Freire GC, Yanchar N, et al. Pediatric moderate and severe traumatic brain injury: a systematic review of clinical practice guideline recommendations. *J Neurotrauma*. 2023;40(21-22):2270–2281. https://doi.org/10.1089/neu.2023.0149.

Centers for Disease Control and Prevention, National Center for Injury and Prevention Control. 2023. *Traumatic brain injury and concussion*. https://www.cdc.gov/traumatic-braininjury/index.html.

Fuentes MM, Wang J, Haarbauer-Krupa J, et al. Unmet rehabilitation needs after hospitalization for traumatic brain injury. *Pediatrics*. 2018;141(5):e20172859. https://doi.org/10.1542/peds.2017-2859.

Hon KL, Leung AKC, Torres AR. Concussion: a global perspective. *Semin Pediatr Neurol*. 2019;30:117–127. https://doi.org/10.1016/j.spen.2019.03.017.

Torres AR, Shaikh ZI, Chavez W, Maldonado JE. Brain MRI in children with mild traumatic brain injury and persistent symptoms in both sports- and non-sports-related concussion. *Cureus*. 2019;11(1):e3937. https://doi.org/10.7759/cureus.3937.

Case 60

Buckle Up!

HISTORY AND PHYSICAL

An 8-year-old, previously healthy boy was traveling in the front seat of a car on his mother's lap with an unfastened seatbelt. The car was hit on the right side by a truck, with both vehicles in transit at high speed. The mother died immediately, and the boy was found unconscious by paramedics. Time to first medical attention was unknown. The patient was hypoxemic, hypotensive, and unconscious (Glasgow Coma Scale [GCS] 3/15). He was intubated and received sedation and analgesia; his cervical spine was stabilized. Upon transfer to a level I trauma center, initial vital signs were heart rate 116/min, blood pressure 89/62, oxygen saturation 100% on FiO_2 50%, and respiratory rate 20/min on ventilator. There were no spontaneous respirations. The patient was unreactive to painful stimuli, and anisocoria was noted with a dilated and unresponsive left pupil. He had left otorrhagia, raccoon eyes, and an ecchymotic area in the anterior right chest wall. Examination of the lungs, heart, and abdomen was unremarkable.

DIAGNOSTIC WORKUP

Initial head CT revealed right temporal epidural/subdural hematomas and stellate fractures of the left parietal, temporal, and sphenoid bones (Fig. 60.1). Rotterdam score was 1. Cervical spine CT was normal. Chest CT revealed bilateral lung contusions. Abdomen CT showed grade 1 laceration of liver segment 4 and pancreatic edema. Liver and pancreatic enzymes were elevated. Arterial blood gas and blood glucose were normal.

The patient was admitted to the pediatric intensive care unit (PICU) and neurosurgery was consulted for intracranial pressure (ICP) monitoring, with first recording of 12 mm Hg. Normal ICP levels were observed during the PICU stay, along with normal video-electroencephalogram (EEG). On day 4 of admission, because of persistent anisocoria and absence of clinical improvement, a brain MRI was ordered. The findings were consistent with moderate (grade 2) diffuse axonal injury (DAI) according to the Adams classification. Multifocal restricted diffusion was seen in the left greater than right cortex and subcortical white matter, left splenium, and left cerebellar hemisphere (Fig. 60.2). Time of flight (TOF) angiography was normal.

CLINICAL DIFFERENTIAL DIAGNOSES

Following acute head trauma, various injuries can occur, including DAI, epidural hematoma, subdural hematoma, subarachnoid hemorrhage, parenchymal hemorrhage, and ischemic and hemorrhagic stroke. Patient status may be complicated by seizures, status epilepticus, hypoxemia, and hypoglycemia. Diagnosis of DAI requires a combination of clinical and imaging findings. The mechanism of head injury is typically high-speed rotation or acceleration-deceleration closed head injury with a GCS <8 for more than 6 consecutive hours. DAI should also be strongly considered in patients who fail to improve after surgical evacuation of subdural or epidural hematomas.

IMAGING DIFFERENTIAL DIAGNOSES

The differential diagnosis includes acute ischemic infarction of the superficial territory of the middle cerebral artery, possibly associated with traumatic dissection or a hemodynamically low-flow state (Fig. 60.3), and extra-limbic autoimmune or infectious encephalitis (Fig. 60.4).

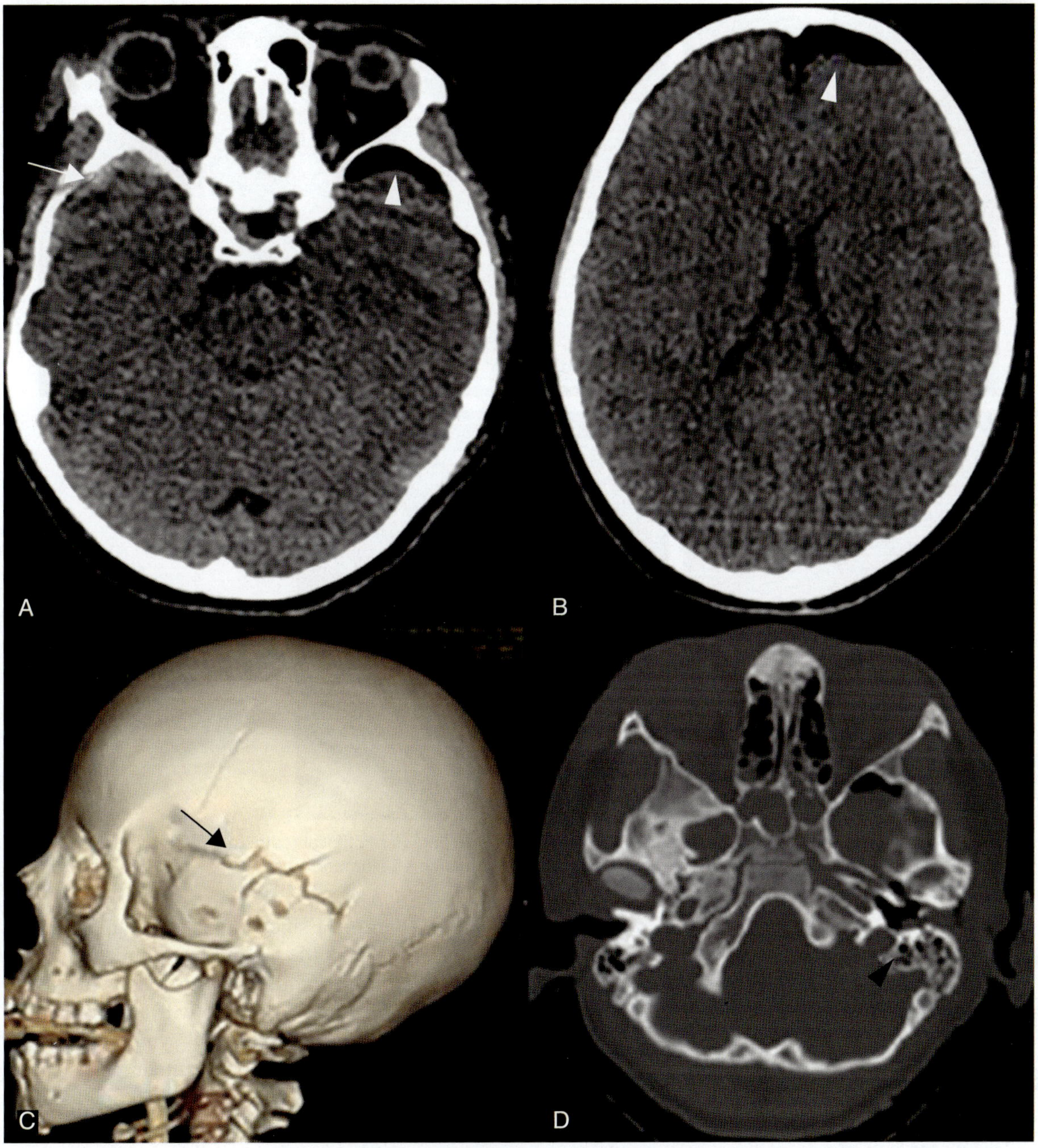

Fig. 60.1 Moderate diffuse axonal injury. Head CT, soft tissue window shows (A) right temporal epidural/ subdural hematoma (*white arrow*) (B) and left frontotemporal pneumocephalus (*white arrowheads*). (C) Sagittal three-dimensional reconstruction and (D) axial bone window show comminuted stellate fractures of the left parietal, temporal, and sphenoid bones (*black arrow*) with hemotympanum (*black arrowhead*).

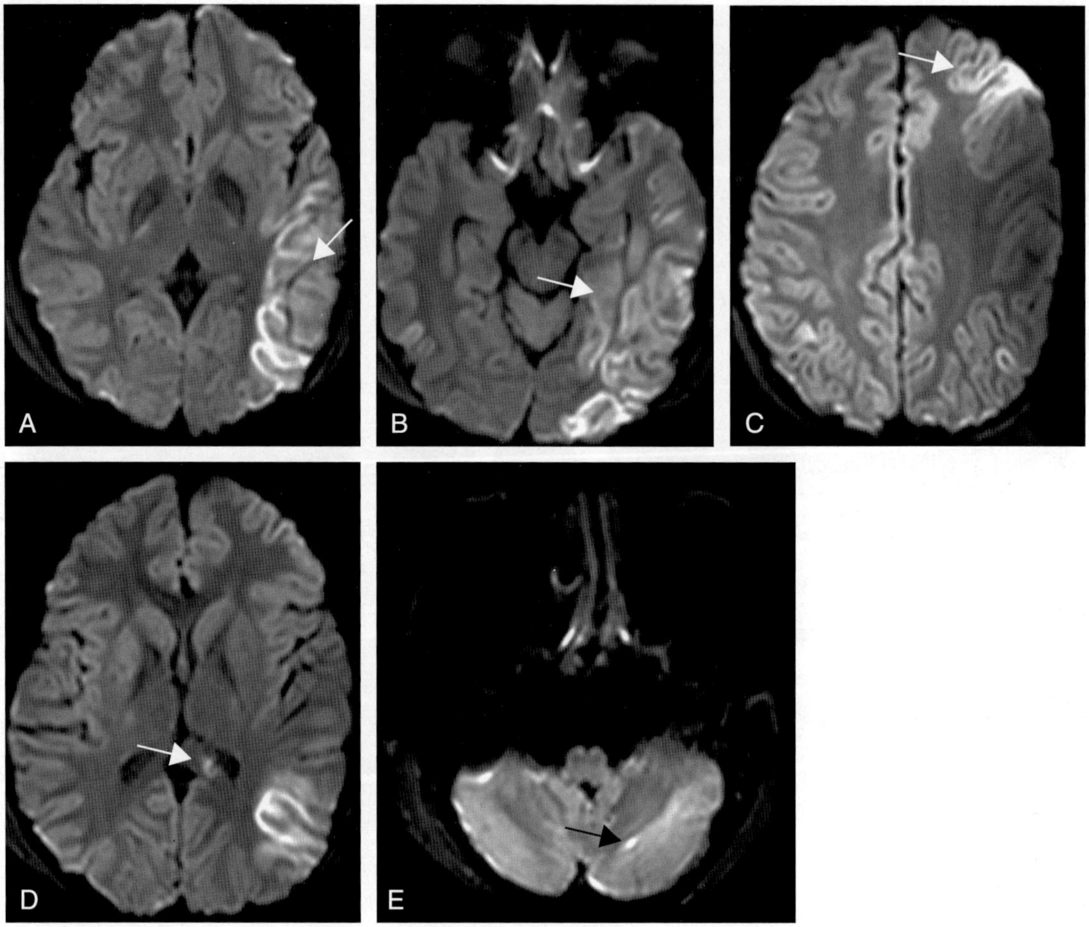

Fig. 60.2 Moderate diffuse axonal injury. Brain MRI, axial DWI shows multifocal restricted diffusion involving the left cerebral cortex, subcortical white matter, splenium, and cerebellum (*arrows*).

FINAL DIAGNOSIS

Moderate (grade 2) diffuse axonal injury.

DISCUSSION

DAI is a type of head trauma that results from a blunt injury to the brain. The most common mechanism involves high-speed motor vehicle accidents causing rotational and acceleration-deceleration forces. This leads to shearing of white matter tracts with gross and microscopic damage to the axons at the gray-white matter junction. More severe DAI can affect deep white matter tracts involved in the corpus callosum and brainstem. Interestingly, DAI can occur in the absence of overlying skull fractures.

The Adams classification is used to diagnose the severity of DAI: grade 1 is mild and limited to the white matter, grade 2 is moderate with lesions of the corpus callosum, and grade 3 is severe with involvement of the brainstem. In grade 1, signs and symptoms may reflect a concussive event with transient or persistent headache, dizziness, nausea, vomiting, and fatigue. In grade 3, patients present with loss of consciousness and a significant risk of prolonged disordered consciousness or death. Dysautonomia can also occur with tachycardia, tachypnea, diaphoresis, vasoplegia, hyperthermia, abnormal muscle tone, and posturing. Head CT is often used for initial screening in the emergency department, but brain MRI is the most sensitive diagnostic imaging study. At present, there are no standardized laboratory tests for diagnosis of DAI, though blood and CSF biomarkers are being evaluated in clinical trials.

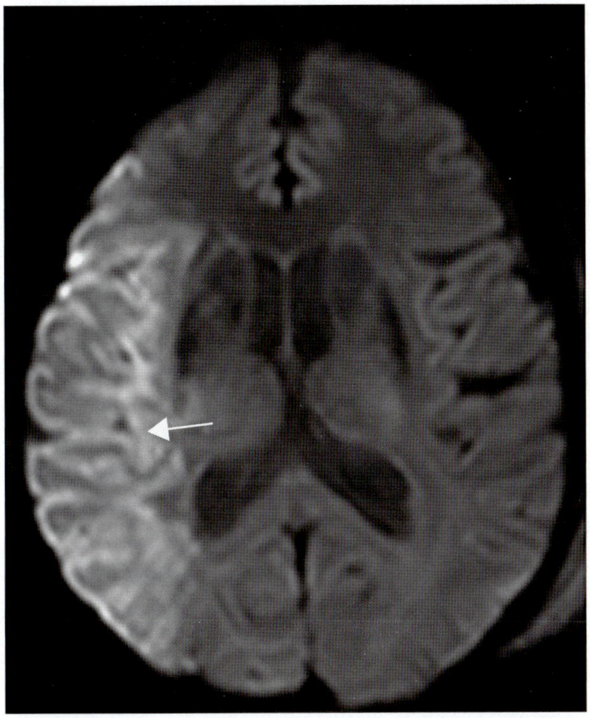

Fig. 60.3 Middle cerebral artery infarction. Brain MRI, axial DWI, shows acute restricted diffusion in the right MCA territory (*arrow*).

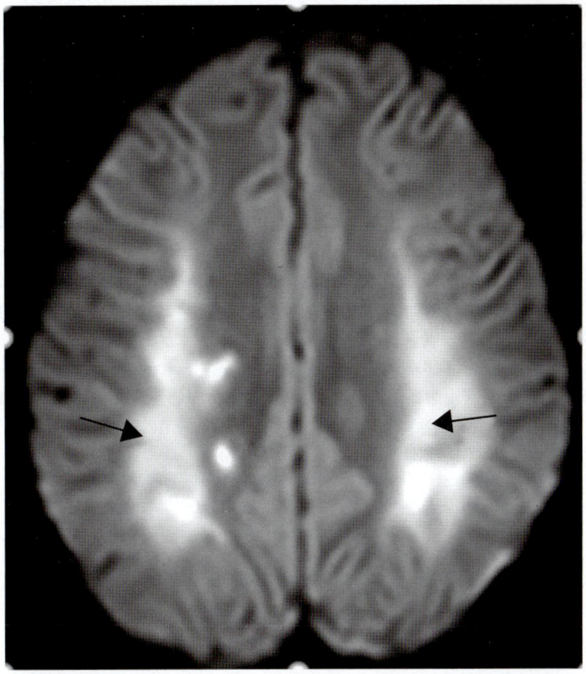

Fig. 60.4 Autoimmune encephalitis. Brain MRI, axial DWI, shows bilateral white matter restricted diffusion (*arrows*).

Treatment of DAI is focused on resuscitation and prevention of secondary injuries. ICP monitoring is indicated in patients with GCS <8 or when continual neurologic examination is infeasible. ICP is an important prognostic variable and allows cerebral perfusion pressure management. Cerebral oxygen saturation monitoring can also be used to assess the degree of oxygenation. Short-term anticonvulsant therapy can be used to prevent early posttraumatic seizures.

CLINICAL RED FLAGS

- Prolonged unconsciousness or confusion lasting >24 hours is concerning for moderate to severe TBI with DAI, especially if findings on CT do not fully explain the clinical picture.
- Hypoxemia or hypotension are risk factors for secondary brain injury.
- Signs of intracranial hypertension, for example posturing, mydriasis, anisocoria, or Cushing reflex (tachycardia or bradycardia, hypertension, and irregular respirations), are important clinical red flags.

IMAGING RED FLAGS

- Discrepancy between GCS and CT findings in a patient with severe head trauma should prompt a brain MRI.
- Susceptibility-weighted imaging (SWI) or gradient recalled echo (GRE) MRI sequences are sensitive to microhemorrhages, which in DAI can involve the gray-white junction, corpus callosum, and brainstem.

CONCLUSIONS

DAI is a severe form of TBI with shearing forces that cause malfunction and/or disconnection of neuronal connections, affecting numerous functional areas. Outcomes are associated with lesion burden at imaging. During the acute phase, hypoxia and hypotension can lead to increased mortality, therefore resuscitation and neuroprotective measures are recommended.

REFERENCES

Adams JH, Doyle D, Ford I, Gennarelli TA, Graham DI, McLellan DR. Diffuse axonal injury in head injury: definition, diagnosis and grading. *Histopathology*. 1989;15(1):49–59. https://doi.org/10.1111/j.1365-2559.1989.tb03040.x.

Izzy S, Mazwi NL, Martinez S, et al. Revisiting grade 3 diffuse axonal injury: not all brainstem microbleeds are prognostically equal. *Neurocrit Care*. 2017;27(2):199–207. https://doi.org/10.1007/s12028-017-0399-2.

Kochanek PM, Tasker RC, Carney N, et al. Guidelines for the management of pediatric severe traumatic brain injury, third edition: update of the brain trauma foundation guidelines [published correction appears in Pediatr Crit Care Med. 2019 Apr;20(4):404]. *Pediatr Crit Care Med*. 2019;20(3 Suppl 1):S1–S82. https://doi.org/10.1097/PCC.0000000000001735.

Mesfin FB, Gupta N, Hays SA, Taylor RS. Diffuse Axonal Injury. *StatPearls*. 2023. https://www.ncbi.nlm.nih.gov/books/NBK448102.

Taylor CA, Bell JM, Breiding MJ, Xu L. Traumatic brain injury-related emergency department visits, hospitalizations, and deaths—United States, 2007 and 2013. *MMWR Surveill Summ*. 2017;66(9):1–16. https://doi.org/10.15585/mmwr.ss6609a1.

van Eijck MM, Schoonman GG, van der Naalt J, de Vries J, Roks G. Diffuse axonal injury after traumatic brain injury is a prognostic factor for functional outcome: a systematic review and meta-analysis. *Brain Inj*. 2018;32(4):395–402. https://doi.org/10.1080/02699052.2018.1429018.

Vieira RC, Paiva WS, de Oliveira DV, Teixeira MJ, de Andrade AF, de Sousa RM. Diffuse axonal injury: epidemiology, outcome and associated risk factors. *Front Neurol*. 2016;7:178. https://doi.org/10.3389/fneur.2016.00178.

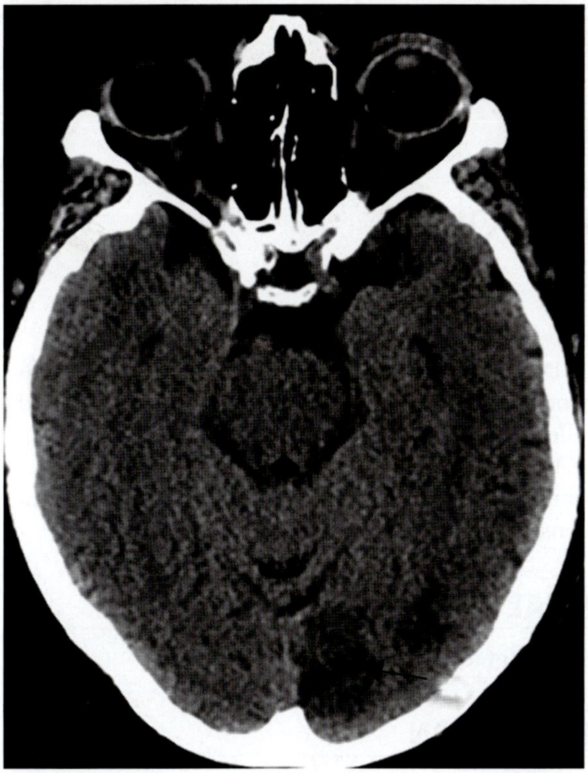

Fig. 61.7 Occipital lobe infarct. Axial head CT shows focal cytotoxic edema in the left occipital pole (*arrow*).

CLINICAL RED FLAGS

- Hypoxemia or hypotension are risk factors for secondary brain injury.
- Monitor for signs of intracranial hypertension (unconsciousness, posturing, motor deficits, Cushing reflex) or dysautonomia (tachycardia, tachypnea, diaphoresis, vasoplegia, hyperthermia, abnormal muscle tone, and posturing).
- Blindness, isolated pupillary changes, or lack of recovery after 48 hours are red flags for optic nerve injury.
- Rhinorrhea raises concern for cerebrospinal fluid (CSF) leak.

IMAGING RED FLAGS

- Optic nerve evaluation should be performed in patients with TBI and mass effect. Other lesions along the visual pathway, for example occipital lobes, can also cause blindness.
- Orbital fractures, particularly involving the sphenoid bone and optic canal, raise the likelihood of optic nerve injury. In the acute phase, edema, hemorrhage, and/or gas surround the optic nerve. In the chronic phase, nerve atrophy develops.

CONCLUSIONS

Traumatic optic neuropathy is a concern in patients following head and facial trauma, especially those who develop intracranial hypertension.

REFERENCES

Bodanapally UK, Van der Byl G, Shanmuganathan K, et al. Traumatic optic neuropathy prediction after blunt facial trauma: derivation of a risk score based on facial CT findings at admission. *Radiology*. 2014;272(3):824–831. https://doi.org/10.1148/radiol.14131873.

Brazis PW. Localization of lesions of the oculomotor nerve: recent concepts. *Mayo Clin Proc*. 1991;66(10):1029–1035. https://doi.org/10.1016/s0025-6196(12)61726-1.

Dinallo S, Waseem M. 2023. *Cushing Reflex*. StatPearls. https://www.ncbi.nlm.nih.gov/books/NBK549801.

Ford RL, Lee V, Xing W, Bunce C. A 2-year prospective surveillance of pediatric traumatic optic neuropathy in the United Kingdom. *J AAPOS*. 2012;16(5):413–417. https://doi.org/10.1016/j.jaapos.2012.04.009.

Gross CE, DeKock JR, Panje WR, Hershkowitz N, Newman J. Evidence for orbital deformation that may contribute to monocular blindness following minor frontal head trauma. *J Neurosurg*. 1981;55(6):963–966. https://doi.org/10.3171/jns.1981.55.6.0963.

Levin LA, Beck RW, Joseph MP, Seiff S, Kraker R. The treatment of traumatic optic neuropathy: the International Optic Nerve Trauma Study. *Ophthalmology*. 1999;106(7):1268–1277. https://doi.org/10.1016/s0161-6420(99)00707-1.

Case 62

Severe TBI: What Is the Outlook?

HISTORY AND PHYSICAL

An 18-year-old, previously healthy woman in her senior year of college failed to return home from an evening outing. She was reported missing by her roommate and subsequently discovered on the roadside as a restrained passenger in an overnight motor vehicle accident. Initial GCS was 5, and she remained in an unconscious state with preserved sleep/wake cycles (unresponsive wakefulness) until day 31 posttrauma. She regained a consistent degree of alertness with reliable following of commands at 64 days and regained orientation at 106 days. At 1 year, she had persistently impaired left motor control, visual and verbal memory deficits, and slowed processing speed. She was able to return to college on a modified schedule 2 years postinjury and was living independently 3 years postinjury. She was able to run a continuous mile by 5 years postinjury and obtained a job as a writer for a nonprofit.

DIAGNOSTIC WORKUP

Head CT and brain MRI at 5 weeks postinjury revealed patchy edema and microhemorrhages in the corpus callosum, basal ganglia and brainstem (Fig. 62.1).

CLINICAL DIFFERENTIAL DIAGNOSES

Posttraumatic seizures with postictal encephalopathy.
Hypoxic-ischemic brain injury.
Substance abuse.

IMAGING DIFFERENTIAL DIAGNOSES

Cerebral edema can be associated with traumatic brain injury (TBI), hypoxic-ischemic injury, acute inflammatory processes such as viral encephalitis, multiple sclerosis, or acute disseminated encephalomyelitis (ADEM).

Diffuse microhemorrhages can be seen in diffuse axonal injury (DAI), small vessel vasculopathies, and following radiation therapy.

Localized macro- and microhemorrhages may be seen in association with underlying vascular malformations or tumors.

FINAL DIAGNOSIS

Severe (grade 3) diffuse axonal injury.

DISCUSSION

Unintentional falls and motor vehicle accidents are the most common causes of moderate to severe TBI. These result in persistently altered consciousness or cognition for at least 24 hours, with sensorimotor deficits and/or cognitive impairments that can persist over time. Along with focal parenchymal injury, DAI is a major cause of neurologic dysfunction after TBI. Disruption of neurofilaments and axonal swelling with impaired cellular transport and electrical signaling contribute to dysfunction of neural circuitry, complicated by toxic neurotransmitter and free radical release. TBI recovery can take place over the course of several years, though the most substantial improvements occur early in the patient's course when medical confounders are addressed.

CLINICAL RED FLAGS

- Exposure to a direct force or blast causing acutely altered consciousness.
- Persistently decreased level of arousal lasting >30 minutes.
- Impaired cognition lasting more than 24 hours.
- Focally impaired motor activation or ataxia.
- Cranial nerve palsies.
- Pupillary asymmetry.

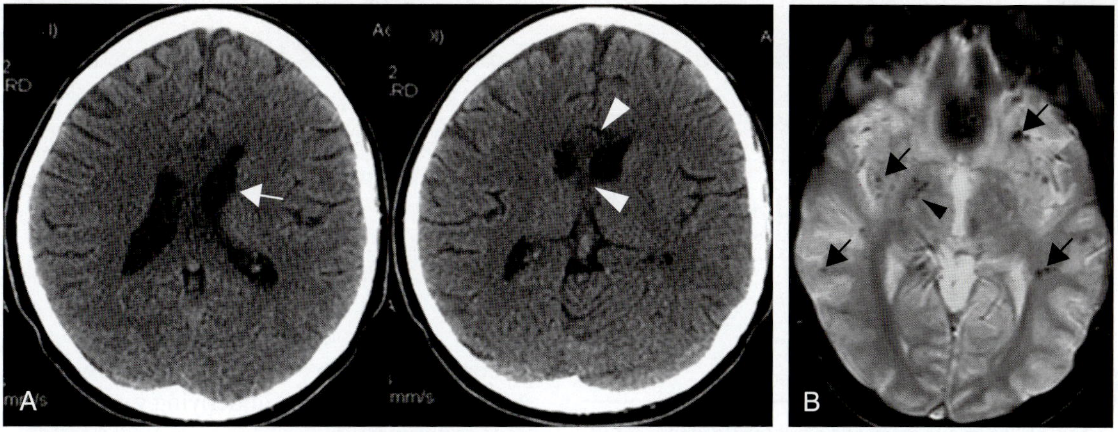

Fig. 62.1 Severe diffuse axonal injury. (A) Head CT reveals patchy hypodensities in the left caudothalamic region (*arrow*), and corpus callosum and fornix (*arrowheads*). (B) Brain MRI, axial SWI, shows multiple bilateral punctate microhemorrhages throughout the subcortical white matter (*arrows*) and basal ganglia (*arrowhead*).

IMAGING RED FLAGS

- Acute epidural, subdural, or subarachnoid hemorrhage.
- Cerebral edema with ventricular or sulcal effacement.
- Acute hemorrhage on CT or MRI involving the gray-white junction, corpus callosum, and brainstem structures.

CONCLUSIONS

Following trauma, immediate impairments in neurologic function and failure to recover baseline mentation within 24 hours should raise concern for moderate to severe TBI. Emergency head CT may reveal findings suggestive of both focal and diffuse traumatic injury, but brain MRI is the most sensitive diagnostic imaging test. Close follow-up can include ICP monitoring and neurosurgical intervention. Though the most profound clinical improvement occurs in the initial months postinjury, significant functional changes and improvements in quality of life are possible years later.

REFERENCES

Centers for Disease Control and Prevention. *Surveillance report of traumatic brain injury–related emergency department visits, hospitalizations, and deaths—United States, 2014*. U.S. Department of Health and Human Services; 2019. https://stacks.cdc.gov/view/cdc/78062.

Katz DI, Polyak M, Coughlan D, Nichols M, Roche A. Natural history of recovery from brain injury after prolonged disorders of consciousness: outcome of patients admitted to inpatient rehabilitation with 1–4 year follow-up. *Prog Brain Res*. 2009;177:73–88. https://doi.org/10.1016/S0079-6123(09)17707-5.

Ng SY, Lee AYW. Traumatic brain injuries: pathophysiology and potential therapeutic targets. *Front Cell Neurosci*. 2019;13:528. https://doi.org/10.3389/fncel.2019.00528.

Case 63

Moderate TBI: How to Tell?

HISTORY AND PHYSICAL

An 18-year-old man experienced a fall while intoxicated. He did not lose consciousness but became immediately disoriented with impaired orientation and ability to follow commands. He was lethargic and required ICU monitoring with frequent neuro checks, not regaining orientation to time until 4 days postinjury. He was able to transition back to his previous living situation but was notably more irritable. His alcohol use increased and he had difficulty verbalizing the potential consequences.

DIAGNOSTIC WORKUP

Brain MRI performed 2 days postinjury demonstrated a left orbital gyrus hemorrhagic contusion (Fig. 63.1).

CLINICAL DIFFERENTIAL DIAGNOSES

Alcohol intoxication or other recreational drugs, as well as prescription medications for pain or agitation, can contribute to altered consciousness after a fall.

Seizures, both early posttraumatic and withdrawal-related with postictal encephalopathy, can occur especially in the first 7 days following injury.

Peritraumatic hypoxic-ischemic injury can occur with a history of unresponsiveness, oxygen desaturation, or respiratory distress.

Clearing of confusion at less than 1 week distinguishes moderate from severe TBI.

IMAGING DIFFERENTIAL DIAGNOSES

Diffuse microhemorrhages can be seen in diffuse axonal injury (DAI), small vessel vasculopathies, and following radiation therapy.

Localized macro- and microhemorrhages may be seen in association with underlying vascular malformations or tumors.

FINAL DIAGNOSIS

Hemorrhagic contusion.

DISCUSSION

Low-impact head trauma tends to involve the fronto-orbital and anterior temporal lobes, with parenchymal contusions and/or hemorrhages. There may be a coup-contrecoup pattern related to the initial impact of the moving brain against the fixed bone and dura, followed by transmission of impact to the opposite side of the brain. Intraventricular hemorrhage may result in early- or late-onset hydrocephalus.

CLINICAL RED FLAGS

- Exposure to a direct force or blast causing acutely altered consciousness.
- Persistent decreased level of arousal lasting >30 minutes.
- Impaired cognition lasting more than 24 hours.
- Focally impaired motor activation or ataxia.
- Cranial nerve palsies.
- Pupillary asymmetry.

IMAGING RED FLAGS

- Acute epidural, subdural, or subarachnoid hemorrhage.
- Cerebral edema with ventricular or sulcal effacement.

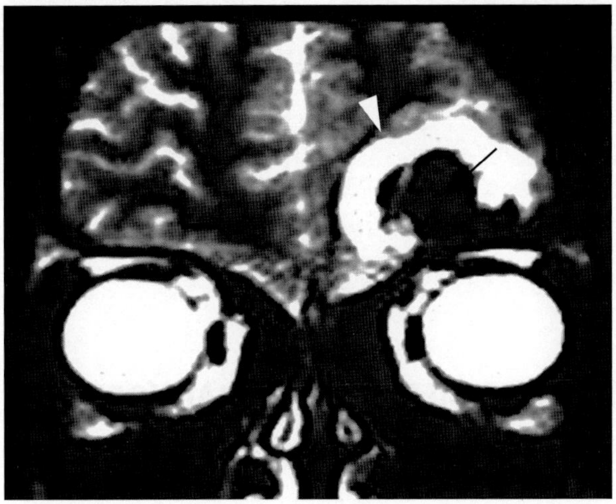

Fig. 63.1 Frontal hemorrhagic contusion. Brain MRI, coronal T2, shows left orbital gyrus contusion with edema (*arrowhead*) and central hypointense blood products (*arrow*).

CONCLUSIONS

TBI is caused by external conditions that result in force transmission to the brain parenchyma. The mechanisms of injury result in structural and functional brain changes of varying severities. This case represents a primarily focal injury resulting in disorientation and behavioral changes. A 1-year follow up of mild to moderate TBI survivors (GCS 9–14) showed a 40% prevalence of cognitive complaints and a 48% prevalence of behavioral problems, correlating significantly with similar complaints persisting at three months postinjury.

REFERENCES

Amin TA, Nerenberg SF, Elsawy OA, Wang A, Johnston JP. Evaluation of levetiracetam for early post-traumatic seizure prophylaxis: a level II trauma center experience. *Surgeon*. 2023;21(2):e78–e82. https://doi.org/10.1016/j.surge.2022.05.001.

van der Naalt J, van Zomeren AH, Sluiter WJ, Minderhoud JM. One year outcome in mild to moderate head injury: the predictive value of acute injury characteristics related to complaints and return to work. *J Neurol Neurosurg Psychiatry*. 1999;66(2):207–213. https://doi.org/10.1136/jnnp.66.2.207.

Case 64

Penetrating Injury

HISTORY AND PHYSICAL

An 18-year-old man was injured by a gunshot wound to the head. He was stabilized in the emergency department and underwent emergency craniotomy, with induced coma for the first 2 days postsurgery. He demonstrated no responsiveness under sedation on day 3, but within 24 hours improved to sustained alertness and could follow commands. He was able to walk without assistive devices and regained full orientation by 7.5 weeks. However, he remained passive, unconcerned with his situation, and predominantly spent his time watching television with irritability whenever interrupted. He required prompts to initiate necessary activities of daily living such as dressing and showering. He was able to learn new information but had poor judgment and problem-solving abilities. He displayed little inhibition when consuming food, new from before the injury. At 13 months post-injury, he was arrested for weapon possession during an outing with friends. In the years to follow, he returned home with the ability to maintain household independence but became paranoid with obsessive-compulsive disorder-like tendencies and a need to constantly check the security features of his residence.

DIAGNOSTIC WORKUP

Head CT showed bifrontal bone defects corresponding to entry and exit wounds, with edema and shrapnel traversing the frontal lobes (Fig. 64.1).

CLINICAL DIFFERENTIAL DIAGNOSES

Patients with penetrating head trauma can present with superimposed hypoxic-ischemic encephalopathy, seizures, medication effects, and vascular complications.

IMAGING DIFFERENTIAL DIAGNOSES

Skull fractures can occur with both blunt and penetrating head trauma.

Cerebral edema may be associated with hypoxic-ischemic brain injury and acute inflammatory and autoimmune processes.

Brain parenchymal tracts can be seen with penetrating trauma and neurosurgical interventions.

FINAL DIAGNOSIS

Penetrating gunshot injury.

DISCUSSION

Penetrating brain injury is a particularly concerning mechanism of TBI and affects thousands of individuals annually, though considerably rarer than nonpenetrating TBI. Of over 400,000 military TBIs tracked through the Department of Defense, only 10,255 were of a severe or penetrating type. The overall survival rate of veterans with penetrating brain injury, even those who present with a GCS score >8, is 18%.

Patients can also experience intracranial pressure changes, epilepsy, vasospasm, ischemic insults, and infection. Concurrent skull fractures are common and can affect both brain parenchyma and cranial nerves. Rare complications can include tension pneumocephalus, wound breakdown, and sinking skin flap syndrome following wide decompressive craniectomy.

CLINICAL RED FLAGS

- Exposure to a direct force or blast causing acutely altered consciousness.
- Persistent decreased level of arousal lasting >30 minutes.
- Impaired cognition lasting more than 24 hours.

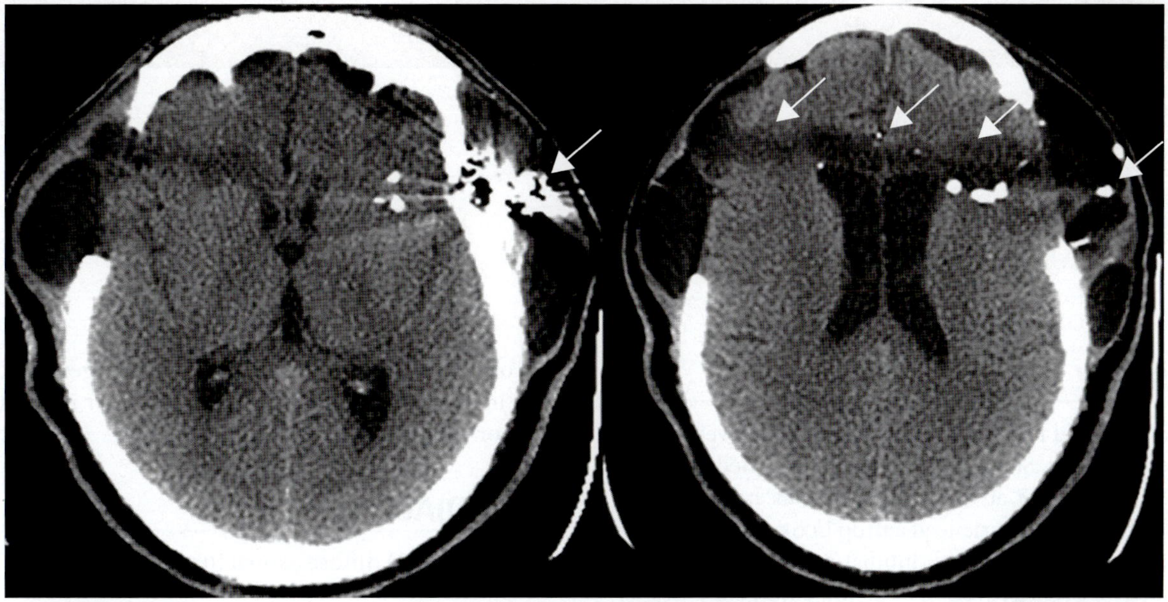

Fig. 64.1 Penetrating gunshot injury. Head CT shows bifrontal bone defects corresponding to entry and exit wounds, with edema and shrapnel traversing the frontal lobes (*arrows*). There are bilateral decompressive craniotomies associated with subgaleal fluid collections.

- Focally impaired motor activation or ataxia.
- Cranial nerve palsies.
- Pupillary asymmetry.
- Signs and symptoms of CNS or systemic infection.
- Symptoms of intracranial hypotension concerning for CSF leak.

IMAGING RED FLAGS

- Acute epidural, subdural, or subarachnoid hemorrhage.
- Cerebral edema with ventricular or sulcal effacement.
- Skull fractures.
- Intracranial foreign bodies.

CONCLUSIONS

Penetrating brain injury adds mechanistic and temporal complexity to the complex diagnosis of TBI. Frontal lobe trauma may feature apathy, abulia, attentional limitations, difficulties with executive function, processing speed, and retrieval, in addition to motor and premotor-based changes in functional performance. Loss of verbal fluency and comprehension, as well as naming inabilities, reflect injury to cortical and subcortical networks associated with the inferior frontal gyrus. Orbitofrontal injury may lead to problems with irritability and aggression.

REFERENCES

Department of Defense. DOD numbers for traumatic brain injury worldwide. 2023. https://health.mil/Military-Health-Topics/Centers-of-Excellence/Traumatic-Brain-Injury-Center-of-Excellence/DOD-TBI-Worldwide-Numbers.

Karras CL, Texakalidis P, Nie JZ, et al. Outcomes following penetrating brain injuries in military settings: a systematic review and meta-analysis. *World Neurosurg.* 2022;166:39–48. https://doi.org/10.1016/j.wneu.2022.07.062.

Case 65

Pedestrian Struck

HISTORY AND PHYSICAL

A 17-year-old female was struck by a motor vehicle and thrown 15 feet. She lost consciousness immediately, and GCS remained 3 at the scene. She was hemodynamically stable but experienced a drop in oxygen saturation, which was remedied with intubation and supplemental oxygen. GCS improved to 7 in the emergency department. By hospital day 3, she began displaying purposeful movements on the right side and localizing sounds. She could track approximately 1 week later and consistently followed commands 12 days after injury. She began participating in rehabilitative therapies, but participation was limited by frequent episodes of agitation. Depakote and Seroquel were added to her medications and improved the behavioral changes. After transferring to an acute rehabilitation facility, she later returned home with 24-hour supervision.

DIAGNOSTIC WORKUP

Brain MRI showed multifocal microhemorrhages throughout the cerebrum and brainstem (Fig. 65.1).

CLINICAL DIFFERENTIAL DIAGNOSES

Global cerebral injury can be seen with trauma, hypoxic-ischemic injury, seizures, recreational drugs, and medication effects. Posttraumatic ischemia and hemorrhage can result from vascular injury, vasospasm, and increased ICP.

IMAGING DIFFERENTIAL DIAGNOSES

Diffuse microhemorrhages can be seen in DAI, small vessel vasculopathies, and following radiation therapy.

Localized macro- and microhemorrhages may be seen in association with underlying vascular malformations or tumors.

FINAL DIAGNOSIS

Severe (grade 3) diffuse axonal injury.

DISCUSSION

The most severe forms of TBI involve DAI secondary to an external force, either direct impact or blast wave. Emergency head CT may show suggestive features, but brain MRI with SWI (3D) or GRE (2D) is more sensitive for microhemorrhages and small areas of parenchymal injury. MRI also helps in detection of underlying lesions, such as vascular malformations or neoplasms, that can be complicated by hemorrhage.

CLINICAL RED FLAGS

- Exposure to a direct force or blast causing acutely altered consciousness.
- Persistent decreased level of arousal lasting >30 minutes.
- Impaired cognition lasting more than 24 hours.
- Focally impaired motor activation or ataxia.
- Cranial nerve palsies.
- Pupillary asymmetry.

IMAGING RED FLAGS

- Acute epidural, subdural, or subarachnoid hemorrhage.
- Cerebral edema with ventricular or sulcal effacement.

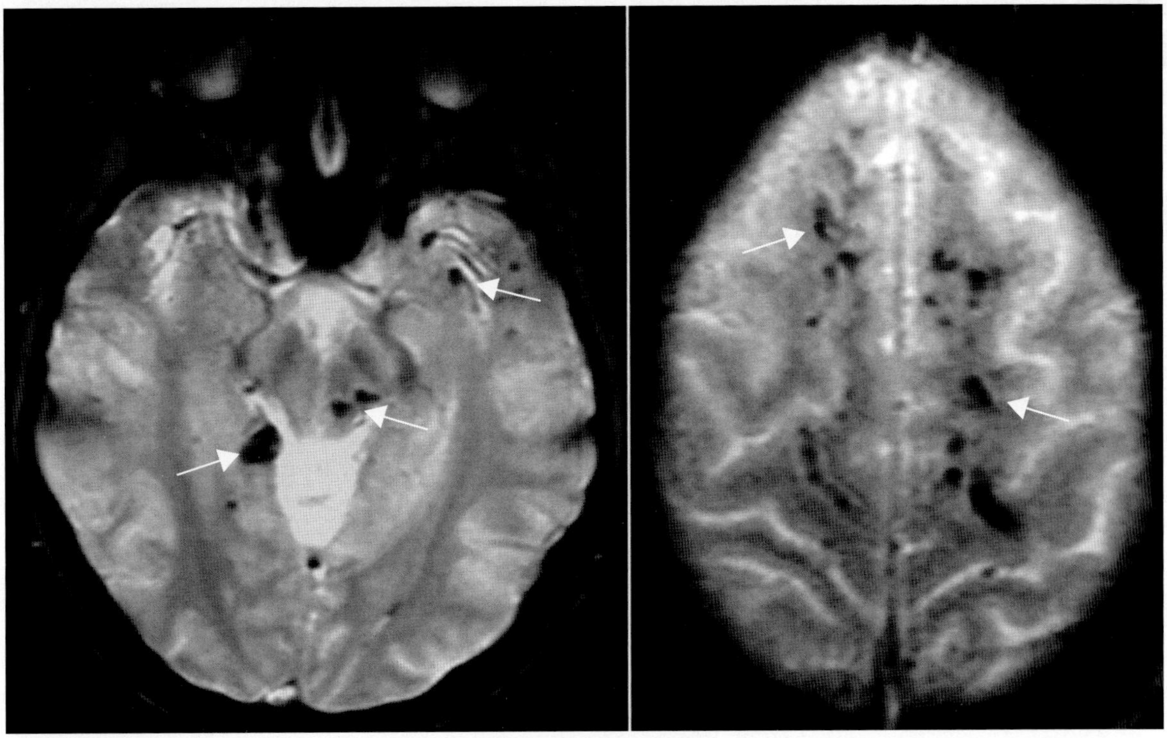

Fig. 65.1 Severe diffuse axonal injury. Brain MRI, axial SWI, shows petechial hemorrhages throughout the left greater than right subcortical white matter and midbrain (*arrows*).

CONCLUSIONS

Moderate to severe TBI, featuring more than 30 minutes of unconsciousness and more than 24 hours of confusion, usually shows multiple abnormalities on imaging. When diffuse subcortical network disruption is present, especially involving the frontal and temporal lobes, patients can experience impaired insight and ability to retain situational understanding and respect safety parameters. Mood-stabilizing or antipsychotic medications may be helpful but should be used appropriately and with care.

REFERENCES

Awad IA, Polster SP. Cavernous angiomas: deconstructing a neurosurgical disease. *J Neurosurg*. 2019;131(1):1–13. https://doi.org/10.3171/2019.3.JNS181724.

Babikian T, Freier MC, Tong KA, et al. Susceptibility weighted imaging: neuropsychologic outcome and pediatric head injury. *Pediatr Neurol*. 2005;33(3):184–194. https://doi.org/10.1016/j.pediatrneurol.2005.03.015.

Han SW, Shin JH, Ihn YK, Yang SH, Sung JH. Comparison of single- and multi-echo susceptibility-weighted imaging in detecting cerebral arteriovenous shunts: a preliminary study. *J Korean Soc Radiol*. 2023;84(1):226–239. https://doi.org/10.3348/jksr.2022.0080.

Katz DI, Dwyer B. Clinical neurorehabilitation: using principles of neurological diagnosis, prognosis, and neuroplasticity in assessment and treatment planning. *Semin Neurol*.2021;41(2):111–123.https://doi.org/10.1055/s-0041-1725132.

Case 66

The Dreaded Epidural

HISTORY AND PHYSICAL

A 16-year-old male fell while skateboarding and lost consciousness for an unknown period of time, with concern for subsequent tonic seizure. He was taken to the nearest emergency room. Initial GCS was 14/15.

DIAGNOSTIC WORKUP

Head CT showed right squamous temporal bone fracture with epidural hematoma and midline shift (Fig. 66.1). He was taken immediately to the operating room for decompression, as his mental status deteriorated overnight.

CLINICAL DIFFERENTIAL DIAGNOSES

Severe headaches can be seen with various conditions including intracranial hemorrhage, infection, tumors, stroke, seizure, migraine, and autoimmune conditions.

IMAGING DIFFERENTIAL DIAGNOSES

Extra-axial hyperdensities with mass effect include epidural and subdural hematoma, tumors, and infection.

FINAL DIAGNOSIS

Epidural hematoma.

DISCUSSION

Epidural hematomas usually occur in the setting of skull fractures with injury to the middle meningeal artery. This condition occurs in 1% to 4% of head injuries and is more common in young male adults. Occasionally, hemorrhage can occur spontaneously or with minor trauma due to a bleeding disorder or vascular malformation. Treatment involves urgent decompressive craniotomy or burr hole to prevent fatal brain herniation.

CLINICAL RED FLAGS

- Focal head trauma and skull fracture.
- History of brief loss of consciousness followed by a lucid interval, usually lasting between 30 minutes and several hours, before becoming somnolent again.
- Abnormal neurological findings include altered mental status, coma, seizures, anisocoria, hemiparesis, hyperreflexia, and Babinski sign.
- Cushing triad: hypertension, bradycardia, and respiratory abnormalities are signs of increased ICP.

IMAGING RED FLAGS

- Head CT showing skull fracture with subjacent biconvex or lenticular hyperdensity that does not cross sutures.
- Cervical spine CT and/or MRI can demonstrate extension of blood products.

CONCLUSIONS

Epidural hematoma is a neurosurgical emergency, and delayed diagnosis is associated with mortality rates over 15%. These are best managed by a multidisciplinary team, with the key prognostic feature being the level of consciousness at time of presentation. Infratentorial or bilateral supratentorial location carries a very high mortality.

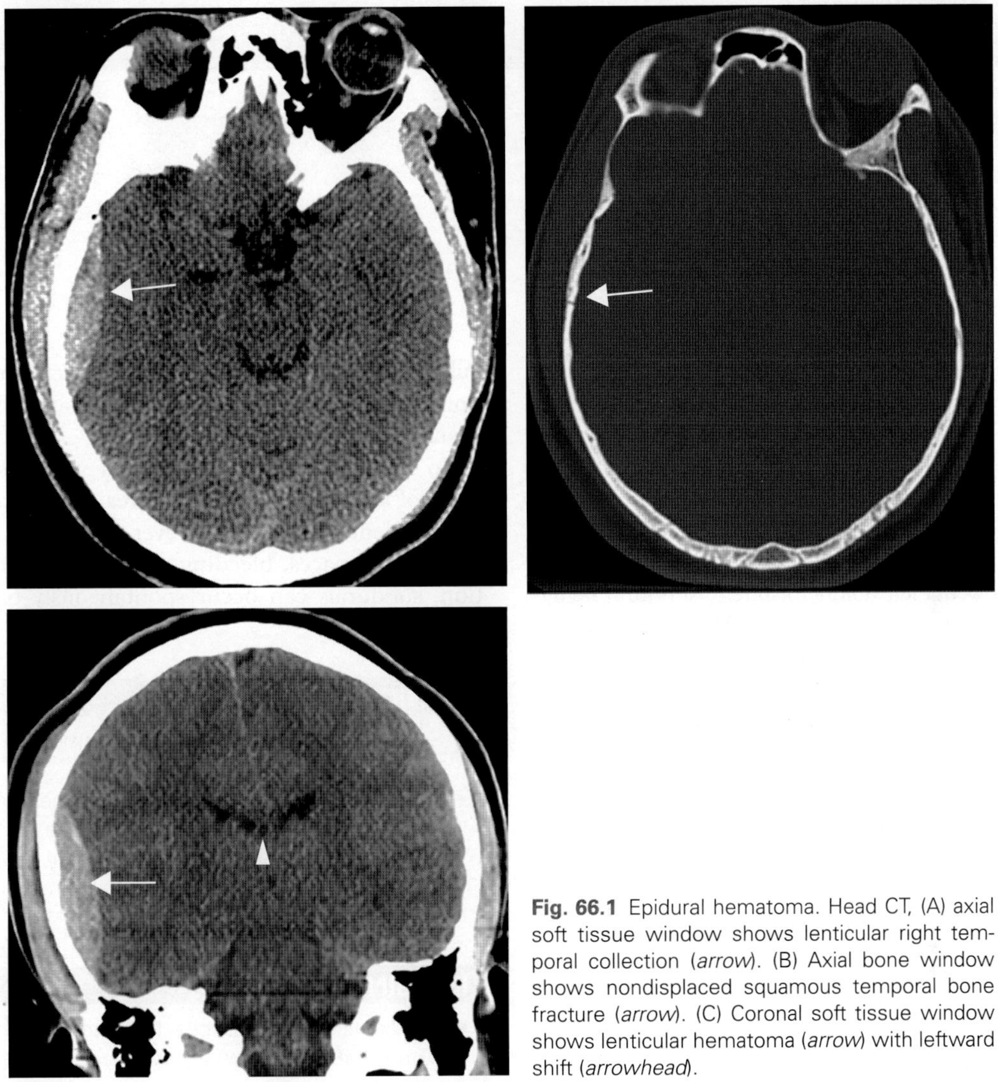

Fig. 66.1 Epidural hematoma. Head CT, (A) axial soft tissue window shows lenticular right temporal collection (*arrow*). (B) Axial bone window shows nondisplaced squamous temporal bone fracture (*arrow*). (C) Coronal soft tissue window shows lenticular hematoma (*arrow*) with leftward shift (*arrowhead*).

REFERENCES

Baker CM, Cox AP, Hunsaker JC, Scoville J, Bollo RJ. Postoperative magnetic resonance imaging may predict poor outcome in children with severe traumatic brain injuries who undergo cranial surgery. *J Neurosurg Pediatr*. 2022. https://doi.org/10.3171/2021.11.PEDS21486.

D'Andrea M, Mongardi L, Cultrera F, et al. Calcified epidural hematoma after conservative treatment of acute epidural hematoma in the pediatric population: a systematic review. *Pediatr Neurosurg*. 2022;57(6):389–395. https://doi.org/10.1159/000527241.

Landart M, Benichi S, Guida L, et al. Cerebral ischemia: a frequent complication of large traumatic epidural hematoma in infants. *J Neurosurg Pediatr*. 2023. https://doi.org/10.3171/2023.1.PEDS22324.

Shope C, Alshareef M, Larrew T, et al. Utility of a pediatric fast magnetic resonance imaging protocol as surveillance scanning for traumatic brain injury. *J Neurosurg Pediatr*. 2021;27(4):475–481. https://doi.org/10.3171/2020.8.PEDS20496.

Young JY, Duhaime AC, Caruso PA, Rincon SP. Comparison of non-sedated brain MRI and CT for the detection of acute traumatic injury in children 6 years of age or less. *Emerg Radiol*. 2016;23(4):325–331. https://doi.org/10.1007/s10140-016-1392-3.

Case 67

Spectrum of Subdurals

HISTORY AND PHYSICAL

A 16-year-old male experienced head injury while playing tackle football, followed by increasing headache.

DIAGNOSTIC WORKUP

Head CT showed a left holohemispheric subdural hematoma with rightward shift (Fig. 67.1). The patient went to the operating room for decompression.

CLINICAL DIFFERENTIAL DIAGNOSES

Posttraumatic headache can be seen with intracranial hemorrhage, infarct, infection, seizures, and autoimmune conditions.

IMAGING DIFFERENTIAL DIAGNOSES

Posttraumatic intracranial hemorrhage can be epidural, subdural, subarachnoid, and/or parenchymal.

Other extra-axial conditions with mass effect include tumors and infection.

FINAL DIAGNOSIS

Subdural hematoma.

DISCUSSION

Subdural hematomas result from cortical venous injury with collection of blood products between the dura and arachnoid mater. They have a crescentic morphology that can cross sutures and track along dural reflections. Subdural hematomas are usually characterized by location, size and mass effect, and time since the inciting event (acute, subacute, chronic).

In children with normal brain volumes, development of subdurals usually requires severe accidental or nonaccidental trauma. However, in patients with large extra-axial spaces, bleeding disorders, or anticoagulation, subdurals can occur spontaneously or following minor trauma.

CLINICAL RED FLAGS

- Subdural hematomas can appear immediately or up to 4 weeks after an injury.
- In infants with malleable sutures, there may be a marked increase in head circumference.
- Abusive head trauma (AHT) can present with subdural hematomas, hygromas, and retinal hemorrhages.

IMAGING RED FLAGS

- Crescentic extra-axial collection that crosses sutures.
- CT and MRI characteristics vary according to the age of the blood products.

CONCLUSIONS

Posttraumatic subdural hematomas can develop with an acute, subacute, or chronic time course. Not every subdural hematoma requires neurosurgical intervention, and management depends on patient age, clinical course, and complications. Mortality rates range from 42% to 90%, and most patients will need long-term follow-up.

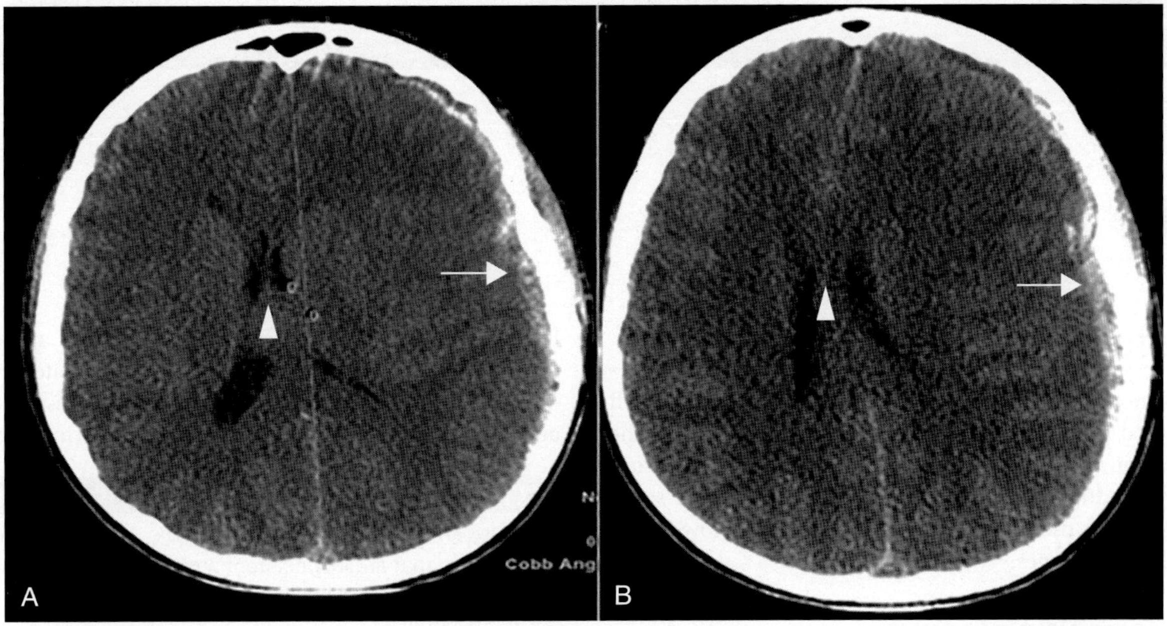

Fig. 67.1 Subdural hematoma. (A-B) Head CT shows left holohemispheric subdural crescentic hyperdensity (*arrows*) with rightward shift (*arrowheads*).

REFERENCES

Akie TE, Gupta M, Rodriguez RM, et al. Physical examination sensitivity for skull fracture in pediatric patients with blunt head trauma: a secondary analysis of the national emergency X-Radiography Utilization Study II Head Computed Tomography Validation Study. *Ann Emerg Med.* 2023;81(3):334–342. https://doi.org/10.1016/j.annemergmed.2022.08.442.

Akutsu N, Nonaka M, Narisawa A, Kato M, Harada A, Park YS. Infantile subdural hematoma in Japan: a multicenter, retrospective study by the J-HITs (Japanese head injury of infants and toddlers study) group. *PLoS One.* 2022;17(2):e0264396.https://doi.org/10.1371/journal.pone.0264396.

Aoki N. Clinical and neuroimaging characteristics in mild-type infantile acute subdural hematoma: report of four cases. *Childs Nerv Syst.* 2023. https://doi.org/10.1007/s00381-023-06089-7.

Iwamura H, Nonaka M, Komori Y, Miyata M, Kamei T, Asai A. Newborn with severe supratentorial subdural hematoma due to laceration of the tentorium cerebelli. *Childs Nerv Syst.* 2023;39(1):261–264. https://doi.org/10.1007/s00381-022-05588-3.

Vilanilam GK, Jayappa S, Desai S, Zuccoli G, Ramakrishnaiah RH, Choudhary AK. Venous injury in pediatric abusive head trauma: a pictorial review. *Pediatr Radiol.* 2021;51(6):918–926. https://doi.org/10.1007/s00247-021-05016-9.

Case 68

The Killer Bed

HISTORY AND PHYSICAL

A 6-month-old, ex-full-term baby girl reportedly fell off her bed from a height of 2 feet. The parents went to the emergency department because of her irritability and poor feeding. Neurological examination showed some bruising in the dorsal thorax. Fundoscopy showed retinal hemorrhages.

DIAGNOSTIC WORKUP

Head CT showed bilateral mixed-density subdural hematomas at the vertex (Fig. 68.1). Skeletal survey showed a left radial fracture.

CLINICAL DIFFERENTIAL DIAGNOSES

Retinal hemorrhages can be seen in AHT but also in 40% of vaginally delivered newborns (resolving within 1 month), coagulopathies, sepsis, osteogenesis imperfecta, glutaric aciduria type 1, and Menkes disease.

IMAGING DIFFERENTIAL DIAGNOSES

Subdural hematomas can be seen in association with AHT, traumatic deliveries, coagulopathies, vasculopathies, vascular malformations, and infections.

FINAL DIAGNOSIS

Abusive head trauma (AHT).

DISCUSSION

Child abuse unfortunately remains common throughout the world. In 2021, there were 588,229 reported cases of child abuse in the United States, with the most common form of maltreatment being neglect. In the first year of life, the incidence of AHT is estimated to be approximately 35 cases per 100,000 infants. Approximately 65% of children experience significant neurological disabilities, and between 5% and 35% of infants die of their injuries.

CLINICAL RED FLAGS

- Delayed clinical presentation, with symptoms and findings that are inconsistent and/or out of proportion with reported mechanism.
- Increased ICP.
- Withdrawal from friends or usual activities, changes in behavior (e.g., aggression, anger, hostility, or hyperactivity), changes in school performance, depression, anxiety or unusual fears, sudden loss of self-confidence, sleep problems and nightmares.

IMAGING RED FLAGS

- Fractures on skeletal survey, particularly in high-probability areas (requiring large forces) and of different ages. In nonmobile children, rib, long bone, and metaphyseal fractures have a high correlation with child abuse. Fractures of the extremities are the most common skeletal injury in children who have been abused, with approximately 80% seen in children under 18 months old.
- Intracranial abnormalities such as cerebral edema or ischemia, subdural and/or subarachnoid hemorrhage, especially if of different ages. Brain MRI can be helpful in identifying blood products, retinal hemorrhages, and hypoxic-ischemic injury, as well as more subtle features including parenchymal, craniovertebral junction, and spinal injuries. The "lollipop" or "tadpole" sign (Fig. 68.2) on SWI represents cortical and bridging venous injury with interruption and thrombosis. Acute dural lacerations and/or chronic hematomas may be associated with serous fluid (hygromas).
- Genetic disorders and vasculopathies can sometimes predispose to brain volume loss and friable vessels with hemorrhage. However, these diagnoses require confirmation with genetic and laboratory testing and also do not exclude the possibility of abuse.

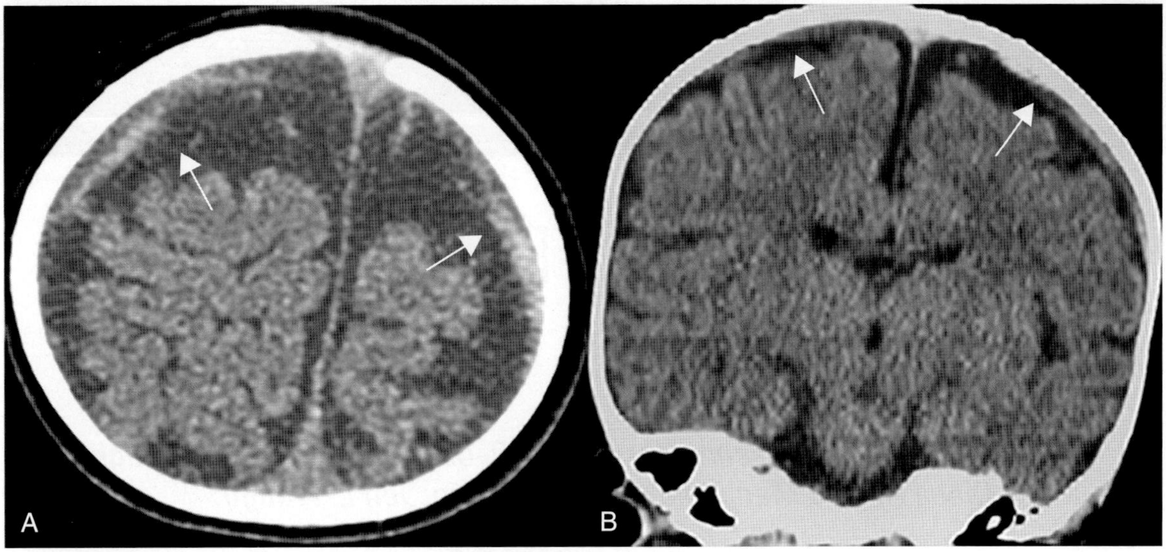

Fig. 68.1 Abusive head trauma. Head CT, (A) axial and (B) coronal show bilateral mixed-density subdural hematomas at the vertex (*arrows*) with irregularity of bridging veins.

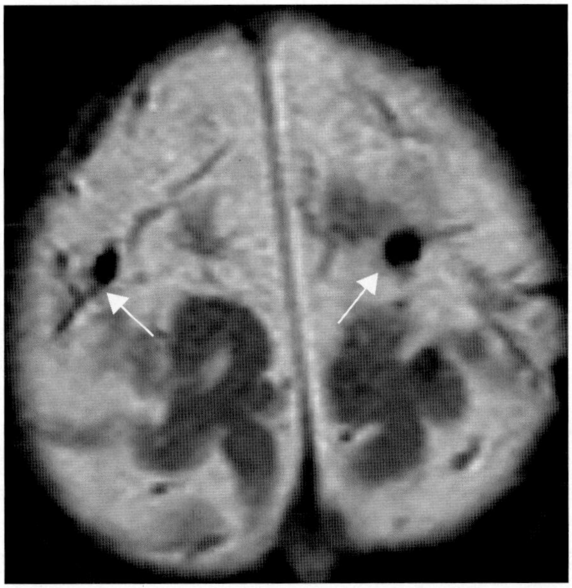

Fig. 68.2 Abusive head trauma. Brain MRI, axial T2, showing bridging venous injury with thrombosis (*arrows*) and interruption.

CONCLUSIONS

AHT is the most common cause of subdural hematomas in children under 2 years of age. The presence of retinal hemorrhages, bone and rib fractures, delayed and inconsistent presentation, and young age are all concerning features.

REFERENCES

Dasgupta D, Elhusseiny AM, Phillips PH, et al. Utility of balanced steady-state field precession sequence in the evaluation of retinal and subdural hemorrhages in patients with abusive head trauma. *Pediatr Radiol.* 2023;53(9):1842–1853. https://doi.org/10.1007/s00247-023-05614-9.

Hahnemann ML, Kronsbein K, Karger B, et al. Characterization of subdural collections in initial neuroimaging of abusive head trauma: implications for forensic age diagnostics and clinical decision-making. *Eur J Radiol.* 2023;159:110652. https://doi.org/10.1016/j.ejrad.2022.110652.

Kato M, Nonaka M, Akutsu N, Narisawa A, Harada A, Park YS. Correlations of intracranial pathology and cause of head injury with retinal hemorrhage in infants and toddlers: a multicenter, retrospective study by the J-HITs (Japanese Head injury of Infants and Toddlers study) Group. *PLoS One.* 2023;18(3):e0283297. https://doi.org/10.1371/journal.pone.0283297.

Pendharkar H, Jabeen S, Pruthi N, et al. Abusive head trauma in India: imaging raises the curtain. *Int J Inj Contr Saf Promot.* 2022;29(1):103–111. https://doi.org/10.1080/17457300.2021.2007955.

Raissaki M, Adamsbaum C, Argyropoulou MI, et al. Benign enlargement of the subarachnoid spaces and subdural collections-when to evaluate for abuse. *Pediatr Radiol.* 2023;53(4):752–767. https://doi.org/10.1007/s00247-023-05611-y.

SECTION 14

Movement Disorders and Ataxia

Angeles Schteinschnaider, Martín D. Carnevale, Micaela Chinigioli, Diana Ángulo Manchola, Rocio E. Alamo, Jeff L. Waugh

INTRODUCTION

Pediatric movement disorders (PMDs) comprise a large group of disorders (tics, myoclonus, tremor, dystonia, chorea, Parkinsonism, ataxia), often with mixed phenotypes. The broad differential diagnosis and complexity of genotype–phenotype relationships can make the diagnostic process time-consuming and difficult.

The diagnostic approach for PMDs includes several steps: recognition of distinct movement disorders (MDs), identification of clinical syndromes, consideration of genetic or acquired causes, and making findings on neuroimaging.

Various neuroimaging alterations have been described for MDs, and MRI findings can assist in ruling an etiological diagnosis in or out. For example, SWI allows for detection of biometal deposition. Diffusion-weighted imaging (DWI) can assess acute energy failure in the setting of metabolic disorders. A few imaging features are pathognomonic for specific disorders. More commonly, the combination of imaging and clinical features helps guide more efficient diagnostic workup. Arriving at an etiological diagnosis is critical for identification of potential targeted therapeutic tools.

In this chapter, we discuss various causes of PMDs, their differential diagnoses, and the importance of neuroimaging in determining etiology.

SUGGESTED READINGS

Barkovich AJ, Raybaud C. *Pediatric Neuroimaging*. Wolters Kluwer; 2019.

Brandsma R, van Egmond ME, Tijssen MAJ, Groningen Movement Disorder Expertise Centre. Diagnostic approach to paediatric movement disorders: a clinical practice guide. *Dev Med Child Neurol*. 2021 Mar;63(3):252–258.

Fernandez-Alvarez E, Arzimanoglou A, Tolosa E. Paediatric movement disorders: progress in understanding. *John Libbey Eurotext*. 2005 1 Jan.ISBN-10 : 2742005420 ISBN-13 : 978-2742005420.

Kurian MA, Dale RC. Movement disorders presenting in childhood. *Continuum (Minneap Minn)*. 2016 Aug;22:1159–1185 (4 Movement Disorders).

Pearson TS, Pons R. Movement disorders in children. *Continuum (Minneap Minn)*. 2019 Aug;25(4):1099–1120.

Petley E, Prasad M, Ojha S, Whitehouse WP. Investigating ataxia in childhood. *Arch Dis Child Educ Pract Ed*. 2020 Aug;105(4):214–221.

Case 69

Ataxic and Metallic

HISTORY AND PHYSICAL

A 10-year-old female with a history of developmental delay since the first year of life developed gait instability and nystagmus at the age of 3, followed by progressive motor and language regression. There was no relevant family or perinatal history.

Neurologic examination revealed horizontal nystagmus, axial hypotonia, dysmetria, and tremor of the upper limbs. Additionally, there was spastic quadriparesis with pyramidal signs. The patient had a visual connection with the environment but lacked verbal language.

DIAGNOSTIC WORKUP

Laboratory testing for ceruloplasmin, copper, alpha-fetoprotein, cholesterol, vitamin levels, and albumin were all within normal ranges. Intermediary metabolism studies showed no significant alterations. Laboratory evaluation, including lipofuscinosis and congenital disorders of glycosylation, was unremarkable.

Genetic consultation was requested. Karyotype was normal 46, XX. DNA methylation and genetic testing for Friedrich ataxia and Fragile X syndrome were negative. Electromyography and nerve conduction studies showed axonal compromise of the sciatic and popliteal nerves.

Serial brain MRI between 2 and 5 years of age demonstrated progressive cerebellar atrophy (Figs. 69.1 and 69.2). By 10 years of age, cerebral atrophy had also developed, with excessive mineralization in the bilateral globus pallidus and substantia nigra (Fig. 69.3). Targeted genetic testing revealed a pathogenic variant in the Phospholipase A_2-group VI (*PLA2G6*) gene.

CLINICAL DIFFERENTIAL DIAGNOSES

Differential diagnoses for degenerative cerebellar ataxia with progressive motor involvement include various genetic conditions: Friedrich ataxia, ataxia with oculomotor apraxia, ataxia-telangiectasia, congenital glycosylation disorders, and Niemann-Pick disease type C.

Pediatric neurodegenerative diseases associated with iron accumulation are known as neurodegeneration with brain iron accumulation (NBIA). Pantothenate kinase-associated neurodegeneration (PKAN), also known as Hallevorden-Spatz syndrome or NBIA type 1, is characterized by dystonic involvement and retinal abnormalities. *PLA2G6*-associated neurodegeneration (PLAN) features variable degrees of psychomotor regression, optic atrophy, and peripheral nerve axonal compromise.

IMAGING DIFFERENTIAL DIAGNOSIS

Progressive cerebellar atrophy followed by global cerebral atrophy can be seen in genetic conditions such as Friedreich ataxia, ataxia-telangiectasia, spinocerebellar ataxia, and neuronal ceroid lipofuscinosis.

Excessive mineralization in the deep gray nuclei can be seen due to iron, calcium, copper, manganese, and other biometals. On MRI, PKAN shows an "eye-of-the-tiger" sign with globus pallidus mineralization and gliosis. PLAN features prominent cerebellar atrophy as the first manifestation, typically followed by mineralization of the globi pallidi and substantia nigra.

FINAL DIAGNOSIS

PLA2G6-associated neurodegeneration, previously known as neuroaxonal dystrophy.

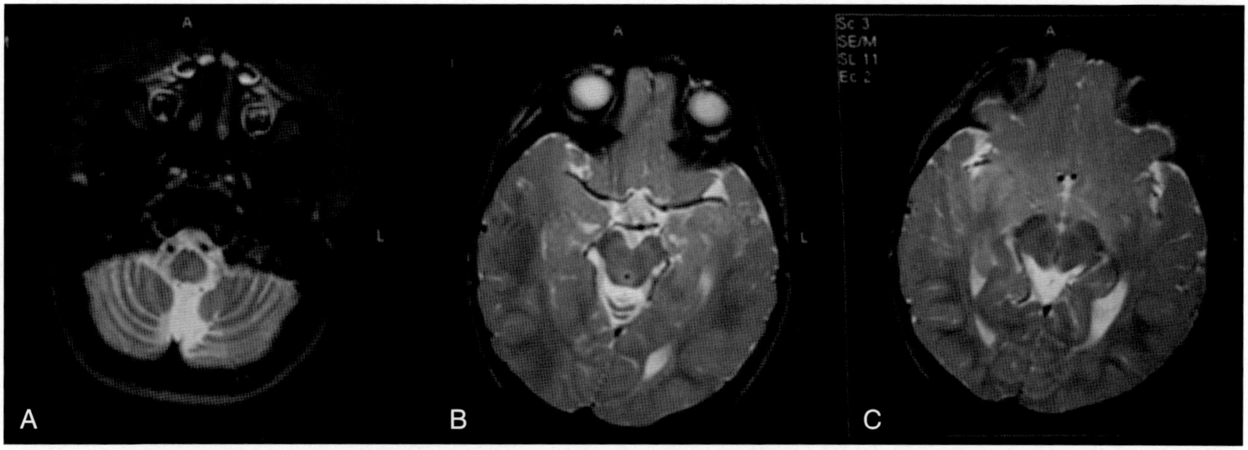

Fig. 69.1 *PLA2G6*-associated neurodegeneration. Brain MRI at 2 years of age. Axial T2 with fat suppression shows (A) cerebellar atrophy and (B and C) mild hypointense mineralization of substantia nigra and globus pallidus.

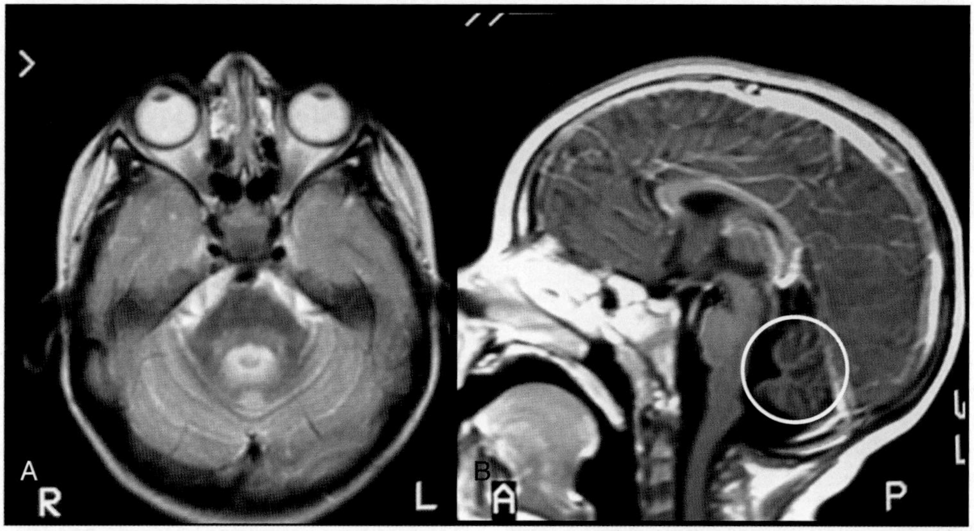

Fig. 69.2 *PLA2G6*-associated neurodegeneration. Brain MRI at 5 years. (A) Axial T2 and (B) sagittal postcontrast T1 show progression of cerebellar atrophy (*circle*).

DISCUSSION

PLAN is an autosomal recessive disorder caused by mutations in the *PLA2G6* gene encoding calcium-independent phospholipase A_2, crucial for cell membrane homeostasis. Depending on the nature and severity of the mutation, there is a broad phenotypic spectrum from early childhood psychomotor regression (infantile and atypical neuroaxonal dystrophy) to adult-onset dystonia-parkinsonism. Peripheral nerve axonal compromise is characteristic. In childhood-onset PLAN, symptoms begin between 6 months and 3 years with developmental regression, cerebellar ataxia, hypotonia, and spastic tetraparesis. Visual deficits and seizures are common.

On imaging, cerebellar atrophy is the earliest manifestation of disease. This can be followed by cerebral atrophy and brain iron accumulation later in the disease course, usually within the globus pallidus and substantia nigra.

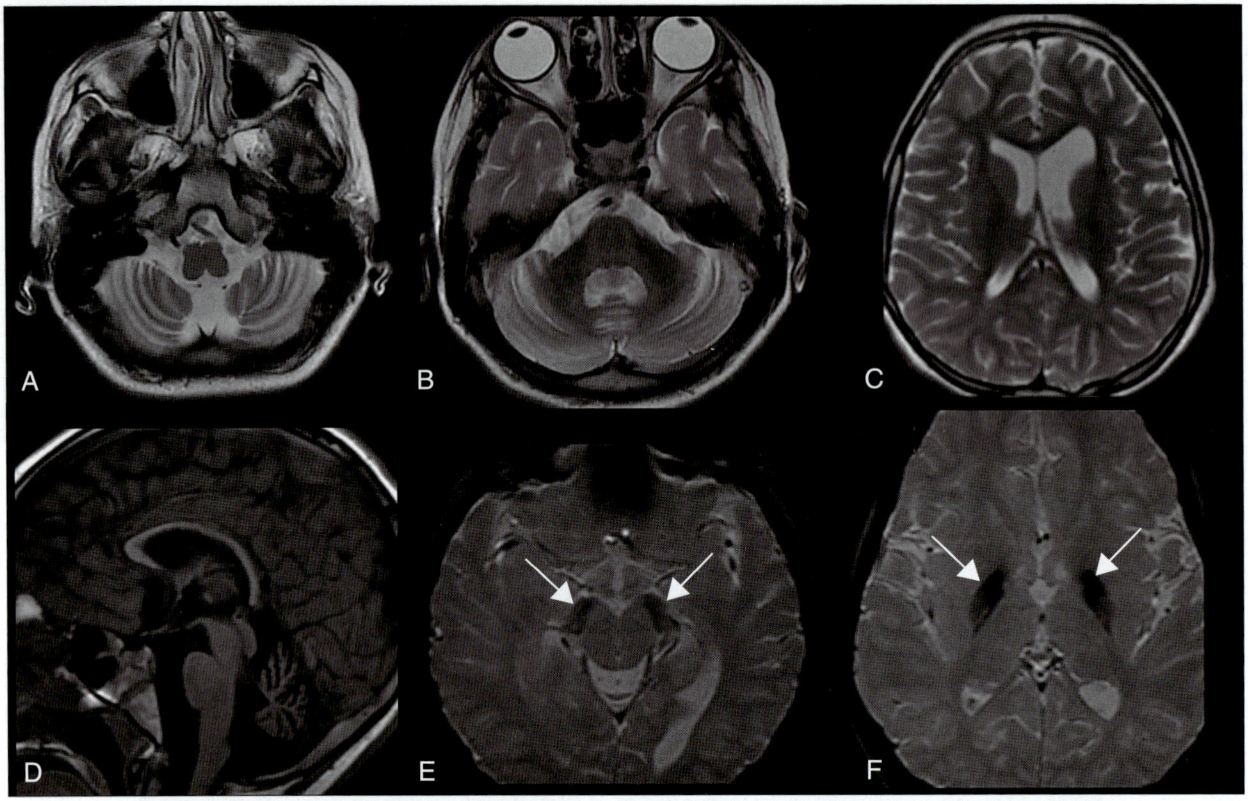

Fig. 69.3 *PLA2G6*-associated neurodegeneration. Brain MRI at 10 years. (A–C) Axial T2 and (D) sagittal T1 show further progression of cerebellar and global atrophy. (E–F) Axial GRE shows susceptibility in the substantia nigra and globi pallidi (*arrows*). *GRE*, Gradient echo.

CLINICAL RED FLAGS

- Cerebellar ataxia accompanied by motor/cognitive neurodevelopmental regression and peripheral axonal compromise.

IMAGING RED FLAGS

- Early cerebellar atrophy.
- Delayed cerebral atrophy.
- Brain iron deposition in the globi pallidi and substantia nigra is a late manifestation.

CONCLUSIONS

Neurodegenerative disorders associated with iron accumulation are rare but should be considered in cases of early-onset cerebellar ataxia with progressive neurodevelopmental deterioration. Peripheral nerve compromise raises clinical suspicion for PLAN. It is essential to recognize that mineral accumulations on MRI may present later in the disease.

REFERENCES

Deng X, Yuan L, Jankovic J, Deng H. The role of the PLA2G6 gene in neurodegenerative diseases. *Ageing Res Rev*. 2023;89:101957. doi:10.1016/j.arr.2023.101957.

Hayflick S, et al. Neurodegeneration with brain iron accumulation. *Handb Clin Neurol*. 2018;147:293–305.

Kruer MC, et al. Neuroimaging features of neurodegeneration with brain iron accumulation. *AJNR Am J Neuroradiol*. 2012;33(3):407–414.

Krygier M, et al. Milestones in genetics of cerebellar ataxias. *Neurogenetics*. 2021 Oct;22(4):225–234.

Kuo SH. Ataxia. *Continuum (Minneap Minn)*. 2019;25(4):1036–1054.

Witek NP, et al. Genetic ataxias: update on classification and diagnostic approaches. *Curr Neurol Neurosci Rep*. 2021;21(3):13.

Yellow and Drooling

HISTORY AND PHYSICAL

A 15-year-old male patient with no relevant family or personal history presented with mild jaundice and fatigue for several months. Subsequently, he developed progressive sialorrhea, dysarthria, motor clumsiness, fine generalized tremors, and declining academic performance.

Physical examination revealed bradylalia, impaired prosody, subtle head titubation, generalized fine tremor, and bradykinesia. He exhibited left-hand dystonia and absence of arm swing during walking.

DIAGNOSTIC WORKUP

Complete blood count (CBC) revealed anemia and thrombocytopenia. Liver function tests (LFTs) were mildly elevated. There were decreased serum copper and ceruloplasmin levels as well as increased 24-hour cupruria.

Ophthalmologic examination with slit lamp revealed bilateral Kayser-Fleischer rings.

Abdominal ultrasound (US) showed splenomegaly.

Brain MRI showed diffuse T2/fluid-attenuated inversion recovery (FLAIR) hyperintensity in the bilateral basal ganglia and brainstem, with increased susceptibility in the putamina, substantia nigra, and red nuclei (Fig. 70.1).

CLINICAL DIFFERENTIAL DIAGNOSES

Jaundice and neurologic signs can be seen in various forms of liver disease.

Acute liver injury has various etiologies including toxic, viral, and autoimmune hepatitis.

Chronic hepatitis can occur with or without cirrhosis. This can be sporadic or genetic, such as in Wilson disease (WD) or hemochromatosis.

Movement disorders can be caused by essential tremor, early-onset Parkinson disease, and generalized dystonia.

Psychiatric manifestations in WD include depression, bipolar disorder, schizophrenia, dementia, and substance use disorder.

IMAGING DIFFERENTIAL DIAGNOSES

Bilateral basal ganglia and brainstem abnormalities are seen in metabolic, infectious, and autoimmune conditions.

Metabolic diagnoses include mitochondrial diseases with basal ganglia involvement, such as Leigh syndrome. In acute episodes, there is usually more diffusion restriction and lactate peak on magnetic resonance spectroscopy (MRS). Disorders of biometal regulation (copper, iron, calcium) can present with increased susceptibility in the deep gray nuclei and variable signal abnormalities.

Viral or autoimmune encephalitis may affect the basal ganglia and brainstem, with mild edema and no or minimal enhancement. Susceptibility is not a characteristic imaging feature, except in cases of hemorrhagic transformation.

FINAL DIAGNOSIS

Wilson disease.

DISCUSSION

WD, also known as hepatolenticular degeneration, is an autosomal recessive genetic disorder caused by defects in the *ATP7B* gene impairing function of the intracellular copper transporter, leading to reduced copper biliary excretion and accumulation in various organs including

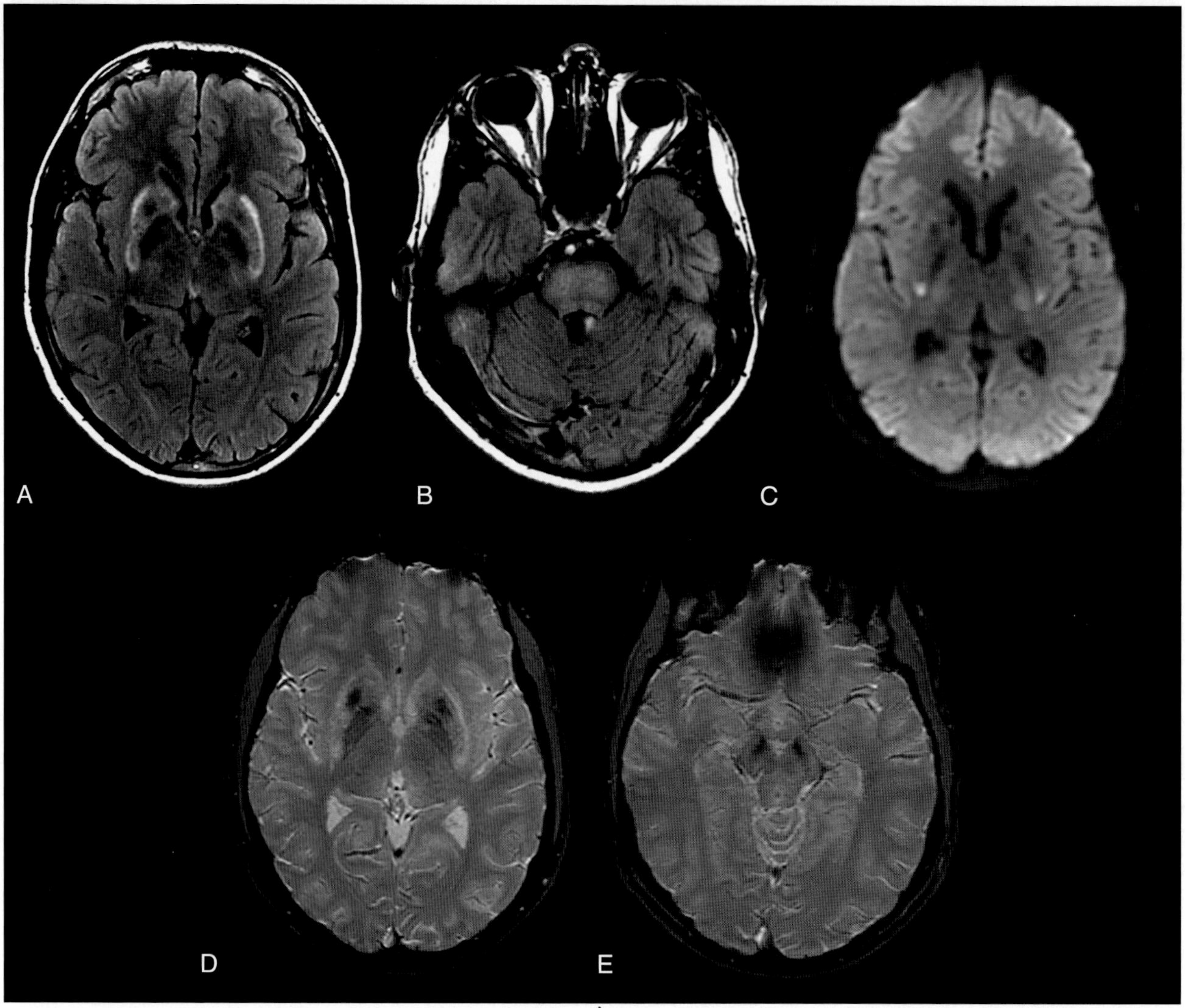

Fig. 70.1 Wilson disease. Brain MRI, (A and B) axial FLAIR shows hyperintensity in the bilateral lentiform nuclei and central pons. (C) DWI shows focal restricted diffusion in the posterior putamina. (D and E) GRE shows increased susceptibility in the putamina, substantia nigra, and red nuclei. *DWI*, Diffusion-weighted imaging; *FLAIR*, fluid-attenuated inversion recovery; *GRE*, gradient echo.

liver, brain, and cornea. Depending on the type and severity of the mutation, disease onset can occur in childhood or young adulthood.

On ophthalmologic examination, Kayser-Fleischer rings are seen with golden-brown copper deposition in the cornea. These are present in most patients with neurological involvement and 50% of patients with hepatic involvement. Less frequently, patients may exhibit renal, cardiac, rheumatologic, endocrinologic, dermatologic, and psychiatric symptoms. Hepatic manifestations include jaundice, hepatomegaly, splenomegaly, ascites, and abnormal bleeding. Neurological symptoms include encephalopathy, dysarthria, ataxia, focal or generalized dystonia, and both resting and action tremors.

Laboratory tests and brain MRI can suggest the diagnosis, with genetic testing for confirmation. Treatment involves copper chelators, such as D-penicillamine or trientine, or agents like zinc that reduce dietary copper absorption. In cases of severe liver failure or decompensated cirrhosis, liver transplantation may be required.

CLINICAL RED FLAGS

- Acute-onset neuropsychiatric symptoms such as personality changes, tremors, dysarthria
- Hepatic abnormalities and hepatomegaly.

IMAGING RED FLAGS

- Bilateral T2/FLAIR hyperintensity and mineralization of basal ganglia and brainstem.

CONCLUSIONS

Wilson disease poses a diagnostic challenge due to its broad clinical spectrum. Patients can present with liver failure, neuropsychiatric symptoms, and clinical features such as jaundice and Kayser-Fleischer rings. Brain MRI helps confirm the diagnosis and facilitate timely intervention.

REFERENCES

de la Vega Bueno A, Carnicer de la Pardina J. Enfermedad de Wilson. *Protoc diagn ter pediatr.* 2023;1:305–316.

Ferenci P. Pathophysiology and clinical features of Wilson disease. *Metab Brain Dis.* 2004;19:229.

Lorincz MT. Neurologic Wilson's disease. *Ann N Y Acad Sci.* 2010;1184:173.

Poujois A, Woimant F. Wilson's disease: a 2017 update. *Clin Res Hepatol Gastroenterol.* 2018;42:512.

Taly AB, Meenakshi-Sundaram S, Sinha S, et al. Wilson disease: description of 282 patients evaluated over 3 decades. *Medicine (Baltimore).* 2007;86:112.

Wiernicka A, Dądalski M, Jańczyk W, et al. Early onset of Wilson disease: diagnostic challenges. *J Pediatr Gastroenterol Nutr.* 2017;65:555.

Case 71

Acute Hemichorea and More

HISTORY AND PHYSICAL

A previously healthy 10-year-old boy presented with acute onset of abnormal involuntary right-sided movements, predominantly affecting the upper extremity. These movements were continuous and undulating, exacerbated by fatigue and stress, and ceased during sleep. There was no history of fever, prior trauma, or toxic exposures. Personal and family history were negative for neurologic disease.

At admission, vital signs including blood pressure were normal. Neurological examination revealed right hemichorea with low muscle tone and increased ipsilateral stretch reflexes, positive right Babinski sign, and subtly hemiplegic gait.

DIAGNOSTIC WORKUP

Lumbar puncture was performed with normal opening pressure. Isoelectric focusing was positive for increased IgG fraction. Plasma IgG was normal.

Laboratory testing of folic acid, thyroid hormone, vitamin B12, collagen, and thrombophilia profile were all normal.

Visual and auditory evoked potentials were normal. ECG and transthoracic echocardiogram were normal.

Doppler US of the neck was normal.

Brain MRI (Fig. 71.1) showed a T2-hyperintense lesion in the left thalamocapsular junction with restricted diffusion. Additional T2-hyperintense, T1-hypointense lesions were noted in the periventricular and subcortical white matter, without enhancement.

Spine MRI (Fig. 71.2) showed multifocal T2-hyperintense signal abnormalities in the spinal cord.

The patient received methylprednisolone pulse therapy and improved completely by the time of discharge. However, he experienced two relapses over the next 3 years.

CLINICAL DIFFERENTIAL DIAGNOSES

Acute-onset chorea has a broad clinical differential diagnosis including inflammatory, ischemic, metabolic, and genetic.

Sydenham (rheumatic) chorea following group A streptococcus infection is the most frequent cause of acquired chorea in children. It is more often bilateral than unilateral but never presents pyramidal signs.

Systemic lupus erythematosus can be associated with chorea in 7% of patients and is associated with the presence of antiphospholipid antibodies. Again, symptoms are more commonly bilateral than unilateral.

Hyperglycemia can cause bilateral chorea, hemichorea-hemiballismus, and/or severe partial seizures. This is more common in older adults with type 2 diabetes and nonketotic hyperglycemia. Cases in children with type 1 diabetes are rare, as they tend to present earlier with hyperglycemia, glycosuria, and ketoacidosis.

Several genetic conditions are associated with chorea, including benign hereditary chorea, Huntington disease, Rett disease, spinocerebellar ataxia, and neurodegeneration with brain iron accumulation (NBIA). In each of these disorders, additional neurologic features are present.

IMAGING DIFFERENTIAL DIAGNOSES

Focal restricted diffusion and T2 hyperintensity in the basal ganglia can be seen with acute ischemia, infection, vasculopathy, demyelination, trauma, or neoplasia.

Multifocal white matter lesions of varying ages in the brain and spinal cord can be seen with demyelinating disease and vasculopathy.

FINAL DIAGNOSIS

Pediatric-onset multiple sclerosis (MS).

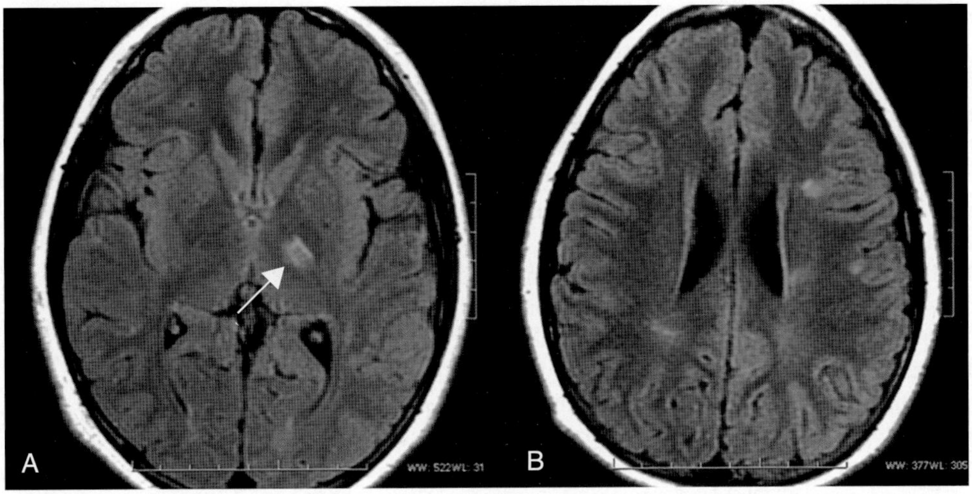

Fig. 71.1 Multiple sclerosis. Brain MRI, axial FLAIR shows (A) hyperintensities in the left thalamocapsular junction and (B) bilateral periventricular and subcortical white matter. *FLAIR*, Fluid-attenuated inversion recovery.

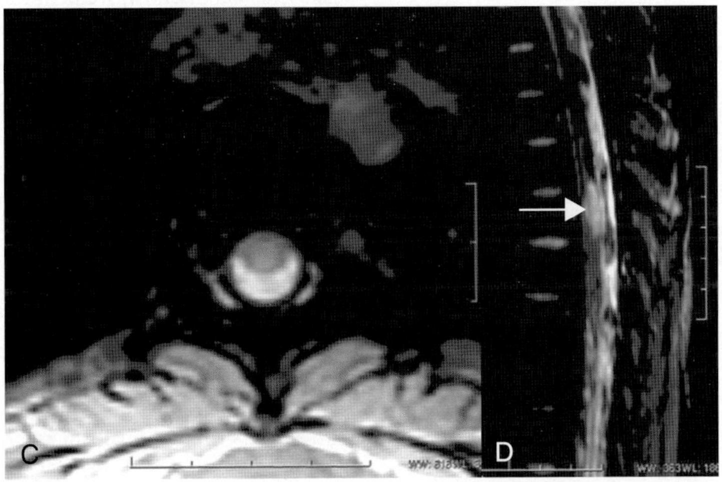

Fig. 71.2 Multiple sclerosis. Thoracic spine MRI, (C) axial and (D) sagittal STIR show multifocal T2-hyperintense signal abnormalities in the thoracic cord, largest at T6 (*arrow*). *STIR*, Short-tau inversion recovery.

DISCUSSION

Multiple sclerosis (MS) is a chronic inflammatory demyelinating disease of the central nervous system. Movement disorders (MD) are occasionally seen in MS, more so as a presenting feature and with pediatric patients. Demyelinating lesions of the basal ganglia may explain the coexistence of MS and MD. The most prevalent MDs in MS include restless leg syndrome (RLS), tremor, ataxia, parkinsonism, paroxysmal dyskinesias, dystonia, chorea, ballismus, facial myokymia, including hemifacial spasm and spastic paretic hemifacial contracture, tics, and Tourettism. More common clinical symptoms include transient pyramidal, sensory, and/or cerebellar signs.

At imaging, the pathology of MS reflects acute inflammation progressing to chronic neurodegeneration over time. Active demyelinating lesions can show restricted diffusion and enhancement in a leading-edge ("incomplete ring") pattern. Chronic disease causes myelin destruction with T1 hypointense signal ("black holes"), volume loss, and lack of enhancement or restricted diffusion. Disease often follows a perivenular pattern radiating out from the lateral ventricles ("Dawson fingers"). There is preferential involvement of periventricular and juxtacortical white matter, as well as callosal-septal junction. Spinal cord lesions are usually small and eccentric with limited craniocaudal extent.

The 2024 McDonald criteria for MS involves dissemination of lesions in space and/or time. At presentation, patients may demonstrate a clinically or radiologically isolated syndrome that does not meet full criteria for MS. Therefore, a definitive diagnosis may require temporal clinical and radiologic follow-up. Over time, patients can show secondary (delayed) progressive or remitting-relapsing disease course. Children almost never present with the primary progressive form of MS without relapses or remissions; therefore progressive neurologic dysfunction is more likely to reflect an MS mimic.

CLINICAL RED FLAGS

- Acute-onset unilateral hemichorea is concerning for a structural lesion.
- Although Sydenham chorea might present unilaterally, it is not accompanied by pyramidal signs.

IMAGING RED FLAGS

- Restricted diffusion and/or enhancement in an active lesion.
- Additional white matter lesions in the brain and spine with chronic features.

CONCLUSIONS

MS symptoms can begin in childhood. Secondary MS is a rare but important manifestation. CSF autoantibody testing and neuraxis MRI are important for diagnosis and follow-up of this lifelong disease.

REFERENCES

Alves C, Sampaio S, Barbosa V, Machado M. Acute chorea and type 1 diabetes mellitus: clinical and neuroimaging findings. *Pediatr Diabetes*. 2012;13(6):e30–e34.

Aquino JH, Spitz M, Pereira JS. Hemichorea-hemiballismus as the first sign of type 1b diabetes during adolescence and its recurrence in the setting of infection. *J Child Neurol*. 2015;30(10):1362–1365.

Athanasopoulos E, Kalaitzidou I, Vlachaki G, Stefanaki S, Tzagkaraki A, Niotakis G, Tritou I, Ladomenou F. Chorea revealing systemic lupus erythematosus in a 13-year old boy: a case report and short review of the literature. *Int Rev Immunol*. 2018;37(4):177–182.

de Seze J, Stojkovic T, Destée M, Destée A, Vermersch P. Paroxysmal kinesigenic choreoathetosis as a presenting symptom of multiple sclerosis. *J Neurol*. 2000;247(6):478–480.

Deuschl Günther. Movement disorders in multiple sclerosis and their treatment. *Neurodegener Dis Manag*. 2016;6(6s):31–35.

Ghosh R, Roy D, Dubey S, Das S, Benito-León J. Movement disorders in multiple sclerosis: an update. *Tremor Other Hyperkinet Mov (N Y)*. 2022;12:14.

Mao CC, Gancher ST, Herndon RM. Movement disorders in multiple sclerosis. *Mov Disord*. 1988;3(2):109–116.

Minagar A, Sheremata WA, Weiner WJ. Transient movement disorders and multiple sclerosis. *Parkinsonism Relat Disord*. 2002;9(2):111–113.

Nociti V, Bentivoglio A, Fasano A, Soleti F, Iorio E. Movement disorders in multiple sclerosis: causal or coincidental association? *Mult Scler*. 2008;14(9):1284–1287.

Waubant E, Simonetta-Moreau M, Clanet M, Berry I, Bonafé A. Left arm monoballism as a relapse in multiple sclerosis. *Mov Disord*. 1997;12(6):1091–1092.

Eye of the Tiger

HISTORY AND PHYSICAL

A 14-year-old boy presented with frequent falls over the past 2 years. These were accompanied by declining gross and fine motor skills with overall clumsiness and changes in hand shape. He had difficulties with handwriting, grasping objects, and dressing.

Prior medical history included development of tics at 10 years old, which improved with age. Family history included a mother with thrombophilia and maternal uncle with intellectual disability.

Physical examination revealed intermittent ulnar deviation of fingers and toes and scoliosis with winged scapulae. Gait was normal with appropriate arm swinging, but some instability was observed during transitions. Motor and sensory exams were normal with preserved reflexes.

DIAGNOSTIC WORKUP

Ophthalmologic evaluation with slit lamp was normal.

EMG/NCS demonstrated mild neuropathy of median nerves.

Brain MRI showed abnormal mineralization and gliosis of the globi pallidi interna (Fig. 72.1).

Genetic panel revealed a pathogenic variant in the *PANK2* gene.

CLINICAL DIFFERENTIAL DIAGNOSES

Dystonia can be primary or secondary. Primary dystonias are thought to be genetic or idiopathic.

Heredodegenerative disorders should be considered when abnormal movements, psychiatric disorders, and changes in motor skills are present.

Metabolic diseases with progressive neurological symptoms include mitochondrial disease, Wilson disease, Leigh disease, and coenzyme Q10 deficiency.

Secondary dystonias result from extrinsic factors causing basal ganglia injury such as drugs/toxins, trauma, infection, inflammation, or ischemia.

IMAGING DIFFERENTIAL DIAGNOSES

Neurodegeneration with brain iron accumulation (NBIA) involves excessive iron deposition in the brain. The pattern of distribution distinguishes the various subtypes of NBIA.

Pantothenate kinase-associated neurodegeneration (PKAN) selectively involves the globi pallidi. The "eye-of-the-tiger" sign is diagnostic, with peripheral and central susceptibility and intervening T2-hyperintense gliosis.

Woodhouse-Sakati syndrome can variably show prominent susceptibility in the globi pallidi without "eye-of-the-tiger" sign. Marked periventricular T2 white matter hyperintensity is present.

Fatty acid hydroxylase-associated neurodegeneration shows susceptibility in the globi pallidi and substantia nigra, with white matter T2 hyperintensity and atrophy of corpus callosum, cerebellum, and brainstem.

Neuroferritinopathy shows mixed T2 signal in the deep gray nuclei, progressing to susceptibility and cavitation.

PLA2G6-associated neurodegeneration shows cerebellar atrophy with variable susceptibility in the globus pallidus and substantia nigra.

Kufor-Rakeb syndrome shows susceptibility in the deep gray nuclei and diffuse cerebral, cerebellar, and brainstem atrophy, particularly corticospinal tracts.

Aceruloplasminemia shows widespread susceptibility throughout the deep gray nuclei and cortex, diffuse white matter hyperintensity, and cerebellar atrophy.

Beta-propeller protein-associated neurodegeneration shows T1 hyperintensity in the substantia nigra with a central hypointense band.

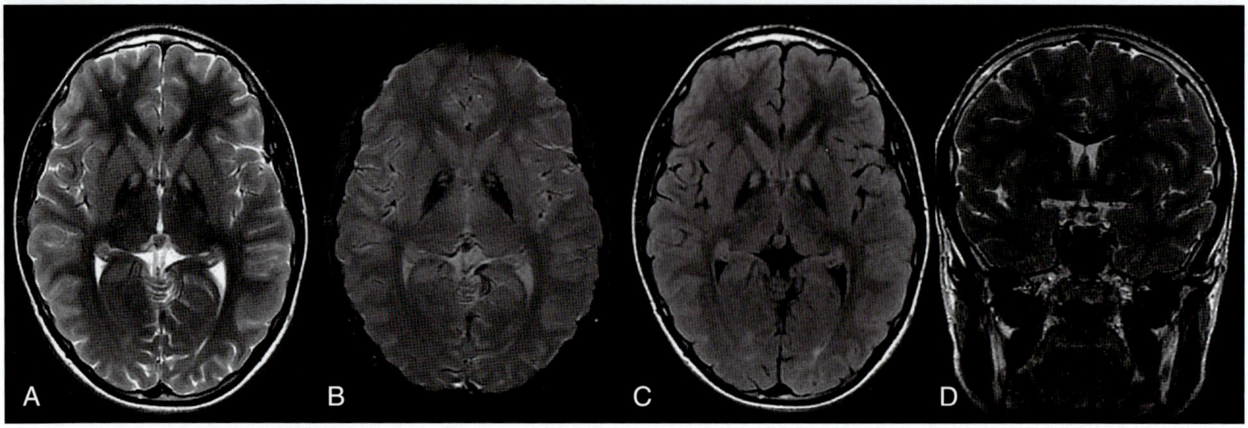

Fig. 72.1 Pantothenate kinase-associated neurodegeneration (PKAN). Brain MRI, (A) axial T2, (B) GRE, (C) FLAIR, and (D) coronal T2 show globus pallidus peripheral and central hypointensity due to iron deposition, with intervening layer of hyperintensity reflective of gliosis. *FLAIR*, Fluid-attenuated inversion recovery.

Basal ganglia susceptibility can be seen with deposition of other biometals, such as calcium, copper, and manganese, as well as gadolinium MRI contrast deposition. Findings will diffusely affect the deep gray nuclei and may show corresponding intrinsic T1 shortening.

Acquired brain injury (neuroinflammation, vascular disorders, radiation) can be associated with premature iron deposition in the basal ganglia. These conditions will show additional imaging findings, with secondary degeneration of the deep gray nuclei.

FINAL DIAGNOSIS

Pantothenate kinase-associated neurodegeneration (PKAN).

DISCUSSION

PKAN is a neurodegenerative disease caused by mutations in the *PANK2* gene encoding pantothenate kinase 2, an enzyme critical for mitochondrial function in various tissues including the brain. PKAN is the most common form of NBIA and presents with abnormal movements, psychiatric symptoms, and cognitive deterioration.

On brain MRI, the globi pallidi are preferentially affected. The classic "eye-of-the-tiger" sign reflects peripheral and central susceptibility with intervening T2-hyperintense gliosis. Other forms of NBIA have distinct patterns of iron deposition and signal abnormality.

Management can include deferiprone, an iron chelator used for thalassemia. The drug crosses the blood–brain barrier and may reverse brain iron deposition. Other supportive treatments to address the movement symptoms include anticholinergics, botulinum toxin, baclofen, and surgical ablation or deep brain stimulation of the globi pallidi.

CLINICAL RED FLAGS

- Dystonia with abnormal movements, alterations in gait and balance, changes in fine and gross motor skills.
- Tics can be an atypical presentation.

IMAGING RED FLAGS

- Susceptibility and gliosis in both globi pallidi ("eye-of-the-tiger" sign).

CONCLUSIONS

Neurodegenerative disorders are an important cause of progressive movement disorders. Brain MRI is important for diagnosis, with the distribution and imaging characteristics supporting the differential diagnosis. The "eye-of-the-tiger" sign is highly suggestive of PKAN and can be confirmed by genetic testing.

REFERENCES

Amaral LL, et al. Neurodegeneration with brain iron accumulation: clinicoradiological approach to diagnosis. *Neuroimaging*. 2015;25(4):539–551.

Gregory A, Hayflick SJ. Neurodegeneration with brain iron accumulation. *Folia Neuropathologica*. 2005;43(4):286–296.

Hayflick SJ, et al. Neurodegeneration with brain iron accumulation. *Handb Clin Neurol*. 2018;147:293–305.

Kruer MC, et al. Neuroimaging features of neurodegeneration with brain iron accumulation. *AJNR Am J Neuroradiol*. 2012;33(3):407–414.

Pohane MR, Dafre R, Sontakke NG. Diagnosis and treatment of pantothenate kinase-associated neurodegeneration (PKAN): a systematic review. *Cureus*. 2023;15(9):e46135.

Schneider SA. Neurodegenerations with brain iron accumulation. *Parkinsonism Relat Disord*. 2016:22(Suppl 1) S21–S25.

Schneider SA, Bhatia KP. Syndromes of neurodegeneration with brain iron accumulation. *Semin Pediatr Neurol*. 2012;19(2):57–66.

Case 73

Boxed In

HISTORY AND PHYSICAL

A 4-year-old girl with normal early development presented with a year of progressive dysarthria. Her speech was "mumbling" with decreased volume and complexity. At 3 years her articulation plateaued and began to decline: speech was 100% intelligible at 3 years, but at 4 she was only 75% intelligible. Three months prior to presentation, her diet shifted from structured meals to softer solids and frequent, small snacks. Swallowing was difficult, with dribbling of liquids. Her gait became progressively more erratic and she began falling. She preferred to crawl and required a stroller for longer distances. She regressed from one-hand dexterity to bimanual tasks. She did not improve with speech and physical therapies.

On exam, her voice was hoarse and trailed off. She drooled while speaking. Her orolingual movements were normal, without tongue atrophy. She had mild proximal weakness in the upper and lower extremities and mild rigidity in the lower extremities. Her reflexes were normal. She struggled with balance and would fall within three steps with minimal protective effort. Her gait was wide-based with irregular pacing. She could not maintain rhythms. There was no chorea, dystonia, or ataxia of the limbs or trunk, but she showed substantial ataxia with fine movements.

DIAGNOSTIC WORKUP

Laboratory testing, including CBC, LFTs, serum chemistry, and creatine kinase, were normal. Genetic testing demonstrated increased CAG trinucleotide repeats within the *HTT* gene.

Brain MRI demonstrated severe volume loss and mild T2 hyperintensity of the bilateral caudate and putamen, with ex vacuo dilation and squaring of the frontal horns. White matter was normal in volume, though there were scattered foci of signal change (Fig. 73.1).

CLINICAL DIFFERENTIAL DIAGNOSES

Progressive neurological symptoms—in this case, dysarthria, dysphagia, ataxia, and rigidity—raise concern for hereditary degenerative syndromes, accumulated toxins (especially heavy metals), acquired brain injury due to infection, inflammatory or autoimmune disorders, and vascular syndromes. The patient's clinical progression was gradual and inexorable, favoring inherited neurodegeneration. There were no occupational or household routes to toxin exposure. For spinocerebellar ataxias, cerebellar and eye movement abnormalities are expected. Striatal atrophy can result from static injury, though typically coincides with other sequelae (e.g., hemosiderin deposition, leukomalacia).

IMAGING DIFFERENTIAL DIAGNOSES

Disorders that produce relatively selective and symmetrical injury to the striatum are unusual and include metabolic, mitochondrial, and neurodegenerative disorders.

Glutaric acidemia type 1 (GA1) typically presents before 18 months. Characteristic features include abrupt onset of encephalopathy with illness, fasting, or hypoglycemia, with severe dystonia following injury. In the acute (encephalopathic) phase, edema and restricted diffusion in the striatum are universal features. Injury may also involve the globus pallidus, substantia nigra, and/or dentate nuclei. Survivors of the encephalopathic phase uniformly have striatal atrophy, and spongiform degeneration of the white matter is common. Children with GA1 typically have macrocephaly

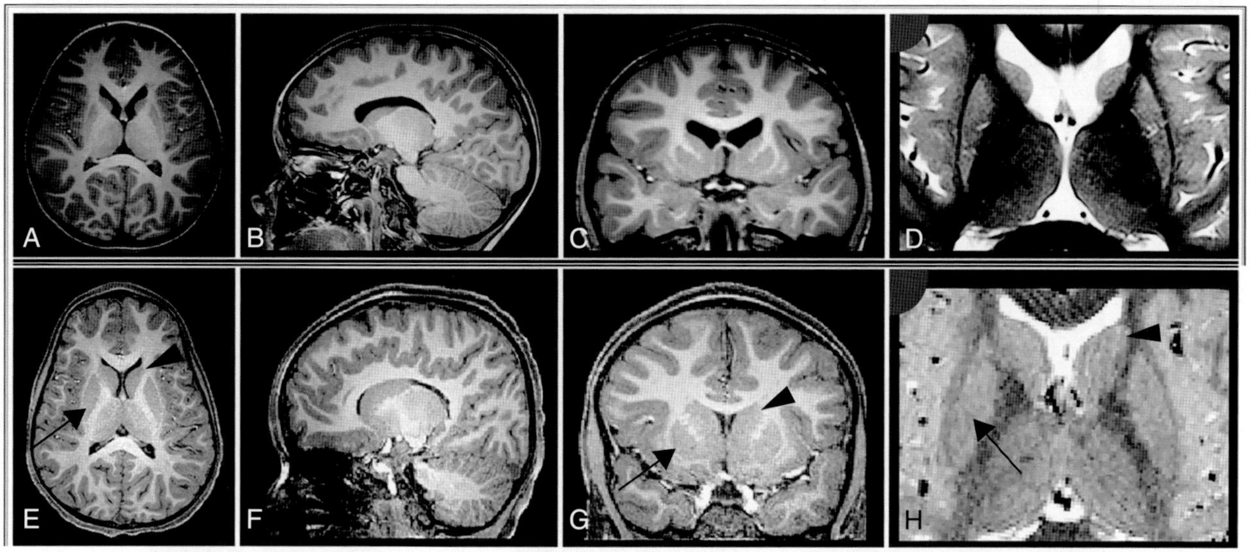

Fig. 73.1 Juvenile Huntington disease. Brain MRI, (A–C) axial, sagittal, and coronal T1, illustrate striatal atrophy with increased distance between the caudate heads, (A and C) thinning of the body of the putamen, and ex vacuo enlargement of the lateral ventricles with boxlike configuration of frontal horns. (D) Axial T2 shows T2 hyperintensity in the striatum and thalamus similar to cortex. (E–H) Comparison to an age- and sex-matched healthy child shows normal size caudates (*arrowheads*) and putamina (*arrows*) with highest T2 signal in the cortex, followed by striatum and thalamus.

at or shortly after birth. Reduced cortical volume, widened Sylvian fissures, and subdural hematomas are common even prior to injury (Fig. 73.2).

Wilson disease (WD) presents throughout childhood, but onset before 3 years of age is unusual. Hepatic injury is near universal in childhood-onset WD; while neuropsychiatric symptoms can occur in childhood-onset WD, finding these features without hepatic injury is uncommon. T1 hyperintensity in the globus pallidus is the most common imaging finding. However, T2 hyperintensity with high frequency of striatal injury and infrequent pallidal injury can occur. Neurologic symptoms are more common in this T2-hyperintense subtype. In both T1- and T2-hyperintense forms, injury to other subcortical structures (especially thalamus and midbrain) is common.

Huntington disease (HD) results from expansions in the number of *CAG* repeats in the HTT gene. While typical HD onset is between 40 and 50 years, in 3–10% of patients, unusually large expansions can yield symptoms before 18 years. Developmental regression and/or dysarthria are far more common at onset than in adult HD. Rigidity and dystonia dominate the movement phenotype. One-third of children with HD develop epilepsy, a rare symptom in adult HD. Striatal atrophy typically lags symptom onset by 1–2 years. Atrophy of the thalamus, pallidum, and cortical grey and white matter is less severe than atrophy in the striatum but still significant.

Recessively inherited mutations in *NUP62* cause infantile bilateral striatal necrosis (IBSN). IBSN onsets from 7 to 15 months with prominent facial chorea, progressing to limbs and trunk. Developmental regression, optic atrophy, and dystonia occur over the subsequent 1–4 years. Brain MRI is often normal early in IBSN. Progressive, symmetrical striatal atrophy with T2 hyperintensities follows later.

Biallelic mutations in *VAC14*, which regulates the level of phosphatidylinositol 3,5-bisphosphate, lead to severe, generalized dystonia with striatal injury. Development is normal prior to onset of dystonia. Early descriptions of *VAC14* described acute-onset dystonia at 18–37 months, but adolescent onset and slower evolution may occur. Early in the disease, susceptibility-weighted hypointensity of the substantia nigra was present in all patients, and of the globus pallidus in two of three cases with MRI. Bilateral, symmetrical striatal

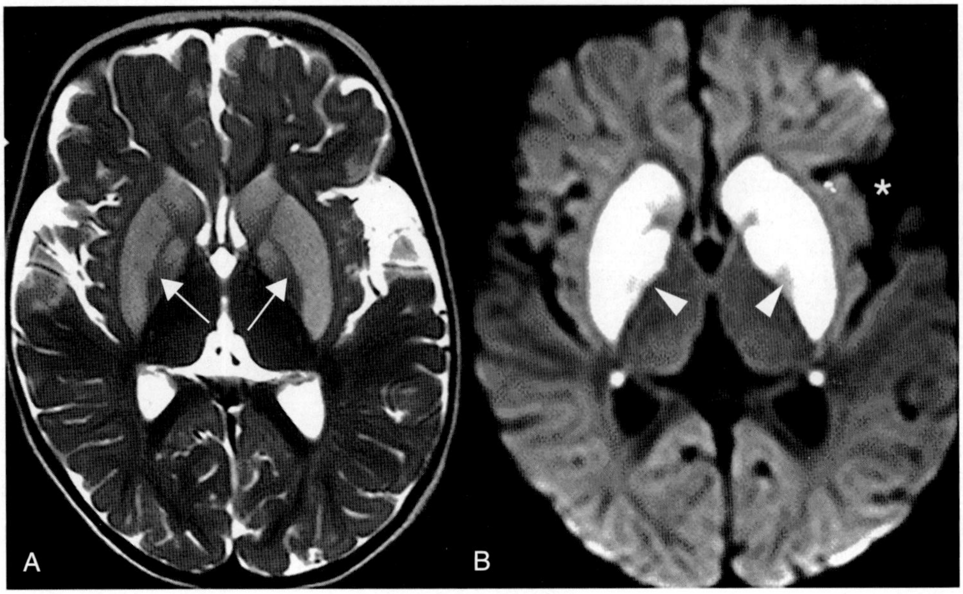

Fig. 73.2 Glutaric aciduria type I. Brain MRI, (A) axial T2 and (B) DWI show restricted diffusion (*arrowheads*) and cytotoxic edema (*arrows*) of the striatum and globi pallidi with enlarged and shallow sylvian fissures (*asterisk*).

T2 hyperintensities were evident at disease onset in the original series, while subsequent cases had diffuse striatal T2 hypointensity.

Bilateral striatal necrosis is a common feature in ADAR1-related neuroinflammatory syndrome. ADAR1 can manifest throughout the first decade of life, though most present by 18 months. Brain MRI typically demonstrates diffuse leukodystrophy and calcifications, primarily in the caudal putamen. Diffuse volume loss is common early in the course, largely due to severe generalized leukodystrophy. ADAR1-related striatal necrosis can occur as an acute, triggered encephalopathy, or as an indolent, progressive disorder. Early developmental delay is common in ADAR1-related disorders and MDs are present at clinical onset in 60% of children.

Mutations in *TUBB4A* lead to hypomyelination with atrophy of the basal ganglia and cerebellum (H-ABC) syndrome. Putaminal volume loss is often evident at diagnosis with subsequent progression to full atrophy. Caudate atrophy is less severe. The thalamus and pallidum are typically spared. Cerebellar (especially vermian) atrophy is common. Symptoms typically manifest at 1 to 3 years, with progressive pyramidal, extrapyramidal, cerebellar, and bulbar features. Progression to spasticity, rigidity, ataxia, dysarthria, and dysphagia are common (Fig. 73.3).

FINAL DIAGNOSIS

Juvenile Huntington disease.

DISCUSSION

CAG repeats in *HTT* are unstable, leading to intergenerational anticipation. Expansion is typically larger when paternally inherited. The patient's paternal grandmother died following a progressive dementia with chorea. However, the patient's father was healthy with no neuropsychiatric symptoms. This presented an ethical dilemma: diagnosing the patient with HD would simultaneously diagnose her pre-symptomatic father. She was found to have 115 repeats (normal: $\leq$35; typical childhood onset: >80) and died 4 years after onset.

Childhood HD is notable for rigidity and/or dystonia rather than chorea, which dominates in adult HD. Children may develop chorea later; this patient did 2 years after onset. Developmental delay/regression is common in childhood HD. Dysarthria and/or psychiatric symptoms are common at disease onset in childhood HD, often preceding motor symptoms. Psychotic symptoms and seizures are more common relative to adult HD. The

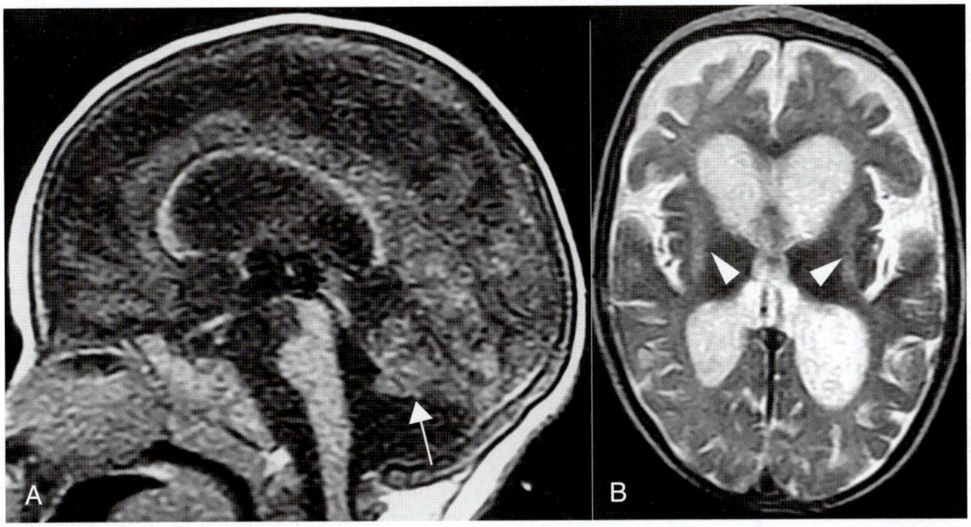

Fig. 73.3 Hypomyelination with atrophy of the basal ganglia and cerebellum (H-ABC). Brain MRI, (A) sagittal T1 and (B) axial T2 show diffuse cerebral and cerebellar atrophy (*arrow*), T2-hyperintense white matter, and small hyperintense basal ganglia (*arrowheads*).

rarity of childhood HD, and the phenotypic differences between childhood and adult HD, often lead to diagnostic delays.

This patient's MRI was notable for the focality of her atrophy, only affecting the striatum. Many children with HD develop atrophy of both grey and white matter, but striatal atrophy precedes other regions. The other disorders in the imaging differential are either much less likely to develop striatal atrophy in isolation or present with acutely injured striata rather than atrophy. A normal MRI does not exclude HD, especially early in the disease.

CLINICAL RED FLAGS

- Dysphagia substantially increases the risk of aspiration and failure to thrive, both of which reduce survival in HD.
- Epilepsy is sufficiently common in childhood HD that proactive screening for seizures is indicated.
- Given the intergenerational impacts of diagnosing childhood HD, partnering with colleagues in ethics and/or genetics is helpful.
- HD is inexorably fatal, and children with HD often have affected parents or grandparents. Caring for the family is critical to optimizing care for the child with HD.

IMAGING RED FLAGS

- Selective atrophy of the caudate and putamen, with box-like dilatation of the frontal horns, is common in childhood HD.
- Inflammatory or contrast-enhanced lesions are uncommon in HD.
- Global atrophy and leukoencephalopathy are not expected in early symptomatic HD.
- In childhood HD, total intracranial volume should be normal or reduced.

CONCLUSIONS

Children with HD present differently and progress faster than adults with HD. Brain MRI is often helpful in diagnosing HD, since few other conditions produce focal striatal atrophy early in the disease course. Inheritance is autosomal dominant, often with anticipation, so confirmatory genetic testing for HD should be performed only after substantial counseling regarding risks and benefits of testing, including the implications for other family members.

REFERENCES

Bakels HS, Roos RAC, van Roon-Mom WMC, de Bot ST. Juvenile-onset huntington disease pathophysiology and neurodevelopment: a review. *Mov Disord.* 2022;37(1):16–24. https://doi.org/10.1002/mds.28823.

Basel-Vanagaite L, Muncher L, Straussberg R, Pasmanik-Chor M, Yahav M, Rainshtein L, Walsh CA, Magal N, Taub E, Drasinover V, Shalev H, Attia R, Rechavi G, Simon AJ, Shohat M. Mutated nup62 causes autosomal recessive infantile bilateral striatal necrosis. *Ann Neurol.* 2006;60(2):214–222. https://doi.org/10.1002/ana.20902.

Boy N, Mühlhausen C, Maier EM, et al. Recommendations for diagnosing and managing individuals with glutaric aciduria type 1: third revision. *J Inherit Metab Dis.* 2023;46(3):482–519. https://doi.org/10.1002/jimd.12566.

Di Lazzaro G, Graziola F, Sancesario A, et al. Movement disorders in ADAR1 disease: insights from a comprehensive cohort. *Parkinsonism Relat Disord.* 2020;79:100–104. https://doi.org/10.1016/j.parkreldis.2020.08.039.

Gonzalez-Alegre P, Afifi AK. Clinical characteristics of childhood-onset (juvenile) Huntington disease: report of 12 patients and review of the literature. *J Child Neurol.* 2006; 21(3):223–229. https://doi.org/10.2310/7010.2006.00055.

Kim TJ, Kim IO, Kim WS, et al. MR imaging of the brain in Wilson disease of childhood: findings before and after treatment with clinical correlation. *AJNR Am J Neuroradiol.* 2006;27(6):1373–1378.

Lenk GM, Szymanska K, Debska-Vielhaber G, et al. Biallelic mutations of VAC14 in pediatric-onset neurological disease. *Am J Hum Genet.* 2016;99(1):188–194. https://doi.org/10.1016/j.ajhg.2016.05.008.

Letort D, Gonzalez-Alegre P. Huntington's disease in children. *Handb Clin Neurol.* 2013;113:1913–1917. https://doi.org/10.1016/b978-0-444-59565-2.00061-7.

Mohammad SS, Angiti RR, Biggin A, et al. Magnetic resonance imaging pattern recognition in childhood bilateral basal ganglia disorders. *Brain Commun.* 2020;2(2):fcaa178. https://doi.org/10.1093/braincomms/fcaa178.

van der Knaap MS, Naidu S, Pouwels PJ, et al. New syndrome characterized by hypomyelination with atrophy of the basal ganglia and cerebellum. *AJNR Am J Neuroradiol.* 2002;23(9):1466–1474.

SECTION 15

Neurologic Complications of Systemic Diseases

Kam Lun Ellis Hon, Quentin Yau Ching Wong, Karen Ka Yan Leung, Mariana Loos, Carlos A. Rugilo, Hugo A. Arroyo, Bindu N. Setty, Alcy R. Torres

INTRODUCTION

Systemic diseases can occasionally involve the nervous system as complications and present as florid neurologic syndromes and entities. Pathophysiology may involve inflammatory versus noninflammatory, immunologic versus nonimmunologic, and infectious versus noninfectious mechanisms of the nervous system. Also, the neurological complications of drugs needed to treat these diseases must be considered.

These mechanisms can occur by multiple pathways, including cytokine-mediated inflammation, antibody-mediated demyelination, immune cell infiltration, mass-like formation, granulomatous inflammation, T-cell–mediated cytotoxic injury, and vasculitic inflammation. Early identification of the underlying systemic etiology of neurological disease is essential, as unchecked inflammation can cause severe neurological disability or even death. Furthermore, proper diagnosis can facilitate a therapeutic approach targeting disease-specific mechanisms.

In this chapter, we report clinical manifestations, diagnostic challenges, and therapeutic recommendations for five types of nervous system involvement resulting from systemic disease: (1) posterior reversible encephalopathy syndrome (PRES); (2) methotrexate (MTX) encephalopathy; (3) hemolytic uremic syndrome (HUS); (4) sickle cell disease (SCD); and (5) progressive cerebellar ataxia associated with vitamin E deficiency. There is a broad differential diagnosis with a paucity of biological markers in pediatric systemic diseases with neurologic complications. As such, multidisciplinary team management creates challenges in terms of complex diagnostic workups and treatment.

We also describe clinical and imaging red flags in children with neurologic manifestations of systemic diseases that should prompt diagnostic testing. A history suggestive of a serious neurological disease and/or abnormal neurological examination are clear indicators for neuroimaging. When ordering an imaging study, providing a detailed and relevant history to the radiologist increases the likelihood of a timely and accurate diagnosis of the underlying systemic disease. Overall, close communication and collaboration among specialists, including neurologists and radiologists, is central to ensuring appropriate diagnosis and management of the neurologic condition and its underlying systemic disease.

SUGGESTED READINGS

Hogg JE. Neurologic complications of acute and chronic renal failure. *Adv Neurol.* 1978;19:637–646.

Kumar N. Neurologic presentations of nutritional deficiencies. *Neurol Clin.* 2010;28(1):107–170. https://doi.org/10.1016/j.ncl.2009.09.006.

Neurologic manifestations of systemic disease. *Neurol Clin.* 1989;7(3):447–679.

Raskin NH, Fishman RA. Neurologic disorders in renal failure (second of two parts). *N Engl J Med.* 1976;294(4):204–210. https://doi.org/10.1056/nejm197601222940406.

Tyler HR. Neurologic disorders in renal failure. *Am J Med.* 1968;44(5):734–748. https://doi.org/10.1016/0002-9343(68)90255-6.

Case 74

White Matter Climate Change

HISTORY AND PHYSICAL

A 4-year-old female patient was diagnosed with relapsing acute lymphocytic leukemia (ALL). She was admitted to the pediatric intensive care unit (PICU) due to septic shock with respiratory failure. During her recovery, after extubation and weaning of sedation, she developed altered mental status, with a Glasgow Coma Scale (GCS) of 12/15, and focal jerks. Her neurological examination was significant for aphasia. She also had features of dysautonomia, with unstable body temperature, labile blood pressure, and profuse sweating, which were noted to be aggravated by urinary retention or constipation.

DIAGNOSTIC WORKUP

CT of the brain showed that the patient had generalized cerebral atrophy. MRI showed patchy to confluent T2/fluid-attenuated inversion recovery (FLAIR) hyperintense signal and restricted diffusion in bilateral centrum semiovale and corpus callosum (Fig. 74.1).

Electroencephalography (EEG) was recorded during a semiconscious state and was abnormal, with diffuse slow background and nonreactivity to painful stimulation. The findings were suggestive of generalized cerebral dysfunction with nonspecific etiology. EEG after thiamine demonstrated excessive intermittent slow waves over the bilateral frontotemporal region with right emphasis and independent right temporal slow waves in awake and sleep states. There were also three episodes of electroclinical seizures (eye staring, frequent eye blinking, and left-hand movement) with bilateral frontotemporal slow waves spreading to frontocentral regions and more prominent over the right temporal region. A lumbar puncture (LP) was performed and showed normal cell counts, differential, Gram stain and cultures were negative, and protein, glucose, lactate, and amino acids were normal. *SLC19A3* gene testing was negative.

The patient was covered with levetiracetam, following which there were no definite further seizures. She was also treated with aminophylline, thiamine, folinic acid, and pyridoxine, and biotin, with improvement in GCS.

CLINICAL DIFFERENTIAL DIAGNOSES

Toxic leukoencephalopathy can be caused by exposure to neurotoxic organic solvents, heavy metals, and drugs. The differential includes CNS infection (either meningitis or encephalitis), inflammatory, vasculitis, vascular, and neoplastic disorders. Methotrexate (MTX)-induced CNS neurotoxicity usually presents days after high-dose intrathecal chemotherapy and may mimic an acute ischemic stroke. Clinical features include subacute encephalopathy with fluctuating course, often followed by improvement of symptoms. Treatment varies, but leucovorin rescue with aminophylline is typically well tolerated to bypass MTX inhibition of dihydrofolate reductase (DHFR), essential for the synthesis of purines and pyrimidines in DNA and RNA.

IMAGING DIFFERENTIAL DIAGNOSES

MTX-associated leukoencephalopathy may coexist with PRES. Treatment involves discontinuation of the culprit medication, and supportive treatment. White matter and basal ganglia involvement can be seen with other toxic and metabolic conditions.

FINAL DIAGNOSIS

Methotrexate-induced leukoencephalopathy.

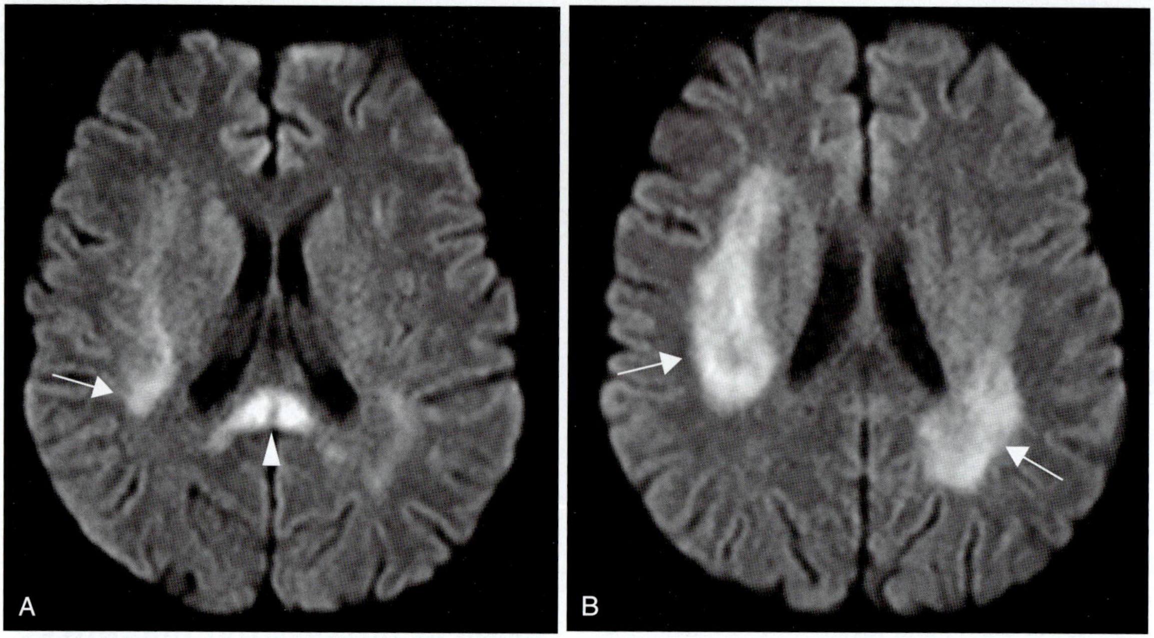

Fig. 74.1 Methotrexate-induced leukoencephalopathy. Brain MRI, (A and B) axial DWI show bilateral asymmetric restricted diffusion in the corona radiata extending into periatrial white matter without mass effect (*arrows*). There is also involvement of splenium of corpus callosum (*arrowhead*). *DWI*, Diffusion-weighted imaging. (Case courtesy Mai-Lan Ho, MD.)

DISCUSSION

Toxic leukoencephalopathy is characterized by damage to white matter and myelin in the brain due to medications, recreational drugs, or environmental toxins. The exact mechanism and underlying pathophysiology of toxic leukoencephalopathy are not well understood. The clinical severity varies with exposure time, drug concentration, and purity. High doses of intravenous or intrathecal chemotherapy, particularly MTX, can be associated with leukoencephalopathy in children and young adults. Cessation of medication with supportive therapy and leucovorin rescue help to minimize neurotoxicity.

CLINICAL RED FLAGS

Encephalopathy in a patient recently administered MTX is a red flag.

IMAGING RED FLAGS

Bilateral white matter signal changes following high-dose intrathecal chemotherapy.

CONCLUSIONS

In cases of MTX leukoencephalopathy, cessation of medication with supportive therapy and leucovorin rescue help to minimize neurotoxicity.

REFERENCES

Baker EL. Chronic toxic encephalopathy caused by occupational solvent exposure. *Ann Neurol.* 2008;63(5):545–547. https://doi.org/10.1002/ana.21394.

Dhariwal N, Roy Moulik N, Smriti V, et al. Clinico-radiological profile, management and follow-up of methotrexate induced neurotoxicity in children with acute lymphoblastic leukemia. *Leuk Lymphoma*. 2023:1–10. https://doi.org/10.1080/10428194.2023.2245093.

Feldman RG, Ratner MH, Ptak T. Chronic toxic encephalopathy in a painter exposed to mixed solvents. *Environ Health Perspect*. 1999;107(5):417–422. https://doi.org/10.1289/ehp.99107417.

Lerner DP, Tadevosyan A, Burns JD. Toxin-induced subacute encephalopathy. *Neurol Clin*. 2020;38(4):799–824. https://doi.org/10.1016/j.ncl.2020.07.006.

Yu T, Yang C. Multifokale Leukenzephalopathie bei Einer Patientin mit etanercept und Methotrexat gegen rheumatoide arthritis (Multifocal leukoencephalopathy in a patient medicated with etanercept and methotrexate for rheumatoid arthritis). *Z für Rheumatol*. 2023. https://doi.org/10.1007/s00393-023-01430-6.

Case 75

When Kidneys and Brain Cry

HISTORY AND PHYSICAL

A 3-year-old girl has had bloody diarrhea for 4 days. On physical examination, the child was afebrile and had normal blood pressure but looked pale and dehydrated. Her skin showed petechial hemorrhages on the buttocks and legs. She was irritable with a fluctuating mental status examination due to lethargy. The rest of the neurologic examination was unremarkable. Hemoglobin was 8.7 g/dl, hematocrit was 29%, and the white blood cell (WBC) count was 39,000/ul, with a marked shift to the left. Blood urea nitrogen was 91 mg/dl, creatinine was 3.6 mg/dl, sodium was 120 mEq/l, and potassium was 4.7 mEq/l. The next day, the hematocrit decreased to 19.7%, and she was transfused with RBCs, after which her level of consciousness improved, but she became oliguric and hypertensive (130/90 mm Hg), so hemodialysis was initiated. She continued to be oliguric and hypertensive, and 8 days after admission she became unresponsive with gasping respirations and developed generalized tonic-clonic seizures. She was intubated and received peritoneal dialysis and anticonvulsant therapy.

DIAGNOSTIC WORKUP

Initial head CT showed bilateral and asymmetric hypodense lesions in the lentiform nuclei and thalami (Fig. 75.1). EEG showed intermittent epileptiform activity without associated motor seizures.

Brain MRI on the 14th day after admission showed hemorrhagic necrosis in the bilateral basal ganglia and surrounding white matter (Fig. 75.2).

The child's renal and neurologic status gradually stabilized, and she was extubated 15 days after admission.

CLINICAL DIFFERENTIAL DIAGNOSES

Infectious diseases such as shigellosis or meningococcemia can present with seizures with or without fever, renal failure, and skin petechiae.

Posterior reversible encephalopathy syndrome (PRES) presents with seizures, visual deficits, and alteration of consciousness that can be associated with renal failure (acute glomerulonephritis, lupus nephritis) (Fig. 75.3).

Immune thrombocytopenia (ITP) and other etiologies of thrombocytopenia can present with hematomas, petechiae, and CNS manifestations due to intracranial hemorrhage.

Henoch-Schönlein purpura is a vasculitis involving the small vessels of the joints, kidneys, gastrointestinal tract, and skin. CNS involvement is rare; however, when present, patients may present with headaches, dizziness, ataxia, seizures, irritability, or intracranial hemorrhage.

Pediatric antiphospholipid antibody syndrome is a systemic autoimmune disorder that presents with recurrent thrombosis, vasospastic, or vasoocclusive events in any organ system with a broad spectrum of involvement ranging from rapidly progressive to clinically silent and indolent. Manifestations include CNS involvement, gastrointestinal, renal, and purpuric or petechial rashes.

Disseminated intravascular coagulation (DIC) is characterized by systemic activation of blood coagulation, leading to microvascular thrombi in various organs and contributing to multiple organ dysfunction syndrome (MODS). Consumption of clotting factors and platelets in DIC can result in life-threatening hemorrhage.

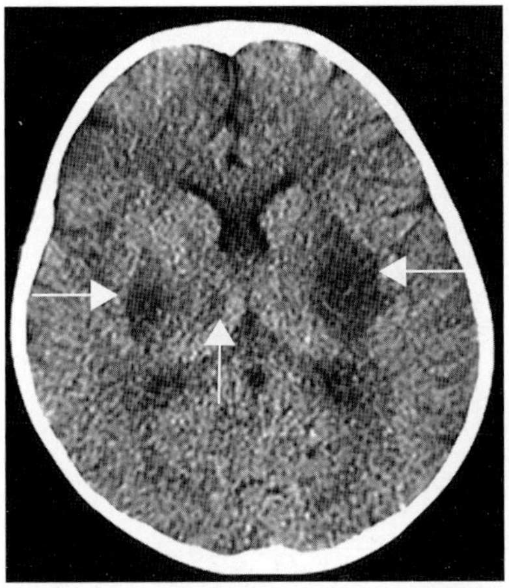

Fig. 75.1 Hemolytic uremic syndrome. Head CT shows asymmetric hypodensities in the bilateral lentiform nuclei and thalami (*arrows*).

IMAGING DIFFERENTIAL DIAGNOSES

PRES can manifest with encephalopathy in patients with renal disorders. In addition to the typical subcortical white matter lesions, PRES can be associated with basal ganglia involvement (Fig. 75.3).

Patients with uremia and acidosis, especially in the context of diabetes, can have basal ganglia lesions on MRI with the lentiform fork sign (Fig. 75.4).

Any disorder associated with thrombocytopenia can produce multiple microbleeds on susceptibility images (Fig. 75.5).

FINAL DIAGNOSIS

Hemolytic uremic syndrome (HUS) with neurologic involvement.

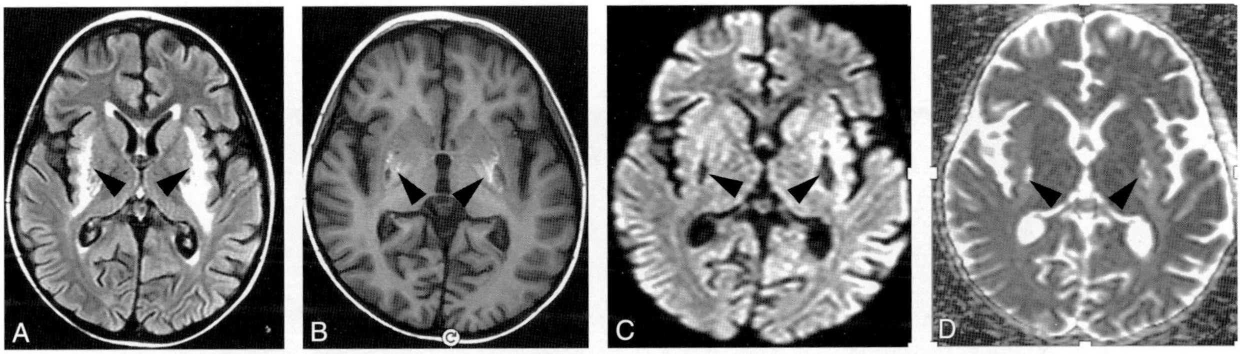

Fig. 75.2 Hemolytic uremic syndrome. Brain MRI, (A) axial FLAIR, (B) T1, (C) DWI, and (D) ADC show edema and hemorrhagic necrosis in the lentiform nuclei and surrounding white matter (*arrowheads*). *ADC*, Apparent diffusion coefficient; *DWI*, diffusion-weighted imaging; *FLAIR*, fluid-attenuated inversion recovery.

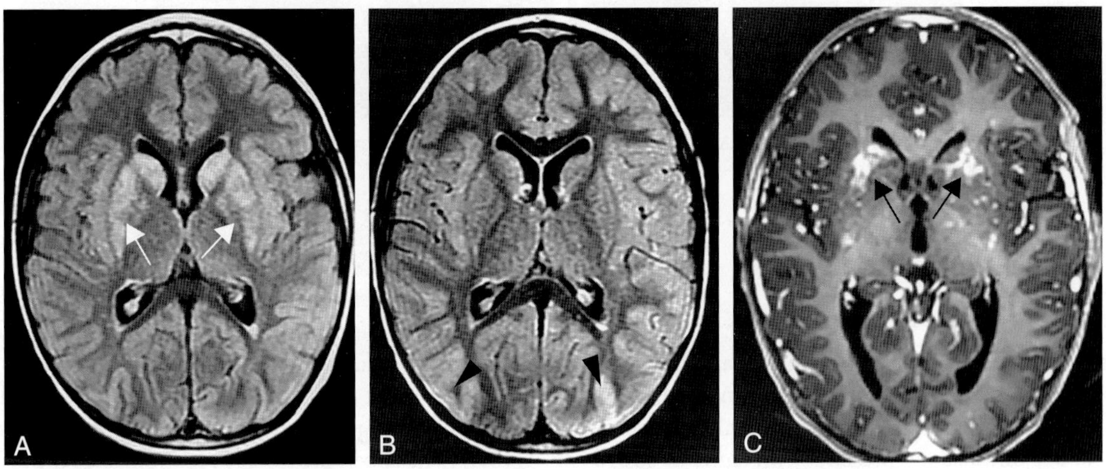

Fig. 75.3 Posterior reversible encephalopathy syndrome (*PRES*). Brain MRI, axial FLAIR shows (A) bilateral lentiform nuclei (*arrows*) and (B) patchy occipital cortical/subcortical hyperintensities (*arrowheads*) with (C) postcontrast T1 showing heterogeneous enhancement (*arrows*). *FLAIR*, Fluid-attenuated inversion recovery.

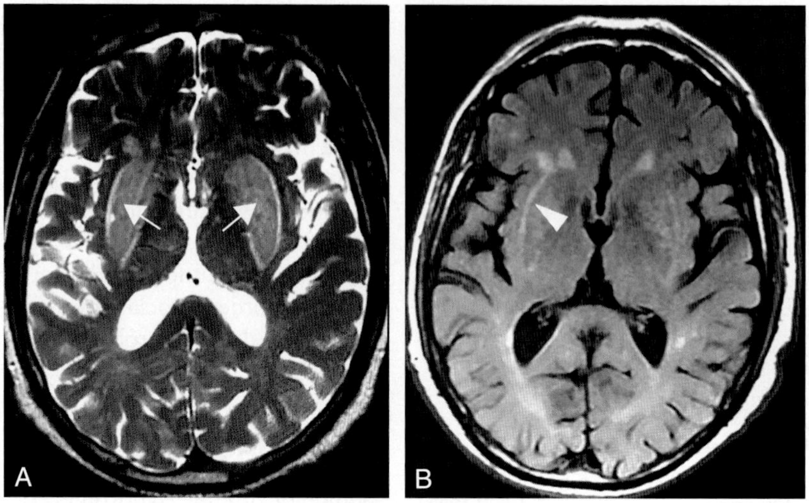

Fig. 75.4 Diabetic uremia. Brain MRI, (A) axial T2 and (B) FLAIR show symmetric hyperintensity of the lentiform nuclei (*arrows*) with intervening white matter edema (lentiform fork sign, *arrowhead*). *FLAIR*, Fluid-attenuated inversion recovery.

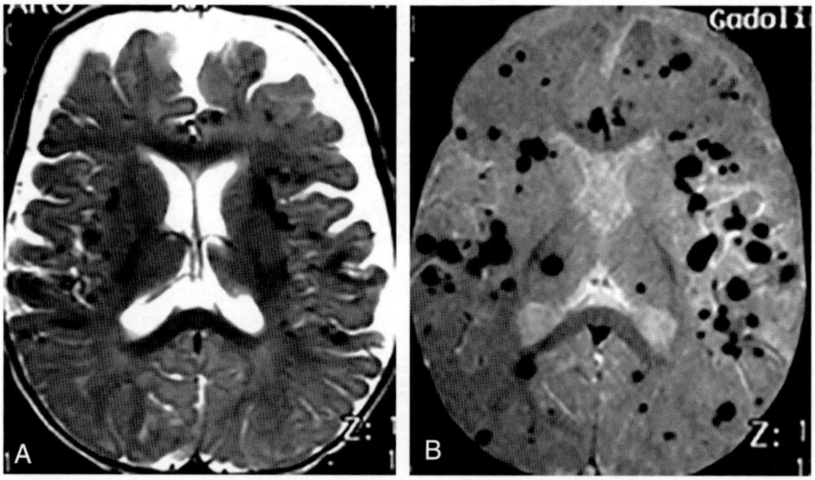

Fig. 75.5 Thrombocytopenia. Brain MRI, (A) axial T2 and (B) GRE show multifocal microhemorrhages with punctate susceptibility.

DISCUSSION

HUS is a complex multisystem disease characterized by microangiopathic hemolytic anemia, thrombocytopenia, and impaired renal function. It affects mainly children of preschool age and usually presents with signs of gastrointestinal disease (diarrhea, often bloody and/or watery) and abdominal tenderness. In the acute phase, 30% of patients are hypertensive, and approximately half require a kidney transplant.

HUS is most often caused in children by Shiga toxin (Stx)–producing *Escherichia coli* (STEC). The serotype O157:H7 has been previously recognized as the predominant cause of HUS worldwide. HUS can sometimes be caused by other infectious agents such as Streptococcus pneumonia, malignancy, drugs, and a type of genetic disorder regulating the alternative pathway of the complement system (atypical HUS).

The CNS is involved in 20% to 50% of cases and indicates a worse prognosis, with increased mortality and morbidity. Common signs of severe CNS involvement are seizures, alteration of consciousness, hemiparesis, visual disturbances, and brainstem symptoms.

The pathogenesis of CNS involvement is not yet fully understood; however, a toxin-mediated vasculopathy involving the small intracerebral vessels similar to the pathological process occurring in the kidneys is thought to be the most probable mechanism. Severe fluid and electrolyte disturbances and hypertension can also be responsible for encephalopathy in HUS patients.

On brain MRI, the basal ganglia are most commonly affected with variable involvement of surrounding white matter, thalami, cerebellum, and brainstem. On follow-up imaging, mild cases may resolve completely. Hemorrhage within an acute lesion is more likely to demonstrate residual abnormalities on follow-up imaging.

The prognosis of children with HUS has improved over time, mostly due to advances in intensive care and dialysis. Eculizumab, a monoclonal C5 antibody, has now been proven to be an effective treatment. Nevertheless, HUS in children is still associated with significant morbidity and mortality.

CLINICAL RED FLAGS

- Seizures, altered level of consciousness.
- Bloody diarrhea.
- Hematuria, oligo-anuric.
- Thrombocytopenia, petechiae, hemolytic anemia.

IMAGING RED FLAGS

- Bilateral basal ganglia edema, evolving to cavitation.
- The cerebral cortex, subcortical white matter, brainstem, and cerebellar vermis may be involved in severe cases.
- Coagulative necrosis may present with T1 hyperintensity, susceptibility, and/or enhancement.

CONCLUSIONS

Gastrointestinal, dermatologic, hematologic, and renal symptoms prompt the diagnosis of HUS. Patients may also present with neurologic symptoms, for which brain MRI helps assess the severity of disease.

REFERENCES

Cody EM, Dixon BP. Hemolytic uremic syndrome. *Pediat Clin N Am.* 2019;66(1):235–246. https://doi.org/10.1016/j.pcl.2018.09.011.

Jenssen GR, Hovland E, Bjerre A, Bangstad H-J, Nygard K, Vold L. Incidence and etiology of hemolytic-uremic syndrome in children in Norway, 1999–2008: a retrospective study of hospital records to assess the sensitivity of surveillance. *BMC Infect Dis.* 2014;14(1):265. https://doi.org/10.1186/1471-2334-14-265.

Steinborn M, Leiz S, Rüdisser K, Griebel M, Harder T, Hahn H. CT and MRI in haemolytic uraemic syndrome with central nervous system involvement: distribution of lesions and prognostic value of imaging findings. *Pediat Radiol.* 2004;34(10):805–810. https://doi.org/10.1007/s00247-004-1289-2.

Ylinen E, Salmenlinna S, Halkilahti J, et al. Hemolytic uremic syndrome caused by Shiga toxin–producing *Escherichia coli* in children: incidence, risk factors, and clinical outcome. *Pediat Nephrol.* 2020;35(9):1749–1759. https://doi.org/10.1007/s00467-020-04560-0.

Case 76

Brain Changes Under Pressure

HISTORY AND PHYSICAL

A 13-year-old female patient with a history of acute lymphoblastic leukemia was admitted to the PICU due to septic shock. She developed two episodes of seizures during her recovery at the age of 12. The first episode started with a 5-second view of a colorful rainbow spot in the midline and lasted for 1 minute. She was noted to have limb and facial twitching, with higher intensity in the right face, that spontaneously resolved. This was followed by a similar episode about 30 minutes later, lasting for 45 seconds, which also stopped spontaneously. One dose of lorazepam was given after the second seizure. She required noninvasive ventilation due to encephalopathic state with decreased consciousness. She was also noted to be hypertensive (BP ~160/101).

After the patient's consciousness improved, she reported that she had no memory of the event except seeing the above-mentioned rainbow spot. She was noted to be lethargic with slow responses; there was no headache, vomiting, or numbness. Pupils were equal and reactive to accommodation and light. Neurological examination showed that no facial weakness or asymmetry; cranial nerves also appeared intact. She had normal tone, and her upper limbs were rated 4/5 with antigravity movement, but she had mild proximal muscle weakness in her lower limbs in the power assessment. On the past-pointing test slight underperformance was observed in the left upper limb. Deep tendon reflexes appeared normal in the upper limbs but were depressed in both knees; these presented after reinforcement but were still absent in ankles. Downgoing plantar reflexes were observed. Sensation was normal.

The patient was initially treated with levetiracetam as an anticonvulsant. Her hypertension was brought down by hydralazine, and labetalol was also administered via IV bolus injection and later changed to oral enalapril and amlodipine. During her recovery, she reported multiple episodes of visual and auditory hallucinations. The former included seeing a rainbow curtain form in both eyes and seeing animals such as a white dinosaur and an orange tiger; the latter included hearing voices from different men talking about buying groceries in a supermarket and having once received a command hallucination asking her to pull away her nasal cannula. Repeated EEG showed no epileptiform discharges.

DIAGNOSTIC WORKUP

LP was performed. The opening pressure was normal, no abnormal cells were seen, bacterial and fungal cultures were negative, and viral encephalitis panel was negative. CT venogram showed no evidence of dural venous sinus thrombosis. EEG was abnormal with a mildly suppressed background, which suggested a generalized cerebral dysfunction of nonspecific etiology.

Brain MRI revealed bilateral and relatively symmetric cortico-subcortical edema. Right parieto-occipital hemorrhage was noted (Fig. 76.1).

CLINICAL DIFFERENTIAL DIAGNOSES

Posterior reversible leukoencephalopathy syndrome (PRES) can be considered if a patient has developed acute neurological symptoms (seizure, altered mental state, headache, visual disturbances) together with one or more known risk factors, characteristic brain imaging, and no other alternative diagnosis. If the abnormalities are reversible, the diagnosis can be confirmed retrospectively. The majority of patients have two or

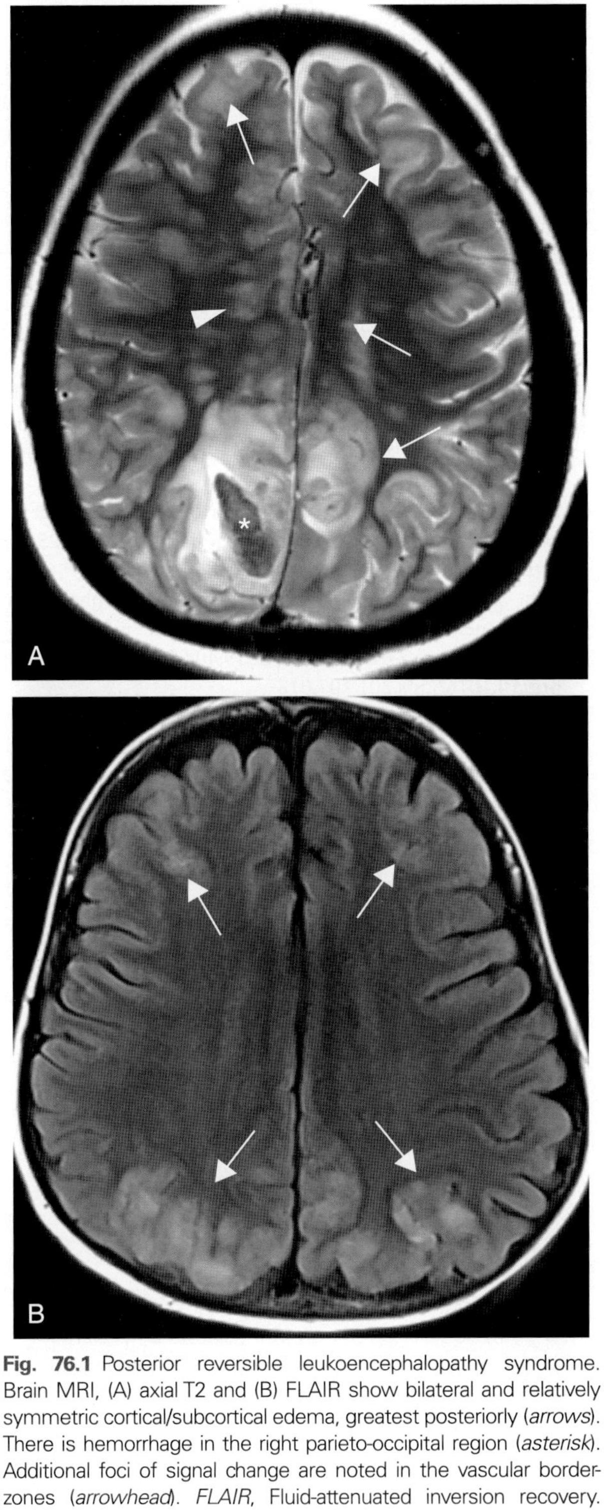

Fig. 76.1 Posterior reversible leukoencephalopathy syndrome. Brain MRI, (A) axial T2 and (B) FLAIR show bilateral and relatively symmetric cortical/subcortical edema, greatest posteriorly (*arrows*). There is hemorrhage in the right parieto-occipital region (*asterisk*). Additional foci of signal change are noted in the vascular border-zones (*arrowhead*). *FLAIR*, Fluid-attenuated inversion recovery. (Case courtesy Mai-Lan Ho, MD.)

more risk factors: hypertension (88%), steroids and immunosuppressors (82%), or steroid therapy alone (71%) are most common, followed by infection (31.4%) and renal failure (14%). CSF may show increased protein levels but no WBCs.

IMAGING DIFFERENTIAL DIAGNOSES

CT may show low-density white matter in the posterior cerebrum and cerebellum.

Brain MRI shows T2/FLAIR hyperintensity in the posterior circulation (parietal, occipital, cerebellum) in more than half of cases. Other patterns include the superior frontal sulcus (SFS) watershed pattern, holohemispheric watershed pattern, and central pattern involving the deep white matter, basal ganglia, thalami, brainstem, cerebellum, and spinal cord. These distinct patterns do not generally correlate with the nature of the symptoms or their severity, although widespread edema may suggest a poorer prognosis. Angiography may reveal transient vascular narrowing, suggesting a possible overlap with reversible cerebral vasoconstriction syndrome (RCVS). Diffusion MRI may be used to identify areas of cytotoxic edema caused by ischemia, seen in about 20% of cases. In 10% to 25% of cases, there is evidence of hemorrhagic transformation. Various types of hemorrhage may occur: intraparenchymal, subarachnoid, and microbleeds.

FINAL DIAGNOSIS

Posterior reversible leukoencephalopathy syndrome.

DISCUSSION

Symptoms of PRES may include headache, changes in vision, seizures, confusion, or limb weakness. Common underlying etiologies are severe hypertension, renal failure, severe infections, certain medications, and some autoimmune diseases. After a hematopoietic stem cell transplantation (bone marrow transplant), the risk of PRES is approximately 8%, whereas the risk is lower (0.4–6%) after a solid organ transplant. Treatment is supportive: removing the cause(s) and treating complications such as seizures or intracranial hemorrhage. Forty percent of patients with PRES are critically ill and require intensive care unit admission for close observation and treatment of complications.

CLINICAL RED FLAGS

PRES may be identical or closely related to hypertensive encephalopathy. The presence of acute neurological symptoms in those with a hypertensive crisis, renal failure, eclampsia, chemotherapy, immunotherapy, autoimmune disorders, thrombotic microangiopathy, sepsis, or fluid overload should be carefully investigated.

IMAGING RED FLAGS

PRES should be considered if the posterior (parieto-occipital, cerebellar) brain is involved with edema in a child with hypertension. Bilateral vasogenic edema extending to the subcortical white matter with sparing of the medial aspects of the occipital lobes is characteristic.

CONCLUSIONS

Triggering factors for PRES include hypertension, pre-eclampsia/eclampsia, renal failure, cytotoxic agents, and autoimmune conditions. A hypertensive crisis must be promptly treated, followed by management of the underlying etiology. Treatment is supportive and involves correcting the underlying cause and managing associated complications, such as seizures.

REFERENCES

Bronina NV, Shchederkina IO, Polushin A Yu, et al. Posterior reversible encephalopathy syndrome in children with hematological diseases. *S S Korsakova J Neurol Psychiatry*. 2023;123(9):33–42. https://doi.org/10.17116/jnevro202312309233.

Fischer M, Schmutzhard E. Posterior reversible encephalopathy syndrome. *J Neurol*. 2017;264(8):1608–1616. https://doi.org/10.1007/s00415-016-8377-8.

Geocadin RG. Posterior reversible encephalopathy syndrome. *N Engl J Med*. 2023;388(23):2171–2178. https://doi.org/10.1056/nejmra2114482.

Hinchey JA. Reversible posterior leukoencephalopathy syndrome: what have we learned in the last 10 years? *Arch Neurol*. 2008;65(2):175–176. https://doi.org/10.1001/archneurol.2007.62.

Liman TG, Siebert E, Endres M. Posterior reversible encephalopathy syndrome. *Curr Opin Neurol*. 2019;32(1):25–35. https://doi.org/10.1097/wco.0000000000000640.

Tetsuka S, Ogawa T. Posterior reversible encephalopathy syndrome: a review with emphasis on neuroimaging characteristics. *J Neurol Sci*. 2019;404:72–79. https://doi.org/10.1016/j.jns.2019.07.018.

Triplett JD, Kutlubaev MA, Kermode AG, Hardy T. Posterior reversible encephalopathy syndrome (PRES): diagnosis and management. *Pract Neurol*. 2022;22(3):183–189. https://doi.org/10.1136/practneurol-2021-003194.

Tell Me How You Eat and I Will Tell You How You Walk

HISTORY AND PHYSICAL

A 15-year-old boy visited the clinic due to a progressively abnormal gait that started 3 years prior. Initially, he experienced an unsteady gait, which gradually worsened and became wide-based and staggering. He presented with difficulties while taking steps, climbing stairs, and running. Additionally, he developed slurred speech and clumsiness in his hands, resulting in deteriorated handwriting. Over the past year, he also developed a head tremor and sensory disturbances in his lower limbs. The pregnancy and birth history were unremarkable, and there was no family history of neurological disorders or other diseases. There was no parental consanguinity.

Prior to the onset of symptoms, his school performance was normal. After the symptoms appeared, he began experiencing difficulties with his writing.

The boy's weight was measured at 56 kg (50%), height 168 cm (50–75%), and head circumference 54 cm (50%). He exhibited normal cognitive function and had no vision or hearing problems. Oculomotor movements were normal. However, an unusual cadence in speech and subtle head tremor were observed. Furthermore, bilateral dysmetria was noted during the nose-finger test. He displayed a wide-based ataxic gait and was unable to walk in tandem. Motor and sensory examinations revealed diffuse areflexia and bilateral Babinski signs. Distal joint position and vibration sense were also affected.

The Scale for the Assessment and Rating of Ataxia (SARA) score was determined to be 12, with the following scores: gait 2.0, stance 2.0, sitting 0.0, speech 2.0, finger chase 1.0 (left 1, right 1), nose-finger test 2.0 (left 2, right 2), fast alternating hand movements 1.0 (left 1, right 1), and heel-shin slide 2.0 (left 2, right 2).

DIAGNOSTIC WORKUP

Initial laboratory investigations, including a complete blood count, glucose, liver and kidney function tests, celiac antibodies, fasting lipids, thyroid function tests, copper and ceruloplasmin levels, vitamin B_{12}, creatinine kinase, alpha-fetoprotein, and immunoglobulins, were normal.

Brain and spinal cord MRIs revealed mild cerebellar atrophy (CA) (Fig. 77.1) and cervical cord thinning with posterior column hyperintensity (Fig. 77.2).

Electrocardiography and echocardiography were normal.

Ophthalmologic examination was significant for myopia.

Friedreich ataxia was ruled out through triplet primed repeat PCR. A comprehensive metabolic profile was normal.

Vitamin E level was low at 3.7 mg/dl (normal range: 6–10 mg/dl). Genetic testing showed two compound heterozygous pathogenic variants in the *TTPA* gene, leading to a loss of α-TTP activity. The variants identified were c.661C>T (p.Arg221Trp) and c.744delA (p.Glu249Asnfster15). The child was put on high doses (1000 mg/day) of oral vitamin E.

CLINICAL DIFFERENTIAL DIAGNOSES

Ataxia is a common clinical sign characterized by impaired coordination of movement and balance, resulting in a lack of muscle control during voluntary activity. It is primarily caused by dysfunction in the circuitry that connects the cerebellum, basal ganglia, and cerebral cortex, known as "cerebellar ataxia."

Acute cerebellar syndromes typically arise as acquired, nongenetic conditions that require prompt

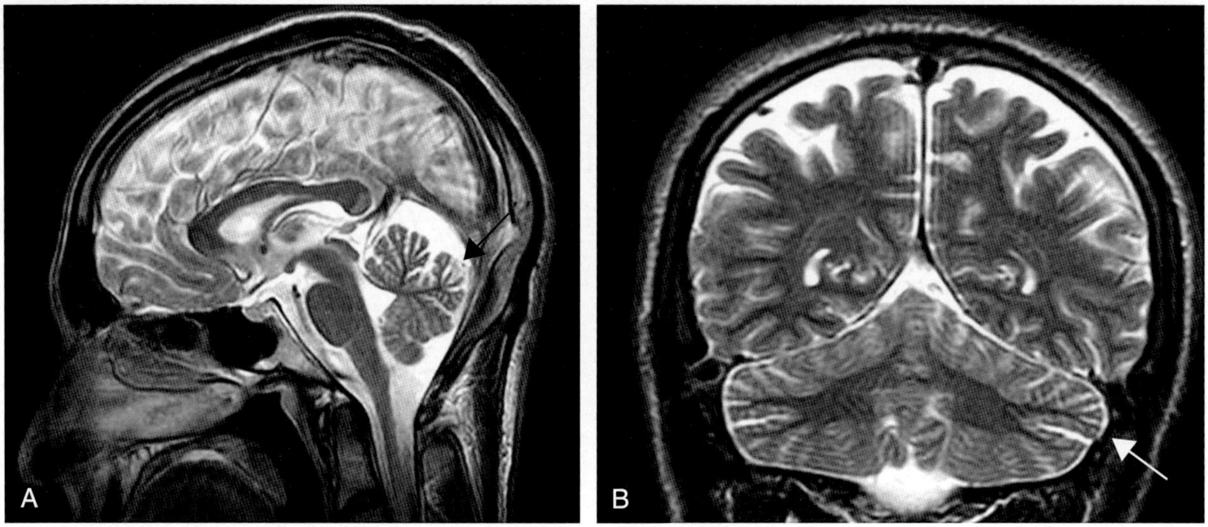

Fig. 77.1 Ataxia with vitamin E deficiency. Brain MRI, (A) sagittal and (B) coronal T2 show mild cerebral and cerebellar atrophy with enlarged interfolial spaces (*arrow*).

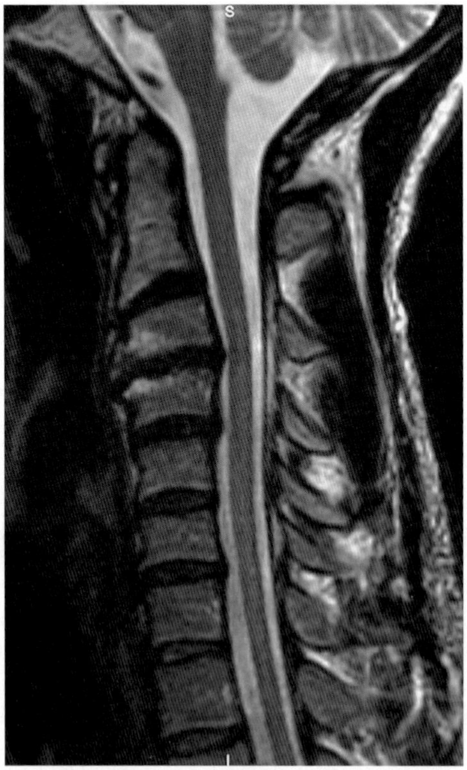

Fig. 77.2 Ataxia with vitamin E deficiency. Cervical spine MRI, sagittal T2 shows mild spinal degenerative changes and gracile cord with faint posterior hyperintensity.

medical attention. It is crucial to consider various conditions including posterior fossa tumors, drug intoxication, postinfectious cerebellitis, meningitis or cerebellar abscess, cerebellar stroke, and inherited metabolic disorders such as nonketotic hyperglycinemia and pyruvate dehydrogenase deficiency.

Chronic cerebellar ataxia can manifest as either nonprogressive or progressive. Nonprogressive ataxia is often associated with cerebral damage, such as hypoxic-ischemic or vascular damage. It can also be linked to brain malformations, such as Arnold-Chiari malformation or Dandy-Walker syndrome.

Progressive ataxia encompasses a heterogeneous group of clinically and genetically diverse neurodegenerative disorders with various inheritance patterns. Among pediatric populations, the most common form is the autosomal recessive type, with Friedreich ataxia being the most prevalent.

Progressive cerebellar ataxia can also be related to inborn errors of metabolism, including ataxia with vitamin E deficiency (AVED), abetalipoproteinemia, Refsum disease, cerebrotendinous xanthomatosis, type 2 gangliosidosis, Niemann-Pick disease type C, and disorders of coenzyme Q10 biosynthesis, among others.

Systemic causes of ataxia and vitamin E deficiency include hypothyroidism, celiac disease, immune disorders

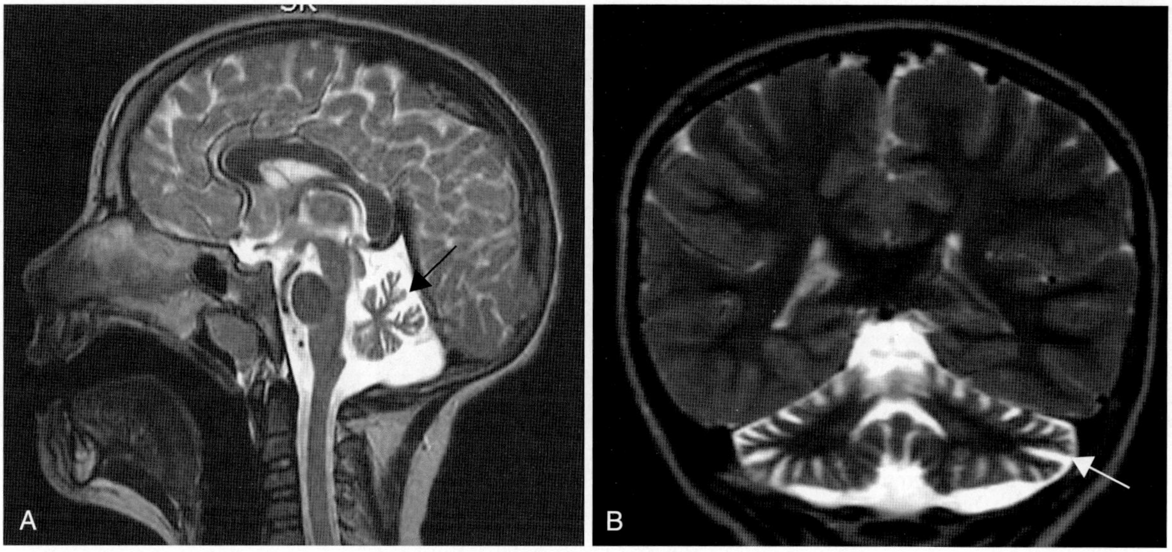

Fig. 77.3 Autosomal recessive cerebellar ataxia. Brain MRI, (A) sagittal and (B) coronal T2 show diffuse cerebellar atrophy with enlarged interfolial spaces (*arrows*).

such as ataxia-telangiectasia, chronic fat malabsorption, and deficiency of plasma lipoproteins. Abetalipoproteinemia can also cause hereditary vitamin E deficiency due to abnormal absorption of fat-soluble vitamins, including vitamin E, in the distal ileum. In AVED, defective alpha-tocopherol transfer protein (ATTP) results in abnormal incorporation of alpha-tocopherol into lipoproteins secreted by the liver. Vitamin E is involved in many physiological processes. In the neurological and immune systems, it has a role as an antioxidant, protecting molecules and tissues against the deleterious effects of free radicals. It also contributes to the stabilization of membranes and regulates many enzymes involved in gene expression and apoptosis. These findings suggest that primary or secondary vitamin E deficiency has an important role in neurodegeneration.

IMAGING DIFFERENTIAL DIAGNOSES

Combining neuroimaging findings with clinical information is essential when investigating pediatric cerebellar ataxia. Brain MRI can identify cerebellar abnormalities such as atrophy or hypoplasia of the cerebellar hemispheres and/or vermis, as well as signal changes and extracerebellar structures.

On neuroimaging, CA is defined as a cerebellum with normal morphology but enlarged fissures (interfolial spaces) (Fig. 77.3). This pattern implies loss of cerebellar parenchyma caused by a progressive disease or a single severe insult such as an infection or toxic exposure.

CA can be isolated or associated with other infratentorial or supratentorial findings such as hypomyelination, progressive white matter abnormalities, involvement of the basal ganglia, dentate nuclei, and cerebellar cortex. FLAIR images are most sensitive for signal changes in the cerebellar parenchyma. Other metabolic causes of CA include mitochondrial disorders (Fig. 77.4), *PLA2G6*-associated neurodegeneration (Fig. 77.5), and Marinesco-Sjögren syndrome, among others.

On the other hand, cerebellar hypoplasia (CH) refers to a reduced volume of the cerebellum with proportionally small and congenitally underdeveloped structures. Global CH may be the neuroimaging feature of nonprogressive cerebellar ataxia. In some cases, atrophy can be superimposed on hypoplasia, as documented in pontocerebellar hypoplasia (PCH) (Fig. 77.6) and congenital disorders of glycosylation (CDG) (Fig. 77.7).

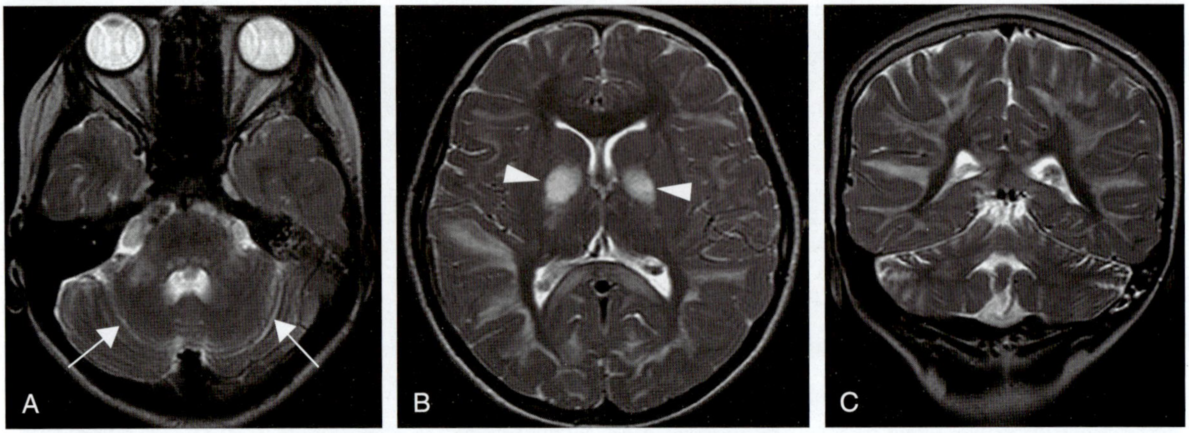

Fig. 77.4 Kearns-Sayre syndrome. Brain MRI, (A–B) axial and (C) coronal T2 show enlarged interfolial spaces (*arrows*), bilateral symmetric hyperintensity in the globi pallidi (*arrowheads*), and widespread white matter involvement, greatest posteriorly.

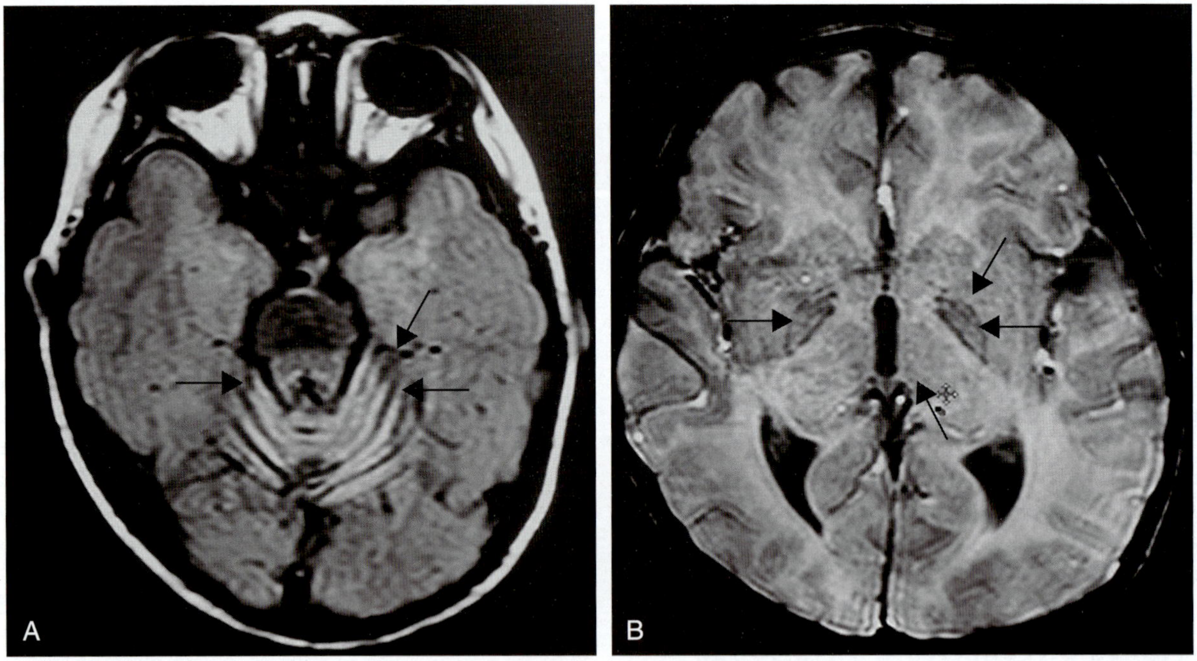

Fig. 77.5 *PLA2G6*-associated neurodegeneration. Brain MRI, (A) axial FLAIR shows hyperintensity and atrophy of the superior cerebellar folia (*arrows*). (B) Axial SWI demonstrates mild hypointensity of the globi pallidi representing iron deposits (*arrows*). *FLAIR*, Fluid-attenuated inversion recovery.

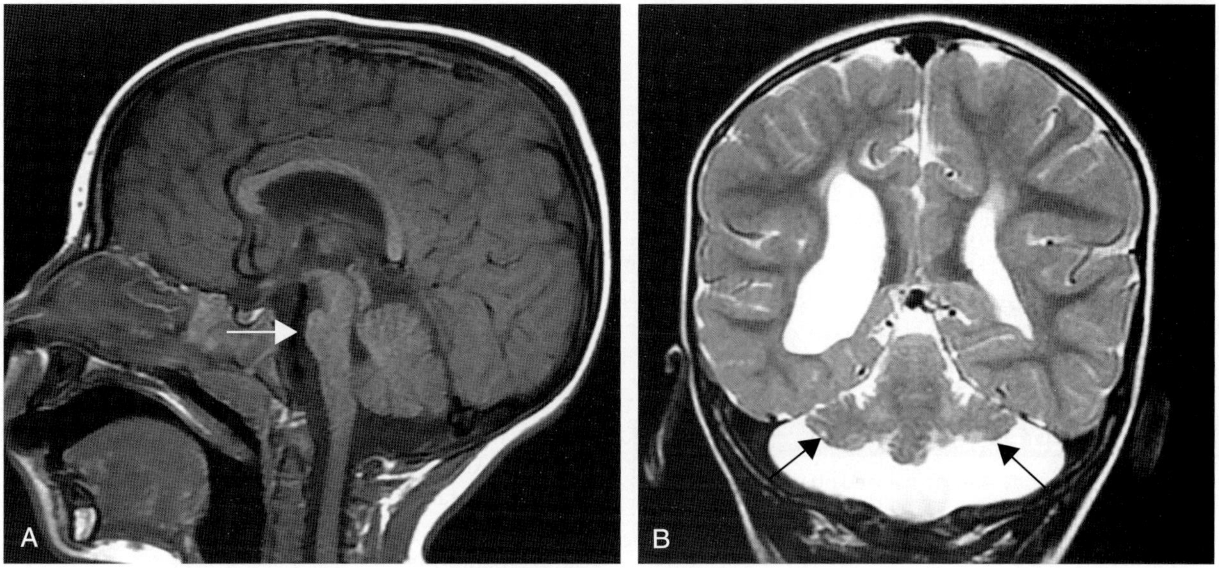

Fig. 77.6 Pontocerebellar hypoplasia. Brain MRI, (A) sagittal T1 and (B) coronal T2 show underdeveloped basis pontis (*white arrow*) and cerebellar hemispheres (*black arrows*).

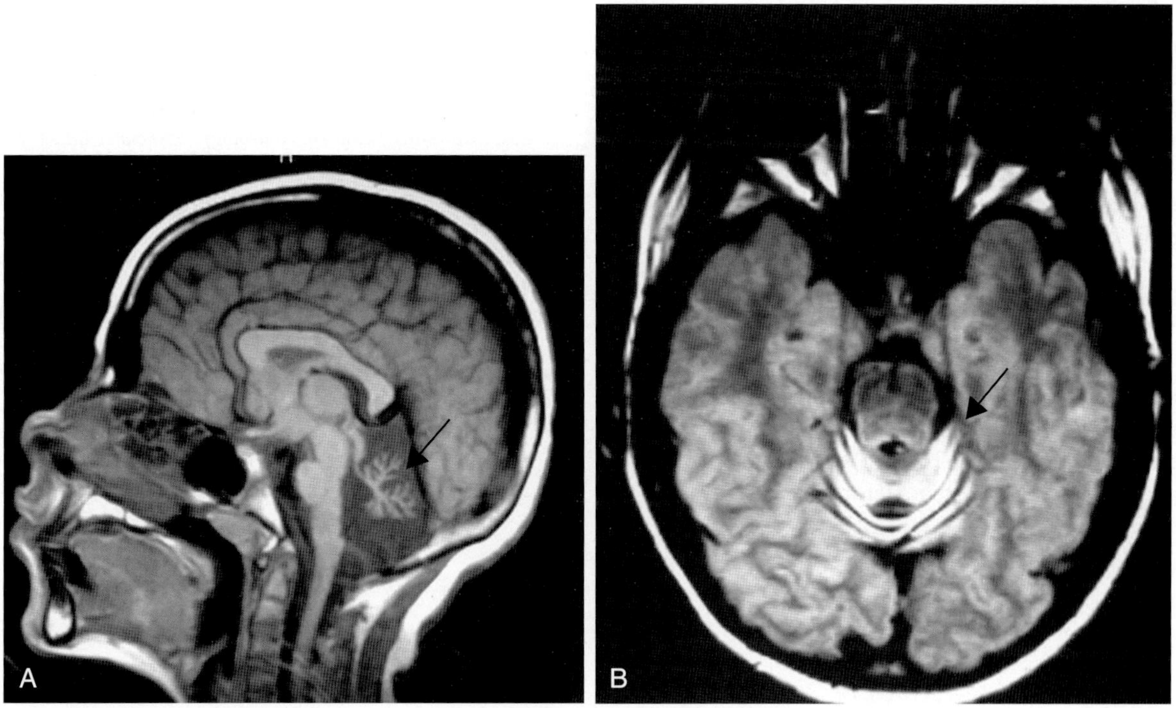

Fig. 77.7 Congenital disorder of glycosylation. Brain MRI, (A) sagittal T1 and (B) axial FLAIR show combined cerebellar hypoplasia and atrophy with FLAIR-hyperintense signal (*arrows*).

FINAL DIAGNOSIS

Ataxia associated with vitamin E deficiency.

CLINICAL RED FLAGS

- Cerebellar ataxia is a relatively common pediatric neurological condition with diverse etiologies and time courses.
- Consider metabolic and potentially treatable causes such as ataxia associated with coenzyme Q10 deficiency, pyruvate dehydrogenase complex deficiency, and vitamin E deficiency.

IMAGING RED FLAGS

- Cerebellar atrophy and spinal findings raise concern for a progressive ataxia.

DISCUSSION

Inherited ataxias comprise a diverse group of neurodegenerative disorders that are clinically and genetically heterogeneous. This group encompasses autosomal dominant ataxias, also known as spinocerebellar ataxias (SCAs), as well as autosomal recessive ataxias (ARCAs). Additionally, X-linked and mitochondrial forms of inherited ataxia are included in this classification.

The spectrum of phenotypes associated with CA is expanding, and the ongoing progress in identifying the genetic basis of these conditions is significant. AVED belongs to the group of ARCAs, caused by genetic variants in the *TTPA* gene coding for the ATTP located on chromosome 8. AVED is characterized by progressive cerebellar ataxia, dysarthria, and progressive clumsiness. Typically, symptoms manifest in late childhood or early adolescence and present with a clinical picture similar to Friedreich ataxia. Skeletal and cardiac deformities are present in Friedreich ataxia, whereas AVED is associated with head titubation or dystonia.

Treatment for AVED administers high doses of D-alpha-tocopherol, a form of vitamin E, which improves most neurological symptoms. The recovery process may be gradual and incomplete, with early supplementation yielding better outcomes.

CONCLUSIONS

Comprehensive evaluation of pediatric patients with cerebellar ataxia requires integration of clinical and neuroimaging findings. Although rare, vitamin E deficiency represents one of the most significant recessive ataxias. An important differential consideration for Friedreich ataxia, AVED can be confirmed by vitamin E levels or molecular testing, and managed with vitamin E supplementation.

REFERENCES

Al-Maawali A, Blaser S, Yoon G. Diagnostic approach to childhood-onset cerebellar atrophy: a 10-year retrospective study of 300 patients. *J Child Neurol.* 2012;27(9):1121–1132. https://doi.org/10.1177/0883073812448680.

Doherty D, Poretti A. Disorders of cerebellar and brainstem development. In: Swaiman KF, Ashwal S, Ferriero DM, et al., eds. *Swaiman's Pediatric Neurology: Principles and Practice.* 6th ed. Elsevier; 2017:199–207.

Poretti A, Wolf N, Boltshauser E. Differential diagnosis of cerebellar atrophy in childhood: an update. *Neuropediatrics.* 2015;46(6):359–370. https://doi.org/10.1055/s-0035-1564620.

Schuelke M. Ataxia with vitamin E deficiency. 2005 [Updated 2023 Mar 16]. In: Adam MP, Mirzaa GM, Pagon RA, et al., eds. GeneReviews®. University of Washington, Seattle; 1993–2023. https://www.ncbi.nlm.nih.gov/books/NBK1241/

Thapa S, Shah S, Chand S, et al. Ataxia due to vitamin E deficiency: a case report and updated review. *Clin Case Rep.* 2022;10(9):e6303. https://doi.org/10.1002/ccr3.6303.

Sickle Cell Disease, Brain, Skull, and Bones

HISTORY AND PHYSICAL

A 21-year-old male with a history of sickle cell anemia (HbSS) and acute chest syndrome presented to the ER with a severe headache. He had been discharged from the pediatric unit for lower extremity pain a few weeks prior.

He required prior exchange transfusions and intubation, with other complications including salmonella osteomyelitis, cholestasis, and nephropathy. He had been on hydroxyurea therapy since he was 13 years old.

The night prior to this admission, he developed a new 10/10 headache. It was located on the forehead and radiated to the entire head. He denied a visual aura. The pain was sharp and aching. There was a history of persistent photophobia and phonophobia but no nausea or vomiting. The headache improved with lying down, dim light, and sleeping. It did not respond to acetaminophen or oxycodone, but responded partially to Toradol, metoclopramide, and Dilaudid and ultimately required a hydromorphone pump. He had no history of fever, trauma, or toxic exposures. A stroke code was called; NIH Stroke Scale (NIHSS) was 0. A noncontrast head CT and computed tomography angiography (CTA) were normal. Brain MRI without contrast was unremarkable.

His review of systems revealed fatigue, chest and right-sided neck pain, myalgia, and weakness.

He denied the use of recreational drugs, including cocaine. His past medical history was also significant for heart valve vegetation, gallstones, and proteinuria. He denied allergy to medications. Vaccinations were up to date.

There was no family history of migraine headaches, aneurysms, or brain tumors.

On physical examination, his weight was 46 kg, height 165 cm, blood pressure 127/74, pulse 75, and temperature 36.2°C. Pain was 6/10. He was lying with his eyes closed and looked ill and thin. His forehead and the right side of the neck were tender, but he had no neck stiffness or lymphadenopathy.

Neurological examination revealed normal mental status for age. Cranial nerves, including fundoscopy exam, were normal. The motor, reflexes, sensory, cerebellar examinations were normal; gait exam was limited due to pain.

DIAGNOSTIC WORKUP

On admission, CTA of the head and neck demonstrated no significant hemodynamic stenosis or large vessel occlusion. Brain MRI showed a right frontal subdural collection (Fig. 78.1). Follow-up MRI demonstrated multifocal bone infarcts (Fig. 78.2) and subperiosteal hemorrhages (Fig. 78.3).

CLINICAL DIFFERENTIAL DIAGNOSES

Headaches and migraines can be seen in sickle cell disease, but their presence during a pain crisis raises other important considerations, including stroke, bone infarct, hemorrhage, and venous thrombosis. With nonfocal exam, a stroke of the brain or ischemia of the optic nerve would be improbable. Subarachnoid hemorrhage was unlikely without nausea or other symptoms of ICP or meningeal inflammation. CNS infection would present with fever or meningismus. Venous thrombosis would be a possibility given photophobia.

IMAGING DIFFERENTIAL DIAGNOSES

Hemodynamic stenosis or large vessel occlusion, including moyamoya disease, was ruled out by CTA. Brain MRV showed extra-axial hemorrhages causing

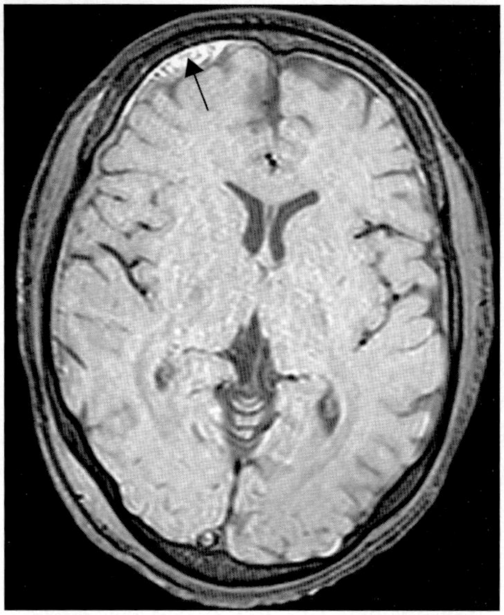

Fig. 78.1 Subdural hematoma. Brain MRI, axial T1, shows right frontal hyperintense crescentic collection (*arrow*).

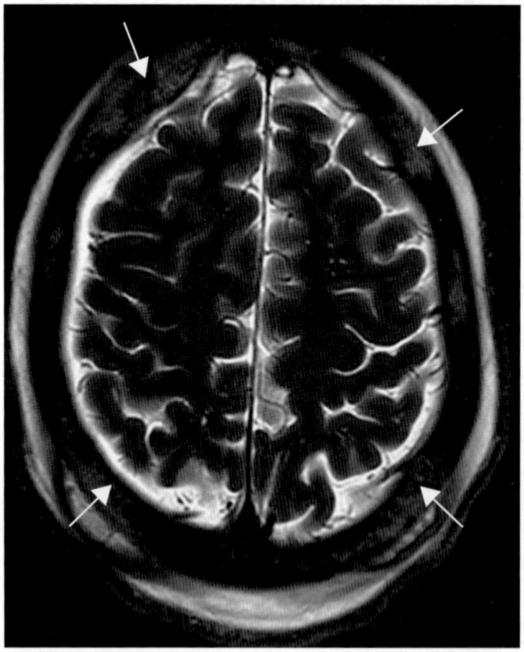

Fig. 78.2 Bone infarcts. Brain MRI, axial T2 with fat suppression, demonstrates multifocal marrow edema (*arrows*) with associated subperiosteal hemorrhages, subdural effusions, and scalp edema.

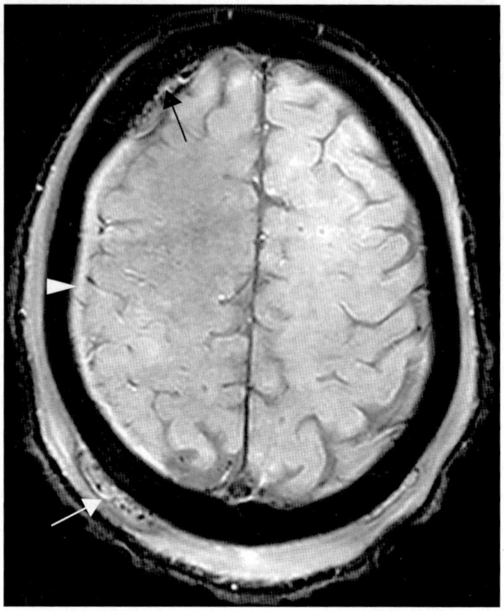

Fig. 78.3 Subperiosteal hemorrhages. Brain MRI, axial SWI, shows crescentic susceptibility along the right parietal calvarial outer table (*white arrow*) with overlying scalp edema, and along the right frontal inner table (*black arrow*) with adjacent subdural effusion (*arrowhead*). *SWI*, Susceptibility-weighted imaging.

extrinsic narrowing of the venous sinuses, but without frank thrombosis.

FINAL DIAGNOSIS

Sickle cell crisis.

DISCUSSION

Acute craniofacial bone infarcts are found in 7% of SCD patients imaged by MRI and in 15% of SCD patients who present with pain. MRI can demonstrate marrow edema, subperiosteal hematomas, and heterogeneous enhancement.

Children and adolescents with SCD have a high prevalence of recurrent headaches (24.0–43.9%). Acute presentation with headache can be diagnostically challenging, as the clinician must consider several potentially devastating conditions, including vascular diseases (stroke, hemorrhage, venous sinus thrombosis, moyamoya, PRES), facial and orbital bone infarcts, dental pain, and osteomyelitis.

CLINICAL RED FLAGS

- Sickle cells can block blood flow in blood vessels that provide blood to bones. When the bone does not get enough oxygen, the bone tissue can die, a complication known as avascular necrosis (AVN). AVN can occur without any symptoms, but as disease progresses, it can result in mild to severe pain in the affected area.

IMAGING RED FLAGS

- Neuroradiological findings in patients with SCD are common and include acute infarction, silent ischemia, and intracranial hemorrhage. Imaging abnormalities are typical but not universal manifestations of the underlying vasculopathy. Coexisting acute and chronic pathology may pose challenges to interpretation.
- Bone infarction, osteomyelitis, and altered marrow signal due to extramedullary hematopoiesis may be observed on neuroimaging. The treatment of SCD can also result in radiological abnormalities.

CONCLUSIONS

At least 25% of individuals with SCD will have a neurological complication over their lifetime, often as early as childhood. Acute presentation with headache can be diagnostically challenging, with a wide differential diagnosis and limited physical exam. Rapid clinical changes and persistent pain should alert clinicians to consider imaging.

REFERENCES

Abreu VS, Xavier S, Santos M, Lopes da Silva R, Kjöllerström P, Conceição C. Neuroimaging findings in paediatric patients with sickle cell disease. *Clin Radiol.* 2023;78(7):509–517. https://doi.org/10.1016/j.crad.2023.02.013.

Nelson CE, Scarfone RJ. A teenager with sickle cell disease and scalp swelling. *Pediat Emerg Care.* 2018;34(9):e168–e170. https://doi.org/10.1097/pec.0000000000001295.

Saito N, Nadgir RN, Flower EN, Sakai O. Clinical and radiologic manifestations of sickle cell disease in the head and Neck. *RadioGraphics.* 2010;30(4):1021–1034. https://doi.org/10.1148/rg.304095171.

Saul D, Pollock AN. Skull Bone/Calvarial infarction and spontaneous epidural hematoma as cause of severe headache in the emergency department. *Pediatr Emerg Care.* 2017;33(12):809–810. https://doi.org/10.1097/PEC.0000000000001338.

Thust SC, Burke C, Siddiqui A. Neuroimaging findings in sickle cell disease. *Br J Radiol.* 2014;87(1040):20130699. https://doi.org/10.1259/bjr.20130699.

Watanabe M, Saito N, Nadgir RN, et al. Craniofacial bone infarcts in sickle cell disease. *J Comput Assist Tomogr.* 2013;37(1):91–97. https://doi.org/10.1097/rct.0b013e3182752967.

CASE INDEX

DIAGNOSIS INDEX

SUBJECT INDEX

Note: Page numbers followed by "*f*" indicate figures, "*t*" indicate tables, and "*b*" indicate boxes.

E

F

G

H

I

T

U

V

W

X

IN THE CLUTCHES OF THE LAW

IN THE CLUTCHES OF THE LAW

Clarence Darrow's Letters

EDITED AND WITH AN INTRODUCTION BY

Randall Tietjen

Randall Tietjen
16 July 2013

UNIVERSITY OF CALIFORNIA PRESS
Berkeley Los Angeles London

University of California Press, one of the most distinguished university presses in the United States, enriches lives around the world by advancing scholarship in the humanities, social sciences, and natural sciences. Its activities are supported by the UC Press Foundation and by philanthropic contributions from individuals and institutions. For more information, visit www.ucpress.edu.

University of California Press
Berkeley and Los Angeles, California

University of California Press, Ltd.
London, England

Library of Congress Cataloging-in-Publication Data

Darrow, Clarence, 1857–1938.
[Correspondence]
In the clutches of the law : Clarence Darrow's letters / Edited and with an introduction by Randall Tietjen.
p. cm.
Includes bibliographical references and index.
ISBN 978-0-520-26558-5 (cloth : alk. paper)
1. Darrow, Clarence, 1857–1938—Correspondence. 2. Lawyers—United States—Correspondence. I. Tietjen, Randall (Matthew), 1961– editor of compilation. II. Title.
KF373.D35A4 2013
340.092—dc23
[B] 2012045889

Manufactured in the United States of America

22 21 20 19 18 17 16 15 14 13
10 9 8 7 6 5 4 3 2 1

The paper used in this publication meets the minimum requirements of ANSI/NISO Z39.48-1992 (R 2002) (*Permanence of Paper*).

For Susan
and our children,
Benjamin and Sophia

CONTENTS

ILLUSTRATIONS

PREFACE

MY SEARCH FOR LETTERS

My interest in Darrow began in 1991 when I was living in Lincoln, Nebraska. I had recently finished law school in Minnesota and was working as a law clerk for a judge. I knew almost no one in Lincoln and had some free time in the evenings and on weekends. I thought about writing an article or possibly a book and then saw an advertisement for the letters of Eugene Debs, which had just recently been published by the University of Illinois Press. I knew that Debs had been one of Darrow's more famous clients and it occurred to me that Darrow's letters had never been published.

I did not know much about Darrow other than what I had read in a few books about him. I knew that most of his fame as a lawyer springs from two cases: the Leopold and Loeb case in 1924 and the Scopes trial in 1925. From what I had read of Darrow's writings, I also knew that he had been a fine writer and speaker. So I started writing to libraries around the country, asking them to look in certain manuscript collections for his letters. Before long, I was receiving photocopies of his letters from the libraries and realized that what I had thought of Darrow as a writer was proving true. His letters—at least some of them—were beautifully written and interesting to read. I forwarded copies of the letters to Darrow's two surviving grandchildren—Mary Darrow Simonson and Blanche Darrow Chase—daughters of Darrow's only child, Paul Darrow, and his wife, Lillian. (Paul's other child, his oldest daughter, Jessie, died in 1968, and Mary and Blanche have also since died.) Mary and Blanche—both of whom were very supportive of my

efforts to unearth their grandfather's letters—were in their twenties when Darrow died in 1938, and they lived just one block from him in the Hyde Park area of Chicago.

Several months after I started looking for Darrow's letters, I drove to Chicago to meet Blanche (Mary lived in Hawaii). Blanche lived in a suburb of the city with her husband, Gordon. The day before I arrived, Gordon had been down in their basement looking through some old boxes. When I arrived, they told me that Gordon had found a box filled with some old papers and they were wondering if I would like to look at the contents. I was excited, of course, but had no idea what was about to come up from the basement. Gordon brought out a box stuffed—there was no order or neatness to it—with 110 or so letters written to Darrow by some of the most famous Americans of the early twentieth century. Inside the box were letters from well-known writers, politicians, labor leaders, and other public figures, including William Dean Howells, Jane Addams, Woodrow Wilson, H. L. Mencken, Henry Ford, Helen Keller, William Jennings Bryan, William Randolph Hearst, Frank Lloyd Wright, W. E. B. Du Bois, John Mitchell, Upton Sinclair, Mother Jones, Eugene Debs, Franklin Roosevelt, F. H. La Guardia, Theodore Dreiser, and Sinclair Lewis.

Also in the box were letters and postcards from lesser-known people, including Robert LaFollette, George Jean Nathan, Arthur Brisbane, Charles Chesnutt, Richard Bennett, William Pinkerton, Anita Loos, Theodore Powys, Zona Gale, Will Durant, Brand Whitlock, Elbert Hubbard, Hamlin Garland, William Allen White, Hutchins Hapgood, Bolton Hall, Fred Gardner, John T. McCutcheon, Algernon Crapsey, Horace J. Bridges, Oscar DePriest, Carl Laemmle, and Harry Elmer Barnes. The letters spanned a thirty-eight-year period, from 1896 (a letter from William Dean Howells) to 1933 (a letter from La Guardia). This was not a random sample of Darrow's mail; someone had selected and saved these letters because of the authors. Blanche told me that she thought her father might have picked them out over the years, as souvenirs, from the piles of letters in the room that Darrow used as an office in his apartment. This is consistent with what Darrow's second wife, Ruby Darrow, told a friend in Los Angeles who was collecting letters and hoping to find some from famous people in Darrow's hands: "One reason for scarcity at close range, is:—Paul Darrow—(son of C—D—) always appropriated, and still does, all that happen along, if noticed,—and if I have remembered to call attention to them . . ."[1]

After Blanche and Gordon and I had gone through all of these letters in their living room, Gordon and I (Blanche had a problem hip and did not want to walk the stairs) went into a large storage area in a corner of their basement to search for more treasure. This was an area of the basement with shelves stacked high with boxes. We spent quite a while searching for more material, and what we found, by the end of our search, was just as exciting as what we had seen so far. In unmarked boxes and a box labeled "Christmas ornaments" we found hundreds of letters to and from Darrow and other members of his

1. Ruby Darrow to T. Perceval Gerson, 17 December 1934, TLS, CLU-SC, Gerson Papers.

family. These included approximately 330 letters written by Darrow to his first wife, Jessie, and to their son, Paul. The boxes also contained many other family letters, including approximately forty letters by Darrow's oldest brother, Everett—most of them written to Darrow from Paris, when Darrow was facing trial for jury bribery in 1911–13 in Los Angeles; letters written by several of Darrow's other siblings, including his two sisters, Jennie and Mary, and two of his other brothers, Hubert and Channing; letters written by his son, Paul; many letters written by Darrow's second wife, Ruby; a few letters and transcripts of letters written by Darrow's mother, Emily, who died when Darrow was fifteen, and by Darrow's father, Ammirus.

We found scrapbooks of newspaper clippings that Darrow's first wife, Jessie, had kept of her husband's career, including many of his early writings published in newspapers as well as news items about speeches and activities that had long been lost or forgotten. We also found nineteen letters written by Darrow's brother-in-law, J. Howard Moore (he was married to Darrow's sister Jennie). These were written to Henry Salt, the English writer and humanitarian reformer. Moore, who lived in Chicago, was a leading advocate of vegetarianism and animal rights. In addition to all of these letters, the boxes also contained many reprints of Darrow's published articles and pamphlets containing his speeches, jury summations, and debates (almost all of these were already generally available in one form or another through libraries).

The letters we found that were written by Darrow spanned nearly his entire adult life. One letter was the earliest of his that I would ever find. It was written by Darrow to his brother Everett in 1873, when Darrow was fifteen years old (it is published here). Darrow's granddaughters were not quite sure how all of these family letters had landed in Blanche's basement, nor were they sure how long they had been down there. They thought that the letters might have been in their mother's hands when she passed away in 1969, and that someone put them away after she died and forgot about them. No biographer of Darrow had ever seen the letters, as far as I could tell, with one exception.

In the basement, Gordon and I found about a dozen letters from Darrow to his son in a small box used for Kodak photographic paper, which had an expiration date on it of October 1952. A note was written on the box: "Returned by Ray Ginger." Ray Ginger (1924–75) was a historian who wrote several books on American history, including a biography of Eugene Debs (*The Bending Cross,* 1949) and an excellent account of the Scopes trial (*Six Days or Forever,* 1958). In *Six Days or Forever,* Ginger mentions that he had been working on a biography of Darrow for eight years. But Ginger never published the book. Ginger's widow told me that he dropped the idea shortly after *Six Days or Forever* was published because he realized that a proper study of Darrow, given the number of cases that Darrow had been involved with, could take the rest of his life. Sometime in the 1950s, Paul Darrow apparently allowed Ginger to see some of the letters that his father had written to him.

In any event, Gordon and Blanche and I went through many of these hundreds of letters that day in their living room, working into the evening. After we had finished

going through them, I packed up all of the papers and—with Blanche and Gordon's permission—took them to a self-service, twenty-four-hour photocopying store. I stayed up all night, carefully copying every letter and envelope. In the morning, I returned everything to Gordon and Blanche, and they fixed breakfast for me. I went back to Lincoln, Nebraska, later that day, exhausted and excited.

Twenty years later, I have located approximately 2,235 letters written by Darrow, including the letters in Blanche and Gordon's basement, and another approximately 1,550 written to him. The originals of the letters are scattered in private and public collections around the country. In fact, a lot of my spare time outside the practice of law—at least before my son was born in 2003—has been spent searching for and researching Darrow's letters. Some of the letters were easy to find, and with the help of many kind librarians, I was able to put my hands on copies of them. Other letters took more work. Darrow's letters to Frank Walsh, for example, are buried throughout Walsh's large and largely unindexed collection of papers at the New York Public Library. Finding them required several days at the library sifting through the collection.

Although 3,785 or so letters is a sizeable amount of correspondence, I always hoped that I would find more. I know that Darrow received an immense amount of mail. In July 1927, for example, he wrote to writer and journalist Mary Field Parton that the "mail is full of letters that I don't want to read and can't answer and my best friends grow discouraged waiting. What can I do?"[2] Just how often Darrow wrote replies to the many letters that he received is unknown. In the later years of his life, when he was very famous, the sheer volume of Darrow's incoming mail must have been overwhelming.

In December 1929, he wrote from Paris to Benjamin Lindsey, a judge and pioneer in the juvenile-courts movement. Lindsey, like Darrow, was a public figure with a lot of incoming mail. Lindsey had written a letter to Darrow wanting to know what Darrow did with his mail. Darrow responded saying that he seldom wrote a reply to any of the usual letters that he received:

> Most of the mail people like you & I receive are from cranks and can generally be told by reading the address. Much of it is from notoriety seekers engaged in getting autographs; they care nothing about us. They don't know the difference between Calvin Coolidge and Bunker Hill Monument. Some are sincere but what can you do about it? These are generally the worst nuisances of all. I seldom reply to any of them nowadays—[3]

As a postscript, Darrow added some advice for Lindsey: "You can't burn it all without looking at it. I once found one with a postage stamp in it."

2. Darrow to Mary Field Parton, 15 July 1927. (Letters cited without a source—like this one—are published in this book.)
3. Darrow to Benjamin B. Lindsey, 17 December 1929.

Still, I can imagine that Darrow must have written many thousands of letters in his life and received many thousands more. He lived a long life and was in the public eye for much of it. Lawyers also tend to write a lot of letters (at least they used to) as part of their work. In addition, Darrow had a political and literary side to his life, which must have generated considerable correspondence. In a preface to the 1932 edition of *Farmington,* a novel about his childhood, Darrow commented that he had "a considerable file of letters [from admirers of his book] running over more than a quarter of a century" (*Farmington* was originally published in 1904).[4] That file is now nowhere to be found. In the manuscript market, Darrow's letters are sought after by collectors and generally sell for thousands of dollars each—but do not often appear on the market.

Darrow's wife, Ruby, gave one explanation for the lack of surviving personal correspondence in a letter to Ella Winter, the widow of the journalist Lincoln Steffens. In 1936, shortly after Steffens died, Winter was working on a book of Steffens's letters. She wrote to Ruby asking if Darrow had kept any letters from Steffens. Ruby wrote back, explaining that when she and Darrow had gone on an extended vacation in Europe several years earlier, Darrow's correspondence had been discarded, apparently by someone in Darrow's law office:

> So sorry to disappoint you, but, when Clarence gave up his office a number of years ago prepatory to the year we spent abroad, he left the dismantling of his offices, storing of papers and personal-communication-assortments, in hands of a secretary who also left the firm at that time, and—when we finally unpacked boxes sent here were surprised and displeased to discover that no letters save of business nature had been saved and sent; so, among those disposed of, must have been the letters from "Steff" which now would be more than ever treasured by us as well as by you.[5]

No one knows what was lost to history in the process of dismantling Darrow's law office.

In a letter to the writer Irving Stone, when Stone was working on a biography of Darrow, Ruby described how some of the letters in Darrow's apartment had gone up in smoke very late in his life. As Ruby explained it, one day when a nurse was taking care of Darrow in the apartment, Ruby had to go downtown. While she was gone, the nurse, along with Darrow's sister (Jennie Darrow Moore) and a friend of Darrow's (George Whitehead), gathered up "boxes of [Darrow's] letters" and "pushed [them] down the incinerator."[6] Ruby told Stone that she and her husband "had the same habit of thinking letters should not be saved to confront one with a sense of obligation toward the senders," and the actions of the nurse and the other two that day had been "a kindness to surprise [her] with the disappearance of

4. Clarence Darrow, *Farmington* (New York: Charles Scribner's Sons, 1932), vii.
5. Ruby Darrow to Ella Winter, 26 October 1936, TLS, NNC, Steffens Collection.
6. Ruby Darrow to Irving Stone, n.d. ("Dear Partner:— | Mrs. McKay telephoned . . ."), DLC-MSS, Darrow Papers.

that bugbear."[7] Despite this loss, Ruby told Stone that she had, "with difficulty at times," "salvaged and secreted" some letters that were worth keeping. I assume that at least some of those letters are now part of the Darrow Collection at the Library of Congress, which is where Ruby's collection of papers, for the most part, is housed. (The collection that Ruby assembled is now split: Ruby sold the papers to Kroch's Bookstores in Chicago in November 1938; Kroch sold the collection to Stone in August 1939 [for five hundred dollars]; Stone sold the collection to Leo Cherne [1912–99] in 1941; and Cherne—a lawyer and economist who had a long and varied career and was an admirer of Darrow—then donated most of the collection to the Library of Congress, but he kept, perhaps inadvertently, an odd assortment, including hundreds of letters and telegrams to Darrow, mostly in 1912 and 1932, that are now among Cherne's papers at Boston University.[8])

Darrow's granddaughters had no intention of being careless with the letters in their hands. They wanted to be sure that their materials would not be lost to history. I encouraged them to find a place for the letters and other papers at a library or some other institution—some place that would keep the collection together and make it available to the public. (Concerned about the fragility of the newspaper clippings in Jessie Darrow's scrapbooks on Darrow, Blanche and Gordon gave them to the Newberry Library in Chicago soon after we found them in the basement.) They did not want the letters sold piecemeal to collectors. In 2005, after many years of looking for a home for the letters, the family sold most of the collection to the University of Minnesota Law School, which, by sheer coincidence, is located just two miles or so from my law office. The sale of the collection was handled for the family by Meyer Boswell Books in San Francisco, which specializes in antiquarian books and manuscripts relating to law. The law school's purchase of the collection served as its library's one-millionth acquisition. Several years after purchasing the collection, the law school launched a marvelous website that includes images and transcripts of the letters and a multitude of other items and information relating to Darrow and his cases.[9]

In 2006, just when the number of Darrow's letters that I was finding was dwindling—suggesting to me that I had nearly exhausted my search—I received a phone call out of the blue from Elva Hamerstrom Paulson, the granddaughter of one of Ruby Darrow's brothers. I had never met Elva, but she told me she had some letters that Darrow had written to Ruby. How many letters, she did not say. But she said that she was trying to decide what she should do with them. I told her that she might want to call the same

7. See also Margaret Parton to Paul Heffron, 8 April 1974, DLC-MSS, Darrow Papers ("I'm disappointed but not surprised at the scarcity of personal correspondence [in the Darrow Papers at the Library of Congress]; my mother [Mary Field Parton] told me once that Darrow almost always threw letters away once he had read and answered them").
8. See, e.g., Leo Cherne to Arthur Garfield Hays, 25 March 1948, TLc, MBU, Cherne Papers, Box 1, Folder 3 (explaining, perhaps mistakenly, in response to Ruby Darrow's concern that the collection had been destroyed, that he had donated the whole collection to the Library of Congress except for a few photographs, a cartoon sketch, and some books).
9. See http://darrow.law.umn.edu, accessed 16 July 2011.

dealer who had handled the placement of Blanche and Mary's collection. She did, and now Elva's collection of letters is also at the University of Minnesota Law School. Elva's collection included some 150 letters written by Darrow to Ruby. As far as I can tell, no one researching Darrow's life had ever seen these letters until Elva brought them to light.

To keep track of the many letters I had been able to collect, I created a database early on in my project. In this database I cataloged details on all of the correspondence, including the size of the stationery, the style of the letterhead, the city that Darrow was in when he wrote the letter, and so forth. The database is not complete in all respects but it has helped me in many ways, including determining the year in which many of the letters were written. The database did not solve all of the difficulties that I had with the letters. Over the years, a great deal of my time on this project has been spent simply trying to decipher Darrow's sometimes terrible handwriting and in making transcripts of the letters. (Darrow himself, in writing about the manuscript for his autobiography, acknowledged that sometimes even he could not "figure out" what he had written on a page.[10]) I have also spent a lot of time researching and writing annotations for many of the letters—too much time, I am sure—including many letters not published here.

CRITERIA FOR SELECTION

Because this book does not come close to including all of the letters that I found, I should say something about the criteria I used to select the letters that are published here. This book publishes in full 502 letters written by Darrow, as well as quotes from others in the annotations. In general, my goal was to reveal as much as possible about Darrow and the events and relationships in his life. At the same time, though, I tried to keep in check my own interest in the minutiae of Darrow's life. I had to remind myself—and I might have failed at this—that some of the letters that I find interesting would not hold the attention of many other people, and that many of his letters have no real historical or literary merit. But sometimes it is hard to predict what might be useful or interesting to other people. Among the letters by Darrow that I have included in this book are thirty-one that were published in books, newspapers, or magazines in Darrow's own day. With one or two exceptions, none of these has since been reprinted.

Because of limitations on space, I have not published any of the many letters written *to* Darrow. There are relatively few sustained back-and-forth sequences of letters in Darrow's surviving correspondence. But if there is a surviving letter to which Darrow was responding or a surviving letter that responded to his, I made a note of that in my annotations. If I thought that a letter written to Darrow provided some context for Darrow's own letter or if I thought it made Darrow's letter more understandable or was revealing in some way of Darrow's own activities or relationships, I often included a quote from the letter in a footnote.

10. *Story*, 323.

In this book, I have included only one letter that was written neither *by* nor *to* Darrow, and that is the first letter—one from Darrow's father to Darrow's oldest brother (Everett), informing his brother that his mother had died. I include this letter because of its beauty and because it reflects on an important event in Darrow's own life.

ARRANGEMENT OF LETTERS

The arrangement of the letters is strictly chronological, from oldest to most recent, with no commentary (other than the notes) in between the letters. I have divided the chronology of letters into five-year increments, with the exception of the first and last sets of letters. The footnote numbers for the annotations begin anew with each "chapter" of letters.

COPY-TEXT

Most of Darrow's extant letters survive in the original manuscript or typescript. Although I have tried to locate the original of each letter, a few letters apparently survive only in some less reliable form, such as carbon copies, typed transcripts, or published versions. By "less reliable," I mean that no one can be sure that the document is an accurate reflection of what Darrow wrote and communicated. Whenever possible, I used the original letter as the copy-text for this edition. If I used a published version as the copy-text, the letter typically does not include the usual greeting, date line, or salutation.

EDITORIAL CONVENTIONS AND EMENDATIONS

In editing these letters, my goal was to make the published version of each letter easily readable, but also to make it correspond as closely as possible to the original text of the letter, with as few emendations as seemed reasonable to me. I have used the following editing principles and conventions.

EDITORIAL HEADING

The heading above each letter identifies the intended recipient of Darrow's letter, the place from which the letter was written, and the day and date of the letter. In the few instances in which the identity of the recipient is unknown or unclear, I have put the recipient's name within quotation marks. I have generally used the name of the person at the time the letter was written. So Mary Field Parton, for example, is listed as Mary Field until after she married, when she became Mary Field Parton. For letters written to people (as opposed to publications), the intended recipient of a letter is identified in the Biographical Register.

The place indicates the city or town from which the letter was written or from which I believe it was written. If the place is not provided somewhere on the letter and cannot

be assumed based on the letterhead or stationery, I provide a brief explanation of my rationale for listing a particular place in the unnumbered note at the end of the letter.

After the name of the place, I provide the day and date of the letter or the estimated date of the letter. If the date or part of the date (e.g., the year) is not listed on the letter itself, I provide a brief explanation for my rationale in the unnumbered note at the end of the letter. Sometimes, the basis for the date is simply a postmark on an envelope. But often the date is based on a combination of things, such as the place from which the letter was written, the content of the letter, or the letterhead or stationery.

LETTERHEAD, PLACE, AND DATE

I have placed all together on one line, flush right and directly below the editorial heading, any main letterhead information printed on the stationery (e.g., the name of the law firm, hotel, or railroad line), the place from which the letter was written (if it was provided by the author anywhere on the letter or if it was printed on the stationery as part of the same line as the date), and the day and date of the letter (if these were provided anywhere on the letter by the author). If the letterhead or place was printed on the stationery—as opposed to being written or typed on the letter by the author—I have reproduced it in small capital letters to distinguish it from information that was handwritten on the letter by the author.

Darrow used a variety of personal and law firm stationery over the course of his life (although he also wrote many of his letters on nondescript pieces of paper). In some instances, the differences between the letterheads on his stationery are slight—sometimes only a difference in the spacing of the letters. Those slight differences have helped me in dating many of the letters, but the differences are not worth trying to depict. So the reader of this book will see, for example, CLARENCE DARROW listed as a letterhead on many letters. This actually represents several different styles of letterhead that Darrow used in the last ten years or so of his life. No matter which personal or business stationery Darrow used, I have reproduced only the first line or two of the letterhead and then always in small capitals. If Darrow wrote the letter, for example, on hotel stationery or some other law firm's stationery, the only information that I have provided from the letterhead is the name of the hotel or law firm and the city and state.

Darrow rarely wrote the place from which his letter was written or sent. He also rarely wrote the day of the week or year. His usual habit was simply to write the month and the day of the month. If he wrote any of this information on the letter, the information is printed flush right on this same line below the editorial heading, regardless of where it was written on the original letter. Thus, if Darrow wrote the place or date at the bottom of the letter, below his signature, which he did on a few occasions, the information is printed here on this first line below the editorial heading. Because the letterhead information is set off in small capital letters, I do not use a vertical line between the letterhead information and the first handwritten element of the letter. Finally, if the stationary

included the first two digits of the year and the author of the letter added the last two digits, the letter contains the full year, as if written in the author's hand.

ADDRESS INFORMATION

If a return address or the name or address of the intended recipient is in the letter itself, this information is placed in the unnumbered note at the end of the letter. In that unnumbered note a vertical line signifies a line break between the elements of the address in the original. If the name alone of the intended recipient is above a salutation in the original and the name is not used in the salutation, the name generally is printed above the salutation and not in the unnumbered note at the end of the letter.

UNNUMBERED NOTES

Immediately at the end of each letter, in an unnumbered note, I provide several items of information about the letter, if the information is available. Following the notation "MS," I provide a short description of the original letter, including the form of the letter (e.g., TLS = typed letter signed) and the owner or source for the letter. If the owner of a letter is an organization, the code that I use for the organization follows the Library of Congress's MARC Code List for Organizations, if the organization has a MARC code. A list of the codes that I used is contained in the list of abbreviations. If the only source that I found for the letter was a publication, I provide a citation to the publication. If the location of the letter is unknown (because the letter, for example, was sold by a manuscript dealer), I use the notation "location of original unknown (copy in editor's files)."

Following the description of the letter and its location, I include information about the date of the letter, the place it was written, any inside address information on the letter, and information on any surviving envelope, including postmark information. If there is any other information about the letter or the envelope that I thought might be significant, I placed that information in this unnumbered note as well, after the word "NOTE."

CAPITALIZATION

In his handwritten letters Darrow often failed to capitalize the first letter beginning a new sentence. Even in the few letters that Darrow himself typed in 1911 and 1912, he would fail to capitalize the first letter. Sometimes, Darrow's poor handwriting makes it difficult if not impossible (especially with the letters *c*, *s*, and *e*) to determine whether he intended an uppercase or lowercase letter. I have used a capital letter to begin each of Darrow's sentences, whether he actually used a capital letter or not. Otherwise, the letters would be difficult to read. In addition to using small capital letters to indicate printed letterhead, I have used them for the text of telegrams, which were often typed in capital letters, as well as for text that appeared in small capitals in published letters.

PUNCTUATION

Many of Darrow's letters were apparently rapidly composed, and Darrow was not very careful with punctuation; in fact, he often did not bother to use it. Just as often as he placed a stop at the end of a sentence, he did not place a stop. He sometimes used commas to set off clauses and parenthetical elements, but usually left them out. Sometimes a stop or pause is suggested in his sentences by a slightly lengthier space than usual between words. Sometimes he seems to have omitted a stop at the end of a sentence if the sentence came to an end at the right margin of the page. Usually it was very hard to distinguish the end and beginning of his sentences, not only because he did not use any stop, but also (as mentioned above) because he often did not capitalize the start of his sentences. He also often did not use apostrophes.

Under all of these conditions, transcribing his handwriting exactly as it appears in his original letters would be nearly impossible without resort to some system of symbols or notation, which would necessarily become excessive and make reading more of a chore and less of a pleasure. To solve this problem, I have added stops and apostrophes as sparingly as possible, but where I believe they will make the letter more readable. Doing this often required some judgment on my part, not only in determining when a sentence ends and when the next one begins, but also in determining *how* to end the sentence. It was not always clear whether a sentence was meant to be declarative or interrogative in nature. I had to decide whether a period or a question mark was more appropriate. In those instances I simply used my best judgment.

Sometimes it is difficult to discern what type of punctuation Darrow intended. Some marks on the page looked to me like they could be dashes or periods. Here, again, I had to use my judgment. I tried to follow conventional rules of punctuation, but sparingly. In general, if Darrow supplied a stop at the end of a sentence and it should have been a question mark, I did not change his punctuation. Sometimes, though, Darrow would use a handwritten dash to fill out the remainder of a line on the page before starting the next line. This cannot be shown very easily in a book and I did not try to include these in my transcripts.

With respect to typewritten letters, if the original included a hyphen or hyphens that would have been an en dash or em dash if typeset, I have converted the hyphens to the appropriate dash. Ruby Darrow often typed letters for Darrow's signature in the last few years of his life and she had a perverse love for hyphens.[11] When she typed Darrow's letters they were often spoiled by her excessive hyphens and her odd phrases. (The writer John Cowper Powys wrote "What a silly letter" in the margin of one of Ruby's letters.[12])

11. Darrow to T. Perceval Gerson, 17 December 1934, TLS, CLU-SC, Gerson Papers ("This is written by Mrs. Darrow, as I am dictating to her at the machine; she has learned to take care of my large mail, and whatever else needs to be moved aside, as I no longer go to any office").
12. Darrow to John Cowper Powys, 9 August 1935, TLS, TxU-Hu, Powys Collection.

I have not included many of the Ruby-typed letters in this book, but her style of writing can be seen in some of the letters.[13]

With typewritten letters I have not reproduced obvious slips of the keys. For example, when the typist inadvertently omitted a space between words or used too many spaces between words I did not try to reproduce this or make a note of this. And at least one odd form of punctuation I have also made no effort to reproduce: Darrow often presented a dollar figure followed by a dash with a dot below it; I have not tried to re-create that here. Finally, any use of parentheses in a letter is from the original, including a few instances of parentheses around a question mark.[14] In some instances, the use of brackets (in previously published letters) is also from the original.[15]

SYMBOLS AND ABBREVIATIONS

With the exception of ampersands and an archaic abbreviation for "et cetera" (&c), Darrow rarely used symbols or abbreviations in his writing. But any that he did use have generally been retained.

SPELLING

Darrow often did not bother to cross the *t* and dot the *i* in his writing. This is an example of something that would be very difficult to reproduce in print but it shows the haste or carelessness with which Darrow wrote. He also often misspelled words and was not consistent in the way that he spelled some words. For example, he sometimes misspelled the names of his friends (e.g., Debbs instead of Debs or Guerson instead of Gerson) and, oddly enough, sometimes misspelled "intelligent" and "literary." On a couple of occasions, Darrow would get someone's name completely wrong. I have retained those types of errors because they might represent more than an inadvertent slip of the pen. But I have silently corrected all other rather obvious inadvertencies in spelling—what I deemed small slips of the pen. There are not many of them, but I decided that little could be gained by retaining them, even if they could all be reproduced—especially when leaving them in might be a distraction or potentially confusing. Still, when I thought Darrow's intent was clear and, in my judgment, the reader would not stumble too much or wonder whether the error was mine or Darrow's, I left the misspellings in.

Given Darrow's poor handwriting, it is not always possible to identify his spelling errors. Sometimes, with handwritten letters, if I thought Darrow *might* have misspelled a word, I gave him the benefit of the doubt and spelled it correctly. In a few instances I have added a word (in brackets) because it seems clear to me that the word was

13. See, e.g., Darrow to Frank Murphy, 9 October 1935.
14. See Darrow to Gertrude Barnum, circa April 1930; Darrow to Charles Mantinband, 23 August 1932; Darrow to John H. Dietrich, 20 September 1932.
15. See Darrow to *Chicago Tribune*, 27 January 1903.

inadvertently omitted by the typist or Darrow. For example, when Darrow himself was typing a letter in 1912 he probably typed the word "of" just off the right margin of the page.[16] I did not comment on most of the typographical errors that have been reproduced here, but a few, I thought, warranted a note. Finally, if a word or set of words was completely illegible to me, I inserted a bracketed "x" for each word that was illegible. Thus, two consecutive illegible words would be signified with "[xx]."

DELETIONS AND INSERTIONS

Deletions in the letters by the writer or the typist, including false starts, have not been retained, unless I thought that the deletion was revealing of an initial thought or something else significant. Interlineations and handwritten insertions by the typist or writer of the letter are not specifically identified as interlineations or insertions.

PARAGRAPHING

All original paragraphing in the letters has been retained. The first line of every paragraph is indented, regardless of whether the original was indented. In his handwritten letters, Darrow often did not divide his writing into paragraphs—the letters are one big paragraph. But sometimes he would suggest or hint at a new paragraph, for example, by leaving more space than usual between his lines of text. I have generally treated these as paragraph breaks, especially if a new paragraph seemed appropriate.

ANNOTATIONS

Through my annotations to the letters, I have tried to make the letters more understandable to the reader today and I have tried to show some of the relationships and events in Darrow's life that have not otherwise received much attention—including cases in which Darrow was involved as a lawyer. The notes (and my separate chronology of his life) show that Darrow's life was much more than the handful of cases and events he described in his own autobiography and that have been reviewed again and again in the literature on him. Because of the period in which he lived and worked—stretching from the Gilded Age to the Great Depression—Darrow is an unusual example of a lawyer who fought for free speech and other civil liberties before as well as after World War I.[17]

In the notes, I have tried to be consistent and to strike a balance in the information provided. For example, for individuals identified in notes, I have provided, in general, more information for historically obscure people and for those who figured prominently in Darrow's life (whether they are obscure or not). Likewise, for those individuals who

16. See Darrow to J. Howard Moore, 28 December 1912.

17. See David M. Rabban, *Free Speech in Its Forgotten Years* (Cambridge: Cambridge University Press, 1997), 8 (noting that many of the progressives who founded the American Civil Liberties Union and who became civil libertarians after the war "had little interest in the subject of free speech before the war").

did not figure prominently in Darrow's life and who are better known today, I have generally provided less information. Of course, the amount of biographical information about the individuals is also limited, in some instances, by the amount of information that I found on each person.

If an individual is mentioned or referred to more than once in the letters, then the biographical information on that person—if I was able to find anything at all—is almost always included in the Biographical Register. If a person's name is mentioned twice or so in close proximity, but never again later, that person is usually not listed in the Biographical Register, but instead is identified in a footnote. Also, whether the person is identified in the notes or in the Biographical Register, I have tried to provide information, especially if relevant, about the person's life at the time of the letter or events involved.

If the first name of the person is given in the letter, I usually state the full name of the person in a footnote. But if the first name of the person is frequently mentioned throughout the letters or the identity of the person should be understood from the context (e.g., "Paul" in letters to Darrow's first wife; "Sara" or "Sarah" in letters to Charles Erskine Scott Wood; and "Lem" in letters to Mary Field Parton), I usually do not provide the full name in the notes. If there is any doubt about who someone is, the Biographical Register will probably clear things up.

I have not listed all of the sources for the biographical information in my notes and the Biographical Register. The number of sources was simply too great and the sources too varied; listing all of them would have cluttered up the notes and the Biographical Register. In many instances, I was able to find listings for the person in traditional reference works, including the *Dictionary of American Biography* and *American National Biography*. In other instances, I used obituaries, manuscript-finding aids, various history books, newspaper articles, interviews with descendants or other people, census forms, and countless online sources.

If a letter in this book was in response to a letter, or if a letter in this book generated a response from the recipient, I have noted it in my annotations, as I mentioned above. If nothing is cited in the annotations, the reader can assume that I did not find any related letters. The same is true for a reference to an enclosure in a letter. If I do not quote from or cite the enclosure, the reader can assume that I was unable to find the enclosure. If Darrow mentions a book or some published item and I was able to identify it, I tried to cite the particular edition or translation that Darrow or his correspondent had in mind (even though a later edition or translation might be available).

MISCELLANEOUS

Finally, I did not include several types of information that might have appeared on a letter: the word "over" at the bottom of a page; any typists' notes; the typist's initials, if any; and any extraneous typographical information on telegrams.

ACKNOWLEDGMENTS

This book has taken a good share of my time over twenty years, but without the generous help of many people I could never have completed the work—no matter how much time I had. Among the people whose help I want to acknowledge are Darrow's granddaughters, Mary Darrow Simonson and Blanche Darrow Chase, and Blanche's husband, Gordon Chase. When I started this book, they were all alive; in fact, Blanche and Mary were the only people alive who had known Darrow well. They all shared my excitement whenever I found some of Darrow's letters and they were kind to me from the start—giving me a great deal of their time for questions and giving me permission to publish the letters. Mary and Blanche had many stories and a lot of information about their grandfather—information that I could never have obtained from any other source. I wish very much that I could have completed this book before they passed away. I am also grateful to William Lyon and Judith Besser—the two children of Mary and Blanche's sister, Jessie Darrow Lyon, who died in 1968—for their permission to publish their great grandfather's letters.

Many dear friends have given generously of their time to this project and they have encouraged and supported me in various ways over the years. Joe Luttrell has been a continual source of support—sharing with me what he knows about Darrow (which is considerable), testing my ideas, and helping me in so many other ways too numerous to mention. I'm also grateful to Joe and his wife, Sherry Goodman, for providing a place for me to stay during several research trips to San Francisco. Arnold Greenberg has shared my excitement about Darrow's letters, helped me decipher some of them, and otherwise given generously of his time for this project—and any time spent with Arnold is such a

delight. Bryan Garner—the most learned lawyer I know—has given me lots of helpful advice and encouraged my work on this book for nearly twenty years, and I sometimes believe that the book would have been delayed by years without him. Dona Munker has been helpful in many ways, sharing with me her research and ideas about Darrow and some of his friends, including Sara Bard Field. (The book that Dona is writing about Sara Bard Field is much needed and sure to be an exciting account of a neglected figure in women's history.) Harriet Lansing and Russ Pannier are two friends who encouraged and inspired my work on this book in similar ways, including by providing me with many stimulating conversations and ideas about how literature, history, law, and philosophy might intersect with a study of Darrow's life.

Whenever I think about all of the varied intellectual subjects that a study of Darrow can entail, I often think about Joel Samaha, the teacher who made me want to become a student—a real student. Joel's undergraduate classes and graduate seminars on the history of criminal justice and criminal law and procedure at the University of Minnesota were a mind-opening experience for me, as they have been, I'm sure, for countless students before and after me. It was in Joel's classes that I first learned about fascinating people like Brand Whitlock, Frederick C. Howe, and Sam "Golden Rule" Jones. From nearly the moment I began this project, Joel listened to me talk about Darrow and my discoveries, and he has been a source of encouragement in more ways than he knows. Every student should be so lucky to have a teacher—even just one teacher—like Joel Samaha.

I would also like to acknowledge the kindness of the many librarians, archivists, scholars, friends, and others who have helped me in one significant way or another over the past twenty years, whether it was with my search for letters and or my research on Darrow's life and the content of his letters. So many people helped in such a wide variety of ways that I could not begin to name all of them. In fact, I never knew the names of most of the librarians and archivists.

But the people I have not forgotten include:

John Ahouse
Paul Avrich
John Q. Barrett
Fred Bauman
Indira Berndtson
Tony Bliss
Peter J. Blodgett
Steve A. Brand
James Bredeson
Martha Briggs
Robert L. Carter
Emmett D. Chisum
Wendy E. Chmielewski
Jan M. Conlin
Timothy Connelly
Helen Corneli
Bernard R. Crystal
Jonathan Dodge
Elizabeth Dubrulle
Gene DeGruson
Alfred H. Edwall Jr.
Kristen A. Earnhardt
John F. Eisberg
Anne Engelhart

James L. Fetterly
Phil Freshman
Dorothy Frye
Mary Gardner
Karolyne Cheng Garner
Janet Goodman
Ann D. Gordon
Kathy Gross Schoen
Marshall Hambro
Michael J. Hannon
Katherine Hedin
George Hendrick
Katie Hensley
Julie Herrada
Martha Hodges
John Hoffman
Joan S. Howland
Kate Hutchens
Karen L. Jania
Drew Kadel
John P. Kaminski
Judith L. Kash
Madeline Kastler
Esther Katz
Thomas C. Kayser
Anne Kintner
Beth E. Luey
Charles Magel
Sylvia Manning
William H. Manning
R. Russell Maylone
Doug McCabe
Laura Micham
Keith Newlin
Grace Palladino
Mary L. Person
Jeannie Pollock
Ben Primer
Paul Pruitt
David M. Rabban
Willis Goth Regier
J. Bridget Reischer
Dorothy Riegel
Damien A. Riehl
Marion Elizabeth Rodgers
Alissa Rosenberg
Herbert K. Russell
Steven J. Ross
Nick Salvatore
Steven A. Schumeister
Dale R. Schwie
Roman M. Silberfeld
Jeffrey L. Sammons
Charles Tamason
Weston T. Thompson
Roberta B. Walburn
Cynthia Wall
Richard Webb
Edward C. Weber
John L. Westphal
Michael Widener
Richard Workman.

I am grateful to Joseph Epstein—whose writing I have long admired—for talking to me early on about this project and for helping me find a publisher. The late J. Anthony Lucas—author of *Big Trouble,* an excellent book about the trials of "Big Bill" Haywood and other labor people in Idaho in 1907—also encouraged my work in the early years of this project. I wish that I could thank him again for taking an interest and giving me advice. Michael E. Stevens, state historian at the State Historical Society of Wisconsin, has been a great help to me over the years, not only in reviewing my manuscript but in giving me advice on the finer points of editing and publishing historical documents.

Three biographers of Darrow—Lila Weinberg (now deceased), Kevin Tierney, and Geoffrey Cowan—and one bibliographer—Willard Hunsberger—were helpful and encouraging in the early stages of my work. My opinions and conclusions about Darrow do not always coincide with theirs (nor with others who have written about Darrow), but I was always aware that the work I was doing was building on the work of other researchers and writers before me. Two biographies of Darrow were published just as I was putting the final touches on the manuscript—one by Andrew E. Kersten (*Clarence Darrow: American Iconoclast* [Hill & Wang]) and the other by John A. Farrell (*Clarence Darrow: Attorney for the Damned* [Doubleday]). I benefited from reading both of those books. They are well-written biographies that reflect a great deal of original research and they warrant attention by anyone interested in Darrow's life. I am especially grateful to John Farrell, who, among other things, brought to my attention a collection of letters and telegrams and other Darrow-related items in the Leo Cherne Papers at Boston University.

I am indebted to three students who helped track down many items relating to Darrow on microfilm and in archives: Madeline Kastler, May Tuyen, and John Zimm. Madeline helped me off and on for several years, and I am especially glad that I had the help of her skillful research. My friend Nathan Kottke helped me in a pinch, when I needed some research at the Library of Congress. I am also indebted to my sister-in-law, Karen Arntzen, who helped me dig through newspaper archives. My niece, Sara Tietjen, also helped me by combing through old newspapers at the Wisconsin Historical Society, and for that I'm grateful.

Barbara Stevens helped me not only in reviewing and proofreading the manuscript but also with organizing all of the materials necessary to bring this book together. I've thanked her repeatedly, but I've never felt it was enough. Her always cheerful attitude and dedicated, careful manner make the law office a very enjoyable place to work.

Four people who are part of Ruby (Hamerstrom) Darrow's surviving family gave very generously of their time, and I would like to thank them for their help: Elizabeth Hamerstrom (now deceased); Frances Hamerstrom (now deceased); Carol Johnstone; and Elva Paulson. Elva gave me a great deal of her time and I certainly benefited from her careful transcripts of Darrow's letters to Ruby, which she and her friend Jeannie Pollock made. Carol kindly sent me copies of all the items in her family collection, including many photographs of Darrow. Both Elva and Carol generously allowed me to use some photographs from their collections in this book.

I would also like to say how glad I am that the Association for Documentary Editing exists. When I started this project, I knew nothing about documentary editing and I wasn't quite sure where to begin. I don't recall how I learned about the ADE, but I remember pouring over back issues of the organization's magazine (*Documentary Editing*) and reading some of the excellent books and other literature written by leaders of the ADE. I also benefitted from a one-week seminar on documentary editing

that the ADE organized for budding documentary editors. Today, I would still not hold myself out as an expert on documentary editing; it has only been an avocation for me, and there are no doubt many flaws or poor choices in this final product. But it was mainly through the ADE that I learned how to go about the task of editing Darrow's letters.

Lynne Withey, now retired as director of the University of California Press, played a very important role in bringing this book about, beginning many years ago when she was an acquisitions editor at the Press. It was only through her help and counsel and after years of patience (both on Lynne's part and on the part of the University of California Press in general) that this book has come about. Many other dedicated people at the Press have also been a great help to me in producing this book, including Naomi Schneider, Stacy Eisenstark, Kate Warne, Christopher Lura, and Mari Coates. The sharp eye and sound advice of copy editor Sue Carter made this a much better book than it otherwise would have been. The Press had two people (anonymous to me) review my manuscript. I am very grateful for the time they took to review the manuscript and help me make it better. I hope that they can see their suggestions reflected in this final product.

Many friends and family spent a lot of time reading and commenting on various drafts of my introduction and other parts of this book and talking with me about this project, and I want to acknowledge their help and support:

Catherine Arntzen
Karen Arntzen
David W. Beehler
Patrick J. Bradley
Michael A. Collyard
Martin J. Costello
Brad P. Engdahl
Mark D. Fiddler
Bryan A. Garner
Robert J. Gilbertson
Arnold Greenberg
Thomas B. Hatch
Harriet Lansing
John Leithen
Rebecca Leithen
Seth J. Leventhal
Martin R. Lueck
Joe Luttrell
Christopher W. Madel
Bruce D. Manning
Richard M. Martinez
Munir R. Meghjee
Joel A. Mintzer
Dona Munker
Russell F. Pannier
Denise S. Rahne
Stephen P. Safranski
Joel Samaha
Ronald J. Schutz
Barbara Stevens
Tara D. Sutton
James Tabor
Aileen Tietjen
Eric Tietjen
Glenora Tietjen
Mary Tietjen
Morris Tietjen
Sara Tietjen
Thomas Tietjen
William R. Wilson Jr.
Matthew L. Woods.

But there is no one to whom I owe more of an acknowledgment of help and support than Susan, my wife. She gave the entire manuscript a careful and intelligent reading—more than once; she helped me think about and work through many of the issues that came up in my research and writing; and, she made sure that I found time to work on the book and encouraged me to work on it when I needed encouragement. But this doesn't begin to describe the many ways in which she has helped and supported me. She and our two children—Ben and Sophie, who make us both smile and laugh every day—make everything possible, and I love them dearly.

ABBREVIATIONS

DOCUMENT CODE

AL	autographed letter unsigned or signature missing
ALS	autographed letter signed
Tele	telegram
TL	typed letter, not signed
TLc	typed letter, copy
TLS	typed letter signed
TT	typed transcript

REPOSITORY CODE

CLL	Los Angeles County Law Library, Los Angeles, California
CLU-SC	Department of Special Collections, Charles E. Young Research Library, University of California, Los Angeles, California
CMalG	The Getty Center for the History of Art and the Humanities, Santa Monica, California
CSmH	Huntington Library, San Marino, California

CSt	Department of Special Collections and University Archives, Stanford University Libraries, Stanford, California
CtW	Wesleyan University, Middletown, Connecticut
CtY-BR	Beinecke Rare Book and Manuscript Library, Yale University, New Haven, Connecticut
CU-BANC	Bancroft Library, University of California, Berkeley, California
DCU	Catholic University of America, Washington, D.C.
DLC-MSS	Library of Congress (Manuscript Division), Washington, D.C.
IaU	University of Iowa, Iowa City, Iowa
ICHi	Chicago Historical Society, Chicago, Illinois
ICN	Newberry Library, Chicago, Illinois
ICU	Special Collections Research Center, University of Chicago Library, University of Chicago, Chicago, Illinois
IdBB	Special Collections, Boise State University, Boise, Idaho
IdHi	Library and Archives, Idaho State Historical Society, Boise, Idaho
IEN	Northwestern University, Evanston, Illinois
IHi	Illinois State Historical Library, Springfield, Illinois
In	Indiana State Library, Indianapolis, Indiana
InTI	Indiana State University, Cunningham Memorial Library, Terre Haute, Indiana
InU-Li	Lilly Library, Indiana University, Bloomington, Indiana
IU-HS	Illinois Historical Survey, University of Illinois at Urbana-Champaign, Urbana, Illinois
KyLoU-L	Law Library, University of Louisville, Louisville, Kentucky
MB	Boston Public Library, Boston, Massachusetts
MBNU	Archives and Special Collections Department, Northeastern University Libraries, Boston, Massachusetts
MBU	Howard Gotlieb Archival Research Center, Boston University, Boston, Massachusetts
MCR-S	Schlesinger Library, Radcliffe Institute for Advanced Study, Harvard University, Cambridge, Massachusetts
MdCpAIP	Niels Bohr Library and Archives, American Institute of Physics, College Park, Maryland
MH-H	Houghton Library, Harvard University, Cambridge, Massachusetts

MiDbEI	Henry Ford Museum, Dearborn, Michigan
Mi-SA	State Archives of Michigan, Lansing, Michigan
MiU	Labadie Collection, Special Collections Library, University of Michigan, Ann Arbor, Michigan
MiU-H	Bentley Historical Library, Michigan Historical Collections, University of Michigan, Ann Arbor, Michigan
MnHi	Minnesota Historical Society, St. Paul, Minnesota
MnU-L	University of Minnesota Law Library, Minneapolis, Minnesota
NHyF	Franklin D. Roosevelt Library, Hyde Park, New York
NIC	John M. Olin Library, Cornell University, Ithaca, New York
NjP	Department of Rare Books and Special Collections, Princeton University, Princeton, New Jersey
NN	Manuscripts and Archives Division, Astor, Lenox, and Tilden Foundations, New York Public Library, New York, New York
NNAF	American Foundation for the Blind, New York, New York
NNC	Butler Library, Columbia University, New York, New York
NNJJ	John Jay College of Criminal Justice, The City University of New York, New York, New York
NSyU	Special Collections Research Center, Syracuse University Library, Syracuse University, Syracuse, New York
OAU	Ohio University, Athens, Ohio
OCAJA	American Jewish Archives, Cincinnati, Ohio
OCU	University of Cincinnati, Cincinnati, Ohio
OHi	Ohio Historical Society, Columbus, Ohio
OKIN	Kinsman Free Public Library, Kinsman, Ohio
OrU	Knight Library, University of Oregon, Eugene, Oregon
OT	Toledo-Lucas County Public Library, Toledo, Ohio
PSC	Swarthmore College, Swarthmore, Pennsylvania
PU-Sp	Special Collections, Van Pelt Library, University of Pennsylvania, Philadelphia, Pennsylvania
SdSifSHM	Siouxland Heritage Museums, Sioux Falls, South Dakota
TxU-Hu	Harry Ransom Humanities Research Center, University of Texas at Austin, Austin, Texas
WaSpHiE	Cheney Cowles Museum, Eastern Washington State Historical Society, Spokane, Washington

WHi State Historical Society of Wisconsin, Madison, Wisconsin

WyU-AH American Heritage Center, University of Wyoming, Laramie, Wyoming

SECONDARY SOURCES

Story Clarence Darrow, *The Story of My Life* (New York: Charles Scribner's Sons, 1932).

INTRODUCTION

In 1928, H. L. Mencken published an essay in the *American Mercury* in which he asked, "How many American lawyers are remembered, *as* lawyers?"[1] Thinking only of dead lawyers, Mencken offered three nominees: John Marshall, Daniel Webster, and Joseph Choate. In 1928, these three might have been the only suitable candidates. But anyone answering the same question today would have to include Clarence Darrow on the list (and remove Choate). Darrow, who died in 1938, is the most celebrated lawyer in American history, and he will likely remain so for a long time.

The number of books and other writings about Darrow or about the cases in which he was involved is considerable, and steadily increasing. Many adult and juvenile biographies have been written about him; the adult biographies began appearing several years before he died. Dissertations and other academic studies have also been written about him, his cases, and his writings. Most of Darrow's own books and many of his speeches and other writings have been reprinted several times, and many are anthologized or otherwise in print today—more than seventy years after his death. Many fictional characters and plots have been based on Darrow or his cases, and Darrow has often been portrayed onstage and on television and in movies (which have played no small part in making him such a celebrated lawyer)—by Spencer Tracy, Orson Welles, Henry Fonda, Jack Lemmon, Christopher Plummer, and Kevin Spacey, among others.

1. H. L. Mencken, "Stewards of Nonsense," *American Mercury*, January 1928, 35–37 (reprinted in H. L. Mencken, *A Second Mencken Chrestomathy*, ed. Terry Teachout [New York: Knopf, 1995], 85–88).

Of course, many lawyers in American history have achieved some degree of fame or attention from the practice of law. In 1907, William Draper Lewis edited an eight-volume set of books titled *Great American Lawyers,* which included essays on ninety-six people. Lewis's goal was to include profiles of all the lawyers and judges who had "acquired [a] permanent national reputation"—"those names with whom educated lawyers and laymen everywhere are alike familiar."[2] With the exception of Daniel Webster, not one of the lawyers profiled in Lewis's eight-volume set has proved to have a permanent reputation as a lawyer.

Both the *Dictionary of American Biography* and the *American National Biography* list hundreds of names under "lawyer" in their occupation indexes. Yet if you exclude from those lists the lawyers who became famous or notable as judges or for reasons other than the practice of law, the remaining names are probably unfamiliar to most Americans. Every major library in the United States has a substantial number of autobiographies and biographies of American lawyers. But how many people today remember the careers, the cases, or even the names of Emory Buckner, Samuel S. Leibowitz, George F. Vanderveer, or William Travers Jerome? Each of those lawyers—excellent lawyers, by all accounts—had cases and careers that a publisher thought warranted a book-length biography. But today they are hardly remembered. William Kunstler, Melvin Belli, and Johnnie Cochran might be names that are better known today, but they have not been dead long enough to stand the test of time (nor do they appear likely to stand the test).

Like many lawyers, Darrow sought attention and fame. In his autobiography, he quipped that in the first half of his life he was "anxious to get into the papers" and in the last half he was "often . . . eager to keep out."[3] Whether he actually made much effort to stay out in the last half is doubtful. Still, no lawyer in American history has found fame on the same level and for such a sustained period of time as Darrow. Oddly, though, whatever place he holds in the history of American law, Darrow would probably maintain that his standing is not much of an accomplishment. Unlike many lawyers (and judges), Darrow did not worship "the law," and he generally did not see the practice of law as an esteemed profession—especially in the latter part of his life (by which time he seems to have held very few institutions or professions in high esteem). He acknowledged that a person in his line of work could do some good for people in need, but he thought this happened far too infrequently.[4]

So why is it that so few lawyers hold any memorable place in American history? More to the point, how is it that Darrow—who professed to care so little for the law or the legal profession—survived the usual wash of time? Mencken argued that most lawyers are quickly forgotten because they waste their "intellectual steam" on "causes and enterprises that live and perish with a day" and that in fact have "no genuine existence at all." He further claimed that most lawyers are forgotten because they "stand on all fours with theologians, and stand in the same shadows"—that is, they make no aim at truth but

2. *Great American Lawyers,* ed. William Draper Lewis (Philadelphia: John C. Winston Co., 1907), 1:iv–v.
3. *Story,* 45.
4. See, e.g., Darrow to William Essling, 15 January 1934.

simply "carry on combats under ancient and archaic rules."[5] Mencken was probably right, at least in part, and his statements help explain how Darrow found a spot in history. Darrow was nothing if not an iconoclast, and many of his causes and enterprises—like his lifelong opposition to the death penalty—have not perished yet. But more would be needed (much more than this introduction can supply) to explain how Darrow came to hold such an exalted position among lawyers in American history. Some insight, though, can be gleaned from his letters.

E. B. White once said that "[a] man who publishes his letters becomes a nudist—nothing shields him from the world's gaze except his bare skin."[6] Darrow's letters may not offer such an unobstructed view of him; after all, they are only fragmentary evidence of his life. Also, the amount of his extant correspondence is not as complete as one might hope. Very little of Darrow's professional correspondence, for example, has surfaced; so the cases on which Darrow worked and his interactions with clients and other lawyers are not well documented. Although no one knows for sure, Darrow was probably not a daily writer of personal letters—at least not on the scale of, say, Mencken, Oliver Wendell Holmes Jr., or Theodore Roosevelt. And he was also not as revealing in his letters as one might hope or expect, especially during the difficult times in his life (although no one knows, of course, what he said in letters that are missing). The surviving letters of Clarence Darrow show him if not nude, then in his skivvies.

Many of his letters are candid and emotional. With the exception of those that he submitted for publication (in newspapers or magazines), there is no reason to believe that Darrow ever planned to have any of his letters published, and—although he surely wrote some of them with the intention of impressing his reader in some way—he probably did not write very many of them, if any, with an eye to posterity. As Darrow once told his friend Fremont Older, "I have little desire for immortality, either personal or in the way of remembrance in the future. The logical thing, and to me the inevitable thing, is to be annihilated by the process of decay, and why should I be interested even in the memory of my life remaining."[7] (This from someone who wrote a novel about his childhood *and* an autobiography.) Many of Darrow's letters were hastily written, in what could sometimes be atrocious handwriting, poorly punctuated, without even a full date on them. But this is not to say that the picture of Darrow that emerges from his unvarnished letters is a particularly embarrassing one; a reader of Darrow's letters should see many of his good qualities. But this is also not to say that every feature of character or detail of life revealed by his letters is admirable. As with most people standing in their skivvies, not everything is pretty.

. . .

5. Mencken, "Stewards of Nonsense," 36.
6. E. B. White to Corona Machemer, 11 June 1975, in *Letters of E. B. White*, ed. Dorothy Lobrano Guth (New York: Harper & Row, 1976), 655.
7. Darrow to Fremont Older, 22 February 1925.

Many aspects of Darrow's personality—his interests and ambitions, his philosophy of life and usual everyday mood, his politics and the events of his day, and his relationships with his family and friends—are revealed to varying degrees in his letters. But one aspect of his personality and attitude toward life stands out among everything else: his pessimism. Especially by the time he was an older man, Darrow believed strongly that life was purposeless and random. In a speech that he gave in Chicago in 1920, under the arrangement of something called the Rationalist Educational Society, Darrow defined his pessimism as accepting life for what it is, without any false hopes, and tempering his happiness with the knowledge that unhappiness will come soon enough:

> The pessimist takes life as he finds it, without the glamor that false creeds and false teachers and foolish people have thrown about it. He knows he must meet this thing day after day, year after year. He knows that it is not good. He knows that it is not entirely bad. He knows it is life. And he adjusts life to meet those conditions. He does not live in the clouds. He does not live with the thought that he will be happy in another world. He lives it from day to day in the knowledge of what it means, and, as a rule, he is a better man and a kindlier man than the optimist.[8]

In his letters, Darrow often expressed his pessimistic view of life ironically or playfully, but his expressions seemed to grow darker as he grew older. In fact, Darrow expressed such a bleak view of life at times that it must have startled (or bemused) his friends when they received his letters.

In a letter to Brand Whitlock in 1910, when Whitlock was ruminating about his job as mayor of Toledo, Ohio, and considering what he would do after holding office, Darrow gave Whitlock no confidence that his political service would have any lasting positive effects: "You will accomplish nothing and it is not possible to accomplish any thing. The people are not ready and after you are done they will return to their vomit; the only thing worth while is to develop your own individuality and leave something that will do a little to liberalize the few who knew and cared because you lived."[9] In 1916, when Darrow heard that a mutual friend had died, he wrote to the poet and lawyer Charles Erskine Scott Wood: "I am glad he is dead & still I will be glad when you are dead and any one else that I love except perhaps my boy."[10] Two years later, he wrote a birthday greeting to Wood that had to be one of the least hope-filled greetings that Wood received on any birthday: "I can not tell you that you will live to be ninety or a hundred for you will not. [He lived to be ninety-two, dying six years after Darrow.] All of us as we grow older think

8. Clarence Darrow, *Pessimism: A Lecture* (Chicago: J. F. Higgins, 1920), 19 (reprinted in *Clarence Darrow: Verdicts out of Court*, ed. Arthur Weinberg and Lila Weinberg [Chicago: Quadrangle Books, 1963; repr., Chicago: Elephant Paperbacks, 1989], 293).
9. Darrow to Brand Whitlock, 17 December 1910.
10. Darrow to Charles Erskine Scott Wood, 6 October 1916.

gravely of the end, and I am quite sure you are like the rest. I am sorry that you are so far along the road though but a step in advance of me. My consolation at death is that I will miss nothing."[11] He wrote in a similar vein to his friend Fremont Older, the journalist and newspaper editor, on Christmas day in 1920: "I gave no presents to any one and wished no one a Merry Christmas. This is one kind of bunk I cut out long ago. I am as fast as possible cutting out all bunk, so if I live a few years longer (as I fear I shall) there will be nothing left in life."[12]

From the earliest date, almost all of his letters to the journalist Mary Field Parton contain some expression of pessimism: "The future will justify us all, but we won't be here."[13] "I did not say to Older that I was not going to Cal. or that I was happy, but he probably inferred both. I will never be happy, no more will you."[14] "No one is happy who is built like you & me."[15] Darrow would sometimes say that his pessimism sprang from the fact that he knew too much—that "weak-minded people" who take "dope" in some form (e.g., religion, political causes) were the only ones who could be happy. He wrote to a woman who had sent him a copy of her self-published book, explaining to her that fools are generally happier than thinkers: "I am also convinced that the book is not true in another regard. It assumes that intelligence and reason tend to happiness. I am satisfied that they do not. The intelligent person is less happy than the fool."[16]

Darrow also sometimes alluded to his work in the law as contributing to his bleak outlook on life. At the age of sixty-three, he told Parton, in a letter in October 1919, that he was "still working like the devil" to keep people out of the "clutches of the law."[17] But a month later, on Thanksgiving Day, he painted such a dreary picture of his law office to Parton that it sounded as though he, too, in his own way, was trapped in the law's clutches:

> I, like you, find nothing new from day to day. My office is filled all the time mainly by poor clients in trouble, people who have got money against the rules of the game & are trying to stay out of jail, people in all sorts of troubles: their wives crying & begging me to help as if I could do any thing if I only tried: how I wish I could but I can't. Lord what an awful mad house the world is, and it is Thanksgiving day and all the damn fools in the world are giving thanks that they are alive. Well I am not.[18]

But Darrow's pessimism was not something that always weighed him down or that even discouraged him. In another letter to Parton, he told her that he liked it when she wrote pessimistic letters to him—that he "thrive[d] on pessimism" and that "[n]o one but

11. Darrow to Charles Erskine Scott Wood, 15 February 1918.
12. Darrow to Fremont Older, 25 December 1920.
13. Darrow to Mary Field, 29 November 1912.
14. Darrow to Mary Field Parton, 31 March [1914?], ALS, ICN, Parton-Darrow Papers, Box 1, Folder 4.
15. Darrow to Mary Field Parton, 4 March 1915.
16. Darrow to Anna Scherff Tzitlonok, 23 September 1921.
17. Darrow to Mary Field Parton, 16 October 1919.
18. Darrow to Mary Field Parton, 25 November 1920.

idiots & dope fiends are optimists."[19] To Parton's sister, Sara Field, whose son had died when a car she was driving rolled off a cliff, he said that "death is better than life" and that for him pessimism was consoling: "In the dark things that come to me, I find that pessimism is the most consoling. Life is nothing but a foolishness, a burden, and a tragedy. Death is peace—it is nothing."[20]

Darrow left some people wondering about the sincerity of his pessimism. Two lawyers who worked closely with him for many years—Peter Sissman and Victor Yarros—considered Darrow's pessimism to be a bit of an act. Yarros wrote that Darrow "loved to pose as a pessimist and a cynic, but he was neither."[21] Peter Sissman, according to Yarros, used to say that Darrow was only a pessimist because he loved life deeply and hated the fact of death: "If Darrow was a cynic, the Hebrew prophets were cynics. He expected little from the average man, and was charitable toward all."[22] The writer Hamlin Garland—whose experiences with Darrow would have been more limited than Sissman and Yarros's—considered the possibility that Darrow's pessimism was simply part of an image that he had cultivated for himself. But Garland concluded, in one of his diary entries, that Darrow's views, for the most part, were genuine:

> Clarence Darrow and his wife came over to supper and we had a great deal of talk. He is a big personality and a most interesting one, but bitter, bitter and essentially hopeless. I can not find that he has any ideals or convictions left. His deep voice booms along on a minor note, a plaintive note, as though life were a mere mechanical going on for him. Part of this might be pose but much of it is, I fear, the truth. What he gets out of life while travelling in this mood I can not understand. His philosophy is essentially destructive, and yet there is something admirable about his honesty of statement.[23]

Eugene Debs did not doubt the sincerity of Darrow's philosophy; he considered Darrow to be "one of the most pessimistic men" he had ever known: "He has few beliefs in the feasibility of movements for human betterment, and but slight faith in the ability of mankind to rise above animal stature. He is skeptical of nearly every social philosophy. He does not think that man is capable of rising much beyond his present mental and spiritual demonstration."[24]

Darrow knew that some people said his "pessimism [was] just a pose." He once dismissed this talk as coming from people who simply thought that he should know better than to hold such a dour view of life.[25] Darrow's letters sometimes give the impression that he was putting on a show or that he was using his pessimism as a means to charm

19. Darrow to Mary Field Parton, 27 April 1916.
20. Darrow to Sara Bard Field, 16 November 1918.
21. Victor S. Yarros, *My 11 Years with Clarence Darrow* (Girard, KS: Haldeman-Julius, 1950), 9.
22. Ibid.
23. *Hamlin Garland's Diaries*, ed. Donald Pizer (San Marino, CA: Huntington Library, 1968), 121–22.
24. David Karsner, *Talks with Debs in Terre Haute* (New York: The New York Call, 1922), 102.
25. Darrow, *Pessimism*, 14.

or otherwise impress his reader with his unusual views—especially in his letters to Mary Field Parton. Some people no doubt saw his pessimism as alluring. The writer Ben Hecht, in one of his columns for the *Chicago Daily News,* said that the opportunity of listening to Darrow's pessimism justified the price of admission to his public debates: "For years and years Mr. Darrow has been gently disproving the intelligence of man, the importance of life, and the necessity of thought. For years and years Mr. Darrow has been whimsically deflating the illusions in which man hides from the purposelessness of the cosmos. God, heaven, politics, philosophies, ambition, love—Mr. Darrow has deflated them time and again—charging from $1 to $2 a seat for the spectacle." Darrow's public debates, Hecht said, "have been always worth $1, $2 and even $5—for various reasons. It is worth at least $5 to observe at first hand what a cheering and invigorating effect Mr. Darrow's pessimism has had upon Mr. Darrow after these innumerable years."[26]

Darrow's pessimistic view of life, if broadly considered, was probably a substantial factor in his life as a lawyer, and might even be said to be one of the reasons for his success as a lawyer. His pessimism certainly colored his view of the legal system. He was not so naive as to think that the law consisted of neutral principles that could be applied equally to everyone; but he also did not see the system as always or as necessarily corrupt, as a true cynic might. His letters suggest that as a younger man, he believed in the law as a means for achieving justice. After meeting with the convicted Haymarket defendants in their jail cells in August 1887, he wrote to the *Ashtabula Democratic Standard,* rejecting the defendants' anarchistic beliefs, saying that he believed the "injustice of this world can only be remedied through law, and order and system."[27] But as he grew older and had more experiences with the law and courts (including the hanging of some of the Haymarket defendants later in 1887 and the injunction and contempt actions following from the Pullman strike in 1894), we see increasing instances of him scoffing at the very notion of justice and challenging the independence of the judiciary. He began to see the courts—as many socialists and radicals did—as part of a system that guarded the ruling class, and judges (who were chosen by that ruling class) as maintaining the status quo: "I do not believe and have never intimated," he wrote to the *Chicago Daily News* in 1900, "either publicly or privately, that judges were influenced by any corrupt consideration—it is simply a result of the environment from which they are chosen, and the tendency to tyranny that goes with arbitrary power."[28]

Pessimism and its close cousin determinism also figured heavily in some of Darrow's jury summations, presumably with some success. In his plea in 1924 to save Leopold and Loeb from the death penalty, Darrow argued his deterministic view of life repeatedly to the judge: "I know that every influence, conscious and unconscious, acts and reacts on

26. Ben Hecht, *A Thousand and One Afternoons in Chicago* (Chicago: Covici-McGee, 1922), 161.
27. Darrow to *Ashtabula (Ohio) Democratic Standard,* 24 August 1887.
28. Darrow to *Chicago Daily News,* 26 February 1900.

every living organism, and that no one can fix the blame. I know that all life is a series of infinite chances, which sometimes result one way and sometimes another."[29] Darrow's pessimism must have often provided a backdrop, too, against which he viewed his clients' cases, especially clients who were charged with crimes. We have relatively few examples of the actual advice that Darrow gave to his clients. But whatever advice he gave and steps that he took to protect their interests were often likely fused with his own grim or realistic view of the matter and the workings of the legal system. He likely never gave his clients false hopes, especially as an older lawyer. In 1929, for example, after he helped obtain a new trial for John Winters, who had been convicted of murdering a woman in Vermont and sentenced to die, Darrow apparently urged his client to see his prospects in the next trial realistically—that he would be convicted again: "There is no doubt in my mind that John should plead guilty. There isn't a chance that the jury will acquit him. To stand against it means death."[30] (For whatever reasons, Winters did not plead guilty and he was convicted again, but not sentenced to death.)

Uncharacteristic, perhaps, for a pessimist, Darrow worked on reform efforts all his professional life, although apparently much more so when he was younger (and more optimistic). His reform work included efforts to improve the legal profession and to aid labor and criminal defendants. Some of that work is reflected in his letters, where he is sometimes shown undertaking the work less than wholeheartedly. He seemed to believe that if matters could be improved at all, it could only be done incrementally. Darrow's letters to Vivian Pierce are an example. In 1925, Pierce started what became known as the American League to Abolish Capital Punishment. She convinced Darrow to serve as president of the league and as a member of its board of directors. Over the course of his tenure as president, Pierce sometimes pleaded with Darrow to get more involved with the organization—to give speeches and participate in the league's efforts to convince state legislatures to either abolish the death penalty or refrain from enacting laws allowing it. Once, in 1931, after Darrow had twice missed board meetings for the league (much to Pierce's frustration), Darrow confessed that he had done nothing recently to try to prevent the Kansas legislature from passing a bill to restore capital punishment in that state: "I did not wire the Kansas legislature. I knew none of the members and I felt that it would do more harm than good. They would have felt it another reason to pass the bill. I get sick and discouraged at the cruelty of man, and often wonder if I should not stop, but I have been at it so long that I can't stop."[31]

· · ·

In his day, Darrow was roundly criticized by some people on the left for charging money—some would simply say, too much money—for his legal talents, and for representing what

29. *The Plea of Clarence Darrow, August 22, 23, and 25, 1924, in Defense of Richard Loeb and Nathan Leopold, Jr., on Trial for Murder* (Chicago: R. F. Seymour, 1924), 83.

30. Darrow to Fred Bicknell, March 1929 or later.

31. Darrow to Vivian Pierce, 8 February 1931.

they perceived as the wrong type of clients. This criticism of Darrow, which continues today, is reflected in an undated typewritten letter that Darrow might have sent to an unknown "Miss S" in 1895.[32] That letter—which appears to be no more than a transcript or draft of something that might have been sent to Miss S—related to two ordinances that the Chicago City Council passed in February 1895 granting utilities-franchise rights to an electric company and a gas company. Many believed that the ordinances were obtained by graft, and a public uproar that followed passage of the ordinances received a great deal of attention in the press. Darrow—who was in private practice at the time and had left his job as a lawyer for the city eighteen months earlier—was hired by the electric company to help obtain some favorable amendments so the mayor would approve the ordinance relating to the electric company. Darrow also defended the electric company against a citizens' lawsuit seeking to enjoin the company from operating its franchise. Miss S wrote to him sometime shortly after learning that he was representing the utility company. She criticized him in some manner for acting as a lawyer for the company and told him that her opinion of him had now changed, and that many of his other friends shared her feelings.

Darrow wrote back to Miss S (or may have written back to her)—in a rambling, not-very-tightly reasoned letter—with no apologies for what he was doing, although he did acknowledge that he was "very sensitive to public opinion, even the opinion of those who are glad to criticize what I do." Darrow told her that he did not know how the ordinance had been passed but he knew enough about municipal affairs to believe that it was "passed for boodle like every ordinance granting valuable privileges in this city." (This is an extraordinary—if not improper—thing for a lawyer to say about a client's conduct.) Darrow refused to rationalize his work to Miss S with the argument that most lawyers might use—that is, that everyone has a right to legal representation, whether good or bad or guilty or innocent. But instead—acknowledging that his "preaching" and his "practicing" had "never been the same"—he explained at length how he had long ago decided that he would work within the system to change it and that he would sell his services to anyone who would buy them, provided that he was not hurting the poor.

Darrow told Miss S that back in Ohio, he and his friend "Swift" (Morrison Isaac Swift) had both had in mind doing some good in the world but they had taken radically different paths to achieve their goals. As Darrow explained it, Swift had destroyed the patent medicine bottles in his late father's drugstore, "left . . . town without money," "refused to compromise with the world," and become "nearly a tramp"—"shunned by most earnest people." Darrow's approach, on the other hand, was a compromise of his ideals; he decided to "take [his] chances with the rest, to get what [he] could out of the system and use it to *destroy* the system." Darrow denied that he cared much about money for himself: "I care nothing whatever for money except to use it in this work and to bring me such comforts as I want and to help my friends."

32. Darrow to "Miss S," March 1895.

This one letter and the circumstances involved are, of course, inadequate evidence alone that Darrow was a greedy lawyer who too often represented the "wrong" clients. The letter appears to represent little more than the personal anguish of a man who could not square his capitalist actions with his radical socialist rhetoric and beliefs or the expectations of his radical friends. Representing the electric company might have made Darrow a hypocrite, a label that he seemed to accept, but his work for the company does not, in itself, show that he was greedy or that he did anything unscrupulous as a lawyer. The fact is that Darrow did not always represent the poor, and he would have had a hard time making a living if he had. The poor, as he sometimes noted, could pay little or nothing for legal services. Serving them exclusively would not enable him to maintain a law office. In a letter to Mary Field Parton, written in a self-pitying tone, he complained of the fact that his friends seemed only to think of him as a lawyer for the poor:

> One of my good friends (formerly of a settlement) came in yesterday panned that I should defend men accused of graft, and wanted to know why I did. I told her for the money and because I hated jails and good people. I said that I had fought for many things that her people believed in, but I had never seen the time that one of them had sent me a case where there was a fee; they had sent many poor to me, that no one else would look after, but if one had money they sent them to a respectable lawyer, which is true. Any how it never occurs to me that I should refuse to defend any one. All I dread about it is the hard work and the long time it will take.[33]

There is other evidence that Darrow was subjected to harsh criticism inside and outside his circle of friends and supporters because of his choice of clients or his fees. In the spring of 1903, for example, after Darrow disappointed some of the labor forces in Chicago with his decision to support Carter Harrison Jr. in the mayoral election, several people who identified themselves as representing labor wrote a stinging public letter to Darrow. They asked him what sacrifice he had ever made for labor and what money he had made representing the American Railway Union in the Pullman matter. They asked whether he had not received fifty dollars a day for defending the labor leader Thomas Kidd in criminal charges arising out of the woodworkers' strike in Oshkosh, Wisconsin, and seventy-five dollars a day from the streetcar employees' union for representing them in an arbitration, and one hundred dollars a day plus expenses representing the striking anthracite miners in Pennsylvania. Darrow's public response to this letter was not inconsistent with his statements to "Miss S."[34]

33. Darrow to Mary Field Parton, 1 February 1923; see also, e.g., Darrow to Harry Elmer Barnes, 12 March 1932 ("I don't know what I should have done if now and then a fairly well-to-do client had not come my way; the ravens have never called on me").

34. Undated, unidentified newspaper clipping, "Darrow Makes Reply to Attack in Letter," ICN, Darrow Family Scrapbooks, Box 3 (quoting text of a letter to Darrow from Hugh M'Gee, William F. Dunn, Edward Quinn, W. E. Kern, H. D. Lighthall, James Curran, John Maloy, N. B. Travis on 4 April 1903).

To the first question put to him, Darrow answered that he had never made a sacrifice for labor because the cause was his as much as it was labor's cause: "I believe in it, and I am not in it for the purpose of getting money." With respect to the Pullman matter, Darrow said that he received one thousand dollars for approximately three months of work. And he acknowledged that he had received fifty dollars a day in the woodworkers' strike and seventy-five dollars a day representing the streetcar employees. But he denied receiving one hundred dollars a day in the anthracite arbitration. With respect to the anthracite arbitration, he said that he would ordinarily charge one hundred dollars a day but that he told the mine workers' union at the outset that they could pay him what they wanted to pay him or nothing at all. When the matter was over, he sent the union a bill for ten thousand dollars, telling the union leaders that he would have sent a corporation a bill for fifty thousand dollars for the same work and that they could pay him less than ten thousand dollars if they wanted to. They promptly paid him ten thousand dollars. Darrow said, in short: "When an organization has the money to pay I let them pay."[35]

Another example of criticism comes a few years later. This was near the end of the trial of "Big Bill" Haywood, after Darrow had given his long closing in defense of Haywood—which moved and infuriated so many people. Joseph Pulitzer's *New York World* published a caustic editorial (which was later republished by the *Chicago Tribune*) suggesting that Darrow's reputation as a defender of the underdog and his real character and life were two different things.[36] The editorial said that Darrow "has grown gray and rich . . . in the service of labor, and no man living has been able to coin more money out of popularity with workingmen than he." The *World* acknowledged that Darrow was a "good lawyer and an effective pleader" who "probably earns all that he gets," but it went on to declare that he cannot "be thoroughly understood unless the fact is borne in mind that he invariably gets all that he earns." The scathing editorial took issue with Darrow's radical writings and utterances, suggesting that Darrow went too far in his attack on the system that made him money, and concluded that Darrow was someone whom no young lawyer should try to imitate:

> An infidel, a misanthrope, a revolutionist, a hater of the rich, a contemnor of the educated and the polite, a hopeless cynic, a man whose soul revolts at every manifestation of intelligent self-interest in others and one who evidently has lost faith in his fellows, Mr. Darrow nevertheless cherishes the idea that he is the champion of the oppressed, and he has persuaded a good many people to think likewise.
>
> Young lawyers will find some phases of this man's career which are worthy of imitation, but more of them against which they should turn their faces like flint. He is able and he is eloquent, but he is otherwise a solecism. A household, a community, a State or a nation of Darrows would be impossible.

35. Ibid.
36. "Clarence Darrow," *New York World*, 27 July 1907.

This editorial is probably typical of the sentiments of some people who were critical of Darrow. But how many people held this view is impossible to say. The praise seems to be just as plentiful as the criticism. There are no opinion polls to help sort it all out, and we know surprisingly little about his day-to-day law practice, so proof of the matter eludes us. We do not have any of his client and law-firm records. They might exist somewhere, but they have not turned up yet. Other than the information revealed or suggested by court opinions, newspapers, and other sources (which shows a great deal of charitable work, much of it for labor or radical causes), we do not know the identity of most of Darrow's many clients during the late nineteenth and early twentieth century. Surely, there were hundreds. And we do not know how much of his time was devoted to clients whom he knew would be unable to pay his usual fee. We do not know how much money his law firms made. We do not know how many people his firms employed (although it was definitely several for many years), and we do not know how much he paid his employees. Ruby Darrow, Darrow's second wife, suggested in a letter to Irving Stone that Darrow, as a general rule, devoted a third of his firm's time to representing people who were unable to afford his services.[37] Much of what Ruby said in praise of Darrow has to be read with skepticism, for she was extremely protective of him. But Darrow himself told a correspondent in 1917 that more than half his time for twenty-five years had been "given to industrial and labor cases . . . without any financial reward."[38] If this is true (or even approximately true), Darrow's devotion to people who were likely unable to afford his services far exceeded the highest pro-bono standards of most law firms today.

We also do not have any detailed financial records for Darrow. In fact, other than many interesting but general statements about his financial condition in his letters and some other more specific bits and pieces about his investments and finances (in his own letters and a few other sources),[39] we have very little detail on this subject. We do not know how much money he made from his law practice each year (he practiced more than fifty years), how much he made and lost from his investments over the years (other than in the stock market crash of 1929), how much he contributed to charitable causes, and so forth. We do not have a personal calendar of his activities, including his lectures and debates. And we do not know how much of his time in these activities was contributed for free (although

37. Ruby Darrow to Irving Stone, 18 September 1940, DLC-MSS, Darrow Papers.

38. Darrow to George P. Costigan Jr., 10 January 1917. See also Transcript, *The People of the State of California v. Clarence Darrow,* Sup. Ct. Calif., vol. 71 (29 July 1912), 5889, CLL (Darrow testifying: "I suppose nine-tenths of my practice has been civil practice and perhaps one-tenth of it criminal and about one-third of it charity for the last twenty years").

39. See, e.g., Darrow to Horace Traubel, 28 January 1903 ("All my life I have been harrassed over money matters, although I make a good income. I have so many people to look after & obligations of all sorts that I am always in debt & unable to do what I would like."); Darrow to Edgar Lee Masters, 29 November 1907 (explaining that he [Darrow] could probably earn one hundred dollars a day in Chicago practicing law and otherwise providing some financial information about the law firm); Darrow to Paul Darrow, 14 May 1911 (revealing that a fee received of twenty-five thousand dollars plus income of three thousand dollars from the gas company would approximately cover his debts, but saying nothing of his assets); Darrow to Charles Erskine Scott Wood, 6 October 1916 ("I am working hard & doing fairly well financially, but there are always so many worthy & unworthy looking for help that it keeps me poor").

it might be safe to assume that it was a great deal of time) or how much income these activities generated. And this is just a sampling of the types of information and documents that we do *not* have on Darrow and that we will likely never have.

We also have only bits and pieces of evidence of how a very few of Darrow's many friends and family members might have felt about him at various points in his life, especially when he was younger—letters here and there, telegrams, diary entries, some memoirs, transcripts of short depositions—nothing that paints a complete picture. There is simply no way to say today how Darrow's friends (if they could all be identified) felt about him at most points in his life. We do not have enough records to make these generalizations. We cannot even say with any certainty how *many* close friends Darrow had at any given point in his life—especially in Ohio (where he spent the first thirty years of his life) and Chicago (where he probably had his longest and closest relationships).[40] Although the names of many of Darrow's friends in Chicago are known through various sources, there are very few surviving letters between those friends and Darrow, which is not surprising, because it is doubtful that Darrow exchanged many letters with people who lived in the same city with him, except when he was away. In his autobiography, Darrow wrote about only a few of his friends from Chicago—including George Schilling and John Altgeld—but many other friendships can be inferred from his law partnerships and newspaper accounts of his cases and other activities. Still, there is just no way of knowing the extent of his circle of friends and how close he really was with them or with various family members—how much time he spent with any particular person, how many ideas they shared in common (politically or otherwise), whether he played poker with the person, whether he confided in the person, and so forth.

Outside Chicago, it is safe to assume that Darrow's frequent correspondents were also good friends—especially Henry Demarest Lloyd, Brand Whitlock, Fremont Older, Charles Erskine Scott Wood, Frank Walsh, Lincoln Steffens, and Mary Field Parton. He spoke fondly of many of them. But we have no idea how many letters to other people have been lost or have yet to be discovered. (Darrow's letters to Parton only came to light in the early 1980s.) Darrow's surviving letters and other evidence suggest that Darrow had a very large circle of friends of varying degrees of intimacy—one that reached far beyond his surviving correspondence. John Francis is a good example. He was superintendent of the Los Angeles schools. From some of Darrow's letters, we can infer that Francis and Darrow were good friends—Darrow and Ruby drove from Iowa to Colorado with Francis and his wife one summer and, for a short while, Darrow employed Francis's son as a lawyer in his office. These are curious facts because no writer on Darrow has ever mentioned John Francis. This omission cannot be because of the lack of a relationship, but, instead, seems to follow from the lack of a record. No letters between the two men seem to have survived. John Randolph Haynes is another example. He was a physician in Los Angeles

40. See, e.g., Darrow to Ruby Hamerstrom, 21 March 1903 ("Besides all of this I hardly believe I have more friends than any one in Chicago, . . . & there are many who love me as devotedly as any one I ever knew").

when Darrow had an operation there in 1908.[41] Haynes was progressive in his politics and probably shared many opinions with Darrow. In 1908, Darrow and Ruby lived for a while with Haynes in his home in Los Angeles. In his autobiography, Darrow mentions Haynes as a good friend. But beyond this, we know almost nothing about their relationship, especially Haynes's thinking about Darrow.

In the end, whether someone was a good friend of Darrow, a mere acquaintance, a critic who never met him, a friend with infrequent contact, or something else entirely, we often cannot assess the accuracy of any statements by that person about Darrow unless we also understand at least a fair amount about that person and his or her involvement, if any, in Darrow's life. The journalist and author Hutchins Hapgood suggests this same thing in his statements about Darrow in *The Spirit of Labor,* published in 1907. Hapgood describes Darrow as a "rich personality, often distrusted, generally inconsistent in all but humanity, too complex to be philosophic, but a gathering point for all the 'radical' notions of the time."[42] Hapgood seemed to recognize, though, that the opinions on Darrow varied greatly according to *who* was expressing them: "[I]n Chicago this interesting man is pretty nearly appreciated at his proper value; for, although he is regarded as 'dangerous' by the ultra-conservative, and as 'crooked' by the pure idealists, and as 'immoral' by the inexperienced ladies of blue stocking tendency, he occupies, nevertheless, a position of sufficient respectability to enable him to work and live to the best advantage."[43]

· · ·

Of course, with Darrow, there is not only the question whether he was ever a greedy lawyer, but also the question whether he was ever a corrupt or unscrupulous lawyer. A few rumors circulated among his opponents about his methods in the Idaho cases in 1906 and 1907 (the reliability of whisperings from the losing side of the cases should not be overestimated), and he was indicted for jury bribery in 1912.[44] The alleged bribery arose out of the trial of James B. McNamara, who blew up the Los Angeles Times Building in 1910, killing twenty-one men and injuring many more. In one indictment, Darrow was accused of bribing a prospective juror named Lockwood. That case went to trial in 1912, and Darrow was acquitted. In the other indictment, Darrow was accused of bribing a juror name Bain. That case was tried in 1913, and there was a hung jury. Darrow was never retried. People close to those events as well as commentators long after have come to a variety of conclusions about Darrow's guilt or innocence and the ethics of his conduct during the McNamara trial. Darrow's biographers offer differing views. Most of the older biographies suggest that he was innocent on the bribery charges, and most of the more

41. See Tom Sitton, *John Randolph Haynes: California Progressive* (Stanford: Stanford University Press, 1992).
42. Hutchins Hapgood, *The Spirit of Labor* (New York: Duffield, 1907; repr., Urbana: University of Illinois Press, 2004), 141.
43. Ibid.
44. See, e.g., J. Anthony Lukas, *Big Trouble* (New York: Simon & Schuster, 1997), 331–33 (discussing rumors that Darrow, in the Idaho trials, had been involved in payments to Steve Adams's uncle to convince Adams to recant a confession; no charges were ever brought or even discussed publicly).

recent ones maintain that he was guilty.[45] Any consensus on whether he was guilty or innocent is made difficult by the incompleteness of the record, misunderstandings about the record, and the many varying interpretations to which the record is subject. Darrow's letters to his friends and family help to establish his state of mind and some of his activities during those years, but they also offer something for an analysis of his guilt or innocence. One letter, in particular, relates to Darrow's alleged bribery of Robert Bain.

The state tried to show in both of Darrow's bribery trials that Darrow had made deep-laid plans with one of his investigators (Bert Franklin) to bribe Bain before he was questioned by attorneys during jury selection in McNamara's trial. In fact, Franklin, who delivered bribe money to Bain, testified on behalf of the prosecution in Darrow's first bribery trial. As part of a plea bargain that allowed him to avoid a prison sentence, Franklin testified that Darrow himself had suggested bribing Bain, that Franklin reported in writing to Darrow about Bain, and that he had many conversations with Darrow on "divers occasions" about bribing Bain—all before Bain was selected for the jury.[46] If Franklin's testimony was true, it seems odd that Darrow would have misidentified Bain as "Bean" in a letter to his son Paul just a few days after Bain was selected for the jury. Darrow's handwriting is difficult to decipher, but he did not merely misspell the name—he got the name wrong.[47] Now, this fact alone does not exonerate Darrow, of course, but it is puzzling. If Darrow and Franklin had conspired to bribe Bain, there should have been very few names that Darrow knew better during jury selection than Bain's.[48] This letter, which apparently remained unnoticed in a pile of Paul's letters from his father for the next eighty years, is consistent with his innocence or at least consistent with a lack of hands-on involvement in the details of the alleged bribery scheme.

The real work and planning behind the bribery scheme could have been carried out, in theory, by any of the more than thirty labor leaders who were indicted in January 1912 and convicted in Indianapolis in December 1912 for conspiring to transport explosives, including those for the Times bombing in Los Angeles. Those labor men—especially the

45. John A. Farrell, *Clarence Darrow: Attorney for the Damned* (New York: Doubleday, 2011), 278 (concluding that Darrow "most assuredly" "participate[d] in the bribery scheme"); Andrew E. Kersten, *Clarence Darrow: American Iconoclast* (New York: Hill & Wang, 2011), 146 ("It seems hard to believe that [Darrow] didn't [know about the bribery]"); Geoffrey Cowan, *The People v. Clarence Darrow* (New York: Times Books, 1993), 434 ("it is fair to conclude that Darrow bribed both Lockwood and Bain"); Arthur Weinberg and Lila Weinberg, *Clarence Darrow: A Sentimental Rebel* (New York: G. P. Putnam's Sons, 1980), 262–64 (providing reasons for believing in Darrow's innocence); Kevin Tierney, *Darrow: A Biography* (New York: Thomas Y. Crowell, 1979), 274 (stating that a review of facts did not show guilt beyond reasonable doubt, "but neither does it give confidence that he was innocent"); Miriam Gurko, *Clarence Darrow* (New York: Thomas Y. Crowell, 1965), 168–80 (implying that Darrow was innocent); Irving Stone, *Clarence Darrow for the Defense* (Garden City, NY: Doubleday, Doran & Co., 1941), 307–42 (written as though Darrow were innocent); Charles Yale Harrison, *Clarence Darrow* (New York: Jonathan Cape & Harrison Smith, 1931), 198–99 (never suggesting that Darrow was guilty and stating that his "acquittal was a popular one").
46. Transcript, *The People of the State of California v. Clarence Darrow*, Sup. Ct. Calif., vol. 5 (28 May 1912), 363–65, CLL.
47. Darrow to Paul Darrow, 11 November 1911.
48. See also, e.g., "Darrow Passes Buck to Davis," *Los Angeles Times*, 14 February 1913 (during his own opening statement in his second trial, "Darrow said his recollection of Bain was slight. He declared that Franklin urged [LeCompte] Davis to retain Bain on the panel.").

San Francisco union leaders among them, who may have been behind the dynamiting of the Times building—would have had an incentive to try to ensure an acquittal in the McNamara case.[49] An acquittal would potentially prevent their own indictments, or so they might have believed. Many of the labor leaders—including Olaf Tveitmoe and Anton Johannsen—were friends or acquaintances of Darrow's.[50] In fact, Darrow himself might have been alluding to their involvement in the bribery when he wrote to his son in early December 1911, after the McNamaras pleaded guilty and while reports were circulating publicly that Darrow might have been involved with bribing jurors. "Try not to worry over me," he told Paul. "I have lots of friends & am all right. They may get me into trouble, but the end will be all right some of these days."[51]

Among many misunderstandings about the facts underlying Darrow's alleged involvement in the bribery is one relating to Bain. One recent biographer (Kersten) claims that Darrow only asked Bain one question during his examination of Bain as a potential juror, implying that Darrow—because he had already bribed Bain—had no need to do a more searching examination. Kersten cites one newspaper article for this proposition (the *New York Times*), which does indeed quote only one question put to Bain by Darrow.[52] But other newspapers show that Darrow asked Bain many more questions than just one. Unfortunately, the transcript of the jury selection process does not seem to have survived. But from other newspaper accounts it appears that Darrow spent approximately two hours examining Bain and one other prospective juror (Roberts) on the afternoon of 16 October 1911, ending the day with Bain and then briefly questioning Bain again the next morning.[53] How much of the time on 16 October was spent with Bain and how much with Roberts and exactly how many questions were asked of each is not settled by the record. But the newspaper accounts of the jury selection process do not provide any basis to support the conclusion that Darrow bribed Bain.

There are other misunderstandings relating to Darrow's Los Angeles years that have arisen from misreadings of Darrow's correspondence. For example, one recent writer

49. Sidney Fine, *"Without Blare of Trumpets": Walter Drew, the National Erectors' Association, and the Open Shop Movement, 1903–57* (Ann Arbor: University of Michigan Press, 1995), 97–98 (explaining why the San Francisco unionist might have been behind the dynamiting).

50. Farrell, *Clarence Darrow*, 279–80 (giving a short analysis of the theory that Tveitmoe—who handled some of the money raised for the defense of the McNamaras—was the architect, without Darrow at "the center of the plot"); Cowan, *The People v. Clarence Darrow*, 435 (summarily dismissing the theory that labor leaders were responsible for the bribery because "no evidence points to [other labor leaders]").

51. Darrow to Paul Darrow, 5 December 1911.

52. Kersten, *Clarence Darrow*, 148 (citing "Too Much Biased against M'Namara," *New York Times*, 17 October 1911).

53. See, e.g., "McNamara Attorneys Win Point," *San Francisco Call*, 17 October 1911 (quoting Darrow asking Bain a question other than the one the *New York Times* reported); "M'Namara Wins Point in Court," *Chicago Tribune*, 17 October 1911 (suggesting several of the questions that were asked); "M'Namara Jurymen," *The (Ogden City) Evening Standard*, 17 October 1911 (reporting that the questioning of Bain continued the next day, 17 October); "Rapid Progress Is Expected in M'Namara Case," *Los Angeles Tribune*, 17 October 1911 (quoting some of the questions Darrow asked Bain and implying that others were asked); "Two Near-Jurors Found in the M'Namara Case," *Los Angeles Examiner*, 17 October 1911 (quoting or implying questions asked by Darrow of Bain).

(Farrell) contends that after Darrow was indicted he wrote a letter to his brother-in-law J. Howard Moore in which he said: "But the evidence against me is strong . . . I may have to leave you all for a time."[54] This is a misreading of Darrow's handwriting (which is easy to do). Darrow often did not bother to dot his *i*'s or cross his *t*'s. If a reader takes this into account, it can be seen that "evidence" is actually "interests." With this correction, the subject and verb agree (Darrow wrote "are," not "is"), and it becomes clear that the sentence as a whole is not an admission about the weight of the evidence against him: "I feel quite sure I can win but the interests against me are strong, & if I fail I may have to leave you all for a time."[55] Similarly, during his first bribery trial, in 1912, Darrow did not write to his son saying "I am afraid there is no way to win," as Farrell reports.[56] Farrell incorrectly assumed that the letter was written in July 1912, but in fact Darrow wrote the letter one year earlier (in July 1911), when he was surveying the prospects of winning the McNamara cases, not his own.

Neither does Farrell's statement that "[i]n his correspondence with his family, Darrow did not assert innocence—only righteousness" seem well supported.[57] Darrow's complete correspondence from those years (and every other year) does not exist, and we have no idea how many letters are missing. But if it is right nonetheless to expect Darrow to have protested his innocence to his own family in his surviving correspondence (which is not necessarily a reasonable expectation), there are letters to family members that can be read as alluding to his innocence (and not just righteousness), and there are letters that have become available since the most recent biographies were published that show that Darrow did, in fact, also expressly deny his involvement in the bribery. Fred Hamerstrom, one of Ruby's brothers, wrote to Darrow, apparently questioning his involvement in the bribery, and Darrow responded by stating outright that he was innocent: "*Of course I didn't,* still there are suspicious circumstances & they are bound to get me & the interests are strong."[58]

Darrow's letters also provide some context for assessing the suggestion by Farrell that Darrow might have been so corrupt as to have actually paid off one of the jurors in his own bribery trial *and* involved his son in the process. Farrell says: "And Darrow, after the trial, would pay [juror Fred] Golding $4,500—some $55,000 in today's currency—or more."[59] At the back of his book, Farrell includes a note regarding the basis for this

54. Farrell, *Clarence Darrow,* 238 (quoting Darrow to J. Howard Moore, 6 February 1912); see also http://darrow.law.umn.edu/letters.php?pid = 37&skey = Moore, Howard J., accessed 16 July 2011 (facsimile of the handwritten letter together with a transcript that includes a similar misreading).
55. See also Darrow to Frederick Hamerstrom, 6 February 1912 (using similar phrasing, about how "the interests are strong" against him).
56. Farrell, *Clarence Darrow,* 248 (quoting Darrow to Paul Darrow, 4 July 1911 [mistaken as 1912 by Farrell]); see also http://darrow.law.umn.edu, accessed 16 July 2011 (facsimile of the handwritten letter together with a transcript, listed under letters to Paul and dated 4 July [1912] on the website).
57. Farrell, *Clarence Darrow,* 278.
58. Darrow to Frederick Hamerstrom, 6 February 1912 (emphasis added); see also, e.g., Darrow to Paul Darrow, 29 December 1911 ("There is no right to get me in trouble . . ."); Darrow to Paul Darrow, 1 January 1912 ("There is really nothing to it except some suspicious circumstances"); Darrow to J. Howard Moore, 6 February 1912 ("They had no right to do this to me & I don't believe it will stick").
59. Farrell, *Clarence Darrow,* 244.

statement: a letter written by Darrow to Paul in 1927—*fifteen years* after the bribery trial—instructing Paul to send Golding $4,500. A reader of the letter will see that Golding was having some financial problems, and Darrow wanted to help him out ("Mr. Golding is one of my dearest friends. He was one of the strongest men on the jury in Los Angeles & seems to need this now. . . . I am sure I will get it back in a year but I would send it just as quickly if I knew I would not").[60] Darrow was trying a case in New York at the time, so he could not send the money himself. He knew that Paul would have cash at hand because they had just sold their gas plant in Colorado.[61] Darrow became good friends with Golding after the bribery trial. In a letter to E. W. Scripps three years after the trial, Darrow described Golding as a "staunch friend," "one of the best fellows that you ever met," and "absolutely honest." Darrow added that "of course my personal feeling toward him is one which would be difficult to describe."[62] In this context, Darrow's instruction to Paul to send $4,500 to Golding should not be viewed with suspicion.

Another letter in Darrow's surviving papers—this one written *to* Darrow and part of the collection of his papers at the Library of Congress—serves as an example of the varying interpretations to which the historical record of Darrow's guilt or innocence is subject. The letter shows that witnesses for the prosecution were apparently hoping that Darrow would pay them off. The letter, which requires some detailed description to appreciate, is from Darrow's friend George Schilling. Schilling wrote the letter from Chicago on 12 February 1913, during Darrow's second trial in Los Angeles for jury bribery. In the letter, Schilling informs Darrow that he has learned from Ed Nockels (an electrician and secretary of the Chicago Federation of Labor and another friend of Darrow's) that one of Darrow's investigators in the McNamara matter—a twenty-two-year-old investigator named Cooney, who had testified against Darrow in Darrow's first bribery trial—had telephoned Nockels some months earlier with a proposition. According to Schilling, Cooney "proposed for a consideration to fix things up so that neither he nor Mr. Harrington [John Harrington, a friend of Cooney's and an alleged accomplice in the bribery, who also testified against Darrow] would be witnesses at [Darrow's] second trial." Cooney told Nockels, according to Schilling, that "it would take considerable money to fix this up and that they would have to be taken care of for the time they would lose."[63] Nockels, according to Schilling, was suspicious of what Cooney was up to when Cooney telephoned him. So later, when Nockels arranged to meet Cooney, he had the secretary of the Milk Wagon Drivers Union (William Neer) stand near him while he spoke with Cooney by the entrance to city hall in Chicago. In his letter, Schilling did not explicitly tell Darrow what

60. Darrow to Paul Darrow, 16 December 1927; see John A. Farrell, "Darrow in the Dock," *Smithsonian* (December 2011): 98–111 (referring to this letter as "another incriminating detail" against Darrow).

61. Darrow to Paul Darrow, 17 December [1927], ALS, MnU-L, Darrow Papers ("I wrote you yesterday about the Draft to Golding. I forgot to tell you what the reason I asked you to do it is that I am here [in New York City] and can not get the money that he needs as easily as you can. Am really glad the plant is sold.").

62. Darrow to E. W. Scripps, 19 May 1915.

63. George Schilling to Darrow, 12 February 1913, DLC-MSS, Darrow Papers.

he should do with this information, but he told Darrow that he had talked the matter over with Nockels and "Thompson" (which is probably a reference to Darrow's old law partner, William O. Thompson) and that they all thought Darrow "ought to know these facts," and "if it [was] desirable for Mr. Nockels to come to Los Angeles in regard to this or any other matter in connection with your case," they wanted Darrow to send a telegram and they would "take care of [Nockels's] coming."

Schilling's letter to Darrow is the only known record of this matter. No response from Darrow exists and there is no other record of how the matter was handled. We know that Harrington testified against Darrow in his second trial (which suggests that Cooney's proposition was not taken up). In fact, Harrington actually testified for the prosecution two days *before* Schilling wrote this letter, which is likely *why* Schilling wrote his letter when he did. (Whether Cooney testified is unclear; newspaper coverage is sketchy, he would have been a relatively minor witness, and no full transcript of the second trial apparently exists.) Darrow's friends probably wanted him to know that if he needed Nockels to testify about Cooney's offer—to discredit Cooney or Harrington or both—they would send Nockels to Los Angeles. If this is a correct interpretation of Schilling's letter, a biographer might reasonably ask: If Cooney and Harrington were trying to extract money from Darrow in exchange for not testifying against him in his second trial, how does that affect the credibility of their testimony against him, especially when Harrington had already made a deal with the prosecution to testify against Darrow? Yet the only biographer to mention this letter interprets it in an entirely different light. Farrell reads it as showing that Darrow's friends and Darrow *himself* (even though no response from Darrow exists) were all willing to consider taking up Cooney's offer: "Schilling's letter," says Farrell, "throws further light on Darrow's ethical standards, and what he and his associates were willing to consider."[64] Given the timing and content of the letter, this interpretation seems doubtful.

In the end, anyone reviewing the matter should concede that it is possible that Darrow was involved with jury bribery. But the evidence against him is not nearly as compelling as some writers have characterized it, especially considering the reliability of the evidence. In my view, for example, the record as a whole and the weaknesses in the prosecution's case, in particular, have been underexplored; too much stock has been put in historical material that should be openly acknowledged for its weaknesses and given the slightest weight, if any; the unfair and corrupt methods of the state and how those should weigh in the mix have been underappreciated, especially when the prosecution's case relied so heavily on the testimony of witnesses who had made plea agreements regarding their own conduct; the number of Darrow's friends whom we can confirm believed that he was guilty has been exaggerated and the number of friends who expressed their confidence in his innocence has been overlooked; the argument that Darrow had lost his moral bearings before the McNamara case, as evidenced by his cases and clients, is deeply flawed

64. Farrell, *Clarence Darrow*, 272.

and misses and misinterprets a wealth of contrary information; the things said and written by various participants and observers, both in those days in Los Angeles and later, have been inadequately analyzed. In short, I believe there is much that can be said yet on the subject of Darrow's innocence, beyond an analysis of some of his letters (which is all that I have tried to do here). Clarence Darrow, the great criminal-defense attorney—renowned for his ability to empathize with his clients and to present compelling explanations for their motives and conduct—has yet to receive, from historians or biographers, the best defense available.

· · ·

Putting questions of Darrow's character and ethics aside, his letters also help to illuminate his relationships with many people in his life. Some writers have been especially harsh on Darrow's first wife, Jessie, whom Darrow married in Ohio in 1880. They have described her in various ways and to varying extents as provincial and domestic by nature, uninterested in the events and movements around her, dull-witted, and unsophisticated—someone who bored Darrow and his friends.[65] Kersten says that "the rumors of other women" (none of whom he identifies) were too much for her and that Darrow's "nastier side [which he also does not describe] . . . made appearances at home."[66] Stone's 1941 biography appears to have started this thinking about Jessie. At the time, Stone might have had sources for his statements. But if he did, he apparently was not willing to reveal them.[67]

There are no surviving letters from Jessie to Darrow. In fact, other than a few bits of recently discovered writings here and there, there appear to be no surviving writings of any kind by Jessie. And except for the rather voluminous newspaper scrapbooks that Jessie kept (which were only made public in the last ten years or so), there are no diaries, no memoirs, and no long letters—certainly nothing on which an assessment could be made of her personality or the intelligence that she exhibited in the 1880s or 1890s, much less of Darrow's manner in their home. The marvelous record of Darrow's early literary, legal, and political activities that Jessie compiled in her scrapbooks is some evidence, though, that Jessie was not as pedestrian and provincial as some writers have suggested. Twenty letters exist that Darrow wrote *to* Jessie. Eleven of them are published here. Most of them are very interesting and help to show something about the relationship between Darrow and Jessie at various times in their lives. But they do not reveal Jessie's personality or her intelligence and interests, which may have been modest compared to Darrow's.

65. Stone, *Clarence Darrow*, 82 (describing Jessie as "lethargic and slow-thinking," lacking "an exciting intellect," etc.); Tierney, *Darrow*, 136–37 ("Clarence for his part was uncomfortable with Jessie's lack of sophistication and distinction. It hurt his pride to be married to a woman who was a living reminder of his past.").

66. Kersten, *Clarence Darrow*, 87–88.

67. William H. Holly, review of *Clarence Darrow for the Defense*, by Irving Stone, *American Bar Association Journal* 28 (1 February 1942): 140–42 (Darrow's friend and former law partner, then a federal judge, reviewing Stone's biography and noting that Stone had "said some things about Darrow's first and his second wife that are unkind and untrue").

All indications in those letters confirm Darrow's short statement about Jessie in his autobiography, where he simply noted that they were divorced (in 1897) "without contest or disagreement and without bitterness on either side, and our son has always been attached to both of us, and she and I have always had full confidence and respect toward each other."[68]

One of the letters from Darrow to Jessie was written in January 1896, before they were divorced but when their marriage was coming to an end. Darrow does not spell out the difficulties in their marriage but suggests that they were incompatible in many ways: "I presume that we never in any way were fitted for each other. Of course we were too young to know it then, and it is always terribly hard to correct such mistakes." Darrow recognized Jessie's equal contribution to what they owned and pledged to always support her: "I have enough, or will within a year, for both and if we did not I could not take it & could not have a moment's peace or comfort unless you had enough. The house you know is yours. Two lots are also yours. You have done as much to get and save what we have as I. It is yours as much as mine and nothing in the world could make me take it from you . . ."[69] Darrow's divorce petition in March 1897 proposed that he pay Jessie "not less than" $150 a month for the rest of her life and that she receive title to their house on Vincennes Avenue in Chicago, Darrow being obligated to pay the property taxes on the house for as long as Jessie lived there.[70]

Jessie did receive the house as part of the divorce, but there are no financial records to show whether Darrow regularly supported her financially throughout his life. All indications, though—including Darrow's letters to Jessie and Paul—suggest that Darrow did support her, even after she remarried. Another letter to Jessie, on the eve of Darrow's marriage to Ruby Hamerstrom in 1903, shows that Darrow continued to care about Jessie a great deal many years after their marriage had failed, which is consistent with his financial support for her: "I am sure of this that always I have meant to think of you as I do more tenderly & gently than of any one else, & I am sure I always shall."[71] (*That* is an extraordinary statement to make shortly before marrying another woman—regardless of whether it was sincere [as it seems to have been] or motivated by guilt [as it might have been]). Of course, there are other angles from which some of Darrow's letters to Jessie can be read. Darrow, for example, seems to exhibit a notable degree of self-pity in them. But the affection and love that he expresses for Jessie in the surviving letters seems deep and genuine.

· · ·

Darrow's relationship with Paul, his only child, is shown in more detail in Darrow's letters than Darrow's relationship with Jessie (Paul's mother). There are 325 extant letters

68. *Story*, 33; see also Darrow to Victor Yarros, 28 May 1930.
69. Darrow to Jessie Darrow, 8 January 1896.
70. Bill (for divorce), *Clarence S. Darrow vs. Jessie O. Darrow*, Circuit Court of Cook County, February Term 1897 (copy in ICN, Arthur and Lila Weinberg Papers, Box 12).
71. Darrow to Jessie Darrow, 14 July 1903.

written by Darrow to Paul (seventy-four of which are published here). Nowhere is there indication of a strained or difficult relationship as adults, as some writers have suggested existed.[72] The letters begin when Paul was a boy—but there are only a few from those early years. They continue much more regularly starting in 1911, when Darrow was in Los Angeles in connection with the McNamara case, and later, during Darrow's own bribery trials beginning in 1912. After Paul moved from Greeley, Colorado, back to Chicago in 1928—moving with his family into an apartment one block from his father (another sign of no serious strain in the relationship)—the letters from Darrow to Paul continue, but these were usually written when Darrow was traveling outside of Chicago.

Darrow's letters to the adult Paul are not written as loving missives from a father to son. The letters usually concern Darrow's travels or lecture activities or their gas business together in Greeley. During the McNamara and bribery-trial years in Los Angeles, Darrow's letters seem to be designed to reassure the son that the father is holding up well under the circumstances, sometimes giving Paul a report on a turn of events. On a few occasions, Darrow's letters involve politics, as when he wrote in some frustration to Paul about the loyalty of Darrow's brother, Everett, to the Harding administration during the Teapot Dome scandal.[73] Just how many of Darrow's political ideas were shared by Paul is unclear. On some points (such as free trade and states' rights), they might have been in agreement. On Prohibition, they were not in agreement. Their interests were not always different: they both liked to play the stock market, they shared some of the same investments, and, of course, they shared the gas plant that Paul managed in Colorado.[74] They spent a fair amount of time together: Darrow often visited Paul in Greeley (as reflected in the letters) and he became friends with many of Paul's friends in that city.[75] In 1915, when a friend of Darrow's was expecting a baby, Darrow told her about the importance of Paul in his life: "Life isn't worth while & still we keep producing it—and there is no joy like a child—perhaps some sorrow too. Through the last thirty years nothing has brought me the consolation that Paul has brought and I have had many loyal & good friends . . ."[76]

No significant record exists of what type of parent Darrow was when Paul was a child. A letter from Paul when he was a young boy and pages from a diary that Paul kept when he was a young man show that he sometimes traveled with his father.[77] But there is not much beyond this. In fact, relatively little is known about Darrow's parenting. Paul reportedly told Irving Stone that his father "was always liberal with his allowance" and that Paul could spend

72. See, e.g., Tierney, *Darrow*, 164 (maintaining that "[n]either father nor son ever fathomed the complexities of their loving but difficult relationship"; and that Paul was embarrassed by Darrow's stand for unpopular causes and Darrow, for his part, was "hurt and mystified to the end" that "Paul wanted neither to follow in his . . . footsteps nor to live in his shadow"), 434 ("In almost every way, father and son contrasted . . .").
73. Darrow to Paul Darrow, 12 March 1924; Darrow to Paul Darrow, 19 March 1924.
74. Darrow to Paul Darrow, 19 March 1924.
75. See, e.g., "Paul Darrow Dies Thursday of Heart Attack," *Greeley Tribune*, 21 December 1956 ("Because of [Paul's] interest in Rotary, the father addressed the club on his frequent visits to Greeley . . .").
76. Darrow to Mary Field Parton, 29 May 1915.
77. Paul Darrow to Jessie Darrow, 25 August 1892, ALS, MnU-L, Darrow Papers; Diary of Paul Darrow (photocopy in editor's files); see also Stone, *Clarence Darrow*, 117.

"any amount of money [he] wanted on books." According to Stone, Paul also described his father as calm and not dictatorial: "He never lost his temper, rarely punished me. He was patient in explaining, even if I had done something wrong. He always took time to reason things out with me."[78] These qualities—especially his non-authoritarian and sympathetic nature—might be fair to assume from his writings. Darrow was decidedly opposed to corporal punishment of children—judging from the views expressed in *Farmington*. That novel—written when Paul was twenty years old—shows an understanding and sympathy for a child's view of the world. Darrow's experience in raising Paul probably contributed to his appreciation of how the world might seem to a child.[79] Like his father before him, Darrow probably placed a high value on his son's education; the fact that Paul graduated from Dartmouth College might be one indication of this. (But Darrow, who was a firm believer in the manual-school movement, did *not* believe that every child should be college bound.)

When Paul was five years old, Darrow signed an autograph book for him that Paul's aunt had given him as a Christmas present. Darrow signed the book with an admonition about caring too much about money: "Paul | Nothing good or great was ever done for money. | Your father | C. S. Darrow, | March 2d—1889."[80] Although there is little contemporaneous evidence beyond a few scraps such as this to support any conclusions about Darrow as a parent, he probably tried to instill noble values in his son. But Paul was surely raised much more by his mother than by his busy father, and how much influence Darrow exercised over Paul is unknown. In one of his letters to Jessie, Darrow acknowledges Jessie's closer relationship to Paul: "He is yours more than mine & he loves you more than he does me. . . . Whatever it would mean to me or him, I would rather die than let you part from him."[81] Jessie, for her part, signed the autograph book with the wish of many parents: "To my little *darling Boy* | Hoping he may grow up to be an honest good man. So that the world may be better for his having lived in it. So that *Papa* & I will both be proud of you. Is the wish of your *mama*."

· · ·

Darrow was married to Ruby (Hamerstrom) Darrow for thirty-five years—from 1903 until his death in 1938. There is probably more of a record of his relationship with Ruby than there is of any other relationship in his life, although this is not saying much; the correspondence between them has great gaps, and it is one-sided. All of the 150-some extant letters between the two were written by Darrow to Ruby. Ruby's letters to Darrow are missing. But a fair amount of information is available about Ruby herself: several

78. Stone, *Clarence Darrow*, 118; see also Handwritten Notes of Irving Stone (apparently from an interview with Paul Darrow), undated, DLC-MSS, Darrow Papers, Box 12 (showing the same statement from Paul Darrow).
79. But see Margaret Parton, *Journey through a Lighted Room* (New York: Viking Press, 1973), 24–25 (the daughter of Darrow's friend, Mary Field Parton, who, as a child, viewed Darrow as someone who "didn't care for children very much").
80. Photocopy in editor's files.
81. Darrow to Jessie Darrow, 8 January 1896.

hundred letters from Ruby to other people exist, as well as some letters written to Ruby by a few of those same correspondents. Ruby's 450-plus pages of mostly undated letters to Darrow's biographer Irving Stone—primarily in the Darrow Papers at the Library of Congress—contain a great deal of information about her life with Darrow, but they require sifting through many idolizing and defensive statements about her late husband. The papers of Darrow's nephew (Karl Darrow) at The American Institute of Physics also contain many letters written by Ruby to Darrow's family members.

Generalizing about the relationship between Darrow and Ruby is difficult. Like many marital relationships, it probably changed over time. There is some indication of a potentially strained relationship at several points.[82] But the early letters from Darrow to Ruby show a man passionately in love. In June 1902, for example, a little over a year before they were married, Darrow wrote to Ruby in rhapsodic tones:

> I want you to know that I love you more than I have ever loved any one in life—that you have been kinder truer & nobler to me than any one else has ever been, that I never can be happy without you. I want you to know that I have never spent a dull hour with you, that I have never for one moment wished to be away and that I have never had an unkind thought of you. I can not think of living without you—the greatest happiness—the only happiness that I can think of is to be with you while I live and near you—*very very* near you in the last long sleep. Any thing else to me now would seem like a sacrifice.[83]

At other points before their marriage, Darrow was not without his doubts about how permanent his feelings were for Ruby, which he openly acknowledged to her, and they were both entangled in other relationships at the time.[84] But the doubts appeared to fade as the months passed, and by late 1902, when Darrow was in the thick of the anthracite coal arbitration in Pennsylvania, he was looking forward to their marriage.[85]

Darrow never publicly—or, apparently, even among most friends—revealed his close relationship and engagement with Ruby before they were married, and their marriage took at least some of his friends by surprise.[86] Why Darrow kept their plans a secret is

82. See, e.g., Darrow to Ruby, 9 November 1911 (Darrow apologizing to Ruby for something he did or said and reassuring her of his love and respect for her); Darrow to Ruby, 7 December 1914 (apologizing for something that he said to Ruby).
83. Darrow to Ruby Hamerstrom, 4 June 1902.
84. See, e.g., Darrow to Ruby Hamerstrom, 20 June 1902; Darrow to Ruby Hamerstrom, n.d. ("Monday"), ALS, MnU-L, Darrow Papers ("There has only been the obstacle of which I told you, the *same* that is in *your* life—I shall try to make this right so I can come to you—I want you & can never be happy without you & can make no-one else happy. I must work this out the best I can to cause the least misery possible but I feel that it must be done & can be—and how anxious I am that it shall be soon").
85. Darrow to Ruby Hamerstrom, 20 November 1902; see also, e.g., Darrow to Ruby Hamerstrom, n.d. ("Friday"), ALS, MnU-L, Darrow Papers ("Really the loveliest picture I can conceive is to have a home & you there. I feel that I would be content."); Ruby Darrow to Irving Stone, 25 January 1941, DLC-MSS, Darrow Papers ("I was afraid for a long time to let him take another chance, for he had so wanted his freedom [in his first marriage], and had so reveled in it, and fully intended never to—again!").
86. "Their Marriage a Surprise to Friends," *Chicago Tribune*, 17 July 1903.

unknown. It might be that he did not want to hurt Jessie or Paul by the news. Or it might be that he simply wanted to keep his private life separate from the whirling public life that he was leading in late 1902 and early 1903—including the coal arbitration in Pennsylvania, his term in the state legislature in Springfield, and the mayoral campaign in Chicago. In fact, with respect to the latter, Darrow's friends probably did not know that his desire to marry Ruby and his hope of enjoying a long honeymoon with her in Europe (where he could write a novel) were probably significant factors in his decision to reject the call to run for mayor of Chicago. "Every day," Darrow wrote to Ruby, "I get some telegram about running for mayor & I am driven distracted by the bother. I think within a few days I will tell them that I will not—for all the time there comes before me a vision of six months at some quiet lake in the north of England or in Italy & with only you—& with it a chance to write a story—a long story—about you & me & every body."[87] After the mayoral election—that is, after Darrow had been "roasted and praised" (his words) for supporting Carter Harrison Jr. for mayor over his friend Daniel Cruice—he longed for his troubles to be over and for his honeymoon with Ruby to begin.[88]

As trying as their relationship might have been at times, surviving letters from later in their marriage show Darrow often longing for home and for Ruby. In addition to the letters published in this volume, here are some of the lonesome, amorous, and teasing statements that Darrow wrote to Ruby in letters:

October 1906: "I want you so I can hardly wait."

November 1906: "I really & truly am wild to see you."

June 1908: "I have been away so long I am anxious to get back. . . . Am getting buggser every minute."

January 1909: "You know how I hate to sleep alone away from you."

May 1909: "Am lonesome without you or any body. . . . K.Y.F.C.T. [i.e., Keep Your Feet Close Together?]."

September 1909: "What I would like would be a good long rest with you, say, from Friday night to Monday morning with the view & the brass bed & not much sleep."

"I am crazy to see you & sleep with you."

December 1909: "Am playing one night stands & sleeping alone & will be glad to get back."

March 1911: "You certainly are a dear girl & I appreciate all you do although I am ashamed to tell you."

April 1911: "D—n it Rube you are a bully girl & I love you & miss you. . . . It is tough to sleep alone—I wake up in the night wanting you. Don't

87. Darrow to Ruby Hamerstrom, 28 January 1903.
88. Darrow to Ruby Hamerstrom, 7 April 1903.

believe I will sleep any the first night after I get home. Do you get the thought?"

May 1911: "I miss you like a house afire . . . I don't like to be away from home."

July 1913: "Love until I see you & then—"

January 1914: "Still I *wish you were here.*"

October 1914: "It is just about bed time & I wish I was at home—or you were here. You know how I hate to sleep alone away from you."

January 1915: "Any how will be glad to get back. Have lots of fun & keep your L[eg]'s crossed."

August 1915: "Honestly Rube I *miss* you & *love you.*"

November 1915: "Am ready to go to bed & wish you were here, or I was there. Nothing [x] happened this afternoon to write about except to tell you I love you & will be home on Thursday."

March 1916: "I shall be glad to get home any how. Go to Mich. with me."

No one can say with much certainty how close or how happy Darrow and Ruby were over the many years of their marriage, especially without detailed diaries or frequent and intimate correspondence or some similar materials to review. But it is probably fair to say that the relationship was complicated by Ruby's personality, which, especially at an older age, is amply reflected in her own correspondence.

Among the papers of some of Darrow's friends and acquaintances, one can find some unflattering statements about Ruby. Brand Whitlock, for example, as Farrell reveals, once referred to her as "wholly uninteresting, crude . . . with no redeeming wit."[89] Perhaps the most sympathetic picture of her complex personality comes from one of her nephews, Frederick Hamerstrom, and his wife, Frances, both of whom knew Ruby well, including while Darrow was still alive. They described Ruby as eccentric and unconventional in a letter to a new physician for Ruby near the end of her life:

> She has always been eccentric, unconventional and intolerant of the commonplace. She used to love the fun of living in a world of books, ideas, excitement and people and sharing those with her husband. She detests sweet domesticity. She cares what the world thinks about her, but doesn't give a hoot about the neighbors' opinions. She likes good clothes, but looks down on mere fashion. She was a delightful hostess, good at setting the atmosphere and generously giving the spotlight to others, especially to her husband. She is courageous and independent. She prides herself on economy and on being practical and managed practical matters for her husband. She strongly dislikes some people and some types and seems to think keeping up with the Joneses a cardinal sin. She takes pride in

89. Farrell, *Clarence Darrow*, 440; see also, e.g., ibid., 124 ("The near-universal opinion of Darrow's pals [was] . . . that his new wife was his intellectual inferior"; they "talk[ed] of her henpecking, of her 'twittering,' and of her insecurity and possessiveness").

> doing some things well, but not the sort of things most people feel strongly about. She would rather accept a challenge than submit to discipline. | She has tremendous spirit. Prides herself on being able to submit to the inevitable. We have never known her to melancholy; she'll fume or cuss or somehow keep going; it does not occur to her to give in to any weakness. | She used to be very witty, but I don't think she ever had much of a sense of humor.[90]

How many of these traits Ruby exhibited as a younger woman, during her marriage with Darrow, is unclear. But some information supporting the description above can be seen in Ruby's own letters throughout her marriage and later, after Darrow's death.

· · ·

On the topic of Darrow and Ruby's intimacy and any discontent in their marriage, the settlement worker and journalist Mary Field Parton will always loom large. Darrow and Parton met sometime in "1907 or 1908" (according to Parton's daughter, many years later, who said that her mother "could never remember the exact date").[91] They were introduced to each other by the suffragist and activist Helen Todd at a "protest meeting [in Chicago] ('Somebody was jailed or somebody was striking or somebody wanted higher wages')."[92] When they met, Parton was unmarried and she was working either as a settlement worker or for the Immigrants' Protective Association in Chicago (she switched from the former to the latter in approximately 1908). Darrow might have had a sexual affair with Parton sometime during this early part of their relationship; their relationship certainly could have developed into a sexual one at some point. A few of Darrow's letters to Parton suggest that type of intimacy: "I miss you all the time. No one is so bright & clever & sympathetic to say nothing of sweet and dear & I wonder how you are & what you are doing in the big city."[93] "I am up here [Montevideo, Minnesota] making a couple of speeches & as lonesome as hell. Little Jay towns & Jay people who never heard of Nietchie or any one else excepting Jesus. What is the use? The radicals are fools. You never can do any thing with the people except to let them wiggle along through the ages. It isn't worth while to butt your head against a stone wall—but still I am blue & lonesome to night & I wish I could see you so I would be bluer & not so lonesome."[94] Other documents and letters also hint at the possibility, including several letters by Mary's sister, Sara, and Charles Erskine Scott Wood that suggest a sexual relationship between Darrow and

90. Frederick and Frances Hamerstrom to Dr. A. H. Wolff, 18 February 1955, TLc, private collection of Elva Paulson (copy in editor's files).
91. Margaret Parton, "Mary Field" (unnumbered pages of a typewritten manuscript of a partial draft, unpublished biography of Parton) [1974], OrU, Margaret Parton Papers, Box 38, Folder 7.
92. Ibid.
93. Darrow to Mary Field, 15 March 1910.
94. Darrow to Mary Field Parton, 4 July 1913, ALS, ICN, Darrow-Parton Papers.

Parton.[95] But determining for certain if and when two people had a sexual relationship one hundred years after the fact is not always easy. When any affair began, how long it lasted, whether and when it was revived from time to time, what was said by each of them to the other about their feelings for each other, and a whole host of other questions of this sort are largely unanswered by the record, despite efforts by some biographers to read into the sparse record a great deal about the relationship.[96]

There was apparently no love lost between Ruby and Parton as the years developed—they each said unkind things about the other in papers that survive.[97] Ruby surely knew about the affection and admiration that her husband and Parton had for each other, but if she knew about any sexual affair between them, there is no definite record of it. In fact, after her husband's death, Ruby denied (or rather seems to have tried to forget) that there was ever any discussion between them about "other women." In a letter to a nephew and his wife—after she heard that Stone's biography of her husband said that Ruby had made life "intolerable" for him with respect to "'other women' so that at times he went on trips to get away from [her]" (Stone did not say this)—Ruby defended herself saying: "In all our years together never, never was there a word about 'other women,' and so there could not have been any absences from me for that reason. I was not beautiful enough to be that dumb!"[98]

Other than the record (such as it is) regarding his relationship with Mary Field Parton, there is, in fact, no reliable evidence of another extramarital affair by Darrow—either during his marriage to Jessie or his longer marriage to Ruby. But there is evidence (of varying reliability) of flirtations with and perhaps propositions to other women. Kevin Boyle, for example, in his history of the Sweet trials in Michigan in 1925 and 1926, brought to light the diary entries of a civil rights activist (Josephine Gomon) who

95. See, e.g., Margaret Parton, "Mary Field" (in the draft of Margaret's book about her mother): "According to Irving Stone, Darrow's biographer, the famous lawyer had many affairs at this period when Free Love had become a cult among radicals; for years I wondered whether my mother had been one of them. It was not exactly a question which any daughter with a sense of delicacy could ask directly, but once during the tape-recording sessions I edged up to it. 'Mother,' I said, 'you went to all those meetings with Darrow and you shared a hundred dinners and sometimes he would walk home with you to your flat. Tell me, didn't you ever talk about anything except politics and suffering humanity? Didn't you ever . . . well, hold hands?' She understood what I was asking, but she was not to be trapped. 'I think if I had been born a Catholic, I would have been a nun,' she answered. This remark left me speechless, which I guess is what she intended. . . . Ruby evidently had reason to be jealous, but whether she had reason to be jealous of Mary I'm not entirely sure, for there are some mysteries in every life which I suppose even the most diligent sleuthing cannot penetrate, and probably should not." See also Farrell, *Clarence Darrow*, 226, 242, quoting letters from Charles Erskine Scott Wood to Sara Bard Field from which details of a sexual affair between Darrow and Parton are inferred; and Cowan, *The People v. Clarence Darrow*, 204 (same).

96. See, e.g., Donald McRae, *The Last Trials of Clarence Darrow* (New York: William Morrow, 2009), 15 (maintaining that Darrow and Parton briefly resumed a sexual relationship in 1924).

97. See, e.g., Ruby Darrow to Irving Stone, undated, TLS, DLC-MSS, Darrow Papers ("Dear Irving Stone:— | You see I did send you . . .") (describing Parton as having "no fine sides"); Weinberg and Weinberg, *Clarence Darrow*, 156–57 ("Against the collective woman Darrow rages as he would like to against the little piss ant wife whose pettiness and jealousies have galled him for years") (quoting Parton's diary entries as quoted by Parton's daughter in her unfinished biography of her mother).

98. Ruby Darrow to Frederick Hamerstrom Jr. and Frances Hamerstrom, undated, TLS, private collection of Elva Paulson (copy in editor's files).

attended the trials and recorded a few of Darrow's amorous overtures to her.[99] Geoffrey Cowan, as another example, writes in his book about a few letters that Sara Bard Field (Mary's sister) wrote to C. E. S. Wood, in which Sara described what can be interpreted as unwanted sexual advances or propositions to her by Darrow during the McNamara trial in 1911 and later in Chicago.[100] Sara Bard Field gave an oral history in her late seventies and early eighties in which she spoke sympathetically of Darrow and mentioned in passing that Darrow had "many affairs" with other women—"always" with "intellectual women."[101] Although she might have been thinking of her sister when she said this, how she knew of "many affairs"—living as far away as she did and with relatively little contact with Darrow—she did not say, nor did she identify any of the women or when the affairs took place. Farrell, in his book, quotes a comment from a pastor (Preston Bradley) in Chicago who knew Darrow to some (unknown) extent, saying that Darrow was "very highly sexed" and that he thought there were many women in Darrow's life "because Darrow did enjoy feminine company, and he looked at it as a conquest."[102] In Farrell's view, Darrow was a "notorious rake." Whether this is accurate is hard to say. The label "notorious" is difficult to support; the record of his extramarital pursuits does not get much wider or deeper than what is described above. Irving Stone may have been the starting point among biographers for generalizations and vagueness on the subject of Darrow's sexual life. When Darrow's friend and former law partner William Holly reviewed Irving Stone's biography of Darrow, he noted that Stone "intimated some things about Darrow's relationship with women that are based on mere gossip" and that "there is always much gossip about an outstanding person such as Darrow was."[103] But one thing is for sure: Darrow's record on women—not just in how he might have treated them in his personal life but also in his public pronouncements—is part of his mixed legacy.

· · ·

In the first half of Darrow's long career he was an ardent promoter of women's rights, including, in particular, the right to vote. He wrote essays and gave many speeches on the subject. In one talk in 1891, at the Universalist church in Englewood, Illinois, he told his audience that society covered up the subjugation of women by chivalry and gallantry, "fine phrases," and talk of "holy relations." He blamed the treatment of women, in part, on the way parents raised their daughters: "The parent . . . who fails

99. Kevin Boyle, *Arc of Justice: A Saga of Race, Civil Rights, and Murder in the Jazz Age* (New York: Henry Holt, 2004), 281, 296.

100. See, e.g., Cowan, *People v. Clarence Darrow*, 174–75; see also Farrell, *Clarence Darrow*, 225 (noting that "Sara had a way of tweaking her lover's jealousy with tales about men who sought to bed her and it is possible that she embellished her encounters with Darrow"), 269, 302.

101. Transcript, Sara Bard Field: Poet and Suffragist, Oral History Interview conducted by Amelia R. Fry (Regional Oral History Project, University of California at Berkeley, 1959–63), 273.

102. Farrell, *Clarence Darrow*, 89.

103. Holly, review of Irving Stone's *Clarence Darrow for the Defense*, 140–42.

to give his daughter an independent calling is doing his part toward making her a slave . . ." But the real problem, he said, was the perpetuation of the idea that the "true destiny" of a woman was to get married.[104] Many years later, in 1915, Darrow made headlines when he became co-counsel in a murder case with a woman lawyer in Chicago, which the *Chicago Tribune* said was "one of the first where a woman [lawyer] has appeared."[105] This may not have seemed like such a notable fact to Darrow, who for many years had employed Nellie Carlin, a graduate of the Chicago College of Law, as a lawyer in his law office.

During or after his trials in Los Angeles for jury bribery, Darrow began reading the writings of Arthur Schopenhauer and Friedrich Nietzsche, and he became enamored with them.[106] In the summer of 1916, he wrote an article on Nietzsche in which he described the philosopher as "old-fashioned" on "modern ideas of feminism."[107] He said that Nietzsche regarded both men and women "in the light of biology and that is all there is to it. . . . Nature has provided certain functions—and with that goes certain tendencies, certain conduct, which does not place woman inferior to man, intellectually, or in any other way." As for himself, Darrow said that he had "no patience" with the notion that women were inferior.[108]

But shortly after this article was published, Darrow seemed to show patience for the idea after all. In a dinner speech for the Chicago Woman's Law League, Darrow told his audience that women did not have "a high grade of intellect" and could never make a living at law unless they became divorce lawyers or defended criminals.[109] This was a demeaning statement, of course, but it did not so much signal a change of heart for Darrow as it did prove his tendency to take a poke at his audience. Still, Darrow seemed to take an increasingly sarcastic attitude toward women in his writings and speeches. This might have been fueled in part by what Darrow saw as wrong-headed opposition to the war by many women leaders and by his belief that too many women were joining with ministers, settlement workers, and other reformers to curtail people's freedoms and liberties.[110] Darrow's fundamental political ideas remained constant most of his life: he believed in free trade, states' rights, individual freedom, and

104. "Woman's Place in Nature," *(Englewood) Daily Evening Call,* 24 January 1891; see also "The Rights of Women," *Rockford (Illinois) Register-Gazette,* 8 September 1891 (reporting on a similar speech by Darrow at the Christian Union Church in Rockford).
105. "Woman Lawyer to Defend Pethick," *Chicago Tribune,* 25 August 1915 (observing that Darrow's co-counsel relationship with Alice Thompson was "one of the first where a woman has appeared in a criminal case").
106. Darrow to Charles Erskine Scott Wood, 19 May 1913.
107. Darrow, "Nietzsche," *The Athena* 1 (June–July 1916), 6–16; see also Darrow, "Schopenhauer," *The Liberal Review* 2 (March 1917): 9–23.
108. Darrow, "Nietzsche," 10–11.
109. "Nothing in Law, Darrow Asserts," *Chicago Tribune,* 17 December 1916.
110. See also, e.g., Darrow, "Attorney for the Defense," *Esquire* 5 (May 1936): 36–37, 211–13 (making harsh statements about women serving on juries); Darrow, "Women and Justice: Are Women Fit to Judge Guilt," *McCall's* (June 1928): 15, 65–66.

limited government. He seemed to view the rise of women, as a political force, as a threat to the latter three.

Darrow's distrust of the "good" people—which included women reformers—runs throughout his later letters and other writings. "All you say about prohibitionists is true," he told Mary Field Parton. "All reformers are cold blooded & cruel to the last degree. They have no imagination & no emotion, else they would not be good."[111] In 1927, Darrow told a reporter, "I'm against whatever the reformers are for."[112] But he was not opposed to all regulation of human behavior: when Mary was going to Albany, New York, in 1910 to protest a law requiring every woman convicted of prostitution to undergo a physical examination for venereal diseases, Darrow, although he had some reservations, told her that he believed a law like that was necessary: "It may not be that the proposed law is any good, probably it is not if the reformers framed it. Still something along that line is necessary & it must not be assumed that it is bad simply because it interferes with the personal liberty of the vendors, or rather the victims. Better think it over & be sure you are right. If there is a big delegation going to Albany probably they are wrong. If there are preachers & settlement workers it is almost surely wrong."[113]

In Darrow's view, biology determined that women would be more conservative than men. He told the writer Alice Beal Parsons that women are simply trying to preserve the species: "I do not like to be too dogmatical about feminists, but I suppose you know what my general view is. I am inclined to think that nature has provided means of perpetuating the fool human species and in that provision, women are much more conservative. Otherwise brats would die young. I think it is biological. Perhaps I am mistaken. If you know anything new on this, I would be glad to see it, for I have no prejudice on the matter."[114] In Darrow's view, this natural conservatism in women, when combined with their new power to vote, led to such legislative evils as Sunday closing laws and Prohibition—the latter of which Darrow saw as "an unmitigated evil and an abominable violation of personal rights."[115] Radical women who advocated for suffrage were apparently not the problem; they were not in favor of these legislative evils. But as he explained to Mary Field Parton, by gaining the right to vote they had unleashed a much more conservative mass of women who supported these measures:

> I see that a campaign has been started to bring back the New England Sunday laws to stop every thing that people want to do. I have been thinking of the woman's party made of Radical women who wanted the ballot. Now they have it and the great mass of conservative women are used by the preachers to suppress life. It would be different if the Y.W.C.A. had

111. Darrow to Mary Field Parton, 26 September 1914, ALS, ICN, Darrow Papers. See also, e.g., *Story*, 106.
112. *Philadelphia Daily Record*, 17 May 1927.
113. Darrow to Mary Field, 27 September 1910.
114. Darrow to Alice Beal Parsons, 13 March 1926.
115. Darrow to H. L. Mencken, 2 May 1924.

> done it; but the radical women did it and now they will get theirs; the only pleasure I have out of it is that I told them so.[116]

. . .

In the end, no simple characterizations of Darrow can be made. But his letters are a good starting place for an examination of him. A careful reader will likely find new insights into his character and some of the events of his life. On the admirable side, Darrow's letters show a lawyer deeply interested and involved in the causes and events of his day, whether they were developments in science, or literature, or politics. They show a sense of humor and wit. They show an almost-always even temper, sympathy for the poor and the underdog, and a commitment to helping clients who could not pay for his services. They show his great ambition as a lawyer and a hint of how shrewd he could be. And they show a basic tolerance, most of the time, for people with opinions and beliefs that differed from his own. They show a lifelong interest in books, which fed his curiosity about a wide variety of subjects. And they also show some trivial but interesting points about Darrow's life, like the fact that Darrow subsidized the first printing in the United States of Oscar Wilde's *The Ballad of Reading Gaol.* They help show, in short, why Darrow is the most celebrated lawyer in American history.

But regardless of what we can learn about Darrow's life through his letters and other research, a conclusive answer to the question to which the *New York World* believed it knew the answer in 1907 will probably always remain elusive: Was Darrow the type of lawyer we should admire? I believe so (with some qualifications, a few of which I allude to above), and I think his letters help to support this conclusion. But a sometimes sketchy historical record will never allow us to answer that question to everyone's satisfaction. One biographer of Darrow (Irving Stone) reportedly said that "everything is findable."[117] This is an indefensible claim. Everything about another person's life is definitely not findable. Janet Malcolm, in her study of Gertrude Stein and Alice B. Toklas, said that biographers have an "arrogant desire to impose a narrative on the stray bits and pieces of life that wash up on the shores of biographical research."[118] Malcolm was probably right. But collections of letters can avoid that charge more easily than biographies. So with no grander ambition (except as displayed above), I offer the reader some stray bits and pieces of Darrow's life.

116. Darrow to Mary Field Parton, 25 November 1920.
117. Cowan, *People v. Clarence Darrow,* xiv (quoting a conversation with Irving Stone).
118. Janet Malcolm, *Two Lives: Gertrude and Alice* (New Haven: Yale University Press, 2007), 56.

CHRONOLOGY OF DARROW'S LIFE

AGE	YEAR	EVENT
	1857	Born 18 April in Farmdale, Ohio, the fifth of eight children (six boys and two girls). Farming supported the family from 1853 to 1855, when Darrow's father started a modest furniture shop.
8	1865	Moves with his family to the nearby village of Kinsman, Ohio, where his father reestablishes his furniture shop and opens a furniture store. Attends country school and the academy in Kinsman.
15	1872	Mother dies. Later in the year, enrolls at Allegheny College in Pennsylvania. Attends one year in the preparatory department of the college.
16	1873	Begins teaching country school in the Kinsman area, which he continues for three years. Works in his father's furniture shop and store during the summer months. Studies law on the side.
20	1877	Enrolls in the law department at the University of Michigan at Ann Arbor and attends one year of classes.
21	1878	Works in a law office in Youngstown, Ohio, where he reads for the law.
22	1879	Admitted to the bar and starts a law practice in Youngstown.
23	1880	Marries Jessie Ohl and moves his law practice to Andover, Ohio, where he also sells real estate and insurance.

26	1883	Darrow and Jessie's son (their only child), Paul, is born.
27	1884	Moves to Ashtabula, Ohio, and continues to practice law. Elected city solicitor, a part-time position that he holds until he moves to Chicago. Speaks and writes on free trade and other subjects.
30	1887	Moves to Chicago, where he rents desk space in a law office. Becomes actively involved in politics and the labor movement.
32	1889	Moves his office to the ten-story Montauk Building. Appointed special assessment attorney for the city and later appointed assistant corporation counsel.
33	1890	Tries many cases involving city matters and provides many legal opinions for the city. Considered by some as a potential candidate for Congress or a judgeship.
34	1891	Loses a contest to become Cook County attorney. Continues speaking on a variety of subjects. Resigns from his position with the city and becomes general attorney for the Chicago & North-Western Railway Company in Chicago.
35	1892	Rejects efforts in political circles to convince him to run for Congress or state's attorney.
36	1893	Resigns from the railroad and accepts a position as assistant corporation counsel for the city. Four months later, resigns that position and forms a law partnership with prominent attorneys and former judges.
37	1894	Represents Patrick Eugene Prendergast, who shot and killed Chicago mayor Carter Harrison Sr. Represents Eugene Debs and several other leaders of the American Railway Union, charged with contempt of a federal court injunction arising out of a strike among employees of the Pullman Palace Car Company.
38	1895	Continues representing Debs and other union leaders when they stand trial again for conspiracy to obstruct the mail. Travels to Europe. After returning, his law partnership dissolves and he establishes a new partnership.
39	1896	Separates from Jessie, who travels with Paul to Europe for several months. Nominated by the Democratic Party for a congressional seat in Chicago but loses the election by approximately three hundred votes.
40	1897	Files a petition for divorce from Jessie, which is granted without contest, on terms agreed to in advance with Jessie.
41	1898	Represents Thomas I. Kidd and other labor leaders who helped organize a strike by the woodworkers at the Paine Lumber Company in

Oshkosh, Wisconsin, seeking higher wages, recognition of their union, and the abolition of child labor.

42 1899 Publishes his first book, *A Persian Pearl: And Other Essays.*

43 1900 Involved in a consumer lawsuit against a utilities company, charging the company with discriminatory pricing.

44 1901 Takes in his friend and former governor of Illinois, John Altgeld, as law partner.

45 1902 Represents, among others, striking machinists in a dispute with the Allis-Chalmers Company, a man charged with defrauding a bank, four men indicted for operating an illegal poolroom and gambling house, three lawyers charged with bribing jurors on behalf of the Union Traction Company, striking members of a streetcar union, a union of striking wholesale grocers, and striking anthracite miners in Pennsylvania. Helps organize a new local bar association. Writes short stories for the *Chicago American* newspaper. Publishes his second book, *Resist Not Evil,* a theory of nonresistance heavily influenced by Tolstoy. Elected to the Illinois House of Representatives on the Public Ownership Party ticket, serving one term.

46 1903 Completes the arbitration hearing for the striking anthracite miners in Pennsylvania. Declines to run for mayor of Chicago. Serves in the state legislature, introducing proposed legislation with a variety of objectives, such as abolishing common-law conspiracy, making it unlawful to raise birds for the purpose of shooting them for amusement, abolishing capital punishment, abolishing prison sentences for debts, and prohibiting free railroad passes and telephones and telegraph franks for members of the legislature. Forms a new law partnership, with Edgar Lee Masters (which lasts until 1911). Continues public speaking on topics such as trade unions, crime, municipal ownership, and the plight of Russian and Polish Jews. Represents many unions in labor disputes. Marries Ruby Hamerstrom and travels to Europe on a three-month honeymoon, where he writes a series of travel essays for the *Chicago Daily News.* Writes an autobiographical novel about his childhood, which is published the following year as *Farmington.*

47 1904 Represents, among others, John Turner, an anarchist speaker from Great Britain threatened with deportation because of his political speeches; the Chicago Teachers Federation, seeking back wages for teachers; and a law clerk accused of killing his wife. Serves as an editor of a short-lived Chicago literary magazine called *Tomorrow.* Serves on a committee investigating voter fraud. Participates in the National

Democratic Convention in St. Louis, giving a speech supporting a motion to nominate William Randolph Hearst as the presidential candidate. Gives speeches on the open shop, crime, and other subjects. Forms a new political club (called the Jefferson Club) with several friends. Darrow's father dies in April.

48 1905 Writes a short naturalistic novel, published as *An Eye for an Eye,* about a man who murders his wife and is sentenced to death. Appointed by the mayor of Chicago as special corporation counsel for the city, with full control of traction litigation and with the goal of achieving municipal ownership of the city railways; resigns from the position approximately six months later after differences with the mayor. Represents, among others, a rector of an Episcopal church claiming that he had been libeled; a physician charged with violating postal laws by selling pills through the mail; a company seeking to copy the indexes, tract book, and records of the County Recorder's office; the Teamsters Union in a strike; seventy-one-year-old Alice Stockham, charged with sending sexual advice through the mail in the form of a pamphlet for newlyweds titled *The Wedding Night;* the International Harvester Company, working up evidence to indict its patent agent for defrauding the company; and an abstract company suing a title company. Continues public speaking on a variety of topics.

49 1906 Following his own investigation into the finances of a bank that he helped to start in Chicago, arranges payment (with reimbursement from bank assets later) of all the small, noncommercial depositors, while the bank itself is placed into receivership. Works with the South Side Woman's Club and others to obtain the right of women to vote in municipal elections. Represents the city in traction cases before the U.S. Supreme Court. Hired by the Western Federation of Miners to represent William "Big Bill" Haywood, Charles H. Moyer, and George Pettibone—all of whom were kidnapped by state authorities and private detectives and taken to Idaho, where they were charged with arranging the murder of the former governor of Idaho. Gives many speeches, including one at an African American church in Chicago urging blacks to avoid employment in positions of servitude and criticizing the methods of accommodation and vocational instruction advanced by Booker T. Washington.

50 1907 Defends Steve Adams, an itinerant miner, in Wallace, Idaho, on the charge of murdering a property claim jumper (authorities prosecuting Haywood, Moyer, and Pettibone hoped to use a conviction of Adams to persuade him to reaffirm his earlier confession that he had been

hired by Haywood and others to kill the former governor of Idaho). Participates in the trial of Haywood. Writes a series of articles about the trial for newspapers. Publishes his closing argument as a pamphlet. Causes a stir in Spokane, Washington, when he refuses to stand during the national anthem. Represents Adams again, in a retrial, which ends in a hung jury. Begins the trial of Pettibone, leaving at the end of the prosecution's case in chief (and after his opening statement to the jury) because of an ear infection. Travels to Los Angeles for possible surgery.

51 1908 Operated on for mastoiditis in Los Angeles. Returns to Chicago, where he and Ruby rent an apartment in the Hyde Park area, where they live for the rest of his life (except for two years in Los Angeles). Delivers many speeches, including speeches against Prohibition and on behalf of unions. Represents, among others, a wealthy married woman who was arrested in a rooming house with a man who was not her husband, sixty-six or more men indicted for election fraud, and a Russian refugee (Christian Rudovitz) whose extradition was sought by the Russian government on the charge that he had murdered three people in a Russian village.

52 1909 Represents, among others, a nineteen-year-old man who killed a policeman, arguing to the governor and pardon board to commute the man's death sentence to life in prison; Sydney Love, a once wealthy stockbroker, in a divorce action; Fred Warren, on trial in Kansas on charges of unlawfully mailing a flyer publicly calling for the kidnapping of the former governor of Kentucky; a banker from Milwaukee convicted of embezzlement and forgery, seeking his release through the parole board; several defendants accused of fixing juries in Cook County; individuals indicted for election fraud; and the receiver for the failed bank in which Darrow had invested, arguing strenuously to the pardon board for *no* clemency for a convicted officer of the bank. Continues delivering public speeches—on Walt Whitman, Abraham Lincoln, Prohibition, and the sentences of Samuel Gompers, John Mitchell, and Frank Morrison for violating a labor injunction, among other subjects.

53 1910 Represents, among others, alleged jury fixers; a man convicted for killing a plainclothes policeman in a gunfight in a bar; a city engineer accused of fraud as part of an excavation project for the city; peddlers objecting to a new city ordinance prohibiting them from crying their wares on the streets; railroad switchmen in an action seeking higher wages before the state board of arbitration; a railroad charged with

bribing members of the Illinois legislature; and the Brotherhood of Locomotive Firemen and Enginemen, who were seeking higher wages in an arbitration. Among many public debates and addresses, speaks on jails and penitentiaries; the abuse of the injunction power by judges against labor; progressive thought in Norway and among writers like Björnstjerne Björnson and Henrik Ibsen; and nonresistance. Spoke on the problems of race at the Second Annual National Negro Conference in New York City (during which the National Association for the Advancement of Colored People was formed). Writes articles, among others, highly critical of Theodore Roosevelt and the November elections and attacking patriotic sentiments as empty and destructive.

54 1911 Appointed by a judge in Chicago to investigate the charge of a citizens' association that city officials had colluded with plaintiffs in settling property-damage claims in track-elevation lawsuits. Represents, among others, a railroad engineer in a personal-injury lawsuit against his employer; a group of distillers convicted of defrauding the federal government of revenue taxes; investors (of which Darrow was one) in a lawsuit against two promoters and agents selling a gold mine in California; directors of the Kankakee Manufacturing Company in a fraud claim brought by an investor and sales representative; and a banker and businessman in San Diego fighting extradition to Oregon, where he was sought on a charge of embezzlement. Serves as an arbitrator selected by a union of striking garment workers in a dispute with Hart, Schaffner & Marx. Moves to Los Angeles to defend John J. and James B. McNamara, accused of blowing up the Los Angeles Times Building and killing some of its occupants.

55 1912 Indicted in Los Angeles on two counts of jury bribery following the guilty pleas of the McNamaras. Represented by Earl Rogers and others, as well as being represented by himself, he is acquitted on the first count after several weeks of trial. Goes on a short speaking tour, talking to labor audiences in the West. Also delivers addresses on Ibsen, John Brown, and industrial conspiracies, among other subjects.

56 1913 Stands trial on the second count of jury bribery and does most of the trial work himself, ending with a hung jury and the indictment eventually dismissed. Appears in *From Dusk to Dawn,* a silent labor film based roughly on recent labor experiences in Los Angeles. Returns to Chicago and attends a banquet in his honor sponsored by the state bar association. Resumes his law business. Lectures on labor, Walt Whitman, socialism, education, the open shop, and Henry George, among other topics. Defends two brothers, both woolen merchants, and an insurance adjuster, all charged with arson in Chicago.

57 1914 Represents, among others, an assistant state's attorney charged with illegally marking ballots in a general election, an assistant cashier of a bank charged with embezzlement, a black man convicted of murdering a white woman, and two brothers and another young man charged with shooting and murdering a man. Involved in efforts to settle a strike in copper mines in Michigan. Gives public addresses on many topics, including Voltaire, eugenics, legislation, child welfare, socialism and labor, and Prohibition.

58 1915 Represents, among others, an attorney charged with embezzling client funds; Frank Lloyd Wright regarding an accusation that Wright violated the Mann Act by his love affair with a woman; the Children's National Tuberculosis Society on a charge that it was operating fraudulently as a nonprofit society; a real-estate dealer before the pardon board who had been convicted of forging deeds and notes; and William Lorimer, former U.S. senator, charged with crimes connected to the failure of a bank that Lorimer had founded and for which he was an officer. Gives public talks on a variety of subjects, including war and personal liberties. Testifies before the U.S. Commission on Industrial Relations, tasked with inquiring into the labor conditions in certain industries and determining the underlying causes of labor unrest.

59 1916 Delivers a moving memorial address for his brother-in-law, J. Howard Moore, who committed suicide. Publishes articles on crime, Nietzsche, and Voltaire, among other topics. Causes a stir by telling members of the Woman's Law League, as a speaker at their meeting, that women can never be good lawyers because they do not have a high grade of intellect and they are not cold blooded enough. Represents, among others, the chief engineer of the *Eastland* (a passenger ship that capsized in July 1915 while docked in the Chicago River, killing over eight hundred crew members and passengers), in federal court in Michigan; the writer and suffragist Crystal Eastman, in her divorce proceedings with her first husband; a man with a long criminal record who was reportedly arrested "on principle" for disorderly conduct; a physician (before the pardon board) who had been convicted of murdering his wife; a gypsy who allegedly sold his daughter for two thousand dollars and was fighting extradition from California to Illinois; a father and son charged with criminal conduct involving a failed private bank they operated in Chicago; several members of an allegedly illegal gambling ring, in federal court in Chicago; and a nineteen-year-old boy convicted of robbing and murdering a woman in her apartment.

60 1917 Publicly lectures on topics such as the war, the French entomologist Jean Henri Fabre, heredity versus environment, Tolstoy, and crime

and criminals. Engages in public debates, usually with friends, on such questions as "Is life worth living?" "Will democracy cure the ills of the world?" "Is there a law of progress in the world?"—with Darrow always answering in the negative. Writes articles on Arthur Schopenhauer and the war, among other subjects. Represents, among others, the striking International Ladies' Garment Workers' union in Chicago, including appealing from contempt orders for violating a labor injunction; Oscar DePriest, a Chicago alderman, on charges of conspiracy to take bribes and extort money, and the former chief of police, Charles Healey, charged as part of the same conspiracy; a pacifist who refused to submit to a medical examination for the draft and was charged with obstructing draft registrations; and twelve-year-old and fifteen-year-old boys charged with murdering a junk dealer by beating him with a baseball bat.

61 1918 Represents, among others, a man who placed a bomb in an opera theatre and who tried to extort money from a banker; a fire-insurance adjuster who was also an arsonist; the stenographer for the insurance adjuster, who perjured herself to protect the adjuster; a ward boss accused of accepting graft money from saloons and others in his ward; a sociologist at the University of Chicago charged in the morals court with disorderly conduct after being arrested in a hotel with a woman who was married to another man; Edward Fielding, head of the Volunteers of America, in a divorce action in which Fielding was alleged to have had a long extramarital affair; and Eugene Debs, seeking his release from prison for violating the federal Espionage Act by a speech against the war. Continues to give public addresses on topics such as the war, crime and punishment, and censorship in films. Participates on a committee to campaign for a state constitutional convention. Meets with the U.S. postmaster general and others to try to convince the government to stop banning publications from the mail. Selected by the federal government, at the request of the British and French governments, to speak in England and France on the war. Writes accounts of his travels that are published in the *Chicago Daily Journal*. Appointed by the board of education in Chicago to serve on a committee to search for a new superintendent of schools.

62 1919 Represents, among others, an alleged forger of municipal and school bonds; a public lecturer who is charged in morals court with disorderly conduct after allegedly engaging in acts of sadomasochism in a hotel room with a woman to whom he was not married; Emma Simpson, who shot and killed her husband in a courtroom during an argument over alimony in their divorce proceedings; a man charged with killing

a detective in a saloon fight; two men convicted of a murder during a bank robbery who were sentenced to die after pleading guilty without the aid of an attorney; the striking Actors' Equity Association, charged with violating an injunction; and a typhoid carrier operating a boarding house who was quarantined by the health department. Serves on a committee to organize a memorial for Theodore Roosevelt. Debates with other public figures on questions such as "Is the human race permanently progressing toward a better civilization?" "Will socialism save the world?" "Are internationalism and the League of Nations practical and desirable schemes for ending war?" (argues in the negative on each occasion). Continues an active public-speaking schedule, addressing topics as diverse as Walt Whitman, the killing of Jews in Poland, the American Medical Association, war prisoners, and the League of Nations.

63 1920 Represents, among others, Benjamin Gitlow, who helped form the Communist Labor Party in 1919 and who was indicted that same year under New York's Criminal Anarchy Act for advocating communism; Arthur Person, a workingman and member of the Communist Labor Party in Rockford, Illinois, charged with violating a state law making it a crime to assist or join any organization that advocates change or overthrow of the government; several relatives of the late widow of one of the owners of the Barnum Bailey Circus, in a dispute regarding the widow's estate; and several officials of a meat-packing company charged with defrauding stockholders. Together with several other lawyers, defends twenty communists in Chicago who are charged with similar offenses, including Henry Demarest Lloyd's son, William Bross Lloyd; together with Frank Walker and another attorney (dubbed "the million-dollar defense"), represents three men, said to be gangsters, charged with the murder of another gangster. Publicly lectures on subjects such as labor, Jean Henri Fabre, pessimism, materialism. Publicly debates questions such as "Is the human race getting anywhere?" "Is life worth living?" "Is civilization a failure?" (always responding in the negative). Speaks to the judiciary committee of the state constitutional convention, advocating against appointment of judges and favoring the election of judges.

64 1921 Writes a book entitled *Crime: Its Cause and Treatment*. Debates Scott Nearing on the proposition that "permanent progress for the human race is impossible." Debates Shirley Jackson Case on the question "Has religion ceased to function?" Addresses the annual meeting of the American Medical Liberty League ("How Liberty Is Lost"). Represents, among others, a stock and bond promoter charged with the

murder of his business associate; several men on trial for conspiracy to illegally transport and sell liquor in Chicago; three officials of the upholsterers' union, including the vice president of the international organization, charged with beatings and bombings during a strike; four men charged with robbing a bank in Indiana and murdering a man in the process of their getaway; Vincent St. John, a mine worker and one of the founders of the Industrial Workers of the World, convicted of violating the Espionage Act of 1917; and Harold McCormick, president of the International Harvester Company, in his divorce from his wife, Edith McCormick, daughter of John D. Rockefeller Sr.

65 1922 Represents, among others, a nineteen-year-old woman labeled in the press as the "boulevard vamp," who allegedly lured a man to a forest preserve where he was attacked and robbed; and three men accused of participating in graft with the public school system. Spends nearly three months traveling in Europe and the Middle East. Opposes a new proposed state constitution for Illinois that followed from a state constitutional convention; among other objections, opposes the provisions that would grant judges the right to deny bail, that would expressly allow public schools to have readings of the bible, and that would politicize the judiciary by allowing the supreme court to select lower appellate judges.

66 1923 Represents, among others, a state official and others accused of selling physicians' and pharmacists' licenses to unqualified people; a president of a bank charged with embezzlement; a Ukrainian schoolteacher who shot a priest during a church service; an inspector of airplanes for the army signal corps charged with misuse of funds; Fred Lundin, a businessman and former Republican congressman, who, along with many other men, including city officials, was indicted and tried for conspiracy to defraud the Chicago school system of some $1 million through bribes, phony contracts and bids, and excessive purchase prices for supplies; four men alleged to be part of a vice ring, accused of murdering a rival in Rock Island, Illinois; and several individuals charged in federal court with violating the Volstead Act in a scheme whereby they sold stock in a company whose assets were liquor, which were then distributed to the stockholders when the company went out of business. Continues his public debates and speeches.

67 1924 Represents, among others, a former president of the board of local improvements in Chicago and an official of a paving company, both charged with fraudulent contracts regarding bridge improvements; a beer runner charged with violating the Volstead Act; Nathan Leopold and Richard Loeb, two wealthy young men who kidnapped and

murdered a fourteen-year-old boy in Chicago and confessed to the crime after their arrest; and an eighteen-year-old boy charged with vehicular manslaughter. Elected as a delegate to the national Democratic convention but does not attend because of his work on Leopold and Loeb's case. Issues a written statement of support for the development of a hospital in New York to treat mental disorders. Speaks at the annual dinner of the Walt Whitman Fellowship in Chicago. Presides at a political debate in New York between Samuel Untermyer and Morris Hillquit. Continues public debates and speaking on a variety of subjects.

68 1925 Represents, among others, a wealthy man charged with vehicular manslaughter after his automobile hits and kills an eighty-year-old farmer driving a truck; a riding master who stands trial for shooting and killing the owner of a riding academy with whom he was romantically involved; the wife of a former minister of a wealthy Congregational church, in a divorce action; John Scopes, a high school teacher who agreed to serve as a defendant to test a recently enacted law that prohibited teaching the theory of evolution in Tennessee public schools; a fourteen-year-old black boy who stabbed a white boy to death in a schoolyard fight; and a black physician (Ossian Sweet) and his family in Detroit, Michigan, who were charged with conspiracy to commit murder and assault after shots were fired from their new house in a white neighborhood, where a hostile crowd had gathered outside. Publicly debates, among other subjects, the responsibility of criminals and the purpose of punishment, and the question "Does the mechanistic theory explain man?" Writes an introduction to the autobiography of Mother Jones and writes articles on eugenics, the methods of salesmanship, and other topics. Speaks at meetings in Harlem to raise funds for the defense of the Sweets.

69 1926 Represents Ossian Sweet's brother, who admitted to shooting from the house, in a separate trial. Testifies before a judiciary subcommittee in the U.S. House of Representatives in support of a bill to abolish capital punishment in the District of Columbia. Publicly debates the merits of the World Court, which he argues is dangerous and futile. On a radio station in Chicago, publicly debates Wayne Wheeler, the leader of the Anti-Saloon League, on whether Prohibition is a failure. Writes book reviews and articles on eugenics, crime, John Brown, Prohibition, and other subjects.

70 1927 Attends a celebration of his birthday at the Palmer House in Chicago, with 1,200 people in attendance. Writes an anti-Prohibition book with Victor Yarros, which is published as *The Prohibition Mania*. Travels

with Ruby to England—where they meet many writers and popular figures, including Thomas Hardy, George Bernard Shaw, James Frazer, and A. E. Housman—and then to Paris and other cities. Represents, among others, a convicted murderer before the Vermont Supreme Court who was sentenced to die, two black men convicted and sentenced to death (before Darrow represented them) for the murder of a grocer during a robbery, and two anti-fascists indicted for the murder of two Italian fascists in the Bronx. Publicly debates Prohibition and questions such as "Is Man a Machine?" "Can the Individual Control His Conduct?" "Is Zionism a Progressive Policy for Israel and for America?" "Will Democracy Give Way to Dictatorship?" Writes book reviews and articles on Prohibition, religion and science, crime, divorce, and education, among other subjects.

71 1928 Blacklisted as a speaker by the Daughters of the American Revolution. Also barred by the National Interdenominational Ministerial Alliance of America from speaking in its members' churches. Continues giving many public lectures and participates frequently in debates with other public figures on questions such as race relations and immigration. Campaigns for Al Smith for president. Writes for several popular magazines, including *Scribner's Magazine, Vanity Fair,* and *McCall's,* on a variety of subjects, including capital punishment, fundamentalism, women on juries, Prohibition, and crime. Defends a man in Jefferson, Ohio, accused of bribery.

72 1929 Testifies in the Illinois state senate in opposition to a bill that would authorize the judiciary (rather than the legislature) to make rules of procedure for courts. Delivers a speech in Boston opposing censorship and the next day reads passages from Theodore Dreiser's *An American Tragedy* to a jury. Travels to Europe with Ruby in July and remains in England, Switzerland, and France until the following spring. Addresses the American Club in Paris. Loses a substantial amount of money in the stock market crash. Writes book reviews and articles, including articles on Prohibition, Herbert Hoover, farmers, and crime. Compiles, with Wallace Rice, an anthology of verse and prose on agnosticism, religion, God, morals, and many other subjects, entitled *Infidels and Heretics.*

73 1930 Represents, among others, two reputed mobsters in Chicago, arrested for violation of vagrancy laws; and a bank clerk charged with embezzlement. Lectures and debates throughout the country in opposition to Prohibition, including a debate tour in many cities with the Rev. Clarence True Wilson. Participates in a radio dramatization of the trial of Benedict Arnold on the charge of treason. Writes several articles on Prohibition and religion, among other subjects.

74 1931 Appears in and narrates a movie about evolution titled *The Mystery of Life,* which was produced by Universal; the movie is banned by some theatres, restricted to adults in others, and criticized as anti-biblical and anti-Christian by ministers and others. Gives addresses on crime, Walt Whitman, and other subjects. Debates the question "Will the world return to religion?" with G. K. Chesterton in New York City. Debates the subject of religion with several other people who support one religion or another. Travels to several major cities in the South debating religion in each one with a Jew, a Catholic, and a Protestant. Writes an editorial on the causes of recent prison riots at the Illinois prisons. Represents, among others, a seventeen-year-old sentenced to death for killing a streetcar conductor during a robbery; a young black woman who worked as a secretary at a bank that failed and who was charged with criminal acts that led to the failure of the bank; and, briefly, at the invitation of the National Association for the Advancement of Colored People, the "Scottsboro" defendants—nine black youths, ranging from twelve to nineteen years of age, all poor and generally illiterate, convicted of raping two white women in a railroad freight car traveling through Alabama.

75 1932 Finishes his autobiography, *The Story of My Life,* which is published by Charles Scribner's Sons. Debates questions such as "Is life worth living?" and "Is religion necessary?" Travels to Hawaii to represent Lieutenant Thomas Massie (an officer in the United States Navy), Massie's mother-in-law, and two enlisted men, all charged with the murder of a native Hawaiian whom they believed had participated in beating and raping Massie's wife. Gives an address to the Chicago Bar Association on race relations and the law in Hawaii. Represents, among others, an owner of some brewing equipment and related materials that were seized in a federal raid; a man who robbed a beauty parlor after losing his grocery business; and a seventeen-year-old youth sentenced to death for murdering a man during a holdup in Chicago. Among other items, writes a supplemental chapter for his autobiography on the Massie trial, an article on the concept of justice for *Scribner's Magazine,* and a short piece on the Scottsboro case for *Crisis* magazine.

76 1933 Speaks at the annual conference of the National Association for the Advancement of Colored People in Chicago and speaks to a large audience in Chicago protesting spending cuts by the school board. Participates in the defense of farmers in Iowa who abducted and threatened to lynch a judge in an effort to halt mortgage foreclosures.

77 1934 Serves as chair of President Roosevelt's new National Recovery Review Board, which issues three controversial reports critical of the National Recovery Administration.

79 1936 Appears before the parole board at Joliet, Illinois, to urge the release of a seventy-one-year-old African American banker who had been convicted of embezzlement.

1938 Dies in Chicago on March 13 at the age of eighty. His ashes are scattered in Jackson Park, Chicago.

LETTERS

• BEFORE 1890

AMMIRUS DARROW TO EVERETT DARROW • KINSMAN, OHIO • WEDNESDAY 17 JULY 1872

17 July 1872

Dear Son:

I wrote you two weeks since and then promised to write every week until there was some marked change in your mother's condition. I delayed in hopes from day to day that I might write something encouraging; but alas! the sad and painful duty devolves upon me to inform you that your mother has changed her state of existence.[1] She has gone; you will see her no more in the flesh; yet I think her spirit lives and she is happy. No one knows the anguish I feel, and my heart bleeds for you, my dear son, away from your home in a foreign land among strangers; yet I trust you have made friends who will sympathize with you in this hour of your greatest need. Know that all your friends here are enquiring concerning you, and expressing their deep heart-felt feeling for your loss; and it seems to me that there will cross the broad ocean, with this letter, like a great wave, the united sympathy of all your friends to sustain you in this trial hour.

1. Everett Darrow was in Europe when his mother, Emily Darrow, died. Fifteen-year-old Clarence—although not out of the country—was also away from home that day: "I never could tell whether I was sorry or relieved that I was not there, but I still remember the blank despair that settled over the home when we realized that her tireless energy and devoted love were lost forever." *Story*, 27.

There are some, I am sure, that think of you and feel for you both day and night. There are some things that should console you. All was done that could be done to save her. No medical man could do it. The proximate cause of her death was a tumor in the duodenum (the small intestine leading from the stomach). This grew so much that no solid food could pass, and she actually died from starvation, although she did not crave food. Nearly all the food she took the last weeks of her life was small quantities of bread coffee at short intervals and nourishment by injection.

It was about ten weeks from the time she gave up work until she passed away. During the first part of her illness she had periods of great pain with intervals of rest. The last two weeks she was more free from pain until about 36 hours before she left—she suffered but not so much as at first. A short time before her departure we turned her on her back and she breathed her life painlessly and peacefully away. Her intellect was strong and clear until a few hours before the last and after that but a short time before her departure she brightened up and kissed her children. She had no fear from the future. From almost the first of her sickness she did not expect to recover. The doctor supposed she would get well until a few weeks before she died. It was weeks after she was sick that she discovered the tumor. Your mother discovered it first. It was too late then for you to reach home. She would have been glad to have seen you and yet she did not express a wish to me that she would like you to give up your plans to come home. She has often mentioned you and seemed to rely on you. You have one great consolation that you have always been kind to her and this she prized above all earthly aid you could have given her. I think you have never given your mother or myself one unkind word. This is remarkable as parents are likely sometimes to be in the wrong.

I think her greatest trial was to leave little Jenny, so young, without a mother. Your sister Jenny[2] is a remarkable pretty, bright and active little girl. She is a great comfort to me. Little Hermy[3] is a good boy. He has been very kind to his mother, always willing to stay with his mother and fan her. I think hard work was not the cause of the tumor. Her stomach has always troubled her more or less. The tumor may have been coming for years. Your mother's spirit left her poor emaciated body on Sunday July 12th about 7 $^1/_2$ o'clock P.M. I bought a nice lot in the cemetery and on Tuesday a large number of sympathizing friends assembled in the house and followed her remains to the place. I had a nice coffin, cushioned the bottom with excelsior; had a rough box made of thick oak boards—placed a double cover of the same material over the top; so it will be many years before it can rot away. The people of Kinsman were very very kind. The sides of her grave were decked with flowers. After the coffin was lowered they strewed it with beautiful flowers. Loren Perkins[4] was particularly kind. He told Hermy we might

2. Viola ("Jennie") Darrow.
3. Herman C. Darrow.
4. Lauren A. Perkins (1847–1923), a florist and the postmaster in Kinsman.

have all the flowers in his summer house if we wanted them. The neighbors sent in beautiful bouquets during her illness. At times her room looked like a floral palace. Your mother was very fond of flowers. Mrs. John Allen[5] sent beautiful bouquets. This was very gratifying to your mother. Mr. Eldred[6] attended the funeral and mentioned you with great sympathy in his prayer. When we returned from the funeral we found your letter to Mary.[7] It was very consoling to us coming when it did. Many other incidents I could tell you but as Mary is going to write you I will forbear as I have but little room left.

This is the most painful letter I have ever written. I know your character so well that I am sure you will bear up manfully. I shall keep house; I shall keep my family together. Nothing could tempt me to do otherwise. Mary will stay this year and I may arrange matters so that she can go to college after the coming year. We all should be very glad to see you, but it is my *deliberate* wish that you do not change your plans but attend some German University the coming year. I think without doubt I can furnish the means. What I live for now is to help my children. My business has been very good; think I will have a good fall trade. You must be careful of your eyes. Know how much it will do to use them, and use them no more than they will bear. I will write again soon. Be brave, my son, there is much to live for yet. From your father, most affectionately,

A. Darrow.

MS: ALS, MdCpAIP, Karl Darrow Collection.

TO EVERETT DARROW • KINSMAN, OHIO • FRIDAY 24 JANUARY 1873

Kinsman Jan. 24th 73

Brother Everett

I thought I would write you a few lines tonight and let you know how wee'r getting along at home.[8] I am studying at home. Recite in Physical Geography Greek and Latin. Am pegging along in the second book of Caesar. Channing[9] went to Cleveland Monday and we got a letter from him today. He has got into business as an agent in some coal company. There is an auction down to Brackin's store. It has been going for about a week. Cheap John is the auctioneer. We have just organized a literary and dramatic club to succeed the old literary society. The small boys (and some larger ones) made such a noise that they nearly broke it up so we started a new one. We had an exhibition

5. Probably Juliette Allen (b. 1819), wife of John D. Allen (b. 1814), a farmer from Kinsman.
6. Henry B. Eldred.
7. Mary Darrow Olson.
8. When this letter was written, Everett was still in Europe, attending the University of Berlin.
9. Channing E. Darrow.

a few weeks ago in the academy and drew a full house.[10] We propose to have an exhibition every four weeks now. We have got a rail road right handy now. We can hear the cars and whistle plain from here. It crosses over by the mule pen on the road to Peabody's and the station is going to be over near Uncle Ezra's[11]: they have got a construction train on the road now. The creek has been so high lately that no one could pass over by the cover bridges; there were three or four persons came pretty near getting drowned a while ago. [. . .][12] Hermy wants you to remember that Steam Nigger you spoke about while you were in London.[13] Pa sent you fifty dollars the other day. The business has been good this Fall & Winter.

Clarence Darrow

MS: ALS, MnU-L, Darrow Collection.

TO THE *ANN ARBOR COURIER* • ANN ARBOR, MICHIGAN • DECEMBER 1877

"His name is Clarence S. Darrow, and his home is Kindsman, Ohio. He is a junior 'law' and has been rooming for some time at Mrs. Foley's, on Huron street.[14] He could not or would not pay for his rooms, and accordingly left them one day last week, telling Mrs. Foley that he had left his trunk and its contents, and those he said would pay his indebtedness to her. She was of course glad to get even this from him. But on opening the trunk it was found to be filled with wood, burnt boots and other things of equal value. Darrow, it is understood, is still in town. This should warn all others from trusting him."

The above article is nearly all an entire fabrication. The club with which I was boarding, at Mrs. Foley's, having been broken up, and not having engaged rooms for any stated period, I proposed leaving and offered her $3.41, her due, which I can prove before witnesses. She insisted on having $2.00 damages which I refused to pay, and accordingly removed my clothing in my chum's trunk, as she refused to allow me to move mine. I subsequently went back and tendered her her due, but discovering that half of the wood

10. In his autobiography sixty years later, Darrow remembered his interest in the literary society: "For several years, while I was in my later teens, the Literary Society met in the schoolhouse. My older brother Everett and my sister Mary were members of the organization, and before I was old enough to join I used to go to hear the essays and debates. It was some very pressing interference that caused me ever to miss one of these meetings. Our father always encouraged us to go, and sometimes he went along. As soon as possible I became a member and participated in the scholarly activities." *Story*, 376.
11. Ezra Lewis (b. 1807), a farmer in Kinsman, married to Ammirus Darrow's sister, Mary Darrow Lewis (b. 1816).
12. Here, one or two sentences—approximately eighteen words—are heavily blackened out with a pencil (the letter itself is in ink) and "taint so" is written in pencil above the blackened-out words.
13. "Hermy" is Darrow's youngest brother, Herman Darrow, but the meaning of the rest of this sentence is unclear. "Steam Nigger" might refer to a steam engine used in hoisting on a ship. See Mitford M. Mathews, ed., *A Dictionary of Americanisms on Historical Principles* (Chicago: University of Chicago Press, 1951), 2:1117.
14. Darrow was enrolled in the law department of the University of Michigan in Ann Arbor. This is apparently a reference to Bridget Foley (b. 1835), who rented out part of her house on Huron Street in Ann Arbor.

I left was missing, I insisted on her paying me for it, which she refused. I never offered her my trunk in payment for my indebtedness. Although poor, I value my reputation too highly to dispose of it for the small sum in controversy. I will prove by witnesses the above facts, as stated by me, to be true, to any one who will call at my present boarding place, at the corner of Fourth and Packard streets.

Clarence Darrow.

MS: *Ann Arbor (Michigan) Courier,* 14 December 1877. PLACE: newspaper in which letter was published. DATE: date of publication in the newspaper.

TO THE *ANDOVER (OHIO) CITIZEN* • NORFALK, VIRGINIA • APRIL 1884

NORFALK, VA.

Editor CITIZEN:—Having a little leisure time, I determined to surprise you by writing a few notes concerning my trip and this portion of the world.[15]

I arrived in Washington on my way to Va., on Sunday, and of course I could not pass through that city without visiting some of the many places of interest that are to be seen at our National Capital.

Washington is a city well worth visiting, and it makes an American's heart beat with pride as he enters this historic place to think that here live the principal part of that body of patriots and noblemen called Federal Officers, who are willing to sacrifice their time, their talents and most of their honor for the love they bear their native land.

But Washington is indeed a beautiful city laid out and built upon a grand scale; its streets are wide and clean, its parks are numerous, and its public buildings are imposing. The Capitol building is located at the head of Pennsylvania Ave., and is a very fine structure; its length is 751 ft. its greatest width is 824 ft. its heighth is 287 ft. and it covers about $3^1/_2$ acres, its cost up to the present time has been about thirteen million dollars; it is built almost entirely of sand stone and marble. In this building the Congress and Senate pass the laws and here also the Supreme Court declares them unconstitutional. I of course visited Congress, every one does who goes to Washington. Like every one else I was somewhat disappointed at the scene. It is said that "distance lends enchantment to the view." It certainly is not unusual that men and institutions lose a great deal of their power to dazzle, upon our near approach. My first view of Congress as it was assembled and doing business in its hall, reminded me very much of a session of the Stock exchange, a sort of cross between a prize fight and a dime social. One would imagine as he looked down on the concentrated wisdom of the Nation, that he saw the workmen at the Tower

15. The purpose of Darrow's trip to Virginia is unknown.

of Bable after the Lord had confused their tongues. Every one talks at once and no one pays any attention to what his neighbor says, unless it is to go and take a drink.

The Senate in the opposite wing of the Capitol is a more reserved assemblage of men, but this body has not half the dignity of a Justices court. As I passed down the marble stairway to the room directly below the hall of Congress, an appalling sight met my view; there within the sacred marble walls of our Capitol buildings, and directly underneath the hall of Congress was a real, living, terrible, saloon. I could hardly believe my eyes; the sight nearly took my breath away, at first I determined to leave the building and never go back again, but then I thought better of it, braced up and went in; I sat down at one of the tables and wept in silence, but even then I felt that I must be in a dream; to make sure of the character of the place, I ordered the drinks. There was no longer any room for doubt; for the first time in my life I was in a saloon. But no one can stop with the first drink, so I went back to the senate chamber, sought out their saloon and entered. There was an other room opened off the main one, and an inscription above the door read, "for senators only", I asked one of the Abasynian waiters what this private room was used for? and he said that in some respects it was like the one we were in, but that it was kept mainly for the benefit of the Republican Senators; the Democrats took theirs in the main room.

I asked the waiter if he was acquainted with any of our Ohio Representatives, and he answered that most of them were members of his bar; I sobbed aloud as I ordered one more glass of beer, and I could not refrain from telling that coon about our Andover Village Council. Gradually, however my indignation over this shameful business cooled down, and then I looked the matter over like a philosopher, and made up my mind that the saloon was a very wise provision, for if every member of Congress was compelled to go down town for a drink, it would be almost impossible to get a quorum together to do business.

I would respectfully commend the institution to the different boards of County Commissioners through the State, as being a time saving, and money saving provision.

The many fine public buildings through out the city, I will not attempt to describe as it would make this letter too long.

Across the Potomac in Virginia, and in plain view of Washington is Arlington heights, which is the nearest point to Washington occupied by the Rebels during the war, there stands the old house in which General Lee lived during the Rebellion, and there in our National Cemetery sleep sixteen thousand of our union dead, many of whose names can not be carved, but all of whom died fighting for the stars and stripes. Sixteen miles below Washington is Mount Vernon which was the home of "the Father of his Country." It is a beautiful estate, located on the banks of the Potomac and commanding a fine view of the river and the Maryland shore beyond; near the landing is the tomb of Washington and his wife, where rest the remains of this illustrious pair, and around the grave from morn 'till night, day after day stand scores of devout Americans paying their tribute of respect to the memory of the dead.

Such is fame, for more than eighty years pilgrims from every land and cline have gathered there each day, drawn by the magic of a great man's name, and neither time

nor distance, nor the changing fancies of a fickle world has made his fame grow less; but all the devotion of the coming world, and all the flattery uttered ore a great man's grave are nothing to the silent dust that lies beneath, while a word of cheer spoken to the living pilgrim as he passes through the world will brighten up his sky, and a kindly act will smooth his rugged path.

The house in which Washington lived and died, stands near the shore of the Potomac, and is kept to-day as nearly as possible in the condition in which Washington left it, much of the furniture contained in the house is a century old, used by Washington and his family; also some of his clothes. In one room dreadful to relate, four or five large bottles in which Washington carried his grog; I closely scrutinized these flasks, but it was no use they were empty. I felt very sorry to think that Washington carried such large sized bottles as the ones I saw, they may however have been necessary in his day, and age, but had they been filled with Ashtabula Co., whiskey, there would have been enough to kill the whole Continental army.

MS: "Notes by the Way, on My Trip to Virginia," *Andover (Ohio) Citizen,* 22 April 1884. DATE: publication date.

TO JESSIE DARROW • ASHTABULA, OHIO • MONDAY 4 APRIL 1887

C. S. DARROW, | ATTORNEY AT LAW. April 4th 1887

Dear Jessie

I am getting very lonesome without you & Paul & will leave here as soon as I possibly can. Shall go next week any how but think I can get three or four cases tried by that time. After I get to Chicago I will either go to Minnesota & stay two or three weeks or will make arrangements to have you come there as soon as I can get suitable rooms.[16] I am getting very tired of boarding around & shall not follow it much longer. Have not stayed two nights in the same place since you left. I spoke at Farmdale yesterday & am going to Warren tomorrow.[17] I have not yet heard from you but hope you & Paul are all right. Hope to hear from you soon. Enclosed you will find Drft. Use all the money you want. Will send you more to come to Chicago.

Kiss Paul for me & remember me to all. Will write again in a day or two.

Yours | Clarence

MS: ALS, Darrow Family. ENVELOPE ADDRESS: Mrs. Jessie Darrow | Edna | Minnesota | Polk Co. POSTMARK: Ashtabula 4 April 1887.

16. Darrow is likely referring to their move to Chicago. Jessie was probably with her sister and brother-in-law, Lizzie (Ohl) and Henry Budd, who lived in northern Minnesota. Interview with Blanche Darrow Chase, Wheaton, Illinois, 29 July 1995.
17. The subject of Darrow's speeches is unknown. The only newspaper account located states that "C. S. Darrow lectured in Root's Hall Monday after noon. The meeting was under the auspices of the Liberals, and they report a good lecture." "Farmdale," *Western Reserve Chronicle,* 6 April 1887.

TO PAUL DARROW • JEFFERSON, OHIO • TUESDAY 19 APRIL 1887

C. S. DARROW, | ATTORNEY AT LAW.

Dear little Paul

I wish I was in Minnesota tonight to see you and ma ma. It is lonesome for me here without you. I went to Chicago the other day and saw Aunt Mary[18] and Uncle Everett.[19] They both wanted to see you and I told them you would come before long. I went to the theater and saw a funny play. Will take you there when we go.

I got your letter & was glad to hear from you. I am going to Chicago in a few days and then I will go to Minn. or send for you & Mamma. Now you must be good to Mamma & mind every thing she tells you and not make her any trouble, and then every body will think you are a nice boy. Write me an other letter when mama does.

from Papa.

MS: ALS, Darrow Family. DATE AND PLACE: "postmarked from Jefferson, Ohio | April 19, 1887" is appended.

TO THE *ASHTABULA (OHIO) DEMOCRATIC STANDARD* • CHICAGO • WEDNESDAY 24 AUGUST 1887

When I left "Benighted Ashtabula" I made you a rash promise that at some future time I would write a letter for THE STANDARD. I had not much idea of fulfilling the agreement when I made it and I have no doubt but you hoped I would not, however this morning I determined to surprise you by keeping my word. I will not bother you with any personal narrative of what I have done since leaving Ashtabula, although a full account of this kind would not add much to the length of this letter.

A few days ago I made a pilgrimage to the county jail (I was not in charge of an officer) and as many of Chicago's most celebrated men are now residing there it might interest some of your readers to tell you what I saw. The sheriff of this county is much more particular than my old friend Latimer[20] for when I marched up to the office and asked to go in, he refused me admittance. I was somewhat surprised at this but when he asked me my name, business and where I hailed from I felt considerably reassured. I told him my name and that I wanted to see the Anarchists, and then, as he still hesitated, I added that I came from the home of Giddings[21] and Wade.[22] Imagine my surprise when he

18. Mary Darrow Olson.
19. Everett Darrow.
20. Starr O. Latimer (1845–1918) was the sheriff of Ashtabula County, Ohio.
21. Joshua R. Giddings (1795–1864), lawyer and antislavery congressman from Ohio (first as a Whig, then a Free Soiler, and eventually a Republican), 1838–59.
22. Benjamin Franklin Wade (1800–1878), lawyer and United States senator from Ohio (first as a Whig and then a Republican), 1851–69, famous for his antislavery stands. Giddings and Wade practiced law together in Jefferson, Ohio, for several years in the 1830s.

looked me over a moment and said, "chestnuts!" This was the first time I had ever known those names to fail one in a public place. As I still insisted that my credentials were good, he looked up at me and said, "who are Giddings and Wade, anyhow?" I was disgusted at his ignorance, but informed him that they were former residents of Jefferson and greatly respected in their day and generation. His next question showed the most dense ignorance, it stunned me like a thunderbolt. "Where is Jefferson?" I told him that it was west of Denmark, east of Eagleville and about three miles from Grigg's Corners. He seemed to locate it by this minute description and after some further parley I succeeded in getting in. I was very much in hopes that I would not have as much trouble in getting out.

About half of the board of Cook County Commissioners are spending their vacation in this retreat; they belong to both the leading political parties, each is about evenly represented; there is perhaps a slight Republican majority, but a full canvass of the jail would doubtless show a sufficient Democratic plurality in the balance of the institution to overthrow any Republican majority here. I will not weary you with a description of these men, all of your readers have seen commissioners.

After looking over these ex-officials I went to another portion of the jail to see the anarchists. As I had never seen an anarchist before coming to Chicago and had heard so much of these, I was naturally very anxious to see them. Perhaps a short narrative of the Haymarket riot for which these men are condemned to death might be of interest as it happened more than a year ago and its details are nearly forgotten. The first day of May, 1887, was the day generally appointed by labor organizations throughout the United States to strike for eight hours work, as righteous an object as any body of men ever tried to achieve. All the large cities were very much agitated, particularly Chicago. On the evening of the 2d a large body of laboring men held a meeting to aid this cause near McCormick's factory. At this meeting a riot took place, some of the union men who had been supplanted by non-union men making a rush upon the McCormick works with stones and bricks. The police were present and opened fire on the crowd dispersing them and killing several. On the 4th a meeting was called to protest against this act of the police. The meeting was held at the Haymarket, which is a wide portion of Randolph street. After the meeting was nearly over and the largest part of the audience had gone home, the police marched up and ordered it to disperse; as they did not obey this order they made a charge upon the crowd when a bomb was thrown from their midst killing eight policemen and wounding several more. Two of the eight men now under sentence were present when the bomb was thrown, one was speaking, and six of them had been there at some portion of the meeting. No one claims to know who threw the bomb and no one pretends that any of the defendants did the throwing. The theory on which a conviction was had, is that the defendants were members of a general conspiracy to overthrow the government by force, and that the bomb was thrown in furtherance of that conspiracy, although there is no evidence to show who threw it. It is not pretended that there was a conspiracy to kill any particular persons or to do the deed at any particular time, but it is claimed that there was

a general conspiracy to use force at some time although there is no evidence that this meeting was called for that purpose. On the trial evidence was offered of the inflammatory speeches of the defendants, going back several years, also evidence of articles published in their papers counselling violence, and covering a space of several years, evidence of the speeches of three of the defendants on the particular evening which were inflammatory and violent, but in all these speeches no particular act was counselled, and no particular persons were designated, but wild, reckless, inflammatory, general statements were made many of them as brainless as Foraker's utterance about the rebel flags.[23] Also evidence was offered showing that one of the defendants had been in the business of making bombs for some time and one the day of the riot. The legal questions raised are numerous, the principal and vital one being whether general statements and advice to murder, without designating any time, place or person, can make one liable for the act of some one else who is supposed to be influenced by these inflammatory utterances. The above I believe is a fair statement of the case and of course there is great difference of opinion as to what will be the outcome. It is now awaiting the action of the Supreme Court, who have arrived at the decision weeks ago but have not made it public.

Eight men have been convicted of the crime, one, Parsons,[24] an American, Fielden,[25] an Englishman, and the rest, Spies,[26] Schwab,[27] Engel,[28] Fischer,[29] Lingg[30] and Neebe,[31] are Germans. Seven are condemned to death and the last mentioned to fifteen years imprisonment. He would doubtless have received the same as the rest had not the States Atty. told the jury he did not consider the evidence strong enough against him to warrant it.

23. Joseph Benson Foraker (1846–1917), Union soldier, Republican governor of Ohio, and United States senator. In 1887, when President Cleveland ordered the return of captured Civil War battle flags to their respective states, Foraker received national attention when he declared: "No rebel flags will be surrendered while I am governor."
24. Albert Parsons (1848–87), Confederate soldier, printer, editor of *Alarm* (a popular radical newspaper in Chicago), and member of the International Working People's Association (IWPA) (a patchwork of revolutionary groups and ideas all with the aim of abolishing the capitalist system). Parsons was hanged on 11 November 1887.
25. Samuel Fielden (1847–1922), English-born laborer, orator, lay minister, and member of the IWPA. Fielden's death sentence was commuted to life imprisonment by Governor Richard Oglesby (1824–99) and he was pardoned by Governor John Altgeld in 1893. He lived out his life on a ranch in Colorado.
26. August Spies (1855–87), German-born editor, writer, orator, manager of *Arbeiter-Zeitung* (a radical German-language newspaper in Chicago), and member of the IWPA. Spies was hanged on 11 November 1887.
27. Michael Schwab (1853–98), German-born bookbinder, reporter and editor of *Arbeiter-Zeitung*, and member of the IWPA. Schwab's death sentence was commuted to life imprisonment by Governor Oglesby and he was pardoned by Governor Altgeld in 1893, after which he operated a shoe store and continued to write for *Arbeiter-Zeitung*.
28. George Engel (1836–87), German-born laborer, owner and operator of a toy store, founder of a short-lived monthly anarchist journal called *Der Anarchist*, and member of the IWPA. Engel was hanged on 11 November 1887.
29. Adolph Fischer (1858–87), German-born compositor for *Arbeiter-Zeitung* and member of the IWPA. Fischer was hanged on 11 November 1887.
30. Louis Lingg (1864–87), German-born carpenter and member of the IWPA. The day before he was scheduled to be executed in November 1887, he committed suicide by exploding a dynamite cartridge in his mouth.
31. Oscar Neebe (1850–1916), laborer, tinsmith, and part owner and operator of a small yeast company. Neebe was pardoned by Governor Altgeld in 1893 and operated a saloon in Chicago after his release.

They are a good looking, intelligent lot of men. At first they were not inclined to talk, but after assuring them that "I was something of a crank myself," although "I knew nothing about dynamite," they entered freely into conversation with me. Parsons is a bright, talkative fellow, about thirty five years old. I told him it was reported in Ohio that he was a delegate to the convention that nominated Hayes, and that he was one who was instrumental in fixing the vote of Louisiana. He indignantly denied both accusations and said that although he had been a leading Republican in Texas he had no hand in that job, and that doubtless the story that he helped count out Tilden in Louisiana came from the idea that he was an anarchist and had no regard for law.[32] I told him I was very glad to know he was not in that affair and explained to him that I thought the idea hurt his case, still I was not sure as I knew John Sherman was in it, and the Republicans of Ohio had indorsed him for President.[33] I had considerable conversation with all these men and on the whole they are very intelligent, earnest men and I could not help feeling sorry for them. Fielden was once a Methodist preacher but it is not thought even by ministers of other denominations that this had anything to do with his present condition.

It is very hard for one who like me believes that the injustice of this world can only be remedied through law, and order and system, to understand how intelligent men can believe that the repeal of all laws can better the world; but this is their doctrine and it is also the doctrine of many men throughout the world. That these men believed that law should be overturned by force is also true. They imagine that wealth is so strong that it controls legislation and elections, and that we can only abolish present evils by wiping out capital and starting over new. Very few men question their sincerity, it is simply to be determined whether one who advocates doctrines that the world believes to be wild and revolutionary, who wildly and generally advises killing and destroying, without however counselling the doing of any particular act against any particular person, can be held guilty of murder if some one does kill when it is supposed that he is influenced by this foolish talk.

For my part, I say now as I always have, that I believe the establishment of such a doctrine would be a vital blow at freedom of speech and of the press, and far more dangerous to human liberty and happiness than all the foolish speeches ever made in America, even including crazy Fairchild's famous advice to the Lord to kill the President

32. In the election of 1876, Democrat Samuel J. Tilden (1814–86), governor of New York, won the popular vote for the presidency over Republican Rutherford B. Hayes (1822–93), governor of Ohio. The electoral college also favored Tilden, but the Republicans claimed that four states rightfully belonged to Hayes (Louisiana was among the four and the integrity of its election returns, in particular, came under a cloud of suspicion). A fifteen-man electoral commission appointed to investigate and resolve the dispute decided the election in favor of Hayes.

33. John Sherman (1823–1900), Republican congressman and senator from Ohio, secretary of treasury under President Hayes, secretary of state under President McKinley, and contender for the Republican presidential nomination in 1880, 1884, and 1888. After the presidential election in 1876, Sherman and a group of other Republicans traveled to Louisiana to observe the work of that state's board of election returns. Democrats sent their own representatives. The board eventually decided the election in favor of Hayes and rumors circulated that members of the board had been bribed or otherwise influenced by the "visiting statesmen." Sherman's conduct was especially scrutinized. See Ralph J. Roske, "'Visiting Statesman' in Louisiana, 1876," *Mid-America* 33 (April 1951): 89–102.

of the United States.[34] There are very few even among anarchists and socialists in Chicago who believe in the use of force, but it is safe to say that three-fourths of all the laboring men of the city believe their conviction was wrong, while very many other honest men and women who have no sympathy with or belief in their doctrines believe that it will be a sad mistake to hang these men.

You will see by this that I still retain my unfortunate habit of looking at many questions in a different light from the majority and of always being ready to express my opinions as it is; but I hope you will not conclude that I am an anarchist, for the more I study, the stronger I am convinced that we need more laws and better rather than fewer, and that although those who believe in anarchy comb their hair and wash their faces and wear as good clothes as most people, still I think their doctrines are wild if their eyes are not.

With best wishes to yourself and readers and assuring you that I will not bore you or them again, I am, as ever,

Your friend, | C. S. Darrow.

Chicago, August 24, 1887.

MS: "Chicago," *Ashtabula (Ohio) Democratic Standard,* 2 September 1887.

TO GEORGE SCHILLING • CHICAGO • SATURDAY 15 OCTOBER 1887

– OFFICE OF– | C. S. DARROW, Oct 15th 1887

Dear Schilling

I suppose you keep an eye on Chicago matters and learned that there is a movement on foot to have a mass meeting for Anarchists on Thursday eve of next week, if the mayor & police do not interfere. Some time ago you asked me if I would speak at such a meeting. I would be glad to if you wished but do not know many of the boys.[35] I think

34. Lucius Fairchild (1831–96), Union soldier, Republican governor of Wisconsin, and foreign diplomat. In a speech in 1887, while serving as Wisconsin commander of the Grand Army of the Republic, Fairchild famously condemned President Cleveland's order requiring the states to return all captured Civil War battle flags: "May God palsy the hand that wrote the order! May God palsy the brain that conceived it! May God palsy the tongue that dictated it!" "Gen. Lucius Fairchild Dead," *New York Times,* 24 May 1896.
35. On 14 September 1887, the Supreme Court of Illinois issued a unanimous decision affirming the judgment of the trial court in the Haymarket case and setting an execution date of 11 November 1887 for the seven men sentenced to death. See *Spies v. People,* 122 Ill. 1, 12 N.E. 865 (1887). Schilling and many others began a clemency movement. Meetings protesting the treatment of the defendants were held in several major cities on 20 October 1887. Some four thousand people gathered in Chicago, with Darrow slated among the speakers. See "Appeal to the People," *Chicago Evening Mail,* 20 October 1887 ("Mr. Darrow is a lawyer, and will give the legal points in the case"); "Mercy for the Reds, It Is Asked by Their Friends," *Chicago Morning News,* 21 October 1887; "Say They Must not Hang," *Chicago Tribune,* 21 October 1887.

I could also get Mr. Salter & perhaps Gen. Trumbull. [. . .][36] adopted by "land and labor" club. They were published in Herald. I prepared them and although they were not as strong as I really felt, I thought they were best that way. They have been sent to George.[37] Am sorry your resolution did not go through at Minneapolis.[38] With best regards

I am yours, | C S Darrow

MS: ALS, IHi, Schilling Papers.

TO JESSIE DARROW • UPPER SANDUSKY, OHIO • TUESDAY 25 OCTOBER 1887

PIERSON HOUSE.

Dear Jessie

I have only a moment to write you now as I take train in ten minutes to go to Marion. Hope I will find a letter there for me. I have spoken every night since coming and am getting tired.[39] Shall go to Columbus Sunday & if they will let me off I will not speak next week. Have had good meetings and pretty good crowds all the time. I spoke at Napoleon. Saw Elsie & the baby.[40] They are both well. The baby has grown a great deal since I saw it. It walks every where & talks a great deal & is a bright smart boy. Looks some like Paul.

I always intend to write longer letters but when I get into a train there are always a lot of fellows to meet me and take my time. But I will try to write more in the future. I do not know as there is any thing else to say. I have been well and having a pretty lively time but I get home sick and will be glad when it is over. Tell little Paul I will write to him next in a day or two. Hope you are having a good time.

Yours | Clarence

MS: ALS, Darrow Family. ENVELOPE ADDRESS: Mrs C. S. Darrow | Chicago | Ill | 2737 Prairie Av. POSTMARK: "Tol & Col.," 25 October 1887.

36. The bottom part of the letter—approximately one-third of the page—is torn off and missing. This might have contained seventy or so words.
37. Here, Darrow is referring to the fact that on 13 October 1887 the club agreed to petition Illinois governor Richard Oglesby to extend executive clemency to the men convicted in the Haymarket bombing. The resolutions of the club—which Darrow prepared—asserted objections to the defendants' trial process, the sufficiency of the evidence, the state supreme court's recent decision, and capital punishment. These resolutions were sent to Henry George.
38. At a meeting of the General Assembly of the Knights of Labor in Minneapolis, Minnesota, Schilling and others urged the Knights of Labor to adopt a resolution that would support commuting the death sentences of the Haymarket defendants. The resolution was strongly opposed by Terence V. Powderly (1849–1924), grand master of the Knights of Labor, and lost on a vote by a three-to-one margin. See "Anarchism," *Minneapolis Tribune,* 11 October 1887.
39. Darrow spoke in Marion, Ohio, and other places against the tariff. In Marion, "the great orator of Chicago" spoke to one hundred fifty Democrats and thirty Republicans for two hours and fifteen minutes: "fifteen minutes preliminary remarks; two hours to show the famous and the poor what a curse the tariff is, and how they had been imposed upon." "'C' Writes from LaRue," *Marion Weekly Star,* 29 October 1887.
40. "Elsie" was Elsie (Welty) Darrow (b. 1864), the first wife of Clarence Darrow's youngest brother, Herman, and "the baby" was Elsie and Herman's first child, Elmer Darrow (1885–1960).

• 1890–1894

TO HENRY DEMAREST LLOYD • CHICAGO • MONDAY 28 APRIL 1890

OFFICE OF THE COUNSEL TO THE CORPORATION April 28 1890

My Dear Lloyd

It seems to me very necessary that we should get up a big "citizens meeting" as you once proposed to give support to the strikers.[1] I fear that their cause will be lost unless we move at once & show that there is something back of them. I see that Franklin Head[2] et al. are getting up what is called a "Patriotic Club" or something of that kind & are to hold a meeting on April 30th. Do you see? This is one more evidence of the truth of Johnston's statement that "Patriotism is the last resort of a knave." Can you not come & see me right away.

As Ever C. S. Darrow.

MS: ALS, WHi, Lloyd Papers.

1. On 7 April 1890, an estimated seven thousand carpenters in Chicago went on strike, seeking an eight-hour day, forty cents an hour in wages, and recognition of their union. Darrow, Lloyd, John Altgeld, William Salter, and others formed a committee to try to bring the carpenters and contractors together to resolve their disputes. By the date of this letter, the strike had developed into a more general strike by many workers in the building trades, which brought to a halt many construction projects in the city. The strike was settled on 6 May 1890 through an arbitration committee, with the carpenters receiving, among other things, an eight-hour day and nearly forty cents an hour. "Dropped Their Tools, *Washington Post*, 8 April 1890; "Intercepting Arrivals," *Chicago Tribune*, 16 April 1890; "Still Another Strike," *Chicago Tribune*, 17 April 1890; "Strike Fever in Chicago," *Washington Post*, 24 April 1890; "Chicago Carpenters," *Washington Post*, 7 May 1890.
2. Franklin Head (1835–1914) was at various times a lawyer, businessman, and banker in Chicago. A wealthy man, Head was active in civic affairs, president of the Civic Federation of Chicago, and a Republican in his politics.

TO PAUL DARROW • MT. CLEMENS, MICHIGAN • WEDNESDAY 7 JANUARY 1891

THE FOUNTAIN HOTEL. Jan 7, 1891

Dear Little Boy

I was glad to get your letter and should have answered it a good while ago. I think I will be home on Sunday or Monday. I am better than when I went away. Have taken a bath every day.[3] The water has salt and iron and lots of other things in it; it is so heavy that you can't sink in it and when you come out your ears are full of salt. When I come back I will see if I can not get some one to give you some lessons on the fiddle. I think you ought to learn to play.

I expect Uncle Hube[4] to come up here from Detroit to see me today. I suppose school has commenced and that you are going every day. I will send a letter with this to mama.

Your father | C. S. Darrow.

MS: ALS, Darrow Family. ENVELOPE ADDRESS: Paul Everett Darrow Esq. | Chicago | 86–53rd. St. POSTMARK: Mt. Clemens, 7 January 1891.

TO JESSIE DARROW • MT. CLEMENS, MICHIGAN • WEDNESDAY 7 JANUARY 1891

THE FOUNTAIN HOTEL. Jan 7 1891

Dear Jessie

Enclosed find $5. I would send more but I borrowed this. Have had no money since I came. Will be home on Monday morning at the latest & will then get some money. I have plenty in the bank. If any thing happens that I stay longer will send for some money & see that you get some. I am sorry I did not do it before. It is no matter about the piano. You had better spend all the time practicing that you can while Helen tends to the house.[5] It is just as well if she wants to do it. Let them do as they please & get along as we will not be there long & if you want to go away for a month when I get back you can do it. I am continuing to get better & think I will be in pretty good shape when I return though not quite well. Am sorry to hear Everett is sick. Have heard nothing from father—

Clarence—

MS: ALS, Darrow Family.

3. The Fountain Hotel—on whose stationery this letter was written—also operated a sanitarium called the New Fountain Bath House.
4. Hubert H. Darrow.
5. "Helen" is probably Helen Kelchner Darrow, Everett Darrow's wife. Darrow and Jessie were apparently staying at the home of Darrow's brother and sister-in-law.

TO HENRY DEMAREST LLOYD • CHICAGO • WEDNESDAY 23 DECEMBER 1891

CHICAGO & NORTH-WESTERN RAILWAY CO. Dec. 23rd '91

My Dear Lloyd

It will not be possible for me to meet you tomorrow so I write you a few lines in answer to your question.[6]

The police are supposed to be appointed to enforce the law nothing more. They & their lords have no more right to do an illegal act than a human being has. The constitution guarantees the right of free assemblage & all kinds of people have the *legal* right to meet & express their views. I know of no limit to this right except the right to disperse a meeting at times of riot or great public excitement, when the gathering of a crowd causes immediate & imminent danger as for instance during a great strike or some great popular excitement. The gathering of crowds might be prevented on the street. This can not be construed to prevent meetings in public halls, certainly at a time when no riot is imminent. Every person has the right to say what he will being responsible for what he says. One may be guilty of murder by directly advising an other to commit it. He may also be guilty of using seditious, or obscene language, but the use of this by a speaker gives no warrant whatever for the breaking up of a meeting. The evidence & decision of J.P. shows that no words were used at the meeting that were actionable, none were charged, but if the speaker instead of saying the Mayor was a dude had advised his hearers to kill him on sight it would have given no warrant for interfering with the meeting. It would have simply justified the arrest of the speaker, & the proper way to have done that would have been to procure a warrant.[7] To say that a meeting may be dispersed because a speaker uses illegal language save in case of riot is absurd. A man with the best of intentions may attend a meeting where some crank uses language he does not indorse. This does not justify a policeman in driving the auditors from the hall. No audience can be made responsible for what the speaker says. A man might attend a meeting with the best of intentions & even you or I might be called on to speak. The raid was illegal without any sort of warrant. This being so, those who occupied the hall had the right to defend their possession with weapons against the police if they wished. The fact that these policemen invaded the hall & violated the rights of the people assembled shows that it

6. Lloyd was scheduled to speak on Saturday, 27 December 1891, at a public meeting of organized labor in Chicago. Six weeks before this letter (on 12 November), approximately one hundred police officers had raided a meeting of the Painters' Union at Greif's Hall in Chicago. Twenty-three men were arrested on charges of resisting arrest and disorderly conduct. Five were also charged with carrying a concealed weapon. The mayor and police came under immediate criticism for the warrantless raid, and they defended their actions by claiming that they had thwarted an imminent uprising of "anarchists." "Anarchy Meets the Law," *Chicago Tribune*, 13 November 1891.
7. During a court hearing the day after the raid, one police detective testified—perhaps before a justice of the peace (which might explain the reference to "J.P.")—that he had heard a man at the meeting say that "they would hang the mayor and that he is a——dude." "Bombs Were to Follow," *Chicago Daily News*, 13 November 1891.

was reasonable for the people to go armed. You might take a hint from this & go prepared on Sunday night.

I do not think of any other points. If there are others send me word or telephone me to no. 618 on Saturday A.M.

Am sorry not to meet you.

Sincerely Yours | C. S. Darrow.

MS: ALS, WHi, Lloyd Papers.

TO HENRY DEMAREST LLOYD • CHICAGO • MONDAY 28 DECEMBER 1891

CHICAGO & NORTH-WESTERN RAILWAY CO. Dec. 28th. '91

My Dear Lloyd

Your speech last night was *great*.[8] In logic & law it can not be disputed. It made me feel that I am a hypocrite & a slave and added to my resolution to make my time of servitude short.

I am glad that you dare to say what is true & know so well how to say it.

Sincerely | C. S. Darrow.

MS: ALS, WHi, Lloyd Papers.

TO HENRY DEMAREST LLOYD • CHICAGO • SATURDAY 12 NOVEMBER 1892

Nov. 12th. '92

My Dear Lloyd

To night Mr. Catlin told me something of today's meeting of the "Labor Committee"—and for that reason I wish to state my position to you.[9] Two weeks ago I sent my resignation to the committe as I became thoroughly convinced that it was organized to *prevent* honest

8. Lloyd delivered a speech condemning the raid on Greif's Hall and urging more active involvement against police lawlessness. The speech was published posthumously in a book of Lloyd's essays. "Free Speech and Assemblage," in Henry Demarest Lloyd, *Mazzini and Other Essays* (New York: G. P. Putnam's Sons, 1910), 125–46.
9. William W. Catlin was a stockbroker in Chicago and a member—together with Darrow, Lloyd, and several others—of what was known as the Labor Committee for the World's Congress Auxiliary. This body was organized to present a series of meetings at the Chicago World's Fair in 1893, covering a wide spectrum of subjects—including medicine, music, literature, engineering, government, religion, labor, education, the press, temperance, "moral and social reform," and "woman's progress." By the end of the fair, the auxiliary had held 1,283 sessions, with 3,817 speakers from around the world delivering a total of 5,978 speeches. The "congress" on religion overshadowed all of the others in the number of speakers and numbers in attendance. Representatives of the world's religions were invited to speak, but freethinkers and mormons were specifically excluded. See David F. Burg, *Chicago's White City of 1893* (Lexington: University Press of Kentucky, 1976), 235–85.

discussion of the "labor question" instead of promote it. I did this as I believed only after a fair trial of the committee and on sufficient evidence to support my theory. More than a year ago at my request & in a meeting when you were present they promised to report to us within two weeks (or at next meeting) the relation between the labor committe & the "so called" Auxilliery. Nothing has been done in a year but to delay & leave the "labor committe" completely in the hands of Mr. Bonney[10] and some more bumptious fanatics with full power to revise and annul every thing the committe does. This after these men have shown their caliber by declaring publicly that they will discuss all phases of the labor question but "Anarchism" and all religions but "Mormanism" *provided no one* says *any thing* ~~*about*~~ against *Christianity*. This committe has set apart six days for discussing labor and six weeks for discussing religion showing that they have the orthodox idea of the relative value of the poor man's body and soul, and which they propose to help.—The result will be that they will spend the six days teaching the poor to be patient in this world and the six weeks in telling them how happy they will be in the next. Mr. Mills—*Rev.* Mills,[11] has tried to quiet the committe by telling them that they need no pledges from Mr. Wordy Bonney but that if they go ahead in their own way the bosses will consent to any programme they make, this after being told in advance what they must not do and after advertising to the world their own narrowness and imbecility.—They have not had the candor to say fairly to the committe what they can do knowing that if they did the committe would resign & go to work on their own account, but instead of that have deceived and misled them believing the Christian doctrine that lying is proper if it results in the glory of God, which of course means his agents. The programme at the Dedicatory exercise was sufficient further evidence of their purpose & caliber.[12] I have never seen or written to any of the members privately about this matter before. I said what I thought in the committe and the rest did not see it my way, so I ~~quit~~ resigned. You were not present and for that reason I desired to give you my views. I believe the committee is being deceived and played with for the purpose of confounding and misleading the cause of

10. Charles C. Bonney (1831–1903), lawyer. Bonney was born in New York, educated at what is now Colgate University, and went to Chicago in 1860, where he practiced law and served for a time as president of the Illinois State Bar Association and as vice president of the American Bar Association. The World's Congress Auxiliary was his inspiration and he organized the efforts behind its establishment. He delivered a speech himself at the opening of each "congress." In politics, he was a Democrat and in religion he was a Swedenborgian. He was also a prohibitionist.
11. Walter Thomas Mills (1856–1942), labor reformer, author, and political organizer. Mills was born in New York, the son of Quaker farmers. After graduating from the College of Wooster and Oberlin College, he moved to Chicago, where he was an ardent prohibitionist, a founder of the Socialist Party, and a social-gospel crusader. He was chairman of the Labor Committee for the World's Congress Auxiliary. He wrote prohibitionist handbooks and other books, including *The Science of Politics* (1887) and *The Struggle for Existence* (1904). After living in New Zealand for several years, 1911–14, Mills returned to the United States, protesting involvement in the war, writing, promoting socialism, and working to establish cooperative communes, among other activities.
12. Darrow might be referring to the religious and patriotic nature of the inaugural ceremony for the auxiliary, which was held on 21 October 1892. See "Congress Auxiliary Inaugural," *Chicago Tribune*, 21 October 1892 (program for the ceremony); "In Oratory and Song," *Chicago Tribune*, 22 October 1892 (text of invocation and speeches at the ceremony). The fair itself did not open until the following May.

labor, and especially to prevent any radical utterances by any independent men or bodies and I am surprised that the committee, composed of individuals who are sincere in their devotion to the cause of the poor can not understand their schemes and tricks.[13]

When I was East last summer I stopped at New Port a day and tried very hard to see you but could not get across, so I contented myself looking at Vanderbilt's home.[14] I have been hoping to see you ever since your return but have been disappointed. I wish you might drop in some time when you are down. I should be very glad of a call. I hope soon to see the book and am sure it will be fine—I have become a great enthusiast over Howells. Remember me kindly to Mrs. Lloyd

Sincerely your friend | C. S. Darrow.

MS: ALS, WHi, Lloyd Papers. PLACE: no reason to doubt Chicago.

TO HENRY DEMAREST LLOYD • CHICAGO • FRIDAY 28 APRIL 1893

CHICAGO & NORTH-WESTERN RAILWAY CO. April 28

My Dear Lloyd

On Saturday night (tomorrow) I am to read a paper to the law club on Judge Gary's article.[15] Would you like to go? If so please come to my office at 5–30. You do not need to go but Judge Gary (high executioner) will be there & the debate will perhaps be lively.[16]

Very truly | C. S. Darrow.

MS: ALS, WHi, Lloyd Papers. DATE: appended.

13. Several weeks after this letter was written, the Women's Labor Committee of the World's Congress Auxiliary, which included Jane Addams, Ellen Gates Starr, and many others, also resigned as a body, apparently because of the authoritative role and conservative approach of Bonney and other managers to the subject of labor. The "religious feature" of the Labor Congress was said to be the "real bone of contention." "Resigns in a Body," *Chicago Tribune*, 29 December 1892. In Bonney's words, the World's Congress Auxiliary had created no "mixed committees" but, in "appropriate cases," had created committees of women, "not to have charge of subjects in general, but to look after the interests of women and children . . . and to cooperate with the general committee of men as occasion may require." Ibid.
14. Lloyd owned a summer house on Sakonnet Point, across the mouth of Narragansett Bay from Newport, Rhode Island. "Vanderbilt's home" is probably the mansion in Newport known as Marble House, which was built for William K. Vanderbilt (1849–1920), of the prominent Vanderbilt family.
15. Joseph E. Gary, who presided over the trial of the Haymarket anarchists, wrote an article defending the trial process. Joseph E. Gary, "The Chicago Anarchists of 1886: The Crime, the Trial, and the Punishment," *Century Magazine*, April 1893, 803–37.
16. The reaction to Darrow's speech at the Chicago Law Club was mixed, as it was for many of his speeches. A few months after the speech, the Republican *Journal*, for example, in commenting on the possibility that Darrow would seek Gary's judicial seat, recalled Darrow as having no "conviction" in his speech: "Only a few months ago, at a meeting of the Chicago Law Club, [Darrow] read a paper purporting to be a review of Judge Gary's article in the *Century*. Judge Gary himself was present as well as most of the lawyers who were engaged in the trial of the Anarchists on either side. Mr. Darrow's paper was merely a reiteration of the time-worn arguments against the justice of the trial. They were presented in good temper, for he is a man of tact, but they failed to carry conviction. Judge Gary was with difficulty prevailed upon to reply, but he did so with a brevity and dignity that elicited tumultuous applause. | That occasion was an epitome of the contest that has been waged for years over the graves of the Anarchists. On one side was a young man of generous feeling, the victim of a dangerous sentimentalism; on the other a tried and venerable Judge, who stood firm as a rock against the enemies of social order." "Gov. Altgeld's Judicial Candidate," *Chicago Journal*, 13 July 1893.

TO HENRY DEMAREST LLOYD • CHICAGO • MONDAY 10 JULY 1893

CITY OF CHICAGO July 10th '93

My Dear Lloyd

Today's mail bring me a notice of a meeting of executive committee at Mr. Barry's[17] office tomorrow Tuesday at 5–30 P.M. I hope you can come as I am anxious to see this committee disband. I do not like to see Barry's name in print in connection with any thing in which I believe and I do not like to be subject to his call at any moment. I am always afraid he will say or do something for the papers & I think we ought to wind up the concern and place it on a new basis. I hope you can come tomorrow. I see by the papers that Mr. Howells is to be here this week. If it should be convenient to you & him I wish I might meet him some where. If you & he were to be down town at lunch hour I wish you could arrange to go to Iroquois Club with me.[18] Of course this matter is of more importance to me than to Mr. Howells.

Very truly | C. S. Darrow.

MS: ALS, WHi, Lloyd Papers.

TO THE *CHICAGO HERALD* • CHICAGO • MONDAY 4 SEPTEMBER 1893

CHICAGO, Sept. 4.—*Editor of The Herald:* It has been the custom of the press to publish the number of paid admissions each day, also the number of admissions by passes.[19] This rule has been universal except as to Sunday, when only paid admissions are given. No doubt this is because no information is given out upon the subject of Sunday admission by passes.

Sunday, by the grace of Judge Goggin,[20] I attended the fair and for some time watched the people enter the grounds. I discovered that the pass gates were crowded

17. Darrow is probably referring to a Charles Bary, who was chairman of the executive committee of the "Amnesty Association of Illinois," which was making an organized effort to get pardons for the remaining anarchists convicted for the Haymarket incident. The committee was made up of dozens of people, including Darrow. "Its Charter Board of Directors," *Chicago Tribune,* 7 August 1892.
18. Howells was likely coming to Chicago for a weeklong session of lectures and meetings among leading men and women in philology, literature, folklore, history, and libraries, as part of the World's Congress Auxiliary of the World's Fair. See "For Men of Letters," *Chicago Tribune,* 9 July 1893.
19. Darrow is referring to admissions to the World's Fair, held in Chicago from 1 May to 29 October 1893.
20. James Goggin (1842?–98), lawyer and judge. Goggin was a judge on the superior court in Chicago and responsible for keeping the World's Fair open on Sundays. The commissioners of the fair had issued an order closing the fair on Sundays. A judge of the superior court (Judge Stein) entered an order enjoining the commissioners from closing the fair. Judge Goggin presided at the hearing on a motion to dissolve the injunction. Before the hearing, Goggin invited two other judges (one of them, Edward Dunne) to sit with him to hear the motion, given the importance of the issue. But before the hearing began, Goggin reportedly learned that the other two judges were in favor of dissolving the injunction. So shortly before the hearing began, Goggin had the clerk enter an order postponing the hearing for sixty days, which effectively left the injunction in place until after the fair was over. See "Quashed the Other Views," *Washington Post,* 1 September 1893; Adolf Kraus, *Reminiscences and Comments* (Chicago: Toby Rubovits, 1925), 86–87.

while the pay gates were poorly patronized. This demonstrated what was before plain to me, that few people had religious objections to attending the fair on Sunday provided they held a pass. It shows conclusively that the paid admissions are comparatively small because people do not wish to pay full price for half a show. It cannot be accounted for on the ground that exhibitors and employees go on Sunday and therefore passes are used. This class of people stay away more generally on Sunday than on any other day. The passes are used by well-dressed, well-to-do people—such as always have passes—and these go on Sunday in spite of the fact that there is less to see than on other days.

If the directors would reduce the price to 25 cents on Sunday with children free, the grounds would be filled. All the other public parks and places of resort are over-crowded on Sunday, better patronized than on week days. Why would not the rule be the same with the fair?

And why should not this be done? No complaint can be made but that the fair management has been very courteous and considerate to princes and princesses, lords and ladies, ra-jays and other jays of high degree, but the people who built the fair and made all its exhibits have not been able to see its wonders.

Everyone knows that the times are very hard, that thousands are out of work, that wages have been reduced, and that a committee is at work in Chicago feeding the hungry. Everyone knows that this year at least the working people and their children cannot afford to visit the fair at the regular price of admission. In addition to this $5,000,000 has been raised by taxation on the citizens of Chicago. This sum in the end comes out of labor, as all burdens must at last come from production. Should not the poor have some benefit from this?

There are thousands of little children in Chicago who cannot see the fair unless they are admitted free. There are thousands of men and women who cannot see it at the regular price. Would it not be wise and generous for the directors to give these little ones some pleasure from the fair, especially when it can be done without expense and when they have paid a large sum by way of taxation to make what it is.

To give these poor children and other less favored people a chance to see the fair will pay. If it does not pay in dollars, it will pay in general culture, in education, refinement, good fellowship and good will among all our citizens, and when the fair is over and the directors confront a bankrupt treasury it will be well to have some of these assets to their credit.

C. S. DARROW.

MS: "Voice of the People. To Make Sunday Opening Popular. Assistant City Attorney Darrow Argues for 25-Cent Admission to the Fair on Sunday—Present Rates a Barrier to the Poor," *Chicago Herald*, 8 September 1893.

TO HENRY DEMAREST LLOYD • CHICAGO • THURSDAY 12 OCTOBER 1893

GOODRICH & VINCENT October 12th, 1893.

My dear Lloyd:—

You will no doubt remember that about a year after the execution of the anarchists Judge Gary made a speech at a bar dinner in which he said that the extortions of capital amounted to very little, but that labor unions were great tyrants, etc.

I well remember your reply to him in the Herald.[21] Can you give me the exact date of this speech, and if you have a copy of it you can spare for a short time. I would be very glad to have it at once. I think it would be a good thing to circulate at this time.

I wish you would call and see me some morning soon at the office.

C. S. Darrow

MS: TLS, WHi, Lloyd Papers. INSIDE ADDRESS: Mr. Henry D. Lloyd, | Winnetka, Illinois.

TO THE *CHICAGO HERALD* • CHICAGO • SATURDAY 18 NOVEMBER 1893

CHICAGO, Nov. 18.—*Editor of The Herald:* If any further evidence were needed to show that man had his origin in the brute creation, the conduct and utterances of the public in reference to the shooting of our mayor has furnished that proof.[22]

Everyone realizes the terrible nature of the deed and the frightful consequences of the act. Nothing can be said or done to make the calamity less or greater or to unmake the facts that are beyond recall. Heaping reproaches upon the miserable being who took his life cannot help the dead or alleviate the sorrows of his family and friends.

It seems as if the whole community had gone mad at the sight of blood and were ready to forget the better instincts that it was supposed civilization had developed in mankind. Some of our papers say that no loophole of the law must be found by lawyer, judge or jury that will permit the prisoner's escape. Others, that all that is now needed is a piece of rope and that no time should be wasted in a trial of the case. We read a graphic description of how the prisoner was told by guards and fellow prisoners that a mob outside the jail were preparing to batter down the walls and put him to death without the aid of law. We are told how he trembled and turned pale

21. On 27 December 1887, Joseph Gary—the judge who presided over the trial of the Haymarket defendants—gave a speech condemning organized labor at a dinner held in his honor by the Chicago Bar Association. The next week, the *Chicago Herald* published a letter from Lloyd criticizing the speech and supporting labor. "Labour and Monopoly: A Reply to the Views of Judge Gary," *Chicago Herald*, 3 January 1888.

22. On 28 October 1893, Patrick Eugene Prendergast (1868–94) called on Mayor Carter Harrison Sr. at the mayor's house and shot him dead.

with fear, and as we realize his exquisite torture we are consoled for the loss of the thumbscrew and the rack and conclude that we can accomplish the same object quite as well without.

Most men admit that the prisoner was insane and yet lawyers, doctors, merchants and men of all classes are almost unanimous in saying that, whether sane or insane, the wretched being ought to hang. In this cry for blood the clergy seem to lead. They are paid for teaching mercy and pity, and it seems as if some of them, at least, might say some kind word of the unfortunate being or, at least, of his mother and his kin. I suppose that from their standpoint even he has a soul that must be saved or lost. The ablest criminal lawyer in the west has been employed to prosecute the case and numberless expert doctors have been hired by the state to prove him sane.

Against this array the voice of justice must be very loud to be heard above the din. Is it possible that the community measures the consequences of its acts?

Here was a young man or boy delivering papers from door to door; he caught the mania of a popular craze; he caught it in the air from those who write and speak; he believed that he was to be made corporation counsel, although a paper peddler who had never read a line of law; he went to the law office of the city and told the corporation counsel that he wished his place. The corporation counsel told him he could have it in a little while, and introduced him to the office force as his successor in the place. He did not get the office; he went to the mayor's house and shot him, then went out onto the streets, no one knowing who he was or what he was, went two miles or more to a police station and placed himself in the custody of the law. Were these the acts of a sane man, responsible for his deeds?

The chief of police, Inspectors Shea, Kipley and Ross are all on record as saying that he is insane, and still it is proposed to kill him whether he is sane or not.

It is urged by nine men out of ten that it makes no difference whether he is crazy or not, he ought to be hanged, and those who protest are called "sickly sentimentalists." Is it not time for a sober second thought? Under the laws of Illinois, if this man were crazy he is not guilty of a crime. Can we afford to sweep away the law because a great majority believe a prisoner has no right to live? Shall a majority say that the law shall be ignored when they believe the necessities demand? If this be the case, then there is no longer need for law. If the law is not strong enough to protect the humblest and weakest citizen it deserves the contempt of all. We cannot use it when we would and ignore it when we will. We cannot sow the wind without reaping the whirlwind.

Can the community afford to say that they hanged a lunatic against the law, because the world was better with him dead? If this were the standard the hangman and the foolkiller would be a very busy pair.

Suppose this man had been ill with typhoid fever and in a moment of delirium had seized a revolver and gone to the mayor's house and shot him down; would the community say he should be hanged, lest if he were locked up the fever might sometime leave him and he would be turned loose? Neither in morals nor in law is he

responsible if he was not himself, and to put a crazy man to death would not be worthy of a savage tribe.

The law of compensation controls the universe. It may not matter much to the unfortunate prisoner or even to his mother and brother whether he shall live or die; but the spectacle of a civilized community pitilessly killing a crazy man will furnish an example of cruelty and fury that in some way must bear evil fruit.[23]

C. S. DARROW.

MS: "The Cry for Blood," *Chicago Herald*, 20 November 1893.

TO HENRY DEMAREST LLOYD • CHICAGO • FRIDAY 12 OCTOBER 1894

COLLINS, GOODRICH, DARROW & VINCENT Oct. 12th '94

Mr. Dear Lloyd

Thanks for your suggestion as to auditorium meeting. I will see that it is carried out.[24]

Can we not do something with the Times? I am told that it must be sold and will be and that it can be had at any price. Don't you think something can be done at once.[25] I am anxious to have some talk with you before I speak, & as early as I can. I am somewhat in doubt as to the line I should adopt. Can you not come in some day to lunch.

Yours C. S. Darrow.

MS: ALS, WHi, Lloyd Papers.

23. Prendergast's trial began in December 1893. His lawyers pleaded insanity as a defense, but he was found guilty and sentenced to hang. Darrow and Stephen S. Gregory represented Prendergast in his post-trial proceedings and eventually obtained an order postponing his execution under a statute that authorized a judge to appoint a jury to inquire into the sanity of a person convicted of a capital crime if the convicted person allegedly became insane after the trial. A trial on that issue—whether Prendergast became insane after his criminal trial—began in June 1894. The jury returned a verdict finding Prendergast sane (again) and he was hanged on 13 July 1894, after Governor Altgeld refused to commute his sentence.
24. The point of Lloyd's "suggestion" is not known, but on 19 October, Darrow would deliver a speech for the People's Party at the auditorium in Chicago. The People's Party, formed in 1892, followed a political platform that included free coinage of silver, direct election of senators, an eight-hour work day, nationalization of communications and railroads, and municipal ownership of utilities, among other reforms. In his speech, Darrow was critical of the policies and actions of both the Democratic and Republican parties. He told his audience that "those who entertain opinions and views such as I hold should no longer affiliate themselves with either of the two great political parties." "Crowd the Auditorium," *Chicago Herald*, 25 October 1894. See also "Pops out in Force: They Besiege the Auditorium to Secure Admittance," *Chicago Tribune*, 20 October 1894.
25. The *(Chicago) Times* was a Democratic daily newspaper that had been owned by the late Mayor Carter Harrison Sr. and Adolf Kraus (1852–1928). After Harrison was assassinated in 1893, Harrison's majority interest in the paper passed to his two sons, who had a difficult time operating the paper profitably. Kraus, *Reminiscences*, 65, 100–101. Darrow—who believed that the "most formidable obstacle" to political reform was the "hostility, indifference and treachery" of the press—was apparently interested in organizing an effort to purchase the paper. Darrow, along with some others, proposed to organize a "People's Press Association," the object of which would be to establish "a great national daily newspaper to be owned and controlled by the people." Darrow et al. to "Dear Sir," 22 October 1894, TLc, WHi, Lloyd Papers. In the end, the *Times* was not sold and Darrow did not establish a national daily newspaper. In 1895, Harrison's sons transferred a majority interest in the *Times* to Kraus. Kraus, *Reminiscences*, 100–101.

TO HENRY DEMAREST LLOYD • CHICAGO • THURSDAY 22 NOVEMBER 1894

863 THE ROOKERY Nov. 22d.

Dear Lloyd

Do you know that they are making history very fast in America, and all the history is against freedom.[26]

Yesterday several A.R.U. men were convicted in Los Angeles—practically for striking.[27] Trials are now on all over the country. Next month some will be convicted here. The people are dead. Can any thing be done to resurrect them, before liberty is dead? I am very much discouraged at the prospect. I can not join the other side but what can be done?

I am also in a quandry about the People's Party. I might be willing to join a Socialists party, but I am not willing to help run an other Socialist movement under the guise of "The People's party." We must take some stand or drop out altogether.

I hoped I might see you before this.

I send you a pamphlet which the Rail roads are circulating everywhere to help make opinion for fools, which is for everyone—What do you think? Can you see any way to do any more to counteract it?

This is one of the days when I feel blue. Will you kindly return the pamphlet as I want it in the case and may not get an other one?

Truly Yours | C. S. Darrow

MS: ALS, WHi, Lloyd Papers. DATE: "[1894]" is appended.

TO HENRY DEMAREST LLOYD • CHICAGO • SATURDAY 24 NOVEMBER 1894

863 THE ROOKERY

Dear Mr. Lloyd,

If I can possibly come tomorrow I will but fear I can not, at least until late.

I think you did not understand my position. I never did and never will believe in banning any one out of any thing least of all the Socialists of whom I am one. My only

26. In the spring of 1894, employees of the Pullman Palace Car Company—manufacturer of railroad cars in the company-owned town of Pullman, Illinois—went on strike when the company refused to negotiate with the American Railway Union over rents on company-owned housing for employees and cuts in employee wages. The strike soon developed into a general railroad strike throughout the West when the ARU's members refused to handle any Pullman cars. This general strike led, in turn, to a federal court injunction in July 1894 prohibiting interference with the mail and interstate commerce. Shortly after this injunction, President Cleveland ordered troops into Chicago to quell rioting and free any blocked trains. In September 1894, several leaders of the strike, including Eugene Debs, were tried for contempt of the injunction and, in early 1895, twenty union men, including Debs, would stand trial for conspiracy to obstruct the mail. Darrow was one of the defendants' lawyers in both matters.

27. Four leaders of the ARU in Los Angeles were convicted on 21 November of conspiracy to interfere with the mail. Lloyd wrote back to Darrow (in a long letter) saying he had been expecting the convictions from the beginning of the strike. Lloyd to Darrow, 23 November 1894, TLc, WHi, Lloyd Papers.

suggestion was as to whether we could claim to commit the People's party to Socialism. I think it was done too much in the last campaign—for instance all the litterature circulated at the meeting was entirely socialistic such as the "People's party" would not indorse and as it was under their auspices it ought not to have been such as was antagonistic to a large portion of the party. I have no objection to the speakers talking Socialism as all of us did but these were understood views, but I must say I think the effort was made to commit the party further than the party ever went.—I am inclined to think that I would be willing to support a straight Socialistic movement and perhaps that is best, but if we intend to work with the great national "People's party" we must keep in line with it, leaving each person to have their own views & express them but not seeking to commit the party to any thing they do not wish to indorse. I believe the Socialists are the best Radicals we have and I always have and always will support and defend them. I only insist that we ought to make the movement stand for just what it pretends or we can not keep it together. I hope I can see you and talk it all over.

Sincerely Yours | C. S. Darrow.

MS: ALS, WHi, Lloyd Papers. DATE: "[24 Nov. 1894]" is appended.

• 1895–1899

TO "MISS S." • CHICAGO • MARCH 1895

My Dear Miss S.[1]

If I did not care for you and your friendship, as well as that of the other members of the "settlement," Hull House, Chicago, I would do as you requested, not answer your letter.[2] I hope you know that I would understand the spirit in which you wrote. I know *you* know and appreciate the feeling of friendship which prompted you to write as you did.

1. The intended recipient might have been Ellen Gates Starr (1859–1940), a settlement worker, social reformer, and cofounder with Jane Addams of Hull House in Chicago in 1889. This is suggested by the salutation ("My Dear Miss S.") and the reference to Hull House, among other indications. But the fact that this document appears to be a typewritten copy of a letter or a draft of a letter (undated and by an unknown typist) leaves some doubt about the identity of the recipient.
2. The letter that Darrow received apparently complained about his representation of the Cosmopolitan Electric Company. In February 1895, the city council for Chicago had passed ordinances granting franchises to the Ogden Gas Company and the Cosmopolitan Electric Company. The ordinances were passed quickly, without any second reading and without being referred to a committee for consideration. One week later, a reported five-thousand-plus people gathered at Central Music Hall to denounce the ordinances and protest against approval by the mayor. On 4 March 1895, despite the protests, the mayor, "amid curses and laughter," approved the ordinance for the Ogden Gas Company and suggested some amendments (encouraged, apparently, by Darrow) for the Cosmopolitan Electric Company, which were then approved by the council. A few days later, some citizens filed a petition in superior court in Chicago, seeking an injunction that would prohibit the companies from using any of the streets and alleys for their businesses. The judge assigned, although "practically [holding] the ordinances were invalid," dismissed the petition on the ground urged by Darrow—that it should have been brought by the state attorney general. "History of the Three Measures," *Chicago Tribune*, 11 April 1895; "Zeisler Picks Flaws," *Chicago Tribune*, 21 March 1895.

Although you may not think it, I am very sensitive to public opinion, even the opinion of those who are glad to criticize what I do. But when it comes to the opinion of those whom I know to be my sincere friends, and well wishers, like yourself, I feel it much more deeply. I should be very sorry to have you change your opinion of me, as I am sorry to have so many other of my good friends feel hurt (almost personally) in reference to the matter of which you wrote. I have always acted legally on my own judgment. I know I have many times made mistakes. I have sometimes admitted them, but I believe I never sought to evade the consequences of anything I have done or to make any defense or excuse for my acts.

I wish to put this matter before you from my own stand point, and in so doing will endeavor not to place myself in the position so frequently occupied by those who wish to excuse something they know to be wrong. An ordinance was passed by the city council granting certain valuable rights to an Electric Co., or to some people purporting to be an electric co. I never heard of this ordinance until after it was passed. The Mayor refused to sign it in the shape in which it passed. I was employed in getting as favorable amendments to the ordinance as I could, and to otherwise act as their attorney.

I did not know how this ordinance was passed, I do not know now. I however know enough about municipal affairs to believe it was passed for boodle like every ordinance granting valuable privileges in this city.

I undertook to serve this company or these people, believing they had an ordinance procured by the aid of boodle. Judged by the ordinary commercial and legal standard of ethics I did right. Every law book and every instructor constantly teaches that all clients have the right to have their cases represented and to receive the benefit and protection of the law. I know that in your mind this is no justification. It is no justification in mine. I do not care a cent for all the ordinary rules of ethics or conduct. They are mostly wrong. I am satisfied that judged by the higher law, in which we both believe, I could not be justified, and that I am practically a thief. I am taking money that I did not earn, which comes to me from men who did not earn but who get it because they have the chance to get it. I take it without performing any useful service to the world, and I take a thousand times as much as my services are worth even assuming they were useful and honest.

This is my position, judged by the high rules of conduct and ethics in which I believe and in which I have in my way and to the best of my ability tried to urge the world to adopt. I came to Chicago about eight years ago, before I came I lived in a small country town.

These modern thoughts about the rights of labor, and the wrongs of the world, had just taken possession of me. My attention was called to these by a friend named Swift, whom I believe you have once met in Boston.[3] We discussed these questions not only abstractly, but as applied to our own life and our own conduct. He took one view and I

3. Morrison Isaac Swift (1856–1946), socialist writer and lecturer. Swift was born in Ravenna, Ohio. He attended Western Reserve University and then Williams College, from which he graduated in 1879. He received a Ph.D. from Johns Hopkins, 1885, concentrating in political economy, and then spent two years studying philosophy at the University of Berlin. Returning to the United States, he performed settlement work in

another, both agreed the ideal life was well nigh unlivable, both had in view doing some good. His father owned a drug store, he died and Swift was appointed administrator of his father's estate. He took all the patent medicines out in the back yard and broke the bottles; he then left his town without money, refused to compromise with the world, lived as best he could, was nearly a tramp. He raised a Coxey army, marched to Washington, is now I believe shunned by most earnest people who cannot follow him. He is no doubt loved by those who know him, but has lived his life as he thought right and best, has perhaps done some good in his way by refusing to compromise with evil, and be a party or participator in wrong. I believed then and I believe now, that society is organized injustice, that business is legal fraud, that a land owner is a pirate, who takes money from the poor for standing on the ground should be free to all, that society consists of two classes, the despoiler and despoiled, that all who directly or indirectly live off the proceeds of labor are enjoying the fruits of robbery, and the poor are their victims.

I determined then to give my energies and ability to help change the system under which all of us are compelled to live. I did not take the course that was adopted by my friend, like him I chose deliberately, and have followed consistently. I came to Chicago. I determined to take my chances with the rest, to get what I could out of the system and use it to *destroy* the system. I came without friends or money. Society provides no fund out of which such people can live while preaching heresy. It compels us to get our living out of society as it is or die. I do not choose yet to die although perhaps it would be the best. Long ago I laid out my course in life. I have followed it without much variation ever since. I care nothing whatever for money except to use it in this work and to bring me such comforts as I want and to help my friends.

After being here a short time I took a position in the law department of the city, where I learned something of municipal affairs. I then served a railroad company for three years. I have since sold my professional services to every corporation or individual who cared to buy, the only exception I have made is that I have never given them to oppress the weak, or convict the innocent. Aside from this I have used them to the best of my ability to serve my clients almost every one of whom are criminals judged by the higher law in which I firmly believe. I have taken their ill-gotten gains and have tried to use it to prevent suffering, sometimes I have succeeded, often I have failed. My preaching and my practicing have never been the same. I have always tried to show a state and a way to reach where men and women can be honest and tender. I have never advised any one not to get a

---

Philadelphia and New York. In 1894, he took a lead role in the march of a Coxey Army of poor and unemployed people from Boston to Washington, D.C. He later moved for a short time to Los Angeles, where he was active in the utopian Alturia Colony. After his return east, he was the chief lecturer and director of the Humanist Forum in Boston, 1907–14, and a frequent contributor of letters to the *Boston Transcript*. See William O. Reichert, "The Melancoly Political Thought of Morrison I. Swift," *New England Quarterly* 49 (December 1976): 542–59. Swift's many books include *The Monarch Billionaire* (New York: J.S. Ogilvie, 1903), *Human Submission* (Philadelphia: Liberty Press, 1905), *Can Mankind Survive* (Boston: Marshall Jones, 1918), and *The Evil Religion Does* (Boston: Liberty Press, 1927).

living out of this society, for I want the best of society to live. I believe that there is absolutely no difference in my conduct whether I serve a corporation conceived in oppression and fraud as all of them are, or whether I take rent from a tenant or sell goods to the poor, all of it is bad, none of it could live in a world that is beautiful and just. My conduct in this matter, if the facts generally believed are true, is nearer right than anything I have ever done for money in a business way. I have harmed no one who cannot afford to loose, and who has the least moral right to their possessions. Now, as when I went to serve the railroad company the only question that is pertinent from my standpoint what are his motives? and what attitude will he assume towards those things he condemns? If I let my professional business change my views of life, or allow it to influence me as a citizen, the support of measures in which I do not believe, I am wrong. Otherwise as I see the light I am doing my duty. It may be that people cannot look at this in the way I view it, I believe the wisest do. I may be condemned and lose influence, this I expected at the time and it hurt me, hurt me grievously. I would have been glad not to have taken the employment, and thus escape the censure which I have received and will receive, and which I knew would come. But had I refused it, I would have done so not because I thought it wrong but because I thought it would not pay. I will not allow myself to be influenced by that consideration. I have defended the poor and weak, have done it without pay, will do it again. I cannot defend them without bread, I cannot get this except from those who have it, and by giving some measure of conformity to what is.

While I am very sensitive to public opinion I have never in my life considered it in determining my course, I hope I never will. I have even dared to do right in face of public opinion, and this is always dangerous. I believe that after a while most of the people, nearly all the laborers, will believe I was right and that I am true to their cause. I hope they will, but I must abide it if they do not. The qualities which you say I possess, and the usefulness which you say might come to me, are due only to taking the same course in other matters that I have taken here. I do not believe that on the whole I would have been as useful in any other way, and yet no one can know. I could have taken the course pursued by my friend Swift, I chose the other. In my mind there is no middle ground. We must take one path or the other. I do not say that he did wrong, but I cannot say that I was wrong. Only infinite wisdom can determine this, and I am inclined to think, that if such a judgment is ever pronounced it will be determined that neither one did wrong. I don't want you to think I did this or anything for the money because I like money, for I do not. I did it as I mean to do all things because I thought it best, because I believe that the only way any person or deed can be judged is by the purpose and the full results.

Sincerely your friend,

MS: TT, DLC-MSS, Darrow Papers. PLACE: no reason to doubt Chicago. DATE: among other things, Darrow's involvement with the Cosmopolitan Electric Company and how those events coincide with the statements in the letter and the statement about having been in Chicago "about eight years."

TO HENRY DEMAREST LLOYD • CHICAGO • THURSDAY 2 JANUARY 1896

DARROW, THOMAS & THOMPSON Jan 2d '95

My Dear Mr. Lloyd

I would like to help Prof. Bemis but do not think I ought to use my money in that way.[4] I have not much to use, and have rather definite plans as to what I must do. I am glad to see Prof. Ely's[5] interest in the matter & think it shows remarkably well in him. I know Aldrich[6] but he is a very hard man to get money from and I would rather pay it than to collect it from him, and that is saying much. When are you to be in town again? Can't we lunch together soon?

Sincerely Yours, | C. S. Darrow.

MS: ALS, WHi, Ely Papers. DATE: letterhead (the firm of Darrow, Thomas & Thompson did not exist in January 1895 but did by January 1896); the letter was likely misdated by Darrow.

TO THE *CHICAGO TRIBUNE* • CHICAGO • MONDAY 6 JANUARY 1896

Chicago, Jan. 6.

THE TRIBUNE this morning contains an editorial based on what I was "reported" to have said on Saturday night at the Review Club.[7] The newspaper report made me say exactly the opposite of what I did say upon the point which the Tribune criticized. Instead of saying that "patriotism was a blind, inhuman cry for blood" I distinctly said that this was not patriotism. In this I fully agree with THE TRIBUNE (strange as it may seem). On that occasion I used substantially the following language: "The human race is always eager for blood. He who advocates war has always been called a patriot, and he who pleads for peace a traitor; patriotism has generally been construed to be a 'blind,

4. Edward W. Bemis (1860–1930), political economist and tenured professor at the University of Chicago, was removed from the faculty in December 1894, probably because of his articles and public statements favoring labor and criticizing utility companies. His removal received a great deal of attention in local newspapers. Lloyd was among Bemis's strongest supporters. See Harold E. Berquist Jr., "The Edward Bemis Controversy at the University of Chicago," *American Association of University Professors Bulletin* 58 (December 1972): 383–93; Chester McArthur Destler, *Henry Demarest Lloyd and the Empire of Reform* (Philadelphia: University of Pennsylvania Press, 1963), 355–72.
5. Richard T. Ely.
6. The identity of "Aldrich" is unknown.
7. The *Tribune* published an editorial sharply critical of a speech that Darrow gave at the Review Club in Chicago, saying that he expressed "an opinion which outrages every instinct of manhood": "For Mr. Darrow was not content with denouncing the Monroe doctrine, nor with attacking President Cleveland, nor with asserting that if England should acquire the whole of South America it would make no difference to the United States. He went very much further than this, though this was far, and vehemently and with every manifestation of emotion said: 'Patriotism? A blind inhuman cry for blood—that is patriotism.' . . . Let Mr. Darrow think again. If he have in his veins a drop of red blood he will make haste to offer apology for the insult he has put upon his own forefathers who 'cried for blood' that he today might enjoy life, liberty, and a right to the pursuit of happiness—including the happiness of sneering and playing cynic in public places." "Patriotism Defined Anew," *Chicago Tribune*, 6 January 1896.

inhuman cry for blood.' If the human race should live long enough it will learn that those who are the truest patriots and best citizens are the ones who advocate peace instead of war." Very truly,

CLARENCE S. DARROW.

MS: "A Distinction without a Difference," *Chicago Tribune*, 7 January 1896.

TO JESSIE DARROW • CHICAGO • WEDNESDAY 8 JANUARY 1896

Dear Jessie

I do not know why I told Paul what I did. I should not have done it and am very sorry that I did—I do not know what to say to your letter. Of course we have not been happy and I suppose neither of us are to blame for this.[8] I know you have done all you could and have always been good & kind to me. I know that I have never made you happy and have always felt that you would have been very much happier if you had never married me. I presume that we never in any way were fitted for each other. Of course we were too young to know it then, and it is always terribly hard to correct such mistakes—I think you know me well enough to know that I could never take Paul away no matter what might be thought best for us to do. He is yours more than mine & he loves you more than he does me; he is young & will be happy in any way: He will soon go away to school and naturally could not be long with me unless he came into my office which of course could not interfere with you. Whatever it would mean to me or him, I would rather die than let you part from him. You also know that I could never be happy unless you were well provided for. I have enough, or will within a year, for both and if we did not I could not take it & could not have a moment's peace or comfort unless you had enough. The house you know is yours. Two lots are also yours. You have done as much to get and save what we have as I. It is yours as much as mine and nothing in the world could make me take it from you—I would give any thing to see you again as happy as you used to be. I know that you would have been if you had not married me and yet I do not know how I could have done differently from what I have. Of course Paul has been compensation for every thing else, and we will always have him in common, so long as we all live. I do not know what is best to do. I think we should stay as we are until you & Paul go to Europe. Then after you have been away six months or a year we can tell better how we feel and what we think is best. I believe that you will be happier & that it will be best to go to Europe for the year and then see how we feel and what is best. I do not want you or Paul to long be far away

8. What Darrow said to Paul is not known. It might have been something about Darrow's relationship with Jessie. In June 1896, Jessie and Paul would travel to Europe and stay there until the fall of that year. When they returned to the United States, they lived in Sharon, Pennsylvania, where Jessie had relatives. In March 1897, Jessie and Paul moved back to Chicago, and Darrow and Jessie were divorced that same month. See Paul Darrow to Irving Stone, 22 February 1940, TLc, MnU-L, Darrow Papers.

from me—for I am sure that whatever we think best to do we will not forget the past or ever have any but the kindest feeling toward each other. Whatever I may do in the future I will never feel that my life is a success unless you and Paul are happy and if there should ever be any bitterness between any of us, I believe you will be happy again, that you can do many things to enjoy life, that Paul will always help make you happy and that you will find a great deal in life. I shall always feel toward you differently than to any one else & shall always do every thing I can for your happiness. I think we should stay as we are until you go abroad. After that we can see how both of us feel. This letter seems cold but I do not intend it to be so & hope it will be no harder for you to read than for me to write. If I had the time to think I might make it clearer & kinder but have written it immediately after getting yours. Always my first wish shall be for your happiness and Paul's.

MS: ALS, MnU-L, Darrow Collection. PLACE: no reason to doubt Chicago. DATE: "Wednesday Jan. 8th 1896" appended in Jessie's hand at the end of the letter.

TO HENRY DEMAREST LLOYD • CHICAGO • THURSDAY 23 APRIL 1896

DARROW, THOMAS & THOMPSON April 23rd

My Dear Lloyd,

I am not like Howells. I can appreciate a joke when it is at my expense—although I enjoy them better when they are on some one else—I never thought that you sent me any thing that you would "want back." The only thing I desired to keep I reluctantly return with this & Mr. Bellamy's letter.[9]

I suppose Mr. Bellamy is not up to us on all lines—of course we must admit that he is good as far as he goes. Still I like Tolstoi's patriotism better than Bellamy's—I feel that Patriotism is one of the fundamental crimes. However I grow more & more willing to work with all kinds of people—who will have me—and more & more am agnostic as to the best way—this without doubting much as to the fact that almost all that is is bad and that the ultimate is about as Wm Morris puts it in News from Nowhere—how to go from here to there—from Hell to Heaven is the problem.[10] I am glad that you are to have a cheap edition of your book.[11] I trust it will still be a "bound" book. I think it will do much more good than ever before. It has been out of the reach of all but parasitical socialists like you & me. I will think of a list of names & send to you. I am sorry to learn that Abbott[12] was the attraction at our Friday luncheons. With the usual vanity of man I had of course assumed that it was I.

9. Edward Bellamy (1850–98), social reformer and author of the popular utopian novel *Looking Backward: 2000–1887* (1888).
10. William Morris (1834–96), English designer, poet, and socialist. Morris's popular novel *News from Nowhere* (1890) described a rural socialist utopia.
11. Darrow is probably referring to Lloyd's *Wealth against Commonwealth* (New York: Harper & Bros., 1894), which criticized the monopolistic practices of the Standard Oil Company and remains the book for which Lloyd is usually remembered today.
12. The identity of "Abbott" is unknown.

Do you suppose you could induce Howells to go to Mrs. Lloyd's summer boarding house for a week or two—I think I shall go if I can get an invitation.

As Ever Your friend | C. S. Darrow.

MS: ALS, WHi, Lloyd Papers. DATE: "[1896?]" appended and 1896 is supported by letterhead.

TO PAUL DARROW • MOUNT MANSFIELD, VERMONT • MONDAY 17 AUGUST 1896

Mount Mansfield Vt | Aug. 17th 96

Dear Paul,

To day I received your letter from Geneva and was very glad to hear from you as I always am. I like to have you tell me all about the places you see and what you learn and whether you are enjoying the trip. How do you get along in traveling with only the English language? and are you learning any thing else. I meant to tell you before you left that "toilet room" in French is "cabinet" I hope it will do you some good to know. I hope you get all my letters. I have sent your mother's letters addressed to you, not knowing whether she would be along. When you get to Paris & London you can get Chicago papers at Thos. Cook & Sons, if you wish.

I have been away from Chicago all this month and shall not return until the first of Sept. Am resting all I can, and trying to get real well. I have made one political speech here, and they want me to make an other but I shall not as I will leave in a few days and go to the Adirondacks. I will not see such high mountains as you have seen in Switzerland. Which mountain did you like the best? What did you think of your trip around the Grand Canall? Do they give you good hotels wherever you go? I have not heard from Uncle Dick[13] since I left two weeks ago but I send them your letters. I presume the billiard table is not very busy. Probably you will be in Paris long before you get this. You must go to Barbazon & Fountainbleau. You can do them both in one day. You take the train to a station about four miles from Barbazon (something like Minn) and then drive through Barbazon (getting dinner there) through to the forest of Fountainbleau to the castle & then you can take the train back from Fontainbleau. You will find carriages at the station and Bedecker's Paris will tell all about it. When you go to London you must see the wax works. I think you can find out about them in Badecker. I want you to see every thing worth looking at and write me all about it. Give my regards to Napoleon Bonaparte when you call on him—I presume he is still there. I sent your mother $100 a few days ago. I hope she got it all right. I can not tell you much news for I have been so long away but will when I get back. Did you write to Frank Brown?[14] He wants you to and will answer your letters.

I presume you are always very kind to mama. I hope so. I want you to be a good boy always as I think you will. I am very glad your mother has been able to go all the way with

13. Richard Fisher.
14. The identity of "Frank Brown" is unknown.

you. I think you will see some things in the British Museum you will like. There are people there who are awful dead. If you stop with Mrs. Young in London it is right near the British Museum.[15] Can you speak French like a Dutchman yet? Write as often as you can and tell me all you see.

Love to mama & all.

Your father, | C. S. Darrow.

MS: ALS, MnU-L, Darrow Collection.

TO THE *CHICAGO TRIBUNE* • CHICAGO • MONDAY 21 SEPTEMBER 1896

That America enjoys greater political freedom than England is one of the chief popular misconceptions of the citizens of this country as well as the rest of the world. For several centuries the rights of the individual have been on a much higher plane in England than in this country. This is not due alone to the law, but to the spirit of independence and personal dignity that is stronger in Englishmen than in Americans.

It would be difficult to name any political right enjoyed by Americans which is not equally enjoyed by the citizens of Great Britain. The fact is, nearly all of our laws and institutions have come directly from England and all that we have in this respect is English. The difference between liberty in England and liberty in the United States is in favor of England, for the reason that guarantees of all kinds are more strictly enforced and defined in that country than in this.

No such injunctions as have been commonly issued by courts in this country in the last year would have been dreamed of in England. The respect for personal liberty and its constitutional guarantees, such as trial by jury, is too great to have even permitted the thought of such aggressions. England has the greatest possible liberty of thought and speech. One may visit Hyde Park a Sunday afternoon, or any of the great busy thoroughfares of London, where the poor people live and congregate, and he will find innumerable meetings of all kinds, in which speakers discuss every conceivable view in the broadest way, without molestation from any official. No such thing as the breaking up of meetings in Chicago a few years ago would have been tolerated for a moment in any English city.

Drunkenness and disorder are probably more prevalent in America than in England, and certainly more so than in continental Europe. This not due to any difference in the law, but to the enforcement of existing legislation. In England, as well as in continental Europe, laws are much more strictly enforced than in the United States. This applies not only to the laws which govern the so-called criminal classes and the poor, but laws which affect the rich as well.

15. "Mrs. Young" might be reference to a boarding house in London.

In this country such as thing as a prosecution or conviction of men in high position, men of wealth, is practically impossible and unknown, although the violations of law by this class is constant; indictments are frequently had of men in these positions, but prosecutions almost never. This and other exhibitions of the laxity of enforcement of law is due to the place that money fills in the United States. Everything else has been subverted to it, much more so than in any of the older countries of the world.

It is not a question of patriotism. There is no term less understood and no word which is so often used as a mask to cover up iniquity as patriotism. Patriotism in the United States has often been used to mean the enforcement of such laws as the privileged classes see fit to use and the arbitrary exhibition of power without law wherever they deem that this is necessary.

An example of sham patriotism may be seen in the idiotic, extravagant, demagogical law passed by the Legislature of Illinois providing for placing an American flag on schoolhouses.[16] This same patriotic Legislature that passed this senseless law is under investigation for bribery. They were not bribed by the dangerous classes who are to be compelled by statute to see the American flag. The only way to make the people love the country is to have the country worth loving. No other manner is possible with intelligent men, and no other ought to be possible.

If England were a republic instead of a monarchy, no one could possibly see the difference so far as political freedom is concerned. If America were a monarchy instead of a republic, it would be equally impossible, so far as the common people are concerned, to notice any difference in the political rights enjoyed. In the Government of France the people have found absolutely no difference between their political rights and privileges and their relations to the State under a monarchy and a republic. The fact is that political governments are not a serious burden upon individual liberty in any of the more enlightened nations of the world. It is very seldom that people have occasion to conflict with any penal law of any country. The lack of freedom all over the world comes not from political institutions but from economic institutions. It comes from those systems of industry and property rights which have grown up through a long series of years, and which have gradually transferred all the opportunities of the world into a very small number of hands, leaving the great mass of the people dependent upon the will of a very few.

It is towards the change of economic institutions, not political ones, that the attention of the world should be directed, and it is only through these that greater freedom can come and better order be preserved. In this connection it might be added that order and peace are not the result of police legislation or restrictive laws, but of liberty and opportunity.

Clarence S. Darrow.

MS: "Clarence S. Darrow," *Chicago Tribune*, 22 September 1896. PLACE: no reason to doubt Chicago. DATE: publication date.

16. In 1895, Illinois was one of six states that passed laws requiring school authorities to display the national flag. The law in Illinois required private schools to comply as well. See Albert Gray, "Notes on the State Legislation of America in 1895," *Journal of the Society of Comparative Legislation* 1 (1896–97): 232–38.

TO RICHARD T. ELY • CHICAGO • THURSDAY 4 MARCH 1897

DARROW, THOMAS & THOMPSON March 4, 1897.

My Dear Mr. Ely:—

It has occurred to me of late that the most important work necessary at this time is some careful compilation showing the rates of wages in the various lines of industry covering a period of perhaps the last 25 years. Also the same sort of compilation as to rents and other costs of living. Together with this, statistics ought to be gathered in relation to the inmates of almshouses, jails and other state institutions.

I am thoroughly convinced that any honest statistics covering these various matters will show that wages absolutely and relatively have constantly declined in the last 25 years, and that they were never as low as at present. It is persistently asserted that wages have increased. This is generally shown by comparisons with periods very remote and regardless of the cost of living. But whatever such facts would show, it is very important to have them carefully gathered and arranged. I think the money could be obtained for paying a good man for the time spent in this work. It ought to be one who approaches it from the right standpoint, and still a person who would state the truth only. Do you know of any such man, and could you make any suggestions as to the amount of time it would probably take and where any money could be had for the work. It might be that such an investigation could be made through some university, which would of course add to its authority; or possibly through some state government, although Michigan is the only one I know of that would probably favor it. If a university would undertake it, I think an amount of money could be raised for the purpose sufficient to defray the expenses. But the most important thing is first to find the right man to gather the statistics.

With kind regards, I am,

Very truly yours, | C. S. Darrow.

MS: TLS, WHi, Ely Papers. INSIDE ADDRESS: Prof. Richard T. Ely, | Madison, Wis.

TO HENRY DEMAREST LLOYD • CHICAGO • TUESDAY 8 MARCH 1898

DARROW, THOMAS & THOMPSON March 8, 1898.

My Dear Mr. Lloyd:—

I have finally determined to go into the trial of the case of the Kingdom Publishing Company.[17] I will not be able to do complete justice to it on account of having practically had no time to prepare it, but am satisfied that we can win the case. From a letter received this

17. In 1897, the Kingdom Publishing Company in Minneapolis, Minnesota, published a pamphlet titled *A Foe to American Schools,* written by George Gates (1851–1912), president of Iowa (now Grinnell) College, 1887–1900. The pamphlet charged that the American Book Company (ABC), a publisher of school and college textbooks out of New York, used bribery and other corrupt and monopolistic business practices to sell

morning from Mr. Gleason,[18] I see his Minneapolis lawyers advise him that it is doubtful whether the plaintiffs can make a legal case, and that he thinks the court will take it from the jury without proof on our side. I am inclined to think his lawyers are right, but at the same time we should not ask for this, but should go ahead with our case. I am satisfied that the evidence we have will be such as to cause a sensation in reference to the sort of work that this company, as well as others of its kind, is constantly doing, and that it will be the means of destroying the combination. I have personally seen several witnesses whose testimony will create a sensation and expose their dealings, and I am very anxious that the case shall be tried and not won on a technicality. I have had a conversation with Mr. Gilson[19] and asked him to write you a letter addressed to Mr. Gleason, promising to stand back of any judgment that may be recovered against them. Of course I cannot otherwise advise the Kingdom to take this stand because it might possibly involve them in the loss of some money which they otherwise would save, but this letter I shall expect you to keep and not even tell Mr. Gleason that you have it, but instead of that, to write him urging him to have the case tried, and telling him that you are confident that if they are beaten that the judgment will be taken care of. I want him to be in a position to say, and say truthfully, that no book company has promised him any remuneration in this matter. As soon as you get the letter from Mr. Gilson, which will be tomorrow, will you please write Gleason immediately?

I wish you could go up to Minneapolis and see the case tried. I am sure it would give you some additional data.[20]

Very truly yours, | C. S. Darrow.

MS: TLS, WHi, Lloyd Papers. INSIDE ADDRESS: Henry D. Lloyd, Esq., | Winnetka, Ill.

---

textbooks to school officials. In May 1897, ABC filed two lawsuits against Kingdom Publishing in state court in Minnesota seeking damages and an injunction prohibiting further publication of the pamphlet. See *American Book Co. v. Kingdom Pub. Co.*, 73 N.W. 1089 (1898). In June 1897, ABC sued Gates for libel in federal court in Iowa. See *American Book Co. v. Gates*, 85 F. 729 (1898). Also in June 1897, ABC sued Kingdom Publishing for libel in federal court in Minnesota. On the eve of trial in federal court in Minnesota, which started on 9 March 1897, Kingdom Publishing's lead attorney became sick and Darrow agreed to serve as its counsel.

18. Herbert Gleason (1855–1937), Congregationalist minister, editor, publisher, and photographer. Gleason was born and raised in Massachusetts. He moved to Minnesota in 1883, serving as pastor of a rural church, 1883–85, and then a church in Minneapolis, 1885–88. Later, he became managing editor of *The Northwestern Congregationalist*, 1888–94, and then its successor, *The Kingdom*, 1894–99 (the associate editors for which included George Gates and Benjamin Fay Mills). After *The Kingdom* stopped publication, Gleason returned to Massachusetts and worked the rest of his life as a nature photographer. See Dale R. Schwie, "Herbert W. Gleason: A Photographer's Journey to Thoreau's World," *The Concord Saunterer* 7 (1999): 150–65. Darrow mentions a letter from Gleason but no letter was found.

19. Tillotson W. Gilson (1849–1914), a partner in Ginn & Company, publisher of school and college textbooks and competitor of the American Book Company. During trial, ABC asserted that Gates's pamphlet had been written with the support of Ginn & Company.

20. At the end of the trial in federal court in Minnesota, the judge instructed the jury to find the Kingdom Publishing Company liable because the company had introduced no evidence to support one of the bribery charges made against ABC in Gates's pamphlet, although evidence was introduced to support other similar charges. The jury awarded ABC $7,500. The following year, *The Kingdom* ceased publication primarily because of the judgment entered against the publishing company. See "Publisher's Announcement," *The Kingdom* 11 (13 April 1899): 1. So Darrow's plan to have any judgment paid by Gilson, as described in Darrow's letter to Lloyd, apparently did not succeed.

TO RICHARD T. ELY • CHICAGO • TUESDAY 27 DECEMBER 1898

DARROW, THOMAS & THOMPSON December 27, 1898.

My Dear Mr. Ely:—

The address I made on the judiciary a few days since will be published in pamphlet form inside the next two or three weeks, and I will surely send you a copy. It was made before the National Trade & Labor Assembly at Kansas City and ordered printed by them.[21]

I send you today a copy of my argument in the Woodworkers strike at Oshkosh, which I think may be of some interest to you.[22] I believe you have my brief in the Debs case.[23] If not, and you care for it, I will send you a copy.

With kind regards, I am,

Very truly yours, | C. S. Darrow.[24]

MS: TLS, WHi, Ely Papers. INSIDE ADDRESS: Prof. Richard T. Ely, | Madison, Wis.

TO RALPH M. EASLEY • CHICAGO • WEDNESDAY 8 FEBRUARY 1899

Chicago, Feb. 8

My Dear Mr. Easley:

The newspapers last night announced that I had been appointed as one of a committee by the federation to recommend various people to the Judges to be appointed to the

21. On 17 December 1898, Darrow delivered an address entitled "Workingmen and the Courts" at the annual convention of the American Federation of Labor. The speech was highly critical of the administration of justice in the courts. A motion was passed at the convention to publish the address as a pamphlet, but Darrow asked to revise it before publication because he had "made it without preparation." AFL, *Report of Proceedings of the Eighteenth Annual Convention of the American Federation of Labor, Held at Kansas City, Missouri, December 12th to 20th Inclusive* (1898?), 113. The pamphlet was apparently never published. The Library of Congress has a typewritten version of the address, partially edited in Darrow's hand. See DLC-MSS, Darrow Papers. Ely probably asked Darrow for a copy of the speech (and for other materials) as part of his research on a history of the labor movement. Ely to Henry Demarest Lloyd, 23 March 1898, TLS, WHi, Lloyd Papers (noting that he would like to have Darrow's legal briefs).
22. In May 1898, woodworkers in Oshkosh, Wisconsin, began a fourteen-week strike for an increase of wages and recognition of their labor organization, among other demands. During the strike, Thomas I. Kidd (1860–1941), general secretary of the Amalgamated Wood-Workers' International Union of America, and two members of local unions were charged in state court with conspiracy to injure the business of the Paine Lumber Company, the largest manufacturer involved in the strike. The case was defended by Darrow and two other attorneys. The defendants were acquitted in November 1898, after a three-week trial. A stenographic report of Darrow's final argument to the jury was published in pamphlet form: *Argument of Clarence S. Darrow in the Wood-Workers Conspiracy Case* (Chicago: Campbell Printers, 1899).
23. Brief and Argument for Petitioners (Clarence Darrow, Counsel for Petitioners), *In re Debs,* 158 U.S. 564 (1895). Darrow's brief and the briefs of his co-counsel and the government are reprinted in Philip B. Kurland and Gerhard Casper, eds. *Landmark Briefs and Arguments of the Supreme Court of the United States: Constitutional Law* (Arlington, VA: University Publications of America, 1975), 11:267–598.
24. Ely replied to this letter a few days later, asking for another copy of Darrow's pamphlet in the woodworkers' case and a copy of Darrow's brief in the case involving the American Book Company against the Kingdom Publishing Company. Ely to Darrow, 4 January 1899, TLc, WHi, Ely Papers.

position of justices of the peace.[25] Since this announcement I have been kept quite busy with callers who would like these positions. I must beg to decline this appointment for the following reasons, amongst others:

In the first place, the Judges have never asked the Civic federation nor me to tell them whom to appoint to these positions, and therefore our advice might be impertinent. If we should give it they probably would not follow it, but would continue appointing men with the strongest political pull, as they have done in the past.

In the next place, I share the general feeling of distrust of your organization. I have observed its various "activities," if that is the proper word, and I cannot recall where it ever undertook to interfere with an individual scheme or project that had either friends or money to sustain it. As far as I can see, it has taken some inconsequential matter, like the appointment of a justice of the peace or the insignificant business of a bucket shop, and busied itself about these affairs as an excuse for living and a reason for officers to draw salaries.

The Civic federation does not seem to be aware that we are forming a new trust every hour of the day and that the rights of the people are more in danger from Judges occupying high positions, who sustain these iniquitous and illegal combinations, than from inferior justices of the peace, who, on the whole, do well. It does not seem to understand that the shyster lawyer who operates around justice courts is comparatively harmless beside the corporation lawyer and the promoter of trust organizations, and that the bucket shop dealer is a person of no consequence compared with the operator on the Board of Trade. On the whole, your body reminds me of a man who would take a great deal of pains to save an old chair when his whole house is in flames.

Truly yours,

C. S. DARROW.

MS: "Raps the Civic Federation," *Chicago Tribune*, 9 February 1899. INSIDE ADDRESS: Ralph M. Easley, Secretary Civic Federation.

TO BRAND WHITLOCK • CHICAGO • THURSDAY 26 OCTOBER 1899

DARROW, THOMAS & THOMPSON Oct. 26th

Dear Whitlock

Your letter & magazine came to hand yesterday.[26] I at once closed my door and read your story. In the evening I took it out where I had a little meeting of friends and read it aloud.

25. The "federation" that appointed Darrow was the Civic Federation of Chicago, of which Easley was the founder and secretary.
26. Darrow might be referring to a recent short story of Whitlock's about a state attorney general caught by the governor borrowing money from the state treasury. Brand Whitlock, "A Secret of State," *Ainslee's Magazine*, November 1899, 447–57.

We all agreed that it was very clever and were glad & proud that you had done it. I really liked it exceedingly well. I feel that ten or fifteen years from now you will be one of our well known men—I feel very confident of this. And I hope you will do as much writing and as little law as you can—the latter will doubtless care for its self. Of course you can improve on your work. Its finish may be made more perfect & it strikes me that you give a little too much detail—still I know this is best and that it will be much easier to cut it down than for one who can [. . . .][27]

MS: ALS, CtW. DATE: letterhead and reference to story.

27. The first page of the letter ends here; what followed is missing.

• 1900–1904

TO DENSLOW LEWIS • CHICAGO • EARLY 1900

My dear Mr. Lewis:

I have read your paper delivered before the American Medical Association and have considered the question whether the publishers of a medical periodical could be convicted of circulating obscene literature in case they published this paper.[1] The United States statutes govern the circulation of obscene literature and are meant to provide for cases where publishers, or purviewors, publish and sell literature which is supposed to appeal

1. In June 1899, Denslow delivered an address titled "The Gynecologic Consideration of the Sexual Act" at the fiftieth annual meeting of the American Medical Association in Columbus, Ohio. In this address, Denslow urged, among other things, that young people receive some education about sex; that the wife, in particular, "should be told that it is right and proper for her to experience pleasure in its performance"; and that the young husband should be made to understand that "he is not the master but the companion of his wife." Denslow also described sexual acts in detail and described his treatment (including clitoral circumcision) of various sexual maladies. See Denslow Lewis, *The Gynecologic Consideration of the Sexual Act* (Chicago: Henry O. Shepard, 1900; Weston, MA: M&S Press, 1970) (the M&S Press edition includes an essay on Lewis by Marc H. Hollender). Lewis was criticized after his address by physicians in the audience. Later, the editor of the *Journal of the American Medical Association* refused to publish Lewis's address (which would have been customary) on the ground that the *Journal* did not publish that "class" of literature. Lewis appealed the editor's decision to the publication committee of the AMA's board of trustees, which refused (by a divided vote) to overrule the editor, with one member suggesting that if they did agree to publish it, the trustees might be convicted of distributing obscene material through the mail. This suggestion prompted Lewis to obtain this legal opinion from Darrow as well as opinions from several other prominent lawyers in Illinois, all of whom agreed that no prosecution was likely. Ibid., 19–40 (citation is to the original Shepard edition).

directly to the passions of the reader for the purpose of making money out of these feelings. Of course, the statute is broad and must be construed with reference to a particular case.[2] There is probably not a medical work of consequence and certainly no piece of literature worth reading, but what verbatim extracts could be made, published and sold in such a way as to meet the condemnation of the jury and the court under our statutes governing obscene literature. On the other hand, it must not be thought that the statutes are meant to provide that any literature relative to the sexual organs, or to what is popularly known as the baser passions, is obscene literature. If so, of course, it would be no longer possible to give medical students and others the specific treatment for venereal diseases and such instructions as have generally been considered necessary regarding the creation of children, their birth and the ordinary relations that tend to the preservation of the species. In short, there is but one test, and that is the obvious intent with which such literature is published and circulated. A paper which is written in good faith to be read before a body of physicians for the purpose of presenting views, which the author sincerely believes are for the best interests of the health, life and morals of the community, is not a paper upon which such author can be convicted for the circulation of obscene literature; and if such paper is published in good faith by a medical journal, and circulated amongst physicians and surgeons as a paper from a man of standing in his profession, given for the obvious purpose of teaching important and necessary truths, whether the statements may be true or false, scientific or unscientific, then no publisher can be convicted for circulating such magazine or article.

I would desire further to add that any physician who did not have the courage to deliver such a paper before an association of scientific men, when he believed it was for the purpose of making people better and happier, and who hesitated for fear that some law might be construed to send him to jail, would not be worthy of the profession to which he belongs. And any publisher who pretends to circulate literature designed to benefit and instruct physicians, who would fear to give out a paper written in good faith, for a good purpose, by a man of standing and ability because of some criminal statute, is not fit to publish a scientific journal.

If the law of the United States will send a doctor to jail for teaching in good faith to the profession what he believes to be the truth, or punish the publisher of a medical journal for circulating literature which comes from a reputable and learned man upon a vital question, and written in the attitude of a teacher, whether such teaching is true or not, then the best work the doctor can do, or that the publisher can do for his profession, or for mankind, is to go to jail in obedience to the law.

2. Darrow is likely referring to United States Revised Statutes, Section 3893, which provided that "[e]very obscene, lewd, or lascivious book, pamphlet, picture, paper, letter, writing, print or other publication of an indecent character, . . . and every article or thing intended or adapted for any indecent or immoral use, . . . are hereby declared to be nonmailable matter." Violation of the statute could result, "for each and every offence," in a fine of not more than five thousand dollars or imprisonment "at hard labor not more than five years, or both."

I believe there is no danger in any civilized or semi-civilized community that could possibly come to any doctor or publisher who in good faith writes and circulates such literature.[3]

Very truly yours, | C. S. DARROW.

MS: Denslow Lewis, *The Gynecologic Consideration of the Sexual Act* (Chicago: Henry O. Shepard Co., 1900), 40–42. PLACE: no reason to doubt Chicago. DATE: other correspondence published in the same book.

TO THE *CHICAGO DAILY NEWS* • CHICAGO • MONDAY 26 FEBRUARY 1900

Chicago, Feb. 26, 1900 .—To the Editor of The Daily News: One of the morning newspapers quotes me as saying at a meeting that "judges are out for what they can get." "They do things that would send the ordinary man to the penitentiary." "Senatorial courtesy protects them."[4] I said nothing of this sort and nothing that could bear any such interpretation. I distinctly said that in almost every instance judges were honest, but that they were chosen from the class whose views were hostile to the interests of the working classes. I did say that lawyers were ready to take any side of any case—it was only a question of what there was in it. While I believe that the tendency of judges to issue injunctions against working men is subversive of liberty and constitutional rights, I do not believe and have never intimated, either publicly or privately, that judges were influenced by any corrupt consideration—it is simply a result of the environment from which they are chosen, and the tendency to tyranny that goes with arbitrary power.

CLARENCE S. DARROW.

MS: "Mr. Darrow Says 'Not Guilty,'" *(Chicago) Daily News*, 26 February 1900.

TO SAMUEL M. JONES • CHICAGO • SATURDAY 14 APRIL 1900

DARROW, THOMAS & THOMPSON April 14th, 1900.

My dear Mr. Jones:—

Thank you very much for the papers and the letter. I was sorry to see that the Council did not stand by you; still I presume it is all right. If I were in your place I should undoubtedly be deluded into making the fight with all the means I had in my power; and still I cannot help

3. Lewis's efforts to appeal to the board of trustees failed, despite the legal opinions he had obtained, so Lewis tried to convince the AMA's membership, in general session at the annual meeting in June 1900, to vote on the matter. At the annual meeting, the president of the AMA referred Lewis's proposal to the general executive committee, which declined to put the matter to a vote in the general meeting. Lewis, *Gynecologic Consideration*, 12–14 (citation is to the M&S Press edition). In 1983, the *Journal* finally published Lewis's address: Denslow Lewis, "The Gynecologic Consideration of the Sexual Act," *JAMA* 250 (8 July 1983): 222–27.
4. The day before this letter, Darrow gave a speech at a meeting of the Chicago Single Tax Club entitled "Government by Injunction," in which he was critical of judges. "Darrow Attacks Judges," *(Chicago) Inter-Ocean*, 26 February 1900. What morning newspaper quoted him is unknown.

but think that you were right and that your whole course has been one that is the best whatever the result may be. If these people want to do what they have started out to accomplish, it had better be done. Meeting force with force is certainly bad, and although it seems the only thing to do I am quite confident that no true success can come in that way; and equally, that no ultimate failure will come the other way. At any rate, and however you choose, I am,

Always faithfully yours, | C. S. Darrow.

MS: TLS, OT, Jones Papers. INSIDE ADDRESS: Samuel M. Jones, Esq., | Toledo, Ohio.

TO SAMUEL M. JONES • CHICAGO • THURSDAY 7 JUNE 1900

DARROW & THOMPSON June 7th, 1900.

My Dear Jones:—

I have been very much interested in your open letters addressed to workingmen.[5] I think it is an excellent plan and that you are doing a great deal of good. I envy you the amount of energy and force and intelligence that you put into this movement. I only wish that I could do more myself along the same line. Since I saw you in Toledo I have made several addresses upon the courts and the poor, similar to the one I made in Toledo. It generally stirs up all the lawyers and judges whereever I go, so in the end I suppose I will be out of a job,—that is my graft will be gone, and I will probably have to come down and go to work in your factory.

I was interested in learning of your trip through the east.[6] I have no doubt that the people in general are ready to listen to intelligent discussion of these important questions, but still the ignorance is very dense and we have a great deal to contend with.

I see by an announcement that you are to speak here in the near future. I want you to make my office your headquarters, and hope to put in as much time as possible with you. I wish we might get Nelson[7] up at the time you come and have a sort of reunion.

Ever with kind regards and best wishes, I am,

Your Friend, | C. S. Darrow.

MS: TLS, OT, Jones Papers. INSIDE ADDRESS: Hon. S. M. Jones, | Toledo, Ohio.

5. In May 1900, Jones began writing a series of open, didactic letters to the men who worked in his machine shops. The letters were delivered to the employees with their wages and carried such titles as "Equality," "Service Brings Its Own Reward," "A Word on Vacations," and "Harmony, the Lesson of Life." Jones continued to write the letters through December 1901. At the end of each year, he collected the letters written that year and had them privately printed. Samuel M. Jones, *Letters of Love and Labor,* 2 vols. (Toledo: Franklin Printing & Engraving, 1900–1901). After Jones's death, these two volumes were published as a single volume with an introduction by Brand Whitlock. Samuel M. Jones, *Letters of Labor and Love* (Indianapolis: Bobbs-Merrill, 1905).
6. Jones had described a lecture trip in a recent letter to Darrow. Jones to Darrow, 28 April 1900, TLc, OT, Jones Papers.
7. Nelson Olsen Nelson.

TO WILLIAM DEAN HOWELLS • CHICAGO • FRIDAY 16 NOVEMBER 1900

DARROW & THOMPSON Nov 16th

Dear Mr. Howells—

Herewith I send you a story of Mr. Whitlock's, which is not what you want but which I think very true to life and exceedingly well done.[8]

He is writing an other story which is more the character of what you want. That will be ready in three or four weeks. I can not tell you how glad I am that you remembered him and his work. Mr. Whitlock is one of the truest young men I ever met and his whole aim is to do some good. I feel that he is sure to succeed as an author. His aims are high & true and his work is constantly improving. It seems to me that no one can write political stories as well.

I have intended writing you long ago and thanking you for your kind letter about my essays. This did me more good than any thing else in connection with them. I would not have ventured to send you the book, as you could not have told me it was bad—and would not have wished to tell me it was good if you did not think so.

Your kind letter encourages me to try to give more time to such work. I can not refrain from sending you a private letter from Mr. Whitlock which he wrote on receipt of yours. It is long & perhaps may not be as interesting to you as to me but it shows the honest feelings of a young man—and also what he thinks of you—[9] Men do not often tell each other what they think as you remark in your sketch of dear Ralph Koeler.[10] But still I think they ought. If you could see me and one or two friends devour your stuff—all of it—if you could see us cry at the almost unconscious pathos—and how, whatever our

8. Howells had written to Darrow after Darrow sent him one of Whitlock's short stories asking if "that Toledo friend of yours . . . has a novel of actual American life in MS" that *Harper's* might consider publishing. Howells to Darrow, 4 November 1900, in *The Letters of Brand Whitlock,* ed. Allan Nevins (New York: D. Appleton-Century, 1936), 31. Whitlock was at work on a political novel that became *The Thirteenth District* (Indianapolis: Bowen-Merrill Co., 1902), but the manuscript was not ready yet. As a substitute for a novel, Darrow likely sent Howells a copy of Whitlock's short story titled "Malachi Nolan," which was going to be published in *Ainslee's Magazine.* See *Letters of Brand Whitlock,* 32–33 (Whitlock to Darrow, 7 November 1900). Howells also wrote to Darrow praising his book of essays, *A Persian Pearl.* Howells to Darrow, 3 June 1900, ALS, MnU-L, Darrow Collection.

9. Darrow probably sent Howells a letter from Whitlock to Darrow in which Whitlock described Howells as his "literary divinity": "For years and years, as you are aware, Mr. Howells has been my literary divinity. I have followed him timorously from afar, I have shivered in the realization that much of my stuff has been a weak imitation of his work, and I have despaired of ever doing anything original. And now I catch my breath to think that I am actually near to attracting his attention, and am fearful that I fail to reward his generous interest by proving worthy." *Letters of Brand Whitlock,* 32 (Whitlock to Darrow, 7 November 1900). On receipt of Whitlock's story and letter, Howells—who later developed a close acquaintance with Whitlock—wrote to Whitlock saying that his letter was "better than the story, . . . though the story is good, too." George Arms, "'Ever Devotedly Yours': The Whitlock-Howells Correspondence," *Journal of the Rutgers University Library* 10 (December 1946): 3.

10. Ralph Keeler (1840–73), journalist and friend of Howells. Keeler died (he might have been murdered) on a steamer en route to Havana, Cuba, where he had been working as a correspondent for the *New York Tribune.* Darrow is referring here to a recent article by Howells in which Howells said of Keeler: "I now realize that I loved him, though I did as little to show it as men commonly do." Howells, "Some Literary Memories of Cambridge," *Harper's Monthly Magazine,* November 1890, 834.

disagreements before, we come together in you and feel with you—you would know how a few people at least love and appreciate you—and how much you are in their lives—

Give my best wishes to Mrs. Howells[11] & Miss Howells[12] and ever with kindest remembrance to you

I am your friend | C. S. Darrow.

MS: ALS, MH-H, Howells Collection. DATE: letterhead and letter from Whitlock to Darrow.

TO SAMUEL M. JONES • CHICAGO • FRIDAY 28 DECEMBER 1900

DARROW & THOMPSON Chicago, Ill., December 28, 1900.

My dear friend Jones:—

Your Christmas present was received for which I am very much obliged to you. I think I read every one of these letters as they came out and fine letters they are too.[13] I am very glad that you have put them in this shape and am sure they will do much good besides the satisfaction it gives to you and your friends to see them.

It is a great pleasure to me to know that you always remember me in this way, and I assure you that I often think of you and value your friendship and esteem very highly.

I was very much pleased with your son who has the management of the Indiana business.[14] He seems to be developing the right way and seems to handle himself well. I was glad also that you succeeded in settling up the difficulty without litigation, for while in justice I have no idea you should have paid anything, still I know you do not like litigation and I feel sure you are right in preferring to suffer some injustice rather than to resort to the courts.[15]

It seems as if you have been a long time away from Chicago. I hope you may be able to come soon. If you think best for me to come to Toledo sometime this winter and speak on Tolstoy's "Resurrection," or something of that sort, I would be glad to come. It will give me an excuse for seeing you.

Ever with best wishes, I am

Your friend | C. S. Darrow.

MS: TLS, OT, Jones Papers. INSIDE ADDRESS: Hon. Samuel M. Jones, | Toledo, Ohio.

11. Elinor Mead Howells (1837–1910), artist and wife of William Dean Howells.
12. Mildred Howells (1872–1966), daughter of Elinor Mead Howells and William Dean Howells.
13. Jones probably sent Darrow the first volume of his *Letters of Love and Labor*. See Darrow to Jones, 7 June 1900, n.5.
14. Darrow is probably referring to Percy Jones (1878–1941).
15. Jones and his son, Percy, apparently had some problem with a contract involving a farm and they considered filing a lawsuit in the matter. Jones to Darrow, TLc, 5 December 1900, OT, Jones Papers.

TO HENRY DEMAREST LLOYD • CHICAGO • WEDNESDAY 2 JANUARY 1901

DARROW & THOMPSON Chicago, Ill., January 2, 1901.

My Dear Mr. Lloyd:—

Dr. Holmes[16] called on me this morning on account of your letter of December 13. He seemed to be considerably agitated concerning it. Of course I do not need to tell you that I will have nothing to do with any matter that is antagonistic to you or to any member of your family, and I know that Miss Stallbohen[17] has been a member of your family for a great many years. I promised the Doctor that I would write you, although I scarcely know why I am doing it or what to say. My relations to him have been about the same as yours have been. I know very little about his business as a physician, although I have supposed that he stood high in his profession. This as you know of itself covers a multitude of sins both in his profession and mine—especially mine.

This letter cannot be regarded in anyway as coming from him, for I do not represent him or would not in case of any difference.

Your communication to him seems to me quite indefinite, but if it means anything it means that Miss Stallbohen believes that his treatment was not proper, and that for this reason she has some either legal or equitable claim against the Doctor. He assures me that he did everything possible and that the case was properly treated. As to his using his best judgment, I presume there could be no doubt—there seldom is with any doctor. At any rate I do not believe he is in any position or any attitude of mind towards this matter so that he would contribute anything to her. He assures me that there is no reason why he should, and I believe that he feels this way. Of course if it is a case where any such complication is to arise I could only pass him on to the mercy of some other lawyer as I would have nothing to do with it myself.

In the meantime if I could be useful to both of you I should be very glad to do it. If you care to write me more fully about this matter I will treat any portion that you wish in the strictest confidence, and you need have no fear that you are communicating anything to the other side, excepting what you may wish me to communicate.

I am very sorry to hear of Miss Stallbohen's illness and condition.

Are you never coming to Chicago again? You are often spoken of here among the radicals, and I suppose equally often in other circles, although I do not hear it. We should all be glad to see you and we are always glad to hear of your contributions to the general cause. My boy is in the freshman year at Dartmouth. I think he

16. The identity of "Dr. Holmes" is unclear, but Darrow might have been referring to Bayard Holmes (1852–1924), a prominent physician and surgeon in Chicago who ran for mayor as the candidate of the People's Party in 1895 (Darrow supported his candidacy).

17. Caroline Stallbohm (1855–1914), longtime secretary and literary aid to Lloyd.

may be in Boston sometime during this term, and I shall ask him to drop in on your family.

Please remember me kindly to Mrs. Lloyd and the boys.

As ever your friend, | C. S. Darrow.

I am trying to get a cast of Wendell Philips and can find none, am obliged to have one made. Would you be interested in it or do you know of any others who would?

D.

MS: TLS, WHi, Lloyd Papers. INSIDE ADDRESS: Henry D. Lloyd, Esq., | 95 Mt. Vernon Street, | Boston, Mass.

TO SAMUEL M. JONES • CHICAGO • TUESDAY 15 JANUARY 1901

ALTGELD, DARROW & THOMPSON Jan. 15

My Dear friend Jones,

Your letter from Pittsburgh was received and should have been promptly answered, but aside from the fact that something seems crowding me every moment, I am the most negligent man in the world. I appreciated your good letter & have always felt that you liked me & believed in me & that you took me for what I am or try to be without explanation or apology, and in return, I think you know how much I respect & love you & how fully I trust & believe in you—I know no one whose spirit is so right, except possibly Nelson[18] & Crosby.[19] I always like to see you, hear you, or read from you & regret that you do not stay longer when you come. Your volume of letters came to hand.[20] They are very touching & beautiful & ought to be useful. They are filled with the right spirit. I hope I may be able to see you soon again—Ever with love

Your friend | C. S. Darrow.

MS: ALS, OT, Jones Papers. DATE: "Jan. 15 [1901]" appended.

TO BRAND WHITLOCK • CHICAGO • TUESDAY 2 JULY 1901

ALTGELD, DARROW & THOMPSON July 2d

Dear Whitlock

Of course I was delighted with Howells' letter, it confirms all the good opinion I have had of Howells.[21] I am sure that even my own success (if such should ever come) would scarcely make me feel better than this of yours.

18. Nelson Olsen Nelson.
19. Ernest Howard Crosby.
20. Darrow is referring to the first volume of Jones's *Letters of Love and Labor*. See Darrow to Jones, 7 June 1900, n.5.
21. Whitlock sent Howells the manuscript for what eventually became Whitlock's first novel, *The Thirteenth District*. Howells praised the novel as "a great, honest, powerful story"—"easily the best political story I know"—and he told Whitlock that he would "gladly do anything" he could to help Whitlock find a publisher

The other letter came today.[22] My instinct is all against changing it. If that fellow knows so much about good art & a novel & good novels why don't he write a novel. Of course Harpers want a book that all the school girls will buy & read—don't write it. I feel that they will not give up this book and if they do another publisher will take it. If it is necessary we will organize a publishing house on purpose. I do not really see how you can go over this thing—you might as well give up your ideals at once.

I feel as if literature is your work. Still perhaps it would do you good to go to the State Senate—think perhaps you had better! In case I do not go to Europe (as I am now figuring somewhat) had we better try to get off together. I would like it better than any thing I know. I must figure out some way to see you all soon.

Kindest regards to Mrs W.[23] & Miss Dowd.[24]

Ever your friend | C. S. Darrow.

MS: ALS, CtW. DATE: references to the letters from Howells and Harpers.

TO BRAND WHITLOCK • CHICAGO • WEDNESDAY 21 AUGUST 1901

DARROW, THOMAS & THOMPSON Aug. 21st

Dear Whitlock

Your letter is just received. I will be there on Saturday evening the 31st and prefer to carry out the programme as you make it.[25]

You are very kind to write me as you did & I assure you I appreciate it. These are the kind of things that make a man like me think that after all it pays to follow his convictions and fight his way through—Of course I will be glad to bring you a picture.

When I come I will tell you how much I liked your last story—of the old member who did not sell out.[26] I read it to my friends and passed it around, they were all delighted. I am going to start a little publishing business with one other "fellow." Shall publish my

---

for it. See Howells to Whitlock, 19 June 1901, in *Life in Letters of William Dean Howells,* ed. Mildred Howells (New York: Doubleday, Doran, 1928), 2:145.

22. Joseph H. Sears (1865–1946), an editor at Harper & Brothers (Howells's publisher) wrote to Whitlock saying that "he found the novel depressing" and he asked Whitlock to "add a chapter of love interest to make the novel salable to young girls." Whitlock revised the novel accordingly but Harper rejected it in the end, leaving the exhausted Whitlock "quite ill, and for two months he was all but unable to function." Robert M. Crunden, *A Hero in Spite of Himself* (New York: Knopf, 1969), 107 (citing letters from Sears to Whitlock, 27 June and 30 September 1901, DLC-MSS, Whitlock Papers).
23. Ella Brainerd Whitlock.
24. Jessie Dowd (Stafford) (1873–1958). Dowd was born in Ohio, educated in the public schools of Toledo, and graduated from the University of Toronto (with a degree in Teutonic Romance languages) and Ohio State University, where she received an M.A. She taught school in Toledo before marrying Frederick Allen Stafford (1856–1918) in 1902 and moving to Arizona to operate a tuberculosis sanitorium. After her husband's death, she returned to Toledo and taught in public and private schools before becoming a professor of English at the University of Toledo, 1926–43.
25. The program to which Darrow is referring is unknown.
26. This is probably a reference to a short story that Whitlock wrote about the fate of a politician who refused to accept the favors of a political boss: "Reform in the First," *Ainslee's Magazine,* July 1910, 545–53.

essays. We thought we would publish a collection of your short stories if you wanted—what do you think?[27]

Truly your friend | C. S. Darrow.

MS: ALS, NNC, Nevins Papers. DATE: letterhead and references to publishing essays and "Saturday evening the 31st."

TO JANE ADDAMS • HANOVER, NEW HAMPSHIRE • WEDNESDAY 11 SEPTEMBER 1901

DC Hanover N.H. | Sept 11th

Dear Miss Addams

In a New York paper I saw about your visit to the mayor in behalf of Isaaks & his friends who have been so cruelly outraged by the mob. Of course I need not tell you how glad I was & that it was no more than I expected from you.[28]

I know both Isaaks & his son also Miss Julia Mechanic, and of course I presume they will be enquiring for me to help defend them. Of course I would gladly avoid this if I could. I have stood in front of mobs so long that my heart is weary and my head sore but I do not see any thing else to do and shall not avoid what seems to me to be my duty. I see by today's paper that Emma Goldman is now under arrest.[29] I never knew her but there is not the

27. The identity of the "fellow" with whom Darrow was going to start a publishing business is unknown. And why Darrow put "fellow" in quotations marks is also unknown. Darrow's book of essays, *A Persian Pearl: And Other Essays* (East Aurora, NY: Roycroft Shop, 1899), contained five essays: four on literary subjects—including Omar Khayyám's "Rubaiyat," Walt Whitman, realism, and Robert Burns—and one on shame and regret entitled "The Skeleton in the Closet." The book was republished in May 1902 by C. L. Ricketts (1859–1941), a Chicago bookseller, calligrapher, and illuminator.
28. On 6 September 1901, President William McKinley was shot in Buffalo, New York, by Leon Czolgosz (1873–1901), an avowed anarchist. He died eight days later. Several anarchists—a few of whom had a slight acquaintance with Czolgosz—were arrested in Chicago after the shooting and charged with conspiracy to assassinate the president. They were held in jail and refused any vistors, including any attorneys. Among those arrested were Abraham Isaak (1856–1937), his wife, Maria (1861–1934), their sixteen-year-old daughter, Mary (1885–1974), their teenage son, Abe Jr. (1883–1953), and several of their friends, including Julia Mechanic (b. 1870), a Russian immigrant and seamstress. Abraham and Mary Isaak were both pacifist Mennonites who immigrated to the United States from Russia in 1889. They settled in Portland, Oregon, where they started *The Firebrand*, an anarchist newspaper, and moved to San Francisco in 1897 after being arrested for publishing a poem by Walt Whitman. In San Francisco, they changed the name of their newspaper to *Free Society*. Three years later, in early 1901, they moved to Chicago, where they were publishing and editing the newspaper at the time of their arrest. See Paul Avrich, *Anarchist Voices: An Oral History of Anarchism in America* (Princeton: Princeton University Press, 1995), 23–28; Steven Kent Smith, "Abraham Isaak: The History of a Mennonite Radical," *Mennonite Quarterly Review* 65 (October 1991): 449–55; and Steven Kent Smith, "Research Note: Further Notes on Abraham Isaak, Mennonite Anarchist," *Mennonite Quarterly Review* 80 (January 2006): 83–94. Jane Addams convinced the mayor of Chicago (Carter H. Harrison Jr.) to allow her to visit the prisoners. Addams described her efforts to help the Isaaks in her autobiography. See Jane Addams, *Twenty Years at Hull-House* (Urbana: University of Illinois Press, 1990), 230–35.
29. Emma Goldman (1869–1940), anarchist and feminist editor, writer, and lecturer. Czolgosz told police that he had heard a speech by Goldman the year before he shot McKinley. From this, police decided that Goldman held some responsibility for the crime and they arrested her in Chicago. Goldman had not conspired with Czolgosz, but she publicly defended him after his arrest. Candace Falk, *Love, Anarchy, and Emma Goldman*, rev. ed. (New Brunswick, NJ: Rutgers University Press, 1990), 33. Thirty years later, in her

slightest excuse for her arrest. Still under the law of the Anarchist case I do not see why it is not possible to convict, if public opinion gives need as it doubtless has & will. I do not know how much you care to do or will feel it your duty to do but it seems to me & *for me* that I have no right to try to save myself when the injustice is so great as here. It may be necessary for every friend of justice to use all our influence in every direction including raising money—for if they try to convict it will be a hard and dangerous fight under the law as it now exists. If a jury believes that a speech of Miss Goldman's or an article of Isaachs or a speech of mine or any other person's caused the shooting they can hold such persons guilty. I know that Isaachs & his boy have worked hard by day & work & set their type at night to keep their little paper running. I know that Miss Mechanic is a dress maker who sews by the day & pays in her small wages to keep the paper alive. I know they are perfectly innocent of any crime and are in great danger of suffering for their opinions—which right or wrong are for the uplifting & improvement of the world. What I specially want from you now is that you see these people especially Miss Mechanic whom I knew particularly in the Kropotkin meeting[30] and if they want me, to say that I shall be ready to do all I can for them. I have planned to stay away until Oct. 1st and do not need to hurry back, but will be there then. I prefer that it be not given out publicly that I am connected with the case & I should gladly help employ others in my place. Still when the time comes, if I am wanted and needed I will be on hand. I have not written any one else about this & shall not but will ask you to see them and I do this because I know you have already seen them & I also know that you believe in justice. I think if a long campaign is needed as in the Anarchist case Miss Johnson[31] ought to be asked to attend to corresponding to raise funds &c. I may be unduly alarmed but I feel that the powers of capital will try to stamp out all radical thought & utterance and will go to any length to accomplish it. Some lawyer not connected with the radical movement could do more to help them, if we could only get such lawyer, but it must be a good one, one with the wisdom of the serpent & the gentleness of the dove, and this is a rare combination—for lawyers. Am here with my boy who is at Dartmouth & will stay for a week or ten days.

Sincerely your friend | C. S. Darrow.

MS: ALS, PSC, Swarthmore College Peace Collection, Jane Addams Papers.

---

autobiography, Goldman said that Darrow had sent a lawyer from his office to visit her in jail. According to Goldman, this lawyer warned her that she was hurting her case by her defense of Czolgosz and that she should admit Czolgosz was crazy. Goldman attributed the advice to Darrow and said that she found the lawyer's talk "repugnant." Emma Goldman, *Living My Life,* vol. 1 (New York: Knopf, 1931), 303–4.

30. Peter Kropotkin (1842–1921), Russian geographer, revolutionist, and anarchist philosopher. Kropotkin visited Chicago in April 1901, during a tour of America, and gave five lectures. The most well attended lecture was on 21 April at Central Music Hall. Darrow was chairman for the event.

31. Probably Amanda Johnson (b. 1871). Johnson obtained an A.B. from the University of Wisconsin, 1893, attended law school at Northwestern University, and was a resident of Hull House for a time. Together with Jane Addams, she served as a garbage inspector for the nineteenth ward in Chicago, 1894–98. Later, she and Darrow were both tenants of a twenty-four-unit tenement house on the South Side known as the Langdon Building. Architect Dwight Heald Perkins (1867–1941) designed the building, which was completed around the turn of the century, and Johnson served as an agent for the developer. Ethel M. Colson, "A Home in the Tenements," *The Junior Munsey* 10 (April 1901): 28–30.

TO BRAND WHITLOCK • CHICAGO • MONDAY 17 MARCH 1902

ALTGELD, DARROW & THOMPSON Mar 17

Dear Whitlock

Of course I know that you too have been mourning over our dear friend who is gone.[32] It has been a great loss to us all especially to us who knew him best & loved him most. Your tribute was very fine. But I write you now on an other matter—I would like you with me if it could be properly arranged. We need a good man who can do all kinds of work. I do not know whether you can or not. Litterary men & dreamers are not generally the ones who can. Still I think so much of you that I wish you could. Do you want to come up at once & talk it over thoroughly with Thompson[33] & me & perhaps make a test. We must make some sort of plan at once though it would not be necessary to permanently come for a little time. If you will come, bring Mrs. W.[34] & both of you come to my flat to put up. Let me know at once—With love to you both

Darrow

MS: ALS, DLC-MSS, Whitlock Papers. DATE: "1902" appended and supported by reference to death of Altgeld.

TO RICHARD F. PETTIGREW • CHICAGO • WEDNESDAY 26 MARCH 1902

ALTGELD, DARROW & THOMPSON March 26, 1902.

My dear Mr. Pettigrew:—

Your kind letter in relation to Governor Altgeld was duly received. It is very generous of you to offer the $500 for a monument. I know what your feelings are in the matter, and that you fully appreciated him and the services he has rendered to the country.[35] At the present time, however, his friends are trying to raise a fund for Mrs. Altgeld. He died without leaving any estate whatever, and we have undertaken to raise $25,000.[36]

I think it would be better to use your donation for this purpose. At the same time I think that maybe you could help us further by subscriptions for this fund. Of course, most of his friends are poor and not able to do much, and we have to appeal to those who are better able to give.

32. John P. Altgeld died on 12 March 1902. He was Darrow's law partner when he died.
33. William O. Thompson.
34. Ella Brainerd Whitlock.
35. Pettigrew had written a letter to Darrow expressing his fondness and admiration for Altgeld and proposing that Darrow approach the *Chicago American* about taking charge of raising funds for a monument in Altgeld's honor. Pettigrew to Darrow, 19 March 1902, TLc, SdSifSHM, Pettigrew Papers.
36. Altgeld's wife, Emma Ford Altgeld (1847–1915), according to one biographer, was "almost always an invalid after the death of her husband." Altgeld's friends eventually raised a fund for her and the Illinois General Assembly, in 1903, voted to give her five thousand dollars to help lift the mortgage on her house. Harry Barnard, *Eagle Forgotten: The Life of John Peter Altgeld* (Secaucus, NJ: Lyle Stuart, 1938), 470.

On the third of April I am to speak at Cooper Union at a memorial meeting to Governor Altgeld, and I will arrive probably in the morning and will stop at the Hoffman House.[37] Mr. Martin[38] will be with me and we shall try to do something amongst the friends in New York.

I wish you would consider it in the meantime and either see me at the hotel or the meeting. If possible I will call on you, but there are so many matters to which I must attend and I may not get the time.

Ever with kindest regards, I am,

Very truly yours, | C. S. Darrow.

MS: ALS, SdSifSHM, Pettigrew Papers. INSIDE ADDRESS: HON. F. S. PETTIGREW.

TO RUBY HAMERSTROM • CHICAGO • WEDNESDAY 4 JUNE 1902

June 4, 1902

My Dearest Girl

This is an answer to your first letter which was the sweetest dearest best letter a man ever received. I shall always be glad you wrote it and shall always keep it even though you may wish it had not been written.

In all the time I have known you I think I have not told you any lies or professed any feelings I did not have or made any statements to any one else that were in conflict with what I say to you. I want you to know that I love you more than I have ever loved any one in life—that you have been kinder truer & nobler to me than any one else has ever been, that I never can be happy without you. I want you to know that I have never spent a dull hour with you, that I have never for one moment wished to be away and that I have never had an unkind thought of you. I can not think of living without you—the greatest happiness—the only happiness that I can think of is to be with you while I live and near you—*very very* near you in the last long sleep. Any thing else to me now would seem like a sacrifice. If I must make it I must, but all the same it could only be that. I am not happy without you I can not be happy without you. Much as I loved you at first it has grown every day & you almost are me. I want you to find some peace & comfort, something to do. I want you again. I was bitterly disappointed that you did not come although I did not ask you to. Still I think it was best. If it can not be it can not, and I presume it is best to know what can be & what had better be, before we place ourselves again when we

37. Public meetings in Altgeld's honor were held in several cities. Darrow was the principal speaker at Cooper Union in New York City. "John P. Altgeld," *New York Times*, 4 April 1902.

38. Probably Joseph S. Martin (1853–1916), who made a lot of money operating a private gambling club in Chicago. Martin had been on Altgeld's staff when Altgeld was governor. Martin was very active in efforts to memorialize Altgeld.

meet. If I could see you now, could take you in my arms, could kiss you I would want no other bliss.

Ever & ever

MS: AL, MnU-L, Darrow Collection.

TO RUBY HAMERSTROM • CHICAGO • WEDNESDAY 11 JUNE 1902

June 11th

Dear Ruby

Your dear letter came yesterday & I of course understand it and know that you are right. I am not satisfied with myself—I probably never can be—and I know how you feel and I am sorry. I love you dearly & appreciate you. I do long & long to see you—but must not ask you to give me more than you do. I want you to be happy & I can not forget how happy you have made me, and I am ever wanting you again & again. I am tired out tonight with the weary grind & can not write what I think or feel.[39] I only want to send a word to tell you I love you & that I appreciate & understand what you say.

Lovingly & hastily | Clarence

MS: ALS, MnU-L, Darrow Collection. DATE: other possible years eliminated.

TO RUBY HAMERSTROM • CHICAGO • FRIDAY 20 JUNE 1902

June 20

My Dear Old Ruben

Your hyphenated letter came to day and your other a day or two ago. Ruben dear you are an artist & the most delightful sweetheart a man ever had, and I would be happy perfectly happy if I could take you in my arms right now. You will think as you read this—but, what about tomorrow? Well what about tomorrow? I put it to myself most seriously—honestly & I wonder if I can never stop thinking & doubting about tomorrow & what terrible fate has made me as I am. Here are you the dearest sweetest loveliest girl in the world—a girl who has given me only the most delicious joy—never a pain or a sorrow and how I do love you & still over & over comes the question that you put. Darling I do think about loving you, about your giving me up & going to some one who can give you more certainty and peace—and my heart almost stands still when I think of it, for I love you so fondly. I wonder could I see you even for a day if I could come, or a week would

39. Darrow was involved in the selection of a jury (which took nine days) for a trial of seven men (including Cyrus Simon) who were charged with bribing a jury on behalf of the Union Traction company in a lawsuit with the City of Chicago in April 1902. The trial of the seven men started on 12 June and continued until 29 June, when all of the defendants were found guilty. "Jury Bribers Found Guilty: Row in Court," *Chicago Tribune,* 29 June 1902.

be so much better any where—any where. My miserable case is dragging its slow length along. It will be finished about Wednesday next week and I am so tired & worn & so anxious to see you—my dearest darling—

MS: AL, MnU-L, Darrow Collection. DATE: other possible years eliminated.

TO RUBY HAMERSTROM • CHICAGO • SUNDAY 29 JUNE 1902

THE ST. HUBERT Sunday

Dearest,

Yesterday my case was finished & I lost—still I saved my men from prison which was a good deal.[40] How I long to see you. I wish I could get a week with you for I need the rest—and you. I would not suggest it again, except for the two letters I got yesterday from you. If you can & want to how happy I would be to go any where. It occurs to me that possibly if you thought best Gretchen[41] & you might put it up together to come here or go somewhere & if so I would send transportation for both. If so wire that you or both will come. If you did I would take a week off & not go to office. Dearest I love you dearly—fondly & want to be with you always & long for the time when I can. Will write tomorrow. How dull it is here at St. H. without you.

MS: AL, MnU-L, Darrow Collection. ENVELOPE ADDRESS: Miss Ruby Stanleigh | 5233 Vernon Ave. | St Louis | Mo. POSTMARK: Chicago, 29 June 1902.

TO RUBY HAMERSTROM • PITTSBURG, PENNSYLVANIA • WEDNESDAY 29 OCTOBER 1902

Wednesday PM

Dearest Ruben

Last night I left Chicago & just arrived on the business that I came East about some time ago.

The worst of it is that I am going from here to Wilksbarre Pa. to meet Mr. John Mitchell who has sent for me to take charge of the miners case before the commission.[42] If I

40. One of the seven defendants convicted in the jury-bribery case received a prison sentence, but the other defendants, including Darrow's three clients, received only fines. On appeal, the convictions of two of Darrow's clients were reversed and their matters remanded for a new trial; the conviction of his other client was affirmed on appeal. See *O'Donnell v. Illinois,* 110 Ill. App. 250 (1903) (reversing conviction of Darrow's clients; affirming conviction of two other defendants), affirmed, *Gallagher v. People,* 211 Ill. 158, 71 N.E. 842 (1904).
41. The identity of "Gretchen" is unknown.
42. In May 1902, anthracite miners in Pennsylvania went on strike, demanding higher wages, shorter hours, and recognition of their union (the United Mine Workers, headed by John Mitchell). In October 1902, as winter approached and anthracite coal became scarce (and prices increased), President Roosevelt obtained an agreement from the striking miners and mine operators to arbitrate their dispute, and he appointed an arbitration commission to hold hearings and decide the matter. The striking miners agreed to return to work while the commission resolved all of the issues between the miners and operators. Darrow and Henry Demarest Lloyd, among others, represented the striking miners in the arbitration.

go as I suppose I must it will take six weeks or two months & be mostly in Washington. I shall no doubt be back in Chicago on Friday noon & I wonder whether under the circumstances you could not come to Chicago over Sunday. If so wire me Friday P.M. there & go right from the train to the place. Would it be possible for you to make a visit to your Swede Brother in Washington while I am there? It would be very lovely if you could. I don't see how I can ever live without seeing you for a month or six weeks & still I don't see how I can get the[43]

MS: AL, MnU-L, Darrow Collection. ENVELOPE ADDRESS: Miss Ruby H. Hammerstrom | 5233 Vernon | St. Louis | Mo. POSTMARK: Pittsburg, 29 October 1902.

TO RUBY HAMERSTROM • SCRANTON, PENNSYLVANIA • THURSDAY 20 NOVEMBER 1902

HOTEL JERMYN Nov. 20th 1902

My Dearest Darling Ruben

I always love you—all the time. It has been a long while since I have had any doubt about it, but sometimes I love you more than others and this is one of the times. It seems as if I must go to you & go at once & take you in my arms & never let you free again.

For two or three days—and nights—I have wanted you so I could hardly think of any thing else—though I have thought of other things—& every night when I went to sleep I dreamed about you—last night that we were to be married that day, realy truly married so you could be with me every day, & all night long in my arms. How anxious I am & how impatient that any thing should keep us apart. In no event will I let it longer than spring & I hope not until then, though I have never heard a word directly or in directly about the only thing that keeps me from it.[44] Still, perhaps I ought to wait until then if I do not hear—but after that I will wait no longer whatever my result.—But this is not what I was going to say.

It looks as if this grind might cease next week for one week & that I might get away for a few days. If so shall I come, & will it be all right to come in a telegram to you, & if so will you come out and meet me on the noon train that we took that delicious day & get the train that you took back—the one I will be on reaching St. L. about 6–30—then we will get our dinner on the train—just you & I together—& then the moon will be up by the time we reach the depot.

Ever with all my love Sweetheart

MS: AL, MnU-L, Darrow Collection.

43. The rest of the letter was cut off.
44. What Darrow was alluding to here, as keeping him from marrying Ruby, is unknown.

TO HORACE TRAUBEL • SCRANTON, PENNSYLVANIA • MONDAY 24 NOVEMBER 1902

Hotel Jermyn, | Scranton, Pa., | November 24, 1902.

Dear Traubel:

I have been trying for a long time to see you, without success.

We have arranged a little party, consisting of Ernest Crosby, Henry D. Lloyd, Senator Pettigrew, yourself and myself to visit John Burroughs on Thanksgiving. Everything is complete excepting the invitation, which we shall try to arrange for. Will you please wire me at once, ~~both here and~~ to the Willard Hotel, Washington, if you can go; and if so I shall wire you where to meet us, unless you know the situation well enough to go there directly.

Sincerely yours, | C. S. Darrow.

MS: TLS, DLC-MSS, Traubel Papers. INSIDE ADDRESS: Horace Traubel, Esq., | Camden, N.J.

TO LOUIS D. BRANDEIS • SCRANTON, PENNSYLVANIA • FRIDAY 28 NOVEMBER 1902

HOTEL JERMYN Nov. 28 1902

Dear Mr. Brandeis—

Mr. Lloyd has told me of your interest in our case and of your willingness to help. We have decided to make an aggressive move along the lines discussed by you and Mr. Lloyd—the extortionate charges for anthracite freight rates as compared with bituminous; the legal and economic wrong in the union of mining and transportation; the relation of over-capitalization to low wages, &c. Mr. Lloyd understood that you would be ready to make an argument before the Commission on this part of our case. Could you do so, and also spend a few days here with us before the Commission in the presentation of the evidence on this subject? We should be glad to have you do so. Kindly let me know what compensation would be expected. If you will be able to join us kindly communicate with me by wire. We hope to be able to open up this matter week after next.[45]

Yours, | C. S. Darrow.

MS: ALS, KyLoU-L, Brandeis Papers.

45. Brandeis agreed to help and he consulted with the lawyers for the miners and toured the coal mines, but he did not make an appearance before the commission. See Lewis J. Paper, *Brandeis* (Englewood Cliffs, NJ: Prentice-Hall, 1983), 65; Melvin I. Urofsky and David W. Levy, eds., *Letters of Louis D. Brandeis* (Albany: State University of New York Press, 1971), 210–23.

TO DANIEL CRUICE • SCRANTON, PENNSYLVANIA • SATURDAY 13 DECEMBER 1902

Your letter is just received. I do not know what to say about the mayoralty. Of course, if I could meet you, I would talk the matter over frankly. I certainly do not want this job. I feel as you do, that there never could be any rivalry between us in a matter of this sort.[46]

If you thought it best to run, I, of course, would be with you. I know that both of us are interested in certain matters and will be glad to do almost anything to bring them about. For my own part, I hate the fight and trouble and worry of a political campaign. I am getting lazy and like my friends, and books, etc., and would rather be left alone.

It seems to me that the only possible chance for either of us to be elected in such a way as we would want to be must come through the laboring man. Of course, I could not think of being a candidate of a faction of democrats who are really not democrats, and I do not believe that a fellow like me could get a democratic nomination. By the time he got it he would be so tied up that he would be like any other political hack.

If there happens to be a ground swell in Chicago this spring and the trade unionists and people of that sort are bent on having an independent candidate, I suppose neither of us would feel as if we had any right to run away in case it was thought that we could get the most votes and somebody needed to do it.

The main thing is to have such independent sentiment as is there started along the line where it may be used at the right time for the right principles, and of course that means the right people. Both of us have been working a long time to get up such an independent sentiment and if we accomplish this we will have done a great deal.

If either of us should be called upon to represent it, I do not see how we should have a right to run away, but the issue can not be forced. If we undertook to do that I think we should fail.

MS: "Darrow's Big Change of Front," *Chicago Journal*, 4 April 1903. RECIPIENT, PLACE, AND DATE: provided in same newspaper article.

TO RUBY HAMERSTROM • PHILADELPHIA, PENNSYLVANIA • LATE JANUARY 1903

THE COLONIAL Thursday

Dearest Ruben

I am getting home sicker & home sicker for you. I am being annoyed too all the time with letters, telegrams & newspaper stuff about running for mayor. I don't want it.

46. The next mayoral election in Chicago would be held April 1903, and there was some talk that Darrow should be a candidate for the office. This letter was published closer to the election (after Cruice had a falling out with Darrow), when Darrow threw his support in the race to Carter Harrison Jr. rather than Cruice.

I am tired & I want to take you & go away for six months and write a book, go away where no one can find us & bother us & I think in a day or two I will write the papers that it is all off—I won't do it. Dearest I love you & want you & want to see you. It may be I can in about two weeks. They are talking about a week's adjournment before the arguments. I might put in a good deal of it with you if F will stand for it.

Ever & Ever

If I come I must work—hard.

MS: AL, MnU-L, Darrow Collection. DATE: reference to running for mayor and the end of the arbitration hearing.

TO JOHN MITCHELL • PHILADELPHIA, PENNSYLVANIA • FRIDAY 23 JANUARY 1903

Philadelphia, Pa. January 23rd, 1903.

My dear Mr. Mitchell:

Everything is going all right. We had a good lively tilt in court yesterday over your statement about the idle miners, and I rather think we did not get the worst of it. The evidence has been more favorable if anything, since you went away.[47] It looks as if the companies would close their case within a week when we shall need about three or four days of rebuttal and will follow with the arguments which have been fixed for five days. I think it would be wise for you to be back if you can.

There is considerable indication that they are coming to us to negotiate for a settlement in which a trade agreement will be fully endorsed. They have all learned a good deal on this line since we commenced this case. Last night, I had a long talk with Major Warren[48] and Mr. Torrey[49] and both of them told me they had become convinced that a trade

47. Mitchell left the arbitration hearing on 17 January 1903 to attend the national convention of the United Mine Workers in Indianapolis. Before leaving, he told the commission that the miners were not responsible for a shortage in the supply of anthracite coal and that three thousand miners were standing idle and ready to go to work. The mine operators, for their part, blamed the shortage of coal on a refusal of the miners to work longer hours. The "lively tilt in court" that Darrow mentions happened when the mine operators challenged the truth of Mitchell's statements during the hearing, through witnesses who maintained that the miners were *not* making an extra effort to produce more coal. Darrow challenged one of the witnesses for the operators (a superintendent of one of the companies) to provide the name of even one miner who refused to make an extra effort. The witness refused on the ground that men he named might then be persecuted by their union. A heated exchange between Darrow and lawyers for the mine operators followed, with Darrow concluding: "I am tired to death hearing the stories of the operators that their poor human slaves drowned out the mines and are responsible for the restrictions upon the output of coal. If I don't prove by their own reports and figures presented to this commission that the operators who are parties to these proceedings have restricted the output of coal, and that their unwarranted attempts to put the blame on the miners' union are for the purpose of throwing dust into the eyes of the American public, then I shall go back to Chicago and request this commission to render a verdict against us." "Lawyers in Hot Dispute," *The (Frederick, Maryland) News*, 23 January 1903.
48. Everett Warren was a lawyer representing the Delaware, Lackawanna & Western Railroad Company.
49. James H. Torrey was a lawyer representing the Delaware and Hudson Company.

agreement was the best, and that they were going to use their influence to have that agreed to by all hands.

This morning, I have a letter from Chicago saying that they engaged the Auditorium for February 5th for a reception to you and to me.[50] I have just written them that I do not believe we will be through in time for the 5th. I want to post you in advance about this matter. As you know, there is considerable effort on the part of various people to have me run for Mayor. I have not made up my mind what I will do but I think the chances are that I will not do it. No doubt some of my friends will try to make this an occasion for booming me in that direction.

Of course, I shall see that nothing is done of that sort at the meeting and shall insist that it shall not be used in any way for that purpose. Still, I have no doubt that the papers and some politicians will say that is the object of the meeting. Now I want you to understand perfectly that I do not consider that you ought to be influenced to go there under friendship to me. Whatever you may think about it personally, you have no right to place your organization in any position that you think might harm it, and if the committee comes to you or if you learn upon investigation through your friends in Chicago, that you might be misunderstood or that the organization might in any way be harmed, you can easily have business to keep you away.

Of course, this reception to you has been talked of since long before this Commission commenced and long before I had anything to do with the case and it would come just the same regardless of me, but we both know how ready the public and politicians are to take advantage of any such matter and of course have to consider it, in making up our minds.

I am under the impression that practically all the Republicans are friendly to me at this time and that nothing would be said in their papers or by their people that would in any way be harmful. This, of course, is due to the fact that they want to aid Mr. Harlan[51] and want to disorganize the other crowd all they can and not through any love for me.

I simply want to tell you all I know about it and advise you to look into the matter and assure you that I consider not only you ought to act independent of any feelings toward me, but that it is your duty to do this on account of your organization.

As ever your friend, | Clarence S. Darrow.[52]

MS: TLS, DCU, Mitchell Papers. INSIDE ADDRESS: John Mitchell, Esq., | Indianapolis, Ind.

50. Six thousand people attended a celebration at the auditorium in Chicago on 16 February 1903. Mitchell, Lloyd, and Darrow all gave speeches. "Labor Honors Mitchell," *New York Times*, 17 February 1903.
51. John Maynard Harlan (1864–1934), lawyer and Republican politician. Harlan was the son of John Marshall Harlan (1833–1911), an associate justice of the United States Supreme Court, and father of John Marshall Harlan II (1899–1971), who was also an associate justice of the Supreme Court. He graduated with an A.B. from Princeton University, 1884, and earned an LL.B. at George Washington University, 1888. He practiced law in Chicago for many years before moving his practice to New York City in 1925. He was active in Republican politics in Chicago, serving as an alderman, 1896–98, running twice as a nominee for mayor, 1897, 1905, and once as a candidate for governor, 1920.
52. In reply to this letter, Mitchell said that he hoped the mine operators would be open to settlement negotiations after finishing with their evidence to the commission. He also said that he would do what he could to help Darrow if he decided to run for mayor. Mitchell to Darrow, TLc, 27 January 1903, DCU, Mitchell Papers.

TO GEORGE SCHILLING • PHILADELPHIA, PENNSYLVANIA • MONDAY 26 JANUARY 1903

PHILADELPHIA, Jan. 26.—George A. Schilling, Ashland Block, Chicago: So many letters and newspaper clippings have come to me in reference to the mayoralty that I feel I ought to say to you that I made no promises of any sort to any person either that I would or would not run for mayor. I have not asked any favors of anyone, and am not under any obligations either to go into the fight or to stay out. I have no personal desire to be mayor of Chicago, and still less to run for that office. I have not asked anybody, directly or indirectly, for his support, and cannot imagine that I ever would. I do not exactly see how it is the business of any man to ask the people to vote for him. As you know I have been absolutely tied up with this case for nearly three months, and have had no time to think of outside matters, and cannot think of it or do anything about it at present. It looks as if this case would be finished certainly in two weeks, and then I shall return, and can say more about it. I do not propose to lose my head over this matter, and shall not be influenced either by those who, on account of some ulterior purpose, desire me to be a candidate or by any who might, for the same reason, wish me not to be.

C. S. DARROW.

MS: Undated, unidentified Chicago newspaper clipping, ICN, Darrow Family Scrapbooks, Box 3.

TO THE *CHICAGO TRIBUNE* • PHILADELPHIA, PENNSYLVANIA • TUESDAY 27 JANUARY 1903

Philadelphia, Pa., Jan. 27.—[Editor of The Tribune.]—I never have been a candidate for the mayoralty nor asked any one's support. I have had no time nor opportunity here to investigate and cannot do so now. The meeting on my return to Chicago would have no political color. I could determine nothing till my arrival in Chicago, and then would be influenced mostly by what I thought best for Chicago. In or out of office, I have always been for municipal ownership and shall continue to be.[53]

C. S. DARROW.

MS: "Darrow States Mayoral Stand," *Chicago Tribune*, 28 January 1903.

53. The publication of this telegram was followed in the *Tribune* by an article reporting that Darrow's attitude had not weakened the belief of his supporters that Darrow would enter the race when he returned to Chicago. The article quoted encouraging statements to that effect from Francis Wilson, who had recently been to visit Darrow in Philadelphia, and it noted that a committee formed to support Darrow's candidacy had placed an order for fifty thousand campaign buttons with Darrow's picture on them and the words "Darrow for Mayor." "Darrow States Mayoral Stand," *Chicago Tribune*, 28 January 1903.

TO HORACE TRAUBEL • PHILADELPHIA, PENNSYLVANIA • WEDNESDAY 28 JANUARY 1903

In Court | Jan 28th

Dear Traubel

Your letter is just received & I will answer it frankly. All my life I have been harrassed over money matters, although I make a good income. I have so many people to look after & obligations of all sorts that I am always in debt & unable to do what I would like. This morning I received a bill for 500. for my publication of essays & I am obliged to wait until I get home to make some arrangements to pay. All of this to say that I do not see how I can do as you request. I am always willing to help out & I feel that you should be helped through, as I should if I needed (and I may) but I don't feel that I can afford to put any considerable amount into the Conservator. I am trying hard to get matters so I can spend 6 months in Europe this summer & must do it if possible. Now as to you. I am sure you know how fully I sympathize with you in all your work & in your present difficulty; but it does not seem to me that it is wise to arrange for the Conservator (valuable though it is) until you arrange for yourself. As to the latter I want to be of assistance, in some way & will do anything that can be done & that either of us can suggest. When it is done, if we can get enough to do some good to take hold of the Conservator I will help, but do not see how anything permanent can be done any other way. If you could get 20 or 30 men to agree to pay a certain amount monthly to keep The Conservator running I would be one, but I am not in position where I could do any considerable amount except for persons & then not very considerable.

MS: AL, DLC-MSS, Traubel Papers. AUTHOR: "[Darrow, Clarence]" appended and letter is in Darrow's hand. PLACE: "In Court" is likely referring to anthracite arbitration. DATE: "[1903]" appended and no reason to doubt.

TO RUBY HAMERSTROM • PHILADELPHIA, PENNSYLVANIA • WEDNESDAY 28 JANUARY 1903

In Court-Room | Philadelphia Jan 28th

Dearest Ruben

I am writing you a line in the court room surrounded by lawyers & miners & maggots of all sorts. I have been cross-questioning witnesses all day & am tired & I wish you were here & I could crawl into your arms & rest & sleep & feel better in the morning. I am sure two weeks more will finish this & then I am going to try & see— Every day I get some telegram about running for mayor & I am driven distracted by the bother. I think within a few days I will tell them that I will not—for all the time there comes before me a vision of six months at some quiet lake in the north of England or in Italy & with only you—& with it a chance to write a story—a long story—about you & me & every body.

Well dearest I still love you—still love you—why don't you write—you always have time.

Your old woozy lover

MS: AL, MnU-L, Darrow Collection. ENVELOPE ADDRESS: Miss Ruby Stanley | ~~3749 Washington~~ | 3949 Washington | St Louis Mo. POSTMARK: Philadelphia | Jan. 29, 1903.

TO GEORGE SCHILLING • PHILADELPHIA, PENNSYLVANIA • THURSDAY 29 JANUARY 1903

Philadelphia, Pa., Jan. 29, 1903.

My Dear Schilling:

Your communications, together with numerous others, have been received, and I have given it such thought as I could while attending to this case. It seems to me that my friends ought to be told explicitly that they should not spend their time and energy circulating petitions and doing political work for me.

Even if I desired to be mayor of Chicago, which I do not, my engagements here will not allow me to give it my attention for two weeks more, and after that time I shall be obliged to go to Springfield and spend four or five days of each week at the legislature. I cannot let any other matter interfere with either one of these duties, which I am bound to perform the best I can.

I do not want to be placed in a position where the efforts of my friends could in any sense influence my judgment or handicap me in determining what I should do on my return to Chicago. If it is thought best for any reason that I should run, I can do it just as well without further petitions or effort until I have determined the question.

I think my friends must appreciate that it is difficult to decide this matter from this distance, and it would embarrass me if they spent too much time and effort in my behalf before I am able to give an answer as to what I think best to do.

C. S. DARROW.

MS: "Agree on Dates for Primaries," *Chicago Tribune*, 1 February 1903.

TO GEORGE SCHILLING • PHILADELPHIA, PENNSYLVANIA • TUESDAY 3 FEBRUARY 1903

Philadelphia, February 3, 1903.

Dear Schilling:

This morning I received another letter from you, and read the newspaper clipping showing that you had published my letter. I am inclined to think that it was the wisest thing to do. Seriously, I believe it would not be wise to run for mayor. I rather think I should be beaten and I would prefer to make as good a record as I can in the Legislature and

even assuming that I wanted to be a statesman, to have a little slower growth—but I don't want to be a statesman.

I am quite sure that my field of usefulness is in another direction and also that I can have more fun following out the course that seems to me easier and more consistent with my tastes. I do not want to say now that I will not run, and perhaps I will, but all the same I think you are right in not having this movement encouraged and leaving it so that I have plenty of chance to refuse.

I wish you would see Lindbloom at once and tell him your doubts about the matter if you still have any and keep him from committing people too far.[54] I think your whole attitude in this matter has been the right one. If there was any great public necessity, we ought not to consider the question of whether we could win or not, but make a red hot campaign on radical lines and let it go at that—but I do not see any such public necessity at this time and it looks to me as if my running was after all more a matter of personal ambition and the good will of my friends.

This does not seem to be the right basis for a fellow of your ideas or mine to go into a political campaign.

On Sunday, I was interviewed by reporters of the Chronicle and the News.[55] I talked to them quite fully and after I got through I got thinking about it, and it began to dawn on me that I had almost entirely overlooked the principles that I have always stood for—that is the bettering of the condition of the common people and had given a very conservative sort of a statement as if I was wanting to get votes, which it seems to be must have been the attitude of my mind at that time.

Now I don't propose to get myself into any such position and rather think the conditions as they exist—my strongest backing would evidently drive me that way, and I don't like it. As to any arrangements that might be made, I rather think we ought to use our position to do something for the cause and for some men—first you, next a friend whose name I will not mention now, and then possibly a few more of the fellows who are right.

Of course, neither of us would trade any of our political opinions for position, but I fully agree with you that we should make the most out of the situation for the future, and that is one of the strong reasons why it seems to me that I ought not now to decline, and I think you will understand how I feel concerning the whole matter.

54. A few days before this letter, Robert Lindblom formally announced that Darrow was, indeed, a candidate in the mayoral race. Lindblom claimed that he had received a letter from Darrow authorizing him to make the announcement whenever Lindblom believed it was proper. "Says Darrow Is in the Race," *Chicago Tribune*, 31 January 1903.

55. The *Daily News* reported Darrow as saying that he would wait to make a decision on his candidacy until he returned to Chicago: "I have decided to withhold any formal announcement in regard to the matter until I return to Chicago and have had time to look into the situation. . . . I want to assure myself that things are as I am told by those who are urging me to become a candidate. I have not been to Chicago for nearly three months except for short visits. I am told that there is widespread dissatisfaction with Mayor Harrison; that I can have the democratic nomination by saying the word and that election would surely follow my nomination. I do not know these things of my own knowledge and for this reason I shall not say anything until I have an opportunity to personally examine the situation." "Darrow Delays Entering the Race," *(Chicago) Daily News*, 2 February 1903.

As to Gunning,[56] I presume what he said grew out of some question over the Unity Bldg—a matter I care nothing about and I am sure would not influence him either after he got sober—if he ever does.[57]

MS: TLS, location of original unknown (copy in editor's files). INSIDE ADDRESS: George A. Schilling, Esq., | Ashland Block, Chicago.

TO GEORGE SCHILLING • PHILADELPHIA, PENNSYLVANIA • FRIDAY 6 FEBRUARY 1903

Philadelphia, February 6th, 1903.

Dear Schilling:

Last night Cruice talked to me over the telephone and said that Harrison[58] had declared for a twenty year franchise and that Lawrence wanted me to stay in a position to run. I got your letter this morning which rather indicates that you too have lost your head over this matter.

You cannot imagine how I dislike to go into it and still I will do it if it needs to be done. I want you to keep cool over it until I get back. In the meantime, find out everything you can.

I have this morning also a letter from Lindbloom[59] telling me I ought not to wait until the 13th as that is too late to make an announcement. I cannot possibly see why this is so. That would be six or eight weeks ahead of the election which is long enough time to be on the rack, God knows.

The leaders are not going to count very much in this fight. If we conclude to go in, I would not care a damn if all the leaders were against me. If the conditions are right, I will win; and if they are not right I will still have a chance to go into the obscurity I desire.

The only advantage in time is to get ahead of the Democratic convention. If this does not come until March, it is time enough for that after the Auditorium meeting. If there is anything in this boom, the leaders and politicians will get out of the way. I think it is well enough to let the people be a little anxious about my running. All there is in it is that they shall not think I am dallying or not able to make up my mind. I can do this too when the right time comes but it does not seem to me to be the time. I do not want to make a mistake about it.

I feel first of all that I ought to know how the press is going to receive it. Lindbloom says that none of them will be hostile. This is more than I could expect, but I do want to have some friends amongst them and, of course, I would like fair treatment so far as I could get it.

56. Possibly Robert J. Gunning (1856–1932), an outdoor display advertiser who also had real-estate holdings in Chicago.
57. The remainder of the letter is missing.
58. Carter Harrison Jr.
59. Robert Lindblom.

The feeling for me if I run will grow very fast and the thing I need to fear is the reaction when the conservative forces get well to work. I do not need a long campaign in order to win. A month is better than six weeks so I feel confident that my absence from Chicago is a good thing even if I conclude to run.

I think the friends out to be urged not to make me declare at this time. I rather believe that I have been in a position to look the matter over carefully than you people who are right with it all the time.

This also should be remembered. Next week is to be a big week here in Philadelphia. I need to give it all my time and attention. The plan is now arranged that Mr. Baer[60] is to make the closing argument for the mine owners and I will follow him and close the case. Mr. Baer will speak Thursday and I will speak Friday and Saturday morning. This is bound to have the center of the stage beyond any doubt.

Is the meeting definitely fixed? It should be fixed at once from Monday the 16th and they had better especially write to Mitchell. It will not be safe to have it before Monday night but it will be absolutely safe on that evening. Please see that our friends at the Langdon get a box and also look after any others that happen to apply.

As ever, | Clarence S. Darrow.

MS: TLS, location of original unknown (copy in editor's files). INSIDE ADDRESS: George A. Schilling, | Chicago.

TO RUBY HAMERSTROM • PHILADELPHIA, PENNSYLVANIA • SATURDAY 7 FEBRUARY 1903

THE WAYSIDE | WINNETKA | ILLINOIS Saturday night

Dearest Ruben

A week from tonight I start back & hope to see you very soon. I want to more than ever. I am worrying about the mayoralty, it looks as if I could not get out of running but shall not decide until I return. There is to be a big reception to Mr. Mitchell & me on Monday night after I return at the Auditorium. I wish you could be there. Fred doesn't happen to be going up that way does he? I wish you both were. It will be a meeting for your life. Well dearest if they would all leave us alone so we could go away it would be all I want. Any how I will not wait—long.

Love C.

MS: ALS, MnU-L, Darrow Collection. ENVELOPE ADDRESS: Miss Ruby Hammerstrom | 3949 Washington | St Louis | Mo. FIRST POSTMARK: only "Feb" and "PA" is legible. SECOND POSTMARK: St. Louis, Missouri, 9 February 1903.

60. George F. Baer (1842–14), lawyer and railroad executive. Baer was born in Pennsylvania and served with the Union army in the Civil War. After the war, he became a lawyer, practiced law, and made a great deal of money rehabilitating businesses that failed in the panic of 1873. This led him to be an adviser to J. P. Morgan (1837–1913), who made him president of the Philadelphia & Reading Railway, which combined railway lines and coal corporations. During the strike and arbitration of the anthracite miners, Baer served as the leader of the mine operators.

TO HENRY DEMAREST LLOYD • CHICAGO • THURSDAY 19 MARCH 1903

STATE OF ILLINOIS | HOUSE OF REPRESENTATIVES Mar 19

My Dear Lloyd

I think it is time for you to be a Socialist. I think we must all come to it, but I think both of us should not come out the same year. You do it now & if the water is not too cold I will jump in next. Really I think it ought to be done, but I do feel that after all the sacrifices you have made you ought to have the glory of coming out first. Don't you?

I want to see you tomorrow or Saturday. Come *down please.* Come down & stay over two trains. I am very lonesome without having seen you for so long & then I am rather blue. I want you to go to Europe & Constantinople & the Hymilayas & Japan with me this Summer & I mean to make you go

Faithfully & Devotedly | Darrow.

MS: ALS, WHi, Lloyd Papers. PLACE: letterhead. DATE: "[1903*]" appended and supported by letterhead.

TO RUBY HAMERSTROM • CHICAGO • SATURDAY 21 MARCH 1903

DARROW, THOMPSON & CROSS Saturday

Dearest Ruben

Your letter came this P.M. I am sorry you are in trouble over the matter.

I think you need not worry. I presume this was some one either on account of politics or some personal enemy of mine, or possibly some news paper who has sent this man. Probably it was political & most likely only to save up in case of need, which case will never come.[61]

I don't believe it had any relation to Mr. O.[62] It might possibly come through the one person on my part whom too I have told you about. Within the last four or five years this has happened before & I rather presume it is a way they have of keeping track of people & using it if occasion requires.

Of course it might be used, but I hardly see how. I think most of the news papers are friendly, and I don't see how such a thing could be used. As to Stewart & Harrison they are both afraid of me,[63] & neither side would dare attack me, & what is there in it any how. Of course it might be carried back to Chicago but still I can't see how it could get in.

61. Something apparently led Ruby to believe that someone in St. Louis was investigating her or her relationship with Darrow. A person might have shown up at her front door. Whether her concerns were founded is unknown.
62. Here, Darrow might have written "Mrs. O" rather than "Mr. O," in which case he might have been referring to his first wife (whose maiden name was Ohl)—somebody Ruby might have feared was behind this incident.
63. This is a reference to Graeme Stewart (1853–1905), the Republican candidate in the upcoming mayoral race in Chicago, and Carter Harrison Jr., the Democratic candidate.

Now my dearest Ruben I know you are brave. You know I love you dearly. You know I have never deceived you in any way. I have enough money to live on & you & I can go alone up into the mountains if we want & no one can harm us. The only thing is if Fred & Geo[64] should go back on you—but even then you & I are of age, & if any thing serious happens we don't need to wait until June 15 and as long as it is all arranged & settled you & I will know it is voluntary & what is the difference about any one else.

But I don't think any thing will happen. Perhaps I had better not be there quite as much in the future but my dear darling sweet heart it won't be long, although it may seem long.

As for me I am 45 years old. I know I have lived an upright life. I know I have been generous & kind & considerate of every one in the world—and I am willing to face any thing that comes, any how if you are with me dearest old Ruben. You can talk with Fred if you think best & you can tell him what I say if you think best. There is nothing in my life that I care much to conceal & I am not afraid & I believe you are not. Besides all of this I hardly believe I have more friends than any one in Chicago, & while I have fought many interests hard & lived a fearless life still I am on the whole respected & there are many who love me as devotedly as any one I ever knew. These could not be effected and they would absolutely destroy any one who would do a miserable cowardly thing like this.

If anyone comes again I think Dr. Smith[65] should treat them as he did before. As for you there is nothing that is any one's business. It is probably some cheap detective—but at any rate dear girl be brave & you know that I will always be ready to come to you or go to you at any time & place & what more is there in it.

Ever Your dearest lover | Clarence S. Darrow.

MS: ALS, MnU-L, Darrow Collection. ENVELOPE ADDRESS: Miss Ruby Hammerstrom | 3949 Washington Av | St Louis | Mo. POSTMARK: Chicago, 21 March 1903.

TO RUBY HAMERSTROM • CHICAGO • SATURDAY 21 MARCH 1903

SHERMAN HOUSE Saturday | Later

Dearest Ruben

Just a word more since writing you—Of course I have a perfect right to go to St. L., & see you at any time. No one is interested or has any business with it. I can't quite see why we should worry or care. At any rate I am sure I only worry at the trouble it makes you. I will not submit to be intimidated by any black guards such as must have been

64. Two of Ruby's brothers, Frederick and George Hamerstrom.
65. Darrow's handwriting is particularly difficult here, and the name might not be "Smith." In any event, the identity of the person is unknown, although Darrow might be referring to someone with whom Ruby was residing.

there. It might have been some small paper—or possibly some matter at the Legislature. Of course there are many bills pending, that the corporations are interested in, & they might perhaps try to get some compromising pictures. It is possible that a telegram from Springfield may have been reported—but all the same I don't think any one would dare do any thing & there is nothing to do. Pure scandal is really of little use & this is not even scandal.

I think dearest Ruben that you need not worry. Any how as long as we love each other what do we care & why? Perhaps we had better make that about the 10th—of June *I mean*

Ever & ever Yours | C.

MS: ALS, MnU-L, Darrow Collection. ENVELOPE ADDRESS: Miss Ruby Hammerstrom | 3949 Washington Av | St Louis | Mo. POSTMARK: Chicago, 22 March 1903.

TO RUBY HAMERSTROM • SPRINGFIELD, ILLINOIS • WEDNESDAY 25 MARCH 1903

FORTY-THIRD GENERAL ASSEMBLY March 25

Dearest Ruben

This is a very pleasant sunshiny day, and of course I am thinking of you. I want to be with you when it is cold & rainy & cloudy, but when the sun shines & it is warm then I want you more than ever. I am dreaming of the time just a few months off when we will get out in the sunshine—& wander over the hills & mountains & through the streets of strange cities until we are tired out & want to come home & go to sleep right off quick—I don't think—Any how it can't come too soon & Ruben darling I am very anxious & very happy over the prospect & shall not try to stretch the time unless to stretch it shorter—for I do want you—want you terribly & am going to have you—

Ever Yours | C.

MS: ALS, MnU-L, Darrow Collection. ENVELOPE ADDRESS: Miss Ruby Hammerstrom | 3949 Washington Av | St Louis | Mo. FIRST POSTMARK: Springfield, 25 March 1903. SECOND POSTMARK: St. Louis, 25 March 1903.

TO HENRY DEMAREST LLOYD • SPRINGFIELD, ILLINOIS • THURSDAY 2 APRIL 1903

Springfield, Ill., Apr. 2nd, 1903.

My dear Lloyd:—

The coal strike kept me away so long that it was not possible for me to introduce the Bills you spoke of.[66] I am very sorry but perhaps we will have better luck some other time.

66. Lloyd had asked Darrow to consider introducing some bills in the state legislature and to help get a bill affecting his hometown of Winnetka, Illinois, out of committee: "Is there any chance of getting the matter of the nationalization of the coal mines before the Illinois Legislature as it has been brought before the

As for the Winnetka matters of course I will do all I can for them. I would like to see and talk with you about the finding of the commission. I think it was a most cowardly document, and in this I complain not of what they did but of what they said and more still of what they did not say.[67] Can't you run down between trains and see me Friday or Saturday?

Sincerely your friend, | C. S. Darrow.

MS: TLS, WHi, Lloyd Papers. INSIDE ADDRESS: Mr. Henry D. Lloyd, | Winnetka, Ill.

TO DANIEL CRUICE • SPRINGFIELD, ILLINOIS • THURSDAY 2 APRIL 1903

Springfield, Ill., April 2.—Daniel L. Cruice, Unity Building, Chicago, Ill.—Friend Dan: Your letter just received and I hasten to answer. When the committee offered me the nomination I felt very badly not to be able to accept it. We were all present at the funeral together, and I did tell you that if you concluded to run I would support you.[68] Afterward I saw you in Chicago and told you that I wanted you to release me from this promise if you could, and your not calling on me led me to hope you had thought it right to do so; however, your letter now asks me to aid you rather than Harrison.[69]

It is not worth while to quibble over small points. Whether you did release me on my request I do not care now to discuss. At the time you accepted the nomination I did tell you that I would support you, but I feel now that I can not do this. I am sure you have known me long enough to know this is due only to one consideration, and that is what I consider to be my duty to the public in this regard. If this were a personal matter, about the loan of money, or any question of personal friendship, I should keep my promise

---

legislatures of Maine and Massachusetts? | If you care to interest yourself in this, I will send you a copy of the Maine and Massachusetts bill. I, myself, think it will be a mighty good stroke of public policy, and personal policy, to do this. | Another popular measure might be to propose a bill authorizing municipalities to establish municipal fuel yards. | We, here in Winnetka, are very much interested in a bill before the legislature, authorizing municipalities in Illinois to own and operate light, heat and power plants. This bill is now buried in committee. Couldn't you help get it out on to the floor of the House? | Let me hear from you." Lloyd to Darrow, 31 March 1903, TLc, WHi, Lloyd Papers.

67. Darrow is referring to the report of the commission appointed by President Roosevelt to arbitrate the dispute between anthracite miners and operators in Pennsylvania. *Report to the President on the Anthracite Coal Strike of May–October 1902, by the Anthracite Coal Strike Commission* (Washington, DC: Government Printing Office, 1903). The commission's award included a ten-percent increase in wages and a reduction in hours but did not result in recognition of the United Mine Workers of America (the commission concluded that the union was not a party to the proceedings and that the commission did not have jurisdiction over the question of union recognition). Ibid., 56, 60–61. Instead, the commission appointed a board of conciliation to resolve future disputes between the operators and miners. Ibid., 67–68. The commission also denounced any efforts by unions to interfere with non-union laborers. Ibid., 75–76.

68. Darrow is probably referring to the funeral for John P. Altgeld. Cruice and Darrow were both pallbearers for Altgeld.

69. Carter Harrison Jr.

absolutely, but it is a promise that does not involve you or me in any way, but only the public. It is a promise which, if I should keep, feeling as I honestly feel, would mean that I would help sacrifice the rights of the people of Chicago for a statement made by me at a critical time without any consideration whatever, and the enforcement of which could not do you any good, and could only result, from my standpoint, in serious injury to the people of Chicago. Under these circumstances I can not carry out this promise.

As to the present political situation, it is not necessary for us to argue. Neither you nor I have ever liked Harrison. I believe that your prejudice against him has absolutely destroyed your judgment as to what is best in this crisis. The facts are perfectly plain. This legislature will not pass an enabling act.[70] Mr. Stewart[71] will not promise that, on failure to pass such an act, he will veto any traction bill that the city council passes; every street railroad company and every stock jobber in Chicago is for Stewart. It is perfectly plain to any one not bereft of his senses, that if this legislature adjourns without passing a bill, and if Mr. Stewart is elected, the city council will at once renew the charters of the street railroad companies. On the other hand, whatever Mr. Harrison's convictions may be, he has deliberately promised that no franchise shall be passed unless over his veto, and that in no event shall any franchise be given street railroads that is not first submitted to the people for their approval. He has deliberately promised this, and so far as traction matters are concerned, he has always kept his promises in the past. In a matter of this sort, every man must choose for himself. I have known you too long, and have too much confidence in you, to believe that you act from any motive except what seems to you to be for the highest good of the people. If I could elect you, I would give anything I have to accomplish it, but you know and I know that I can not, and that any support that I might give you would simply mean that I was helping Mr. Stewart to become mayor of Chicago, and deliver the interest of the people into the hands of the traction companies. Seeing and feeling in this matter as I do, I am sure you must know that much as I regret it, there is no other course open for me.

Ever, with kind regards and best wishes, your friend, C. S. DARROW.[72]

MS: "Darrow Is Here for the Fray," *Chicago Journal*, 3 April 1903.

70. The central issue in the mayoral campaign involved several private streetcar franchises that had operated in Chicago for many years. Many people believed that municipal ownership of the franchises—a goal that Darrow supported—might be possible if the legislature passed an enabling act authorizing it, which would give the city leverage in negotiating with the private franchise operators. At the outset of the legislative session in 1903, "the prospects for any legislation opposed by the street railway companies were far from bright." But shortly after the mayoral election, the state senate passed what was known as the Müller bill, which authorized any city in Illinois to own and operate local street railways under certain conditions. The bill was signed by the governor near the end of the session after a dramatic showdown between supporters and opponents of the bill in the legislative house. John A. Fairlie, "The Street Railway Question in Chicago," *Quarterly Journal of Economics* 21 (May 1907): 385–87.
71. Graeme Stewart, the Republican candidate for mayor, became a supporter of the Müller bill. Ibid., 385.
72. Cruice, who ran for mayor himself as an Independent Labor Party candidate, was unwilling to accept Darrow's explanation for supporting Harrison. Cruice was the principal speaker at a meeting of "Altgeld

TO RUBY HAMERSTROM • CHICAGO • TUESDAY 7 APRIL 1903

DARROW, THOMPSON & CROSS Tuesday

Dearest Ruben

I have been having the time of my life—a hot time—been roasted and praised—newspapers both way but I shall stand it and come out all right. Had to take a hand in election as it got in such a shape I could not keep still & they rather put me in the center, but any how I know the little girl down at St. Louis loves me & is with me & that is the most I care. I know too that within *about* two months we will have a nice suite of rooms somewhere in a pleasant place on the English lakes or near London & our troubles will be over for a while. Any how it is all I look forward to. Don't think I am discouraged—but I have been working very hard & am tired but it is over today. Shall be in Springfield tomorrow morning & shall look for a letter on my desk from my dearest dearest sweet heart.

Ever Yours

MS: AL, MnU-L, Darrow Collection. ENVELOPE ADDRESS: Miss Ruby Hammerstrom | 3949 Washington Av | St. Louis Mo. POSTMARK: Chicago, 7 April 1903.

TO RUBY HAMERSTROM • CHICAGO • TUESDAY 7 APRIL 1903

DARROW, THOMPSON & CROSS April 7

Dearest Ruben

This is a postscript just to say that my candidate has won and I am now feeling all right—& although I have been through a pretty hard fight, am now strictly in it.[73] But still what do I care for that. I am only thinking of that June day & the cozy rooms somewhere in England & my dear old sweet heart.

Ever & ever

MS: AL, MnU-L, Darrow Collection. ENVELOPE ADDRESS: Miss Ruby Hammerstrom | 3949 Washington | St. Louis. POSTMARK: Chicago, 8 April 1903.

---

followers" on 2 April 1903, where he apparently made this letter available to newspapers and, at the same time, publicly denounced Darrow: "Darrow has broken faith with me, and if he has done it with me he will do it with you. I want to say, and in as certain tones as may be, that Clarence S. Darrow in taking the stump for Harrison is guilty of a breach of trust to the independent labor party and to myself, who counted him as my friend." "Darrow Branded a Labor Traitor," *Chicago Tribune*, 3 April 1903.

73. On 7 April 1903, Carter Harrison Jr. won his fourth consecutive election as mayor, receiving 143,323 votes to Graeme Stewart's 138,485 votes. The Socialist candidate received 11,207 votes and Daniel Cruice, as the Independent Labor candidate, received 9,989 votes. "Mayor Harrison Re-Elected," *Chicago Tribune*, 8 April 1903.

TO RUBY HAMERSTROM • SPRINGFIELD, ILLINOIS • SPRING 1903

FORTY-THIRD GENERAL ASSEMBLY Tuesday

Dearest Ruben

How are you? It seems an age since I have seen you & you don't know how I want you—how I want you every day & every night & all day & all night. I am really getting batty on the subject. Dearest what about your going to Chicago? I can't go to St. L. this week as Paul will be back but *can't you can't you* come up? I am really counting the days until we are together.

Last week I made a bargain to write one letter a week while away, for $250 per month.[74] So you see I can let you help me & we can pay our expenses around the world—How is that? I will make you read all the guide books & get all the stuff while I am flirting &c. Do you see? I wish you could write short hand, then I could dictate them in about half an hour & go out & play while you did the rest. But dearest—can you come up & do you love me?

MS: AL, MnU-L, Darrow Collection. DATE: letterhead, impending marriage, and reference to Paul being back from Dartmouth. ENVELOPE ADDRESS: Miss Ruby Hammerstrom | 3949 Washington Av | St. Louis Mo. POSTMARK: illegible.

TO RUBY HAMERSTROM • CHICAGO • SATURDAY 20 JUNE 1903

DARROW & MASTERS June 20th

Dearest Ruben

It has been a long time since I wrote or had a letter but this is not because I am not thinking of you but because I am so dead tired every night & so D—n busy all day. But all the same it is just the same & I want you as much as ever & now it is only a little more than two weeks & I don't seem to shudder MUCH and am not figuring on putting it off or anything & am coming right up to the scratch. Any how you dear old girl I love you & every thing is all right *so far* & will be further.

Ever & Ever

MS: AL, MnU-L, Darrow Collection. DATE: letterhead and implied reference to impending wedding.

74. While Darrow and Ruby were on their honeymoon in Europe, Darrow wrote a series of twelve travel essays, mostly on labor and politics in Europe, that were published weekly in the *Chicago Daily News* (and other newspapers): "English Trade Unions in Politics," 22 August 1903; "Labor Politics in England," 29 August 1903; "Present Day Socialism in England," 5 September 1903; "Tariff Agitation in England," 12 September 1903; "England's Rich and Poor," 19 September 1903; "Where the British Earnings Go," 26 September 1903; "Success of the German Socialists," 3 October 1903; "Wilhelm Liebknecht and His Work," 10 October 1903; "Results of Bismarckian Socialism," 17 October 1903; "Among the Toilers of Switzerland," 24 October 1903; "Switzerland and Its Reformers," 31 October 1903; and "Switzerland's Political Life," 7 November 1903.

TO JESSIE DARROW • CHICAGO • TUESDAY 14 JULY 1903

DARROW & MASTERS July 14th 1903

My Dear Jessie

I trust you will not be in any way disappointed or saddened by this letter. I tried to tell you & Paul but somehow I could not. I am going to be married Thursday before starting to Europe.[75] I think that you will feel as I do and realize that I have worked so very hard for several years & been through so much that I feel as if my health will not stand the strain unless I find a regular quiet home, again. I want to do some work. Something that will live for Paul & all of us & as I am my time is so destroyed that it is almost hopeless. For many reasons which I can not go into fully I feel that I really must & my only or rather my chief trouble in it all is the fear that you & Paul especially Paul may think I have done wrong. All my life I have tried as hard as I could to be considerate & kind to all who came near me. I may have failed, but if I were to die tonight I could say honestly that I have tried and have never meant to let my selfish desires keep me from doing my duty to others as I have seen it. You have always been so true & gentle & loyal to me that I feel that I could not live, I know I could not be happy, if you censured me or disapproved of me. I am sure of this that always I have meant to think of you as I do more tenderly & gently than of any one else, & I am sure I always shall. I remember that you once told me you wished I would marry. I presume you then felt as I do now that it was absolutely necessary for me to have a steady home as I grow older. Of course a woman can have a home but a man who works & fights as I have done must rely on some one else for that.

The woman I am to marry is Miss Ruby Hammerstrom a name I presume you never heard though Paul has met her brother. I have known her three years, met her first at the White City Club when I read my paper.[76] For two years she has lived in St. Louis. She is kind & good & feels right toward you & Paul & wants me to be happy & I know will look after me well. She is a friend of Mrs. Gregg whom you know & is about 33 years old. I hope you will think I am doing right & will make Paul think so for this is of the first importance to me. And above all things else I want things to be as they always have been. You know how I love Paul & how miserable I should be if he did not love me.

Ever & ever Your friend Clarence

MS: ALS, Darrow Family.

75. Darrow and Ruby Hamerstrom were married on 16 July 1903 by Edward F. Dunne (then a judge), in the home of John R. Gregg (1867–1948), publisher and inventor of the Gregg shorthand system. Ruby Darrow to Irving Stone, TL, n.d. ("We were married on . . ."), DLC-MSS, Darrow Papers.

76. The White City Club was an intellectual club of artists, writers, and musicians. Darrow lectured on Omar Khayyam the night that he met Ruby Hamerstrom. Ibid.

TO JESSIE DARROW • ZERMATT, SWITZERLAND • TUESDAY 8 SEPTEMBER 1903

HOTEL DE ZERMATT Sept 8 1903

Dear Jessie

I have been on the move all the time since leaving America but have settled down here for a few days. Have not written many letters & have had very few so don't know just how things are going at home. Though I had a letter from Paul in which he said you were all having a good time & of course I was glad of this.

I rather think I shall come home soon. The stock market has been so bad that I feel as though I ought to look closely after my business for an other year. I did think that I had enough to keep us all but don't want to risk any thing now on account of any of us. Still I am in hopes that things will look better soon so that I will have enough with what money I have on hand to finish paying for 200 shares.

Before I left I told Frank[77] to give you all the money that come in or to give it to Baker[78] to be paid on stocks. There should have been some in but I have not heard. I wish you would telephone him & if there is let him send it to you or to Baker, whichever you choose. I would not send Baker less than $1,000 but would rather keep it.

I want you to know that when I return I shall live where I did before or in some cheap house near buy & shall not spend money or be extravagant in any way. I should not do this even if we were all provided for but this must come first. I do not know whether the land was sold. I thought it would be & I left word to have all the money paid to you or Baker. If this were sold it would make things easy.

Ruby understood every thing in advance & knew how much I thought of you & Paul & that I should always consider that I must first look out for both & she believes in it fully & wants it that way. You will find that I will not be changed in any way & that so long as I live you will both come first. This is all I will need to say for I want you to be happy & there is no occasion for our discussing things. You will find that always every thing will be done without asking. I hope your mother is with you & that you are both well. I think you ought to keep a girl if you are back in the house. Really the expense is very little & I would feel much better to have it that way.

Ever with love | Clarence

Love to your Mother.

MS: ALS, MnU-L, Darrow Collection.

77. Francis S. Wilson.
78. The identity of "Baker" is unknown but he was probably a stockbroker for Darrow.

TO JESSIE BROSS LLOYD • CHICAGO • MONDAY 19 OCTOBER 1903

VICTORIA HOTEL, | CHICAGO Oct. 19th

My Dear Mrs. Lloyd

This morning I returned from Europe & was told of the death of my dear friend Mr Lloyd.[79]

You can imagine what a shock it was to me. I loved him as I have few people & trusted him as I did almost no one else. I can scarcely think of any thing today but this. The only consolation I have over it is the fact that I was with him so much last winter.

I can not tell you how sorry I am for you & all the rest left behind. I only wish that there was something that I can do, but what can one do in the presence of death?

I am so glad that you & your son are taking up his work; it at least is some little consolation.

With sincerest regards

Your friend | C. S. Darrow.

MS: ALS, WHi, Lloyd Papers. DATE: "[1903]" appended and supported by reference to death of Lloyd.

TO BRAND WHITLOCK • CHICAGO • SUNDAY 6 NOVEMBER 1903

DARROW & MASTERS Nov. 6

Dear Whitlock

Of course I will put your friend up at the club.[80] I was glad to hear from you & know that you were well & progressing with your work. I would like very much to see what you have done.

I have completed my story.[81] If I will send it to you right away, will you read it at once & return telling me exactly what you think & where it can be improved either by burning or otherwise making all sorts of honest suggestions just as I have about yours?

I know this is a hard thing to ask of a friend, for suppose you don't like it at all. Still you can write so well that you can tell me so without hurting much & besides I should then think you did not know.

Any how I want you to do it and do it now. Will you?

Ever with the same regard & love to you & Mrs W. Darrow.

MS: ALS, CtW. DATE: letterhead and reference to the book that became *Farmington.*

79. Henry Demarest Lloyd died of pneumonia on 28 September 1903 while working on a campaign to secure municipal ownership of Chicago's street railways.
80. The identity of Whitlock's friend is not known.
81. Darrow is likely referring to his novel *Farmington* (Chicago: A. C. McClurg, 1904), which was based on his childhood in Ohio. Darrow worked on the novel while in Europe on his honeymoon.

TO JESSIE DARROW • CHICAGO • THURSDAY 10 MARCH 1904

DARROW & MASTERS March 10th 1904

Dear Jessie

Your letter is received. I shall go to Washington alone. I would not ask him to go any where any other way. Any thing more must be by his own choosing & yours. Of course you know that I have *always* thought of you first in relation to Paul & if he ever must choose between us I want him to choose you although I have always cared for him more than any thing on earth.

You know too that I always have appreciated all you have done for me & that I never in any way have failed to recognize & remember it. And that I never would have proposed the step we took however I might have believed it best for both.

I have tried to live an unselfish life, have tried to do what good I could in the world, have tried to consider others & do all in my power for their happiness. I can not now see where I could have done any different & when I have not done my very best. Paul is too young to judge me. And neither to him nor any one else shall I make any effort to be judged or understood. I shall go on with what is left of my life & try to live it as honestly & courageously as I can & pay no attention to the rewards or punishment which the world always gives without any regard to merit. However in all I do I shall always remember you & Paul first, & *shall* always appreciate most deeply all of your kindness & generosity to me.

Sincerely | Clarence.

MS: ALS, MnU-L, Darrow Collection.

TO JESSIE DARROW • CHICAGO • WEDNESDAY 20 JULY 1904

DARROW & MASTERS July 20th

Dear Jessie

As I have not yet been quite able to get my matters arranged as I want I thought I ought to make a will before I went away for my summer vacation. I send it to you & as it leaves Paul to settle matters you can put it in his papers after looking it over if you wish.[82]

As to Paul I rather think it best to start him along the line of some publishing business. He likes books & so far has not shown any great liking for law. He has a good business head & I think will get along all right after about a year of studying the business. When he comes back in the fall I will raise the amount sent to you to $75 if you think this will

82. Darrow's will—written in his own hand and witnessed by his law partner, Edgar Lee Masters, and by Harlan K. Saunders Jr. (b. 1878), a clerk in their law office—provided for a rather simple division of his estate, with his books as the first item:

cover Paul's board & I think he will earn enough to pay for clothes &c. If not of course he & you can have all you want.

I am bound to get things right next season but want to try to have things fairly economical for one more year. Of course I have had pretty heavy expenses. Last year cost about $1,000 for father. Another at least $1,000 for Paul, & the stock market cost a good deal more. I am sure Paul is all right & will not need to cause either of us any worry. Will buy him a life membership in the Yacht Club if you don't object. This is good exercise & will get him into a good crowd of young people. Paul is very cautious & any how I don't think it is dangerous—but we will be obliged to take some chances & if any thing ever does happen [to] him we will know that we have done all we could to make him enjoy himself. Will send you an other $60 before I go away. Expect to spend about a month at Cassells Colorado & if you should need any thing more call up Frank.[83] When I return will give you the money to go to St Louis for a while if you want to go—or any where else you wish. If any thing should happen to me I am sure there is enough to make you all fairly comfortable. You know the two houses & the two lots on Collins St. are now in your name—these with the stock now in your hands at present low prices are worth at least $15,000 or $16,000 above the mortgages on the houses. Each of them you know have $3,000 mortgages on them.

As Ever | Clarence.

MS: ALS, Darrow Family.

I; Clarence S. Darrow being in my usual condition of mind make this my last will

Item 1st I give and bequeath to my son Paul my library.

Item 2d I give and bequeath to Ruby H. Darrow all house hold & office goods & property.

Item 3rd The balance of my property real & personal I give devise and bequeath to be equally divided between Jessie Ohl Darrow Paul E. Darrow and Ruby H. Darrow, requesting that said Jessie O. and Paul E. shall give any reasonable assistance (such as I might have given) to any of my relatives needing aid at any time.

Item 4th I nominate and appoint Paul E. Darrow as executor of this my last will and testament and request that no bond shall be required and that any property I may leave shall be amicably divided.

Clarence S Darrow

Signed by Clarence S Darrow & acknowledged as his last will and testament in our presence and by us signed in his presence the 20th day of July 1904

Witnesses | Edgar L. Masters. | Harlan K. Saunders Jr

83. Probably Francis S. Wilson.

• 1905–1909

TO BENJAMIN FAY MILLS • CHICAGO • THURSDAY 23 FEBRUARY 1905

DARROW, MASTERS & WILSON Feby 23rd 1905

My Dear Mills

I want to come next summer & have planned to do so.[1] Still I don't want to put it out of my power to go to Europe in case I have the time (which I do not now expect to have.) You may put me down if you are willing to leave me the right to notify you later of a change of my plans. I think the chances are decidedly that I will be with you.

Ever with best wishes | C. S. Darrow.

MS: ALS, CLU-SC, Theodore Perceval Gerson Papers (Collection 724).

TO JESSIE DARROW • CHICAGO • THURSDAY 16 MARCH 1905

DARROW & MASTERS Mar 16

Dear Jessie

Of course you had better stay where you are. I thought the lease expired this year & it might be easier to rent the 29th St house. But I want you to have the best. I will pay for

1. Mills had probably invited Darrow to speak in California at the "Los Angeles Fellowship," an independent liberal congregation led by Mills after his break with Unitarianism.

fixing it just as you want it or I will send someone down to give you an idea of the best way to fix it. Will also see that enough is paid to take care of the mortgage.

A short time ago I bought 100 shares of biscuit common which is good & pays 4%.[2] Will doubtless pay more sometime. I shall arrange to put this in your hands paid up soon, certainly before summer. This will bring $400 every year. Sometime I presume the Republic will bring $700 & I am sure the Gt Western will bring $400 within the next two or three years & sometime more. This would be 1,500 a year or $125 a month. As soon as I deliver the 100 shares of biscuit I will arrange so your income shall be then $100 a month until the other stock commences paying again & of course will take care of Paul. If he stays here he will go into some business & can pay something at home. Let me know when you want the house fixed up & if I had better send a decorator out. Can do it as well as not.

One more word as to Paul. He has some feeling that he wants to go to Oxford for a year. I sometimes think it would be good for him to have a year in England away from his own country, but this you & he must settle & unless you consent I will not let him have the money. If you think best for him to go, I will also give you enough extra so you can go over there & stay half the time if you want—although I presume it would be better to stay in Italy or France or London, as I know that boys at school do not want to live with their parents. However he could see you every few weeks, as Europe is very small, but you would not enjoy a long stay alone.[3]

I shall always consider Paul's feelings & yours in every way, especially not to hurt them & not to urge any one to do any thing. Of course I wish Paul would sometime feel like coming & putting in an evening with me as the office is a poor place to visit, but I shall not ask it or suggest it. I only want you to know that always & at all times I shall do every thing to keep you first with Paul & I know you need never doubt his loyalty to you. Neither I nor any one else shall ever forget that you are always entitled to him first.

As Ever | Clarence.

MS: ALS, MnU-L, Darrow Collection. DATE: letterhead and the suggestion that Paul had graduated from Dartmouth College and was living in Chicago.

TO EDWARD F. DUNNE • CHICAGO • WEDNESDAY 1 NOVEMBER 1905

My dear Mr. Dunne:

In view of the present condition of the traction question I desire to resign my position as traction counsel.[4]

2. Darrow is probably referring to common stock in the National Biscuit Company (later to become Nabisco, Inc.), which, since 1899, had paid a regular quarterly dividend on its stock at a rate of four percent.
3. Paul Darrow did not go to Oxford.
4. Darrow had been appointed "special traction counsel" for Chicago by Dunne on 12 April 1905, shortly after Dunne was inaugurated as mayor. As a candidate for mayor, Dunne had pledged to seek municipal

You are well aware that I have never wished this or any other political position and that the interference with private business costs much more than any compensation received from the city. Beyond this it occasions a great deal of annoyance, which I am anxious to avoid as far as possible. Neither the loss of money nor the annoyance would affect me in any way if I felt that I could be of any further use at this time in settling the question of municipal ownership.

Since my appointment a considerable portion of my time has been taken up with quo warranto cases and the cases now pending in the United States Supreme court in reference to the construction of the franchise ordinances. The balance of the time that I have given to the city has been employed in the plans before the council and the traction committee looking toward municipal ownership of street car lines.

We are now engaged in the hearing of the quo warranto cases and the argument in the Supreme court cases is set for Jan. 2, 1906. The briefs in this case must be filed before that day and therefore within a few days of that time these actions will be disposed of, except the possibility of a brief in the Supreme court of this state on the quo warranto cases, which brief can be prepared from the investigation already made without any great expenditure of time. During the arguments of the quo warranto and preparations of the briefs it is not possible for me to attend committee meetings, and so far as any attendance by your representatives is necessary, no doubt some member of the law department could take my place.

It is now perfectly plain that no steps can be taken toward municipal ownership until after the spring election, when the whole question, together with the election of half of the city council must be submitted to the people. In the meantime I can see no occasion for spending any time on any of these matters, excepting as above indicated. If I will take any part in the election in the spring, I feel that I should be entirely free from any political position, and for that reason I desire to be released from any further duties in the matter of special counsel, excepting so far as the present hearing of the quo warranto case and the writing and preparation of the brief and argument in the Supreme court. Yours respectfully,

C. S. DARROW.

MS: TL, "Darrow Retires, Mayor Consents," *Chicago Tribune*, 8 November 1905. INSIDE ADDRESS: Hon. Edward F. Dunne, | Mayor of the City of Chicago—PLACE: no reason to doubt.

---

ownership of the city railways, and Darrow's role as special counsel was to help Dunne achieve that goal. Later, according to Ray Ginger, Darrow became "fed up" with Dunne's indecisiveness on how to achieve municipal ownership and believed that Dunne had underestimated the obstacles involved. Ray Ginger, *Altgeld's America: The Lincoln Ideal versus Changing Realities* (New York: Funk & Wagnalls, 1958), 296–97. Many Democrats had expected Dunne to accomplish some significant municipal reforms—including public ownership of the streetcar lines—and they were disappointed with his results. See Richard Allen Morton, *Justice and Humanity: Edward F. Dunne, Illinois Progressive* (Carbondale: Southern Illinois University Press, 1997), 16–49. Darrow wrote an earlier letter of resignation for Dunne, in June, but whether that letter was ever delivered is unknown. See Darrow to Dunne, 19 June 1905, TL, DLC-MSS, Darrow Papers.

TO CAROLINE LLOYD WITHINGTON • CHICAGO • THURSDAY 9 NOVEMBER 1905

DARROW, MASTERS & WILSON November 9, 1905.

My dear Madam:-

Mr. Leon Vincent is at Boulder, Colorado. I do not know where his brothers are, but you can doubtless get their address from him. I should presume that they might have some of Mr. Lloyd's letters.[5]

I remember the meeting at Tattersall's very well. Mr. Lloyd marched with us from the hall down to the Coliseum. We had a great crowd; it looked as if all of Chicago was there but if it was, most of them forgot to vote, although we got 30,000. He tried to speak, as I did, but neither of us could be heard. In fact, nothing but a trumpet or a fog horn could make any impression.[6]

The best meeting at which he spoke during that campaign was at Central Music Hall; at this meeting, he and Ex-Senator Trumbull[7] made the addresses of the evening and I had the pleasure of being Chairman.[8] I have a copy of his speech, which, like all of his, is a good one. I presume you also have it, if not, I can send it to you.

It was my good fortune to be with Mr. Lloyd during all the time of the coal strike trial and I know how much he did in that case; and, in that cause, I know what he did, not only for the men but for me personally. I presume you have pretty full data as to the coal strike case, but, if anything more is needed, I should be glad to give you all the information I can.

Mr. Carroll D. Wright[9] especially saw him very frequently during those days. His address before the Commission I presume you have seen. It was very carefully worked

5. Leo Vincent and his brothers (Cuthbert Vincent and Henry Vincent) were populist reformers who helped found the People's Party and who published a radical newspaper in Winfield, Kansas, 1886–91, called *The American Non-Conformist and Kansas Industrial Liberator*. Henry Vincent later published another populist newspaper in Chicago called *The Searchlight*. William E. Connelley, *A Standard History of Kansas and Kansans* (Chicago: Lewis Publishing, 1918), 2:1159; Robert C. McMath Jr., *American Populism: A Social History, 1877–1898* (New York: Hill & Wang, 1993), 132–34, 190; Walter T. K. Nugent, *The Tolerant Populists: Kansas Populism and Nativism* (Chicago: University of Chicago Press, 1963), 49–50.
6. Darrow is referring to a demonstration and meeting of the People's Party on 3 November 1894, at Tattersall's Hall in Chicago. Lloyd, Darrow, and many others were speakers. "Pops Wild with Joy, Great Enthusiasm Is Manifested at Tattersall's," *Chicago Tribune*, 4 November 1894.
7. Lyman Trumbull (1813–96), lawyer, judge, and politician. Trumbull practiced law in Belleville, Illinois, and served in the state legislature, 1840–41, as secretary of state for Illinois, 1841–43, and as justice of the Supreme Court of Illinois, 1848–53, before serving in the United States Senate, 1855–73. At various times, Trumbull was a Democrat and a Republican. After his third term in the Senate, he resumed the practice of law in Chicago. In his final years, he was involved with the Populists in Illinois.
8. Darrow is referring to a meeting on 6 October 1894 at the Central Music Hall in Chicago, on the opening of the People's Party's campaign in the city. Trumbull was billed for this meeting as a recent convert to the party. "To His New Allies, Lyman Trumbull Signalizes His Political Conversion," *Chicago Tribune*, 7 October 1894.
9. Carroll D. Wright (1840–1909), Union officer, lawyer, statistician, and social economist. Wright served as chief of the Massachusetts Bureau of Statistics of Labor, 1873–88, and as the first commissioner of the United States Bureau of Labor, 1885–1905. He chaired the federal commission to investigate the nature and causes of the Pullman strike in 1894, and he was commissioner and recorder of the Anthracite Coal Strike Commission, appointed by President Roosevelt in 1902.

out and was very strong. If I were publishing his life, I should work in as many of his addresses and essays as I could. He was much more brilliant in these matters than in his books. His books were so careful and laborious that one missed the brightness of his mind. I never have seen such a master of epigrams, and one with such a scathing wit. Even yet, I can hardly think of him as being dead.

With kindest regards, I am,

Yours very truly, | C. S. Darrow.

MS: TLS, WHi, Lloyd Papers. INSIDE ADDRESS: Mrs. C. L. Withington, | 2 Malcolm St., Boston.

TO JOHN MITCHELL • CHICAGO • TUESDAY 13 MARCH 1906

DARROW, MASTERS & WILSON March 13, 1906.

My dear Mr. Mitchell:

I have been called upon in the case of the Idaho Miners.[10] This is a matter which I would rather avoid if I could on account of the hard fight and the serious odds. However, I do not see how I can get out of it. I presume that they are trying to railroad these fellows because they want to get rid of them.

Could you write me in confidence whether you think organized labor would support them as far as possible in this matter? I am interested in two ways.

First, as to the public sentiment which is very necessary in a great case of this kind.

Second, that a successful fight cannot be made so far from the home without considerable resource. I will keep anything you say in strictest confidence.

How are you coming on in the strike? I still feel as I did when I write you from Washington, that these fellows cannot afford to fight.[11]

Yours very truly, | C. S. Darrow.

MS: TLS, DCU, Mitchell Papers. INSIDE ADDRESS: Jn. Mitchell, Esq., | Indianapolis, Ind.

10. In late December 1905, Frank Steunenberg, former governor of Idaho, was killed by the explosion of a bomb rigged to the gate of the fence around his house in Caldwell, Idaho. State authorities and mine owners believed that the murder had been commissioned by officials of the Western Federation of Miners in retaliation for Steunenberg calling in federal troops several years earlier to quell a violent strike by mine workers in northern Idaho. Their investigation focused in particular on three men associated with the WFM: William "Big Bill" Haywood, Charles H. Moyer, and George Pettibone. In February 1906, state authorities and their private detectives kidnapped these three men in Denver, Colorado, and took them to Idaho to stand trial. The WFM hired Darrow to represent them.

11. This might be a reference to the strike by coal miners in Lethbridge, Alberta, Canada. The strike started in early March 1906, lasted for nine months, and was sometimes violent. The United Mine Workers of America represented the strikers. Mitchell responded to Darrow with a long letter saying that he had "no doubt" that labor would support the three men and describing efforts already made to raise money. Mitchell to Darrow, 14 March 1906, Tc, DCU, Mitchell Papers.

TO BOLTON HALL • CHICAGO • TUESDAY 8 MAY 1906

DARROW, MASTERS & WILSON May 8th, 1906.

My dear Hall:

I was very glad to receive your letter with reference to the Idaho matter.[12] If you feel like going out and assisting in the trial of the case I personally should be glad to have you there and have your help, and will take the matter up with Mr. Richardson,[13] who is an attorney and is associated with me in the case.

We need a good deal of money, and it is pretty hard to get funds. I believe you could help us materially in that direction in New York, and of course we would like to have you and all the other friends take a hand in it. I think it would be worth while for you to be connected with the case on account of your interest in these matters, and although I have the impression that you do not like court trials, if you would care to do it, nothing would give me more pleasure than to have you there.

Are you going to spend the summer in the Catskills? If anything happens that this case is not reached until fall, I have been considering going there for a few weeks.

With kind regards I am,

Yours very truly, | C. S. Darrow

MS: TLS, NN, Hall Papers, Box 1. INSIDE ADDRESS: Bolton Hall, Esq., | 58 Pine st., New York, N.Y.

TO RUBY DARROW • WASHINGTON, D.C. • MONDAY 8 OCTOBER 1906

THE NEW WILLARD Oct 8th

Dearest Ruben

Here I am at the place where we had such a happy time & I am about to go to bed. How I wish you were here. If you were we would sleep late in the morning & order a breakfast to be served in our room,

Virginia ham, eggs, potatoes, coffee. Any how I wish you were here my dear dear girl—

Paul came with me which is next best—but only next best. We have been to the theater & he is taking a bath. My case is set for tomorrow but I am not sure it will

12. Hall had written Darrow a short note offering to help in the case against Haywood, Moyer, and Pettibone: "If there is anything I can do about the Idaho outrage on the Colo. miners I would be glad to do it. I feel strongly about that matter. | If there is not, this needs no answer." Hall to Darrow, 3 May 1906, ALS, MnU-L, Darrow Collection.
13. Edmund F. Richardson.

be reached then, but hope it won't be long for I am anxious to get back to Colorado & you.[14]

With love & kisses to you always | Clarence

MS: ALS, MnU-L, Darrow Collection. ENVELOPE ADDRESS: Mrs. C. S. Darrow | Manitou | Colorado. POSTMARK: Washington, D.C., 9 October 1906.

TO CHARLES MOYER, WILLIAM HAYWOOD, AND GEORGE PETTIBONE • CHICAGO • MONDAY 5 NOVEMBER 1906

DARROW, MASTERS & WILSON November 5th, 1906.

Dear friends:

Enclosed find copy of letter which I have just sent to Mr. Richardson.[15] You may write him about it if you wish, or you may write me about it if you prefer. If you ask me to I will see that Mr. Dickson is discharged, although I deem it both unfair and unwise. If you prefer you may indicate to Mr. Richardson that he may do it, or, as I have stated in my letter, he may do it on his own account. But whatever you or he may conclude to do in this matter I want to assure you that it would take much more than this, or more than anything that I can conceive,—except your own suggestion—to cause me to do anything that would in any way injure the case, or imperil your safety. None of us have any right to consider anything else at this time.

With best wishes, believe me, | Your friend,

MS: TLc, MnU-L, Darrow Collection. INSIDE ADDRESS: Messrs. Moyer, Haywood & Pettibone, | Boise, Idaho.

TO RUBY DARROW • CHICAGO • THURSDAY 8 NOVEMBER 1906

DARROW & MASTERS Thursday

Dearest Ruben

I am propped up in bed—all alone—in the Windsor Clifton. This is the third day I have been here but expect to be out tomorrow. I have been trying hard since I left you to side step an attack of rheumatism but I got it—some & for three days it kept me in bed but am so much better today that I am sure tomorrow I can get out & will be almost

14. Darrow and other defense attorneys had sought writs of habeas corpus on behalf of Haywood, Moyer, and Pettibone from state and federal courts in Idaho. The petitions were denied by the lower courts, and the United States Supreme Court heard arguments in the matter on 10 and 11 October 1906. Darrow and Edmund Richardson argued in favor of the petitions. On 3 December 1906, the Supreme Court affirmed the lower courts. *Pettibone v. Nichols,* 203 U.S. 192 (1906); *Moyer v. Nichols,* 203 U.S. 221 (1906).

15. Darrow and Edmund Richardson had a contentious relationship and bitter disagreements as co-counsel. On this occasion, they were having a disagreement about whether an investigator (George Dickson) should remain on the case or be let go. See Richardson to Darrow, 1 November 1906, TLS, MnU-L, Darrow Collection; Darrow to Richardson, 5 November 1906, TLc, MnU-L, Darrow Collection.

as good as new in a week or ten days. Have missed you all the time but still I guess it was best for what I do & how would I feel if you were lying here in bed with me with your legs & arms & every thing right up by me? You can see yourself Ruben what would happen & I simply couldn't so it has been just as well to have you a thousand miles away for you don't do me any harm except when I get to thinking to minutely & vividly about you—I try to just think of your noble soul & that doesn't hurt me—just about as good as not thinking. But my dear sweet luscious girl one of these days I won't do a thing to you. Am really almost ashamed to write this way about my wife & to my wife. I consider it a real scandal & still I want you so bad. I suppose you are rushing through this for me to say just when now whether I am all right or not. I am going to see you next week (probably near the last). If I do not come there will have you come here if you will. Tomorrow I will send over for the fare so you can have it ready. The trouble is this place is no good for you, & I don't care to go any where else for a short time. Still I will if necessary. Any how I am going to have you & the way looks now I don't believe I will let you leave me again for a long while. I am thinking that I would rather get a place, a house or flat & fix it up as nice as we can & have good things to eat & some of our friends—and loafing & sleeping with & now & then a dinner and theater down town than to go to Europe after the blooming case is done.

As to the case I have not heard—court convenes in Wallace on Nov. 9th tomorrow that may or may not come soon, but at any event I ought to be in Colorado getting things ready.[16] And I should have been there before if I had been well. Still I have been very busy here. There were so many things in the office to attend to & then there was Paul's business too[17] & I have had several cases since I came back. Got one man off for murder &c &c. Saw Fred[18] for a few minutes the other day. He is looking fine & feeling well. Have seen George[19] several times & he called me up yesterday. Well dearest sweet heart—have a good time; you won't have a chance to be alone long. Still be sure & keep you L.C. for I am—

Ever & ever | C.S.D.

MS: ALS, MnU-L, Darrow Collection. ENVELOPE ADDRESS: Mrs. C. S. Darrow | Denver | Colorado | Savoy Hotel. FIRST POSTMARK: Chicago, 8 November 1906. SECOND POSTMARK: Denver, 10 November 1906.

TO RUBY DARROW • CHICAGO • FRIDAY 9 NOVEMBER 1906

DARROW & MASTERS Friday Evening

Dearest Ruben

Am still at Windsor Clifton & have not been out since Monday. Could have gone today but thought I would wait one more. Don't worry about me for I am all right & will be OK. P.D.Q.

16. Haywood's trial did not begin until 9 May 1907.
17. This is probably a reference to the fact that around this time Darrow was purchasing a gas plant in Greeley, Colorado. Paul eventually moved to Greeley and operated that business until 1928.
18. Frederick Hamerstrom.
19. George Hamerstrom.

On Monday I will return your pass. Have not yet had a chance to get it. I think I will send for you to come next week as it begins to look as if I might not go back then, possibly not at all.

Richardson & I are having some disagreement about the case & if the fellows will let me I shall leave it.[20] Any how I shall not stop in and be told what to do by him. If he or Mrs. R. are giving you any attention there don't let it make the least bit of difference & don't let him know that any thing has been said to you. If not I would not bother to look them up.

In one way I would be awfully glad to be out of it. I hate the work & the responsibility & the discomfort of it all, and if I am out we can get a flat right off & go to house keeping which would seem to me the happiest thing in the world. I have learned to appreciate the home I had & you. I am sorry for the men & would like to help them if I could but I do dread to go and I am awfully fearful of the result. We are in the hands of unfriendly people.

I have not heard from you since you got to Denver & have been anxiously looking for a letter every day.

Any how dearest I love you & want to see you.

Clarence.

MS: ALS, MnU-L, Darrow Collection. ENVELOPE ADDRESS: Mrs. C. S. Darrow | Denver | Colorado | Savoy Hotel. FIRST POSTMARK: Chicago, 9 November 1906. SECOND POSTMARK: Denver, 10 November 1906.

TO BRAND WHITLOCK • CHICAGO • MONDAY 8 APRIL 1907

DARROW, MASTERS & WILSON April 8th, 1907.

My dear Whitlock:

I got your book on Saturday and read it half through yesterday, and will finish it in a day or two.[21] Will write Bobbs-Merril about it. It is a great book. It has been a long time since I read anything that did me as much good. I only hope it will have a big sale. You can see your finish as a lawyer, and I hope that you will not long need to be bothered with your profession.

I wish we might get together some where this summer after my Idaho case is over. Have you any vacation plans for the summer?

I note what you say about Dunne.[22] You have evidently been deceived by those radicals who have no judgment. Nothing has made me so happy in politics in recent years as the

20. A few days later, Darrow thought he was out of the case. See Darrow to Ruby Darrow, 13 November 1906 (mistakenly labeled "Wednesday"), ALS, MnU-L, Darrow Collection ("Dearest Ruben | It looks as if I was out of the case & you can come back Saturday or Sunday bringing everything with you, if you are ready. Wire me the train. I am dying to see you—almost— | Ever with love | *Clarence.*").

21. Darrow is likely referring to Whitlock's *The Turn of the Balance* (Indianapolis: Bobbs-Merrill, 1907), a novel published in March 1907.

22. Darrow might be referring to a letter from Whitlock when he says, "I note what you say about Dunne," but no letter was found. Edward F. Dunne was defeated on 2 April 1907 in the Chicago mayoral election by Republican Fred Busse (1866–1914) after serving one two-year term.

defeat of Dunne. He is a man without brains, back-bone or guts. He is unfaithful to every person and every thing. He is the nearest to nothing of any man that I ever knew, and while municipal ownership and progressive ideas lost something in his election, they have lost nothing in his defeat. Every body who knows Dunne knows that this is true, but still there are some people who have been eating pie at the expense of the city, and others who have received offices who are not yet ready to admit it. Radical ideas could never be benefitted by any such man as Dunne in public places. And I am glad we are rid of him and rid of him forever.

I am going back to Idaho the last of this week to begin the fight of my life in the Moyer-Hayward case.[23] No one can tell how it will come out, but it will surely be interesting. I hope I may see you this summer, some time at least.

With best wishes to yourself, and regards to Mrs. Whitlock, I am,

Your friend, | C. S. D. | C. S. Darrow.

MS: TLS, DLC-MSS, Whitlock Papers. INSIDE ADDRESS: Hon. Brand Whitlock, | Mayor of Toledo, | Toledo, O.

TO WILLIAM BORAH • EN ROUTE TO CHICAGO • FRIDAY 9 AUGUST 1907

THE COLORADO SPECIAL August 9th

Hon W. Borah

My Dear Senator

Am just leaving Denver. Senator Patterson[24] was away at Grand Lake, Colo. & I could not see him. Every one at the office is your friend & so is Patterson.

I expect to be back in Denver in two weeks & will see him then if you wish even if I have to go to Grand Lake. If you want me to do any special thing in Chicago or the east

23. Darrow had recently returned to Chicago from Wallace, Idaho, where he defended Stephen W. Adams (b. 1867), an itinerant miner and union member, on the charge of murdering a property claim jumper. The trial of Adams ended with a hung jury. Idaho authorities had hoped to use a conviction of Adams to persuade him to reaffirm his earlier confession that he had been hired by Haywood and others to kill Steunenberg. Adams's confession would have provided corroboration for the confession of Harry Orchard (1866–1954), the central witness for the prosecution. Orchard—who had been arrested shortly after the murder of Steunenberg—signed a confession stating that Haywood and others had hired him to kill Steunenberg. Darrow was returning to Idaho "to begin the fight of [his] life" in defending Haywood, whose trial was scheduled to begin on 9 May 1907.
24. Thomas Patterson (1839–1916), United States senator from Colorado, 1901–6, and owner of the *Rocky Mountain News* and the *Denver Times*. During the trial of Haywood, a sealed federal indictment was brought against Borah and many others by a grand jury in Boise, Idaho, charging Borah and the others with conspiracy to defraud the federal government in connection with the sale of land to timber companies. The indictment might have been politically motivated (he was acquitted of the charges following a trial in the fall of 1907). Borah had been elected to the United States Senate by the Idaho legislature in January 1907 and he was to take his seat in December. The indictment threatened his political future and Borah, according to a biographer, "made an effort to rally support from every quarter possible." Marian C. McKenna, *Borah* (Ann Arbor: University of Michigan Press, 1961), 71. Darrow was likely trying to contact Patterson as part of this effort.

wire or write to Ashland Blk Chicago as soon as possible, as you are making me come back early.

That Ass formerly my associate has been trying to make more trouble, but I think he is out of it.[25] If you can consistently I wish you would have the Boise papers treat me fairly in the matter. I am sure both you & they can work with me the best & especially the next time, if there is any next.

Don't fail to let me know if there is anything I can possibly do. If I cannot do it I won't try. Ever with best wishes

Your friend | C. S. Darrow.

MS: ALS, IdHi, Borah Papers. DATE: implied reference to Richardson and to going back to Idaho as well as other letters.

TO HUGO MÜNSTERBERG • CHICAGO • FRIDAY 16 AUGUST 1907

DARROW, MASTERS & WILSON August 16 1907

My dear Sir:—

Your letter to Boise was duly received but I did not have a chance to answer at that time.[26] I don't know that I understand the letter. I don't know whether you mean to say in your letter that your final article or report was going to be favorable to Haywood or not. Neither do I know whether I care. As a scientific man I think that you cannot afford to put yourself in such position as you have already placed yourself in by your statements to the press. You came to Boise at the request of Mr. McClure. Mr. McClure had already published or had in his possession the autobiography of Harry Orchard.[27] It is entirely possible that you

25. Darrow is referring to Edmund Richardson.
26. Münsterberg had recently traveled to Idaho for the trial of Haywood at the request of S. S. McClure (1857–1949), editor and publisher of the popular *McClure's Magazine.* McClure—who later said that he was acting on the suggestion of Darrow himself—wanted an eminent psychologist to conduct an examination of Harry Orchard. Münsterberg observed Orchard on the witness stand and met Orchard in his jail cell, where he subjected Orchard to a battery of tests to determine if his confession was truthful, including word-association tests and observations about Orchard's physical appearance (Münsterberg later stated that Orchard had "the profile of a murderer"). Back in Boston, Münsterberg—who had originally intended to keep his "scientific" conclusions to himself until after the trial—allowed two interviews with newspapers that later reported Münsterberg's firm conclusion that Orchard had been telling the truth in his confession. These newspaper stories spread across the country and Münsterberg immediately came in for a barrage of criticism; Darrow issued a statement saying that Münsterberg's opinion was no more than a testimonial bought by a magazine publisher. Darrow maintained, among other things, that Münsterberg had had no opportunity to hear Orchard testify and that Münsterberg had been paid for his efforts by McClure. See J. Anthony Lukas, *Big Trouble: A Murder in a Small Western Town Sets off a Struggle for the Soul of America* (New York: Simon & Schuster, 1997), 594–601. Münsterberg wrote Darrow complaining that Darrow had treated him unfairly in the press by misrepresenting the facts relating to his work. See Münsterberg to Darrow, 14 July 1907, AL, MB, Münsterberg Papers.
27. Orchard, who confessed to a total of some eighteen murders—including Steunenberg's—had a sensational story to tell. As early as April 1907, McClure became interested in publishing an autobiographical essay that Orchard had written, and he assigned one of his reporters, George Kibbe Turner (1869–1952), to polish and edit the work. Lukas, *Big Trouble,* 591–92. The "autobiography" was eventually published in five parts in *McClure's Magazine*: "The Confession and Autobiography of Harry Orchard," *McClure's Magazine,* July 1907, 296–306; August 1907, 367–79; September 1907, 507–23; October 1907, 658–72; November 1907, 113–29.

did not intend to boom that article or be used by McClure, but the inference that it was done wittingly or unwittingly will always remain if you proceed further in this matter.

So far as your statements of observing Orchard in Court, they are not true. Orchard was on the stand about eight days. He was recalled one day when you were there to ask a few impeaching questions; at that time he was not on the stand over thirty minutes and the questions were unimportant and could in no way test him, and the record will show that my statement is true.

You consorted and associated with the enemies of the defense and the friends of Orchard and the prosecution. You got no information whatever from us and made no investigation of our witnesses or our clients, and in my humble opinion you are in no more position to give any intelligent judgment upon the truthfulness of Orchard's story than the man in the moon, and whatever you say upon this question does not interest me especially, excepting to give my view that you are saying it at your own risk of your reputation and whatever there may be in the science you profess to serve.

If you could tell by the measurements of Orchard's head whether he was an honest man or not it might have been well to take some measurements of our witnesses and see whether they were liars too.

I did not seek any controversy with you upon this question and am not anxious to have any now, but if any article is published in reference to it I shall feel as if I ought to publish my views upon it the same as I did before, and in my former interview the only injustice I could possibly have done you was to say that you were employed by McClure. This may not have been true. It may have been simply that you were used by him, but you were called by him to my certain knowledge, and you went at the matter in the same way he did, in a one-sided and partial manner.

Yours very truly, | C. S. Darrow.

MS: TLS, MB, Münsterberg Papers. INSIDE ADDRESS: Prof. Hugo Minsterberg, | Clifton, Mass.

TO JAMES HAWLEY • SAN FRANCISCO • WEDNESDAY 23 OCTOBER 1907

HOTEL ST. FRANCIS | SAN FRANCISCO Oct 23rd

My Dear Mr. Hawley

A consultation of Drs. have decided this morning that I must have an operation called a "mastoid" which is cutting into the skull back of the ear. It will be done tomorrow. They say it will take three or four weeks before I can go to work.[28]

28. On 29 July 1907, following a nearly two-month trial, the jury found Haywood not guilty. After Haywood was acquitted, prosecutors were going to try a second time to convict Steve Adams on the charge of murdering a property claim jumper in northern Idaho. Their object, as with the first trial, was to force Adams to corroborate Harry Orchard's testimony in the cases now remaining against Moyer and Pettibone. Darrow planned to defend Adams again, but when he returned to Boise from Chicago he suffered the flu and developed a severe infection in his left ear.

Now I feel that I must have Adams case put over until I am able to go into it, unless he voluntarily releases me, which I don't believe he will. The terms of court up there may make it necessary to let it go to Jan. & if you people are insisting on trying Adams first it would mean Pettibone must go beyond that. There is no alternative with me & if my fellows wish to have me in the case and these are your conditions they must accept. If they are willing to try them without me I will feel relieved, but if they will accept the time that the Court will fix up north, I want you to help me continue it until I am able to go. I would go now if I could be moved. As to Pettibone's case our fellows will have to agree to what you want within reason on this.

Thanking you in advance.[29]

I am truly yours, | C. S. Darrow.

MS: ALS, IdHi, Hawley Papers, Box 37. DATE: reference to "mastoid" and Adams and Pettibone cases.

TO EUGENE V. DEBS • RATHDRUM, IDAHO • NOVEMBER 1907

HOTEL ST. FRANCIS | SAN FRANCISCO Rathdrum | Idaho

My Dear Debbs,

Your nice letter came to hand some time ago & I assure you that I appreciate it and prize it. You are one who has never disappointed me & I know never will. I feel that I know you & you are always the same. I appreciate all you have done & all you have tried to do & wanted to do. I don't know as either of us are entitled to any sympathy for what we have lost for our convictions. We have likewise gained much & perhaps are better off than the rest.

I am just now trying the Adams case and am very hopeful about it.[30] I shall try to go back through Girard & meet you all & talk business to you about my books.[31]

How about the pamphlet of the Haywood argument? It ought to be out & I am getting a little impatient at the delay. If it is not coming right away I wish you

29. Darrow was not able to delay Adams's trial and he did not have an operation. Instead, as he describes it in some detail in his autobiography, he traveled to Rathdrum, Idaho, to defend Adams. *Story*, 157–63. (Prosecutors, according to Darrow, changed the venue of Adams's second trial to Rathdrum—where there were "few miners or laboring men"—because "[t]hey did not want to risk another trial [of Adams] in Wallace." Ibid., 157.) In Rathdrum, where there was no hospital or nurse, Ruby took responsibility for regularly irrigating Darrow's ear in the evening, after trial, and injecting Darrow with codeine when the pain became too severe ("When my memory roams over the West I try to skip Rathdrum. It was one continuous orgy of pain."). Ibid., 160. In his autobiography, Darrow says that he traveled to San Francisco *after* the Adams trial for consultation with Dr. Kaspar Pischel (1862–1953), who "sent [him] to the St. Francis Hotel and put [him] under his observation and treatment for a week." Ibid., 163. The stationery of this and the next letter suggest that Darrow might have remembered the order of events and other details incorrectly; his consultation with Dr. Pischel and stay at the St. Francis Hotel probably preceded Adams's trial.
30. The second trial of Steve Adams, like the first one, ended in a hung jury. Prosecutors gave up trying to convict Adams, and Adams never testified for the state against Pettibone.
31. Debs was part of the editorial staff of the *Appeal to Reason*, and Darrow might have been considering republishing some of his books and pamphlets.

would send me the proof as I never have had the full proof—but if it is coming quickly let it go.

I enclose some names to which please send copies.

Always with love & devotion

Your friend | Clarence S. Darrow.

MS: ALS, InTI, Debs Papers. DATE: "1907" appended.

TO EDGAR LEE MASTERS • BOISE, IDAHO • FRIDAY 29 NOVEMBER 1907

THE | IDAN-HA | BOISE, | IDAHO. Nov 29th

Dear Ed,

Your letter came to hand at Rathdrum just as I was finishing the Steve Adams case. Am now in Pettibone case which will last until Jan. Then I think I will be through.[32] I could see no way to stop—there was none. As to money I think $100 per day is all I could earn there, & while I know that it hurts the business to be away still I have been earning money. I am inclined to believe that if you look the books over you will find that the amount of money I have put in from business I got & did has more than paid what I took out, all the expenses of the office & one at least of Frank or Cy.[33] I want to be fair about this matter & I regret my absence & still I feel as if the individual members have had good dividends ever since I left. I am sure both Cy & Frank have had twice as much as they ever got any where else, & at least twice as much as they could get any where else. I don't know what you were earning before but I trust the last year has paid fairly well. As to immediate matters when I was back in August I got in a fee of 2,750. This was divided in Oct. This of course I got myself in Oct. As I recall it you drew about 1,000, Cy & Frank 500 each—& 500 was credited on my indebtedness. I don't think so much should have been drawn out if the office is hard up. Certainly Frank or Cy would have to work for $150 a month if thrown on their own resources & Frank would be very lucky to get that. Why should they draw so much if money is scarce. I think you ought to go to N.Y. & see Hearst if the bill is crawling up so fast. It is perhaps best to keep the work but some arrangement should be made for pay.

I will write Paul not to ask for money & will send him what I can get here. You know how we have been pressed & I suppose he has felt he could not help it.

32. The trial against Pettibone started almost immediately after the second trial of Adams, and ended with an acquittal in January 1908. After the trial, the charges against Moyer were dropped. Darrow was only able to stay in the trial of Pettibone until the prosecutors had finished presenting their evidence. The pain from his ear infection had become unbearable and he could no longer stand in the courtroom. On the advice of doctors, he went to Los Angeles to see some specialists, including the well-known John Randolph Haynes (1853–1937), who became a friend of Darrow's and who took Darrow into his home while Darrow was in Los Angeles. Eventually Darrow was operated on for mastoiditis, which left him deaf or near deaf in his left ear for the rest of his life. *Story*, 168–71.

33. Francis S. Wilson and Cyrus Simon.

I do not mean by this to write any way except in the most sympathetic & kindly spirit. I would not give up our association in the office for money. It is worth much more than that. Still unless I can keep for the present, what I can get ~~there~~ here, I will stand to loose all I have, & the necessities are such that if the firm can not get along on the amount received there I will be obliged to pull out for I ~~must~~ can not at any time of life afford to loose what I have. If you can pull it along there until I am back I believe we can put it on its feet all right & can soon adjust any differences for overdrafts &c. You might talk with the other fellows about it & I want to assure them & you that I would feel very badly if it was necessary to quit the game, but I am absolutely obliged to hold what I get here until the pinch is over. However don't send any to Paul & I will write him not to ask. I am sure you will understand this & know too well how deep is my feeling of regard & love for all of you to doubt but what I would do the very best I can. I believe I can be back by Jan 1st.

Ever Your friend | C. S. Darrow.

MS: ALS, TxU-Hu, Masters Collection. DATE: reference to Adams and Pettibone cases.

TO RUBY DARROW • JARDINE, MONTANA • TUESDAY 21 JULY 1908

KIMBERLY MONTANA GOLD MINING COMPANY July 21/1908

Dearest Ruben

You do not know how sorry I am that you are not here to enjoy this scenery.[34] It is a very beautiful place and I have all the "Comforts of Home"—pretty near—good meals, good bed, type-writer with high heeled shoes, but even under these circumstances I think of you pretty much of the time: I can't help it.

D.

MS: TLS, MnU-L, Darrow Collection. ENVELOPE ADDRESS: Mrs. C. S. Darrow | 218—60th Street, | Chicago, | Ills. POSTMARK: illegible.

TO BRAND WHITLOCK • CHICAGO • FRIDAY 23 APRIL 1909

DARROW, MASTERS & WILSON April 23, 1909.

My Dear Whitlock:—

Since I saw you in Toledo I have been thinking over the question of your being a candidate for another term as Mayor of Toledo, and although it is none of my business, I feel as if I ought to write you about it.[35] You know about how much interest I have always had in you and your work, and this is the only excuse I have to offer. It may have been all right

34. Darrow was in Montana on business.
35. Later in the year, Whitlock ran for reelection as mayor of Toledo.

for you to be Mayor up to this time, but I want to say frankly that I think you are wasting your life to keep the job any longer. You can accomplish nothing specific in this place. You will get a street railway fight on your hands if you continue another term, and you will be beaten.

A lot of people who do not know, will tell you that you are the Moses who will lead the people to Municipal Ownership, but if you could lead they will not follow. You have only to witness the fate of Tom Johnson,[36] who is far better equipped for this job than you can possibly be. If you quit now you quit with a fair record; if you stay, you will go out of the office in the end discredited, and with little following. If you were to run again and enter this battle for Municipal Ownership you will not live long enough to see it finished, even should you be successful. You will waste your life in a vain effort to accomplish something that the people are not ready for, and would not do any good if you succeeded.

You know I have always thought that your writing was worthwhile. This is your long-suit; anything else is a side line, which is only valuable for recreation, the same as running an automobile. You are now in a position where you can do more in the way of writing than you ever could, where you can be heard by the people, or where you can make a living out of it, which is perhaps more to the point. People have got to read, and perhaps even think and study before they will be able to accomplish anything along the lines in which we are interested. If you stay where you are you must give up your writing; you may now and then write something which will be of some value, but your whole time will be devoted to politics, which is a useless, thankless task. If you quit the job you can go where you please, and do as you please and give all your time to literature, which is the thing you are most fitted for.

If I did not feel this so clearly and so deeply, I would not take the responsibility of advising you because it is not generally worth while to do that. Anyhow, I would quit the job at the earliest possible moment, and before it is too late to inform your friends that flattery, etc., etc., have no effect on you, and that they had better look around for some other man who likes to follow rainbows.

Ever with best wishes,

Your friend, | Clarence Darrow.

MS: TLS, NNC, Nevins Papers.

36. Tom L. Johnson (1854–1911), inventor, businessman, congressman, and mayor of Cleveland, Ohio. As mayor of Cleveland, 1901–9, Johnson, a Democrat, was well known for his municipal reforms and fights with street-railway interests, but he never accomplished his goal of municipal ownership of the street railways. He served eight consecutive terms as mayor, losing the election in November 1908 to a Republican, in part because of voter dissatisfaction with some of his reforms and continuing disputes with street-railway interests.

TO LILLIAN (ANDERSON) DARROW • CHICAGO • MONDAY 14 JUNE 1909

DARROW, MASTERS & WILSON June 14

Dear Lil

Well I suppose it is all over. You got a lot of advertising here.[37] They raked up some of Lilian Russell's old pictures & published them for you. They looked pretty well & said you were a graduate of Vassar.[38] Paul's pictures were taken when he was about ten years old, so it looked like a case of cradle snatching on your part. Well if you don't get enough to eat send word to me & I will send you the money to come home & you can tend the telephone—

With love | C. S. Darrow

MS: ALS, Darrow Family. DATE: appended and reference to marriage.

TO VICTOR BERGER • CHICAGO • FRIDAY 6 AUGUST 1909

DARROW, MASTERS & WILSON August 6, 1909.

My dear Berger:

I would like to help your damn preacher if I could but I am so financially involved at present that I cannot do any more than I am doing; I hope sometime I can do more.[39] However, people sometimes pay money to hear me talk. If your crowd could get up a meeting any time after October 1st, I would come to La Cross, pay my own expenses and give them the money. I might talk on the "Open Shop" or almost any old thing. If there are not enough people to pay twenty-five or fifty cents a head to look at me and hear me talk, they aren't yet ready for Socialism.

Your Friend, | Clarence Darrow.

MS: TLS, WHi, Berger Papers. INSIDE ADDRESS: Mr. Victor Berger, | Milwaukee, Wis.

37. On 10 June 1909, Paul Darrow married Lillian Anderson in Denver, Colorado. Lillian had worked as a telephone receptionist in Darrow's law office. Their marriage was written up in at least one Chicago newspaper, with pictures of Lillian and Paul. See Plate 20 of the illustrations.
38. Darrow often told Lillian Anderson that she looked like Lillian Russell (1861–1922), the American singer and actress. Lillian Anderson did not attend Vassar. Interview with Mary Darrow Simonson, Wheaton, Illinois, 29 July 1995.
39. The identity of the "damn preacher" is unknown. It might have been Winfield Gaylord (1870–1943), a Congregational and Methodist minister who served as a socialist in the Wisconsin Senate, 1909–1913, and ran unsuccessfully for Congress several times. It also might have been Carl D. Thompson (1870–1949), a Congregational minister who served as a socialist in the Wisconsin Assembly, 1907–1909. Both were acquainted with Berger. See Victor Berger to Meta Berger, 30 June 1912, in *The Family Letters of Victor and Meta Berger*, ed. Michael E. Stevens (Madison: State Historical Society of Wisconsin, 1995), 140–42. Michael E. Stevens, personal communication, Madison, Wisconsin, June 1996.

TO BRAND WHITLOCK • CHICAGO • WEDNESDAY 22 DECEMBER 1909

DARROW, MASTERS & WILSON Dec. 22d.

Dear Brand

Thanks for your letter. I wonder if there would not be a chance for me to come down & talk on "Crime" or something so I could see you. I am getting very lonesome.

I have a friend who is in a clerical position with one of the big religious, prohibition reform organizations. A while ago I received a letter from her saying, "I feel like a horse thief I have just been sending out a lot of letters against dear Brand Whitlock. They are gathering all kinds of data to show that the criminals paroled &c. went back to their old life." I don't care much about these religious crooks & I know you don't—still I hoped you would be beaten & get through with it, although I did want to see one good man stop before he was obliged to quit the fool game of politics.[40] I was at Haverhill Mass. the other day. My friend Rev. M. L. Powers[41] (who is not reverend enough to trust) says you promised to talk for him. I told him I would write you to go. He is a bully fellow & I hope you can go. But I don't care for all this. When will I see you again.

Ever your friend | Clarence Darrow.

Love to Mrs W.[42]

MS: ALS, NNC, Nevins Papers. DATE: Whitlock's reply, letterhead, and Darrow's whereabouts in December of other years in which Whitlock was reelected.

40. Whitlock had just won the third of four consecutive terms as mayor of Toledo.
41. Darrow's friend was Levi Moore Powers.
42. In Whitlock's reply to Darrow's letter, Whitlock, among other things, encouraged Darrow to come to Toledo and give a speech: "I want you to come down here soon and I shall take up the question of having a speech from you. I should like to hear you and so would several thousand other persons in this town. But speech or not, I want you here." Whitlock to Darrow, 3 January 1910, in *The Letters of Brand Whitlock*, ed. Allan Nevins (New York: D. Appleton-Century, 1936), 123–24.

PLATE 1

Darrow's boyhood home in Kinsman, Ohio—an octagon-shaped house that was built in the 1840s or 1850s.

PLATE 2

Ammirus Darrow, Clarence Darrow's father, ca. 1860s. A well-educated and bookish man, Ammirus was active in the abolitionist movement in Ohio. He was a farmer and later a furniture maker by trade. According to an obituary written by his oldest son, Everett, Ammirus "stood consistently for freedom from the beginning of his career to the end—free trade, free thought, free speech, free men."

PLATE 3

Emily (Eddy) Darrow, Clarence Darrow's mother, ca. 1860s. She died when Darrow was fifteen years old. According to surviving descriptions of her, she was a caring mother and an industrious and intelligent woman who took an active interest in political matters. (Photo: AIP Emilio Segre Visual Archives, Darrow Collection)

PLATE 4

Darrow as a young man, probably in Ohio, ca. 1880.

PLATE 5
Three generations of Darrows: Ammirus, Paul, and Clarence, ca. 1887. (Photo: AIP Emilio Segre Visual Archives, Darrow Collection)

PLATE 6

Jessie, Paul, and Clarence, in what might have been the last studio portrait of them together before Clarence and Jessie divorced, ca. 1893.

PLATE 7

Ruby Hamerstrom, when she was approximately thirty years old, ca. 1900. This photograph was published by newspapers when she married Darrow in 1903.

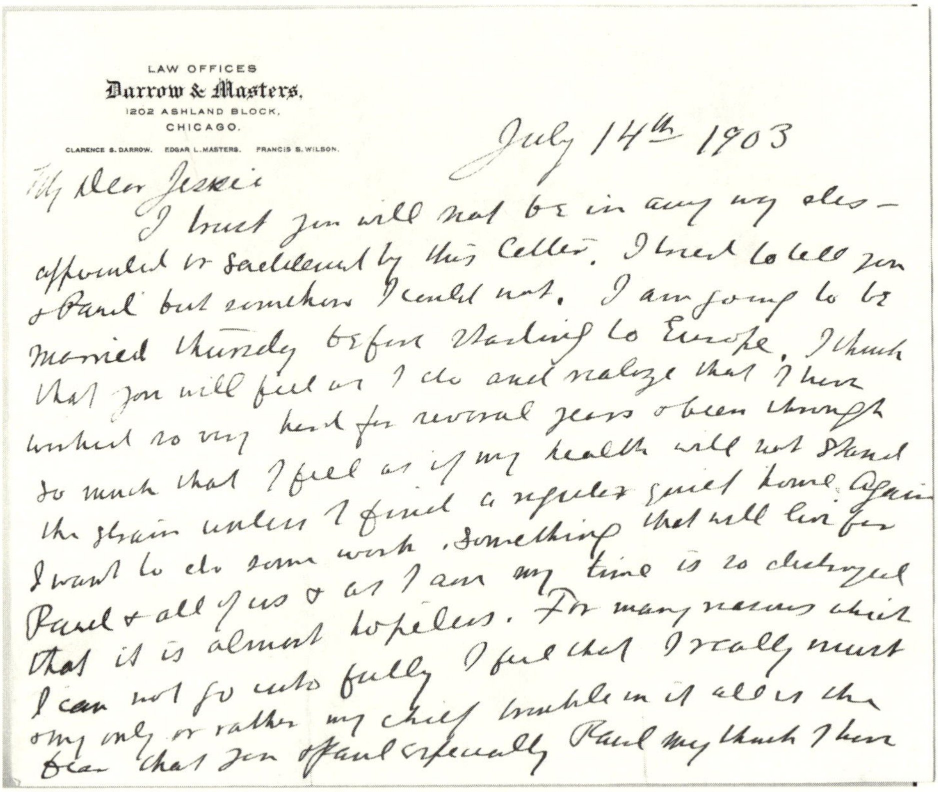

LAW OFFICES
Darrow & Masters,
1202 ASHLAND BLOCK,
CHICAGO.
CLARENCE S. DARROW. EDGAR L. MASTERS. FRANCIS S. WILSON.

July 14th 1903

My Dear Jessie
I trust you will not be in any way dis-
appointed or saddened by this letter. I tried to tell you
& Paul but somehow I could not. I am going to be
married Thursday before starting to Europe. I think
that you will feel as I do and realize that I have
worked so very hard for several years & been through
so much that I feel as if my health will not stand
the strain unless I find a regular quiet home. Again
I want to do some work, something that will live for
Paul & all of us & as I am my time is so destroyed
that it is almost hopeless. For many reasons which
I can not go into fully I feel that I really must
The only or rather my chief trouble in it all is the
fear that you & Paul especially Paul may think I have

PLATE 8

The first page of Darrow's letter to his first wife, Jessie, on the eve of his marriage to Ruby, written on the stationery of the Darrow & Masters law firm, 14 July 1903.

PLATE 9

George Schilling, a socialist, single-tax advocate, and one of Darrow's earliest friends in Chicago, ca. 1910s. (Photo: Labadie Collection, University of Michigan)

PLATE 10

Eugene Debs, 1912. Debs and Darrow had a long friendship, beginning in 1894–95, when Darrow represented Debs after he was accused of violating an injunction arising out of the Pullman strike and charged with conspiring to obstruct the mail. (Photo: Library of Congress, Prints & Photographs Division, reproduction no. LC-DIG-hec-01584)

PLATE 11

Henry Demarest Lloyd, 1903, the year Lloyd and Darrow represented striking anthracite miners in Pennsylvania. (Photo: Library of Congress, Prints & Photographs Division, reproduction no. LC-USZ62–103845)

PLATE 12

John Mitchell, ca. 1910s. Mitchell was president of the United Mine Workers of America. Darrow represented the UMWA in the arbitration hearing for striking anthracite miners in Pennsylvania in 1902–3. (Photo: Library of Congress, Prints & Photographs Division, reproduction no. LC-DIG-ggbain-18153)

PLATE 13

Darrow in a formal portrait in Chicago that was often used in newspapers and publicity materials, ca. 1903. This copy was inscribed on the back to the anarchist and labor organizer Joseph Labadie: "To my friend, Jos. A. Labadie from Clarence Darrow." (Photo: Labadie Collection, University of Michigan)

PLATE 14

Lawyers in the extradition hearing for Christian Rudovitz, 1908: Darrow is on the far right and Peter Sissman—who became Darrow's law partner several years later—is in the middle (third from the right). (Photo: DN-0006760, *Chicago Daily News* negatives collection, Chicago History Museum)

PLATE 15
Richard Pettigrew, ca. 1913. Pettigrew, who served in the United States Senate, was considered a radical by many of his fellow Republicans: he advocated the single tax, unlimited silver coinage, government ownership of railroads and telegraph lines, and anti-imperialism. (Photo: Library of Congress, Prints & Photographs Division, reproduction no. LC-DIG-ggbain-05072)

PLATE 16
The poet and lawyer Edgar Lee Masters, ca. 1908. Darrow had one of his longest law partnerships with Masters. In his 1936 autobiography, Masters led his readers to believe that he had always despised or distrusted Darrow. But his earlier writings and other evidence suggest that Masters held Darrow in very high esteem during some periods of their relationship

PLATE 17

Darrow's clients in the Steunenberg murder trials in Idaho: George A. Pettibone, William D. Haywood, and Charles H. Moyer, 1907. (Photo: Library of Congress, Prints & Photographs Division, reproduction no. LC-USZ62–59678)

PLATE 18

Mary Field Parton, ca. 1915 (Photo: Margaret Parton Papers, Special Collections and University Archives, University of Oregon Libraries)

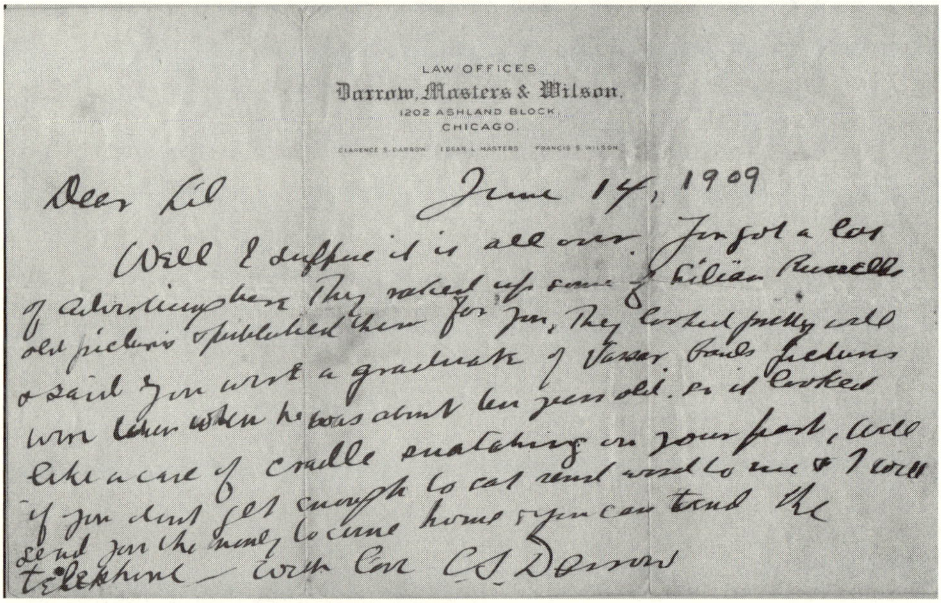

PLATE 19

"Well I suppose it is all over. You got a lot of advertising here. They raked up some of Lilian Russell's old pictures & published them for you. They looked pretty well & said you were a graduate of Vassar. Paul's pictures were taken when he was about ten years old, so it looked like a case of cradle snatching on your part. Well if you don't get enough to eat send word to me & I will send you the money to come home & you can tend the telephone—" Darrow to Lillian (Anderson) Darrow, 14 June 1909.

SON OF CLARENCE S. DARROW WEDS

His Bride Miss Lillian Anderson—They Will Live at Greeley, Col.

Paul Darrow, son of Attorney Clarence S. Darrow, married Miss Lillian Anderson of Chicago yesterday in Denver, Col. The

MRS. PAUL DARROW.
[Photo by Lavecchia, Chicago.]

PAUL DARROW.
[Photo by Dyer, Chicago.]

SON OF CHICAGO LAWYER AND HIS YOUNG BRIDE, ALSO OF THIS CITY, WEDDED IN COLORADO WHERE THE GROOM IS EMPLOYED.

PLATE 20

"Son of Clarence Darrow Weds," *Chicago Daily News* clipping enclosed with Clarence Darrow's letter to Lillian (Anderson) Darrow, 14 June 1909, announcing the wedding of Paul Darrow and Lillian Anderson. Lillian worked as a telephone receptionist in Darrow's law office before her marriage to Paul.

PLATE 21

Brand Whitlock, 1912, who became lifelong friends with Darrow in the 1890s, when Whitlock worked in Governor Altgeld's administration. (Photo: Library of Congress, Prints & Photographs Division, reproduction no. LC-DIG-ggbain-20434)

PLATE 22

J. Howard Moore, ca. 1900s, a leader in the vegetarian and animal-rights movements, who was married to Darrow's sister Jennie. Darrow gave a stirring memorial address honoring Moore's life after Moore killed himself in 1916.

PLATE 23

A flyer advertising Darrow's many lecture subjects, both literary and political. (Photo: University of California, Los Angeles, Charles E. Young Research Library, Department of Special Collections)

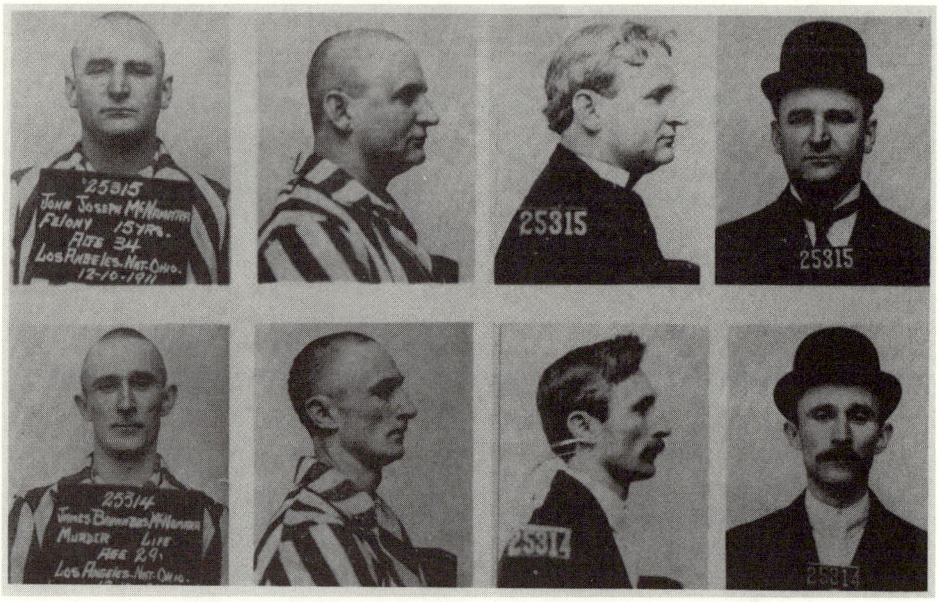

PLATE 24

John J. and James B. McNamara, in their arrest photos (right), April 1911, and their prison photos (left), December 1911.

PLATE 25

Lincoln Steffens, ca. 1912, around the time of his involvement in the McNamara case. (Photo: Library of Congress, Prints & Photographs Division, reproduction no. LC-DIG-ggbain-05710)

PLATE 26
Samuel Gompers testifying before the United States Commission on Industrial Relations, 1915. (Photo: Library of Congress, Prints & Photographs Division, reproduction no. LC-B2–3361–1)

• 1910–1914

TO MARY FIELD • CHICAGO • TUESDAY 15 MARCH 1910

March 15

Dear Mary

I am staying a few minutes after the rest & after a rush day to write you a line. I miss you all the time. No one else is so bright & clever & sympathetic to say nothing of sweet and dear & I wonder how you are & what you are doing in the big city. I don't hear from you—please write.

Helen[1] came in Saturday & turned the office topsy turvy telephoning to every one on earth about a Russian Meeting. They were trying to hunt up a revolutionist who was a prominent citizen and *not* a *radical*. I scoffed a while to her & Friedman.[2] F. began singing the praises of Hull house & other conservatives mentioning Calhoun.[3] I asked him

1. Probably Helen Todd.
2. Probably Isaac Kahn Friedman (1870–1931), who was born in Chicago of wealthy parents, obtained a degree from the University of Michigan, 1893, became a socialist and interested in settlement house work, and operated a florist business in Chicago for several years. He later traveled extensively, worked as a journalist for the *(Chicago) Daily News*, and wrote radical novels, including *By Bread Alone* (1901).
3. William J. Calhoun (1848–1916), lawyer and diplomat. Calhoun practiced law in Danville, Illinois, and later Chicago. He held a variety of foreign affairs positions for Presidents McKinley, Roosevelt, and Taft. He also served as a commissioner of the Interstate Commerce Commission, 1898–99, appointed by President McKinley.

what he did & he said he kept Rudowitz from going back to Russia.[4] I thought of you & how mad you would be. I didn't care. I just thought I was a damn fool. But I am really going to NY to live & not far from now. I am to speak at the Auditorium on Booze April 2d. Wish you could be there.[5] Am tired & hungry & wish you were here to eat & drink with me & talk to me with your low, sweet kind sympathetic voice. I will send you some money next week.

Ever | C. S D

Shall I send the young woman I told you of to meet you. I know you would be friends.

MS: ALS, ICN, Parton-Darrow Papers, Box 1, Folder 2. ENVELOPE RETURN ADDRESS: 1202 Ashland Blk. ENVELOPE ADDRESS: Miss Mary Field | 331—W. 31st St | N.Y. POSTMARK: Chicago 16 March 1910. NOTE: Mary Field Parton wrote on the envelope: "precious letter | a kind friend who helped me when I needed. Glad I repaid debt."

TO MARY FIELD • EN ROUTE TO CHICAGO FROM NEBRASKA • MONDAY 4 APRIL 1910

ATLANTIC COAST LIMITED | DENVER—CHICAGO April 4

Dear Mary

Am just returning from Lincoln Neb where I made a speech. You should have been there. The meeting was in a great rush & set for 3 P.M. At two o'clock all the women from the churches filled most of the lower floor, all the best seats. They wore "Dry buttons" as big as the head light of a locomotive. My friends were in the back of the room & the galleries. Nothing for me to do but trick them. So I started in. I admit that Whiskey has done lots

4. In late 1908 and early 1909, Darrow represented a Russian refugee named Christian Rudovitz. Rudovitz's extradition was sought by the Russian government on the charge that he had murdered three people in a Russian village in 1906. The Department of State's commissioner in Illinois granted the application for extradition, but Secretary of State Elihu Root reversed the decision and Rudovitz remained in the United States. Jane Addams and other residents of Hull House and prominent citizens of Chicago such as Edward F. Dunne actively supported Rudovitz. In their brief to the Department of State, Rudovitz's lawyers argued that even if Rudovitz had been involved in the murders (the Russian government presented some evidence that he was), he should not be extradited because the victims had been spies for the government and their murders were political crimes. See William J. Calhoun [Of Counsel], Clarence S. Darrow, Peter Sissman, and Charles Cheney Hyde [Counsel for the Accused], "Before the Department of State in the Matter of the Demand of the Imperial Russian Government for the Extradition of Christian Rudovitz," Statement and Argument in Behalf of the Accused [(1909)].
5. Prohibition advocates in Chicago had filed a petition to place the question of whether Chicago should be a dry city on the local election ballot on 5 April 1910. Darrow and former mayor Carter H. Harrison Jr. were scheduled to speak against the measure at the Chicago Auditorium on 26 March 1910 (Darrow might have had the date wrong in his letter, or maybe the date was moved up). The day before the meeting, local election commissioners ruled that the issue would not be on the ballot because the petition had an inadequate number of signatures. Darrow showed up for the meeting at the auditorium but the mootness of the issue and the resulting poor turnout led to the cancelation of the meeting. "Ballot to Omit Saloon Question," *Chicago Tribune*, 26 March 1910; "Societies Pass on Ward Candidates," *Chicago Tribune*, 27 March 1910.

of evil in the world. (great applause) Let's prohibit it. (applause) Tobacco is useles & shortens life & is vile & a nuisance. (applause) Let's prohibit it. (great applause) Let's prohibit Sunday base ball. (applause) Let's prohibit Tea & Coffee. (applause) Let's prohibit Cards. applause. Dancing ruins your girls. (applause) Let's prohibit it. (applause) Theaters are evil. (applause). Let's prohibit them. (applause) Corsets injure the born & unborn. (applause) Let's prohibit them. (applause) Man's body is nothing compared with his soul. (applause) Let's make laws on Earth to save men's souls in heaven. (great applause) Then I turned to the galleries & now what do you people in the galleries think about placing your lives & your liberties in the hands of this bunch (wild cheers in the galleries). I had a running fun with them for two hours & a half & they never will take the front seats again when I go to Lincoln.

I have just finished the finest, loveliest book, "The Thief of Virtue."[6] You are in; some of my thoughts & feelings are in it; Hull house is in it, all the hypocrisy & cant is in it. The bad are all good & the good are all bad. I will send it to you at once. I wish we could have read it together. Perhaps we will the second reading or the third.

Ever | C. D.

MS: ALS, ICN, Parton-Darrow Papers, Box 1, Folder 2. ENVELOPE ADDRESS: Miss Mary Field | ~~335 E. 31- St~~ | ~~N.Y.~~ | Care C. Darrow | Ashland Blk. | Chicago | Illinois. POSTMARK: Chicago, 4 April 1910; New York City, 16 April 1910. NOTE: in Field's hand on back of envelope: "A prohibition | speech in | Lincoln Neb | Thief of Virtue."

TO CHARLES ERSKINE SCOTT WOOD • CHICAGO • TUESDAY 28 JUNE 1910

DARROW, MASTERS & WILSON June 28th

My Dear Wood

Am glad to get your letter saying that the Wilde case is ended.[7] Still I wanted to go back for I had such a pleasant time in meeting you & your friends. I hardly think I am justified in sending a further bill. I feel that you are the one who prevented this indictment and that it would have been returned without you, and that it would have caused serious damage to Wilde to say nothing of the danger incident to it. Of course I don't know just how you fix fees there, but I think Wilde is worth from $500,000 to $1,000,000 & it should

6. Eden Phillpotts, *The Thief of Virtue* (New York: John Lane Co., 1910). This was one of Phillpotts's many novels, plays, and short stories set in the wild upland area of Dartmoor, in southwest England.
7. Louis J. Wilde was facing the possibility of being indicted by a grand jury in Portland for embezzlement in connection with the sale of some bonds to the failed Oregon Trust and Savings Bank in Portland. Darrow and Wood represented Wilde, who was eventually indicted in June 1911. "Wilde to Face Heavy Charge," *Los Angeles Times*, 15 April 1910; "Property of Alleged Embezzler at Portland Attached in Suit," *Los Angeles Times*, 2 July 1911.

stand a good fee & whatever you send I will feel is right although I do not want to be quoted. If it was here & I had done what you have I should probably send a bill of about $2,500 although I might make it bigger. Of course the law is a con game & there is no way to tell what a thing is worth—and yet the service has been valuable to him & I feel that no one else could have done it.

I wish I could come out this summer but it is a long ways, & very dreary until you get there. Any how I hope I may see you again soon. Give my kindest regards to Mrs. Beck[8] & any one else who inquires. I got the book and enjoy it.

Your friend Clarence Darrow.

MS: ALS, CU-BANC, C.E.S. Wood Papers, Carton 2. DATE: reference to Wilde case.

TO WILLIAM ENGLISH WALLING • CHICAGO • THURSDAY 14 JULY 1910

DARROW, MASTERS & WILSON July 14th

My Dear Walling

I have been in a hard struggle for two or three years on account of some very heavy losses, & am paying up debts to hold my gas plant in Colorado. As soon as I am out of the woods I intend moving to N.Y. but I have been obliged to refuse to make contributions for some time & don't see how I can constantly do it until I am out of debt. Then too it cost me about $125 for expenses for the trip to N.Y. & that ought to be considered.[9] Before my speech is published in any form I want to go over it both for clerical & grammatical errors & also to make a little clearer my statement about race amalgamation. I shall take nothing

8. Kathryn (Kitty) Seaman Beck (1884–1924), stenographer and secretary. Beck was born in Sacramento. She married a man named John Beck at a young age, but the marriage soon ended in divorce, after which she became a stenographer and secretary for Wood. She held radical ideas, like Wood (who may have influenced her in that regard). She married twice more, in 1911 and 1920. The last marriage was to George W. Vanderveer (1875–1942), a prominent radical lawyer. She died by committing suicide.
9. Walling had probably asked Darrow to make a contribution to the National Association for the Advancement of Colored People (NAACP), which was formed at the second annual National Negro Conference in New York City in May 1910. Darrow was one of the speakers at the Conference. His speech was a wide-ranging criticism of the state of race relations in the country. See Transcript of Darrow's Speech at the National Negro Conference, Cooper Union, New York City, 12 May 1910, NAACP Papers, Part I, Reel 8, Frames 54–66. He argued, for example, that whites in the South were slowly reconquering the North and driving blacks into ever lower positions of standing and servitude, and that no one was raising a voice against this: "Deprived of the ballot, deprived of any influence in the councils of the state, not permitted in good society, which is white society—lynched and burned—and no one to raise their voice against it—while the optimist stands like a jack ass in a grave yard and says 'I am not a pessimist. God is in heaven and all is well.'" Ibid. He told the audience to put no faith in the notion that the races could be separate yet equal: "I think it is a false philosophy to teach that humanity are like the fingers on the hand—the various races and nations separate but joining together for a complete hand. If they are separate, I know where you come in—way down at the bottom, just where you have always been." Ibid.

back but I want it perfectly clear.[10] We are going to some point in White Mountains for Aug. Wish we could see you.

Regard to Mrs W.[11]

Truly | Clarence Darrow.

Your brother[12] knows all about my financial affairs & has materially helped me & I think he would say that I ought to pay my debts first.

D.

MS: ALS, DLC-MSS, NAACP Administrative Files. DATE: "[1910?]" appended and reference to speech.

TO FREMONT OLDER • CHICAGO • WEDNESDAY 21 SEPTEMBER 1910

DARROW, MASTERS & WILSON Sept. 21st

My Dear Mr. Older

I have been thinking of you often since the late insurgent wave & especially of your triumph in Cal. It was fine & I know how it must have pleased you. I am glad if Johnston is the kind of man you spoke of & I trust he will win.[13] It almost gives me some hope. Roosevelt seems to be running crazy and saying things.[14] Perhaps the world will jog up a little bit before the people forget it all. I should like to see you & have a long visit with you. There is some chance that I may be out this fall or winter. I want to very much. If I had the courage I would move to California, but I still have to earn some money & am a little afraid to make the change. However I hope it will come. Tell Mrs. Older we often

10. In his speech, Darrow told his black audience that their progress toward equality would be slow and imperceptible and that eventually race problems would be "worked out by race amalgamation, as the difference between the Irish and the German and the American and all the others who used to build up a barbed wire fence to keep the sheep from the goats." Ibid. Darrow's speech resulted in an Associated Press account that interpreted Darrow as advocating the marriage of blacks and whites. See "Advises Negroes to Marry Whites," *Chicago Tribune*, 13 May 1910. Darrow later denied this and said that he was simply pointing out that race amalgamation seemed inevitable and that laws against it would have no effect. He also stated that he did not personally believe in or advocate the marriage of blacks and whites. "Darrow Says He Never Said Blacks Should Wed Whites," *Chicago Tribune*, 20 May 1910. Darrow's speech was apparently never published.
11. Anna Strunsky Walling (1877–1964), author and lecturer. Anna Strunsky Walling was active in the socialist movement in the United States in the early 1900s. She was known for her collaboration with Jack London (1876–1916) on *The Kempton-Wace Letters* (1903), an epistolary novel on the subject of love.
12. Willoughby George Walling.
13. Older supported Hiram Johnson as a candidate for governor of California. In mid-August 1910, Johnson handily defeated his Republican competitors in the primary election.
14. In August and September 1910, Theodore Roosevelt, trying to resolve the split between the conservative and progressive elements in the Republican party, made a series of speeches and statements that one day showed support for the party regulars and the next day showed support for the progressives. In the end, he was lampooned in the press as a "man on two horsebacks." George E. Mowry, "Theodore Roosevelt and the Election of 1910," *Mississippi Valley Historical Review* 25 (March 1939): 532.

speak of her & remember her visit which we both enjoyed. Should be glad to hear from you at any time.

Truly | Clarence Darrow.

MS: ALS, CU-BANC, Older Papers, Box 1. DATE: letterhead and reference to Johnson and Roosevelt.

TO MARY FIELD • CHICAGO • TUESDAY 27 SEPTEMBER 1910

DARROW, MASTERS & BAILY Sept. 27

Dear Mary

I have been thinking of your going to Albany on the Social diseases law.[15] I believe in a fair show for women & they never have had a fair show, & I don't know just what this law is. Still there are some things to remember. Of course prostitution is all wrong & of course it is caused by poverty & can not be cured except by curing poverty. Still it is here & will stay in substantially its present condition until people get down to fundamentals which will be a D–n long while yet. This being so what safeguards are best to throw around the business.

It is a menace to men & women both to have anyone in this occupation spreading disease—for instance a man gets an occupational disease, his wife gets it, the preacher gets it, most any one gets it. Society ought to provide against it. Those who have it ought to be withdrawn from business in some way or by some process—either killing or segregating or treating or branding or something.

You might say why not the men. Of course why not, it ought to be equal. If there is any difference the women should have the best chance if there is a way to give it to them—but is there? The men are not in business. They are customers. It might be all right to provide a law for examining men each time they go to such an emporium, but this is hardly feasible, or to examine all men (except settlement workers) every day. This would be an invasion of liberty that would hardly be justified. Only a limited proportion of men go to such places. Whereas of course all women who are in the business, are in the business—and may properly be subject to restriction. Of course it should be the wisest & humanest possible, but that some means should be taken seems to me to be not only wise but humane even to those in business. Then too if men were assured that everything was all right it would largely increase the business & revenue of this trade, it would give them a chance to demand a better scale of prices, something more like "union"

15. The "social diseases law" is the Inferior Criminal Courts Act of the City of New York (also known as the Page Act), which became law in June 1910. See 1910 N.Y. Laws Ch. 659. The act required that every woman convicted of prostitution had to be examined by a physician and, if the physician determined that she was afflicted with a venereal disease, the judge was required to commit her to a public hospital for treatment, for a period not to exceed one year. If she was eventually certified as "free of any venereal disease," she was to be released, provided that a minimum-detention period had expired. If her minimum-detention period had not been served, she was to be transferred to the workhouse. Many reform groups were strongly opposed to this law, on a variety of grounds. See Barbara Meil Hobson, *Uneasy Virtue: The Politics of Prostitution and the American Reform Tradition* (New York: Basic Books: 1987), 169–70.

conditions—shorter hours—time & a half for over time & what not. D–n it girl don't you see how it works out. It may not be that the proposed law is any good, probably it is not if the reformers framed it. Still something along that line is necessary & it must not be assumed that it is bad simply because it interferes with the personal liberty of the vendors, or rather the victims. Better think it over & be sure you are right. If there is a big delegation going to Albany probably they are wrong. If there are preachers & settlement workers it is almost surely wrong. Ask Ida Raugh[16]: It is not that I am not for helping women. I sure am & especially this kind of women but how? I would know how but the world won't do it—& every thing considered perhaps this is the wisest that can be had.

They are trying to form an organization to help the Negro here. Miss Belascer[17] has been here for several days & I have seen her a good deal. She is a bully good woman. Some of the settlement parties are worried about having to do with Walling since the last newspaper stories—why not. He ought to keep away from ladies.[18] D—n the ladies. They are always raising the devil with people, but what are we going to do about it. Say Mary you are all right. I wish you was here right now, at least that's the way I feel now.

C. S. D.

MS: ALS, ICN, Parton-Darrow Papers, Box 1, Folder 2. ENVELOPE ADDRESS: Miss Mary G. Field | 418—E. 65th St | N.Y. POSTMARK: Chicago 27 September 1910. NOTE: In Parton's hand on the envelope is written, among other notes and doodles, "Page Bill Social diseases | Prostit."

TO CAROLINE LLOYD WITHINGTON • CHICAGO • THURSDAY 8 DECEMBER 1910

DARROW, MASTERS & BAILY December 8, 1910.

My dear Mrs. Lloyd:

Your letter received and so far as the Warren case is concerned, I am writing you in confidence, permitting you to show it to the lawyer you mentioned, if you think you can trust him, and you can trust most any lawyer you have to.

16. Ida Rauh (1877–1970), actress, artist, and poet. Rauh came from a wealthy family and graduated with a law degree from New York University in 1905, but she never practiced law. She was one of the founding members of the Provincetown Players, the American theatrical organization that first introduced the plays of Eugene O'Neill, and she acted in many of the plays put on by that organization between 1915 and 1920. After this period, she concentrated on painting, sculpture, and poetry (publishing one volume in 1959). She was a strong advocate of equal rights for women and active in the birth control campaigns. She was arrested in 1916 for distributing birth control pamphlets and received a suspended sentence.
17. Darrow is probably referring to Frances Blascoer (b. 1873), an organizer and executive secretary for the National Association for the Advancement of Colored People, 1910–11. Blascoer had been a social worker in Chicago and active in the women's movement. Later, as a special investigator for a committee on schoolchildren's hygiene for the Public Education Association of the City of New York, she was author of a study on African American schoolchildren titled *Colored School Children in New York* (New York: Public Education Association of the City of New York, 1915).
18. William English Walling was being sued in state court in New York by Anna Berthe Grunspan, a Jewish Russian immigrant whom Walling had met in France in 1905, before he married Anna Strunsky. Grunspan claimed that Walling had breached a promise to marry her. Her lawsuit received a great deal of attention from newspapers, but the jury rejected her claim in March 1911. See James Boylan, *Revolutionary Lives: Anna Strunsky and William English Walling* (Amherst: University of Massachusetts Press, 1998), 72–74, 165–80.

I was employed by Warren in this case. He was charged in the indictment with having mailed a letter, on the outside wrapper of which was a matter of a scurrilous, defamatory and threatening nature. The outside wrapper contained in bold red letters an offer of a reward of a thousand dollars to anyone who would kidnap Ex-Governor Taylor and return him to Kentucky.[19] So far as the facts of the publication and letter there was no question, so the case really was whether this came within the meaning of the law. The offence was rather technical and the evidence not serious.

The matter was delayed for many months. The government offered to take a fine of $25. in case of a plea of guilty, which he was advised to pay. As a matter of fact, what he wanted was not an easy way out, but advertising notoriety for the paper and himself. I soon found that I was employed to sell newspapers, which is a disagreeable job and one which is not governed by my license. I went down and helped try the case. There was nothing to try except to make the argument that there was no crime charged in the indictment. Associated with me was a good lawyer, Ex-Attorney General Boyle[20] of Kansas City.

There was no question between us as to the law or the method of conducting the case. Under a holding of the court that this was within the purview of the Statute, the jury returned a verdict of guilty. Warren was dissatisfied with both of us. He thought he could make a national case out of a matter that was really for the Police Court, a sort of drunk and disorderly charge, and he thought we could spend at least a month in trying it. Immediately upon the verdict of the jury we entered a motion for a new trial and I argued it. There was nothing in it but a question of law, as I have said. The court overruled it. The court would have been glad to give him a small fine if he would have dared to.

Warren, dissatisfied with his lawyers, prepared a speech and delivered it to the court. I told him it was a good speech, but would probably give him a year in jail. It only gave him six months so I was wrong. Both Boyle and I were practically dismissed from the case. We did write a brief for the United States Circuit Court of Appeals, and argued it of course, as lawyers, on the question as to whether this matter was governed by the Statute. That was the last we had to do with it. Then Warren picked up a one-horse lawyer down in his own town and he and that lawyer went to St. Paul where Warren made another

19. William S. Taylor (1853–1928), lawyer, judge, state attorney general, and Republican governor of Kentucky, was elected governor in 1899 by a narrow margin over Democrat William Goebel (1856–1900). The Democratic majority in the state legislature appointed a committee to investigate the election, but before its work was complete, Goebel was shot by an unknown assassin. A short while later—after several judicial rulings on the election—Taylor was removed from office. Facing possible arrest for conspiracy to assassination Goebel, Taylor fled to Indianapolis, where he worked as a lawyer and vice president of an insurance company. In 1907, after Haywood, Pettibone, and Moyer were kidnapped in Colorado and taken to Idaho to stand trial, *The Appeal to Reason*, the socialist newspaper edited by Fred D. Warren, offered a reward for the kidnap and return of Taylor to Kentucky. Warren apparently did this to draw attention to himself and the *Appeal* and to draw a contrast between the treatment of the kidnapped union men and Taylor. See Elliott Shore, *Talkin' Socialism: J.A. Wayland and the Role of the Press in American Radicalism, 1890–1912* (Lawrence: University Press of Kansas, 1988), 175–81.

20. Louis C. Boyle (1866–1925), lawyer. Born in Canada, Boyle graduated from the law department of the University of Michigan, 1889. He practiced law for several years in Fort Scott, Kansas, and served as county attorney there for four years. He was elected as a Populist candidate to one term as attorney general of Kansas, 1897–99, and then continued his law practice in Kansas City, Missouri, until his death.

speech, which—of course—from a lawyer's standpoint was wholly irrelevant and insulting to the court. I do not mean to say that courts ought not to be insulted, but if a man insults them, he ought to be ready to take the consequences.

Some time after the upper court confirmed the holding of the lower court.[21] He has no legal advice that is of any value. No lawyer could advise him any differently from the advice given him by Mr. Boyle and myself. No one could have tried the case any differently. While I presume the case was largely got up because of the character of the paper, still the court did not stretch it much to say that it was a technical offence and on the whole, it was not in very good taste to print the matter on an envelope and circulate it.

At once after the trial of the case Warren commenced a series of attacks again that were irrelevant and scurrilous against various Judges of the United States Courts. These Judges were proper subjects for criticism, but the attacks were largely of a personal nature, which he had no right to make.

I have no idea that the Supreme Court of the United States would entertain a petition for a Writ of Habeas Corpus. It has never been discussed with me and probably it has not with any competent lawyer. It is possible that a Writ of Habeas Corpus might lie on the theory that the matter charged in the indictment did not constitute a crime, but even were that true, I doubt if the Supreme Court of the United States would entertain it, although they would have a right to do so. They would probably relegate it to one of the Circuit or District Courts in the country.

I am helpless to do anything in the matter for the reason that I have been "fired". What I would suggest is that if you or any other socialist wanted to help in the case, you ought not to be misled and the people ought not to be and it might be well for a "bunch" to get together and ask the opinion of a good lawyer who holds our view if any such can be found. I think Mr. Morris Hilquit is a man of good sober judgment who could write a fair opinion to circulate to Socialists in this matter, if he would undertake it, but—of course—I would not want it known that I had anything to do with suggesting this myself. Socialists are fooled so often that probably once more won't hurt.[22]

As to the Moyer, Heywood and Pettibone case, the law is not an exact science, as probably your lawyer friend will tell you, unless he is too orthodox, and in the pay of too many corporations. Of course, he is right that the crime was in the conduct of the Governors of Idaho and Colorado. An affidavit was filed in Idaho alleging that Moyer, Heywood and Pettibone were guilty of murder and on the night that Steunenberg was killed they were corporally in the state of Idaho. This the States Attorney, Attorney General and Governor knew was a lie. On this charge the Governor of Idaho issued a requisition asking the Governor of Colorado to give them up. The Governor of Colorado also knew that this was a lie; that on that day

21. See *Warren v. United States*, 183 F. 718 (8th Cir. 1910).

22. Warren's conviction resulted in a $1,500 fine and a sentence of six months in prison. He refused to pay the fine or surrender himself. On 1 February 1911, President Taft—not wanting to make a martyr out of Warren—reduced his fine to one hundred dollars and canceled the prison term. Shore, *Talkin' Socialism*, 181.

they were in Colorado, yet, knowing it, he honored the requisition, and they took the men without giving them a chance to appeal to any court and sent them to Idaho.

The petition for Habeas Corpus was filed in the Supreme Court of the United States on the theory that the whole thing was a fraud, that they had never had a day in court and that they should be sent back to Colorado where they belonged before the legal machinery could reach them. Before this case was heard, they were regularly indicted in Idaho and were held under warrants from this indictment. The Supreme Court held that although the arrest and kidnapping might be illegal, still they had no right to inquire into anything except the fact that they were then held under indictment in Idaho.[23]

Justice McKenna dissented and held substantially the views which I have already expressed.[24] There are authorities by the United States Supreme Court which have held as the Supreme Court did in this case on nearly the same state of facts. Whether it was law or not, I do not know. It certainly wasn't justice. Of course, it is the law because the Supreme Court says so.

So long as I am writing you this much, I ought to apologize for failing you so many times, in what you asked me about your brother. One reason was my carelessness; another was because really I could not think of anything substantial that you did not already have. Of course, I do not need to tell you how much I thought of him. I have considered him the best and most valuable friend I had, and he was of the greatest assistance in the case in Pennsylvania.[25] You asked me for incidents connected with him in that case and I couldn't then, nor can I now, recall much that would seem to be of value in a biography. Mr. Lloyd went down there before I was retained in the case, and I think it was mainly through him that I was asked in. He did all he could through the newspaper and through council and advice to place the case right before the public, and this work was very valuable. So far as his participation in the court work was concerned, it was not great. While he had been admitted to the bar, as you know, he never practiced and had never pretended to be proficient in court matters.

In court he had practically nothing to do with the examination of the witnesses or the conduct of the trial. At our rooms in the preparation of the case he was always present with all the aid he could give and with very valuable suggestions. He made one of the arguments in the case, which you have, and which—of course—is very able, and which is one of the sort of literary productions which only he could make, full of humanity, but

23. See *Pettibone v. Nichols*, 203 U.S. 192 (1906); *Moyer v. Nichols*, 203 U.S. 221 (1906).

24. Justice Joseph McKenna (1843–1926), an appointment of President McKinley, believed that the conduct of the government officials who abducted Haywood, Pettibone, and Moyer was indefensible: "Kidnapping is a crime, pure and simple. It is difficult to accomplish; hazardous at every step. All of the officers of the law are supposed to be on guard against it. All of the officers of the law may be invoked against it. But how is it when the law becomes the kidnapper? When the officers of the law, using its forms, and exerting its power, become abductors?" *Pettibone*, 203 U.S. at 218.

25. The "case in Pennsylvania" is the arbitration of the strike by anthracite coal miners in 1902. See Darrow to Ruby Hamerstrom, 29 October 1902, n.42.

at the same time full of biting sarcasm and keen criticisms of things as they are.[26] All through the trial he was watchful and solicitous about the health of Mr. Mitchel and myself and insisted on our taking long walks, and in doing everything for our comfort. He also frequently sent dispatches to the newspapers, who would use these, when they would not have used them if they came from anybody else, and in this way did more than anybody else towards bringing about a public opinion which was certainly very essential to the ultimate outcome.

You may have an impression that his work in the court was very much more than it really was. I know you are sure enough of me to know that I would not belittle it in any way, and that I fully appreciate the value of his services. As a matter of fact, the record would not show any considerable participation in the court outside the argument. I believe you are familiar with the record. I gave my copy to the library of the Wisconsin University and I think John Mitchel has one.

I am glad to hear from you again and to know of your interest in all these matters.

With kindest regards I am,

Yours very truly, | Clarence Darrow.

P.S. Please forgive such a long letter. I never did it before and never will again.

D

MS: TLS, WHi, Lloyd Papers. INSIDE ADDRESS: Mrs. Caro D. Lloyd, | 22 Grand Avenue, | Nutley, New Jersey.

TO BRAND WHITLOCK • CHICAGO • SATURDAY 17 DECEMBER 1910

Chicago Dec. 17

My dear Whitlock

I have heard a good many literary fellows say that they could write better by using a type writer; so it has recently occured that this was just what I lacked, so I am practicing on my friends and here goes with you. I had intended to write you before when you sent me the book, but I have been away a good deal and so put it off.[27] I was glad to get the volume, it awoke memories too with me of a time when you were not famous and I was sure that you some day would be. Incidentally I thought I might be Too. Well I am glad I did not miss it on you. Then too I was glad to get the "Gold brick" because it is the only one I ever got for nothing although many is the one I have had

26. Lloyd delivered one of the closing arguments for the miners, urging an annual trade agreement between miners and operators and recognition of the miners' union. His argument was published posthumously in a collection of his speeches and essays. See Henry Demarest Lloyd, *Men, the Workers* (1909; reprint, with an introduction by Leon Stein and Philip Taft [New York: Arno Press, 1969]), 201–52.

27. Darrow is referring to Whitlock's *The Gold Brick* (Indianapolis: The Bobbs-Merrill Co., 1910), a collection of short stories originally published in popular magazines.

handed to me. I have praised the stories so many times when they came out that I don't need to say any thing about that but I hope they will sell. I have not read Arnold Bennett's Story.[28] I have tried but will try again. I would like to see you mighty well and have been thinking of taking Mrs. D. and going down on purpose for a long time. But if I do it will certainly be the last time unless you people come and stay with us the next time you come even if you do come to speak to the Pharisees. Any way I would like to see you, and it would be worth a trip down. I have been thinking that if you have any liberal or labor organizations that are interested in Tolstoi I might come down and talk to them about him. I would like to talk to you about what you will do after that job is done; you know my views about it. You should have left it long ago. There is nothing in being "Sam Jones succesor." You will accomplish nothing and it is not possible to accomplish any thing. The people are not ready and after you are done they will return to their vomit; the only thing worth while is to develop your own individuality and leave something that will do a little to liberalize the few who knew and cared because you lived.[29] I am strongly thinking of leaving here before very long and going probably to N.Y. Would have done it before if I had not lost all my money a few years ago and did not dare risk it, but I can do it very soon.

With kindest regards to Mrs. W.[30]

As ever your friend, | Clarence Darrow

MS: TLS, DLC-MSS, Whitlock Papers, Box 29. DATE: the day is struck out ("Dec. ~~17~~") and "[13]" is appended, apparently as the year, but Whitlock's letter and his book and the reference to him as mayor make 1910 the only possible year.

TO CAROLINE LLOYD WITHINGTON • CHICAGO • WEDNESDAY 8 FEBRUARY 1911

DARROW, MASTERS & BAILY Feby 8

My Dear Mrs Lloyd

I was very glad to receive your note: As to Warren I have no doubt he is sincere in his advocacy of Socialism & that he is honest or thinks so. He is small & ignorant & likes to be in the lime light. Some people can not get notoriety without going to jail & many are willing to do this rather than not have it. The whole thing amounted to nothing. The Socialists as a class are honest but not students, not acquainted with history or

28. Whitlock told Darrow in his letter that if he had not read any of the works of Arnold Bennett, he should read Bennett's *The Old Wives' Tale* (1908). Whitlock to Darrow, 12 December 1910, DLC-MSS, Whitlock Papers.
29. In his letter to Darrow, Whitlock had ruminated about his job as mayor of Toledo and his future in general: "I am very busy; the street car fight is approaching a crisis, one which I hope will dispose of it so that I can get out of this office. What I am to do then I don't know, whether to give up the law and devote myself entirely to literature or to try to carry water on both shoulders and do both. At any rate I shall not give up writing. This is one of the things I want to talk to you about when I see you." Ibid.
30. Ella Brainerd Whitlock.

science or philosophy, are typical fanatics knowing little & believing little & therefore believing it very strongly. Of course this is necessary. If one knows too much they believe nothing & know that nothing is worth while & so do nothing. Your brother was a rare exception. I will search carefully for letters of your brother's & will write you Monday.

Sincerely | Clarence Darrow.

MS: ALS, WHi, Lloyd Papers. DATE: "1911" appended.

TO RUBY DARROW • NEW YORK CITY • TUESDAY 28 FEBRUARY 1911

HOTEL BREVOORT Tuesday Eve

Dearest Rube

The D—n case hangs on and I can't leave this P.M.[31] I am not sure about tomorrow but am getting very impatient to get back. I am awfully sorry I did not have you leave Sunday, but thought surely another day would be all. I am not trying the case but the Wallings insist on my staying & consulting them. Have been in court all day & wish you were here for the night. It is really lonesome & I would like to be at home. I hope your foot is better & that you are all right. Will wire date of my return.

Ever | D.

MS: ALS, MnU-L, Darrow Collection. ENVELOPE ADDRESS: Mrs C S Darrow | 1537 E. 60th St | Chicago. POSTMARK: New York, 28 February 1911.

TO BRAND WHITLOCK • CHICAGO • WEDNESDAY 26 APRIL 1911

DARROW, MASTERS & WILSON April 26

Dear Brand

I am sorry your telegrame got into print.[32] I showed it to the fellows who were dependent and gave them a copy without thinking of publication—still I suppose you don't care.

31. Darrow was helping William English Walling defend himself against a lawsuit from Anna Berthe Grunspan. See Darrow to Field, 27 September 1910, n.18.
32. On 23 April 1911, newspapers reported that John and James McNamara and Ortie McManigal had been taken by train from the Midwest to California (without the use of any extradition process), under arrest for dynamiting the Los Angeles Times Building on 1 October 1910, killing twenty-one people in the explosion and fire that followed. Newspapers also soon began to report that Darrow had been retained as chief counsel to represent them. See, e.g., "Retain Darrow in Times Cases," *Chicago Tribune,* 25 April 1911. Whitlock, who was then mayor of Toledo, sent a telegram to Darrow after learning that Darrow would be involved in the case, and the telegram ended up in one of the local newspapers: "Clarence S. Darrow, Esq., Indianapolis, Ind.—Glad you have been retained in the McNamara case and that labor has you once more to defend. I wish there was something I could do to help, but I seem to have nothing but sympathy for the cause and indignation at the methods that are used to crush it. Good luck to you. Brand Whitlock." "Mayor Wires Good Luck to Darrow, Defender of Labor," *Toledo Blade,* 25 April 1911.

It was nice of you to wire me and there is no one I would rather have with me at this time. I go at it if I go with fear & forebodings—I dread the fight & am in the dark. If I could avoid it I would, but how can I: they are my friends & in trouble & have an insane faith in me & I don't see how I can disappoint them much as I tremble at the plunge. I wish we could see you before we go. It may be in a week or two. I may get out of it but probably not. I feel like one going away on a long & dangerous voyage.

Ever Your friend | Clarence Darrow.

Love to Mrs W.[33]

MS: ALS, NNC, Nevins Papers. DATE: reference to telegram.

TO PAUL DARROW • CHICAGO • SUNDAY 14 MAY 1911

DARROW, MASTERS & BAILY May 14th

Dear Paul

I expect to start to Los Angeles on Saturday the 20th. Shall go direct there & will probably return for a short time about June 10th when I will stop at Greeley. Within the present year I expect about $50,000 from this & about $25,000 within 30 days. Of course I want to get all my debts off my hands as soon as possible. The first $25,000 will just about do this including the $3,000 for the Gas Co which I got of Fred.[34] Of course I can let you have some of this & you will have what you need, but prefer to go a little slower there, & make it look out for its self as far as possible & put the surplus into some good stocks like Atchison, paying for it in full. Still I will not invest in any thing without consulting you & whatever you need will come first.

Hastily | C. S. D.

You can address me at L.A. at Alexandria Hotel.

D.

MS: ALS, MnU-L, Darrow Collection. DATE: letterhead and reference to travel to Los Angeles.

TO SAMUEL GOMPERS • CHICAGO • SATURDAY 20 MAY 1911

DARROW, MASTERS & BAILY May 20, 1911.

My dear Mr. Gompers:

I am leaving to-night for California and will write you after I get there. Expect to stay about three weeks and will return to look matters up here.

33. Ella Brainerd Whitlock.
34. Frederick Hamerstrom.

I have concluded not to do anything about Eastern lawyers until I see what the situation is there. The question of lawyers is very difficult. There are many who want to go into the case but unless a man is a really big lawyer there is no object in taking one from this section of the country. Of course, I would like to get the best there is any where in this fight. If we could only get some such man as Ex-Governor Black of New York,[35] it would be taking great responsibility off my shoulders. You might consider this matter. If you see any way or have any suggestions to make I will be glad to hear from you about it. I know there are enough who would not be of any great assistance and what I really want is some one that I know is the equal of any one. I hope to come out of this all right.

Ever, | Your friend, | Clarence Darrow.

P S—Mr. Rappaport[36] has been the attorney of the organization for so long it seems to me it would be fitting to have him go. I think him a very good lawyer and, of course, he can be useful in the matter, although I would like some one of the description I gave you if it is possible to do it. I know what to expect and would prefer not to take the responsibility alone, although I will take it if I have to.

D

MS: TLS, WHi, AFL Records: Gompers Era. INSIDE ADDRESS: Samuel Gompers, Esq., | American Federation of Labor | Washington, D.C.

TO RUBY DARROW • EN ROUTE TO SAN FRANCISCO • TUESDAY 23 MAY 1911

SAN FRANCISCO | "OVERLAND LIMITED" May 23rd

Dearest Rube

We are just passing through the snow sheds in California where we were tied up so long on that tough trip to San Francisco when you were so good to me—as you always have been. Maybe some time I will be good to you. I am always trying & falling down. How I long for you on this trip. Reach San Francisco at five this afternoon. It has been a very easy trip.

Ever lovingly | D.

MS: ALS, MnU-L, Darrow Collection. PLACE: letterhead. DATE: letterhead and partial date. ENVELOPE ADDRESS: Mrs. C S Darrow | 1537—E 60th St | Chicago. POSTMARK: illegible.

35. Frank S. Black (1853–1913), lawyer, Republican congressman from New York, and governor of New York. Black graduated from Dartmouth College, 1875, worked for newspapers in New York for a few years, and then practiced law, 1879–94, before serving in Congress, 1895–97. He resigned from Congress to become governor, 1897–99, after which he resumed a successful civil and criminal law practice in New York City, from which he retired in 1913. According to one obituary, Black announced in early 1912 "that he had amassed a fortune of $500,000, which was ample to keep him for the remainder of his life," and that "[j]ust before his retirement [in 1913] he would not take a case unless there was a large fee attached." "Ex-Gov. Black Dies at His Troy Home," *New York Times*, 22 March 1913.

36. Leo M. Rappaport (b. 1879), an attorney in Indianapolis who had long been counsel for the International Association of Bridge and Structural Iron Workers, the union for which John McNamara was treasurer.

TO RUBY DARROW • LOS ANGELES • SATURDAY 27 MAY 1911

HOTEL ALEXANDRIA Saturday PM

Dearest Rube

Just a line to say I will be there about 4 days after you get this. I will stay in & around Chicago about a week & then *you must come back* with me. I am D—n lonesome & need you every day & night. It looks fine here & I think you will like it. Have seen every one & they all ask for you, but I want you most. Get ready to come. Saw some beautiful apartments today—3 & 4 rooms with fine views—where they do all the work but getting meals. They do cleaning, dish washing &c. every thing else. You might like this as we would get most of meals down town. Still I don't want you to work any. I know we can get something to suit. If Christine[37] doesn't come, I wouldn't urge her, as we can get a girl here—have seen several & they seem fine. Still D—n it Rube, you are the nicest & dearest & sweetest of all.

Ever | D.

MS: ALS, MnU-L, Darrow Collection. ENVELOPE ADDRESS: Mrs. Clarence Darrow | 1537 E 60th St | Chicago Ill. | Fulton St. | Galesburg, Ills. FIRST POSTMARK: Los Angeles, 28 May 1911. SECOND POSTMARK: Chicago, 31 May 1911. THIRD POSTMARK: Galesburg, 31 May 1911.

TO FRANK L. MULHOLLAND • LOS ANGELES • MONDAY 29 MAY 1911

HARRIMAN, RYCKMAN & TUTTLE, | ATTORNEYS-AT-LAW May 29, 1911.

My Dear Mr. Mulholland:

I was in here about a week getting a line on things and have employed two lawyers whom I am quite sure are the right ones for the case and men of standing—Mr. Davis[38] and Mr. Scott.[39]

I have got together considerable information and am going back east in a few days to make some investigations there, when I will possibly see you.

So far there are four of us in the case, with a possibility of Rappaport being in. While I would enjoy having you with me I cannot see where we would be justified in spending any more money for lawyers, unless there was somebody of preeminent ability and standing. Of course, something of this sort I would gladly welcome to relieve me of responsibility and also make more sure of the case. It might be possible that some one

37. The identity of "Christine" is unknown, but she was apparently a domestic helper for the Darrows.
38. LeCompte Davis.
39. Joseph Scott.

else will be wanted on the Pacific coast, but I don't see where any one from the east could add greatly in this fight, as I now look at it.

With kind regards, I am,

Very truly yours, | (Signed) Clarence Darrow.

MS: TT, WHi, AFL Records: Gompers Era. INSIDE ADDRESS: Mr. Frank L. Mulholland, | Toledo, Ohio.

TO SAMUEL GOMPERS • LOS ANGELES • MONDAY 29 MAY 1911

HARRIMAN, RYCKMAN & TUTTLE May 29, 1911.

My Dear Mr. Gompers:-

Your letters have been duly received and very glad to hear from you. I have been getting a line on things here and have employed two lawyers of high standing, whom I think will be able to furnish us about all the assistance we need. There will be so many directions for money to go that I don't feel we are justified in spending more money on eastern lawyers, unless, as I once suggested, that some man of preeminent ability could come, and this I think very doubtful as these men are all employed to defend the interests and they would not care to go into a case like this.

I want to discuss this case fully with you, not only as regards my clients but as regards the cause which both of us have so much at heart.

The day of pleading has been set over until July 5th, so I will return to the east in a very few days, and, if you can meet me in New York, I will come on there. Please write me a line to my office in Chicago on receipt of this and let me know whether you can meet me. I will get this line about the time it reaches Chicago.

With kind regards,

Your friend, | Clarence Darrow

MS: TLS, WHi, AFL Records: Gompers Era. INSIDE ADDRESS: Samuel Gompers, Esq., | Washington, D.C.

TO PAUL DARROW • LOS ANGELES • TUESDAY 4 JULY 1911

RAMPART July 4th

Dear Paul

Received your letter O.K. By this time you have heard from Fred.[40] I did not give him the 3,000 bonds. Let me know what were your receipts for June & the no. of meters. We are having a hot time here and so far have been very busy but think it will let up some this

40. Frederick Hamerstrom.

week. Have not yet got McManagel but have hopes.[41] The weather here is fine, not a single hot day so far. We have a crowd of good fellows on the case so that part of the thing is pleasant. Still I am afraid there is no way to win, but I can't help it. Shall do the best possible. We are both well. Don't know when I shall get back east. Think a little later we will have to try and arrange for you & Lil to come out, if you can leave the business for a while. Is Jacobs coming?[42] Tell him I am anxious to see him & the climate is fine.

C. S. D.

MS: ALS, MnU-L, Darrow Collection. DATE: reference to trial and McManigal.

TO SAMUEL GOMPERS • LOS ANGELES • SATURDAY 8 JULY 1911

RAMPART July 8

My Dear Gompers

No doubt you keep posted in a way in the papers. We are having a fierce time—all the powers seem to be bent on getting blood & it is a fearful fight. Of course there is nothing to do but fight. I received your telegram today that a second 15,000 on the way. I hate to urge you about money but none of the lawyers here have had any thing—except I was given $5,000 by the Structural Iron Workers at first & took 5,000 of the 15,000—but I must do something for them. Then we have a first class man for the detective work, who will need help. He is from Chicago & trusty.[43] We have the ablest evidence gatherer I ever saw from Chicago—he needs help.[44] We have a first class gas &c expert laying out that part of the case—& he will help about getting the others.[45] Then the McManagel matter, has cost & is costing money.[46] It goes every way & I am as careful as can be. We will need all we talked about between now & Jan 1st & half ought to be here very soon. I can not promise all these without knowing & can not be too much worried over it. Please let me know just what arrangements are made & how soon & fast it will come. I want to win if there is a way & must leave nothing undone & still can not make promises I can't keep. Better send a night wire.

Truly | Clarence Darrow

41. Ortie McManigal confessed to his involvement in blowing up bridges and buildings for the International Association of Bridge and Structural Iron Workers shortly after his arrest in Detroit in April 1911, and he implicated the McNamaras in his confession as well. Many people believed that McManigal had been coerced into making his confession and that the confession was not true. The McNamaras' defense team worked hard to convince McManigal to repudiate his confession, including using the influence of his wife and uncle, who visited him in jail.
42. John T. Jacobs.
43. Darrow might be referring to P. J. Cooney, a detective from Chicago who was employed by the McNamara defense in July 1911. "Bars Down to New Evidence," *Los Angeles Times*, 11 June 1912.
44. Here, Darrow is probably referring to John Harrington.
45. Darrow might be referring to James H. Levering (1859–1942), a civil and hydraulic engineer in California who was hired as an expert by the McNamara defense to reconstruct what happened in the explosion of the Los Angeles Times Building. (He would later complain that he was not fully paid for his work.)
46. Darrow might be referring to the costs associated with bringing McManigal's wife and uncle to Los Angeles to see if McManigal would repudiate his confession.

MS: ALS, WHi, AFL Records: Gompers Era. DATE: references to defense work for the McNamaras.

TO SAMUEL GOMPERS • LOS ANGELES • SATURDAY 15 JULY 1911

RAMPART | LOS ANGELES July 15th

My Dear Gompers

The case (as you know) has been set for trial for Oct 11th. It is necessary that the money matters must be clearly understood at least so far as possible—There is no way to try this case with a chance of winning without a great deal of money—The other side are spending it in every direction; Then they have all the organized channels of society: the states Atty—grand jury ~~judge~~—police force, Mayor, Manufacturers Association. Every one is afraid of the line-up—& there is little light any where. Burns'[47] whole force utterly regardless of personal rights is everywhere in evidence: intimidating, hounding, and buldozing—the grand jury kept constantly in session to awe every one who comes as our witness. No one will do any thing without money. It is a tough game & I want you to understand it. You know I never wanted to come. It is filled only with trouble for me. If I could only be relieved I would gladly sacrifice my fee, even the $10,000 already received. If some one would come & take charge of the money end I would be glad for there is too much worry and work about it any how.

I am expecting next week the best chemist & explosives expert in the country from N.Y. Wired him a thousand & his charge is $100 per day & expenses but not to exceed 3,000 all together. After he reports on the theory I will need more experts. The witnesses & policing & looking after it takes money all the time, but I need not go further into details although I can & will. Raising money is a disagreeable task but it is the pleasantest job in this work. The work & worry & responsibility and danger of defeat is mainly here. This will need all together $350,000 to $400,000 between now & Jan 1st—& we should have $100,000 now & the balance at about 35,000 or 40,000 a month until that time. After this I should say it would need $20,000 a month until it is done. In this I am not thinking much of myself. Out of that I doubt if I could possibly take what I said—still that is all right. I can't get away even though I wish I might, & then there are so many to pay that it ought to be easily & cheerfully done & can be if the right organization is made. But still I must know & at once. If the necessary things can not be done I must know that, & do what I can & leave the rest undone. I am not going through with it & leave a lot of promises & obligations on my hands. Please let me know at once & definitely. I am very sorry to put any extra trouble on you—but what can we do. We all seem to think that organized labor must make this fight & I suppose it must—

Ever Your friend | Clarence Darrow

MS: ALS, WHi, AFL Records: Gompers Era. DATE: stamped: "RECEIVED: | July 20 1911." NOTE: on the last page of the letter, Darrow struck out the name on the letterhead and wrote "Higgins Building."

47. William J. Burns.

TO FREMONT OLDER • LOS ANGELES • THURSDAY 26 JULY 1911

CLARENCE DARROW | HIGGINS BUILDING July 26th

My Dear Mr. Older

The editorial is beautiful in spirit & I believe it is true.[48] You don't know how I enjoy hearing you talk & reading these things which you at least inspire. I have studied & talked & worked along these lines for many years until I am growing tired—but you come nearer to it all than I have ever come. At least I never have been able to get over the dread of being poor & the fear of it & you have passed that with all the rest seemingly without an effort. Still I can't help wishing you could get free from it all—I am so bound to do it when this is over, as I suppose it sometime will be.

As to the Governor I was much disappointed.[49] I had heard of him from you & others, had felt that he was honest & narrow—and had seen little & probably never would see much—but I think I could judge him in the hour I spent with him. He is worth all you have said and done for him. I have seldom been so well impressed with a man. He may not see all we think we see but what of it—we might not see it right—but his mind is clear & vigorous & alert—& he acts regardless of consequences & with an independence that is almost never seen in a public man. Then too he is human. I watched him in the Wilde case[50] which called for conflicting emotions, & could see how his human side entered into it, how he acted with complete independence—moved no doubt somewhat by his human feeling. By the way I am going to see that man before long & urge him to arrange his business & go up there & try his case. I know the Governor would have made more friends by deciding it the other way, & so did he. Then too he is so simple & free from humbug & knows so well that almost every one is trying to humbug society & even themselves. I am not worried any more about his radicalism or his narrowness of vision. He has got it all in him, & with his keenness & courage he will be right—at least so near

48. Darrow is likely referring to an editorial the day before in Older's *San Francisco Bulletin* that explained the *Bulletin's* attitude toward Abraham Ruef (1864–1936). Ruef was a political boss who helped maintain corrupt control of San Francisco until he was convicted of bribery in 1908 and sentenced to fourteen years in prison (which he began serving in 1911). Older, through the *Bulletin,* and William J. Burns helped to convict Ruef. Later, Older sought Ruef's release from prison. In the editorial to which Darrow refers, Older explained his change of heart and his sympathy for any person suffering in prison conditions. "Concerning the Bulletin's Attitude toward Abe Ruef," *San Francisco Bulletin,* 25 July 1911.
49. The governor was Hiram Johnson.
50. Louis J. Wilde was indicted by a grand jury in Portland, Oregon, in June 1911, on the charge of embezzlement from a failed bank in Portland. The prosecutor sought to have Wilde, who lived in California, extradited to Oregon. A few days before this letter, the prosecutor and Darrow, who represented Wilde, met with Governor Johnson in Sacramento, California, to discuss Wilde's extradition. Despite an initial opinion from the attorney general for California that Wilde was not guilty and letters and statements of support for Wilde from many people, the governor ordered his extradition, and Wilde went to Portland on 28 July. He stood trial in January 1912 (he was not represented by Darrow then) and, at the end of the trial, the judge ordered the jury to acquit him on the grounds that the prosecution's evidence failed to support the charge and that the indictment failed to meet the statute of limitations. "Wilde Fighting for His Rights," *Los Angeles Times,* 19 July 1911; "Wilde's Extradition," *Los Angeles Times,* 23 July 1911; "Wilde Makes Statement," 29 July 1911; "A Verdict of not Guilty in Banker Wilde's Case," *Los Angeles Times,* 4 February 1912.

as we poor d—n fools can tell the right. But he won't get very much further in politics. Place & power are for sycofants & humbugs & cowards. Here is a really independent, right thinking, right acting, courageous man, who has been given a commanding position, for the smallest, & cheepest, & easiest & most ignoble act of his life. He will do good things & will loose political power & influence as he does them.

We both enjoyed our visit. I always do, no where more than with you & Mrs. Older & your friends. We will come back for a day or two soon. I will let you know & see if we can't take that trip.

Your friend | Clarence Darrow

MS: ALS, CU-BANC, Older Papers, Box 1. DATE: letterhead.

TO FREMONT OLDER • LOS ANGELES • THURSDAY 17 AUGUST 1911

CLARENCE DARROW | HIGGINS BUILDING Aug 17

My Dear Older

The editorial is fine. I will try to have it copied here.[51] Also that was a bully article of Barry's.[52] I will use it in my argument if I live that long. We have been trying to get up there. I may come this week—but may not. You remember the bearer Mr. Davis.[53] I want you to see him & give him any advice you can. The District Atty made a queer remark to us this morning—& at the time of McNamaras arrest Burns[54] made a strange one to Clancy,[55] which has set me thinking & made me suspicious. I hate to be suspicious. I thought I had better find out if you knew Clancy & get your opinion. Met Burns today & he said he was going up to S.F. tomorrow & would see you. He said you were getting clear on my side & wanted Rufe[56] pardoned. You might get something out of B. Still you might not.

Your friend | C. S. D.

MS: ALS, CU-BANC, Older Papers, Box 1. DATE: letterhead.

51. Darrow is likely referring to an editorial in Older's *Bulletin* that criticized the use of the grand jury by the Los Angeles county attorney to intimidate witnesses and gather evidence for the prosecution of the McNamaras. The county attorney had subpoenaed many witnesses to give grand jury testimony, including a private detective employed by the defense. See "Otis Transforms His Grand Jury into Detective Agency," *San Francisco Bulletin*, 16 August 1911.
52. Darrow might be referring to an article by John D. Barry in the same issue of the *Bulletin* as the editorial referred to above. In this article, Barry lamented the fact that so many people seemed to have lost their capacity for enjoying life. "Ways of the World," *San Francisco Bulletin*, 16 August 1911.
53. Possibly LeCompte Davis.
54. William J. Burns.
55. Eugene A. Clancy (b. 1876) was a vice president of the International Association of Bridge and Structural Iron Workers, the union for which John McNamara was treasurer. Clancy lived with his wife and children in San Francisco. He was convicted together with thirty-seven other leaders of the IABSIW in Indianapolis in December 1912. See Darrow to Field, 22 October 1912, n.104 (describing the trial). He served a seven-year sentence in prison. See "San Quentin Gates to Open for Clancy," *Los Angeles Times*, 21 September 1918.
56. Abraham Ruef.

TO J. HOWARD MOORE • LOS ANGELES • FRIDAY 6 OCTOBER 1911

CLARENCE DARROW | HIGGINS BUILDING Oct 6th

My Dear Mr. Moore

Am glad you got the tenant. Tell him to use the books & every thing else. I am sure they are all right. The battle begins soon & I wish it was over. It doesn't look good to me, but I shall take care of myself. After this I will join you on a farm, either in the east or California which is a delightful climate.

Love to Jennie.

Hastily | C S Darrow

MS: ALS, MnU-L, Darrow Collection. ENVELOPE ADDRESS: J Howard Moore Esq | 6260 Jackson Pk Av | Chicago. POSTMARK: Los Angeles, 7 October 1911.

TO FREMONT OLDER • LOS ANGELES • THURSDAY 2 NOVEMBER 1911

CLARENCE DARROW | HIGGINS BUILDING Oct 2d

My Dear Older

I am glad you are back & wish you could come down. Don't see when I can get away. I am getting a raw deal, but don't believe they can "get away with it." Am "sawing wood" all the time.[57] Scripps[58] wired for Russell[59] so it is up to him. I hope he comes. We must have our side represented. Harriman's vote was great, & it helps.[60] I wonder if some of your rich friends (not you) wouldn't help him out. Got a wire from Steffens[61] that he is coming later. Mrs Jacobson[62] is here. Spent last night with us. Will help her out. She is all right.

Ever yours | Darrow

MS: ALS, CU-BANC, Older Papers, Box 1. DATE: reference to "Harriman's vote" suggests that Darrow used the wrong month in his date.

57. Darrow is probably referring to the long and difficult process of selecting jurors for the trial of James McNamara, which had been under way for three weeks.
58. E. W. Scripps.
59. Charles Edward Russell.
60. Job Harriman, Darrow's co-counsel, was also the socialist candidate for mayor of Los Angeles. On 31 October, he won the vote in the primary, with 20,157 votes, well over the 16,790 votes of the incumbent, George Alexander (1839–1923). But Alexander went on to win the general election on 5 December 1911.
61. Lincoln Steffens.
62. The identity of "Mrs. Jacobson" is unknown.

TO RUBY DARROW • LOS ANGELES • THURSDAY 9 NOVEMBER 1911

CLARENCE DARROW | HIGGINS BUILDING Thursday morning

Dearest Rube

There was nothing whatever about that matter different from what you saw, & no intention on any one's part that there ever should be. I told her several times how much I thought of you & how good & kind & clever you are—as I always tell every one with whom I talk. I am very sorry that my fool jokes ever cause you annoyance or humiliation & I will see that it is never done in the future.[63] I don't suppose I can ever change my nature or my feelings but it has been many years since I ever respected or loved any one else as I do you—& this will never change.

Clarence.

MS: ALS, MnU-L, Darrow Collection. ENVELOPE ADDRESS: Mrs. Ruby Darrow | 803 North Bonnie Brae St | Los Angeles | Cal. POSTMARK: Los Angeles, 9 November 1911.

TO PAUL DARROW • LOS ANGELES • SATURDAY 11 NOVEMBER 1911

CLARENCE DARROW | HIGGINS BUILDING Nov 11th

Dear Paul

In this state they get twelve men in the jury box who have passed both sides with no excuse for cause & then they challenge what they wish—the state has ten peremptory challenges & the defense 20.[64] We got 12—& they used 2 & we used 5—leaving 5 in the box. Then we excused 2 of these by agreement leaving 3 sworn to try the case. They are Bean, Green & one more.[65] We are well satisfied with them. We then started out to fill it & have passed three more for cause. After the panel is full we will both challenge peremptorily again. They have been d—n raw but have not got the best of us in any particular. Still I feel about the ultimate outcome just as I have—although Harriman's big vote has helped. It will take to Christmas to get a jury & probably until April to finish the case. When Baer[66] comes I want you to talk with him about some deal on the plant such as I wrote you about. They can afford to give more for it than we because they can save a lot of money running it. I suppose it will turn out all right some time, but it will be a long time before any dividends can be taken out. Am well & we wish you could both come out & see us.

C. S. D.

MS: ALS, MnU-L, Darrow Collection. DATE: reference to jury selection.

63. What Darrow did is unknown and can only be surmised from this letter.
64. The prosecution decided to try James McNamara first, and his trial started on 11 October 1911. Some fifty days were spent trying to select a jury.
65. The three jurors, selected and sworn for service on 8 November, were Robert D. Bain (b. 1842), a carpenter (the district attorney would later allege that Darrow had bribed Bain); F. D. Green, an orange grower; and Byron Lisk (b. 1850), a retired mill owner.
66. Darrow likely means William A. Baehr.

TO SAMUEL GOMPERS • LOS ANGELES • FRIDAY 1 DECEMBER 1911

Los Angeles, Calif., Dec 1.,11

There was no avoiding step taken today.[67] When I see you I know you will be satisfied that all of us gave everything we had to accomplish the best. Hope you will believe we realize our responsibility and did the best that could be done. Will wire.

Darrow. | 1022 PM

MS: Tele, WHi, AFL Records: Gompers Era. TELEGRAM ADDRESS: Samuel Gompers | American Federation of Labor, G. St., | Washington, DC.

TO ANDREW GALLAGHER • LOS ANGELES • FRIDAY 1 DECEMBER 1911

LOS ANGELES, CAL., DEC-I–II

ON FULL CONSIDERATION BY ALL COUNSEL EXCEPTING HARRIMAN[68] WE WERE SATISFIED THAT THERE WAS NOTHING ELSE TO DO. HARRIMAN WAS NOT CALLED IN BECAUSE OF POLITICAL AFFILIATIONS AND IT WAS DONE WITHOUT HIS KNOWLEDGE.

CLARENCE S DARROW.

MS: Tele, CU-BANC, San Francisco Labor Council, Box 8. INSIDE ADDRESS: ANDREW GALLAGHER, | 510 METROPOLIS BANK BLG., SAN FRANCISCO.

TO PAUL DARROW • LOS ANGELES • TUESDAY 5 DECEMBER 1911

Dec 5

Dear Paul

It has been so strenuous I have not written.[69] Try not to worry over me. I have lots of friends & am all right. They may get me into trouble, but the end will be all right some of these days. You know me better than any one else & love me more & my chief anxiety is over you, & I know you will be brave as I will be. I think things will come out right but

67. On 1 December 1911, James McNamara confessed to blowing up the Los Angeles Times Building and pleaded guilty to first-degree murder of a machinist who died in the explosion. His brother, John McNamara, pleaded guilty to conspiring to dynamiting the Llewellyn Iron Works in Los Angeles on 25 December 1910 (where a strike had been in progress).
68. The election for mayor of Los Angeles was to be held in four days, on 5 December 1911. This telegram was cited by the *Los Angeles Times* as confirmation that Harriman, the socialist candidate, had not been part of the plea deliberations. "McNamara Pleads Guilty to Murder," *Los Angeles Times,* 2 December 1911.
69. The McNamaras were sentenced on the day of this letter. James McNamara received life in prison. John McNamara received a fifteen-year sentence. Many reports of Darrow's potential involvement with the bribing of jurors were circulating and one newspaper heard reports (later confirmed to be untrue) that Darrow had been arrested. "Tensest Moment of the Century's Trial," *Los Angeles Times,* 5 December 1911.

if they don't you will never find that your father is not brave & true & has not acted as was best & right.

With lots of love to you & Lil

C. S. D.

MS: ALS, Darrow Family. PLACE: no reason to doubt Los Angeles. DATE: reference to strenuousness and possible trouble.

TO PAUL DARROW • LOS ANGELES • TUESDAY 12 DECEMBER 1911

CLARENCE DARROW | HIGGINS BUILDING Dec 12

Dear Paul

I don't want you to worry.[70] I am very sure no one can make me serious trouble or that they even will try. Of course it causes us all lots of worry & I am sorry for you—but you know me & know all the motives of my life. I have lots of good friends here & enough money to look after me and when I am done with it will make my plans. Ever with love to you & Lil

C S D.

MS: ALS, MnU-L, Darrow Collection. DATE: letterhead.

TO PAUL DARROW • LOS ANGELES • FRIDAY 29 DECEMBER 1911

LAW OFFICES | HARRIMAN RYCKMAN & TUTTLE Dec 29

Dear Paul,

I am no doubt in some danger here & don't know how things will turn—There is no right to get me in trouble—but I am ready for any thing that comes. My health & spirits are all right & don't worry over me. You know me but we must wait & be content. I still feel if you could make a turn of the property you ought to do it. I don't need the money but if I got into trouble it might hurt the business. Talk it over fully with Jacobs.[71] I wrote and wired asking him to come & see me—Would like him to know the full situation. I think of you all a great deal & fear you worry over me, but my mind is at ease & any thing that comes is all right. With love to you & Lil

C. S. D.

MS: ALS, MnU-L, Darrow Collection. DATE: reference to danger and trouble, suggesting the imminent indictment.

70. Stories about Darrow's potential involvement in bribing jurors continued. "Now Names Darrow in Bribery Tale," *New York Times,* 12 December 1911.
71. John T. Jacobs.

TO PAUL DARROW • LOS ANGELES • MONDAY 1 JANUARY 1912

CLARENCE DARROW | HIGGINS BUILDING Jan 1st

Dear Paul

I think I was too pessimistic when I wrote you last—Of course there is danger here but I don't believe there is one chance in twenty that they could get me even if they try which they might. There is really nothing to it except some suspicious circumstances. My worry over you was the effect on the business if they did & whether if you could not sell it. I had not better turn over my stock to you & Jacobs & Tew,[72] & have it go out that they owned the control. I don't want you or the business to suffer. As for your trouble I know you will feel badly but you know that every step I have taken has been out of devotion to the cause & that I have done nothing wrong.

I have about 9,000 here with a chance to get 5,000 more if I don't get into serious trouble. Shall make no plans now for the future, but will keep you posted. We have just moved to a little flat & Ruby is doing her own work & all our expenses will be inside 90 a month. I have been thinking of your mother. Last month I sent her 75. Shall do the same for Dec. She told me she thought of moving into the house. We can finish paying that (about 600) & then can't she get along on about 50 a month until we are out of the woods or know how we are? I want to be careful of money now, & shall do my part. I should think within another 30 days I will know whether I shall have to make an other fight for myself. If I do I think sure I will win, & so do my friends—All the other matters will come out right in time for every thing was right & for the best. Don't take things too much to heart. Of course the business is the chief thing & we ought to have enough to make us all comfortable.

C. S. D.

Our house address is Ocean Park, Los Angeles Co. Cal.

CSD.

MS: ALS, MnU-L, Darrow Collection. DATE: letterhead and reference to allegations of jury bribery.

TO JOHN J. AND JAMES B. MCNAMARA • LOS ANGELES • TUESDAY 2 JANUARY 1912

Jan 2d

Dear J. & Jim

I have intended to write & hoped to come up before now, but so many things are happening that I can't just yet. I don't know when they will stop, but they will get enough

72. John T. Jacobs and Charles F. Tew.

sometime. The boys all seem friendly & are understanding better but it has been tough for us all. Any how don't think that you are forgotten or ever will be. And when I can I shall write or see you.

Your friend | Clarence Darrow

MS: ALS, OCU, McNamara Papers, Box 8. PLACE: other letters. DATE: reference to difficulties.

TO PAUL DARROW • LOS ANGELES • THURSDAY 4 JANUARY 1912

LAW OFFICES | HARRIMAN RYCKMAN & TUTTLE Jan 4

Dear Paul

There is nothing new here, but may be soon. Anyhow I am not afraid or worried about the future whatever it may be.

I wrote Willie Carlin[73] to send you my stock &c. He may send the tin boxes with it or may pick it out & send it. Use your best judgment about transferring it to Jacobs & Tew in case of trouble. Am sorry your mother is ill. Write me more about it if it is serious. I hope she may recover soon. Will write often.

Ever | C. S. D.

MS: ALS, MnU-L, Darrow Collection. DATE: letterhead and reference to possibly transferring stock to Jacobs and Tew.

TO PAUL DARROW • LOS ANGELES • TUESDAY 9 JANUARY 1912

Tuesday

Dear Paul

I feel that you ought to see Conley[74] *now* & see if here is a chance to dispose of the plant. You will not need to sell it unless it is best but I feel if we could get 75,000 or even 60,000 we ought to do it. It looks to me that improvements &c. will make it a long time before we can ever get an income above bonds & that more money will be needed—and that you could do better if you had the money to invest where it would bring regular returns. I won't insist on your selling but I think you should see at once if there is a chance. It looks like I will never earn any more & while it will take very little to live on still I don't want to put too much on you. Then too I may be put to expense in my defence if I am indicted as I probably will be. Any how look into it, go over it with Jacobs & make some little effort in the matter.

C. S. D.

I feel that I had better not leave here now. Will wait a little any how.

73. William Carlin.
74. The identity of "Conley" is unknown.

MS: ALS, MnU-L, Darrow Collection. DATE: reference to expecting indictment and the content of other letters.

TO PAUL DARROW • LOS ANGELES • SATURDAY 13 JANUARY 1912

LAW OFFICES | HARRIMAN RYCKMAN & TUTTLE Jan 13

Dear Paul

I do not like to worry you but feel I ought to keep you posted about the worst. They are making every effort to indict me & I would not be surprised if they accomplished it at any time. If they do it will be a fight. I ought to win, but in this place I don't know. Do not be surprised at any thing you hear. As for me I don't care much, my mind & conscience are at ease & I only worry about you & the effect on your business & about Ruby though she is game. If you are doing any thing in the direction I urged keep me posted. It seems best to do it if you can. Again I am afraid hard times are coming on & I would not expand any more than needed.

Love to Lil | D.

MS: ALS, MnU-L, Darrow Collection. DATE: reference to efforts to indict.

TO PAUL DARROW • LOS ANGELES • WEDNESDAY 17 JANUARY 1912

Jan 17

Dear Paul

I have very direct information that I will be indicted tomorrow. I believe I will win—but may not. I got good letters from Jacobs yesterday & Tew today & they assure me that every thing will be all right there whatever happens so I am content. I know that all I did has been for the poor & the highest motives & I am content & want you not to worry. Enclosed is check which send to your mother with my love. I am living economically and am afraid we must ask her to adjust her expenses on a smaller basis until we know where we are. It seems to me that with the house if they take it she could get along comfortably on 50 more, but you & she adjust that. Both of you know that I think of you both first.

One thing more. If the baby is a boy be sure & name it Paul. I know neither you or Lil would care for yourself but this is a child that can't choose, so do as I say.[75]

Ever with love to both | C. S. D.

Ruby is a brick & neither blames or worries. There is no one like her.

D.

MS: ALS, Darrow Family. DATE: reference to imminent indictment.

75. Paul Darrow's second child, Mary, was born 13 February 1912.

TO MARY FIELD • LOS ANGELES • THURSDAY 25 JANUARY 1912

Thursday Eve

Dear Mary

Things are as they were when you left. It looks sure for an indictment early next week. Of course there might be a slip but I don't think so. Will keep you posted. I believe I can win & of course shall give them a good fight. Am getting back my spirits & my grit, but somehow I can't help the thought, that if it comes it will be for the best & will then do my best work—perhaps it is necessary. Still I shall resist.

Hastily | C. S. D.

MS: ALS, ICN, Parton-Darrow Papers, Box 1, Folder 3. ENVELOPE ADDRESS: Miss Mary Field | c/o Fremont Older | "The Bulletin" | San Francisco | Cal. POSTMARK: Los Angeles, 26 January 1912.

TO PAUL DARROW • LOS ANGELES • THURSDAY 25 JANUARY 1912

Thursday

Dear Paul,

Your last letter just came: it did me lots of good. I am so glad you look at everything as you do. I have not lost ambition. If I go I will do my greatest work see if I don't. I have the feeling that it would be the greatest thing in my life & find myself wanting it to happen. Still I shall fight to avoid it & believe I shall win. Franklin[76] is on their side—but I feel as I always have that this will make my case better. My lawyer friends feel the same. I wrote Walling[77] to send the bonds & stock & money for coupons to you. If you haven't got them let me know & when you get them you had better pay the balance on the house. Ensign[78] will send you the account. It seems to me that if your mother takes the house 50 a month would make her very comfortable if Mr. B[79] is able to do any thing. Of course

76. Bert H. Franklin (1868–1927), a former deputy United States marshal and longtime resident of Los Angeles, had been working as a private detective for Darrow as part of the team of lawyers and investigators defending the McNamara brothers. During the selection of jurors for the trial of James McNamara, Franklin was arrested for attempting to bribe one of the jurors and one of the veniremen. Within a few days after this letter, newspapers reported that Franklin had confessed and was cooperating with prosecutors. "Darrow's Detective May Confess All," *New York Times,* 31 January 1912. Franklin, who pleaded guilty the following month and received a fine of four thousand dollars (the amount found on him at the time of his arrest), eventually became the prosecution's principal witness against Darrow. "Darrow Detective Confesses Bribery," *New York Times,* 28 February 1912; "Darrow Sleuth Fined $4,000," *Chicago Tribune,* 2 March 1912.
77. Probably Willoughby George Walling.
78. This could be a reference to Charles B. Ensign (1860–1942); his brother, Adelbert L. Ensign (b. 1850); or their Chicago firm, C. B. Ensign & Co., which served as an investment bank for Darrow and his son's gas plant in Colorado.
79. This is a reference to Mungo Brownlee (1843–1925), Jessie Darrow's second husband. Brownlee was born in Scotland and emigrated to the United States with his family at the age of five. He grew up and lived in Trumbull County, Ohio, and worked as a schoolteacher and justice of the peace in the area of Vernon, Ohio. He lived in Chicago from 1908 (after his first wife died) until 1920, when he moved to Burg Hill, Ohio (where Jessie was born); there he worked as a farmer. He and Jessie were married in Chicago in 1912.

if I was not in trouble it would be different. The indictment has not yet come but it seems sure that it will probably the first of next week. As I have said I really believe I can win but possibly not. Probably you had better leave money matters as they are for a time.

C. S. D.

Just received word from Walling that he has sent you the bonds but has not got the stock. It must be somewhere in the office. I had two boxes—or it might be in my desk or somewhere else in vault. Write Willie[80] at once & have him look it up & send to you.

MS: ALS, MnU-L, Darrow Collection. DATE: reference to imminent indictment and statements in other letters.

TO PAUL DARROW • LOS ANGELES • THURSDAY 1 FEBRUARY 1912

Feby 1st

Dear Paul

I have been feeling very well since the thing broke.[81] My health & spirits are good & shall go to work to win. I think I will but of course no one knows. Somehow I do not feel worried about the whole thing. My life has been pretty full of experiences & I am not done & will not be whatever the result & I know I can do more good & probably better work if I am stuck—still I am quite confident I shall not be. Probably before the trial you had better come out for two or three days, although I know you are needed there—the only thing I care about is that probably some of the Greeley people will think it strange if you do not. I suppose the trial will come in two or three months. Love to Lil

C. S. D.

MS: ALS, MnU-L, Darrow Collection. DATE: year appended and supported by reference to indictment and impending trial.

TO EDGAR LEE MASTERS • CHICAGO • SATURDAY 3 FEBRUARY 1912

Feby 3rd

Dear Ed

As you know the ax has fallen—but I feel very confident I shall win—though of course, it is a hard blow—Well I chose my life & must stand the consequences. I understand that a friend in San Francisco wrote you about money without my knowledge.[82] Don't do any thing about this now. I can't make any general appeal & can only write to a few I know

80. William Carlin.
81. The grand jury in Los Angeles County returned two indictments against Darrow on 29 January 1912: one alleging bribery of Robert Bain and the other alleging bribery of George Lockwood.
82. The identity of Darrow's friend in San Francisco is unknown.

unless the Unions help which I fear they will not. Of course if you could get something on the bank case or any other matters, I would like it. Will write fully soon. I appreciate your devotion & loyalty—[83]

Ever Yours | C. S. Darrow.

MS: ALS, TxU-Hu, Masters Collection. DATE: "the ax has fallen" probably refers to the indictment.

TO JENNIE DARROW MOORE • LOS ANGELES • SUNDAY 4 FEBRUARY 1912

DARROW, MASTERS & WILSON Feby 4

Dear Jennie

Thanks for your good letter & kind offer.[84] I don't need any thing now but if I do later might let you help some—but I don't expect to. Don't worry over me. I have it all settled in my mind which is clear & tranquil & if any thing happens it won't hurt & I am sure under the circumstances will develop & help me. Have many good friends here—and if it was an other in my place I would say nothing else can be as good for you. Still for all that they can't do it without a fight & I see little chance for me to lose.

With love from both to both of you

Clarence.

MS: ALS, MnU-L, Darrow Collection. ENVELOPE ADDRESS: Mrs Jennie More | 6260 Jackson Pk Av. | Chicago. POSTMARK: Los Angeles, 5 February 1912.

TO PAUL DARROW • LOS ANGELES • SUNDAY 4 FEBRUARY 1912

DARROW, MASTERS & WILSON Feby 4

Dear Paul

I would guess that the trial would come in about two months. It looks very favorable, but I will keep you posted. I really don't see how I can lose—but of course. And then if I

83. All of the ways in which Masters had shown devotion to Darrow by this date may not be known. But several weeks before this letter, Masters had sent a telegram to Darrow acknowledging receipt of Darrow's letters and sending his love to Darrow and Ruby. Darrow to Masters, 10 January 1912, Tele, MBU, Leo Cherne Papers, Box 2, Folder 1. Masters had also publicly shown his support for Darrow by sending a telegram to Fremont Older's newspaper on the day Darrow was indicted: "Darrow has given his whole life and all his great ability to the cause of liberty and particularly to the emancipation of labor from unjust laws and conditions. He has done this deliberately and with a full understanding of the flattery, the riches and the worldly power that would have been his had he given his talents to the service of capitalism. This supreme self dedication speaks so conclusively for the fundamental trust of the man's nature and for the largeness of his vision that no one who takes these things into account will countenance any charge which lowers his stature." "Chicago Judges Telegraph Esteem for Labor Lawyer," *San Francisco Bulletin,* 30 January 1912.
84. This is probably a reference to a long letter from Jennie to Ruby in which Jennie had, among other things, expressed her concern in some detail for Darrow's health and offered to help financially and by coming to Los Angeles. Jennie Darrow Moore to Ruby Darrow, 1 February 1912, ALS, MBU, Leo Cherne Papers, Box 2, Folder 1.

should I have that all settled—somehow I hardly care. I know the truth and am satisfied & feel sure that nothing better could happen to me or to you & that it would do more for me & the cause than any thing I could do—and that it would make me almost no pain—then too I would have much time to write. My spirits are bully now—& although in my heart I don't care, still I expect to win. Got good letter from Baer[85] about business. It seems to me to be coming on all right. I hope your assistant won't ask for an other raise. Baer should tell him his salary is high enough if he does.

Hastily | C. S. D.

MS: ALS, MnU-L, Darrow Collection. PLACE: despite letterhead, Los Angeles is supported by biographical evidence. DATE: reference to impending trial.

TO J. HOWARD MOORE • OCEAN PARK, CALIFORNIA • TUESDAY 6 FEBRUARY 1912

Ocean Park | Feby. 6

Dear Howard

Your good letters just came—you are kind & generous & true. I don't need the money either of you or Jennie now. Save it & sometime I may. They had no right to do this to me & I don't believe it will stick. I feel quite sure I can win but the interests against me are strong, & if I fail I may have to leave you all for a time—not long—I believe, but I think that even then I will adjust my life & come out of it all stronger than before—Still I think & hope I shall win—although perhaps losing would be best. Any how I love you both & thank you both & don't want you to mourn for me—for my mind & soul are adjusted to what comes.

Ever your brother | Clarence.

MS: ALS, MnU-L, Darrow Collection. DATE: place and reference to impending trial.

TO FREDERICK HAMERSTROM • OCEAN PARK, CALIFORNIA • TUESDAY 6 FEBRUARY 1912

Ocean Park | Feby 6

Dear Fred

Your good letter just came.[86] I appreciate all you say. Of course I didn't, still there are suspicious circumstances & they are bound to get me & the interests are strong. In spite

85. Darrow is referring to William A. Baehr.
86. Fred had sent a telegram to Darrow one week earlier, seeking more information and offering to drum up publicity for Darrow, but no letter to Darrow was located. Frederick Hamerstrom to Darrow, 30 January 1912, Tele, MBU, Leo Cherne Papers, Box 2, Folder 1.

of that I think I shall win. If I don't I will adjust myself to that & believe will grow by it all—but it is awful hard. More than any thing else I am heart broken on Ruby's account. She is so fine & strong & brave & devoted.

As to publicity, it seems better to let them have their stay now. The storm is too high to stem it, but I have many good friends & some strong ones & I believe their time & mine will come. After all Fred we are helpless in the hands of fate & if it is needed that I go through this, I must go. Please don't worry too much for me. If I fail Paul may need your counsel & help to keep things together, but he too is brave & strong. Love to Helen.

Yours Ever | Clarence Darrow

MS: ALS, MnU-L, Darrow Collection. DATE: place and reference to impending trial.

TO EDWARD BOYCE • LOS ANGELES • MONDAY 12 FEBRUARY 1912

CLARENCE DARROW | HIGGINS BUILDING Feby 12

My Dear Boyce

You know of my serious trouble. I must have help. The money I received paid my debts & only a little more & I must have considerable amounts for my defense. There are but a very few I can ask. Won't you let me have $1,000. I would not ask it if I did not need it & need it badly. Please do this for me & the cause I have long worked for.[87]

Truly | C. S. Darrow.

MS: ALS, WaSpHiE, Boyce Papers. DATE: letterhead and replies from Boyce.

TO SAMUEL GOMPERS • LOS ANGELES • FEBRUARY 1912

HIGGINS BUILDING | LOS ANGELES

My Dear Gompers

In every crisis I have stood by labor & my convictions & always given my best of devotion & brain. I am in serious trouble as you know. The money I received only a little more than paid my debts & I have no other available means, & I need help to protect my liberty. They ought to help, won't they? Of course I don't want a general appeal but some of the Unions ought to stand by me in this time of trial & give

87. Boyce replied one week later, saying that he was "sorry to read of the serious trouble [Darrow had] to face" and that he would write to him in two or three days. Boyce to Darrow, 21 February 1912, ALS, WaSpHiE, Boyce Papers. Several weeks later, Boyce sent Darrow one hundred dollars, saying: "Am sorry I cannot send you the amount you ask; it is unnecessary for me to enter into details as to why I cannot send it: suffice to say if I had the money you could have it." Boyce to Darrow, 2 April 1912, ALS, WaSpHiE, Boyce Papers.

substantial aid. If they will & you can let me know. You understand what it means at least to me.

Truly | Clarence Darrow.

MS: ALS, WHi, AFL Records: Gompers Era. DATE: "[Feb., 1912]" appended.

TO PAUL DARROW • LOS ANGELES • TUESDAY 20 FEBRUARY 1912

Feby 20

Dear Paul

Yours containing Ensign letter & answer is received. I have written quite a number of friends asking financial assistance, am getting some. I tell them the truth that most that I got went to pay my debts, that while I have the main interest in the plant subject to bonds, still I could not get money on it, & that any how those in sympathy ought to help. Of course I may never be able to make any more money, whatever the outcome. I don't want you to write any one that we can give security or any thing like that. You can say that you think I am hard up & in a general way tell them the truth just as I tell you.

There is nothing new since I last wrote. Am feeling well & in fighting mood & ready for whatever comes.

C. S. D.

MS: ALS, MnU-L, Darrow Collection. DATE: reference to impending trial.

TO SAMUEL GOMPERS • LOS ANGELES • TUESDAY 20 FEBRUARY 1912

LAW OFFICES | HARRIMAN RYCKMAN & TUTTLE Feby 20th

My Dear Gompers

A letter today from Pettigrew says that you told him an interview was once published from me in which I said you knew the McS were guilty from the start. I never said such a thing & never knew such a thing was in print. I or you can deny it as you please. Of course it is silly, & you know the reliability to be placed in such things.[88]

Truly | Clarence Darrow

MS: ALS, WHi, AFL Records: Gompers Era. DATE: "[1912]" appended and reply from Gompers.

88. Gompers responded in one letter to these last two letters from Darrow, saying that it would be impossible to raise any money for his defense: "For the life of me I can not see how we can raise any money . . . for you. Believing, aye, almost firmly convinced of the innocence of the McNamaras, we strained every nerve to raise as near as possible the amount of money you suggested would be necessary for their defense. Upon learning that they were guilty, the first intimation of which was conveyed to the rank and file as well as to the officers of the labor movement through their confession, I am free to say to you that in my judgment any general appeal for funds to defend you . . . would fall upon indifferent ears and elicit little, if any, response at this time." Gompers to Darrow, 16 March 1912, TLc, WHi, AFL Records: Gompers Era. On the subject of whether Darrow ever said that Gompers knew the McNamaras were guilty from the start, Gompers told Darrow that he was "gratified at the receipt of [his] letter." Ibid.

TO JOHN MITCHELL • LOS ANGELES • TUESDAY 20 FEBRUARY 1912

Higgins Building, LA. | Feby 20

My Dear Mitchell

I thought I would drop you one more line to tell you how much I need assistance at this time. So many people think I have money when really I have been in debt all my life & now have very little available & it will cost 25,000 to make the defense. It seems to me by consulting Gompers & Morrison[89] & some others some plan could be made to get the help without making it public & also get it soon. Surely I have served long & faithfully & I am certain that the unions would not let me go to prison without a defense, especially when the case was one growing out of their fight. I know you will do all you can & as fast as possible.

Truly | Clarence Darrow

MS: ALS, DCU, Mitchell Papers.

TO CHARLES ERSKINE SCOTT WOOD • LOS ANGELES • TUESDAY 20 FEBRUARY 1912

Feby 20

My Dear Wood

You asked if you could do any thing for me.[90] I believe you have not much money but I need it badly. Could you let me have 500 or 1,000. The money I got nearly all went to pay debts & this is an expensive fight. If I win I am sure you will get it back. If not I don't know. If you could I wish you would. The man you wrote about is openly with the other side. If he turned up against me could you testify to any conversation with him?

Sincerely | C S Darrow.

Higgins Bldg | Los Angeles

MS: ALS, CU-BANC, C. E. S. Wood Papers, Carton 2. DATE: reference to "fight" and address in "Higgins Bldg."

89. Frank Morrison (1859–1949), secretary of the American Federation of Labor, 1897–1935.
90. Three weeks earlier, after Darrow's indictment, Wood had written to Darrow, predicting that the prosecution would likely fail, but he sympathized with Darrow and offered to help in any practical way that he could. He also asked whether Larry Sullivan, one of Darrow's investigators in the McNamara matter and an acquaintance of Wood's, had been "straight and true." Wood to Darrow, 29 January 1912, ALS, MBU, Leo Cherne Papers, Box 2, Folder 1.

TO BRAND WHITLOCK • LOS ANGELES • TUESDAY 20 FEBRUARY 1912

Feby 20

Dear Brand

I learned yesterday that Mrs D. had written you a letter.[91] I did not know it & was sorry to hear it. You know her love & loyalty to me & will understand.

Of course I am going through deep waters almost alone—as one must always do. But I know you so well that I know that whatever you think or feel about it all you are always governed by your conscience, & you will again believe the same of me.

Truly | Darrow

MS: ALS, CtW. DATE: reference to Ruby Darrow's letter to Whitlock.

TO CHARLES ERSKINE SCOTT WOOD • LOS ANGELES • FRIDAY 23 FEBRUARY 1912

Feby 23

My Dear Wood

I have been thinking I should not have asked you for money, as I have the impression you are like me & always live close to your income. Unless your circumstances warrant it I don't want you to send any. I will get along in some way.

Truly | C S Darrow

MS: ALS, CU-BANC, C. E. S. Wood Papers, Carton 2. DATE: reference to request for money.

TO CHARLES ERSKINE SCOTT WOOD • LOS ANGELES • FRIDAY 1 MARCH 1912

Mar 1st

My Dear Mr. Wood

I feel as if I ought to return your generous check & still I need it so badly I will keep it. I hope you will get the money back, & I believe you will.

91. Ruby Darrow had written a long letter to Whitlock seeking an explanation for why he had not contacted her husband and pleading for Whitlock to write and show his support: "*How can* you have remained silent so long!! You men in the east fairly *shoved* this man out here, and these men in the west came to our house and almost *dragged* him here—and were *horrified* when I replied to their whispers of 'traitor' that I would rather have him that and *alive*. . . . Are you *all going* to sit on the fence and see this man marched *past* you *to prison?* . . . *Please write to him at once*—tell him you have been ill anything—*anything* but *write at once* and it will be remembered *with gratitude* til death *by* R—D—." Ruby Darrow to Brand Whitlock, 14 February 1912, ALS, DLC-MSS, Whitlock Papers, Container 25.

As to the case, you are wrongly advised. Every thing is being done possible to convict & I shall have a hard fight.

As to the fellow we have talked so much of the only thing that could help would be testimony to the effect that he was never asked to do any thing crooked & knew of nothing of the sort.[92]

Thanking you

Your friend | C S Darrow

MS: ALS, CSmH, Wood Papers, WD Box 126 (41). DATE: reference to "hard fight" ahead.

TO RICHARD F. PETTIGREW • LOS ANGELES • MONDAY 4 MARCH 1912

EARL ROGERS | COUNSELOR AT LAW March 4

My Dear Senator Pettigrew

Yours saying you will come just received. Both my wife & I are very thankful. If I did not need it badly I would not put you to the trouble. The case has not yet been set. It probably will begin about May 1st.

I wish you would see if Gompers will not raise me some money. Many of them think I am rich but I am poor & you know my circumstances. It will take $25,000 to defend me besides I must stay here Lord knows how long & what will I do afterward? They ought not to desert me at this crisis after all the years I have stood by their cause. See what you can do.

Faithfully | C. S. Darrow

MS: ALS, WHi, AFL Records: Gompers Era. DATE: enclosed with letter from Pettigrew to Gompers dated 12 March 1912.

TO JENNIE DARROW MOORE • OCEAN PARK, CALIFORNIA • MONDAY 11 MARCH 1912

Dear Jennie—

If the flat is not rented & we are obliged to store the goods send the following sets to Adain's book Store (2d hand) 43 Van Buren St. I think they will send for them—& let them sell them on commission. Smollet & Hume's History of England.—"Edmund Burke's Works," Franklin's Works—The fine Edition of Walt Whitman.—None of these are of any value. If you want any of them take them. Then if Miss Carlin, Miss Wood,

92. This might be another reference to Larry Sullivan.

Jessie or any of our other friends want to take any of them on storage & any of our things, it will save that much bother of storage—[93]

Vaughn[94] is a piker & I don't like to let him chissel me out of $100 though I might some one else. If you can't rent it furnished let the owner take it, though I would rather keep it. I am feeling hopeful about things—though I may lose. But somehow that doesn't look so bad. I am really convinced that it would do me good—though I don't want it— Any how it will be all right however it turns. My health was never better than now.

Your brother | C. S. D.

MS: ALS, MnU-L, Darrow Collection. ENVELOPE ADDRESS: Mrs. J—H—Moore— | #6260 Jackson Park Ave. | Chicago—Illinois. POSTMARK: "California" and "March 1912" but the rest is illegible.

TO PAUL DARROW • LOS ANGELES • WEDNESDAY 13 MARCH 1912

March 13

Dear Paul

Things have been progressing rather favorably. Don't be alarmed by report of Dictafone—[95]I feel quite sure that I will win—but of course might fail. If I do shall not consider it a waste of time or much loss of happiness. Still I think I shall win. How long would you like to be here? I should think a day or two would be all right & any time between now & May 14th when trial is scheduled. Ruby wants to know how little Pauline is.[96] Billy[97] is here tonight comes nearly every night, & is mighty good. Get lots of letters

93. "Miss Carlin" is Nellie Carlin. "Jessie" is Jessie (Ohl) Brownlee. But the identity of "Miss Wood" is unknown.
94. "Vaughn" was a prospective sublessee of the Darrows' furnished apartment in Chicago. He wanted one month free rent.
95. A "dictograph" or "dictofone" (as it was sometimes called) was a relatively recent invention that allowed someone to listen by wire to someone else talking in another room, using an audio amplifier. Dictographs were starting to be used around this time by private detectives and law enforcement officials and, in this case, the National Erectors' Association (NEA), an anti-union employers' organization that helped investigate and prosecute Darrow. In February 1912, the NEA and prosecutors lured Darrow to John Harrington's hotel room in Los Angeles to try to trap Darrow into making some incriminating statements that could be recorded by a stenographer listening next door through a dictograph. The day before this letter, the NEA revealed the use of the dictograph to the *New York Times,* and the commissioner of the NEA told the newspaper that the evidence obtained through the dictograph would have an "important bearing" on Darrow's case. "Dictograph Near Darrow," *New York Times,* 13 March 1912. But later, during Darrow's trial, the prosecution never used the stenographic transcript or any other related evidence, and the prosecution refused to provide a copy of the transcript to the defense. "Dictograph Is Nut to Crack," *Los Angeles Times,* 5 July 1912.
96. Darrow had insisted that if Paul's next child was a boy the baby should be named Paul. The baby was a girl, so "Pauline" is apparently how Darrow or Ruby referred to the baby.
97. Probably William Cavenaugh, a stonecutter who became Darrow's friend in 1907 in Boise, Idaho, during the trial of William Haywood. By the time of the McNamara trial, Cavanaugh was a policeman in the Los Angeles area.

from all kinds of people & think my friends stick O.K.[98] Had a fine letter from Debbs today, have had several.[99]

Hastily | C. S. D.

MS: ALS, Darrow Family. PLACE: no reason to doubt Los Angeles. DATE: reference to trial beginning in May.

TO PAUL DARROW • LOS ANGELES • WEDNESDAY 1 MAY 1912

May 1st

Dear Paul

The trial will no doubt begin the 15th of May. It seems as if I would win without much doubt. Still one never knows & if I am disappointed in the outcome, I still think that it will in the end have many compensations. I should think you would not be able to stay here long, so perhaps it might be as well for you to come in the beginning while we are getting the jury. If you want to you might get here one or a few days before the 15th. We move tomorrow to The Mayhew Apartments corner of Orange & Valencia Av. Take 6th St. car or 7th St. If you get here before nine in the morning come there if after come to Earl Roger's office, California Building 2d & Broadway. We are both well. I have never had better health & spirits in my life. Love to Lil

C. S. D.

MS: ALS, MnU-L, Darrow Collection. PLACE: no reason to doubt Los Angeles. DATE: reference to impending trial.

TO PAUL DARROW • LOS ANGELES • FRIDAY 12 JULY 1912

LAW OFFICES, | BERRY STURGEON Friday

Dear Paul

So far every thing looks good. Most every one expects me to win & I don't see much danger. Still you never can tell until the end & it will be all right any how. Ruby & I are both well & I am feeling all right in every way.[100]

Hastily | C. S. D.

MS: ALS, MnU-L, Darrow Collection. DATE: appended.

98. The Leo Cherne Papers (Box 2) at the Howard Gotlieb Archival Research Center at Boston University contain several hundred letters and telegrams of support to Darrow during his time in Los Angeles after his indictment. The Darrow Papers (Box 2) at the Library of Congress also contain many letters and telegrams to Darrow during this same period.
99. Darrow might be referring to a long letter from Debs that was dated nearly one month earlier, relaying several criticisms of Darrow but expressing his personal sympathy and support for him. See J. Robert Constantine, ed., *Letters of Eugene V. Debs* (Urbana: University of Illinois Press, 1990), 1:460–62 (letter from Debs to Darrow, 19 February 1912). But it seems more likely that if Darrow had just received a letter from Debs on this date, a further exchange of correspondence followed after that earlier letter.
100. On 17 August 1912, the jury, after thirty minutes of deliberation, acquitted Darrow of the charge of participating in the attempted bribery of George Lockwood. The indictment charging him with participating in the bribery of Robert Bain remained to be tried.

TO STEPHEN S. GREGORY • LOS ANGELES • THURSDAY 22 AUGUST 1912

Los Angeles, California, | August 22nd, 1912.

My dear Gregory:—

I received your telegram.[101] Am very thankful to you for your loyalty to me in all this trouble.

I don't know yet whether I will be tried on the other charge or not, but I see no danger in it, only trouble and expense.

I notice by the papers that a movement has been taken up to disbar Harrington. You know about what my philosophy is—Harrington lied on the witness stand, he tried to trap me in the most cowardly manner, if one is responsible for their conduct, I don't know anyone whose conduct is worse, at the same time he was scared, and taking into consideration his nature, I don't see that he could help it.

Anyhow, it would give me no satisfaction to see any trouble made for him, and if this movement is being pushed by my friends for the sake of me, I will just as soon you would say to them, I have no desire to injure anybody, however much they may have injured me.

As ever, with kind regards, I am

Your friend, | Clarence Darrow

MS: TLS, location of original unknown (photocopy in the editor's files). INSIDE ADDRESS: S. S. Gregory, Esq., | 100 Washington Street, | Chicago, Ills. NOTE: at the bottom of the letter, apparently in Gregory's hand, is written: "I showed this letter to [name illegible] Chicago Bar Assn Sept 18th 1912."

TO JOHN J. AND JAMES B. MCNAMARA • LOS ANGELES • WEDNESDAY 28 AUGUST 1912

Aug. 28th

Dear J. J. & J B

I know you were glad of my acquittal. Of course I was, but it looks as if they might try it again. It is now set for Oct. 21st. I will be in S.F. on labor day & it has been my intention to see you the first thing. When I get through with my trouble I shall give my time & work to making you understood. Any how at all times you have my best thoughts & wishes. I am sure things are getting understood better every day.

Ever your friend | Clarence Darrow

MS: ALS, OCU, McNamara Papers, Box 8. PLACE: implied by mention of traveling to San Francisco. DATE: reference to acquittal.

101. Gregory had sent a telegram to Darrow three days earlier, congratulating him on his great closing argument and his acquittal. Gregory to Darrow, 19 August 1912, Tele, MBU, Leo Cherne Papers, Box 2, Folder 4.

TO PAUL DARROW • SAN JOSE, CALIFORNIA • WEDNESDAY 4 SEPTEMBER 1912

Wednesday

Dear Paul

Am taking an automobile trip through northern Cal. with Older & Fay Lewis & we are having a good time. Spoke at S.F. labor day & had the biggest crowd they ever had & the reception was fine, they went wild—so things are now right with labor—[102] I believe I have more friends than ever & I am not worrying in the least. The case is set for Oct. 21st. Whether it will be tried again I can't tell, but I doubt it—most people think it will not. If it is it should be a hundred to one shot that I win & if I don't it will only put them in deeper without really hurting me. If I get through without a trial I will of course go back that way. If I have a trial probably you had better make me a visit. Any how I will write again in a few days.

Love to Lil. | C. S. D.

MS: ALS, MnU-L, Darrow Collection. DATE: "9/4/12" appended.

TO MARGARET HALEY • SPOKANE, WASHINGTON • SATURDAY 14 SEPTEMBER 1912

THE BULLETIN | SAN FRANCISCO Spokane | Sept 14

My Dear Mrs Haley

I am making a short speaking tour & shall return to Los Angeles on the 21st.

I received your kind telegram signed by you & the Kiefers[103] & I was glad to hear from you. No one knows how much such things are appreciated. I have had a hard time & have so far come out victorious & am quite sure I will again if they still try to get me. Sometime the people will understand it all & know that there was no other course to

102. Darrow stepped off the steamship from Los Angeles to San Francisco on 31 August 1912. The *Bulletin* ran a front-page story and picture of Darrow standing at the railing of the steamship, with Ruby on one side and Mary Field on the other, while they were greeted with a brass band and hundreds of well-wishers, including local labor leaders. "Rousing Welcome for Darrow," *(San Francisco) Bulletin,* 31 August 1912. Later, he gave a Labor Day speech in San Francisco that was attended by a great throng of people. "'Labor's Friend' Makes Great Speech at Park," *(San Francisco) Bulletin,* 3 September 1912.

103. Haley and Daniel Kiefer (1856–1923) and his wife Rosa Kiefer (b. 1863) had sent a telegram from Cincinnati praising Darrow and congratulating him (and Ruby and Lincoln Steffens, who testified extensively on Darrow's behalf) on the verdict. Haley and Kiefer to Darrow, 17 August 1912, Tele, MBU, Leo Cherne Papers, Box 2, Folder 4. Daniel Kiefer was a businessman in Cincinnati who became wealthy in the wholesale clothing business. Later, both in Cincinnati and Chicago, he became a political reformer and very active in the single-tax movement.

take hard though it was. Any how it helps me wonderfully to know that my old friends are with me.

Sincerely & Thankfully Your friend | Clarence Darrow

MS: ALS, ICHi, Chicago Teachers Federation Records. DATE: location and reference to speaking tour.

TO FREDERICK HAMERSTROM • LOS ANGELES • SATURDAY 21 SEPTEMBER 1912

~~THE SEMLOR | SALT LAKE CITY | UTAH~~ Sept. 21st 1912

Dear Fred

Have just returned from a short speaking trip & find your letter. I really think it would be a good thing to sell & you might look into it & see what can be done. I am not sure about an other trial. They are a crowd of crooks & it may happen. Don't worry about it any how. I will be all right & Ruby is a brick. We are very sorry we can not get there to spend vacation with you.

Hastily | C S Darrow

MS: ALS, MnU-L, Darrow Collection. DATE: reference to speaking trip and another potential trial.

TO MARY FIELD • LOS ANGELES • TUESDAY 22 OCTOBER 1912

Oct 22d

Dear Mary

Yours just received. Am sorry about your position but it is about as I feared.[104] I will send you $100 tomorrow & you can always call on me. Tell Tvietmoe[105] that you don't want to be a burden & can't, that you want to help him but must leave and that you think you had better go back to Cal, that you will help on organized labor all you can &c &c & then come. Don't be discouraged about yourself. You don't need them. None of us *need any* one *except* Still you don't need them, & you must work out your own life. I do miss you. My case went over until Nov 25 at their request.[106] I don't believe it will be tried, but still it may be. Any how Mary I don't care much. What can we do with fate & then too

104. On 1 October 1912, the federal court in Indianapolis began a trial of forty some members of the International Association of Bridge and Structural Iron Workers, including many of its leaders. They were charged with being part of the dynamiting conspiracy involving Ortie McManigal, the McNamaras, and others. Field covered the trial for *Bridgemen's Magazine*, a monthly publication of the IABSIW. Field's "position," as Darrow referred to it, might have related to money problems that she was having.
105. Olaf A. Tveitmoe.
106. The trial on the remaining indictment against Darrow, which was set for 21 October 1912—after Darrow's motion to dismiss the indictment was denied—was postponed several times before the trial finally began in January 1913. "Darrow Case Postponed," *Los Angeles Times*, 12 October 1912; "Darrow Hearing May Be Delayed," *Los Angeles Times*, 13 November 1912; "'To Be Continued,'" *Los Angeles Times*, 20 November 1912.

Even the weariest river, winds somewhere safe to sea.[107]

Have been to S. F. for several days. There are good true people in the world & what of it all?

Ever.

MS: ALS, ICN, Parton-Darrow Papers, Box 1, Folder 3. ENVELOPE ADDRESS: Miss Mary Field | Indianapolis | Ind | 412 American Bank Bldg | c/o O A Tveitmoe. POSTMARK: Los Angeles, 22 October 1912.

TO MARY FIELD • LOS ANGELES • THURSDAY 24 OCTOBER 1912

THE GOLDEN PRESS Oct 24

Dear Mary

If you have any trouble getting money on the enclosed go to Wm E Henley[108] a lawyer & an ex Judge & a friend of mine—for this or any thing else. I talked at a church last night at Pasadena on Ibsen—had a good audience kind & enthusiastic.[109] Poor Mary don't stay there & worry. Make a sneak the best way you can & don't ever worry about money while I have any or can get any. Send to me for more if you need it. If you haven't enough to get back tell Judge Henley to loan it to you & I will send it to him. He has been in trouble & is all right.

Ever | C. S. D.

MS: ALS, ICN, Parton-Darrow Papers, Box 1, Folder 3. ENVELOPE ADDRESS: Miss Mary Field | Indianapolis | *Ind* | c/o 412 American Life Bldg | Care O A Tveitmoe. POSTMARK: Los Angeles, 24 October 1912.

TO PAUL DARROW • LOS ANGELES • WEDNESDAY 30 OCTOBER 1912

October 30

Dear Paul

I can't tell when I will be east. The trial is now set for Nov 25. I doubt if it will be tried but don't want to go east until it is over. Have been taking trips into the country &

107. Darrow is quoting from "The Garden of Proserpine," a poem by Algernon Charles Swinburne (1837–1909), one of Darrow's favorite English poets.
108. Darrow is referring to William J. Henley (1863–1944), a lawyer and former judge on the Indiana Court of Appeals, 1896–1903. Henley resigned his judgeship to become general counsel for the Chicago Railway Terminal Company. In May 1910, after serving for a time as president of the Chicago & Western Indiana Railroad, Henley, who was then practicing law in Indianapolis, was indicted in Chicago on charges that he had bribed members of the Illinois legislature to secure passage of legislation favorable to the railroad. Darrow represented Henley before leaving for Los Angeles. In December 1912, Henley's indictment was dismissed because of insufficient evidence. In early 1912, Henley went through a divorce and prompt second marriage that also landed his name in the newspaper. "Henley Defense Gets into Action," *Chicago Tribune*, 10 May 1910; "Sues for Divorce from W. J. Henley," *Chicago Tribune*, 26 January 1912; "Wayman Explains 'Nolles,'" *Chicago Tribune*, 21 December 1912.
109. Darrow spoke on the playwright Henrick Ibsen (1828–1906) at the First Universalist Church in Pasadena, California, at the invitation of the men's club of the church. "Clarence Darrow Interpreter of Ibsen," *Pasadena Star*, 24 October 1912.

having a good time. Am not worrying about things. Sometime it will be all right & I seem to have more friends than ever. You did not say any thing about receiving the 500 I sent from Butte. Suppose you got it all right. Am glad the Gas business is looking up, think it will be all right some time. Don't let any of them ever worry about me. Whatever may happen it is all right now, & I don't believe they could beat me, but if they did it would not hurt. Shall be glad to hear how you come out for Oct. Love to all

C. S. D.

Send the Mark Twain to E C Rockwell Belvue—Idaho.[110]

C S D

MS: ALS, MnU-L, Darrow Collection. DATE: reference to impending trial.

TO MARY FIELD • LOS ANGELES • FRIDAY 29 NOVEMBER 1912

THE GOLDEN PRESS Nov 29th

Dear Mary

Your letter just received. I am sorry for you dear girl, but what the hell. We just have to stand things and you are doing more than any of the rest.[111] The further they go now the greater the reaction will be. Suppose they get me—I am no different from all the others who have been persecuted by the world. As to me I shall insist on a trial Jan 6th. I don't know what they intend doing & don't trust them & do not think I am yet out of the woods, but I have all my nerve & fortitude & will stand any thing all right. I am really glad you are out of that mess. I didn't want you to go, but I presume it is for the best. Any how it is all right. I think the work you are on now is all right & I am glad you are doing it. You will get a hearing and the persecution will only help you get it. I know how you hate notoriety—I know how I hate it. But it can't be avoided if one is true to any high ideal. Every body & every thing here is the same, all want to see you again & all are for you. I shall not go back east until this is over whenever & however that may be. I am going to San Francisco to see the old friends in a few days, & I am sure to have a good time there. Still take it all around I haven't had such a bad time the last year. I have lived and life at the worst is short, & why not live. The future will justify us all, but we won't be here.

110. Darrow might be referring to Irwin E. Rockwell, but what Twain item Darrow wanted Paul to send to Rockwell is unknown.

111. On her typewritten transcript of this letter, Mary's daughter (Margaret Parton) wrote an explanation for Darrow's comment: "Note by M.P: Mary had been evicted from Judge Anderson's courtroom in Indianapolis—I think because of audible remarks of derision—and had been branded an 'anarchist' in the newspapers. She was covering the trial for 'The Bridgeman's Magazine.'" Darrow to Parton, 29 November 1912, TT, ICN, Parton-Darrow Papers, Box 1, Folder 19.

Yesterday (thanksgiving) I went out to Jim's.[112] We read & talked & ate. That is about all there is to it any how. I am sorry for the situation in Indianapolis but they are only sowing the wind. What fools they are. Write often & you will hear from me regularly.

Ever yours,

MS: ALS, ICN, Parton-Darrow Papers, Box 1, Folder 3. ENVELOPE ADDRESS: Miss Mary Field | 180 Charlotte Av | Detroit | Mich. POSTMARK: Los Angeles 29 November 1912.

TO PAUL DARROW • LOS ANGELES • THURSDAY 12 DECEMBER 1912

Dec. 12

Dear Paul,

They are going to try me again beginning Jan. 6. Of course it is wrotten but it can't be helped. I hope it won't make you feel badly. I am really not worrying about it; however it comes out it will help me and if any thing should happen as it might it would hardly discomfort me while they never could recover from it; any how I am all right and don't worry a bit.

C. S. D.

MS: TL, MnU-L, Darrow Collection. PLACE: no reason to doubt Los Angeles. DATE: "1913" is appended, but reference to impending trial makes 1912 more probable.

TO RUBY DARROW • SAN FRANCISCO • SATURDAY 14 DECEMBER 1912

THE LARK | SOUTHERN PACIFIC Saturday Night

Dearest Rube

Just before going to bed I want to say that I am very sorry. That I love you dearly. Better than all the world & I don't care for any thing much if I have your love & devotion. Don't worry dearest over me. Sometime & somewhere in the world all things will come right—for I have ever tried to do right.[113]

Ever & Ever | Clarence.

112. Probably James H. Griffes (1868–1919), single-tax advocate, writer, and magazine publisher. Griffes was born in New York and moved to California from Chicago in 1890, first living in San Francisco and then moving to Los Angeles in approximately 1909. For the last ten years or so of his life, Griffes published and wrote (under the pseudonym Luke North) for a magazine called *Everyman,* which was devoted to advocating for single-tax ideas. Griffes published pieces by Darrow and Parton (and one by Ruby Darrow) in the magazine.

113. What Darrow was sorry about is unknown, but he might have been sorry for the fact that Ruby would have to endure another trial.

MS: ALS, MnU-L, Darrow Collection. ENVELOPE ADDRESS: Mrs. C. S. Darrow | Mayhew Apartments | Orange & Valencia Sts, | Los Angeles | Cal. POSTMARK: San Francisco, 14 December 1912.

TO PAUL DARROW • LOS ANGELES • SUNDAY 22 DECEMBER 1912

Dec. 22

Dear Paul:

I have been in San Francisco for a week and find your two letters, and am glad to hear from you and to know that every thing is going so well. I have no doubt that my case will go to trial on Jan. 6. I am not worrying about it; and am ready to take whatever comes. Of course with this bunch I might get stuck, but don't see how; still I realy don't care much on my own account; so far as I am concerned I honestly think it would be best for me and I absolutely have no fear or worry over it. I never felt better in my life, and Ruby is all right too. There may be scare things in the paper from time to time as that is their system but I will keep you posted if there is any thing serious; nothing has been done by the Grand Jury and I hardly look for any such thing; if they tried further it would do them no good. I have lots of friends and if any thing should happen I would have more and then I could get my book written; so you see it is all right any way. Love to Lill. Rockwell's address is Belvue Idaho; you might send me an extra copy of the Mark Twain if you have one.

C. S. D.

I have money enough for this fight.

MS: TL, MnU-L, Darrow Collection. PLACE: implied that Darrow just returned to Los Angeles. DATE: "'12" appended and supported by reference to impending trial.

TO J. HOWARD MOORE • LOS ANGELES • SATURDAY 28 DECEMBER 1912

Dec. 28

My Dear Mr. Moore;

Your letter with enclosure from Mr. Salt[114] received, am very much oblijed for both. Your philosophy is exactly right and it is the way I look at it. I really am not wor-

114. Darrow is probably referring to a letter from Henry Salt. Moore and Salt were both strong proponents of vegetarianism and animal rights, and they corresponded with each other often during the last years of Moore's life. See J. Howard Moore, *The Universal Kinship*, ed. Charles Magel (Fontwell, Sussex: Centaur Press, 1992), 333–40 (includes several of Moore's letters to Salt).

rying at all. It is of no consequence nothing is; So far as it matters it would be best if I am beaten after a fight. I hope Jennie and the rest understand it that way. I am perfectly serene and have no regrets for any thing. Nothing else is worth while—even if this is.

Did you ever read Plutarch on meat eating? It is as good as any thing you moderns have done, and seems to cover every thing that has been written in the last two thousand years. All of which seems to show we don't move. You will find it in his volume [of] essays. Love from both to all of you.

C. S. Darrow

MS: TL, MnU-L, Darrow Collection. ENVELOPE ADDRESS: J Howard Moore | Chicago | Ill. | 6260 Jackson Pk Av. POSTMARK: Los Angeles 30 Dec 1912.

TO PAUL DARROW • LOS ANGELES • THURSDAY 9 JANUARY 1913

Jan. 9

Dear Paul;

The case went over to the 20; it will be a sure shot then; every one thinks I will win still you never know and really it is mighty little I care. From time to time I will keep you posted as to how things are going; don't believe it is worth while for you to come unless you are anxious to do so. Powers[115] of Salt Lake is just opening offices here and he was willing to go into the case regardless of fees, and as R[116] is always uncertain at critical times, I was glad to have him. He is one of the best lawyers in the west; he was the lawyer who defended Mrs. Bradley in Washington for killing Senator Brown a few years ago.[117] Both Ruby and I are well and happy. You will note my improvement in type-writing.

C. S. D.

MS: TLS, MnU-L, Darrow Collection. DATE: "'13" appended and supported by reference to continuation of case.

115. Orlando W. Powers.

116. This is a reference to Earl Rogers, who eventually withdrew for health reasons from representing Darrow in his second trial. "Rogers Quits Darrow Case," *Chicago Tribune*, 8 February 1913. Two months earlier, Rogers had been in a private sanitorium for a month and was unable, for that reason, to participate in a trial. "Darrow Hearing May Be Delayed," *Los Angeles Times*, 13 November 1912. During Darrow's first trial, Rogers was also absent at times. See, e.g., "Illness Halts Darrow Trial," *Chicago Tribune*, 18 June 1912; "Rogers not There," *Los Angeles Times*, 6 July 1912.

117. In December 1906, Anna Bradley (d. 1950) shot Arthur Brown (1843–1906) in his hotel room in Washington, D.C. Brown, a former Republican senator from Utah, later died from the wounds. Brown's mistress, Bradley, had two children with him (although he denied this). She was tried for murder and Powers was her chief defense counsel. She was eventually acquitted of the murder charges by a jury. See "Ex-Senator Brown Shot by a Woman at Capital," *New York Times*, 9 December 1906; "Judge Locks up the Bradley Jury," *New York Times*, 3 December 1907.

TO PAUL DARROW • LOS ANGELES • SUNDAY 2 FEBRUARY 1913

Feb. 2

Dear Paul:

We have begun taking the evidence and so far things look favorable; still I don't want you to think that it is sure; I am very well satisfied with the jury and the opinion is nearly universal that I will win: I am realy caring very little about it but of course doing all I can. It looks as if it would not take over two or three weeks more. Will keep you posted if there is any indication of importance.

C. S. D.

MS: TL, MnU-L, Darrow Collection. DATE: reference to the trial.

TO PAUL DARROW • LOS ANGELES • SATURDAY 15 FEBRUARY 1913

Feb. 15

Dear Paul;

Received your letter to day and was glad to get it; I am surprised to know how much business you did in Jan. I don't quite understand it; The case is getting along faster than before. It will be finished in three weeks more at least. It looks much better than before; in fact there is nothing to it and I think no one believes I will loose. Most of them are confident I will win and most of them want me to. I am not loosing any thing by Rogers absence and am saving some money; I am doing most of the work myself. Of course there is nothing certain in this world and I may loose but still I don't care a dam.

C. S. D.

MS: TL, MnU-L, Darrow Collection.

TO CHARLES H. MOYER • LOS ANGELES • MONDAY 24 FEBRUARY 1913

Feby 24

My Dear Mr. Moyer

Your letter with P.O. Order for $3 is received. I must return this to you. I want you to know how I appreciate it, & how good you were to send it, but I feel that it is wrong to take so much from a man who must work as you do, especially after you sent me $5 before. While this thing has cost me most all that I have & could borrow still I have enough now to fund this trial & if I have more trouble you can then do as you please. I think I will win easily & I know I can make

money easier than you can. I shall always keep your letter and never forget your kindness and generosity.[118]

Ever Your friend | Clarence Darrow.

MS: ALS, DLC-MSS, Darrow Papers. DATE: reference to trial and possibility of more trouble. RECIPIENT: Moyer's other correspondence with Darrow and the name in the salutation (Darrow's handwriting is difficult and he might have included an "s" at the end of Moyer).

TO PAUL DARROW • LOS ANGELES • SATURDAY 8 MARCH 1913

Saturday PM

Dear Paul

The jury started in 6 & 6, & wound up 4 to 8 against me.[119] No one in town expected any such thing. It was a fluke all around. There really was no evidence. I am quite sure it could not happen again. I am not sure whether I will be tried again, but would not be surprised if I was made more trouble—Still somehow I don't care. I think I will get the unions to help me in the next if there is a next so don't worry about me. I am in good fighting shape & they will never get me. Will write tomorrow—

D

MS: ALS, MnU-L, Darrow Collection. DATE: "3/8/13" appended and supported by reference to verdict.

TO JOHN NOLAN • LOS ANGELES • MONDAY 10 MARCH 1913

March 10th

My Dear Nolan,

Thank you very much for the copy of the resolution which you have sent me.[120] It is a least one ray of hope & comfort. I am sure I have always been true to the cause of labor

118. Although Moyer's letter to Darrow was not located, a telegram from Moyer after Darrow's acquittal in the first bribery trial survives. Moyer to Darrow, 17 August 1912, Tele, MBU, Leo Cherne Papers, Box 2, Folder 4 ("Accept my congratulations on your acquittal. Knowing your past record as I do there has never been a doubt in my mind as to your innocence.").

119. The judge in Darrow's second trial discharged the jury on this day after forty hours of deliberations. The jury was divided with eight votes to convict Darrow and four votes to acquit him. Several explanations for the divided jury circulated in newspapers, including a common one (reportedly confirmed by an anonymous juror) holding that Darrow had angered some of the jurors by saying that the McNamaras were not murderers but workers in a great cause. "Darrow Remark Lost Him Liberty," *Chicago Tribune*, 9 March 1913; "Sting of Conviction Comes Near Darrow," *Los Angeles Times*, 9 March 1913.

120. Archived with this letter is a copy of the following recitals and resolution of the Varnishers & Polishers Local Union No. 134, in San Francisco:

WHEREAS:—The acquittal of Clarence S. Darrow, Labor's foremost champion at Los Angeles has met with the approval of all true Unionists;

& given my best ability & devotion to the poor. I am glad to have you & your council appreciate. Please thank them for me.

Truly | Clarence Darrow.

MS: ALS, CU-BANC, San Francisco Labor Council Papers, Box 8. PLACE: no reason to doubt Los Angeles. DATE: reference to resolution.

TO CHARLES ERSKINE SCOTT WOOD • LOS ANGELES • WEDNESDAY 19 MARCH 1913

CALIFORNIA STATE FEDERATION OF LABOR March 19

My Dear Mr. Wood

Miss Field has just told me of your letter & it touches me deeply. These are the ordeals that bring men together & I can't now tell you how much I value your love & friendship & how thoroughly I reciprocate both; I can't let you give me any more money at least not now. Some of the people that I have worked for so long have got busy to raise money & they are producing results & I believe I will get enough to carry me through. Of course if it came to the point that I must have something it might be a different matter, but I don't believe it will & if it does I will tell you but I am glad you wrote the letter.

As to the case there should not have been the slightest doubt. I never saw a defense so overwhelming. It is only the prejudice that has been pound in day by day through the Times & the M & M.[121] Still I don't think it is possible that they could ever again come so near to beating me. I don't want you to have any trouble but I hope before either of us die I may be able to show that my friendship & love for you would take me as far in your aid as yours has carried you—

Ever Your friend | Clarence Darrow

MS: ALS, CSmH, Wood Papers, WD Box 126 (42). DATE: reference to the nearness of defeat at trial places this after the second trial.

WHEREAS:—Clarence S. Darrow has lived a life for man's betterment with unswerving fidelity, his arms outstretched in succor, his voice in thunderous tones spoke; his pen always wielded with master strokes in behalf of Labor's rights; liken unto the lowly Nazarene was he.

THEREFORE BE IT RESOLVED:—By Varnishers & Polishers L.U. #134 in meeting assembled Tuesday evening August 27th, 1912. That we extend our most sincere and hearty congratulations to Clarence S. Darrow in his acquittal, hoping that many years be allotted him to continue on in his life's work and the accomplishment of his high ideals "Equality, Justice & Right" and further that the dark clouds over shadowing his path will disappear as does the melting snow before the sun.

121. The "Times" is the *Los Angeles Times* and "M & M" is the Merchants and Manufacturers Association, a well-funded, aggressively anti-union organization of employers in Los Angeles formed in 1896 at the suggestion of Harrison Gray Otis (1837–1917), owner and editor of the *Los Angeles Times* and militant opponent of unions.

TO PAUL DARROW • LOS ANGELES • MONDAY 24 MARCH 1913

March 24

Dear Paul

To day I had a talk with Dist. Att'y. He offers to let case be continued until June 15 at which time he practically promises to dismiss it. There will really be no doubt about this. In the mean time I can go back to Chicago & will not need to return unless I wish. As I think they would not try it any how & the best I can get in the end is a dismissal. I have no doubt I will accept it & go in to court in a day or two & continue it, & if you see that it is continued you can expect to see me about April 6th to 10th. Will send you word in advance. I suppose I am coming out of a hard fight all right—& it doesn't worry me in the least. If it had not been for two or three put over on me & the D–n champions of fairness[122] there would have been nothing to the last trial—but what of it all—Don't say that you know the case is to be dismissed.

Hastily | C. S. D.

MS: ALS, MnU-L, Darrow Collection. DATE: "'13" appended and supported by reference to trial and expected dismissal.

TO CHARLES ERSKINE SCOTT WOOD • GREELEY, COLORADO • THURSDAY 17 APRIL 1913

THE GREELEY GAS & FUEL CO. April 17th

My Dear Mr. Wood

I am on my way to Chicago & stopping a few days here to visit my son. Shall leave tonight. I am quite sure that the case will be dismissed. The Dist. Atty has assured me that it will. Still I shall not be sure until it is done. I have little fears however of an other trial, but prefer not to go through it. There was really nothing to the last case. No one thought there could be any doubt of its outcome but a series of accidents such as sometimes comes in a case caused the disagreement. In the first case the jury was very bad and it could not be helped. Next the Indianapolis case doubtless had something to do with it. Then I really had no lawyer. Rogers broke down the first day & Powers[123] is not a fighter. I tried it myself but while I could do that, still it is hard to fight all the while for yourself. It doesn't look good. I have heard of some Irishman in Portland that is supposed to be a successful criminal lawyer. Is he good & would he come if I needed him which I am quite sure I shall not?

122. Darrow's handwriting is difficult here; he might have intended "champs of fairness" rather than "champions of fairness."

123. Orlando W. Powers.

When in San Francisco I had two visits with Mr E.[124] Before that I had sympathy for him, while of course my whole feelings were the other way. But after my interview I felt convinced that no woman of intelligence & feeling could possibly live with him whatever the consequences. He is small, narrow, & self righteous to the last degree & he can not be changed. The fact that he means to be good & thinks he is only makes it the more hopeless. I wish I saw some way out, but one can only take one step at a time & wait developments for the rest. Any how she is away from him and can not be brought back. He knows she went to Nevada & has consulted a lawyer though I do not know who. Of course the situation is not easy but we are all used to difficulties. He was in a threatening attitude as to any one coming in to trespass on his rights. Spoke of her in the same way that men do of property, which I told him, but still protested that he should not interfere with her unless she took some action or some one "invaded" his rights. He gave me to understand that he should insist on the children being kept together & she would be compelled to take his choice in the situation. I advised Mary that she had better get the girl back to her mother the easiest & quickest way. If you think of *any thing* more that I can do for either of you at any time let me know, for there is almost nothing I would not do to help. I am uncertain as to the future. I feel that I shall go back to the Pacific coast to live probably San Francisco. Am not worrying about making a living when the troubles are over as I think they are. I like the climate of the Pacific coast & then I have so many friends there who have stood so close by me in my trouble that I feel I can not stay away from them. Somehow they seem more to me than the friends of a life time who have been friends under other conditions. Should be glad to hear from you. My address will be Ashland Block Chicago.

Your friend | Clarence Darrow.

MS: ALS, CSmH, Wood Papers, WD Box 126 (43). DATE: reference to second bribery trial.

TO FREDERICK HAMERSTROM • CHICAGO • SUNDAY 4 MAY 1913

THE LARK Ashland Block | Chicago May 4

Dear Fred

We are back in the old apartment & old office. I think the matters out west are finished. I have their assurance & yet am not certain until they are dismissed. Can you get along without your money until I know. If I must go back & fight I need all I have & more, but I have no right to hold you up. If I am through I am sure I can make as much as ever perhaps more.

124. Albert Ehrgott (1863–1929), Sara Bard Field's first husband. Ehrgott was a Baptist minister and Sara was seeking a divorce from him, which she would eventually receive in November 1914.

Paul is getting along all right but it is rather slow. I know that your affairs & ours will be fixed to our mutual satisfaction. Ruby & I will try to get east & see you as soon as I am definitely out of the woods. We would be very glad to see you both again.

Ever | Clarence Darrow

MS: ALS, MnU-L, Darrow Collection. DATE: reference to being back in Chicago and the case in California.

TO PAUL DARROW • CHICAGO • MONDAY 5 MAY 1913

JOSEPH R. W. COOPER | LAWYER May 5

Dear Paul

Am back at the old place for a time. Don't know what I will do yet until I am sure about L.A. Every one glad to see me & I believe I have more friends than ever before—any how it is all right & I presume an other trial would make almost every one with me.[125] Any how if I go through an other will have help enough to pay all bills. Several people want me to go into business with them & many have come to see me & the telephone is busy most of the time. Am glad you are doing well now. I bought 50 shares Southern Pacific at 97. Will write when I hear any news & if I go back will stop on the way.

Hastily | C. S. D.

Have considerable hopes of the Camfield Greeley Recorder deal.[126]

D.

MS: ALS, MnU-L, Darrow Collection. DATE: reference to return to Chicago and possible retrial.

TO PAUL DARROW • CHICAGO • WEDNESDAY 14 MAY 1913

DARROW & BAILY May 14

Dear Paul

I got a telegram from L.A. today saying that tomorrow they would strike my case from the calendar. This indicates that they will make good & dismiss it next month. Any how it is not now set for trial so I presume there is little chance that it will ever come up again. Shall decide in a few days about going into business. Have about 25 lecture engagements for July & Aug. Will write in a few days about the Greeley deal which looks hopeful. We

125. On his return from California, the Lawyers' Association of Illinois organized a celebratory banquet for Darrow at the Hotel Sherman in Chicago, with more than two hundred in attendance. "C. S. Darrow Shies from Sympathy," *Chicago Tribune,* 11 May 1913.

126. "Camfield" is Daniel A. Camfield, but the "Greeley Recorder deal" to which Darrow refers is unknown.

are back in the old place. Every one here seems glad to see me & I am beginning to feel at home.

Love to Lil | C. S. D.

Gurley just telephoned he would be at Brown Palace Hotel Sat. P.M. next at 4:30. Better have Tew & Camfield there & you had better go.[127]

C. S. D.

MS: ALS, MnU-L, Darrow Collection. DATE: "13" appended and supported by reference to dismissal of indictment.

TO CHARLES ERSKINE SCOTT WOOD • CHICAGO • MONDAY 19 MAY 1913

DARROW & BAILY May 19

My Dear Wood

Your letter was duly received, and your kindness is fully appreciated though I have been long in acknowledging it. It seems hard to ask you to do so much for me. I am very confident now that the case will not be tried. Last week it was stricken from the docket which was in pursuance with their agreement to strike it off now & dismiss it next month. Have not yet determined what to do. I long for the west & still my friends are good & kind here & want me to stay. It is probably necessary for me to make some more money so I may stay. Shall determine soon. I shall at least go back in the early fall & will then see you. I presume you are not coming this way this summer. I wish I might see you again & wish I could be of more service to you and your friends. Have had a letter from Mary which tells me matters are in the same condition there as to her sister. What a lot of trouble a D–n fool can make in this world with its rules & conventions and narrow views of life. Still somehow I have come to think one's happiness or sorrow is not much changed by externals. One's life is mostly inside & somehow we are obliged to adjust our thoughts & feelings to conditions and if we really can externals do not so much count. This sounds like the canting slave morality of the christians but there is a large grain of truth in it just the same. We all long for freedom but there is no freedom except within ourselves. I sent Mary a letter from Nevada which had some good suggestions in it. If I see that I can do any good I will go there. I do not know what I would not do for you or them.

I am to speak on Nietzsche next Sunday & have been reading him industriously. I am getting quite enamored of him & he is doing me good, before I am through I shall stand about as you do on the whole scheme. I have been going that way fast in the last year. I believe if I could be left alone & go into the mountains with a few friends & books I should never

127. "Gurley" is possibly William W. Gurley (1851–1923), a corporate lawyer and general counsel for traction companies in Chicago, including the Union Traction Company. He was a friend of Darrow's. "Tew" is Charles F. Tew. The Brown Palace Hotel is in Denver, Colorado. What they were all involved in with Darrow or his son is unknown.

want to come out again, but I can't do that now. It is a little hard to adjust myself again to internal and external changes, but I have always had plenty of turbulence of soul & body. As we grow older I think we all feel that a few friends that we know are friends is about all there is to the whole scheme, and I feel sure of a few friends in fact many, and on the whole have no complaints against the world. Should be glad to hear from you at any time that you see fit to write and if you ever need me for any thing, the distance will not be too great.

Ever Yours | Clarence Darrow.

MS: ALS, CSmH, Wood Papers, WD Box 126 (44). DATE: reference to case stricken from docket.

TO EUGENE V. DEBS • CHICAGO • SATURDAY 14 JUNE 1913

DARROW & BAILY June 14th 1913.

My Dear Friend:—

I have just mailed a copy of the Los Angeles argument to Mr. Roach,[128] it is the only one I have in the office and is soiled, but it is all there.[129]

I have none of the Haywood argument at hand, but will try to get one the first of the week and send it.[130] In a few days I will get some other copies of the Los Angeles one and send them to you, of course, I am glad to do it.

It was very kind of you to write me as you did in reference to Mr. Winter,[131] as one likes to hear those things.

When am I going to see you again? Are you never coming to Chicago? If not I have almost a mind to go down on purpose to see you.

I am feeling very well and have got down to work again.

As ever your friend, | Clarence Darrow.

MS: TLS, InTI, Debs Papers. INSIDE ADDRESS: Mr. Eugene V. Debs, | Terre Haute, | Indiana.

TO MARY FIELD • CHICAGO • FRIDAY 27 JUNE 1913

June 27th

Dear Mary

I don't know why in hell I haven't written before. Not for lack of thinking of you for I always do that. I have been away on a speech making tour once & had good audiences &

128. The identity of "Mr. Roach" is unknown.
129. Darrow is likely referring to a pamphlet containing his final argument to the jury in his first bribery trial: *Plea of Clarence Darrow, in His Own Defense to the Jury That Exonerated Him of the Charge of Bribery at Los Angeles, August–1912* (Los Angeles: Golden Press, 1912). Darrow's final argument in his second trial was published in a magazine: "Second Plea of Clarence Darrow in His Own Defense," *Everyman (Los Angeles)*, May 1913, 3–24.
130. Darrow's final argument in the trial of Haywood was published in toto and in excerpts in a variety of forms, including "Darrow's Speech in the Haywood Case," *Wayland's Monthly*, October 1907, 4–111.
131. The identity of "Mr. Winter" is unknown.

have been trying a case but for the most part have been loafing & not feeling like doing any thing worth while.[132] Guess I am getting old. Don't you think so? Have seen Mrs. Hamilton[133] a number of times. She is all right & have had a good time. Helen[134] has flown in or rather flutterred in & out. I think she has gone east & we have lady suffrage here. Soon there will be no haven in all the wide seas. Mr. Wood was here a few minutes the other day and as a consequence I wrote a letter to your town. Hope things will come out all right. I am very anxious to see Sarah get away from that little priest. I don't see how she has stood it so long. How is she & how are you and are you to be married soon? I hear nothing more from L.A. but I am going back to California in Oct. any how. I am anxious to see all of you and to see San Francisco & I want to live there. Have not yet determined any thing in the way of future plans and don't know as I shall or if it is worth while. Will do what comes along which is about all any one can do. I see Dr. Foster quite often. Have made three different addresses since I returned. He has been to all of them and he is as fine as ever. He has just given me a wonderful new book to read, & I have read it through once & am reading it again. "The Significance of Existence," by an Englishman named Harris.[135] He says it hasn't any significance but it takes a big volume to say it & it is fine. My Nietchie talk was a success. The same old crowd largely Jews were there. I said a few things you would have liked. Mary your letters are fine. You can write. Why don't you write a Goldfield story for the eastern magazines.[136] I do wish I could see you & will one of these days.

Ever your friend | C. S. D.

MS: ALS, ICN, Parton-Darrow Papers, Box 1, Folder 4. ENVELOPE ADDRESS: Miss Mary Field | Goldfield | Nevada. POSTMARK: Chicago 28 June 1913.

TO T. PERCEVAL GERSON • "IN MINNESOTA" • FRIDAY 4 JULY 1913

THE OLYMPIAN | CHICAGO, MILWAUKEE & ST. PAUL RAILWAY In Minnesota | July 4th

My Dear Dr. Guerson

I am making two or three speeches up in this country. Have been delivering a few and have tried one case since my return to Chicago. Every one there has been most kind & yet you don't know how I miss you all & want to see you again. With all of my trouble

132. Darrow is probably referring to a recent case in state court in Chicago in which he defended two brothers, both woolen merchants (Edward and Paul Cotiz), and a third man, an insurance adjuster (Joseph Clarke). They were charged with arson and were all found guilty by a jury two days after Darrow wrote this letter. "Three Convicted on Arson Charge," *Chicago Tribune*, 30 June 1913.
133. The identity of "Mrs. Hamilton" is unknown.
134. Probably Helen Todd.
135. I. Harris, *The Significance of Existence* (London: Longmans, Green, 1911).
136. Mary was in Goldfield, Nevada, with her sister, Sara Bard Field. Sara was living there temporarily so she could obtain a divorce from her husband, Albert Ehrgott.

those were fine days and evenings in Los Angeles and I think they were worth the pain. Have not yet made any plans for the future except that up to Christmas I expect to lecture. I can make some money this way which I need to repay some I borrowed & really one thing is about as satisfying as an other. It is all inside, any how. Hope you will go carefully with the cooperative scheme & be sure you can make good on all the promises that are made.[137] I believe in the people, but to make good in a business matter is not easy & you will get only the money of the poor. The plan is good & I know I am going to be with you all some of these times. I have been reading a book which I wish your circle could get. It is very strong, biological & scientific: "The Significance of Existence" by I. Harris—an English scientist. He develops the thought that has been growing on me for several years, that reason is of little value in human actions, that it is the poorest grade to truth & right living, that instinct is almost all. Hope you will get it & tell me what you think of it.

With best love always to you & Mrs Gerson.[138]

Your friend | Clarence Darrow.

Ruby is very well & I think quite happy. I am glad for her that we are in Chicago a while & yet to me the California people are nearer & dearer.

MS: ALS, CLU-SC, Theodore Perceval Gerson Papers (Collection 724). DATE: reference to returning to Chicago. ENVELOPE ADDRESS: Dr T. Perceval Guerson | Story Bldg | Los Angeles, Cal.

TO MARY FIELD PARTON • BELLEVILLE, KANSAS • FRIDAY 8 AUGUST 1913

THE YANKEE INN Aug 8 1913

Dear Mary

Your letter followed me here where I have been in a blistering state talking to Chatauquas (God save the world). How stupid they all are, and yet always come some enquiring young men & women looking for light, ready to drink in anything like the parched soil of Kansas. And what is the use of all of it. I do want you to write the book—to begin it now. I want it partly for me & those who are to come after me but mostly for you. I am so glad that Lem doesn't want marriage like death to end all, for I know you can do wonderful things, things he and all of us will be proud of. I want you to come soon & to see all of us in Chicago on your way. We all want to see you again. When shall it be? Poor Sarah, tell her all of it life & all is not worth while, but how I want her to be rid of the blatant conceited fool of a person. I know she would rather die than go to him again & I would rather that she did. How I wish I could help her. I shall be back in Chicago on the morning of the 14th. Let me hear from you & know when you are coming. Poor Older. I

137. The nature of Gerson's "cooperative scheme" is unknown.
138. Harriet Anna (Thompson) Gerson (d. 1922) was Gerson's first wife. They were married in 1899.

wish I could help him, & I want to go back. Poor every body. How lucky we will be when the tragic farce is done.

Ever your friend | C. S. D.

MS: ALS, ICN, Parton-Darrow Papers, Box 1, Folder 4. ENVELOPE ADDRESS: Mrs Mary Field Parton | ~~1623 Lake St~~ | ~~San Francisco~~ | Cal | Quincy | Gen. Delivery. POSTMARK (first postmark illegible): San Francisco 18 August 1913.

TO MARY FIELD PARTON • BROWNSVILLE, PENNSYLVANIA • SUNDAY 30 NOVEMBER 1913

PENNSYLVANIA HOTEL Nov 30th 1913

Dear Mary

Am in this little Jay town where I am to speak tonight.[139] Have been doing a good deal of it of late. Get good crowds & would like it if it were not for the moving around and if I could do it for nothing. Think about the Holidays I shall stop making a business of it. I was in N.Y. several days and had a fine time. Every one was glad to see me. Went to dinner &c. more than I ever ate before. Saw Gertrude,[140] Inez Mulholland,[141] Ellis Jones,[142] Leonard Abbott,[143] Allen Benson[144] and others. We talked a great deal of you, & I read them your Goldfields letter & your and Lem's *poem* over & over again.[145] They think you are great stuff and I encouraged them in it. Gertrude is going to Cleveland for a time. She is not now with the Garment workers but seems to be busy. I wish she had a man too.

What you say about the case is true but I am quite sure it will soon be dismissed. If not I shall go out & see that it is done or tried.[146] I am very sure they will never try it. It really doesn't worry me much, there are too many living things. I am sorry about Sarah.

139. Darrow spoke at the Brownsville Opera House on 30 November 1913. A local newspaper summarized the speech as wide-ranging and sarcastic: "The address was full of radicalism and Mr. Darrow spoke in sarcastic disparagement of lawyers, doctors, preachers and bankers. He made light of the constitution, played dangerously with religion and made organization of laboring men the burden of his message. "Sarcastic Address by C. S. Darrow to Labor Men in Brownsville," *(Union Town) Daily News Standard,* 1 December 1913.
140. Gertrude Barnum.
141. Inez Milholland Boissevain.
142. Ellis O. Jones (1874–1967), journalist. Jones was an editor for the original *Life* magazine and later editor for the *Ladies' Home Journal.* A pacifist during World War I, Jones became a fascist during World War II.
143. Leonard Dalton Abbott (1878–1953), English-born socialist editor. Abbott came to the United States in 1897. For twenty years he was an associate editor for *Current Literature* (later, *Current Opinion*), 1905–25. He was also president of the Free Speech League, 1910–14, and one of the founders of the Rand School and Intercollegiate Socialist Society (later known as the League for Industrial Democracy).
144. Allan Benson (1871–1940), journalist, newspaper editor, and writer. Benson received a public school education in Michigan and worked as a reporter and editor for various newspapers around the country, until approximately 1907. Later, he wrote for magazines and socialist publications. He was the author of many popular socialist books and booklets, as well as other books. In 1916, Benson was nominated by the Socialist Party as a candidate for president.
145. Darrow is likely referring to a letter that he received from Parton while she was in Goldfield, Nevada. The poems to which Darrow is referring are unknown.
146. Darrow is referring to the second indictment against him in Los Angeles.

I told either her or you that I didn't believe a divorce could be granted on the grounds of incompatibility, but hope she will get it somehow & somewhere. I wish she could get untangled. I like to see every life get untangled so we can tangle them up again—to hell with life any how. Geo West[147] has been staying with us & I have been trying to do something for him. He is a fine chap & I am glad to have him around.

I am preparing an address on Voltaire which I believe will be the best I have ever done in that line.[148] You will hear it some time, for I am coming. I would be so glad to see you again.

Ever Yours | C. S. Darrow

Love to Lem.

MS: ALS, ICN, Parton-Darrow Papers, Box 1, Folder 4. ENVELOPE ADDRESS: Mrs Mary Field Parton | ~~c/o Fremont Older Esq~~ | 1623 Lake St | San Francisco | Cal | ~~The Bulletin~~ POSTMARK: Brownsville 1 December 1913; San Francisco 5 December 1913.

TO JOHN D. FREDERICKS • CHICAGO • DECEMBER 1913

Chicago, Ill., Dec. 23, 1913

Dear Sir—

I have just learned that the case which has been pending in the State of California against me has been dismissed, and that there is now pending no further charges or indictments against me there.[149]

147. George West (1884–1943) was a writer or editor for many different newspapers and magazines, including the *San Francisco Bulletin* and later the *San Francisco News*. He lived with Darrow and his wife for several weeks while Darrow tried to find employment for him.
148. Darrow delivered an address on Voltaire before the Chicago Society of Rationalism in Chicago on 11 January 1914. The address was later published: "Voltaire," *(Los Angeles) Everyman* 9 (January–February 1914): 19–31.
149. In December 1913, Fredericks was considering or planning a candidacy for governor of California and he was apparently concerned that his campaign would have difficulty with labor forces because of the way in which Fredericks had handled the McNamara case and Darrow's bribery trials. On approximately 15 December, according to Darrow, someone (unidentified) who was a friend of Fredericks and Darrow presented this letter to Darrow in Chicago for his signature. The letter had no date on it, but Darrow was told that if he signed it the still-pending indictment against him for jury bribery would be dismissed. Darrow signed the letter and Fredericks dismissed the indictment on 20 December 1913. The date on the letter (23 December) was apparently added after Darrow signed the letter (Darrow was not in Chicago on that date), so the letter could be dated *after* the indictment was dismissed. The *Los Angeles Tribune*, which published this letter, reported that supporters of Fredericks had been "quietly" showing this letter to "various labor leaders." The *Tribune* accused Fredericks of abusing his power as district attorney to extort Darrow's signature, to serve Fredericks's own political ambitions. "Who Wrote 'Darrow Whitewash Letter?'" *Los Angeles Tribune*, 14 October 1914. Before this letter, Darrow and Fredericks had corresponded about the pending indictment, but Fredericks had put off giving any answer to Darrow on the matter because he said that he wanted to talk to Darrow in person in Chicago. See Fredericks to Darrow, 15 September 1913, TLS, MBU, Leo Cherne Papers, Box 2, Folder 5. (In May 1914, Fredericks announced that he would be a Republican candidate for governor. He went on to win the primary election in August but lost the general election in November to Hiram Johnson.)

I wish to take this opportunity to thank you for your action in dismissing the case. It is a great relief to me, and I am further glad to say to you some things which I could not say before for fear of being misunderstood.

Now that this entire matter is terminated, I wish to say that when I came to California to undertake the defense of the McNamaras, I expected some battle, and I think I know what battles are. But you gave me the battle of my life, and through the case it may be some satisfaction for you to know that I felt and feel now that while your actions were strenuous in the extreme, you were simply doing your duty as you saw it, and that you were absolutely fair, both to me and my clients.

Of course we were on opposite sides and saw things from a different point of view, but I never found you taking advantage of me or my clients or my associates. And I know you had no personal animus or feeling, either against my clients, whom I was defending, or the great army of labor unions who were assisting them. You personally refused at all times to adopt any measures or follow any course for the purpose of creating public sentiment against labor unions.

You might also be interested in knowing that there is no one in your office who went through that fight with you who was untrue or disloyal. We had our sources of information, it is true, but never broke through your line of integrity and loyalty, with which you surrounded yourself in the person of your assistants.

Very truly yours, | Clarence Darrow.

MS: "Who Wrote 'Darrow Whitewash Letter?,'" *Los Angeles Tribune*, 14 October 1914. INSIDE ADDRESS: J. D. Fredericks, Esq., | District Attorney, | Los Angeles, Cal.

TO CHARLES ERSKINE SCOTT WOOD • CHICAGO • SUNDAY 4 JANUARY 1914

DARROW, BAILY & SISSMAN Jan 4

My Dear Wood

Just received your letter & was glad to hear from you. It is some satisfaction to know that the case has been dismissed and I shall always appreciate all you did, and your friendship & devotion to me when I needed friends. I am lecturing some—writing some, practicing law some. In my trouble there, I got about $8,000 from my friends which I shall pay the first thing I do, or nearly so. They were in the main people like you who would never want it, if I could not do it, but I can & will. I have however my interest in the gas plant in Colorado which I could not sell & which my son & I own, at Greeley Colorado. This is now doing well & I think in an other year will support me moderately and any how I can make a living even without practicing law. So what I must do is to settle in my own mind where and how I want to live. The Pacific coast around San Francisco appeals to me more & more & my old-time friend Senator Pettigrew wants to go there and like you, I want to try to do something before I die. I believe I will go out in the next two months probably coming to Seattle, Tacoma & Portland &

on down to California. Any how I want to see you. As to Sarah I hope things will come out. Of course I don't wonder that the dominie would not want the charges made that seem to be necessary. If only one could deal with him and he would agree to get it himself on desertion when the time is up that would do, but I presume he would not. I don't just see how she stayed with him all those years. His little goodness is deadly. If he had big faults & weaknesses one could stand it: poor girl I wish I could help. If a crowd of us could get reasonably close together out there it would be a comfort. That is about all there is in life & really we ought to do something before the end—even if that was the end. I have been greatly influenced of late by Nietchie. Activity and fight is about all there is to life—in fact all there is to life, and any scheme to get out of it can bring no satisfaction.

I feel that if there is any difference I shall fight more in the future than in the past, but very likely it will be on a different line. Have you read "Talentyres" life of Voltaire? It is very inspiring.[150] Jean Christophe too tells the whole story. It is a wonderful book. If ever there is a chance to be of any special use to you or any that are near to you, I want you always to call on me. I was greatly impressed with Chapman.[151] I wish he could be counted in if we ever do any thing but dream. Please give him my kindest remembrances.

Your friend | Clarence Darrow

MS: ALS, ICN, Parton-Darrow Papers, Box 1, Folder 5. ENVELOPE ADDRESS: *Personal* | Mr C. E. S. Wood | Portland | Oregon | Atty at Law. POSTMARK: Chicago 5 January 1914.

TO SAN FRANCISCO LABOR COUNCIL • CHICAGO • FRIDAY 16 JANUARY 1914

DARROW, BAILY & SISSMAN January 16, 1914.

Gentlemen:—

Some money was raised to assist me while I was in Los Angeles. This, I understand, is in your hands. So long as my case was dismissed, I shall not need it and would be glad if you would see your way clear to turn it over to the defense of the men who were convicted in Indianapolis.[152]

150. S. G. Tallentyre [Evelyn Beatrice Hall], *The Life of Voltaire,* 3rd ed. (New York: G. P. Putnam's Sons, 1910).
151. Possibly Charles C. Chapman (1876–1956), civic leader in Portland, Oregon, and founder and editor for forty years of the *Oregon Voter,* a weekly political publication.
152. In December 1912, thirty-eight of the defendants in the federal conspiracy trial in Indianapolis, all leaders or members of the International Association of Bridge and Structural Iron Workers, were found guilty. Thirty of the men who were convicted appealed (six of them successfully). Sidney Fine, *"Without Blare of Trumpets": Walter Drew, the National Erectors' Association, and the Open Shop Movement, 1903–57* (Ann Arbor: University of Michigan Press, 1995), 125.

So far as I have any interest in this matter, I am glad to release it for this purpose.

Very truly yours, | Clarence Darrow.

MS: TLS, CU-BANC, San Francisco Labor Council Papers, Box 8. INSIDE ADDRESS: San Francisco Labor Council, | San Francisco, Calif.

TO MABEL DODGE LUHAN • CHICAGO • TUESDAY 31 MARCH 1914

1202 ASHLAND BLOCK Mar 31st

My Dear Mrs. Dodge

I had intended writing you long ago about coming to N.Y. but so many things have got in the way that I had no chance to go. It was nice of you to wire me to come, & I wanted to start at once for the lure of N.Y. is still on me. It is a dangerous place for me to visit.

I have an invitation to be there April 10th and am trying to arrange to go. Shall do it if I can, and will write or wire you in plenty of time if I can get away. I wish I lived there & I hope I can arrange to move, but there are so many things to think of after my long years here. Still I could do it if I only did it. The habit of procrastination is so strong and old with me that I am always intending to do things and never doing them. Any how when I come I shall come & see you.

Truly | Clarence Darrow

MS: ALS, CtY-BR, Luhan Papers, Box 7, Folder 220. DATE: "D Misc | 1914 | Darrow" appended and supported by letterhead and reference to speaking in New York.

TO RUBY DARROW • EN ROUTE TO NEW YORK CITY • MONDAY 7 DECEMBER 1914

PENNSYLVANIA RAILROAD | BROADWAY LIMITED 1 P.M. | Monday

Dearest Rube

I am so sorry about this morning.[153] I suppose I should not have said any thing but I really had not an unkind thought. I don't want to stifle you in any way & no doubt what you say is worth as much as any of the rest of us. I do feel very badly to make you suffer. For I do love you very dearly, more than I ever have any one else, and I want to do all I can to make you happy. You have been through so much for me & with me, that I could never think of being without you. And I appreciate all that you have done & are doing for me. I am proud of my house & I know it is you & what you do more than me that makes people like to come. I only thought that it would be best for you to say what I did, and no doubt I could have said it better but meant it only in kindness and the fact that I have waited so long shows that it was harder for me to say it than for you to listen to it. You

153. What Darrow is referring to is unknown and can only be inferred from this letter.

have often had occasion to tell me unpleasant things about myself & no doubt will many more times—as you ought to. But nothing of this should in any way effect our love, which I am sure is deep & genuine. Whatever I may do, or not do I never think of any one else as fondly as I do of you & am already missing you—

Ever with deepest love | D.

MS: ALS, MnU-L, Darrow Collection. PLACE: letterhead and other letters referring to business in New York. DATE: "Dec 7—1914" appended, probably by recipient. ENVELOPE ADDRESS: Mrs. C. S. Darrow, | 1537 E 60th St | Chicago. POSTMARK: illegible.

• 1915–1919

TO MARY FIELD PARTON • CHICAGO • THURSDAY 4 MARCH 1915

1202 ASHLAND BLOCK March 4th

Dear Mary

For some reason I am feeling in the dumps today, so I write you. I haven't heard from you for a long time and I enjoy your letters & miss them when they don't come. I wish I could see you and hope you are happy, but you are not. No one is happy who is built like you & me. I have been sorry about those two arrests and am doing all I can to raise some money.[1] Shall give all I can myself and send some this month. I do hope nothing very serious will happen to them. Well it is the way of the world and I presume nothing matters much, but still some days we feel blue especially temperamental people like you & me. I hear a great deal about the fair & wish I could see it.[2] I have had a number of letters from Steffens. He is the same dear man always. Am just writing Older a letter because

1. Darrow is referring to the arrest of Matthew Schmidt and David Caplan. They had been indicted in 1911 for the dynamiting of the Los Angeles Times Building, but they evaded arrest until February 1915. "Dynamite Conspirator Is Caught in New York," *Los Angeles Times,* 14 February 1915; "Last of Indicted Dynamiters Now in Jail in Los Angeles," *Los Angeles Times,* 28 February 1915.
2. The Panama-Pacific International Exposition was held in San Francisco from 4 February to 4 December 1915, marking the opening of the Panama Canal and celebrating the European discovery of the Pacific Ocean. Some 19 million people attended.

of what you wrote Fay[3] about his illness. I do hope it isn't very serious. I can't think of any thing happening [to] him and yet sometime it will happen to us all.

With all best wishes

Ever Your friend | C. S. D.

MS: ALS, ICN, Parton-Darrow Papers, Box 1, Folder 6. ENVELOPE ADDRESS: Mrs Mary Field Parton | 2 Alta Vista | Russian Hill | San Francisco | Cal. POSTMARK: Chicago 4 Mar 1915.

TO E. W. SCRIPPS • CHICAGO • WEDNESDAY 19 MAY 1915

DARROW, BAILY & SISSMAN May 19, 1915.

My Dear Mr. Scripps:—

I presume you get tired of having your friends write you asking you to do things for them through your papers, but I am going to take a chance anyhow, knowing that you can always turn a person down if you feel that you ought to.

I am very much interested in Professor Francis,[4] who is the head of the schools of Los Angeles, as you know. He is a very able and broad minded man and more than that, was always my friend. They are running a special ticket to support him. I am interested in all of it, but especially interested in Mr. Fred E. Golding, who was on my first jury and of course is a staunch friend of mine and one of the best fellows that you ever met. He is absolutely honest and is always ready to help in the cause in which you are interested and of course my personal feeling toward him is one which would be difficult to describe.

If you can see your way clear to help the Ticket and especially him, I would appreciate it more than anything you could do and I feel sure that the cause that they represent, is your cause.

I often see your people here and always enjoy being with them and sympathize with the work they are doing. They are making a success and are going to win.[5] Of course I am anxious to see the paper grow faster than it does, but I presume it will come along in good time.

I wish you would come out here and see us. We appreciated your visit at our house and thoroughly realized the compliment of your having taken dinner with us for the first time in many years away from home.

Ever with kindest regards, I am

Your friend, | Clarence Darrow.

MS: TLS, OAU, Scripps Collection, Box 35, Folder 7. INSIDE ADDRESS: Mr. E. N. Scripps, | San Diego, Calif.

3. Fay Lewis.
4. John H. Francis.
5. Darrow is likely referring to people associated with the *Day Book,* an advertisement-free newspaper that Scripps started in Chicago in 1911 that was designed for the working-class reader. The editor of the newspaper, which folded in 1917, was Negley Cochran. See Duane C. S. Stoltzfus, *Freedom from Advertising: E. W. Scripps's Chicago Experiment* (Urbana: University of Illinois Press, 2007).

TO MARY FIELD PARTON • CHICAGO • SATURDAY 29 MAY 1915

May 29

Dear Mary

It has been a long time since I wrote and I am ashamed. Still it will punish you for waiting so long before you wrote me the last time. Jo was here & told me the news that Lem was expecting a baby.[6] Well I am glad for you both. Life isn't worth while & still we keep producing it—and there is no joy like a child—perhaps some sorrow too. Through the last thirty years nothing has brought me the consolation that Paul has brought and I have had many loyal & good friends—you, especially. It is the order of nature to bring forth & it must be done & it satisfies one of the strongest instincts & emotions. Love to you & Lem & the stranger.

I had them send you a book which discusses it and every thing else & which will delight you some—"The Second blooming."[7] Shall send you an other one which will give you special joy as soon as I can get it. How I wish I could see you but when I don't know. Was in Washington & had a fine time, telling the Commission about every thing on earth,[8] and also seeing your friend Inez Gilmore[9] who is a bully bully girl—wish she lived nearer or I did—also Crystal Eastman[10] & then too Miss Younger[11] was especially nice.

6. Parton and her husband, Lem, were expecting a child, Margaret Parton (1915–81), who became a journalist and author. The "Jo" who relayed the news to Darrow was likely Anton Johannsen.
7. Darrow is referring to Walter Lionel George's novel, *The Second Blooming* (Boston: Little, Brown, 1915).
8. Darrow is referring to his testimony before the United States Commission on Industrial Relations, which was established by an act of Congress in 1912 to inquire into the general condition of labor in principal industries and to determine and report on the underlying causes of labor unrest. Frank Walsh was chair of the commission, which traveled to several cities and heard testimony from over seven hundred witnesses. Darrow testified on 18 May 1915. Senate, *Industrial Relations: Final Report and Testimony Submitted to Congress by the Commission on Industrial Relations Created by the Act of August 23, 1912*, 64th Cong., 1st sess., 1916, S. Doc. 415, 11: 10769–815.
9. Inez Haynes (Gilmore) Irwin (1873–1970), suffragist and writer. Irwin earned a two-year degree at Radcliffe College, 1896, and became active in the suffrage movement, cofounding the National College Equal Suffrage League, 1900, and later joining the Congressional Union for Woman Suffrage. She worked as a war correspondent in Europe for American magazines, 1916–18, and lived in New York City most of her life. Her first marriage, to a man named Gilmore, ended in divorce, and she later married Will Irwin, a writer. She wrote *The Story of the Woman's Party* (1921) (a history) and many novels, children's books, short stories, and murder mysteries. She was the president of the Authors' League of America, 1931, and the Authors' Guild, 1925–28.
10. Crystal Eastman (1881–1928), reformer, writer, suffragist. Eastman graduated from Vassar College, 1903; she received a master's degree in sociology from Columbia University, 1904, and a law degree from New York University, 1907. She investigated workplace accidents for the Russell Sage Foundation, 1907–08, and served as the only woman on New York's Employer's Liability Commission, 1909–10. She cofounded the Congressional Union for Women's Suffrage, 1913, the Woman's Peace Party in New York, 1914, and the Civil Liberties Bureau, 1917, which became the American Civil Liberties Union. She wrote many articles on women's issues, social reform, and other subjects, and cofounded and edited the *Liberator*, 1918–22, a socialist magazine, with her brother, Max Eastman (1883–1969). Darrow represented her in her divorce from her first husband.
11. "Maude" is written in pencil (the letter is in ink) with the initials "MP" (Mary Parton) next to the name "Younger." Maude Younger (1870–1936), trade union activist and suffragist. She was active in trade unionism, in particular, the waitresses' unions, in New York City and San Francisco before becoming involved in suffrage work. She was a member of the Congressional Union and later the National Woman's Party, and active in both organizations.

If I could write like you I would go on forever & if I could see you I would, but you don't always need to see those who are close to you & you have always been very close.

I often think too of Sarah the dear girl & want you to give her my love. It looks as if I would be terribly tied up all summer trying the Lorimer bank case.[12] Am working like a dog & now & then snatching some one from the cruel jaws of the law & the mob. I am just learning one reason why the number of criminals are increasing. Fifty years ago we had about a hundred crimes on our Statute book now about 1000. D—n the cruel good people. You noticed about Jane Adams & the bunch going to Europe to stop the war.[13] Immediately the Lucitania was blown up & Italy went in. Great is Jane & the rest—

Ever your friend | C. Darrow

MS: ALS, ICN, Parton-Darrow Papers, Box 1, Folder 6. ENVELOPE ADDRESS: Miss Mary Field Parton | 2 Alta Vesta—Russian Hill | San Francisco | Cal. POSTMARK: Chicago 29 May 1915.

TO CHARLES ERSKINE SCOTT WOOD • CHICAGO • THURSDAY 3 JUNE 1915

DARROW, BAILY & SISSMAN June 3rd, 1915.

My dear Mr. Wood:—

I received your book and letter and was very glad to hear from you.[14] I have not had time to look at the book as yet, but will go over it on Sunday. Several people have picked it up in the office and have been delighted with it, and I am sure I shall like it. As quick as I read it, I will do what I can to it. There are two or three of the smaller book stores here whom I know would like to take it, and do what they can for it. I presume McClurg's would not care to handle it, although I will see them. They are conservative and very little would be done there for it.[15]

If I like the book, as I am quite sure I will, I will write a review for William Marion Ready's publication, THE MIRROR. I would suggest that you send him a copy, and I will

12. Darrow is referring to William Lorimer (1861–1934), politician, banker, and businessman. Lorimer served as a Republican congressman from Illinois for several terms, 1895–1901, 1903–08, and later as United States senator, 1909–12, until the Senate removed him from his seat after an investigation into corrupt methods and practices in his election. In June 1914, after Lorimer was removed from the Senate, a bank that he had started in Chicago failed and Lorimer was charged with criminal conduct in connection with the failure. Darrow represented Lorimer early on in the criminal proceedings, but he did not represent him when the matter when to trial in March 1916. See "Trial for Lorimer and Aids Ordered by Judge O'Connor," *Chicago Tribune*, 10 April 1915; Joel Tarr, *A Study in Boss Politics: William Lorimer of Chicago* (Urbana: University of Illinois Press, 1971), 311–13.
13. In April 1915, Addams made a widely publicized trip to the Netherlands to chair the International Congress of Women at The Hague. During the meeting, several resolutions were passed calling for international peace. Afterward, in May and June, Addams and several other delegates personally delivered those resolutions to the warring countries. Addams was in London in early May 1915 urging peace two days after the British passenger ship *Lusitania* was sunk by the Germans, killing 1,198 passengers, including 114 Americans. Allen F. Davis, *American Heroine: The Life and Legend of Jane Addams* (New York: Oxford University Press, 1973), 217–24.
14. Probably *The Poet in the Desert* (Portland, OR, 1915), Wood's best-known work.
15. The bookstore called "A. C. McClurg" was founded in Chicago in 1844.

write him before your book arrives.[16] I will also write Mr. Howells. He is thoroughly radical and does not dare express his opinion. This is not slandering him, for he told me that himself. He is a great admirer of Zola[17] and of all radical literature. I do not think he would be afraid of it, and still he might be afraid to do much for it. I have some other literary friends, and may write you to send a book to them.

I am mailing you a book today which was written by my former partner, which has attracted a great deal of attention, and think you will enjoy it.[18]

I note what you say about the Los Angeles case and shall be glad to see you in it.[19] I do not know how you can get along with the lawyers. Davis[20] is a good fellow and both he and Appel[21] are hard fighters. Of course they have no vision to look to and no idea of defending a case along the lines of principle, even though the defense should be more or less veiled. I am sure it will do a great deal of good to have you in the case. As you know I am very much interested in it and am contributing what I can towards the defense.

I have intended writing you for a long time. I have taken up life about where I left it when I went to California. Have been very busy, although there are a good many lawyers who make more money. I also appreciate what you did in my behalf in the West and will soon be in shape to return the financial part, which I know is a matter of no great interest to you, but still it is to me.

I wish you would happen this way again. I should be glad to see you.

With kind regards, I am as ever

Your friend, | Clarence Darrow.

MS: TLS, CU-BANC, C. E. S. Wood Papers, Carton 2. LETTER ADDRESS: Mr. C. E. S. Wood, | Yeon Building, | Portland, Oreg.

TO T. PERCEVAL GERSON • CHICAGO • TUESDAY 29 JUNE 1915

DARROW, BAILY & SISSMAN June 29

My Dear Dr. Guerson

I was glad to get your note & Mrs. D. was glad to hear from Mrs. Guerson. We miss you both & would give any thing to see you. Whatever happens you will both always be very

16. No review of Wood's book was published in *The Mirror*.
17. Émile Zola (1840–1902), French novelist, critic, and founder of naturalism in literature.
18. Edgar Lee Masters, *Spoon River Anthology* (New York: Macmillan, 1915).
19. Darrow is referring to the cases of Matthew Schmidt and David Caplan. Schmidt was tried in late 1915 and Caplan was tried in late 1916. Wood considered representing them, but they could not reach an agreement on fees. Robert Hamburger, *Two Rooms: The Life of Charles Erskine Scott Wood* (Lincoln: University of Nebraska Press, 1998), 220–22.
20. LeCompte Davis.
21. Horace Appel (1860–1922), a criminal-defense attorney in Los Angeles who was involved in many prominent cases in his day, including as part of the defense team for Darrow's first trial in Los Angeles for jury bribery. Appel was defense counsel for David Caplan during his trial in 1916. In 1919, Appel was committed to the Norwalk Asylum for the Insane (in Los Angeles County), and for a time was in the same ward as Earl Rogers, his co-counsel on Darrow's defense team.

dear to us. I can't say that I was disappointed at Mills.[22] He is not solid & I have no doubt that the love of new things & applause had much to do with his joining the liberal ranks at first and I am very sure that he would never have left if he had seen a good living with the Rationalists. You remember that in the last Campaign he joined the Socialists & a few days later left them for the progressives. It is hard for him to stand grief. I have no idea that he ever changed his views or his real attitude toward life. All this seems like a criticism on Mills but I really do not mean it this way. I know he is filled with charity & good feeling which are the main things. I know that he is never successful in business. He is intensely emotional, and I am sure that the financial temptations were great. No doubt he believes he can do as much where he is & perhaps he can. It does not change my views of any thing. None of us can stand only a certain amount, & the amount is proportioned to the elements that make us up. Under the same conditions I might have done as he did. I know how many times I fall short, and it is only a question of how much I can stand. Any how I shall always admire him & wish him well & feel that he has done & will do good in the world.

I have been very busy at the old trade. I find a good many chances—every day—to help some one out of trouble & try always to do it especially as I remember how you & others helped me. I believe that I am [x] than I ever was before, & it too pays. Then I do some work that I get real money for. I long to go back & see my old friends at L.A. & believe I sometime shall, though I don't know when. No one ever knows when in this world. If you & Mrs. G. haven't read Jean-Christophe I want you to do it. How you two would love it! I was terribly disappointed not to see Mr. Williams[23] & if I could drop in on the heart to heart club, I would be almost happy. I love you all, & so many times feel the need of you all. If only you would come here & see us. You would all get a warm welcome. Write me a line when you can & give my love to all especially the Williams & the Blights[24] & Mrs. Guerson. Ever your friend—

Clarence Darrow.

MS: ALS, CLU-SC, Theodore Perceval Gerson Papers (Collection 724). DATE: "1915" appended.

22. Darrow is probably referring to Benjamin Fay Mills and his conversion in 1915 to a more conservative form of Christianity.
23. Probably Edwin M. Williams and his wife, Della.
24. Reynold E. Blight (1879–1951) and his wife, Lydia (Walters) Blight (1879?–1922). Reynold Blight, born in England, emigrated to Canada at an early age and settled in California in 1903. He was partner in an accounting firm in Los Angeles and active in church and civic affairs. He was editor for many years of the *New Age Magazine* and other publications of the Scottish Rite of Freemasonry. Lydia Blight was born in Racine, Wisconsin. She attended normal school in Long Beach, California, and taught school in Los Angeles. The Blights, along with the Gersons and the Williamses, were members of the Severance Club, a cultural club in Los Angeles. Darrow was an occasional speaker and guest at meetings of the club when he was in Los Angeles.

TO FRANK LLOYD WRIGHT • EN ROUTE TO NEW YORK • FRIDAY 19 NOVEMBER 1915

PENNSYLVANIA RAILROAD | BROADWAY LIMITED Nov. 19

Dear Frank

Am on my way to N.Y. for two or three days. It looks like most everyone has forgotten you & your troubles & I hope you are forgetting them to.[25] Really we all take ourselves too seriously. Hope you will be down soon & come & see us. Our house is always open—

Your friend | C. S. Darrow.

MS: ALS, CMalG, Wright Papers. DATE: reference to Wright's "troubles" together with the partial date.

TO MARY FIELD PARTON • CHICAGO • MONDAY 6 DECEMBER 1915

DARROW, BAILY & SISSMAN Dec 6th

Dear Mary

If I could write letters as you can, I would write all the time, and if you knew how I like to get them & read them you would send them to me. Really no one can write as you do & it is always a joy to get them.

Life moves on the same way with me, most of the time is spent trying to get some poor person out or keep them out & I often think it does no good, for the everlasting flood moves on, & one or a hundred doesn't count. Still what does do good, & if here & there you can help one specific case, it may be just as good, as good as working everlastingly for a cause which recedes as fast as you approach it. What an everlasting enigma is life, & how we do get lost in its dark maze. No sooner do we plant our feet on something that seems like solid ground, than we find the sand shifting under us & we look for something else. I wonder how much of truth [x], these the things that I have been frantically working for through all the years. Well it has furnished me an interest in life & made me forget myself and I guess this is its chief value. Any how I am starting all over new. We have organized a Biology class, meeting once a week. Prof Foster & a good number of other philosophers & near philosophers belong & we have an expert talk to us & it is very interesting. I feel that I am finding out some real things that shed a little ray of light here & there. Any how the evenings are interesting & as life is flying past this is the main

25. In October 1915, a disgruntled former housekeeper of Wright's tried to convince federal authorities in Chicago to prosecute Wright for violation of the Mann Act. Wright had been traveling back and forth from Chicago to his home in Spring Green, Wisconsin, with Maude Miriam Noel (1869–1930), who would become his wife many years later. The Mann Act made transportation of women across state lines for an "immoral purpose" a federal crime. Darrow represented Wright during the investigation, which was covered extensively by newspapers. See, e.g., Meryle Secrest, *Frank Lloyd Wright: A Biography* (New York: Knopf, 1992), 244–46; "Bungalow Life Defended by Frank Wright: Complains His Love Affairs Have Been 'Flung under Foot,'" *Chicago Tribune*, 7 November 1915.

thing. I was glad to see Sarah & shall be glad to see her again when she returns. Her name is in the News Papers day by day & she is getting a taste of fame or notoriety as the case may be and I wonder what it tastes like. Probably not like what she expected.[26]

Yesterday I spoke in Cincinnati on "The War." Saw Kiefer & the rest of the Single Tax fanatics who mourned that I was traveling in new fields, & losing my usefulness. All they want is Henry George & him crucified. I wonder if I know any more than I used to or is just a phase of life & my heart is going slower—probably that. Any how I am interested in the same things but know the world won't change. I wish you would look through the library there & see if you can get a wonderful book "Folk Ways" by Prof Sumner of Yale.[27] If you can't I must buy it & send it to you.

I had an invitation to go in the Ford ship but told some of my friends that I could make a D—n fool of myself without leaving Chicago.[28] But I saw Barry as he passed through on his noble errand & had a pleasant visit & heard from you all.

Am going east during the Holy days & hope I can see Sarah there. Any how dear Mary I love you & all the rest of my friends out there & would dearly love to see them. Please write often & I will do better with my answers, & give my love to all.

Ever | Clarence Darrow

MS: ALS, ICN, Parton-Darrow Papers, Box 1, Folder 6. ENVELOPE ADDRESS: Mrs Mary Field Parton | ~~Corde Madero~~ | 1607 Taylor St | San Francisco | California. POSTMARK: Chicago 6 December 1915.

TO LEVI MOORE POWERS • CHICAGO • WEDNESDAY 15 DECEMBER 1915

DARROW, BAILY & SISSMAN Dec. 15

My Dear Powers

It was good to hear from you this morning and I am glad you liked the War talk.[29] I believe it will stand close analysis. Of course there are only a few people who really think about

26. In September 1915, Parton's sister, Sara Bard Field, and a few other women began an automobile trip across the country, from San Francisco to Washington, D.C. The object of the trip was to garner support for the suffrage movement and deliver a suffrage petition to Congress and President Wilson, symbolizing an offer of political power from women in the West (where several states had granted suffrage to women) to women in the East (where no states had granted suffrage). Half a million signatures were gathered on the petition at the Panama-Pacific International Exposition in San Francisco in 1915. The automobile trip was the idea of Field's friend, Alice Paul. All of the major cities along the route (including Chicago) held parades and rallies when the automobile with Field arrived, and the trip received considerable attention in the newspapers. Amelia Fry, "Along the Suffrage Trail: From West to East for FREEDOM NOW!" *The American West,* January 1969, 16–25.
27. William Graham Sumner, *Folkways: A Study of the Sociological Importance of Usages, Manners, Customs, Mores, and Morals* (Boston: Ginn & Co., 1906).
28. On 5 December 1915, a "peace ship" sponsored by Henry Ford set sail from New York for Oslo, Norway, carrying Ford, some sixty to eighty other "peace delegates" and opponents of the war and preparedness, and approximately half as many journalists. Many of the people invited on this pacifist mission declined to go, including Darrow. Among the delegates who accepted Ford's invitation were many writers, editors, feminists, and politicians, including John D. Barry, Benjamin W. Huebsch, Inez Milholland Boissevain, and Benjamin B. Lindsey. The mission received considerable criticism and ridicule in the press. Allan Nevins and Frank Ernest Hill, *Ford: Expansion and Challenge, 1915–1933* (New York: Charles Scribner's Sons, 1957), 26–54.
29. The speech (or written account of a speech) to which Darrow is referring is unknown.

any thing, and this war is bound to bring more than the usual crop of fool talkers & writers. I have long lost all conceit of the wisdom or honesty of the mob and am coming to believe that Democracy is a failure. I was awfully sorry not to see you when I was in Boston, but got tied up & couldn't go. We are going to N.Y. in the holidays. I wonder if you would happen to be there. It would seem good to have another visit with you. Mrs. D is well & I am at the old game. Remember me to Mrs. Powers.

Your friend | Clarence Darrow

MS: ALS, location of original unknown (copy in editor's files). DATE: letterhead and reference to war.

TO MARY FIELD PARTON • CHICAGO • THURSDAY 27 APRIL 1916

April 27th.

Dear Mary

I would have written you sooner but was punishing you for leaving my last letter so long unanswered. I am always happy to get your letters. No one else writes such letters as you do and then I like to hear from you. If you are pessimistic I like that too, for I thrive on pessimism. No one but idiots & dope fiends are optimists. I have been talking on Nietchie & Schopenhauer & had a good time over it & I think the audience liked it too. Life goes on in the same way. Many emotions, lots of troubles to listen to, some money, but is hell to be the Genl Counsel to the poor. Still I have had my share & more, and am glad I can afford to help. I am trying some cases, get paid for some, with real money, get paid for all in some way. Any how I *do* some of the things that the others talk about doing & here & there are a few people that I help out of hard places. Yesterday I was down to the penitentiary pleading with the pardon board for a number, generally go down every month—& the board seems to like to have me talk & to listen to my queer ideas, that they are no better than the fellows inside—really they are a pretty good bunch. One of them a country banker & merchant, wants to let them all out. He says he knows they are as good as he is. He told me that when he was a young man he went west with a little money & a bible, that he worked as hard as he could & had bad luck & found himself out of a job, & made up his mind he would have to either beg or steal and that he swore he wouldn't beg. I just got a check of 250 from Julius Rosenwald[30] to pay the expenses in appealing a colored man's case,[31] so we must remember that for Julius.

30. Julius Rosenwald (1862–1932), president of Sears, Roebuck in Chicago, 1908–24, and then its chairman, 1924–32, was an active Republican and one of the great philanthropists of the early twentieth century. He donated millions of dollars to museums, schools, YMCAs, and Jewish charities. Influenced by Booker T. Washington's autobiography, *Up from Slavery* (1901), Rosenwald was particularly interested in helping African Americans, and he helped build several thousand schools and libraries in the rural South.

31. This is likely a reference to the case of Isaac Bond, a forty-year-old black man who was convicted of murdering Ida Leegson, a white woman who worked as a nurse, artist, and art teacher. Several witnesses testified that they had seen Bond or someone who resembled him in the company of Leegson in the area of the murder in Chicago on the day that she died. Other witnesses testified that they had seen Bond with Leegson's

I was awfully glad to see Sarah although we nearly fought. Imagine Sarah & I fighting when either one of us would go to hell for the other. It was about the war & she was defending the doctrines I used to teach.[32] Well Mary it is this way with me about the war. When an orthodox socialist or anarchist with a full fledged theory finds that his theory runs up against a fact he says to hell with the fact. I try to be right and I know I can't change a fact so I modify my theory. Here was Germany preparing for years to destroy civilization (such as it is) to make the world Prussian. They trampled Belgium under foot violating their written word. They invaded France & Poland. They ran their submarines under ships & destroyed them without warning. The world had to submit to Germany & to go back to barbarism or fight for what they had. There can be no peace while Prussian militarism lives & I want to see it destroyed because I don't believe war is ideal. Unless the Allies can lick Germany there can be no peace on earth, and I want to see them licked if it takes the whole world to do it. Then too it is a world of war from the lowest to highest: all life living on other life & it can't be changed. In fact the emotions of hate & fear have preserved life as much as the emotions of love & sympathy, & we can't get out of it. Human nature has not changed since man came upon the earth. It will not change, except ever so slowly extending over ages. The Catholic dopes himself with Religion. The Christian Scientist does the same. The Humanitarian takes his dope. We have been taking labor dope. Some take whiskey some opium. It is all dope, and man does not live by facts but by dope & I fear I am waking & can't find any other dope. So what in hell am I to do. I still find a little activity in my old dope, but I know it gets no where & will come to nothing. Still I go on & on in the dark, with only a few like you & Older who have the strength to stagger along. I am glad of what Mr. Wood sd. He should not sell his soul to those people.[33] I will sometime tell you a story, but I try not to think of it, for I know the limitations of men, & I am sorry for them all. But dear girl it is a dark hard world, & I get the most ~~satisfactions~~ out my friends—it is better than reforming—but I never will close my eyes again until I shut them for the last long sleep.

I was disappointed not to see more of Sarah. She sd. she was coming again soon & I hope she will & I hope she won't come with a brass band so all her time will be taken. She is like you dear & loyal & sweet & clever, & I have been glad of all the attention she has had, still it isn't worth while. It is a hollow sham. Saw Helen[34] a little while as she went to California to be disillusioned again. Dear Helen. I wish she would light (or *lite*).

---

watch and a pin attached to it or jewelry that resembled those items shortly after she was murdered. On the other hand, seven witnesses testified that Bond was in Gary, Indiana, on the day of and the day after the murder, which would have made Bond's guilt impossible. The prosecution attacked the credibility of Bond's witnesses, all of whom were friends or acquaintances of Bond. Darrow represented Bond in his trial and on appeal, which ended with his conviction and a life sentence affirmed on appeal. *People v. Bond*, 281 Ill. 490, 118 N.E. 14 (Dec. 19, 1917) (affirming conviction).

32. This is probably a reference to a heated argument about the war that Darrow and Sara Bard Field had in New York City at a New Year's party. Dona Munker, personal communication, New York City, September 2007.

33. What Charles Erskine Scott Wood said is unknown.

34. Probably Helen Todd.

Any how Mary write me quick and give my love to Older & tell him I *think* I will write him today.

Ever Your devoted friend | Clarence.

MS: ALS, ICN, Parton-Darrow Papers, Box 1, Folder 7. PLACE: implied. DATE: "1915" appended but 1916 is more likely given the apparent reference to the Bond case and the reference to nearly fighting with Sara over the war.

TO MARY FIELD PARTON • CHICAGO • FRIDAY 14 JULY 1916

DARROW & SISSMAN July 14

Dear Mary

This isn't a letter just a note to tell you that I am going East to the White Mountains & Quebec for a little over two weeks and am then coming back to go to Colorado for a month:—a vacation. God knows for what—except to spend some money. I had the best visit with Sarah[35] never so good before. When she had been here at other times she was in the mad whirl with other fool world saviors, like we once were. How I do like to get your letters & wish I could write like you. I would write all the time—I think. I know you will devour the little volume of poems that Sarah took back with her. How I wish we could read them together—some time we will.

The world drags on the same way—work most of the time, read some, frivol a little. Haven't written much but shall commence tomorrow morning & see if I can't. How lazy I am & how it seems not worth while—we are so long dead—and what if they should read our stuff when we are not there to know it—D–n the thinking any how. As Hauseman says "Thinking lays lads underground."[36] Well Mary I will think of you in Quebec,—& the White Mountains & down the St. Lawrence & will write you & want to see you.

As ever— | Always, | Clarence Darrow

MS: ALS, ICN, Parton-Darrow Papers, Box 1, Folder 7. ENVELOPE ADDRESS: Mrs Mary Parton Field | ~~c/o Mr. Fremont Older~~ | 1146 Green St | San Francisco | Cal. | ~~c/o The *Bulletin*~~. POSTMARK: Chicago 14 July 1916.

TO FREMONT OLDER • CHICAGO • MONDAY 25 SEPTEMBER 1916

DARROW & SISSMAN Sept 25

Dear Fremont

Your letter makes me sad. I too would have quit the game long ago except for cowardice—but I don't want you to quit.

35. Sara Bard Field was in Chicago in early June 1916 to speak and otherwise participate in a convention of women who were forming the National Woman's Party.
36. Darrow is quoting a line from A. E. Housman's *A Shropshire Lad:* "Oh, 'tis jesting, dancing, and drinking / Spins the heavy world around. / If young hearts were not so clever, / Oh, they would be young for ever: / Think no more; 'tis only thinking / Lays lads underground."

I will be 60 also on my next birthday. And I believe I feel more like living than ever for I know that it can't last long.

For people who are made like you & me, there is nothing in life except a few brief moments of companionship & pleasure, which in no way make up for the anguish of soul at the injustice of the world, to say nothing of physical pain. I do not regret that the path ahead is short. Still you have as much as any one. You know you have done your best, done it lovingly, loyally & with a great courage, & you have many devoted friends who would almost die for you.

When the Hearst papers attacked you for being morally responsible for the bomb, you ought to have quoted Root's speech holding him morally responsible for the death of McKinley.[37] The whole press of the country took the same view. In a sense we are morally responsible for such things but how can we help it. If the world is to move it must be brought about by everlasting agitation & some people must die. The weak minded are always with us. The inventors of the alphabet are morally responsible for many deaths & revolutions, but they are likewise responsible in the same way for whatever good has come through agitation & enlightenment. But you know all this & philosophy don't help when our feelings are keen. You have often philosophized to me but it did not drive away the pain, but your love & loyalty & that of others did help. I wish I could help you now. I don't know any thing I would not do for you. This will pass away as all things pass away, and as you told me once when I needed it, we can't indulge in self pity. What you say of the labor fellows is true & that hurts the most. Still it couldn't be otherwise. The fact is you & I have both over played the labor question, placed it clear out of its proportion to all the rest of life. I am for the poor and shall always be but there are other things in life. I do wish you could come east. I wouldn't leave you a minute. I am just now using my emotions on the cause of The Alies in Europe and on Wilson. I never felt more anxious for a man to win than I do for Wilson, & I believe he will loose. No end of money will be used to beat him. I am glad to know the Bulletin is for him. What can those Congressional Union people be thinking of to help the common enemy?[38]

Ever with all love to you & Mrs O | Clarence Darrow

MS: ALS, CU-BANC, Older Papers, Box 1. DATE: reference to birthday.

37. The bomb to which Darrow is referring exploded on 22 July 1916 during the Preparedness-Day parade in San Francisco. Ten people were killed. Two of the people arrested—Tom Mooney and Warren Billings—were convicted in what became one of the most sensational radical-labor prosecutions of the early twentieth century. Two days after the bombing, William Randolph Hearst's San Francisco *Examiner* published a scathing editorial claiming that the bombing had been incited by three "political and journalistic demagogues"—which was meant to include Older. The *Examiner* urged the city to rid itself of "these mean and loathsome vermin." Richard H. Frost, *The Mooney Case* (Stanford: Stanford University Press, 1968), 88–99. The speech by Elihu Root (1845–1937) to which Darrow refers occurred in 1906, when Hearst ran for governor of New York. Root, who was then Roosevelt's secretary of state, gave a widely publicized speech denouncing Hearst as a demagogue whose "incendiary abuse" of political leaders had "wrought out its natural consequence—in the murder of President McKinley." Elihu Root, *The United States and the War, the Mission to Russia, Political Addresses,* comp. and ed. Robert Bacon and James Brown Scott (Cambridge: Harvard University Press, 1918), 222–23.

38. The Congressional Union for Woman Suffrage, formed in 1913, was made up of militant suffragists who sought an amendment to the federal Constitution that would allow women the right to vote. The Congressional Union merged with the National Woman's Party in 1916. Here, Darrow might be referring to the Congressional Union's efforts against Democratic candidates in the fall of 1916 who opposed an amendment.

TO SARA BARD FIELD • CHICAGO • FRIDAY 6 OCTOBER 1916

DARROW & SISSMAN Oct. 6

Dear Sarah

I owe Mr. Wood $500 to say nothing of interest. I wrote him that I would begin paying him soon. He said if it was ever convenient I could do if not I need not but when (or if) I did to send to you. So dear girl here is $200. The rest will come before Jan 1st. How I wish I could do more for you & Mary, but Lord how many beggars there are & how many know my address.

Aren't you ever coming this way. I want to see you. Love to Mary & Lem.

Clarence Darrow

MS: ALS, CSmH., Wood Papers, WD Box 126 (52). PLACE: letterhead. DATE: letterhead and reference to Wilson in letter on this same date to C. E. S. Wood.

TO CHARLES ERSKINE SCOTT WOOD • CHICAGO • FRIDAY 6 OCTOBER 1916

DARROW & SISSMAN Oct. 6th

My Dear Mr. Wood

I have just mailed Sarah a check for $200 & will send the rest between now & the Holidays. I am glad you wrote me for I might have delayed a little longer. Mary wrote me about what you did for Marion.[39] I am sorry you give so easily and wish I could help you. Perhaps I can when I get this paid. I am working hard & doing fairly well financially, but there are always so many worthy & unworthy looking for help that it keeps me poor. Still it may be just as well it doesn't last long any how. I don't know what to think about Wilson's chances. I am afraid of the money. It is still all up to N.Y. and money is all powerful. Of course the working man & every one but the big thieves should vote for him but they won't. I am glad you say that Sarah is working for Hughes to earn some money.[40] I should hate to think that she didn't know better. She does. But with me she never could do wrong—even if she was for Germany. I hear indirectly that Jim Caslin[41] is dead. Is it so & have you Mrs. Caslin's address? Poor Caslin. I am glad he is dead & still I will be glad when you are dead and any one else that I love except perhaps my boy. Don't think

39. "Marion" is Marion Field Greene, the younger sister of Mary Field Parton and Sara Bard Field. Marion, who had two children, was in some financial straits, and Wood had helped her out. Dona Munker, personal communication, New York City, September 2007.
40. Sara Bard Field and other suffragists supported Republican Charles Evans Hughes (1862–1948) in the presidential campaign in 1916. Hughes (unlike Woodrow Wilson) endorsed the idea of a federal suffrage amendment to the Constitution.
41. The identity of "Jim Caslin" is unknown.

that I ever forget all your goodness to me & others or that I don't understand & admire you to the limit.

Clarence Darrow.

MS: ALS, CU-BANC, C. E. S. Wood Papers, Carton 2. DATE: letterhead and reference to Wilson.

TO GEORGE P. COSTIGAN JR. • CHICAGO • WEDNESDAY 10 JANUARY 1917

Chicago, Ill., Jan. 10, 1917

I undertook the McNamara case without any knowledge whatever as to whether the defendants were in any way involved in the destruction of the Times building with its incidental loss of life.[42] At the time I went into the case I had never seen the defendants and had not visited Los Angeles and the matter had been under investigation and in progress for several months. I did not know the facts until weeks after I undertook the case. I then believed as I do now that no intention was in the mind of any one to kill any person; the purpose being only to scare the owners of the Los Angeles Times—a paper then conducting a hostile campaign against the strikers in the city. Sixteen sticks of dynamite (as I now recall it) were placed in an alley leading into the building. The explosion did not even stop the machinery, but unfortunately the sticks were hastily dropped near some barrels of ink which were converted into vapor, spread through the building, and thus set on fire the building, and the lives were lost through the fire. Legally the crime of murder was complete for the reason that the placing of dynamite was an unlawful act and the defendants were therefore guilty of the act whether the result was intended or not. Five lawyers were associated in the case and a large corps of investigators gathered information from many cities covering the whole United States. Most of the money to defray the expenses was collected before the real facts were known, but I then and now considered it my duty when in the case to give the defendant the best defense I could, and of course could not give out that I really believed he placed the dynamite. Under the laws of California one convicted of murder in the first degree could be punished by death or life imprisonment as the jury might determine, and in any event I felt it my duty to get the lowest punishment possible. I

42. Costigan was writing a book on legal ethics and a section of it was devoted to the McNamara case. In particular, Costigan focused on the ethical issues raised by Darrow having encouraged labor organizations to raise money for the defense of the McNamaras, while at the same time, according to newspaper reports in December 1911 (after the McNaramas pleaded guilty), Darrow knew of their guilt when he undertook their defense. George P. Costigan Jr., *Cases and Other Authorities on Legal Ethics* (St. Paul, MN: West Publishing, 1917), 343–52. John Wigmore (1863–1943), dean of the law school at Northwestern University, where Costigan taught, had been highly critical of Darrow in a well-publicized law-journal article written along these same lines, published shortly after the guilty pleas of the McNamaras. Ibid., 348–49. Costigan noted that Darrow, "[i]n view of the contemplated publication" of Costigan's book, had handed him this "statement" on 10 January 1917. Ibid., 351.

always abhorred the idea of the state taking life and then as always like the physician I felt it my duty to save life if I could. Then, too, I recognized that in labor and political cases the motives of men are far different than in cases that are generally designated as criminal. Neither did I ever believe in the doctrine of free will, but I think that every act is governed by conditions and circumstances which make the act absolutely necessary. I judged this case, as I do all other acts in court and out, from what I consider uncontrovertible rules of logic and philosophy.

As to fees, five lawyers were associated with me with numerous investigators and the necessary expenses involved in such a case were large. The amount collected for the defendants was less than that paid by the state and all lawyers' fees and most detectives' services for the state were paid through regular salaries and did not come from the fund. I closed my office and went to Los Angeles and was engaged in that case for six months and received less than $50,000 as a fee, which would not be mentioned as extravagant for a lawyer engaged in any important case. Especially is this true in my case, as much more than half my time that has been given to industrial and labor cases for twenty-five years has been without any financial reward.

I have thought this case over from every angle and am sure that whatever the responsibilities involved no conscientious lawyer could have performed them in any other way.

MS: George P. Costigan Jr., *Cases and Other Authorities on Legal Ethics* (St. Paul, MN: West Publishing, 1917), 351–52.

TO DUNCAN C. MILNER • CHICAGO • SATURDAY 16 JUNE 1917

DARROW & SISSMAN June 16th

My Dear Mr. Milner

I have just received & read your address on war & was very much pleased with it.[43] I feel that you are entirely right on the main thing & I wish that more ministers would do what you have done. The war must be fought until Prussian Militaryism is destroyed. I presume I might not fully agree with all you say. I feel that Jesus was like all other men. All he said & did perhaps can not be harmonized—much less all that was attributed to him. It is not at all necessary that it should be harmonized. For the subjects he spoke about few if any have ever spoken so truly & a literal enactment of every thing he said is in no way necessary nor ever possible. I feel too that you over emphasize liquor & do not go to the foundation of "vice" but still

43. Milner delivered a sermon at the Ravenswood Presbyterian Church in Chicago on 3 June 1917 that was designed to reconcile the tenets of Christianity with acts of war. The sermon was published as a pamphlet: Duncan C. Milner, *May a Christian Be a Soldier and Fight?* (1917).

I did not write this as a criticism but as an appreciation & I am glad you said it and published it.

Very truly | Clarence Darrow

MS: ALS, IU-HS, Milner Papers. DATE: "1917" appended. INSIDE ADDRESS: "Rev. Duncan C. Milner."

TO FRANK WALSH • CHICAGO • THURSDAY 12 JULY 1917

DARROW & SISSMAN July 12, 1917.

My Dear Walsh:—

I have promised to go to Washington, reaching the Shoreham Hotel next Monday morning for breakfast.

The National Organization of the Socialist Party have asked me to see what I could do toward giving their papers access to the mails. In my opinion, they have clamped the lid on too tight and it seems to me the right kind of talk will produce results. They also want you to go with me.

An appointment has been made for some hour Monday. Hope you can do it. Anyhow, I shall be very glad to see you.[44]

Very truly yours, | Clarence Darrow

MS: TLS, NN, Walsh Papers, Box 4. INSIDE ADDRESS: Hon. Frank Walsh, | Shoreham Hotel, | Washington, | D.C.

TO SAMUEL GOMPERS • CHICAGO • THURSDAY 9 AUGUST 1917

DARROW & SISSMAN Aug 9

My Dear Mr Gompers

I want to tell you how much I appreciate your stand in the war. You have done a lot of good. Germany *must* be beaten before the world can move on. If I can be of any help to you in any meetings or any thing else in the East let me know & I will respond.[45]

Truly Yours | Clarence Darrow

MS: ALS, WHi, AFL Records: Gompers Era. LETTER STAMPED: "RECEIVED | AUG 10 1917."

44. On 16 July 1917, Darrow, Walsh, Morris Hillquit, Seymour Stedman, Roger Baldwin, and others spent the morning in Washington, D.C., with Assistant Attorney General William C. Herron (1864–1922) and the afternoon with Postmaster General Albert S. Burleson (1863–1937), trying to convince them that the government should stop banning *Masses* and *Mother Earth* and "[s]ome thirteen or fourteen other publications" from the mail. Frank Walsh to Emma Goldman, 18 July 1917, TLc, NN, Walsh Papers. See J. L. Engdahl, "Press Has Right to Oppose Draft Law, Postmaster General Tells Socialists," *American Socialist*, 21 July 1917.
45. Gompers responded with a brief note: "I greatly appreciate and thank you for all that you said and for your offer of services. I may yet call upon you." Gompers to Darrow, 27 August 1917, TLc, WHi, AFL Records: Gompers Era.

TO NEGLEY D. COCHRAN • CHICAGO • THURSDAY 9 AUGUST 1917

DARROW & SISSMAN Aug 9

Dear Neg

I wrote the President & Mr. Kent[46] according to Mr. K's suggesting I telling them that I would be willing to speak in N.Y. or elsewhere. The fact is I would like to make some speeches on the war. I know what to say about it & how to say it & if you can push the game along I would appreciate it. It isn't often that I ask any one to do any thing for me—but then I have done it.

I was lonesome after leaving you. I shall not try to tell you how much I think of you. These are the things that women do & we men bluff along pretending that we have no feelings. But my dear friend (if you will excuse me) I want to say that I have found very few friends whom I love & respect more than you. Remember me to Mr. Scripps. He is a real fellow & I am very fond of him.

Truly yours, | Clarence.

MS: ALS, OT. DATE: letterhead and reference to speeches for the war.

TO HARRY WEINBERGER • CHICAGO • FRIDAY 10 AUGUST 1917

DARROW & SISSMAN August 10, 1917.

Dear Mr Weinberger:-

I told Mr. Nathanson[47] that if you would send me the abstract after it was printed, I would go over it carefully and make any suggestions or render any help I could on the brief and if it did seem as if I could be of any assistance in an oral argument, I would probably do that.[48]

I would not want my name on the brief at this time. Of course I prefer not to be in this case. I have had so many of this sort that I would rather not do it unless it was necessary. It probably would be better for the defendants to have some one else do it. However, if I felt that it was in any way necessary in order to obtain justice, I would do so, but I would not want to have anything said in reference to it or have my name used in connection with it until after I had examined the abstract.

46. William Kent (1864–1928), a businessman and politician, was one of the founders of the Municipal Voters League in Chicago, 1896, and later a three-term congressman from California, 1911–17, as well as a member of the United States Tariff Commission, 1917–20, appointed by President Wilson.
47. William Nathanson (1883–1963) was an author, anarchist, and Yiddish writer who lived in Chicago for approximately fifty years before moving to Los Angeles shortly before his death.
48. Weinberger represented Emma Goldman and Alexander Berkman (1870–1936), anarchist editor, organizer, and Goldman's friend and comrade. Goldman and Berkman were convicted by a jury in federal court in New York in July 1917 for conspiring to induce eligible men to resist the draft. Weinberger had written to Darrow after he heard from Nathanson that Darrow might be willing to help with the appeal in the Supreme Court: "Mr. Nathanson of Chicago wire[d] me that you would be willing to be associated in the case of United States vs. Emma Goldman and Alexander Berkman on the appeal. | They and myself would be glad to have you. If you will help, as soon as the case is printed I will send you a copy and submit my plans for the appeal to you." Weinberger to Darrow, 8 August 1917, TLc, CtY-BR, Weinberger Papers, Box 28, Folder 4.

Please mail it to me when you have it ready. I will look it over and communicate with you.

Very truly yours, | Clarence Darrow[49]

MS: TLS, CtY-BR, Weinberger Papers, Box 28, Folder 4. INSIDE ADDRESS: Mr. Harry Weinberger, | 261 Broadway, | New York, | N.Y.

TO FRANK WALSH • CHICAGO • MONDAY 10 SEPTEMBER 1917

DARROW & SISSMAN September 10, 1917.

My Dear Mr. Walsh:—

They are starting a campaign down here on the war business and I have just had a meeting with people who are doing it and are all right and they want you to come and speak.

We will have several meetings between Friday night and three weeks from now and I want you to speak at a good one. Let me know if you can do it.

I have tried my best to get you into society and now I shall try to make you famous.

As ever, | Yours, | Clarence Darrow

MS: TLS, NN, Walsh Papers, Box 5. INSIDE ADDRESS: Hon. Frank P. Walsh, | Kansas City, | Missouri.

TO PAUL DARROW • CHICAGO • SATURDAY 29 SEPTEMBER 1917

DARROW & SISSMAN Sept 29

Dear Paul

Have you heard any thing from Byllsbee's man?[50] Since returning I have sent Noyes & Jackson 1,000 and have an other $500 or $1,000, to send either to them or you.[51] Am waiting a few days to see how market jumps. Am very busy. Am going into Healey case,[52] &

49. In a short response, Weinberger assured Darrow that his name would not be used: "Your name will not be used. I will communicate further with you, and certainly will be glad of your advice and help in whatever form it takes." Weinberger to Darrow, 13 August 1917, TLc, CtY-BR, Weinberger Papers, Box 28, Folder 4. The extent of Darrow's involvement in the appeal is unknown (his name did not appear on the brief), but the appeal—which, among other points, challenged the constitutionality of the draft—was unsuccessful. See *Goldman v. United States*, 245 U.S. 474 (1918).
50. Darrow is probably referring to someone who either worked for Henry M. Byllesby or H. M. Byllesby & Co., a large utility holding company owned by Byllesby and located in Chicago. Byllesby or his company was apparently a prospective buyer for Paul and Clarence Darrow's gas plant in Greeley, Colorado.
51. Noyes & Jackson was a stock brokerage firm in Chicago.
52. This is a reference to the criminal trial of Charles C. Healey (1856–1925), a former police chief in Chicago. Prosecutors alleged that Healey had been a member of a conspiracy to take bribes and extort money from several businesses in the city, including prostitution and gambling operations. Healey and two others (a saloon keeper and a police detective) were indicted and tried together in Chicago starting on 15 October 1917. Darrow and another lawyer represented Healey. Healey's trial followed after the trial of Oscar DePriest (1871–1951), a Chicago alderman (and later Republican congressman from Illinois) who was indicted, on several counts, for being part of the same conspiracy. Darrow also represented DePriest, who was acquitted in June 1917 after a trial on one of the counts against him.

have also been doing a good deal on the war. After I get through with this case I may spend a good deal of time speaking, for which I will be paid. Have made a good many speeches on the war—Minneapolis, St Paul, N.Y., Philadelphia &c. Shall have a big meeting here soon. Have been appointed member of the Security board having charge of things here & am "right in it" with the fellows who have always been against me. I am sure that I can get any help we need there if we need any. If you think it best to sell, I think I can do it.

Hastily | C. S. D.

Am very anxious that we should be in good shape by next Summer which we will be if we have no bad luck either with stock market or otherwise.

MS: ALS, MnU-L, Darrow Collection. DATE: "1917" appended and reference to war effort.

TO FRANK WALSH • CHICAGO • MONDAY 8 OCTOBER 1917

DARROW & SISSMAN October 8, 1917.

My Dear Walsh:—

Some time ago I promised Johansen that I was going to New York on the 13th to have a meeting with various people with reference to raising a fund. You were also to go and we were to meet Steffins.[53] The Supreme Court, much to my surprise, has selected Saturday the 13th for the argument of a case where the defendant got a life sentence.[54] I ought to say that I did not defend him, otherwise he might have been hanged. Anyhow, I took the case up, prepared the briefs and promised to make the oral arguments and of course I cannot leave him in this situation. I am very sorry, as I would like to be there with you. You will understand how it is and that it will be impossible to get away. Next week I go into a case that will last for six weeks, so I see no chance of going.[55]

I don't know whether I could be of any use there. I certainly believe the organization ought to be kept alive and am anxious to see the money raised.

I trust that you can do as much without me.

When are you coming this way again?

As ever, | C. S. Darrow

MS: TLS, NN, Walsh Papers, Box 5. INSIDE ADDRESS: Hon. Frank P. Walsh, | Kansas City, Mo.

53. Darrow is probably referring to "raising a fund" for the National Labor Defense Council, which had been formed a few months before this letter. Anton Johannsen was general organizer for the council and Walsh was chairman. The object of the council was to give aid and publicity in labor cases "to all persons prosecuted or discriminated against through the courts and other avenues of the law." Walsh to Fay Lewis, 13 June 1917, TLc, NN, Walsh Papers. The council had two staffs: a legal staff that included Walsh, Darrow, and Charles Erskine Scott Wood, among others; and an editorial staff that included Lincoln Steffens, Fremont Older, John Reed (1887–1920), George West, and several other journalists.
54. Darrow is referring to the appeal of Isaac Bond to the Supreme Court of Illinois. See Darrow to Parton, 27 April 1916, n.31.
55. The Healey case lasted three months, from 16 October 1917 to 12 January 1918, and ended with an acquittal for all three defendants.

TO PAUL DARROW • CHICAGO • SUNDAY 9 DECEMBER 1917

DARROW & SISSMAN Dec 9

Dear Paul

Got your statement a few days ago, and am glad to see the healthy growth of business. Of course I know it is hard to make much money now & don't expect it, but I believe it will come all right when the war is over or when there is a change of rates. Any how you are certainly showing a good gain. Send me Nov. as soon as it is out. Mr. Bylsbee[56] sent me the report of his man from Pueblo & it was a mighty good one. Good for the town & the business. He says you have a real gas plant—finely managed & that it will show good profits soon. He says the plant & the management are both popular & that it will soon show handsome profits. I will send it to you but am writing from the house & it is at the office. Bylsbe is no doubt having difficulties of his own & does not seem inclined to buy, but feels that it is O.K. and I know if we ever needed help I could now get it of him & others, but I am inclined to think it is all right to keep except that I would like to have you in something bigger & nearer here. I expect to go to N.Y. after the case is finished & shall talk with Dougherty[57] about it. Am now on good terms with him. I have a call to speak at Independence Kansas the middle of Feby & if I accept it will postpone going to Greeley until then. If not shall go soon after the case is over which will be about Jan 15. Don't know how I will come out. Am getting some surprises & jolts & don't get my pay as was promised & perhaps will not get it all (probably not). So far have only had 2,000 out of it. Still my receipts have been fair. Since July 1st to Dec. 1st have received net 6,500.

Have done a great deal of War speaking. Am called for every where & by all kinds of people from preachers & bankers & Governors up to working men & burglars. Could get money but have not yet taken it. If I conclude to spend a month or two after this case in speaking, shall have to take money for it & will be willing to. Am not able to send you any money yet. Have not paid what I borrowed to take care of stocks but will get it finished by the first of the year *I think*. The National Security League are publishing one of my speeches in pamphlet for general circulation.[58] Will send you some when they are ready soon. Any how I am coming out soon.

Love to all | C. S. D.

MS: ALS, MnU-L, Darrow Collection. DATE: "1917" appended and supported by reference to trial.

56. Henry M. Byllesby.
57. Henry L. Doherty.
58. *The War Address by Clarence Darrow, Noted Labor Lawyer, under the Auspices of the National Security League at Chicago, November 1, 1917* (New York: National Security League, Patriotism through Education Series No. 26, [1918]). The National Security League was a preparedness group organized in 1914 and funded by several powerful industrialists. After the United States declared war in April 1917, the league became increasingly conservative, shifting its "emphasis from military preparedness to the formulation of standards for the achievement of complete national unity of thought and action." Robert D. Ward, "The Origin and Activities of the National Security League, 1914–1919," *Mississippi Valley Historical Review* 47 (1960): 51, 58.

TO CHARLES ERSKINE SCOTT WOOD • CHICAGO • FRIDAY 15 FEBRUARY 1918

DARROW & SISSMAN Feby 15th

My Dear friend Wood

Sarah writes me that you will be sixty-six years old on Feb. 20th. And so I send you a few lines of greeting. I can not tell you that you will live to be ninety or a hundred for you will not.[59] All of us as we grow older think gravely of the end, and I am quite sure you are like the rest. I am sorry that you are so far along the road though but a step in advance of me. My consolation at death is that I will miss nothing. Yours may not be and if not I can see none. Anyhow my dear friend it is inevitable & there is nothing that we can say or do. I want to tell you how much I have always loved and admired you, and how gladly I remember that you were one who came to me in deep affliction & showed your sympathy and understanding. You have fought a brave fight & in spite of many friends have lived alone & this to me is the test of true greatness & sublimity. For those of us who know you & who shall be left behind the world will be colder and darker. I hope before that time we may meet again & snatch a few moments of companionship from the ocean of time that is needlessly sailing bye.

With sincere assurances of my gratitude & love, I am always your friend.

Clarence Darrow

MS: ALS, CSmH, Wood Papers, WD Box 126 (45). DATE: reference to Wood's age.

TO NEGLEY D. COCHRAN • CHICAGO • THURSDAY 9 MAY 1918

DARROW & SISSMAN May 9th

Dear Neg

I have been invited to go to England & France to make some speeches & think I shall try to go in June or July.[60] Wish you could go. Ruby wants to go & strange as it may seem, I would rather like to have her go. It isn't easy for any one to go unless they are needed, and I don't know whether she is needed. What I was thinking of was this: I wonder if you couldn't have her go for one of the papers if I go. She has done news paper work & does it well, but of course she doesn't want any money, she only wants to go. What do you think about it.[61] Wish you could come out. We miss you.

Your friend | Clarence Darrow

MS: ALS, OT, Cochran Papers. DATE: reference to expected travel to England and France.

59. Wood lived to be ninety-two, dying six years after Darrow.
60. Darrow was one of several people selected by the United States government, at the request of the British and French governments, to speak in England and France on the war. "Darrow to Tell of Our War Policies," *New York Times*, 20 July 1918.
61. Ruby did not take the trip with Darrow.

TO PAUL DARROW • CHICAGO • WEDNESDAY 17 JULY 1918

DARROW & SISSMAN July 17

Dear Paul

You will find the enclosed without my mentioning it. I expect to leave for England on Saturday & will be gone about two months. Sorry that I can't see you all before I go but won't stay away long after I get back. I expect to make some speeches in England & to go to France & get as near to the line as will be safe. You can write me there c/o U.S. Embassy, & shall be glad to hear from you when you have time. Shall keep you posted. Expect to write weekly letter to the papers & hope the Denver Post will take them.[62] Was glad to get the pictures of the kids. They look O.K. Will try to keep away from the submarines & bullets. When I get back I am going to try to get rid of the indebtedness out there as fast as possible on my return.

C. S. D.

MS: ALS, MnU-L, Darrow Collection. DATE: "1918" appended and supported by reference to trip.

TO JESSIE BROWNLEE • EN ROUTE TO NEW YORK CITY • SATURDAY 20 JULY 1918

DARROW & SISSMAN July 20

Dear Jessie

I am on my way to N.Y. & expect to sail tomorrow. Will be gone about two months. In my hurry I overlooked sending you the money I should have sent. Am writing Paul to do it. If you can conveniently get it of Mary & Dick[63] until my return, you might do it that way & write Paul to that effect, otherwise he will send it. An other thing. While both Paul & I are alive you are all right. But in case any thing should happen to me, you had better ask Paul to fix you either by will or otherwise so that if he should die you will be safe. There is no need as long as we both, Paul & I, are alive. Will let you know on my return.

Ever your friend | Clarence

MS: ALS, MnU-L, Darrow Collection. DATE: letterhead and reference to traveling to New York.

62. Darrow's account of his trip was published as a thirteen-part series in the *Chicago Daily Journal*, appearing every couple of days from 21 October to 15 November 1918.
63. Richard Fisher and his wife, Mary.

TO EUGENE V. DEBS • EN ROUTE TO NEW YORK CITY • SATURDAY 20 JULY 1918

DARROW & SISSMAN July 20th

My Dear Debbs

I am on my way to England & France & will be gone about two months. I want to send you this line from the train to say, what I know I do not need to say, that I am sorry for your indictment & that you now as always have my deepest love & sympathy & that if I can ever be of any assistance to you I will give all the aid in my power.[64] I know you always follow the right as you see & no one can do more.

With love always | Clarence Darrow

MS: ALS, InTI, Debs Papers. DATE: "July 23/18" appended.

TO PAUL DARROW • LONDON • THURSDAY 8 AUGUST 1918

RITZ HOTEL Aug 8th

Dear Paul

Got to Liverpool after an ocean voyage of 12 days. We had [. . .][65] Saw nothing of submarines except the day before reaching Liverpool when I was wakened by a bombing some 20 deep. No bombs were fired. The rumor was that they got two sub-marines but I don't know as no information of these matters are given out either through the press or otherwise. I see by the papers that the age is to be increased for conscription in America to 45. This of course will take you in. I have never talked with you about it & don't want to influence you in any way as to what you should do. Of course I can't help feeling sorry about it but presume the government should do it. I presume none of your age would be called until next year though they might be. If you decide to go in case you are called I should think the best way would be to go to an officers training camp: It will be better to be an officer & you can do the most good there. I would think that the artilery would be the best place for you. I don't believe you could do bayonet work. I am very sure you would have no trouble to be an artilery officer. If you were to go of course something must be done about the business. I think you ought to see if it is not possible to make a combination. This should be done any how. If not it might be best to try to get Fred Hammerstrom to run it. I know he could hold the business & I don't know any one else who could. He would have to take more out than you but it would be run right & taken care of. Still I presume that part can await my coming. Still I think you ought to see if you can't figure out a way to consolidate. I expect to leave on Monday or Tuesday to go to France. Am to

64. On 29 June 1918, Debs was indicted under the federal Espionage Act for his speeches against the war. He was convicted the following September and sentenced to ten years in prison.
65. Approximately fifteen words are scratched out here, probably by the federal board of censorship.

be taken in special trip over France by automobile. Am to visit trenches & every where I want to go also to go from there to the Italian Front & then to go to see the fleet and any thing else I wish. It will be a great trip, if I don't run into a shell—or if I do.

Every one here thinks the war will be finished next year, if not sooner. Have talked with many well posted people. I have felt that way for some time. You can write me a line to this hotel if you have time

As ever | C. S. D.

MS: ALS, MnU-L, Darrow Collection. DATE: "1918" appended and references to the war.

TO SARA BARD FIELD • CHICAGO • SATURDAY 16 NOVEMBER 1918

Nov. 16 | 140 N. Dearborn St

Dear Sarah

I was terribly shocked at the news of the accident.[66] Poor girl, I wish I could say something consoling about Alfred. I can't, except that death is better than life. In the dark things that come to me, I find that pessimism is the most consoling. Life is nothing but a foolishness, a burden, and a tragedy. Death is peace—it is nothing. I hope you will try to console yourself with what you have left & get all you can out of life. According to the law of your maker there is nothing else to it. All the rest is a delusion and a dream. If you can find some illusion it is good to take. But I fancy that you are so made that you can't find one. Are you ever coming this way? If you do don't hurry through and spend all your time with the reformers.

Any how dear girl, I am always for you, as you have been for me. I know that you are glad that the war is over & I am sure that I am, & I do not want to see any bitterness against one's old enemies. They for the most part are like the rest of us. If there are any books you want which you can't get there let me know and I will send them. I sent one to Mrs. Edsen[67] that I want you to read.

With Sympathy & love

Your friend always | Clarence Darrow.

MS: ALS, CSmH, Wood Papers, WD Box 126 (53). DATE: references to war and death of Field's son.

66. In October 1918, the brakes failed on an automobile that Field was driving in the hills of Marin County, California, and the automobile rolled backward over a cliff. Field's two children—Albert Jr. (Darrow gets his name wrong) and Kay—and Charles Erskine Scott Wood were also in the automobile. Albert Jr., who was seventeen years old, was pinned under the automobile and killed. Margaret Parton, *Journey through a Lighted Room* (New York: Viking Press, 1973), 32.
67. The identity of "Mrs. Edsen" is unknown.

TO WOODROW WILSON • CHICAGO • TUESDAY 29 JULY 1919

Washington, D.C., July 29, 1919.

Dear Mr. President:

I earnestly petition the Government for the release of Eugene V. Debs from the Federal prison at Atlanta, Georgia, where he is now held for violation of the Espionage Act. This I do as a friend of Mr. Debs for more than twenty-five years and after full consultation with him in prison.

I am aware that Mr. Debs did violate the Act and in his argument to the jury and address to the court, he fully and freely stated that he did. I know that Mr. Debs, like many other sincere men and women, did not believe in war and that he could not bring himself to think that the United States was justified in entering the conflict.

From the time the German army invaded Belgium, I believed that the civilized world should unite to drive it out and that this country must ultimately do its part. When the United States entered the war, I gave my time and energy without reserve to support the Allies' cause. I was sorry for many men and women who were sent to jail for speaking what they believed to be the truth in opposition to the act of Congress in declaring war. I believe that many of these were guilty of no moral wrong, but I likewise know that self-preservation is the first law of nations as well as of men and that while the war was on we could not weigh individual motives, but were bound to take all necessary measures to protect ourselves, even from those who committed no moral wrong. This course the Government followed—not with malice or hatred, but as a stern duty in meeting a grave emergency. Any Government, however liberal, would have done the same.

But the war is over and it is right to examine the motives of men; and to keep in prison one who felt it his duty to disagree, after the need has passed, would not be self-defense but a punishment undeserved.

I confess to the deepest affection for Mr. Debs, an affection which has made me glad to travel hundreds of miles in trying weather and to sacrifice a much needed rest and vacation, that I might aid in obtaining his release from prison. He is courageous, honest, emotional and loving. He has freely given his life to help his fellow men and proclaimed the truth as he saw the truth. More than this no man can do, for it is not given to any of us to be sure that the opinions we hold are right. He is sixty-four years old and in prison for speaking what he believed to be the truth and now, when the war is over and the danger is passed, he should be released.

I am very sure that I do not ask this alone for my friend. The work of the world today is to heal the deep wounds of war, and I am most anxious that this Government, which has always tolerated differences and upheld the freedom of thought and speech, should show that stern measures were only used for self-protection and that it has acted without malice or hatred and is willing and anxious not only to be just, but

forgiving. I know of nothing that could make this so plain to intelligent men as the pardon of Eugene V. Debs.

Very respectfully, | Clarence Darrow[68]

MS: TLS, DLC-MSS, Wilson Papers. INSIDE ADDRESS: The President, | The White House.

TO CHARLES ERSKINE SCOTT WOOD • CHICAGO • TUESDAY 26 AUGUST 1919

DARROW & SISSMAN August 26, 1919.

My Dear Wood:—

I received your brief and have read it carefully and passed it around.[69] It is a very able document and I do not know of anyone who could have written it better. I wish I could have done it. If I could, I certainly would have. If you have others to spare I wish you

68. This letter was delivered to the president with a memorandum (also in the Wilson Papers) from the attorney general, A. Mitchell Palmer. Palmer believed that Debs's sentence was too long and ought to be commuted but that the time for commutation was not right:

OFFICE OF THE ATTORNEY GENERAL

July 30, 1919.

MEMORANDUM FOR THE PRESIDENT.

I promised Clarence Darrow to hand you the attached letter.

Debs' sentence of ten years is too long and ought to be commuted, but I am firmly of the opinion that the time is not yet ripe for such action. He has been in prison only a couple of months, is absolutely unrepentant, will not personally make any application for clemency, and a pardon now would be bitterly resented by a very large portion of the population who consider him a dangerous leader in the ultra-radical class war movement.

When we release Debs, we shall have to release also two or three other leaders of the same class. Their release now would be used by many opponents of the peace treaty as evidence of too great leniency toward law violators of the radical element in the labor classes, in a way that would prejudice many people against the liberal labor provisions of the treaty.

My own judgment is that we should wait until the peace treaty is ratified and out of the way and conditions in the country have settled down somewhat before we seriously consider executive clemency for these leaders. We have already commuted the sentences of more than a hundred persons convicted under the Espionage Act and my plan is to make recommendations to you with respect to the remainder of the cases (including Debs) at or about the time of the actual going into force of the treaty of peace.

A. Mitchell Palmer | Attorney General.

69. Wood wrote a long letter to Darrow and enclosed a copy of a brief that he had written on behalf of Marie Equi (1872–1952), a physician and suffragist in Portland, Oregon. See Wood to Darrow, 22 August 1919, CSmH, Wood Papers. Equi was an outspoken and controversial figure: she performed abortions as part of her practice; she was active in the Industrial Workers of the World (IWW); and she did not try to hide that she was a lesbian. In 1918, she was convicted of violating the federal Espionage Act of 1917 because she delivered an anti-war speech in an IWW hall in Portland. Wood represented her in her appeal, challenging the constitutionality of the act. The appeal failed and her conviction was affirmed in an opinion written by Frank Rudkin (who was sitting temporarily on the federal appellate court). See *Equi v. United States,* 261 F. 53 (1919). A portion of Wood's brief was published as a pamphlet, a short section of which is reprinted in *Wood Works: The Life and Writings of Charles Erskine Scott Wood,* eds. Edwin Bingham and Tim Barnes (Corvallis: Oregon State University Press, 1997), 256–58. Wood used most of his letter to Darrow to comment and ask for Darrow's view on a variety of political subjects, including the League of Nations, the Treaty of Versailles, President Wilson, the Democratic Party (Wood said that he was of a mind "to come out and speak in favor of the Socialists"), Great Britain, the federal government's repression of free speech, "the assault on Russia," "universal militarism coming in as a preparation to control Labor and invade Mexico," and human beings in general ("How seriously we do take ourselves, we little two-legged ants").

would send them to me and I will see that they are put in the hands of people who appreciate them. As a lawyer trying a case, I presume the brief will do no good. I wish it would, but what is the use in arguing with the mob.

I feel about as you do as to the present administration. I went to Washington about three weeks ago to see what I could do for the military prisoners and Debs and the rest confined on like charges. I took the trouble to go from there to Atlanta to see Debs, and then back to Washington and believed that when I was through, that these men would be released. I think so now but I do not know. If they are not soon released, I shall say what I think about it in a public way.

I presume I am not as much disturbed by the situation of the world as you are, although I look at it in the same way, but I have long since ceased to have any illusions about the human race. They are more uncertain and less important than bees, or perhaps any other animals.

I cannot feel that the Shantung matter and even the Saar Valley is very bad.[70] Of course I believe Russia should be left alone. I believe that the free speech that we once had should be resurrected. I never believed in universal militarism or any other kind, excepting that man is a fighting animal and will fight. I do not believe in invading Mexico, neither have I had the same feeling against Great Britain that many radicals have. I recognize her on the whole as being the leading nation of the world and standing better for human liberty than any other country. This, in spite of the fact, that she has subjugated peoples and spread her dominion over the world. Nations, of course, are like individuals—they are born and grow and die. Syria, Babylon, Persia, Egypt, Greece, Rome, Constantinople, France and now Great Britain, have ruled the world. Great Britain will die like the rest and I presume all that we say or do has little to do with either its growth or its death. When we get to a certain age we die, no matter how carefully we look after ourselves and when nations reach a certain age, they too die.

I perhaps judge Wilson more leniently than you do. I think the United States took itself entirely too seriously; that its sacrifices in the war were small; that it had no right to expect to shape the policy of the world and that Mr. Wilson was unable to do things he thought he ought to do. I have no doubt that his influence on the world was moderate and progressive, but I think we should have nothing to do with European affairs, excepting that now and then we might be drawn into a war.

70. This is a reference to two issues relating to the Versailles treaty, both mentioned by Wood in his letter to Darrow. Shantung (or Shandong) is a northeast coastal province of China. Germany had a naval base there before the war, which Japan took control of during the war and, through a provision in the treaty, continued to control after the war. President Wilson's acquiescence in this provision of the treaty angered Chinese nationalists and many Americans, and it became an issue when ratification of the treaty was being considered by the United States Senate. Two days before Darrow wrote this letter, a committee of the Senate, which was considering ratification of the treaty, voted to require that Shantung be returned to China as part of the treaty. Margaret MacMillan, *Paris 1919: Six Months That Changed the World* (New York: Random House, 2001), 325–44, 490. The Saar Valley is a region in southwest Germany, on the border with France, that was rich in coal. The Treaty of Versailles made the coal mines there the property of France for fifteen years, as reparations for Germany's destruction of France's coal mines during the war.

I have never believed in the League of Nations. I think it is evil in its inception and cannot be made good. I am one of the old-time democrats who believe in states' rights and abhor strong centralized governments and now it is proposed to virtually make one government that will reach around the world. It would be the death of liberty for a long time to come. Of course I think peace should be proclaimed and at once, and it should not be mixed with any other question. I cannot help being sympathetic with the Bolsheviks of Russia, as I am for all people who are fighting for what they think is liberty with the more or less confused idea of what it means.

You seem to hit it when you speak about the human race. It takes itself too seriously. It cannot think and still it tries to think. If it was like the bees and the ants and did not try, it would probably get on better.

I see no immediate hope in the Democratic party. Most of the men in control are hopeless reactionaries, but what to do is another question. I do not see how men like you or me can enter very seriously into a fight with any political party. So far as I know Socialists are just like the rest. I know there is growing up a very deep-seated hatred of Wilson and the administration. It comes from these who have been his friends in the past and who are the only ones who could help him. Nothing the administration can do can get them the Wall Street bunch. They have a party of their own and will stick to it. The Democratic party is now driving out the others.

To return to your brief, it is true and it is not true. I used to swear off on a lot of things on New Year's and write a constitution of my own. Sometime it would last a week,—generally about a day—than the old time habits came back. I fancy you and everyone else have done the same. Constitutions are only good when you do not need them. When they run up against the deep-seated feelings and emotions of man, they are powerless. They help the strong, but they cannot help the weak. The majority in force and power always has its way regardless of its constitutions or laws. I think as a legal proposition, the constitution of the United States applies the same in war as in peace, but it is only an academic matter as to what the law says or what it means. In times of great stress, constitutions are always swept away. While the United States never was in serious danger in this last war, still they were earnestly in the war and using every effort to win and it could not be expected that people could oppose the war at home with any safety to themselves. If they had not been prosecuted in the courts, the mobs would have taken care of them, which to my mind would have been much better. They did this in England. They did it in the United States in the Civil war. I fancy they have always done it and always will do it. These are the fundamental things and the law really is an abstraction. Human nature is a thing which persists and it is impossible to curb it by laws and constitutions. It only needs a strong enough inciting cause to have it over-throw the laws and constitutions and institutions. I have been worried more about prohibition, than I have these repressive measures that you write of, for the modern policy of our government in the way of prohibition, national factory laws, national women's suffrage has entirely wiped out the State rights and brought on an era of centralization and power which is rapidly crushing the individual.

Substantially, my views are like yours, as they have been ever since I knew you and I fancy that while I might at times disagree on immediate things, still our turn of mind and our instinctive love of liberty makes it pretty certain we would look at big questions the same way.

I wish you would come East soon. I would be very glad to see you again. I often think of you and of your long friendship to me.

With kind regards, I am, as ever,

Your friend, | Clarence Darrow

MS: TLS, CSmH, Wood Papers, WD Box 126 (46). INSIDE ADDRESS: Mr. C. E. S. Wood, | 1310 Yeon Bldg., | Portland, Oregon.

TO PAUL DARROW • CHICAGO • SOMETIME AFTER 1 OCTOBER 1919

CLARENCE DARROW Sept 4

Dear Paul

Yours just arrived, had heard nothing about what had been done. How much raise are you to get & was every one satisfied at home?

Where did you get that stuff about my loosing Simpson case.[71] I won it. The jury returned a verdict of not guilty of murder finding she was insane at the time & still insane. She has gone to the asylum at Elgin and as soon as she recovers she will be released.

Hastily | C. S. D.

MS: ALS, MnU-L, Darrow Collection. DATE: letterhead and reference to Simpson having gone to Elgin.

TO MARY FIELD PARTON • CHICAGO • THURSDAY 16 OCTOBER 1919

140 NORTH DEARBORN STREET Oct. 16th

Dear Mary

What in the devil is the reason I haven't written sooner? I don't know. I was always intending to but you know about good intentions. It was fine to see you again after so many years and I enjoyed every minute of the time I was able to see you and was sorry when you had to leave. It does seem as if you should come oftener and I am not the only one in Chicago who thinks so. Gussie was complaining because you didn't see her when you passed

71. Emma D. Simpson (1875–1929?) shot and killed her husband, Elmer Simpson, in the spring of 1919 in a courtroom in Chicago during an argument over alimony in their divorce proceedings. Emma Simpson was the niece of John M. Roach (1851–1924), a wealthy railway official who had been president of the Chicago Railways Company. She was tried for murder in September 1919. Darrow represented her. The jury found her not guilty due to insanity. The judge sent her to the state asylum at Elgin, Illinois, on 1 October 1919. She was released fifty-one days later, having been determined sane by another judge after hearing expert testimony.

through on your way home & of course the Johansens are always crying for you.[72] Well life is very strange—here you are a long way from most of your old time friends & the fates never seem to care any thing about the sentiments or feelings of man. They just throw us around without reason or purpose. Still some talk of the goodness of god. Joe tells me you & Lem are both talking of going to N.Y. or here or somewhere in the world.[73] Why don't you? I am sure this is the best place. The city is dirty & brutal & crass, but it is fairly free and there are lots of good people here. Still there are some there. How I would like to come to S.F. if I could only get my mind adjusted to it. How I would like to see Older & Sarah & Mr. Wood & many others. Well may be I will—I really want to. Say Mary I have been wondering if our friend Tom O'Connor couldn't do something for J.J. McN.[74] He should be out. There is no excuse for holding him longer. It could be done if the outstanding indictments at L.A. were dismissed which were long ago promised & should be done. I wish you would get him to go over & see J.B. & J.J. & see if he could do something. I will manage to raise some money for him if he can & any how pay him myself for going over. I would like to help them. Let me know. I am sorry you wrote me about the "Young friends."[75] I was going to send it to you. It is a peach. I rather doubt the twelve year old girl part or any other girl part. It is too clever. I am still working like the devil snatching people out of the clutches of the law, whose only function is to break and destroy. Well I generally manage to cheet it. How people do like to make others suffer! If I don't come soon again you must come out here. Joe & I will manage to figure out [xx] I will without Joe.[76] We started our biology class again & I am loading up my brain with more stuff for the worms to get "belly ache" on. I am getting weary & discouraged over the suppression of freedom: the keeping of men & women in jail &c &c. I am going to say something publicly the second sunday in Nov.[77] Will try to dig you up a new book & send. Am glad you liked Henry Adams.[78] It is one of the best things I have seen for many a day—

Ever as of old | Clarence Darrow

72. "Gussie" is probably Augusta ("Gussie") Rosenwald (1869–1929), who was married to Julius Rosenwald. She was active in the suffrage movement and involved in many philanthropic activities in Chicago, including at Hull House. The "Johansens" are Anton and Margaret Johannsen.
73. "Joe" might be a misspelling and reference to the sculptor Jo Davidson (1883–1952), who was a friend of Darrow and Parton's. But in an earlier letter to Parton, Darrow spelled Davidson's first name correctly. See Darrow to Parton, 14 March 1917, ALS, ICN, Parton-Darrow Papers, Box 1, Folder 7. "Lem" is Parton's husband, Lemuel Parton.
74. Whether the end of this sentence actually reads "McN" is unclear, given damage to the letter. But "J.J." and (later in the letter) "J.B." are referring to John J. and James B. McNamara. "Tom O'Connor" is Thomas H. O'Connor (d. 1920), a prominent criminal-defense attorney in San Francisco and friend of Fremont Older's.
75. "Young friends" is probably a reference to a book, but the book has not been identified.
76. Part of this sentence is illegible because the letter is damaged.
77. On 9 November 1919, Darrow gave an address at the Garrick Theatre in Chicago describing his philosophical attitude toward the war and criticizing the government's prosecution and continued punishment of civilians under the Espionage Act of 1917 and the government's treatment of members of the military who were court-martialed during the war. The address was later published in a pamphlet titled *War Prisoners* (Chicago: Maclaskey & Maclaskey, 1919).
78. Darrow is probably referring to *The Education of Henry Adams,* by Henry Adams (1838–1918), which was published in late 1918 by Houghton Mifflin. In another letter later in the year, Darrow asked Field if she had read *The Education,* apparently forgetting this earlier correspondence. Darrow to Field, 22 December 1919, ALS, ICN, Parton-Darrow Papers, Box 1, Folder 7.

MS: ALS, ICN, Parton-Darrow Papers, Box 1, Folder 7. DATE: "around | 1920" is appended but 1919 is more likely because of Darrow's reference to his upcoming speech and his reference to Adams's book.

TO EDGAR LEE MASTERS • CHICAGO • MONDAY 10 NOVEMBER 1919

DARROW, SISSMAN & POPHAM November 10, 1919.

Dear Ed:—

Your letter was just received. Glad to hear from you.[79] Of course you know me well enough to know that I would never start suit against you or try to make you any trouble in court or out. My first impression was when the matter came to me, that I should say that I would have nothing to do with it, but on second thought, I did not know but that my relations with both parties might make it possible for me to assist both of you, which of course, I will do, without any thought of compensation, except friendship, if the matter can be worked out.

I do not see any need for your hurrying back. I have no doubt that everything will remain in status quo until you come. When you do come, let me know, and we will go out and have lunch together and talk the whole matter over.

I should be very glad if I could be of assistance to both.

As ever, your friend, | Clarence Darrow.

MS: TLS, TxU-Hu, Masters Collection.

TO FREMONT OLDER • GREELEY, COLORADO • SATURDAY 27 DECEMBER 1919

THE GREELEY GAS AND FUEL COMPANY Dec 27th

Dear Fremont

I am here spending the holidays with my boy & his family. I have three grand daughters, the oldest getting along toward the age that suggests an other generation to crowd one out. Any how, I am quite reconciled although it makes me feel old. I am enclosing a letter to Judge Rudkin of the Federal court. He is now in San Francisco I believe. I have

79. Masters had recently left his first wife, Helen Jenkins Masters (1874–1958), and was pursuing a relationship with Lillian Wilson (1887–1950?), a wealthy thirty-two-year-old widow in Marion, Indiana. Masters wrote to Darrow from out East, apparently knowing or believing that Darrow was involved in the matter in some way on behalf of his wife. Masters explained that he hoped Darrow—who himself had gone through a divorce and who Masters said should have "much common understanding" with him—could "prevent the statement of things, particularly things not well founded but also things unnecessary to state." Masters to Darrow, 8 November 1921, TLc, TxU-Hu, Masters Collection (quoted in Herbert K. Russell, *Edgar Lee Masters: A Biography* [Urbana: University of Illinois Press, 2001], 141). In his autobiography, Masters would later contend that Darrow acted as a lawyer for Helen in the divorce. See Edgar Lee Masters, *Across Spoon River* (New York: Farrar & Rinehart, 1936), 396; see also Russell, *Edgar Lee Masters*, 140–68. But this letter suggests that Darrow, at least initially, was trying to serve as a mediator of some sort. Whatever role Darrow played, Masters eventually came to bitterly resent Darrow.

been urging him to recommend a pardon or commutation for the men who were convicted at Sacramento.[80] He writes me that he feels he ought not to, but will not oppose it. He is really a good fellow with fairly liberal ideas. He went to school to me for three years in Ohio, & we have been friends a long time. I thought if you would see him he might do it. The people in the east think that this is the only thing that prevents a general release of the war prisoners. Any how if you think it worth while, try it.

Always your friend | Clarence Darrow.

MS: ALS, CU-BANC, Older Papers, Box 1. DATE: other evidence of Darrow in Greeley and reference to convictions at Sacramento.

80. In September 1917, federal agents conducted a nationwide raid on the offices of the anti-war IWW. Hundreds of members of the IWW were arrested and charged with subversion. In Sacramento, California, the government brought forty-six Wobblies to trial in 1919. Most of the defendants refused to defend themselves and sat mute in the courtroom without lawyers. Rudkin presided at the trial and, although he reportedly conducted the proceedings in a fair manner, the jury returned a conviction. See David C. Frederick, *Rugged Justice: The Ninth Circuit Court of Appeals and the American West, 1891–1941* (Berkeley: University of California Press, 1994), 152.

• 1920–1924

TO EUGENE V. DEBS • WASHINGTON, D.C. • WEDNESDAY 14 JANUARY 1920

THE NEW WILLARD Jan 14 1920

My Dear Debs,

I am down here to see if I can do a little on this mad crusade against freedom.[1] I did not go to the Attorney General on your case. In my frame of mind I couldn't ask him to do any thing. At the same time I felt that I had no right to talk about individuals, and I knew perfectly well that you would feel the same way. Incidentally I am lead to believe that your case & others will be disposed of when the treaty is signed by U.S. I don't know. I hope so, but it is no time to bother about individuals—much as I care for you. Any how I want you to know how I feel about this madness, & that nothing can happen which can make me overlook you for long.

With regards & affection

Your friend | Clarence Darrow[2]

MS: ALS, InTI, Debs Papers.

1. Debs was still in prison for violating the federal Espionage Act.
2. On the bottom of the page is a note in Debs's hand to his brother, Theodore: "Pls. acknowledge with thanks. Tell him we know he'll do the best he can and all he can & that's enough. His fidelity and his unforgetfulness is everything."

TO CHARLES ERSKINE SCOTT WOOD • CHICAGO • FRIDAY 11 JUNE 1920

DARROW, SISSMAN, POPHAM & CARLIN June 11, 1920.

My Dear Mr. Wood:—

Your letter was just received. I have sent the note to Mr. Bryan, so that I know it will reach him. I read it carefully. Of course I approve of it. I have no confidence in Bryan. Anyhow, the note was all right.

I observed your postscript which asked for press seat for you and Sarah.[3] Mr. W.W. Marsh[4] is the Treasurer of the National Committee and he is a close friend of mine and a fine fellow. I suppose he is in California by this time and stopping at the Palace. He was here a week or so ago and is driving through. Anyhow, he told me he would be glad to do anything for any of my friends in San Francisco, so I am enclosing a letter for both you and Sarah and I am sure he will take care of you. In addition to this, he will be thoroughly posted on what is going on and will give you any information you want. He is not a radical. He is just a good fellow and an able man and my friend. He is really Palmer's[5] friend, which will not commend him to you, but with him it is largely a question of personal liking and loyalty.

I want you to see him. If it comes in the way for you or a crowd to entertain him, I wish you would. I am sure you will enjoy him.

I am glad you speak as you do of my letter to Reidy in reply to yours.[6] I really felt that something could be said for Wilson and I tried to say it. I, of course, thoroughly agree with everything you said in your article. At the same time I felt that it was not quite fair to Wilson. Your article was a wonderful piece of workmanship and I admired it greatly. Was sorry that mine fell so far short of yours in this regard.

I have been terribly depressed over the tyranny and injustice that has grown out of the war, but I fancy we had no reason to expect anything else.

I often think of you both and wish I might see you again.

As ever, | Your friend, | Clarence Darrow

MS: TLS, CSmH, Wood Papers, WD Box 126 (48). INSIDE ADDRESS: Mr. C. E. S. Wood, | 1601 Taylor Street, | San Francisco, | Calif.

3. The Democratic National Convention would be held in San Francisco in late June and early July 1920, and Wood apparently was seeking press seats for himself and Sara Bard Field. William Jennings Bryan sought the nomination at the convention, but he failed to get the necessary votes.
4. Wilbur W. Marsh (1862–1929), businessman. Marsh was an owner of many different businesses in Waterloo, Iowa, including a cattle ranch, an insurance business, and the manufacturer of a dairy-separator machine. He was also the director of several banks and the organizer of a local hospital. Although he never sought office, he was very active in political campaigns and served as treasurer of the national Democratic Party, 1916–24.
5. A. Mitchell Palmer.
6. Wood wrote an article for William Marion Reedy's magazine that was highly critical of Woodrow Wilson's foreign and domestic policies. C. E. S. Wood, "Woodrow Wilson," *Reedy's Mirror,* 25 March 1920, 247–49. Darrow wrote a defense of sorts for Wilson, which Reedy published the next month. Darrow, "Woodrow Wilson," *Reedy's Mirror,* 15 April 1920, 311–13.

TO PAUL DARROW • CHICAGO • MONDAY 28 JUNE 1920

DARROW, SISSMAN & POPHAM June 28th

Dear Paul

I should have written you long ago but it has been a busy spring and summer and I have been putting it off and then too you are not much of a writer yourself. I got the May report & I thought it very good. Still I am sure we should have a higher price and if the electric ask for more I think we should too. You can afford to let them make their own estimate.

I have been doing well and am now trying the Lloyd & others case.[7] We have so far been two months getting a jury & it will take a week or two longer & then a month to try the case so you see I am pretty closely held. I wish you would try to come. Don't believe you will loose much by leaving for a week or two. Have seen Lilian & the children twice. They are all looking well and seem to be happy. There will be plenty of room for you to stay here such time as you can. Everett is here but stopping at Mr. Dawson's.[8] I tried running an automobile & the first day I drove fifty miles without much trouble & then drove down town. Am doing pretty well at it now. I also went up in the flying machine that made the record flight from Omaha to N.Y.[9] So you see I am pretty lively. I am hoping that the Democrats will nominate McAdoo[10] at San Francisco. He is by far the ablest man in either party. Harding is absolutely nothing but one of the cheepest of cheep politicians. I had a good visit with Doherty also with Gilchrist.[11] Tell G. that he is a poor guesser on what the convention would do. Any how let me hear from you & come if you possibly can, and any time you want to.

As Ever | C. S. D.

MS: ALS, MnU-L, Darrow Collection. DATE: "1920" appended.

7. William Bross Lloyd (1875–1946), wealthy son of Darrow's late friend Henry Demarest Lloyd, and nineteen other members of the Communist Labor Party were tried together in Chicago for felony conspiracy to violate Illinois's anarchy and sedition laws, which were enacted in 1919. These statutes were typical of many statutes passed by states in the red-scare aftermath of the war, to suppress and punish speech. See Robert K. Murray, *Red Scare: A Study in National Hysteria, 1919–1920* (Minneapolis: University of Minnesota Press, 1955), 231–35. Lloyd and the other defendants were all convicted during a trial that lasted from 10 May to 2 August 1920. Darrow represented several of the defendants. With the exception of two of the defendants (one disappeared and the other died before sentencing), all of the defendants received sentences with varying terms of imprisonment. The defendants raised a variety of constitutional and other defenses to the charges, but the Supreme Court of Illinois affirmed their convictions two years later. See *People v. Lloyd,* 136 N.E. 505 (1922).
8. "Everett" is Everett Darrow. The identity of "Mr. Dawson" is unknown although it might be a reference to Charles W. Dawson of Kankakee, Illinois. See Darrow to Lindsey, 4 May 1922, n.52.
9. By this, Darrow probably means that he took a ride on the same type of airplane that had made a record nonstop flight the day before this letter was written, a "JL-6," the world's first all-metal passenger (six-seater) airplane. "Larsen Makes New Nonstop Flight Record," *Chicago Tribune,* 28 June 1920.
10. William G. McAdoo.
11. Paul Darrow had friends in Greeley by the names of Gilchrist and Doherty but their identities are unknown. Interview with Mary Darrow Simonson, Honolulu, Hawaii, 15 September 1999.

TO FREMONT OLDER • CHICAGO • TUESDAY 13 JULY 1920

DARROW, SISSMAN & POPHAM July 13th

My Dear Fremont

I have been intending to write ever since I got your letter. But I have been working hard against the mob in one of the Syndicalist cases. It took nine weeks to get a jury and I have put off every one, you with the rest. It gives me a thrill to think of seeing you again, really I had been wondering if I ever should. Somehow I once in a while get it into my head that I won't stick around so very long, and it rather gives relief. I have seen about all I want of it. There is nothing in the scheme. We have always been foolish to think that any thing could be made of a man—except a man. Still I presume we will keep on trying. I noted what you said about J.J.[12] but I really don't know what to think about it. Of course I couldn't go there without seeing them & I would not want to be insulted—perhaps I would not be, although Walsh was here today and did not seem very reassuring. If I knew they would want to see me I would come, for I would dearly love to see you all. I don't know how you could find out any more than you have. I don't want them to think that I am anxious to be invited. Of course something will need to be done for J.J. to get his indictments dismissed between now & next May and I believe I might help. I feel that you & Lem[13] could do more for him than any one else, and then Frank Walsh thinks that his friend in L.A. would help. I don't know what to think about it all and I want to come. I don't want them or any one else to think that I am worried for I am not. I would never think of it except for the nightmare that I went through, and still one thing is about as good as an other in this world. I don't know whether you have any reason to go there again & if you did whether any thing more would come of it. You necessarily must handle it very gingerly. With it all I would like to help them. I know as well as any one else can how much I did for them and at what a sacrifice, but these things don't count. If I came it would be around the middle of August probably a little later. How I would like an other ride with you down the Santa Clara Valley.

Ever your friend | Darrow

MS: ALS, CU-BANC, Older Papers, Box 1. DATE: letterhead and reference to "Syndicalist cases."

TO MARY FIELD PARTON • CHICAGO • THURSDAY 25 NOVEMBER 1920

140 NORTH DEARBORN STREET Thanksgiving day

Dear Mary

I came down this morning to write you a letter but I don't know as there is anything to say. I got yours yesterday and it was like all of them, the best any one ever wrote. Why

12. John J. McNamara.
13. Probably Lemuel Parton.

don't you pick out a few people and subjects & write into the air and have them published. No one can do it like you and they would make a great hit. I read it to Frank Wolfe who was crazy about it and said what a shame it was that you didn't write. He said that he couldn't write but made a living out of it while you could beat any one, & did nothing. Go on and do it.

I, like you, find nothing new from day to day. My office is filled all the time mainly by poor clients in trouble, people who have got money against the rules of the game & are trying to stay out of jail. People in all sorts of troubles: their wives crying & begging me to help as if I could do any thing if I only tried: how I wish I could but I can't. Lord what an awful mad house the world is, and it is Thanksgiving day and all the damn fools in the world are giving thanks that they are alive. Well I am not.

Sunday I am to debate with Starr[14] on the question is civilization a failure. It ought to be easy to show. How any one can think any thing else I can't conceive. I don't know why I do these things. I never convert any one and don't want to. I am getting more and more convinced that if any one has any dope they ought to keep it. The only trouble is they insist that we shall take their dope or go without. Chicago is now on a mad hunt for criminals, the big ones are after the little ones as usual except worse. People are getting more cruel all the time more insistent that they shall have their way. I wish I was either younger or older. If I was younger I would go to the South Seas or somewhere east of Suez. If I were older I shouldn't care so much. Any how it wouldn't have the same personal meaning for me. I have grown quite convinced that the happiest time of the human race was in Barbarism and likewise convinced that we are going back to it, although I presume I shall not be able to go. I have been thinking of the civilized cattel & hogs & horses. Take a Berkshire hog for instance. All fat. It can hardly waddel. Stays in its pen and drinks swill. All the good people think that this shows that civilization has improved the hog. Still turn out a Berkshire to run wild in competition with one of the primitive Razor backs and which would win. There can't be a doubt the Berkshire would die. Of course the men have only considered hogs from the standpoint of their use to men: they have not thought of it from the standpoint of hogs. The human race are going the same way. We are getting so civilized that we can't live. The old time savage chased the game & digested its food. We have it brought to us and take pills. The civilized man can't live. The race is only replenished by the primitive people. Nature is boss and when we get too far away she just snuffs us out. I am for the snuffing. Still it won't be snuffed out. We will just go over the same old ground that civilization has traveled over before. I have no doubt but what the human race is going back, neither have I any regrets. All we need to do is to teach the good women birth control & we will get rid of them & their kind, and repopulate the world with those who don't know any thing about birth control; in fact don't know what causes birth. I see that a campaign has been started to bring back the New England Sunday laws to stop every thing that people want to do. I have been thinking of the woman's party made of Radical women

14. Frederick Starr.

who wanted the ballot. Now they have it and the great mass of conservative women are used by the preachers to suppress life. It would be different if the Y.W.C.A. had done it; but the radical women did it and now they will get theirs; the only pleasure I have out of it is that I told them so. Steffens is to be here next month. Suppose he will go from here to California speaking on the way; he and I are to debate in [x] Dec 19th. We do it to get money for the Socialists, so they can help suppress people. When he gets out there perhaps he may fix it so I can come. I would really like to come, would like to see you and all the rest. Gee Mary you are about the only one that knows any thing;—you and I. But see what advantage you have had. I presume when the Soviets get to boss the world they will snuff out what little freedom is left. The fact is I am getting afraid of everyone who has convictions. When one loves a theory more than they do human beings they are dangerous. I hope I won't believe in any theories again. I was interested in the things you are doing. In your rosy faced lady with five children, all older than the mother, but what does it prove? The children will not be rosy faced, will not lure men; will understand birth control, will die. The rosy faced women who grade 10 mentally will keep on populating the world. It would be all right if the wise ones could destroy life, but they can't. There will be some left with low intellect & big busts, and they will breed. Which kind are the best and what are the Eugenists doing any how. Nature is always working for the normall which are the low grade intellectually. They have no imagination. The present moment is all there is to life with them, and so they enjoy the process of having children & only suffer for a short time. This is the law of life and it can't be changed. It is interesting to study it for people like us who get interest from ideas; but all their fads prove the opposite from the conclusions that they reach. Write often. You always have something to say & can say it. I will try to do better in the future for I do miss you.

Your friend always | Clarence

MS: ALS, ICN, Parton-Darrow Papers, Box 1, Folder 8. ENVELOPE ADDRESS: Mrs. Mary Field Parton | 184 Edgewood Av. | San Francisco | Cal. POSTMARK: Chicago 26 November 1920.

TO MAX SEHAM • CHICAGO • MONDAY 6 DECEMBER 1920

December 6, 1920.

My dear Doctor:

I remember our conversation at Mr. Leonard's[15] and am glad to write to you.

The best article I ever saw on the subject was written by Alfred Russell Wallace, in a volume published more than twenty years ago. I think its title is "Some Great Illusions"

15. George Leonard (1872–1956), an attorney in Minneapolis, Minnesota, was a good friend of Seham. Telephone interview with David Seham, Brooklyn, New York, 15 October 2000. Darrow had met Seham at Leonard's house, and during this meeting, Darrow brought up the subject of vaccination. As Seham later recalled, Darrow was then "engaged by the Illinois Anti-Vivisectionist groups to oppose some medical legislation." Seham told one of Darrow's biographers that he believed "[t]his letter gives you an idea of a blind-spot in an otherwise brilliant and rational mind." Seham to Irving Stone, 3 March 1941, TLS, DLC-MSS, Darrow Papers.

or something of that sort.[16] I believe you can find it. It is a very thorough article and it seems to me quite conclusive on the question.

There is an excellent article in the Encyclopedia Britannica. I have not examined the latest edition, but it was in the former edition, which you can easily find. This does not take sides, but it shows plainly that most of the things claimed for vaccination are uncertain, if not untrue. I have taken pains to find out what there is on the other side, both by reading books and talking to physicians, and I am surprised to see how little the physicians really know about the subject and also how little literature there is on their side of the question.

In the first place, I never yet found a physician who could tell me just what takes place in the blood or any other part of the human system, as a result of vaccination. If they could tell this, it might throw some light on the further question, assuming that it does something toward making one immune from smallpox, how does it effect other diseases? We are getting so much of this vaccination business on different diseases, that it is hard to tell what will become of the human system after they get through with it. Nature herself is some artist in the way of making one immune. She tempers man through successive generations to the place where they live and makes them more or less immune from the things that are most liable to kill them. The human system, through time, has been adapted by nature to the condition of life of the individual. Some people live in countries where miasma is prevalent, and the native inhabitants are not bothered with it as a stranger would be who moves into that part of the country. I suppose a vaccine could be found for five or six of the diseases which cause most of the deaths of mankind. For instance—tuberculosis, cancer, pneumonia, diphtheria and typhoid fever. Suppose this vaccine is given and it really makes the man immune from any of these diseases, would he then live forever, or would he die in operation. I am inclined to think he would die. He at least would probably fall a victim to something else that otherwise he would not have had.

Alfred Russell Wallace in this book says that the human system is something like a garden. You may destroy all the pigweed in the garden, but some other weed would grow up to take its place. We who have lived in the country, know this is the truth.

The fact is, the human system is a stone house for germs of all sort and I have no idea that the system can get rid of all germs and stay rid of them. Every position that the believers of vaccination have taken has been found tenable. It was first claimed that it made one immune forever, but cases of smallpox were found after vaccination. It was then

16. Darrow is probably referring to Alfred Russel Wallace's *The Wonderful Century: Its Successes and Its Failures* (New York: Dodd, Mead, 1898), which contains a long chapter titled "Vaccination a Delusion—Its Penal Enforcement a Crime." Wallace (1823–1913), an English naturalist, was a leading figure in the anti-vaccination crusade in the late nineteenth century. See Giacomo Scarpelli, "'Nothing in Nature That Is not Useful': The Anti-Vaccination Crusade and the Idea of *Harmonia Naturae* in Alfred Russel Wallace," *Nuncius (Italy)* 7 (1992): 109–30; Arthur Allen, *Vaccine: The Controversial Story of Medicine's Greatest Lifesaver* (New York: W.W. Norton, 2007), 66–68.

claimed that it was good for fifteen years, then for ten, then for seven and now they think that one should be vaccinated every time it enters their head. Under modern systems of sanitation, smallpox is a matter of very little consequence. Very few people die of it and to say that one in health shall introduce something into his system, where the chances are not more than one in a thousand that he would ever have smallpox, it seems to me to be absurd and probably very injurious.

Anyhow, Wallace has collected a vast amount of facts and I am sure the book will interest you.

With kind regards, I am,

Very truly yours, | (signed) Clarence Darrow

MS: TT, DLC-MSS, Darrow Papers. PLACE: no reason to doubt Chicago. INSIDE ADDRESS: Dr. Max Seham, | 538 LaSalle Building, | Minneapolis, Minnesota.

TO FREMONT OLDER • CHICAGO • SATURDAY 25 DECEMBER 1920

140 NORTH DEARBORN STREET Dec 25th

Dear Fremont

I am a very poor letter writer as you already know, but today being Christ's birth day and not going to the office I am writing a few letters. I gave no presents to any one and wished no one a Merry Christmas. This is one kind of bunk I cut out long ago. I am as fast as possible cutting out all bunk, so if I live a few years longer (as I fear I shall) there will be nothing left in life. I am still working hard though I don't know why except habit, a habit that at my age is hard to break. What I should do is to take the small amount I have and go to the South Seas and wait, but I presume I shan't do this. Of course I get some consolation and satisfaction from my friends and I have gathered around me a good many, (more probably than I deserve) and we spend some rather pleasant evenings together. Then too I read some, but hardly ever find any thing really new, only more or less new ways of saying old things. Chicago is now in the throes of a fierce, brutal, unthinking, and foolish fight with criminals. That is one class of them is trying to terrorize an other. We are having a good many shootings by gun men, mostly boys, and the good people are hanging indiscriminately. Last week we hanged a boy eighteen years old; which should have terrorized every one into virtue but which hasn't done it.[17] Of course no one studies the causes of things or tries to cure the cause and I presume no one ever will. It does not seem to occur to them that the slaughter of millions in the last four years could have any thing to do with jarring people loose from their old mores, but it has jarred the public loose as well, for they too like murder, if it is only the right ones. I got a little bit interested in politics & made a few

17. Darrow is likely referring to the hanging of Nicholas Viana (1901–1920) on 10 December 1920, Viana's nineteenth birthday. Viana was hanged for participating in the murder of a saloon keeper in Chicago. In the press, he was often referred to as the "choir boy" because he sang for the other prisoners in jail. He sang Rudyard Kipling's "Mother o' Mine" for his mother shortly before he was hanged.

speeches for Cox.[18] Don't know exactly why except on account of Harding. The election added its evidence of proof of the wonderful intellect of man, and also confirmed my prophesy of the censuring effect of woman's suffrage. In Chicago where they take the votes of men & women and put them in separate boxes (no doubt for moral purposes) I figured out that 48% of the prohibition vote was women, 39% of the Republican vote was women, 30% of the Democratic vote women, 25% of the Socialist women, about 20% of the Farmer labor vote women. Those who thought that the women's vote would help radicalism or progressive ideas ought to know, but probably never will. I can see nothing in voting but generally go to the polls as a matter of habit. For amusement I now & then have a debate in which I take the pessimistic side—I really can see no other. The only optimistic thing that I can see is death; but surely this is a very permanent hope, and one that for all is soon reached. A week ago I debated with Steffens on Does the Russian Revolution show there is permanent progress in the world. I of course said "no." It was not really a debate. He made his speeches for Russia & I said what of it. Steffens goes west in Feby & will be in California early in March. How I wish I could be there with him. We could at least have some companionable times together. I hear nothing more about the McNamaras & wonder sometimes what will happen when JJ gets out. You will probably keep an eye on it & do anything that needs to be done if it can be. I am not seriously worrying about it all. I did the best I could in what the world would class as an unselfish way & that is all there is to it, and then I can really see how any thing could befall. It looks as if there was a determined fight on the Unions and I am afraid that big business is making some progress in it. 100% American is a good camaflage for a scoundrel, and it does seem as if all idealism and aspiration for freedom is dead. It is hard to realize that the phisical laws control much the same as blind matter, and that action and reaction are equal; but I think they are absolutely equal. We have been through four years of drunkenness and now comes the depression of the morning after. I am very much disappointed that I have not been able to see you this year, but I shall not let an other year pass without it, we are both getting too old. My health in the main is pretty good but I find myself out of geer quite often and not coming back as I once did. I don't suppose I could stand as hard a jolt as I once could & the truth is I don't want to. Of course I would be sorry to have you think that all of this means self pitty. I believe I have conquered this form of egoism, and then when I look things over as an intellectual process I am quite sure I have had as much as any one else, and would not change places with those who seem to have had the most. I am always glad to hear from you. One of your letters always gives me a thrill. Perhaps it is unmanly to say it but my acquaintance with you has been enough to compensate me for any pain I have had in the years I have known you.

Ever your friend | Clarence Darrow.

MS: ALS, CU-BANC, Older Papers, Box 1. DATE: "1920" appended and reference to speeches for Cox.

18. James Middleton Cox (1870–1957), newspaper publisher, congressman from Ohio, 1909–13, governor of Ohio, 1913–15, 1917–21, and Democratic nominee for president in 1920. He lost to Warren G. Harding.

TO CHARLES ERSKINE SCOTT WOOD • CHICAGO • TUESDAY 18 JANUARY 1921

140 NORTH DEARBORN STREET Jan 18th

My Dear Mr. Wood

I received the book and have acknowledged it and thanked Mr Nash for sending.[19] It is a beautiful peace of work & I prize it highly and thank you for having it sent. I will mail you some stuff tomorrow. Don't know how good it is or how much you will care for them. They are stenographic copies of debates &c and really not done well enough to publish. I would have sent some things before if I had known your address. I wish I might see you once in a while. I hear that Sarah is coming this way & hope I can see her. I am glad to see that the public is slowly finding out that you are a poet and I hope this is some pleasure to you. I don't know any thing that brings much more satisfaction than turning out some work you like to do. So far my life does not change a great deal. I still live in Court & always hope to stop & never find the place. In the natural course of events I will soon find the place.

Ever with regards and best wishes

Your friend | Clarence Darrow.

MS: ALS, CSmH, Wood Papers, WD Box 126 (47). DATE: reference to Nash's book.

TO SINCLAIR LEWIS • CHICAGO • WEDNESDAY 9 FEBRUARY 1921

DARROW, SISSMAN, POPHAM & CARLIN Feby 9th

Dear Mr. Lewis

I got your address from Mr. Ben Huebsch.[20] Now and then some D—n fellow writes a book that costs me about $100. You are the last. When I get the right book I feel I must send it to my friends, so you see I like the book about $100 worth. Really you have done a wonderful job. I don't want to over-do my praise, but I do wish I could have done it. But I couldn't & no one else could. I want to write a page review mostly quotations if one of the Chicago papers will take it. If not I will get some one to.[21] I wonder if I ever met you.[22] I don't remem-

19. Darrow is referring to *Ecclesiastes, or, The Preacher* (San Francisco: J. H. Nash, 1920), a limited-edition book sent to him by John Henry Nash (1871–1947), typographer and printer of fine books in San Francisco. Darrow's letter to Nash survives: "I received your beautiful book Ecclesiastes. I am quite sure that no one will appreciate your work more than I do. I wish I could write something good enough for you to print. I am sure you must have great joy in your work else you could not do it. | It was very kind of you to send it to me and I shall always prize it." Darrow to Nash, 17 January 1921, ALS, CU-BANC, Nash Collection.
20. Benjamin W. Huebsch was publisher of the third edition of Darrow's *Farmington*, and a friend of Sinclair Lewis.
21. Darrow is referring to Lewis's *Main Street*. No review was located.
22. A handwritten note in the margin, with lines drawn to this sentence and to Darrow's name on the letterhead, states: "Isn't this the socialist lawyer | Didn't you breakfast with him in New York?" A biographer of Lewis suggests that Darrow and Lewis met at the Cosmos Club in Washington, D.C., sometime in the winter or spring of 1919–20, when Lewis was writing *Main Street*. Mark Schorer, *Sinclair Lewis: An American Life* (New York: McGraw-Hill Books, 1961), 261.

ber that I have but wish I might. The book was so popular I didn't read it for a long time. I am a confirmed pessimist & I think the people have no brains. Now I must either revise my opinions as to the people or give up the idea that I am a judge of litterature. I don't like to do the latter. If you are ever this way I wish you would let me look at you. Still perhaps I should leave it entirely with the book. Any how I put you down in the top shelf of litterary men. I am very thankful that you did the job & wonder if you can ever do an other.

Sincerely Yours | Clarence Darrow

Am enclosing a part of a letter from a very clever woman to whom I sent a copy.[23]

D.

MS: ALS, CtY-BR, Lewis Papers, Box 46, Folder 479. DATE: *Main Street* was published in October 1920 and other letters confirm that Darrow had read the book by early 1921.

TO PAUL DARROW • CHICAGO • SUNDAY 20 FEBRUARY 1921

DARROW, SISSMAN, POPHAM & CARLIN Feby 20th

Dear Paul

You probably haven't seen me yet. I am like your Grand father: "next week." I have refused to make any Sunday speaking engagements through March & the last tour in Feby thinking I could get away but so far haven't had a chance. Am now in the trial of a case which will take two weeks more & shall then try again to come.[24] Any how shall take the first chance.

We are obliged to move this spring as the building is to be cut up into small apartments & I don't think I shall take an other place *before fall* and am thinking of my books. How would you like to have me send the following to you

Fine edition Oliver Wendel Holmes—14 vol.

Balzac—(Gebbie edition) about 30 vol.

Thackrey—(limited edition) about 35 vol.

R. L. Stevenson—The old edition—26 vol.

Ben Franklin—(old edition) 10 vol.

Stoddard's Lectures 10 vol.

Jefferson—10 vol.

De Musset—(Limited edition) 10 vol.

23. No enclosure exists.

24. From 15 February to 8 March 1921, Darrow was involved as defense counsel in the federal trial of Michael Heitler, a saloon keeper, and eleven codefendants who were charged with conspiracy to transport and sell two hundred thousand dollars worth of Kentucky whiskey in Chicago. Many other prominent local attorneys were involved in the case, which resulted in guilty verdicts for Heitler and five of his codefendants. "Mr. Heitler Now, not Mike De Pike, Court Decides," *Chicago Tribune*, 16 February 1921; "Supreme Court Will Pass on Heitler Case," *Chicago Tribune*, 9 March 1921.

Then there are 42 vol. Voltaire—good edition. I can sell them for about $1 per vol. They would cost probably $3 now. I shall never use them & I can sell or send to you whichever you wish. Will also put in some other things that will interest you. You might write me about it. If there are any others you want let me know.[25]

Hastily | C. S. D.

MS: ALS, MnU-L, Darrow Collection. DATE: letterhead and reference to trial.

TO DUNCAN C. MILNER • GREELEY, COLORADO • WEDNESDAY 23 MARCH 1921

THE GREELEY GAS & FUEL CO. March 23rd.

My Dear Mr. Milner

I am here for a few days with my son and grand children and your letter was forwarded and just received. I am very glad that you thought of me. I have read your sermon and find it good and kindly like yourself.[26] Of course I can not see all things as you do, but I know and admire & so far as I can try to practice your spirit. I am glad that you grow more charitable to others as you grow old—that you don't bar any out. The longer I live the more I try to understand, that all are the product of their heredity and environment and that no one has the right to judge. I am quite sure that there is no one in the world to whom I bear ill will or who I would try to injure & who I would not really like to help. But I didn't mean to brag so much about myself. Ever since I knew you I have loved you and believed in you & have never thought about any difference in any views that we might hold. I hope I can see you when we both return to Chicago.

Ever with the warmest personal regards,

Your friend Clarence Darrow

MS: ALS, IU-HS, Milner Papers. DATE: letterhead, Darrow's presence in Colorado in March, and the reference to a sermon.

TO PAUL DARROW • CHICAGO • MONDAY 18 APRIL 1921

DARROW & SISSMAN April 18th

Dear Paul

I have not heard from you since my return, nor have I written so I guess we are even. I have today paid the bank the balance I owe them & sent Noyes & Jackson

25. The apartment building in which the Darrows lived was divided into smaller apartments, but the landlord allowed the Darrows to keep their full apartment and they did not move.
26. Darrow is probably referring to a sermon that Milner delivered on his eightieth birthday. See "Portion of a Sermon Preached by the Rev. Duncan A. Milner on His Eightieth Birthday at a Union Meeting in Mt. Dora, Florida," IU-HS, Milner Papers, Folder 68.

$500 on acct. Am just now in the trial of a case that will last a month.[27] Just returned from St Paul where I made a talk yesterday, raking in $150.[28] We are all well, & I don't know any thing new to report. Am hoping you are getting busy on coal rate. It looks as if there would be a general reduction of freight rates soon, but ours is out of line.

Regards to all | Clarence Darrow.

MS: ALS, MnU-L, Darrow Collection. DATE: reference to "talk" in St. Paul.

TO MARY FIELD PARTON • CHICAGO • FRIDAY 10 JUNE 1921

DARROW, SISSMAN, POPHAM & CARLIN June 10th

Dear Mary

When I got your letter I felt sure that I would answer it at once but I haven't. Probably I never will do anything on time. I have been busy at the same game, trying cases here. Then I went down to a small town in Indiana to defend four young fellows who tried to get money out of a bank without having deposited any. They took revolvers & masks &c and one citizen was killed in the affray. They were indicted for murder & I worked 10 days to save their lives—nothing else—and the jury did it much to the regret of the whole community. The court house was packed the whole time. I had not seen any thing of the sort since I was a youth.[29] Still it was tough on me. The fact is Mary I have not been well for two months—my digestion is racing the devil with me, and I have been taking it as easy as I could and am going away to a country place in Wisconsin for two months to try to get well (why in hell should I). If the spirit moves me I will write a book while I am gone. So far as I can make plans I am not going to work so hard any more, and I am going out to California for a while this winter. Tomorrow I am going up to Wisconsin to look at a place where I hope to spend the summer and

27. Darrow was defense counsel for three officials of an upholsterers' union who were charged with conspiring to commit acts of violence—namely, bombings and beatings—during a strike by the union that began in 1919. The jury returned a verdict on 10 May 1921, finding two of the three men guilty. "2 Union Chiefs Found Guilty of Slugging Plot," *Chicago Tribune*, 11 May 1921.
28. Darrow spoke at the auditorium in St. Paul, Minnesota, on labor unions and the "closed shop." "Darrow Tells Aims of Trade Unionism," *Minneapolis Journal*, 18 April 1921; "Closed Shops Selfish Institution and not Idealism, Declares Darrow," *St. Paul Pioneer Press*, 18 April 1921.
29. The trial was in Warsaw, Indiana, from 10 to 19 May. Darrow and two other lawyers (with Darrow in the lead) defended four men in their early twenties who had robbed a bank in Culver, Indiana. (A fifth robber was never caught.) In a shootout during their getaway, a townsman who tried to stop them was shot and killed, which led to the four defendants being charged with first-degree murder. They were found guilty and could have been sentenced to death, but the jury fixed their punishment at life in prison. The courtroom was packed every day of the trial, especially during Darrow's closing argument. One newspaper reported that Darrow's presence was "a greater attraction than the features of the murder itself." "Bandits May Know Fate Tomorrow," *Warsaw Daily Times*, 19 May 1921.

am just rushing this off before I go. When I get back will send you a letter at least twice as long as this.

Ever | C. S. D.

MS: TLS, ICN, Parton-Darrow Papers, Box 1, Folder 8. DATE: "1929" is appended but the letterhead and reference to the Indiana case places this in 1921.

TO JOSEPH LEWIS • CHICAGO • TUESDAY 21 JUNE 1921

DARROW & SISSMAN June 21st

Dear Mr. Lewis

Sometime ago I received a copy of your little book "The tyranny of god."[30] I just read it. The book is well done. It is a very clear statement of the question, bold & true, beyond dispute. Of course it seems foolish that people should write books to prove that a man is not living when he is dead. That you could take a live fly and put it in the fire and the fly would still live. But men cling to these delusions in spite of facts. I am quite sure that reason has nothing to do with beliefs & next to nothing to do with conduct, perhaps failing to recognize this fact is the fundamental mistake of all "rationalists." I am not sure that your book will convert any one or that the world would be any happier if it converted every one, or that it makes any substantial difference whether men are happy or not, or whether any thing makes any difference. But I am glad you wrote it & it is as plain & true as the multiplication table, which does not mean that any one will believe it. I am glad too that it is well printed. If you will send me your address I will send you a few things of mine more or less along the same line. And if you live in N.Y. will try to hunt you up sometime when I am there. With thanks to you for writing the book and to the company for sending it I am

Very truly yours | Clarence Darrow.

MS: ALS, IEN, Leopold-Loeb Collection, Box 39, Folder 26. DATE: letterhead and publication of *The Tyranny of God.*

TO PAUL DARROW • FISH CREEK, WISCONSIN • TUESDAY 19 JULY 1921

DARROW, SISSMAN, POPHAM & CARLIN July 19th

Dear Paul

I got your letter the other day telling your gross for June. I am glad to see it growing. Hope you will get a freight reduction but I know the roads never do any more than they are obliged to do. I feel as if we ought not to wait any longer than this fall, we should

30. Joseph Lewis, *The Tyranny of God* (New York: Freethought Press, 1921).

be making more money and you should not be working so hard. Your time is worth too much to spend it on the things clerks can do. I would like to go to Greece; Italy; Spain; Egypt & Constantinople this winter, but I don't like to leave business for three or four months at that time of year until I feel that the business out there is in such shape that it will keep on improving and with a good fair income in sight say at least 1,000 per month. Of course I don't want to hurry you but I really think we should face the situation & do the best possible about it. I have been here a week and hope to stay until the middle of September if possible.[31] Am gradually getting better. We have a house & Fay Lewis & Mr. & Mrs. Eldridge[32]; backers from Rockford are with us. It is a very beautiful country. I am writing a book on Criminology. Have made a good start & will have it done subject to revision by the first of Sept. About 80,000 or 100,000 words.[33] Ask Jessie why she didn't copy The Hen with One Chicken. She mustn't grow up like her Grand father & great grand father & put things off. Tell her I want it. You can write directly here.

Fish Creek—Door Co.—Wisconsin

C. S. D.

MS: ALS, MnU-L, Darrow Collection. DATE: "1921" appended and supported by reference to criminology book.

TO MARY FIELD PARTON • FISH CREEK, WISCONSIN • THURSDAY 25 AUGUST 1921

Fish Creek—Wisconsin | Aug 25

Dear Mary

Your letter duly arrived yesterday and made my conscience (what is left of it) prick me for my indolence in not writing. I have been here for two months, loafing, driving a machine, writing and vegetating. It is a very beautiful country tucked in between Lake Michigan and Green Bay, cut up with hills and promontories and covered with woods. The people have not really discovered it so thoroughly that the rich have driven all comfort and simplicity away, but they are finding it and getting the best places, and fencing them away from the poor. Still it is a beautiful spot and I wish you could see it which you can't. I have been working on a book on Criminology. Have written about 60,000 words, a damn lot of words, and am nursing it. Don't know what it will look like or who will print it but there is some good stuff in it. One of my chief reasons in coming here was my health. The truth is I have not been well for about five months. Don't know yet just what

31. Darrow was spending his summer vacation in Door County, Wisconsin.
32. Seba Eldridge (1885–1953) and his wife, Catherine Eldridge (b. 1890). At the time of this letter, Seba Eldridge was an assistant professor of sociology and economics at Rockford College, 1919–21. Later, he became a professor of sociology at the University of Kansas, 1921–53, and author of several books of political sociology. Catherine Eldridge was a trained nurse and lay social worker.
33. Darrow is referring to what became his book, *Crime: Its Cause and Treatment* (New York: Thomas Y. Crowell, 1922).

it is but some lack of elimination is depositing some poison in my system. It shows mainly by indigestion &c. I didn't know but this would cure me but it hasn't. So when I go back will find out just what it is and possibly some cutting will need to be done; guess not much. You will probably still know me if at all. Any how it doesn't worry me any. I really believe that now nothing would seriously worry me. I am so sure that there is nothing in it all—and then I have so nearly *finished* the foolishness—but this isn't very serious. I shall leave here the 6th of Sept. and go back to work & to the Drs. and the old grind of five little mosquito bites that I have got used to and I will surely write you as soon as I get a more definite line on myself. You said you were going to give up your job & write. You should have done that long ago and you should do it *now*. Nobody can write like you. No one feels so much & knows so well and can do it. So do it. I want to see it, some of it in print, before Jesus calls me home.

Ever with love | Clarence Darrow

MS: ALS, ICN, Parton-Darrow Papers, Box 1, Folder 8. DATE: "1921" appended and supported by reference to book on criminology.

TO ANNA SCHERFF TZITLONOK • CHICAGO • FRIDAY 23 SEPTEMBER 1921

DARROW, SISSMAN, POPHAM & CARLIN September 23, 1921.

My Dear Mrs. Tzitlonok:—

I received the book "The Children of The Universe" and I have read it.[34] I have been away on a long vacation and did not get it until last week, which is the reason I have not written sooner. Of course, I like this book, but I have no idea as to whether it would sell. My guess would be that it would not. I doubt whether it is a proper subject for a play and do not know of any form in which science and sense can be made attractive to the world made up of fools. Neither am I sure that the book is true. Am inclined to think it is not. It makes too much of healthy reason. There is no such thing. There is not even reason, let alone healthy reason.

As a matter of strict science, I am convinced that the brain is about the last organ to develop and the least use in life. It has almost nothing to do with life or action. If it did, the human race would have been dead long ago, which would have been a very good thing.

I am also convinced that the book is not true in another regard. It assumes that intelligence and reason tend to happiness. I am satisfied that they do not. The intelligent

34. Darrow is referring to a five-act allegorical play that was written and published by Tzitlonok's husband, Schevel Tzitlonok: *The Children of the Universe* (New York: privately printed, 1921). Schevel Tzitlonok (b. 1880) immigrated to the United States in 1913 after escaping from czarist Russia, where he was imprisoned as a revolutionist. After arriving in the United States, he peddled fruits and vegetables in South Bend, Indiana, before attending Toledo University, where he received a B.A. When he published his play, he and his wife lived in Brooklyn, New York. Later, they lived in Milwaukee, Wisconsin, where he continued working as a produce merchant.

person is less happy then the fool. The truth is, nature did not make people to be happy, but just out of a whim she insists on preserving life and for that reason takes little account of the brain.

The misery of life is not caused by superstition or ignorance, but it is instinct in life itself and cannot be cured. The only amelioration to living, is dope in some form—religious, political or physical. Some take it in Catholicism, some in Methodism, some in Christian Science, some in Socialism, some in Single Tax. The brain that will receive this dope is lucky, but not strong. With some of us, the only dope that ever works is some form of opium and this is carefully guarded from those who need it most. This may sound like a joke, but I am satisfied that it is true; but nobody can live on the fact.

However, the book is good in the sense that anything is good. That helps to destroy superstition. At least, it meets my emotional nature and I would like to see it sell.

I am enclosing the price of the book, not because you expect it, but because I printed books that way myself and I know they do not sell.

I wish I might see you and your husband. I am going to be in New York Monday next and possibly Tuesday at the Prince George. If you get a chance to be that way, will be glad to see you.

Very truly yours, | Clarence Darrow

MS: TLS, WHi, Tzitlonok Papers. INSIDE ADDRESS: Mrs. Anna Scherff Tzitlonok, | 137 Bay 25th St., | Bath Beach, | Brooklyn, N.Y.

TO FRANK WALSH • CHICAGO • SATURDAY 8 OCTOBER 1921

DARROW, SISSMAN, POPHAM & CARLIN October 8th, 1921.

Dear Frank:—

I was very glad to get your letter this morning and glad to know that you are back in America.[35] Somehow I like it better when you are here. I was down in New York the day before you arrived and would have stayed and waited for the boat, but I knew there would be so many shouting Irishmen around you, that I would not have any chance, so I went on my way.

I see you have got me down for an A.P.A. and a lover of England.[36] When I do anything in politics here that does not agree with some of the Irish, they always put me down that way, but I do not know why, for in spite of their damned imperfections—perhaps on account of them—I have always been strong for the Irish. They are an emotional, sympathetic, law hating bunch and all this appeals to me. I would be glad to see Ireland get

35. Walsh was chairman of the American Commission on Irish Independence and he had just returned from a trip to Ireland.

36. "A.P.A." is probably a reference to the American Protective Association or perhaps the American Protestant Association, both of which were anti-Catholic fraternal organizations formed in the mid- to late-nineteenth century. Alvin J. Schmidt, *Fraternal Organizations* (Westport, CT: Greenwood Press, 1980), 37–38.

Home Rule, which I think they are going to get. If they get it and both sides behave themselves, which they will not, they would be in good shape. I am quite sure that Ireland is better off as a part of the British Empire, but they do not know it and perhaps never will. Any how, I like to see a row and they are always good at stirring up a row.

I am glad to see that you have got over your delusion of prohibition. I do not know whether you have begun drinking, but your size and weight would indicate it. This is the best kind of dope I know of, so long as I cannot take religious dope.

I would not blame you if you went to Ireland to live. Anywhere is better than America. They are so damned pharisaical and good, that if I was not too old to move and any other country would have me, I would go on the first ship.

Am glad to hear what you say about the Cole estate and I am inclined to think we will win.[37] I will read the briefs in this case, not because I like to read a fool brief, much less write one, but I am very much interested personally in the outcome.

The next time I am down I will see if I can get hold of Daugherty.[38] I want to do it and I want you to get in touch with him. Glad to see you get into politics and I do not know but what it is as good to be with the Tammany bunch as any other.

By the way, I am interested in a case here where the City of Chicago has forbidden the sale of the Ford papers on the streets on account of their malicious attacks on the Jews.[39] In this I am helping the City and have been reading some of Ford's truck against the Jews. They are bad enough, but his stories are slightly exaggerated. For instance, one of the last numbers contained a story showing how the Jews had debauched Tammany Hall. I remarked to a friend of mine that the charge of the Jews debauching Tammany Hall would be about like charging a fifteen year old boy with debauching the madam of a pleasure house. You having lived in Kansas City in the good old days would know what I mean.

37. The "Cole estate" is a reference to litigation over the estate of Margaret C. Cole (d. 1920), which was reportedly valued at $1 million. Cole was the widow of William Washington Cole (1847–1915), a well-known circus proprietor. When Margaret Cole died, she left the bulk of her estate to her personal physician in New York City. Both Walsh and Darrow were lawyers in the litigation, which involved several parties claiming entitlement to assets of the estate. Darrow represented two nieces of Margaret Cole and a daughter of one of those nieces, all of whom lived in Chicago. Darrow reportedly settled the matter involving his clients for two hundred thousand dollars. "Chicago Women Get $200,000 of Cole Estate," *Chicago Tribune,* 20 December 1920. The Walsh Papers contain many items relating to the litigation. See "Margaret C. Cole Estate," NN, Walsh Papers, Boxes 62–63.

38. Darrow might be referring to Henry L. Doherty (rather than Harry M. Daugherty), who probably had an office in New York at the time.

39. In 1920, the *Dearborn (Michigan) Independent,* a weekly newspaper owned by Henry Ford, began publishing a long series of anti-Semitic articles. These articles maintained, among other things, that Jews were responsible for the recent war and plotting to destroy Christian civilization. The newspaper found a strong reaction against it in several large cities where it tried to increase its street sales. Allan Nevins and Frank Ernest Hill, *Ford: Expansion and Challenge, 1915–1933* (New York: Charles Scribner's Sons, 1957), 315; see also Neil Baldwin, *Henry Ford and the Jews: The Mass Production of Hate* (New York: Public Affairs, 2001). In Chicago, in July 1921, the chief of police had two newsboys arrested for selling the *Independent* and he ordered a ban on the sale of the newspaper. In August, the ban was lifted by a court injunction, which the city fought unsuccessfully against. "Chief's Ban on Ford's Weekly Lifted by Writ," *Chicago Tribune,* 5 August 1921; "Ford's Weekly Menaces City, Court Is Told," *Chicago Tribune,* 6 January 1922.

I am to be in New York on November 27th to debate with Scott Nearing[40] on one of my favorite topics involving a grouch against the world. Do you want to be chairman? We got to do something to get out a crowd and I think this would help. If you do, I will tell them you must be chairman. I may be there before, but I am not certain.[41]

With all good wishes,

Your A.P.A. friend, | Clarence Darrow.

MS: TLS, NN, Walsh Papers, Box 10. INSIDE ADDRESS: Hon. Frank P. Walsh, | Woolworth Building, | New York City, N.Y.

TO NEGLEY D. COCHRAN • CHICAGO • FRIDAY 14 OCTOBER 1921

DARROW, SISSMAN, POPHAM & CARLIN October 14, 1921.

Dear Neg:—

Am much obliged for your letter with the enclosure from Daugherty.[42]

I was down to Washington a week or ten days ago in reference to the pardon of St. John and it seems that all they need is a little more urging in order to get him released. You will remember St. John.[43] He was that brick of a fellow that visited you at your booze parlor in the Sherman House one day, on his road to Leavenworth. You remember we talked about getting him out after he got in. He has been there altogether about two years and really for nothing. He was tried with one hundred others, the I.W.W. bunch. He was one of the original organizers and he was its first President, but had severed all

40. Scott Nearing (1883–1983), socialist economist, writer, and reformer. Nearing received a Ph.D. from the Wharton School at the University of Pennsylvania, 1909, and taught at many universities. He was fired by Wharton in 1915 for his socialist views and by the University of Toledo in 1917 for his pacifists views. He was prosecuted under the federal Espionage Act in 1919 and acquitted. He wrote fifty some books and many pamphlets and articles.

41. Darrow and Nearing debated the proposition "Permanent Progress for the Human Race Is Impossible" at the Manhattan Opera House on 27 November 1921. Walsh served as chairman for the event.

42. Cochran told Darrow that he would be in Washington soon on newspaper business and that he would probably see Harry Daugherty. Cochran to Darrow, 11 October 1921, TLc, OT, Cochran Papers. Daugherty's letter to Cochran said that Daugherty would be pleased to see Darrow when he came to Washington. Daugherty to Cochran, 1 October 1921, TLS, OT, Cochran Papers.

43. Vincent St. John (1876–1929), mine worker and labor leader. St. John, who was born in Kentucky, began working in the mines in Colorado and other western states in 1894. He was an active labor organizer and held various offices in the Western Federation of Miners, 1900–6. He was one of the founders of the Industrial Workers of the World, serving as its general organizer, 1907–08, and later as its general secretary-treasurer, 1909–14. In 1915, he started his own copper-mining venture in New Mexico and became ineligible for membership in the IWW (which was limited to wage workers). In September 1917, the United States Department of Justice conducted a nationwide raid on the offices of the IWW, seizing papers and arresting hundreds of people connected with the organization. St. John was arrested in New Mexico, where he was working in his mine. He was taken to Chicago and stood trial in federal court with William Haywood and some hundred other defendants, charged with conspiracy to violate the Espionage Act of 1917. Even though he was not a member of the IWW or active in the IWW during the period of time covered by the indictment, St. John was convicted along with the other defendants in August 1918 and sentenced to twenty years in prison. Darrow began representing St. John shortly after his trial. In April 1919, he obtained St. John's release on bail pending appeal. Two years later, the judgment of the trial court was affirmed and St. John returned to prison. In 1922, President Harding commuted St. John's sentence and he was released.

connection with the organization more than two years before anything happened upon which he was indicted. He went because the rest went. He is probably like you and me—got over his illusions that he could do much good and had embarked in the laudable business of getting money, and in that way was engaged in mining where he had got a claim that he thought he would make money out of. He still thinks so, if he was not so far away as Leavenworth.

There is really no evidence of any substantial sort against him. He wrote a letter or two in which he said that he would be willing to give any help he could in reference to finding out spotters in the mine where he lived, but this had no reference to anything that was charged in the indictment.

I am sending you a copy of the brief, which is very short and which states all there is in the case.

When I was down there, Mr. Daugherty was away. I went to see his First Assistant, Mr. Goff,[44] who seemed to know a great deal about the case and was rather favorably impressed with the matter. From there I went to the Pardon Attorney on the same floor and had a long conference with him. I have the feeling that he thinks St. John has been there long enough, but he did not say so. The custom is for the Pardon Attorney to go over the matter and report the facts to the Attorney General.

I think a little urging to the Attorney General or Mr. Goff to bring the papers out of the Pardon Office will result in at least a parole and I am darned anxious to have it done.

While you are there, will you see what you can do. I will probably have some one from New York call and see you and if you have time, you might write me where you will be in Washington and if possible, I may come down. Will if I can.

Forgot to thank you for the books you sent to Fish Creek. "The Mirrors of Washington" is a peach.[45] I have read it many times, especially the one about our noble President. I have had a good deal of fun reading it to my friends. Wish I knew who wrote it. I am inclined to think that it was not Samuel Blythe.[46] If you get any line on it, let me know.

I often think of the days at Fish Creek and the good times we had and wish we could get together again soon.

44. Guy Goff (1866–1933), lawyer and United States senator from West Virginia. Goff held various government positions before serving in the Senate, 1925–31, including United States attorney for the eastern district of Wisconsin and several appointments between 1920 and 1923 as an assistant to the attorney general, Harry M. Daugherty.

45. *The Mirrors of Washington* (New York: Knickerbocker Press, 1921) contains critical and satirical essays about fourteen political and public men in Washington, including Warren G. Harding, Woodrow Wilson, Edward M. House, Herbert Hoover, Elihu Root, and Hiram Johnson. The book, published anonymously, caused a public sensation and became a best seller. The author was Clinton Gilbert (1871–1933), a writer and journalist who worked for the Washington bureau of the *Philadelphia Public Ledger*.

46. Samuel Blythe (1868–1947), writer and journalist. Blythe was the author of several books and worked for many years as a political writer for the *Saturday Evening Post*.

While you are in Washington, I wish you could get General Sherwood to send me a copy of that magnificent speech he made in Congress where he compared the Civil War with the War in Europe.[47] The part that was carried by the Associated Press was one of the best things I ever saw. Incidentally, remember me kindly to both Mr. Sherwood and his wife.[48]

As ever, | Your friend, | Clarence Darrow.

MS: TLS, OT, Cochran Papers.

TO NEGLEY D. COCHRAN • CHICAGO • TUESDAY 27 DECEMBER 1921

DARROW, SISSMAN, POPHAM & CARLIN Dec. 27

Dear Neg

Sorry, but I expect to go the P.M. of the 28th to see Paul. I would put it off but I only have a few days. Too D—n bad. Call up Ruby & Dwight & May.[49] They will all be glad to see you & get you a drink. I wish I could go with you & E.W.[50] It would be better than going to Europe, but I am intending to sail Jan 21st for two months. If it doesn't go I will be glad to go to Florida. I am glad you are going to let up so am I. Probably we can loaf together for a part of the time that's left. We can get a place in an Old Man's home for 500 or same price in an Old Lady's home.

Ever | Darrow

MS: ALS, OT, Cochran Papers. DATE: letterhead and reference to trip to Europe.

TO FREMONT OLDER • PARIS, FRANCE • WEDNESDAY 22 MARCH 1922

Paris | March 22d.

Dear Fremont

Ever since I left America I have intended to write you but have been working pretty hard—sight seeing &c. I sailed from N.Y. the 21st of Jan. and have done Italy, been to Cairo & have seen the Pyramids, the Sphynx, the Nile, the desert &c &c and been to

47. Isaac R. Sherwood (1835–1925), newspaper editor, Civil War veteran, and congressman from Ohio. Sherwood was a pacifist during World War I and often referred to the Civil War in his congressional speeches. Here, Darrow might be referring to a speech that Sherwood gave in opposition to a bill to make appropriations for a large standing army. See *Congressional Record,* 66th Cong., 2d sess., 1920, 59, pt. 9:8928–31. But he also might be referring to a speech in April 1917 in opposition to the resolution of war. See *Congressional Record,* 65th Cong., 1st sess., 1917, 55, pt. 1:335–40.
48. Katherine Brownlee Sherwood (1841–1914), poet and newspaper editor. A native of Ohio, Sherwood helped manage newspapers with her husband, translated French and German poems, and wrote poetry of her own, including *Campfire and Memorial Poems* (Chicago: Jensen, McClung & Co., 1885). For fifteen years, she was also a contributing editor of the women's department of the *National Tribune* in Washington, D.C.
49. "Ruby" is Ruby Darrow but the identities of "Dwight" and "May" are unknown.
50. E. W. Scripps.

Jerusalem and shall be back home by April 5th. So you see I have thoroughly done three continents, leaving nothing more to do but S America & Australia before I die. Still I am not anxious to wait for the other two continents. Think I have had enough of the game. Rome did not impress me. There are some ruins of past splendor, considerable new in the way of buildings and art, plenty of Religious Junk, but still I left without any desire to return. I lingered longer in Naples with its wonderful view over the bay with Vesuvius on the other side. The view is very fine, some like your own Golden gate. After all nature appeals to me most where man leaves it alone. The ragged people—the beggars, the religious bunk and all that defaces it makes you weary if not sad. The Nile is interesting & beautiful. The Pyramids & Sphynx, not much. The people a motley throng of all the nations on earth are an ever interesting picture. One gets an idea of what we have called the "backward" people. The Arabs from the desert & the Turks &c. can beat the Jews out of their eye teeth in trade. We westerners haven't a chance with them. They are industrious, alert—smart. They know all our tricks and many more. Egypt is farmed to the last foot of land. Our farmers can teach them nothing, either in raising or selling. The idea that has been created of their backward and primitive ways is bunk. An American farmer could not live beside them. They are too smart & too industrious. There is more evidence of prosperity & push in Egypt than I saw in Europe.

I went to Jerusalem too. This was different from the Jerusalem I expected to see. Of course all the Religious junk was there, but no one seemed to notice it, except a few of us ignorant civilized people. With all that has been done to convert the benighted heathen, nine tenths are still Muhammedans & Jews, the latter being about 10% of the whole population. The child of the [x] is the man. There he is wide awake smart and he or she breeds. The panorama in the streets is most interesting with its people of all races in all kinds of costumes. Its camels, donkeys and goats. The place is barren windy and a desert, but they know what they are doing & neither the Christian or the Jew is a match for the Arab. Zionism is a foolish dream, where it isn't a fake. In the main it is useful to help Jews get offices in America, but they have as much chance [to] control Palestine as the Socialists have to control America. One is impressed with the age of it all, with the fact that man has not changed and can not change. That he is as important as the fly & no more so, that he is a fool to take himself so seriously. I wish you could have been with me. Our moods would have fitted the surroundings. We have been disillusioned, but all of this old stuff, the march of generations from birth to death makes it somehow more real, and helps put you where you belong. What difference whether you manage to live until next week or not. How I would like to see you once more. I presume you have the same struggles as the rest of us, but you always impress me as one who knows the vanity and futility of it all and who has helped me to know it better than any one else.

Always your friend | Clarence Darrow.

MS: ALS, CU-BANC, Older Papers, Box 1. DATE: Reference to trip and an unpublished letter to Paul Darrow on same day with year appended.

TO BENJAMIN B. LINDSEY • CHICAGO • THURSDAY 4 MAY 1922

DARROW, SISSMAN, HOLLY & CARLIN May 4th, 1922.

My Dear Judge Lindsey:—

Your letter of May 2nd is received.[51] I know John R. Randolph, if that is his name. I do not suppose even he remembers what his name is, and I likewise know his wife. I think you know me well enough to know that I will be very careful not to do an injustice to anyone who might suffer on account of it.

Randolph was in the penitentiary in Missouri, if I recall it, for burglary. His wife and his wife's mother whom I have known for many years, were instrumental in getting him out.[52] He then married the young woman. Her mother later came to see me because she could not get track of the daughter. I looked him up and found the evidence to show that he was a professional burglar. I advised her mother that he would turn up sooner or later to see the outcome of things. Not long after that, early in December last, the wife came to me in great trouble because her husband had been arrested and was in the lock-up for burglary. I told her that there was nothing that could be done for him and that she ought to get a divorce and get it at once. There were many charges against him here at the time and there was no sort of question about his profession, but she succeeded in getting bail for him and they came to my office, together. I told him what I had told her, that it would be impossible for him to change and that if he really cared anything about his wife he should leave her. He said if he ever got into trouble again he would. I urged him to do it at the time but of course he did not. I am not certain what was done with the cases here in Chicago. The chances are there were some bonds put up and he went somewhere else to ply his trade. If he is released in Denver, we will hear of him in some other State. I say all this without the slightest feeling against him. I am sorry for him, but it is out of the question for him to change. If he were sixty years old and somebody would take care of him, he might not have ambition enough to engage in business any further, or if there should be such a change in society that he would get as much as I do in a safer trade, he would follow that, but with society as it is, he never can do anything else.

He seems to me to be a nice fellow and under other environment in his early life, might have been a good respectable hod carrier, getting $50.00 a week and being satisfied, but

51. Lindsey wrote to Darrow about a case that was before him involving a small-time criminal who told Lindsey that his name was John R. Randolph (b. 1895?) (Randolph had sometimes gone by the name David Hill). Randolph had been arrested in Denver, Colorado, along with his wife, for robbing an apartment. His wife was Elizabeth Calhoun Randolph (b. 1892?), a graduate of the University of Chicago and an occasional newspaper and short-story writer. Elizabeth Randolph had asked Lindsey to write to Darrow to explain her and her husband's plight to him. Lindsey told Darrow that he would do what he could to have the charges against Elizabeth dropped, but he was seeking any suggestions that Darrow might have for Elizabeth. Lindsey to Darrow, 2 May 1922, TLc, DLC-MSS, Lindsey Papers.

52. Elizabeth Randolph's mother was Catherine Dawson (b. 1869). She lived in Kankakee, Illinois, and was active in prison reform work. Catherine's husband, Charles W. Dawson (1838–1921), was a wealthy automobile and real estate dealer in Kankakee.

he is too ambitious to hold any job that is recognized by society, with the attainments he has. Of course there is no other place for him than prison, although I wish there was.

His wife is all right. She comes of a good family, has been in newspaper work; has written some good short stories. She has ability and is a fine person. Of course she is not guilty of any crime. I am certain of it. It may be that any wife of the right sort would get remotely implicated with something the husband did, if the husband was this sort and she most certainly will if she sticks to him, but everything ought to be done that is possible to help her to leave her husband. I told her this when she was here and I told it to her in his presence, with the best intentions to both of them. If he had the right kind of feeling, he would tell her the same. He has absolutely no business to have a wife.

I am willing to do anything I possibly can to help her in her difficulty and if there is any danger of her suffering any through this, let me know and I will see that anything that I can do is done.

You are at perfect liberty to show her this letter and to show it to her husband. She has no chance whatever unless she quits him.[53]

I expect to be out your way this summer and shall call and see you.

With kindest regards, as ever,

Your friend, | Clarence Darrow

MS: TLS, DLC-MSS, Lindsey Papers. INSIDE ADDRESS: Hon. Ben B. Lindsey, | Denver, Colo.

TO MELVILLE E. STONE • CHICAGO • WEDNESDAY 17 MAY 1922

DARROW, SISSMAN, HOLLY & CARLIN May 17, 1922.

My Dear Mr. Stone:—

Some time ago, Mr. George Schilling wrote you a letter concerning a publication in your book about the anarchist case and his connection with it.[54] He has not heard from you regarding it. Thinking you had not received it, I am sending you herewith a copy.

This article seems not only to make out that Mr. Schilling was a part of the physical force party, but also that he betrayed his companions, and of course this is distressing him a great deal.

I am not writing to you professionally about this matter, but I feel that I know you well enough to know that you would not do anybody any injustice knowing it

53. Randolph eventually pleaded guilty to burglary and robbery and was sentenced to at least five years in prison. His wife was released without charges. Lindsey to Darrow, 24 May 1922, TLc, DLC, Lindsey Papers.

54. Stone reported in his autobiography that during the days of the famous Haymarket bombing (1886), "[w]hile the anarchists were plotting," George Schilling "frequently called at [his] office and told [him] of the progress of 'the impending revolution.'" Melville E. Stone, *Fifty Years a Journalist* (Garden City, NY: Doubleday, Page, 1921), 174. As editor of the *Chicago Daily News,* Stone had done much to build up hostility against the anarchists before their trial. Paul Avrich, *The Haymarket Tragedy* (Princeton: Princeton University Press, 1984), 338. Schilling, on the other hand, was always an active supporter of the Haymarket defendants, and he would have been bothered by the implication in Stone's autobiography that he had covertly worked against them.

and if you did one without knowing it, you would be glad to make it good so far as possible.

I think you will remember Mr. Schilling well enough to know that he was always a non-resistant and that the last thing in his nature would be to betray any person.

He was a member of the Free Trade Club, as I was, with you and many others, and his ideas are pretty well known. He has received letters from Lyman Gage,[55] Andrew Adair[56] who was formerly in your composing room for many years, whom you will remember, Judge E. O. Brown,[57] Dr. William Salter[58] and others, concerning his views and activities.

Of course Mr. Schilling is not looking for money and has no purpose, except to protect his name.

Won't you take this up seriously and see what you think is right about it in the way of satisfying his feelings. I think most anything that would set him right would be entirely satisfactory.

Very truly yours, | Clarence Darrow.

MS: TLS, ICN, Stone Papers, Box 1, Folder 95. INSIDE ADDRESS: Mr. Melville Stone | 51 Chambers Street, | New York, | N.Y.

TO BENJAMIN SCHLESINGER • CHICAGO • THURSDAY 3 AUGUST 1922

Chicago, August 3, 1922.

Dear Mr. Schlesinger:—

I am just sending you a wire that you may use my name in the matter of the prosecution in Russia against Socialists.[59]

55. Lyman Gage (1836–1927), Chicago banker and secretary of the treasury under President McKinley. While working as vice president of the First National Bank in Chicago, Gage was an active supporter of the Haymarket defendants.
56. Andrew Adair (1851?–1936), printer. Adair started as an apprentice printer at the age of twelve and worked for the next seventy years as a printer in Chicago, working for several Chicago newspapers.
57. Edward Osgood Brown (1847–1923), lawyer and judge. Brown obtained an A.B. from Brown University, 1867, attended Harvard Law School, and began practicing law in Chicago in 1872. He served as a judge on the Circuit Court of Cook County, Illinois, 1903–15, and then returned to the practice of law. He was active in the single-tax movement and wrote papers and pamphlets on political and historical subjects.
58. William Salter.
59. Schlesinger was trying to garner public support for leaders of the Socialist Revolutionary Party in Russia who were on trial by a tribunal of the Soviet government for treasonous crimes. The tribunal refused to allow the defendants to present witnesses and documents in their defense and otherwise conducted the trial in an extremely biased manner. A few days after this letter, on 7 August 1922, the tribunal announced the death penalty for twelve of the defendants. Shortly after this announcement, the defendants' sentences were stayed on the condition that there be no acts against the Soviet regime by the SRP. Fourteen years later, in 1936, Joseph Stalin ordered the survivors executed and "[t]hey were shot in a routine fashion without public announcement." David Shub, "The Trial of the SRs," *Russian Review* 23 (October 1964): 362–69. Many Western intellectuals and socialists voiced their support for the defendants during the proceedings, including Anatole France, H. G. Wells, George Bernard Shaw, Eugene Debs, Albert Einstein, and Bertrand Russell. See Marc Jansen, *A Show Trial under Lenin: The Trial of the Socialist Revolutionaries, Moscow 1922* (The Hague: Martinus Nijhoff, 1982), 166.

Of course I do not want to see these people executed. It may be that they have been conspiring against the government and perhaps connected with some killings, but I know what their purpose was. However, it demonstrates that radicals are just like other people which I have known for a good many years. I think it would be unwise to send anything in the way of criticism either of the trial or the accusation. Very likely these people are just like anybody else who conspires against the government and no doubt they are doing it from high motives. Still, all governments act alike to protect themselves. However, their lives should be saved and then before very long, they would be pardoned. Anyhow, whatever you do is satisfactory to me and you may use my name.

Truly yours, | Clarence Darrow

MS: TLS, NIC, Schlesinger Papers. INSIDE ADDRESS: Mr. Benjamin Schlesinger, | 3 W. 16th Street, | New York, N.Y.

TO MARY FIELD PARTON • EN ROUTE TO NEW YORK CITY • FRIDAY 8 SEPTEMBER 1922

PENNSYLVANIA SYSTEM | BROADWAY LIMITED Sept 8th

Dear Mary

Am on my way to N.Y. for a few days. Shall send you a book from there which I hope you will like. Have been loafing all summer. Took an automobile trip of 2,500 miles through Canada & then went to Colorado & loafed with my boy & grandchildren. Seems as if I had grown weary of work & the world, but suppose it is time. Any how I have seen the show, & have no desire to see much more and certainly not to do it again here or elsewhere. Your letter from California was forwarded to me at Colorado. Yes I have read Berman.[60] It is a remarkable book. The scientists generally think it is too emphatic & positive, still it is one the people are reading & all the better for being strong and lucid. The scientific world is rapidly solving the origin & method of life & learning all about the conduct of man. Of course we are only a machine responding to stimuli, good & bad. Moral concepts are going into the descent with intelligent people and either praise or blame have no longer any justification. It is all very interesting but it will never effect the mass of people who are not moved by scientific conceptions, but work automatically and more through mass psycology. I don't know that the world will ever be any better or kindlier—we must take it as it is and excuse the human animal as we do all others.

I am growing a more confirmed pessimist all the time. Nothing is worth while except to keep the emotions at work so we can forget life, at least my part of it. How I wish I could talk it all over with you. Sometime I hope I shall. What you say about the cooling of the passions is likewise true. They have a distinct function & when they have finished their work we should rejoice. I do for one. Nirvana is the only thing that is really alluring.

60. Darrow is likely referring to Louis Berman's first book, *The Glands Regulating Personality* (New York: Macmillan, 1921).

As I grow older I think I grow more reconciled to life & death, and neither expect or hope for any thing. The desire for rest and peace comes over me as a premonition of the endless rest & peace. Of course the mountains and woods & water are beautiful, and give a certain pleasure. Still it is not the peace of Nirvana. I am anxious to see your book.[61] I know you can write. If you don't get a publisher let me try. I hope you too are getting peace & quiet as you grow older.

I never can be thankful enough for our long & helpfull friendship. It has been a great deal in my life & will be to the end. I always love your letters and get everything from them. I hope Sarah[62] will sometime find rest. Life is terribly hard while one tries to do things and imagines they can. When [I] look in the glass to comb my hair I can see the grey slowly coming on & it gives me pleasure. It is a part of the whole premonition.

Love always | Clarence D.

MS: ALS, ICN, Parton-Darrow Papers, Box 1, Folder 9. ENVELOPE ADDRESS: Mrs. Mary Parton | San Francisco | Cal. | 1607 Taylor St. POSTMARK: New York City, 8 September 1922.

TO E. W. SCRIPPS • CHICAGO • MONDAY 30 OCTOBER 1922

DARROW, SISSMAN, HOLLY & CARLIN October 30, 1922.

My Dear Mr. Scripps:—

I was glad to get your letter and know what you thought about the book.[63] If it agrees with your opinions, I am pretty well satisfied it is all right. If you and I can agree, we ought not to need anything else.

I wish I could go to Wood's Hole some time. I do not know whether I could get in with the bunch or not, but would go if I thought I could.[64]

The biological part of the book ought to pretty nearly reflect Conklin's views. I have certainly read him more than any other biologist and in the main, I think he is right, although I do not especially admire his last book.[65]

61. The book to which Darrow is referring is unknown. Parton edited *The Autobiography of Mother Jones* (Chicago: Charles H. Kerr Pub. Co., 1925), but her work on that book probably did not begin until 1923 or later. See Elliott J. Gorn, *Mother Jones: The Most Dangerous Woman in America* (New York: Hill & Wang, 2001), 281.
62. Sara Bard Field.
63. Scripps had complimented Darrow on his recent book, *Crime: Its Cause and Treatment*. Scripps to Darrow, TLc, 18 October 1922, OAU, Scripps Papers, Box 20, Folder 11.
64. Scripps told Darrow that he had spent a few days in August "with a whole bunch of biologists at Woods Hole," a marine biological laboratory on the coast of Massachusetts.
65. Darrow is referring to the prominent biologist Edwin Grant Conklin (1863–1952), whose "last book" was probably *The Direction of Human Evolution* (New York: Charles Scribner's Sons, 1922). Conklin obtained his Ph.D. from Johns Hopkins University, 1891, and taught biology at Ohio Wesleyan University, 1891–94, Northwestern University, 1894–96, the University of Pennsylvania, 1896–1908, and Princeton University, 1908–33, where he was also chairman of the biology department. Conklin spent most of his summers at the marine biological laboratory in Woods Hole.

I am not quite certain what I said about the subnormal settling in America and the West. I have read the book so many times that I hate to look at it again. My impression is, however, that I did not put it that strong.[66]

Let us see whether we can agree on the people who are constantly going West from the centers of population. Barring the spirit of adventure, which no doubt attracts some strong men, the people who really settle in a new country are those who are poor and who have given up the race in favor of the stronger and the richer. I well remember those that went from a little country town in Ohio where I lived and who settled in Kansas in the early days. They were all poor, coming from a class of shiftless and often regarded as worthless. California has a little different history, due to the gold excitement in '49 and perhaps since that, due to the lure of climate, which has taken many strong men, although I am not stuck on the Iowans who make up the larger part of Southern California. I still believe that the people who migrate to a new country are in the main, weaker physically, intellectually and certainly financially than the ones who stay at home. I cannot understand why they would take the hardships of pioneering, except for this. Of course, as I have said, allowance must be made for the minority who are moved by the spirit of adventure. Assuming, what is no doubt true, that the average wealth is greater in California and probably in a number of other Western States, that the number of college graduates are greater, this does not prove that those sections were settled by the strongest people. One cannot discuss questions of human conduct without making due allowance for environment, as well as heredity. The environment for getting rich, was very much easier in the West and men of inferior capacity could accumulate wealth there, while superior men would be poor in the East. This has happened in thousands of cases. This in turn would place their sons in college and raise both the level of property and the level of intelligence. Then too, you must distinguish between native intelligence and the results real and seeming that come from education. The well educated man of poor intellect shows up much better than a strong man with no education. Many college graduates are not much over the moron class, although by means of their education and association and wealth, they have the reputation of intelligence and may doubtless do many things much better than a more intellectual man without education. You have seen this in your daily experience through life and it seems to me to be entirely in accordance with biology and the nature of things.

Much of the work of the world, in business and the professions, is purely routine and cannot be done successfully without education. It does not require a great amount of

66. Scripps told Darrow that he was "surprised" by Darrow's "general statement that it was the sub-normal men that first migrated to America, and second, that it was the sub-normal men who were adventurers and pioneers and had settled the West." Scripps said his own experience had been that "the best men and women of the country are those living farthest west" and that "when one travels east," including all the way to Russia, "one finds men and women of constantly decreasing stature, constantly decreasing all-around mentality, and constantly decreasing per capita wealth." Scripps maintained that the wealth of the people in California was three time greater per capita "than that of the people of the states east of the Mississippi" and that more people in California attended colleges and universities than in the eastern states. Scripps to Darrow, 18 October 1922, TT, OAU, Scripps Papers, Box 20, Folder 11.

strength to get a conventional education that enables one to get by, especially where such persons also have money.

As you suggest in your letter, there are many captains of industry who have less intelligence than their employees.[67] A close examination would show why and it would generally show that the employers have had a better chance.

It would hardly do to say that the men who carried down the fortunes of the Astors, the Vanderbilts and the Fields were men of unusual mental strength, but with education and association and understanding the routine of affairs, they were able to do what the more intelligent men could not possibly do. We have had, probably now have, for Presidents of the United States, men who would grade rather low in tests as to native ability, but fortuitous circumstances have placed them where they could get by without ability.

I am glad you like the chapter on "Luck and Chance". It seems to me to be responsible for most of the good and ill that befall man in the world.

I do not know whether you are familiar with the story of Jonathan Edwards.[68] This is quoted by the eugenists as an example of breeding. The number of Supreme Court judges, both Federal and of the various States, college professors and presidents, bankers and lawyers and one vice president, is very startling. Eugenists write of the Edwards family as if Jonathan Edwards had no ancestors, but that he was specially made by the Lord to raise up strong men, which of course means, mainly conventional men. I find that Jonathan Edwards' grandmother, Elizabeth Tuthill,[69] was a woman who would now be classed as not much different from a harlot. She had a brother who murdered one of the family and a sister who killed another. She was divorced from the Edwards branch, I presume, for adultery and remarried. Little came of the descendants of the second marriage, which shows that the second husband did not contribute much, if it shows anything, of which I am doubtful. One of her sisters started another line and from that line came Grant, Grover Cleveland and Mrs Theodore Roosevelt, as well as a number of other strong people, so Elizabeth with all her tendencies to violate traditions, must have carried down

67. Scripps told Darrow: "I have written a number of disquisition[s] besides formulating several hundred pages of autobiographical notes, the whole purpose of all these being to disabuse the minds of at least many of the several thousands of my employees of the idea that I was in any way better equipped than the general run of them, and that therefore none of them had any poorer chances of making a successful life than I have had. I deem it an outrage for any young man to excuse himself, to himself and others, for lack of accomplishment on the ground that he, as a machine, as you call him, is in anyway inferior to the machine that happens to be his employer." Ibid.

68. Jonathan Edwards (1703–58), Congregational preacher, renowned colonial figure, and considered the greatest theologian of American Puritanism. Among his many prominent descendants was his grandson Aaron Burr (1756–1836), vice president of United States.

69. Elizabeth Tuttle (1645–1718), paternal grandmother of Jonathan Edwards. Elizabeth married Richard Edwards (1647–1718) in 1667, when she was pregnant with another man's child. In 1688, Richard tried unsuccessfully to divorce Elizabeth. Two years later he succeeded. The grounds included frequent adultery and Elizabeth's threat to kill Richard in his sleep. Before the divorce, Elizabeth's brother, Benjamin, murdered one of his other sisters, Sarah, with an axe, and another sister of Elizabeth, Mercy, killed her own son, also with an axe. Darrow states in this letter that Elizabeth remarried after her divorce, but there is apparently no record of her marrying again. Sybil Smith, "What Is It with Those Tuttles?" *Ancestry Magazine*, May–June 1995, 4–8.

the germplasm. Where she got it, I do not know. I do know that the modern eugenists would have said that Elizabeth should not have had children. I think this would have been best, for Jonathan Edwards was nowhere near as good for the race as the elder Jukes.[70] I am quite distrustful of the whole eugenists idea. I would rather trust nature with all her vagaries, than to submit the question of ancestry to a town meeting.

I had a fine time with Neg[71] last summer. He told me he was going to visit you after our vacation. I have not heard from him lately, because I have not written him. I expect to go to Miami some time in January for two or three weeks. I wish I might run on to you.

I share your views as to the good that a book like mine will do and as to the insignificance of one man and for that matter the whole damn race.

With kindest personal regards, I am,

Your friend, | Clarence Darrow.

MS: TLS, OAU, Scripps Papers, Box 39, Folder 7. INSIDE ADDRESS: Mr. E.W. Scripps, | United Bank Building, | Cincinnati, | Ohio.

TO E. W. SCRIPPS • CHICAGO • MONDAY 4 DECEMBER 1922

DARROW, SISSMAN, HOLLY & CARLIN December 4, 1922.

My Dear Mr. Scripps:—

I have just received your letter and still think I can go.[72] I am very thankful to you for giving me a chance.

From what you state about inviting Ritter and some others,[73] something occurred to me which perhaps I should not mention. I have learned enough about polite society to know that it is not polite to ask for anything from one who is doing what you are for me, but I am not asking that. If you have the room and want it, Professor Starr[74] who is one

70. The "elder Jukes" is a reference to "Max Jukes," a fictitious name for a real person who was the subject—together with seven generations of his supposed descendants in upstate New York—of a famous study of criminality, poverty, and other social problems within a family. The study was done by the social scientist Richard L. Dugdale (1841–83) and published as *"The Jukes": A Study in Crime, Pauperism, Disease and Heredity* (New York: G.P. Putnam's Sons, 1877). Dugdale's (now discredited) study showed a high incidence of social problems within the "Jukes" family, which Dugdale attributed to genetic and environmental causes. His study was often cited by eugenicists as evidence that "bad blood" caused these problems, and "Max Jukes" and his descendants were contrasted with Jonathan Edwards and his descendants in eugenics literature.

71. Negley D. Cochran.

72. Scripps wrote to Darrow from Florida explaining that he would probably arrive with his yacht in San Diego by 1 February 1923, that he would leave for the Sandwich Islands on about 1 March, and that he would probably not continue his cruise more than six months after leaving San Diego. Scripps to Darrow, 20 November 1922, TT, OAU, Scripps Papers, Box 20, Folder 11.

73. Scripps told Darrow that he had invited William Emerson Ritter (1856–1944) and two other scientists to join him on the cruise. Ibid. Ritter was a professor of zoology at the University of California, Berkeley, an author of several scientific and philosophical books, and a good friend of Scripps. Together, in 1903, Scripps and Ritter founded what has been known since 1925 as the Scripps Institution of Oceanography, in La Jolla, California.

74. Frederick Starr.

of the leading anthropologists of the world and an all around well-informed man, has been in Japan many times and is a great traveller and knows all about the kind of people we are to meet and a very interesting and well informed man. I know he would fit in well, but of course I have not mentioned it to him and would not want it unless it would be convenient and I thought you would like to do it, in which event I will take it up with him. He is leaving the University in spring, as he is eligible to pension, at which time he proposes to keep on travelling, as he has done all his life.

With thanks and best wishes, I am,

Your friend, | Clarence Darrow

P. S. I hope you will be able to persuade Neg to go.

MS: TLS, OAU, Scripps Papers, Box 39, Folder 7. INSIDE ADDRESS: Mr. E.W. Scripps, | United Bank Building, | Cincinnati, O.

TO PAUL DARROW • CHICAGO • MONDAY 4 DECEMBER 1922

DARROW, SISSMAN, HOLLY & CARLIN Dec 4

Dear Paul

I have been away a good deal lately trying to beat the new constitution which will be voted on the 12th. I think we will beat it.[75]

Your report was mighty good for Oct. especially the net which is *important.*

I have got my note in the bank paid so I can no doubt help if you need it.

I am to speak in Denver on the 24th of Dec. Shall arrive there in the morning unless I go direct to Greeley. If I go there first will wire you & you might come down & call for me at Savoy. Shall speak for the Open Forum. Am not sure whether afternoon or evening. You can find out by writing Judge Lindsey.[76] Can stay only a short time probably until the 30th.

C. S. D.

MS: ALS, MnU-L, Darrow Collection. DATE: reference to vote on state constitution.

75. From January 1920 until September 1922, a constitutional convention was assembled in Illinois for the purpose of considering amendments to the state constitution. The convention—which was labeled "a conservative body"—produced a whole new document (instead of select amendments), which united some otherwise diverse groups against the proposed constitution. Among the more controversial features were provisions that would authorize income taxes, consolidate the courts and give the state supreme court authority to make rules of practice and procedure, provide Chicago the power to frame its own charter and obtain powers of municipal home rule, and permanently limit Cook County's representation in the state senate to one-third of the seats (regardless of the county's percentage of the state's population). The proposed constitution was rejected at a special election on 12 December, by a margin of nearly five to one. See Walter F. Dodd, "Illinois Rejects New Constitution," *American Political Science Review* 17 (February 1923): 70–72. Darrow gave several speeches against the proposed constitution. See, e.g., "Darrow Debates Basic Law with Colored Framer," *Chicago Tribune,* 27 November 1922 (noting that in this debate, Darrow's opposition "was centered on the provisions granting to judges the right to deny bail to persons charged with crimes").
76. Benjamin Lindsey.

TO MARY FIELD PARTON • CHICAGO • THURSDAY 1 FEBRUARY 1923

Feby 1st

Dear Mary

If I ever delay writing so long again, I won't expect you to answer a letter. The fact is I began one two weeks ago. In the mean time I have been to N.Y and have tried a case and rushed around like mad—for what—D–n fi-kno.[77] Life has moved or rather rushed along with me without much change. I scarcely feel that it is going yet it is. Some one is always waiting in the outside office until some one else goes, and I hear an endless sound of troubles & sorrows from morning until night. Talk of *Grand* Juries, Courts, Jails, Penitentiaries &c. &c. until I wish I was on a desert Island where none of these signs of progress have ever appeared. I have been pretty busy in court this winter and am now going into the school graft cases (so called) which will probably take forever.[78] One of my good friends (formerly of a settlement) came in yesterday panned that I should defend men accused of graft, and wanted to know why I did. I told her for the money and because I hated jails and good people. I said that I had fought for many things that her people believed in, but I had never seen the time that one of them had sent me a case where there was a fee; they had sent many poor to me, that no one else would look after, but if one had money they sent them to a respectable lawyer, which is true. Any how it never occurs to me that I should refuse to defend any one. All I dread about it is the hard work and the long time it will take.

I was in New York not long ago where I debated again the old question is life worth living, which it isn't. Still all the dope fiends profess that it is. They think that one is not only foolish but wicked if he is a pessimist. Every one of them takes dope and yet they send men to jail for peddling the only kind of dope that will work on me. Really there are a lot of fools in this world, and it is getting no wiser.

I saw Dudley Malone & Doris[79] in N.Y. They are just as lovable as ever. Doris is still trying to find out things that females can complain about, with Alice Paul[80] & the rest of them really grieving because they got the amendment for it took away one of the emotions

77. The case that Darrow tried involved William H. H. Miller, a state director of registration and education in Illinois. Miller and three other defendants, represented by Darrow and another lawyer, were charged with conspiracy to sell physicians' and pharmacists' licenses to unqualified people. Miller and one other defendant were found guilty. "Miller Guilty of Grafting," *Chicago Tribune,* 29 January 1923.

78. By the "school graft cases," Darrow is referring to the trial of some twenty men, including many city officials, who were indicted and tried together in 1923 for conspiracy to defraud the Chicago school system of about $1 million through bribes, phony contracts and bids, and excessive purchase prices for school supplies, among other acts. The most prominent of the defendants was Fred Lundin (1868–1947), a business man and former Republican congressman from Illinois, 1909–11. Lundin was a confidant of William "Big Bill" Thompson (1867–1944), the mayor of Chicago from 1915 to 1923 and then again from 1927 to 1931. Thompson declined to seek reelection as mayor in 1923 because of the controversies surrounding the indictments.

79. Doris Stevens (1888–1963), suffragist. Stevens graduated from Oberlin College, 1911, worked in a settlement in Cleveland, Ohio, taught high school, and then became an organizer for the Congressional Union for Woman Suffrage. Later, she was also very active in the National Woman's Party. In 1917, she was arrested for demonstrating for suffrage outside the White House. She was represented by Dudley Field Malone, to whom she was married from 1921 to 1929. After 1920, she devoted more of her time to international feminist activities.

that made life bearable. It is awful to have nothing to do but to think about yourself. It is better to love money and try to get it. I was out to Greeley over the holidays to see my boy & his family. The three girls are growing fast, the oldest beginning to suggest a new generation to push me further toward oblivion, and might. It beats the devil how we pushed the others off & are now being pushed. What a senseless fool thing the march of the generations of men to nothingness. And how damn foolish to think any of it has any meaning to one who thinks and does not take dope. I still have many friends, but am not so ambitious to go out of my way to find them, like them when they come where I am, which they often do, & sometimes hunt them up. Some people think that this means growing wisdom & virtue but I know better. I know exactly what it means & somehow have no regrets. I read a good deal. I wonder if you have seen the novels of Jerald O'Donell.[81] He was a Catholic Priest, in Ireland but left them & his stories tell why. They are very good & beautiful. If you haven't seen them I will send you one. Of course I read Berman[82] and believe it is true even if perhaps exaggerated. I like science more & more; especially those branches which deal with life and its manifestations. I have quite a fever for George Moore[83] whom I had somehow overlooked. Have been reading quite a number of his. As soon as I finish this case I am going to begin an other book, this I hope to make much better than any of the others, it may & may not be. Any how I think I can do it. The Crime book is selling very well, have had the very best reviews, but people don't seem to really buy books, they borrow them or wait until the author sends them one. Still I write for fun of it, so I am not disappointed. I don't wonder people do not read. It is much more thrilling to live a story than it is to read about it.

Margarett Johansen was in yesterday and we both had a good deal to say about you & both wished we might see you perhaps some time we will—Perhaps.

Any how, always with best thoughts & wishes and always your friend

Clarence Darrow

MS: ALS, ICN, Parton-Darrow Papers, Box 1, Folder 9. PLACE: no reason to doubt Chicago. DATE: "1923" appended, probably in Parton's hand.

In the late 1920s and early 1930s, she was a member of the national executive committee of the American League to Abolish Capital Punishment, of which Darrow was president. She wrote an account of the final years of the militant struggle for female suffrage in *Jailed for Freedom* (New York: Boni & Liveright, 1920).

80. Alice Paul (1885–1977), suffragist. Paul graduated from Swarthmore College, 1905, earned an M.A. in sociology from the University of Pennsylvania, 1912, a J.D. from Washington College of Law, 1922, and a Ph.D. from American University, 1928. She was a founder of the Congressional Union for Women's Suffrage in 1913, which eventually became the National Woman's Party. She devoted much of her life to campaigning for the rights of women.
81. Darrow is no doubt referring to Gerald O'Donovan (1871–1942), Roman Catholic priest and novelist. O'Donovan was born in Ireland and served as the priest for a parish there for eight years, 1896–1904, until a strained relationship with a conservative bishop made him quit. He left the priesthood, moved to London, married, and became a novelist. His best-known work was the semi-autobiographical *Father Ralph* (London: Macmillan, 1913), which was highly critical of the Catholic Church and the priesthood in Ireland in the early 1900s.
82. Louis Berman.
83. George Moore (1852–1933), Irish writer and author of many novels, including *Esther Waters* (London: Walter Scott, 1894), *Evelyn Innes* (New York: D. Appleton, 1898), and *Sister Teresa* (Philadelphia: J.B. Lippincott, 1901).

TO EDWARD BOYCE • CHICAGO • SATURDAY 10 FEBRUARY 1923

DARROW, SISSMAN, HOLLY & CARLIN Feby 10

My Dear Boyce

For years I have been intending to write you. I am afraid I did not even write when you were good enough to help in the most trying time of my life.[84] In spite of that I have always appreciated and valued your friendship and only regret we live so far apart. I have been working hard as always & although the years are accumulating I am well and strong & do not take life to heart. Mrs. Darrow too is well. I would be glad to know how you are and trust this will reach you. If I am ever your way I shall hunt you up. Senator Pettigrew told of having a nice visit with you some time ago.

Always Your friend | Clarence Darrow

MS: ALS, WaSpHiE, Boyce Papers. NOTE: at the bottom of the letter in another hand is written "Answered Oct. 21, 1923"; no letter from Boyce to Darrow was found.

TO E. W. SCRIPPS • CHICAGO • FRIDAY 16 FEBRUARY 1923

DARROW, SISSMAN, HOLLY & CARLIN Feby 16

My Dear Mr. Scripps

I am heart broken over not going with you also a little ashamed. I had expected to be sea sick all the way for I generally am on a big ship but wanted so much to go that I was willing to be sick (and I hate sea-sickness). The fact is I couldn't afford to miss the trial of this case which will be long & hard.[85] I have seen so many radicals broke in their last years that I always had a foolish & unholy fear of alms, and inconvenience. Perhaps it was a sort of foolish pride. And while I could afford to take the trip & lose the time as it is still I would have been obliged to come back to work & I didn't want to after this case. With what I have I can live comfortably (and will probably die at once in consequence) and I thought I ought to do it. If you are lingering around China or Japan when my case is finished I will go there at once and take the rest of the trip with you. Prof Starr is going to leave Seattle about July 15th going directly to Japan. He has been there many times & knows the leading men & I want you to meet him there, if you will be there about that time.

I want you to know how much I appreciate your kindness & how disappointed I am.

Your friend | Clarence Darrow.

Love to Neg, hope he goes.

MS: ALS, OAU, Scripps Papers, Box 39, Folder 9. DATE: reference to trip.

84. Boyce sent Darrow one hundred dollars shortly before the beginning of Darrow's first trial for jury bribery in Los Angeles. See Darrow to Boyce, 12 February 1912, n.87.
85. Darrow is referring to the trial of Fred Lundin, who had recently posted a bond for his release pending his trial (which didn't start until April). "Lundin Free on $10,000 Bond," *Chicago Tribune,* 3 February 1923.

TO THE *CHICAGO TRIBUNE* • CHICAGO • WEDNESDAY 4 JULY 1923

Editor of The Tribune:

I was very much interested in Mr. Bryan's letter to THE TRIBUNE and in your editorial reply.[86] I have likewise followed Mr. Bryan's efforts to shut out the teaching of science from the public schools and his questionnaires to various college-professors who believe in evolution and still profess Christianity. No doubt his questions to the professors, if answered, would tend to help clear the issue, and likewise a few questions to Mr. Bryan and the fundamentalists, if fairly answered, might serve the interests of reaching the truth—all of this assumes that truth is desirable.

CREATION OF THE EARTH

For this reason I think it would be helpful if Mr. Bryan would answer the following questions: Do you believe in the literal interpretation of the whole Bible? Is the account of the creation of the earth and all life in Genesis literally true, or is it an allegory? Was the earth made in six literal days, measured by the revolution of the earth on its axis? Was the sun made on the fourth day to give light to the earth by day and the moon made on the same day to give light by night, and were the stars made for the benefit of the earth? Did God create man on the sixth day? Did God rest on the seventh day?

GARDEN OF EDEN

Did god place man in the Garden of Eden and tell him he could eat of every tree except the tree of knowledge? Was Eve literally made from the rib of Adam? Did the serpent induce Eve to eat of the tree of knowledge? Did the eating of this fruit cause Adam and Eve to know that they were naked? Did God curse the serpent for tempting Eve and decree that thereafter he should go on his belly? How did he travel before that time? Did God tell Eve that thereafter he would multiply the sorrows of all women and that their husband should rule over them?

WHAT ABOUT FLOOD?

Did God send a flood covering the whole earth, even the tops of the highest mountains, and destroy "all flesh that has the breath of life," excepting the inmates of the

86. Darrow is referring to an exchange that apparently started with an editorial by the *Tribune* that mocked Bryan's opposition to the sale of alcohol and teaching of evolution in schools. "Bow to Bryan," *Chicago Tribune*, 10 June 1923. Bryan replied to the editorial with a long letter, arguing that the *Tribune* had misrepresented his views and that his actual views "are held by a large majority of the church members of all the Christian churches." "W.G.N. Put 'on Carpet'; Gets a Bryan Lashing," *Chicago Tribune*, 20 June 1923. This was followed by another editorial reprinted from the *Peoria (Illinois) Transcript*. "Mr. Bryan's Definitions," *Chicago Tribune*, 29 June 1923.

ark? Did God command Noah to build an ark for him and his family and to take on board a male and female of every living species on earth? Did he build the ark and gather the pairs of all animals on the earth and the food and water necessary to preserve them? As there were no ships in those days, except the ark, how did Noah gather them from all the continents and islands of the earth? Did he then cause it to rain forty days and forty nights and destroy every living thing on the earth? Did all these living things enter the ark on the second month and 17th day of the month? Were all the high mountains on all the earth covered? Did the waters prevail on the earth for 150 days?

ARARAT AND THE RAINBOW

Did the ark rest on Mount Ararat in the seventh month and the tenth day of the month? Did God set a rainbow in the heavens for a token that the world would not again be destroyed by flood? Was this the first rainbow that ever appeared? According to the old testament, was this not about 1,750 years B.C.? Is not history full of proof that all colors and kinds of people lived over large and remote parts of the earth within fifty years after this time? Were the pairs of animals sent to every quarter of the earth after the flood? How could many species that are found nowhere but in Australia or other far off places get there and why did they not stop on the way? Was there any more water on the earth in Noah's day than any other time before or since? Is not all the water that falls drawn from the reservoirs of water on the earth? Is it possible to increase the amount of water on any part of the earth without drawing it from another part? Does not water seek its level? Shortly after the flood was the whole earth of one language? Did the inhabitants begin to build the Tower of Babel so they might reach the heavens? Did God confound their language so they could not complete the tower? How high would the tower have had to be built to reach the heavens? Was the confounding of tongues at the Tower of Babel the cause of the many languages spoken by the people of the earth? Did the Lord prepare a big fish to swallow Jonah and did he lie for three days and three nights in the whale's belly when he was spewed out on dry land? Was Lot's wife turned into a literal pillar of salt for turning back and looking at Sodom and Gomorrah when she was fleeing from their destruction? Did Balaam's ass speak to him in human language? Did the walls of Jerico fall down flat from the soldiers and priests marching around it and blowing on the ram's horn?

JOSHUA AND THE SUN

Did the sun stand still to give Joshua time to fight a battle? If the sun had stood still, would that have lengthened the day? If instead of the sun standing still, the earth had stopped revolving on its axis, what would have happened to the earth and all life thereon? Under the biblical chronology, Was not the earth created less than 6,000 years ago? Were there not many flourishing civilizations on the earth 10,000 years ago? According to the same chronology, Was not Adam created less than 6,000 years ago? Are there not

evidences in writing and hieroglyphics and the evidence of man's handiwork which show that man has been on the earth more than 50,000 years? Are there no human remains that carry their age on the earth back to at least 100,000 years? Does not geology show by fossil remains, by the cutting away of rock for river beds, by deposit of all sorts, that the earth is much more than a million years and probably many million years old? Did Christ drive devils out of two sick men and did the devils request that they should be driven into a large herd of swine and were the devils driven into the swine and did the swine run off a high bank, and were they drowned in the sea? Was this literally true, or does it simply show the attitude of the age toward the cause of sickness and affliction? Can one not be a Christian without believing in the literal truth of the narrations of the Bible here mentioned? Would you forbid the public schools from teaching anything in conflict with the literal statement referred to?

Questions might be extended indefinitely but a specific answer to these might make it clear what one must believe to be a "fundamentalist."[87]

Very truly yours, | Clarence Darrow.

MS: "Darrow Asks W. J. Bryan to Answer These," *Chicago Tribune*, 4 July 1923. DATE: publication of letter.

TO FREMONT OLDER • CHICAGO • SATURDAY 14 JULY 1923

Chicago, July 14, 1923

Dear Fremont:

Your letter just came to hand. I am sorry you have been ill and glad you are getting better, and likewise I am interested in the way you treated your sickness. So far as you are personally concerned, I am sure I would not mourn over your death, but would feel relieved to feel that you got through with it and it was not still before you. I would feel very sad about it, but that would be purely personal, because I would miss you. Of course my

87. Bryan, who was attending a Christian conference at the Billy Sunday Tabernacle in Winona Lake, Indiana, replied to this letter in an interview the same day that it was published: "I know Mr. Darrow's attitude towards religion and I can give you an interview before reading his questions as well as after. | Mr. Darrow is one of two atheists with whom I am acquainted. I am not worried about an atheist who admits he is one. The man who denies the existence of God is not likely to have much influence, because evidences of a creator are so plain and innumerable that atheism when avowed is not nearly so dangerous as so-called theistic evolution. | Theistic evolution lulls Christians to sleep. It is an anaesthetic which deadens pain while religion is being removed. The theistic evolutionist assumes the existence of God, but puts him so far away that the influence upon life is weakened when not entirely destroyed. | The evolutionist claims that evolution was God's method, but the method, when carried to its logical conclusion, eliminates all that is vital in the Bible. Evolution has no place for the miracle and the supernatural. That leaves the Bible merely a man made book, and the Bible, shorn of its divine authority, would be hardly as influential as a book that never claimed to be divine. If it is convicted of being an imposter, it is the greatest of imposters. | My controversy is not with atheists like Mr. Darrow, but with those who claim to be Christians and who substitute the guesses of evolution for the word of God. | I decline to turn aside to enter into controversy with those who reject the Bible as Mr. Darrow does." "Bryan Brushes Darrow Bible Queries Aside," *Chicago Tribune*, 5 July 1923.

philosophy is practically the same as yours. Intellectually I know that life is a damned humbug and not worth while. I am quite certain I would not care to be born again, or go through it again, yet I know I will fight as hard as you will when it is coming to an end. Man is just like every other organism, whether a tree, a rabbit, or the Socialist Party. It fights to preserve itself. It is instinctive in the organism and we cannot help it. Life must be preserved by those who fight death. In fact I think everybody fights, even the man who suicides does not do it until the will to live has been overcome. I am quite sure that you cannot do anything with your mental equipment, whatever that is, to prevent your physical reaction which makes you fight death. I often have been told in my debates that if I really believed that annihilation was preferable to life, I would suicide. Of course I know this is not so and that one's thoughts and philosophy have nothing whatever to do with his conduct. His reactions are purely mechanistic and cannot be changed. These people are like the pacifists who get up organizations to prevent the war and who think they can educate man so that he will not fight. I used to believe it, but I know that I was ignorant and silly as they are. Pacifism is a good philosophy when you don't want to fight, but when you get mad you fight, because the instinctive side of man is in absolute mastery of it. But anyhow, I am glad you are better and hope you keep well.

I am always wishing I could see you. I would like to take another look at the California hills from your veranda, but I presume I never shall. There are a good many things that impel me to do it, and likewise not to do it, so that I have pretty much given up the idea that the forces that urge me to do it will ever predominate. This I regret, but so far cannot help it. I wish you would come here, or meet me some time in Colorado.

I have just got out of a big case, where I have had a three months' fight to keep twenty men out of prison.[88] We had a terrible man-hunt and a fierce public opinion, but we managed to overcome it and got a verdict of not guilty. This gives me some satisfaction which may last for forty-eight hours, and then I will have to look for some new emotion.

A few days ago Abby Scott Baker[89] went to California to see what she could do with Judge Rudkin to get him to show some consideration to the men he sentenced to prison.[90] I have known him since he was a boy and he is a good fellow and I cannot understand why he does not do it. I hope she will be successful. I know she will go and see you. She is a very interesting person.

Give my best wishes to Mrs. Older and let me hear from you when you feel like writing.

Always your friend, | Clarence Darrow. (Signed)

MS: TT, CU-BANC, Older Papers, Box 1.

88. On 13 July 1923, Fred Lundin and his codefendants were acquitted by the jury after less than four hours of deliberation.
89. Abby Scott Baker (1871–1944) was active in the suffrage movement and a leader in both the Congressional Union for Woman Suffrage and the National Woman's Party.
90. Darrow is referring to the members of the IWW who were convicted in Sacramento in January 1919 for subversive activities. See Darrow to Older, 27 December 1919, n.80.

TO PAUL DARROW • CHICAGO • SATURDAY 14 JULY 1923

July 14

Dear Paul

Your mother has concluded to go to Greeley next month and I just finished my case & shall go next week. Will be there around the 21st or 22d. Just finished Lundin case yesterday & it was a wild time when they were acquitted. I never saw such a happy crowd.

Mr. & Mrs. John Frances[91] are here and are driving through to California, & want Ruby & me to go with them as far as Colorado, so we shall do it. He will start Monday & we will start about two days later & we will pick them up in Iowa or at Omaha. They want to stay a few days in Greeley, perhaps a week & go to Estes Park. If you know a convenient place near bye where they can get one or two rooms you might arrange it. If not perhaps the Sterling would be all right. They naturally haven't much money to waste. Will keep you posted so you will know when we shall get there.

Hastily | C. S. D.

MS: ALS, MnU-L, Darrow Collection. DATE: reference to Lundin trial.

TO EDGAR LEE MASTERS • CHICAGO • THURSDAY 16 AUGUST 1923

DARROW, SISSMAN, HOLLY & CARLIN Aug 16th

Dear Ed

Sometime ago you spoke to me about getting into a good law office on a salary. A few days ago, such a position happened to be presented to me with the request that I find some one so I immediately thought of you, and made the suggestion, telling them that I was not sure whether you would take it. I was just called up & asked if I had seen you. It is in the corporation counsel's office. Frank Bush[92] has the swing of the place. The salary would be somewhere from $6,000 to 7,500 probably even more could be got later. It would be a fine place where you would be put in the way of business, and would not be obliged to work too hard. I don't know whether you would want to take it or whether you

91. Darrow is referring to John H. Francis and his wife, Lou Hott Francis (b. 1870). Darrow and Ruby did drive with them to Paul's house in Colorado. Interview with Mary Darrow Simonson, Honolulu, Hawaii, 15 September 1999.

92. Francis X. Busch (1879–1975), lawyer, educator, and writer. Busch was educated at the Illinois College of Law and DePaul University. He was admitted to the bar in 1901 and began private practice in Chicago. He was a private attorney in criminal and civil cases except when he was assistant corporation counsel of Chicago and attorney for the Chicago Civil Service Commission, 1904–6, master in chancery of the circuit court of Cook County, Illinois, 1920–23, and corporation counsel of Chicago, 1923–27, 1931. He was an instructor and lecturer in the evening division of the Illinois College of Law, 1901–12, and later dean of the evening law school at DePaul University, 1912–23. He wrote several books, including *In and out of Court* (Chicago: DePaul University Press, 1942), which contains some reminiscences of cases involving Darrow.

should take it, but if I wanted a good place with a good prospect for the future in the law line, I would take it. Mr. Bush wants to know tomorrow.

Yours | C. S. Darrow.[93]

MS: ALS, TxU-Hu, Masters Collection. DATE: letterhead and suggestion that Busch had just become corporation counsel and that Masters was still in Chicago (he moved to New York City in late 1923).

TO FREMONT OLDER • CHICAGO • WEDNESDAY 22 AUGUST 1923

DARROW, SISSMAN, POPHAM & CARLIN Aug 22d

Dear Fremont

Have you read G. Stanley Hall's book on Senescence.[94] If you haven't, get it. I am sure you would find it worth while. I did. Of course it is none too funny for us old fellows & still you & I have a habit of looking things in the face & somehow this didn't hurt me. Do you think your will to live grows stronger or weaker as you grow older? I believe mine weakens but am not quite certain.

I trust you are better & will be able to fairly enjoy the 10 or 12 yrs which are probably still to come. I am not sure that I hope for any more for you. Love to Cora—

Your friend always | Darrow.

MS: ALS, CU-BANC, Older Papers, Box 1. DATE: "[1923]" appended.

TO FREDERICK STARR • CHICAGO • FRIDAY 12 OCTOBER 1923

DARROW, SISSMAN, HOLLY & CARLIN Oct 12 1923

My dear Mr. Starr:

We were very much worried about you until we found in the newspapers and later by your postcard, that you were all right and in this country. As long as you got away without serious injury, it must have been a wonderful experience.[95] I shall try to get hold of a copy

93. The following note in Masters's hand—which might have been a draft of his response to Darrow's letter—is written at the end of the letter: "How can I think of such a thing with all on my mind that there is now? I'd have to be two gentlemen at once like Cerberus. What is the future? Shall I live with reference to food at 65 or write now and let the future rip? You ought to have some idea of this yourself. I shall be all right to-day anyway, except for the assaults of Envy, and the Dullness of those who didn't know, and the Greedy Gnats. E. L. M." Masters had recently gone through a bitter, very public, and costly divorce (in which Darrow had played some part), and his law business and literary career were in steep decline, all of which might account for the content and tone of this note. See Herbert K. Russell, *Edgar Lee Masters: A Biography* (Urbana: University of Illinois Press, 2001), 146–201; Darrow to Masters, 10 November 1919, n.79.

94. G. Stanley Hall, *Senescence: The Last Half of Life* (New York: D. Appleton, 1922). Older responded that he had enjoyed the book "immensely" and had recommended it to many friends. Older to Darrow, 27 August 1923, Tc, CU-BANC, Older Papers.

95. Starr had been in Japan when the great Kanto earthquake struck Tokyo, Yokohama, and surrounding areas on 1 September 1923. For nearly two weeks, there was no news on whether Starr had survived the earthquake. "Prof. Starr Safe in Japan," *Chicago Tribune*, 12 September 1923.

of the University paper to read an account that I hear you have given them, and if you should speak or write more fully on it, I wish you would send me a copy. Although I am a pessimist, I am glad you got out all right and your many friends feel the same.

Mrs. Darrow's brother, Bert Hamerstrom,[96] has located in Seattle and will call you. He is a fine young man, interested in all things that will interest you. I hope he won't bore you.

With best regards, I am | Your friend, | Clarence Darrow

MS: TLS, ICU, Starr Papers, Box 4, Folder 8. INSIDE ADDRESS: Dr. Frederick Starr, | 5727–35th Ave., N.E., | Seattle, Wash.

TO JULIUS F. TAYLOR • CHICAGO • WEDNESDAY 24 OCTOBER 1923

DARROW, SISSMAN, HOLLY & CARLIN Oct. 24, 1923.

Dear sir:

I desire to protest against the unfair treatment received by Edward H. Morris[97] at the hands of the Chicago Bar Association and its committee. It is unfortunate that such a direct insult should be offered to the colored people of Chicago. It does no good to the feeling that already exists due to very narrow views of many people.

The committee's report on the candidates for judges stated that Edward H. Morris was a colored man. They might as well have given the nationality or race of every other candidate on the ticket, and the ticket is made up of various nationalities. They stated that he was a man who had a large practice, mainly in criminal cases. I know of no reason why a lawyer engaged in the defense of those charged with crime should not be a good judge, but, as a matter of fact, Mr. Morris' practice has been mainly civil for many years, which fact must have been known to this committee and certainly should have been known had they wished to make a point of the question of his line of practice. We have

96. Albert Hamerstrom (b. 1884) was Ruby Darrow's youngest brother. Ruby described Bert as a wanderer. Ruby Darrow to Irving Stone, n.d. ("Neither you nor the Los A. attorneys . . ."), TLS, DLC-MSS, Darrow Papers. He apparently held a variety of jobs over the course of his life, including, as a young man, working and studying law in Darrow's office in approximately 1903. Later, he worked for a railroad in San Francisco, as an advertising manager and reporter for newspapers, and as a salesman. According to Ruby, during the trial of William Haywood in 1907, he showed up in Boise, Utah, "unannounced and unexpected" and stayed for much of the trial, and then during the McNamara matter in Los Angeles, he "again quite unexpectedly . . . appeared" and Darrow "had him help with investigating" and "just whatever he could by way of being one more helper." Ibid.

97. Edward H. Morris (1858–1943), lawyer. Morris was born in Kentucky, the son of a slave. His family moved to Chicago in 1867. He graduated from St. Patrick's College, studied law, and was admitted to the Illinois bar in 1879. He became a prominent and successful lawyer in Chicago. He was elected to the state legislature in 1881, serving a total of eight years. He was very active in the Grand United Order of Odd Fellows. In the election in November 1923, Morris, a Republican, sought a seat on the Superior Court of Cook County. The Chicago Bar Association, through a committee, refused to endorse him. He also did poorly in a "primary" in which members of the bar association voted, and the *Chicago Tribune* wouldn't endorse him. "Foell Tops List in Bar Primary on Judge Timber," *Chicago Tribune*, 21 October 1923; "Bar Indorsements and Little Ballot Recommendations," *Chicago Tribune*, 4 November 1923.

had many judges who came directly from the State's Attorney's office and whose sole experience had been in the criminal courts, and this is the first time I have ever known this matter to be referred to in a report of the committee.

The report also says that he would not be a fit man for the bench. Every man familiar with Mr. Morris' attainments and practice of the law in the City of Chicago knows perfectly well that in legal ability, disposition and everything else that goes to make a judge, he is the peer of any man on either ticket. This must have been known both to the committee and the members of the bar who voted at the bar primary.

The statement of the committee that he would not make a fit judge must have been prompted solely by his color. The small vote he received at the bar primary was due solely to his color. I guarantee that if any one doubts this and will ask the lawyers whom they meet in Chicago indiscriminately, 90 per cent of them will say of Mr. Morris what I said. I say it not only from his general reputation as a lawyer, but from a long personal acquaintance, friendship, and experience with him in court. Aside from his ability as a lawyer, he was for many years a member of legislature. During one session, I was a member with him and I can say emphatically that there was no abler man in the legislature than Mr. Morris.

I know of no man on either ticket who is better qualified or whom I believe that would make a better judge, and I trust that the colored voters of this City will give him such a vote as emphatically to show their disapproval of the report of the committee and the action of the bar.[98]

Very truly yours, | Clarence S. Darrow

MS: "Hon. Clarence S. Darrow, One of the Most Eminent Lawyers in the United States, Champions the Candidacy of Hon. Edward H. Morris for Judge of the Superior Court of Cook County," *The (Chicago) Broad Ax*, 23 November 1923. INSIDE ADDRESS: Julius F. Taylor, Editor, | The Broad Ax, | Chicago.

TO BRAND WHITLOCK • CHICAGO • WEDNESDAY 19 DECEMBER 1923

DARROW, SISSMAN, HOLLY & CARLIN December 19th 1923.

Dear Brand:—

Some days ago I receive your book from the publishers and since that, your welcome letter.[99] I have read the book. It is a bully one. The best you have written, as a matter of art, and I am delighted that your views of life have undergone no change. You have done

98. In the end, Morris lost the election. "Chicago-Cook County Election," *Chicago Tribune*, 7 November 1923.

99. Whitlock wrote to Darrow to explain that he had asked his publishers to send Darrow a copy of his latest novel, *J. Hardin and Son* (New York: D. Appleton, 1923), and to ask Darrow, among other things, if he had read *The Diary of Samuel Pepys* or Lothrop Stoddard's *The Revolt against Civilization: The Menace of the Under Man* (New York: Charles Scribner's Sons, 1922). Stoddard's book, drawn mainly along racial lines, maintained that civilization is threatened by a biologically unfit, mentally inferior class of people. Whitlock told Darrow that he read it "with deep interest" and "despair" for he "fear[ed] it is all too true." Whitlock to Darrow, 19 November 1923, TLS, MnU-L, Darrow Collection.

a fine job. It is true and pessimistic. It must be pessimistic if true. Your picture of the cruelties of human judgments—the futility and foolishness of the law, delights me. You also know the love psychology better than I feared you did. (Has Nellie read it? If so, she will want a divorce). You picture the junior Harding true to life. Likewise the senior, and the knocks about the prohibition fanaticism and the fanaticism of all virtue are fine. The junior could not follow his instincts, but was bound by his heredity and environment and went back to the fool bank and the fool wife. This is as it should be and is. The wives will approve it. I have found that there is no other trade unionist who hates a scab as much as the members of the married woman's union. Life is a deadly thing about nothing. Happiness and the following of emotions is the unforgivable sin. You have done it all remarkably well.

As to myself, life moves on as it always has. I am very busy. Never was so busy in my profession as the last two years. Am trying to get enough money ahead to live and will succeed by the time I am so old that I will not be able to buy any fun with my money. This time has almost arrived. My best emotions come from fighting the law and the good and I generally manage to cheat the mob. I am sending you some miscellaneous stuff that you may care to read, and which will give you a picture of what I think I am thinking in these later days. I am also asking my publishers to send you a book which I managed to write and which I believe you will find interesting and I think you will agree with. It is on crime and stands pretty nearly alone amongst the books on the subject.[100] Needless to say, it is written from the standpoint of the criminal that I like and sympathize with and somehow understand. I am quite sure that the scientific part is true, as well as the rest. To me the life of man is like the life of a fly—a buzzing about nothing. Life itself is only an unsatisfactory and brief interruption of nothingness. I think I have no illusions left (mores the pity). I still have good health and while I probably am not as alert and responsive, and my mind does not work as well as it once did, still I do not know it. God is very good to me and every one. I was discussing it the other day with a Christian. I told him that after one was sixty, the Lord made up his mind to take away about ten teeth and to show his goodness he took five from the east side of his upper jaw and five from the west side of his lower jaw, so he might as well have taken twenty if he had that many left. I am intending to take a trip to Europe next summer unless the Lord interferes. Charlie Russell and I have planned a walking tour through Switzerland and the writing of a book at the same time. Wish you could join us. If not, hope we can see you there. I rather envy you living abroad where there is some freedom left. There is no chance in Protestant countries, although England is better than America.

I sympathize fully with your views of England and the English. I have never read Peppys' Diary, but shall. I wonder if you have read "Of Human Bondage".[101] It is one of

100. The book that Darrow sent must have been his *Crime: Its Cause and Treatment* (1922).
101. W. Somerset Maugham, *Of Human Bondage* (Garden City, NY: Garden City Publishing, 1915).

the best things I have seen for years. Also "The Growth of the Soil".[102] I have read "The Revolt Against Civilization". I do not like it. There is much truth in it, but I think the author is a snob. I have read a great deal on this subject and I do not believe Stoddard is scientific. If you can get "The Mind of the Original Man" by Bvaz,[103] who is a Columbia professor, I think you will find it a good antidote for Stoddard. I do not mean by that the human race is of any value, or that it is capable of improvement, but that the "backward people" are the equal of the "forward" assuming that we could tell what is backward and what is forward.

This is the longest letter I have written for many months. I wish you would write again and often.

Love to Nellie.[104]

Best wishes, | Always, | Clarence Darrow.

MS: TLS, NNC, Allan Nevins Papers.

TO PAUL DARROW • CHICAGO • WEDNESDAY 16 JANUARY 1924

DARROW, SISSMAN, HOLLY & CARLIN Jan. 16

Dear Paul

Just got your statement. It is very encouraging. Am glad to see how many heating stoves you are selling. It may be the solution of the gas business in spite of the fact that involves lower rates. I thought I sent Mary the book she wanted. If she will return it, with the name of the one she wants I will get it.

Ned Oakley[105] has been to see me several times of late. He has made up his mind he must work. Sort of awakened from a dream. I got an interview for him with a news paper & he worried so much over it that I made up my mind that he couldn't do it, and told him he should try something simpler first. As to contact with life he is a child. He then thought he ought to go to work at manual labor, in the stock yards or on a farm, (not a bad idea if he would do it). I told him if he really wanted to try working on a farm he could probably get a job in Colorado when the season opens up. So he said he was going to write you. Now I know you can't give your time to looking up jobs; and I know Ned will not

102. Knut Hamsun, *Growth of the Soil*, trans. W. W. Worster (New York: Knopf, 1921).

103. Darrow meant *The Mind of Primitive Man* (New York: Macmillan, 1922), by Franz Boas (1858–1942), a professor at Columbia University and one of the founders of modern anthropology. *The Mind of Primitive Man* was first published in 1911 and revised or reprinted many times. Boas maintained in this classic work that "blacks could progress on an equal level with all other races, if given the opportunity," and that "people who advanced theories of black inferiority spoke from ignorance." Marshall Hyatt, *Franz Boas, Social Activist: The Dynamics of Ethnicity* (Westport, CT: Greenwood Press, 1990), 97.

104. Ella Brainerd Whitlock.

105. Darrow probably means Edwin ("Ned") Oakford (1879–1955), from Peoria, Illinois. Interview with Mary Darrow Simonson, Honolulu, Hawaii, 13 September 1999. Oakford graduated from Dartmouth College in 1908, a few years after Paul Darrow. He studied in Europe after graduation. He never worked in a steady job. He was a writer but apparently never published anything. Telephone interview with Richard Oakford, Peoria, Illinois, 13 December 1999.

expect it. He is one of the most considerate & independent fellows I ever met. He has stayed over night at the house a number of times and is always reluctant to do it, and always refuses to come back the 2d night, so if he does go there I know he will make you no trouble. He really should try to do something & must try for himself & he knows it perfectly well. Of course you know his father is well to do and always helps him but naturally wants him to do something for himself & Ned is bound to do it.[106]

Truly | C. S. D.

How did you come out with Shoemaker?[107]

MS: ALS, MnU-L, Darrow Collection. DATE: "1924" appended.

TO PAUL DARROW • CHICAGO • WEDNESDAY 12 MARCH 1924

DARROW, SISSMAN, HOLLY & CARLIN March 12, 1924.

Dear Paul:—

Was glad to get your letter with Everett's enclosure. Everett has gone plumb crazy. I never write to him any more about the question that obsesses him. The fact that a member of the cabinet took a bribe of $100,000 to make conveyance of government property, does not seem to effect or even interest him.[108] This man was always a crook and Harding knew it when he appointed him and appointed him for that reason. Only a small part of his work has come to light or ever will come to light, most likely. About half of Harding's cabinet and all of his friends are the same sort, as everybody knows who cares about knowing.

As to Coolidge, I regard him as simply nothing. His tariff on the farmer's wheat shows how much he amounts to and likewise what he thinks of the farmer. As to the latter, he is undoubtedly right. Of course Everett would not have the Senate or any one else make any investigations as to fraud. No matter what crooked thing the employer or capitalist did, he would think is all right. I was surprised he classed Adams[109] as a red. It gives me a better opinion of Adams, although I notice Adams has been doing something of late.

106. Edwin Oakford's father was Aaron Oakford (1845–1933), founder in 1868 of the Oakford Company, a large wholesale distributor of groceries in Peoria, Illinois.

107. The identity of "Shoemaker" is unknown, but he might have been someone connected to the possible sale of the gas plant in Greeley.

108. The subject that "obsessed" Darrow's brother, Everett, was apparently the Teapot Dome scandal, the worst of the many scandals of President Harding's administration, which continued long after Harding's death in 1923. Albert Fall (1861–1944), Harding's secretary of the interior, 1921–23, was accused of accepting bribes in the form of large, interest-free loans from Edward L. Doheney (1856–1935), president of the Pan-American Petroleum Company, and Harry F. Sinclair (1876–1956), president of the Mammoth Oil Company. These loans were allegedly in exchange for leasing government oil reserves to Doheney and Sinclair's companies. Fall and Doheney were tried on fraud and conspiracy charges in 1926 and Sinclair was tried on the same charges in 1928. Both trials resulted in acquittals, although an earlier civil lawsuit against Pan-American resulted in a finding that the oil reserve leases had been fraudulently obtained. Fall was convicted of bribery in 1929 and Doheney was acquitted on the same charges in 1930.

109. Darrow might have been referring to John T. Adams (1862–1939), who was chairman of the Republican National Committee, 1921–24.

LaFollette, I regard as the outstanding, honest man in politics. He has never wavered in his fight on the crooked men who control political and business life. Of course it is wrong for the farmers and laborers to have a bloc, but every one else has and always have had it. Lenroot[110] has always been a tool of the corporation. I think he admires Phipps who was elected Senator because he had money to pay for it as everybody knows. Of course I admire his stand on the soldier's bonus, but that is all I ever saw about him to admire.

Every lawyer that Coolidge has appointed to represent the government is a man tied up with big business and one who is on their side, no matter what they do. Of course he is dreaming when he thinks all of this is going to seriously effect any half-way decent business.

Much that he says about the railroads in reference to regulations and rates and combination, is due entirely to railroads. The working man had nothing whatever to do with it. The Union Pacific, for instance, was built entirely with government money. They had a land grant in addition, which was large enough to build it and they repudiated both their bonds and obligations to the government and they bonded and stocked it for many times its value. The same is true of the Southern Pacific and largely true of all other railroads. Their freight rates, as you know, are simply a specie of grand larceny. They have no regard whatever for the rights or justice of anybody who pays them, but simply get all they can.

As to the labor unions, of course I know more about their good and bad things than he ever dreamed of. They do a great many unwarranted things, most of which they learned from the employer. Even at that, the working man would be helpless without them. The truth is that all business is a hodge podge where every fellow is grabbing all he can. There is no method or system or sense of justice in any of it and I do not know how it can ever be changed. I don't see how anybody who thinks can believe that coal and oil and lumber, to say nothing about air, should be privately owned. The trouble with the question is to know how to own it and operate it some other way, but I have never seen the way.

As to the Coolidge oil business, it is perfectly plain that he was trying to shield Fall and the rest of them from the beginning. It does not admit of question. I don't know how far organizations of capital or organizations of labor are either immutable or natural laws. They are probably neither one, but grow out of a phase of life and in that sense are natural.

Of course McAdoo[111] did not go to Mexico to do anything to Doheny's rights in Mexico. This could only have been done in Washington. He either went there or sent his partner, which is the same thing.

110. Irvine L. Lenroot (1869–1949), lawyer and politician. Lenroot served as a Republican congressman, 1909–18, and senator from Wisconsin, 1918–27, and later as a judge on the United States Court of Customs and Patent Appeals, 1929–44. He was a moderate progressive and one-time close ally of Robert La Follette. But during the Teapot Dome scandal, when he was a member and later chairman of the Senate Committee on Public Lands and Surveys, he was attacked for being too close to the administration and too slow in finding the corruption behind the scandal, all of which led to his defeat in the Republican primary in 1926.

111. In January 1924, when William McAdoo was a front-runner for the Democratic presidential nomination, he was thought to be implicated in the Teapot Dome scandal after Doheney revealed that McAdoo was on his company's payroll.

I wonder how soon we would get cheap transportation or cheap freight rates if the railroads were left to manage it without the interference of government. The truth is, the railroads have always owned the government.

I see that Everett misunderstood your letter as to business in Colorado. I presume you have written him about it since. Of course he is a fine fellow and would do anything we wanted him to do, but I don't like to have him even worry about the amount of bonds he has. I could take them up if you can't.

I am not certain as to what you write me about the tariff and the balance of trade as shown by the imports of plate glass. Of course the tariff on farmer's wheat is nothing but a reflection on the farmer's brains. The farmers last year exported about two hundred and fifty millions of wheat, most of which went to Europe. Canada exported about one hundred and fifty millions, but I have not the figures, most of which went to Liverpool. A small amount of Canadian wheat was sent to Minneapolis, because their wheat is hard wheat like the Red River Valley wheat and there was a shortage in the Red River Valley last fall. This is not in any way influenced by the tariff and of course the extra 12¢ that the politicians in the White House put on, will not raise the price of wheat. There was already a tariff of 30¢ on wheat and the farmer has never received this because he takes the Liverpool price after paying the freight. I presume this was the sense in which you made your reference—the tariff on wheat—that it would have a tendency to keep Europe from buying it. One trouble with us has been that our exports have so far exceeded our imports and I am glad that we are importing more glass than we once did. It shows that we are selling more wheat. Of course trade is a good thing. If it was not, we ought to exclude it.

I am not writing all this because I want to seriously influence your thought on the matter. I have always wanted you to do your own thinking, which I know you do. If for any reason you are a little doubtful on the tariff question, you might reread one of the books that treat on that subject.

I am glad to see that business is doing so well this year.

Truly, | C. S. D.

MS: TLS, MnU-L, Darrow Collection.

TO PAUL DARROW • CHICAGO • WEDNESDAY 19 MARCH 1924

DARROW, SISSMAN, HOLLY & CARLIN March 19, 1924.

Dear Paul:—

Replying to your letter of March 15th, I would say I do not remember exactly what I wrote you about McAdoo, but there is no question about the facts.

Doheny employed four of Wilson's cabinet members immediately on their retirement. It is perfectly obvious that they were not employed for law business, but to help him in his graft on account of political influence. As to McAdoo, he resigned from the cabinet, stating that he had to make some money. He had never been a lawyer to speak of—was really a

promoter and a soldier of fortune. Within one year of his resignation, he received a million dollars from Doheny and others, which was paid purely as political graft. He says he went to Mexico to spend about two weeks in reference to Doheny's interests in Mexico. This I am sure is not true and if the Senate Committee had seen fit to cross-examine him, the facts would have been brought out. He received $100,000 with the prospective contingent fee of $900,000 more. He never made an entry in his books, nor prepared a paper, nor filed one, nor entered a court room. He could be of no use in Mexico. The only lawyer that could help him there would be some Dago who spoke their language and knew their men. When he went to Mexico, his partners went to Washington. Of course Doheny could be helped from Washington and nowhere else. It was undoubtedly a case of the recognition of the Mexican government by providing that oil should be protected. McAdoo had been the Secretary of the Treasury for six or seven years. He was a son-in-law of the President; he knew all the departments and the men connected with them. He not only got this money from Doheny, but some three or four hundred thousand dollars on coal shipped to Italy and several hundred thousand dollars by getting a rebate of taxes for the Republic Iron & Steel Co., from his own department. He got many other sums which have not yet come out. The Federal statutes provide that it is an offense for any clerk in any department to practice law within two years after leaving the department. This statute does not apply to the heads of the department, for it would be presumed that they would not do such a thing. One of my friends said that McAdoo was not a lawyer, but a son-in-lawyer.

There is absolutely no defense for him, and to nominate him would be certain defeat, otherwise he would have been cross-examined by the Republicans on the investigating committee.

The whole situation revealed in Washington by the investigating committee is rotten in the extreme. Nothing like it has ever been shown in American politics, with the possible exception of Grant's administration.

As to Coolidge, he sent his Secretary to Palm Beach to see Fall and he spent several weeks with him. Three telegrams were sent from the White House cautioning Fall and Doheny and informing them of the situation. He has not acted in the Daugherty case.[112] He has appointed investigators whom he knew would not investigate. He is simply a small-sized New England politician.

I feel about as you do as to Mellon.[113] It would require a very strong necessity to make me vote for Coolidge. As between him and McAdoo, I would have no choice.

112. In early 1924, several senators and others were increasingly trying to link Attorney General Daugherty to the Teapot Dome scandal. The pressure on Daugherty to resign mounted and on 28 March 1924, at the request of President Coolidge, Daugherty resigned. See James N. Giglio, *H. M. Daugherty and the Politics of Expediency* (Kent, OH: Kent State University Press, 1978), 163–73.

113. Andrew Mellon (1855–1937), financier and statesman. Mellon acquired large interests in the oil and steel industries, aluminum manufacturing, and banking. He was a generous contributor to Republican politicians and causes before serving as secretary of the treasury and a powerful figure in the administrations of presidents Harding, Coolidge, and Hoover, 1921–32. How Darrow and his son felt about Mellon is not clear, but there were some Democrats, at the time of Daugherty's resignation, who especially wanted to investigate Mellon. Giglio, *H. M. Daugherty*, 174.

I am rather expecting to be a delegate to the National Democratic Convention for Al Smith. Don't know whether I will succeed or not.

I did not know about Phipps on the Volsted Act. In fact, I know very little about it. I presume my view of him is largely prejudiced. About all I know of him is that he was a very wealthy Pittsburgh man who had never been known as anything but a business man. He went to Colorado, either for his health or his family's and on account of his money alone, this man who was practically a carpet bagger in Colorado, was elected to the United States Senate. He might be better than I think, but it was a rotten thing for Colorado to do and it shows the effect of money in politics.

I see you have the free trade idea of the traffic, which I believe is absolutely sound. As you know, I am not very well posted on exchange. You know much more about this than I do. However, you are probably in error in thinking that the tariff on wheat caused a drop in exchange. I can readily see how it would do this if it effected the export or import of wheat, which it does not—at least only slightly, due to a sentiment in Europe against the United States on account of our selfishness. I noted the drop of the price of wheat after the increase in tariff, but I would rather assume that this was due to the law of supply and demand which causes a constant variance of price, instead of to the tariff.

I was interested in my radio talk reaching Greeley.[114] I don't look for any improvement in stocks until the campaign is far enough along to see who will win. Still I don't expect much further decline.

C. S. D.

MS: TLS, MnU-L, Darrow Collection. NOTE: The last paragraph is written in Darrow's hand.

TO NEGLEY D. COCHRAN • CHICAGO • SUNDAY 6 APRIL 1924

DARROW & SISSMAN April 6th

Dear Neg

It is a devil of a long time since I heard from you. I have been trying to get down, perhaps I can in two or three weeks. My main reason is to see you. Are you figuring on any thing for this summer. I mean to take a good vacation but don't know where. Wish I could be with you. These days must furnish you a lot of excitement. Things are d—n wrotten down there and I wish they could all be cleaned out. I am running for delegate to National Convention. Election on Tuesday. Rather think I shall win.[115] If I go I want to do what I can for Al Smith—he might help us get a drink. Should be glad to hear from you—Love to family

Always yours Darrow.

MS: ALS, OT, Cochran Papers. DATE: "1928" appended but reference to convention makes 1924 more likely.

114. The "radio talk" to which Darrow is referring is unknown.
115. Darrow was elected as a delegate to the Democratic National Convention from the second district in Illinois. The convention was held in New York City from 24 June to 9 July 1924. John W. Davis was nominated on the 103rd ballot.

TO H. L. MENCKEN • CHICAGO • FRIDAY 2 MAY 1924

DARROW, SISSMAN, HOLLY & CARLIN May 2, 1924.

My Dear Mr. Mencken:—

Enclosed you will find the copy that you requested. I have revised it, as you wished, and also cut out some of the paragraphs. I have no doubt you have readers who understand punctuation and grammar and will find many corrections to make. I shall be glad to see this in the July number.[116]

I wonder if arrangements could be made to have it printed by itself for circulation? I am willing to pay for some of this. I would like to get it before some of the delegates to the National Convention which meets in New York on the 20th of June. By the way, I am one of the delegates and hope to see you in New York at that time. I have long wanted to know you and have read most everything you have written and find little of your stuff I do not believe is true. This of course, will show you that your views are logical and correct.

You ask me about further manuscripts. I have some in mind and will get them ready. I want to write one about Eugenics. In fact, I have one practically finished. This is one of my pet abominations. Also I am preparing one on the Jukes family and the Edwards family, in which I seek to show the Jukes family was much the better family.[117] I think you will be interested in this.

These articles will be livelier than I one I enclosed. Will use the axe in them. I purposely wanted to make this dull and stupid so that I might deceive some yokels into believing that it is judicial and fair. Of course I have no judicial attitude toward prohibition. I think it is an unmitigated evil and an abominable violation of personal rights. I like to hit it in every way it can be hit.

You will find me amongst the subscribers to your magazine from the first and there is no other I like as well.

Wishing you a long life and more power, I am,

Your friend, | Clarence Darrow

MS: TLS, NN, Mencken Collection. INSIDE ADDRESS: Mr. H. L. Mencken, | 730 5th Avenue, | New York, N.Y.

116. Darrow is referring to an article he wrote doubting that Prohibition statutes could be repealed and predicting (or hoping) that the laws would fall into disuse instead, like the laws supporting the Inquisition and prosecution of witches and the blue laws prohibiting theaters, dancing, etc. Mencken published the article as "The Ordeal of Prohibition," *American Mercury,* August 1924, 419–27.

117. On the Edwardses and Jukeses, and Darrow's view of those families, see Darrow to E. W. Scripps, 30 October 1922 and nn. 69, 70.

TO H. L. MENCKEN • CHICAGO • SUNDAY 11 MAY 1924

DARROW & SISSMAN May 11th

My Dear Mr. Mencken,

It has occurred to me that you have a Who's Who business in the back of your magazine giving a sketch of the contributors. Less said about me the better. Please *don't* say I am a "labor lawyer." If any thing you can say I am a lawyer. If necessary, that I am well known & live in Chicago. If more is needed, I have written several books. The last on "Crime, its cause & treatment"—also that I have given many addresses on political economy and other subjects. Please *don't* say I am a criminal lawyer—although I am both. Still, as to law, I have done *all sorts*.[118] Shall hunt you up at the convention or Biltmore & adjourn to your celler, and let the convention go hang, unless I see a chance for a bigger part in the bunk game than I expect to play.[119]

Yours | Clarence Darrow.

MS: ALS, NN, Mencken Papers.

TO JESSIE BROWNLEE • CHICAGO • TUESDAY 10 JUNE 1924

DARROW & SISSMAN June 10th

Dear Jessie

Have been so busy I have had no chance to write letters. Do just what you think best about the house either keep it or sell it. I want you to live as you wish and go where you want to go. Both Paul & I can afford to give you what you want at any time and of course we want to do it. If you wish to go back by Ohio you should do it. Let me know about what you want & I will see that you get the money promptly. This case is quite perplexing & will most likely be a hard struggle to save the lives of the boys.[120] Was intending to go to NY. as a delegate to the convention but may not be able to get away. Don't know about going to Paul's this summer but hope I will find time. Let me know at once when & where you will go & also if you need more money to repair house. Have not called up to see if Mary is at Frank's but will in a day or so—

Always your friend | C. S. D.

118. Mencken sent a short reply to this letter, saying, among other things, that he had already instinctively avoided what Darrow did not want him to say. Mencken to Darrow, TLS, 15 May 1924, MnU-L, Darrow Collection. The biographical note published on Darrow in the back of the *American Mercury* stated: "Clarence S. Darrow is the well-known Chicago lawyer and libertarian. He has been counsel in many celebrated cases, mainly involving the constitutional rights of the individual. He is the author of a novel and of several volumes of essays." *American Mercury*, August 1924, 511.

119. Mencken had written a letter in reply to Darrow's earlier letter describing some changes to Darrow's article and proposing that he and Darrow meet for a drink at the upcoming Democratic National Convention in New York. Mencken to Darrow, 9 May 1924, TLS, MnU-L, Darrow Collection.

120. On 21 May 1924, Richard Loeb and Nathan Leopold kidnapped and murdered fourteen-year-old Bobby Franks. Within two weeks, they were arrested and confessed to the crime. Their parents hired Darrow to represent them and their case became one of the most sensational murder cases in American history.

[In Jessie Brownlee's hand, to Paul Darrow:] I wrote your father about selling the house last mo. but he's forgotten it. He may never have gotten it altho. it was sent to his office instead of house. So queer about the long letter I wrote Lillian & mailed to 1537—E—60th Chic. c/o your father &c.

MS: ALS, MnU-L, Darrow Collection. DATE: "1924" appended.

TO FRANK WALSH • CHICAGO • FRIDAY 13 JUNE 1924

DARROW, SISSMAN, HOLLY & CARLIN June 13, 1924.

Dear Frank:—

I have seen your name mentioned in the papers a number of times as likely to be in the Franks case here.

Of course I do not need to tell you that I would be very glad to have you in it, more than any one else, with me. It would soften up a hard job to have you around.

I have not heard any one connected with the case speak of it and do not know just how it got into the press. Their present intention now seems not to have any one outside of Chicago and probably no one else, but if it was thought best to get outside assistance, of course I would be for you.

With best wishes, | Always, | Clarence Darrow

MS: TLS, NN, Walsh Papers, Box 13. INSIDE ADDRESS: Hon. Frank P. Walsh, | 55 Liberty Street, | New York, N.Y.

TO PAUL DARROW • CHICAGO • WEDNESDAY 25 JUNE 1924

DARROW, SISSMAN, HOLLY & CARLIN June 25

Dear Paul

Just got your statement. It is certainly good. It looks as if things are now all right with you. I have been so busy that I have hardly had time to think of any thing but this wierd case. Don't know how I will come out. It is very hard to get a fair hearing. As to fees I will of course get a fair & substantial fee, as yet I have no idea how much time it will take. The families are fine people and will do what is right & of course you know I will. You might write me just what you think of various stocks & when you think is the right time. B & O looks good to me so does Gt Northern and Northern Pacific. Haven't thought much about others. Will try to write oftener after this.

Love to all | C. S. D.

Don't know when I will get out there probably not until this case is finished.

MS: ALS, MnU-L, Darrow Collection. DATE: reference to Loeb and Leopold case.

TO PAUL DARROW • CHICAGO • SUNDAY 20 JULY 1924

Sunday | July 20

Dear Paul

You have no doubt been surprised at the turn we have taken in the Loeb-Leopold case.[121] We have concluded it is the most hopeful way of saving the boys' lives. It is doubtful if any way will accomplish it.

Hastily | C. S. D.

MS: ALS, MnU-L, Darrow Collection. DATE: "1924" appended.

TO PAUL DARROW • CHICAGO • SUNDAY 3 AUGUST 1924

DARROW & SISSMAN Aug 3rd

Dear Paul

The last report is mighty good. It begins to look as if you were coming out all right with the Co. It seems as if we ought to get in on the oil, but do as you please about it. I don't know how I shall come out in the case. It is an awfull hard fight and the papers have been so rotten that the feeling runs high. However I am hopeful of succeeding in saving their lives. It will probably be over in about two weeks and I shall be out sometime this fall. Am not going to stick so closely to work any more. So I will have more time for visiting & writing. How is Blanche?[122] Tell her that Marie[123] has looked for a letter for a long time and has given up hearing from her. Love to all

C. S. D.

MS: ALS, MnU-L, Darrow Collection. DATE: reference to Loeb and Leopold case.

TO PAUL DARROW • CHICAGO • MONDAY 4 AUGUST 1924

Aug. 4th

Dear Paul

I suppose you know that the case will be decided the tenth of this month. I am very hopeful that I will win, but may not. Will send you 25 copies or more if you want as soon as

121. On 21 July 1924, Darrow announced that his clients were withdrawing their not-guilty pleas and changing their pleas to guilty. Many people had expected the defendants to argue insanity as a defense at their trial. The guilty pleas eliminated a trial and placed responsibility for sentencing the defendants in the hands of the trial judge alone, rather than a jury.
122. Blanche Darrow Chase.
123. Marie Thompson, live-in housekeeper and cook for Clarence and Ruby Darrow for sixteen years, until Clarence Darrow's death in 1938. Interview with Blanche Darrow Chase and Mary Darrow Simonson, Wheaton, Illinois, 29 July 1995; Ruby Darrow to Irving Stone, n.d. ("The constant reminders of other wars . . ."), TL, DLC-MSS, Darrow Papers.

it is ready which will be in a few days.[124] If we win I shall go away for a little time & later go out to Colorado, but have your mother stay as long as she wishes. Any how it will be some time before I go. If we loose shall probably stay here for a while to figure out something else to do, but I do not really expect to loose. Can't just see how the judge can beat us.

I think you are having a good year & I presume you will continue making a better showing than last year. I had a visit with Davis[125] for about an hour yesterday. He is a fine fellow: he seems thoroughly posted and speaks square out and has a good sense of humor. He is to be in Denver the 11th & I told him I was going to have you call if you could get up there. You will find with him, no doubt, Jack Nevins[126] who is one of my best friends & who will be delighted to see you. I think you will find it worth while to go up.[127]

Truly | C. S. D.

Tell the girls there was a paper here that had my picture in last month.

MS: ALS, MnU-L, Darrow Collection. DATE: "1924" appended and supported by reference to Loeb and Leopold case.

TO FRANK WALSH • CHICAGO • MONDAY 8 SEPTEMBER 1924

DARROW, SISSMAN, HOLLY & CARLIN September 8, 1924.

Dear Frank:—

Of course I am very much obliged to you for your kind letter.[128] My argument will be out in pamphlet form in a few days and will send you one. I am hopeful of winning. I hope it will do some good outside of those involved.

124. Darrow is referring to the pamphlet containing his plea for Leopold and Loeb: *The Plea of Clarence Darrow, August 22, 23, and 25, 1924, in Defense of Richard Loeb and Nathan Leopold, Jr., on Trial for Murder* (Chicago: R. F. Seymour, 1924).
125. John W. Davis.
126. John ("Jack") E. Nevin (d. 1933), journalist. Nevin was an organizer of William Randolph Hearst's International News Service and chief of its Washington Bureau for some time. During Davis's campaign, Nevin—who was described by the *New York Times* as "astute and jovial" and as a man who "knew every politician and statesman between Paris and Pocatello"—served as Davis's press representative.
127. With this letter, Darrow enclosed a brief letter of introduction to Davis, stating simply: "This will introduce my son Paul of whom I told you while you were in Chicago. He lives in Greeley Colorado."
128. Walsh had sent a letter congratulating Darrow on his effort in the Leopold-and-Loeb case and expressing concern that Darrow might not support Robert La Follette for president: "First, I want this to be a belated note of congratulation upon your magnificent effort just concluded. It vindicated what I have said to unnumbered hundreds with whom I talked that you were the only man in America fitted to conduct that case. | I believe you will win the issue but if you do not your speech will save many human lives, because it carried your philosophy through the nation in an incomparable way. | I notice in the Associated Press dispatches that you had called upon Mr. Davis, Mr. [J. P.] Morgan's messenger boy. For God's sake do not break my heart by going back on La Follette. That's all." Walsh to Darrow, 5 September 1924, TLc, NN, Walsh Papers.

I called upon Mr. Davis when he was here and was very much taken with him. He is a very likeable fellow and exceedingly intelligent and has a sense of humor, which always appeals to me. At the same time, you need not worry about me going back on La Follette. I would like to see him win. First of all, I want to see Coolidge beaten, if it is possible and I assume that Davis will get the South and possibly some of the East, including New York. In the West it is divided between La Follette and Coolidge and it ought to result in throwing the election into the House. If my vote or influence could do him any good, it would all be cast for him.

I wish you would give me your ideas from New York and the East. I do not see how Coolidge can be defeated if he carries New York and I have been thinking that Davis has a much better show there than La Follette. What do you think of the other States in that section?

This may impress you as a sort of two-sided position, but to me it seems logical. Any how, I want to see La Follette win.

I have been trying for a long time to get to New York and hope I make it pretty soon.

Always, | Your friend, | Clarence Darrow

MS: TLS, NN, Walsh Papers, Box 13. INSIDE ADDRESS: Hon. Frank P. Walsh, | 55 Liberty Street, | New York, N.Y.

TO H. L. MENCKEN • CHICAGO • TUESDAY 9 SEPTEMBER 1924

DARROW, SISSMAN, HOLLY & CARLIN Sept 9th

My Dear Menkin

I am sending you c/o Knopf a book that I wrote years ago. It is I am quite sure an overlooked classic. You can tell from the first page whether it is worth reading through. It went through two editions only by McClurg's. Then Huebsch published it in a bum way. Knopf wrote me that when I had an other MSS he wanted a look at it.[129] I feel pretty sure that this book would sell if it had a chance. If I had been some other sort of a fellow it would have sold better. I am not much better now, still I think there are more people who would read it. Won't you look it over and if you think it worth while pass it on to Knopf.

Faithfully | Clarence Darrow

MS: ALS, NN, Mencken Papers. DATE: "1924" appended.

129. Darrow is referring to *Farmington,* the autobiographical novel of his childhood, which was first published by A.C. McClurg in Chicago (1904) and later by Benjamin Huebsch in New York (1919). Alfred A. Knopf never published any edition of the book.

TO HAROLD ICKES • CHARLEVOIX, MICHIGAN • WEDNESDAY 17 SEPTEMBER 1924

MRS. ALBERT H. LOEB | LOEB FARMS Sept 17th

My Dear Mr Ickes

It was mighty good of you to write me.[130] I hope you will write Judge Caverly.[131] I am particularly glad that you agree with me on crime & punishment. I am very anxious to have the legislature abolish capital punishment, and if you will join it will be a great help.

With kind regards | Your friend | Clarence Darrow

MS: ALS, DLC-MSS, Ickes Papers. DATE: letter from Ickes.

TO NATHAN LEOPOLD • CHARLEVOIX, MICHIGAN • SATURDAY 20 SEPTEMBER 1924

CHARLEVOIX, MICHIGAN Sept 20th

Dear Nathan

I have been up here for about ten days getting some rest.[132] Shall be back in Chicago on Monday & will arrange to go & see you soon after arriving. I won't take the trouble to give you advice now & any how I presume I know less about it all than you do. Although I am not a christian scientist (or any thing else) I know that the most of life "is within" us and man is a wonderfully adaptable animal. I think you know this too. Of course you will be there for a long time & will naturally figure out the best way to make things tolerable, as I have tried to do, with poor success, on the outside. I can help you figure this out & will make it my business to do it both for you & Dick.

I am ambitious for you to write your bird book. I have had a good deal of pleasure, or rather forgetfulness in writing books which no one reads, & I want you to write one which will be read. Any how I won't forget you and I am sure I can help you in many ways.

Always Your friend | Clarence Darrow.

MS: ALS, ICHi, Leopold Collection. ENVELOPE ADDRESS: Nathan Leopold Jr | Joliet | Ill. | 1900 Collins St #9306.

130. On 10 September 1924, the judge announced that Loeb and Leopold would each be sentenced to life imprisonment for murder and ninety-nine years for kidnapping. Ickes had written to Darrow to congratulate him on the result: "I want to congratulate you on the outcome of the Loeb-Leopold trial. I read every word of your argument as it appeared in the public press and it was great throughout. I may say also that I agree with your point of view on crime, criminals and punishment. It was in every way a crowning achievement and the credit due you is none the less because Judge Caverly bravely withstanding the cry of the mob for blood rendered a just and proper judgment." Ickes to Darrow, 11 September 1924, TLc, DLC-MSS, Ickes Papers.

131. John R. Caverly (1861–1939), judge who presided over the hearing for Leopold and Loeb. Born in London, Caverly came to the United States as a boy, received a law degree from the Chicago College of Law, 1897, worked in the Chicago city attorney's office, 1897–1903, and as justice of the peace and police magistrate, 1903–6, before being appointed city attorney, 1907–9. Later, he became a judge of the municipal court, 1909–20, and then was elected judge of the circuit court, 1921–39.

132. Darrow was staying at a summer estate owned by Richard Loeb's parents.

TO FRANK WALSH • CHICAGO • MONDAY 6 OCTOBER 1924

DARROW, SISSMAN, HOLLY & CARLIN October 6, 1924.

Dear Frank:

I will probably be down to New York for a few hours to act as chairman in the debate between Untermeyer[133] and Hillquit. I suppose they want me for an ornament and to draw a crowd, and I no doubt will serve very well for both purposes.[134]

I hope you will be there and I will see you. That is another reason for coming. I am also going to debate capital punishment with some New York judge on the 26th of October and I probably will have a chance to see you.[135] Anyhow, I want to see you.

As always,

Call me at Belmont Hotel 10–30 am.

MS: TL, NN, Walsh Papers, Box 13. INSIDE ADDRESS: Mr. Frank P. Walsh, | 55 Liberty street, | New York, N.Y.

TO PAUL DARROW • CHICAGO • WEDNESDAY 29 OCTOBER 1924

DARROW, SISSMAN, HOLLY & CARLIN October 29, 1924.

Dear Paul:—

Just got your letter and statement and think business is holding up remarkably well. Wish I could come out to Greeley before the campaign is over, but cannot do it.

As to the La Follette matter, I guess you understand how it is. I think Davis is probably the best in the lot, but I am confident that he cannot win, and neither can La Follette unless it goes into the House. I talked the matter over fully with the Democratic National State Committee and they agree with my point of view and are quietly doing what they

133. Samuel Untermyer (1858–1940), lawyer and civic leader. Untermyer was a well-known and wealthy lawyer in New York City. He participated in many prominent cases. In 1912, he was appointed as counsel to a congressional subcommittee known as the Pujo Money Trust Investigation, which resulted in the Federal Reserve Act of 1914, among other legislation. He was also counsel to the "Lockwood committee" of the New York legislature, 1921–22, which investigated abuses in the building trades and statewide housing conditions. He advocated regulating the stock market and public utilities and government ownership of railroads, among other reforms. He was a leader against anti-Semitism and an early American opponent of the Nazi government in Germany.

134. The debate between Untermyer and Morris Hillquit, with Darrow presiding, was held at Madison Square Garden on 12 October 1924. It was a political event under the auspices of the National Labor Forum, with Untermyer urging the audience to vote in the upcoming presidential election for Democratic candidate John W. Davis and with Hillquit advocating for independent candidate Robert M. La Follette. Darrow told the audience that he was neutral: he "didn't care who licked Coolidge." "10,000 Fill Garden at Political Debate," *New York Times*, 13 October 1924.

135. On 26 October 1924, Darrow debated the subject of capital punishment with Alfred J. Talley (1877–1952) at the Metropolitan Opera House in New York. Talley was judge of the Court of General Sessions in New York, a court of exclusively criminal jurisdiction. Their debate was published later that year as a pamphlet: *Resolved: That Capital Punishment Is a Wise Public Policy. Clarence Darrow, Negative; Judge Alfred J. Talley, Affirmative* (New York: League for Public Discussion, 1924).

can in the same direction. Of course I have refused to speak in any State where Davis has a chance, but I am satisfied that in the Western states, with the possible exception of Colorado, La Follette has the only chance to win.

I note what you say about Senator Phipps. I think I should vote for him as against any wet Democrat, unless there were some exceedingly good reason for not doing it.

Truly yours, | Clarence Darrow

MS: TLS, MnU-L, Darrow Collection.

• 1925–1929

TO ROGER BALDWIN • CHICAGO • WEDNESDAY 21 JANUARY 1925

DARROW, SISSMAN, HOLLY & CARLIN January 21, 1925.

My Dear Baldwin:—

I know a good deal about Metzen's case.[1] I have been trying to help him. He is rather a hard man to help. He has the faculty of making enemies where he ought to make friends. If you and I had his disposition, we would be hanged long ago without any special cause, but on general principles.

My opinion is that if he really wants to get back, instead of making his grievances public, that he had better confine his attention to his friends here.

You know I am willing to do anything I can for him and have done something for him. By this I do not mean that they should have disbarred him. I do not think they should, but of course you know how pure we have to keep the profession.

1. Baldwin had written to Darrow asking if he knew anything about the disbarment of John L. Metzen (1880–1940?), a lawyer in Chicago with radical connections and (apparently) a difficult personality: "What do you know about the disbarment of John L. Metzen, presumably for his championship of the I.W.W. and strikers, but I guess in reality for a pugnacious and disagreeable personality? Have you had occasion to hear anything about it, and if you haven't may we tell you what we know? | He wants to get reinstated and from all I can learn, he deserves. I talked it over with Stedman [probably Seymour Stedman] when I was in Chicago in November and he seems to think that Metzen got a raw deal." Baldwin to Darrow, TLc, 17 January 1925, NjP, ACLU Archives.

I have been disappointed in not seeing you on my visits to New York. I never managed to find you. Anyhow, I will try again some time in March.

Always, | Your friend, | Clarence Darrow

MS: TLc, NjP, ACLU Archives. INSIDE ADDRESS: Mr. Roger N. Baldwin, | 100 Fifth Avenue, | New York City, N.Y.

TO FREMONT OLDER • MIAMI BEACH, FLORIDA • SUNDAY 22 FEBRUARY 1925

Miami Beach—Florida.

My dear Older:

Your letter followed me here where I am loafing and trying to make myself young again (with poor success).

I do not see how I could be of much assistance in the Wolfgang case, though I wish I could.[2] It seems to me that it was not a hanging case, and that the Governor should have commuted the sentence, still he didn't. I am not certain about the right of the U.S. Supreme Ct. to pass on the case, as it seems to have been pretty thoroughly settled in the California court, and the margin of the Federal Court is not great on review. Still there may be something in the points. Spagnoli[3] seems to be a good worker and to have raised every point that could be conjured up. I would guess that he would write a good brief. If he cares to send me a copy of his abstract and brief in the U.S. Supreme Ct. I will go over them and see if I can think of anything else. Of course the case is a long way off, and I am reluctant to go into anything now that seems too desperate—although I am always sorry for the poor devil fighting for his life. Doubtless he was not responsible at the time of the shooting and was dazed with what he had gone through, and acted automatically as all of us do most of the time.[4]

You can always remember my age by your own, and the years are beginning to tell on me, both in physical vigor and mental alertness. I know it won't be long until I will be out of commission entirely, and yet somehow I don't seem to regret it. Somehow I look forward to it with considerable consolation. I have had a long life of activity, and in the main used it to help others who needed it, not overlooking much that I could get for my own satisfaction on the way, and I think I have had enough. I feel reluctant and rather humorous about anything new, and grow lazier all the time; in fact rather like

2. In 1922, Isaac Wolfgang—fifty-four years old, unmarried, and living in a rooming house in Los Angeles—was seen stealing two bottles of milk early one morning from a box in front of a building near where he lived. A special watchman, joined by a policeman, chased Wolfgang and a struggle ensued at Wolfgang's rooming house. Conflicting stories were later told about how severe of a beating (if any) Wolfgang received during this struggle, but the encounter ended with Wolfgang shooting and killing the policeman with a revolver that he pulled from his dresser drawer. Wolfgang was convicted of first-degree murder and sentenced to death. See *People v. Wolfgang,* 221 P. 907 (1923).
3. Ernest B. D. Spagnoli (1885–1972), a lawyer from San Francisco who represented Wolfgang.
4. On 25 January 1926, the United States Supreme Court affirmed the denial of a writ of habeas corpus and on 10 September 1926 Wolfgang was hanged at San Quentin Prison in California.

to vegetate and neither use my body or my mind. I can get up a burst of speed now and then, but don't like to. I begin feeling that some of the responsibilities I have taken (I don't know why) must be passed to others. I am hoping to write one more book which will probably be rambling and pointless, but which I wish to do. I look back as old men do, and I can't see that anything permanent has been accomplished by me or the race, since I was a child, and of course I have no doubt but what it has always been so, and will be until the race is "snuffed out". More than anything else I would like to see man get some sympathy, kindness and understanding of his fellow man, but I do not see that he is any different or that he can ever be. He is bound by his machine, which acts and reacts according to stimuli, and he is not to be blamed even for his cruelty. I have little desire for immortality, either personal or in the way of remembrance in the future. The logical thing, and to me the inevitable thing, is to be annihilated by the process of decay, and why should I be interested even in the memory of my life remaining. The truth is the whole race has taken itself too seriously and this of course applies to each individual unit, myself included. I do love my friends, and more and more as I grow older I dwell on them. I have the greatest longing to see you again, also Steffens. If you could get away I would go to Europe with you and see him, but I am not so much interested in crowds, in cities, in the ocean or even the mountains which I have loved so passionately all my life. I get some occupation in putting myself under observation and studying the causes that drove me here and there and my reactions to things while I am growing old. I fear that I am fast growing into indifference. The things that interest me and others are really nothing, and the fate of the race and all its units is seldom worth thinking about. I know that my own fate is not worth troubling over to me or any of my friends. Yet I can see myself in spite of all my reason and philosophy struggling up to the last second to keep alive for further perplexity and pain. The will to live is with us to the end. I speak a great deal, but why; only because people ask me and urge. Almost always I get the criticism of newspapers and the crowd for what I say, but I still go on. I can't help it, but one day soon I can't do it. I hope sometime we may have one more visit, one more communion—we can't have many more and perhaps none. Anyhow my gratitude and love to you does not dim.

With best wishes to Mrs. Older and yourself,

Your friend always,

MS: TT, CU-BANC, Hiram W. Johnson Papers. DATE: "[ca. Feb. 22, 1925]" appended. NOTE: "COPY" appended.

TO FREDERICK STARR • MIAMI BEACH, FLORIDA • TUESDAY 24 FEBRUARY 1925

Miami Beech Fla

My Dear Mr Starr

Your letter followed us here where we are taking a rest & dodging Realtors. The climate is warm and sunny and the air balmy. Still it is a Bedlam. Everybody crazy and shouting

at the top of their voice "For God sake buy my land." I marvel at what a dam fool I used to be to think that the world could be changed. I have had a few chances to speak and you know how I like to hear myself talk and how the preachers and other [x] tear me to pieces afterward. I know better but am a congenital dam fool, & shall never recover. I am sorry I did not see more of you when you were in Chicago & that I couldn't do more for you. The next time you come if I can know ahead I hope I may be able to get up a meeting or two which might bring some real money. We always enjoy your letters and always like to see you.

With best wishes always | Your friend | Clarence Darrow

I appreciate all you say about the Japanese. I have always been for them as well as for the rest. The truth is our selfish Americans are afraid of them. They think & work—we do neither.

D.

MS: ALS, ICU, Starr Papers, Box 1, Folder 1. DATE: month and day appended but this might be the date of receipt or reply by Starr.

TO JOSEPH JASIN • MIAMI BEACH, FLORIDA • FRIDAY 27 FEBRUARY 1925

Miami Beech | Feby 27th

My Dear Mr. Jasin

I have written LaFollette asking him to speak for you. Have also told him that I thought he should be paid as I really do. Senator Lafollette is a poor man, who has made a hard fight all his life & has no means of living except his little salary & speaking. Of course I want you to know that I don't mean that I wanted to be paid. I was glad to go.[5] I am a visitor here & while I am not rich I can live as long as I ought to & I considered it a great pleasure to meet your people & do something for you. I think however you ought to offer to pay Senator Lafollete.

With best remembrances & wishes | Clarence Darrow

I am leaving Saturday.

MS: ALS, OCAJA, Jasin Collection, Folder SC-5682. DATE: month and place from which letter was written and speech by Darrow in Miami.

5. Darrow spoke on the subject of crime and punishment to Jasin's congregation at Temple Israel in Miami on 15 February 1925. "Crime and Punishment to Israel Temple Congregation," *(Miami) Illustrated Daily Tab,* 16 February 1925. This letter followed after a letter from Darrow accepting Jasin's offer of an honorary membership in Temple Israel. Darrow to Jasin, 23 February 1925, ALS, OCAJA, Jasin Collection.

TO JAMES H. KENNEDY • CHICAGO • SATURDAY 21 MARCH 1925

DARROW, SISSMAN, HOLLY & CARLIN March 21, 1925.

My Dear Mr. Kennedy:—

I was very glad to receive your letter this morning. I have just looked you up in "Who's Who" and find that you have been in the business of giving others publicity instead of yourself. I think your business is the best. Anyhow, the whole matter is familiar to me.

I was born in Kinsman, Ohio, which is in Trumbull County about twenty miles from Farmington. I did not want to wish my book on my own town, so I chose your town and likewise changed the State. However, it is a Trumbull County story and of course I knew Farmington very well as a boy. I remember the Western Reserve Seminary which was a sort of Mecca to the people in that benighted land. I presume it has served its usefulness and gone its way.

I had an uncle or two who lived in Farmington—not very prominent. They were engaged largely in fiddling and drinking whiskey, which is not a bad way to kill time while we are here. Their name was Darrow. My father who had a different frame of mind and is well described in the book, once lived in Farmington. I also had an Aunt Sally who married a Mr. Oatley, whose first name I have forgotten. He had two sons—William and Edmund and some girls, whose names I have forgotten, being cousins.[6]

I often used to drive to Farmington and knew a number of people there fairly well. One of them especially, whose name I cannot now just recall, but you will know him. He was quite a prominent man and an active spiritualist, which was in vogue in those days. Washington Hyde[7] has been a life-long acquaintance of mine. I saw him a year ago when I was back in Warren and like the rest of us, he is growing old, I think some ten years older than I. He and my brother Everett were classmates at Ann Arbor and were lifelong friends afterwards.

Squire Allen was really patterned after John Kinsman[8] who was one of the patriarchs of our town and who has a wonderful monument, about six feet high, enclosed by an iron fence, in the Kinsman burying ground. I have not seen either him or the monument for about ten years, but I understand he is still there under the monument.

The river and the hills were patterned after Meadville where I once took a college course for nine months at Allegheny and learned to play a pretty good game of baseball

6. Darrow is referring to one of his father's older sisters, Sarah Darrow Oatley (1815–96), her husband, Joshua Oatley (1814–62), and their children: William, Edwin, Sophia, Ellen, and Mary. The Oatleys were farmers in Farmington, Ohio. In addition to the two boys mentioned by Darrow, the Oatleys also had two other boys who died, one at the age of two (Plimpton) and the other at six months (Charley).
7. George Washington Hyde (1847–1940), lawyer and businessman. Hyde was born and raised in Farmington, Ohio. He was educated in the district school, attended the Western Reserve Seminary, and then went to the University of Michigan, where he obtained a B.A., 1870, and graduated from the law school, 1872. He practiced law in Warren, Ohio, for more than sixty years and was one of the organizers of a local telephone company, serving as its president and treasurer for many years. He was also president and director of a local rubber company and one of the organizers of a local furniture manufacturing company.
8. John Kinsman (1753–1813), the man after whom Darrow's hometown of Kinsman was named.

and likewise learned to decline "mensa". This is about all the Latin I remember and I never had a chance to use this until a few days ago, when I was working a cross-word puzzle, so Latin is worth while after all.

I have no doubt I am the one your father spoke about, for I was frequently in Farmington. I also had some doubt as to whether I ought to have named my book after your town, but you are the first man from Farmington who has called my attention to it and you do not seem to object, so we will have to let it go at that.

I presume you come this way occasionally and if you ever come again, I shall be glad to see you. Once in a while I go back to Trumbull County, but most all the names I used to know are chiseled on gravestones, so I do not get much kick out of it. The last time I was there, I intended to spend a week. I got into Kinsman on a morning train and in an hour or two, thought I would want to spend two or three days. Along toward noon, I found there was an afternoon train out so I went away the same day. I was back there about two months ago for an evening when the people got together and gave me a dinner, which they would not have done if I had stayed. There were a few ghosts present whose names I remembered, but could not figure any likeness. I probably looked the same to them, but somehow I have a feeling for the old place and may possibly go back again this summer.

Warren, you know, has grown to be quite a City, with its modern improvements, such as steel mills. I have not heard that Farmington has stirred any. Could not even find the old corner where I used to turn down the road to Farmington. I did not go over to Mecca. I did not even hear of it.

Anyhow, I am very much obliged for your letter and recognition and for the kind things you have said about the book. I thought it was pretty good when I wrote it, but not many people found it out. It seems to have been printed for private circulation. Perhaps after I am dead and they are well rid of me, some of them will look it up and read it.

With kind regards, I am,

Very truly yours, | Clarence Darrow

MS: TLS, OHi, VFM 2021, Clarence Darrow Papers. INSIDE ADDRESS: Mr. James H. Kennedy, | 1841 Otley Street, | South Pasadena, Calif.

TO H. L. MENCKEN • CHICAGO • SUNDAY 22 MARCH 1925

DARROW, SISSMAN, HOLLY & CARLIN March 22d

My Dear Menken

I am afraid you will begin to think I am a liar. I have not written the two contributions, "The Edwards & Jukes families" and "Eugenics." I have been so tied up that I couldn't get to it. I have however accumulated the material & fairly well digested it and on my return from the east shall write them. Will have one or both ready to send you in April.

I think I shall prove, (to my own satisfaction at least & I hope yours) that the Jukes family was the better family and that the Eugenicists are half baked dreamers.

With all good wishes, | Clarence Darrow.

MS: ALS, NN, Mencken Papers. DATE: "1925" appended.

TO VIVIAN PIERCE • NEW YORK CITY • THURSDAY 11 JUNE 1925

HOTEL BELMONT June 11

Dear Vivian

The enclosed will seem small & it is but I feel I should not do more now. I have so many calls & so little income. Mr. Hearst is very strongly against capital punishment & if you could get his attention the right way I feel sure you could get a good deal of aid from him, in various ways. I am awfully glad you are going into it & I will help all I can & in every direction.[9] I assume you are not going after a Federal amendment. I should not be for this. Would rather keep capital punishment.

Truly | Clarence Darrow

MS: ALS, MBNU, Sara Ehrmann Papers, Box 16, Folder 91. DATE: suggestion that Pierce was forming an organization against capital punishment.

TO VIVIAN PIERCE • CHICAGO • MONDAY 15 JUNE 1925

DARROW, SISSMAN, HOLLY & CARLIN June 15th 1925.

My Dear Vivian Pierce:-

I just received a letter from your Chicago friend and I will see her. Do not know how much I can help, but will try.

I am glad you are in this work and I believe we can make things go after we get started.

The best man on the psychiatrist end is Dr. William A. White,[10] St. Elizabeth Hospital, Washington. He has been for many years the head of the government hospital, and has written more on the subject than any other man. He is all on our side. You can tell him that I suggested that you write him.

9. This letter was apparently in response to a letter from Pierce requesting help for what became the American League to Abolish Capital Punishment. Darrow was part of the organizing committee for the league, which was formed in 1925. The league was later incorporated in New York and called the American League to Abolish Capital Punishment. William Randolph Hearst did contribute to the organization; in its first year, he distributed ten thousand copies of an anti-death-penalty article from *Cosmopolitan* in states that used electrocution. Pierce to League Members, 8 June 1926, TLS, MBNU, Sara Ehrmann Papers, Box 32, Folder 27.
10. William A. White (1870–1937), psychiatrist, hospital administrator, and author. White was superintendent of the Government Hospital for the Insane in Washington, D.C. (later called St. Elizabeth's Hospital), 1903–37, and a pioneer in the field of psychiatry and treatment of the insane. He wrote widely on medicine and psychiatry as well as crime and eugenics and many other social issues. He testified for the defense in the hearing for Nathan Leopold and Richard Loeb in 1924.

An eminent man in New York is Dr. Bernard Gluick.[11] You can find his name in the telephone directory and my name will go with him.

Dr. William A. Healy[12] is another good man. He is connected with the courts in Boston and a letter addressed to him in care of the court will get him.

When I get time, I will try to help you.

Very truly yours, | Clarence Darrow

MS: TLS, MBNU, Sara Ehrmann Papers, Box 16, Folder 91. INSIDE ADDRESS: Miss Vivian Pierce, | 448 W. 24th Street, | New York, N.Y.

TO H. L. MENCKEN • CHICAGO • WEDNESDAY 5 AUGUST 1925

DARROW, SISSMAN, HOLLY & CARLIN August 5, 1925.

My Dear Mr. Mencken:—

If you think best, change the title as you suggested—"Edwardses and Jukeses" or "Edwards vs Jukes." I think the former is better. I want you to make sure of the grammar of the first title. I have very few prejudices about grammar and am never quite sure.[13]

It was nice to see you and get so well acquainted down in the benighted South. I wonder how you people kept the Baltimore Sun in such good shape so near the dead line. In fact it is dead enough anywhere. I enjoyed your stories and I hope you will publish them in some permanent form.[14]

Am sorry you missed my examination of Bryan. I made up my mind to show the country what an ignoramus he was and I succeeded, but I only had two hours of him and wanted another day. However, the judge came in court in the morning without any

11. Bernard Glueck (1884–1972), psychiatric criminologist. Born in Poland, Glueck earned his medical degree from Georgetown University Medical School, 1909, and worked at St. Elizabeth's Hospital before leading a psychiatric clinic at Sing Sing prison in New York. Later, he worked as director of New York's Bureau of Child Guidance, served in the Army Medical Corps during World War I, and taught at the New York School of Social Work. In 1927, he was one of the organizers of Stony Lodge, a private psychiatric hospital in Ossining, New York. After his retirement from there in 1946, Glueck started outpatient clinics for the Veterans Administration and served on the faculty of the University of North Carolina at Chapel Hill, 1956–64. Glueck, like White, testified for the defense during the hearing for Leopold and Loeb.
12. William Healy (1869–1962), psychiatric criminologist, medical psychologist, and author. Born in England, Healy earned an A.B. from Harvard, 1899, and an M.D. from the University of Chicago, 1900. In 1909, he became the director of the Juvenile Psychopathic Institute in Chicago (later called the Institute for Juvenile Research), which was the first child guidance clinic in America. In 1915, he wrote *The Individual Delinquent,* an influential book that described social and developmental factors in delinquency. In 1917, he moved to Boston, where he helped found the Judge Baker Foundation (later called the Judge Baker Guidance Center). He was the coauthor of many books on delinquency, mental testing, psychoanalysis, and crime. Healy, like White and Glueck, also testified for the defense in the hearing for Leopold and Loeb.
13. Darrow is referring to his article on eugenics that was published in Mencken's magazine: "The Edwardses and the Jukeses," *American Mercury,* October 1925, 147–57.
14. Mencken was among 225 newspaper reporters who gathered in Dayton, Tennessee, for the trial of John T. Scopes. His reports on the trial have been called "some of the most brilliant dispatches in the history of journalism." *The Impossible H. L. Mencken: A Selection of His Best Newspaper Stories,* ed. Marion Elizabeth Rodgers (New York: Doubleday, 1991), 561; ibid., 562–611 (reprinting Mencken's dispatches).

motion on the part of anybody and dragged him off the stand. Of course the judge had been seen the night before.

Lipmann evidently has not any sense.[15] I wonder what was to be done. Scopes was indicted and it either had to go by default or somebody had to make a fuss about it. I was interested in waking up to the country as to what they had to meet and think we succeeded so far. I do not know how much farther they can get, but they will never pull off anything else without a fight in the first instance and I think science should lead and I think will. However, life is nothing else but a fight, if you believe in any kind of freedom and they will edge in on us some where all the time. Prohibition was the first thing that caused all the difficulty and I knew it would, but although I can get along without booze myself, I looked on it as an outside fortification of freedom.

I shall surely hunt you up when I come to New York again.

I am mighty glad you like the Edwards-Jukes story. I hope it will stir up some thought on the subject of letting a committee determine who should do the propagating. Of course it does not concern me much personally any more, but at the same time, I do not want the Methodists or the Baptists to pick out the fathers and mothers of the fool race.

Always, | Your friend, | Clarence Darrow

MS: TLS, NN, Mencken Papers. INSIDE ADDRESS: Mr. H. L. Mencken, | 730 Fifth Avenue, | New York, N.Y.

TO THE *(CHICAGO) DAILY NEWS* • GREELEY, COLORADO • TUESDAY 11 AUGUST 1925

Judge Raulston was elected on a fluke and is now campaigning for reelection this fall.[16] The trial was part of his campaign. He called the grand jury and asked them to indict Scopes

15. Mencken may have relayed to Darrow something that Lippmann said to him or he may have made some statement about Lippmann's editorials in the *New York World*, which were criticial of the Scopes defense. In one editorial, the *World* complained that the defense had made a mistake in trying to show through expert testimony "that science can be reconciled with the Bible" rather than challenging the Tennessee law outright as a "breach of the American doctrine of the separation of church and state." "A Blunder by the Scopes Defense," *New York World*, 21 July 1925. In another piece, Lippmann complained that Darrow had turned the trial into a contest about whether one "was for or against the Christian religion" and that it was now "dawning upon the friends of evolution that science was rendered a wretched service" by the trial. Edward J. Larson, *Summer for the Gods* (New York: Basic Books, 1997), 207 (quoting Lippmann, "Darrow's Blunder," *New York World*, 23 July 1925).
16. John T. Raulston (1868–1956), the judge in Tennessee who presided at the trial of John T. Scopes, gave a speech in Chicago on 10 August 1925 at a conference of Christian fundamentalists, held under the auspices of the Illinois Christian Fundamentals Association. He praised the conduct of William Jennings Bryan during the trial and criticized Darrow. He said, "There was much effort on the part of the defendant's counsel to make Mr. Bryan and the things for which he stood the real issue," and Bryan "calmly and serenely" suffered many "gibes, taunts and sneers." Raulston also told his audience how he had cited Darrow for contempt after Darrow became upset with his ruling that Scopes would be prohibited from putting any experts on the witness stand to testify about the scientific basis for evolution. See "Champions of Bible Push Chicago Drive" and "Opens Campaign for Memorial to Bryan," *Daily News*, 10 August 1925. The *Daily News* might have sent this story to Darrow, who was staying with his son in Colorado. The next day, the newspaper published the full text of this telegram. Raulston was seeking reelection as a judge but he did not win.

in a hurry so the case could be tried in his district. The indictment was illegal, as it was brought too soon after convening of a special grand jury, so the judge had him reindicted a month later, on the day of the trial.

On Sunday, three days before the case was closed, Mr. Bryan spoke twice in Dayton. Raulston was present at both meetings and sat on the platform at one. He paraded his fundamentalism all through the trial and has given the people of Chicago a chance to see what sort of trial could have been had before him.

It was perfectly proper to call Mr. Bryan a recognized expert on the Bible, to testify as to meaning of story of creation. The questions asked him were perfectly civil, but when the examination had only commenced the judge came in to court in the morning and took Mr. Bryan off the stand without any motion being made in court to that effect.

The judge may be glad he has a limited education. One cannot always avoid being ignorant, but few boast of it.

The incident citing me for contempt is absurd. I did feel a contempt for his unfairness. I did show it, as often happens by lawyers in court. I did apologize as I should have done. This constantly happens in court and the judge knows it, although it never happened to me before.

Clarence Darrow.

MS: (Telegram) "Darrow Criticizes Raulston as Unfair," *The (Chicago) Daily News*, 11 August 1925. DATE: telegram was reported by the *Daily News* as sent on this date.

TO SAMUEL D. SCHWARTZ • GREELEY, COLORADO • WEDNESDAY 12 AUGUST 1925

THE GREELEY GAS AND FUEL COMPANY Aug 12th

My Dear Mr. Schwartz

I don't think I would be the right one to debate with Dr. Stratton.[17] I would suggest Dr. Shirley Jackson Case of the University or Dr. John Thompson[18] or the Evanston minister whose name I can't recall but you can find out about him. You doubtless know

17. Schwartz had written to Darrow saying that he had a letter from John Roach Straton proposing a debate on the subject of fundamentalism versus modernism. Schwartz asked if Darrow wanted to debate Straton. See Schwartz to Darrow, 10 August 1925, TLc, ICN, Arthur and Lila Weinberg Papers. Straton had also been publicly challenging Darrow to debate the subject of evolution, "assailing" Darrow in his speeches and saying that "the moral decline of the present day started two generations ago when the 'dark and sinister shadow of Darwinism fell across the fair field of human life.'" "Straton to Debate Darrow, He Hopes," *New York Times*, 4 August 1925.
18. John Thompson (1862–1944), pastor. Thompson was born in England and came to the United States in 1893. He graduated from Northwest University and Garrett Biblical Institute in Evanston, Illinois. He was a well-known figure in Chicago and, for more than twenty years, pastor of First Methodist Church (The Chicago Temple).

others. Dr. Will Durant[19] is one of the ablest debaters I ever met. I would be willing to debate with him on Feby 8th but I want it billed on condition that you may substitute some one else in case I can't be there. I don't like to promise absolutely so far ahead. Will be in Chicago Aug 25.

Very truly | Clarence Darrow

MS: ALS (copy), ICN, Arthur and Lila Weinberg Papers. DATE: letters from Schwartz to Darrow.

TO SAMUEL D. SCHWARTZ • GREELEY, COLORADO • THURSDAY 20 AUGUST 1925

THE GREELEY GAS AND FUEL COMPANY Aug 20th

My Dear Schwartz

From your letter it would seem that Bishop McConnell and I have nothing to debate.[20] I like what you said about his letter and would like to debate with him if there is some question on which we honestly disagree, and which at the same time will be worth while to the public. I never debate just for the sake of debating, don't think it is fair to the audience or a dignified thing to do, and I judge the Bishop feels as I do, for that reason it would be a pleasant thing to meet him. I am perfectly willing to state my views frankly to you about the subject. I believe that all organic and inorganic has always been in a state of change one from growing out of an other which I call Evolution. I believe that man as he is today is a product of Evolution. I have no theory of how the Universe came into being and am inclined to think that this will forever be a sealed book to man. I have no quarrel with the God idea although I can not conceive of it as an explanation, for the reason that I can get no mental image of God and if I could the question would still exist as to his or its origin. However I think, that it is just as admissable to say that God created

19. Will Durant (1885–1981), writer and lecturer. Durant attended seminary, taught at the Modern School in New York, lectured at other Modern Schools and at an adult education project in New York City before obtaining his Ph.D. in philosophy from Columbia University, 1917, after which he taught extension courses at Columbia and became director of the Labor Temple School in New York. Durant's *The Story of Philosophy* (1926), which had been published as a "little blue book" by the radical publisher E. Haldeman-Julius (1889–1951), became a best seller and helped to make Durant a popular lecturer. Over the course of the next almost fifty years, Durant, in collaboration with this wife, Ariel Durant (1898–1981), wrote a popular eleven-volume history of the world entitled *The Story of Civilization* (1935–75). Durant and Darrow debated on stage several times before and after Durant became famous. See Will Durant and Ariel Durant, *A Dual Autobiography* (New York: Simon & Schuster, 1977), 91, 96, 110, 114. In Schwartz's letter to Darrow, he had suggested Durant as another person whom Darrow might want to debate.

20. Schwartz had written another letter to Darrow, proposing a debate between Darrow and Francis J. McConnell (1871–1953), a Methodist bishop in Pittsburg who became well known for his liberal views and activism in liberal causes. In his letter to Darrow, Schwartz quoted a letter from McConnell in which McConnell seemed to say that he could only debate an evolutionist who refused to conceive of an involvement by God: "The only phase of the debate in which I have ever been interested is that between the scientist who maintains that evolution cannot be conceived in terms of God, and the believer who maintains that it can thus be conceived. I simply would not know how to go about it to debate with a man who did not accept evolution. I think I can say some things to the man who believes in Evolution and yet does not believe that Evolution can be interpreted in terms of Divine procedure. I do not pretend to be a scientist but rather an interpreter of the results of science." Schwartz to Darrow, 15 August 1925, TLc, ICN, Arthur and Lila Weinberg Papers.

the Universe in some form as to say that it created it self or that it existed forever. I am satisfied that there are things that human beings must be satisfied not to know. Neither have I any quarrel with the religionist. I am inclined to think that life is so hard and insoluble that the race must needs have some religion. More than that I can see little in Evolution that conflicts with a rational interpretation of Christianity. I think I could pretty well agree with most of the modernists position. I wish that Dr. McConnell would debate with someone like Stratton. I would be glad to sit amongst the bleachers and hear it. It is only the dogmatists and cock sure fellows that I can't get along with. It seems to me that the student is always modest and willing to say that he does not know but is willing to use some theory as a working hypothesis that he thinks will help him and others, without being sure that he is right.

This is not much of an answer to your letter but I don't see how I can do any better. I am quite sure that in the main you have somewhat the same attitude that I have, and will understand me.

By the way Dr. John Stratton has challenged me for a debate. I wish you would find out something about him, whether he really represents anyone, or is a man that it would be worthwhile to debate with. I am like Dr. McConnell, I am not an expert in Evolution, merely a student, there are thousands of men who know much more about it than I do. I am a pretty fair Evolutionist for a lawyer as Dr. McConnell is for a preacher. And I will not assume to know more about Evolution than I think I do. You can write the Bishop giving my views, sending him a copy of my letter if you wish but it is personal to him & you, I wouldn't want it in print as it is written hastily. I will be in Chicago the 25th or 26th of this month & would like to see you then when you will have had a chance to hear from Bishop McConnell and perhaps have some information about Dr. Stratton. I think it would be a fine thing for you to have Bishop McConnell on your programme for an address. Still better to have a debate between him and a fundamentalist. I am not trying to get up a row between Christians, but it seems to me, that the progressive ones must make a stand for religious freedom, and more & more I find myself in sympathy with them and coming to feel that they are the only ones who can preserve liberty of conscience and speech. With kindest appreciation & regards,

Clarence Darrow

MS: ALS (copy), ICN, Arthur and Lila Weinberg Papers. DATE: letters from Schwartz to Darrow.

TO H. L. MENCKEN • GREELEY, COLORADO • TUESDAY 25 AUGUST 1925

THE GREELEY GAS AND FUEL COMPANY Aug 25th

My Dear Menkin

Your letter reached me here where I am taking a short loaf with my son and three grand children who live here. You see I am afraid the germ-plasm will play out and it would be

a calamity not to help keep the fool race going. Any how I won't be going very long and intellectually I am glad of it, though emotionally I presume I shall fight to the last.

I am interested in what you say about fundamentalism. I am sure we are in for a long fight and if it is ever finished we will be in for others. The human animal is like any others; his brain doesn't count, he acts of course through emotion and it is as easy to stir him up now as it ever was. His life too is as aimless as ever was, in fact all life is aimless except for our kidding. I am satisfied too that the Catholics of this country are with the fundamentalists although they like to keep the crowd fighting in self protection.

However I have much more hope of Europe than America, and the pope & all the cardinals (nearly) come from Europe. Europe is much more civilized and as the Catholics will not act together until the church acts, the Catholic scientists and scholars in Europe may keep them from acting. You know somehow I would like to spend a day or two with you better than anything I can think of and would rather spend it in Baltimore than N.Y. for I wouldn't be interfered with by as many people. Got your check and am glad you liked my stuff on the Edwardses & the Jukeses. I will probably need space and perhaps help to answer some of the critics that I am sure won't like it. I want to write an other on Eugenics. It is strange how the fool notion has taken hold of the Semi-civilized. Because a man can make a fat hog out of a lean one by regulating their love affairs, they think we can make a fatter headed man by doing the same thing & perhaps we can. Still I know who will pick out the fathers & mothers of the race—It will be the fundamentalists in some sections and the Catholics in others. We wouldn't have a [xx]. Then too I am prepared to show that a razor back hog is better than a Berkshire—of course I am considering the hog.

Always with appreciation & regard | Clarence Darrow

MS: ALS, NN, Mencken Papers. DATE: "1925" appended.

TO FRANK WALSH • CHICAGO • SATURDAY 29 AUGUST 1925

DARROW, SMITH, CRONSON & SMITH August 29th, 1925

Personal

Dear Frank:—

This is for your private consumption.[21] Reverend Stratton has been making a good many cracks of a nasty sort to the Newspapers, to which I have so far paid no attention. You know of him and have heard him debate. I don't want to debate with a man who cannot treat

21. Darrow wrote another letter to Walsh (not labeled "personal") on this same date, saying that he would be willing to publicly debate Straton on a question like "Was the Earth Developed by a Process of Evolution and Is Man the Product of Evolution?" Darrow also proposed a way to divide the debate time, suggesting that the first debate be held in Chicago and any second debate ("if I live through the first one") in New York. Darrow to Walsh, 29 August 1925, TLS, NN, Walsh Papers.

the matter in a gentlemanly way, and not resort to personalities. I could do it but it isn't a pleasant job, and I don't care to be annoyed.

I want you to assure yourself without telling him my views, that a debate could be so conducted.

If we come to New York, I hope you can act as Chairman. I am sorry I haven't seen you for so long. Next time I am there I will surely hunt you up. I haven't at hand your new address but trust this will reach you.

Always your Friend, | Clarence Darrow

MS: TLS, NN, Walsh Papers, Box 14.

TO FORREST BAILEY • CHICAGO • FRIDAY 4 SEPTEMBER 1925

DARROW, SMITH, CRONSON & SMITH September 4, 1925.

My Dear Mr. Bailey:—

Your letter is more than satisfactory.[22] I never had any doubt about you or the rest of the boys. Of course we have to expect criticism if we do what we think we should do and I get used to it. I know perfectly well that the case was handled in the proper way and I doubt whether many people could have brought the attention of the country to it as we did, and after all, this is the main thing.

I urged Dr. Neal to take in a leading Tennessee lawyer and even got one of the very best lawyers in Tennessee to consent to argue this case with him. I told Dr. Neal I would be very glad indeed not to argue it if he would get a representative Tennessee lawyer. He replied that there would be no reason why all of us could not argue it, which is probably true and that he would get the lawyer. This he has not done. It is somewhat embarrassing to me and I am very anxious to have it done. Dr. Neal knows the man. He lives in Chattanooga and I think it very important to have him or some one equally as good.

I might as well be frank about Dr. Neal, although, of course, I prefer that he should not know it. He is a fine man and an able man and could have been a good lawyer if he had given his time to it, but he has chosen to be a professor and is not equipped to take the leading part in arguing a case. Mr. Hays,[23] I am sure, knows all about it. It is very

22. Bailey and others with the American Civil Liberties Union wanted Darrow to take a less prominent role in the appellate proceedings of the Scopes case; they also wanted to replace him with a more conservative lawyer with a national reputation. They were sensitive to criticisms of the defense at trial as too theatrical or disrespectful of religious beliefs, and they saw Darrow as too radical for their cause, all of which was affecting the ACLU's fund-raising for the case. Ray Ginger, *Six Days of Forever? Tennessee v. John Thomas Scopes* (Boston: Beacon Press, 1958), 193–202. Darrow apparently learned of some of this through Arthur Garfield Hays (who might have learned of it through John R. Neal, lead local defense counsel in the case). In any event, Bailey wrote a letter to Darrow to reassure him that the executive committee of the ACLU had the "highest esteem" for him and that they were "unanimously of the opinion that he should not be invited to withdraw" from the case, but they also believed that he "ought to be made aware that a problem existed," and they thought the "proper person to do it was Dr. Neal." Bailey to Darrow, 2 September 1925, TLc, NjP, ALCU Archives.

23. Arthur Garfield Hays.

hard to get Dr. Neal in any matter. I do not know quite how we can accomplish it, but I am very strongly of the opinion that a Tennessee lawyer of experience who stands well with the court should make the main argument in this case and I think it might be worth while for Mr. Hays to go and see him and if he does, to attend to it while he is there. Otherwise it may not be done.

The lawyer's name, whom I think should argue this case, is Spurlock[24] and every one knows his standing in Tennessee. However, I am not insistent on any special one, but feel very strongly that some one should be in and I would be glad to forego an argument myself, if it is necessary, in order to bring him in.

Of course I understand your position as well as I do my own. We have to be interested first of all in the result of this case and I would resent any lawyers outside of Tennessee coming in, but I am emphatic in my belief that some one there should be in this case. I have already said that to Mr. Hays and I have felt that from the beginning it should have been done down there. We did have a fairly good one who lived in Dayton, but at the last minute he got cold feet. I suppose he was afraid of the fundamentalists in his County, but this man I told you about, I know will do it.

There is another good lawyer there whom I think is the equal of any of them, but a younger man, and probably not quite as well known to the court. He would be perfectly willing to go in and I think Neal is rather more friendly to him than to Spurlock. This is Mr. Robert S. Keebler,[25] Memphis, Tenn. He is very able and an evolutionist and has made a good fight.

There is no use of any of us expecting that a man can take up a case like this and make a fight without criticism and I imagine nobody knows it better than your people.

I feel just a little mean about writing you in reference to Neal and asking you not to tell him about it. I think he should make an argument, but I know that one of these other lawyers would have more influence with the court and the people.

I want you to know that I thoroughly understand the situation and know that your letter states the facts just as they are and also understand your high esteem for me and I want you to know that it is fully reciprocated.

Very truly yours, | Clarence Darrow

24. Frank Spurlock (1854–1947), a lawyer from Chattanooga, Tennessee, was well known as a local lawyer who championed civil liberties, including the repeal of Prohibition laws. Although he was always in private practice, he was also general counsel for many years for the *Chattanooga Times*, the city water company, a local railroad, and other companies.

25. Robert S. Keebler (1889–1976), a lawyer from Memphis, Tennessee, had been a vocal critic of the law under which Scopes was prosecuted. In June 1925, before the trial, he denounced the law in a speech during a meeting of the Tennessee bar association, and his speech was removed from the record of the proceedings by the association. He was a graduate of Washington and Lee University and received a master's degree and law degree from Harvard University. Keebler eventually joined Scopes's defense team in the appeal to the Tennessee Supreme Court. In 1934, he moved to Washington, D.C., to work as counsel for the National Recovery Review Board, for which Darrow was the chairman, and he later worked as a lawyer for the federal government in other capacities.

P.S. You are at liberty to show this letter to Mr. Hays or Mr. Malone.

MS: TLS, NjP, ACLU Archives. INSIDE ADDRESS: Mr. Forrest Bailey, | 100 Fifth Avenue, | New York, N.Y. ENDORSEMENT: noted as received on "9/8/25" and reviewed by "FB."

TO ARTHUR GARFIELD HAYS • CHICAGO • THURSDAY 17 SEPTEMBER 1925

September 17, 1925.

Dear Arthur:—

I cannot help worrying some about the situation of the case. I hear nothing from Neal and this morning I received a letter from the Bureau and find that you have received no word. He is absolutely hopeless.[26]

I am not at all sure that he has the record in shape, to start with, and if he has, he has probably done nothing in the way of preparing the matter for argument. It will be too late to get another Tennessee lawyer when we get down there. Don't you think you should go down and straighten things out and if you do, do not leave until it is done.

I know this is a big job for you, but I feel that it cannot be accomplished any other way.

This case ought to be won in the Supreme Court of Tennessee and I think can be with the right handling. When I was there, he promised me to at once get one of the Tennessee lawyers that was suggested, but I am sure he has done nothing except to prevent it. I think Spurlock of Chattanooga would probably be the best man, although Keebler of Memphis is an exceedingly good lawyer and would be perfectly satisfactory to me.

I note what Mr. Bailey says about the case being placed at the end and I want to say that before I left Tennessee, Mr. Neal did speak to me about trying to have the case specially set with two days for argument, at the end of the docket, but since that, I have heard nothing.

Always, with best wishes, | Your friend,

P.S. I have heard from some source that Mr. Neal has been very much disturbed because he was not put on as one of the lecturers for the Daughters of the Revolution. He is probably being boycotted down there and it is possible he has got cold feet with all the rest.

MS: TLc, NjP, ACLU Archives. INSIDE ADDRESS: Mr. Arthur Garfield Hays, | 43 Exchange Place, | New York, N.Y. AUTHOR: references to Spurlock and Keebler, among other points.

TO VIVIAN PIERCE • CHICAGO • FRIDAY 18 SEPTEMBER 1925

DARROW, SMITH, CRONSON & SMITH September 18, 1925.

Dear Miss Pierce:-

Your letter is just received. I will do the best I can to get down there in October, but cannot come this month.

26. Darrow is probably referring to the letter referenced above from Forrest Bailey.

I am very much pleased with the progress you are making. I have great confidence in your bunch.[27]

I think we ought to get a few Christian Science people on this list, as they all seem to be our way. I would suggest Alice Thompson[28] who is a lawyer here. She is very intelligent and is very strong for us. You may address her in my care, if you wish.

I wonder if Willis Abbott[29] would not go on the committee. He is the editor of the Christian Science Monitor. I believe this committee is going to accomplish something. It is the first time I have felt very hopeful about doing it.

You will find my taking more active interest before long.

Very truly yours, | Clarence Darrow

MS: TLS, MBNU, Sara Ehrmann Papers, Box 16, Folder 91. INSIDE ADDRESS: Miss Vivian Pierce, | 70 Fifth Avenue | New York, N.Y.

TO OSWALD GARRISON VILLARD • CHICAGO • FRIDAY 2 OCTOBER 1925

DARROW, SMITH, CRONSON & SMITH October 2, 1925.

My Dear Mr. Villard:—

Replying to your letter about coming to New York on the 10th, I would say I would like very much to come and of course I will be satisfied to simply take my expenses. I like you and your crowd and the paper, and feel that you are doing a great deal for the cause of liberal thinking. You are about as open-minded a bunch as I know, and likewise fearless.

I must add, however, that I do not like the subject you propose—"Is Science the Enemy of the Church." I do not think that science is the enemy of the Universalist Church or the Unitarian, or most of the Congregational churches. Neither do I think it is the enemy of churches like the one where Fosdick talks, nor John Haynes Holmes, nor of many Methodists that I know, and even some of other denominations.

I must confess, that beyond this, my experience in Dayton where I saw the dense ignorance of what we call Fundamentalists and their persistent endeavor to destroy all freedom of thought, it caused me to draw nearer to those who are fighting bigotry and intolerance from the inside of some church organizations, and with some church organizations.

27. By "bunch" Darrow is apparently referring to the members of the organizing committee for what became the American League to Abolish Capital Punishment, which included Darrow.
28. Alice H. Thompson (1892–1969), lawyer. Thompson was a graduate of the law school at the University of Valparaiso. She had a general practice in Chicago. Darrow had known Thompson for a long time. He was co-counsel with her in 1915, when they defended a man charged with murdering a woman and her baby.
29. Willis J. Abbott (1863–1934), newspaper editor. Abbott received an LL.B. and L.H.D. from the University of Michigan. He was managing editor of the *Chicago Times* in the early 1890s and an editor or editorial writer for many other newspapers and periodicals, including the *New York American*, the *Chicago American*, and *Collier's Weekly*. He was editor of the *Christian Science Monitor* from 1922 to 1927 and later a member of the newspaper's editorial board. He also wrote a column for the paper.

Of course many of the so-called progressives cannot avoid finding some hang-over of the old time theology which is mixed with their tolerant ideas and their belief in science, and I fancy perhaps the same thing might be said of you and me. All of us are to a certain extent bound by the past and in spite of ourselves, we use much of the language of the past and intuitively accept many old ideas without investigation, assuming they are correct.

I believe a large part of the church is very rapidly alligning itself with scientific thought, and personally I do not feel like doing anything to drive them away.

I presume you have got your mind set on the subject, but if you have not, I would suggest "Is man a Mechanism". I am certain that Mr. Fosdick, or most any of the liberal ministers are not ready to accept that idea. Without being dogmatic, however, I am pretty sure that man is simply a piece of mechanism. Under such a question, we could say most anything regarding present day ideas. If that would not do, we might think of something else, but I would hate to put myself openly in the way of declaring that the church is an enemy of science. I am not at all sure that religion is an enemy of science. Life is so hard that I am satisfied for some time to come, perhaps forever, the great mass of men will turn to some kind of faith to make it easier. I am not at all certain that humanity at large could live without it.

Anyhow, write me your ideas on the matter and I will certainly be glad to come. Preparing something in advance is pretty hard for me, but I might even do that.

With kind regards and best wishes, I am,

Your friend, | Clarence Darrow

MS: TLS, MH-H. INSIDE ADDRESS: Mr. Oswald Garrison Villard, | 20 Vesey Street, | New York, N.Y.

TO *THE SURVEY* • CHICAGO • JANUARY 1926

I have no doubt but what the world war is largely responsible for the reactionary tendency of the day.[30] This is a condition that has followed all great wars. To engage in such a contest requires a cultivation of intense patriotism. When nations begin mobilizing, they start with the liars. They write about their enemies and they write about themselves. Everything is good at home and bad with their enemies. Some fairly intelligent people do not know any better than to believe it. I believed part of it myself, but am gradually getting over it. After the war, the spirit of super-patriotism remains. This is easily used

30. This letter was part of a symposium titled "Where Are the Pre-War Radicals?" The editors of *The Survey* said that this symposium had been inspired by a similar question in the autobiography of Frederick C. Howe (1867–1940): "Fred Howe asked the question in his *Confessions of a Reformer* [1925]. We broaden it to include progressives, insurgents, liberals, socialists, single-taxers, 'muck rakers,' civic campaigners, and labor leaders who in the early years of the century fought for the common good as they variously saw it, and dramatized it before the people. We have asked: 'Who succeeds them?' and put the questions to men and women who were in the thick of the fight then, or who are active now." "Where Are the Pre-War Radicals," *The Survey* 55 (1 February 1926): 556–57.

to the advantage of the strong. Religious superstitions likewise grow; the leaders have a positive doctrine which involves unlimited promises. Then too, people are generally prosperous, or seem to be, during a great war. All the slack is taken up. Every man is busy. Production is great. Wages and commodities are high. Every one likes it until they wake up, which is several years after.

Following the War of the Rebellion, it was eight years before the people began to realize that somebody had to pay.

One must always remember that human beings do not reason—enough to hurt. They live from their emotions and so far as they do reason, this is controlled by their emotions. They are patriotic when they are getting plenty to eat and begin to grumble when times are hard. The grumbling will come later—not very much later; and after that, again will come bragging, blustering and one hundred per cent patriotism, and so on—world without end.

CLARENCE DARROW.

MS: "Where Are the Pre-War Radicals," *The Survey* 55 (1 February 1926): 556, 566. PLACE: no reason to doubt Chicago. DATE: publication date.

TO ALICE BEAL PARSONS • CHICAGO • SATURDAY 13 MARCH 1926

DARROW, SMITH, CRONSON & SMITH March 13, 1926.

My Dear Mrs. Parsons:—

I was glad to get your letter and glad you finished your book. I shall certainly read it and if possible write something about it myself, which might do it a little good here. If I cannot praise it, I will not say anything.[31]

I think there are a few things that I believe in that do not correspond with your views. I do not like to be too dogmatical about feminists, but I suppose you know what my general view is. I am inclined to think that nature has provided means of perpetuating the fool human species and in that provision, women are much more conservative. Otherwise brats would die young. I think it is biological. Perhaps I am mistaken. If you know anything new on this, I would be glad to see it, for I have no prejudice on the matter.

I get down to New York once in a while, but have not had your address, or would have tried to see you.

Best wishes, always, | Very truly yours, | Clarence Darrow

MS: TLS, NSyU, Alice Beal Parsons Papers, Box 1. INSIDE ADDRESS: Mrs. Alice Beal Parsons, | 71 Bedford Street, | New York, N.Y.

31. Darrow is probably referring to what became Parsons's *Woman's Dilemma* (New York: Thomas Y. Crowell, 1926), which appeared in April 1926. No review of the book by Darrow was located.

TO H. L. MENCKEN • CHICAGO • WEDNESDAY 17 MARCH 1926

DARROW, SMITH, CRONSON & SMITH March 17, 1926.

My Dear Mr. Mencken:—

Enclosed I am sending you a story on Eugenics. You have been publishing so much on this question that I am not sure that you will feel that you can use it. If you do not, send it back without the slightest hesitation. I am not even sure that it is worth publishing, but anyhow, here it is.[32]

I hope to be in New York around the 1st of April, and if so, I am going to make an effort to see you.

That was a corking letter you sent out last Sunday on Tennessee. I am glad there is somebody that knows how to do it and is not afraid.[33]

Your friend, | Clarence Darrow

MS: TLS, NN, Mencken Papers. INSIDE ADDRESS: Mr. H. L. Mencken, | 730 Fifth Avenue, | New York, N.Y.

TO SINCLAIR LEWIS • CHICAGO • THURSDAY 15 APRIL 1926

April 15, 1926.

Dear Sinclair:—

I am awfully glad you got the book started. I want to help you. I know you need it.[34]

You have got to go down to the Ozarks with us. I do not know just when it will be, but some time after the 10th of May. My case starts in Detroit on the 19th and I will know better after it is started and then I will let you know.[35]

32. Darrow's "story on Eugenics" was an article mocking the claims of eugenicists that the human race could be improved through better breeding. Mencken published it as "The Eugenics Cult," *American Mercury*, June 1926, 129–37.
33. Mencken wrote a column arguing that newspapers in Tennessee helped to sustain the "intellectual darkness" in that state and that an "intelligent and courageous press" could have prevented "the Scopes obscenity," which put "Tennessee all over the first pages of the world" and made it "a joke state, laughed at even by Haitians and Dominicans." H. L. Mencken, "The Sad Case of Tennessee," *Chicago Tribune*, 14 March 1926.
34. This is the only letter from Darrow to Lewis that survives from an exchange of several letters between the two of them in April and May 1926. Darrow was trying to get Lewis to join him on a trip to the Ozarks and Lewis was begging off because he was working on his "preacher book" (which became *Elmer Gantry* [New York: Harcourt, Brace, 1927]). See Lewis to Darrow, 5 April, 7 April, 17 April, 10 May 1926, TLS (all), MnU-L, Darrow Collection.
35. The case to which Darrow is referring is known as the second "Sweet" trial. In 1925, Ossian Sweet (1894–1960), a black physician, bought a house in a white neighborhood of Detroit. Shortly after he moved into the house, a hostile crowd gathered outside. Some people in the crowd began throwing stones and other objects at the house. Several shots were fired from the house, killing one person in the crowd and injuring another. Dr. Sweet and ten other family members and friends who were in the house were all charged with conspiracy to commit murder and assault. They were tried together in late 1925; the trial resulted in a hung jury. Ossian Sweet's brother, Henry Sweet—who admitted shooting—was tried again, separately, in April and May 1926. His trial ended in an acquittal. Darrow was lead defense attorney in both trials. He was recruited and paid by the National Association for the Advancement of Colored People.

You and that pulpit-pounder Jenkins are a damn fine pair of friends.[36] I could tell the lady where she could do better than taking a shot at me. Anyhow, you will hear from me.

Best wishes. Truly,

MS: TLc, MnU-L, Darrow Collection. PLACE: no reason to doubt Chicago. INSIDE ADDRESS: Mr. Sinclair Lewis, | Ambassador Hotel, | Kansas City, Mo.

TO FRANK MURPHY • CHICAGO • THURSDAY 27 MAY 1926

DARROW, SMITH, CRONSON & SMITH May 27th

My Dear Judge Murphy

I am sending you today the books I told you about, and I hope you may like them.[37] I think of you a great deal and miss you a lot. You were so kindly and human that it made a troublesome case easy to try. I wish you could come over for a few days. I think we could make you comfortable and I know you would make us happy. Tell Frank[38] I shall write him in a few days. Tomorrow I go to Tennessee to argue the Scopes Case in the Supreme Court.[39]

With gratitude and affection

I am your friend always | Clarence Darrow

Mrs. D. sends kind regards—

MS: ALS, MiU-H, Frank Murphy Papers. DATE: reference to Scopes argument.

TO NEGLEY D. COCHRAN • CHICAGO • SUNDAY 6 JUNE 1926

DARROW, SMITH, CRONSON & SMITH June 6th

Dear Neg

It has been a long time since I have written you, but I often think of you & I always shall. We are going to Colorado the last of June and shall stay two months or more, at Greeley mainly. I wish you could go. Scripps died and was buried in a characteristic way.[40] I hope

36. This is a reference to Burris Jenkins (1869–1945), a clergyman, educator, and author. Jenkins was pastor of the Christian (Campbellite) Church in Kansas City, Missouri. He wrote many books on religious subjects and he was publisher of a weekly journal on religion. In Lewis's letter to Darrow, Lewis had said: "And, damn you, you will probably seduce me into going off with your infidel and criminal friends to the Ozarks, at that! This noon I talked it all over with Burris Jenkins and we agreed that the lady who tried to assassinate Mussolini had a good idea but she would have contributed much more to human progress if she had taken a shot at you instead." Lewis to Darrow, 7 April 1926, TLS, MnU-L, Darrow Collection.
37. Darrow might have told Murphy about some books during or after the second Sweet trial, which ended with an acquittal of Henry Sweet on 13 May 1926, but what books Darrow sent to Murphy is unknown.
38. The identity of "Frank" is unknown.
39. John Scopes was appealing to the Supreme Court of Tennessee from his conviction the year before in Dayton.
40. On 12 March 1926, E. W. Scripps died on his boat while anchored off Monrovia, Liberia. He was buried at sea. Oliver Knight, ed., *I Protest: Selected Disquisitions of E. W. Scripps* (Madison: University Wisconsin Press, 1966), 87.

his death will not affect your business affairs any. I hoped he would do something for you in his will. Still every one holds onto their property as long as they can and don't want to do much when they die. Still he was a remarkable man and I thought a great deal of him. I just got home from Tennessee where I argued the Scopes case in the Supreme Court. They gave what seemed like a good hearing, but you can't guess. I wonder if by any chance you will be here soon. We ought to have a few weeks together before long. Whatever we do must be "before long."

Always your friend | Clarence Darrow

Best always to Mrs. Cochran.

MS: ALS, OT, Cochran Papers. DATE: "1926" appended.

TO RICHARD F. PETTIGREW • CHICAGO • FRIDAY, 18 JUNE 1926

DARROW, SMITH, CRONSON & SMITH June 18, 1926.

My Dear Pettigrew:—

Glad to get your letter addressed to Mr. Lewis.[41]

On account of your postscript, I want to say that most people probably have an idea that Evolution means constant progress. I say this without knowing what the word progress means. I am satisfied that no well informed evolutionist now believes this. I am sure I do not. I think man has not changed since he became man.

Evolution simply means that one form of organized matter grew out of another. The horse is a gradual growth from a little animal called the Eohipus which can be found in various stages down through the rocks. The bird has grown out of the fish or reptiles. Man developed, perhaps, from the Lemur, a little animal which probably inhabited the earth several million years ago and was at the dividing line between ape and man. The structure of apes and monkeys to say nothing about horses and dogs, is practically the same as that of man.

Evolution does not mean perfection or an approach to perfection. It simply means that form of matter is not a separate creation, but that one grows out of another.

If you want me to, I will send you a book on the subject.

I wish you would come back to Chicago some time. I do not know just when I could get out there. I am going to Colorado the 1st of July to spend about two months.

I see in your letter to Mr. Lewis you refer to China and the United States. I am satisfied there is more what we call crime in the United States than in China, but I have been

41. Darrow might be referring to his friend Fay Lewis.

looking for figures on the question of criminology in China and have been unable to find them. I wish you would tell me where I could get hold of some.

Best wishes to you and Berta,[42] I am,

Your friend, | Clarence Darrow

MS: TLS, SdSifSHM, Pettigrew Papers.

TO H. L. MENCKEN • GREELEY, COLORADO • TUESDAY 27 JULY 1926

Greeley Colorado | July 27th

My Dear Mr. Menken

Enclosed is the old check. I am very sorry that I put you to the trouble of looking it up, but it had entirely faded from my mind.

I have been greatly impressed with [x] Wheless' book.[43] He has done a fine job and I wrote him a line about it. I wish that in some way it could be put into the hands of the general public, but they can't pay $5 for it. Still I am hoping that it will start discussion on the subject. Every one seems to be buffaloed by the preachers. I must put a word of criticism to you on Wheless' book. His God business is bunk. There is no sort of evidence of God any where and can't be. No one knows what the word means and if there were a God we would need to explain where he came from. Then where does he get the stuff on the last page or two that the bible is the greatest book. I think pound for pound it doesn't compare with any of the world's greatest litterature. Still I have no desire to criticise, for he did a great job and I hope it will sell.

Mrs. Darrow enclosed a check for $1.00 to pay for sending your copy to me. I hope it found the right person. I wanted it quick & I appreciated the kindness of your office in sending it so I returned it as soon as I got an other.

I am putting in my time loafing and writing, don't know what I shall bring forth. Of course I would rather you take any of my stuff than any one else, although I have sent a story to Harpers on their request on crime.[44]

I shall go back to Chicago the first of Sept. and I am coming East toward the end of the month and want to have a visit and a drink with you; keep me posted as to where you

42. Roberta ("Berta") Hollister Smith Pettigrew (1866?–1952), second wife of Pettigrew and a resident of Chicago when she married him in 1922.

43. The indecipherable word in this sentence might be "with," mistakenly written a second time by Darrow. The book to which Darrow is referring is Joseph Wheless's *Is It God's Word? An Exposition of the Fables and Mythology of the Bible and of the Impostures of Theology* (New York, Knopf, 1926). Wheless (1868–1950), a lawyer in New York who specialized in Latin American matters, was also active as a lawyer for freethinking causes and organizations. Darrow might have learned of Wheless's book from Mencken's recent review of a private, limited printing of the book: H. L. Mencken, "Counter-Offensive," review of *Is It God's Word?* (New York: Wheless Publishers, 1926), *American Mercury*, May 1926, 123–25.

44. See Clarence Darrow, "Crime and the Alarmists," *Harper's Magazine*, October 1926, 535–44.

will be and I will find you. I haven't been quite so well as usual. Guess I have been going a little too lively. I seem to forget that I am almost 70 but it gives me no concern. I don't want to do it over, and I am satisfied with my rather firm conviction that when we are through we are through. Sorry to send you so long a letter written by hand

All good wishes always | Clarence Darrow

MS: ALS, NN, Mencken Papers. DATE: "1926" is appended and supported by reference to Wheless's book.

TO HENRY FORD • CHICAGO • THURSDAY 14 OCTOBER 1926

DARROW, SMITH, CRONSON & SMITH Oct 14th

Dear Mr. Ford,

I feel that I should write you a line telling you how glad I am that you expressed your views on crime.[45] Every one seems to believe in cruel punishments, which is really vengeance, but still the students have always taken the view that you have expressed so well. If boys were trained to make a living and had a chance to earn good wages most of the crime would disappear, and I believe nothing can be done in any other way. The state tries to educate every one to be scholars; it can be done for only a few, and those who can not be scholars, or do not wish to be, should be educated to be useful in other lines; most of them could work with their hands and would enjoy it, if they could receive fair wages. I am so glad for what you have said and hope you will say more.

Sincerely Yours—Clarence Darrow.

MS: ALS, MiDbEI. DATE: letter is stamped received on 18 October 1926.

TO HENRY FORD • CHICAGO • SUNDAY 24 OCTOBER 1926

DARROW, SMITH, CRONSON & SMITH Oct 24th

My Dear Mr. Ford,

I was very glad to receive your letter today.[46] I am sending you a copy of a book I once wrote, which has McGuffe's school readers in it and the old time country school,—I think possibly you may enjoy.[47] I would be glad indeed to get the readers which you said you

45. Earlier in October, Ford had announced in a long interview published in Hearst's newspapers that he planned to hire five thousand young men between sixteen and twenty years of age as a means of curbing the prevailing "crime wave" in the country. "Henry Ford to Employ 5,000 Boys as a Crime Cure Experiment," *San Francisco Examiner*, 3 October 1926.
46. Ford responded to Darrow's earlier letter saying how gratifying it was to receive Darrow's endorsement of his statements and asking if he could quote from Darrow's letter. Ford also said that he would forward reproductions of the first four books from the McGuffey Readers series. Ford to Darrow, 20 October 1926, TLS, MnU-L, Darrow Collection.
47. Darrow is referring to *Farmington*, his novel about his childhood.

would send. If you wish to I should like to have you use what I said about your position on crime. I have often wanted to drop in and see you when I was in Detroit, but I know how busy you are and then I fancy that a very large percentage who call to see you want you to do something for them in some cause which may or may not be wise, and I don't want to be put in that class.

With best wishes—| Clarence Darrow—

MS: ALS, MiDbEI.

TO KATHERINE DEBS • ATLANTIC CITY, NEW JERSEY • FRIDAY 5 NOVEMBER 1926

THE SHELBURNE Nov 5th

My Dear Mrs Debbs

I have been here for my health trying to recover from a long illness. Of course I read of dear Jene's death.[48] It was a hard blow to me. I never knew a man whom I loved more than I did him. No better, kindlier man ever lived than Jene. I shall miss him as I have missed few others. You have my deepest love & sympathy in your affliction.

Your friend always | Clarence Darrow

MS: ALS, InTI, Debs Papers. DATE: reference to death of Eugene Debs.

TO JOSEPH MORO • CHICAGO • SATURDAY 4 DECEMBER 1926

DARROW, SMITH, CRONSON & SMITH Dec. 4th.

Dear Mr Moro

I feel that it would not be wise to hold meetings while the matter is before the Supreme Court, especially if the lawyer in the case does not desire it.[49] If they are beaten I am quite sure that there will be time enough on appeal to the Governor & I shall then be glad to do all I can.

Very truly | Clarence Darrow.

MS: ALS, MB, Felicani Sacco-Vanzetti Collection.

48. Eugene Debs died on 20 October 1926. Darrow sent a similar letter to Debs's brother. See Darrow to Theodore Debs, 5 November 1926, ALS, InTI, Debs Papers.
49. Darrow is referring to the case involving Nicola Sacco (1891–1927) and Bartolomeo Vanzetti (1888–1927), Italian immigrants and anarchists who were convicted and sentenced to die for the murder of a paymaster and guard during the robbery of a shoe factory in Massachusetts. Their case became one of the most famous and controversial of the 1920s. Moro had written to Darrow from Boston asking if Darrow would speak at meetings in Boston and New York on behalf of the convicted men and asking if Darrow thought the meetings were advisable. Moro noted that William G. Thompson (1864–1938), Sacco and Vanzetti's lawyer, was opposed to the meetings but that the defense committee for the two condemned men disagreed with Thompson. See Moro to Darrow, 2 December 1926, TLc, MB, Sacco-Vanzetti Collection.

TO FREMONT OLDER • CHICAGO • TUESDAY 14 DECEMBER 1926

DARROW, SMITH, CRONSON & SMITH Dec. 14

Dear Fremont

Yours of 10th just received.[50] I want to do any thing possible for J.B. but he must call in some one to advise him and not expect his friends to take a hopeless position. His position as shown by Coyle[51] is that he did not have any thing to do with the matter. What do you suppose the L.A. people and the governor would do on that statement. Remember he plead guilty. He was fully advised by his lawyers, Davis,[52] Scott[53] & myself. Steffens also knew the facts & as I remember it you sat in with us. Not only did he plead guilty but he made a written statement telling how it was done which of course they had. He was for weeks in San Francisco. Was identified by the people who sold the powder. He registered in San Francisco. McManigal[54] I suppose is in L.A. A number of people saw him in L.A. that day and one of them in the building. The evidence was taken in Schmidt's case and it is all there.[55] Large amounts of Dynamite were found in two places in Indianapolis one being in the vault of the bldg where the headquarters was located. The evidence of the Indianapolis case is still preserved & in the files of the U.S. Court. There are 20 more indictments undisposed of in L.A. J.B. could not explain his presence in San Francisco or L.A. It is absolutely out of the question to succeed on that line. On the other hand he never intended killing any one. His statement shows that it was only for a scare. He has been there long enough. He does not even need to say any thing about it. If such a position as he suggests is taken before Steffens sees Chandler,[56] there wouldn't be a chance of even keeping them neutral. No steps should be taken in any direction without full conference. When Steffens comes we could all get together there. I know how determined he is but you must make it clear to him. You had probably better go over there and perhaps take Brennan[57] with you. Of course I don't want him to put the load on me and prefer that you do not show him this letter. There has never been a time and never will be that I won't help but it must be on lines that have a chance of success.

I shall not go to Europe this winter. I really do not feel able. Could not make a long trip. The Drs tell me to go to Louisiana but I hate even to do that but probably shall.

50. No letter from Older to Darrow on 10 December 1926 was found, but a carbon copy of a letter dated 3 December 1926 exists. In this letter, Older expressed his desire to see James McNamara released from prison. See Older to Darrow, 3 December 1926, TLc, CU-BANC, Older Papers, Box 2.
51. Albert F. Coyle was editor of the *Brotherhood of Locomotive Engineers Journal* and a friend of James McNamara.
52. LeCompte Davis.
53. Joseph Scott.
54. Ortie McManigal.
55. Matthew Schmidt.
56. Harry Chandler (1864–1944), publisher of the *Los Angeles Times* after Harrison Gray Otis died in 1917 (Chandler was married to Otis's daughter).
57. The identity of "Brennan" is unknown.

Yesterday I wired to the Herald Tribune but have not had a reply. This in reference to the review of the book. If they don't take it The Chicago News will and I have the book, and want to do a good job. I fancy no one knows you or understands you or loves you more than I and I want to do it.[58]

Always your friend | Clarence Darrow.

MS: ALS, CU-BANC, Older Papers, Box 1. DATE: reference to reviewing Older's book.

TO FREMONT OLDER • CHICAGO • WEDNESDAY 15 DECEMBER 1926

DARROW, SMITH, CRONSON & SMITH Dec. 15

Dear Fremont

I wrote you a letter yesterday. You may get this first. If so don't act on this until you receive the other. I went into the matter fully in that. I hate to see J.B. make a mistake and there is only one way to win which I indicated. I have been thinking that I *could* go out there and have a conference with you and him in Jan. I hate to go. It is not easy for me to make so long a trip but I can and will if thought best. Of course Steffens will be here in the Spring and I may need to go again then. What I was thinking is for you to go & see J.B. after reading my letter written yesterday and if you can't get him to leave things until Steffens comes. Suggest on your own account that you try to get me out when we three can go over the situation. He is not easy to handle but you may do it. Otherwise he has no chance. Am reading your book. It is beautiful. The Tribune wired me that they already had a review, but the Chicago News will take it.

Faithfully Clarence Darrow

I wonder if by mistake I sent the other to the Bulletin.

MS: ALS, CU-BANC, Older Papers, Box 1. DATE: reference to Older's book.

TO LINCOLN STEFFENS • CHICAGO • SUNDAY 26 DECEMBER 1926

DARROW, SMITH, CRONSON & SMITH Dec 26th

Dear Lincoln

Your letter just arrived, the day after christ's birthday. In the same mail was one from Older with an enclosure from J.B. In this J.B. seems to take a reasonable view. Of course

58. Darrow is referring to his review of Older's autobiography, which was eventually published in the *Daily News*. See Clarence Darrow, "Crusader's Progress," review of *My Own Story*, by Fremont Older, *(Chicago) Daily News*, 19 January 1927.

it is utterly idle to make a contention that J.B. did not place the dynamite. The evidence is overwhelming and is preserved in the record of Schmidti's case,[59] also Indianapolis—also in a hundred other ways, lastly his over written statement at the time of the plea. He should be out as he never intended to kill any one or blow up any building. It was simply a misfortune so far as that is concerned. You know that the dynamite did not even stop the presses right under the place where it was deposited. All were killed by the fire that unfortunately was kindled from some barrels of ink in the alley. He is now willing that it be handled in our own way. I feel that it will be all right for you to come in the Spring, although I would not want him to know I advised it. I do not feel able to go there this winter. Shall go south in a few days, am really in bad shape, but think I will improve. Would be awfully happy to live to see him released. Will write more fully in a few days. I think we could get up some meetings for you. Perhaps a *real* debate here, out of which you could get something. Any how we will do it some way. This is just a note to tell you I got your letter and feel as if there is no need to give up your house this winter, but let me know what you think as to time. My fool friends are getting up a dinner for me April 18th—my 70th birth day if I stay that long which I presume I shall. It would be wonderful to have you here.[60]

Always Yours | Clarence Darrow.

MS: ALS, NNC, Steffens Papers. DATE: "[1926]" appended.

TO JOHN T. SCOPES • MOBILE, ALABAMA • MONDAY 17 JANUARY 1927

Jan. 17

My Dear Scopes

I suppose you have seen all about the decision.[61] As a matter of fact, it was more our way than theirs. Still, all of us here agreed that we should ask for a reassignment of the case as only four judges participated and they were really evenly divided. All the lawyers are agreed that this is what we should do, so I assume you will approve. I am pretty well satisfied that the law is dead but we want to be sure if possible. One of the four decided that it was unconstitutional and another that a teacher could teach any scientific doctrine of man's origin except materialism. I am trying to

59. This is a reference to the trial of Matthew Schmidt.
60. A dinner in celebration of Darrow's birthday was held at the Palmer House in Chicago on 18 April 1927, with 1,200 people in attendance. See Carroll Binder, "Darrow's Friends Meet to Laud Him," *(Chicago) Daily News,* 19 April 1927.
61. On 17 January 1927 the Supreme Court of Tennessee, in a split decision, upheld the constitutionality of the "Anti-Evolution Act" under which Scopes had been convicted but reversed the judgment because the trial judge rather than the jury—as required by state constitution—had imposed the fine on Scopes. See *Scopes v. State,* 289 S.W. 363 (Tenn. 1927).

recover my health and will probably not be back in Chicago till March. Will keep you posted.[62]

Truly— | Clarence Darrow

MS: John T. Scopes and James Presley, *Center of the Storm* (New York: Holt, Rinehart & Winston, 1967), 238–39.
DATE: reference to the court decision.

TO H. L. MENCKEN • MOBILE, ALABAMA • SATURDAY 22 JANUARY 1927

THE BATTLE HOUSE Jan. 22, 1927.

My Dear Mr. Mencken:

I am here loafing, dodging winter, trying to get young again. It is very doubtful whether I will succeed in the last endeavor.

I have been thinking of something that ought to make a good story, if you have not already published anything like it on the subject:

The Lord's Day Alliance, with Headquarters in New York, are raising H—l generally, especially in the Bible belt.[63] Wherever they see anyone having any fun on Sunday, they are introducing laws to prevent it; theaters, Sunday baseball, etc., etc. They have a good deal of literature that could be used to good effect. If you want me to do it, and can manage to get hold of their literature in New York and send it to me, I will see what I can make out of it.

This morning I received a letter from my old time friend, Brand Whitlock, whose name you will no doubt remember. The letter is all about a book of which I have never heard before, written by a Frenchman named Proust, and published in fifteen volumes, of which thirteen have already appeared.[64] Whitlock thinks it is the greatest thing he ever read. You probably know something about it. He says it is pessimistic in the extreme and that the author set his task to do this work and died immediately after it was finished. The first volume is entitled "Swan's Way," but I did not write specifically to tell you about this book; you have probably heard of it.

62. The court recommended in its decision that the state attorney general abandon the suit because Scopes was no longer working for the state. The court saw no reason to continue the prosecution: "We see nothing to be gained by prolonging the life of this bizarre case. On the contrary, we think the peace and dignity of the state, which all criminal prosecutions are brought to redress, will be better conserved by the entry of a nolle prosequi herein." Ibid. at 367. The state complied by entering a *nolle prosequi* and the case came to an end. Ray Ginger, *Six Days or Forever? Tennessee v. John Thomas Scopes* (Boston: Beacon Press, 1958), 209.
63. The Lord's Day Alliance, originally called the American Sabbath Union, was founded in Washington, D.C., in 1888 by representatives of several Protestant denominations. The purpose of the organization was to promote Sunday "Blue Laws" and otherwise encourage strict observance of Sunday as a religious day.
64. The letter that Darrow had just received ("this morning") was probably one sent by Whitlock from Cannes in early January 1927, recommending Marcel Proust's *Remembrance of Things Past* (1913–27). See Whitlock to Darrow, 2 January 1927, TT, DLC-MSS, Whitlock Papers, Container 45. But here, Darrow is describing and quoting an earlier letter sent by Whitlock from Brussels in October 1926, also recommending Proust. See Whitlock to Darrow, 13 October 1926, *The Letters and Journal of Brand Whitlock: The Letters*, ed. Allan Nevins (New York: D. Appleton-Century, 1936), 390–92.

However, my friend Whitlock says, "I have been tempted to write an essay on Proust, but I don't know who would publish it if I were to do so. Mencken might print it in the *Mercury*, but I have lost touch with Mencken these many years. I never met him, in fact, although when I was Mayor of Toledo he used to write now and again in approval of my endless and unequal conflict with neo-puritanism, with it's cant and bigotry and intolerance. . . . "

It occurred to me that you would like this article from Whitlock. I am sure you are familiar with his work and his ideas. He feels about as we do about most matters. If you want to send me a line here I would be glad to write him, or better still, if you care to, you can write him at Hotel des Anglais, Cannes, A.M., France.

I will be stopping here for some time and shall be glad to hear from you whenever it is convenient.

With best wishes always, | Sincerely yours, | Clarence Darrow

You can write me at Fairhope, Ala. This is across the bay from Mobile.

MS: TLS, NN, Mencken Papers. INSIDE ADDRESS: Mr. H. L. Mencken, | c/o Alfred A. Knopf, | New York City, N.Y.

TO MARTHA BENSLEY BRUÈRE • MOBILE, ALABAMA • MONDAY 24 JANUARY 1927

THE BATTLE HOUSE Jan 24th

My Dear Mrs. Bruere

Your letter followed me here, where I will be until the middle of March. I would be glad to see you & will when I come to N.Y. but I don't see that it would do any good.[65] The settlements are evidently lined up with the preachers who believe in forcing people to obey laws that have no reason for existence. They propose to help make this country the home of cowards. I don't know why you should say my views are "unusual." Every inteligent person who ever read history and knows any thing about the subject knows that always and every where obnoxious laws are got rid of because the people will not obey them. Suppose you read Sumner's Folk Ways.[66]

With best wishes | Clarence Darrow.

MS: ALS, ICN, Parton-Darrow Papers, Box 1, Folder 1. DATE: stationery and other letters from Alabama.

65. Bruère was director of a study conducted by the National Federation of Settlements on the effects of Prohibition on urban life, which was published in 1927: *Does Prohibition Work?* (New York: Harper & Bros., 1927). Bruère probably sought Darrow's help or advice in connection with this work.

66. William Graham Sumner, *Folkways: A Study of the Sociological Importance of Usages, Manners, Customs, Mores, and Morals* (Boston: Ginn & Co., 1906).

TO HORACE LIVERIGHT • FAIRHOPE, ALABAMA • FRIDAY 4 MARCH 1927

DARROW, SMITH, CRONSON & SMITH Fairhope Ala | Mar 4th

My Dear Liveright

I have been here for the cold weather and shall return soon. Shall be in N.Y. Mar. 15th. While here I have written my share (about 30,000) words of a book in collaboration with Mr. Victor Yarros of Chicago which is an answer to Dr. Irving Fisher's "Prohibition at its worst."[67] You probably know the book. It has had a big run and is quite generally quoted. Dr. Yarros is a very able fellow & a good writer. Mine is as good as any thing I ever did. It is a live book and we leave nothing of Dr. Fisher's book. Do you want to see it? We want to get it out soon. The MSS will be ready by April 15th. What do you think about it? I will bring a copy with me to N.Y. I shall be in Chattanooga Tenn. Mar 9 & 10. Can be got by Western Union or telephone. Will be in Washington from 11th to 15th at New Willard Hotel.[68]

Truly Clarence Darrow

MS: ALS, PU-Sp, Liveright Collection. DATE: "[1927]" appended. NOTE: street address and city on letterhead are struck out.

TO H. L. MENCKEN • NEW YORK CITY • 23 MARCH 1927

HOTEL BELMONT March 23

My Dear Mencken

Sorry to miss you again. I am going from here to Washington. I wonder if I could see you Sunday or Monday if I stopped at Baltimore. Would like to see Dr Pearle[69] too. Arthur[70] says he would go over with me Sunday, or rather Saturday night. I want you to know how much I appreciated your kind words for me which were published in Vanity Fair.[71] You know a fellow that gets so many stones &c can't help appreciating the other especially from you. If you can see me probably better wire.

Your friend | Clarence Darrow.

MS: ALS, NN, Mencken Papers. DATE: "(1927)" appended and supported by reference to *Vanity Fair.*

67. Irving Fisher, *Prohibition at Its Worst* (New York: Macmillan, 1926).
68. Liveright eventually published Darrow's book, and Fisher later wrote a sequel in defense of Prohibition. See Clarence Darrow and Victor Yarros, *The Prohibition Mania: A Reply to Professor Irving Fisher and Others* (New York: Boni & Liveright, 1927); Irving Fisher, *Prohibition Still at Its Worst* (New York: Alcohol Information Comm., 1928).
69. Probably Raymond Pearl (1879–1940), professor of biology at Johns Hopkins and member of Mencken's music-playing, beer-drinking "Saturday Night Club."
70. Probably Arthur Garfield Hays.
71. H. L. Mencken, "The Great Defender—Clarence Darrow," *Vanity Fair,* March 1927, 44.

TO ELMER GERTZ • CHICAGO • FRIDAY 3 JUNE 1927

DARROW, SMITH, CRONSON & SMITH June 3rd

My Dear Mr Gertz

Won't you send this letter to Mr Harris.[72] If he concludes to come I will do any thing I can to help him. Still he should think it over carefully. There is no doubt whatever that the book is obscene under our law. It would not be possible to defend that part of the case. All that is left is the question, did he have any thing to do with its circulation. In the first place it was printed in English. Then copies were sent here. I don't know whether it was advertised or how, or who sent them or what relations he had with his publishers. The book has been talked about so much that the government is almost sure to act and they are liable to turn up any evidence there is. If he had any connection with their circulation they would stick him. Merely writing it is not enough. Still that would furnish a legal presumption. It would be assumed that it was written to sell and was published in English to sell in English speaking countries. It would take very little beyond that to connect him with the circulation here. He should be slow to put himself in danger. I think the chances would be decidedly against him. Tell him I expect to be over this summer or fall and can talk with him more specifically about the facts. Please forward this.[73]

Very truly, | Clarence Darrow.

MS: ALS, IEN, Leopold-Loeb Collection. DATE: "[1927]" appended.

TO PAUL DARROW • CHICAGO • SUNDAY 5 JUNE 1927

CHICAGO June 5th

Dear Paul

Was automobiling yesterday and today & just returned and found your letter. When I was down to Dartmouth, one of the boys came to me and told me the lady wanted to see me and told me what it was all about. I told the boy that she must be crazy, that no such thing could have happened, but I told him to bring her to me, she

72. Frank Harris's notorious autobiography, *My Life and Loves,* 3 vols. (1923–27), was banned in the United States and England for many years because of its sexual frankness. Harris had asked Gertz to consult with Darrow about defending him in any criminal proceedings if he were to come to the United States. See Elmer Gertz, "Clarence Darrow: An American Legend," *Progressive,* May 1957, 13. Earlier, in late 1926 and early 1927, Harris, from France, had exchanged letters directly with Darrow. Harris explained where his autobiography had been written, published, and distributed, and sought advice on whether he could avoid prosecution if he came to the United States. See Harris to Darrow, 14 November 1926, TLc, TxU-Hu, Harris Papers; Harris to Darrow, 8 January 1927, TLc, TxU-Hu, Harris Papers. Darrow's side of this exchange has not been located.

73. Harris came to the United States secretly and did not have difficulty with the government. See Gertz, "Clarence Darrow," 13.

came & showed me your letter (it was a very nice letter). She said that you were in no way to blame.[74] She told me that her nephew had been convicted and given a death sentence in an adjoining county; and I had her telephone the lawyer who came over to see me. It is very doubtful if any thing can be done. But it is pending on appeal and as soon as the lawyer has the record perfected he is to send it to me and I will see what I can do with an argument in the supreme court. If they are beaten I will go with them to the Governor. She said that they could raise a little money, and I told her I didn't want any. Of course I will do all I can for her. It is a matter that will not take much time or energy. I am sorry that this has bothered you all these years. Of course there was nothing you could have done to prevent it. Hope you can go there next year and I should be glad to go with you. I had a fine time there. Want to get this off to-night.

Hastily | C. S. D.

MS: ALS, MnU-L, Darrow Collection. DATE: reference to Dartmouth.

TO JAMES WELDON JOHNSON • CHICAGO • MONDAY 6 JUNE 1927

DARROW, SMITH, CRONSON & SMITH June 6th

My Dear Mr Johnson

I am delighted with your new volume of poems "God's Trombones."[75] It is the only Fundamentalists output I ever did like. It is a fine interpretation of the Negro preacher and his standard fables and sermons. These have of course been a large part of Negro life in the south and for that matter of all life in Dixie. It deserves a large circulation and I hope will receive it. This book is another evidence of the growing power and artistic sense of the Negro. I look for this sort of talent to ultimately win the long and cruel fight for race equality.

Always your friend | Clarence Darrow

MS: ALS, CtY-BR, Johnson Collection Files. ENDORSEMENT: stamped received: "JUN 8–1927." INSIDE ADDRESS: Mr. James Welden Johnson.

74. In 1904, Paul Darrow, then a senior at Dartmouth, was driving a horse-drawn carriage when the horse suddenly ran wild, trampling to death a five-year-old boy. Paul wrote a letter to the boy's parents saying that if any member of the boy's family ever needed help, they only needed to ask and Paul's family would help if they could. Twenty-three years later, on 11 May 1927, the boy's mother approached Darrow after a lecture at Dartmouth. She showed him the letter that Paul had written in 1904 and explained that her nephew, John Winters (b. 1894), had been convicted of murder in Vermont and sentenced to die. "Darrow to Help Save Winters from Hanging," *Boston Globe,* 3 June 1927.

75. James Weldon Johnson, *God's Trombones: Seven Negro Sermons in Verse* (New York: Viking Press, 1927).

TO UPTON SINCLAIR • CHICAGO • FRIDAY 10 JUNE 1927

DARROW, SMITH, CRONSON & SMITH June 10th

My Dear Sinclair

I have not yet had a chance to read your book but I know it is not obscene, and I know that the reasons for prohibiting it are just the ones you state.[76] I rather expect to be in the Boston case where they have forbidden Dreiser's book, An American Tragedy. Boston is the laughing stock of the U.S. in this matter. They have forbidden the sale of many books and the publishers should join in fighting them.[77] While in N.Y. go and see Arthur Garfield Hayes 43 Exchange Place. He knows the case better than any other lawyer, so far as I have heard.

With best wishes | Clarence Darrow.

MS: ALS, InU-Li, Sinclair Papers. DATE: reference to Boston case.

TO UPTON SINCLAIR • CHICAGO • THURSDAY 30 JUNE 1927

CLARENCE S. DARROW Chicago June 30th

My Dear Sinclair

I have just finished reading your last book Oil. Few novels have impressed me as much as this. 1st It is intensely interesting from the beginning. 2d It should help the public to see how constant and insidious have been the encroachments upon thought and speech since the war. If it is not already too late your book should be a great help in awakening the people to the imminent danger. 3d You know about the production and institutions of oil and still more important the production and distribution of "oil stock."

I hope the book will be one of the best sellers.

Very truly | Clarence Darrow.

MS: ALS, InU-Li, Sinclair Papers. DATE: "[1927]" appended.

76. Sinclair's *Oil!* (New York: Grosset & Dunlap, 1927), a novel about the scandals of the Harding administration, was banned in Boston, reportedly because it contained a reference to birth control. See Paul S. Boyer, *Purity in Print: The Vice-Society Movement and Book Censorship in America* (New York: Charles Scribner's Sons, 1968), 186.
77. In April 1927, the district attorney in Boston announced that the sale of Theodore Dreiser's *An American Tragedy* (1925) or Sinclair Lewis's *Elmer Gantry* (1927) could be grounds for prosecution because both books contained obscenity. Donald Friede (1901–1965), a partner in Dreiser's publisher (Boni and Liveright), went to Boston to test the ban by selling Dreiser's book. Represented by Arthur Garfield Hays, Friede was convicted and fined by a municipal court judge. His appeal to the superior court was not heard until two years later, in April 1929. Darrow participated in the superior court trial and read a chapter of Dreiser's book to the jury. Boyer, *Purity in Print*, 185–86, 192–93. The jury brought in a verdict of guilty, and the conviction was upheld on appeal. See *Massachusetts v. Friede*, 171 N.E. 472 (Mass. 1930).

TO T. PERCEVAL GERSON • CHICAGO • MONDAY 11 JULY 1927

CLARENCE S. DARROW July 11th

My Dear Dr. Gerson

I have long been intending to write you, but am a very poor letter writer. My resolution was jogged by seeing your son in N.Y. He showed up at one of my meetings and it did me good to see him, although I only had a few minutes to talk with him. Life has jogged along fairly well since the long years between my stay in L.A. and now. Of course I am older, just passed my 70th birthday. Still I have hardly known that except that my health and strength are some what impaired. I had a quite a serious illness last summer but am better excepting that my engine is not as steady as it once was,—but what can you expect. I look forward without the slightest fear or worry or doubt, with the almost sure conviction that I am done when I am dead. The last fifteen years on the whole have been as pleasant as I have ever had. I have no longings for place or power, and need have none for notoriety or fame which ever we may call it. I have tried to take things quietly as they came along helping where I could to those who need it most, and getting my pay in my work. It is strange how the fates have thrust notoriety on me without my seeking. Wherever I go I am so drown with calls & telephones that I have no rest. I don't know whether I like it or hate it. I only know that I can't avoid it. I have few delusions about myself. I can see the accidents that brought it all about and I try to do the best I can with it. One thing it has done. It has assured me an audience wherever I go, and I always say what I believe and if it is not true, I think it is and is certainly not the stuff that they get in Congress, Churches, Rotary Clubs and the like. Mrs. Darrow is very well. I almost always take her with me. In fact I couldn't get along with all the calls away from home without her. We expect to go to Europe this summer and I presume I will not be so much disturbed.—Still I am to make some talks in England. I want to compare their audiences with ours. You probably heard something of the birth-day party they gave me on my 70th anniversary. I couldn't help being gratified as no one was obliged to come. I had no punishments to give and no benefits to bestow. Fay[78] is the same good, true, faithful friend as he has always been. We seldom meet without talking of you. No one is closer to us in thought and feeling. I do wish I could see you again. Aren't you never coming East. I would very much like to see Mrs Gerson too. You know how much both of us thought of the first Mrs. Gerson but I was very glad to hear that you married, and I am sure it was the thing to do.[79] The world is lonely enough at the best and no one should be alone. With all my good wishes always & love from both of us to both of you—Your friend

Clarence Darrow

MS: ALS, CLU-SC, Theodore Perceval Gerson Papers (Collection 724). PLACE: "Chicago, Ill. | Chicago Temple Bldg" appended. DATE: "1927" appended and reference to seventieth birthday.

78. Fay Lewis.
79. Gerson's first wife, Harriet, died in 1922. Gerson married Vera Madeline Daniels in 1923.

TO MARY FIELD PARTON • CHICAGO • FRIDAY 15 JULY 1927

July 15

Dear Mary

Nellie[80] came in with your good letter which of course I was glad to get. Why haven't I written before? I don't know. The outside office is always a stream of people waiting & I am tired before I can get away. I don't want them to come but I can't help it. I go somewhere else for relief & there they are the same crowd forever and forever. The mail is full of letters that I don't want to read and can't answer and my best friends grow discouraged waiting. What can I do?

I am weary of days and hours, &c. The old beautiful stanzas that you taught me, weary of "Every thing but sleep."

This isn't entirely an excuse,—my eyes always brighten and my heart gladdens at a letter from you which is always delivered to me when it comes at the office and once in a long time I am made glad by seeing you. But life is a weary drag and I like all others seem willing to let it drag, which it won't forever.

How I wish I could come out and see you but I don't see how I can. I haven't been to New York for a long time and shall not go until I sail for Europe around Aug 1st. Will be gone two or three months. It may be in the heart of the Alps I will find some rest. Still I will be there with myself—O dam. Philpot[81] makes one of his characters say of one who is old and ill and afraid he would spend his last days in the "Union." You need a good bottle of medicine. He answered no what I need is church yard mold. Dear Mary I am not blue but it is now toward the evening, and around the close of day I am weary. I should write you in the morning when I am young & fresh.

I have just read and returned the proof to Boni and Liveright's of my book on prohibition which I hope you will like.[82] I am trying to get an article off for Mencken on the stuff you gave me, "The Lords day Alliance."[83] Am writing a little on my life story which I hope will be readable, if not true. I still have ambition. I like to speak and debate, but writing means a little more work than I like to do. One thing ought to please me, I have enough money to live on comfortably to the end. Still it is harder to keep than it was to get it. But what can I buy with my money. You know what Hausman says

80. Possibly Nellie Carlin.
81. Eden Phillpotts (1862–1960), British novelist, poet, and dramatist. Phillpotts was a friend and admirer of Darrow. He dedicated *Minions of the Moon* (London: Hutchinson, 1934), one of his many novels, to Darrow.
82. Clarence Darrow and Victor Yarros, *The Prohibition Mania: A Reply to Professor Irving Fisher and Others* (New York: Boni & Liveright, 1927).
83. Darrow submitted an article on the Lord's Day Alliance to Mencken's *American Mercury*, but Mencken declined to publish it. See Darrow to Mencken, 28 November 1927, ALS, NN, Mencken Papers. Two articles by Darrow on the Lord's Day Alliance were later published separately in *Vanity Fair* and *Plain Talk*. See "Our Growing Tyranny, *Vanity Fair*, February 1928, 39, 104; and "The Lord's Day Alliance," *Plain Talk*, March 1928, 257–70.

When first my way to fair I took
Few pence in purse had I
And long I used to stand and look
At things I could not buy.
But times have changed and if I wish
To buy a thing I can
I have the pence and here's the fair
But where's the lost young man.[84]

Hell Mary I am sorry not to be cheerful. I really am cheerful. I am eternally saying things witty & clever, and laughing at fate. Still I don't seem to be in that mood today. I will sure see you when you get back to N.Y. in the fall even if I can't see you in the country.

It must be nice to see Dr. Beard.[85] He is a fine fellow (I was about to say soul). I love him and he is so like the dear dead loving Foster.[86]

Well they won't stay outside the office any longer, this stream of poor crippled useless people on the way to the grave. Good bye dear girl. I always think of you & love you.

Clarence D.

MS: ALS, ICN, Parton-Darrow Papers, Box 1, Folder 9. ENVELOPE ADDRESS: Mrs Mary Parton | Palisades | Rockland County | N.Y. POSTMARK: Chicago 15 July 1927.

TO FRANK WALSH • CHICAGO • MONDAY 25 JULY 1927

CLARENCE S. DARROW July 25th

Dear Frank

I am tonight mailing you my picture.[87] I have never told you how much I think of you and most likely never shall. Several years ago when I came back from California with the feeling that I hadn't a friend in the world, when those for whom I had done the most through the best years of my life turned their backs upon me, I found you almost a total stranger, greeting me as a friend who knew what I had always tried to be. Since then you have showed your loyalty in many ways. And while I have never felt resentment toward

84. Darrow is quoting—actually, misquoting—A. E. Housman, who wrote: "Now times are altered: if I care / To buy a thing, I can; / The pence are here and here's the fair, / But where's the lost young man?" A. E. Housman, *Last Poems* (New York: Henry Holt, 1922), 69.
85. Charles Beard (1874–1948), teacher and historian. Beard taught at Columbia University and then helped found the New School for Social Research, where he also taught. Beard was one of the leading progressive historians.
86. George Burman Foster.
87. Another letter suggests that Walsh had asked Darrow for a photograph. See Darrow to Walsh, 21 July [1927], NN, Walsh Papers.

those who should have been my friends, I have year by year felt a growing affection for you. I am sure that there will never be a time when I shall not feel that I am

Yours with the deepest grattitude | and affection | Clarence Darrow

MS: ALS, NN, Walsh Papers, Box 15. DATE: placement in Walsh Papers.

TO JOSEPH MORO • CHICAGO • FRIDAY 29 JULY 1927

CHICAGO ILL. | JOSEPH MORO. | 259 HANOVER ST BOSTON MASS.

NEVER CAREFULLY EXAMINED SACCO VANZETTI CASE BUT KNOW THAT MEN OF THEIR VIEWS COULD NOT HAVE HAD FAIR TRIAL SO SOON AFTER THE WAR.[88] SO MANY PERSONS OF INTELLIGENCE AND STANDING HAVE INTERVENED IN THEIR BEHALF THAT FEEL SURE IT WOULD BE A TERRIBLE MISTAKE NOT TO GRANT A PARDON.

CLARENCE DARROW.

MS: Tele, MB, Felicani Sacco-Vanzetti Collection. ENDORSEMENTS: date stamped: "1927 JUL 29 AM."

TO FRANK MURPHY • CHICAGO • FRIDAY 29 JULY 1927

Chicago, July 29, 1927.

My dear Judge:

Some time ago Frank sent me your address on capital punishment.[89] I have read it carefully and it is a very fine piece of work. I wish you would have it printed in pamphlet form.

If you will permit me to make some suggestions about it, I think the lawyers who know little about this subject and care less have overworked the idea of swift and speedy justice, as they call it, not swift and speedy justice but speedy trial or what they call speedy justice. They have talked themselves hoarse on the law's delays and technicalities. I know something about the administration of law in criminal cases. There was a time when there was a chance to reverse a case on what people are pleased to call technicalities, although they were not technicalities, they were substantial rights. The modern statutes and the rulings of courts have wiped away everything that savors of a technicality in a criminal case. A lawyer hardly needs to read an indictment. He knows it is good. But, if it is not good, the State can get a new one.

It has been a long time since I made any motions in court in the way of quashing indictments. If the indictment is so bad that it cannot possibly sustain a verdict, I go ahead

88. For a short description of the Sacco-Vanzetti case, see Darrow to Moro, 4 December 1926, n.49. Sacco and Vanzetti were executed in the electric chair on 23 August 1927.
89. The identity of "Frank" is unknown. The address that Murphy sent to Darrow might have been part of a well-publicized radio debate in which Murphy participated shortly before the legislature in Michigan failed to pass a bill to reinstate capital punishment. See Sidney Fine, *Frank Murphy: The Detroit Years* (Ann Arbor: University Michigan Press, 1975), 137–38.

with the trial, and if it is informal, I know that an objection will not avail me. The courts now even uphold double jeopardy in many forms for fear that some persons whom the newspapers accuse may escape punishment.

There is no delay in criminal cases. In Chicago, if one files a civil suit it will be two years before it reaches a hearing but in a criminal case an indictment may be found the next day after the commission of the offence, providing popular clamor demands it, and the defendant put on trial without sufficient time to prepare his case. In most of the states there is no stay of writ of execution as a matter of right in a capital case. One may be hanged while his case is pending in the Supreme Court. Judges are very slow to grant a supersedas, especially where there is great public clamor. The whole docket is cleared for the trial of a criminal case and the defendant, who is most always poor, practically helpless, must go into court without proper counsel or proper time for preparation.

I would say there is nothing whatever today in the point that what we need is swift and certain justice. Nobody knows what is justice, let alone swift or certain. There are cases where prosecutions have been long delayed but these are almost invariably cases where the States Attorney did not want to press them for trial. In a case of public clamor one is fortunate if he does not need to be in court defending his client within thirty days of bringing an indictment.

Whether justice is swift and certain or not, trial and condemnation travels at lightening speed. In fact, the defendant is condemned almost immediately on an indictment and no chance is given for feelings to cool so that he may have a fair trial.

Comparisons with English justice are beside the point. No public outcry can be raised by the newspapers against the man accused of crime in England, and he can at least get a trial by a jury which has not pre-judged his case.

I think if you would let this address be published you might consider this question. For I know the corporation lawyers, the big interests and the newspapers are persistently educating people to the old call of speedy and certain justice, which only means speedy and certain vengeance, and a denial of justice.

However, this letter is not meant to criticise this magnificent address which is true and brave and human like everything that you have done. I am going to keep this copy unless you want it back. I want some of my friends to see it. But I would like to have you re-write it if you desire to and have it published in pamphlet form. I am quite sure that Haldeman-Julius would get it out in one of their five cent books which insures a large circulation. I have so many calls for that sort of literature that I wish I had something to recommend. I feel that you personally won a victory in standing off capital punishment in Michigan, and I hope the tide will turn before long so that the voice of humanity can be heard. I was going to say justice, but I have not been able to find out what that word means.

We are sailing for Europe on the 6th. I have been disappointed that you are not going along. I wish you were. If you can go wire me and I will let you know the name of the ship we take. Of course, I was deeply gratified at the dismissal of the Sweet case. I shall

always look back with pleasure and satisfaction to that trial. Perhaps it was the most important one I ever participated in and, aside from that, it gave me the great pleasure of knowing you as you are.

With deep regard and abiding affection, I am

Your friend, | Clarence Darrow

Love to Frank

MS: TLS, MiU-H, Frank Murphy Papers. INSIDE RETURN ADDRESS: 77 West Washington street, | Chicago, Illinois. INSIDE ADDRESS: Hon. Francis Murphy, | Recorder's Court, | Detroit, Michigan.

TO PAUL DARROW • LONDON • SUNDAY 25 SEPTEMBER 1927

HOTEL METROPOLE Sept 25

Dear Paul

Am sailing Oct 8th arriving in NY about the 17th. If you get this in time write me to The Belmont Hotel so I will get it about that time. Have had a very good time here in London. Have seen Sir John Frasier.[90] Shall see Hardy tomorrow, and Edward Carpenter[91] on Wednesday & I hope to get Shaw and Arnold Bennette. Have also spoken at American Chamber of Commerce here and the American Club is giving me a dinner Tuesday night. Have got so far into things that I have more requests than I can take care of. Still I am ready to get back to America. I don't know that it is the best country but I feel more at home there. Have had one letter from you here in London & had one in Paris. Hope to get an other before I leave.

Love to the rest | C. S. D.

MS: ALS, MnU-L, Darrow Collection. DATE: "1927" appended.

TO EDWARD A. ROSS • CHICAGO • WEDNESDAY 26 OCTOBER 1927

77 West Washington street, | Chicago, Illinois,
October 26, 1927.

My dear Doctor Ross:

I received a letter from Percy Ward[92] at Milwaukee, Wisconsin, wanting me to come to Milwaukee and debate with you on Prohibition. I don't want you to think I had anything

90. Darrow must have meant James Frazer (1854–1941), British anthropologist and classical scholar.
91. Edward Carpenter (1844–1929), English writer identified with social reform and the anti-industrial Arts-and-Crafts Movement.
92. Darrow is probably referring to H. Percy Ward (b. 1875), a member of the Chicago Rationalist Society and other liberal or agnostic organizations. He lived in Chicago and made his living as a public lecturer and debater.

to do with this. I never tried to get up a debate with anybody. My personal view is that it would not be well handled even if we wanted to do it. It would be necessary for us to look after it ourselves. As far as I am concerned, I prefer not to and I presume you feel the same way. However, I might do it if you saw any reason for it.

With kind regards, I am | Very truly yours, | Clarence Darrow.[93]

MS: TLS, WHi, Ross Papers. LETTER ADDRESS: Dr. E. C. Ross, | c/o University of Wisconsin, | Madison, Wis.

TO PAUL DARROW • CHICAGO • FRIDAY 18 NOVEMBER 1927

CLARENCE S. DARROW Nov. 18th

Dear Paul

Got your letter this morning. It looks as if the deal will go through. Is that your idea about it? I wrote Fred to have the bonds sent here, and it will be done promptly.[94] Would like to know if you think it will be a sale. If it is not I shall arrange to go and see you this winter. Would go over the holidays but I am to argue that case in Vermont on Jan 2d.[95] Delivered a number of talks in the east, and am going back for a half dozen early in Dec. I don't over work and take it easy. Am not doing any law work except to take something easy once in a while without going into court. Am writing some (I think Jan Mercury will have a story). I read a good deal and loaf more and work some cross word puzzles. Am feeling better than I have for a year or more. Haven't bought any stocks lately. I wonder what has happened to Brazillian Traction. It was quoted yesterday at 207 to 208. Haven't notice today. I got an autographed book from Thos Hardy, also one from Jas. Frazier, Arthur Keith,[96] and A. E. Hausman, which I will give you when you come, or when I go there. Had fine visits with all of them. Of course I am quite anxious for you to come here. I am sure that we can sell the plant if Hazeltine[97] doesn't take it. Hope you won't tie yourself up out there. I am sure you will enjoy life better here.

C. S. D.

MS: ALS, MnU-L, Darrow Collection. DATE: "1927" appended.

93. Ross agreed that they should not debate: "I agree with you about joint debates. Generally, I observe, the opponents glide past each other on different tracks. There is no real collision of facts or argument. That would be the case if we debated prohibition. You would establish your contention from your point of view and I would do the same for my contention from a different point of view. So I agree that it is just as well for each to advance his ideas in his own way as occasion offers." Ross to Darrow, 1 November 1927, TLc, WHi, Ross Papers.
94. "Fred" is likely Fred Hamerstom. The "deal" to which Darrow is referring was the potential sale of the gas plant that he owned with Paul (and that Paul managed) in Greeley, Colorado.
95. Darrow participated in the argument for John Winters in the Vermont Supreme Court. See Darrow to Paul Darrow, 5 June 1927, n.74.
96. Arthur Keith (1866–1955), Scottish anthropologist and author.
97. The identity of "Hazeltine" (a prospective buyer for the gas plant) is unknown.

TO PAUL DARROW • NEW YORK CITY • FRIDAY 16 DECEMBER 1927

HOTEL BELMONT Dec. 16

Dear Paul

I want you to send a Draft or Cashiers check to Fred. E. Golding on receipt of this Via Air Mail to 608 Central Bldg. Los Angeles Cal for $4500. Mr. Golding is one of my dearest friends. He was one of the strongest men on the jury in Los Angeles & seems to need this now. He has considerable property but it is more or less encumbered. I am sure I will get it back in a year but I would send it just as quickly if I knew I would not. Holly wired me that the deal went through all right.[98] Of course I am very glad, and am anxious for you to come to Chicago as soon as possible. I am trying a case that has already taken a week & will take an other one. This is my last one.[99] Wire me here that you have sent the check.

Always | C. S. D.

MS: ALS, MnU-L, Darrow Collection. DATE: "~~1928?~~ probably 1927" appended.

TO VIVIAN PIERCE • CHICAGO • TUESDAY 3 JANUARY 1928

CLARENCE DARROW January 3, 1928.

Dear Vivian:

I am glad you are doing something on the idea of looking up cases where the wrong people have been convicted. I think it would be a strong card to play. There is much more need of an organization to fight the ferocious changes in criminal statutes in the various states than there is for an anti-capital punishment league. I have been wondering whether we could take it on among other duties.

I will be in New York arriving about one o'clock p.m. on the afternoon of the 7th and go to the Belmont.[100] I will call you up at that time or you can call me. With best wishes, I am

Very truly yours, | Clarence Darrow

MS: TLS, MBNU, Sara Ehrmann Papers, Box 16, Folder 91. INSIDE ADDRESS: Miss Vivian Pierce, | League to Abolish Capital Punishment, | 104—5th avenue, New York City, N.Y.

98. Darrow's former law partner, William Holly, helped with the sale of the gas plant.
99. Two Italian fascists were murdered in the Bronx in May 1927 and two well-known anti-fascists, Cologero Greco and Donato Carillo, were indicted for the murders. Darrow and Arthur Garfield Hays defended them, at the urging of Norman Thomas and Italian American anarchist Carlo Tresca (1879–1943). The defendants were acquitted by a jury in late December 1927.
100. This is probably a reference to Darrow's plan to speak in New York City at a fund-raiser for the American League to Abolish Capital Punishment. The speech was postponed until 19 February 1928.

TO LINCOLN STEFFENS • CHICAGO • MONDAY 16 JANUARY 1928

CLARENCE DARROW | 1537 East 60th St. | Chicago | January 16, 1928.

My dear Steffens;

I returned yesterday from about a month's absence in the east where I managed to try one case and argue another in the Supreme Court and made a number of so-called speeches, so I am breeding dissension and doubt as far as I can.

I was glad to hear what you said about J.B. and Smithy.[101] Of course I do not need to tell you that I will help in any way I can that seems at all feasible. My opinion is that you have made a very good start and the important thing in the future is to keep the friends that you already have. I think we would have very hard work accomplishing it without, and with these friends we are bound to win before long even though it involves a new pardon board and a new governor. I do not see exactly how the committee that you spoke of could render us any assistance at this time. Of course, there is a good deal of force in the idea that these men are kept along because of their being labor men. Still if that was urged too hard, wouldn't there be danger of our very influential people in Los Angeles going the other way, if it involves any publicity which would bring any serious criticism to them? I would be afraid of the consequences, and there is no doubt but what the friendship of those associated with him will be worth a great deal. From what you tell me I have no doubt but what he is sincere in his position.

The matter that I have told you about several times I think should be urged, that no one intended to kill any person in the explosion; it was meant only for a scare. The bomb was meant to be placed where it would not injure life. I believe that Joe Ford[102] would verify this, as the statements taken show it is absolutely true, and likewise the evidence shows the same. I think it would be a good plan for you to see Joe when you go down there. I want him to know that I have never felt unfriendly to him and will be glad to see him myself if I come there. His help would be very valuable and I believe he would aid us. I am glad to know what you say about the kind of feeling of the parties concerned. There is nothing that I have been more desirous to get.

I would like very much to come to California and may persuade myself to go. There is a very strong urge to have me go there in the coming summer, but we will have plenty of time to consider it and write back and forth about it before that time. I trust you are happy, at least as happy as an intelligent man can be in an damn fool world. I send you

101. "J.B." was James B. McNamara and "Smithy" was Matthew Schmidt, usually called "Schmidty" or "Smitty." What Steffens said about them is unknown.

102. W. Joseph Ford (1877–1932), lawyer. Born in Oakland, California, Ford was chief assistant district attorney for Los Angeles County, 1907–1914, when he helped John Fredericks, the district attorney, prosecute the McNamara brothers for the Los Angeles Times bombing and Darrow for jury bribery. Ford participated in both of Darrow's bribery trials. He entered private practice in 1914 and became well known as a criminal-defense attorney in Los Angeles and occasionally served as a special prosecutor. He was also dean of the law school at Loyola University in Los Angeles, 1925–30.

my kindest regards and Mrs. Darrow's to your wife. We hope we will see her again some of these days.

Ever, your friend, | Clarence Darrow.

This turned over to me to sign, seal and send—so—please permit me to add my own friendly goodwishes—, and regret that *the effort* has not yet succeeded,—with hope for the future.

yours faithfully— | Ruby D.—

MS: TLS, NNC, Steffens Papers. INSIDE ADDRESS: Dr. Lincoln Steffens, | P.O. Box 835, | Carmel, Calif. NOTE: The last paragraph is in Ruby Darrow's hand.

TO WILLIAM C. EWING • CHICAGO • MONDAY 23 JANUARY 1928

CLARENCE DARROW | 1357 East 60th St. | Chicago
January 23, 1928.

My dear Mr. Ewing:

Your letter in reference to capital punishment was duly received. I somehow feel the urge to write you further about it. I think you are absolutely wrong on prohibition, if you believe in prohibition. In the first place, the old time chaplains and people of that ilk who hunted around prisons, were always interested to say that all the inmates were there on account of drink. The truth, as I believe, is that it has always been less than one in a hundred and probably one in a thousand would be much nearer correct. I have been defending people charged with murder for a good many years. I have never yet found a case where the homicide was due to drink. I found one case where I hesitated some time between making that defense and self-defense, but decided on the latter. The way the chaplains have made up the figures, is to ask a man if he drank. Pretty nearly all of them did drink as they likewise ate, and then inmates of prisons know what please chaplains so they give the answer wanted. Likewise they all want alibis and whiskey always furnishes an excellent one.

I would say that certain things go with most homicides, in fact, with most of the things we call crime, although I do not like the use of the word. There is no such thing in the world. I would say ignorance, lack of opportunity, no early training, no trade or calling and the fact that a criminal career commences in early youth. Most men who go to prison also drink. However, half of them are subnormal. When several things go together it is seldom possible to say which one is the cause or whether any one is the cause. Cause and effect are not easy to locate in human activity. The most that can be said is that certain conditions affect it. Almost all people who go to prison are poor and always have been poor. If a man begins a course of crime when young, if he has no education, if he is subnormal, if he has no trade and if he drinks, what was the cause of the killing? Nobody can tell. There are such things as proximate cause and remote cause. But, drinking

cannot be a cause excepting in the case of drunkenness or a long course of overdrinking which weakens the structure. This can come much more easily from over-eating and perhaps from over-working, or from any one of perhaps a thousand things. I know perfectly well that men have committed homicides while drunk who would never have committed them while sober. These things are also in the realm of uncertainty because if a man drinks and intends to rob or kill, the chances are he will drink before he performs the act. You can hardly imagine a man who would do it without bracing up on coffee, whiskey or something else. But this does not demonstrate any causal connection.

Of course, I am very bitterly opposed to prohibition. This is not at all because I care for liquor, for I do not care for it. You could probably put all of the liquor I ever have drank in a ten gallon container, but I am opposed to it because I am opposed to interference of people with individual conduct. I would not be opposed to arresting a man if he was drunk, or possibly arresting him, if, through drunkenness or shiftlessness, he did not support his family. But, to say that I, who seldom drink, cannot take a glass of wine or whiskey because some "damn" fool abuses it, is to me indefensible.

I think you can understand my position because you evidently do not like meddlers. Freedom is a hard thing to preserve. In order to have enough you must have too much. Nobody can draw the line in matters where Government should begin or individual freedom leave off. They are purely imaginary and subject to ebb and flow. We do not know that some people have a more scientific idea of the function of the state than others, but we know you can divide men into two classes: One which is always trying to more and more control the conduct of its fellows, and the other class which is always trying to get more freedom. I belong to the latter class and would not be a prohibitionist even if I thought liquor caused a good deal of homicide, because I think that a large degree of liberty is necessary to any sort of human enjoyment. But then I do not like prohibitionists. Of course, there are exceptions everywhere. I have seen some "damn" good fellows who were prohibitionists. Of course, there are not many. Mencken defined a prohibitionist as a man you wouldn't want to take a drink with if he drank. I have found that out in my life that the fellows who believe in prohibition believe in Sunday laws; they would believe in burning heretics; they believe in making the use of tobacco criminal; they set themselves up as authorities on morals and conduct and they have not the slightest tolerance for anyone who differs with them.

Any liberal minded man who deals with a prohibitionist is playing with fire. It is hard enough to preserve liberty as it is, and we do not preserve it. Look at Boston where you cannot go to a theatre on Sunday; you cannot have games and sports where admissions are charged; you cannot buy books that are fit to read; you cannot do much of anything unless it appeals to a lot of old maids and blue-nosed emotionless men. I do not like it and I believe you ought to think it over. You will never find anybody who will lay down any scientific rule as to where the individual's rights might be stopped. The single-taxer would probably think he could, but then he thinks he can lay down rules for everything. I have laid one down to my own satisfaction.

The theory of criminal statutes is that men may be sent to prison for doing something that is morally wrong, and which they knew was morally wrong. Now, of course, there is no way to tell what morals mean excepting custom and habit. Morals are based upon folk-ways. But anything that is done, where one-fourth or even one-tenth of the population adhere to that sort of conduct without any feeling of guilt is not a proper subject for a penal statute.

I would guess that much more than half the people of the United States take a drink without the slightest feeling of moral guilt. There are a few of such men who believe in prohibition, but they are absolutely inconsistent with any sane idea of the function of a criminal statute. To say that everybody who takes a drink and believes in it, should be sent to jail, would shock most men unless they were utterly lost to any sane ideas of human freedom. Of course, it could be carried into eating as well as drinking. I am not at all sure there is any standpoint from which drinking is wrong. Some people think it produces poverty. I do not. Poor people would not have any more money if they did not drink. There may be a few exceptions to the rule, but not many. The person who drinks excessively would waste his money some other way. The amount of money spent in drink would never in any way compare with the money spent on automobiles, gasoline, tobacco, silks and satins, extravagant houses and foolish luxuries. Of course, enough could be produced and more to take care of everybody with comfort and a large degree of luxury, if only the question of distribution were solved. Taking a drink from a man simply means lessening his relaxation and his power of release from the drudgery of everyday life without in any way bettering his condition.

However, I do not mean to preach an intemperance sermon to you, but I feel called upon to talk a little about it. You say that the homicides in the United States have increased since 1900. How do you know this? I do not pretend to know. I used to be a hound for gathering statistics. I pay no attention to them in Illinois; they are not worth anything.

Let me make a few suggestions for you to think of. There are no reliable statistics on homicide anywhere in the United States. You may write to Washington, but you will find none. You may get English statistics and Canadian statistics, but not American statistics. Of course, some sort of statistics might be gathered by writing to the various states. Only a certain portion of them keep any and these are very imperfectly kept. True, in the last ten or fifteen years an effort has been made to keep criminal statistics. If the statistics show that homicide has increased since 1900, it could doubtless more than be accounted for by the greater care in gathering statistics. To my mind there is not a question but what it could.

But, that is not the only way to account for it. What is homicide, anyway? Homicide does not necessarily imply any evil intent. It means the unlawful killing of a human being with or without malice. Killing by gross carelessness or disregard of human rights like shooting off a gun in a crowded street. In all tables of statistics for the past few years there are a large number of automobile accidents included. I saw a while ago that twenty-five thousand people were killed from automobile accidents in the United States last year.

This is more or less correct. So far beyond the homicides in number that there cannot be any comparison. But where an automobile accident caused a death and the accident is due to gross carelessness or to disregard of rights of others, which amounts to about the same thing, these are included in homicides. They are included everywhere in the United States so far as I have any knowledge of the subject, which is considerable. Automobiles have increased to an alarming extent of late. There were none to speak of in 1900. Do these people who parade their "fool" statistics ever stop to analyze them? I shall send you in a few days a careful analysis that I have made of the figures of the Crime Commission in Chicago where there are reported as much as six times as many murders as really take place, and you will see from my article, which is a reprint from Harper's Magazine, that there is no answer to it and cannot be any.[103] The newspapers and preachers, and other respectable people, never try to find out causes. They want to sell papers and sermons. The unsuspecting public gets into a white heat of anger so that somebody will be punished. It is pure sadism.

There are an infinite number of causes that enter into homicide. For instance, the growth of Ku Klux Klanism has produced a good many by intensifying religious differences. Prohibition has been the cause of many of them. The jails in many places are filled with violators of the prohibition law, some of them for murders as between different gangs of bootleggers. They will increase as long as there is prohibition. At least I don't want people to stop bootlegging. Liberty is worth fighting for. Strikes and lock-outs cause them. The cheapening of the value of life by the great war undoubtedly causes many, and a surprising number by returned soldiers. But, the psychology was not confined to returned soldiers; it affected all classes. In this country the mixture of races and creeds has been a prolific cause of homicide. Our figures have been compared with England but of course the people who talk about it, as a rule, know nothing about England. As nearly as I can get at it, there have been for the last few years one hundred and fifty murders reported in England and Wales, with about thirty-five convictions carrying the death penalty. Of these thirty-five, twenty were reprieved so the executions were about fifteen where this country probably has had three or four hundred, with a population of two and one-half times as great.

If examples would do anything, nobody would kill any more. English courts probably have trials quicker, but that does not mean justice, neither does it mean a deterrent. Nobody would dare say a word about a criminal case in England, in any way reflecting upon any person connected or allowed to be connected with it until after the trial. Papers try all the cases and convict all of the defendants within a week of the time the thing has happened, and it is almost impossible to get a fair trial in this country.

Another thing is that newer countries produce more violations of law than older countries. A violation of law simply means getting out of the old rut, which is violating a

103. See Clarence Darrow, "Crime and the Alarmists," *Harper's Magazine,* October 1926, 535–44.

custom, and the ruts are not as deep in newer countries as in older ones. Someone may call your attention to Canada. This is no exception. Take out the large cities and the mining districts and the manufacturing centers in Canada and America and the results will be the same. Canada has few large cities and a fairly homogenous population. I do not like the idea of our fellows accepting the "fool" statements that are made by the sadists. People get punished quickly enough.

You suggest to me that if everybody knew that every crime would be punished wouldn't they stop? Probably they would, but if everybody gave up committing them, they would likewise stop. Nobody knows that every crime would be punished. In the first place, they don't know what the word means. Everybody who robs or kills prepares an escape and generally succeed in making it. That is true the world over and always will be true. Only the timid can be kept from it by fear of punishment and the people who commit crimes are not timid. I use the word crime because other people use it. That word never should be used. Crime is only a violation of custom and habit that has become the subject of a penal statute, and that is all there is about it. For instance, we have statutes against cheating, but there is not a newspaper in the world that does not carry lying advertisements and not a merchant who does not cheat. Advertisers write for the purpose of imposing upon "damn" fools and making them buy something they do not want and cannot pay for. Over-reaching is business. Selling real estate and services,—all sorts of things are alike. But, only the poor get hooked under such statutes.

I have never had as much sympathy as I might with many of the books against capital punishment. They have taken a religious attitude which is of no value. I would do as you do, I would use it where I could get any result, but a man cannot submit to it in his own thinking, at least.

The tendency is to make penalties worse instead of better. There are some such things in your book, good as it is.[104] People argue there would be more convictions if we got rid of the death penalty. Probably there would but penalties are too hard anyhow, and prisons are too horrible. This is much more important than capital punishment because there are tens of thousands in prison where there is one who is executed. And, anyway, to a sane person a long term of imprisonment is worse than death. It does not shock we sensitive people so much, but it is really worse. I have an idea that if you had a choice to die from some natural cause or to go to prison, you would want to die. If you knew you were liable to go to prison for a long term of years, when you went to bed, you would hope you would not wake up. That does not mean that a person would hasten to land himself in the frying pan.

I hope you will excuse the length of this letter. Perhaps it will not be of any value to you, but I think it may possibly give you a little different slant on some things. With kind regards, I am

Very truly yours,

104. The book to which Darrow is referring is unknown.

P.S. I note on re-reading your letter that you refer for statistics to Dr. Haufman[105] of the Babson Institute and the Prudential. I wish you would have them send me copies. I still think I can explain them if I see them.

CSD

MS: TT, ICU, Darrow Papers, Box 1, Folder 13. INSIDE ADDRESS: Mr. Wm. C. Ewing | c/o Mass. Council for the Abolition of the Death Penalty | 4 Park Street | Boston, Mass.

TO VIVIAN PIERCE • CHICAGO • FRIDAY 17 FEBRUARY 1928

CLARENCE DARROW February 17, 1928.

Dear Vivian:

I will be in New York without fail on the 19th, probably arriving in the morning.[106] Don't you suppose the papers would carry this as a news item which would undoubtedly result in filling the house? If so, let it be known that the proceeds of the meeting are to go to the League to help in carrying on the campaign.

I also think after we get the people in the house the occasion should be used to take up a collection. I don't know whether you ever attended a Methodist meeting where they raised money for the church. Some barker tells what it is all about and the need for money and then asks for contributions, not by passing the hat but asking how many will give say a thousand dollars apiece or maybe five hundred or anyhow a hundred first. And then gradually runs it down until he gets to five dollars.

I believe quite a lot of money could be raised this way after the meeting. You are the one to do this because you can state rather briefly what the work is all about and its needs and the sacrifice being made for it. You may not be used to this sort of thing but you could do it. We must try to get some money. You better call me up at the Belmont soon after my arrival.

With best wishes, | Very truly yours, | Clarence Darrow

MS: TLS, MBNU, Sara Ehrmann Papers, Box 16, Folder 91. INSIDE ADDRESS: Vivian Pierce, | 104 Fifth avenue | New York City.

105. Frederick L. Hoffman (1865–1946), German-born statistician, author, and lecturer. Hoffman immigrated to the United States in 1884. He worked as an insurance agent and superintendent of an insurance office, 1887–94, before working as a statistician for the Prudential Insurance Company and (eventually) as a vice president for Prudential, 1895–1922, and later as a part-time consultant for the company, 1922–1934. He was a member of the faculty at Yale University for one year, 1917–18. He served as dean of advanced research at the Babson Institute (now Babson College) in Wellesley Hills, Massachusetts, 1922–27, specializing in economic and industrial research. Later, he worked as a consultant with the Biochemical Research Foundation of the Franklin Institute in Boston, 1934–38. He was responsible for the founding of the American Society for the Control of Cancer in 1913, which later became the American Cancer Society. Throughout his life, he wrote and lectured extensively on a wide variety of subjects related to public health, insurance, and demographic subjects (including widely read reports on suicide and murder rates), and he published some sixteen books. He was a member of many organizations and societies, including the American League to Abolish Capital Punishment, of which Darrow was president.

106. Darrow, Frank Walsh, and Lewis Lawes were all speakers for the American League to Abolish Capital Punishment at Hampden's Theatre in New York on 19 February 1928. "Would Force Jury to View Execution," *New York Times,* 20 February 1928.

TO JOSEPH S. LABADIE • CHICAGO • SUNDAY 26 FEBRUARY 1928

CLARENCE DARROW February 26, 1928.

My dear Labadie:

Glad you like the story in Plain Talk.[107] I get a kick out of going after such damn bigots. If we don't go after them there would be no living with them. There is always something that can be found fault with by them. I think we have to fight.

Sorry to hear that you have been laid up. With best wishes, I am

Your friend, | Clarence Darrow

MS: TLS, MiU, Labadie Collection. INSIDE ADDRESS: Mr. Joseph Labadie, | Detroit, Mich.

TO FRANK WALSH • ST. PETERSBURG, FLORIDA • SATURDAY 24 MARCH 1928

PRINCESS MARTHA March 24, 1928

My dear Mr. Walsh:

I just wired you but think I better write more fully. The matter you propose has its allurements.[108] I would be glad, if it would do any good to the movement that interests you and me so intensely. The money, too, is not without its attraction. Still, I hesitate to do it. I am afraid it would come to a very crass noteriety that would cause me a considerable amount of pain. A picture of this sort would cost a considerable amount of money. I could not expect anyone would undertake it except for the money to be made out of it. It would cover bill-boards with advertising matter that would embarrass me and my friends. It would be subject to all sorts of interpretations, and I am afraid of it.

I wish you would thoroughly consider all of this, and if it is to be done, see just what kind of provisions could be made for a dignified presentation of the matter. I do not expect there can be a great deal of idealism in it. I cannot expect men to pay in large amounts of money without the hope of large profits in return. I am afraid the scenario would not be what you or I would like. It would make all kinds of appeals which would disturb, if not disgust us. I could not think of it without knowing just what was to be said in the scenario, and just how it would be advertised, and just what

107. Clarence Darrow, "The Lord's Day Alliance," *Plain Talk*, March 1928, 257–70. See Darrow to H. L. Mencken, 22 January 1927, n.63.

108. Walsh's son, Jerome Walsh (1902–71), was a defense lawyer in a celebrated murder trial in Los Angeles, California, in early 1928. His argument to the jury on the appropriate punishment for the defendant—for which he said that he "took great liberties" with Darrow's ideas—resulted in life imprisonment for his client rather than the death penalty. After the trial, a representative of the Warner Film Company approached Jerome with the idea of producing a movie that "would be a preachment against capital punishment," and he asked if it could be arranged to have Darrow appear in the movie. Frank Walsh to Darrow, 27 March 1928, TLc, NN, Walsh Papers.

I was expected to do; and then we could try to see whether it could all be brought about in a dignified way. This would involve a conference which I might have with you and the others in Chicago or New York (preferably in Chicago) around the middle of April. Anyhow, I would not want to be committed to the matter until I knew, to the smallest detail, what it would involve.

I know you are as sensitive as I, and am prepared to let you take up the preliminary matters and then we can check up and confer.

I want to convey to your son how much I admire the course he has taken and what he has been through. It has been a tough job for a young man, but I think he will always look back to it with satisfaction. I do not know another young man who would have carried himself so well.[109]

With kindest wishes to both of you, I am, as always,

Your friend, | Clarence Darrow

MS: TLS, NN, Walsh Papers, Box 15. INSIDE ADDRESS: Hon. Frank P. Walsh | Jefferson Hotel | KANSAS CITY MO.

TO JAMES WELDON JOHNSON • CHICAGO • TUESDAY 17 APRIL 1928

CLARENCE DARROW April 17, 1928.

My dear Johnson:

When I was in Florida someone sent me a newspaper report from Washington which contained a resolution of the colored preachers that I was not to speak at any of their churches when I came there.[110] Somehow, I do not find fault with it. I do not blame them for feeling that my talks, which always slam the preachers, generally do not exactly fit a temple of god. The only excuse I could see for their having me in a church is that you

109. Darrow later wrote to Walsh saying that he had "thought a good deal of the movie matter" and that he wanted to do it if they could "arrange it to hold [the movie company] down to something that will not be too raw." Darrow said that he wanted Jerome Walsh and his associate in Los Angeles to receive twenty-five thousand dollars from the movie company as part of the deal, and he had "some ideas about the disposition of [his] part of the money that would make it easier for [him] to do it." Darrow to Frank Walsh, 4 April 1928, ALS, NN, Walsh Papers. Walsh believed that Darrow would give his part of the money to the American League to Abolish Capital Punishment. See Walsh to Vivian Pierce, 26 April 1928, TLc, NN, Walsh Papers. The movie was apparently never made.

110. On 6 April 1928, the National Interdenominational Ministerial Alliance of America, holding a convention at the Metropolitan Baptist Church in Washington, D.C., passed a resolution understood by many to be aimed at Darrow (but not mentioning him by name), barring any speaker with atheistic or agnostic views from speaking in its members' churches. "Pastors Bar Pulpits to Unbelievers," *Chicago Defender,* 7 April 1928. W. E. B. Du Bois described this resolution as the most "unfortunate" thing to happen "in the recent history of the Negro race": "There is not a Negro church in the United States that ought not to throw wide its doors to Clarence Darrow and beg him to come in. . . . Clarence Darrow does not believe many things that Orthodox Christians believe; but he respects the beliefs of any sincere person and in turn he deserves respect for his own honest opinions. If the Negro race is going to start hunting Heretics, let it pause and remember that William Lloyd Garrison, Abraham Lincoln and Frederick Douglass were nearly as radical religious freethinkers as Clarence Darrow." W. E. B. Du Bois, "Postscript," *Crisis,* June 1928, 203.

have often told me that a large part of the money for paying for churches was given on the theory that they really did use their places for halls, at least you said something like this, and something like this is probably true. If they take the money for that purpose, it seems to me they ought to admit a fellow like me whom they know is speaking for the negroes, and if they feel they cannot, why it ought to be understood when they raise money.

However, I had no feeling about the matter. I have promised to go to Washington and am also going to Springfield. I have heard from Washington since but no information as to where I am to speak. I have been embarrassed several times in speaking in halls for the negroes by having some damn fool preacher start the thing off with a prayer and close with a benediction. I don't have this even among white christians who are bad enough, if I am speaking in their churches. I can see some point in conforming and would not raise the question, but I wish you would tell them that when I speak in a hall I don't want them to do it. I am not interested in God and he is not interested in the colored people. I don't think they ought to impose it on me.

Mind, this does not go as to the churches but tell them that if a meeting is held in a hall that I resent it. I don't believe in their forcing themselves on a fellow like me and shall be apt to say something about it in my remarks if it is done.[111]

I expect to be in New York in the forenoon of the 23rd and also a part of the time at least on the 24th and 25th. With all good wishes, to yourself and wife, I am as ever

Your friend, | Clarence Darrow

MS: TLS, DLC-MSS, NAACP Administrative Files. INSIDE ADDRESS: Mr. James Weldon Johnson, | c/o N.A.A.C.P., | 69—5th Avenue, | New York City.

TO BLANCHE DARROW CHASE • NEW YORK CITY • MONDAY 23 APRIL 1928

HOTEL BELMONT April 23rd

Dear Little Blanche

Just got in this morning and thought I would rite you a nice letter. I hope you are having a good time, and not picking on deer Mery[112] two much. It may be that Mery is healthier than you are and possibly Jesie[113] is prettier. But don't think that health or beauty is every thing. Helthy people can get sick and butie is only skin deap and

111. Darrow did not speak in a church the next time he spoke in Washington, D.C. On 27 April 1928, he spoke at an amusement park in Washington called Suburban Gardens, talking on the subject of race and religion. "Darrow Rips into Church," *Chicago Defender*, 28 April 1928.
112. Mary Darrow Simonson.
113. Jessie Darrow Johnston.

sometime Jessie might be skinned and then where would she be. Even if you get sick or skinned you are good and that will be left, but see what would happen to them other kids if they got sick or skinned. I really think that you take after me morn either of the other kids. I never cared so much about buty or helth but I like to be good. I suppose you have been to Holly-would before now and probably Mary has followed off some of them sloppy movie actresses, that she bies the pictures of. They ain't so much, they just get drest up to get their pictures took to send to foolish girls and men. You ought to see them in the morning when they ware kumonos and dressing gowns and don't look so nice.

I am counting on meating you in N.Y. and going to Mount Vernon where Geo Washington grew up and got to be the father of his country and Gettesburg and Boston, and New Orleans, and Montreall and Quebeck and Kinsman and all them other fine cities.

Well I must cloze.

With lots of luv | Your *Grand* dad | C. S. D.

I spose you stil want to get back to Evans & Nun[114] and that other dump that I can't think of the name of.

MS: ALS, Darrow Family. DATE: "(1928)" appended.

TO JOSEPH ISHILL • CHICAGO • THURSDAY 7 JUNE 1928

CLARENCE DARROW June 7, 1928.

Dear Sir:

For many years I have been an ardent admirer of Havelock Ellis and his work. As a young man he began his great work of teaching the facts about sex. Every line of his work has been serious, thoughtful, honest and brave. During a long life he has worked on what seemed a hopeless task. He has never been swerved from his cause by criticism, jibes, ridicule or the law. If I were an optimist, I should believe that the world would someday pay homage to his learning, bravery and devotion.[115]

Yours truly, | Clarence Darrow

MS: TLS, MH-H. INSIDE ADDRESS: Mr. Joseph Ishill, | The Oriole Press, | Berkeley Heights, N.J.

114. Evans and Nunn are towns near Greeley, Colorado, where Blanche lived before moving to Chicago with her father and mother.

115. Ishill published the body of this letter in a limited-edition book of tributes to Ellis: Joseph Ishill, ed., *Havelock Ellis: In Appreciation* (Berkeley Heights, NJ: Oriole Press, 1929), 265. Among other contributors to the book were H. L. Mencken, Benjamin B. Lindsey, John Haynes Holmes, Bolton Hall, and Horace Traubel.

TO C. RUSSELL PREWITT • CHICAGO • SATURDAY 9 JUNE 1928

CLARENCE DARROW June 9, 1928.

Dear Mr. Prewitt:

I was very glad to receive your letter. Without attempting to answer it, I am writing this in reply. You state that my position in regard to the Christian church is not correct in 1928 but would apply to the middle ages, still in the same letter you tell of your troubles within your group and your experience on account of being a progressive minister, and about how hopelessly conservative the ordinary minister is. Don't you think these two statements are in conflict? It seems to me that you confess my position by your letter. I believe I know what Christianity means today. It means the old story of the creation of man, the temptation and fall on account of the terrible sin of eating from the tree of knowledge; it means the serpent speaking in Hebrew to Eve; it means that unborn generations of women were condemned to bring forth children in pain and anguish, all on account of this terrible sin; it means the flood and the whale and all the rest of it; it means that Jesus was born of a virgin, and that on account of his terrible sacrifice those who do not know better can accept the myths and keep out of hell and get into heaven, although it does not seem to provide that woman shall not still suffer in childbirth but to indicate that the Lord overlooked a point.

I know that you and Fosdick and a considerable group of intelligent ministers do not believe these stories. I believe your group is growing but not so rapidly as I wish. I do not believe that you are Christians although Fosdick manages to work in a good deal of nonsense together with many excellent statements.

I know the Apostles Creed and the Westminster Catechism and the creeds of most of the churches state Christianity as I stated it. Am I to take your definition of Christianity against the whole Christian world? Of course, I am for you, Fosdick and the rest of them as against the fundamentalists, but it is impossible for me to see how you can accept and practice what is called Christianity, without accepting it all. You can accept what, for lack of a better word, we call the moral precepts but this is no more Christian than Pagan. In my opinion Marcus Aurelius was way ahead of any Christian conception of life. Then, of course, nobody knows anything about Jesus, whether he ever lived or what he said. There are not over ten lines that by any process of reasoning or evidence could be attributed to Jesus and I have just been sent a book by Dr. Clark of Harvard who holds that St. Paul was the first Christian.[116] I know, of course that some of his letters came before the gospels. Clark says that Paul was the founder of Christianity and the disciples' stories were

116. Darrow might be referring to James Freeman Clarke's *The Ideas of the Apostle Paul* (Boston: James R. Osgood, 1884). Clarke (1810–88), a Unitarian minister, author, and scholar, attended Harvard College and was appointed to the faculty of Harvard Divinity School in 1867. His *Ideas of the Apostle Paul* maintained that St. Paul had "emancipated Christianity from its Jewish form" and that he "was the founder of Liberal Christianity, believing that there might be many members and yet one body." Ibid., 5.

written to fit the doctrines Paul announced. I have not carefully read the book and perhaps my judgment would not be good even if I did, but I am satisfied that no man who ever lived has had a copyright upon what may be said to be the chief, moral doctrines of the world. These most likely imply imagination which carries with it kindness, with the determination not to judge, and perhaps some other things whose origin would probably go back almost to primitive man. It does seem to me that you people who are claiming to be Christians and religious ought to make some statement that is definite and specific as to what you mean by religion and what you mean by Christianity. Perhaps this has been done but if so it has escaped my notice. I have no doubt that some definition of religion could be made which would include men of my opinions, but, all the same, the overwhelming mass of Christians believe in an inspired Bible, not in the sense that Marcus Aurelius was inspired, but as a special gift of God to man to guide their conduct. They believe that Jesus had no father; they believe in a personal God and I see no chance to believe in a God unless it is a personal God; they believe that man, unlike every other form of life is immortal. I do not object to changing dictionary definitions but I do object to men using ambiguous words, of taking a word with a well known definition as accepted by the public, and claiming some other definition for the word without stating the matter clearly.

How am I to determine whether you are a Christian or John Roach Stratton,[117] or whether Dr. Case is a Christian, or Riley[118] of Minneapolis? It is not up to me to settle it. I know who has the most followers. I know that even the liberal ministers are today not raising their voices against the fundamentalists who literally believe in the cardinal tenets of Christianity as contained in the Westminster Catechism and the Apostles Creed which are about the most immoral, impossible and degrading beliefs that have ever been given to man. As to the freedom of the will, it is too long a subject to discuss in a letter. I doubt if any scientific man any longer believes in it. It is a purely religious doctrine. As Neitszche said, it was invented to give God an excuse for damning man.

I am unable to see how you can ask me the question why I was interested in getting my grand daughter in Smith College. I certainly explained this thoroughly in my talk, but evidently you did not agree with me or did not get it. If I believed in free will I would not be interested because I would know that whatever her education she would act under her free will. I believe in education because I believe that knowledge opens up more avenues for enjoyment and also teaches the things to avoid. One does not choose some avenue of pleasure and avoid some avenue of pain because they have free will, but because they balance them up and decide according to their weight in their own mind.

117. John Roach Straton.
118. William Bell Riley (1861–1947), Baptist preacher and fundamentalist leader. Riley was pastor of the First Baptist Church in Minneapolis, Minnesota, and an active organizer of grassroots fundamentalism in the Midwest.

I can hardly imagine you could have thought I said anything for effect excepting perhaps in the way it was put. It has been a long time since I have said anything that I did not believe in a public meeting. I have sense enough to know what it means to fight the mob. I have done it all my life. I do it because I cannot do anything else. I would not be happy if I did.

I think I said something about the law. Perhaps my humor was either too coarse or too subtle for you to get it. I think the preachers are as honest as the lawyers, which is not saying much for them. I think that there is more injustice in the administration of law than you can find most anywhere else in the world; in fact, man does not know the meaning of the word justice, too many things are involved and it would be utterly absurd for you to judge me or for me to judge you. It requires a knowledge of many things, that even the subject knows nothing about.

However, having said all this I am very much pleased with your letter. I was very glad you took the pains to write me. I am willing to believe that you want to be right which is more than most of us do. I have not read Dr. Ayers' book[119] although I have it and shall do it, but from others who have read it, I think he must be as far from being a Christian as I am, myself. You speak of Dr. Case. I wonder if you have read anything of his but his Life of Jesus? This is, I think, an exceedingly good work but he has discussed Christianity from all standpoints. For instance his book on the Social Origins of Christianity and the Historicity of Jesus are very valuable books.[120] I have read all of the books he has written and I do not believe that he would agree with you on free will, and I doubt if I would disagree with him in anything he says or has written excepting possibly I might be more pessimistic than he is. However, Dr. Case is a thorough scientist in the treatment of his subjects, he never uses a word that has not a fairly definite meaning. I doubt if you would find the word "God" or "soul" in any of his books. If you are familiar with him and will call my attention to anything he has said that is in conflict with what I have said, I would be very glad to examine it and would guess in advance that he was right.

I would enjoy having a good visit with you. I will probably be in Northampton again. If I do you will see me. If you should ever come to Chicago, you would be very welcome at my home. With kind regards, I am

Very truly yours, | Clarence Darrow

MS: TLS, location of original unknown (copy in editor's files). INSIDE ADDRESS: Rev. C. Russell Prewitt, | First Methodist Church, | Northampton, Mass.

119. Darrow is probably referring to *Science: The False Messiah* (Indianapolis: Bobbs-Merrill, 1927), by Clarence Edwin Ayres (1891–1972). Ayers taught at the University of Chicago, Amherst College, and other schools after receiving his Ph.D. from Chicago in 1917. Most of his professional life was spent as a professor of economics at the University of Texas, 1930–68.

120. The books of Shirley Jackson Case to which Darrow is referring are *The Historicity of Jesus* (Chicago: University of Chicago Press, 1912), *The Social Origins of Christianity* (Chicago: University of Chicago Press, 1923), and *Jesus* (Chicago: University of Chicago Press, 1928).

TO C. RUSSELL PREWITT • CHICAGO • SATURDAY 23 JUNE 1928

CLARENCE DARROW June 23, 1928.

My dear Mr. Prewitt:

Your letter was duly received and I have read it carefully. I am afraid it does not pay us to discuss the questions that have grown out of our correspondence.

Your definitions of religion and Christianity and all the rest are so changeable and unique that one does not know where he stands. In the last letter you said: "I regard religion as the attitude of mind we assume toward 'all' the facts in the universe". If this is a correct definition of the word religion then all the dictionaries ought to be called in and burned. Your statement that both the scientist and the religionist walk by faith is, I believe, without justification in fact. Another definition which shows the uncertainty of discussing with one who makes the dictionary over anew, is as follows: "The data of religion consist in any discovery of beauty, whether it is the beauty of art, mind, or body, either intrinsic or extrinsic".

Likewise: "It" (I suppose you mean religion) "consists in the practice of goodness, in the love of truth, wherein we enter into that larger freedom and thus make the startling discovery that truths defend us, rather than vice versa". I tried to find out what that meant but can not. If this is a definition of religion, then it cannot be discussed. Again you say: "Religion consists in the experience of love". I wonder if Christians have any patent on any such experience?

You say also that "when reason no longer walks by sight it walks by faith". Well, I suppose that would sound good in a sermon, but it does not to me. Aren't you obscessed of the word Jesus? Who was he, anyhow, and why do you have to spend so much time thinking about him and talking about him? He was certainly one of the lesser people of the earth so far as we are able to find out anything about what he said or thought, which is almost nothing. He is credited with saying some good things but also saying "he that believieth not shall be damned", or words to that effect. However, this was after he had been resurected and he might not have been quite responsible.

You told me that the soul psychology is coming back. Coming back from where and to whom? I am still of the opinion that no scientist ever uses the word when he is discussing any problem and wants to be understood. I do not know why the virgin birth was not spoken of by Matthew. The four disciples wrote at different times, probably without having been acquainted. Probably Mark is the oldest and the others were taken largely from his, and, perhaps there is a manuscript still older that has been lost. But, why fuss about it all? It is important simply because people make it important. The reason anybody like Fosdick wastes his time talking about Jesus is not because he sees anything in Jesus any more than in any other person but because he inherits the tradition that Jesus was born of a virgin, that he came here to appease his God who was his father or uncle or something like that, so that men would not be obliged to go to hell because Adam ate the apple. You do not believe that and neither does Fosdick, but it travelled across from Rome, was adopted by Constantine and became the religion of Western Europe and was imported into America and our whole

literature is so filled with it that intelligent men try to warp truth and science and philosophy to correspond with the word of an individual that they know nothing whatever about.

I think you at least said one thing in your letter that is true. If the people got over this religion they would get another one. I think they would. If you cut all the weeds out of a garden some others will grow. But that furnishes me no excuse for harboring weeds.

Judge Kavanagh[121] is about like the other judges and the people in general, on the subject of crime. He has never made any scientific examination of it but he believes like you, in free will, and supposes a man is responsible because he got born. I think if you still have my letter you will find I referred to Neitszche's statement wherein I told you he agreed with you, that the question about Christianity was not whether Christ lived but whether his religion was good.

I would be the last one to quote very much from Neitszche although if we did not quote crazy men we probably would have little to quote. Men are crazy or sane in spots and at times. Neitszche was certainly a brilliant man.

When you say to read Genesis in terms of poetry, I suppose you mean the first and second chapter, certainly not all of it. What is the use of talking about Christ's being divine if his divinity is like that of every other person's?

In looking through your letter here is another one which may be the fault of the typing: "When God as an intellectual concept is subsidized by the personal experience of God in the sense of love, then and only then can personal religion be born." I do not know what that means and I do not care. There is no reason why one cannot use simple and ordinary expressions when he wants to convey real ideas.

I must say that I wish you would approach this question as you would any other because you certainly have too good a mind and equipment, in my opinion, to go to waste on metaphysics. With best wishes, I am

Your friend, Clarence Darrow.

MS: TLS, location of original unknown (copy in editor's files). INSIDE ADDRESS: Rev. C. Russell Prewitt, | c/o First Methodist Episcopal Church, | Northampton, Massachusetts.

TO T. PERCEVAL GERSON • CHICAGO • SATURDAY 23 JUNE 1928

CLARENCE DARROW June 23, 1928.

My dear Mr. Guerson:

Your good letter received and some of these times I will write you in reply. Just now I want to call your attention specially to the meeting of the National Association for the

121. Marcus Kavanagh (1859–1937), lawyer and judge. Kavanagh was a judge for many years on the Superior Court of Cook County in Chicago, 1898–1935, and author of *The Criminal and His Allies* (Indianapolis: Bobbs-Merrill Co., 1928), which was probably what prompted the discussion of Kavanagh by Darrow and Prewitt.

Advancement of Colored People which is now being held in Los Angeles. I have told some of my friends that I wanted them to see you. I wish you would find Dr. Du Bois who is a wonderful man and also James Weldon Johnson who has done some fine literary work and Arthur Spenga[122] who has done a great deal for the organization although he is not a negro. They will introduce you to any others you want to meet and I am sure you will think a great deal of these people.

Your friend, always, | Clarence Darrow.

MS: TLS, CLU-SC, Theodore Perceval Gerson Papers (Collection 724). PLACE: letterhead. INSIDE ADDRESS: Dr. Persival Guerson, | Roosevelt Hotel, | Hollywood, California.

TO OSWALD GARRISON VILLARD • CHICAGO • MONDAY 25 JUNE 1928

CLARENCE DARROW Personal June 25, 1928.

My dear Mr. Villard:

Yesterday a story came to me from a business man who is thoroughly reliable. He told me that Curtis the nominee for vice president has a son who is practicing law in Chicago, and that some time ago this son had been employed by Sinclair.[123] Of course, I know nothing about the facts and my informant did not want to be known in the matter. He and all his friends are Republicans and he is a business man who is well known. I feel confident, however, that he knew what he was talking about.

This matter is important if it is true, and I should say it ought to be investigated. Offhand, my idea would be unless you can handle it yourself the World should send a reporter to the young man and ask him whether the statement is true. After that it could be investigated.

Of course, as I say, I am giving it to you as it comes to me. I did not even know that Curtis had a son practicing law in Chicago but I could verify it, however, if I tried.

With kind regards, I am | Very truly yours, | Clarence Darrow

P.S. I prefer not to be known in this matter as it is all hearsay to me. That does not mean that I would not give any assistance I could to investigate it.[124]

CD

MS: TLS, MH-H. INSIDE ADDRESS: Mr. Oswald Garrison Villard, | c/o The Nation, | 39 Vesey street, New York City.

122. Darrow must mean Arthur Spingarn.
123. Harry F. Sinclair, an American businessman, was indicted in 1925 as part of the Teapot Dome scandal of the Harding administration. Charles Curtis (1860–1936), a lawyer and public official, was the Republican running mate of Herbert Hoover in 1928. Curtis's son, Harry King Curtis (1890–1946), was also a lawyer. He worked as a member of the legal department of the Sinclair Consolidated Oil Corporation, in New York and Chicago, 1923–29.
124. *The Nation* did eventually do a story on the subject, interviewing Curtis's son. See "Curtis's Oily Hands," *The Nation*, 26 September 1928, 288–89.

TO BRAND WHITLOCK • CHICAGO • WEDNESDAY 4 JULY 1928

CLARENCE DARROW July 4, 1928.

My dear Brand:

I have been intending to write you ever since I got back but as you know I never do anything I ought to do. We had a fine time visiting you last summer, and wish we might see you again. I read your story, Transplanted, which you sent to me, and I thought it was an excellent piece of work.[125] I always meant to write something about it, but I just didn't do it. Since then I have received your Big Matt which I think is one of the best things you ever did.[126] I took it up one evening and got through reading it after midnight and then wrote a review for the News, which was published with a good display.[127] I think you have received it, but if not, I will send you a copy. This book ought to sell and I believe it will.

I am thinking of going to southern Europe sometime this winter, probably around the holidays. Are you going to be at Cannes? If you are, we will try to come and settle somewhere in that neighborhood for a time. I will try not to be with you so much as to interfere with your work, but at the same time I would be glad to be somewhere near you. I have a little stuff of my own that I ought to do but probably will never complete it. At any rate, let me hear from you. With best wishes from both of us to you and Nell, your friend,

Clarence Darrow | 1537 East 60th street, | Chicago, Illinois.

MS: TLS, DLC-MSS, Whitlock Papers, Box 45. INSIDE ADDRESS: Hon. Brand Whitlock, | c/o American Embassy, | Brussells, Belgium.

TO JOHN T. FREDERICK • CHICAGO • WEDNESDAY 4 JULY 1928

CLARENCE DARROW July 4, 1928.

My dear Mr. Fredericks:

As today was the birthday of our glorious republic, I have stayed at home trying to clean up some work. I hadn't got very far until I ran onto two copies of the Midland which you sent me long ago. These had been buried with such other periodicals as the Nation, the New Republic and other ungodly stuff. I had often thought of you since then and wondered where in the devil I had put the magazines. So, when I found them, I read them and enjoyed them very much indeed. I think the story, Effie, in the January-February number, is a bully piece of work. I wonder what the author is doing now?[128] It is certainly

125. Brand Whitlock, *Transplanted* (New York: D. Appleton, 1927).
126. Brand Whitlock, *Big Matt* (New York: D. Appleton, 1928).
127. Clarence Darrow, "Read Whitlock's Book and Wonder, Says Darrow," review of *Big Matt*, by Brand Whitlock, *(Chicago) Daily News*, 20 June 1928.
128. Darrow is referring to a short story by Paul T. Coonradt: "Effie," *Midland* 14 (January–February 1928): 7–24. Coonradt (1897–1954) was a writer and journalist in Utica, New York. He later worked as a teacher at a boarding school for boys in Cooperstown, New York.

very promising. There are other good stories in the magazines which I will not stop to discuss, and of course, I enjoyed your book reviews and your other contributions.

As I indicated, I have often thought of you and the pleasant day I spent in your sleep town. I have lived so long in a big city that I am getting at that time of life when I feel that I would like to live in a sleepy town myself. Still it is just possible that I would have the longing to hear the street cars and elevated trains and to dodge automobiles for my life in our crowded thoroughfares. Habits are awfully strong and I presume that I will go a while on habit after everything else is lost. But, in a way, I sort of envy you in a scholar's office, surrounded by books and magazines and not pestered by the things that are always coming to one who has lived the life that I have lived. When you are interrupted, it is usually by some school boy or school girl anxious to learn something although they forget it after it is learned.

I haven't forgotten that I promised the Unitarian minister that I would come and speak for him. I am always thinking of promises that I have made which not only follow me from every appointment I keep but have tagged me up all through life, most of them broken, although they were made in good faith. However, this is one I mean to keep. If you will see him and tell him to put me down as soon as the scholars come back to the school, I will come and talk for him. I want him to charge as much as you think the traffic will bear and take the profit. I get my pay in seeing you and the rest of them, most of whose names I have forgotten, but I have not forgot the day nor the people.

I wonder whether I promised you something and didn't make good? If so, send me a line and if there is anything I can do, I trust it will be done. Enclosed you will find a check for your magazine for a year. I know it will be worth the money but I am not sure what I will read it. My intentions are good enough but I am growing old and lazy. If nothing else is done, it will be piled up with the Nations and New Republics and sent to the hospitals where the patients can not do anything else but read.

It seems to me that if I lived as close to Chicago as Iowa City I would be drawn here once in a while. Don't you ever come to buy paper or something? If you do, come and see me. Let me know long enough ahead so I will be here. I would like to have you come to my house.

With kind regards, I am

Your friend, | Clarence Darrow

MS: TLS, IaU, Frederick Papers. INSIDE ADDRESS: Mr. John T. Fredericks, | c/o University, | Iowa City, Iowa.

TO THOMAS J. MOONEY • CHICAGO • TUESDAY 24 JULY 1928

CLARENCE DARROW 1537 East 60th Street Chicago, Ill. | July 24, 1928.

My dear Mooney:

I hope you will excuse me for keeping your papers so long. I have been terribly tied up and only just had the opportunity to go through them.[129]

129. Mooney had apparently asked Darrow's advice about publishing and circulating documents that were part of his pardon petition.

I am surprised to see how complete the case is. It is hard to imagine the Governor keeping you in prison after reading these documents. I would suggest this: I would cut out the report signed by William Wilson and others.[130] It does not add anything to the other documents. I would also cut out the affidavit of Alfred H. Spink.[131] The only purpose of this affidavit is to show that someone else might have done it, presumably some Germans who were interested in helping Germany in the war. While this may be true, it is simply a theory and in my mind has not enough force to overcome the position that it would cause many German citizens to take.

These papers are all sufficient without the two that I have noted. They ought to result in a release. However, there is something that is keeping you beyond what applies to the ordinary prisoner. When the judge, the state's attorney, the police department and the jurors confess that they were mistaken and ask for your pardon, it ought to be enough.

I think this should be printed after leaving out the portions that I referred to. It ought to be placed in the hands of everyone in California so far as it can be done. It is not at all likely that the people understand the situation. I hardly know what they could get out in reply. I don't see how they could do anything that could overcome a Judge and a State's Attorney and the case made against Oxner.[132] When it is printed I would put all of the jurors together. You can arrange it as you think best. I presume the question of money will cut some figure. Let me know what it will cost and I will see if I cannot raise the money here. It seems to me if the people hear this case they will demand your release.

Give my kindest regards to J.B.[133] I am still hoping that something can be done to help him before long.

Very truly yours, | Clarence Darrow

P.S. I will keep the papers unless you want me to return them.

MS: TLS, CU-BANC, Mooney Papers, Box 7. INSIDE ADDRESS: Mr. Tom Mooney, | San Quentin Penitentiary, | San Quentin, Calif.

130. Darrow is probably referring to a report in 1918 of a "Mediation Commission" appointed by President Wilson to investigate Mooney's case. William B. Wilson (1862–1934), secretary of labor under President Wilson, was chairman of the commission.

131. Alfred H. Spink (1854–1928), sports journalist and founder-editor of *The Sporting News* in 1886. Spink lived in Oakland, California, in 1916, next door to a former German consular for the Marshall Islands. In 1926, Spink described in an affidavit how this former consular's talk and activities led him to believe that some of the consular's friends or cohorts were behind the Preparedness-Day bombing. Mooney honored Spink's request that his affidavit not be made public until after his death. See Curt Gentry, *Frame-Up: The Incredible Case of Tom Mooney and Warren Billings* (New York: W. W. Norton, 1967), 467–68.

132. Darrow means Frank C. Oxman (d. 1931), a cattleman who served as an important prosecution witness against Mooney and whose testimony was later shown to be perjured. Ibid., 196–206.

133. James B. McNamara.

TO HARRY ELMER BARNES • CHICAGO • THURSDAY 2 AUGUST 1928

CLARENCE DARROW Aug 2d.

My Dear Barnes

I am going to Woods Hole for a little vacation leaving here about Aug 10th. I wonder if you have been there and if you don't want to go. It has been a long time since I have seen you. I think my son has decided to send the girl to Northampton and has written for catalogue of the preparatory school.[134] That may make another excuse for coming up now and then. Any how I hope I may run in to you somewhere one of these days. I shall have a "piece" in October Forum on the great delusion which I am afraid will loose me a number of the friends I already have left.—[135]

With kindest regards to you and Mrs. Barnes

Your friend | Clarence Darrow

MS: ALS, WyU-AH, Barnes Collection. DATE: reference to "piece" in *Forum*.

TO PAUL DARROW • CHICAGO • THURSDAY 2 AUGUST 1928

CLARENCE DARROW Aug 2d

Dear Paul

I have been looking at apartments in the vicinity that you want to locate. There are plenty of them. Good ones ranging from $100 to $200 per month, the latter are the better. You can get something very nice for 140 to 150. Any how it won't be hard to find a place when you come. I have been looking for a location where a movie can be reached with not over two changes of elect. cars or three quarters of an hour in traveling. I think we can find it. Any how I shall be glad to see all of you again. Am going to take a trip to Woods hole starting about the 10th. Probably shall be gone two weeks.

Love to all | C. S. D.

MS: ALS, MnU-L, Darrow Collection. DATE: "1928?" appended and supported by reference to Woods Hole.

TO PAUL DARROW • CHICAGO • SATURDAY 4 AUGUST 1928

CLARENCE DARROW Aug 4

Dear Paul

On the 13th of Aug we are going East to Woods Hole for about ten days. On Sept 4th we are going to Yankton S. Dakota where I speak to the bar association & from there to the

134. Two of Paul Darrow's daughters attended (and graduated from) Northampton School for Girls in Massachusetts: Jessie Darrow Lyon enrolled in 1928 and Mary Darrow Simonson enrolled in 1929. Interview with Mary Darrow Simonson, Honolulu, Hawaii, 16 September 1999.

135. Clarence Darrow, "The Myth of the Soul," *Forum (New York)* 80 (October 1928): 524–33.

Black Hills for about ten days.[136] Hadn't you better try to get here late in August or Sept 1st at the latest so I can help you some about "choosing" an apartment. Let me know your idea on the subject soon as possible.

Hastily | C. S. D.

MS: ALS, MnU-L, Darrow Collection. DATE: "1928?" appended and supported by reference to trip to Woods Hole and South Dakota.

TO WALTER LIPPMANN • CHICAGO • WEDNESDAY 29 AUGUST 1928

CLARENCE DARROW August 29, 1928.

My dear Lipmann:

If you send over to the "Lord's Day Alliance" for the series of tracts they are distributing to morons on the Sunday and other questions, and likewise get hold of the same series that are now running into the hundreds, issued from the "Methodist Vatican," adjoining the Capitol Building in Washington, you will find two mines of good stuff.

The public ought to know what these fanatics are trying to do to curtail the liberties of the people in all directions. It would be interesting to many people to inform them about the pamphlets that have been issued from the Methodists on the dangers of dancing, the necessity of an old time Sunday, and everything else that goes to bring back the old Puritan days.

The World has done a great work in this campaign and I am quite certain you will find something here you would like to give attention to.

With best wishes, I am | Very truly yours, | Clarence Darrow

MS: TLS, CtY-BR, Lippmann Papers, Box 7, Folder 318. INSIDE ADDRESS: Mr. Walter Lipmann, | c/o New York World, | Editorial Department, | New York City, N.Y.

TO HARRY ELMER BARNES • CHICAGO • WEDNESDAY 29 AUGUST 1928

CLARENCE DARROW August 29, 1928.

My dear Dr. Barnes:

It is too bad that I did not see you in Northampton. That is one of the reasons I went there but I could not stay any longer. However, I will probably be back one of these days. I suggested your name to Stratford & Company for a history of punishment.

136. A stenographic account of Darrow's speech to the bar association was published in its annual report. See *Report of the Twenty-Ninth Annual Meeting of the South Dakota Bar Association held at Yankton, South Dakota, September* 5th and 6th, *1928*, 110–27.

I have just received a letter from them saying you are going to do the work. I am very glad of it.[137]

I brought back with me from England a book entitled "A History of Penal Methods," with the sub-title, "Criminals, Witches, Lunatics", written by George Ives, and published by Stanley Paul & Company, London.[138] The book shows every evidence of investigation and scholarship. It is well indexed and so forth, and contains some four hundred pages of reading matter. I met Mr. Ives when I was in London last fall. He is a typical student and his whole life seemed wrapped up in this subject. This book takes up every country and age. I have not read the book. It is one of several thousand that I am going to read when I get to it. However, I have looked into it considerably and know it is worth while. If you want it, I will send it to you. I have an idea that you can go through a book pretty fast and sort out what you want.

With best wishes, I am

Always, | Your friend | Clarence Darrow

It was nice of you to send those Methodist pamphlets on dancing and other horribles, but I don't dance. I am going to send for the whole set and have something to say about them.[139]

CSD.

MS: TLS, WyU-AH, Barnes Collection. INSIDE ADDRESS: Dr. Harry Elmer Barnes, | 108 Maynard Road, | Northampton, Mass.

TO JOHN H. DIETRICH • CHICAGO • SATURDAY 22 SEPTEMBER 1928

CLARENCE DARROW September Twenty-Two,
Nineteen Hundred Twenty-Eight.

My dear Mr. Dietrich:

I was very glad to meet you and get so well acquainted. You do not need to bother about giving me any evidence on your view of evolution; after my talk with you, I am sure we agree on this subject. The word evolution has become so mixed up with the idea of progress that it is very common to hear the statement that the world is growing better through evolution, but I know you could not take it that way after what you told me of your views. Of course, determining what is better and what is worse, is not easy, but if it is growing better there must be a God inside of matter instead of outside, but it all comes to the same

137. The book was published with this dedication by Barnes: "To Clarence S. Darrow, foremost American opponent of juristic savagery." Harry Elmer Barnes, *The Story of Punishment: A Record of Man's Inhumanity to Man* (Boston: Stratford, 1930).
138. George Ives (1867–1950), English author and criminologist. Darrow is referring to Ives's *A History of Penal Methods: Criminals, Witches, Lunatics* (London: S. Paul, 1914).
139. What pamphlets Barnes sent Darrow is unknown.

thing. It means purpose, and nobody can read this into the universe. I would be glad to get the book and will read it with interest.[140]

Sincerely, your friend, | Clarence Darrow

MS: TLS, MnHi, Dietrich Papers. INSIDE ADDRESS: Rev. John H. Dietrich, | 1506 Harmon Place, | Minneapolis, Minn.

TO NATHAN LEOPOLD • CHICAGO • WEDNESDAY 3 OCTOBER 1928

CLARENCE DARROW October 3, 1928.

Dear Nathan:

I have expected to come and see you long before now but I am awfully lazy and quite busy and then I am not as ambitious as I once was. You can guess the reason. I often think of you and especially when the people got a brain storm lately over the deep laid plans to procure your freedom. It is strange the satisfaction people get over tormenting someone. The rest of the animal kingdom do not indulge in these pleasing past-times which shows, of course, that man is the apex of creation. But, the apex is not very high. I saw your interview and Dick's and thought they both were very good.[141] I don't know how anybody else feels about it, but I shall always cling to the idea that sometime you will be out but it will not be very near, still, at that, you have a longer time to live outside than I have. I don't know whether it is a consolation to you; it is to most people, especially the shortness of my time. Of course, we all learn to adjust ourselves in this world no matter what the circumstances are, and I presume that you are doing it fairly well, and automatically, if no other way. You know I am no preacher or moralist. I don't know what the Devil to say to make life any easier to you or to any other person. Anyhow, I think of you often and would be glad to help you. I am going to be quite busy in this campaign but when I get through I shall make you a visit.[142]

Always, your friend, | Clarence Darrow

MS: TLS, IEN, Leopold-Loeb Collection, Box 39, Folder 21. INSIDE ADDRESS: Nathan Leopold, | 1900 Collins street, | Joliet, Ill.

140. Dietrich probably offered to send Darrow his recent book, *The Fathers of Evolution and Other Addresses* (Minneapolis: First Unitarian Society, 1927).

141. In late September 1928, Hinton G. Clabaugh (1882–1946), the chairman of the Illinois board of pardons and paroles, complained that Leopold and Loeb were "pampered pets" of the prison at Joliet, Illinois. He also complained that Leopold and Loeb might not remain in prison for life because "an error in the records made [their sentence] concurrent rather than consecutive," making them eligible for parole after twenty years. Darrow publicly agreed that they would be eligible for parole after twenty years but doubted they could ever obtain parole. "Doubt Chances of Leopold and Loeb for Parole," *Chicago Tribune*, 26 September 1928. The warden of the prison denied that Leopold and Loeb were pampered and the Associated Press published an interview of sorts with Leopold and Loeb in which they both denied that they were being given any special treatment. "Warden Green Answers Attack of Parole Head," *Chicago Tribune*, 28 September 1928; "Loeb and Leopold Deny They Are Pets," *Washington Post*, 1 October 1928.

142. Darrow actively campaigned for Al Smith against Herbert Hoover in the presidential election in 1928.

TO THOMAS J. MOONEY • CHICAGO • WEDNESDAY 3 OCTOBER 1928

CLARENCE DARROW October 3, 1928.

Dear Tom:

I have been out of town a great deal lately and was not here when your letter came, which is the reason for my not answering it sooner. My own opinion in this matter is that so long as your case has been presented to the Governor it might be best not to get out any literature until his decision is delivered. Someone there who knows the situation ought to be able to judge better than I can. He might resent the idea of going to the people while it was under his consideration. I had thought, as I wrote you before receiving your telegram, that this was your plan.[143]

I am going to New York next week and shall see Frank Walsh and get his opinion on it and write you from there and also take up there the question of raising the money for publication and circularization of your statement. I don't know how I shall succeed but I think I can get some money in the east. I know that I will make a substantial contribution whether I get anybody else or not, but I am very anxious to help you all I can. Suppose you write a letter to Mr. Walsh regarding it so there will be no danger of our not taking it up. You can address him at the Fifth Avenue Hotel, New York City.

With best wishes, I am | Your friend, | Clarence Darrow

MS: TLS, CU-BANC, Mooney Papers, Box 7. PLACE: implied. LETTER ADDRESS: Mr. Tom Mooney, | San Quentin, Calif.

TO GEORGE W. OAKES • CHICAGO • WEDNESDAY 3 OCTOBER 1928

CLARENCE DARROW October 3, 1928.

Dear Mr. Oakes:

I hardly know what to say about your letter. I have always enjoyed my visits to Princeton and shall be glad to come again. Still, it is hard for me to make dates. I am seventy-one years old and not in very good health, still as good as I could expect for an antediluvian. My time is pretty fully taken up, but in spite of these excuses I am inclined to think I will make it some way.

I assume from your letter you would want me in the evening. If I were doing as I would like I would do it in connection with other engagements in the east but matters have not

143. Darrow had cautioned Mooney against sending out printed material or otherwise immediately publicizing his case: "I think this printing should not go out unless the Governor denies your petition. It will be time enough to get it printed then in a general appeal to the people of the country. I do not believe anything could be done on the radio until after election. People are only listening to political speeches. However, I will do anything I can with the people here as soon as it is out of the way." Darrow to Mooney, 27 September 1928, TLS, CU-BANC, Mooney Papers.

sufficiently cleared up for me to know just when this would be the handiest. I shall be in New York City for about two weeks, arriving around the 12th or 13th and will be at the Belmont Hotel. From there I shall probably speak every night in Pennsylvania, New York, New Jersey, and perhaps Massachusetts. I am engaging in the laudable occupation of trying to help convince the American people to elect a Catholic and a Wet as the next President of the United States.

Suppose you write me a letter addressed to the Belmont Hotel around the 15th. It is just possible I could fix a date. I don't imagine I could do it on this visit, as I presume every evening will be taken, but anyhow, I enjoy speaking to the young college boys; they, at least, know what you are talking about and are interested. Of course, they will probably get over it later, but the speaker gets a kick out of it, and then I like boys, anyhow. One of my Pennsylvania dates may be in Philadelphia, so I could drop in and have a visit with you at least. I have been thinking of making a few talks this year on "Looking Life in the Face." This ought to be easier for young people than older ones because death seems so far off.

With best wishes, I am

Very truly yours, | Clarence Darrow

MS: TLS, location of original unknown (copy in editor's files). INSIDE ADDRESS: George W. Oakes Jr., | 733 Pyne Hall, | Princeton University, | Princeton, N.J.

TO H. L. MENCKEN • CHICAGO • SUNDAY 7 OCTOBER 1928

CLARENCE DARROW October 7, 1928.

My dear Mr. Mencken:

I am enclosing a copy of a letter that I sent to Mr. King, which will be self-explanatory. I am going to be in New York between the 12th and 16th and perhaps a week or ten days. I am going to make talks for Al Smith. I am glad you are going into it too. The United States has reached a hell of a pass when they would elect Hoover rather than Smith. I think Smith is a little too cultured for the job. The kind you suggest is what we ought to have, and perhaps would be better at that.

I have running in my head a story which I shall call "The Confessions of a Near Patriot." It is in reference to the war and the hysteria of the day. I must admit that I was a near patriot and this little story will be rather biographical. I am going to show it to you when I finish it. If it looks like the thing you want you shall have it.[144]

I will call you up as soon as I get to New York.

With best wishes, | Your friend, | Clarence Darrow

MS: TLS, NN, Mencken Papers. INSIDE ADDRESS: Mr. Henry L. Mencken, | c/o American Mercury, | 730—5th avenue, | New York City, N.Y.

144. Nothing like this was published in Mencken's *American Mercury*, and whether Darrow ever wrote the story is unknown.

TO JOHN F. KING • CHICAGO • SUNDAY 7 OCTOBER 1928

October 7, 1928.

Dear Mr. King:

A few days ago I received a copy of your letter. Your case ought to be fairly easy to determine. If you will send a copy of the opinion of the Attorney-General and a statement of the facts and anything there that you have in reference to it, to Arthur Garfield Hays, attorney at law, 43 Exchange Place, New York City, or rather to me in his care, I will be in New York about the 13th or 14th of the month and will see what can be done.

As to compensation, I would not like to take the small savings of the unfortunate people who are in prison. If I make up my mind that I can win it, I will make no charge whatever for my services.

I would like to have Mr. Hays with me and he may think we may need to spend a little money for some one in his or some other office to brief the case but this would not be very much.

Very truly yours,[145]

MS: TLc, NN, Mencken Papers. INSIDE ADDRESS: Mr. John F. King, | c/o State Prison, | Tranton, N.J.

TO HARRY ELMER BARNES • CHICAGO • SATURDAY 10 NOVEMBER 1928

CLARENCE DARROW November 10, 1928.

My dear Doctor Barnes:

I hope you will not be too disappointed over the election. I have been with the losers so long on every question that it never bothers me.[146] I am going to take up your last book, which I know will be interesting.[147]

I wonder if you are going to New York much this winter? I expect to be down there sometime early in January or possibly in December. If you know about when your dates will be, I might try to make it convenient to go at that time.

I shall be glad to see you again. With all good wishes, I am

Your friend, | Clarence Darrow

MS: TLS, WyU-AH, Barnes Collection. INSIDE ADDRESS: Dr. Harry Elmer Barnes, | 108 Mainard Road, | Northampton, Mass.

145. Neither the court opinions nor the available appellate briefs in King's case list Darrow or Hays as counsel, and it is unknown whether Darrow or Hays represented him.
146. Al Smith lost the presidential election to Hoover on 6 November 1928.
147. Darrow is probably referring either to Barnes's *Living in the Twentieth Century* (Indianapolis: Bobbs-Merrill, 1928) or *The Evolution of Penology in Pennsylvania* (Indianapolis: Bobbs-Merrill, 1927).

TO D. C. STEPHENSON • CHICAGO • SATURDAY 10 NOVEMBER 1928

CLARENCE DARROW November 10, 1928

Dear Mr. Stephenson

It is rather difficult for me to get down there at present. I wonder if there is not someone who knows the facts that could come to see me? If not, I will try to come and see you about it before long. While I have not believed in the Klan, I think that the conviction was absolutely wrong.[148]

Very truly yours, | Clarence Darrow

MS: TT, In, Stephenson Papers. INSIDE ADDRESS: Mr. D. C. Stephenson | P.O. Box 41 | Michigan City, Indiana. NOTE: At the top of the letter transcript is typed: "Copy made November 12, 1928 MIM."

TO HELEN KELLER • CHICAGO • SATURDAY 1 DECEMBER 1928

CLARENCE DARROW December 1, 1928.

My dear Miss Keller:

I would have answered your letter long ago excepting that I have been away. I appreciate being put on the board or acting in any capacity with you in the work. The only objection I have is seeing the name of Hon. Calvin Coolidge above mine, but when I remember that you probably object to it as much as I do, I do not mind.[149] Amongst the others, I see some who mean little to me excepting money but you need the money and you have to get it where it is, if possible. You can forward the enclosed to the office. It would not do for them to know what I think of all of them.

I often remember my pleasant afternoon with you and in spite of the fact that you are so far out of the world, I am coming again.

With all good wishes, I am

Your friend, | Clarence Darrow

MS: TLS, NNAF, Helen Keller Archives. INSIDE ADDRESS: Miss Helen Keller, | 93 Seminole avenue, | Forest Hills, N.Y.

148. Stephenson asked Darrow if he would represent him in his post-conviction efforts to get released from prison. Stephenson to Darrow, 2 November 1928, TT, In, Stephenson Papers.
149. Darrow might be referring to the possibility of serving on the board of directors for the American Foundation for the Blind (AFB). Calvin Coolidge was honorary president of the AFB, and Keller was then an active fund-raiser for the organization. But Darrow never did serve on the board. Telephone interview with Allison M. Bergmann (information specialist with the AFB), January 1996.

TO VIVIAN PIERCE • CHICAGO • SATURDAY 1 DECEMBER 1928

CLARENCE DARROW December 1, 1928.

Dear Vivian:

Replying to your letter of November 26th, I would say if you don't know what else to do, you can make me chairman. Of course, I don't want it, for I don't like responsibility or work, and I will probably not do either, anyhow, but I am very much interested and glad to do whatever I can.[150]

I don't know whether I wrote you before, but I have been thinking what we should do is to get up a list of well authenticated murder cases where the wrong man has been convicted. I don't know just how to get at it, but I do know some cases myself. Such a list would have to be well verified.

Yours truly, | Clarence Darrow

MS: TLS, MBNU, Sara Ehrmann Papers, Box 16, Folder 91. INSIDE ADDRESS: Miss Vivian Pierce, | 104—5th avenue | New York City, N.Y.

TO GEORGE W. OAKES • CHICAGO • THURSDAY 13 DECEMBER 1928

CLARENCE DARROW Dec. 13

My Dear Mr. Oakes

I always think of you and your club when I am in the east and want to go and see you again. So far I haven't been able to do it. Don't like to ask for money from you for I know that most of you have none to spare and if you had I think you should spend it on first—ball, automobiles &c. &c. I am inclined to think that pleasure is the most important thing in life and there are more things you can get at your age than mine. Of course as this might be shown to a preacher or fundamentalist professor I must add that every thing should be taken in moderation and with care, and fortunately the young don't need to be urged not to over look the main things in life. I don't know what connection all this has with the real answer. I am to debate with Mr. Lothrop Stoddard on the Supreme importance of the Nordic over all other life at Wilmington, Del. on Jan 23rd.[151] I wonder if you could take

150. Pierce wanted Darrow, who had been chairman of the executive committee of the League to Abolish Capital Punishment, to be chairman of what would be called the American League to Abolish Capital Punishment. (He eventually served as president of the organization and as a member of its board of directors). Pierce told Darrow that she would be grateful just to use his name even if he did no work for the organization: "I need not tell you that it would be an enormous help to the organization to have your name at the heart of our committee, even if you do nothing more. And, of course, as you know, you always have done more than many on our executive committee." Pierce to Darrow, 10 December 1928, TLc, MBNU, Sara Ehrmann Papers, Box 16, Folder 91.

151. A sold-out crowd at the Shubert Playhouse in Wilmington, Delaware, on 23 January 1929, heard Darrow and Stoddard debate on "whether the present immigration policy of the United States discriminating in favor of the North European races at the expense of the South European races is to the best interest of the

the 22 or 24th. I would even make it the 20 or 21 because I really want to go. What do you want me to talk about at the dinner & will there be other speakers? Of course I can talk about any *thing*, whether what I shall say will be worth while is an other question—

With best wishes | Clarence Darrow

MS: ALS, location of original unknown (copy in editor's files). DATE: reference to debate with Stoddard.

TO LINCOLN STEFFENS • CHICAGO • FRIDAY 28 DECEMBER 1928

CLARENCE DARROW December 28, 1928.

Dear Lincoln:

I wonder where you got the story of the Cleveland judge who sentenced two people to prison for three years for practicing birth control. It is a good illustration of history making. Judge Harrison Ewing of Cleveland is an oldtime friend of mine and a very intelligent, progressive man. A divorce case was pending in his court where two people were getting about twenty-four dollars a week and had three children in about as long a time as it took to get them. He made no order whatever about birth control, but what he said was that people with the slender income they had should learn to practice birth control. I don't know what this story will do after a while. It now seems to be that the people were sent to the penitentiary for three years because they practiced it, when in fact the judge is entirely on the other side of the question. If you look carefully at what you said of Father Ryan's interview, you will see that he understood the case as it was; his objection to the judge's remark was because he advised birth control, and his interest in bettering the economic condition was somewhat due to speak moderately of the ordinary Catholic antagonism to birth control.[152]

I am not sending this for the purpose of getting you to publish it or even to make a corrected statement. One never can catch up with things, anyhow.

It was a great disappointment to me to miss you the last time you were through. I cannot realize you were here and that we had such a short opportunity to visit. I hope we will have a chance again before long.

With good wishes always to you and to Peter and little Pete.[153]

Your friend, | Clarence Darrow.

MS: TLS, NNC, Steffens Papers. INSIDE ADDRESS: Mr. Lincoln Steffens, | Carmel, | Calif.

United States." *Wilmington News,* 24 January 1929. A transcript of the debate was later published as a little blue book: *Is the U.S. Immigration Law Beneficial? A Debate: Clarence Darrow vs. Lothrop Stoddard,* Little Blue Book No. 1423 (Girard, KS: Haldeman-Julius, 1929).

152. The birth control sentence of Judge Harrison W. Ewing (1874–1955) of the Court of Common Pleas in Cleveland was widely reported as Darrow described it. See, e.g., "Birth Control Sentence Stirs Legal Criticism," *Decatur (Illinois) Evening Herald,* 5 December 1928 (United Press account); "Birth Control," *Time,* 17 December 1928. What Steffens said about a "Father Ryan" is unknown.

153. "Peter" was Steffens's nickname for his wife, Ella Winter Steffens (1898–1980), and "little Pete" is Steffens's son, Pete Steffens (1924–2012).

TO VIVIAN PIERCE • CHICAGO • TUESDAY 29 JANUARY 1929

CLARENCE DARROW Jan. 29

My Dear Vivian

It is a long way to N.Y. and I don't want to go. Then, too, I have nothing new to say on the subject.[154] An organization has asked me to speak in N.Y. in February at a dinner given in commemoration of Voltaire, which I promised to attend. The man who is getting this up is an infidel named Lewis.[155] Arthur Garfield Hayes knows him and has his address. If you will get him at once and fix the two meetings for consecutive nights not more than *one day* between I will come. Of course I want to help you & the cause, but really I am afraid I won't draw in N.Y. on this subject.

Best wishes always | Clarence S. Darrow.

MS: ALS, MBNU, Sara Ehrmann Papers, Box 16, Folder 91. PLACE: no reason to doubt.

TO JOHN MACRAE • CHICAGO • SATURDAY 2 FEBRUARY 1929

CLARENCE DARROW February 2, 1929.

Dear Mr. Macrae:

Thank you very much for the beautiful copy of the Ballad of Reading Gaol.[156] I just received it today. It is a fine piece of work. I am glad to know what you say about your reactions toward what we call glibly the criminal. I have always been against the orthodox treatment of the unfortunate and especially against capital punishment. I don't know whether you have ever seen any of my stuff on the subject. If you have not and care to, I will send you some.

I think I ought to call your attention to the fact that the first edition of Oscar Wilde ever printed in this country was printed by Tucker of Boston.[157] He used to run an anarchist weekly paper. I had read the book in an English edition and I told Tucker if he would get it out I would pay for it, which I did. He got out a very nice edition. Since then, of course, there have been many published, most of which I think I have. It is a wonderful piece of work.

154. Pierce wanted Darrow to speak at the Hampden Theatre in New York City as a fund-raising event for the American League to Abolish Capital Punishment. She had already leased the theatre and advertised the event. Pierce to Darrow, 29 and 30 January 1929, TLc, MBNU, Sara Ehrmann Papers, Box 16, Folder 91. Darrow did give a speech at the event, saying, among other things, that he believed Americans were living in the most reactionary period since the Civil War and that a quarter of the people in prison were there for offenses that were not considered crimes fifteen years earlier. The novelist Kathleen Norris (1880–1966) also spoke at the event. See "Darrow Lays Crime to Curb on Liberty," *New York Times*, 18 February 1929.

155. Joseph Lewis.

156. Macrae sent Darrow a copy of Oscar Wilde's *The Ballad of Reading Gaol*, which E. P. Dutton published in 1928, with illustrations by the Greek American artist John Vassos (1898–1985).

157. Darrow is referring to Benjamin R. Tucker (1854–1939), an anarchist publisher who is best known for a newspaper that he published from 1881 to 1908 called *Liberty*. Tucker published an edition of *The Ballad of Reading Gaol* in 1899.

You are quite right in considering what great things could come from what society believes a poluted source. I have seen hundreds of so-called criminals and known many of them very well, and have found instances of greatness and goodness amongst them that you never could find amongst the ~~rich~~ good. I would guess that the common idea that you refer to, about the horrible crime of homosexuality, has been pretty well knocked to pieces. I think it is universally regarded by intelligent men as pathological today. Of course, the Courts treat it as a crime, but you cannot expect much from Courts. They only read law books and the older they are, the better.

With best wishes, and thanks, I am

Very truly yours, | Clarence Darrow

MS: TLS, NsyU, E. P. Dutton & Company, Inc. Records. INSIDE ADDRESS: Mr. John Macrae, | 286 Fourth avenue, | c/o E. P. Dutton & Co., Inc., | New York City, N.Y.

TO HELEN KELLER • CHICAGO • THURSDAY 21 MARCH 1929

DARROW, SMITH, CRONSON & SMITH March 21st 1929

My Dear Helen Keller

Our good friend Edna Porter[158] wrote me that she received a letter from you in which you suggested that I probably consented to be a member of the Association for the blind on your account and not through any interest in the other blind, which really includes almost all the people in the world. There are so many ways of being blind. The main difference between the physically blind and the mentally blind is that the physically blind would like to see, while the mentally blind prefer to stay blind. The mentally blind prefer not to see because it would make them unhappy, the same reason should make the physically blind contended with their lot. But that is an other story: No one can tell just why they do any thing unless it is rising suddenly when one sits on a pin. Of course I would have done it for you, not only that but almost any thing else. I could even strike out the *almost.* But I would rather you should not think it was the only reason. For many years I was one of the directors of "The Industrial home for the blind" in Illinois.[159] I gave of a good deal of time, for no salary and no graft but why did I do that? It was because I was once a close friend of a beautiful and inteligent woman (Miss Hyman)[160] of Chicago. I used to go to

158. Edna Porter (1882?–1946), actress and writer. Porter lived in New York City and was an actress in many plays. She had a deep interest in the blind and she compiled a short anthology of writings about Helen Keller, including a short entry by Darrow. See *Double Blossoms: Helen Keller Anthology* (New York: L. Copeland, 1931), 13.

159. The Illinois Industrial Home for the Blind was created by Illinois in 1887 for the purpose of providing a home and training and employment for the blind. Both men and women lived at the home, which was located at Marshall Boulevard and Nineteenth Street in Chicago.

160. Belle Hyman Egler (1863–1926), whose parents were German immigrants, was born in Chicago. Her father was a prominent jeweler in Chicago. She was blind from the age of four, as a result of an illness. She studied at the State School for the Blind in Jacksonville, Illinois, and later studied music in Chicago and

her home and read to her and take her to art gallerys and tell her about the pictures, take her to the lake, and the parks and I always enjoyed being with her. She died a few years ago. I liked all the residents of the home. The board of directors were once greatly shocked to learn that one of the girls was in the way of having a child. They met in special session to consider where to send her. I made a fight to keep her where she was, and finally won. I was indignant that all pleasure should be denied the blind. I even argued that one who saw too much could get no comfort out of life. To get back to the girl, (Miss Hyman) she too was on the board and of course stood with me. I was interested in her at first because I was sorry for her, but I learned that she had so many things to do that she was as happy as I or any one else. I know that you have more handicaps than that poor girl (now dead). I stayed away from you for many years after I wanted to see you because I was sorry for you and did not want to give myself pain by seeing you. But my visit has taken all of that away. I do not pitty you any more. I found that your life was so full in helping others and trying to make the blind world see, that I almost envied you. I wonder if you ever read Tolstoi's Master & Man.[161] If not I would like to send it to you. That and life has taught me that the greatest joy comes in trying to help some one else. I have lived up to it the best I could but am always sluffing. My visit to you did me lots of good and has brought me happiness. So much that when I am in N.Y. again I will go and see you. Please remember me to Miss Sullivan[162] whom I am sure is happy too.

With all good wishes and affection—

Your friend | Clarence Darrow

MS: ALS, NNAF, Helen Keller Archives.

TO FRED BICKNELL • CHICAGO • MARCH 1929 OR LATER

My Dear Bicknell[163]

This letter is for you & John.[164] There is no doubt in my mind that John should plead guilty. There isn't a chance that the jury will acquit him. To stand against it means death. It is a serious responsibility for any one to take. I would not think of taking it. The case is now where John's life can be saved & sometime he will get out. Under the circum-

---

Europe. She was an accomplished musician and well known in Chicago for her efforts to benefit the blind and poor. She was an important influence in the establishment of the Illinois Industrial Home for the Blind in 1887 and she served as one of its trustees until 1897.

161. Leo Tolstoy, *Master and Man* (1895).

162. Anne Sullivan Macy (1866–1936), teacher and lifelong companion of Helen Keller.

163. The handwriting of Bicknell's name—if, in fact, he is the person to whom this letter was addressed—is very poor. The first letter of the name could very well be a *T* or an *F* rather than a *B*, but the last letters are almost surely *l*. Given the subject and confidential nature of the letter, Bicknell was probably the intended recipient. But whether this letter was actually sent is unknown.

164. "John" is no doubt John Winters. Darrow and Bicknell represented Winters, who had been convicted of murder in the Vermont Supreme Court. See Darrow to Paul Darrow, 5 June 1927, n.74. On 22 March 1929, the Vermont Supreme Court issued an opinion setting aside the judgment and verdict against Winters and granting him a new trial. See *State v. Winters*, 145 A. 413 (1929).

stances I would not think of going there and taking such a chance. I don't know how Mr. Tupper[165] feels but he is convinced as I am that there is no chance to win, and I would think that he would not want to go into it when he is offered a chance to save life. Think it over seriously and quick while there is a chance.[166]

With best wishes.

Your friend | Clarence D

MS: ALS, DLC-MSS, Darrow Papers. PLACE: probable date of this letter and other letters and information. DATE: reference to Winters having a chance to plead guilty.

TO WALTER WHITE • CHICAGO • TUESDAY 30 APRIL 1929

CLARENCE DARROW April 30th

Dear Walter

As you know I am getting damn old. And like all people who have no other out door sport I am making a will. I want to include your association in it. There won't be enough to make it of any great consequence. But still enough to show how I feel and possibly attract some others to do likewise. Won't you kindly send me a letter stating the legal name of the association, so you will get it all right.[167] By the way I made some money out of you. The Tribune sent me a check of 27.[168]

Always your friend | Clarence Darrow

MS: ALS, DLC-MSS, NAACP Administrative Files. ENDORSEMENT: stamped received, "~~W.W.~~ C.T.F. 5–1-29 pm"; and replied to, "W.W. 5–1-29."

TO ROGER BALDWIN • CHICAGO • TUESDAY 30 APRIL 1929

CLARENCE DARROW April 30th

Dear Roger

When a fellow gets old there is nothing else to get any fun out of excepting making wills. I want to leave a little to the Civil Liberties Bureau. It may induce others. Any how I shall

165. Herbert G. Tupper (1877–1932) was a lawyer with a general practice in Springfield, Vermont. He was co-counsel with Darrow and Bicknell for John Winters. Darrow had a high regard for Tupper and they became friends as a result of their work together on Winters's case.
166. John Winters did not plead guilty but was later tried again, convicted of second-degree murder, and sentenced to life in prison. Darrow did not participate in the trial. Winters was paroled from Vermont State Prison at Windsor in 1949. See John Stark Bellamy II, *Vintage Vermont Villainies* (Woodstock, VT: Countryman Press, 2007), 129.
167. Darrow prepared at least one or two wills during his life, but none was probated. Interview with Blanche Darrow Chase and Mary Darrow Simonson, Wheaton, Illinois, 29 July 1995. See Darrow to Jessie Darrow Ohl, 20 July 1904, n.82 (transcript of one will).
168. Darrow is referring to the payment for his review of White's study of lynching: "The Shame of America," review of *Rope and Faggot: A Biography of Judge Lynch* (New York: Alfred A. Knopf, 1929), by Walter White, *New York Herald Tribune*, 21 April 1929.

have the fun of thinking of it for a little while. Please send me the legal name so there will be no mistake about it.

Your friend | Clarence Darrow[169]

MS: ALS, NjP, ACLU Archives. DATE: Baldwin's response.

TO VIVIAN PIERCE • CHICAGO • TUESDAY 30 APRIL 1929

CLARENCE DARROW April 30th

Dear Vivian

The main sport of old age is making wills. I want to leave something to the league that may induce others to follow my example. Please write me the legal name so there will be no trouble in getting what little will be going to you if I die soon enough to leave anything.

With best wishes | Your friend, | Clarence Darrow

MS: ALS, MBNU, Sara Ehrmann Papers, Box 16, Folder 91.

TO VICTOR F. CALVERTON • CHICAGO • FRIDAY 3 MAY 1929

CLARENCE DARROW May 3rd

My Dear Calverton

I *just* ran into your *first* letter, which was overlooked when I wrote the review.[170] I see I made a mess of it and wrote about Bryan—instead of our friend Walter! How the h—l could I get him mixed up with a *Nordic Stiff like B.* I had just written a Bryan review for the New Republic.[171] Now you can publish the Bryan one or return it as you please and I can no doubt find some one else that wants it, and if you still want a review of Walter's book let me know *at once* and you shall have it. Will be in N.Y. about the 15th or 16th and try to see you.

All good wishes | Clarence Darrow

MS: ALS, NN, Calverton Papers, Box 4. DATE: "[1929]?" appended and confirmed by reference to *The New Republic.*

169. Baldwin replied: "I find making wills an interesting occupation almost any time. It gives a fellow a sense of having something, even when he hasn't got much. Anyway we are touched by this thought of us in that connection, though we hope that you will have won the liberties of the American people in time for us to go out of business before you do." Baldwin to Darrow, 6 May 1929, TLc, NjP, ACLU Archives.
170. Calverton had apparently asked Darrow to write a review of Walter White's *Rope and Faggot* for the *The Modern Quarterly,* for which Calverton was the editor. Darrow mistakenly submitted a review of a recent biography of William Jennings Bryan instead.
171. Clarence Darrow, "Bryan," review of *Bryan* (1929), by Morris R. Werner, *The New Republic,* May 1929, 363–64.

TO MARY DARROW SIMONSON • CHICAGO • FRIDAY 10 MAY 1929

CLARENCE DARROW May 10th

Dear Mary

Enclosed you will find a V. This is sent you on condition that you shall buy nothing useful with it. Don't spend any of it for stockings,—or food or tuition. Don't give any of it to poor people. Don't let any of [it] go to any old poverty stricken widows who are hungry. Don't give any of it to any lame children. Don't give it to any blind people or any deaf & dumb or any one legged people or anyone without an arm. Don't put any of it in any contribution box at church. Don't send any of it to foreign missions. The heathens are bad enough as they are. Don't buy any books, at least none that are good and dull. You can use it for movies, except don't use it on any animal movies or any landscapes or any news of foreign countries or any one where you can possibly learn something. Go to some moveys where there are boy and girl sheiks or where the censors have tried to stop them or some show in an old building that has been condemned as a fire trap or something like that. You can buy Esquimaux pie, for that is unhealthy and will make you look sick and interesting. You can buy chocolate creams for these will rot your teeth and then you can get some nice new white ones with gold lining and can put them on the mantel for ornaments and attract attention. I said you could buy stockings but I don't think you need them. It is warm enough without stockings. I have just been over to the park and I couldn't tell whether the girls had legs or stockings except a few of them that had been darned. Don't use any of it to ride in street cars or in buses. If you want to go any where take a car and go as far as you can for 2.50. and then you can get back. You don't need to save any to tip the driver; he will probably cheet you any how, if he doesn't it will show that he hasn't been raised right.

I go over to 5844 most every nite to see the park, it saves walking and the view is better any how. Blance[172] is getting all right again. She is hie-hatting every body about her operation. I had one once myself on my hed. My brains were growing so fast that they crowded into my skull and I had to have some of them cut out. But I don't think you will be bothered that way. Jessie[173] is getting along fine, she is pretty near into a sorority. I suppose she is getting in on her looks. I don't know how else.

O yes don't spend any money sending flowers on Mother's day. It is so far away that they would be wilted before they got here and if they were not they would look pretty punk by the time Lil[174] got back from the north side. Anyhow that day was just got up for the florists. They think more of their mothers than any one else does, but they think more of other peoples mothers than they do of their own. If they didn't they would send the flowers to their own mothers instead of selling them. I don't think it is very nice any how

172. Blanche Darrow Chase, Mary Darrow Simonson's sister, had surgery to correct a congenital hip disorder.
173. Jessie Darrow Johnston, Mary Darrow Simonson's older sister.
174. Lillian (Anderson) Darrow, Mary Darrow Simonson's mother.

to buy a lot of flowers for mothers day and then go and sell them. They tried to get up a father's day too so as to sell more flowers but they couldn't get any one to go to father's day. Well this is about enough for this time. If I knew what you was studying (if any thing) I could write you something about your studies which you couldn't find in your old books. I suppose you will [be] back after a while and I am trying to arrange some engagements so I won't be here while you are home.

This is from your Grand dad.

Clarence Darrow

MS: ALS, Darrow Family (TLc, DLC-MSS, Darrow Papers).

TO ROGER BALDWIN • CHICAGO • SUNDAY 19 MAY 1929

CLARENCE DARROW May 19, 1929.

Dear Roger:

Replying to your letter of May 5th I would say all the states in the union, so far as I know of, have had a good many bills introduced into the legislatures to seriously deprive citizens of rights.[175] Amongst others, many states have a bill providing that if the defendant does not testify the state can comment on that fact as raising a presumption against him. Likewise, there are bills asking that less than the unanimous vote be necessary to convict. Likewise, increasing penalties and permitting the judges to give oral instructions and comment on the evidence, making our courts like federal courts in which there is no jury trials. I don't know what the American Law Institute suggested in the way of a revised code. I know about the lawyers who make it up and would expect it to be reactionary, but whatever they suggested, it is not binding upon the legislatures of the various states. They have had some bad ones introduced in Illinois. I managed to get together a few fellows and we have been fighting them and I think the bills will not be passed. I would suggest it would be well to find out what is going on in Albany and anywhere else that you have representatives. You may be sure that the powers of reaction and despotism never sleep and in these days when conservatism is in the saddle, we have to be very watchful. Anyway, I am glad you are interested.

With best wishes, always, | Your friend, | Clarence Darrow

MS: TLS, NjP, ACLU Archives. INSIDE ADDRESS: Mr. Roger Baldwin, | 100—5th avenue, | New York City, N.Y.

175. This letter is a reply by Darrow to a letter from Baldwin that reminded Darrow of their earlier conversation about recent inroads on the rights of criminal defendants: "You remember when we talked some time ago about the new inroads upon defendants' rights in criminal trials that I told you we would take this subject up and see what we can do about it. | I got the report of the American Law Institute with the revised Code of Criminal Procedure, which they are recommending all over the country, and I had Art Hays examine it. He has just reported that none of the provisions which you called our attention to is contained in the draft. There is no suggestion that defendants be compelled to take the stand or that juries bring in a three-quarters verdict, or that the judge may comment on the evidence as well as the law. | Do you know from what source these suggestions come and how we can get the dope in print? When we get wind of just how the attack is being made, we can act." Baldwin to Darrow, 8 May 1929, TLc, NjP, ACLU Archives.

TO GEORGE T. BYE • CHICAGO • SUNDAY 19 MAY 1929

CLARENCE DARROW May 19, 1929.

My dear Mr. Bye:

Your telegram was duly received. Won't you let the Saturday Evening Post have the manuscript.[176] It beats the devil that a big publication is afraid of a few sentences on religion, but as it is no essential part of my manuscript, of course I don't care. Sorry there are one or two sentences early in the article. I don't see why they should object to those. There is a little more about it toward the end and I can understand how somebody might object to those. I hope you will see that nothing is put in their place and also leave the first one in if possible. I would have been glad to fix it up myself if it was not to be published too soon. I shall be in New York on the morning of the 6th of June. I may have some more stuff for you, but anyhow, I am sailing on the evening of the 7th for Europe and I think I can dig up something while I am gone. Won't you get in touch with me at the Belmont as soon after my arrival as possible?

Always, with kind regards, your friend,

Clarence Darrow

MS: TLS, NNC, James O. Brown Papers. INSIDE ADDRESS: Mr. George Bye, | c/o Saturday Evening Post, | New York City, N.Y.

TO THE EDITOR OF *THE NATION* • CHICAGO • WEDNESDAY 22 MAY 1929

Chicago, Illinois, May 22

TO THE EDITOR OF THE NATION:

SIR: Mr. Hoover is no doubt a good civil engineer. Still, this fact, if true, does not make him a statesman. How little he really appreciates the value of freedom and the vigilance necessary to preserve human liberty was shown by his remarks at a luncheon of the Associated Press.[177] In referring to prohibition Mr. Hoover, following in the lead of the orthodox prohibition fanatics, used this language: "Whatever the value of any law may be, the enforcement of that law, written in plain terms upon the statute books, is not to my mind a debatable question. Law should be observed and must be enforced until it is repealed by the proper processes of our democracy." These words would have gladdened the hearts of the witch-hangers of New England when juries were refusing to send old women to death in obedience to a tyrannical and fanatical law.

176. Darrow is probably referring to Clarence Darrow, "At Seventy-Two," *Saturday Evening Post,* 6 July 1929, 23, 109, 114.
177. President Hoover delivered an address titled "Respect for Law a National Duty" at an annual luncheon of the Associated Press in New York City on 22 April. See William Starr Myers, ed., *The State Papers and Other Public Writings of Herbert Hoover* (Garden City, NY: Doubleday, Doran, 1934), 1:42–47.

To mark the progress in government in two thousand years, these words of Mr. Hoover might be compared with an utterance of Trajan, the Emperor of Rome, made in the year 112. Pliny was then the governor of a Roman province, and the prosecution of the Christians was in full swing. The law provided death for becoming a Christian—Senator Jones, please note.[178] Men and women, however, continued to stand by their faith in spite of terrible torture. Under the circumstances Pliny who was shocked by the Joneses of his day, wrote to Trajan for instructions. The Emperor, after recommending clemency and toleration, instructed Pliny about violations of the act. He did not say that a hideous law must be enforced so long as it is a law. In speaking of the violators of the statute, he said: "Do not go out of your way to look for them." Had the Roman Emperor determined to enforce all laws while they were laws Christianity would have been wiped out of the Roman Empire and therefore of all Europe.

Who was right, the Roman Emperor two thousand years ago or the chief magistrate of the American Republic? The truth is that it is impossible to repeal a criminal statute until it is generally violated.

Emerson said that the good citizen must not be too obedient to the law. There is no limit to which fanaticism will not go. To teach the sacredness of the statutes, and to prefer the strict obedience to law to the preservation of freedom, is a cowardly doctrine that would inevitably lead to slavery. A criminal statute to be enforced requires the overwhelming support of the people. The first Adams used every possible effort to enforce the obnoxious Alien and Sedition laws, but all over the land American citizens defied the jail, and the laws were finally disregarded. When Jefferson was elected to follow Adams, he did not announce that whether the law was good or bad it should be obeyed. He found that the people would not submit to such legislation, and he used all his influence to have the tyrannical statutes repealed, which was promptly done.

To enforce obedience to an obnoxious law that is held in general contempt by a large percentage of the citizens is not law-enforcement; it is tyranny. To awe men and women by threats of persecution and jail is to destroy independence, to degrade citizenship and belittle man. The statesman who discovered that a law was odious to good citizens would not seek to club them into submission. Instead of that he would recognize and respect the feelings of a free people and use his influence to repeal the law.

CLARENCE DARROW

MS: "Emperor or President," *The Nation* 128 (5 June 1929): 672–73.

178. Wesley L. Jones (1863–1932), congressman and senator from Washington, was a staunch supporter of Hoover as well as an advocate of Sunday-closing laws, Prohibition, and other measures that Darrow found repugnant. On 2 March 1929—three months or so before this letter was written—Congress enacted what was popularly known as the Jones Act, which amended the National Prohibition Act to allow increased fines and imprisonment for anyone making, selling, or transporting liquor. Jones sponsored the bill in the Senate. See Jones Act, ch. 473, § 1, 45 Stat. 1446 (1929).

TO T. PERCEVAL GERSON • MONTREUX, SWITZERLAND • SUNDAY 1 AUGUST 1929

HÔTEL BEAU-RIVAGE, MONTREUX (SUISSE) Aug 1st 1928

My Dear friend Guerson

It was good to get your letter that was forwarded here. We left Chicago the 3rd of May and came almost directly here. Have been in this place six or seven weeks and have felt no inclination to leave. I am sleeping and loafing and writing a little and waiting. Shall go to London in about ten days. Don't know when we will go back to America probably not until November. It was good of you to take so much interest in Miss Ruben. She wrote me how kind you were.[179] That you are coming to Chicago in the spring is the best news we have heard for a long time. It will be so fine to see you and I hope Mrs. Guerson will be with you. We can take care of you fine at our place and then we can be together all the time and we will invite in the people you will like. I am really loafing here on account of my health which is not so bad for one who has been on the Earth as long as I have. Somehow no matter what we think we hang on as long as we possibly can. For me I feel convinced that this life is all and I cannot feel any regrets that there is no more, and still I am bound to say that it has not been so bad. I have been blessed with hosts of friends which is about the best that can come to one on his journey. I am not sure whether you have ever been in Europe or not. You should come. Switzerland especially is a beauty spot wherever you go. I may write you again from Europe. I don't suppose you can ever realize how much you have ever meant to us. I am sure the memory of all your kindness will be with me to the end. It will do us so much good if you come and stay with us.

With love to both of you from Ruby & me

Devotedly | Clarence Darrow

Will I never get your name spelled right.

MS: ALS, CLU-SC, Theodore Perceval Gerson Papers (Collection 724). DATE: letter is misdated as 1928.

TO PAUL DARROW • LONDON • SATURDAY 31 AUGUST 1929

HOTEL METROPOLE Aug 31st

Dear Paul

Got an other letter from you today which had been on a long journey. Think I told you to address me at American Express—*London* which you can do at present. I wrote you some

179. Darrow had asked Gerson to help Edythe Rubens (1897–1957), Darrow's stenographer for many years, find a job in Los Angeles. Darrow to Gerson, 4 June 1929, TLS, CLU-SC, Theodore Perceval Gerson Papers (Collection 724).

days ago about selling my U.P.[180] I can't help thinking that we will have a smash soon and I feel sure that you should reduce indebtedness. When things go down you will want some money instead of scrambling around to borrow. It is certain that things can't keep going up forever. You can sell any thing I have if you think it better to sell mine. Of course I don't mean to insist that you shall take my advice but I don't like to see you owe so much with every thing so high. I was interested in what you said about the bank. I suppose while you are in debt and I am away you don't want to give up a job. But when I get back, I will certainly urge you to quit them. I don't see a chance there.

Hastily | C. S. D.

MS: ALS, MnU-L, Darrow Collection. DATE: "1929" appended.

TO PAUL DARROW • LONDON • FRIDAY 27 SEPTEMBER 1929

HOTEL METROPOLE Sept 27th

Dear Paul

Received your letter with the 100£. Also information of sale of 50 shares of U.P. Am glad you sold it. Hope you won't load up any more until you materially reduce indebtedness. I don't know just how my account stands, but if there is any money there would rather you take it and pay .06% on it than to buy more stock. Would rather see you reduce your indebtedness than get more stock. I still believe things are going lower. They are ridiculously high. A falling off of earnings would surely make things go down. Shall probably be here ten days & then go to France & drive from there to Cannes—*France* & stay a few weeks. My friend Mr. Kellogg[181] of Jamestown N.D. has been here with his car. We have driven four thousand miles in England, Scotland and Wales, and I feel as if I had seen it all. It is very beautiful. We will drive from Paris to Southern France and see most of it along the Riviara. Shall avoid playing in Monte Carlo as the stock market is enough. Will cable *Darro* Chicago next address which will probably be Cannes France c/o American Express. When I get back we will consider new job for you. If you were out of debt or nearly so I would not bother with any job now. Will reach Chicago probably before the first of the year. Tell Blanche she will have a letter a few days after you get this. I am trying to get some information for her. Got letter from Mary yesterday and was glad to hear from her.

Love to all | C. S. D.

MS: ALS, MnU-L, Darrow Collection. DATE: "1929" appended.

180. Darrow is likely referring to stock in Union Pacific.
181. William Ross Kellogg (b. 1857), editor of the *Alert* newspaper in Jamestown, North Dakota. Kellogg was born in Pittsfield, Illinois. He obtained a B.S. from Illinois College, 1876. In 1882 or so, he moved to Fargo, North Dakota, and worked for the *Argus* newspaper. In 1886, he bought the *Alert* and worked as its publisher and editor until 1925.

TO PAUL DARROW • LONDON • SUNDAY 29 SEPTEMBER 1929

HOTEL METROPOLE Sept 29th

Dear Paul

Have just sent you a cable. I don't like the looks of things. All stocks are far too high. It is the same thing over & over again. You should reduce, where you can even if you take losses. The more stock you get the heavier the load and it is no time to buy. I think you ought not to owe more than $100,000 or 125,000 at the most. If there are big drops you might get caught very badly. Why not sell some brazilian Traction. Of course you owe so much that a little doesn't seem worth while. Still I would get some from Colorado if I could, and I am willing to let any or all of mine go although it will add to income tax. Still you can't afford to go broke at this time or to keep on selling at a falling market and things are too awfully high, this condition exists all over the world. Any of my bonds that have been bought in the last year could be sold at a small loss. Of course, I am far ahead of the game on all stocks. The Anaconda & Gt. Northern and N.P. could be sold at big profits, but you can't tell how long the profits will last. Earnings may go down, and the condition may get steadily worse for a year. I have been thinking some of going back home on account of the market. I may do it but will cable you if I do. On receipt of this you might send cable to me here Metropole Hotel or American Express, just Darrow, at either place. I won't bother you with further S.O.S. stuff, but you know how I feel, and you should not take long chances. I will cable before I go to Cannes or home. You can send 25 word cable here deferred for $1.50. If we clean up there should be enough left for all, but I don't know that you need to reduce below a safe margin, but reduce and don't buy no matter how cheep until the indebtedness is down to decent figures. All this is of course only advisory, but I think it is very important advice.

C. S. D.

MS: ALS, MnU-L, Darrow Collection. DATE: "1929" appended.

TO PAUL DARROW • LONDON • FRIDAY 4 OCTOBER 1929

HOTEL METROPOLE Oct 4th

Dear Paul,

Yesterday I received your letter of Sept 30th indicating that you had sold some stuff and would sell more. I am hoping that you hurried the sales after my second cable. I noted the slump yesterday & cabled you this morning to use all or any part of the stuff you have that is in my name in your safety deposit vault. I want you to do this. Probably some of mine should be sold rather than some of yours. I have no confidence in the market. It has been going up for several years and every body is crazy and most of them will lose their money. No doubt many of your bonds will not fall much, but I know you have a considerable amount of shaky stuff. You should owe very little in these times and I presume you realize it now. So far as I am concerned, my stuff has not gone down very much. Including about

$60,000 that Ruby has I have at this price what amounts to 225 to $240,000 worth, and we can save something out of it all so we will be all right. One trouble with people is that they can't realize that things are going to pieces and instead of selling enough to be perfectly safe they sell a little at a time in a falling market. There can't be any doubt about the thing. I think it will be at least a year before it stops going down so I hope you will clean up thoroughly, then there will be no more worry. I feel as if I should go back home but unless you wire me I probably won't be there before Dec 1st.

Hastily | C. S. D.

MS: ALS, MnU-L, Darrow Collection. DATE: "1929" appended. ENVELOPE ADDRESS: Paul Darrow | 111 W. Jackson Boul | Chicago | Ill | U.S.A. | Amalgamated Bank. POSTMARK: London 4 October 1929.

TO PAUL DARROW • LONDON • WEDNESDAY 30 OCTOBER 1929

HOTEL METROPOLE Oct 29th

Dear Paul

This is the day after the second big break in American market.[182] It must have left you in bad shape. You will probably need to get things adjusted so you won't be bothered with stock fluctuations. Don't take the matter hard. We will be just as happy & live just as long. I rather estimate that you and I will have around $300,000 which is really enough, and of course I think we ought to quit the gambling business. I have thought so before and done it for a time. I will probably wire you before you get this the date of my return. Will doubtless be there by Dec 1st. We will then go over our affairs and get our expenses inside of our income. I am afraid Fred[183] will be in bad shape, but he must take a traveling-man's job. I really do not care a damn about it. The speculating business is a hectic business any how. So don't give yourself a bit of worry about it all.

Ever | C. S. D.

MS: ALS, MnU-L, Darrow Collection. DATE: "1929" appended.

TO PAUL DARROW • LONDON • THURSDAY 31 OCTOBER 1929

HOTEL METROPOLE Oct 31st

Dear Paul,

I see that after a few hours today the stock exchange will be closed the rest of the week. Well I am not figuring on how you came out of the tornado. Any how don't worry about

182. Darrow probably misdated this letter. If he was writing the day after the "second big break" in the American stock market, he was probably writing the day after what is often called "Black Tuesday," 29 October 1929. Black Tuesday was the most catastrophic day in the history of the New York Stock Exchange. Black Tuesday followed an earlier collapse of the market on 24 October 1929, known as "Black Thursday."
183. Fred Hamerstrom.

any of it. We will live just as long & have as much fun. It was sure some land slide. We might think of the millions who came out worse than we did. Of course if you need any of my stuff as security to first National use it, but I would not unless it seems safe. You may have used it before in which case it is all right. We sail for home on Nov 28th "The Geo Washington" will be 9 days to N.Y. Shall stay there two days at Belmont. You might have a letter there for me.

Hastily | C. S. D.

MS: ALS, MnU-L, Darrow Collection. DATE: "1929" appended. ENVELOPE ADDRESS: Paul Darrow | 111 W Jackson Boul | Chicago | Ill | U.S.A. | Bank. POSTMARK: London, 31 October 1929.

TO GEORGE T. BYE • LONDON • WEDNESDAY 20 NOVEMBER 1929

HOTEL METROPOLE Nov 20th

My Dear Buy

I don't see how I could write that article on Jesus, or something that you wanted for "The Homely Ladies Journal" or something. I don't know him and he don't know me. And I am convinced that when I am dead I won't be compelled to live again. Ingersoll, I know, said that in the "night of death hope sees a star &c," but I haven't got that far yet.[184] I may see a comet, in which case I shall think it is hell (and try to send back an article about it,) I don't know, but why not get a preacher to write it; that is their job. Any how I would like to do it, but how can I?

I have just finished a story on Justice and now that it is done I feel as I always do, that I don't know whether it is mighty good or damn poor:—probably neither, but I shall send it along. If you don't think it is good, don't offer it.

I just received a letter from Eaton[185] saying that his magazine is being consolidated with Literary Guild and he expects it to boom, and he wants something, P.D.Q. for March. I wrote him to have you show him that Prohibition story. It is true that I and others have said a good many of the same things before, but I can't find anything new to say. The trouble is that Socrates and Plato and Jesus Christ and Judas Iscariot and the rest of the great got here first. Still the one I am sending you is very new. I doubt if there is a single

184. Darrow is quoting from Ingersoll's eulogy for his brother in 1879: "Life is a narrow vale between the cold and barren peaks of two eternities. We strive in vain to look beyond the heights. We cry aloud, and the only answer is the echo of our wailing cry. From the voiceless lips of the unreplying dead there comes no word; but in the night of death hope sees a star and listening love can hear the rustle of a wing." Robert G. Ingersoll, "A Tribute to Ebon C. Ingersoll," in *The Works of Robert G. Ingersoll* (New York: Dresden, 1912), 12:391.

185. Darrow is likely referring to Geoffrey D. Eaton (1984–1930), the editor of the monthly *Plain Talk*, a magazine that made its first appearance in 1927. Darrow was a contributor to the first issue. Eaton was the author of many magazine articles himself and he wrote a novel. Before editing *Plain Talk*, he had been literary editor for the *(New York) Morning Telegraph*. He also had worked for several newspapers in Detroit and on the staff of the Associated Press.

idea in it that ever occurred to anyone before. In fact, I doubt if there are any in it. I am leaving in a day or two for Cannes, France where I will be until some time around March 1st when I will go back if the stock market and the literary market improve. You can reach me there c/o American Express Co.

Your friend | Clarence Darrow

MS: ALS, NNC, James O. Brown Papers. DATE: letterhead and reference to stock market.

TO PAUL DARROW • CANNES, FRANCE • FRIDAY 6 DECEMBER 1929

HOTEL MAJESTIC Dec 6

Dear Paul

The last letter I had from you was written Nov. 14th right after there seemed to be a turn in the market. I have been looking for one all the time since. Hadn't you better write oftener?

The market seems to have gradually improved especially the last two days, and I am wondering how it is going with you. I don't know whether you sold the stuff you bought for me [or] not. There should be some profit in it and if you have sold or think best to sell you had better take the profit and pay in as far as it goes. Of course you haven't had much chance to do any thing since the slump began, but you could easily get wiped out with all you owe, but you know all about it now. I think it might happen again, and I wish I could see you get out of debt or somewhere near out. I have for a long time expected you to go broke and of course if it happens, we will get along and make no fuss over it. Still we must do the best we can with a situation and you will be obliged to take some very substantial losses if you ever get out. The market will not go up again for a long long time, and it may not go down. It is very nice down here, the climate is good and the scenery fine. Brand Whitlock lives here and I have seen him twice in the last week. I could just as well come home and if things look bad again I think I should go. There will be no trouble about keeping warm. Write often if only short letter.

C. S. D.

MS: ALS, MnU-L, Darrow Collection. DATE: "1929" appended. ENVELOPE ADDRESS: Paul Darrow | 111 Jackson Boulevard | Chicago | Ill | U.S.A. | Bank. POSTMARK: Cannes 6 December 1929.

TO PAUL DARROW • CANNES, FRANCE • SATURDAY 14 DECEMBER 1929

THE AMERICAN EXPRESS CO., INC. Nov 14th

Dear Paul

Just to tell you that if you need to cable at any time use just Darrow—Cannes. Don't know whether France is needed or not. This last week I see has had lower prices but

considerably above the former low. Don't think the Pullometer will get them up much for a time. There will be plenty of chance when I get back, which will be soon after March 1st. This is really a very beautiful place and quite warm so I am feeling much better. I was wondering if you shouldn't call on Baehr.[186] I feel that when I get back at least we should be considering something else. You know I think a regular business beats all stock speculation. One is never at ease in his mind, and one misses the best chances to enjoy life by being worried over the turn of a card. Any how we will see about it when I get back. Wish I could be there with all of you for Christmas. Love to all.

C. S. D.

MS: ALS, MnU-L, Darrow Collection. DATE: year is appended and in Paul Darrow's hand "Nov." is struck out and "Dec" is written.

TO BENJAMIN B. LINDSEY • CANNES, FRANCE • TUESDAY 17 DECEMBER 1929

HOTEL MAJESTIC Dec. 17th 1929

Hon. Ben. Lindsey

My Dear Judge

The Paris paper carried some account of the decision of the Colorado court.[187] I am very sorry and believe that the whole campaign has been inspired by the desire to destroy your influence. Of course you mustn't take it too seriously. It is the way of the world—always has been and always will be. There are many young boys and girls in Denver whose lives you have made easier, and many others whom you have caused to think—and this must be your consolation. As a matter of fact, you are so well known that I fancy a thing like this would not hurt you except in your feelings, but you are used to this.

With love from Mrs Darrow and me to you and Henrietta—

Your friend | Clarence Darrow

186. William A. Baehr.

187. In 1926, while Lindsey was a judge in Colorado, he had done some legal work in New York in the matter of a contested will. On 9 December 1929, the Supreme Court of Colorado issued a decision disbarring Lindsey from the practice of law on the ground that this work violated state laws prohibiting a judge from acting as an attorney in any court or cause and prohibiting a judge from receiving any compensation for legal services except a government salary. See *People ex rel. Colorado Bar Assoc. v. Lindsey*, 283 P. 539 (Colo. 1929). Disbarment proceedings were instigated by a former district attorney who had had public disagreements with Lindsey. Some members of the state supreme court also had a history of political disagreements with Lindsey. (The court reinstated Lindsey in 1935.) See Charles Larsen, *The Good Fight: The Life and Times of Ben B. Lindsey* (Chicago: Quadrangle Books, 1972), 204–17, 236–37. This letter from Darrow is in response to a letter that Lindsey wrote (to other people as well) seeking advice about the matter of his disbarment. Lindsey's letter was addressed to Darrow in Chicago, not Cannes. See Lindsey to Darrow, 14 December 1929, TLc, DLC-MSS, Lindsey Papers, Container 164.

AMERICAN EXPRESS CO., INC.

Your inquiry about mail has no answer satisfactory to myself.[188] Most of the mail people like you & I receive are from cranks and can generally be told by reading the address. Much of it is from noteriety seekers engaged in getting autographs; they care nothing about us. They don't know the difference between Calvin Coolidge and Bunker Hill Monument. Some are sincere but what can you do about it? These are generally the worst nuisances of all. I seldom reply to any of them nowadays—

C. S. D.

You can't burn it all without looking at it. I once found one with a postage stamp in it.

MS: ALS, DLC-MSS, Lindsey Papers.

188. Lindsey had written to Ruby Darrow asking what Darrow does with his large volume of mail, and he described the difficulties that he had in keeping up with his own large correspondence. Lindsey to Ruby Darrow, 21 November 1929, TLc, DLC-MSS, Lindsey Papers.

PLATE 27
Frederick Hamerstrom, Ruby (Hamerstrom) Darrow's brother, ca. 1900.

PLATE 28
Darrow at a portrait studio in Los Angeles, 1911.

PLATE 29
Paul Darrow, ca. 1920s.

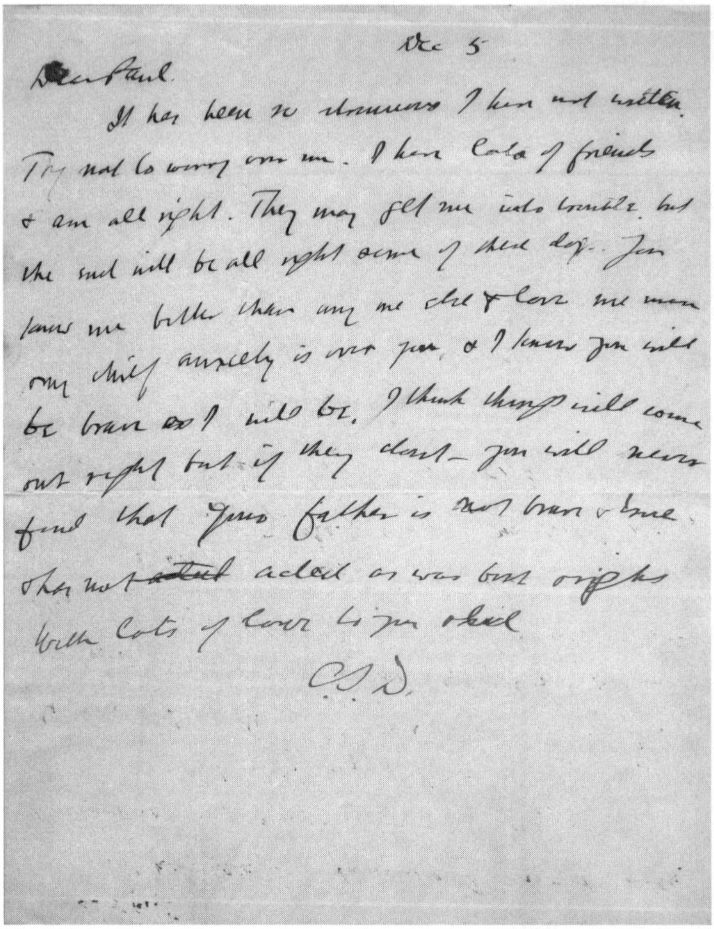

Dec 5

Dear Paul.

It has been so strenuous I have not written. Try not to worry over me. I have lots of friends & am all right. They may get me into trouble but the end will be all right some of these days. You know me better than any one else & love me more — my chief anxiety is over you, & I know you will be brave as I will be. I think things will come out right but if they don't — you will never find that your father is not brave & true & has not ~~acted~~ acted as was best or right.

With lots of love to you old kid

C.S.D.

PLATE 30

Darrow's letter to his son on 5 December 1911, the day the McNamara brothers were sentenced; at that time, rumors were circulating that Darrow had been involved in bribing jurors.

PLATE 31

Upton Sinclair, ca. 1930s, reformer and writer. Sinclair knew Darrow as early as 1905, when he asked Darrow to review his now-famous novel, *The Jungle,* to determine whether it might be libelous. (Photo: Library of Congress, Prints & Photographs Division, reproduction no. LC-DIG-gg-bain-06185)

PLATE 32

Vivian Pierce, ca. 1910, when she was a suffragist and approximately fifteen years before she formed the League to Abolish Capital Punishment. (Photo: Women of Protest: Photographs from the Records of the National Woman's Party, Manuscript Division, Library of Congress)

PLATE 33

Frank Walsh, 1915. Darrow testified before the United States Commission on Industrial Relations—for which Walsh was chairman—the year this picture was taken. (Photo: Library of Congress, Prints & Photographs Division, reproduction no. LC-USZ62–117861)

PLATE 34

Darrow at a hearing for Nathan Leopold and Richard Loeb, 1924. Benjamin Bachrach, Darrow's co-counsel, is on the left and Leopold and Loeb are between Bachrach and Darrow. (Photo: DN-0078021, *Chicago Daily News* negatives collection, Chicago History Museum)

PLATE 35
A bookplate with an Arts-and-Crafts design that Darrow used for many of his books. The bookplate was likely designed by someone associated with C. L. (Coella Lindsay) Ricketts (1859–1941), a Chicago calligrapher and illuminator who republished Darrow's book of essays (*A Persian Pearl*) in 1902.

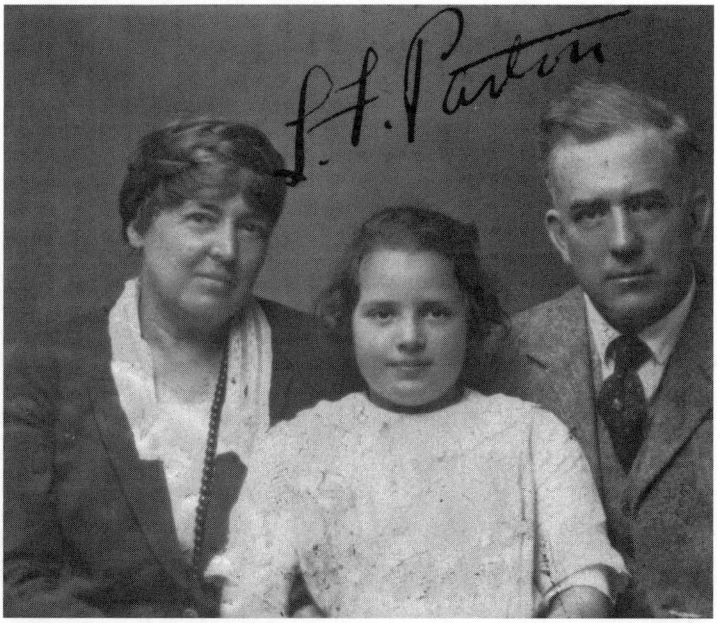

PLATE 36
Mary Field Parton and Lemuel Parton with their daughter Margaret, in a passport photo, 1923. (Photo: Margaret Parton Papers, Special Collections and University Archives, University of Oregon Libraries)

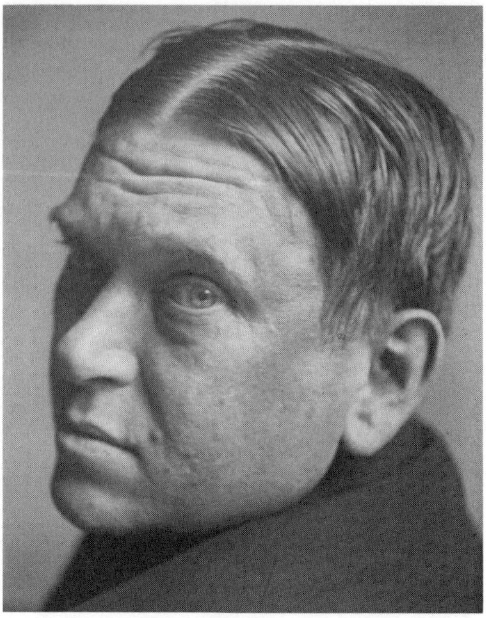

PLATE 37
H. L. Mencken, 1928. (Photo: Enoch Pratt Free Library, Maryland's State Library Resource Center, Baltimore, Maryland)

PLATE 38
Frederick Starr, an anthropologist at the University of Chicago, 1909. Darrow and Starr would publicly debate questions such as "Is the Human Race Getting Anywhere?" and "Is Civilization a Failure?" Darrow always took the pessimistic position. (Photo: Library of Congress, Prints & Photographs Division, reproduction no. LC-DIG-ggbain-01258)

PLATE 39
Sara Bard Field and Charles Erskine Scott Wood, ca. 1926 (Photo: Oregon Historical Society Research Library, bb002909; © The Ansel Adams Publishing Rights Trust)

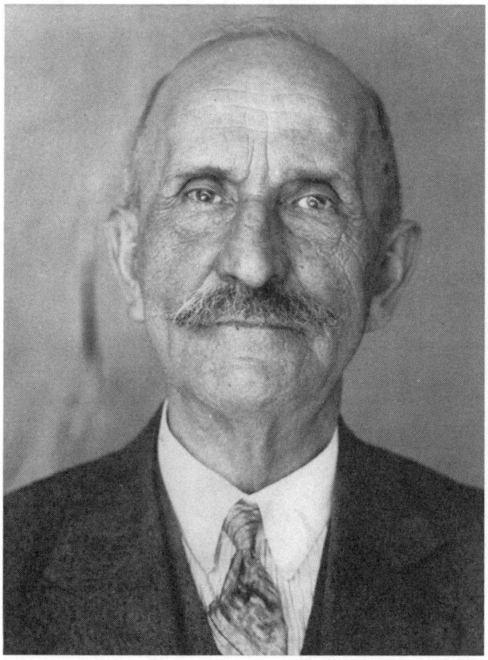

PLATE 40
Fremont Older, editor of the *San Francisco Bulletin* and later editor of the *San Francisco Call* and then the *Call-Bulletin,* 1930. (Photo: San Francisco History Center, San Francisco Public Library)

PLATE 41
Darrow and William Jennings Bryan during the Scopes trial, July 1925. "I made up my mind to show the country what an ignoramus [Bryan] was and I succeeded, but I only had two hours of him and wanted another day." Darrow to Mencken, 5 August 1925.

PLATE 42
Darrow and John T. Raulston, the judge who presided over the Scopes trial in Tennessee, 12 July 1925. "The judge may be glad he has a limited education. One cannot always avoid being ignorant, but few boast of it." Darrow to the *Daily News*, 11 August 1925. (Photo: Library of Congress, Prints & Photographs Division, reproduction no. LC-USZ62–95411)

PLATE 43
Darrow in the Ozarks, 1926. (Photo: Carol Johnstone, from the estate of her mother, Joan Hamerstrom Hawley).

PLATE 44
Darrow and Sinclair Lewis in Kansas City, 1926, where Lewis was writing *Elmer Gantry*. The photograph was taken on the roof of the Muehlebach Hotel. (Photo: Carol Johnstone, from the estate of her mother, Joan Hamerstrom Hawley).

PLATE 45

James Weldon Johnson, December 1932. "I am delighted with your new volume of poems 'God's Trombones.' It is the only Fundamentalists output I ever did like." Darrow to Johnson, 6 June 1927 (Photo: Library of Congress, Prints & Photographs Division, reproduction no. LC-USZ62–42498)

PLATE 46

E. W. Scripps, ca. 1920–24. "I have seen so many radicals broke in their last years that I always had a foolish & unholy fear of alms, and inconvenience." Darrow to Scripps, 16 February 1923. (Photo: E. W. Scripps Archive, Mahn Center for Archives and Special Collections, Ohio University Libraries)

PLATE 47
Negley Cochran, the editor for E. W. Scripps's ad-less Chicago newspaper, *The Day Book*, ca. 1920. (Photo: E. W. Scripps Archive, Mahn Center for Archives and Special Collections, Ohio University Libraries)

PLATE 48
Darrow with a stack of mail during the Scopes trial, 18 July 1925. "Most of the mail people like you & I receive are from cranks and can generally be told by reading the address. Much of it is from noteriety seekers engaged in getting autographs; they care nothing about us." Darrow to Benjamin Lindsey, 17 December 1929.

PLATE 49
Darrow in Jackson Park, Chicago, near his apartment building, 1932. The first half of the inscription to Darrow's brother-in-law, Frederick Hamerstrom, is in Darrow's hand; the second half is in Ruby's hand.

PLATE 50
Harry Elmer Barnes, 1929. "The calendar and various other hunches constantly warn me that there are only a few more speeches and debates left in me, and I am so relieved when I look at you." Darrow to Barnes, 8 February 1931. (Photo: Henry Elmer Barnes Collection, American Heritage Center, University of Wyoming)

PLATE 51
Calvin Coolidge and Helen Keller, 11 January 1926. "I appreciate being put on the board or acting in any capacity with you in the work. The only objection I have is seeing the name of Hon. Calvin Coolidge above mine, but when I remember that you probably object to it as much as I do, I do not mind." Darrow to Keller, 1 December 1928. (Photo: Library of Congress, Prints & Photographs Division, reproduction no. LC-USZ62–111737)

PLATE 52
Lewis Lawes, warden at Sing Sing Prison, ca. 1910–15. "I want to get your stuff a wider circulation, and then it will help me to have the public know that I know you. It is a sign of social standing to be a friend of a warden . . ." Darrow to Lawes, 16 January 1932. (Photo: Library of Congress, Prints & Photographs Division, reproduction no. LC-DIG-ggbain-16342)

PLATE 53
Frank Murphy, 1930. Darrow told Murphy, who presided at the Sweet trial in 1926, that "the Detroit case . . . was the first time in all my career where a judge really tried to help, and displayed a sympathetic interest in saving poor devils from the extreme forces of the law, rather than otherwise." Darrow to Murphy, 9 October 1935. (Photo: Walter P. Reuther Library, Wayne State University)

PLATE 54
Ruby and Darrow in their passport photo, ca. 1929.

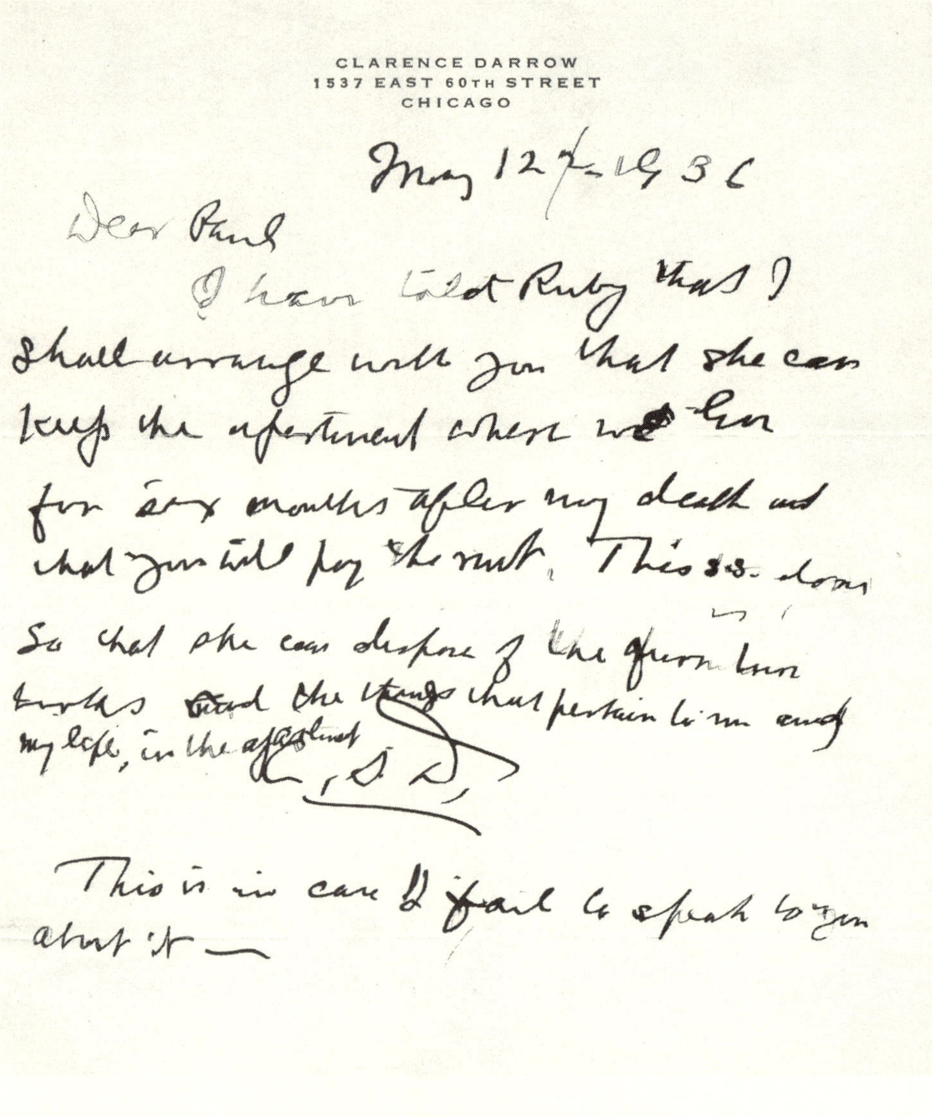
CLARENCE DARROW
1537 EAST 60TH STREET
CHICAGO

May 12 – 1936

Dear Paul

I have told Ruby that I shall arrange with you that she can keep the apartment where we live for six months after my death and that you will pay the rent. This is done so that she can dispose of the furniture books and the things that pertain to me and my life, in the apartment

C. D.

This is in case I fail to speak to you about it —

PLATE 55

Darrow's letter to Paul on 12 May 1936: "I have told Ruby that I shall arrange with you that she can keep the apartment where we live for six months after my death and that you will pay the rent. This is done so that she can dispose of the furniture, books and the things that pertain to me and my life, in the apartment."

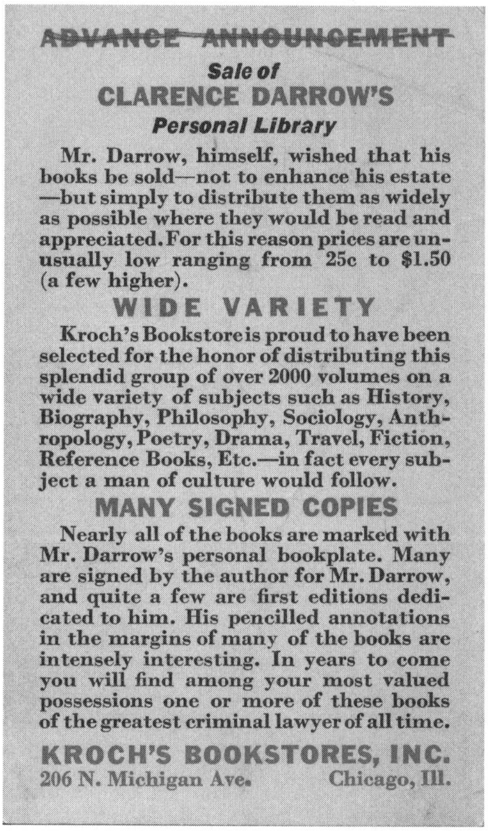

~~ADVANCE ANNOUNCEMENT~~

Sale of

CLARENCE DARROW'S

Personal Library

Mr. Darrow, himself, wished that his books be sold—not to enhance his estate—but simply to distribute them as widely as possible where they would be read and appreciated. For this reason prices are unusually low ranging from 25c to $1.50 (a few higher).

WIDE VARIETY

Kroch's Bookstore is proud to have been selected for the honor of distributing this splendid group of over 2000 volumes on a wide variety of subjects such as History, Biography, Philosophy, Sociology, Anthropology, Poetry, Drama, Travel, Fiction, Reference Books, Etc.—in fact every subject a man of culture would follow.

MANY SIGNED COPIES

Nearly all of the books are marked with Mr. Darrow's personal bookplate. Many are signed by the author for Mr. Darrow, and quite a few are first editions dedicated to him. His pencilled annotations in the margins of many of the books are intensely interesting. In years to come you will find among your most valued possessions one or more of these books of the greatest criminal lawyer of all time.

KROCH'S BOOKSTORES, INC.

206 N. Michigan Ave. Chicago, Ill.

PLATE 56

A card announcing the sale of Darrow's library after his death. The sale was handled by Kroch's Bookstores in Chicago, as an agent for Ruby.

• 1930–1934

TO FRANK WALSH • CANNES, FRANCE • TUESDAY 28 JANUARY 1930

HOTEL MAJESTIC Jan. 28th 1930

Dear Frank

I was very glad to get your letter and especially glad that you are connected with the Roosevelt Administration. I am hoping that he may be able to run for President. If Al Smith does not run, I see nobody else excepting Roosevelt or Jim Reed,[1] unless possibly Claude Bowers,[2] who I think is able and a real Democrat. Jim Reed should run for Senator this fall if they elect a senator in Missouri. Any how he should get into the campaign. Can't you help get him in? I believe the country will repudiate prohibition before long and it is time to start a real fight. There is nothing else to do. I should think

1. James Reed (1861–1944), lawyer and politician. Reed began practicing law in Kansas City, Missouri, in 1887. He was elected county prosecutor, 1898–90, and mayor, 1900–4, before being elected to the United States Senate as a Democrat, 1911–29. He continued practicing law in Kansas City after serving in the Senate, and he made unsuccessful bids for the presidency in 1928 and 1932. He opposed Roosevelt's New Deal and supported Republicans for president after 1932.
2. Claude Bowers (1878–1958), journalist, historian, and diplomat. Bowers was an editorial writer for the *(New York) Evening World,* 1923–31, and a political columnist for the *(New York) Evening Journal,* 1931–33, before serving as United States ambassador to Spain, 1933–39, and minister to Chile, 1939–53. He was also the author of many historical and biographical works, including *Jefferson and Hamilton* (1925) and *The Tragic Era: The Revolution after Lincoln* (1929). At the national Democratic convention in 1928, Bowers gave a keynote address attacking Harding and Coolidge.

the Hoover boom should be pretty flat by this time. Even Coolidge looks big by comparison. I have been away a long time and seen a lot of Europe and am now on the Riviera, which is well worth seeing, and certainly is much warmer than the U.S.A. according to the papers. We are leaving here on the Saturnia, an Italian line, on March 8th arriving in N.Y. on the 17th. I will be there several days and I want one evening with you, with no one else present. I want to talk with you about things in general and something in particular. Can't we fix it now for the 18th? A letter leaving N.Y. any time up to Feby 20th will get me before leaving. Will go to the Belmont when we reach N.Y.

With best wishes always—

Your friend | Clarence Darrow

MS: ALS, NN, Walsh Papers, Box 17.

TO HENRY FORD • CANNES, FRANCE • SATURDAY 22 FEBRUARY 1930

CLARENCE DARROW Cannes, France

My Dear Mr. Ford:—

I have just read a story of your plan to use 100,000,000 dollars for founding trades schools for boys in the United States.[3] I am delighted to see it. I believe this is the most intelligent way of spending a large sum of money that has ever come under my observation. If schools of this sort could reach all the youth of America, in time it would result in the abolition of crime and poverty, both of which are a disgrace to our civilization.

Our prisons, almshouses and streets are filled with the unadjusted derelicts that are the product of our unscientific way of living and doing. The schools and colleges of the world do not even try to reach that class that more than any others needs training. The courses of study in our institutions are useless in a practical world.

No one knows as well as you do how most men can be adapted to useful and remunerative work. I feel sure that you have found the right way, and that the time will come when every one will appreciate the great work which you are undertaking.

With best wishes for your success,

Very truly yours, | Clarence Darrow

MS: TLS, MiDbEI. INSIDE ADDRESS: To Mr. Henry Ford, | Dearborn, Michigan. ENVELOPE ADDRESS: Mr. Henry Ford | DEARBORN—Near Detroit | Michigan | *U.S.A.* POSTMARK: Cannes, 22 February 1930.

3. The Associated Press reported that Ford had announced he would devote the remainder of his life to education, including building schools in which young men could learn a trade (to keep them "active and out of trouble"), and that he would spend perhaps $100 million in this effort. "Ford Will Give Rest of His Life to Education," *New York Times*, 14 February 1930.

TO GERTRUDE BARNUM • CHICAGO • CIRCA APRIL 1930

CLARENCE DARROW

Dear Gertrude

I was awfully glad to get your letter. I was away a while in Europe and then I lost your address & always meant to telephone your brother but day after day slipped by, and I didn't do it.[4] Still I hope you will forgive me. And I won't let it happen again (?) I received your letter telling of the death of your mother and your aunt and the main thing I thought about was that it might be some relief for you. Still there is no relief in this world for those who are imaginative and feel the sorrows of the rest. So I am afraid you will never be free. As to me I am just growing older year by year and day by day. I don't mind it. I really want it, for while I have had a great deal in life, more love than is given to most people, still life is a terrible burden, and nothing can alleviate its pain. I am sure I would not want to call back any friend of mine who has finished it all. Chicago has not changed much, except that we have some beautiful drives, but there is the same enmity and hatred and quarreling and bickering that is always present here and every where.

Aren't you ever coming here again. I wish you would. The clipping that you enclosed from the paper interested me. He really was quite [x]; if I knew his name I would write to him. No body but a friend like you would ever have taken the [x]. It is the first time it ever happened to me. Still isn't it strange that any one could ever think that I would be a prohibitionist and that I would become one on account of debating. I wish I could see all my friends in LA again, but I suppose I never shall. Won't you give my love to Blanche.[5] I wonder if you ever met the Gersons.[6] You should. He is a wonderful man. He is at the Roosevelt hotel in Hollywood and he would be so glad to see you. He is just your sort. I keep traveling over & over the world speaking and debating and I can't see that any good comes of it all,—or from any thing. It is too bad we couldn't have been more [x] like the rest so long as the world won't change.

Any how always with love

Your friend | Clarence Darrow

Write to this address when you can.

MS: ALS, DLC-MSS, Darrow Papers. DATE: "about 1935 | I think" is written in an unknown hand on the letter but letterhead and reference to returning from Europe and Prohibition make sometime after April 1930 and before April 1933 more probable.

4. Barnum's brother, Harry Hyde Barnum (1879–1951), was a lawyer in Chicago.
5. The identity of "Blanche" is unknown.
6. T. Perceval Gerson and his wife, Vera.

TO D. C. STEPHENSON • CHICAGO • TUESDAY 15 APRIL 1930

CLARENCE DARROW April 15th

D. C. Stephenson
My dear Sir:

I have been out of the country more than a year since I promised to go and see you, and have many times thought of you and my broken promise to go and see you. On my way home I stopped to see a friend of mine in New York.[7] He is an Indiana man well known and influential in Indiana. He felt as I do that there was no possible excuse for you being in prison on the charge under which you were convicted. He also said that if I would undertake the case he would help me, which he could do.

If you want me to go and see you about it, I will drive down to Michigan City. For this there will be no charge. The ideas that you have apparently stood for are as far away from my views as one can possibly imagine, but I believe in fair play and I have a very strong feeling that you have not had it.

Very truly yours, | Clarence Darrow

MS: TT, In, Stephenson Papers. DATE: reference to being out of the country for more than a year. INSIDE ADDRESS: Clarence Darrow | 1537 East 60th Street | Chicago, Illinois.

TO *THE NEW YORK TIMES* • CHICAGO • TUESDAY 22 APRIL 1930

Chicago, Ill., April 22, 1930.

To the Editor of The New York Times:

On April 18 THE TIMES published an excerpt from a letter that I wrote regarding the great need of working for freedom in these days. The letter was published in connection with a story of a May Day meeting which, to some extent as least, could be turned into a criticism of Russia and communism.[8]

I had no idea that my letter would be used in any such connection. I feel that Russia is the only nation in the world that holds the high purpose of helping those who need it most. While I have no opinion as to whether her ideals can now or ever be worked out, I still wish she might succeed.

As to communism, it has been a high ideal from the first century of Christianity and no doubt long before.

7. The identity of Darrow's friend is not known.
8. The story in the *New York Times* reported that at a recent meeting to put together a patriotic May Day parade, the organizers had announced that Russian war veterans would be marching in the parade for the first time. The story also reported that a letter from Darrow was read at the meeting, which said: "It is time that everyone who really loves his country should rally to its defense." "Russian Veterans to March on May Day," *New York Times,* 18 January 1930.

Whether human nature can ever admit of putting such an ideal into practice I very much doubt. Still I think the Communists have as good a right under the Constitution and laws of this country to propagate their ideas as the Socialists or the Republicans.

I presume that I would be one of the last persons in America to join in any crusade against them, even though I thought they could not or should not succeed.

CLARENCE DARROW.

MS: "Mr. Darrow's Views," *New York Times*, 26 April 1930, p. 18.

TO JAMES M. BECK • CHICAGO • SUNDAY 18 MAY 1930

CLARENCE DARROW May 18th.

Hon James Beck
My Dear Mr Beck

If I am not much mistaken you were one of the assistants in the office of the Attorney General when Hon Richard Olney was there and I argued the Debs case.[9] And if I am right you and I had long visit about books and I fully expected to see you often but I never did. Any how if it was you, then you certainly made a strong impression on me then—and even if you are not you, then you have made a strong impression on me since. First in your argument in the Smith case and your stand for the right of the states to send whom they wished, without consulting the other Senators who might feel poluted and did not want to resign,[10] and *Secondly* in your speech against prohibition where you said what every lawyer should know, that it is not necessary to get rid of the Eighteenth Amendment to get a legal drink.[11] The Eighteenth Amendment is of no value without the statute and I believe that congress is under no obligation to pass a statute. They certainly are under no legal obligation. Of course there are other ways. It can be done in the way that The House of Commons in England freed its self and the people from The House of Lords. I am not writing to tell you any thing but to tell you how I liked your address as reported

9. Darrow is referring to the Pullman strike in 1894, which resulted in the imprisonment of Eugene Debs. See Darrow to Henry Demarest Lloyd, 22 November 1894, n.26. In January 1895, Darrow and other lawyers argued in Debs's case before the United States Supreme Court.
10. Frank L. Smith (1867–1950), a Chicago businessman and Republican Congressman from Illinois, 1919–21, won a seat in the United States Senate in November 1926. He was also appointed the following month to fill out the last few months of the term of the recently deceased Senator William B. McKinley (1856–1926). Smith's election and appointment were embroiled in charges of fraud and corruption, which stemmed mainly from a $125,000 campaign contribution from Samuel Insull (1859–1938), the well-known Chicago utilities magnate. In the end, the Senate refused to seat Smith. See Carroll H. Wooddy, *The Case of Frank L. Smith* (Chicago: University of Chicago Press, 1931). Beck defended Smith before a Senate investigating committee and also wrote a book (*The Vanishing Rights of the States* [New York: Geo. Doran, 1926]) that "challenged the constitutional right of the Senate to decide upon the moral fitness of a member-elect or the means by which he gained that status." Morton Keller, *In Defense of Yesterday: James M. Beck and the Politics of Conservatism* (New York: Coward-McCann, 1958), 193.
11. Beck delivered a speech against Prohibition in the United States House of Representatives in February 1930, which was later published as a pamphlet: *The Revolt against Prohibition* (New York: Association against the Prohibition Amendment, 1930).

by the papers, and also to urge you to do more. It is amazing that the prohibitionists can mislead so many wets. I have thought of this especially since Morrow says he is in favor of repealing the Eighteenth Amendment.[12] In all human probability that can not be done in a hundred years, but the Volsted Act can be repealed in five, and as it gets nearer repeal the politicians will jump onto the band wagon and stop spending all our money to have thugs shoot down Citizens in cold blood or to put poison in liquor. While I think that Hon. Geo. Tinkham[13] has done some very useful work, I am specially interested *now* in your position. I have written a magazine article on the subject and when it appears I shall send it to you although you don't need it.

Wishing you more power

I am | Your friend | Clarence Darrow

MS: ALS, location of original unknown (copy in editor's files). DATE: letterhead and references to Beck's speech and Morrow.

TO "WINIFRED MORONEY" • CHICAGO • WEDNESDAY 11 JUNE 1930

CLARENCE DARROW June 11, 1930.

Dear Miss Moroney:

I presume it is too late to reply to your letter of June 2 which has just come to my notice. Mr. Gitlow was indicted for the violation of an Espionage act which was passed in New York after the war.[14] The same sort of an act, conceived by the same brains and written by the same hand, was passed in nearly every state of the Union. It was an outrageous act and an outrageous law, which was purposely meant to strangle the freedom of discussing political questions.

Mr. Gitlow was a member of the communist party and was one of the committee who prepared the platform of that party in New York which, in turn, endorsed the communist manifesto of Russia declaring in favor of the proletariat taking control of the government,

12. Dwight Morrow (1873–1931) was a lawyer, banker, diplomat, and United States Senator (Republican) from New Jersey, 1930–31. He attracted considerable attention by urging repeal of the Eighteenth Amendment during his campaign for the senate in 1930.
13. George Tinkham (1870–1956), Republican congressman from Massachusetts. Tinkham graduated from Harvard University, 1894, and held several local and state political offices before his election to the United States House of Representatives, where he served fourteen consecutive terms, 1915–43. He was a strong opponent of Prohibition.
14. Benjamin Gitlow (1891–1965) was active in the Socialist Party's militant left wing when he helped form the Communist Labor Party in 1919. That same year, he was indicted under New York's Criminal Anarchy Act for advocating communism. The act prohibited advocating the overthrow of organized government by force or violence. Darrow was Gitlow's defense attorney in the trial court. Gitlow was found guilty in February 1920. The United States Supreme Court rejected his constitutional challenge to the state law but held that the free-speech protections of the First Amendment of the Constitution should restrict state actions. See *Gitlow v. New York*, 268 U.S. 652 (1925). Gitlow was released from prison in 1922, while his case was on appeal. Shortly after the Supreme Court's decision, he was pardoned by Governor Al Smith. By the end of his life, Gitlow was a committed anti-communist.

even though it was a minority. Of course, minorities have always controlled every country and probably will continue but the courts held, as courts are apt to do, that this was virtually a declaration of war on democratic government and Gitlow was convicted for this, and nothing else.

He was not convicted for his writings. He was convicted as one who wrote and supported this platform.

You asked what the results have been. A number of men were convicted in Chicago under the same law and they were pardoned before they went to prison. A number of others have been convicted, some sent to jail and some pardoned. As a matter of fact, this law is now practically a dead letter in most of the States of the union and yet there are still many people in jail who were sent to prison under this statute.

Very truly yours, | Clarence Darrow

MS: TLS, ICU, Miscellaneous Manuscripts. INSIDE ADDRESS: Winifred Moroney, | 3715 W. Polk Street, | Chicago, Illinois.

TO JAMES M. BECK • CHICAGO • WEDNESDAY 11 JUNE 1930

CLARENCE DARROW June 11, 1930.

My dear Mr. Beck:

Immediately upon receiving copy of your speech, I wrote you a letter but concluded not to send it as I did not feel quite sure about some things I said.

I want to say first of all that this was a magnificent argument. I do not know anything better you could do than to join in this fight, which is very far-reaching. I have all of my life been a believer in state's rights and I think it is most important for the preservation of any sort of individual liberty. I think it would be pretty hard to do any good work that was not based upon this principle. That was a special reason that appealed to me so strongly in your argument before the Supreme Court for seating Smith in the Senate. If any number of senators who happen to have a certificate of election can pass on the qualifications of those who have not already been seated, then it will not be long until the Senate can become a permanent body. I have no doubt but what passing upon the qualifications meant simply examining the papers to see whether they were regular.

I have just sent a contribution to New York which I presume will appear in one of the magazines. In this I discussed the question of the best means of getting rid of prohibition. Of course, I am convinced that the first step, so far as we can say at present is the repealing of the Volstead Act.[15]

15. Darrow told his literary agent in May 1930 that he was working on an article that had as its theme the "best method of getting rid of prohibition." Darrow was worried about the market for his writings, and he hoped that this particular article would be published "without many refusals." Darrow to George Bye, 13 May [1930], ALS, NNC, James O. Brown Collection. Whether the article was ever published is doubtful.

I am taking the position that this would leave the whole matter with the states and put the federal government out of business so far as having anything to do with prohibition is concerned. I am aware that there may be some question on the line you raise, that the first part of the Eighteenth Amendment explicitly forbids the manufacture and so forth of intoxicating liquors. I can conceive that a state law which permitted the sale of intoxicating liquors might possibly land in the Supreme Court of the United States and perhaps be declared unconstitutional. However, as against that view, I can not see how the Supreme Court can take judicial notice of what constitutes intoxicating liquor.

I am inclined to think that a court must base its opinion upon the definition given by either Congress or the Legislatures of the States. They may say fifty per cent. if they wish or any other per cent. of intoxicating liquor by volume. It is certainly in keeping with their previous holding that one-half of one per-cent. is intoxicating because Congress has so declared. I am not quarreling with this decision. Everybody knows that one-half of one per cent. is not intoxicating within every reasonable meaning of the word. But, so long as Congress has fixed it perhaps the Supreme Court must be guided by that alone. If so, there is no reason why any Legislature cannot fix the percentage it sees fit.

Then, of course, there are various ways of framing bills by legislative bodies. They most likely would side-step this question.

I am inclined to think that with the repeal of the Volstead Act the Legislatures could work out a plan that would give them full control. However, perhaps nobody is sure in advance.

There are many other ways to get rid of prohibition, but perhaps the time is not ripe for adopting them. However, before we can destroy this terrible law, the country must make up its mind to get rid of it, and it cannot be too particular about the means.

Both Congress and the Senate must approve of appropriation bills, and, I for one, am tired of having so large a portion of my income tax given to the enforcement of a foolish and brutal statute. Any time that either Congress or the Senate should refuse to appropriate or cut the amount down to the minimum, we would get rid of prohibition, and then the statesmen, such as we have left, could find the proper way of returning the whole matter to the States, where it belongs. If we need any authority for this, we have only to examine English history which shows how the people, through Parliament, overcame the House of Lords. Under Charles I, as I believe, they tied up the government until it surrendered, and ever since that date, the people of Great Britain have been reaping the reward of the courage of their representatives.

What appealed to me in your speech in Congress was exactly what you say: The problem of the man against the state. As far as I read history that seems to have been the everlasting struggle in organized government. It has generally gone on until it was solved in one way—by revolution with its accompanying destruction. I would like to see it solved in a less violent manner.

Guessing on the future, I would say that when we do get rid of Volsteadism, it would be by refusing to appropriate money for the odious law. I am satisfied that you could not get men to shoot down their fellow men in cold blood unless they were paid for it, although it is possible that you could get preachers who would pour poison into the liquor so that the man who took a drink would meet certain death or at least blindness or paralysis. That is one of the kind of things that those class of preachers could specially do because it is done in silence and with an odor of sanctity which surrounds all their activities. However, perhaps the poison squad in the Senate will gradually diminish; some of them may even take some of the liquor that the preachers have poisoned.

The sooner we can get the country to understand that this is a real fight, and that it involves the whole question of human freedom, the sooner we will get rid of it.

I am interested in one clause of your letter referring to your criticism of Morrow's position. Everybody in the world should recognize the unlimited right of the State to impose restrictions upon private conduct. This is a question I have thought a great deal about. Perhaps with little effect. I am inclined to think the word right does not mean anything. In its last analysis it has to be translated, I suppose, into the word power.

We are in the hands of the majority and whenever they say a thing is right, it at least becomes the rule of action for the majority, however tyrannical that may be. I have never been able to satisfy myself that there could be any clear distinction between the word right and the word power as applied to legislative bodies. I have read Mill on liberty several times over, but it seems to me he does not make a very good case in the way of exact reasoning.

All I can see is to try to teach tolerance and do our best to get people to respect the habits, ideas and conduct of their fellow men. The great majority of any country is not much above the morons and easily swept away. That, I presume, is the reason that no question is ever settled and that we, in the twentieth century, are discussing over again all of the things that have plagued man since the beginning of what we call civilization.

I would have sent you a copy of my article, which I have just sent east, not so you might read it, but so you might criticize it, for I want it to be pretty nearly correct, but I knew you were busy and did not feel that I should take your time. However, I am coming to Washington one of these days, and shall endeavor to see you.

With kind regards, I am | Your friend, | Clarence Darrow

It is too bad to plague a busy man with so long a letter.

D

MS: TLS, NjP, Beck Papers. INSIDE ADDRESS: Hon. James W. Beck, M.C., | Washington, D.C. NOTE: under the letterhead is written (not in Darrow's hand) "1537 E. 60th St. Chicago Ill"; on the first page is also written "Acknowledged | June 14th."

TO GEORGE T. BYE • CHICAGO • SUNDAY 15 JUNE 1930

CLARENCE DARROW June 15th

My Dear Bye

"The early bird" had been sent to a publisher, but I would guess it would be back.[16] What do you think about "Liberty" any how since the new management. I am beginning to think I can't write and should not try but when I have time I rather like to do it. I suppose one trouble with me is I don't believe any thing that any one else believes in and I can't help saying it.

Best Wishes Always | Clarence Darrow

MS: ALS, NNC, James O. Brown Papers. DATE: letter from Bye (cited below).

TO HARRY ELMER BARNES • CHICAGO • SUNDAY 15 JUNE 1930

CLARENCE DARROW June 15th

My Dear Barnes

I am to speak at East Aurora where they are unveiling a monument to Elbert Hubbard.[17] In the evening I shall be with that bunch of good fellows with the Scripps-Howard papers in Buffalo. I don't imagine that you will be in that neighborhood at that time but I was hoping that you might be. I will write about your book for the Scripps Howard people, about 1,200 words.[18] I may go to N.Y. at the same time that I am east. If I come I want to talk with you about some of my stuff. I am beginning to doubt if I know how to write. In fact I think that I don't. If you have the time won't you see George Bye 535—5th Av who has some of my stuff. I would like especially to have you read "The Early Bird" and tell me what is the matter with it.

Your friend | Clarence Darrow

MS: ALS, WyU-AH, Barnes Collection. DATE: speech and unveiling of monument to Hubbard.

16. "The early bird" was probably a short story. According to Bye, one magazine later turned it down because it was too "pessimistic." Bye to Darrow, 21 October 1930, TLc, NNC, James O. Brown Papers.
17. Darrow presented "Life and How to Live It" to some 2,500 people in East Aurora, New York, on 19 June 1930, the anniversary of the birth of Elbert Hubbard (1856–1915). See "News from the Birthday Celebration," *The Roycrofter*, July 1930, 1–3. Hubbard, an author and publisher, founded an artists' colony and the Roycroft Press in East Aurora, which published fine, handmade books in the Arts-and-Crafts tradition. His press published Darrow's first book, *A Persian Pearl*, in 1899. Hubbard died on the *Lusitania* when it was torpedoed by a German submarine in 1915.
18. Darrow is probably referring to Barnes's recent book on punishment: *The Story of Punishment: A Record of Man's Inhumanity to Man* (Boston: Stratford, 1930). No review of the book by Darrow was located.

TO HARRY ELMER BARNES • CHICAGO • SATURDAY 5 JULY 1930

CLARENCE DARROW July 5th

My Dear Mr. Barnes

I will be in N.Y. the fourteenth or fifteenth and I want to see you. I will try to get you at your office but I shall stay at The Murray Hill Hotel.

I have just read your Twilight of Christianity.[19] It is really a wonderful book—I wonder how you do it all. It has been a long time since I have read a book that compares with it. Its depth and thoroughness are marvelous. I don't see why I did not read it before. It would have invited, (both the book and the author,) burning two hundred years ago.

With all good wishes | Your friend | Clarence Darrow

MS: ALS, WyU-AH, Barnes Collection. DATE: letterhead and reference to late reading of Barnes's book.

TO FREDERICK HAMERSTROM • CHICAGO • SATURDAY 12 JULY 1930

CLARENCE DARROW July 12

Dear Fred

I have intended to write you before this but I never seem to get to it, and really there is nothing much to say. I have been quite well and fairly active since I saw you, but I have grown so used to loafing that I neglect many things that I should do. I don't want you to think that I have lost any interest I have in you and the family, for I have not. When I got back from Europe things were in none too good a shape. Of course I had been spending money for a year with nothing coming in except from the dividends of my stock. While I did not owe anything when I went away, if I should sell what I have today or any part of them I would not get over 60% of what they were worth about the time I left America. Paul was worse hit than I for he had improvidently accumulated some debts from new purchases of stocks and bonds, many of them not doing well. So I took hold of it with him to try to straighten things out. Neither of us have wasted any money. I have made some, but neither of us have bought any thing since my return and we are slowly working it out. I am now sure that we will not be obliged to sell at low prices and believe that within the next year stocks will increase in value and we can get the debts paid and not need to do any more worrying about a fair income. It may come sooner, but I am not optimistic. Every one has been crazy and in the midst of the distress our horrible politicians are letting the captains of finance take what little there is left. Of course I necessarily was obliged to first turn my attention to our own affairs. Paul's indebtedness has been materially reduced. I don't know just how soon we will have all this done but I would say within a year, and

19. Harry Elmer Barnes, *The Twilight of Christianity* (New York: Vanguard Press, 1929).

when we are on safe ground again I shall feel like doing any thing for you that can be done. I have never changed my mind in any way and don't expect to, and I am sure that Paul feels just as I do about the matter. I am sorry you are obliged to be in the South for any part of this hot weather, and that you haven't any thing better to do, but we are obliged to take things as they come. We are going East in a day or two. Shall spend about ten days in Toronto and then go across to New England for two or three weeks. Ruby will keep you posted of our whereabouts and we may be able to meet some way. With love to Helen & the boys—

Your friend | C.S.D.

MS: ALS, MnU-L, Darrow Collection. DATE: "1930" appended and reference to stock market and Europe.

TO VICTOR YARROS • CHICAGO • MONDAY 28 JULY 1930

CLARENCE DARROW July 28

My Dear Yarros

The first Mrs. Darrow's name was Jessie Ohl. She lived in an adjoining town and we are substantially the same age and were married a few months after we were twenty one years old. She is still living and spends her time between here and Florida. She has been married since and her husband is now dead. We have been good friends all of our lives. My son Paul is 47 years old.

Please excuse me for not writing sooner.[20]

With best wishes always, | Your friend | Clarence Darrow

MS: ALS, NNC, Charles Harrison Papers. DATE: letterhead and Harrison's biography.

TO ALLEN CRANDALL • CHICAGO • SUNDAY 17 AUGUST 1930

CLARENCE DARROW Aug 17th

Dear Mr Crandall

Have been in the east on a vacation and find your letter on my return. I was in Estes Park at the time the war broke out in Europe. I was not able to get very full reports for some days. I read the dispatches between the warring countries and was convinced that Germany wanted the war. I felt that she at least could have prevented it. When Germany invaded Belgium I had the same emotional reaction that one feels when a big dog attacks a little one. I wanted to see Germany driven back. I never had any feeling against the

20. This was apparently for Charles Yale Harrison, who was writing a biography of Darrow. In the upper-right corner of the letter is a handwritten note from Yarros to Harrison: "Dear Mr. H:— | This answers your last queries. | V. S. Y."

German people in fact I always liked them better than any others. They were always more skeptical and tolerant, at least so it seemed to me. I did not like the bluster and brag of the Kaiser on going into the war. I did feel that we should go into it. I am nowhere near as sure now as I was then. I am now inclined to think that it was none of our affairs. I also feel that Germany was not so much to blame in starting it as I once felt. I still think that Germany was responsible for the cause of the war, but I doubt if she was the cause of the cause! At this time I feel that no one was responsible. I think it was a capitalistic war for markets, and I have said so many times since. I did not pretend to be patriotic in the war neither did I tell any fool stories about German atrocities. I took the ground that she should be driven back home. I am confident that I took my position purely from an emotional reaction in the first days. I never approved of any of the terrible persecution of pacifists and did all I could to help them, and any one else who was cruelly and ruthlessly sent to jail for long terms. I was a Tolstoyan [. . .][21]

MS: ALS (facsimile), Allen Crandall, *The Man from Kinsman* (Sterling, Colo.: [by the author], 1933). DATE: letterhead and reference to return from East.

TO MARIE SWEET SMITH AND "MRS. PHELPS" • CHICAGO • SATURDAY 23 AUGUST 1930

CLARENCE DARROW August 23rd

Dear Mrs. Smith | and Mrs. Phelps

As I don't like to write, I am trying to make this letter do for both of you. Enclosed find check for 250, which is part of my promise to put in 1000. I believe this will make 750. This goes to the Vermont campaign.[22] I really can not do more now. For one of my limited means, who is no longer in business, I am doing all I can afford. I was interested in your letter in reference to our combining with other organizations and getting the support of Wall St. et al., as suggested by Mr. Reis.[23] I would want to know more about it before I would personally be in favor of it.

21. Allen Crandall's biography only includes a facsimile of the first page of this letter, and the transcript ends here.
22. The "Vermont campaign" was an effort by the American League to Abolish Capital Punishment to organize opponents of the death penalty in Vermont and to pursue state legislation that would abolish the death penalty. Darrow's representation of John Winters before the Vermont Supreme Court in 1928 (see Darrow to Paul Darrow, 18 November 1927, n.95) provided at least part of the impetus for the league's campaign in Vermont. See ALACP, Annual Report of 1930 at 2–3, MBNU, Sara Erhmann Papers, Box 32, Folder 5.
23. Roger William Riis (1894–1953), a publicist, writer, and magazine editor, was the league's treasurer and a member of its board of directors. This letter (and the next letter from Darrow to Smith) was read in Darrow's absence at a meeting of the board and copies were distributed to board members. The minutes of that meeting show only that Marie Sweet Smith had "incorrectly" represented the league's proposed money-raising plan to Darrow. See Meeting Minutes, Board of Directors, ALACP, 24 October 1930, NN, Walsh Papers.

These Crime Committees that are raising money, so far as I know them, have no sympathy with our ideas. They are behind such horrible legislation as the Baumes law.[24] They are not interested in any humane ideas, such as abolishing crime by abolishing poverty and giving children a useful and workable education. They get out the rotten statistics about how much crime costs the country, which means only how much the burglars, et al. cost the country. They of course do not include brokers, bankers, promoters, the issuers of fake stocks, who fleece the people &c &c who are really responsible for our topsy-turvy system. They are interested in "working their side of the street." Of course, there may be some men in the organization who are different, but I must be shown. Of course, you know that I don't want to be president, and would be glad to let anyone else take it off my hands so I would not stand in the way of anything that the rest want to do. Their stuff about the cost of crime is the bunk. If crime costs what they say how much does the stock market, the land lords, the fake bonds and stocks under which the country staggers, cost the people? How much does general unemployment cost? Crime costs nothing except to the victims. Talk this over with Mr. Walsh, Arthur Hays, Roger Baldwin, or any of the others. By the way, I wish you would get me one of their pamphlets telling of the cost of crime. I am sure Mr. Reis could get one. I want to analyze it. So far these committees have only produced more hangings—longer and more cruel punishments. They are doing exactly what our people are against. If they have any new light on the subject and are really undertaking what these reformers call "constructive work" I shall be glad to change my view. I don't know that our organization is doing any good. I am doubtful if anything does good, and even more doubtful about the meaning of "good." But I am in favor of fewer prisons and shorter terms, if any, and a chance for the submerged to get a living in an easier way than burglary, and not so easy a way as by issuing stocks and bonds for me to play.

I really would appreciate it if you could send me their litterature. After I get it I will tell you what I think of it. I know what a hard time Miss Pierce has gone through, and I am afraid she is wasting her time and herself in a hopeless cause.[25] People are not much moved by speeches and pamphlets; their urges are too primitive for that. They are moved by food and drink and bonds and sex and theatres, &c. I am sorry to write so long a letter. Show this to Mr. Reis who is a thoroughly sincere and intelligent young man and see

24. "Baumes laws" were state statutes that provided increased punishment for repeat criminal offenders, imposed mandatory sentences ranging from five to twenty-five years for anyone armed with a weapon when committing a felony, and life in prison for anyone who had a fourth conviction for a felony. The laws originated in New York. See NY Penal Law §§ 1941–44 (1930). The laws were named after their state legislative sponsor, Caleb H. Baumes (1863–1937), a state senator and chairman of the New York State Crime Commission.

25. Vivian Pierce had recently worked for several months on the league's "preliminary organization campaigns" in Arizona, California, Colorado, and Indiana. Pierce to Walsh, 17 October 1930, TLS, NN, Walsh Papers.

what he thinks of it. Anyhow I am sending the check which should go to Vermont, to make good a part of my promise.

I expect to be in N.Y. around Sept. 1st and will try to see you.

With best wishes, | Clarence Darrow

MS: ALS, MBNU, Sara Ehrmann Papers, Box 16, Folder 91. DATE: typed transcript of letter in papers of Frank Walsh, NN.

TO MARIE SWEET SMITH • CHICAGO • WEDNESDAY 27 AUGUST 1930

August 27, 1930

Dear Mrs. Smith:

Your letter of August 25th is just received. It is very strange that you do not understand that the people who believe in saving money by abolishing crime are all for capital punishment. They would laugh at you if you even suggested that getting rid of capital punishment would prevent crime. Of course it would not, and if it would, you could not make them believe it. All this talk about the cost of crime is bunk and nonsense gotten out by people who are interested in running banks and collecting money. The growth of crime such as it is has come from the passing of endless new statutes and from prohibition, and it cannot be cured excepting by educating children and making life easier for the masses.

I certainly would have nothing to do with such a scheme. The people who run banks and boiler factories and oil wells are not the people who are against capital punishment. To tie up with them would be virtually to tie up with the hang-man. They now control every Legislature in the country. If they want capital punishment abolished, why don't they do it?

This proposition is still worse. The men who are promising to raise this money are doing it on the basis of getting a percentage for the money they raise. They are not interested one way or the other. They probably don't know themselves what the money-bags would say about it, but *I* know, and *you* should. They are all on the other side. If anything is to be done, it must be done through the poor and the humane and the idealists. I would have nothing to do with any kind of a showing that crime is costly and expensive and that abolishing capital punishment would decrease crime. There isn't a bit of sense in it and you could not put it over.

You know I have never wanted to be connected with this organization in an official way. I have not the time nor energy to give to it, or any considerable amount of money, and I do not want to stand in anybody else's way. But I would at once resign as chairman if any such thing should be undertaken. I don't want them to think I haven't got any sense or that I don't know who my enemies are and that I don't know what the rich men think about things; or who runs the Legislatures; or who is

responsible for hangings. I do know and I would have no dealings with them. I don't think Arthur (referring to Mr. Hays) understands the situation or he would not consider it.[26]

How would it be to call together such of the Board as are in New York and give them my views? If they think I am wrong, let me out of the presidency which will not mean I will stop working to abolish capital punishment. I am still for it but I know my friends from my enemies.

Very truly yours, | (Signed) Clarence Darrow

MS: TT, NN, Walsh Papers, Box 17. INSIDE ADDRESS: Mrs. Marie Sweet Smith | New York, N.Y.

TO LLEWELYN POWYS • CHICAGO • TUESDAY 2 SEPTEMBER 1930

CLARENCE DARROW Sept 2d

My Dear Mr. Powys—

I have read your book, "An hour on Christianity", and it is *a fine piece of work:* True—and beautiful. I feel *greatly honored* that it should have been dedicated to me.[27] I have never had anything so well done, dedicated to me, and probably it will not happen again. I wish people would read the book, but they read little that *is* of *any value.* We often think of the pleasant time we had at your home on the high point fronting on the sea. We may get back next year and—if so—will see you once more. The Powys family have some how been allotted more than their share of the brains—if not the money, but one shouldn't expect too much. I was much taken with Theodore.[28] He does not hedge or run away from facts. John[29] is a genius, but he has a hopeless streak of mysticism about him which does not bother me, but why should intelligent men talk of something that they know nothing about. That sort of thing should be left to men like Eddington[30] and Jeans.[31] I wonder if you are never coming back to the states. We should be so glad to see you both!

With love to both from

Mrs. Darrow & Clarence Darrow

MS: ALS, TxU-Hu. DATE: publication of Powys's book. NOTE: letter and signatures are in Darrow's hand, not Ruby's.

26. Arthur Garfield Hays, who was also a member of the board of directors for the ALACP, received a copy of this letter from the league and wrote to Darrow, saying he agreed with him "one hundred percent and told Mrs Smith the same thing." Hays to Darrow, 11 September 1930, TT, NN, Walsh Papers, Box 17, Folder: 1930, August.
27. Powys dedicated his *An Hour on Christianity* (Philadelphia: J. B. Lippincott, 1930) to Darrow with the statement: "Dedicated to Clarence Darrow with affection and appreciation."
28. Theodore Francis Powys (1875–1953), English novelist and short-story writer. Theodore and Llewelyn were brothers.
29. John Cowper Powys (1872–1963), novelist, essayist, poet, and lecturer. John was also Llewelyn's brother.
30. Arthur Stanley Eddington (1882–1944), English astronomer, author, and Cambridge professor.
31. James Hopwood Jeans (1877–1946), English physicist, astronomer, and author.

TO H. L. MENCKEN • CHICAGO • FRIDAY 5 SEPTEMBER 1930

CLARENCE DARROW Sept 5th

My Dear Mr Menken—

The announcement of your marriage has been received; of course I had read of it in the papers long before, so the blow was softened.[32] I knew it would happen. It always does. Still, I want to compliment you on the long brave fight you made. That is all that a man can do, for the fool race must be preserved, and this is the way that has been ordained for its preservation. Any how I hope to see both you and Mrs. Menken before very long. Give her my kindest regards and best wishes; also my sincere sympathy. With all good wishes to you jointly and severally—

Your friend | Clarence Darrow.

MS: ALS, NN, Mencken Papers. DATE: "1930" appended.

TO MARK SULLIVAN • CHICAGO • FRIDAY 5 SEPTEMBER 1930

CLARENCE DARROW Sept 5th

My Dear Mr. Sullivan

I want to thank you for your letter.[33] Men like me who seem to have been made to oppose almost every established belief find it none to easy. We are fair game for almost every one, and it is so easy to discolor all that is said and done. The story you quoted from was a very prejudiced one. Still one of fair inteligence looks for this and I have seldom tried to have any thing changed or amended so it was a relief to get your letter. I am sending you a copy of my address in the Loeb-Leopold case which you may care to read.

Very Sincerely | Clarence Darrow

MS: ALS, location of original unknown (copy in editor's files). DATE: another letter from Darrow to Sullivan. INSIDE ADDRESS: Mr Mark Sullivan.

32. On 27 August 1930, Mencken married Sara Powell Haardt (1898–1935), a writer and native of Alabama.
33. This letter followed an exchange of correspondence between Sullivan and Darrow when Sullivan was preparing his multivolume *Our Times*. Sullivan had asked Darrow to comment about some events associated with the trial of William Haywood in 1907, including Darrow's final argument to the jury, where Darrow said that he did not care how many wrongs labor had committed or how many brutalities for which labor was guilty, he believed that labor's cause was just. At the time of the trial, Darrow received a great deal of criticism for that statement. After reviewing some of the proofs for Sullivan's book, Darrow wrote back to Sullivan explaining that he meant *regardless* of how many wrongs labor committed, labor's cause was still just: "I don't believe anybody can fairly interpret it in any other way." Darrow to Sullivan, 27 August 1930, TLS, location of original unknown (copy in editor's files). Sullivan revised his book and referred to Darrow's letter in a footnote. Mark Sullivan, *Our Times: The United States 1900–1925*, vol. 3, *Pre-War America* (New York: Charles Scribner's Sons, 1930), 493–94.

TO WALTER WHITE • CHICAGO • TUESDAY 16 SEPTEMBER 1930

CLARENCE DARROW Sept. 16

Dear Walter

I was interested in what Mrs. Eleanor Rowland Wembridge[34] says about the good manners of the Negroes.[35] I had never thought of it before but came to reflect on my experience. I think Mrs. Rowland is right. I remember that southern generals very polite and dignified used to come and talk to our political meetings in the North and invariably they told us how they like the negro. These men were much more courteous and polite than were we Northerners and I didn't know why their manners were so good. Now I distinctly remember that all of them told us that they were raised by their old black Mammy and that they loved her as much or more than their own mother. Funny, I didn't understand it then.

Truly | Darrow

MS: ALS, DLC-MSS, NAACP Administrative Files. DATE: stamped received "SEP 18 1930."

TO UPTON SINCLAIR • CHICAGO • SATURDAY 27 SEPTEMBER 1930

CLARENCE DARROW September 27-th, 1930—

Dear Sinclair:—

Of course I should be glad to debate with you, and of course it would be satisfactory for you to take the extra for coming here and doing the work.[36] Still, I don't believe it could be done.

34. Eleanor Harris Rowland Wembridge (1883–1944), teacher, writer, and psychologist. Wembridge earned a Ph.D. from Radcliffe College, 1905, taught psychology at Mount Holyoke College, later became dean of women at Reed College in Oregon, and still later, in 1922, moved to Cleveland, where she performed psychological work for the Women's Protective Association and served as a referee of the Women's Department of the Juvenile Court. She wrote many books, including *The Right to Believe* (1909), *Other People's Daughters* (1928), and *Life among the Lowbrows* (1931).
35. Darrow is likely referring to an article that Wembridge wrote while she was a referee in the juvenile court in Cleveland. In this article, Wembridge commented on differences that she observed between blacks and whites in court on misdemeanor charges and, in particular, on the exceptional manners and dignity of the African American grandmothers who appeared with their grandchildren. Wembridge, "Negroes in Custody," *American Mercury*, September 1930, 76–83.
36. Sinclair had written to Darrow explaining, in a rather confusing way, that he had been approached by Albert Rogell (1901–88), a film director in Los Angeles, who wanted Sinclair and another person to "write a debate"—with Sinclair advocating Prohibition and the other person (Darrow) arguing against it. This written debate would then be incorporated into a script for a movie to be produced by Rogell, with the characters using lines from the debate. The storyline for the movie, according to Sinclair, was to involve "a boy who is lured by . . . bootleggers and becomes a murderer, and the debate on prohibition and what was to be done about it was to come in as a part of the trial scene of this boy." Sinclair reminded Darrow that "there are restrictions imposed by the moving-picture censorship which there is no escaping if you are going to work for the movies. You cannot swear, . . . you cannot be obscene, and you probably cannot ridicule the church, and you certainly cannot call for the overthrow of the government." Sinclair to Darrow, 25 September 1930, TLc, InU-Li, Sinclair Papers.

First:—I wouldn't have anything to do with a play where a boy was lured away by a boot-legger and became a murderer. If it was to be a boy who was lured by a prohibition agent, or a prohibitionist, it might be another thing. I have known some boot-leggers, and have known none who did any luring. Of course it is the law that makes the boot-leggers. It is this that I am after. I could have nothing to do with a play that was formed on any such conception.

Second:—I could not take the part of a preacher. Imagine putting words of philosophy and understanding into the mouth of a preacher! I could get along without being obscene,—at least any more obscene than the movies; but really I don't know what the word means. I might get along without swearing, although I always feel like cursing when I think of prohibition.

I don't believe I could get along without ridiculing religion. Prohibition is really religion, and no one can intelligently discuss it without showing how the protestant church is seeking the destruction of freedom. I really don't believe a play could be written on the subject that would be fair.

I would no more ridicule the boot-legger than you would the socialist, and I have as strong a feeling against prohibition as you have against capitalism. So what can we do?

Sincerely yours, | Clarence Darrow

MS: TLS, InU-Li, Sinclair Papers. INSIDE ADDRESS: Mr. Upton Sinclair : | Pasadena, California.

TO MARY FIELD PARTON • CHICAGO • WEDNESDAY 1 OCTOBER 1930

CLARENCE DARROW Oct. 1st

Dear Mary

I am sorry to seem to worrying over that bank loan.[37] The truth is I got pretty hurt with all the rest in the last year's failure and the disappointments since. Won't you send me word as to just how much is still owed the bank and the rate at which it is being paid and whether you have any difficulty keeping it up. I have up as security one hundred shares of Southern Pacific which now is worth $11,800. If it is reduced far enough to be sufficient security I am going to have Mr. Thompson[38] get it cut into two certificates so that one can be returned. An other reason is that I am not so very well and I don't want any one else to have the trouble and expense of fixing up any business in the New York Courts. I am sorry to write you about [it]. Of course I am not seeking [to] have you

37. In 1928, Darrow had pledged some securities as collateral for a loan for Mary and her husband, Lem, so they could borrow four thousand dollars to buy a brownstone townhouse in New York City.
38. The identity of "Mr. Thompson" is unknown.

pay it. I am wanting to put it into the easiest way I can in view of contingencies that are not far off.

You might enclose your answer to Joe Hamilton who lives next door.

With best wishes to Lem Your friend always | Clarence Darrow

MS: ALS, ICN, Parton-Darrow Papers, Box 1, Folder 10. ENVELOPE ADDRESS: Mrs Mary Parton | 7 Charles St | New York City | N.Y. POSTMARK: Chicago 1 October 1930.

TO UPTON SINCLAIR • CHICAGO • THURSDAY 2 OCTOBER 1930

CLARENCE DARROW October 2-nd, 1930—

Dear Sinclair:—

Your letter was received last night.[39] I understood you to say that your idea in the matter of bringing out the discussion was to have some preachers argue as to how the boy happened to get into the scrape. I have no doubt that you could overcome the objections I raised. I understand that the MOVIES are bound by certain restrictions that come from the moralists and other fanatics. Like you, I can usually manage to get my ideas across, and I never try to teach profanity or obscenity, so it is not a matter of propaganda.

I would not start with an assumption that liquor produced murder, or any other sort of evil or wrong. If you want to argue it, it is all right with me; you will find many who will agree with you—but what a bunch! I don't quite see how all this is to be accomplished when we are so far apart, but, if you do, all right.

When the story is written it might be sent to me, and I will make no more changes than absolutely needful. I was hoping that you were coming out as would like to see you again. It would do me good, for a dry radical is so rare.

With all good wishes, | Clarence Darrow

MS: TLS, InU-Li, Sinclair Papers.

39. Sinclair responded to Darrow's last letter with a long letter explaining that no preacher would be a character in the proposed story and that the story would not involve a boy lured by bootleggers but rather a boy "who is lured into the bootlegging business and becomes a murderer": "What is desired is to have a story in which a boy commits murder as a result of our present intolerable liquor situation. We both agree that the situation is intolerable, and we differ only as to what is to be done. . . . Whether the boy is to be lured by a bootlegger, or whether he is to be lured by a prohibition agent, or whether he is lured by high-jackers—surely we could find some device by which the boy could be lured which we could agree was characteristic of the present situation, and which caused the boy to commit murder." Sinclair assured Darrow that he would be free to say in the script what he said in his letter about how "prohibition is really religion," but "[w]here the objection would come in would be if you should start to use abusive terms about the church and clergy, calling them 'wowsers' and 'blue noses' and all the other terms of ridicule which our friend, Mencken, employs." Sinclair to Darrow, 29 September 1930, TLc, InU-Li, Sinclair Papers.

TO UPTON SINCLAIR • CHICAGO • WEDNESDAY 8 OCTOBER 1930

CLARENCE DARROW Oct. 8

My Dear Sinclair

I utterly disagree with you on the whole subject of Crime.[40] What we call crime is the result of poverty, which in turn comes from economic questions that you understand better than I do. Except when thugs employed as prohibition agents shoot down men and women on the street, and where, men are attacked by officers for doing what they should have the right to do there are no killings and of course no robberies growing out of liquor. Such crimes will only end when we get rid of the "Infamous Volsted Act." There is no chance to compromise with me on the cause of crime, although it may be subject to argument along with other questions. Liquor as liquor has no more to do with crime than ham and eggs. If you care to know my views in detail you can probably find a book that I wrote some years ago "Crime: its Cause and Treatment." Most Universities and some librarys have it.

I don't see why a story could not be written stating facts & events and leave the field open for you who have been brought up on such songs as "Father dear father come home with me now" & I who have no such allusions, make our own argument. I don't see any reason why we need to dispute on such details. I am leaving tomorrow for the N.W. and will be back in about two weeks.[41]

Truly | Clarence Darrow.

MS: ALS, InU-Li, Sinclair Papers. DATE: "[1930]" appended.

TO W. E. B. DU BOIS • CHICAGO • WEDNESDAY 8 OCTOBER 1930

October 8, 1929

My dear Du Bois:

I suppose you might as well go at the question of religion. I imagine that the preachers do nothing of any consequence for our organization and probably never will. They and

40. Sinclair wrote to Darrow again trying to work out the premise of the story and saying that they both should agree that Prohibition was producing crime: "Forgive me if I am inept in expressing to you what I am trying to get across. We would both agree, I presume, that the present condition of tolerated outlawry leads to murder. In other words, existence of an illegal traffic in the hands of gangsters, preyed upon by high-jackers, leads to murder, and the condition is getting worse, because the prizes offered are increasing." Sinclair to Darrow, 6 October 1930, TLc, InU-Li, Sinclair Papers.

41. Darrow and Sinclair continued through an exchange of several letters to have misunderstandings about the proposal for a film. The producers sent Darrow a proposed contract in November, and Darrow responded to one of Sinclair's final inquiries with uncertainty about the whole matter: "I would like to do what you wish, but, the business is new to me, although I have a number of propositions before me now. How far one would interfere with another I don't know. Of course I want to be governed as much by what is fair and just as by what is legal. I would not think it right to sign a contract without telling what other ideas I have in my mind. I am getting to that time of life that I don't believe in hurrying or being hurried." Darrow to Sinclair, 4 December 1930, ALS, InU-Li, Sinclair Papers. With that, the idea for a film involving Darrow and Sinclair apparently faded.

their churches are a terrible load on the poor workers. Of course sooner or later the preachers will be shaken off but it is a hard job. I am going west for about two weeks. I will try to figure out something for you on my journey.[42]

With best wishes always | Your friend | Clarence Darrow

MS: Herbert Aptheker, ed., *The Correspondence of W. E. B. Du Bois: Volume 1, Selections, 1877–1934* (Amherst: University of Massachusetts Press, 1973), 408. DATE: the letter is misdated in the book; Darrow was in London in 1929 but he was in Chicago in 1930, and about to travel West.

TO BOLTON HALL • CHICAGO • FRIDAY 31 OCTOBER 1930

CLARENCE DARROW Oct. 31

My Dear Hall

I am always glad to see you or hear from you or read what you write. I have been one of your most ardent admirers for lo these many years, and am glad that you keep at it. I think I am about like you. I read and speak and write a good deal, but don't practice law. It is too strenuous for one of my years, and besides I think the whole system is more or less a humbug. I have never claimed to be an Atheist. I am too modest for that. I class myself as an Agnostic which is at least a doubter. I think one can not believe without evidence and I have no evidence on the subject.

Your friend always | Clarence Darrow

MS: ALS, NN, Hall Papers, Box 4. DATE: year uncertain; could also be 1928, given letterhead and other letters, but statement about no longer practicing law makes 1930 more likely.

TO VIVIAN PIERCE • CHICAGO • THURSDAY 4 DECEMBER 1930

CLARENCE DARROW Dec 4th

Dear Vivian

Except for a few hours on Sunday the 7th when I speak in the evening at Dr. Holmes' church,[43] I will not be in New York until January 11th. I do hope that Dr. Van Waters may be there then. I would like to see her, as I always do.

Hastily | C.S.D.

MS: ALS, MBNU, Sara Ehrmann Papers, Box 16, Folder 91. DATE: other letters and reference to speech at church.

42. Du Bois might have asked Darrow to write something for *Crisis* magazine on the subject of religion. The following year, *Crisis* published two competing views—one by Darrow and one by Robert Elijah Jones (1871–1960), a bishop of the Methodist Episcopal Church—on what benefit organized religion had been for African Americans. "The Religion of the American Negro," *Crisis,* June 1931, 190–92.
43. John Haynes Holmes's church was the Community Church of New York. Darrow's speech at the church was announced as "Free Will, the Doctrine of Despair," which is what Darrow requested. Holmes to Darrow, 11 November 1930, TLS, DLC-MSS, Darrow Papers.

TO JAMES WELDON JOHNSON • CHICAGO • THURSDAY 1 JANUARY 1931

CLARENCE DARROW Jan 1st.

Dear James

Your unknown soldier is a peach, and *awfully clever*.[44] More power to you! Of course, you should get out a cheaper edition—although I got this very cheap. But if it was widely circulated a few d—n fools might see the point. Shall be in N.Y. for a few days about 12th of Jan. Always with affection and regard

Your friend | Clarence Darrow

MS: ALS, CtY-BR, Johnson Collection Files. DATE: "1921" is appended but letterhead, reference to "unknown soldier," and New York make 1931 the more likely year. INSIDE ADDRESS: Mr Jas Weldon Johnson.

TO LEWIS E. LAWES • WASHINGTON, D.C. • SUNDAY 4 JANUARY 1931

THE WILLARD Jan 4th

Dear Laws

When I left home yesterday I put in your book, "Life & death in Sing sing",[45] and it kept me awake most of the night & I have finished it this morning. You know we authors talk about other people's books but seldom read them. Why should we, so long as we know more about the subject than any one else? But I can now say honestly, that I have not only read your book but have lived it through the reading. I don't want you to think that I am exaggerating, for I am too much interested in the subject to say something I do not believe. I am, as you know, pretty well familiar with the subject and have read many of the important books and have written and talked about it for years. No one else has done anything that compares with this book. Of course this is partly due to your long experience and largely to your deep feeling and wonderful imagination. I know of no book that would have the tendency to make people feel and

44. Darrow is referring to Johnson's poem "Saint Peter Relates an Incident of the Resurrection Day," which was printed in an edition of two hundred copies in 1930 by Viking Press, for private distribution. Darrow probably received a copy directly from Johnson or Benjamin Huebsch at Viking. In the poem, Saint Peter tells how the Unknown Soldier, on Resurrection Day and in the presence of all the patriotic groups (including the Grand Army of the Republic, the Daughters of the American Revolution, Confederate veterans, and the Ku Klux Klan), rose from his grave and—to the horror of everyone present—turned out to be a black man. The poem was inspired in part by news accounts of the federal government sending a group of Gold Star mothers to France in 1930 to visit the graves of their sons who died in World War I and making the black mothers travel on a separate, second-class vessel.

45. Lawes's *Life and Death in Sing Sing* (Garden City, NY: Doubleday, Doran, 1928) describes his experiences with prisoners at Sing Sing prison and his views on criminology.

understand like this one. I feel that I know you now. Let me also say that the style is marvelous. I can't praise it enough. I don't see how any human being can believe in capital punishment after reading this book. You are right in saying that prisoners are just like other men. Of course they won't average as high in intelligence, and of course in the main have had no chance. The book makes me hate good people more than I ever did before. Your analysis of crime and the fool distinctions of men is remarkable, but I mustn't rave on. What can we do about it? I don't know what kind of sale this book has had, or how much has been done to promote, but every one should read it, and I want to do all I can to make them read it. I think the 7th & 8th Chapters should be published in pamphlet form and circulated by the League—*everyone* ought to have it.[46] I don't know what the publishers would do about it, but I think some arrangement could be made. It would carry advertising for the whole book. I am preparing a thirty minutes talk for the movies and I think I can help advertise it to the movie fans. I shall be here until Jan 10th. On the 12th I go to New York where I will be at the Murray Hill for several days. If you are down that way I hope I can see you. By the way—there is one little paragraph that I think should be removed when a new edition is printed, and that is the one about the Jews putting Jesus to death.[47] I think I can show you that the passages that give that impression are interpolations that are not in the original texts. Any how, I think it should not be in.[48] Still, it is wonderful book and it should do good

With regards & affection, | Your friend | Clarence Darrow[49]

MS: ALS, NNJJ, Lawes Papers, Box 4 (correspondence scrapbook). DATE: reference to Lawes's book and Ruby Darrow's partially dated note.

46. By "the League," Darrow is probably referring to the American League to Abolish Capital Punishment, for which Darrow and Lawes were officers and directors.
47. Darrow is probably referring to a passage by Lawes in which he maintained that public sentiment alone is no justification for allowing something to happen or to exist: "Frankly, I do not think that the mere fact that a large part or even most of the public 'wants something' is justification for furnishing it if the something is essentially detrimental and destructive in character. The South wanted slavery, the Jews of Jerusalem wanted Jesus crucified, and a large part of the public wants suggestive plays and books." *Life and Death in Sing Sing*, 260.
48. Lawes wrote to Darrow explaining that he simply meant to draw an analogy by his statement: "I note your remark about the paragraph referring to the Crucifixion. It was not intended to confirm the traditional view. I cited it as an outstanding example of the application of the death penalty. Authority, popular or legal, no matter which, decreed its infliction. What might have been the course of history had there been no capital punishment in those days, can only be imagined. In a more limited way and perhaps less devastating—does not every execution involve its particular social upheaval?" Lawes to Darrow, TLS, 12 January 1931, DLC, Darrow Collection.
49. Ruby Darrow enclosed a note with this letter (dated "Sunday—January fourth"), wishing Lawes well with his book and "echo[ing] all that [Darrow] says."

TO HARRY ELMER BARNES • NEW YORK CITY • SUNDAY 8 FEBRUARY 1931

Murray Hill Hotel | February 8th

My dear Dr. Barnes:—

I am very sorry not to see you again before I leave, but I am starting tonight for Florida to see if a little rest, where I can get out of doors, may not help the machine a little. I shall be back sometime the last of March or the first of April.

I am returning your article from the *Scientific Monthly*.[50] It is very fine. I have been thinking of you a good deal of late. Somehow I have been called on so much to defend the Devil against the Christians that I have been trying to get some of my friends to take some one else. When infidelity is to be preached they seem to look to me. I have been wondering who can meet these fellows in "immortal" combat. The calendar and various other hunches constantly warn me that there are only a few more speeches and debates left in me, and I am so relieved when I look at you.

I want you to do me the credit to think that I know that you know infinitely more about these subjects than I ever can know. You can meet the enemy on any and every ground. I have never heard you and do not know what your method of discourse is. It may be that my long practise in speaking to morons has given me a simpler and more direct style—I don't know. Of course, added to this, is the fact of my notoriety which draws crowds. I have heard one suggestion, namely, that you speak too rapidly. You must remember that ordinary minds go by "slow freight" and *give them time*. But please excuse me for this suggestion, which you may not need at all.

I hope you will gradually take up a good deal of this work. It is sorely needed. I know I am a damn fool to worry about what will happen to the world when I cash in. Of course, I know that nothing will happen, but a fair degree of intelligence combined with some courage is so rare. I am sorry I had to write this in very poor long hand, but I wanted to say it to you while I am here.

With kindest regards, always,

Your friend, | Clarence Darrow[51]

MS: TT, WyU-AH, Barnes Collection. DATE: place and reference to Florida.

50. Darrow might have been returning an article of Barnes's that had been published eighteen months earlier by *Scientific Monthly* on the conflicts between religion and science. See Harry Elmer Barnes, "The Role of Religion in a Secular Society," *Scientific Monthly*, May 1929, 430–45.
51. In Barnes's long response to this letter, he said that he was flattered by the "suggestion that [he] might fittingly wear even a patch of [Darrow's] mantle." Barnes to Darrow, 21 February 1931, TLS, DLC-MSS, Darrow Papers.

TO VIVIAN PIERCE • NEW YORK CITY • SUNDAY 8 FEBRUARY 1931

MURRAY HILL HOTEL Feby. 8th

Dear Vivian,

I am terribly sorry and ashamed at the way I have treated you, but I have had a wretched time. Very foolishly I made a number of engagements before coming East and it was terribly wearisome especially as I have been suffering from the "Flu." Every time I got back here I went to bed and staid until I had to leave again. The date of the meeting I did not know, but I could not have been here anyhow—as was in Boston that day.[52] I am terribly sorry not to have seen Dr. Van Waters. I surely would not have missed a chance to see her, if I could possibly have helped it. I did not wire the Kansas legislature. I knew none of the members and I felt that it would do more harm than good. They would have felt it another reason to pass the bill.[53] I get sick and discouraged at the cruelty of man, and often wonder if I should not stop, but I have been at it so long that I can't stop. I am leaving today for a rest in Florida. I shall be at

Dunedin—Florida c/o Fenway Hotel

Remember me kindly to Miss Van Watters; hope she will stay in the East.

Your friend always | Clarence Darrow

MS: ALS, MBNU, Sara Ehrmann Papers, Box 16, Folder 91. DATE: Pierce's letter to Darrow.

TO HARRY ELMER BARNES • DUNEDIN, FLORIDA • FRIDAY 6 MARCH 1931

HOTEL FENWAY March 6th

My Dear Mr Barnes

One of the companies (the Ayer Newspaper adv. Co) are putting on some historical incidents as trials. They are to start with Benedict Arnold. James S. Beck is to represent the state, I the defendant, and what I am to do is to ask for clemency on account of former devotion and service, and my opposition to capital punishment. When it came to me I did not think anything about the feeling of the public against Arnold any more than I had

52. Pierce had twice set a date for a board meeting for the league and Darrow had apparently been unable to meet either date, which greatly disappointed Pierce: "The reason it was important—*is* important—to get you occasionally to a Board meeting is because of *the effect you have on the Board*. . . . With all your faults, we are all crazy about you. I told Dr [Miriam] Van Waters I was never going to send you another appeal or speak to you again. I had put a lot of people, including herself, to enormous inconvenience, over our meeting. But I knew I would weaken. We just can't get along without you. And of course you know it." Pierce to Darrow, 17 February 1931, TLc, MBNU, Sara Ehrmann Papers, Box 16, Folder 91.

53. The Kansas legislature was considering a bill that would restore capital punishment in that state. Pierce disagreed with Darrow's assessment of the effect he would have on legislators if he made an appeal to them: "I do not agree with you that your very name would have antagonized the Kansas Legislature. These little lawyers that make up Legislatures are opposed to you perhaps. But don't forget you have an immense effect on them. To them you are Success and Fame with a capital S." Ibid.

not ever thought of such matters. But there are so many papers who would like to criticize that I have been wondering. The Co. thinks there would be no criticism as to them or me, but I don't know or how much.

Of course there is a considerable fee offered for the two evenings but that is not of controlling motive, or any motive with me. Won't you think of it, and, if you wish, talk with one or two of the boys there and see what they think and wire me at Houston Texas at my expense, what you think. I will be there March 13th and shall probably be governed by your judgment—although I would not think of holding you responsible.[54]

With kind regards | Clarence Darrow

MS: ALS, WyU-AH, Barnes Collection. DATE: reference to mock trial of Benedict Arnold.

TO VIVIAN PIERCE • DUNEDIN, FLORIDA • FRIDAY 6 MARCH 1931

HOTEL FENWAY April 10

Dear Vivian:—

I don't see how I could possibly go to Albany this month. Anyhow, I wouldn't want to undertake it unless I knew something about how I would be received.[55] This is a bad time for our cause—but I feel quite sure that another year will make quite a difference. You can't hold people up to their present pitch of anger and hatred for too long a time. I have been reading Warden Law's book "Life and Death in Sing Sing." I think it is a wonderful book; by all odds the most important and thorough one I have ever read. We could do no better work than to get this circulated. We would be obliged to have a cheaper edition printed, and get some of the news-papers, like the Scripps-Howard, to take hold of it—and I believe it would have a good effect. That little book "The Hand book of hanging" too should be circulated.[56] Shall leave here soon for Texas. Will be in N.Y. about April 1st.

Sincerely your friend | Clarence Darrow

MS: ALS, MBNU, Sara Ehrmann Papers, Box 16, Folder 91. DATE: Pierce's letter to Darrow.

54. The dramatization of the trial was broadcast on radio station NBC-WEAF on 22 March 1931. The state was represented by James Montgomery Beck, not "James S. Beck." "Darrow and Beck to Participate in the 'Famous Trials of History,'" *New York Times,* 15 March 1931.

55. Pierce wanted Darrow to speak at a public hearing before a joint committee of the state legislature in Albany, New York. The bill under consideration by the committee would have substituted life imprisonment for the death penalty and lessened the severity of the Baumes law. Pierce to Darrow, 10 March 1931, TLc, MBNU, Sara Ehrmann Papers, Box 16, Folder 91; "All Albany Bills in One Committee," *New York Times,* 18 March 1931; Darrow to Marie Sweet Smith and "Mrs. Phelps," 23 August 1930, n.24 (describing the Baumes law).

56. Charles Duff, *A Handbook on Hanging: Being a Short Introduction to the Fine Art of Execution, and Containing Much Useful Information on Neck-Breaking, Throttling, Strangling, Asphyxiation, Decapitation and Electrocution* (London: The Cayme Press, 1928). Pierce was in favor of trying to get a wider circulation for Lawe's book but told Darrow that she thought *The Handbook on Hanging* was "a little highbrow for popular reading" and that she did "not think that satire on this subject appeals to a large number of people." Pierce to Darrow, 10 March 1931, TLc, MBNU, Sara Ehrmann Papers, Box 16, Folder 91.

TO PAUL DARROW • NEW YORK CITY • TUESDAY 24 MARCH 1931

MURRAY HILL HOTEL March 24th.

Dear Paul,

You will not need to save any money out of what you have. I shall get $5,000 more early in the week from the Arnold case, and $1,500 is enough to keep in bank. If needed you can use all of it in your matters. If not perhaps it had better be kept in bank until my return which will be about April 10th. I am now working on the evolution film, which I want to finish before I leave.[57] Am also to do some other talks called shorts, for the movies—or talkies. Shall be glad to get back and will stay a while when I come—

C. S. D.

MS: ALS, MnU-L, Darrow Collection. DATE: "1931" appended.

TO PAUL DARROW • NEW YORK CITY • SATURDAY 4 APRIL 1931

MURRAY HILL HOTEL April 4th.

Dear Paul

Mencken wants me to write an article on who is responsible for the hard times and I want to do it. I think the Hoover bunch is. He was elected on the promise of still wilder prosperity than under Coolidge. He was elected before the panic. Stocks went up probably 25 to 50 after his election. In the mean time no hint from Hoover, Mellon or any one else of danger. Then of course the tariff was raised long after the panic. Will you take some 10 of the most active stocks? Find what they sold at when Hoover was elected. How high they went afterward. There was some falling off before the panic. Find the price then. Give the price after the panic say 20 or 60 days after. The low since. I want it to be a representative list like General Motors, Genl Elec, U.S. Steel, Int. T.T. & T. also a short list of what are now supposed to be cats & dogs that come all to pieces. These of course in a separate item.

What do you think of stocks now. They look rather scary to me. Do you think we will pull through all right. Also if you think best to lighten do so. Sell any of mine you wish and pay in the money. I don't want to see us go broke.

Hastily | C. S. D.

MS: ALS, MnU-L, Darrow Collection. DATE: "1931" appended.

57. In addition to participating in the mock trial of Benedict Arnold, Darrow was one of the narrators of a motion picture about evolution called *The Mystery of Life,* which was produced by Universal.

TO PAUL DARROW • NEW YORK CITY • TUESDAY 7 APRIL 1931

MURRAY HILL HOTEL Tuesday—7th

Dear Paul

I am of course somewhat alarmed over the market. I don't know how we stand assets and liabilities. I don't know whether we are in better or worse shape than at the first of the year or even at the low point before the first of the year. I believe every thing is low and will be higher. But the country is D—n sick. Of course I don't want to loose all we have, would rather sell some stuff now. Would suggest B & O, my U. P. and your S.P. perhaps International T. & T. possibly some bonds. Any how do what you think best. If we had $2^1/_2$ or 3 for every dollar of indebtedness I would say all right. Perhaps it doesn't need that much. I am obliged to stay longer than I thought. I am finishing the evolution picture and I think there is some money in it. I would guess that I will get $25,000 out of it before the year is out and perhaps more. Of course I have put nothing in it and do not have to. I am of course willing to risk what I have in holding our stocks but want you to figure it out the best you can and keep me posted. Hope you won't worry too much. I think we will pull out some way. I had a good time with Schoolcraft.[58] Spent a day together driving. He told me you were the best asset that N. & J. had. I am sure he is your friend. One of Arthur Hay's rich friends (for whom he is attorney) is in the business of buying Utilities. He (Arthur) thought you might get a line on some of them & make good money by it. Any how keep me posted. You might write often. Shall not be home (most likely) until May 1st. Shall not draw *more* than 1,000 from my account and probably not that much. So use what there is if you want to—

Hastily | C. S. D.

MS: ALS, MnU-L, Darrow Collection. DATE: "1931" appended, letterhead, and the seventh of the month falling on a Tuesday.

TO VIVIAN PIERCE • NEW YORK CITY • FRIDAY 10 APRIL 1931

MURRAY HILL HOTEL April 10

Dear Vivian

I have been tied up very closely since I have been in New York, but have a little more chance now. I don't feel like asking for money from Mr. Brooks.[59] I don't know him nor anything about him except the incident you mention. It is not in the least a question of time. I am willing to do what you want about the committee. Send me the letter you wish

58. Darrow might be referring to Henry L. Schoolcraft (1868?–1936), a neighbor of Paul Darrow who taught at colleges in the East and then became a real estate investor.
59. Pierce apparently wanted Darrow to solicit money for the American League to Abolish Capital Punishment from a "Mr. Brooks," but his identity is unknown.

me to sign and I will do it.[60] I am no less interested in the work than ever. I just feel its hopelessness. Men are insane with cruelty and nothing *can* be done. I think I see some faint signs of the pendulum swinging back which comes about from the revolt of prisoners, but all we can do now is to wait. Will be here nearly a month and hope I can see you.

Truly | Clarence Darrow

MS: ALS, MBNU, Sara Ehrmann Papers, Box 16, Folder 91. DATE: Pierce's letter to Darrow.

TO PAUL DARROW • NEW YORK CITY • SATURDAY 18 APRIL 1931

MURRAY HILL HOTEL April 18th

Dear Paul,

I shall be home the 12th or 13th of May. I have stayed so long partly on account of the pictures I have been doing while I stayed. Any how I thought I might as well do the Aaron Burr thing which takes three Sunday nights beginning April 26th at 10:15 N.Y. time.[61] Shall leave immediately after the May 10th one but am going to Birmingham and from there home. Shan't travel much more for a time. I don't like the looks of the stock market but it may come out. Handle it all just as you think best. Any thing I have can be used & if you think best to get out do that. I rather think I shall make some money out of what I am doing but not much will come before fall. Shall be glad to get back.

Love to all | C. S. D.

MS: ALS, MnU-L, Darrow Collection. DATE: "1931" appended.

TO CHARLES YALE HARRISON • NEW YORK CITY • MONDAY 20 APRIL 1931

MURRAY HILL HOTEL Apr. 20, 1931.

My dear Mr. Harrison:—

I am sorry to say that I must insist, so far as I can, on finishing my autobiography and giving it to a publisher and also negotiating for serial rights before yours comes out.[62]

When you first called to see me, a short time ago, I told you about what progress I had made in my work and that I did not want to have any one else do it until I had finished

60. Pierce believed that the membership of the league should be changed in order to replace members who were uninvolved, and she wanted Darrow, as president of the league, to appoint a committee to review potential nominees. Pierce to Darrow, 13 April 1931, TLc, MBNU, Sara Ehrmann Papers, Box 16, Folder 91.

61. On 26 April 1931, radio station NBC-WEAF broadcast the "trial" of Aaron Burr, with Darrow defending Burr and George Gordon Battle (1868–1949), a prominent lawyer in New York City, representing the opposition.

62. Harrison was working on a biography of Darrow, which was published—despite this letter—before Darrow's autobiography. See Charles Yale Harrison, *Clarence Darrow* (New York: Jonathan Cape & Harrison Smith, 1931).

mine. You told me that you had made up your mind to do it anyhow. I said I had seen your book, "Generals Die in Bed,"[63] and considered you an excellent writer and that I would rather see you do it than any one else that would be likely to take it up, and that I did not know how I could prevent any one from writing it, although I did not want it done, and I would rather give you the facts if you must do it than to put you to the trouble of looking them up and probably getting some things wrong. In that connection, we talked of your going to my childhood home. You also told me of your work in the New York Public Library.

Since then, some of my friends, including Mrs. Darrow, have insisted that I should publish mine at once; that mine should be the first one published, and I realize that they are right. I am very sorry for any disappointment that may result. You have generously consented to give up the book until I have a chance to publish mine, which I think will not be long. I write you so that you can explain to your publisher that you had talked with me about it, and that while I raised an objection, I did not perhaps sufficiently discourage you.

With all best wishes, | Very truly yours, | Clarence Darrow.

MS: TLS, NNC, Harrison Papers.

TO PAUL DARROW • NEW YORK CITY • WEDNESDAY 22 APRIL 1931

MURRAY HILL HOTEL April 22—3 PM

Dear Paul

It looks pretty bad for stocks: I don't see any need of writing for I don't know what to advise. I presume if we cleaned out every thing, Ruby & I together would have $125,000 and probably including your Greeley stuff and your apartment you would have $100,000. Perhaps not. If you sold half or perhaps a third of your holdings & some of mine at N. & J. we would have a lot of stocks with a chance for a fair comeback and we would be pretty well fixed. Still I hate to see you do it but perhaps it should be done. I would advise you if I knew what to say. Perhaps you had better take Sturgess[64] and Sydney Love[65] into your confidence and get their advice. If you want to I am sure that the Pres of first Natl would give you the best advice he can. I don't need to tell you that whatever you decide to do goes with me. Every one else seems to be broke and I don't see how we can be blamed for doing

63. Harrison's novel *Generals Die in Bed* (New York: Wm. Morrow, 1930), which is generally considered his finest book, is a realistic account of war told by a private in the Canadian army in World War I.

64. Solomon Sturges (1865–1940) was an associate for many years at the brokerage firm of David A. Noyes & Co. in Chicago, until he retired in 1938 and moved to California. Sturges was the adopted father of the screenplay writer and film director Preston Sturges (1898–1959).

65. Sidney Love (1872–1952) was once a wealthy stockbroker in Chicago. He lost his fortune through the market in 1909. Darrow later represented him in his divorce, which garnered a lot of attention in newspapers. See, e.g., "Love Quits after Market Mishaps," *New York Times,* 28 January 1909; "Wife Calls Love Now Unlovable," *Chicago Tribune,* 16 June 1911; "Name Mrs. Roy in Love Case," *New York Times,* 18 July 1911.

what all the rest have done. I think I am going to get rather a substantial amount of money in the fall, and perhaps a fairly good income will come along for a year or two but I never feel any certainty until it comes. I may be able to send about $2,000 next week and of course you can use what is in the bank, leaving not more than $1,000. Any how I think you should talk with Sturgess & Sydney Love who are both our friends, and *keep me posted.*

C.S.D.

MS: ALS, MnU-L, Darrow Collection. DATE: "1931" appended.

TO PAUL DARROW • NEW YORK CITY • WEDNESDAY 29 APRIL 1931

MURRAY HILL HOTEL April 29

Dear Paul

I don't know of any thing new to say. Every one is pretty blue and discouraged. It looks as if every one would be broke if it went much further. If you want to use any of those bonds of mine or all, that you have taken out from time to time, or any that I bought in stock, either do it. I don't know whether it is wise or not. I think it would surely stop before it is all gone but what it would be worth or is now worth I don't know. I don't see how any body could have foreseen all this, and of course no one did. I think if I had ready money I would buy but that might be wrong. All the publishers want my book which I shall finish when I get home. They all think it will be a good seller and that the serial rights will bring a good amount. I feel sure that I will make some money out of all these things very soon. I don't want you to get discouraged over things. I am inclined to think you can turn it to a good end. Shall be glad to get back home—which will be about May 13th. Leave here the 10th but go via Birmingham though Ruby will go straight back.

C.S.D.

MS: ALS, MnU-L, Darrow Collection. DATE: "1931" appended.

TO VIVIAN PIERCE • CHICAGO • SATURDAY 16 MAY 1931

CLARENCE DARROW May 16th

Dear Vivian

At your suggestion I am going to appoint the following nominating committee to nominate officers for our league: Dr. Miriam Van Watters, Louis E. Lawes; Doris Stevens; Arthur Garfield Hays, and Vivian Pierce. I also appoint Miss Mary Dubrow as active Treasurer.

I suggest that you put the wits of the Committee at work to find a new name for our League. I have got *so tired* writing that D—n name that I have sworn never to do it again. Cut out *American.* No one would look for that. I would call it Anti Capital Punishment League, even if someone else had the name. I don't think it would matter; if they tried to

stop us it would advertise the League—or call it Anti Killing League, or Life Saving League or anything else without more than three words or so—

Truly | Clarence Darrow

MS: ALS, MBNU, Sara Ehrmann Papers, Box 16, Folder 91. DATE: other letters regarding a nominating committee. INSIDE ADDRESS: Miss Vivian Pierce | Executive Secretary.

TO MARY DUBROW • CHICAGO • SUNDAY 14 JUNE 1931

CLARENCE DARROW June 14th

Miss Mary C. Dubrow
Dear Miss Dubrow

I just appointed you at Vivian's request to be treasurer of the League and you sit right down and ask me for money. This, in spite of the fact that I think I have done more for it by way of contributions and paying own expenses to speak for it in N.Y. Etc. than any of the rest (especially in view of the fact that I never have had any money worth talking about) except by some one like Vivian who never has enough to eat. Well, I feel that I don't owe the League anything—that it probably isn't doing any good—and can't do any good. The world is dead and the people are already damned, I with the rest, who can't help thinking of money. Still, you look like a good treasurer. I can't comply with your request now, but if you don't get anything by 15th of September write me again. I shall not make any pledge, but don't give me up.[66]

Best wishes to you and Vivian— | Clarence Darrow

MS: ALS, MBNU, Sara Ehrmann Papers, Box 16, Folder 91. DATE: appointment of Dubrow as treasurer and other correspondence.

TO GEORGE T. BYE • CHICAGO • MONDAY 15 JUNE 1931

CLARENCE DARROW June 15th

My Dear Buy

A day or two ago I sent you my prohibition story.[67] I think the Forum or Vanity Fair would like it. It seems to me that Vanity Fair would take "The Early worm." I am really a little disappointed at the failure to find publishers for the last two or three things. I am not

66. Pierce read this letter as confirmation that the organization had to find someone to replace Darrow as president of the organization: "As a matter of fact, there are members of the Board who contribute far more than [Darrow] does, but it is not tactful to tell him so. | This letter confirms me in the belief that Doris [Stevens] has: that we should get Dr. [Miriam] Van Waters to agree to take the Presidency of the League." Pierce to Dubrow, 17 June 1931, TLc, MBNU, Sara Ehrmann Papers, Box 16, Folder 91.

67. Darrow is probably referring to an article that was eventually published in *Vanity Fair*. See Clarence Darrow, "Why the 18th Amendment Cannot be Repealed," *Vanity Fair*, November 1931, 62–63, 84.

attributing any blame to you. Is it because they have had too much of my stuff. Is it that they think I am not popular with the readers? Is it that I don't know how to write? I suspect the latter, or perhaps all of the reasons. I of course have never had the training for writing. Any how I want you to consider where you offer things, although I told you I thought that Harpers would take the story. I don't want them peddled too much. If they don't like my stuff then they don't and you can't help it. I may be in N.Y. next week and if so of course I shall see you. I think the one on "Justice" you had better return. I should probably rewrite it. The idea is good but I presume it is too draggy.[68]

Your friend | Clarence Darrow.

MS: ALS, NNC, James O. Brown Papers. DATE: reference to articles that were eventually published.

TO VIVIAN PIERCE • CHICAGO • FRIDAY 26 JUNE 1931

CLARENCE DARROW June 26

Dear Vivian

I am sorry not to respond to your drive, but the truth is I am obliged to curtail all the expenses I can. The stock market smash did not help me, and of course I am not doing any more business—and don't want to. I am not broke but want to take care that I don't get dependent on anyone. I shall get the balance of that thousand out of the way (most likely).[69] If you go back this way come and stay with us.

With love, | Clarence Darrow

MS: ALS, MBNU, Sara Ehrmann Papers, Box 16, Folder 91. DATE: letterhead and reference to stock market crash makes 1931 likely.

TO LINCOLN STEFFENS • CHICAGO • MONDAY 13 JULY 1931

CLARENCE DARROW July 13

Dear Lincoln

I was slow in starting to read your book.[70] I had so many things taking my time in N.Y. that I couldn't do it until I got back to Chicago. However I did begin it soon after my return and went through it very rapidly. I am sure I did not miss a word. It is a remarkable piece of work and I am so glad that you wrote it. I have never read a braver, truer, more understanding book, and there isn't a dull place in it all. You have dodged nothing.

68. Darrow is probably referring to an article that was eventually published in *Scribner's Magazine*. See Clarence Darrow, "Who Knows Justice?" *Scribner's Magazine*, February 1932, 73–77.
69. After Darrow agreed to help John Winters in the Vermont Supreme Court, he pledged to send one thousand dollars to the American League to Abolish Capital Punishment to support the organization's effort to abolish capital punishment in Vermont.
70. Lincoln Steffens, *The Autobiography of Lincoln Steffens* (New York: Harcourt, Brace, 1931).

I know of no other book so true and brave and frank and I am delighted that you have done it. It is so new and true that it is hard to understand how it could be so well accepted by a world that knew nothing about your point of view. I wonder if it is too late for me to give it a review and if so if you can give me any idea where.[71] I want you to stop and see us on the way back. Please don't disappoint us. I am working quite steadily on my book. In a way yours has discouraged me but I shall not even try to do what you have done. I can't. I shall try to make mine honest and as fearless as I can bring myself to do it, and if it gets few readers I shall not be disappointed. Give my love to Fremont.[72] How I wish I could see you both.

Always your friend | Clarence Darrow

MS: ALS, NNC, Steffens Papers. DATE: letterhead and references to New York, Steffens's book, and Darrow's own book.

TO D. C. STEPHENSON • CHICAGO • TUESDAY 21 JULY 1931

CLARENCE DARROW July 21st, 1931

Dear Mr. Stephenson

Your letter duly received. Even if I wanted to help a newspaper, and there are some I would like to help, even if I wanted to, I could not for a moment consider anyone but you—otherwise, I could not have entered your case. A lawyer should forget his own interests in the service of his client and I am sure I have always done it. Of course, I want the paper to give you a fair show sometime but if that happens it can not be by playing favorites. It must be done openly. Of course, the first question is getting you out of your trouble.

I think I am justified in saying that I have been very much impressed with your straight forward way of talking and looking at life. It is quite unusual for one in your station. I don't want to over state anything but I feel that you have the right attitude toward life. There is no other way to play the game. People do not care for denials or explanations. All of them have plenty to explain themselves. I have had several very nice and intelligent letters about you which I will show you when I come which will probably be sometime this week. A man who cannot learn something by such an experience as you have had, could not be helped by anything.

With kind regards, | Clarence Darrow

MS: TT, In, Stephenson Papers.

71. In Steffens's response, he said that he would take up the question with his publisher of where Darrow might place a review: "As to the book and a review thereof—it is almost enough for me that you like it, and so explicitly. And you, Clarence, have about all you should do to get on with your own book. But I will take it up with Harcourt and see if he has a suggestion to offer for a publication to exploit a review by you." Steffens to Darrow, 21 July 1931, TLS, DLC-MSS, Darrow Papers. No review of Steffens's book by Darrow was located.
72. Fremont Older.

TO HARRY ELMER BARNES • CHICAGO • SATURDAY 1 AUGUST 1931

CLARENCE DARROW Aug. 1st

My Dear Barnes

I suppose you know that you and I are on the programme to debate with Rabbi Mann and Preston Bradley at Sinai Temple Nov 10th.[73] They are a fine pair of hot-air artists without any ideas, and we should have a good time of it. I have insisted that we have the last say.

I have been doing pretty steady work on my book (for me!). I will have the first draft finished this week,[74] so I am safer to die now for that matter. I am not at all sure about how good it will be, or how much of it can be called biography and how much propaganda. I have fully discussed my ideas on law, Courts, Crime, Religion, Heaven, God, Etc. Shall be interested in showing it to you. Most of it has been gone over twice. And I think once more will be about all I can do for it until I have some expert read it.[75]

I prefer that you should not say any thing about it—as I don't want to be troubled with publishers now. My plan is to see what I can do about serial rights this fall and winter and publish it for the spring trade, if there is any. The book will be about 150,000 words, which is words enough.

All good wishes, | Clarence Darrow

MS: ALS, WyU-AH, Barnes Collection. DATE: reference to debate and book.

TO JOSEPH ISHILL • CHICAGO • FRIDAY 7 AUGUST 1931

CLARENCE DARROW Aug 7th

My Dear Mr Ishill

Thank you very much for sending me Mr. Salt's volume of ~~poems~~ "verses and epigrams." It is a beautiful piece of printing and book making, of which you have the right to feel

73. Darrow and Barnes debated with Preston Bradley and Rabbi Louis I. Mann (1890–1966) at the Sinai Temple in Chicago on 19 October (not 10 November). The title of the debate was "Can the Church Meet the Needs of Our New Age?" "Sinai Temple Lecture Series Opens Tonight," *Chicago Tribune*, 19 October 1931. Rabbi Mann was the leader of the Chicago Sinai congregation from 1923 to 1962. Born in Kentucky, he had a B.A. from the University of Cincinnati and a Ph.D. in psychology from Yale. He was one of the founders of the National Conference of Christians and Jews (now called the National Conference for Community and Justice) in 1927. Among his many activities, he was a strong proponent for birth control, an opponent of what was known as companionate marriages, a promoter of the theory of evolution, and a believer (at least in the 1930s) in the forced sterilization of certain criminals.
74. Here, "–?–" is written in Ruby Darrow's hand.
75. Here, "in confidence" is written in Ruby Darrow's hand.

proud. Mr Salt's verses are very clever, as they always are. I have read them with pleasure; especially the one that concerns me![76]

With thanks and good Wishes | Clarence Darrow

MS: ALS, MH-H. DATE: publication of Salt's book.

TO DAVID H. CRAMER • CHICAGO • SEPTEMBER 1931

My Dear Mr. Cramer:

Thanks for your kind letter. I did not know that the big white church is so old. It came to Kinsman before I did, which was a long time ago.

I used to hear Rev. Eldred[77] preach, and I presume there are few people in the town now who were there so long ago. While I heard him preach, I cannot say I knew what he told us, or meant to, for I was fussing and fidgeting and wishing he would stop and let me go home.

Mr. Eldred pastured his cow in a field back of our place, and I remember meeting him as the sun was setting, one night. I was afraid of him, but he did not have on his Sunday clothes, and he talked to me like a human being, kindly and understandingly, without a word of religion, and so, boy-like, after that I thought of him as a different man.

The old church is associated with all my early life. I supposed that it was the biggest, most wonderful building in the world, and the bell, the largest one anywhere. Since then I have been to London and have seen and heard "Big Ben," the great clock in the tower of Westminster; at every hour, and even at the quarters and halves, by day and night, its musical tones roll out over the great city. Often have I heard it in the quiet of the night, thunder out its peals, telling the time, but it has never sent forth such a voice as the bell in the high steeple up in the big church on the hill in Kinsman.

I never think of Kinsman without the dim vision of the church floating through my mind. As a boy, I used to run past the graveyard that flanked two sides of that great building. I hurried by, fearing the dead would be awakened by my fleeting feet. An older brother, who died when I was a little child, lies in his grave in the old yard, and beside him sleeps my mother, whom we placed there one sad, endless day when I was about 14.

Strange it is about these old memories. Somehow, my thoughts are always roaming back to the old, peaceful, pretty village, and in its midst, towering over all the rest, I see the big white church keeping guard over the living and the dead.

76. Darrow is referring to Henry Salt's *Cvm Grano, Verses and Epigrams* (Berkeley Heights, NJ: Oriole Press, 1931), in which Salt published a poem about Darrow titled "Darrow and the Sinner": "Old preachers once, if heaven we hoped to win, / Bade us beware the Unpardonable Sin; / A threat that over-anxious minds would harrow, / Till wise Compassion found her spokesman, Darrow; / Darrow, so suave of speech, so nimble-witted, / His clients ever went their ways acquitted. / And now no needless fears our feelings rend; / For this we know: with Darrow to defend, / No court will be too harsh, no heart too hardened:—/ He'd get the Unpardonable Sinner pardoned!"

77. Henry B. Eldred.

With kind regard to you and the congregation,

Very truly yours, | Clarence Darrow.

MS: clipping from unidentified Ohio newspaper titled "Clarence Darrow Native Son of Kinsman Writes Tenderly of Church of His Childhood." PLACE: no reason to doubt Chicago. DATE: dated material on back of newspaper clipping.

TO ARTHUR SPINGARN • CHICAGO • FRIDAY 25 SEPTEMBER 1931

CLARENCE DARROW Sept. 25th.

Dear Arthur

I have been making you a lot of trouble, but I am anxious to fix up that matter with Liveright Co. if I can. In spite of what they told you they did not advertise Farmington according to the agreement.[78]

They searched their files while Arthur Hays was present and to their seeming surprise found nothing except one ad. in the Chicago News. The option on publishing reminiscences was made six years ago in connection with Farmington and they have spent neither time nor money on the book. If you or I had been employed as lawyers and our client had changed his mind and wanted some one else I am sure we would tell him to go in peace which is what they should do here. It is absurd that they should try to hold me when I do not want to stay. I dislike trouble about anything but I want to be left free in this matter. I have made no bargain with any one—nor is the book finished but I would like to try to do it. The stock market has left me with very little but I will raise One Thousand dollars if they will cancel the contract. I shall harbor no feeling about this matter, but I trust that they will see the justice of the matter. Please let me know as soon as possible—I want to get through with it.

With best Wishes | Clarence Darrow

MS: ALS, private collection of Kevin Tierney. DATE: "[1931]" appended.

TO FREDERICK STARR • CHICAGO • TUESDAY 29 SEPTEMBER 1931

CLARENCE DARROW Sept. 29th

My Dear Dr. Starr,

I think I remember Connelly's letter. If I am right he had a weird and extravagant claim for damages. I felt sure that his mind was affected.[79] I get so many of these from all over the country that I can spot them quite easily, and the trouble is there is nothing can be

78. Darrow is referring to Horace Liveright's publishing firm, which published an edition of his *Farmington* in 1925.
79. The identity of "Connelly" is unknown.

done for them. Of course if he was all right I could not go to Washington to start a damage case; they need endless time, and I would be dead before the litigation was over. Generally I do not answer these letters as I get *so many* that I haven't the time or strength. I am sorry for the poor fellow, but one letter only brings an other if my diagnosis is correct.

Your Liberia address was excellent.[80] What horrible people our Americans have come to be! They have been terribly chastined but this doesn't seem to effect them. *I hope* we *shall be here* in March. There is no one we would rather see. All good wishes from both of us.

Your friend | Clarence Darrow

MS: ALS, location of original unknown (copy in editor's files). DATE: letterhead and reference to address on Liberia. NOTE: "Oct.5" is appended in the upper right corner and, in Ruby Darrow's hand, at the bottom of the letter is written "Greetings from Ruby D.—to your sister. Our house phone is:—Hyde Park—5657—."

TO WALTER WHITE • CHICAGO • THURSDAY 31 DECEMBER 1931

CLARENCE DARROW December 31, 1931.

Dear Walter White:—

I left Birmingham on Tuesday noon, after putting an evening and part of next day with the Communist bunch.[81] Arthur was the originator of the idea that we might take Chamlee[82] in with us if the Communist bunch would get out. I thought it was a good idea. Of course the Communists are interested in propaganda only. You know of their getting the boys to sign a wire to me that they did not want me unless I would leave the

80. Darrow is probably referring to an address on Liberia delivered by Starr at the University of Oregon in July 1931 entitled "The Crisis in Liberia." In this address, Starr reviewed the harmful effects of the rubber plantation established in Liberia in 1926 by the Firestone Tire and Rubber Company. He also criticized the recent demands of the United States State Department and League of Nations on the government of Liberia, seeking far-reaching reforms that Starr believed would result in the destruction of Liberia's government. Starr's address was published in *Unity* on 17 August 1931.

81. Darrow is referring to his involvement in the Scottsboro cases. In late March 1931, nine black youths, ranging from twelve to nineteen years of age, all poor and generally illiterate, were accused of raping two white women in a railroad freight car traveling through Alabama. In early April 1931, the accused—represented by inept lawyers in a tense and hostile courtroom atmosphere—were convicted and all but the youngest were sentenced to death after brief trials in Scottsboro, Alabama. In September 1931, Darrow (and later, Arthur Garfield Hays) was retained by the National Association for the Advancement of Colored People to represent the defendants in their appeal to the Alabama Supreme Court. The NAACP was competing, in effect, for the right to represent the defendants with the International Labor Defense, a legal arm of the Communist Party in the United States. See Dan T. Carter, *Scottsboro: A Tragedy of the American South,* rev. ed. (Baton Rouge: Louisiana State University Press, 1979), 97–103.

82. George W. Chamlee (1872–1958), lawyer. Chamlee graduated from Mercer College, 1891, and opened a law office in Chattanooga, Tennessee in 1893, with three of his brothers. He was city attorney for Chattanooga, 1902–08, and later elected district attorney for Hamilton County, Tennessee, 1918–29. He was the most prominent of the ILD-sponsored lawyers representing the defendants in the Scottsboro cases, and he was not affiliated with the Communist Party.

N.A.A.C.P. and come in with them. I told them at once that under no circumstances would I work in this case with them, and neither would fight for a case. If they wanted to undertake the case, so long as the boys had sent me the wire, I would be glad to be relieved, and they could go on with the case. With this Arthur agreed.

They don't want to take the responsibility. But they got in touch with the New York office, and consulted during the night, and the next morning, at which time I left. I have word from Arthur that he gave it up, too, and went to Mexico. However, I still think they will be afraid to go on. As it is, I don't see how any of us can fight to get in. It is a very dangerous case, and it seems as though we can hardly afford to take the responsibility in the face of the telegram from the boys.

Will keep you posted, and if you hear anything let me know. Anyhow, it was nice to have the meeting in Birmingham.

With all good wishes,

Your friend, | (Signed) Clarence Darrow

MS: TT, CtY-BR, Walter Francis White and Poppy Cannon Papers, Box 2, Folder 46.

TO LEWIS E. LAWES • CHICAGO • SATURDAY 16 JANUARY 1932

CLARENCE DARROW Jan. 16th.

My Dear Warden Lawes—

You may have seen that I am publishing what I call an Autobiography. Any how, to make it interesting, and instructing, I have quoted about a page from your excellent book "Life and Death in Sing Sing." This is in the chapter on Capital Punishment. You might like to read again what you said. I did not write to you about it because I was afraid you would object, but I want to get your stuff a wider circulation, and then it will help me to have the public know that I know you. It is a sign of social standing to be a friend of a warden, but any how you won't need to buy my book to read what you said because the publishers have been instructed to send you a copy; So that you can find what you said without reading a lot of things that I said *on my own* you will find yours on pages 373–4.

With kindest wishes to your family, and a long and happy life to you and all your guests! I am as always

Your friend | Clarence Darrow.

Whenever I make any statement about crime I always refer to you for corroboration of my statement. I trust you will always come through.

D.

MS: ALS, NNJJ, Lawes Papers, Box 4 (correspondence scrapbook). DATE: reference to Darrow's autobiography.

TO RALPH JOHNSON • CHICAGO • SATURDAY 30 JANUARY 1932

CLARENCE DARROW January 30-th, 1932.—

My Dear Mr. Johnson;—

After receiving your wire in Topeka, I did not have a chance to answer it until I reached Chicago. I appreciated your kind invitation, but it was not possible to accept it at that time.[83]

My local residence in McPherson did not exceed four hours, but I remember the town now in spite of the fact that it was 54 years ago. I was looking for a place that seemed promising for opening a law-shop. I stopped a few days at Newton with old friends and drove one day from Newton to McPherson, about fifty miles, I should judge. I looked the town over, and thought it was all right; so I rented an office, but did not take possession; when I got back to Newton, I decided to go on to Denver, so I never did go back to take that office. I don't know whether they have held it for me all these years, but I have been a little afraid to go back for fear I would be sued for the back rent.

You see, however, what a narrow escape McPherson had from getting me fastened onto its population, and it was best, for Kansas has had a hard time as it is. During all these years I have thought I would sometime see McPherson again, but somehow never found the chance. I am going to be in Kansas City some time in early March, and I might go over there then, if it is not too far, and I can spare the time, and you really want to see what I look like.

Anyhow, with thanks and good wishes,

Very truly, | Clarence Darrow

MS: TLS (copy), DLC-MSS, Darrow Papers. INSIDE ADDRESS: Mr. Ralph Johnson;— | McPherson, Kansas.—.

TO FRANK WALSH • CHICAGO • WEDNESDAY 10 FEBRUARY 1932

CLARENCE DARROW Feby. 10th

Dear Frank

I have been asked to review the Mooney case over the telephone.[84] I should like to do this. They have promised a Nation wide "hook up." If you think well of it won't you send me some literature, *not too much,* and dictate a letter covering the high spots, especially the people who were in some way connected with the prosecution who have petitioned to have Mooney released, and the grounds for it. Also, the names of those who have confessed that they prejured themselves, and how important was their testimony? Anything you think worth while will help. I hate to burden you too much, but it might help.[85]

83. Johnson reportedly had written to Darrow asking him to come speak in McPherson. See *The McPherson (Kansas) Sentinel,* 6 September 1974.
84. Walsh was Thomas J. Mooney's principal attorney from 1923 to 1939.
85. These efforts to persuade California governor James Rolph (1869–1934) to pardon Mooney were unsuccessful. On 21 April 1932, the governor denied Mooney's application for a pardon, saying he was convinced of Mooney's guilt. Richard H. Frost, *The Mooney Case* (Stanford: Stanford University Press, 1968), 409.

I think of you often and admire & love you as much as ever. I do wish I saw you oftener. I am wondering how much time you give to political matters. It seems to me as if Roosevelt is the most available democrat in sights, and still from all sources I am told that he really lacks "guts"—but of course most men do. The interests are conspiring to beat him, which commends him. I hope you will be an important man with him. If he is elected he will need some men close to him who can not be fooled.

Always with admiration and devotion

Your friend | Clarence Darrow.

MS: ALS, NN, Walsh Papers, Box 19. DATE: placement in Walsh Papers.

TO JULIA PORTER • CHICAGO • WEDNESDAY 17 FEBRUARY 1932

CLARENCE DARROW Feby 17th.

My Dear Mrs. Porter

I am sending you a book by express for the Kinsman *"free"* public library. Don't you think they could afford to *buy* another Farmington. I don't think anyone else who ever lived in Kinsman ever wrote about the town but me. I doubt if any one could. And then, there are a number of people in the town who have more money than I. This might not have been true three years ago, but it is now. But any how I have a warm feeling toward Kinsman and no animosities against anyone who lives there or ever did. I knew all of your husband's family; I don't know whether I knew yours or not, for girls loose their names, if not their identity, and you are now a Mrs. You must be very careful to whom you loan this new book. No one under sixty should be permitted to read it, for while it is very religious in spots, in fact all-through, it is not orthodox in anything—and I know Kinsman: I can hear the old Presbyterian bell ring now as I write this letter and expect to hear it amongst the last sounds that ever reach my ears. Your husband and family came from Champion. I only remembered the town for two things, your husband's family and the poor house. I used to think that someday I would go there to live and am beginning to think so again. I really should not have the least feeling about the town not *buying* my books. I ought to be pleased that any of the people would read them. I never thought they would. Perhaps in another hundred years they will have a crayon portrait of me hanging in the public library. Then if I should see it, which I will not, I shall think how lucky I was that it was the portrait instead of I that was hanging there. But again I want to say that I have nothing against Kinsman. I like the town, and the memories of those that I once knew always bring a sad and kindly feeling. And I can never write of the town (as I do in the book) without rambling on—and on as I am doing now

With kind regard to you and your husband—if he is living—

Clarence Darrow[86]

86. In Porter's reply to Darrow's letter, she told Darrow of her family (she was raised in nearby Burghill, Ohio), and she recalled memories of people whom they knew in common, including Darrow's first wife's family

MS: ALS, OKIN. DATE: "(1932)" appended and confirmed by Porter's reply.

TO CHARLES ERSKINE SCOTT WOOD • CHICAGO • THURSDAY 18 FEBRUARY 1932

CLARENCE DARROW Feby. 18

My dear Mr. Wood

Was glad to hear from you as I always am. I am enclosing a statement for the paper. The trouble with these fellows is that they think only of the cause. The lives of twelve boys or any regard for the truth.[87] They may be right but no lawyer can accept this doctrine. The client of course comes first. All they cared for me was to exploit me for the sacred cause. I am getting rather old and very lazy. Doing little excepting having a bout with a preacher or Rabbi now and then. How they do like to cling to illusions. I wonder if they really fool themselves. All good wishes to you and Sarah.

Your friend | Clarence Darrow

MS: ALS, CSmH, Wood Papers, WD Box 126 (49). DATE: reference to the Scottsboro case.

TO ELMER GERTZ • CHICAGO • THURSDAY 18 FEBRUARY 1932

CLARENCE DARROW Feby. 18th (1932)

Dear Mr. Gertz:

I did not receive the copy of your book on Harris.[88] If by any chance one was sent me I must have overlooked it, and it has been scrambled in with many others. I would not want to speak at a memorial for Harris or to help raise funds.[89] In fact, I never admired him. I always felt that he was unreliable, untruthful and not honest. He was likewise an egotist to the point of paranoia.

I don't like the book about Shaw.[90] The only thing I could say for him is that he was brilliant but this is not a virtue unless coupled with other things. I don't believe he

---

(the Ohls) and Hubert Darrow and Herman Darrow (Darrow's brothers). She told Darrow that she believed he would find a broader, more tolerant, and kindlier class of people in Kinsman today than when he had lived there. Porter to Darrow, TLS, MBU, Leo Cherne Papers, Box 3, Folder 10.

87. Darrow probably intended to write this sentence as "*Not* the lives of twelve boys . . ." He is likely referring to the Scottsboro cases, although only nine youths were involved in Scottsboro. See Darrow to White, 31 December 1931, n.81.

88. Elmer Gertz and A. I. Tobin, *Frank Harris: A Study in Black and White* (Chicago: Madelaine Mendelsohn, 1931).

89. Harris died in August 1931 and Gertz, who had been his lawyer, was planning a memorial meeting in Harris's honor. See Elmer Gertz, "Clarence Darrow: An American Legend," *Progressive*, May 1957, 12, 13.

90. Harris's last book was a biography of Bernard Shaw (*Bernard Shaw* [New York: Simon & Schuster, 1931]).

will be remembered long. I may be very wrong in my estimate but this is the way I sized him up.

Very truly, | /s/Clarence Darrow

MS: TT, DLC-MSS, Gertz Papers.

TO HARRY ELMER BARNES • CHICAGO • SATURDAY 5 MARCH 1932

CLARENCE DARROW March 5th.

My dear Barnes

Before receiving your letter I had gone over the subject fully and already within that I felt that I could not go into the case and gave my reasons for it. I knew practically nothing about it except that such a case was to be tried in Honolulu, and I really wanted to go.[91] Without expressing any opinion on the matter I learned that one who tried, the [x] could scarcely avoid discussing race conflict in the trial of the case. I had so long and decidedly been for the Negro and all so-called "foreigners" that I could not put myself in a position where I might be compelled to take a position, even in a case at variance with what I felt and had stood for. In the mean time I had got all the "news papers" that I could and knew how the case would inevitably line up. The defendants are entitled to counsel who could not be handicapped by his opinions and former statements and I felt that I might handicap them by former trials and opinions. So, I shall not be in the case and have so written them. They will have the letter in their hands by the time this is written. Won't you please keep this confidential, as it will no doubt be known before you receive this, and I do not want to seem to express any views that could possibly effect the defendants.

I want you to know how thoroughly I appreciate your friendship and devotion.

Always your friend— | Clarence Darrow

MS: ALS, WyU-AH, Barnes Collection. DATE: reference to Massie case.

91. Darrow is referring to the Massie case—a case rife with racial implications, which concerned both Darrow and Barnes. In September 1931, Thalia Massie (1911–63), the wife of Thomas Massie (1904–87), a lieutenant in the United States Navy stationed at Pearl Harbor in Hawaii, and daughter of a prominent mainland family, told police in Honolulu that she had been beaten and raped by five dark-skinned Hawaiians. Her accusation led to the arrest and indictment of five men (two Hawaiians, two Japanese, and one Hawaiian-Chinese) whose trial ended in a mistrial in December 1931, when the jury was unable to reach a verdict. The accused men were released on bail pending retrial. One morning in January 1932, police officers in Honolulu stopped a speeding automobile occupied by Thomas Massie, an enlisted man, and Thalia Massie's mother. In the automobile with these three was the dead body of one of the accused men. The three occupants of the automobile and another enlisted man were indicted on 26 January 1932 for murder in the second degree, and they wanted Darrow to defend them.

TO HARRY ELMER BARNES • CHICAGO • SATURDAY 12 MARCH 1932

CLARENCE DARROW March 12-th, 1932—

My Dear Barnes:—

Thank you for being interested in me and my best welfare, as well as those that I have so long and so honestly championed, and ever intend to, you may be sure. Nothing is ever going to change that in me.

As I told you, at the time I agreed to go to Honolulu I had not thought of a race issue. As soon as it began to suggest itself and the question was brought up I at once wrote to the parties concerned relating my attitude on this point and sent my argument in the Detroit Sweet trial.[92] I told them that I could not [x] from the position I have taken so long and that I thought it would be better for them to employ someone else.[93]

After a day or two they wrote me that they thought I was right in my position on the race question, and they wanted that attitude maintained in court, and all would be as I wished. Which left nothing for me to do but go. I should hate to hurt your feelings and faith and to disappoint you, as you know. However, I feel that had I known about it at the start there would have been no impropriety in my taking the case, assuming that I stick by my convictions in the trial of the case, which I shall do; of course I have occasionally in the past represented people of wealth, and there have always been criticisms when I have done this; especially was this true in the Loeb-Leopold case. I don't know what I should have done if now and then a fairly well-to-do client had not come my way; the ravens have never called on me. Still,—I am sorry that the matter came along. I am especially sorry that it pains you, as you know that my affection for you is genuine and deep. I want you to watch the case and see if you can criticise anything I do in the matter. And I do want you to keep your faith in me.[94]

Always your friend, | Clarence Darrow

MS: TLS, WyU-AH, Barnes Collection. INSIDE ADDRESS: Mr. Harry Elmer Barnes— | Scripps-Howard Co.— | 230 Park Ave., New York City.

92. Clarence Darrow, *Argument of Clarence Darrow in the Case of Henry Sweet* (New York: National Association for the Advancement of Colored People, 1927).
93. The bracketed "x" in this sentence is not an illegible word; there is a half-inch of blank space on the line between the typewritten words "not" and "from."
94. On 29 April 1932, the jury in the Massie case returned a verdict of manslaughter for each defendant, with a recommendation for leniency. On 4 May 1932, the trial judge sentenced each of the defendants to ten years in prison and their sentences were immediately commuted to one hour by the territorial governor, Lawrence M. Judd (1887–1968), under pressure from the federal government.

TO BOLTON HALL • CHICAGO • MONDAY 16 MAY 1932

CLARENCE DARROW May 16

My Dear Hall

So glad to hear from you. Yes, I have known Swift[95] for many years. He is intelligent and a fine fellow. I will send for his book. He is a very good thinker but a bit woozy. However he is a good student and interesting.

It was good to hear from you again. I read a book of fables of yours years ago and have read several others from time to time.[96] They are always good and I enjoy them. I always expect to see you when I go to New York but seldom do. When I get there I am overwhelmed by all sorts of people, and finally come back to Chicago to rest. Of course I have known you from the days of Henry George, when I always mentioned and thought of you and Crosby together.[97] I am running a race with you to see who will stay on the fool Earth the longest. Any how I will try to see you the next time I am in N.Y.

Your friend | Clarence Darrow.

MS: ALS, NN, Hall Papers, Box 4. DATE: uncertain; letterhead makes 1932 likely. INSIDE ADDRESS: Mr Bolton Hall.

TO GRAHAM TAYLOR • CHICAGO • MONDAY 16 MAY 1932

CLARENCE DARROW May 16th

Dr. Graham Taylor

It was good of you to write me as you did about the case of Russell McWilliams.[98] The powers seemed bent on taking his life. I just can't understand them. I am much alarmed for fear they will cut down what we have so far made the limit of taking life which is still eighteen. I am sure it will take the effort of all of us to keep back the tide of hatred that

95. Darrow may not have written "Swift"; his handwriting is difficult to read. If he did mean "Swift," he might be referring to Isaac Morrison Swift. Darrow had known him for more than forty years.
96. The book of fables to which Darrow is probably referring is Hall's *The Game of Life* (New York: A. Wessels, 1902), a collection of short parables on labor, religion, politics, and other subjects.
97. Hall and Ernest Howard Crosby were both advocates of the single-tax ideas of Henry George. They often worked on reform activities together, including cofounding the anti-imperialist American League of New York City in 1899.
98. Russell McWilliams (1914–1997) shot and killed a streetcar conductor during a robbery in Rockford, Illinois, in August 1931. He had just turned seventeen. Darrow began representing him after he pleaded guilty and was sentenced to death. In his first appeal, the Supreme Court of Illinois, in April 1932, remanded the matter for further proceedings because the trial court judge had not heard and (to some extent) had not allowed evidence of McWilliams's character, background, habits, etc., before sentencing him to death. See *People v. McWilliams*, 348 Ill. 333, 180 N.E. 832 (1932). On remand, McWilliams was sentenced to death again. In his second appeal, decided in December 1932, the court remanded the matter for a change of venue. See *People v. McWilliams*, 350 Ill. 628, 183 N.E. 582 (1932). On remand, before a different judge, McWilliams was sentenced to death a third time, in February 1933. Finally, in April 1933, Henry Horner (1879–1940), democratic governor of Illinois, 1933–40, acting on the recommendation of the state pardon board, commuted McWilliams's sentence to ninety-nine years in prison. McWilliams was paroled in 1950.

seems to be overwhelming us. Any how I hope you will long be spared to carry on your good work.

With good wishes always | Clarence Darrow.

MS: ALS, ICN, Taylor Papers, Box 7, Folder 148. DATE: reference to McWilliams case.

TO MIRIAM VAN WATERS • CHICAGO • SATURDAY 28 MAY 1932

CLARENCE DARROW May 28-th, 1932—

My Dear Miriam Van Waters;—

Thanks for the kind words about my book. I believe it is honest, but I presume no one can judge his own. Sometimes I wonder if it may possibly be that I am crazy and all the rest are sane; of course a word like this from you helps me to feel surer that I am right and the rest wrong.

I argued the McWilliams case in the Supreme Court and got the reversal of the case. Still, the judge who sentenced him before seems bound to hold that the plea of guilty shall stand and that he will re-sentence. I am afraid that nothing can be done before the trial judge, but I shall get it before the Supreme Court once more, and if we fail there we must go after the Governor. I think you can help in this. I don't think they can execute him until another election passes,—and both candidates for Governor are friends of mine; one of them, at least, is a crook, and therefore human; the other is rather close to me. We may need you then.

I have never seen the boy, and don't like to. Just now he has got religion, but I am informed that he relies more on me than he does on Jesus,—but probably he needs us both.

Somehow, I can't get my mind away from that young woman in Arizona. She is plainly insane, and whatever one may think it is decidedly more cruel to put a woman to death than a man.[99] The Governor of Arizona is a fine, liberal fellow.[100] I wonder if anything can be done?—but I am not equal to any such undertaking, and must not be urged into it.

With most friendly regards from Mrs. Darrow and myself,

Sincerely yours, | Clarence Darrow

MS: TLS, MCR-S, Van Waters Papers, Box 49, Folder 610.

99. Winnie Ruth Judd (1905–98) was convicted of murder and sentenced to death in February 1932 in Phoenix, Arizona. She had been charged with the murder of two young female friends whose bodies were found in Judd's luggage trunks. One of the victims had been dismembered to fit in the trunk. Judd's case received nationwide attention. In April 1933, shortly before her scheduled execution, the warden of the state prison petitioned the court to determine Judd's sanity, and a jury found that she was insane. She was committed to the state hospital for the insane, where she remained for the next nearly forty years (except for several periods during which she escaped). See Jana Bommersbach, *The Trunk Murderess: Winnie Ruth Judd* (New York: Simon & Schuster, 1992).

100. George W. P. Hunt (1859–1934), Democratic governor of Arizona. Hunt served seven two-year terms as governor, 1912–19, 1923–29, 1931–33. Before becoming governor, he was (at various times) a rancher, businessman, mayor, and member of the Arizona territorial legislature.

TO VIVIAN PIERCE • CHICAGO • SATURDAY 25 JUNE 1932

CLARENCE DARROW June 25-th, 1932.—

Dear Miss Pierce:—

Yours received, but don't see how can do anything about the Judd case. Even if wanted to, am not at all well, and am as broke as the rest of the old world, and so is everybody else, I guess. I have no "wealthy friends" that I know of; if I did I'd probably be selfish, like most of mankind, and try to get them to help me first. Anyhow, it's too bad about the poor parents, and I'd like to make it easier for them if I knew how, but I don't.

I know of no one who has received any "Fees" in the McWilliams case,—nor expecting to,—though Miss Binford[101] may be somehow using money for some of expenses. You might explain it to me if you want to. I don't see why you should try to send any more money. We do not expect that the McWilliams boy will ever be executed; we are very sure that he will not be.

Sorry that we all are so helpless about doing anything for you there, but personally am doing more than should have to, but cannot escape it,—and cannot undertake anything more.

Best wishes for better luck sometime.

As ever your friend, | Clarence Darrow.

MS: ALS, MBNU, Sara Ehrmann Papers, Box 16, Folder 91.

TO VIVIAN PIERCE • CHICAGO • SUNDAY 3 JULY 1932

CLARENCE DARROW July 3rd.

Dear Vivian

I did not know that you had left the league until I received your letter. I am glad and sorry. I am sure you can do better, but I know how deeply interested you are in the league. It is almost impossible to get money these days. Everyone is broke and their courage is gone.[102]

As to the case of the boy in Illinois, I have been to Springfield twice and paid my own expenses and shall do this same thing at least once more.[103] I suppose the money has been mostly used in getting the record and printing the brief. Still, I think it should be raised here. As to Miss Binford, she is a very fine, devoted person. She has some position in the juvenile court, but is far ahead of the people she works with, and could probably

101. Jessie Florence Binford.
102. Pierce had intended to resign from her position as director of the American League to Abolish Capital Punishment two years before this letter because she was "worn out with the growing responsibility" and thought "a new office group and new or additional board members would be a good thing." Pierce to Darrow, 26 August 1930, TLc, MBNU, Sara Ehrmann Papers, Box 16, Folder 91. She apparently had a change of heart both then and in 1932, because she remained in her position.
103. Darrow is referring to Russell McWilliams's case.

get no money from any of them. Miss Binford has no money. She undertook it in connection with Miss Lathrop[104] who was connected with welfare work with the National Government. Miss Lathrop had money and used some to help in this case but she died a few weeks ago. If you are asked for any more you had better refer them to me. I hope things will go well with you, now you are on your own.

With good wishes always— | Your friend | Clarence Darrow.

MS: ALS, MBNU, Sara Ehrmann Papers, Box 16, Folder 91. DATE: reference to McWilliams case and death of Lathrop.

TO CARL ERIC LINDEN • CHICAGO • MONDAY 4 JULY 1932

CLARENCE DARROW July 4th

Dear Carl—

It is a pure accident that I should be writing you on this "glorious" day. The anniversary of the date that made us "*free.*" However, it was good to get your fine letter. I am so glad that you liked the book. If you hadn't I don't know who would have stood for it. Often we think of you and talk about you. I do wish we could see you once in a while. Have you left the Catskills? If not I might stop off some time on the way to N.Y. Why don't you try an autobiography. You can write much better than I, and have much to tell, and it is really some town to put into a book. Of course you know that I don't really think that I can change the world. I have been fighting like Hell to keep the world from changing me. You realize what a job that is. I think I shall now pull through and go down into the grave defiant and unrepentant. It seems as if that is something in a world where they turn out human beings with all similarity and perfection of Hart Schafner & Marks clothes. Of course I know why I haven't conformed. It is because it would have made me miserable to do as others do—and think as others think—if they think. Will you be this way sometime, or where will you be this summer & fall?

With all good wishes from Mrs Darrow and me—

Your friend | Clarence Darrow

MS: ALS, location of original unknown (copy in editor's files). DATE: letterhead and reference to book (i.e., Darrow's autobiography).

104. Julia Lathrop (1858–1932), social worker. Born in Rockford, Illinois, Lathrop attended Rockford Female Seminary, 1876–77, and then graduated from Vassar College, 1880, after which she worked in her father's law office in Rockford. In 1890, she moved to Hull House to work with Jane Addams. In 1892, she was appointed by the governor to the State Board of Charities, in which capacity she was responsible for many reform efforts. In 1899, she helped establish a juvenile court in Chicago, the first of its kind in the United States. In 1912, President William Howard Taft appointed her chief of the Children's Bureau in the Department of Commerce and Labor, a position she held until 1921. In the remaining years of her life, she continued her reform efforts, including as a member of the Child Welfare Committee for the League of Nations.

TO "MY DEAR PATTERSON" • CHICAGO • SATURDAY 9 JULY 1932

CLARENCE DARROW July 9

My Dear Patterson

Was glad to get your letter after so many years. I often think of you and wonder if you are not coming this way again, especially about the time of the "stock yards" show. I can find no one who seems to know anything about the difficulty between Al Smith and Roosevelt. I would guess it was simply because Al thought a Democrat could be elected and so he wanted to run. This was, of course, encouraged by big business that seems to control Al. He was all right when he came from Fulton St. Fish Market but Roosevelt and the rest of the moneybags are too much for him.[105]

I have no information as to Harding's death. This story of Gaston Means doesn't seem reasonable and it comes from a rotten source, but all the bunch were rotten. No doubt they knew that exposure was close by.[106] As to the farmer, I know of nothing that can help him, but giving him a chance to buy where he sells. He always was an Ass, which is shown by the Republicans gratuitously insulting him by giving him about 40¢ protection a bushel on wheat. I would guess, however, that the troubles of the world are deeper than tariff. Men are competing against machines. Nothing except something like Socialism can ever materially help the great mass of men.

I think Roosevelt is quite a fellow, he seems to read and study. Perhaps he is a little wishy washy, but he is really a radical and the good people say his wife is a "red". It looks as if the pious sham of prohibition is on its way to the Guilotine. No doubt I shall get out on the hustings after awhile. I think I can stand one more campaign. Hoover must be beaten, no matter what happens. The U.S. has had many afflictions but none like this *package* that the English handed us. I don't blame the English, either. Let me know a little ahead of time when you come I shall be glad to see you. I don't go down town much. I live at 1537 E 60th St Telephone Hyde Park 5657. Take Ill. Central to 59th

105. The Democratic Party had recently held its national convention in Chicago and nominated Roosevelt over Smith on the fourth ballot.

106. President Harding's death in 1923 was probably caused by a heart attack or a cerebral hemorrhage. But widespread and persistent rumors followed his death, claiming that he had not died by natural causes. These included rumors that Harding's wife, Florence Harding (1860–1924), had murdered him with poison. Gaston Means (1879–1938) contributed to these rumors with the publication in March 1930 of his as-told-to book, titled *The Strange Death of President Harding* (New York: Guild Pub., 1930). Means had worked for William J. Burns's detective agency and was also employed briefly during Harding's presidency as an agent under Burns in the Justice Department's Bureau of Investigation, until Harry M. Daugherty fired him. Means had a lifelong history of criminal conduct. One historian has described him as "an out-and-out scoundrel, in almost any way one might have imagined." Robert H. Ferrell, *The Strange Deaths of President Harding* (Columbia: University of Missouri Press, 1996), 40. Means's book on Harding claimed that Florence Harding had hired him to investigate her husband's adulterous connections with Nan Britton (1896–1995), and that Florence Harding murdered the president with poison sometime after Means reported the results of his investigation to her. Ibid., 30–49.

St and you are within a block and a half of my house.[107] Remember me kindly to Mrs Patterson.

Your friend | Clarence Darrow

MS: ALS, location of original unknown (copy in editor's files). DATE: reference to the election.

TO LEWIS E. LAWES • CHICAGO • SATURDAY 23 JULY 1932

CLARENCE DARROW July 23

My Dear Lawes

I finally got to your book—and what a book![108] I stayed with it all night and finished it after dawn. If people would only *feel,* but damn them—they only hate! I hope you will have a good sale—but you won't. They don't want to know—: That is the trouble about helping. Human beings are cold and grasping and cruel. We could influence other animals much easier.

I haven't been to N.Y. for some time. I am broke, about like the rest, and not throwing away money. When I go again I will try to see you.

With best wishes to you and love to the rest of the *family.*

Your friend | Clarence Darrow.

MS: ALS, NNJJ, Lawes Papers, Box 4 (correspondence scrapbook). DATE: "(1932)" is appended and at the bottom of the page is written: "(answered July 29–1932 | see General File)."

TO CHARLES MANTINBAND • CHICAGO • TUESDAY 23 AUGUST 1932

CLARENCE DARROW Aug 23rd

My Dear Rabbi—

Of course I remember you and your organization and many of its members.[109] I remember that I felt as if I wanted to stay there and take your place—I have wondered (?) why I never got an other "call." I didn't tell near all that I knew. I would have written you on my own hook, but I couldn't remember the name. How could I? It is a hell of a name! Still, while I forgot your name I didn't forget you. I broke, at least, one of my rules, in your town, I went to hear you preach.

107. Here, in the margin, in Ruby Darrow's hand, is written: "write first | am away good deal."
108. Lewis E. Lawes, *Twenty Thousand Years in Sing Sing* (New York: R. Long & R. R. Smith, 1932) (largely devoted to describing Lawes's experiences as warden of Sing Sing prison).
109. Darrow might be referring to his visit to Williamsport, Pennsylvania, four years earlier, during which he gave a public lecture on crime.

Well out I will come—not for charity, except to myself.[110] *I can't afford it.* I will take a chance with you on the meeting or fix a price. About how many does your temple seat, and what do you think should be the admission? and how should we divide? I could tell you right off what I would charge, except that people are so broke. I will send you a book as soon as I get some, which won't be long. If I sent it now, and you read it, you wouldn't debate with me. About what time would you want it? Give me a week or two leeway so I can arrange something else somewhere near it. Remember me to such members of the congregation who *ask about* me,—if any.

Very truly | Clarence Darrow—

MS: ALS, OCAJA, Mantinband Collection, Folder SC-7729. INSIDE ADDRESS: Rabbi Chas. Mantinband—. DATE: "1933?" is appended but 1932 is more likely given the date of the debate.

TO E. M. HOUSE • CHICAGO • WEDNESDAY 24 AUGUST 1932

CLARENCE S. DARROW August 24th

My Dear Mr. House

I wonder if it has come to Mr. Roosevelt's ears that many Catholic Priests sent letters to all sort of their parishioners that Mr. R. had joined the "Klan" in Georgia. This packed the galleries with the Irish and others who did all in their power to defeat Roosevelt. I knew it before I was told, for all the Irish were against him, whether in the convention or on the streets. I am inclined to think that the priests were honest about it—and really felt about as I would, had I believed the story. But it came very near defeating Mr. R. I have no doubt but what it was inspired by the *Interests,* as he was the only candidate that had not surrendered to them. Any how, those in charge of the campaign should know about it, as they doubtless do.[111]

I wonder if you can tell me what is the best time to visit New England—when the leaves are turning—as I am expecting to go to the White Mountains then, unless it will be so late as to prevent me from doing any talking in the Campaign. We should win, but it is a desperate bunch who will take any means to win.

110. Darrow and Mantinband debated the question "Is Religion Necessary?" on 30 November 1932 at the Majestic Theatre in Williamsport, Pennsylvania. The debate was sponsored by the Jewish Civil League in Williamsport and presided over by a rector of a local Episcopalian church.

111. In late 1930, some political promoters in the South began organizing "Roosevelt Southern Clubs" and soliciting memberships at one dollar apiece. The clubs were not sanctioned by Roosevelt's campaign, and in early 1932, the campaign disavowed any association with the clubs and refused to reimburse the promoters for their expenses. In retaliation, the promoters revealed that they had the backing of the Ku Klux Klan in Atlanta, Georgia, and they tried to connect Roosevelt publicly to the Klan. The charges against Roosevelt spread throughout the country. See Frank Freidel, *Franklin D. Roosevelt: The Triumph* (Boston: Little, Brown, 1956), 276–77. Darrow is apparently referring to the effect that these charges had on some attendees of the Democratic convention in Chicago in late June and early July 1932.

With kind regards to you and Mrs. House—

Clarence Darrow.[112]

MS: ALS, CtY-BR, House Papers, Box 35, Folder 1106. DATE: "[1932]" appended and response by House. NOTE: Darrow's address is written in another person's hand above the letterhead: "1537 East 60 St | Chicago, Ill."

TO E. M. HOUSE • CHICAGO • THURSDAY 1 SEPTEMBER 1932

CLARENCE DARROW September 1-st. 1932.—

My Dear Friend:—

Thanks for your kind and interesting letter. When I visit New York I shall indeed take pleasure in seeing you again.

A few days ago I received a letter from a bank-president in New England, who, a Democrat, tells me that everything possible is being done by *the interests* to defeat Roosevelt. I know this is true. I shall not be surprised if the Republicans carry New York, and that the Democrats must depend on the west. This means that a radical campaign should be carried on against the enemy, the big interests. These are responsible for the graveyard we are wandering about in, and they have not the common decency to admit it. Nothing but radical measures in the interests of the people can prevent future disaster. Plainly,—our whole system must be changed. This is no time for pussy-footing. I find many of my best friends, especially instructors in the University, will vote for Norman Thomas. Mr. Roosevelt points no way. He is a man of ability and human sympathies. Has he the courage? It would be interesting to know what the Scripps-Howard crowd would advise. The west is against the "money-bags" of the east.

Forgive me for troubling you,—but I am not so sure of the wisdom of anyone else. Unless what I say seems worth while, just disregard it.

I trust your summer is proving a happy and beneficial change. I look forward to being able to say "Hello" to you from The Murray Hill before long.

With warmest regards, truly yours,

Clarence Darrow.

MS: TLS, CtY-BR, House Papers, Box 35, Folder 1106. INSIDE ADDRESS: Col. E. M. House:— | Beverly Farms, Mass.

112. House's response to Darrow said that he was sending a copy of Darrow's letter to Roosevelt and explained that Darrow had hit on "one of the serious problems of [the] campaign." According to House, the "*Big Interests*" had "fanned the flame in the only direction that would produce results unfavorable to Roosevelt": "They were never more bent on beating a man for the nomination than they were Roosevelt. The *Boston News Bureau* and the *Wall Street Journal* both had items a few days before the Convention stating that the betting was five to one against Roosevelt's nomination. We ran this down and found that there were no such betting odds but that it was merely propaganda." House to Darrow, 26 August 1932, TLc, CtY-BR, House Papers, Box 35, Folder 1106.

TO JOHN H. DIETRICH • CHICAGO • TUESDAY 20 SEPTEMBER 1932

CLARENCE DARROW September 20-th, 1932.—

My Dear Mr. Dietrich:—

Like you, I have had a bombardment of calls from reporters here.[113] The first told me that the information was given out by Dr. Potter,[114] of New York, that I had "joined the Unitarian Church"—and was going to lecture through the east on "humanitarianism, or, humanism." Of course labels don't count in a sense, but I have so long been known as an agnostic, or whatever it may be, that I don't want them to think that I have "joined the church"—!!

I was under the impression that your crowd call themselves a HUMANIST SOCIETY, but I see by your letterhead that it is THE FIRST UNITARIAN SOCIETY, and you are shown as the "Minister". I probably should have more carefully observed all this before. I have too much sense to be really worried by this, or about names of things, but I want it to be given out *clearly* so that there will be no mistake by any one who seeks to know. I would like to know if there is any creed, or any sort of statement used. So far as I am concerned, your name is creed enough in itself to me, because I understand your attitude, which harmonizes with my own, of course.

I have an idea that it is best to let the whole matter stand on your explanation, now,—and a little later I can give out a definite one that will leave no ambiguity. It is silly (?) to make so much fuss and to-do about my name, etc. I had always indulged the hope that, like the other "infidels", my deathbed repentance would be postponed until after my cremation, but—

However, I am not fretting over it, and trust you are not.

With kind regards, | Very truly yours, | Clarence Darrow

MS: TLS, MnHi, Dietrich Papers. DATE: John H. Dietrich:— | Minneapolis, Minn.—.

TO JANE ADDAMS • CHICAGO • FRIDAY 21 OCTOBER 1932

CLARENCE DARROW Oct 21st

My Dear Miss Addams

Thank you very much for the book and the good letter.[115] I am sure that Miss Binford overestimated the argument, but all the same I am glad she did. I took up the book

113. Newspapers reported in September 1932 that Darrow had joined the First Unitarian Society of Minneapolis, where Dietrich was minister. See "Darrow Joins Unitarian Church and Will Lecture on Humanism," *New York Times*, 19 September 1932.

114. Charles Francis Potter (1885–1962), minister, author, and lecturer. Potter started his career as a Baptist minister, converted to Unitarianism by 1914, and eventually became a Humanist. He established the First Humanist Society of New York in 1929. He also served as a consultant for the attorneys for John Scopes in 1925. Potter wrote several books in the last thirty or so years of his life, including an autobiography and a popular study of the Dead Sea Scrolls.

115. The book to which Darrow is referring is *The Excellent Becomes the Permanent* (New York: Macmillan, 1932), a collection of Addams's memorial and funeral addresses. Addams sent the book to Darrow with a note saying that Jessica Binford had told her of his recent "fine address" for Russell McWilliams before the state supreme court. Addams to Darrow, 20 October 1932, ALS, MnU-L, Darrow Collection.

immediately on its receipt, and ran it through trusting that I got it fairly well. I was sorry that you had not included the Altgeld address with the others. It was especially good. In a way, I like everything you write.—In a way, I do not. Of course, I like the human side, the charity, the kindness, but I don't like the mysticism. If I know any thing, I know that I am not alive after I am dead, and that the same applies to every other form of life. I am inclined to think that no one believes in a future life. It is not only unbelievable, but unthinkable. I can not see that you affirm or deny. You can prove death by all of your reasoning faculties, and most of your senses. If one believed in a future life he would not travel over the world in agony, and be cut up, until he has no semblance of himself, just to stay here a week longer. He does it because he dreads and fears death—. He will continue to do it as long as he dreads and fears—and believes; I think when he gives up belief he will give up fear. I really don't like the title of the book for the excellent does not become permanent. The permanent (if there is any such thing) becomes excellent, because it survives, and in no other way. Who knows what is excellent or what is permanent? I knew a considerable number of those you mention in your book. I knew Henry D. Lloyd the best, and loved him most. I am afraid this letter is too critical. *I appreciate* all that *you have been* and *done,* but I have so long been striving for realities, and seeking to look life in the face, that I can not do otherwise, even with one I respect and admire as much as I do you.

Always with regards and good wishes,

Your friend | Clarence Darrow

MS: ALS, PSC, Swarthmore College Peace Collection, Jane Addams Papers. DATE: "[1932]" appended.

TO RICHARD BENNETT • CHICAGO • SUNDAY 15 JANUARY 1933

January 15, 1933

Dear Mr. Bennett:

Thank you ever so much for your fine letter. It is always so good to hear from you. I do wish we could go and see you, but doubt if I can get that far away from Chicago again. If I did, I should likely go to Europe, but I don't see much prospect of that. I often feel ashamed that I got you all "het up" to get me some money in Hollywood. After I got a good chance I felt that I should not do it.[116] I think I had rather be a good actor than do most anything else (and I am some actor in my profession!) but the idea of accepting a contract to be an actor because I am a lawyer seemed too much for me. I really had no right on the stage just because I had gained some "notoriety" in my profession. Anyhow, that is the way it looked to me after you and your friends had found a good contract!

116. Bennett had arranged for some type of contract for Darrow in the movie industry. Joan Bennett and Lois Kibbee, *The Bennett Playbill* (New York: Holt, Rinehart & Winston, 1970), 229.

Anyhow, I wish I could see you again and hope you will come this way soon.

With Admiration and Affection, | Your friend, | Clarence Darrow

MS: Joan Bennett and Lois Kibbee, *The Bennett Playbill* (New York: Holt, Rinehart & Winston, 1970), 229–30.

TO T. PERCEVAL GERSON • CHICAGO • SUNDAY 15 JANUARY 1933

CLARENCE DARROW Jan. 15th

My Dear Gerson—

I am returning the $1—. Of course I am always only sorry that I can't send my best friends books, without their spending money to buy them. But really the book is expensive and I *have* a *good many* friends (luckily) and I just can't do it. Of course I am glad you liked the book. I was sure that most of it concerns your own ideas. I am of course a radical as I have always been and hoping that our industrial system will be changed. No permanent good can come from the old. If there is any recovery it will last but a short time. I am working some on Technocracy and am glad to see how it is being taken up.[117] If we were not Barbarians no one in the world would be poor. We often talk of you and wish we could see you, and love you as much as ever. You will ever be close to us. I often think of Judge Lindsey and hope he will make a place for himself in L.A. I can't help thinking that he should not return to Denver. Give him my love.[118] It is a terrible plight into which our captains of industry have thrown the world. They would rather that the people should starve than to give them a chance. I am hoping much for Russia, and have but little knowledge about it.

With good wishes always | Your friend— | Clarence Darrow.

MS: ALS, location of original unknown (copy in editor's files). DATE: "'33" appended and "Ans. 1/19.'33. t.p.g." noted in the bottom margin, probably in Gerson's hand.

TO "MY DEAR RABBI" • CHICAGO • FRIDAY 17 FEBRUARY 1933

CLARENCE DARROW February 17-th, 1933—

My Dear Rabbi:—

I was in Rockford the whole of last week trying to save the life of a 17-year-old boy.[119] Twice I have argued, and twice reversed his death sentence in the Supreme Court, and

117. Technocracy was a political movement that became popular in the early 1930s. Its adherents believed that technicians, especially engineers—and not politicians or businessmen—were the ones most capable of making the changes in the economic order that were necessary to respond to the Great Depression. William E. Akin, *Technocracy and the American Dream: The Technocrat Movement, 1900–1941* (Berkeley: University of California Press, 1977), x.
118. Benjamin Lindsey had moved to Los Angeles in 1931, after the disbarment proceedings against him in Denver. See Darrow to Lindsey, 17 December 1929, n.187.
119. Darrow is referring to his defense of Russell McWilliams. See Darrow to Taylor, 16 May 1932, n.98.

think I shall be obliged to go again. On my return from Rockford I found six letters from penitentiaries pleading that I take their cases; every day they come, and I simply cannot do them; for physical and financial obstacles make it a long, hard job to try to save one of these unfortunates, and it takes money and strength, and I have little left of either, of course. I have undertaken to try to save another 17-year here.[120] So it goes, in spite of myself; but, I try not to read these letters from prisoners, if can avoid that. I can't, and bear to tell them how it is; and I can't assume these matters and live. I would like to take this fellow's case, as I would so many others, but I simply cannot.

To do anything for these fellows requires several trips to the penitentiaries; often cases which require costs of courts, etc. In this one I am assuming in Rockford I have paid $200.00 to $300.00 of my own,—going back and forth to prisons and courts, and it is absolutely useless and hopeless to venture into them without. Sorry to disappoint this one or any others, but you can see how impossible it is for me.

With most friendly regards, etc.

MS: TLc, ICN, Arthur and Lila Weinberg Papers.

TO PAUL GOLDBLATT • CHICAGO • SATURDAY 18 MARCH 1933

CLARENCE DARROW March 18th '33—

Dear Mr. Goldblatt

I was delighted with your fine letter and of course I was very glad that you liked the book. Praising one's book is like praising his child and no one can get too much of either sort. I have often thought of you and the pleasant time I had at your meeting and your home. I generally think of you with a little tinge of pity, because of the cruel ignorant bigotted city which you are trying to soften and humanize. I have always thought that it was the most hopeless place in America and I came away with my feelings confirmed. It was a rotten place to have a meeting; I think the worst in which I have ever spoken. But of course I liked you and the little group who waited with me in your little home until the

120. In December 1932, Darrow joined the defense of seventeen-year-old James ("Iggy") Varecha (1915–78). Varecha, who had an extensive juvenile record, had pleaded guilty to the charge of murdering a man during a holdup. He confessed not only to the murder but also to raping the niece of a deputy police commissioner on the night of the murder. He was sentenced to death on 16 December 1932. Darrow began working with Verecha's lawyer a week later, but all of their post-sentencing efforts to have the death sentence vacated in the trial court failed. See, e.g., "'Iggy' Varecha Must Die, Is Court Ruling: Darrow Loses Plea to Vacate Sentence," *Chicago Tribune*, 6 January 1933. In June 1933, the Illinois Supreme Court ordered a new trial for Varecha because he was an escapee from the state hospital at the time of the crime and had been placed there after a juvenile court determined that he was "feeble minded." *People v. Varecha*, 353 Ill. 52, 186 N.E. 607 (1933). Before his new trial, Varecha was judged by the court to be sane and he pleaded guilty again. This time, he was sentenced to one hundred years in prison. One of Darrow's former law partners (William W. Smith) represented Varecha in his appeal and later in the trial court. Darrow apparently did not participate in the appellate proceedings or in later trial court proceedings. Ibid. (listing attorneys for Varecha); "Varecha's 2d Murder Trial Starts Dec. 4," *Chicago Tribune*, 19 November 1933; "Varecha Gets 100 Years for Holdup Killing," *Chicago Tribune*, 5 December 1933.

train came along and rescued me. I don't like the history of Harrisburg with its Matt Quay,[121] its Penroses,[122] its Camerones[123] and its Pinchots[124] and of these I like the Penroses the best and the Pinchots the worst. I prefer the smell of brimstone that hangs around the sinner better than the soap and sapolio that comes from the person of the self-conscious saint. Still, I have no doubt that the average is not so much worse in the State house with the high brows and the penitentiary with its unwashed and often lousy inmates. Any how, you don't know how often I have thought of you and the little crowd that do all they can to redeem Harisburg.

Sometime around the 15th of April I am going to hold a few meetings in Scranton—perhaps Wilkesbarry—Reading, & maybe Allentown. I was just thinking if you thought that a fair sort of meeting could be gotten up, or a debate, say, with a Rabbi on "Is Religion Necessary?" and you thought it would get a good fair audience, I wouldn't want any guarantee, but would make some sort of a division of the proceeds—no doubt—whatever you would suggest. Possibly it would not be worth while to ever try this.

Any how, do just what you want to and don't go into the trouble of getting up a meeting *unless* it sounds *feasible.*

With best wishes to you and those who sat up with me

Your friend | Clarence Darrow

MS: ALS, ICU, Darrow Papers, Box 2, Folder 13a.

121. Matthew Quay (1833–1904), politician. Quay was a Republican political boss in Pennsylvania. He served in the Civil War with distinction and later owned and edited a newspaper He was secretary of the commonwealth of Pennsylvania, 1873–78, 1879–82, managed the presidential campaign of Benjamin Harrison in 1888, and served in the United States Senate, 1887–99, 1901–02, with an interruption in service caused by corruption charges.

122. Boies Penrose (1860–1921), politician. Penrose, a political lieutenant of Matthew Quay and later a political boss himself, served as a representative, 1884–86, and senator, 1886–97, in the state legislature in Pennsylvania before serving four terms in the United States Senate, 1897–1921. He was an isolationist, a friend of big business, a staunch conservative, and a strong opponent of many reforms, including Prohibition, female suffrage, federal income tax, and labor rights. One of his brothers, Richard Penrose (1863–1931), was a geologist who taught for a time at the University of Chicago and another brother, Charles Penrose (1862–1925), was a surgeon in Philadelphia.

123. Simon Cameron (1799–1889), businessman and politician. Cameron invested in banks, railroads, and other businesses before he was elected to fill a vacancy for Pennsylvania in the United States Senate, 1845–49. Later, he was reelected as a Republican, 1857–61, before becoming secretary of war, 1861–62, in the cabinet of Abraham Lincoln (1809–65). After a brief stint as United States minister to Russia, 1862, he was reelected to the United States Senate, 1867–77. He lived in Harrisburg, Pennsylvania, and had a scandalous career, often facing charges of corruption. Cameron controlled the Republican political machine in Pennsylvania (until Matthew Quay took charge), and this control benefited Cameron's son, J. Donald Cameron (1833–1918), who was secretary of war, 1876–77, in the cabinet of Ulysses Grant (1822–85), and who succeeded his father in the United States Senate, 1877–97.

124. Gifford Pinchot (1865–1946), conservationist and politician. From 1898 to 1910, Pinchot was in charge of the federal government's forest work. His last position was chief of the United States Forest Service. He was also a professor of forestry at Yale University, 1903–36. For two terms, he was a Republican governor of Pennsylvania, 1923–27, 1931–35. While governor, he strongly supported Prohibition and other Progressive-era causes. His wife, Cornelia Pinchot (1881–1960), was a suffragist, proponent of Prohibition, supporter of trade unions, and twice an unsuccessful candidate for Congress, in 1928 and 1932. His brother, Amos Pinchot (1873–1944), was a lawyer in New York City. He helped organize the Progressive Party in 1912 and established himself as a liberal reformer, campaigning for labor and civil liberties, among other causes.

TO IRVIN E. ROCKWELL • CHICAGO • MONDAY 15 MAY 1933

CLARENCE DARROW May 15th 1933

My Dear Rockwell—

Was glad to get your letter, as I always am.[125] Of course it was a hodge-podge of Christianity, Masonic Christian Science, and nothing, but still I read it and fancied the intellectual bunch of masons in Idaho listening to it and seeming to know what it was all about. I don't know why you do such things anyhow. Of course no one of any learning believes that Jesus was the greatest man who ever lived on this fool planet. In fact, he would hardly be in the first grade now. Instead of knowing all science, he knew none whatever. If he ever existed, he was a pretty good sort of a fellow and of course a religious fanatic. The world was full of such people, especially Eastern Asia. Not one word is recorded as coming from Jesus—in the way of principles or ideals that was not in the old testament, which he knew and had read thoroughly. Most likely he was trying to be a Rabbi and some doubt of parentage made it impossible. John the Baptist was his cousin and he was a ranting maniac. The world was full of such people then—; read the first chapter of Luke. Christianity is not helped by running in Christian Science dope, statements about PRINCIPLE and a lot more of things that might sound all right up in the hills of Idaho, but which are utterly devoid of meaning. You know I am very fond of you and, you are a wonderful friend, but why do you send me such senseless stuff? Take your speech and read it backward, and I would guarantee that it would read just as well. The trouble is that none of you believe any of the bunk you send out. You just *want to* believe something. You don't want to die—and so you gibber about God and principle and, law and love, and infinity &c &c &c. How in hell can you get any consolation out of all that raving—? Any how, in spite of all the trash you pour out on the Idaho stiffs, I like you,

125. Rockwell explained his concept of God in his letter to Darrow:

> You have kidded me about "God" and Jesus a lot, and I am coming back at you in this brief comment, declaring my concept of God, with the odds of about 1000 to 1, against me that I can convert you to reason!
>
> My God is self existant perfect life, perfect intelligence, The Creative Principle, ageless, diseaseless, free whole and end endless. Infinite Mind and its Infinite manifestation, hence ever & always present, and available, all same as the law or "principle" of music or mathematics. Old Habakkuk whom you have read and disected also has "declared" saying: "(God) Thou art of purer eyes than to behold evil and canst not look on iniquity. It must be obvious then, even your hardened encysted burl of unrighteousness, that Perfection cannot know of imperfection. Perfection and Principle are Siamese twins, cannot be separated; Cause & Effect as self existant Law cannot be reversed,—just IS.
>
> Now the honest simple Truth about your activity in mixing with things during your long life, is that you have proven a thousand times and more, that you DO love God! "God" used to have four letters in His name GOOD—the Icelanders still say it that way. And you have loved Good; you not only love it, but you have been doing good for the 40 years more or less that I have known you. I know of a single Good deed that you did, that cost you a $100,000 and bankrupted you for ten years or twenty? And you didn't have to do it; no compulsion at all, and nobody asked you to do it—and ALL be cause you loved GOOD more than you did safety or security or any other one thing in life. So your "two foot rule" goes out of the window.
>
> Now dear Clarence, all you need to do is to keep right on loving and doing "Good" and I'll meet you another day in the Kingdom of heaven!
>
> Lovingly Rock (Himself). | Affectionate regards to Ruby.

Rockwell to Darrow, 14 May 1933, TLS, IdBB, Rockwell-Darrow Collection.

and them, but *I don't want to go to your heaven.* I don't want to live for ever. I don't know what you mean by principle. I don't want to be deluded. I still believe that two an two is four, and that a dead man *is dead* &c &c.

All the same—Your friend | *Clarence Darrow.*

MS: ALS, IdBB, Rockwell-Darrow Collection.

TO JOHN T. FREDERICK • CHICAGO • MONDAY 15 MAY 1933

CLARENCE DARROW May 15-th, 1933—

My Dear Mr. Frederick:-

Enclosed find my check for $1.50, for *The Midland.* I am very sorry to learn that you have been obliged to abandon the further publication of your periodical. I suppose it is too high-class for the public. I imagine that a paper that has individuality can not compete with the department-store publications. They can only live by catering to the advertisers, and this source of revenue is beyond your reach.

What are you going to do now? Will you remain in Chicago? It is strange how our plans go up in vapor. I was delighted when you came here, and expected to see you often,—but, with failing health, and growing years, I have been losing mental and physical ambition, and have been putting off most things that I meant to do, for a day, a week, a month, and then putting them off again and again, until—I haven't seen you since we dined together at the home of Mr. and Mrs. Lllewellyn Jones,[126]—so long ago.

But you have been treated no worse than my other friends, and I am coming to the time of having a good excuse for all seeming lapses. Anyway, I hate exertion, now,—and it is mighty convenient to put things off till tomorrow.

Won't you kindly write me a letter as to whether you are going away, or shall stay in Chicago,—and where and when? I am sure that I want very much to see you; enough, so that I can overcome the habit and ennuie which for the most part limits my journeys to the stretch between the bedroom and frontroom and diningroom,—not to mention the bathroom.

Kind regards to you and your wife, from

your affectionate friend, | Clarence Darrow

MS: TLS, IaU, Frederick Papers. INSIDE ADDRESS: Mr. J. T. Frederick:— | 447 Monadnock Building, | Chicago, Illinois.—.

126. Llewellyn Jones (1884–1961), author and literary critic, and his wife, Susan. Llewellyn Jones was literary editor of the *Chicago Evening Post,* 1914–32, on the editorial staff of the *Chicago Herald-Examiner,* 1933–34, and later, after he moved to Boston, editor of the *Christian Register,* 1938–41, a weekly journal of the Unitarian churches. He was the author of several books, including *How to Criticize Books* (1928) and *How to Read Books* (1930), as well as many articles and reviews, including a favorable review of Darrow's autobiography: "Clarence Darrow Is a Don Quixote Who Can Go on without Illusions," *Chicago Evening Post,* 5 February 1932.

TO WILLIAM O. BLASE • CHICAGO • FRIDAY 7 JULY 1933

CLARENCE DARROW July 7-th, 1933—

My Dear Sir:—

I knew Henry George very well, and was one of his enthusiastic followers from the first. However, he now seems to be as dead as Julias Caesar. I am sorry. Of course I am always ready to aid any radical movement that seems to have a ghost of a chance. Perhaps sometime something may happen—but not very likely during my lifetime.

Very best wishes and regards, from | Clarence Darrow.

MS: TLS, location of original unknown (copy in editor's files). INSIDE ADDRESS: Dr, W. O. Blase:— | Youngstown, Ohio.—.

TO ABRAM E. ADELMAN • CHICAGO • SATURDAY 2 SEPTEMBER 1933

CLARENCE DARROW September 2-nd, 1933—

My Dear Mr. Adelman:—

Thank you very much for sending me the copy of your address. It is exceedingly well done.[127] In spite of the fact that you have mentioned me, I feel like saying something more specific about the speech.

I, like you, have been almost a worshiper of Ingersoll. Few, if any, men have done more toward liberalizing the world on the question of religion. He had a wonderful power over audiences; he was a past master in his use of words; he was fearless, and paid the price of his courage; and, still I must say—"But—" his oratory was largely "bunk"—tinkling bells and sounding cymbals. He ruined a whole generation of would-be speakers who tried to copy his style; but, still I must admit that he gave a great deal of pleasure to his listeners, and his oratory must be judged in remembrance of the time when he lived and spoke. I doubt if people would go to hear him now, although they are much more unfriendly toward religion than they were then.

Ingersoll, in spite of his oratory, was a good reader and a good thinker, and he seldom consciously posed. In politics, he was a blind man; he could turn his oratory loose on Blaine,[128] a plain corruptionist, as well as on Voltaire. The words you quote from him have made me no end of trouble. In the night of death, hope does not see a star, and listening love hears no rustling of a wing. There is no hope, and neither is there any wing. And still less should he have said, after quoting his brother, who might have said while dying: "I am better now." Either he did feel better, which was not a miracle, or he thought

127. What address Adelman sent to Darrow is unknown.

128. James Gillespie Blaine (1830–93), politician. Blaine was a Republican congressman, 1863–76, and senator from Maine, 1876–81, and secretary of state in the cabinets of Presidents Garfield and Arthur, 1881, and Harrison, 1889–92. He was also the Republican nominee for president in 1884 and several times an unsuccessful candidate for the nomination. Charges of corruption dogged Blaine much of his political career.

he would make some one else feel better by saying it. And why should we believe in spite of doubts and dogmas that the dying and the dead "feel better now."

You have spoken very kindly of me, and of what I have said and done, and I thoroughly appreciate that. I can say with perfect honesty that I have never knowingly catered to anyone's ideas, and have expressed what was within me, regardless of consequences.

There is nothing so silly as the talk about immortality. You are quite right in saying that the resurrection is more tenable than the soul stuff,—although the resurrection is absolutely impossible, and requires especial attention of God for the re-assembling of every atom of every one who ever lived,—and of all other animals, too. And, as live animals have kept themselves going by eating other animals, it is evident that corpses have been well mixed through all eternity.

Neither have I any use for the cowardly people who say that there is no proof on either side of the question of immortality. It is not a question that needs proof; it is self-evident. It can be proven by every one of the senses, except, possibly, hearing. It is only a short time after death when the nose is convinced of putrefaction; if people looked death in the face they would probably not worry about their souls. I believe that I can say honestly that I have had enough of life, and would regard it as a sound of doom if I should be condemned to immortality.

I like your talk for the reason that you do no dodging; It ought to be beneath any intelligent man to quibble. But most people are terrible cowards about death.

Having thoroughly absorbed your article, am returning it,—feeling that you may be glad—sometime—to have the extra copy.

Always your friend, | Clarence Darrow.

I hesitate to return your article,—in case you mean for me to keep it,—and yet,—perhaps you wanted me to do so?

MS: TLS, IEN, Leopold-Loeb Collection, Box 39, Folder 23.

TO GEORGE MURPHY • CHICAGO • THURSDAY 7 SEPTEMBER 1933

CLARENCE DARROW September 7-th, 1933—

My Dear Mr. Murphy:—

I am sorry I cannot recall your first name, but am sure you will excuse that.

Am enclosing a letter from a young woman who is very anxious about her brother,—who is in the penitentiary in Jackson, Michigan.[129] From her story, it would seem a

129. Murphy's notes written on this letter and his response show that the "young woman" was Stella Pukas (b. 1912?), who was writing about her brother, Edward Pukas (1914–1969), who had been sentenced to prison for "12 1/2 to 25" years for armed robbery in 1930. The Pukases lived in Chicago with their mother. Their parents, both Lithuanian immigrants, were divorced. Among other notes written on Darrow's letter were some facts of the case: "No record in Chicago. Stopped for gas and used guns. Recd no money. 16 yrs old when sentenced."

terrible miscarriage of justice, as it generally is when anyone goes to prison. If this boy's age is stated correctly, it is a shame that he should ever have gone there. I am sorry to bother you, but, won't you please look into this matter and find out what the facts are, and what can be done?[130]

Did the committee in Washington make any finding on the matter we presented to them concerning work for the inmates of prisons?[131]

Give my kindest regards to Mr. O'Brien.[132] and, when you reply, please return letter from Miss Pukas. With appreciation for anything you may do for her,

Your friend always, | Clarence Darrow.

MS: TLS, MiU-H, George Murphy Collection.

TO ROBERT R. GROS • CHICAGO • SATURDAY 4 NOVEMBER 1933

CLARENCE DARROW November 4-th, 1933—

My Dear Robert R. Gros:—

Your letter received a few days ago, and was glad and interested in all you say. We are always glad to hear from you, and to learn about what you are doing, etc.

What you say about your summer work is especially interesting. The world is so ignorant and cruel that one likes to be able to look at a bright side—or spot—once in awhile. The fact that this news came from the Mormon element makes it so much better—so far as I am concerned. The Mormons have been so ungodly religious that it has been very hard to get a modern idea into their heads; they seemed to be almost hopeless. Still, I have found a good many worthwhile people in Salt Lake City, at that,—and I should like

130. Murphy assured Darrow that he would look into Pukas's case: "You may be assured that I will be very happy to take a person[al] interest in this case and call upon Miss Pukas' brother in Jackson Prison. After I talk with Mr. Pukas and the parole commissioner I will again communicate with you." Murphy to Darrow, TLc, 8 September 1933, MiU, Murphy Collection. Whether Darrow and Murphy's interest in Edward Pukas had any effect on his sentence is unknown. Pukas was paroled to Chicago in December 1936. Prisoner Record for Edward Pukas, Serial No. 27997, Mi-SA, Jackson Prison Archives.

131. In late August 1933, Darrow, at Murphy's apparent urging, spoke at a hearing of the National Recovery Administration in Washington, D.C., to encourage the NRA to remove a clause in its tentative code that would have prohibited merchants from buying prisoner-made goods. Darrow argued that prisoners should be made to feel useful: "A man must do something besides pounding rocks if our penitentiaries are ever to be more than crime factories. . . . What he does must be useful." "Use of Prison-Made Goods," *Washington Post,* 29 August 1933. See Murphy to Darrow, 8 September 1933, TLc, MiU-H, George Murphy Collection ("You were so considerate, as usual, in speaking before the N.R.A. committee in Washington. . . . Before I left Washington I was given to understand from parties in the legal department of the N.R.A. that the clause in the code you spoke about would be at least modified and possibly eliminated.").

132. Patrick H. O'Brien (1868–1959), lawyer and judge. O'Brien practiced law in Wisconsin and Michigan before becoming a state court judge in Michigan, 1912–22. He moved to Detroit in 1922, where he was active in the local operations of the American Civil Liberties Union. He was a Democratic candidate for governor of Michigan, 1932, before being elected state attorney general, 1933–34. Later, he was elected to a probate judgeship, 1939–56.

to meet any of your friends -(and converts?-!-) especially Judge Clark,[133] and if I ever visit Salt Lake City again I shall look him up.

I assume you are intending to practise law when you finish your college-course. It is a bum profession, as generally practised. It is utterly devoid of idealism, and almost poverty-stricken as to any real ideas. Of course, however, there is a lot of chance to do some good in this profession if you can get along without making money your ambition. If you enter the field of law with the idea of helping those who need it most you will have a very interesting life, full of hard work and misunderstandings and misrepresentations,—but you will be able to do something toward alleviating the miseries and sorrows of unfortunates. I don't know whether I shall ever again go so far west as California; probably not. If, however, I should, I will arrange to meet you again.

The hurried visit we managed to have last time I was there seems to have (somehow-) been worth the trouble you went to.

Friendly regards and good wishes from

Yours Very Truly, | Clarence Darrow

MS: TLS, CSt, Robert R. Gros Papers, Cont. 1, Folder 4. INSIDE ADDRESS: Robert R. Gros:—| Stanford Univ.—| California:—.

TO FREMONT OLDER • CHICAGO • FRIDAY 15 DECEMBER 1933

CLARENCE DARROW December 15-th, 1933—

My Dear Fremont—

Your letter to Mrs. Darrow was appreciated by us both. Since that I have read your editorial in THE CALL, which is exceedingly good,—although I am quite certain that you did not let yourself out fully on the matter. Neither do I. As you know, I've always had some liking for the Governor, though I know perfectly well that he is not a profound man, and his influence about the same as the average man along the street; probably nine tenths of that class were delighted with what the Governor said.[134] You and I have long since

133. The identity of "Judge Clark" is unknown. He might have been a retired judge; no sitting federal, state, or local judge in Salt Lake City in 1933 with the name of "Clark" was identified.

134. In late November 1933, two men were arrested in San Jose, California, in connection with the kidnapping and murder of Brooke Hart, a twenty-two-year-old son of a wealthy department store owner in San Jose. While the suspects, who had reportedly confessed to the crime, were waiting in jail, a mob of people stormed the jail and lynched them. After the lynching, California governor Rolph issued a statement praising the work of the mob, which prompted a rebuke from President Roosevelt. Older later published an editorial describing the lynching and doubting whether mankind was any less cruel now than in ancient times: "Two cold-blooded murderers were taken from the jail in San Jose, by a mob, a gay, laughing, joking mob, and hanged to trees in St. James Park. Before they were killed their clothes were stripped from their bodies, their faces were stamped upon by the heels of the lynchers and an attempt was made to burn one of them. The women laughed merrily and applauded each cruel act. While one of the murderers was writhing in agony some of the women shouted a line from a coarse play, 'Come up and see me sometime!'" Fremont Older, "Man's Advance Is Slow," *San Francisco Call-Bulletin*, 6 December 1933.

learned that "the people" are morons, and never so happy as when they see some one else suffering. Of course, the lynching in San Jose was a horrible thing!—and was inspired by the brutal nature of primitive men; they like blood, and they delight in the torturing of sinners.

In these primitive emotions there is no distinction between sex and age. But, in spite of the fact that the majority of rich and poor seem to be with him, he is doomed politically. We are not going to revert to savagery where each man redresses his own wrongs, and where there are no general rules that have some power back of them; it would mean chaos to those who have lived in a semi-organized society during the past 5,000 years.

Of course I am not writing any of this for publication. I don't need to tell you how I really feel.

Clarence Darrow

Steffens was with us one evening this week, and next day papers reported his departure for California, because taken ill. Hope he recovered when he and the boy were reunited. He seems the same as ever, entertaining as ever,—and we thought he seemed as well as ever, but—?—

Do write from time to time, and take care of yourselves. My health seems better than a few years ago, but I haven't the vitality of once-upon-a-time. My pet vice is loafing.

MS: TLS, CU-BANC, Older Papers, Box 1.

TO WILLIAM ESSLING • CHICAGO • MONDAY 15 JANUARY 1934

CLARENCE DARROW January 15-th, 1934—

My Dear Mr. Essling:—

I am so sorry that I did not recall and recognize you yesterday, until after you had left. Of course I remembered the fine letter you wrote, and the note attached, from your friend, Paul; and for some reason or other, in the congestion and confusion of so many to talk with, it entirely escaped my mind for the moment.[135] I should have been very glad to talk with you as to your ambitions to practise law, etc. The highest wish of most of the boys who are studying law is to get on the payroll of some big corporation, and, after being servants to the rich for a long enough time, to be "elevated" to a judgeship where they

135. The day before Darrow wrote this letter, Essling had heard Darrow speak at a convention of the Northwest Shoe Retailers in Minneapolis, Minnesota, and he had a brief conversation with Darrow after the speech. See "Many Faults in NRA, Clarence Darrow Tells Shoe Men," *Commercial Bulletin and Apparel Merchant,* February 1935, 38–39 (text of Darrow's speech). Sometime before the convention, Essling had sent a letter to Darrow complimenting him on his autobiography and enclosing an appreciative note from Paul Stauff (1887–1983), a chemist and friend of Essling's who worked for the Eveleth Water Company in Eveleth, Minnesota. Telephone interview with William Essling, St. Paul, Minnesota, 3 June 1996.

can still serve the rich. Those that you find in college with you will think you mad to want to do anything for the common man.

I wonder if you ever come to Chicago?—I hope you will sometime, and want you to come to see me; the above is my address,—a re-conditioned old building, converted into an apartment-hotel where comfortable and inexpensive accomodations are easily found any time. Anyhow, Mrs. Darrow will help me remember about you another time without fail. Of course if you had been a bit more aggressive and less considerate of me and the rest, the circumstances would have quickly cleared up with me. I shall always appreciate your letter and all you seem to feel in sympathy with my views and attitudes, and I look forward to knowing you better some day, here or elsewhere. If ever again we are in the same city, do come and make yourself known to me.

In regard to the speech you inquire about, made at that—(to me) memorable Henry George meeting:—It looks as if that is lost to posterity.[136] Perhaps that is just as well, or better. It might not have been so great as I now think it was, and the applause of the audience may have been because it was not worse or longer, and was at last over with!

My best regards to your appreciative "Paul" and yourself, and, since you seem specially interested in my "efforts"—say—am sending you my closing address in the Loeb- Leopold case,—and maybe something else, if find anything around that think you will care for.

Sincerely yours, | Clarence Darrow

MS: TLS, location of original unknown (copy in editor's files). INSIDE ADDRESS: Wm. Essling:— | 1200 Powderhorn Terrace:— | Minneapolis, Minn.

TO RUBY DARROW • WASHINGTON, D.C. • MONDAY 22 JANUARY 1934

THE WILLARD HOTEL

Dear R.

I am none too well, and things are lively here. I am quite sure that I shall never make an other tour like this. I realize that I can't stand as much as I once could. And there are too many people here. I can't say what day I shall be back but I won't stay more than two days more.

Love | CSD

MS: ALS, MnU-L, Darrow Collection. DATE: postmark. ENVELOPE ADDRESS: Mrs. Clarence Darrow, | 1537—E 60th St | Chicago. POSTMARK: Washington, D.C., 22 January 1934.

136. Essling had asked Darrow for a copy of a speech that Darrow delivered on the subject of tariffs during a "Free Trade Convention" at Central Music Hall in Chicago in 1889. Ibid. Henry George spoke at the same meeting. In his autobiography, Darrow described this speech as being very favorably received by his audience. *Story*, 46–48. See "The Workingmen and the Tariff," *Chicago Herald*, 21 February 1889 (text of Darrow's speech).

TO JOHN J. MEEHAN • CHICAGO • TUESDAY 30 JANUARY 1934

January 30th, 1934.

My Dear Mr. Meehan:—

Regarding yours about Governor Altgeld, I am quite sure that he was not a member of the Chicago Bar Association—or any other; he always considered this organization, as I do, one of the many aids to monopoly. Late in his life, we organized another organization, for which we got a good many members; this organization of lawyers was meant to combat the capitalistic ideas of conventional Bar Associations; in the course of time we found it hard to keep going, and it was dissolved.[137]

If you had been the President of our Bar Association, we would not have felt the need of a new one, I feel sure.

With kind regards, etc. | Very truly yours, | signed Clarence Darrow

MS: Tlc, IHi, George Schilling Papers.

TO HUGH S. JOHNSON • CHICAGO • FRIDAY 16 FEBRUARY 1934

Hon Hugh F. Johnson— Administrator N.R.A. Washington D.C.—

I appreciate the compliment and confidence shown by your telegram received today.[138] Am sure that the N.R.A. was not meant to aid and encourage monopolies but to protect those who need it most.

Of course I am no longer young and my health is not altogether reliable but am inclined to accept your invitation if after interview you decide that I can be of value to the board and the cause. Unless you think best to be there earlier will arrive morning of twenty fifth or sixth and go to Willard until decide on most suitable place.[139]

MS: TT, DLC-MSS, Darrow Papers.

137. Some forty attorneys, including Darrow, Altgeld, Daniel Cruice, and Edgar Lee Masters, met in March 1902 to organize a local bar association. The aim of the organization was reportedly to "do work [that the Chicago Bar Association had] neglected." The desired reforms included raising "the limit of $5,000 indemnity for a human life, the revision of government by injunction, . . . the selection of better men for the judiciary, . . . uplift[ing] the character of the bar and . . . see[ing] that men who commit offenses worthy of such punishment [are] disbarred." "Lawyers to Form New Body," *Chicago Tribune,* 8 March 1902.

138. Johnson had sent a telegram to Darrow explaining that Gerald P. Nye (1892–1971), United States senator (Republican) from North Dakota, had recommended that Darrow serve as a member of President Roosevelt's new National Recovery Review Board. Johnson invited Darrow to accept the position. See Johnson to Darrow, 16 February 1934, Tele, DLC-MSS, Darrow Papers. Nye also sent a telegram encouraging Darrow to accept the position. See Nye to Darrow, 16 February 1934, Tele, DLC-MSS, Darrow Papers. The NRRB was conceived by Nye as a means of studying the National Recovery Administration (NRA), a federal agency established in mid-1933 to develop and administer a system of fair-competition codes for a variety of industries. The NRA was supposed to encourage industrial recovery and combat widespread unemployment. But by late 1933, the agency (and Johnson) had been accused of being authoritarian and its five-hundred-some codes were considered by many as encouraging monopolies and thwarting competition and labor unionization. See John Kennedy Ohl, *Hugh S. Johnson and the New Deal* (Dekalb: Northern Illinois University Press, 1985), 138–217.

139. The last ten words of this sentence were added in the hand of Ruby Darrow.

TO FLOYD E. ECKERT • CHICAGO • SATURDAY 17 FEBRUARY 1934

February 17-th, 1934—

Dear Mr. Eckert:—

Yours about a meeting with Preston Bradley and myself to help your hospital, etc.—in Woodstock—has awaited my return and a let-up in the congestion,—and meantime have talked with Dr. Bradley, and have his word that he would write you about it, as he seemed to prefer.

You know, Floyd, that there are a great many hospitals in the country, and I have had a great many invitations to speak for their benefit, and I have always declined. I really don't think there is any reason why Mr. Bradley and I should go to Woodstock and speak for nothing in order to make money for others.

Of course you know that I like to hear my speeches, but I can hear them at home, and I am growing old and tired, and even slightly lazy—or something.

Thank you for wanting me to come there, anyhow,—and I trust I shall be able to arrange for some other kind of a visit with you all again one of these days.

Your friend, | Clarence Darrow

MS: TT, DLC-MSS, Gertz Papers.

TO PAUL DARROW • WASHINGTON, D.C. • SATURDAY 10 MARCH 1934

THE WILLARD HOTEL March 10th

Dear Paul

There has not been much to write about. It took *ten* days to get the appointment made and we have been pretty busy since getting the machine running. You will see Mr. Mason[140] before you get this and if you think it worth while to undertake what he has on his mind I shall be glad to see you for a few days and you might enjoy seeing it for a while. We have been having pretty rough weather but it hasn't been cold. It looks as if every body in America was on the payroll which does not give me a very optimistic outlook. Most every one I ever heard of is coming and few if any are going. I don't know how much if any thing we can accomplish probably very little if any thing. The main occupation is spending money. Many of them seem incompetent and

140. Lowell B. Mason (1893–1983), lawyer. Mason was the son of William E. Mason (1850–1921), Republican senator from Illinois, 1897–1903, and a friend of Darrow. He obtained an LL.B. from Northwestern University, 1914, and practiced law in Chicago before Darrow hired him as general counsel for the National Recovery Review Board in 1934. In Chicago, Mason had worked with Darrow on some criminal law matters. He had been made nearly penniless by the stock market crash of 1929. See Stephen J. Sniegoski, "The Darrow Board and the Downfall of the NRA," *Continuity*, Spring/Fall 1990, 69 (citing author's interview with Mason).

extravagant. The whole effort seems to be to find something new to tax. Still of course there are a lot of people in the country who are not here. I guess Washington has always been this way and probably will be so long as so many people are so poor. It looks like it would be hard for prices of commodities to go up, and of course for stock and bonds to reach any higher level. I wish I could come back to the dinner to Holly but I don't now see how I can. You and Lill should go. I think it would be a good plan for you to go over and see him—but of course I know he will not forget. I feel that if you see a good chance to take something else you should do it for things *don't look good* to me from here. No one whom I have seems to have any idea which way we are going or how long any thing will last. Love to Lill and the kids.

C. S. D.

MS: ALS, MnU-L, Darrow Collection. DATE: "1934" appended.

TO ANTON JULIUS CARLSON • CHICAGO • SUNDAY 11 MARCH 1934

Dr. A. J. Carlson:[141]

I am sorry a reply to your letter has been so long delayed. When I was much younger I was interested in antivivisection but have had no connection with it for a good many years. I have been pretty well convinced that the operation is now performed with care as to anaesthetics, which really takes away the horror of its contemplation. Then, too, at the very best the death of most animals is a horrible one, if death comes from natural causes. So I am satisfied that vivisection does not add to the pain of animal life.

Then, too, I can see no difference between that and killing and eating meat, from which I abstained for a number of years. If the other animals were cared for as humans they would soon drive us off the earth. While I do not place the value of a man far above that of any other animal, still we have a better brain and we will not let the other animals destroy us. Long ago I made up my mind that with strict adherence to anaesthetics the

141. This letter was published by the *Chicago News* during a controversy involving Carlson and Irene Castle (1893–1969), a popular dancer and actress who was active in the anti-vivisection and animal-rights movement. Castle (then Irene Castle McLaughlin) wanted the city council of Chicago to stop allowing unclaimed dogs and other animals at the city pound to be used for scientific experimentation. See "Anti-Vivisection Move Assailed as Blow to City," *Chicago Tribune*, 28 November 1934. Carlson asked the *Chicago News* to publish this letter after Castle claimed that Darrow was among her supporters. The letter was introduced with the following note from Carlson: "Irene Castle McLaughlin lists Clarence Darrow as an antivivisectionist. In order to correct that will you kindly print the inclosed letter from Clarence Darrow to me March 11, 1934. I have Mr. Darrow's permission to publish this letter." Carlson was a strong supporter of animal research at the University of Chicago and one of the people who used the animals from the pound in experiments. (In 1946, Carlson founded and organized the National Society for Medical Research, for the purpose of ensuring that medical researchers could use animals in their work.)

terrors and pain of animals is rather diminished than increased by vivisection. So, long ago I stopped advocating antivivisection.

CLARENCE DARROW

MS: "Darrow on Vivisection," *Chicago News*, 20 January 1935.

TO FRANKLIN D. ROOSEVELT • WASHINGTON, D.C. • FRIDAY 27 APRIL 1934

NATIONAL RECOVERY REVIEW BOARD April 27th, 1934.

My dear Mr. President:

Articles are appearing in the public press from time to time that assume to reveal or to forecast the report that is to be made to you by the Review Board you created to inquire into certain alleged practices and conditions under the National Recovery Act. May I assure you that I have neither authorized nor ever given the least occasion for any such publication? We all feel strongly and adhere strictly to the obligation to make our report, when we shall find it, to you and to you alone. Any other course would be a betrayal of duty. But it is, of course, impossible to foresee or to restrain the journalistic imagination.

Very truly yours, | Clarence Darrow

MS: TLS, NHyF. INSIDE ADDRESS: The President, | Executive Mansion, | Washington, D.C.

TO FRANKLIN D. ROOSEVELT • WASHINGTON, D.C. • TUESDAY 1 MAY 1934

NATIONAL RECOVERY REVIEW BOARD May 1st. | 1934

Dear Mr. President:

In the interest of harmony and of the effective dispatch of the duties you have entrusted to us, we feel regretfully constrained to suggest that if Mr. Sinclair[142] does not resign his place on this Board it would be well if other employment were found for him.

We do not disparage his ability nor his worth, but the unavoidable though painful truth is that for some weeks he has not functioned as a member of this Board. He has attended upon fewer than half of our hearings,—he has declined in writing to join with us in such a report as alone could be of the least service to you or the nation, and for other

142. John F. Sinclair (1885–1950), banker and writer. Sinclair obtained an A.B., 1906, and LL.B., 1909, from the University of Minnesota and worked in banking, 1912–22. He also worked as a newspaper editor and writer in New York City, 1923–31, and wrote a syndicated column on business for newspapers, 1927–31.

reasons we have so lost confidence in him, that it is no longer possible for us to cooperate with him or he with us.

The task assigned to us we feel to be so vital and momentous that the fact that Mr. Sinclair and we are at hopeless odds renders it highly inadvisable for the present relation to continue.[143]

Your respectfully, | Clarence Darrow | Samuel C. Henry[144]
W. O. Thompson | Fred P. Mann Sr.[145] | W. W. Neal[146]

MS: TLS, NHyF. INSIDE ADDRESS: To the President, | Executive Mansion | Washington, D.C.

TO FRANKLIN D. ROOSEVELT • WASHINGTON, D.C. • THURSDAY 28 JUNE 1934

THE WILLARD HOTEL June 28th

Hon. Franklin Roosevelt
My Dear President

Our board is sending you our third report, and I feel that I can no longer be burdened with the work, so I hereby resign from the National Recovery Review board and its presidency to take effect July 1st.[147]

Wishing you all kinds of success for yourself and the country,

I am Very Truly Yours, | Clarence Darrow

MS: ALS, NHyF. DATE: reference to report and resignation.

143. Darrow apparently did not know that Sinclair had tendered his resignation to President Roosevelt two days earlier. Sinclair told Roosevelt that the National Recovery Review Board, under the chairmanship of Darrow, was "really a one-man institution" that showed an "utter disregard for fair play or the basic facts." Sinclair to Roosevelt, TLS, 28 April 1934, NHyF. According to newspaper reports, Sinclair "was opposed to the board's policies because it made recommendations on specific codes without getting the views of code authorities or NRA officials." "J. F. Sinclair Quits the Darrow Board," *New York Times,* 8 May 1934. Sinclair submitted a report dissenting from the findings of the NRRB. "Text of Sinclair Report," *Washington Post,* 21 May 1934.

144. Samuel C. Henry (1869?–1949) was a former president of the National Retail Druggists Association. Henry and the other signatories of this letter were appointed by President Roosevelt to the NRRB by executive order on 7 March 1934.

145. Fred P. Mann Sr. (1869–1942) was the owner of a successful department store in Devil's Lake, North Dakota.

146. William W. Neal (1896–1946) was owner of the Marion Hosiery Mills in Marion, North Carolina.

147. In a series of three reports sharply critical of the National Recovery Administration, the NRRB concluded that the "fair-competition codes" established by the NRA promoted monopolistic practices and oppressed small businesses. The NRRB's first report was followed by scathing replies from Hugh Johnson and the NRA, criticizing the substance of the report and the investigative methods of the NRRB. "Darrow Board Finds NRA Tends toward Monopoly: Johnson Condemns Report," *New York Times,* 21 May 1934; "Reply of the Recovery Administration to the Criticisms by the Darrow Board," *New York Times,* 21 May 1934.

TO RUBY DARROW • NEW YORK CITY • SATURDAY 17 NOVEMBER 1934

HOTEL NEW YORKER Saturday Evening

Dear R.

I just got in from Connecticut where I spoke last night—stopped with my friends there and had a good meeting. Shall go tomorrow to Eastern Pa. I am quite tired of it all but am feeling all right. I just wired to see if I can get out of the Salem date. It is along way to go for just one date. I have met a good many interesting people and had a pleasant time, but you know I don't like to be obliged to go somewhere and think I will do very little of it in the future. I will like to get back home where we can loaf around in spite of the fact that I go to bed at eight o'clock and you tell me "in a few minutes" and then show up about day light. Don't worry about me I will come through all right but it seems like a long time.

Love | C.S.D.

MS: ALS, MnU-L, Darrow Collection. ENVELOPE ADDRESS: Mrs. Clarence Darrow, | 1537 E. 60th St | Chicago | Ill. POSTMARK: New York, 17 November 1934.

TO THE *BUFFALO (NEW YORK) TIMES* • UNKNOWN • SATURDAY 15 DECEMBER 1934

I feel pretty well convinced that Millard Crow, who was killed by the policemen, was shot without any reasonable justification.[148]

In the first place, this was a young boy 15 years of age; he was not in the act of molesting or resisting the policemen, or any one else, and under the circumstances the officers had no right to shoot him.

The policemen saw the boy running away; they either shot at him, or were grossly careless in the handling of their guns.

Human life is regarded as of such importance that it cannot be taken wilfully without grave and sufficient provocation. Even if the boy was running away from the policeman, this was no justification for shooting him. He could have been arrested the next day, if necessary.

The character and standing of the boy makes it almost impossible to suppose that the lives of the policemen were in any danger from him—and nothing short of such danger could justify this act on part of the police.

148. In late November 1934, unarmed, fifteen-year-old Millard Crow, of Buffalo, New York, was shot and killed outside an apartment building by policemen who said that they suspected him of being a burglar. In early December, the district attorney, Walter Newcomb, conducted an investigation and announced that there was no wrongdoing on the part of the police. "Newcomb Avoids Controversy over Boy's Death," *Buffalo Courier-Express*, 2 December 1934. Several years later, a new district attorney cleared Crow of any criminal activity. "Prosecutor Thanked," *Buffalo Courier-Express*, 13 November 1940.

It seems obvious that a great deal of effort has been made to shield the police; the testimony of the maid (Rose Lakatos) when she was recalled shows plainly the attempt made to place the guilt on the boy. It seems that a thorough investigation should be made of this whole case by someone to be specially appointed by the governor or some other official competent to act.

Clarence Darrow

MS: "Killing of Millard Crow Unjustified, Darrow Says," *Buffalo (New York) Times*, 15 December 1934. NOTE: a facsimile of Darrow's signature appears at the end of the publication.

• AFTER 1934

TO FRANK MURPHY • CHICAGO • WEDNESDAY 9 OCTOBER 1935

CLARENCE DARROW Oct. 9-th, 1935.

My Very Dear Friend:—

It was indeed a pleasant treat to receive your letter, to know that you are recovered,—even though disappointing that you could not come to see us on your way from Detroit, and to learn of the many really remarkable accomplishments to your credit in your present world! I appreciate the many things you say about my influence in your life, and whatever that may have to do with what you are able to now see as the right way, etc. but I don't feel sure that you are not giving me too much praise; perhaps sometime I may climb up to it,—but in the Detroit case it was the first time in all my career where a judge really tried to help, and displayed a sympathetic interest in saving poor devils from the extreme forces of the law, rather than otherwise. Although I have known some humane judges, I have found very few really wanting to really help any of the victims.

I am delighted to know of your work in the Philippines. Think of a Governor taking a real interest in "the people"! I never knew but one other:—John P. Altgeld,—and eventually he gave his life in the pursuit of his splendid ideals. Most men receiving the appointment you are occupying would have spent the time seeking out the influential ones and coddling them. It is glorious that you should have so devoted yourself to improving and liberalizing that section, and once begun it will forge forward on momentum surely.

How I would enjoy going over there and visiting you and your interesting ventures and land, but I am getting along in life, and my health is not what it once was. Of course you could have received anything you had wanted in Michigan, but what you are doing is of far greater importance and value. I do not know of anyone in the state at present concerning himself very deeply in the welfare of its people.

I presume you keep a fair watch of the politics of the United States. I cannot remember any time when political affairs were at such a low ebb. One who feels as I do wonders if it will be worth while to cast a vote at the coming election. As you know, I have always been a democrat, but I am satisfied that Roosevelt is thoroughly incompetent; so far as money is concerned, he has the mind of a child; it is hard to understand how he would throw away money as he has during his management of matters. While many things in the country are in a critical condition he goes a-fishing and playing on land and see, at all kinds of distances. I heard a great deal about him while he was Governor of New York State, but somehow I doubted the stories then; now I know that he has an army of people on the payroll who have no work to do, with the country swamped in debt. The republicans are making the most possible of the situation, although they have no good timber in sight. The Supreme Court has declared almost the whole of the N.R.A. unconstitutional, but he still keeps the old crowd on the payroll, doing nothing, which was about what they did before it was declared unconstitutional. He has made some inane remarks, criticising the Supreme Court, and the republicans have seized on the opportunity to proclaim that the constitution is a sacred instrument, and that the campaign must be waged on this issue. If they win, the most reactionary bunch of high-binders and republicans will be in power, and I am inclined to think that will be worse. So far as I am concerned, I probably shall vote for Roosevelt again, although it looks now as though he will be defeated. At any rate, it will be a lively campaign, and I hope you will happen to be here, and then come here to see us in Chicago, where a never-ending warm welcome awaits you. For your own sake, and outside the point of holding an honorable position, I cannot help thinking that it will be a good idea for you to remain in The Philippines until after election, however. I shall read at leisure the documents you so kindly sent, but know in advance they are all that anyone can wish and hope for. You are busy, of course, but, any time you spare the time for a letter to me it will give me much pleasure to hear further about your activities and successes. And always come whenever possible to the fireside of your fond and faithful friends,

Clarence Darrow | and Ruby D.[1]—-

MS: TLS, MiU-H, Frank Murphy Papers. INSIDE ADDRESS: Hon. Frank Murphy:— | Philippine Islands:—.

1. Ruby's signature is in her hand.

TO WILLIAM MCKNIGHT • CHICAGO • WEDNESDAY 15 APRIL 1936

CLARENCE DARROW April 15-th, 1936.

Dear Bill McKnight:[2]

Young men are ambitious to get into the law game largely because it is a showy profession, and is one that lets a man enjoy the limelight; this has attracted so many that the lawyers who already are admitted to the bar go to all kinds of trouble to keep others out, making preliminaries difficult, and examinations harder than ever.

Young aspirants dream of one step up after another,—good earnings, political position, glory, etc—that the field already is overcrowded. With such competition, unless a young man is especially fitted and gifted, what chance has he? With any thought of helping his fellow man, the law is the last field he should venture into. City and County departments, and towns are overflowing with both old and new lawyers, all struggling to get ahead of each other. Psychiatry, on the other hand, is not yet quite so overcrowded, and is by far a more interesting field, but, of course requires years of study and preparation.

It is practically impossible to advise anyone about such a life-scheme as you need to choose; you will need to try to gauge your own ability and resources,—environment and circumstances of all sorts enter in to whether you will succeed; the cost of either of the above ventures would cost enough to buy a good farm, and I think the farmer has a happier time, and in many ways is a greater benefit to others,—if that interests you. As a matter of fact, it seems to me that, in this day, the choice of law as an avenue of future well being is about the poorest you can undertake; however, if you risk it, I hope you may make a "go" of it,—or, anything else you decide upon. This will not help you much, I fear, but there is no way of furnishing a recipe—or prophesy.

Shall send you a picture, if you care to have it, and appreciate your complimentary attitude toward me.

Very sincerely yours, | Clarence Darrow

MS: TLS, Kevin Tierney. INSIDE ADDRESS: To Bill McKnight:— | Brookville, Pa.—.

TO PAUL DARROW • CHICAGO • TUESDAY 12 MAY 1936

CLARENCE DARROW May 12th 1936

Dear Paul

I have told Ruby that I shall arrange with you that she can keep the apartment where we live for six months after my death and that you will pay the rent. This is done so that she

2. The identity of "William McKnight" is unknown. He was apparently a young man interested in becoming a lawyer and he wrote to Darrow for advice.

can dispose of the furniture, books and the things that pertain to me and my life, in the apartment.

C. S. D.

This is in case I fail to speak to you about it—

MS: ALS, MnU-L, Darrow Collection.

TO RUBY DARROW • WARREN, OHIO • TUESDAY 25 MAY 1936

May 25th

Dear R.

I am sorry I haven't written you before but, I have been tired out every night.[3] I shall be home in two or three days & will be glad to get back. Shall leave here tomorrow a.m. and stop probably over night at Canton and then go straight back. I stayed longer in Kinsman than any other place. There was a crowd every day. They all seemed to want to see me. Shall not make any long stop again *until I get home.*

With love | C.S.D.

MS: ALS, MnU-L, Darrow Collection. ENVELOPE ADDRESS: Mrs. Ruby Darrow | 1537—E 60th St | Chicago | Ill. POSTMARK: Warren, Ohio, 26 May 1936.

TO FRANK MURPHY • CHICAGO • MONDAY 29 MARCH 1937

CLARENCE DARROW March 29-th, '37

My very Dear Mr. Murphy:—

Enclosed find letter from Vivian Pierce which please read carefully; then I will refrain from restating the situation. The U.S. Gov't figures show that Capital Punishment is not the remedy. We know that Capital Punishment laws are not based on up-to-date estimates and scientific treatments. The record of Michigan speaks for itself in comparison with neighboring states inflicting capital punishment, and much of what Miss Pierce alludes to as "recent crimes" in no way applies to Michigan especially, but is a part of the hard-times prevailing everywhere, with increased difficulty of getting anywhere against terrific competition; and people will steal, commit almost any crime, lose self-respect when facing starvation and extreme self-denial of every sort; uneven distribution is responsible for much of the waywardness of youth today.

But, morons who vote,—even in Legislative bodies,—public representatives, politicians, and people in general, do not think, or really care, beyond punishing those who have not

3. Darrow was traveling in the Western Reserve area of Ohio, visiting friends and acquaintances from when he lived in the area as a child and young man.

the material or mental equipment for getting along. Most cases are mental cases, at that, if understood. I have just received a report from England showing that authorities there are recognizing this and reshaping their laws accordingly. I hope you will use your power at once to prevent the barbaric reinstatement of Capital Punishment. The reactionaries surely cannot be permitted to put Michigan on the black list of civilization,—if there is any!

Ever devotedly your friend, | Clarence Darrow

MS: TLS, MiU-H, Frank Murphy Papers. INSIDE ADDRESS: Hon. Frank Murphy:— | Detroit, Michigan:—.

TO VICTOR HACKLER • CHICAGO • WEDNESDAY 14 APRIL 1937

CLARENCE DARROW April 14-th— | 1937.

To Mr. Victor Hackler—News Editor

Associated Press—Chicago—Illinois

Replying to your submitted questions, I am answering:

No. 1— Do I wish that I had done differently?—: I am fairly well satisfied with the way I have lived and acted.

No. 2— What do I regard as having done the most good?—: My strong feeling of tolerance toward all things, and my constant belief that no one is responsible for his makeup and his acts; this, of course, is hostile to the unscientific belief in free will. Granted that we are burdened with many abnormal and misfit humans, who are the victims of their own conduct, nevertheless they deserve to be treated as patients in institutions instead of imprisoned and punished.

No. 3— What has brought me the most satisfaction?—: My efforts in behalf of unfortunates has brought me the greatest and most lasting gratification.

No. 4— What appears to have been my most difficult task?—: Trying my hardest to help overcome the cruelties of the world. Worst of all, the horrible punishments, tortures and injustices inflicted; like lynching, the rankest vengeance; capital punishment, which does not deter others, etc.

No. 5— Have I a guide to offer those entering the legal profession?—: I would like to see a crop of lawyers developed with more genuine, humane ambition to benefit the poor and unfortunate clients, rather than mainly themselves.

No. 6— Regarding my attitude toward religion:—I feel as I always have, that the Earth is the home, and the only home, of man, and I am convinced that whatever he is to get out of his existence he must get while he is here.

Signed by:— | Clarence Darrow

MS: TLS, IEN, Leopold-Loeb Collection, Box 39, Folder 24.

BIOGRAPHICAL REGISTER

Addams, Jane (1860–1935). Social reformer and author. In 1889, Addams, together with Ellen Gates Starr *(q.v.)*, founded the social settlement in Chicago known as Hull House, which served as a center of civic activity and a forum through which Addams and other reformers carried out their efforts to help the urban poor. She also wrote many books and articles, including her autobiographical *Twenty Years at Hull-House* (1910).

Adelman, Abram E. (1882–1977). Lawyer. Adelman was born in Lithuania and came to the United States in 1888. He obtained an LL.B. from Northwestern University, 1904, and practiced law in Chicago, specializing in real estate and corporation law. For several years, he had an office on the same floor as the Darrow & Masters firm at 1202 Ashland Block in Chicago.

Altgeld, John P. (1847–1902). Lawyer, judge, businessman, and politician. Altgeld was born in Germany and came to the United States when he was an infant. He moved to Chicago in 1875, where he practiced law and became wealthy through real estate. He served as a judge of the Superior Court of Cook County, 1886–91, and as Democratic governor of Illinois, 1893–97. As governor, he was both lauded and reviled for pardoning the surviving Haymarket defendants in 1893 and for protesting federal intervention in the Pullman strike in 1894. After reelection defeat, he lost his fortune and returned to practicing law, joining Darrow's firm a year or so before his death. His writings include *Our Penal Machinery and Its Victims* (1884) and *Oratory: Its Requirements and Rewards* (1901).

Baehr, William A. (1873–1943). Businessman. Born in Oshkosh, Wisconsin, Baehr received a B.S. from the University of Wisconsin, 1894, and spent most of his life in the Chicago area. He worked as a consulting engineer for gas-utility companies and eventually became a highly successful investor and owner of many different utilities and chemical, mining, and ice-and-refrigeration companies. He acted as a consultant to Darrow and his son Paul on their gas plant in Greeley, Colorado.

Bailey, Forrest (1881–1933). Teacher and civil libertarian. Bailey was born in San Jose, California, and received an A.B. and M.A. in English from Stanford University. He taught high school in Los Angeles for several years before moving to France after World War I, where he organized schools to prepare veterans for civilian life. In 1925, he became codirector of the American Civil Liberties Union, with Roger Baldwin *(q.v.)*, a position he held until 1932.

Baily, Jacob L. (1850–1921?). Lawyer. Baily was educated at Oberlin College and Northwestern University. He practiced law in Macomb, Illinois, 1876–1900, before moving to Chicago, where he headed his own firm and worked as trial attorney for several elevated railway companies. He practiced law with Darrow from approximately 1910 to 1914, with the exception of the two years that Darrow spent in Los Angeles (May 1911–April 1913).

Baldwin, Roger (1884–1981). Civil libertarian and reformer. Baldwin received an A.B. and M.A. from Harvard University, 1905, and later worked as a teacher and probation officer. During World War I, he served one year in prison for refusing to register for the draft. In 1920, a few months after his release, he helped found the American Civil Liberties Union and served as executive director of the organization for the next thirty years.

Barnes, Harry Elmer (1889–1968). Educator, historian, and sociologist. Barnes received a Ph.D. from Columbia University, 1918, and taught history, sociology, and economics at many different colleges and universities. He also worked as a general editorial writer for the Scripps-Howard newspapers. Barnes, who became known as a revisionist historian, wrote many books, including *The Social History of the Western World* (1921), *The Genesis of the World War* (1926), and *Perpetual War for Perpetual Peace* (1953).

Barnum, Gertrude (1866–1948). Social worker, labor reformer, and writer. Barnum, a graduate of the University of Wisconsin, worked in Chicago's settlement houses, including Hull House, and as national organizer for the National Women's Trade Union League, 1903–6. She was also a publicity agent for the International Ladies' Garment Workers' Union, 1911–16. She wrote short stories and many articles for reform magazines. She served briefly as an assistant director of investigations for the United States Department of Labor, 1918–19, after which she retired and lived in Los Angeles.

Barry, John D. (1866–1942). Novelist and journalist. Barry was born in Boston and graduated from Harvard University, 1888. He worked as a drama critic for *Harper's Weekly* and *Collier's* and in 1910 began as a staff writer for the *San Francisco Bulletin.* During the last sixteen years of his life, he was a columnist for the *San Francisco News.* He wrote several novels and some nonfiction books.

Beck, James Montgomery (1861–1936). Lawyer and politician. Beck graduated from Moravian College and Theological Seminary in Pennsylvania, 1880, and was admitted to the bar in 1884. After working in private practice, he became an assistant United States attorney in Pennsylvania, 1888–92, United States attorney in Pennsylvania, 1896–1900, and later assistant to the United States attorney general, 1900–3. After that period of government service—during which he changed political affiliation from Democratic to Republican—Beck practiced law privately, 1903–21, before being appointed solicitor general, 1921–25, by President Warren G. Harding *(q.v.)*. Beck was later elected as a Republican congressman from Pennsylvania and served several terms, 1927–34, before resuming the practice of law.

Bennett, Arnold (1867–1931). English playwright, critic, and novelist. Bennett wrote in a realistic manner about provincial and lower-class life. His novels include *Anna of the Five Towns* (1902) and *The Old Wives' Tale* (1908).

Bennett, Richard (1870–1944). Actor. Bennett starred in many popular Broadway productions and sold-out stage tours, and he occasionally appeared in movies. He was the father of actresses Constance Bennett (1905–65) and Joan Bennett (1910–90).

Berger, Victor (1860–1929). Socialist editor and politician. Berger was born in Transylvania and emigrated to the United States in 1878. He worked as a schoolteacher in Milwaukee, 1880–90, founded and edited the *Wisconsin Vorwärts,* 1892–98, and later edited the *Social Democratic Herald,* 1901–11, and the *(Milwaukee) Leader,* 1911–29. He helped establish the Social Democratic Party, 1898, with Eugene V. Debs *(q.v.)*, and was the first socialist elected to the U.S. House of Representatives, 1911–13. He was elected again, twice, during World War I but was denied his seat because of his anti-war views. His later conviction for sedition was reversed on appeal. In 1922, he was elected to the House again and served three terms.

Berman, Louis (1893–1946). Physician and author. Berman received an M.D. from the College of Physicians and Surgeons, Columbia University, 1915, and then went into private practice. Later, he taught biological chemistry for several years at the college, 1921–28. He became a well-known endocrinologist and published many books and articles on glands and the effects of glands on human behavior.

Bicknell, Fred (1872–1934). Lawyer and judge. Bicknell was born in Johnson, Vermont. He worked for a time as a school principal, attended the University of Vermont for one year, and then studied law. He was admitted to the bar in 1900. He practiced law in Johnson for twelve years, also serving as town clerk, town

treasurer, state representative, 1906, and county attorney, 1902–6. Later he practiced law in Chester, Vermont, 1912–17, and then in Windsor, Vermont, where he was again elected as a state representative, 1928. In 1929, he was elected as superior court judge for the state of Vermont and held that position until his death.

Binford, Jessie Florence (1876–1966). Social worker. Binford graduated from Rockford College in 1900 and lived at Hull House in Chicago from 1905 until 1963. She worked for United Charities and the Legal Aid Society, 1906–9, but most of her career was spent working for the Juvenile Protective Association, 1906–52—a child-welfare organization in Chicago—including as superintendent of the organization, 1916–52. The JPA provided services for the juvenile courts and worked with juvenile delinquents and their families.

Blase, William O. (1873–1937). Optometrist and reformer. Born in Wilkes-Barre, Pennsylvania, Blase graduated from Kingston Seminary and Needles Institute of Optometry. He was a failed investor in oil fields in Texas before moving to Youngstown, Ohio, in 1901. There, he was active in business, civic, and charitable affairs and operated a business as an optometrist. He was an ardent Christian Scientist, an advocate of the single tax, and an organizer and president of the Henry George School of Social Science. After an illness of several months, he committed suicide by shooting himself.

Boissevain, Inez Milholland (1886–1916). Lawyer, reformer, and suffrage activist. Boissevain graduated from Vassar College, 1909, and the law school of New York University, 1912. She worked for a law firm in New York and promoted many causes, including prison reform, labor, and, in particular, suffrage. She was an active pacifist during World War I. She collapsed in Los Angeles while speaking for suffrage, died ten weeks later, and became a martyr for the suffrage movement.

Borah, William (1865–1940). Lawyer and politician. Borah was born on a farm in Illinois. He attended the University of Kansas for two years and then studied law and was admitted to practice in 1887. Three years later, he moved to Boise, Idaho, and continued the practice of law. He was elected as a Republican to the United States Senate in 1907 and served in that position until his death, developing a reputation as a progressive and defender of civil liberties. Borah was the prosecutor in the trial of William ("Big Bill") Haywood *(q.v.)* in 1907. He and Darrow became friends during the trial.

Boyce, Edward (1863–1941). Labor leader and businessman. Born in Ireland, Boyce emigrated to the United States in approximately 1882. He worked on railroads and then in the mines, in Colorado and Idaho. He held various positions with miners' unions and was a founder of the Western Federation of Miners in 1893, serving for several years as its president, 1896–1902, and as editor of its journal, the *Miners' Magazine,* 1900–2. He became wealthy through his wife, whose father and

brother struck a rich silver-lead vein in their mine. He eventually moved to Portland, Oregon, where he operated a mine and later a hotel.

Bradley, Preston (1888–1983). Clergyman and civic leader. Bradley founded and served as pastor of the People's Church in Chicago, 1912–68, which functioned as an independent church until 1923, when it became part of the Unitarian Church. He was a longtime director of the Chicago Public Library, a pioneer in religious radio broadcasting, a founder of the Izaak Walton League of America, and a member of the Chicago Commission on Human Relations.

Brandeis, Louis D. (1856–1941). Lawyer and judge. Brandeis graduated from Harvard Law School, 1877, taught and wrote on legal subjects, and enjoyed a thriving law practice in Boston before serving as the first Jewish justice on the U.S. Supreme Court, 1916–39. He was devoted to free speech, believed that law should reflect society's needs, and was an advocate for a variety of public-interest, labor, and employment-law causes and reforms.

Brownlee, Jessie (Ohl) (1857–1953). Darrow's first wife. Brownlee was born in Burghill, Ohio, and raised in the same area of Ohio as Darrow. She was one of six children born to Michael and Eliza Ohl. Her father died in 1865 from injuries caused by falling from a bridge that he was helping to build. She married Darrow in 1880 and they lived in Andover and Ashtabula, Ohio, before moving to Chicago in 1887, where they divorced in 1897. She continued living in Chicago, most of her years, until her death. Darrow and Jessie had one child together, Paul Darrow *(q.v.)*. In 1912, Jessie married Mungo Brownlee.

Bruère, Martha Bensley (1879–1953). Writer, editor, lecturer, and illustrator. Bruère wrote articles for popular magazines and wrote and edited several books, including *Laughing Their Way: Women's Humor in America* (1934), with Mary Ritter Beard (1876–1958). Bruère's husband, Robert Bruère (1876–1964), was also an author and editor. The Bruères were neighbors of Lemuel Parton *(q.v.)* and Mary Field Parton *(q.v.)* in Palisades, New York.

Bryan, William Jennings (1860–1925). Lawyer, lecturer, congressman, three-time Democratic nominee for president, and secretary of state under President Woodrow Wilson *(q.v.)*. Bryan, hostile to the theory of evolution, was one of the prosecuting attorneys in the trial of John T. Scopes *(q.v.)*.

Burns, William J. (1861–1932). Detective. Burns's father was a police commissioner in Columbus, Ohio, and Burns started detective work at a young age. He worked on many cases of government fraud and corruption—including as a member of the Secret Service—before starting a private detective agency in 1909. Burns and his detectives investigated the bombing of the Los Angeles Times Building in 1910, and their work led to the arrests of James B. McNamara *(q.v.)* and John J. McNamara *(q.v.)*. Burns worked for three years or so in the U.S. Department of Justice as director of the Bureau of Investigation, 1921–24, the forerunner of

the Federal Bureau of Investigation, and then continued working as a private detective.

Burroughs, John (1837–1921). Naturalist and author. Burroughs worked as a farmer and rural schoolteacher and contributed many articles to newspapers and magazines before working for the U.S. Treasury Department in Washington, D.C., 1863–72. After that, he worked briefly as a bank examiner and then moved to southern New York, where he built a house and cabin near the Hudson River and continued writing. He was deeply influenced by the Transcendentalism of Ralph Waldo Emerson (1803–1882) and Walt Whitman (1819–1892) and wrote many popular essays and books on nature and other subjects, including studies of Whitman.

Bye, George T. (1887–1957). Literary agent. Bye was born in Kansas and started his career as a newspaper reporter, first in Kansas and later Chicago and New York. In New York, he began working as a literary agent and founded George T. Bye & Company for that purpose in 1923. Bye's list of clients over his career included many notable people. He was Darrow's literary agent for a time.

Byllesby, Henry M. (1859–1924). Engineer and utilities owner. Byllesby worked early in his career as a draftsman for Thomas A. Edison (1847–1931) and then took a job in management for the Westinghouse Electric Company. Later, he formed his own business in Chicago, called H. M. Byllesby & Co., which acquired many gas and electric-power generating and distribution companies in several states.

Calverton, Victor F. (1900–40). Socialist writer and editor. Calverton, whose real name was George Goetz (Calverton was his pen name), graduated from Johns Hopkins University, 1921, pursued graduate studies, and taught public school for a while. He edited, published, and wrote for the *Modern Quarterly* (known for a time as the *Modern Monthly*), 1923–40, a radical magazine that covered a wide range of political, social, literary, and scientific topics. He also wrote many books, including history, fiction, and literary criticism.

Camfield, Daniel A. (1863–1914). Builder, developer, and businessman. Camfield was born in Rhode Island and moved to Greeley, Colorado, in 1881, where Darrow's son Paul resided. Camfield became a large landowner in northeast Colorado. He was actively involved in large irrigation projects, including in the Platte Valley, from Greeley to Nebraska. He was responsible for building and renovating several buildings in downtown Greeley. He also helped organize a bank and was part owner of a publishing company.

Caplan, David (d. 1934?). Laborer. Caplan was indicted in Los Angeles in 1911, along with John J. McNamara *(q.v.),* James B. McNamara *(q.v.),* and Matthew Schmidt *(q.v.),* for his role in purchasing and transporting the dynamite and nitroglycerin that were used to blow up the Los Angeles Times Building. Caplan wasn't captured until 1914, when he was found working as a barber under an alias in Washington.

He was first tried in Los Angeles in April and May 1915, but the result was a hung jury. He was tried again later in the year and convicted of voluntary manslaughter. He was sentenced to ten years in prison, but his sentence was reduced for good behavior. He was released from prison in 1923.

Carlin, Nellie (1869–1948). Lawyer. Carlin graduated from the Chicago College of Law, 1896. She worked as a lawyer in Darrow's law offices between 1896 and 1910 (although not continuously), and began a private practice of her own, 1910–13, before being appointed public guardian of Cook County, 1913–18, by Governor Edward F. Dunne *(q.v.)*. Later, she became the first woman appointed as an assistant state's attorney for Illinois, 1918–19. She was a member of the Single Tax Club in Chicago. She was also a vice president of the National Women's Lawyers Association and president of the Women's Protective Association in Chicago. She was the author of many essays on social and legal reforms, which were published in various magazines. Her nephew, William L. Carlin *(q.v.)*, also practiced law with Darrow.

Carlin, William L. (1887–1963). Lawyer. Carlin's parents died when he was a boy in Chicago and he was raised by his aunt, Nellie Carlin *(q.v.)*. He began working for Darrow's law firm as an office boy in 1910 (and eventually married Darrow's secretary). Darrow convinced him to go to law school and he graduated from Chicago Kent Law School, 1915. He became a law partner of Darrow's after he graduated and remained his partner until approximately 1928. Later in his career, Carlin worked for many years as an assistant state's attorney for Illinois, in the appeals division.

Carlson, A[nton] J[ulius] (1875–1956). Physiologist and educator. Carlson was born in Sweden and came to the United States when he was sixteen. He attended Augustana College and Theological Seminary in Rock Island, Illinois, where he obtained a B.A., 1898, and an M.A., 1899. He worked as a minister and then obtained a Ph.D. in physiology, 1902, from Stanford University. Later, he joined the faculty at the University of Chicago, where he conducted research and taught physiology, 1904–40. He was also a consultant to the U.S. Food and Drug Administration. He performed pioneering research in hunger and nutrition. His research on diabetes led to the use of insulin. He was an ardent civil libertarian and active in many professional organizations.

Case, Shirley Jackson (1872–1947). Educator and writer. Case was a Baptist scholar of the New Testament and early church history and professor at the University of Chicago Divinity School, 1908–38. He wrote many books on early Christianity.

Chase, Blanche Darrow (1913–2006). Darrow's granddaughter and the youngest daughter of Paul and Lillian (Anderson) Darrow *(q.v.)*. Chase was born in Greeley, Colorado, and lived there until her father moved with his family to Chicago in 1928, taking an apartment near Jackson Park, two blocks from Darrow's apartment. In

1938, she married Gordon Chase (1914–2009). They always lived in the Chicago area.

Cochran, Negley D. (1863–1941). Journalist. Cochran was born in Martin's Ferry, Ohio, and graduated from the University of Michigan, 1883. After working for his father (a lawyer) for a while, Cochran eventually became a reporter for the *Toledo Blade,* then managing editor of the *Toledo Commercial,* and editor of the *Toledo Bee,* which he later purchased. When the *Bee* merged with the *Toledo News,* after being bought out by a syndicate controlled by E. W. Scripps *(q.v.)* in 1903, Cochran continued working as an editor and developed a close relationship with Scripps. In 1911, Scripps made Cochran editor of an experimental, ad-less tabloid newspaper in Chicago called *The Day Book,* 1911–17. Cochran retired as editor of the *News-Bee* in 1922 and became an editorial and feature writer for Scripps's chain of newspapers.

Coolidge, Calvin (1872–1933). Thirtieth president of the United States, 1923–29.

Costigan, Jr., George P. (1870–1934). Lawyer and law professor. Costigan was born in Chicago and received an A.B., 1892, A.M., 1894, and LL.B., 1894, from Harvard and an LL.D., 1913, from the University of Nebraska. He practiced law in Salt Lake City, 1894–99, and later worked as a professor at Denver Law School, 1904–5, and the University of Nebraska College of Law, 1905–7, where he was also dean, 1907–9. Later, he was a professor of law at Northwestern University, 1909–21, and the University of California at Berkeley, 1922–34. He was the author of books on mining law, contracts, and legal ethics and a frequent contributor to legal periodicals.

Cramer, David H. (1873?–1940). Minister. Cramer was a pastor at the Presbyterian Church in Darrow's hometown of Kinsman, Ohio, from 1931 to 1936.

Crandall, Allen (1896–1973). Proofreader, printer, writer, and farmer. Crandall worked for many years as a proofreader for the *Sterling (Colorado) Advocate* and the *Denver Post.* He also operated his own small printing press, on which he printed advertisements, pamphlets, and his own books, including a short biography of Darrow, *The Man from Kinsman* (1933), which he published while working for the *Advocate.* He lived the last years of his life operating a small farm in Kansas.

Cronbach, Abraham (1882–1965). Religious leader, author, and educator. Cronbach was a rabbi at Reform Jewish synagogues in Indiana, New York, and Ohio, 1906–19, and chaplain of the Chicago Federation of Synagogues, 1919–22, before becoming a professor at Hebrew Union College in Cincinnati, Ohio, 1922–50. He was the author of many books and articles, many of which addressed Judaism or advocated a pacifist philosophy.

Crosby, Ernest Howard (1856–1907). Lawyer, author, and social reformer. Crosby graduated from New York University, 1876, and Columbia University Law School, 1878. He practiced law in New York, 1878–88, and served two years in New York's

state assembly before serving as a judge on the international court at Alexandria, Egypt, 1889–94. In Egypt, he fell under the influence of Tolstoy's writings and returned to New York, where he became a disciple of Henry George *(q.v.)*. He founded and served as the first president of the Social Reform Club of New York City, 1894, and the Anti-Imperialism League of New York, 1900. He wrote poetry and several books, including an anti-imperialism novel, *Captain Jinks: Hero* (1902).

Cruice, Daniel L. (b. 1868). Postal worker and lawyer. Born in Buffalo, New York, Cruice, whose parents were poor, worked as a messenger boy for a telegraph office and later as a sailor on rivers and the Great Lakes during breaks from attending the University of New York, where he earned a degree in 1888. After graduating, he worked for the U.S. post office and took an active part in the union organization of post office clerks. Later, he was transferred to the railway mail service and worked a route from Buffalo to Chicago, while also earning an LL.B. from the Chicago College of Law, 1894. After graduating, he opened a general law practice in Chicago but kept his mail route for some time to supplement his income. He was involved in many labor and progressive reform efforts in Chicago. He ran unsuccessfully for mayor in 1903, as an Independent Labor Party candidate. He was president of the Referendum League, which advocated for public ownership of the street railways and gas and electric utilities, among other reforms.

Darrow, Ammirus (1818–1904). Furniture maker and Clarence Darrow's father. Ammirus was born in Henrietta, New York. He married Clarence Darrow's mother, Emily (Eddy) Darrow *(q.v.)*, in 1845. As a young man, he considered entering the ministry, graduating from Western Unitarian Theological School in Meadville, Pennsylvania, 1850, and Cleveland University in Ohio, 1852, but later began farming in Farmdale, Ohio. He attended one year in the law department at the University of Michigan, 1864–65, and then started and operated a furniture factory and store in Kinsman, Ohio, with his brother-in-law. In about 1881, he sold the business and moved to Youngstown, Ohio, where he worked with his sons Channing E. Darrow *(q.v.)* and Herman C. Darrow *(q.v.)*. He ran unsuccessfully for the state senate in Ohio in 1883. Later, he lived with his son Clarence and his family in Ashtabula, Ohio, moving to Chicago the same year as Clarence, 1887, and probably at the same time. He lived with his children in Chicago when he married Katherine Donahue (b. 1855) in 1897. He died in Chicago.

Darrow, Channing E. (1850–1911). Darrow's brother and the second child of Ammirus and Emily (Eddy) Darrow *(q.v.)*. Little is known about Channing's early adult life. But during his last twenty years he was a second-hand furniture dealer and auction house operater in Denver, San Francisco, Los Angeles, and Arizona. He married three times and apparently had no children.

Darrow, Emily (Eddy) (1823–72). Clarence Darrow's mother. Born in Windsor, Connecticut, Emily met Darrow's father, Ammirus, when they were students at a school academy in Mahoning County, Ohio. They married the following year, 1845, and

had eight children (six boys and two girls), with one son dying in infancy. By all surviving accounts, she was an industrious and intelligent woman who took an active interest in political matters and was an ardent advocate for women's rights. She died in Kinsman, Ohio.

Darrow, [Edward] Everett (1846–1927). Teacher, Darrow's brother, and the first child of Ammirus and Emily (Eddy) Darrow *(q.v.)*. Everett was born in Meadville, Pennsylvania. He attended the Kinsman Academy, 1862–64, and graduated from the high school in Ann Arbor, Michigan, 1866, and the University of Michigan, 1870. He later spent two years traveling and studying in Europe, 1871–73, listening to lectures at the Sorbonne and attending one school year at the University of Berlin. After returning from Europe, he taught school for two years at Andover, Ohio, 1875–77, worked as a high school teacher in Springfield, Illinois, 1877–83, and then taught the rest of his career at South Side High School in Chicago, where he was also assistant principal. After he retired from teaching, he lived in New York City. He married Helen Kelchner Darrow *(q.v.)* in 1889 and they had one child, Karl K. Darrow *(q.v.)*.

Darrow, Helen Kelchner (1865–1954). Teacher and wife of Everett Darrow. Helen was born in Pittsburgh, Pennsylvania, but spent her youth in Springfield, Illinois. She received a B.A. from the University of Chicago, 1899, and continued there as a graduate student for two years, studying Greek. Later, she worked as a high school teacher and church organist in Chicago. She met Darrow's brother, [Edward] Everett Darrow *(q.v.)*, when she was his student in high school in Chicago. They lived in Chicago until they moved to New York City in 1917, where they lived the rest of their lives.

Darrow, Herman C. (1862–1933). Darrow's brother and the seventh child of Ammirus and Emily (Eddy) Darrow *(q.v.)*. Herman worked with his father in his furniture business in Kinsman, Ohio. In 1893, he moved to Chicago and worked for the city and as a teacher. The last nine years of his life, he worked as a proofreader for the *Chicago Tribune*.

Darrow, Hubert H. (1860–1905). Darrow's brother and the sixth child of Ammirus and Emily (Eddy) Darrow *(q.v.)*. Hubert taught in country schools near Kinsman, Ohio, for several years and was the leader of Kinsman's community band. He later moved East, where he worked as a musician and band leader at eastern resorts, including in Saratoga, New York. He married and had two children, from whom he was estranged for many years. In 1901, he started a business selling and renting music supplies in New Orleans, which he later moved to Chicago, where he lived during the last fifteen years of his life. He organized the Fenten Ladies Band, an attraction at the World's Fair in 1893. He died of tuberculosis in Tucson, Arizona, where his brother Channing lived.

Darrow, Jessie (Ohl). *See* **Brownlee, Jessie (Ohl).**

Darrow, Karl K. (1891–1982). Physicist, author, lecturer, and son of Everett and Helen Kelchner Darrow *(q.v.)*. Karl received his Ph.D. in physics from the University of Chicago, 1917, and also studied at the University of Paris, 1911–12, and the University of Berlin, 1912. He worked as a research physicist at Western Electric, 1917–25, and later as a physicist and member of the technical staff at Bell Laboratories, 1925–56. He wrote several scientific books and textbooks, including *Atomic Energy* (1948) and *Introduction to Contemporary Physics* (1926), and more than two hundred articles for professional and technical journals.

Darrow, Lillian (Anderson) (1887–1969). Wife of Paul Darrow *(q.v.)*. Lillian worked in Darrow's law office as a telephone receptionist before she married Paul Darrow in 1909. They had three children: Jessie Darrow Johnston *(q.v.)*, Mary Darrow Simonson *(q.v.)*, and Blanche Darrow Chase *(q.v.)*. Lillian's sister, Annie Anderson Lund, was Darrow's dentist.

Darrow, Mary. *See* **Olson, Mary Darrow.**

Darrow, Paul [Everett] (1883–1956). Businessman and Darrow's only child, from his marriage to Jessie (Ohl) Brownlee *(q.v.)*. Paul attended the McCosh School in Chicago, the Chicago Manual Training School, and the Melville W. Fuller Public School in Chicago before graduating from Dartmouth College, 1904. After college, he worked for a book publisher in Chicago before moving to Greeley, Colorado, 1907, to manage a gas plant that he owned with his father. He married Lillian (Anderson) Darrow *(q.v.)*, 1909, and they had three children. In 1928, Paul and his father sold the gas plant and Paul and his family moved to Chicago, taking an apartment close by his father's apartment, near Jackson Park. In Chicago, he worked as vice president for a bank, 1928–30, and then as a stockbroker, 1930–35. In 1935, William Holly *(q.v.)* appointed him as a trustee of two large real estate investment companies, and he held that position until 1943.

Darrow, Ruby (Hamerstrom) (1870–1957). Second wife of Clarence Darrow. Ruby Darrow—whose given name at birth was Hannah, not Ruby—was born in Galesburg, Illinois. Her mother and father were Swedish (her father came to the United States when he was a boy). She had six brothers and no sisters. She left high school at the age of fourteen to take care of her invalid mother. She worked as a feature writer for newspapers in Chicago before she married Darrow in 1903. She also wrote for magazines. She did not work outside the home after their marriage. After Darrow's death, she remained living in their apartment for a short while and then moved into a residential hotel in Chicago, where she remained until the last two years of her life, when she lived in a nursing home in Wisconsin.

Darrow, Viola ("Jennie"). *See* **Moore, Viola ("Jennie") Darrow.**

Daugherty, Harry M. (1860–1941). Lawyer and politician. Daugherty graduated from the University of Michigan Law School, 1881, practiced law in Washington Court House, Ohio, served as a city councilman, 1886–87, and as a Republican member

of the state house of representatives in Ohio, 1891–95. Later, he continued practicing law in Columbus, Ohio, as a corporation lawyer, and he worked as a lobbyist. He became very influential in Republican politics in Ohio, helping in 1920 to secure the presidential nomination for Warren G. Harding *(q.v.)*, who rewarded him with the position of attorney general, 1921–24. Daugherty proved inept and corrupt and President Coolidge demanded his resignation, after which he returned to practicing law in Ohio.

Davis, John W. (1873–1955). Lawyer, solicitor general, ambassador, and politician. Davis practiced law in West Virginia and served in the U.S. House of Representatives, 1910–13, before serving as U.S. soliciter general, 1913–18, and then ambassador to the Court of St. James's, 1918–20. He worked as a lawyer on Wall Street before being nominated as the Democratic presidential candidate in 1924. He faced a third-party contest from Robert M. La Follette *(q.v.)* and was defeated by Calvin Coolidge *(q.v.)*. He devoted the rest of his life primarily to his legal practice and he argued many cases in the U.S. Supreme Court challenging New Deal legislation.

Davis, LeCompte (1864–1958). Lawyer. Davis was a native of Kentucky and graduate of Centre College in Danville, Kentucky. He spent most of his professional life in Los Angeles, where he became a well-known criminal-defense attorney. His entire career was in private practice, except for a two-year stint in the early 1900s as an assistant district attorney in Los Angeles. Davis was part of the legal team representing John J. and James B. McNamara *(q.v.)*.

Debs, Eugene V. (1855–1926). Labor leader. Born in Terre Haute, Indiana, Debs worked for a railroad in Indiana as a young man and helped organize a local union in 1875. In 1893, he helped found and became first president of the American Railway Union. He was sentenced to six months in prison for his role in leading the Pullman strike in 1894. He helped establish the Social Democratic Party, 1898, the Socialist Party of America, 1901, and the Industrial Workers of the World, 1905. He was a socialist presidential candidate in 1900, 1904, 1908, 1912, and 1920. He worked as an editor and promoter for the *Appeal to Reason,* a socialist newspaper, 1907–12. In 1918, he was convicted under the federal Espionage Act, sentenced to prison, and pardoned in 1921, after which he tried to rebuild the Socialist Party.

Debs, Katherine (1857–1936). Wife of Eugene V. Debs *(q.v.)*.

Dietrich, John H. (1878–1957). Unitarian minister. Dietrich was a minister in the Reformed Church in Pittsburg, Pennsylvania, 1905–11, until he became a Unitarian minister, first in Spokane, Washington, 1911–16, and then with the First Unitarian Society in Minneapolis, Minnesota, 1916–38. He was one of the founders of and a spokesperson for the Humanist movement in Unitarianism.

Doherty, Henry L. (1870–1939). Engineer, inventor, and businessman. Largely self-educated, Doherty worked as an engineer for and manager of gas and electric companies before forming his own company in 1905, to provide engineering and

financial services to utilities companies. In 1910, he formed a holding company called Cities Service Co., which became publicly traded and had vast holdings, including dozens of subsidiaries with gas, electric, and oil operations throughout the United States. As an inventor, Doherty was awarded 140 patents in a variety of fields. He kept a Wall Street office and also invested heavily in real estate in New York City and Florida in the 1920s.

Du Bois, W. E. B. (1868–1963). Author, educator, and civil rights leader. Du Bois received a B.A., 1890, an M.A., 1891, and a Ph.D., 1895, from Harvard University. He taught history and economics at Atlanta University, 1897–1910, and later was head of the sociology department at Atlanta University, 1932–44. He was a founder of the Niagara Movement in 1905, one of the organizers in 1909 of the National Association for the Advancement of Colored People, and long an advocate of Pan Africanism. From 1909 until 1932, Du Bois served as editor of the NAACP's journal, *Crisis*. His many books include *The Suppression of the African Slave-Trade to the United States 1638–1870* (1896), *The Souls of Black Folk* (1903), *Black Reconstruction in America* (1935), and *Dusk of Dawn* (1940), an autobiography.

Dubrow, Mary C. (1897?–1984?). Teacher and suffragist. Dubrow attended the University of New York and taught school in New Jersey before she became an organizer and speaker for the National Woman's Party. She was among the suffragists arrested during the watch-fire demonstrations in Washington, D.C., in January 1919. Dubrow later lived in New York City and became treasurer of the American League to Abolish Capital Punishment in 1931.

Dunne, Edward F. (1853–1937). Lawyer, judge, and politician. Dunne graduated from Union College of Law in Chicago, 1877, and practiced law in Chicago before he was elected to the circuit court of Cook County, 1892–1905. A Democrat, Dunne was elected to one term as mayor of Chicago, 1905–7, after which he practiced law again, 1907–11, and then was elected Democratic governor of Illinois, 1913–17. After his reelection defeat in 1916, he returned to the practice of law.

Easley, Ralph M. (1856–1939). Journalist and reformer. Born in Illinois, Easley moved to Kansas in 1875 and taught school and served as a postmaster before founding, publishing, and editing the *Hutchinson (Kansas) News*, 1883–87. He left Kansas in 1887 and moved to Chicago, where he worked as a reporter for the *(Chicago) Inter-Ocean*, 1887–90. In 1893, he helped found and served as secretary of, 1893–1900, the Civic Federation of Chicago, a reform organization that, among other things, worked to accomplish municipal reforms and mediate labor disputes. In 1900, Easley moved to New York, where he founded the National Civic Federation and served as chairman of its executive council, 1900–39. The national organization, in addition to its reform work, at Easley's direction opposed all socialistic efforts in the United States and abroad and fought against radical labor organizations like the Industrial Workers of the World.

Eckert, Floyd E. (1893–1971). Lawyer. Eckert obtained an LL.B. from Chicago-Kent College of Law, 1915, and practiced law in Woodstock, Illinois, until approximately 1965. He was also public administrator for McHenry County, 1917–42.

Eldred, Henry B. (1810–1895). Presbyterian minister. Eldred obtained a B.A. and M.A., 1934, from Yale Divinity School. He served as an ordained minister of the Presbyterian church in Darrow's hometown of Kinsman, Ohio, 1838–74.

Ellis, [Henry] Havelock (1859–1939). Writer, editor, and physician. Ellis spent most of his professional life studying and writing about human sexual behavior. He was well known as an advocate of women's rights and sex education. His best-known work is the seven-volume *Studies in the Psychology of Sex* (1897–1928).

Ely, Richard T. (1954–1943). American economist, progressive reformer, and professor at Johns Hopkins, 1881–92, the University of Wisconsin, 1892–1925, and Northwestern University, 1925–33.

Essling, William W. (1915–1998). Lawyer. Essling graduated from the University of Minnesota and later, 1939, from the St. Paul College of Law. He served in the navy during World War II and worked as a prosecutor for a time in the U.S. attorney's office in Minnesota before starting a long career in private practice in St. Paul, Minnesota. He also taught trial practice and family law at William Mitchell College of Law in St. Paul, Minnesota, for several years.

Ewing, William C. Ewing was the first executive director of the Massachusetts Council for the Abolition of the Death Penalty.

Field, Mary. *See* **Parton, Mary Field.**

Field, Sara Bard (1882–1974). Poet, suffragist, and sister of Mary Field Parton *(q.v.)*. Field married Albert Ehrgott, a Baptist minister and friend of her parents, in 1900. They lived in Rangoon, Burma, 1900–1902, where they worked for the church, before moving to Cleveland, Ohio, 1903–10, where Ehrgott was in charge of a parish. Field became active in reform activities in Cleveland and continued these activities throughout her life. She moved to Portland, Oregon, in 1910, after her husband was dismissed from his post for supporting Christian socialism. In Portland, she was introduced by Darrow to C. E. S. Wood *(q.v.)*. Eventually, she lived with and married Wood. She was active in the suffrage movement and active in the anti-war movement during World War I. She wrote three volumes of poetry, including *Barabbas* (1932).

Fisher, Richard (1849–1926). Physician. Fisher was born in Pittsburg but spent much of his childhood in Sharon, Pennsylvania, graduating from a local school there. He was married to Mary (Ohl) Fisher (b. 1853), an older sister of Darrow's first wife, Jessie (Ohl) Brownlee *(q.v.)*. Fisher worked in the local mills in Sharon until he was thirty-eight years old, after which, having long been interested in medicine, he obtained an M.D. from a medical school in Washington, D.C. He practiced medicine in Washington for several years thereafter, with many prominent patients in

civic circles and government, including President Grover Cleveland. He later moved to Chicago, where he continued his practice. He was well known for including fasting among his treatments for various ailments. In 1919, he and his wife moved to Melbourne, Florida, to retire on a large estate.

Ford, Henry (1863–1947). American automobile manufacturer.

Fosdick, Harry Emerson (1878–1969). Minister, educator, and author. Fosdick received a B.A. from Colgate University, 1900, a B.D. from Union Theological Seminary, 1904 (where he later worked as a professor), and an M.A. from Columbia University, 1908. Fosdick, a Baptist, was supported throughout his career as a minister by John D. Rockefeller (1839–1937). He served as a minister at the First Presbyterian Church in New York City, 1918–25, then Park Avenue Baptist Church in New York City, 1925–1931, and finally Riverside Church in New York City, 1931–46. He wrote many popular religious books and was widely known as a liberal protestant minister.

Foster, George Burman (1858–1918). Baptist theologian and educator. Foster taught systematic theology and philosophy of religion at the University of Chicago for the last twenty-three years of his life. A theological modernist, Foster believed in the necessity of religion and the importance of personal faith but fought against religious authority and traditions. He was often denounced by more orthodox clergymen and fundamentalists.

Francis, John H. (1866–1934). Educator and school administrator. Francis was born in Greenbush, Ohio, and graduated from San Joaquin Valley College, 1890, and Otterbein University, 1895, after which he taught in the rural schools of Ohio, at San Joaquin Valley College, and in public high schools in Los Angeles and Stockton, California. While in Los Angeles, he developed schools for immigrants and founded the Los Angeles Polytechnic High School (which is now named after him), serving as its first principal. From 1910 to 1916, he was superintendent of schools in Los Angeles, during which time Los Angeles built the first junior high school and the first agricultural high school in the country. Francis's son, George H. Francis, worked for a time (circa. 1924–25) as a lawyer in Darrow's law office.

Frederick, John T. (1893–1975). English professor, author, and editor. Frederick was born in Iowa, graduated from the University of Iowa, 1915, where he also received his M.A., 1917. He was the founder and editor of *The Midland,* a regional literary magazine published from 1915 to 1933. He taught English at the University of Iowa, 1921–30, and later at other schools, including Northwestern University and the University of Notre Dame, before returning to the University of Iowa in the 1960s. He was the author of several novels and scholarly books and articles.

Fredericks, John D. (1869–1945). Lawyer and politician. Born in Pennsylvania, Fredericks obtained an LL.D. from Washington and Jefferson College, 1891, and was admitted to the bar in Los Angeles in 1895. He served as district attorney for

Los Angeles County for twelve years, 1903–1915, and also as president of the Los Angeles Chamber of Commerce. As district attorney, he was well known as a prosecutor of liquor offenders, and he (unsuccessfully) prosecuted Darrow on jury bribery charges. In Darrow's first trial, Fredericks was the lead prosecutor. In Darrow's second trial, he was a witness and did not serve as a prosecutor in the courtroom. He was a Republican candidate for governor of California in 1914 and later was elected to Congress to fill a vacancy, 1923–27, after which he resumed the practice of law in Los Angeles.

Gallagher, Andrew. Union leader. Gallagher was secretary of the San Francisco Labor Council, 1907–12.

Garland, Hamlin (1860–1940). Writer. Garland was born in Wisconsin. His mother and father were farmers. Largely self-educated, he abandoned farm life in 1884 and moved to Boston to become a teacher of literature. He eventually established himself as a writer of realistic fiction. From 1893 to 1916, he lived primarily in Chicago and later moved to New York, where he lived until 1930, when he moved to California. Garland's writings and many books include literary essays, novels, autobiographies, and memoirs. His best-known novel is probably *Rose of Dutcher's Coolly* (1895) and his best-known autobiographical work is probably *A Son of the Middle Border* (1917).

Gary, Joseph E. (1821–1906). Lawyer and judge. Gary was born in New York, worked as carpenter, and eventually started reading for the law. He moved to Missouri in 1843, where he was admitted to the bar the following year. He practiced law in Nevada and California before settling in Chicago in 1856, where he continued his practice. In 1863, he was elected as a judge on the Superior Court of Cook County, a position that he held until his death. He presided over the celebrated trial of the Haymarket defendants in 1886.

George, Henry (1839–1897). Economist, reformer, and journalist. George presented his single-tax theory in his classic work, *Progress and Poverty* (1877–79).

Gerson, T[heodore] Perceval (1872–1960). Prominent physician and surgeon in Hollywood, California. Gerson obtained his M.D. from the University of Pennsylvania, 1895. He had internships in the East and practiced medicine in Pennsylvania before moving to Los Angeles in 1903. He was active in local political, civic, and cultural affairs, including the founding of the Hollywood Bowl. He was a close friend of Darrow's when Darrow stood trial for jury bribery in Los Angeles.

Gertz, Elmer (1906–2000). Lawyer and author. Gertz was born in Chicago and raised in orphanages after his mother died, when Gertz was nine. He graduated from the University of Chicago with a Ph.B., 1928, and J.D., 1930, and practiced law in Chicago from 1930 until his retirement late in life. He was involved with many civil liberties cases and had several famous clients, including the writer Henry Miller (1891–1980) and Nathan Leopold *(q.v.)*, whose parole he helped obtain. Gertz wrote

several books, including two autobiographies: *A Handful of Clients* (1965) and *To Life* (1974).

Goldblatt, Paul (1898–1986). Social worker and community leader. Goldblatt was born in New York, graduated from New York University, and for many years served as the executive director of the Jewish Community Center in Harrisburg, Pennsylvania.

Golding, Fred E. (1879–1942). Lumber wholesaler. Born in Los Angeles, Golding worked as the treasurer of a lumber company before starting his own lumber wholesale business in Los Angeles. He served as a juror in Darrow's first trial for jury bribery in 1912, after which they became lifelong friends. Golding's lumber business was ruined in the depression of the 1930s. He later worked selling real estate and tires. He enjoyed writing poetry, and he loved books and nature.

Gompers, Samuel (1850–1924). Labor leader. Born in London, Gompers emigrated to the United States with his family in 1863. He worked as a cigar maker and helped reorganize the Cigarmakers International Union in the 1870s. He helped found the Federation of Organized Trades and Labor Unions in 1881, which was reorganized in 1886 as the American Federation of Labor. He was elected president of the AFL that same year and every year thereafter (except one, 1895) until his death.

Gregory, Stephen S. (1849–1920). Lawyer. Gregory earned an LL.B. from the University of Wisconsin, 1871, and practiced law in Madison, Wisconsin, 1871–74, before moving to Chicago. Gregory and Darrow, in 1894, represented Eugene Prendergast, the assassin of Carter Harrison Sr. *(q.v.)*, and Eugene V. Debs *(q.v.)* and other leaders of the Pullman strike. Gregory was highly regarded as a lawyer. He served as president of the Chicago Bar Association, 1900, the Illinois State Bar Association, 1904, and the American Bar Association, 1911.

Gros, Robert R. (1914–1997). Public relations director and lecturer. Gros graduated with a B.A. from Stanford University, 1935, and worked for the advertising and publicity department of the Pacific Gas and Electric Company in San Francisco, California. He became manager of the department in 1944 and eventually vice president of public relations, 1955–76. He took an active interest in world affairs and often sought interviews with prominent or influential people. He was also a frequent lecturer on a variety of subjects.

Hackler, Victor (1906–1975). Journalist and editor. Hackler graduated from the University of Nebraska, 1927, and began working for the Associated Press the same year, in Omaha, Nebraska. He eventually became bureau chief for the Associated Press in Milwaukee, Chicago, and New York, and worked as a news editor for the organization in London.

Haley, Margaret (1861–1939). Teacher and organizer. Haley taught in country schools in Illinois and, in 1882, began teaching in Chicago-area schools. She was an early member of the Chicago Teachers Federation, formed in 1897, and soon became a

full-time leader of the CTF. She was instrumental in making the CTF a powerful organization. On the national level, her activism—including her work as president of the National Federation of Teachers—forced the National Education Association in the early 1900s to become more responsive to and representative of elementary school teachers. She edited and wrote most of the monthly *Chicago Teachers' Federation Bulletin*, 1901–8, and *Margaret Haley's Bulletin*, 1915–16, 1925–31.

Hall, Bolton (1854–1938). Lawyer and author. Born in Ireland, son of a Presbyterian clergyman, Hall obtained an A.B. from Princeton University, 1875, and an LL.B. from Columbia Law School, 1881. He was active in social reforms, including the single-tax movement and model-tenement housing. He wrote many works of fiction and nonfiction and edited a version of the King James Bible called *The Living Bible* (1928). He practiced law in New York City until shortly before his death.

Hamerstrom, Frederick (1873–1948). Businessman. Hamerstrom grew up in Galesburg, Illinois, and was a younger brother of Ruby (Hamerstrom) Darrow *(q.v.)*. Although his business successes fluctuated widely, for many years (in the 1910s and 1920s) he was vice president of a rubber manufacturer in Trenton City, New Jersey. He was married and had two children—Davis Hamerstrom (an architect) and Frederick Hamerstrom Jr. (a naturalist)—both of whom Darrow and Ruby helped through college. He was living in Winchester, Massachusetts, when he died.

Hamerstrom, George (b. 1876). Newspaperman. Hamerstrom was one of Ruby's younger brothers. Like his siblings, he was born and raised in Galesburg, Illinois. As a young man, when he lived in Galesburg, he worked as a bookkeeper. At some point in his thirties, he worked as a newspaper editor in Texas. But then later, for many years, he was on the staff and then director of the advertising department of a daily newspaper in Oklahoma.

Hamerstrom, Ruby. See **Darrow, Ruby (Hamerstrom)**.

Harding, Warren G. (1865–1923). Twenty-ninth president of the United States, 1921–23.

Hardy, Thomas (1840–1928). English poet and novelist.

Harriman, Job (1861–1925). Socialist politician, lawyer, and utopian colonist. Harriman was born in Indiana, studied religion at Northwest Christian University, and served three years after graduation as a minister in the Disciples of Christ Church. In 1886, he moved to San Francisco, where he eventually became a member of the Socialist Labor Party and ran as the party's candidate for governor in 1898. At the same time, he studied for and was admitted to the bar in California. By 1900, Harriman had switched his political allegiances to the Social Democratic Party and he was the running mate of Eugene V. Debs *(q.v.)* in the presidential election. Harriman was one several lawyers working with Darrow in 1911 on the defense of James B. and John J. McNamara *(q.v.)*. At the same time that he worked

on the case, he ran a campaign for mayor of Los Angeles on the socialist ticket. He lost the race that year and again in 1913. In 1914, he founded a short-lived utopian colony known as "Llano del Rio" in the desert northeast of Los Angeles. He died in Los Angeles.

Harrington, John R. (1860–1916). Lawyer. For many years, Harrington was the chief investigator for the Chicago City Railway Company, and it was in this capacity that he first met Darrow, when Darrow was representing the company in the mid-1890s. Many years later, Darrow hired Harrington—who had been fired by his employer—to gather evidence for him in preparation for the trial of James B. and John P. McNamara *(q.v.)* in Los Angeles. Although he was a lawyer, Harrington apparently never practiced law.

Harris, Frank (1856–1931). Irish-born journalist, editor, biographer, and novelist. Harris moved to the United States at the age of fifteen and later moved to England, where he edited a series of magazines, including the *Saturday Review,* 1894–98. Among his many books are *The Bomb* (1908), a novel based on the Haymarket bombing in Chicago in 1886; *Oscar Wilde: His Life and Confessions* (1916), a biography; and *My Life and Loves* (1923–27), his scandalous multivolume autobiography.

Harrison, Sr., Carter (1825–1893). Lawyer, politician, newspaper editor and publisher. Harrison, the son of a plantation owner, was born in Kentucky. He received an A.B. from Yale University, 1845, and a law degree from Transylvania College in Lexington, Kentucky, 1855, after which he moved to Chicago, where he practiced law and speculated in real estate. He was elected as a Democrat to Congress for two terms, 1875–79, and then served four two-year terms as mayor, 1879–87, declining the renomination in 1887. He was a popular mayor who enjoyed support across a broad spectrum of people. In 1891, he ran again for mayor (unsuccessfully) but then was reelected in 1893, during the year of the World's Fair in Chicago. During the period out of office, he was editor and part owner of the *(Chicago) Times,* 1891–93. He was assassinated by a deranged office seeker while serving his fifth term. His son, Carter Harrison Jr. *(q.v.),* also served as as mayor of Chicago.

Harrison, Jr., Carter (1860–1953). Lawyer, politician, newspaper publisher and editor. Harrison received a law degree from Yale University, 1883, and was elected mayor of Chicago four years after the assassination of his father, Carter Harrison Sr. *(q.v.).* Like his father, he was elected to five terms as mayor of Chicago, 1897–1905, 1911–15, as a Democrat. Before his election, he practiced law, worked in the family real estate office, and, for several years, worked as editor and publisher of the *(Chicago) Times,* which his father had owned and edited.

Harrison, Charles Yale (1898–1954). Journalist and novelist. Harrison was born in Philadelphia and was largely self-educated. He worked for a newspaper in Montreal and then enlisted in the Royal Montreal Regiment and served as a machine gunner in France and Belgium during World War I. After the war, he worked as a theatre

manager and newspaper reporter before moving to New York City, where he worked as a public relations consultant and radio commentator while he pursued a writing career. Among other works, he wrote the first full-length biography of Darrow and several sociological novels.

Hawley, James (1847–1929). Lawyer and politician. Hawley was born and raised in Dubuque, Iowa. After high school, he lived in Idaho and then California, where he attended the City College of San Francisco, 1864–67, and read law. He returned to Idaho and was eventually admitted to the bar, 1871. He served in a variety of elected and appointed positions, including in the Idaho territorial legislature, 1870–78, as county attorney, 1878–82, U.S. attorney, 1885–89, mayor of Boise, 1903–1905, and governor of Idaho, 1911–13. Together with William Borah *(q.v.)*, Hawley served as prosecutor of Steve Adams and of William ("Big Bill") Haywood *(q.v.)* and George A. Pettibone *(q.v.)* for the murder of Idaho's former governor, Frank Steunenberg.

Hays, Arthur Garfield (1881–1954). Lawyer and author. Born in Rochester, New York, Hays lived most of his life in New York City. He graduated from Columbia University with a B.A., 1902, and an M.A. and LL.B., 1905, and shortly thereafter opened his own law office. He maintained a large commercial practice, but combined this work with high-profile cases involving free speech and other civil liberties. He worked with Darrow on many matters, including the Scopes trial, 1925, the Sweet cases, 1926, the trial of Greco and Carillo, 1927, and the Scottsboro case, 1932. Hays was one of the founders of the American Civil Liberties Union in 1920 and served as its general counsel from the late 1920s until his death. He wrote several books, including *Let Freedom Ring* (1925), *Trial by Prejudice* (1933), and *City Lawyer* (1942).

Haywood, William ("Big Bill") (1869–1928). Miner and labor leader. Haywood was born in Utah. His father, an itinerant worker, died when Haywood was three years old. Haywood received a rudimentary education and worked primarily as a miner from the age of fifteen until 1901, when he went to work as the secretary-treasurer of the Western Federation of Miners. In 1905, Haywood and other socialists and trade unionists formed the Industrial Workers of the World (IWW). In 1907, Darrow successfully defended Haywood for the murder of Frank Steunenberg, the former governor of Idaho. After the trial, Haywood campaigned for the Socialist Party of America and served as a member of its national executive committee, until he was removed by the SPA in 1913. Haywood then returned to the IWW as a national organizer. In 1918, he was convicted in Chicago along with more than one hundred other members of the IWW, charged by the federal government with sedition and espionage. In 1921, while out on bail pending appeal, Haywood escaped to Russia, where he wrote an autobiography and lived out his life.

Hearst, William Randolph (1863–1951). Publisher. Hearst was born in San Francisco, the son of a wealthy mine developer and United States senator. He attended

Harvard University, 1882–85, and then operated the *San Francisco Examiner,* a paper owned by his father. He turned the rundown paper into a commercial success and eventually built a newspaper and magazine publishing empire—often using color printing and sensational tabloid techniques—that included the *New York Morning Journal, Cosmopolitan,* and *Good Housekeeping.* Hearst started the *Chicago American* newspaper in 1900 and the *Chicago Examiner* in 1902 and employed Darrow as legal counsel for the newspapers. Hearst was also active in Democratic politics. He served two terms as a congressman from New York, 1903–7, and sought several other offices, including mayor and governor of New York.

Hillquit, Morris (1869–1933). Labor leader, lawyer, and author. Hillquit was born in Russia and emigrated to New York with his family in 1886. In 1887, he became active in the Socialist Labor Party and the labor movement. In 1893, he graduated with an LL.B. from New York University Law School. By 1901, he had split with the SLP and formed the Socialist Party of America, eventually becoming one of the best-known socialists of his time. He maintained an active law practice in New York City, representing individuals and trade unions, and worked as general counsel for the International Ladies' Garment Workers' Union. He was involved in several significant cases involving socialist activities. Between 1906 and 1920, he was five times a socialist candidate for Congress and, in 1917 and 1932, twice a candidate for mayor of New York City. He wrote several works on socialism, including *History of Socialism in the United States* (1903) and *Socialism in Theory and Practice* (1909).

Holly, William H. (1869–1958). Lawyer and judge. Holly was born in Bellefonte, Pennsylvania, and received an education in public and private schools in Macomb, Illinois. He read for the law and practiced in Macomb (for a time with Jacob Baily *[q.v.],* 1891–1902) before moving to Chicago, where he continued in private practice, 1902–14. He worked several years as an assistant state's attorney, 1914–16, and then returned to private practice, 1916–1933. He worked in Darrow's law office for many years and for a while was a named partner in the firm, 1922–25. In 1934, he was appointed by President Franklin D. Roosevelt *(q.v.)* as a district court judge, a position he held until his retirement in 1943.

Holmes, John Haynes (1879–1964). Holmes graduated from Harvard University in 1902 and became an ordained Unitarian minister in 1904. He was pastor for many years of the Church of the Messiah in New York City (later, starting in 1919, called the Community Church of New York), 1907–49. Holmes worked for many liberal causes and he was active in many organizations, including the Urban League, the National Association for the Advancement of Colored People, and the American Civil Liberties Union, among other civic and political organizations. He was also editor of the journal *Unity,* 1921–46.

Hoover, Herbert (1874–1964). Thirty-first president of the United States, 1929–33.

House, E[dward] M[andell] (1858–1938). Businessman and presidential advisor. Born in Texas to a wealthy family, House attended Cornell University and then returned to Texas to pursue a variety of business activities, including farming and real estate. He eventually moved to Boston and New York. Always interested in politics, House formed a close friendship with Woodrow Wilson *(q.v.)* in 1911 and became Wilson's closest advisor on many matters. After the Wilson presidency, House remained active in the Democratic Party and he became a supporter of Franklin D. Roosevelt *(q.v.)* in the 1932 election.

Howells, William Dean (1837–1920). Novelist, editor, and literary critic. Howells was born in Ohio to parents with Quaker and radical beliefs. His father was a small-town newspaper publisher. Howells supplemented his meager formal education with wide reading and a variety of work for newspapers. By the time he was in his twenties, Howells was publishing poetry, fiction, and criticism in popular magazines. He wrote a campaign biography of Lincoln that led to his appointment as consul to Venice, 1861–65. He became assistant editor and then editor-in-chief of the *Atlantic Monthly*, 1866–81, but resigned to devote himself to fiction, which was often serialized in *Century* magazine. He wrote a monthly column for *Harper's* for many years and served as its editor from 1886 to 1892. Howells, who held Tolstoy in great reverence, played an important role in the development of American realism. His literary output was large, including thirty-six novels, ten travel books and as many volumes of short stories and sketches, and several books of poetry, memoirs, drama, and hundreds of uncollected essays, reviews, editorials, etc.

Huebsch, Benjamin W. (1876–1964). Publisher. Born in New York City, Huebsch was largely educated at home and, at a young age, began working in the printing business. In the early 1900s, he turned a family printing business into a book publishing firm known as B. W. Huebsch. The firm became well known as a publisher of new and experimental writers and translations of European and Russian writers, including works by James Joyce, D. H. Lawrence, Thorstein Veblen, Gerhart Hauptmann, and Maxim Gorky. Huebsch published the third edition of Darrow's *Farmington* in 1919. Huebsch's firm merged with Viking Press in 1925, with Huebsch remaining on as vice president and editorial director.

Ickes, Harold (1874–1952). Lawyer, political organizer, and secretary of the interior. Born in Pennsylvania and raised in Chicago, Ickes graduated from the University of Chicago, 1896, worked as a newspaper reporter, got involved in local Republican politics, obtained a J.D. from the University of Chicago, 1907, and then practiced law in Chicago while continuing his political activities, rising in prominence in the progressive wing of the Republican party. Ickes's wife, Anna (d. 1935), a wealthy divorcée, served three terms in the Illinois General Assembly, 1928–34. In 1932, Franklin D. Roosevelt *(q.v.)* asked Ickes to help with his campaign. He did, and after the election, Ickes asked for and received an appointment as secretary of the interior, a post that

grew in importance during Ickes's tenure. Ickes served in this position throughout the Roosevelt presidency and briefly in the administration of Harry S. Truman.

Ingersoll, Robert G. (1833–99). Soldier, lawyer, orator, and author. Ingersoll, the son of an itinerant Congregational minister, had little formal education but was well read in the classics. He read for the law and was admitted to the bar in Illinois in 1854. He started a law practice with his brother in Peoria, Illinois, in approximately 1858. He raised and commanded a volunteer cavalry regiment from Illinois during the Civil War and later served as attorney general of Illinois, 1867–69. In 1877, he moved his successful law practice to Washington, D.C., and then, in 1885, to New York City. A Republican, Ingersoll was a popular political stump speaker, but he became particularly famous as an agnostic lecturer and author of works criticizing religious beliefs.

Ishill, Joseph (1888–1966). Typographer and anarchist printer. Ishill emigrated to the United States from Rumania in 1909 and worked as a typesetter in New York City. Influenced by anarchists like Emma Goldman, he became one of the original members of the Ferrer Colony in Stelton, New Jersey, in 1915. He taught printing to the children at the Modern School in Stelton and printed *The Modern School* magazine. Ishill published more than two hundred books and pamphlets in his life, all hand produced, and he became one of the finest printers and typographers of the twentieth century.

Jacobs, John T. (1869–1939). Lawyer and judge. Born and raised in New York, Jacobs obtained a law degree from the University of Denver and moved to Greeley, Colorado, in 1887, where he practiced law and became active in Republican politics and various businesses. He was very involved in forming Colorado's irrigation laws and he served briefly as a county judge, 1899–1902. He was fond of books and had an extensive private library. He committed suicide after suffering from what might have been cancer.

Jasin, Joseph (1883–1968). Rabbi. Born in Poland, Jasin came to the United States when he was ten years old. He attended Hebrew Union College and the University of Cincinnati. He was ordained a rabbi in 1904 and served congregations in Texas, Florida (Temple Israel in Miami), and California. He was also a national secretary of the Zionist Organization of America.

Johannsen, Anton (1872–1951). Woodworker and labor leader. Johannsen was born in Germany and arrived in the United States in 1882. As a young man, he worked odd jobs until he became a woodworker in Chicago, where he joined the carpenters' union. He eventually moved to San Francisco, where he was an organizer for the California Building Trades Council, 1909–14, and later an organizer for the carpenters' union, 1914–17. When he moved back to Chicago in 1918, he worked as an agent for the carpenters' union, 1918–25, and served eight years on the Illinois Industrial Commission. He also worked for the Chicago Federation of Labor for many years, including eleven years as its vice president, 1935–46. When Johannsen

was in San Francisco, he was indicted in federal court in Los Angeles in December 1911, together with Olaf Tveitmoe *(q.v.)* and other labor leaders, for conspiracy to transport explosives, but he was never tried for the offense. Johannsen and Tveitmoe were active in organizing labor support for the defense of John J. and James B. McNamara *(q.v.)* in 1911. Johannsen was a central character in *The Spirit of Labor* (1907), Hutchins Hapgood's account of labor and radicals in Chicago at the turn of the century.

Johannsen, Margaret (b. 1876). Born in Germany, Margaret Johannsen, like her husband, Anton Johannsen *(q.v.)*, immigrated to the United States in 1882.

Johnson, Hiram (1866–1945). Lawyer and politician. Johnson studied law in his father's law office in Sacramento, California, and he was admitted to the bar in 1888. He practiced in Sacramento and later, 1907, moved his practice to San Francisco. In 1908, he gained fame as an assistant district attorney when he successfully prosecuted the political boss Abraham Ruef (1864–1936) for bribery of city officials. He was elected governor of California as a Republican in 1910 and won reelection as a Progressive in 1914. As governor, he gained a national reputation as a speaker and accomplished many reforms, including regulation of the railroads and installation of a civil service system. He was the running mate of Theodore Roosevelt (1858–1919) on the Progressive ticket in 1912. In 1917, he resigned the governorship after winning election to the United States Senate, where he was a staunch isolationist. He served in the Senate until his death.

Johnson, Hugh S. (1882–1942). Army officer and government administrator. Johnson was born in Kansas and raised in Oklahoma. He graduated from the United States Military Academy at West Point, 1903, and received an A.B. and J.D. from the University of California Law School, 1916. He resigned from the army in 1919, having attained the rank of brigadier general, and for the next several years worked on business ventures. In 1933, President Franklin D. Roosevelt *(q.v.)* appointed him to head up the National Recovery Administration, which developed a system of compulsory fair-competition codes (which were declared unconstitutional in 1935 by the Supreme Court). Johnson was eased out of this position in October 1934 and, after a brief stint as head of the Works Progress Administration in New York City, spent his final years as a syndicated columnist and radio broadcaster.

Johnson, James Weldon (1871–1938). Teacher, lawyer, songwriter, civil rights leader, poet, and novelist. Johnson was born in Jacksonville, Florida, graduated from Atlanta University, 1894, and worked as a schoolteacher before practicing law in Jacksonville, 1897–1901, after reading for the law. Theodore Roosevelt appointed Johnson consul to Puerto Cabello, Venezuela, 1906–9, and then to Corinto, Nicaragua, 1909–12. After resigning as consul, Johnson worked as an editor and writer for the *New York Age*, 1914–16, after which he joined the staff of the National Association for the Advancement of Colored People, where he became executive

secretary, 1920–30. In 1930, he accepted a professorship at Fisk University and held that position until his death in an automobile accident. Johnson was one of the leading African American literary figures of his time: he edited several anthologies of poetry and songs and wrote several books of his own, including both poetry and fiction, most notably *The Autobiography of an Ex-Colored Man* (1912), as well as his autobiography, *Along This Way* (1933).

Johnson, Ralph (1903–73). Civic leader and postmaster. Johnson graduated from the University of Kansas, 1928, worked for thirty years as manager and secretary of the chamber of commerce for McPherson, Kansas, 1928–58, and later worked as postmaster. He was a community organizer and very active in civic affairs in McPherson.

Johnston, Jessie Darrow (1910–68). Darrow's granddaughter and the oldest daughter of Paul and Lillian (Anderson) Darrow *(q.v.)*. Johnston was born in Greeley, Colorado, and lived there until her father moved with his family to Chicago in 1928. She married twice, with two children from her first marriage. She died from cancer.

Jones, Samuel M. (1846–1904). Oil producer, manufacturer, and politician. Jones and his parents emigrated to the United States from Wales when Jones was nearly four years old. He had little formal education and worked menial jobs before starting an oil business. After selling his business to Standard Oil Company in 1889, Jones settled in Toledo, Ohio; there he secured a patent on an iron rod for pumping oil and started manufacturing drilling appliances. Jones instituted labor policies at his manufacturing plant that were remarkable for the time, including policies allowing eight-hour work days and paid vacations. He was elected mayor of Toledo as a Republican in 1897, and served in that office until his death. Jones was a controversial mayor: he established a minimum wage and an eight-hour work day for municipal employees, sought public ownership of utilities and streetcar operations, and (in his capacity as police judge) exercised a lenient attitude toward criminals. After his first two-year term in office, the Republican party refused to support him, and he won reelection each successive term as an independent. He failed in an independent bid for governor in 1899.

Keller, Helen (1880–1968). Author and lecturer. Keller was made blind and deaf by an illness at the age of nineteen months. She learned to speak and read Braille and graduated from Radcliffe College, 1904. A socialist and pacifist in her politics, she often lectured on political subjects and advocated many causes, including female suffrage and anti-militarism. She often campaigned for the blind and promoted the work of organizations for the blind, especially the American Foundation for the Blind. She was the author of many books, including *The World I Live In* (1908) and *Teacher* (1955).

Kennedy, James H. (1849–1934). Editor and journalist. Kennedy was born in Farmington, Ohio, and educated at the Western Reserve Seminary. He worked as

an editor for the *Cleveland Leader* and as managing editor for the *Cleveland Herald* before becoming editor of the *Magazine of Western History*, 1889–1902. He also worked as the editor of *Hardware Dealers* magazine and for ten years as the New York correspondent for the *Cleveland Plain Dealer*. For some period of time he was also one of the owners of the *Cleveland Voice*.

King, John F. (b. 1903?). King was convicted in New Jersey of first-degree murder after he shot and killed the proprietor of a saloon in 1926, during an attempted robbery. He was sentenced to life in prison and served his sentence in the New Jersey State Prison in Trenton; he was paroled in 1944.

Labadie, Joseph (1850–1933). Anarchist and labor organizer. Labadie was born in Paw Paw, Michigan. His father was an Indian interpreter for Jesuit missionaries. Labadie received virtually no formal education and was apprenticed to a printer in Indiana when he was sixteen years old. He became active in a typographical union and participated as an organizer for the Knights of Labor in 1878. In 1880, he helped establish the Detroit Council of Trades and Labor Unions. He was also a founder and first president, 1889–90, of the Michigan Federation of Labor. In the 1880s, he worked as a journalist for several labor papers, and in the early 1880s he became an anarchist and frequently contributed to the anarchist journal *Liberty*. Because of poor health, Labadie took a job in 1893 as a clerk with the Detroit Water Works, which he held until approximately 1920.

La Follette, Robert (1855–1925). Lawyer and politician. Born in Primrose, Wisconsin, La Follette graduated from the University of Wisconsin at Madison, 1879, studied law and was admitted to the bar, 1880. That same year, he was elected district attorney of Dane County, Wisconsin, 1880–84, and then elected as a Republican congressman, 1885–91. After losing reelection, he returned to the practice of law in Madison, remained active in Republican politics, and was eventually elected governor of Wisconsin, 1901–6. He resigned after being elected to the United States Senate. He was reelected to the Senate in 1911, 1917, and 1923, and served in that office until his death. La Follette unsuccessfully sought the Republican and Progressive presidential nominations several times.

Lawes, Lewis E. (1883–1947). Penologist and author. Lawes was born in Elmira, New York, the son of a prison guard. Lawes became a prison guard himself after a three-year stint in the army and then studied sociology at the New York School of Social Work. He returned to prison work, eventually becoming superintendent at the New York City Reformatory, 1915–19. Governor Alfred E. Smith *(q.v.)* appointed Lawes warden at Sing Sing in 1919, and Lawes continued in that position until 1941. He became well known as penal reformer and outspoken opponent of capital punishment, and he wrote several books about the penal system and his life.

Lawrence, Andrew M. (1864–1942). Newspaper reporter, editor, and publisher. Lawrence began his career as a reporter in 1884 for William Randolph Hearst's

San Francisco Examiner, later becoming the managing editor of the paper. He served briefly in the California legislature, 1887–88. He became the managing editor of Hearst's *Chicago American* when that paper was founded in 1900. Later, he became president of Hearst's *Chicago Examiner.* In 1920, Lawrence and a group of other investors bought the *San Francisco Journal,* which Lawrence managed and published before the *Journal* merged with the *San Francisco Bulletin* in 1924.

Leopold, Nathan (1904–1971). Student and hospital technician. Leopold was born in Chicago, the son of a wealthy box manufacturer. A brilliant young man with a strong interest in ornithology, he graduated from the University of Chicago, 1923, at the age of eighteen. He planned to enter Harvard Law School in the fall of 1924 but then committed the kidnapping and murder with Richard Loeb *(q.v.)* that made the two men famous. In prison in Illinois, Leopold studied a variety of subjects, organized the prison library, tutored other prisoners, volunteered for medical experiments, and otherwise became a model prisoner. He was paroled in 1958 and moved to Puerto Rico, where he worked as a hospital technician. He married in 1961.

Lewis, Denslow (1856–1913). Physician. Lewis was born in New York City. He graduated from the medical department of the University of Michigan, 1878, after which he did three years of postgraduate work in France and Germany before starting a private medical practice in Chicago. During his career in Chicago, he was chief of the attending staff at Cook County Hospital, chairman of the hygiene and sanitary science section of the American Medical Association, vice president of the Illinois State Medical Society, and professor of gynecology at the Chicago Policlinic (a clinical school for medical practitioners). Lewis wrote many articles for medical periodicals on the science of medicine as well as other topics like prostitution, abortion, and venereal diseases.

Lewis, Fay (1857–1949). Businessman. Lewis was a lifelong resident of Rockford, Illinois. He started work in a cigar shop at the age of seventeen, purchased the business the following year, and, from that beginning, developed a large corporate enterprise, including a successful wholesale tobacco business. Active in charitable and civic affairs, Lewis was an organizer and officer of the local humane society and an elected member of the local park board. He often campaigned for penal reforms and published a book on the subject, *The City Jail: A Symposium* (1903), which included an excerpt from Darrow's *Resist not Evil* (1902). Lewis and Darrow were close friends for many years. Lewis traveled to Los Angeles in 1912 to be with Darrow during his first trial for jury bribery.

Lewis, Joseph (1889–1968). Writer, publisher, and promoter of atheism. Lewis was born to a large family in Montgomery, Alabama, and educated in public schools until he left school at the age of nine. He lived most of his life in New York City. He founded the Thomas Paine Foundation, the Robert G. Ingersoll Memorial

Association, the American League for Separation of Church and State, and the Freethinkers of America. Lewis instigated many lawsuits that sought to increase the separation between religion and government. He edited an atheistic paper called *The Age of Reason* and wrote many books, most of them promoting atheism, published by the Freethought Press in New York City, which Lewis founded.

Lewis, Sinclair (1885–1951). Novelist. Lewis was the author of many well-known works, including *Main Street* (1920), *Babbitt* (1922), and *Elmer Gantry* (1927), and he was the first American to receive the Nobel Prize for literature, 1930.

Lindblom, Robert (1844–1907). Stockbroker. Lindblom was born in Sweden and came to the United States in 1864, first working in the grain business in Milwaukee, Wisconsin, and then moving to Chicago in 1877, where he became a stock broker and, for more than twenty-five years, a member of the Chicago Board of Trade, where he achieved some prominence. He was also president of the Chicago civil service commission, 1898–1902, having been appointed by Mayor Harrison, and a director of the Chicago World's Fair in 1893.

Linden, Carl Eric (1869–1942). Painter. Linden was born in Sweden and came to the United States in 1887, settling in Chicago. He studied at the Chicago Art Institute and later in Paris. He had an association with Hull House in Chicago before moving to the area of Woodstock, New York, in 1902. He lived the rest of his life there and became one of the founding members of the Woodstock Artists Association in 1920.

Lindsey, Benjamin B. (1869–1943). Lawyer and judge. Lindsey was born in Jackson, Tennessee. His family moved to Denver, Colorado, in 1880. Lindsey held various jobs in Denver, studied the law, and was admitted to the Colorado bar in 1894. He practiced law in Denver and became active in the Democratic Party. He was appointed public administrator and guardian for orphans, 1899–1901, and then county judge, a position to which he was reelected repeatedly and held for twenty-six years, 1901–1927. Lindsey organized his court as an informal juvenile court—a novel idea, with the object of protecting and rehabilitating juveniles. He was outspoken and often generated publicity for himself and the court over which he presided. He unsuccessfully sought the governorship in 1906. He became a leading figure in the Progressive Party and a public advocate of birth control, female suffrage, and "the companionate marriage" (the title of a popular and controversial book by Lindsey in 1927 that advocated legalized birth control and divorce by mutual consent). He moved to Los Angeles in 1930, where he had been admitted to the bar two years earlier, and served as county judge from 1934 until his death.

Lippmann, Walter (1889–1974). Journalist and author. Born in New York City to a wealthy family, Lippmann attended private schools and Harvard University, and then started writing for a socialist newspaper. Lippmann was one of the founding

editors and writers for the *New Republic,* 1914–22, and then an editorial writer, 1922–29, and editor, 1929–31, for the *New York World* newspaper. When the *World* went out of business, he joined the *New York Herald-Tribune* as a syndicated columnist, 1931–67. He was the author of many books, including *Public Opinion* (1922), *A Preface to Morals* (1929), *The Good Society* (1937), and *Essays in the Public Philosophy* (1955).

Liveright, Horace (1886–1933). Publisher. Liveright was born in Osceola Mills, Pennsylvania. His family moved to Philadelphia when he was thirteen. He dropped out of high school and became a stockbroker. In 1917, using money from his father-in-law, Liveright, with a partner, started the book publishing firm of Boni & Liveright, which became one of the most important publishers of literature in the 1920s. Liveright took many stands against censorship, lived an extravagant life, and had a talent for generating publicity about his books. The Modern Library series was first published by Boni & Liveright, as were two of Darrow's books: an edition of *Farmington* in 1925 and *The Prohibition Mania* in 1927 (with Victor Yarros *(q.v.)*. Liveright suffered financial problems in the late 1920s and resigned as president of the firm (then known as Horace Liveright Inc.) in 1930.

Lloyd, Caroline. *See* **Withington, Caroline ("Caro") Lloyd.**

Lloyd, Henry Demarest (1847–1903). Journalist. Lloyd was born in New York City, graduated with a B.A. from Columbia College, 1867, and attended Columbia Law School. He was admitted to the bar in New York in 1869 and worked as a public relations agent for the American Free-Trade League, 1869–72. He moved to Chicago in 1872 and became literary editor, financial editor, and eventually chief editorial writer for the *Chicago Tribune,* 1872–1885. He married the daughter of one of the owners of the newspaper in 1873. He resigned from the newspaper in 1885, after political differences with the principal owner, and spent the rest of his life working independently as a writer and political reformer. Lloyd is often referred to as the first muckraking journalist in America. He wrote several articles and books aimed at exposing business corruption and unfair practices, including *A Strike of Millionaires against Miners* (1890) and his best-known book, *Wealth against Commonwealth* (1894).

Lloyd, Jessie Bross (1844–1904). Wife of Henry Demarest Lloyd *(q.v.)* and daughter of William Bross, wealthy part owner of the *Chicago Tribune.* Lloyd was born in New York and came to Chicago with her parents as a young child. She was active in philanthropy work throughout her life, including as a leader in the Chicago Relief and Aid Society after the great Chicago fire of 1871.

Loeb, Richard (1905–1936). Student. Loeb was born in Chicago, the son of a wealthy executive for Sears, Roebuck and Company. Like his friend Nathan Leopold *(q.v.),* Loeb was a brilliant student. He graduated from the University of Michigan in 1923 at the age of eighteen. He planned to enter the University of

Chicago Law School in the fall of 1924, but then, with Leopold, he committed the kidnapping and murder that made both men famous. Loeb was murdered in prison by another inmate.

Luhan, Mabel Dodge (1879–1962). Arts patron and writer. Born Mabel Gaston to a wealthy family in Buffalo, New York, Luhan's first husband died shortly before her twenty-fifth birthday. During a trip to Europe for solace she met and eventually married her second husband, Edwin Dodge, a wealthy architectural student. They moved to Florence, Italy, where she entertained many illustrious guests in their villa. In 1912, they moved to New York City, where Luhan held gatherings in their apartment for artists, writers, social agitators, and reformers, among others, many of whom she helped financially. Luhan divorced Dodge in 1916 and the following year married Maurice Sterne (1878–1957), an artist. They moved to New Mexico, where she (again) operated her house as salon for prominent people. In 1922 she divorced Sterne and married a Taos Pueblo Indian, Antonio Luhan. She wrote several volumes of memoirs.

Macrae, John (1867–1944). Publisher. Macrae was born in Virginia and started as a young man sweeping offices for the E. P. Dutton publishing firm in New York. He eventually worked his way up in the firm to salesman, junior partner, and vice president. In 1923, when the founder of the firm died, he became president and eventually owner of the publishing section of the business. He also served as president of the National Association of Book Publishers, 1924–27.

Malone, Dudley Field (1882–1950). Lawyer and government official. Malone graduated from Francis Xavier College, 1903, and obtained a law degree from Fordham University, 1905. He was active in the first presidential campaign of Woodrow Wilson *(q.v.)* and served for seven months in 1913 as an assistant secretary of state in the Wilson administration before being appointed collector of the port of New York, 1914–17. Malone was active in many civil liberties cases and liberal political causes, and he practiced law for a time with Arthur Garfield Hays *(q.v.)*. He lived part time in Paris for a while and maintained a lucrative divorce practice. He was one of the lawyers for John T. Scopes *(q.v.)* in 1925. During the last years of his life, he worked as counsel for Twentieth Century-Fox Film Corporation and sometimes as an actor, portraying Winston Churchill in *Mission to Moscow* (1943). He was married three times. His second wife was Doris Stevens and his third wife was the actress Edna Louise Johnson (d. 1972).

Mantinband, Charles (1895–1974). Rabbi and civic leader. Mantinband grew up in Norfolk, Virginia, attended City College of New York and Hebrew Union College in Cincinnati, obtained an M.S. from Columbia University, and was ordained at the Jewish Institute of Religion in New York City. He served as rabbi of many congregations in the North and South over his career, including at least seven years in Williamsport, Pennsylvania, where he debated with Darrow in 1932. Mantinband

was very active in the civil rights movement in the late 1950s and early 1960s in Mississippi.

Masters, Edgar Lee (1869–1950). Lawyer and writer. Masters attended public schools in western Illinois, where he also read for the law in his father's law office. He moved to Chicago in 1892 and started practicing law. He was Darrow's law partner from 1903 to 1912. During much of his life, he tried to balance his literary pursuits with the practice of law. His greatest literary achievement and most popular success was *Spoon River Anthology* (1915), a series of free-verse monologues from people who lay buried in a small-town cemetery. He published many other works of poetry and fiction as well as essays and biographies, but never repeated the success of *Spoon River Anthology*.

McAdoo, William G. (1863–1941). Lawyer, railroad executive, and politician. McAdoo practiced law and developed and operated a company that built a system of rapid-transit tunnels under the Hudson River, between New York and New Jersey, before serving as secretary of the treasury in the cabinet of President Wilson, 1913–18. He was an unsuccessful candidate for the Democratic nomination for president in 1920 and 1924, but later was elected as a Democrat to the United States Senate from California, 1933–38.

McManigal, Ortie (1873–1964). Laborer. McManigal was born in Ohio and left school at the age of ten. He worked in stone quarries in the Midwest starting at the age of twelve and later operated a hoisting engine for a steel-erecting business. He joined the International Association of Bridge and Structural Iron Workers union in the early 1900s and traveled from city to city in his work. After his confession in 1911 to the bombing of the Los Angeles Times Building, as well as other bombings, he was kept in Los Angeles by the government as a witness for other trials, including the trials of David Caplan *(q.v.)* and Matthew Schmidt *(q.v.)*. After those trials were completed, McManigal moved to Honduras for several years, where he changed his name to W. E. Mack. He later returned to Los Angeles, where he worked as a watchman in the Hall of Records, 1932–44, after which he retired.

McNamara, James B. (1882–1941). Printer. McNamara, younger brother of John J. McNamara *(q.v.)*, was born in Ohio, worked as an apprentice printer, and was a member of a typographical union. In 1911, represented by Darrow, he pleaded guilty to the dynamiting of the Los Angeles Times Building in October 1910. Twenty men were killed in the blast. McNamara was sentenced to life in prison and died in San Quentin prison.

McNamara, John J. (1876–1941). Ironworker and union official. McNamara, older brother of James B. McNamara *(q.v.)*, was born in Ohio, worked as an ironworker, and joined the International Association of Bridge and Structural Iron Workers, serving as vice president, 1903–4, and secretary-treasurer, 1904–11, of the union. He pleaded guilty in 1911 to conspiring to dynamite the Lewellyn Iron Works in

Los Angeles. He was released from San Quentin prison in 1921. After his release, he worked as financial secretary and business agent for the union, 1922–27.

Meehan, John J. (1884–1936). Lawyer and law professor. Born in New York, Meehan received an LL.B. degree from Syracuse University, 1906, and had a private law practice in New York and Chicago before becoming a professor, 1924, and later law librarian at De Paul University in Chicago. Meehan served as president of the John P. Altgeld Society at De Paul University.

Mencken, H. L. (1880–1956). Journalist, editor, writer, and critic. Mencken was born in Baltimore and completed his formal education at the Baltimore Polytechnic High School. He worked for the *(Baltimore) Herald* as a reporter and eventually managing editor. In 1906, he became Sunday editor for the *(Baltimore) Sun.* For fifteen years, he worked as an editor of the *Smart Set,* 1908–23, a monthly magazine in New York. In 1923, he cofounded and edited the monthly *American Mercury* with drama critic George Nathan (1882–1958). He edited this magazine until 1933. publishing several articles by Darrow. Mencken discovered and encouraged many writers in his career, and his influence on American literature and politics, especially in the 1920s, was considerable. In addition to his journalism, he wrote many volumes of literary and social criticism, including *Prejudices* (1919–27), and several memoirs, including *Happy Days* (1940), *Newspaper Days* (1941), and *Heathen Days* (1943). He also wrote a highly regarded philological study, *The American Language,* which was published in its fourth edition in 1936.

Mills, Benjamin Fay (1857–1916). Evangelist and religious leader. Mills was the son of a Presbyterian minister. He attended Phillips Andover Academy and graduated from Lake Forest University, 1879. Ordained as a Congregationalist minister in 1878, he served as a pastor in small parishes in Minnesota, New York, and Vermont before working several years as an itinerant, interdenominational evangelist. In the early 1890s, he became interested in the Social-Gospel thinking of George D. Herron (1862–1925). In 1899, he continued his ministry in Oakland, California, at the First Unitarian Church. In 1904, he moved to Los Angeles, where he served as minister of an independent religious group known as the Fellowship. Later, he presided over a similar group in Chicago, 1911–16. In 1915, Mills reconverted to a more conservative form of Christianity and sought ordination in the Presbyterian Church.

Milner, Duncan C. (1841–1928). Presbyterian clergyman and reformer. Milner was born in Ohio and fought in the Civil War with the Union army. He graduated from Washington and Jefferson College, 1866, and Union Theological Seminary, 1868. He was a pastor in Missouri and Kansas, 1868–92, and active in the temperance movement in Kansas before moving to Chicago, where he was superintendent of the Armour Mission, 1893–98. From 1899 until his death, he led congregations in the Chicago area and in Florida. He was a director of the conservative Chicago Law and Order League and an active crusader for civil rights for African Americans.

Mitchell, John (1870–1919). Labor leader. Mitchell was born in Braidwood, Illinois, the son of a coal miner and farmer. He began working in the mines as a boy and joined the Knights of Labor. He became a founding member of the United Mine Workers of America in 1890, rising through the ranks of the union to become president, 1899–1908. He was also one of the founders of (and a longtime leader in) the National Civic Federation in 1900, which was organized to improve relations between businesses and labor. He served as chair of the New York State Industrial Commission, 1915–19. He died from pneumonia following a gallstone operation.

Mooney, Thomas J. (1882–1942). Labor leader. Mooney was born in Chicago, the son of a coal miner. He left school at the age of fourteen and worked as a laborer. He became a socialist in 1907, during a trip to Europe. Eventually, he moved to California and, in 1913, became involved in a bitter strike against a gas and electricity company, which led to charges against him for illegal possession of explosives. Mooney and his alleged accomplice, Warren K. Billings (1893–1972), were eventually acquitted of the charges. In July 1916, the two men were arrested again after a bomb exploded during a Preparedness-Day parade in San Francisco, killing ten people. Both men were convicted for the crime but the prosecution's case was eventually thoroughly discredited. Mooney's persistent efforts for release from the state prison in San Quentin became a *cause célèbre* among labor leaders, liberals, and others. All of Mooney's repeated appeals to the courts and government officials for a new trial or release failed until finally, in 1939, he was pardoned by the governor of California.

Moore, J[ohn] Howard (1862–1916). Teacher, author, lecturer. Moore was married to Darrow's sister Viola ("Jennie") Darrow Moore *(q.v.)*. A graduate of the University of Chicago, Moore taught biology and ethics at the Crane Technical High School in Chicago during the last twenty years of his life. He was a prominent advocate of vegetarianism and animal rights. He lectured on temperance and other reforms and wrote several books, including *Better-World Philosophy* (1906), *The Universal Kinship* (1908), and *The New Ethics* (1909). Suffering from poor health, Moore, apparently in a fit of despondency, committed suicide by shooting himself in Jackson Park in Chicago.

Moore, Viola ("Jennie") Darrow (1868–1955). Teacher, Clarence Darrow's sister, and the eighth and last child of Ammirus and Emily (Eddy) Darrow *(q.v.)*. She was married to J. Howard Moore *(q.v.)*. They had no children. Jennie worked as a teacher at the McCosh Grammar School in Chicago, where her sister, Mary Darrow Olson, was principal.

Moro, Joseph (1894–1995). Shoemaker. Moro was born in Italy and came to the United States in 1911, settling with his mother in Massachusetts. He worked in shoe factories and became an anarchist. He was friends with both Nicola Sacco and Bartolomeo Vanzetti and served as secretary of their legal defense committee.

Moyer, Charles H. (1866–1929). Union leader. Moyer worked as a miner in South Dakota in the 1890s and was active in the miners union, eventually serving as a member of the executive board of the Western Federation of Miners, 1899–1902. He moved to Denver, Colorado, and was elected president of the WFM in 1902, a position he held until 1926 (the WFM changed its name to the International Union of Mine, Mill, and Smelter Workers in 1916). He was a cofounder of the Industrial Workers of the World, 1905, and a member of its executive board until he was arrested in 1906, together with William ("Big Bill") Haywood *(q.v.)* and George A. Pettibone *(q.v.)*, for the murder of Frank Steunenberg, former governor of Idaho. After the trials, Moyer led the WFM out of the IWW, 1908, and helped re-affiliate it with the American Federation of Labor, 1911.

Mulholland, Frank L. (1875–1949). Lawyer. Mulholland was a prominent lawyer in Toledo, Ohio. He served as counsel for unions and labor leaders in many cases. He was active in Rotary International and served as its president, 1914–15. He also served as general counsel for the Railway Labor Executives Association in the 1940s.

MÞnsterberg, Hugo (1863–1916). Psychologist, educator, and writer. Born in Danzig, Germany, Münsterberg received a Ph.D. from the University of Leipzig, 1885, and an M.D. from the University of Heidelberg, 1887. He taught for three years at Harvard University, 1892–95, at the invitation of the American psychologist William James, and eventually accepted a permanent position there. Through his books and articles in popular magazines and by frequent lectures throughout the country, Münsterberg became a well-known authority on applied psychology. He was elected president of the American Psychological Assocation in 1898. He published some thirteen books, including *On the Witness Stand* (1908), a collection of essays on topics such the reliability of eyewitness testimony and the use of hypnotism in courts.

Murphy, Frank (1890–1949). Lawyer, judge, and politician. Murphy, the son of an attorney, received his LL.B. from the University of Michigan, 1914. He practiced law in Detroit before serving in the military during World War I. After the war, he served as United States attorney in Michigan, 1919–22, ran unsuccessfully for Congress on the Democratic ticket, 1920, and three years later was elected to a judgeship in the recorder's court in Detroit, a position to which he was reelected in 1929. While serving in this capacity, Murphy presided over the trial of Ossian Sweet and his codefendants. Darrow was their defense counsel. In 1930, Murphy was elected mayor of Detroit. A few years later, he was appointed governor-general and later high commissioner of the Philippines, 1933–36. Murphy returned from the Philippines to run for governor of Michigan, at President Roosevelt's urging. He won the election and served as governor until his defeat in 1938. He then served one year as United States attorney general before Roosevelt appointed him to a position as associate justice of the United States Supreme Court, 1940–49, where he established a reputation as a defender of civil liberties.

Murphy, George (1897–1961). Lawyer and judge. Murphy practiced law in Detroit and later served as a judge on the Detroit recorder's court, 1936–61. He was a brother of Frank Murphy *(q.v.)*.

Neal, John R. (1893–1959). Legal educator. Neal received an A.B. from the University of Tennessee, 1893, an A.M. and LL.B. from Vanderbilt University, 1896, and a Ph.D. from Columbia University, 1899. He taught law at the University of Denver, 1899–1917, and he was a part-time and later, 1917, full-time professor of law at the University of Tennessee, 1909–23. The university terminated him on the grounds, among others, that he was frequently absent from class and failed to give examinations. He had a reputation for eccentric behavior. In 1923, he founded and operated his own law school in Knoxville, Tennessee, called John Randolph Neal College of Law, which he operated for twenty years. In 1925, he volunteered his services as counsel for John T. Scopes *(q.v.)* and served as Scopes's local counsel.

Nelson, Nelson Olsen (1844–1922). Businessman. Born in Lillesand, Norway, Nelson emigrated to the United States with his family in 1847. They settled on a farm in Missouri. Nelson enlisted in the Union army at the outbreak of the Civil War and served through the war's duration. In 1877, he started a business manufacturing building and plumbing supplies in St. Louis. The company grew to become one of the largest such manufacturers in the country. He introduced a program of employee profit sharing at his plant in 1886 and promoted the idea of profit sharing for other businesses. He was involved in many civic and social affairs, including serving as a member of the city council in St. Louis, 1887–90. He was well known for philanthropic activities.

Nolan, John I. (1874–1922). Labor leader and politician. Born in San Francisco, California, Nolan became an iron molder as a young man, later an officer of the local union of iron molders, and eventually an officer of the International Molders' Union of North America. In 1911, the mayor of San Francisco named Nolan to the Board of Supervisors for the City and County of San Francisco. In 1912, he became secretary of the San Francisco Labor Council. In November 1912, he was elected to Congress as a Republican and, after being reelected six times, served in that position from 4 March 1913 until his death.

Oakes, George W. (1909–65). Journalist and author. Oakes obtained an A.B. from Princeton University, 1930, and a B.A. and M.A. from Queen's College, Oxford, England, 1930–32. At Princeton, he was president of the literary and debating societies. He worked as a journalist for the *Chattanooga (Tennessee) Times,* 1933, and then in the advertising department of the *New York Times,* 1934–42, which his uncle, Adolph S. Ochs (1858–1935), owned. He served as an officer in the United States Army, 1946–48, founded and published a weekly newspaper in London, 1946–48, worked for the Central Intelligence Agency, 1949–55, and as a freelance writer and journalist, 1956–65.

Older, Cora Miranda Baggerly (1875–1968). Journalist, magazine writer, author of several books of fiction and nonfiction—including a biography of William Randolph Hearst *(q.v.)*—and second wife of Fremont Older *(q.v.)*.

Older, Fremont (1856–1935). Journalist and reformer. Born in Wisconsin and raised with little formal education, Older started work at a young age as a printer's devil and eventually moved West, where he worked for various newspapers in Nevada and California before settling in San Francisco in 1884. Ten years later, he became editor of the *San Francisco Bulletin,* a position he held for the next twenty-four years. He became famous for his crusade against San Francisco's corrupt municipal politics and he actively promoted state and municipal reform candidates, including, in particular, Hiram Johnson *(q.v.)*. He took a strong interest in penal reform and worked for many years to secure the release of Thomas J. Mooney *(q.v.)*. Older's controversial efforts on Mooney's behalf eventually led to his split with the owners of the *Bulletin* and, in 1918, he became editor of the *San Francisco Call,* which was owned by William Randolph Hearst *(q.v.)*. Approximately ten years later, Hearst acquired the *Bulletin* and Older worked as president and editor of the *Call-Bulletin* until his death.

Olney, Richard (1835–1917). Lawyer, attorney general, and secretary of state. Educated at Brown College and Harvard Law School, Olney was a successful railroad attorney in Boston when he was appointed United States attorney general in 1893 by Grover Cleveland. As attorney general, Olney worked to suppress the Pullman strike in 1894, led by Eugene V. Debs *(q.v.),* and he personally argued against Darrow and other lawyers working for Debs in the United States Supreme Court in 1895. After serving two years as attorney general, Olney was appointed United States secretary of state. He retired after two years in this position and returned to the practice of law.

Olson, Mary Darrow (1851–1909). Teacher, Clarence Darrow's sister, and the third child of Ammirus and Emily (Eddy) Darrow *(q.v.)*. Mary Darrow was born in Cleveland, Ohio, when her father was attending the University of Cleveland. She received a B.A. in 1882 from Allegheny College in Meadville, Pennsylvania, and worked as a teacher most of her life, in Kinsman, Vernon, and Youngstown, Ohio. She taught Latin and Greek briefly at Northeastern Ohio Normal School, 1882–83. Later, she worked as an assistant to a professor of modern languages at the University of Illinois at Urbana, 1883–85. She began teaching school in Chicago in 1889. She worked briefly as the principal of a private school in 1890. In 1894, she became the principal at McCosh Grammar School in Chicago, where she remained until she retired. She was an officer on the board of trustees of the public school-teachers' pension and retirement fund in Chicago, and she was an active worker for female suffrage and anti-cigarette laws. She was married to Olaf G. Olson (1851–1906), a Swedish-born tailor.

PALMER, A. MITCHELL (1872–1936). Lawyer and politician. Born in Moosehead, Pennsylvania, Palmer graduated from Swarthmore College, 1891, and then studied law with a judge before being admitted to the bar in 1893. He practiced law in Stroudsburg, Pennsylvania, and served three terms as a Democrat in the U.S. House of Representatives, 1909–1915, after which he lost a race for the U.S. Senate. During World War I, he served as Alien Property Custodian, 1917–1919. Later, Woodrow Wilson *(q.v.)* appointed him attorney general, a position he held from March 1919 to March 1921. As attorney general, he became well known for leading attacks and "Palmer raids" on labor and radical organizations and individuals, as part of the "Red Scare" in the U.S. after the Bolshevik revolution in Russia in 1917. Palmer unsuccessfully sought the Democratic presidential nomination in 1920. After leaving government service, he practiced law in Washington, D.C. and Pennsylvania.

PARSONS, ALICE BEAL (1886–1962). Author. Parsons graduated from Rockford College in Illinois, 1908, managed a family farm in Vermont, pursued graduate studies in social work at the University of Chicago, and worked as a freelance writer and book reviewer for several magazines and newspapers, including *The Dial, The Nation,* and the *New York Herald Tribune.* She also wrote eight books, including *The Trial of Helen McLeod* (1938), which is reportedly a slightly fictionalized but largely autobiographical account of her own experience as one of several defendant members of the Communist Labor Party who were tried and acquitted on sedition charges in Rockford, Illinois, in 1920, with Darrow as their lawyer.

PARTON, LEMUEL F. (1879–1943). Journalist, husband of Mary Field Parton. Parton graduated from the University of Colorado, 1903, and worked as a writer for the Chicago City Press Association that same year and then for the *Chicago Tribune* for three years. Parton moved to Nevada in 1907 to prospect for gold and then traveled in South America. He later became city editor for the *Los Angeles Herald,* 1910–11, then associate editor of the *San Francisco Bulletin,* 1917–19, before moving to New York in 1926. He was married to Mary Field Parton *(q.v.)* in 1913. From 1931 to 1942, Parton wrote a syndicated column called "Who's News Today." He was known as a supporter of liberal causes. Parton and his wife had one child, Margaret Parton (1915–1981), who (like her parents) became a journalist and writer of books and magazine articles.

PARTON, MARY FIELD (1878–1969). Journalist. Parton was born in Cincinnati and raised in Detroit with a Quaker mother and a fundamentalist Baptist father. She rebelled against her strict father, graduated from the University of Michigan, 1900, and taught school in Ovid, Michigan, before moving to Chicago, where she worked in settlement houses and then for the Immigrants' Protective Association. Later, she began working as a labor reporter. In 1907 or 1908, she met Darrow, introduced to him by Helen Todd *(q.v.)*. Throughout her career as a journalist, Parton covered many labor trials, including the trial of James B. and John N. McNamara *(q.v.)*. She

wrote many magazine articles from the 1920s through the 1940s and played a substantial role in writing *The Autobiography of Mother Jones* (1925) (Darrow wrote an introduction to the book), although she only listed herself as editor of the work. She and her husband, Lemuel F. Parton *(q.v.)* lived much of their married lives in Palisades, New York.

Pettibone, George A. (1863–1908). Laborer. Pettibone worked as a miner in the lead and silver mining region of Coeur D'Alene, Idaho. He was imprisoned for his role there in the strike of 1892, which resulted in the arrests of hundreds of miners and sympathizers. He also worked as a printer's apprentice, owned a saloon in Montana, and sold electrical appliances and worked as a superintendent for American Wringer Company in Denver, Colorado. He had many close ties with members and leaders of the Western Federation of Miners. When he was arrested in 1906, with William ("Big Bill") Haywood *(q.v.)* and Charles H. Moyer *(q.v.)*, for the murder of Idaho's former governor, Frank Steunenberg, Pettibone was operating a household appliance store in Denver, Colorado, which also served as a meeting place for members of the WFM. Pettibone was tried after Haywood and died shortly after his acquittal in January 1908.

Pettigrew, Richard F. (1848–1926). Businessman, lawyer, and politician. Pettigrew was born in Vermont and grew up on a farm in Wisconsin. He attended Beloit College and studied law at the University of Wisconsin but did not obtain a degree at either institution. In 1870, he settled in Sioux Falls, South Dakota, where he became active in civic affairs and several businesses, including surveying, banking, milling, and manufacturing. He was admitted to the bar in 1871. He was active in politics and elected as a Republican territorial delegate to Congress for the Dakota Territory, 1881–83, and later to the United States Senate, 1889–1901. Pettigrew was considered a radical by many Republicans. He advocated the single tax, unlimited silver coinage, government ownership of railroads and telegraph lines, and anti-imperialism. He joined the Silver Republicans in 1896 and was defeated in the election of 1900, after which he moved to New York City and practiced law. Mining investments brought him a fortune and he returned to Sioux Falls in 1911, where he became active again in politics and business. Pettigrew's opposition to the First World War led to his indictment under the Espionage Act, but he was never tried for the crime.

Phillips, Wendell (1811–1884). Lawyer, social reformer, and orator. Phillips was a prominent abolitionist and advocate of Prohibition, female suffrage, labor, corporate regulation, and the abolition of capital punishment, among other causes.

Phipps, Lawrence C. (1862–1958). Businessman and politician. Phipps was born and raised in Pennsylvania. He attended common schools and worked for Carnegie Steel Company, advancing from clerk to first vice president. In 1901, he retired from the steel business and moved to Denver, Colorado, where he was engaged in

an investment business before he was elected as a Republican to the United States Senate, 1919–31.

Pierce, Vivian (b. 1890?) Suffragist and reformer. Pierce was a native of San Diego, California. In 1915, she served as press chairperson for the Congressional Union. Later she became an active member and organizer for the National Woman's Party and an editor and writer, 1917–18, for *The Suffragist,* a publication of the NWP. In 1925, Pierce organized the League to Abolish Capital Punishment (which was incorporated several years later and then called the American League to Abolish Capital Punishment). She said that the league "grew out of the loud and ignorant clamor of protest following the Leopold-Loeb trial." The object of the league was to eliminate the death penalty in all of the states where it was still being used and to prevent it from being reinstituted in other states. The methods employed by the league, which usually had a meager budget, included publicity campaigns, political lobbying, and distributing literature. Pierce, who served as executive secretary for the league for many years, was the driving force behind the organization. The league eventually joined with the Massachusetts Council for the Abolition of the Death Penalty in 1949 and stopping operating some twenty years later. Robert Morss Lovett, one of the leaders of the league, described Pierce has having a "vivid" personality and a "burning zeal" for the work.

Porter, Julia (Smith) (1868–1946). Librarian. Porter was head librarian of the Kinsman (Ohio) Free Public Library (in Darrow's childhood town) from the early 1920s until late in her life. She was born in Burghill, Ohio (near Kinsman), where Darrow's first wife, Jessie (Ohl) Brownlee *(q.v.)* was born. Her husband, Byron Porter (1857–1950), was a photographer and postmaster in Kinsman.

Powers, Levi Moore (1864–1920). Powers graduated from Tufts University in 1890 and was ordained as a Universalist minister the same year. From 1890 until his death, he was a minister at several Universalist churches in Massachusetts, New York, and Washington, D.C., including the First Universalist Church in Haverhill, Massachusetts, 1905–13, and the Independent Christian Church of Gloucester, Massachusetts, 1913–19. Powers was active in many liberal reform activities during his life.

Powers, Orlando W. (1851–1914). Lawyer and judge. Born in New York, Powers graduated from the University of Michigan Law School, 1871. He started a law practice in Salt Lake City, Utah, in the late 1880s and later served briefly as an associate justice on the territorial supreme court of Utah, 1885–86, and as a state court trial judge. He was active in Democratic politics in Utah and served in the Utah legislature in 1893. In late 1912, he moved to Los Angeles to start a law office with his son. He was a lawyer for Darrow in his second trial for jury bribery in Los Angeles in 1913.

Powys, Llewelyn (1884–1939). Writer. British writer of travel books, essays, and memoirs. Born in Dorchester, England, son of a church rector, Powys was educated at

Cambridge University. He wrote thirty-four books, including books of essays, travel books, a biography of the explorer Henry Hudson, a novel, and memoirs. Among his better known books are *Black Laughter* (1925) and *Love and Death* (1939), which was published posthumously. For much of his life, he suffered from tuberculosis, which is what caused his death.

Prewitt, Charles Russell (1900–1980). Methodist minister. Prewitt was born and raised in Iowa. He became a deacon in the Methodist Church in 1925. He obtained an S.T.B. from Boston University School of Theology in 1926, at which time he became an elder in the church. He also obtained an A.B. from Iowa Wesleyan, 1932. He served as a pastor for many local congregations in the Methodist Church—in Rhode Island, Massachusetts, New Jersey, New York, and California (where he spent the last thirty years of his life). He was active in the Salvation Army and Freemasonry, and also served as a member of the board of regents of the University of the Pacific.

Richardson, Edmund F. (1862–1911). Lawyer. Richardson taught school and was employed in a mercantile business in Massachusetts before moving to San Francisco and working as a bookkeeper for a manufacturer, while reading law at night. He was admitted to the bar in California in 1885 and the following year moved to Colorado, eventually settling in Denver, where he was a member of a prominent firm and provided legal services for the Western Federation of Miners. He was co-counsel with Darrow for William ("Big Bill") Haywood *(q.v.)*, Charles H. Moyer *(q.v.)*, and George A. Pettibone *(q.v.)*.

Rockwell, Irvin E. (1863–1952). Businessman. Rockwell was born in Sun Prairie, Wisconsin, the son of a farmer. As a young man, he worked in the newspaper business in Minnesota and Wisconsin and as a court reporter. In 1887, he started an accounting firm in Chicago. In 1889, he purchased an interest in a mine in Idaho. In 1901, he sold his interest in the accounting firm and moved to Idaho, where he worked as an operator of the mine. He was active in Masonry and political affairs, including serving on the Idaho Board of Education, 1920–25, the state welfare board, 1939–41, and in the Idaho legislature, 1915–19, 1929–30.

Rogers, Earl (1870–1922). Lawyer. Born in New York, the son of a Methodist minister, Rogers was educated at Ashland College in Ohio and the University of Syracuse in New York (graduating from neither) before he began studying in a law office in Los Angeles in 1893, where he was eventually admitted to the bar. He became famous as a criminal-defense attorney but also worked in other capacities, including teaching law at the University of Southern California. By special appointment, he served as a prosecutor conducting the grand jury investigation of the bombing of the Los Angeles Times Building in 1910, which led to the arrest of James and John McNamara *(q.v.)*. Two years later, he was one of the defense attorneys in Darrow's first trial for jury bribery in Los Angeles, in 1911. Married twice, Rogers was a Democrat in his politics. He was also an alcoholic and died at the age of fifty-two.

Roosevelt, Franklin D. (1882–1945). Thirty-second president of the United States, 1933–45.

Ross, Edward A. (1866–1951). Sociologist and writer. Ross was born in Virden, Illinois, the son of a farmer and a schoolteacher. He received an A.B. at Coe College, 1886, and a Ph.D. from Johns Hopkins, 1891, concentrating on economics. He taught at several universities, including Stanford and the University of Nebraska, before accepting a position in 1906 with the University of Wisconsin, where he taught with Richard T. Ely *(q.v.)*. In addition to his academic work in sociology, Ross became well known for his public lectures and popular writings on a variety of social and reform topics and for his foreign travel books.

Rudkin, Frank H. (1864–1931). Lawyer and judge. Born and raised in Vernon, Ohio, Rudkin was a student under Darrow for three years when Darrow taught school in rural Ohio. Rudkin attended Washington and Lee University and then read for the law in 1887. He worked in private practice in Ellensburg, Washington, 1887–90, and then in North Yakima, Washington, 1890–1901. He served first as a judge on the Superior Court of Washington, 1901–5, and then as justice and chief justice of the Washington Supreme Court, 1905–1910. Nominated by President Taft, he later served as a judge for the United States District Court for the Eastern District of Washington, 1911–22, and then as a judge of the United States Court of Appeals for the Ninth Circuit, 1923–31.

Russell, Charles Edward (1860–1941). Journalist, author, and socialist political candidate. Russell worked as a newspaper reporter and editor, at various times, for several Midwest newspapers and in New York City, as well as for the Newspaper Enterprise Association, which served Scripps-owned newspapers. He also wrote magazine articles of a muckraking sort, as well as many biographies and books of travel and poetry. He was a socialist candidate for governor of New York, 1910 and 1912, mayor of New York City, 1913, and the United States Senate, 1914.

Salt, Henry (1851–1939). English classical scholar, author, and naturalist. Salt was born in India, the son of an officer in the Royal Bengal Artillery. He was a King's scholar at Eton College, 1866–71, and attended King's College, Cambridge, gaining a first in the classical tripos, 1875. He later taught classics at Eton, 1875–84. He left Eton to live a simple life in a cottage and follow his humanitarian interests. He wrote many books, pamphlets, and articles, on a variety of people and subjects, including his own life story, vegetarianism, animal rights, and Henry David Thoreau. He also translated and published Lucretius and Virgil. In 1891, he founded the Humanitarian League and first met Darrow there in 1903, with a letter of introduction from their mutual friend, Ernest Howard Crosby *(q.v.)*. Salt was also a friend and admirer of Darrow's brother, [Edward] Everett Darrow *(q.v.)*, and his brother-in-law, J. Howard Moore *(q.v.)*. Salt founded the *The Humane Review* in 1900, a journal devoted to humanitarian subjects, which published essays by Darrow and Moore.

Salter, William M. (1853–1931). Lecturer and author. Salter was born in Burlington, Iowa, the son of a clergyman. He graduated from Knox College, 1871, studied at Yale Divinity School, 1871–73, obtained a B.D. from Harvard Divinity School, 1876, and later attended the University of Göttingen in Germany, 1876–77, and Columbia University, 1881–82. In 1881, Salter became involved in the newly founded Ethical Cultural Society in New York City. In 1883, he founded a branch of the ECS in Chicago, where he also served as editor of the ECS's magazine (*The Cause*) and as a lecturer, 1883–92, 1897–1907. He worked in the same lecturer capacity for the ECS in Philadelphia, 1892–97. Before his retirement, he was an adjunct professor in philosophy at the University of Chicago, 1907–13. Salter published many philosophical lectures and books.

Schilling, George A. (1850–1938). Socialist and trade unionist. Schilling was born in Germany and emigrated to Ohio with his parents in 1852. He moved to Chicago in 1875 and became active in labor and anarchist circles and eventually an advocate of the single-tax ideas of Henry George *(q.v.)*. He was commissioner of the Illinois Bureau of Labor Statistics, 1893–97, during the administration of John P. Altgeld *(q.v.)*, and later served as a member, 1903–5, and president, 1905–7, 1911–15, of the Chicago Board of Local Improvements. Schilling met Darrow at a single-tax meeting in Chicago in 1888 and they remained good friends the rest of their lives.

Schlesinger, Benjamin (1876–1932). Labor leader and journalist. Schlesinger was born in Lithuania and emigrated to the United States in 1891. He worked in a garment factory in Chicago and became active in his trade union. He helped to organize the International Ladies' Garment Workers' Union in 1900 and served for many years as its president, 1903–4, 1914–23, 1928–32. In the 1890s, he worked as a journalist for Jewish daily newspapers in New York City and later as business manager of the *Jewish Daily Forward*, 1907–12. He also managed the Chicago office of the *Jewish Daily Forward*, 1923–26.

Schmidt, Matthew (1881–1955). Laborer. Schmidt was a woodworker and building tradesman before he was indicted in early 1911, along with John and James McNamara *(q.v.)*, for his role in delivering the dynamite that was used to blow up the Los Angeles Times Building. He eluded authorities after his indictment until he was captured in 1915. He stood trial that same year and was convicted of first-degree murder and sentenced to life in prison. Schmidt's sentence was eventually commuted to time served and he was paroled from San Quentin in 1939. He lived out his life in San Francisco.

Schwartz, Samuel D. (1890–1968). Social service worker and lecture organizer. Schwartz obtained a Ph.B., 1912, and M.A., 1913, from the University of Chicago. He worked as a director at the Chicago Hebrew Institute, 1911–14, and as assistant superintendent at the Sinai Social Center in Chicago, 1914–16, before becoming a long-term executive director of the Emil G. Hirsch Center in Chicago in 1916. He

was also secretary and trustee of the Sinai Temple, 1917–68, and founder and executive director of the Sinai Temple Forum, 1914–64.

Scopes, John T. (1900–1970). Teacher and geologist. Born in Paducah, Kentucky, Scopes graduated from the University of Kentucky, 1924, and then taught school in Dayton, Tennessee. In 1925, he became the defendant in the celebrated test case challenging a statute in Tennessee that made it a misdemeanor to teach evolution in the state's public schools. Darrow was lead counsel for Scopes. After the trial, Scopes obtained a master's degree in geology from the University of Chicago, at the encouragement of Darrow (with whom he remained lifelong friends), and he later worked in the oil business in Venezuela.

Scott, Joseph (1867–1958). Attorney. Scott was born in England and educated there and in the United States. His degrees included an M.A., LL.D., and Ph.D. He came to the United States in 1889 and taught rhetoric and English literature at St. Bonaventure College in New York before moving to Los Angeles in 1893, where he was admitted to the bar the next year. Throughout his long career as an attorney in Los Angeles, he was active in Republican politics and civic matters. When he joined Darrow as co-counsel for James B. and John J. McNamara *(q.v.)* in 1911, he was a member of the Los Angeles Board of Education (of which he was president for five years); president (and one of the founders) of the Los Angeles Chamber of Commerce (a post he held from 1910 to 1920); and a member (and original organizer) of the Knights of Columbus in California.

Scripps, E. W. (1854–1926). Journalist and newspaper publisher. Scripps was born in Illinois, the son of farmers. As a young man, he worked for a while on the farm and then began working for newspapers in Detroit, including a daily newspaper established by his half-brother. Eventually, he began to establish and purchase his own newspapers, which he expanded into a chain in the 1890s. Over the course of his life, Scripps established or purchased twenty-nine newspapers throughout the United States. His newspapers emphasized short news articles, favored working-class interests and progressive reforms, operated on tight budgets, and obtained a great deal of their material from shared news services that Scripps had created (one of which became the United Press Association). Scripps's newspapers were highly profitable and made him very wealthy.

Seham, Max (1888–1974). Physician, educator, and author. Seham was born in Russia and came to the United States with his parents as a young boy. He graduated from the University of Minnesota Medical School, 1910, and served during World War I in the United States Army Medical Corps, 1917–18. He spent most of his career practicing medicine in Minneapolis, specializing in pediatrics. He also taught pediatrics at the University of Minnesota and served for a period of time as chief of staff at Abbott Hospital in Minneapolis. Seham was active in liberal politics and performed a great deal of charitable work in medicine. He

wrote many articles, on a variety of subjects, and two books: *The Tired Child* (1926), a study of the effects of fatigue on children's behavior; and *Blacks and American Medical Care* (1973), a discussion of the poor medical care that African Americans receive and the unfair opportunities for African Americans entering and working in the field of medicine.

Shaw, George Bernard (1856–1950), British playwright and critic.

Simon, Cyrus (1872–1915). Lawyer. Simon, whose parents were Prussian immigrants, was born in Brookfield, Missouri, but came to Chicago with his parents shortly after he was born. He began working in a law office at the age of sixteen and was admitted to the bar in Illinois when he was twenty-one. He began working for the West Chicago Street Railroad Company in approximately 1895 and then continued working for the Chicago Union Traction Company when it combined with West Chicago in 1899, usually handling small claims and employee matters for the company. In 1902, Simon was convicted along with several other men of participating in a jury bribery scheme on behalf of Union Traction. He paid a fine of two thousand dollars and continued practicing law. Darrow was one of the defense lawyers in the case (although not for Simon), and the following year, he hired Simon to work in his law office. Several years later, Darrow learned that Simon was settling cases on the side and pocketing the proceeds for himself rather depositing the money with the firm, and Simon was fired.

Simonson, Mary Darrow (1912–2003). Darrow's granddaughter and the middle daughter of Paul and Lillian (Anderson) Darrow *(q.v.)*. Simonson was born in Greeley, Colorado, and lived there until she and her family moved to Chicago in 1928, where they lived in an apartment near Jackson Park, two blocks from Darrow's apartment. In 1953, she married Burton Simonson (1899–1989), a building contractor in Chicago. They later lived in Honolulu, Hawaii.

Sinclair, Upton (1878–1968). Writer and social reformer. Sinclair was born in Baltimore, Maryland, the son of a wholesale liquor salesman. He obtained a B.A. from the City College of New York, 1897, and attended graduate school at Columbia University. He began writing stories at a young age and became a prolific author. In all, he wrote some ninety books, fiction and nonfiction, and hundreds of pamphlets, articles, essays, and book reviews. His writing often advocated some type of social reform. His most famous and influential novel was *The Jungle* (1906). He was twice a socialist candidate for Congress, 1920, 1922, and for governor of California, 1926, 1930. In 1934, he received the Democratic nomination for governor and was narrowly defeated. Between 1940 and 1953, he wrote an eleven-volume series of novels depicting contemporary American history, one volume of which won the Pulitzer prize.

Sissman, Peter (1868–1941). Lawyer. Sissman was born in Horodishtch, Russia. He was educated in private schools and under private tutors in Russia. He came to the

United States in 1886. He obtained an LL.B. from the Chicago College of Law, 1894, and began his law practice in Chicago. He specialized in real estate law and he was an active member of the Socialist Party. He was also Darrow's law partner from 1913 to 1925.

Smith, Alfred E. (1873–1944). Politician. Smith was born in New York City. His parents were laborers. He had little formal education. He became part of the Tammany Hall organization and served several years as a Democrat in the New York legislature, 1903–15. He served briefly as sheriff of New York County, 1915–17, and as president of New York City's board of alderman, 1917. He was elected four times as governor of New York, 1919–20, 1923–28. He was the Democratic candidate for president of the United States in 1928, the first Roman Catholic to run for that office.

Smith, Marie Sweet. Smith served for three months in the summer of 1930 as the organizing secretary for the American League to Abolish Capital Punishment. Darrow was the president of the league and Vivian Pierce *(q.v.)* was its organizing force.

Spingarn, Arthur (1878–1971). Lawyer and civil rights leader. Spingarn was born in New York City, the son of an Austrian Jewish immigrant and successful tobacco merchant. He obtained three degrees from Columbia University: a B.A., 1897, an M.A., 1899, and an LL.B., 1900. He also received an LL.D. from Howard University, 1941, and an L.H.D. from Long Island University, 1966. He began a private legal practice in New York City in 1900 and became active in civil rights work. Spingarn served for several years as vice president and chairman of the National Legal Committee for the National Association for the Advancement of Colored People, 1911–40, and later for many years as president of the NAACP, 1940–66, replacing his brother, Joel Spingarn (1875–1939). Spingarn was also president of the NAACP Legal Defense and Educational Fund, 1940–57, and he was at the center of the NAACP's legal activities for many years. In 1925–26, he helped coordinate the defense team for Dr. Ossian Sweet, which was led by Darrow.

Starr, Frederick (1858–1933). Anthropologist. Starr was educated at the University of Rochester and obtained a Ph.D. in geology from Lafayette College, 1885. After serving in various academic posts, he taught for most of his career at the University of Chicago, 1892–1923, where he helped organize an anthropology department and served as curator of the university's museum of natural history, 1895–1923. As an anthropologist, he made many trips to Africa, the Far East, and Mexico. After retiring from teaching, he lived in Seattle, Washington.

Stedman, Seymour (1871–1948). Lawyer and socialist politician. Stedman graduated from Northwestern University Law School, 1891, and practiced law in Chicago. He helped Eugene V. Debs *(q.v.)* and the American Railway Union during the Pullman strike, 1894. He was a founder of the Social Democratic Party, 1898. He

served one term as a socialist in the Illinois legislature, 1912–14. He defended socialists prosecuted under the federal Espionage Act of 1917, including Debs and Victor Berger *(q.v.)*, and he was Debs's running mate for the presidency in 1920. After the election, he became trustee of some chain stores in receivership and later an officer and director of a bank. After the bank went into receivership, 1929, Stedman and other officers were convicted of embezzlement, 1931. His conviction was reversed on appeal, 1935, and he practiced law in Chicago until his death.

Steffens, Lincoln (1866–1936). Journalist and author. Steffens graduated from the University of California at Berkeley, 1889, and studied in Germany and France, 1890–92. He worked as a reporter with the *New York Evening Post*, 1893–96, as city editor of the *New York Commercial Advertiser*, 1897–1901, as managing editor for *McClure's Magazine*, 1901–6, and later as an associate editor for *American Magazine* and *Everybody's Magazine*. He wrote many articles of a muckraking variety and several books, including *The Shame of the Cities* (1904).

Stephenson, D[avid] C[urtis] (1891–1966). Ku Klux Klan leader. Stephenson, a salesman by occupation, was a leader of the Indiana Klan, 1922–25, chief organizer or recruiter for the Klan in most midwestern states, and Grand Dragon of the Realm of Indiana, 1923–25. He served a prison term (1925–56) for the murder of Madge Oberholtzer (1896–1925), a romantic acquaintance. The evidence against Stephenson included a deathbed declaration by Oberholtzer accusing him of kidnapping and raping her and testimony by pathologists that the cause of death was an infection from a human bite mark.

Stoddard, Lothrop (1883–1950). Writer. Stoddard obtained a B.A., 1905, M.A., 1910, and Ph.D., 1914, from Harvard University, and a J.D., 1908, from Boston University. He practiced law for one year in Boston and then devoted himself to writing, including many articles on world affairs, and twenty-three books. He was a believer in the supremacy of the white race and in eugenics, and his writings often expressed his racist and anti-immigration views.

Stone, Melville (1848–1929). Journalist. Stone was a founder of the *Chicago Daily News*, 1875, where he worked as the paper's editor, 1875–88. The *Daily News* made him wealthy. He also worked as general manager of the Associated Press, which, under his management, 1893–1921, became the dominant domestic news service.

Straton, John Roach (1875–1929). Baptist preacher and author. Born in Evansville, Indiana, the son of a Baptist preacher, Straton attended Mercer University and was ordained a Baptist minister himself in 1900, while attending the Southern Baptist Theological Seminary in Kentucky. He received a Doctor of Divinity degree from Shurtleff College, 1906. He taught at Baylor University, 1906–7, and worked as a pastor in Chicago, Baltimore, and Norfolk, Virginia, 1908–17, before becoming pastor of Calvary Baptist Church in New York City, 1918–29. He was an outspoken

fundamentalist—loudly condemning dancing, divorce, art, alcohol, atheism, etc. He generated a great deal of attention after the trial of John T. Scopes *(q.v.)* by denouncing evolution and engaging in public debates on the subject. He was the author of several fundamentalist books, including *The Menace of Immorality in Church and State: Messages of Wrath and Judgment* (1920) and *Fighting the Devil in Babylon* (1929).

SULLIVAN, MARK (1874–1952). Journalist, author, and editor. Sullivan worked as a journalist for small newspapers before obtaining an A.B., 1900, and an LL.B., 1903, from Harvard. He practiced law only briefly and then returned to journalism, first for the *Ladies' Home Journal,* 1904–5, and then for *Collier's* magazine, where he was editor of the magazine from 1914 to 1919. After leaving *Collier's,* he worked as a correspondent for the *New York Evening Post* and later the *New York Tribune,* which consolidated with the *New York Herald* in 1924. He started a popular syndicated column around this time that he continued until his death. Sullivan also wrote a popular six-volume history of the United States, titled *Our Times* (1926–35), starting with the period of 1900 and ending with 1925.

TAYLOR, GRAHAM (1851–1938). Clergyman, settlement house director, author, and educator. Graham graduated from Rutgers College, 1870, and a theological seminary in New Jersey, 1873. He served as pastor at churches in New York, 1873–80, and Connecticut, 1880–92, before accepting a faculty position at the Chicago Theological Seminary, 1892–1924. He also taught classes in social work at the University of Chicago and founded a school for training social workers in 1908. In 1894, he started the settlement house known as Chicago Commons, which he directed until 1922. He helped publish the *Commons,* a monthly magazine, 1896–1905, which eventually became the *Survey,* for which he was an associate editor, 1909–19. He wrote a weekly column for the *Chicago Daily News,* 1902–1938, and three books, including an autobiography.

TAYLOR, JULIUS F. (1854–1934). Newspaper editor and publisher. Born in Virginia, the son of a slave, Taylor lived in several cities in the East and Midwest, including Chicago, before settling in Salt Lake City, Utah, in 1895, where he founded *The Broad Ax* newspaper, a small tabloid weekly that was liberal and Democratic in its politics. Taylor and the paper moved to Chicago in 1899, where he continued to edit and publish the newspaper until 1931.

TEW, CHARLES F. (1871–1927). Lawyer. Tew was born in Blair, Nebraska, and moved to Cheyenne, Wyoming, in 1890, where he was admitted to the bar in 1893. He moved to Greeley, Colorado, in 1897, where he became friends with Darrow's son, Paul, after Paul moved to Greeley. Tew was actively involved as a lawyer in irrigation projects, representing the developers of those projects, including, in particular, Daniel A. Camfield *(q.v.)*. Tew was also active in the Democratic party, serving as a delegate to the national convention in 1912 and once as a candidate for Congress.

In approximately 1917, Tew and his wife moved to Denver, Colorado, which is where he was living when he was killed in an automobile accident.

Thomas, Morris St. P. (1862–1943). Lawyer. Thomas obtained his LL.B. from the Union College of Law in Chicago, 1883, and an LL.D. from St. Ignatius College, 1895. He served as assistant corporation counsel for the City of Chicago in the early 1890s, when Darrow was also in that office, and he was Darrow's law partner for approximately four years, 1896–1900. Otherwise he maintained a general law practice in Chicago for most of his career.

Thomas, Norman (1884–1968). Socialist activist, political candidate, and author. Born in Ohio, Thomas was a graduate of Princeton University, 1905, and Union Theological Seminary, 1911. He served as a Presbyterian minister in Harlem, 1911–17, and helped found the organization that became the American Civil Liberties Union. He edited the pacifist magazine *World Tomorrow,* 1918–21, and was an associate editor of *The Nation,* 1921–22. In the 1920s, he became a perennial candidate for office, including state and local offices and every presidential election beginning in 1928. Thomas wrote many books related to his socialist and pacifist causes and served as the leading voice for the Socialist Party for much of his life.

Thompson, William Ormonde (1870?–1942). Lawyer and businessman. Thompson was born in England. He was Darrow's law partner from 1896 to 1903. He left the partnership after he married a wealthy widow. Later, he often served as an arbitrator in labor disputes and for many years he was president of the American Cotton Oil Company in New York City. He was also counsel for many years to the Illinois Industrial Commission. In 1933, Darrow selected him to serve as a member of the National Recovery Review Board, for which Darrow was chair. Thompson refused to sign the second report of the NRRB and wrote his own separate report condemning the National Recovery Administration, which resulted in Darrow severing his long relationship with Thompson.

Todd, Helen (1870–1953). Reformer and suffragist. Todd worked as a settlement worker at Hull House in Chicago and later as a deputy inspector of factories for the state of Illinois for six years, 1905–11, while at the same time devoting a great deal of time to campaigning for suffrage for women, primarily in Illinois and later in California, where she lived for several years before moving to New York. She worked for much of her life on issues affecting labor, children, and women, and she wrote on the subjects of suffrage and child labor for the *American Magazine* and *McClure's Magazine.* Among other activities, she was involved in the International Child Welfare Bureau and in providing low-cost housing for artists and writers in New York City.

Traubel, Horace (1858–1919). Author, editor, journalist, and publisher. Traubel founded and edited the monthly magazine *Conservator,* 1890–1919, which provided

him with a meager and uncertain income, and he worked as a freelance journalist. He was also an associate editor for *The Artsman,* 1903–07. He was a friend and biographer of Walt Whitman (1819–92), writing and editing several works about him.

Trumbull, Matthew Mark (1826–1894). Soldier, lawyer, and author. Trumbull was born in London and emigrated first to Canada, 1846, and then the United States, 1847. He fought in the Mexican War, taught school and studied law in Virginia, practiced law in Iowa, and served in the Union army, rising to the rank of brigadier general. After the war, he was a state district attorney in Iowa and then a federal collector of revenue. In 1882, he moved to Chicago and wrote books and articles, usually on political issues, including on behalf of the Haymarket anarchists.

Tveitmoe, Olaf A. (1863–1923). Labor leader. Born in Norway, Tveitmoe was a schoolteacher and newspaper editor in Oregon and Minnesota (where he served time in a state penitentiary in 1894 for fraud) before moving to San Francisco. There he helped organize a cement workers' union, served as secretary of the California State Building Trades Council, 1900–1922, and edited the magazine *Organized Labor,* 1900–1920. He was also a founder and president of the Asiatic Exclusion League, 1904–12, a racist organization that fought against Asian immigration. In 1912, Tveitmoe and thirty-seven other labor leaders were convicted in federal court in Indianapolis on charges of conspiring to transport explosives, including in connection with the bombing of the Los Angeles Times Building in 1910. Tveitmoe obtained a new trial on appeal but he was never retried. Tveitmoe and Anton Johannsen *(q.v.)* also were active in organizing labor support for the McNamara brothers *(q.v.)* in 1911.

Tzitlonok, Anna Scherff (b. 1889?). Teacher. Tzitlonok was born in Ohio, married Schevel Tzitlonok in approximately 1921, and worked as a public schoolteacher in Brooklyn, New York, in the 1920s. Later, she and her husband lived in Milwaukee, Wisconsin.

Van Waters, Miriam (1887–1974). Prison superintendent and reformer. Van Waters obtained a B.A., 1908, and M.A., 1910, from the University of Oregon and a Ph.D., 1913, in anthropology from Clark University. She worked in the juvenile justice systems in Boston and Portland and then supervised an experimental county home for juvenile delinquent girls in Los Angeles, 1919–31. Later, she was superintendent of the Massachusetts Women's Reformatory at Framingham, 1932–57. She was sometimes a controversial figure and always committed to liberal penal reforms.

Villard, Oswald Garrison (1872–1949). Editor, author, and social reformer. Villard earned an A.B. from Harvard University, 1893, and went to work as an editor for his father's *New York Evening Post,* eventually inheriting control of the paper and its weekly supplement, *The Nation,* in 1900. He sold the paper in 1918 but kept *The Nation*—which he converted from a literary review to a political journal—until the

1930s. He was active in many liberal causes, wrote some twenty books, and contributed many editorials and articles to magazines.

Walling, William English (1877–1936). Writer and socialist reformer. Walling earned a B.S. from the University of Chicago, 1897, and inherited considerable wealth from his parents. Around 1900, he and Darrow lived in the same tenement building in Chicago, known as the Langdon Building. Later, Walling worked for a settlement house in New York City, became involved in trade unionism and socialist causes, and worked as a freelance labor journalist. In 1909, he played an important role in organizing the National Association for the Advancement of Colored People and remained active in the organization throughout his life. He also wrote books on labor and politics.

Walling, Willoughby George (1878–1938). Walling was a banker in Chicago and the brother of William English Walling *(q.v.)*.

Walsh, Frank P. (1864–1939). Lawyer and government official. Walsh practiced law in Kansas City, Missouri, and held a variety of positions there in city government. In 1913, President Woodrow Wilson *(q.v.)* appointed Walsh chairman of the Commission on Industrial Relations, which was charged with investigating the causes of labor-management unrest. He moved to New York City in 1919 and worked for many labor and civil liberties causes, including as chief counsel for Thomas J. Mooney *(q.v.)*. In 1931, Franklin D. Roosevelt *(q.v.)*, then governor of New York, appointed him chairman of the New York State Power Authority.

Warren, Fred D. (1872–1959). Printer, editor, and stockbroker. Warren worked odd jobs in Missouri and Kansas before learning the printing trade. In 1890, he started a small, short-lived Republican newspaper in Rich Hill, Missouri, and then operated a job-printing business. He converted to socialism and founded and published a local socialist newspaper, 1898–99. In 1900, he moved to Girard, Kansas, to work for the socialist *Appeal to Reason* as a printer and, eventually, assistant editor. In 1902, he tried to revive another socialist paper, *Coming Nation,* which consolidated with the *Appeal* in 1904, after which he became managing editor of the *Appeal,* 1904–14. After World War I, he moved to Chicago and became a stockbroker. After the stock market crash in 1929, he moved back to Girard, worked for the Haldeman-Julius Publishing Company for a time, and became increasingly more conservative politically.

Weinberger, Harry (1888–1944). Lawyer. Born in New York City, Weinberger graduated from New York University Law School, 1908, and distinguished himself as a defender of civil liberties, including free speech, in particular. In 1918, he defended four anarchists who were convicted under the federal Espionage Act of 1917 for distributing leaflets opposing American military intervention in Russia, which, on appeal, led to the famous dissent by Oliver Wendell Holmes (1841–1935) in *Abrams v. United States* (1919). He defended Emma Goldman and Alexander Berkman

(1870–1936) when the federal government deported them in 1919. He defended the playwright Eugene O'Neill (1888–1953) in a plagiarism lawsuit in 1931. In 1923, Weinberger produced a play in New York City that resulted in his arrest on the ground that the play was indecent and immoral.

WHITE, WALTER (1893–1955). Author and civil rights leader. White was born in Atlanta, Georgia, and graduated from Atlanta University, 1916. He took a job with a life insurance company after graduation but within two years became assistant executive secretary of the National Association for the Advancement of Colored People, 1918–29, and, eventually, executive secretary, 1931–55.

WHITLOCK, ELLA ("NELL") BRAINERD (1876–1942). Brand Whitlock's second wife and the sister of his deceased first wife, Susanne Brainerd Whitlock (1874–92), who died four months after she married Whitlock.

WHITLOCK, BRAND (1869–1934). Journalist, lawyer, writer, mayor, diplomat. Whitlock was a journalist in his native Toledo, Ohio, before moving to Chicago, where he worked for the *Chicago Herald* and later as a clerk in the administration of Governor John P. Altgeld *(q.v.)*. He returned to Toledo to practice law in 1897, and later served four terms as mayor of Toledo, 1905–13. President Woodrow Wilson *(q.v.)* appointed him minister to Belgium in 1913. During World War I, he gained considerable fame through his Belgian relief work. When Belgium was invaded, he went with the government into exile. He wrote about his own life and experiences in *Forty Years of It* (1914) and *Belgium: A Personal Narrative* (1919). He also wrote many short stories and novels, including *The Turn of the Balance* (1907) and *Her Infinite Variety* (1904).

WILDE, LOUIS J. (1865–1926). Businessman, banker, and politician. Wilde was born in Iowa and was employed as an auctioneer in New York and Philadelphia before moving West and eventually settling in San Diego in 1903. There, he organized several banks and became a very successful and wealthy businessman, builder, and civic booster. He was elected mayor of the city in 1917 and served two two-year terms, after which he moved to Los Angeles.

WILLIAMS, EDWIN M. (1861?–1948). Court reporter. Williams started as a court reporter working for William Howard Taft (1857–1930) in Cincinnati, Ohio (when Taft was a judge) and later moved to Los Angeles, where he continued to work as a court reporter for the county court.

WILSON, FRANCIS S. (1882–1951). Lawyer and judge. Wilson's mother was an aunt of Jessie (Ohl) Brownlee *(q.v.)*, Darrow's first wife. Wilson shared an apartment with Darrow in the Hull House area of Chicago before Darrow married Ruby (Hamerstrom) Darrow *(q.v.)* in 1903, and he was Darrow's law partner from 1903 to 1911. After the partnership dissolved, Wilson worked as county attorney for Cook County, 1911–12, and then returned to private practice (interrupted by service in the army during World War I) until he became a judge of the Circuit Court of Cook

County in 1920. He was appointed justice of the state appellate court in 1927 and later, in 1935, justice (and chief justice in 1939) of the Illinois Supreme Court.

Wilson, Woodrow (1856–1924). Twenty-eighth president of the United States, 1913–21.

Withington, Caroline ("Caro") Lloyd (b. 1859). Journalist and author. Withington was the sister of Henry Demarest Lloyd *(q.v.)* and a graduate of Vassar College. She wrote for newspapers and magazines, edited her brother's papers, and was the author of a two-volume biography of her brother: *Henry Demarest Lloyd, 1847–1903: A Biography* (1912).

Wolfe, Frank E. (b. 1869). Union organizer, writer, editor, and filmmaker. Born in Illinois and raised in Kentucky, Wolfe began working on a flatboat as a boy and then worked for a railroad, where he helped unionize telegraph operators and station agents. Before moving to Los Angeles in approximately 1902, he lived and worked in a number of cities, including Boston, where he worked for approximately ten years as a writer and telegrapher for the *Boston Herald* and the *Boston Globe.* In Los Angeles, he was the managing editor of the *Los Angeles Herald* for a time, which was secretly owned by Harrison Gray Otis, and later, 1912–13, he was editor of the short-lived *Municipal News,* a municipal-owned newspaper in Los Angeles. In 1911, he wrote a pamphlet about the McNamara case titled *Capitalism's Conspiracy in California,* and he testified at Darrow's bribery trials. He wrote and directed a (now lost) silent pro-labor film titled *From Dusk to Dawn* in 1913, which featured Darrow. The next year, he became editor of *The Western Comrade,* a newspaper that Job Harriman *(q.v.)* purchased for his socialist colony (Llano del Rio). Later, he served as director of press service for the American Alliance for Labor and Democracy, a pro-war propaganda organization created in 1917, supported by Samuel Gompers (among others) and financed by the federal government.

Wood, Charles Erskine Scott (1852–1944). Army officer, lawyer, and writer. Wood graduated from West Point, 1874, served as an officer in the United States infantry for several years, and graduated from Columbia University with a Ph.B., 1882, and an LL.B., 1883. He resigned from the army in 1884 with the rank of colonel and practiced law in Portland, Oregon, 1884–1919, specializing in maritime law. In the later years of his practice, he became interested in civil liberties and social and political reforms. In 1919, he retired to Los Gatos, California, where he concentrated on literary work and lived with Sara Bard Field *(q.v.),* who became his second wife. He published many articles, stories, and poems. His best-known books are *The Poet in the Desert* (1915) and *Heavenly Discourse* (1927).

Wright, Frank Lloyd (1867–1959). Architect and author. A leading figure in the Prairie School of architecture and widely regarded as the greatest of American architects, Wright was born and raised in Wisconsin and practiced for many years in Chicago, creating some of the most striking residential and public buildings

in the United States. He was author of an autobiography and several books on architecture.

Yarros, Victor S. (1865–1956). Journalist, lawyer, and educator. Yarros emigrated to the United States from Russia in the early 1880s. He settled in the East and contributed to many anarchist publications, including *Liberty*. Later, he moved to Chicago with his Russian-born wife, Rachelle Slobodinsky Yarros (1869–1946), an obstetrician who became a longtime member of the medical faculty at the University of Illinois. Yarros and his wife lived at Hull House for twenty years. He wrote editorials for Chicago newspapers, including the *Daily News*, and he was a frequent contributor to national magazines. He worked part time in Darrow's law office, mainly researching and writing, 1914–25. He later lectured at the Lewis Institute and taught at John Marshall Law School in Chicago.

INDEX

Clarence Darrow is abbreviated CD. Page numbers in bold refer to the main biographical information for individuals. Three subentries precede all others: "CD's letter(s) to," "letter(s) to CD," and subentries for photos or other illustrations (which are numbered plate 1 through plate 56). Darrow's written works are gathered under his name (e.g., Darrow, Clarence, WORKS [BOOKS AND PAMPHLETS]) and are not listed as separate entries. The following are not indexed: the places from which Darrow's letters were written; letterhead information; the unnumbered notes at the end of each letter; newspapers cited in footnotes.